Countries, Peoples & Cultures

Central, South & Southeast Asia

Countries, Peoples & Cultures

Central, South & Southeast Asia

First Edition

Volume 2

Editor
Michael Shally-Jensen, PhD

SALEM PRESS
A Division of EBSCO Information Services, Inc.
Ipswich, Massachusetts

Grey House
Publishing

∞ The paper used in these volumes conforms to the American National Standard for Permanence of Paper for Printed Library Materials, Z39.48-1992 (R1997).

Publisher's Cataloging-In-Publication Data
(Prepared by The Donohue Group, Inc.)

Central, South & Southeast Asia / editor, Michael Shally-Jensen, PhD. – First edition.

pages: illustrations; cm. – (Countries, peoples & cultures; v. 2)

Includes bibliographical references and index.
ISBN: 978-1-61925-792-4 (v. 2)
ISBN: 978-1-61925-800-6 (set)

1. Asia, Central – History. 2. Asia, Central – Economic conditions. 3. Asia, Central – Social life and customs. 4. South Asia – History. 5. South Asia – Economic conditions. 6. South Asia – Social life and customs. 7. Southeast Asia – History. 8. Southeast Asia – Economic conditions. 9. Southeast Asia – Social life and customs. I. Shally-Jensen, Michael. II. Title: Central, South and Southeast Asia

DS33.C46 2015
950

First Printing
PRINTED IN CANADA

Contents

Publisher's Note

Countries, Peoples & Cultures: Central, South & Southeast Asia is the second volume of a new 9-volume series from Salem Press. It follows volume one, *Central & South America*, published earlier this year. *Countries, Peoples & Cultures* offers valuable insight into the social, cultural, economic, historical and religious practices and beliefs of nearly every country around the globe.

Following the extensive introduction that summarizes this politically and physically complex part of the world, this volume provides 20-page profiles of all 24 countries that make up the vast region that is Central, South and Southeast Asia. Each includes colorful maps—one highlighting the country's location in the world, and one with its major cities and natural landmarks—and a country flag, plus 10 categories of information: General Information; Environment & Geography; Customs & Courtesies; Lifestyle; Cultural History; Culture; Society; Social Development; Government; and Economy. Each profile also includes full color photographs, valuable tables of information including fun "Do You Know?" facts, and a comprehensive Bibliography.

Each country profile combines must-have statistics, such as population, language, size, climate, and currency, with the flavor and feel of the land. You'll read about favorite foods, arts & entertainment, youth culture, women's rights, health care, and tourism, for a comprehensive picture of the country, its people, and their culture.

Appendix One: World Governments, focuses on 21 types of governments found around the world today, from Commonwealth and Communism to Treaty System and Failed State. Each government profile includes its Guiding Premise, Structure, Citizen's Role, and modern-day examples.

Appendix Two: World Religions, focuses on 10 of the world's major religions from African religious traditions to Sikhism. Each religion profile includes number of adherents, basic tenets, major figures and holy sites, and major rites and celebrations.

The nine volumes of *Countries, Peoples & Cultures* are: *Central & South America; Central, South & Southeast Asia; Western Europe; Eastern Europe; Middle East & North Africa; East & Southern Africa; West & Central Africa; North America & the Caribbean;* and *East Asia & the Pacific.*

Introduction

The three regions covered in this book, Central Asia, South Asia, and Southeast Asia, occupy a vast expanse of land ranging from Iran and the Caspian Sea at the western edge to Australia and the Pacific at the eastern edge. The identification of these three regions, though longstanding, is something of a matter of convenience. Significant geographical, cultural, and historical differences separate them—and yet there are notable similarities and linkages among them as well. In any case, the three regions and their outlines have by now become widely accepted among scholars and observers of Asia.

Regional Outlines

Central Asia, in contemporary usage, refers to the countries of Kazakhstan, Kyrgyzstan, Tajikistan, Turkmenistan, and Uzbekistan—all former republics of the Soviet Union. In previous decades the term was used more broadly to mean these Muslim and partly nomadic regions as well as adjacent areas of central Russia, Mongolia, and regions of far western China (in particular, Tibet and what is now the Xinjiang Uyghur Autonomous Region). Afghanistan, to the south, was also sometimes included. A variety of researchers continue to prefer the broader designation, and for good reason. The famed Silk Road passed through "greater" Central Asia, and for a time in the 19th century the region was considered politically pivotal, connecting East and West. Although Islam remains the majority religion in the five "stans" making up modern-day Central Asia, Buddhism has been a factor in the easternmost regions that traditionally were included under the designation.

South Asia denotes the Indian subcontinent and adjacent areas. Besides India, the region includes Pakistan and Bangladesh at the flanks, Nepal and Bhutan in the Himalayas to the northeast, and the island nations of Sri Lanka and the Maldives (in the Indian Ocean) to the south. Afghanistan, in the northwest, is again usually included. The oldest civilizations in the region developed under Hinduism, but Buddhism and Islam have been and remain major cultural forces. Today, as always, South Asia remains culturally and historically complex. Over a hundred languages are regularly spoken in India alone, and the distribution of languages does not always correspond with the distribution of ethnicities, religions, and other markers of cultural identity. Social subdivisions, based on kinship and historical status, are at times more meaningful than any of these broader categories. Despite its diversity, size, and complexity, South Asia is widely recognized as a distinct region with its own unique character.

Southeast Asia is a combination of mainland countries and island nations extending from Myanmar/Burma in the west to the Philippines in the east, and from the southern borders of China in the north to the scattered islands of Indonesia in the south. The countries it includes are Myanmar, Thailand, Laos, Cambodia, Vietnam, Malaysia, and Singapore on the mainland, and Brunei, Indonesia, the Philippines, and East Timor in the maritime area. Like South Asia, this region is substantially populated and characterized by ethnic, religious, and linguistic pluralism. Although Buddhism and Islam make up the majority religions in most of the countries of the region—the notable exceptions being the predominately Catholic Philippines and East Timor—various indigenous religions exist alongside these world religions. Southeast Asia, too, is culturally and historically complex.

Habitats and Histories

Central Asia

The terrain of Central Asia features both highlands—principally the Hindu Kush and the Kazakh Hills—and lowlands—mainly around the Caspian and Aral seas. The region is drained by the Syr-Darya and Amu-Darya, both of which flow into the Aral. Much of the area is made up of desert basins, salt flats, rocky hills, and relict lakes formerly connected to oceans but now cut off and gradually shrinking and becoming more saline. There is little rainfall, and the region's vegetation consists mostly of tough grasses and low shrubs that thrive in a steppe environment.

Before the 19th century, the area was occupied by nomadic Turkmen tribes and ruled, in part, by local Muslim khanates. Around 1865 the nomadic tribes were largely brought under the control of the Russian czar, Alexander II, who eventually also subdued the khanates as well but allowed them a degree of autonomy. The region was established under Russia as a province called Turkestan. After the Russian Revolution of 1917, the area was reorganized as five constituent republics of the Soviet Union: Kazakhstan, Kyrgyzstan, Tajikistan, Turkmenistan, and Uzbekistan. Later in the century the Russians invaded Afghanistan (1979) and installed a puppet regime there in hopes of bringing the country into the Soviet sphere, but after a taxing ten-year conflict the Russians withdrew. With the breakup of the Soviet Union in 1991, the five Central Asian republics became independent states. In Afghanistan, an Islamic fundamentalist political movement, the Taliban, launched a civil war and gained control of the capital and other areas by 1996. The group was ousted from power in 2001 by the United States, however, in response to the 9/11 terrorist attacks by the al-Qaeda terrorist organization, whose members had been given safe haven by the Taliban. Since then, Afghanistan has continued to experience ongoing war and political division, although in recent years some advances toward stability have been made.

South Asia

The Indian subcontinent is sharply delineated by the Himalaya and Karakoram ranges on the north, the Hindu-Kush and Sulaiman ranges on the west, and the Arakan Yoma range on the east. Major subregions within South Asia are delineated, in the northern half, by three great rivers: the Indus, the Ganges, and the Brahmaputra, each with its own valleys, floodplains, and drainage basins. The summer monsoon, moving primarily up the Ganges Valley, becomes less potent by the time it hits the upper reaches of the Indus Basin, which leaves most of the latter area semiarid or even desert. These drier regions yield to tropical conditions in the lower Ganges. The floodplains of all three rivers are quite fertile. In the valleys, the summers are long and hot and the winters are short and mild.

The southern half of South Asia, consisting of the Indian peninsula, is made up of a vast plateau known as the Deccan. It is flanked by the Western and Eastern Ghats (mountain ranges). In each case a coastal plain lies between the Ghats and the sea. Both of these plains are affected by monsoon rains, particularly in the east, while the interior of the Deccan remains relatively dry. The vegetation of the plateau is primarily scrub and trees able to withstand heat and drought. To the south of India is the island of Sri Lanka. Its northern half is somewhat dry while its southern tier is wetter and marked by tropical forests.

Early cultures in the region include the 3rd millennium B.C.E. Indus civilization of northern India, whose decline may have been brought about by the arrival of invading Aryans from the Iranian plateau in the 2nd millennium B.C.E. The Aryan's ancient Vedic religious tradition, which spread to the south and southeast, produced the system of Brahmanism with its accompanying caste system. The religions of Buddhism and Jainism emerged in the 6th and 5th centuries B.C.E., Buddhism eventually migrating to other areas of Asia (but remaining in Sri Lanka). In the 4th century B.C.E. the Punjab region of northwestern India was invaded by the Macedonian conqueror Alexander the Great, but the entire northern region (including parts of Afghanistan) and middle India were subsequently consolidated into the Maurya Empire (322 B.C.E.-185 B.C.E.). Later dynasties variously broke up or united these areas. By about 1,000 C.E. Muslim invasions in the north brought a change, even while some Hindu kingdoms continued to flourish in the south. Portuguese explorers opened the region to trade with Europe in the late 15th century, followed by increased competition for influence among European powers. The Mughal (Mogul) emperors ruled most of India between 1526 and 1707. They were challenged in turn by the Hindu Marathas. A period of dynastic struggle led to the growing power of British and French commercial interests, and to the ascendency of the British after 1757. Parts of India not under direct British control remained protected states under local rulers. After World War I, the self-rule movement under Mahatma Gandhi developed. Varying degrees of autonomy were granted by the British overlords to different provinces, but the movement pushed ahead and by 1947 British rule in the subcontinent had been broken.

In the making of Indian independence, and in India's division from Pakistan in 1947, conflicts and military exchanges erupted between the two countries over the provinces of Jammu and Kashmir in the far north. Clashes continued to occur in later years (1965, 1971); Bangladesh split from Pakistan in 1971 in a bloody war. Today, India and Pakistan remain testy neighbors, each possessing nuclear capabilities. Pakistan's tribal areas bordering Afghanistan have become strongholds of radical Islamist groups, which feed Afghanistan's ongoing internal struggles and continue to bedevil the Pakistani government. There were attacks on the Indian city of Mumbai in 2008. Sri Lanka, with its own long history (albeit related to India's), emerged from a lengthy civil war that pitted Hindu Tamils against Buddhist Sinhalese only in 2009. Nepal has had struggles with Maoist factions. Throughout South Asia in the modern era, religious violence, terrorism, political instability, and poverty remain problems, even while significant gains have been evident.

Southeast Asia

Mainland Southeast Asia—that is, Myanmar, Thailand, Laos, Cambodia, Vietnam, and the Malay Peninsula—is separated from neighboring India and China by a string of mountains extending out from the great Himalayan range. The region is marked by four major rivers and their associated valleys, floodplains, and deltas: the Irrawaddy in Myanmar, the Chao Praya in Thailand, the Mekong in Cambodia and southern Vietnam, and the Red River in northern Vietnam. Extensive alluvial plains, used for rice cultivation, exist in the lowlands, while upriver are mountain crests, gorges, and plush forests. Upland Thailand and central Myanmar are drier than the rest of the region, which receives monsoonal rains and has a tropical climate The Malay Peninsula features lower mountains and numerous streams rather than a large river.

In insular Southeast Asia, the Indonesian and Philippine archipelagos comprise thousands of small and large islands, some of which are active volcanoes (as in Java). Most of the islands feature a mountainous "spine" or core, from which run many small streams and valleys. Traditional maritime culture, as well as modernized sea transport and air travel, link the islands together—although some remain relatively remote and not all of the smallest ones are inhabited.

The long and complex history of Southeast Asia is generally regarded as falling into five major periods. (1) the ancient era, to about 800 C.E.; (2) the classical Hindu-Buddhist era, from the 9th to the mid-13th century; (3) the pre-modern "middle" period—1250 to about 1700—marked by the spread of both Islam and Theravada Buddhism and the emergence of early states; (4) the colonial era, extending from about 1700 to about 1940 and characterized by the growth of European influence; and (5) the modern, postcolonial era of the 20th and 21st centuries.

During the 18th and 19th centuries, the expansion of Western colonial empires brought the whole region—except Thailand—under European or American rule. The driving force behind this expansion was the need to protect and expand commercial markets in the east and to best one's global rivals in the region. Although Spain, Portugal, and the Netherlands were the main players in earlier eras, by the 1800s the contest was primarily between the British, the

French, and, to a lesser extent, the United States. The economic and political transformation of Southeast Asia under colonial rule penetrated deeply into the lives and welfare of the indigenous populations. Communities that previously had been largely self-sufficient became specialized in the production of a single food crop or raw material for export to the global market. By the late 19th century, the region saw the emergence of anti-colonial nationalist movements, one of the first arising in the Philippines in 1896 as Filipinos revolted against Spanish rule. The United States would use the Spanish-American War of 1898 to insert itself into the Philippines as a political "savior." The French in Vietnam and the British in Burma (Myanmar) would face similar insurgencies aimed at casting them out.

During World War II much of Southeast Asia was occupied by the Japanese. Following Japan's defeat by the United States and its allies in 1945, efforts to restore colonial rule met with resistance in most areas. By 1965 most countries in the region were again independent, although Brunei remained a British protectorate until 1983. Vietnam split into northern and southern states, the former under communist rule and the latter not. The United States fought a bitter war in Vietnam against communist forces in the south and north between 1965 and 1975. Ultimately, it was compelled to pull out and watch the south be overtaken by the communists. Burma, for its part, pursued a policy of nonalignment and isolation; it was run for 40 years (until 2011) by a military junta. Cambodia suffered (1975–79) a murderous transition to communist rule (under Pol Pot) and back again. Indonesia, too, fought a bloody battle with communist elements in the 1960s and 70s, using an iron hand that left many communities scarred. The Philippines has suffered from secessionist movements, and Thailand has faced political wrangling and military assertions of power. Malaysia has come under the sway of political Islam in recent years. Only tiny Singapore is often viewed as a shining light in the region, and yet its reputation has been won only through the application of strict civil measures. Throughout Southeast Asia, a shift has been seen in recent decades to increased industrialization and economic expansion, even as political instability, corruption, and the maintenance of human health and welfare remain vexing issues.

Michael Shally-Jensen, PhD

Bibliography

Adams, Kathleen M., and Kathleen A. Gillogly, eds. *Everyday Life in Southeast Asia.* Bloomington, IN: Indiana University Press, 2011.

Bose, Sugata. *Modern South Asia: History, Culture, and Political Economy.* New York: Routledge, 2011.

Dilip, Hiro. *Inside Central Asia.* New York: Overlook Duckworth, 2009.

Golden, Peter B. *Central Asia in World History.* New York: Oxford University Press, 2011.

Keay, John. *Midnight's Descendants: South Asia and Its Peoples from Partition to the Present Day.* London: Harper Collins, 2014.

Ludden, David E. *India and South Asia: A Short History.* London: Oneworld, 2014.

Ricklefs, M.C., et al. *A New History of Southeast Asia.* New York: Palgrave Macmillan, 2010.

SarDesai, D.R. *Southeast Asia: Past and Present.* Boulder, CO: Westview Press, 2013.

CENTRAL ASIA

Ascension Cathedral in Almaty, Kazakhstan. The cathedral, completed in 1907, is the second tallest wooden building in the world/iStock photo © Dmitry Chulov

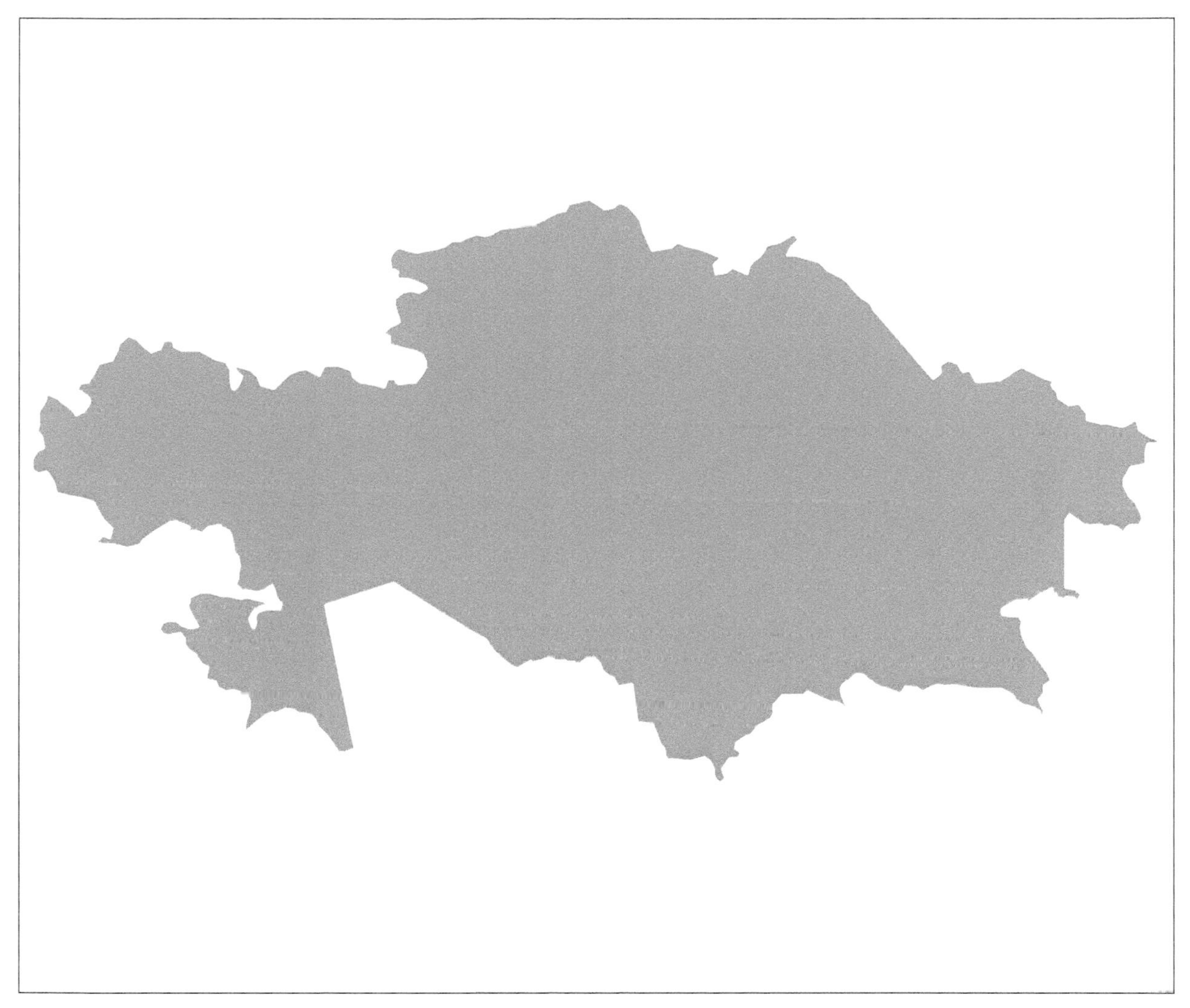

KAZAKHSTAN

Introduction

Kazakhstan, lying between northwest China and southern Russia, is geographically the largest of the former Soviet republics (excluding Russia itself). Ethnic Kazakhs represent a mix of ancient Turkic and Mongol nomadic tribes who migrated to the region before the 13th century. The Kazakh tribal area, where Islam was the main religion, was conquered by Russia in the 18th century; in 1936 Kazakhstan became a Soviet Republic. During the Soviet era an influx of immigrants produced a situation in which native Kazakhs became a minority, but by the mid-1990s that trend had started to reverse.

Kazakhstan's economy is larger than those of the other Central Asian states. It possesses substantial fossil fuel reserves and other minerals and metal. Being a landlocked country, it relies on its neighbors, particularly on Russia, to export its oil, grain, and other products. Kazakhstan is known as the home of Russia's Baykonur space launch facility, the land for which it leases to its larger northern neighbor.

Because livestock was central to the Kazakhs' traditional nomadic lifestyle, most of their customs and arts relate in some way to livestock—particularly to horses and horse-riding.

GENERAL INFORMATION

Official Language: Kazakh
Population: 17,949,000 (2014 est.)
Currency: Tenge
Coins: The tïin (1/100 tenge) comes in denominations of 1, 2, 5, 10, 20, and 50.

Land Area: 2,724,900 square kilometers (1,052,128 square miles)
Water Area: 25,200 square kilometers (9,730 square miles)
National Anthem: "Meniñ Qazaqstanım" ("My Kazakhstan")
Capital: Astana
Time Zone: GMT +6
Flag Description: The flag of the Republic of Kazakhstan features a sky-blue background with a central image of a golden sun with 32 rays extending outward, sitting above a soaring steppe eagle. The flagstaff edge has a vertical line of traditional ornamentation.

CUSTOMS & COURTESIES

Greetings

There are different modes when greeting strangers and friends in Kazakhstani culture. Since society is quite hierarchical, greetings among

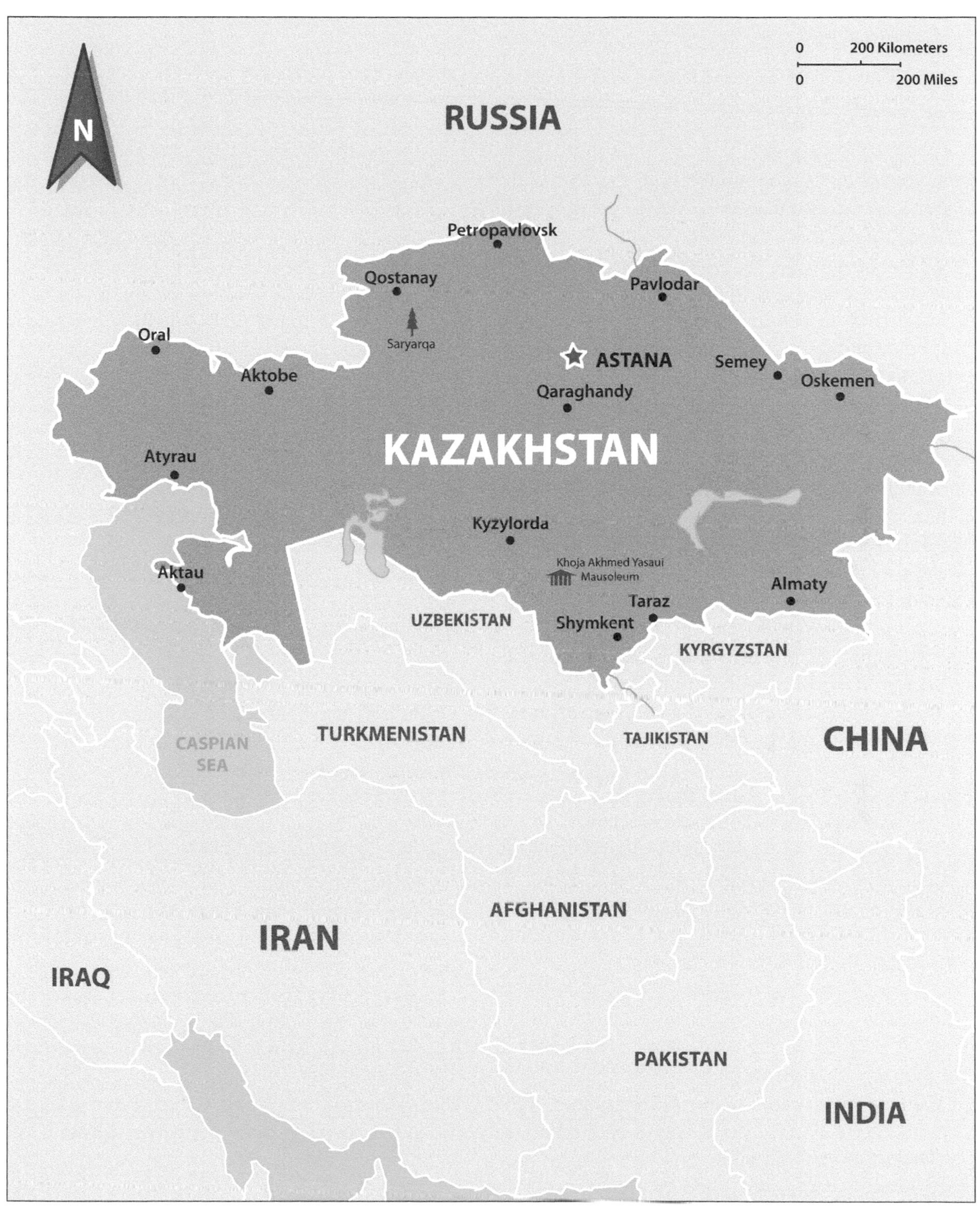
0 200 Kilometers
0 200 Miles
N
RUSSIA
Petropavlovsk
Qostanay
Pavlodar
Saryarqa
Oral
ASTANA
Semey
Aktobe
Qaraghandy
Oskemen
KAZAKHSTAN
Atyrau
Kyzylorda
Khoja Akhmed Yasaui Mausoleum
Aktau
Almaty
Taraz
UZBEKISTAN
Shymkent
KYRGYZSTAN
CASPIAN SEA
TURKMENISTAN
TAJIKISTAN
CHINA
AFGHANISTAN
IRAN
IRAQ
PAKISTAN
INDIA

Principal Cities by Population (2012 estimate):

- Almaty (1,400,000)
- Shymkent (476,066)
- Taraz (427,469)
- Astana (425,806)
- Qaragandy (421,250)
- Pavlodar (360,050)
- Oskemen (349,713)
- Semej (311,687)

people who are not close or related tend to be formal. It is typical for men to shake hands with both hands when meeting. While Kazakhstan is far less religious than other Central Asian nations, it is still considered polite to keep a certain distance between the sexes. Therefore, a man should allow a woman to initiate a handshake, as some women may be uncomfortable greeting a male stranger in this manner. The formal way to address someone in Kazakhstan is to refer to them by their first name and then their father's name, followed by the suffix -ich" ("son of") or "-ovich" ("daughter of").

In contrast, friends tend to be very informal with one another. In fact, informality is considered a sign of closeness. Friends and relatives tend to show physical affection quite readily, and often embrace instead of shaking hands. Because of Kazakhstan's past as home to nomadic herdsmen, it is still customary to greet a friend by asking about the health of the family livestock. Once people know one another fairly well, it is typical to use informal first names. However, it is important to be sure that this is acceptable before doing so.

Gestures & Etiquette

Due to Kazakhstan's hierarchical society, older people are typically the most revered members of society. Traditionally, they are always consulted with important decisions, and it is rude to criticize or contradict what an elder says. Among people of the same age group, hierarchy is largely based on professional qualifications. Hence, it is considered good behavior to refer to people by their titles and surnames. Among devout Muslims, it is considered improper for a woman to talk informally with a man she does not know. Additionally, Kazakhstani Muslims may also be cautious about shaking hands with members of the opposite sex. Similarly, public displays of affection between men and women may cause offense and are typically avoided.

Kazakhstanis have somewhat different priorities regarding the use of time. For example, it is perfectly normal to not be punctual, and arriving somewhat late to an engagement is not considered impolite. People also spend a larger amount of time engaged in leisurely activities, and taking time to relax several times a day is considered healthy behavior.

Eating/Meals

Meals are an extremely important part of Kazakhstani social life. They are times for family members and friends to sit down together and exchange information in a casual setting. This means that they usually take a good deal of time. Meals typically begin with tea, dried fruits, and nuts. Teacups are customarily only filled half way, which is a sign of being welcome to stay for more. Bread usually follows the first course.

Breakfast consists of tea, dried fruits, nuts, and bread. Lunch and dinner are much larger meals, featuring a variety of shared dishes. Common dishes include shashlyk (kebabs), noodle soup (kespe), and dumplings. Beshbarmak is considered the national dish, and consists of noodles with horse, mutton, or beef.

Since bread is considered sacred, it is important to not waste bread or set a loaf face down. Guests to a meal are traditionally served on a tablecloth called a dastarkhan, which is also considered sacred and should be treated with respect. Food is generally eaten with the right hand, and eating with gusto is a sign of appreciation. When finished eating, a guest should leave a little food on the plate, to indicate that he or she is done with the meal.

Visiting

As is the case throughout Central Asia, guests are deeply revered in Kazakhstan. It is common to be invited into a Kazakhstani family's home for tea or a meal. People give graciously, sometimes to the point of exhausting their meager resources for casual guests. As such, it is polite to contribute in some way, often in the form of gifts or cash. In Kazakhstan it is considered polite to bring something to the table, such as sweets or a bottle of wine or vodka. Due to Islamic custom, alcohol is not appropriate when visiting Muslim Kazakhstanis.

Guests to a Kazakhstani home are customarily greeted with tea served in a half-filled cup, which is a sign of welcome. Sitting around a tablecloth called a dastarkhan, they will be served dried fruit and nuts, bread, and then a number of shared dishes. The hosts might refill a guest's plate every time it is emptied, so it is appropriate to signal that one is done eating by leaving a small amount of food on the plate. A particularly honored guest may be called upon to carve and serve a boiled sheep or horse head to the assembled group. There is a symbolic protocol for doing this. For example, the ear of the animal is traditionally served to the youngest child as a reminder to listen to his or her elders.

LIFESTYLE

Family

Family is extremely important to the people of Kazakhstan. It forms the basic social unit, and people have historically depended on family connections to make a living in the rather harsh climate. Historically, all members of the family participated in the work needed to sustain the traditional nomadic lifestyle. Even children were expected to work. Daughters were taught to look after younger siblings, and sons were trained to tend the family's flocks. Making carpets, which was a primary method in which nomadic people stored their wealth, was also traditionally a task performed by the entire family.

Family is also the key to gaining respect within the wider society. A family's position in the social hierarchy is based partially on material wealth, but mostly on honor. Elders are to be consulted whenever there is a major decision to make, and it is considered impolite to contradict an elder. The generosity a family shows toward guests is also central to the esteem it receives from other members of the community.

Housing

Housing in Kazakhstan varies significantly between urban and rural areas. In urban areas, most people live in apartments. There are extensive blocks of apartments in major cities, many of which were built during the Soviet period and are currently in disrepair. New apartment buildings are also being constructed, evidence of increasing urbanization and relative prosperity brought about by the sale of fossil fuels. Wealthier people in cities are flocking to these new housing blocks on the expanding borders of cities, leaving the crumbling apartment buildings in urban centers.

The traditional form of housing in Kazakhstan, still in use throughout the countryside, is the yurt (sometimes called yurta). The yurt is form of tent made from a wooden frame covered with animal hides. The floors of a yurt are typically lined with decorative carpets, making the interior warm and aesthetically appealing. There is a stove in the middle of the yurt, providing enough heat to make the structure livable in cold weather. The material goods of the household are stored in decorative wooden chests, which are positioned along the walls of the yurt. The yurt is an ideal design for nomadic herders, as it collapses for easy transportation.

Food

With a cultural history that was largely shaped by nomadic herding, the cuisine of Kazakhstan is undoubtedly associated with livestock. Sheep, cows, and horses are slaughtered for meat. These animals are highly venerated, and no part of them is wasted. As a result, people in Kazakhstan consider certain unusual cuts great delicacies. For example, one choice cut is zhal (fat from a horse's neck), and another is karta (cut from a horse's rectum). Animals also provide milk, which is consumed in various forms, and many dishes include cream or sour cream. A dried milk curd called irimshik is eaten as a snack. Fermented horse and camel milk, called kumys and shubat, respectively, are favored beverages.

Because the climate varies significantly throughout the country, there are many different crops grown throughout Kazakhstan. Therefore, each region is particularly well suited to one or two crops. For example, the area around Almaty is especially known for apples, while other areas produce different kinds of dried fruits, such as raisins and apricots. Vegetables are consumed in large quantities in Kazakhstan, including carrots, onions, and beets. The most common grain crops are types of rice and wheat.

There are several typical Kazakhstani dishes. One is plov (or pilaf), a rice casserole made with chunks of meat, carrots, onions, and dried fruits. Meat filled dumplings called manti are also very popular. The dish which is said to best represent Kazakhstani cooking is beshbarmak, a noodle dish made with meat and vegetables. There are several kinds of soup, including borscht made with beets and sour cream, a fish or meat soup called sorpa, and a rich noodle soup called kespe. Meat is often served as a dish. For instance, there is a popular kind of smoked horse sausage called kazys. Various sorts of kebabs called shashlyk are also enjoyed throughout the country.

Life's Milestones

The people of Kazakhstan celebrate changes from one part of life to another with a good deal of ceremony. Important events such as the birth of a son, marriage between two families, and death of an elder, are traditionally celebrated with large social gatherings and massive feasts. These feasts serve as opportunities to display family honor and the ability to serve large quantities of meat to friends and neighbors is considered a point of pride—the more honorable the family, the better the feast. Gatherings to celebrate change from one stage of life to the next are therefore socially significant, as they give families the opportunity to bolster their status within the community.

One of the most significant moments in the life of a male child is when he is circumcised. This generally takes place between the ages of five and eight, and it is typical for groups of boys from the same family to go through the circumcision ceremony together. Marriage was historically a very important rite of passage, not just for the individuals involved, but for all their relatives since it represented the coming together of two families. It is traditional for the groom's family to pay a bride price in livestock, and for the bride's family to provide a dowry of wooden chests filled with household goods. It used to be normal for a groom to select his bride by kidnapping her, in a practice known as alyp qashu. While alyp qashu was banned in the Soviet era, it is enjoying a small resurgence in rural areas.

CULTURAL HISTORY

Art

Kazakhstan's rich artistic traditions underwent significant changes during the Soviet period. The Soviets provided free education in Moscow to aspiring artists, which had the dual effect of encouraging more young people to get into the arts and changing their thinking about aesthetic matters. One of the most notable changes was that the arts were taken out of the traditional social context of festivals and family celebrations, and put into a stage setting. With funding from Moscow, several new institutions flourished. One such institution was the Zhambyl Philharmonic Society, founded in 1935, which intentionally integrated traditional music and dance with Western approaches to performance. The government-funded Kazakh State Musical Theater (later renamed the Abay State Academic Opera and Ballet), founded in 1934, popularized ballet and opera within Kazakhstan.

On the other hand, the Soviet government was opposed to what it considered expressions of

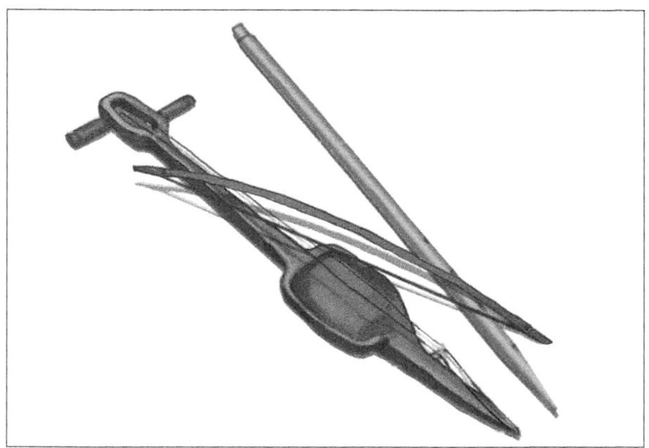

Traditional Kazakhstan wooden musical instruments (left Dombra; right Sybyzgy)

religion. Since the festivals traditionally celebrated in Kazakhstan have been associated with spirituality since ancient times, the government in Moscow discouraged them, thus removing the defining context of the Kazakhstani performance arts. Since achieving independence in 1991, the people of Kazakhstan have revived the traditional festivals as a means of asserting cultural pride. Among the most important festivals that have been revived is Nauryz, a celebration of the coming of spring. The celebration of Nauryz is considered a means of renewing interest in the pre-Soviet past.

Since the return of festivals to the social life of the people of Kazakhstan, there has been an increased interest in musical competition. Traditionally, duels between musicians have been a beloved form of entertainment at festivals. Aitys, as these competitions are called, usually feature two dombra players who try to outdo one another with masterful playing and witty lyrics. This tradition nearly vanished during the Soviet years. Aitys events are now wildly popular among people of all ages, spawning a renewed interest in studying Kazakhstan's musical and poetic past. Other organized competitions have also helped to inspire a prolific musical scene in present day Kazakhstan. The best folk music competitors in the country come together for the now legendary Zhas Kanat Music Festival, held each year in Almaty, which offers a national stage and exposure to young musical artists. The popular music industry is also growing and following a similar pattern. Televised musical competitions such as *SuperStar KZ* have a huge following, helping Kazakhstan develop a unique pop sound.

Architecture

As Kazakhstan was home to nomads throughout its past, it is not particularly known for its historic architecture. However, in the 20th century Kazakhstani architects produced some very impressive religious buildings. This trend was started by Russian architect Andrei Zenkov (1863–1936), who was active just before the Soviet era. His masterful Orthodox church, Svyato-Voznesensky Cathedral, has been considered a national treasure since it was built in 1904. Since independence, the government has encouraged several massive building projects. Due to these efforts, the country now boasts several structures that rival any in Central Asia. Many new mosques have been built in this period of independence. One example of this new trend toward building monumental structures is the Central Mosque, built in Astana in 1999. Featuring a glimmering turquoise blue dome and grand minarets, the Central Mosque is considered one of the most beautiful buildings in the region. It has become a major pilgrimage site for Muslims throughout Central Asia.

Since the end of Soviet rule, the people of Kazakhstan have also come to consider the material goods associated with nomadic living to be valuable expressions of national pride. Traditional pieces such as carpets, clothing, jewelry, and horse-riding gear have come to be appreciated as artistically significant objects. Older pieces are now carefully preserved and displayed in museums throughout the nation. Kazakhstanis also have a renewed interest in producing traditional nomadic arts, both for actual use and as increasingly valuable trade goods. This revival of interest in the nomadic arts has created an important cottage industry, which has been especially helpful for female artists that experienced economic hardships during the transition from Soviet rule to independence.

Kazakhstan has rich artistic traditions which reflect the country's ancient history. The first known settlers to the area, dating back to the second millennium BCE, left a record of their creative nature in the form of elaborately carved metal ornaments. Kazakhstan has always been a land of nomadic herders. Around 300 BCE, Kazakhstan also became part of the Silk Road, a network of important overland trade routes that connected Europe with Asia. Trade caravans continuously traversed the Silk Road for centuries, spreading ideas and artistic techniques into what is now Kazakhstan.

The nomadic nature of the Kazakhstani people had an effect on their arts. As nomads, they lived in transportable and impermanent housing. Unlike its Central Asian neighbors, Kazakhstan is not particularly well known for its architecture. However, there are a few excellent examples of uniquely Kazakhstani architecture, mainly memorials to the dead. The oldest of these are the ancient burial mounds of warriors on the Saryarka Plains, which date back to 500 BCE. Another example of Kazakhstani architecture is the mausoleum of Islamic scholar Khoja Akhmed Yasaui (1106–1166), which dates to the twelfth century CE. This mausoleum is heavily decorated with elaborate mosaics, showing the influence of Islamic art on the country. In 2003, the United Nations Educational, Scientific, and Cultural Organization (UNESCO) designated the famous mausoleum as a World Heritage Site, one of three recognized sites in Kazakhstan.

The nomads of Kazakhstan excelled in other crafts, imparting a rich material culture to their descendants. They have long been known for their textiles. Carpet making has always been extremely important, providing a practical way to store the wealth provided by the sheep herds that were central to life in Kazakhstan. Kazakhstani carpets are still produced the same way they have been for centuries. Once the wool is harvested, spun, and woven into carpets with characteristic geometric designs, the carpets are felted. This is accomplished by wetting the carpet and having each member of the household walk on it, starting with the eldest and finishing with the youngest. Kazakhstanis also produce other textiles, such as finely embroidered and beaded clothing. These goods were popular trade goods in the days of the Silk Road. Kazakhstanis have also been known throughout history as masterful silversmiths, making jewelry and silver-encrusted saddles decorated with geometrically patterned plant and animal motifs.

Drama, Dance & Music

Kazakhstan has a rich, overlapping tradition of performance arts. It is difficult to clearly distinguish between music, dance, drama, and literature within Kazakhstani culture. Performance served a number of important social functions, including shamanic divination, social entertainment, and the recounting of tribal history. It also helped create cohesion within individual tribal groups. It was also a form of diplomacy, allowing people of different backgrounds to come together in a context of artistic celebration. This was especially important during the Silk Road period, as the previously isolated nomads began to interact with the wider world.

The people of Kazakhstan have always enjoyed dancing. Lacking formal rules or steps, dance was traditionally an opportunity for people to show off their bravado, acrobatic fitness, and ability to devise moves in real time. Themes typically included artistic renditions of aspects of the nomadic lifestyle. Dancers often acted out scenes of hunting and animal husbandry. One of the most impressive forms of dance takes place on horseback, with groups of performers executing elaborate improvised steps while standing in their saddles.

The people of Kazakhstan have long been known as great musicians, and developed a number of popular instruments and performance techniques. The most common is the stringed dombra, which is played like a lute. Others include the cello-like kobys, the double flute called a sybyzghy, and a mouth harp called a shankobyz. Music is usually played to accompany the telling of epic poems, which form the cornerstone of what can be considered traditional Kazakhstani literature. There were several categories of poetic performers who recounted verses along with musical accompaniment. Singers called zhyraus sang epic poems about history, akyns recited florid poetry at weddings and funerals, and akyndars competed with one another at festivals to come up with the wittiest lyrics.

Literature

Although written literature is relatively new in Kazakhstan, the rich tradition of poetic creativity has inspired some notable writers. Chief among these was Abay Kunanbayev (1845–1904), who pioneered Kazakhstani literature in the late nineteenth-century. Drawing inspiration from the epic poetry that defined the culture since ancient times, he helped renew a sense of Kazakh pride in a time when the influence of the modern world began to complicate life for the historically nomadic people. He was emulated by an equally talented writer, Mukhtar Auezov (1897–1961), whose compassionate biographical exploration of Kunanbayev furthered interest among a new generation in traditional ways of life.

CULTURE

Cultural Sites & Landmarks

Visitors to Kazakhstan generally come through Almaty, the former capital and the largest city in the country. An elegant and prosperous city, Almaty holds many important cultural destinations. Citizens of Almaty are particularly proud of the green spaces in their city. One of the finest parks is the Central Park, also known as Gorky Park. Another beloved green space is Panfilov Park, which is known for its cultural monuments. Within Panfilov Park there is a memorial to the Kazakhstani soldiers who fought off Nazi tanks during World War II. The Zenkov Cathedral, a Russian Orthodox church designed at the turn of the twentieth century, is also found on the grounds of this park. Almaty is also home to the country's largest museums, including the Central State Museum, the Kazakhstan Museum of Arts, and the Museum of Kazakh Musical Instruments.

The city of Shymkent, located in southern Kazakhstant, was originally an outpost on the Silk Road. In the nineteenth century, Shymkent was rebuilt as a fortress town, making it one of the most important cities in the southern region. It still houses an impressive bazaar, where visitors can browse local crafts and foods. There are also several important historical sites nearby, including two associated with the Islamic scholar Khoja Akhmed Yasaui. His mother is buried at the thirteenth-century Karash-Ana Mausoleum, and his father is entombed at the nearby fourteenth-century Ibragim Ata Mausoleum. Khoja Akhmed Yasaui's mausoleum, a UNESCO World Heritage Site, is located in the city of Turkistan

In addition to the Mausoleum of Khoja Akhmed Yasaui, Kazakhstan is home to two other World Heritage Sites: the petroglyphs within the Archaeological Landscape of Tamgaly, and a natural site, Saryarqa, which features the steppe and lakes of northern Kazakhstan. The petroglyphs (rock images or carvings) at Tamgaly date to the Bronze Age. The site shows multi-layered human development since the second millennium BCE. The natural heritage site of Saryarqa is comprised of two nature reserves—the Naurzum State Nature Reserve and Korgalzhyn State Nature Reserve—and contains endangered species and important wetlands.

Youth Culture

Young people have always been very important to the culture of Kazakhstan. They have been integral to the economic success of their families, and boys were taught to take care of the livestock. Girls were educated in domestic duties and were expected to look after younger siblings and relatives. Young people were also very important since marriage was the means by which families could forge bonds with one another, ensuring mutual economic benefits. Traditionally, young people were married at a very early age. This was especially true for daughters, who were usually married as soon as they reached puberty.

Culture and traditions drastically changed for young people during the Soviet era. Basic education became available for both boys and girls, and those who wished could attend college in larger cities or in Russia. As this happened, the tradition of early marriage began to wane. However, funding for education suffered after Kazakhstan achieved independence in the late twentieth century. Funding has since improved, and education is now compulsory. Since the country suffers from a lack of qualified professionals because of these initial educational problems, young people of both genders are strongly encouraged to go to university.

With this increase in educational opportunities, coupled with increasing urbanization of the country, youth in the early 21st century are experiencing a rapid change in lifestyle. They are becoming better educated and more financially independent than any other generation in Kazakhstan's history. Additionally, with the advent of the Internet and its associated technologies, Kazakhstani youth are also becoming more globally oriented.

SOCIETY

Transportation

Since independence, travel in and out of Kazakhstan has become remarkably easy. There are international airports in the capital Astana and the largest city, Almaty. The airport in Almaty is the busiest, with regular flights to over twenty cities throughout Asia and Europe. The airport at Astana has flights to several cities in Europe. It is also possible to travel overland to and from Kazakhstan by bus and train. Bus is the most common form of overland transportation between Kazakhstan and other Central Asian nations. Rail travel connects Kazakhstan with China and Russia, and although schedules can vary, service is generally reliable. There is also a ferry across the Caspian Sea to Azerbaijan.

Travel within Kazakhstan is also relatively simple. Domestic flights are affordable and connect most major cities. Buses are inexpensive, and are the preferred choice for medium distances. However, they can be somewhat uncomfortable, and may not be ideal for long trips. It is more comfortable to go longer distances by rail, and train travel is available between larger cities. However, some rail routes pass through Russian territory, requiring a special visa that must be purchased in advance. For shorter distances and within cities, there are several viable options. Taxis and minibuses are available for hire in most cities, and can be shared to save money. Marshrutkas, or minibuses running along fixed routes, are also popular.

Media & Communications

According to the Kazakhstani constitution, the press is allowed ample freedom. However, there have been frequent allegations that the government exerts a good deal of influence over the press. The media monitoring organization Reporters Without Borders, for instance, claims that media outlets are routinely pressured and intimidated. Journalists have been jailed and even killed in very suspicious circumstances, allegedly for daring to speak out against government corruption.

Despite press censorship and the recent closing of independent newspaper *Pravadivaya Gazeta*, there are many media outlets that operate in the country. Government newspapers include the Russian-language *Kazakhstanskaya Pravda* and the Kazakh-language *Yegemen Qazaqstan*. *Liter* and *Zhas Alash* are among the most popular Kazakh language private papers, and *Ekspress-K* is an independent paper published in Russian. The main government radio station is Kazakh Radio. Private radio stations include Europa Plus, Russkoye Radio-Aziya, and Khabar Hit FM. Television networks Eurasia TV, Khabar TV, and Kazak TV are the main government-run networks. They are complimented by a number of private television channels, such as Kazakh Channel 31 TV, and Caspionet TV.

Telecommunication infrastructure in Kazakhstan is still developing. According to a 2007 report on Internet access in the nation,

Internet users are faced with high costs. In addition, the government routinely restricts user access to social media and blogs. As of 2012, 53 percent of the population was using the Internet.

SOCIAL DEVELOPMENT

Women's Rights

The women of Kazakhstan face many serious challenges in the twenty-first century. Women have always been very important to the economy of Kazakhstani families, and unlike other Central Asian nations, Kazakhstan boasts many historical female heroes. In the past several generations, however, the role of women in society has become a divisive issue. Men traditionally held public roles and made community decisions, while women were mainly expected to be in charge of the home and family life. During the Soviet era, Moscow imposed its ideals of gender equality, which many Kazakhstani conservatives considered an offensive intrusion. Since independence, there was something of a backlash against this externally imposed ideal.

After the end of Soviet rule, Kazakhstan faced significant economic shortfalls that had several negative effects on the country's female population. Since it could not afford to maintain the educational system that the Soviets had put into place, the new government cut funds for schools. While both sexes suffered from this lack of funding, female students were put at a particular disadvantage, since educating girls was considered a secondary priority. Educational funding has since increased and several organizations are working to ensure literacy and English language skills among girls and women who came of age during the initial years of independence.

Although the situation has improved dramatically in recent years, women had great difficulty finding high paying jobs in the first decade of independence. Non-governmental organizations (NGOs) contend that women are underrepresented in higher positions, while forming the majority in lower-paying industries. There has also been a shortage of female representatives in government. As a result, women have not had peers in government to look out for their interests and concerns.

Domestic violence is a widespread problem in Kazakhstani society. Women are often abused by husbands and relatives when families experience economic difficulties. Although this abuse is illegal, the authorities are usually reluctant to do anything about it, as they feel it is a private matter. Trafficking in women is also a major problem. Kazakhstan is mainly considered a source and transit country for human trafficking. In particular, economically disadvantaged women have been tricked or coerced into working abroad as prostitutes, sometimes with the alleged complicity of government officials. The conviction of traffickers increased in 2007, and the government provided funding that same year to increase public awareness of trafficking.

GOVERNMENT

Foreign Policy

Kazakhstan was under Russian control since the middle of the eighteenth-century. When Russia formed the Soviet Union, Kazakhstan became a satellite state dependent on the government in Moscow. During this period, it was almost entirely closed off from the outside world. Kazakhstan achieved independence in 1991 when the Soviet Union collapsed. Since gaining independence, Kazakhstan has made great efforts to open itself to the outside world. Although the country has faced serious allegations of political corruption and human rights abuses, it has largely been successful in its attempts to develop normalized relations with the world community.

Part of the reason that Kazakhstan has enjoyed such success in normalizing relations with the outside world is the fact that it had many nuclear weapons at the end of the Soviet era. Through its willingness to halt its nuclear weapons program, it gained the confidence of the United States, which has been a strong ally ever since. Kazakhstan and the US have a policy of mutual cooperation with regard to military and economic issues. Kazakhstan supports the US-led "war on terror," and has diplomatically backed the campaigns in Afghanistan and Iraq. As a regional neighbor to Afghanistan, Kazakhstan has actively assisted war and rebuilding efforts in that country, guaranteeing continued financial assistance from the US.

Kazakhstan's foreign policy strategy of reaching out to the US and other Western powers is based on its desire to fully integrate with the world community. It joined the United Nations (UN) in 1992 and holds membership in the Commonwealth of Independent States (CIS) and the Organization for Security and Cooperation in Europe (OSCE). Kazakhstan has managed to establish friendly relations with most of the world's nations, including those of Central Asia and Russia. Given its long history of Russian domination, Kazakhstan had been long wary of slipping back under Russian influence. In recent years relations with Russia have grown increasingly close.

Kazakhstan has pursued a liberal economic policy, and embraced the concept of globalized trade as it diplomatically joined the world community. Since the country has ample fuel and metal reserves, but relatively little development capital, this policy has been a prudent way for Kazakhstan to increase its national wealth. In fact, Kazakhstan has emerged as a regional leader in pursuing global economic integration. In 2005, it proposed a Central Asian organization designed to further regional investment and economic cooperation, the Central Asian Union. In 2011, Kazakhstan signed an agreement with Russia and Belarus to establish a Eurasian Union trade zone by 2015, and in 2012, signed an agreement with Russia and Kyrgyzstan to build a hydroelectric power plant.

Human Rights Profile

International human rights laws insist that states respect civil and political rights, and also promote an individual's economic, social and cultural rights. The United Nations Universal Declaration on Human Rights (UDHR) is recognized as the standard for international human rights. Its authors sought the counsel of the world's great thinkers, philosophers, and religious leaders, and were careful to create a document that reflects the core values of every world culture. (To read this document or view the articles relating to cultural human rights, visit: http://www.udhr.org/UDHR/default.htm.)

Since achieving independence, Kazakhstan has done an excellent job of integrating into the global community, but continues to face many serious human rights problems. The country's constitution guarantees free and fair elections, but there are consistent allegations that this does not actually take place. President Nursultan Nazarbayev (1940–), who has served as Kazakhstan's de facto ruler since the Soviet era, has established such a firm grasp on power that he is in effect leader for life. Opposition candidates are routinely disqualified from elections on technicalities, and the most powerful rival party was overtaken by those loyal to Nazarbayev. The president has deflected criticism of his administration by suggesting that a full democracy would be too disruptive, and that he plans a more gradual approach to establishing a representative government.

Freedom of speech is significantly curtailed in Kazakhstan, and the state routinely uses violence as a means of social control. Opposition voices in the press are routinely silenced with threats, violence, and imprisonment. For instance, in 2012, Vladimir Kozlov, a prominent opposition leader was sentenced to seven years in prison on charges of orchestrating unrest among oil workers. As a result, self-censorship is widely practiced. Additionally, when opposition political groups do meet, they are constantly at risk of being beaten or arrested by police. Corruption is also rampant among police and other authorities, and there is little recourse for those people who have been arrested on politically motivated charges. Despite international pressure to cease using torture as a means of social control, it remains a major human rights issue. Occasionally, mistreatment leads to the death of prisoners in government custody. Although the government has in theory agreed to address this problem, it has taken few concrete steps to discourage law enforcement officers from committing acts of violence against those in custody.

Adam Berger

Bibliography

Aitken, Jonathan. *Kazakhstan: Surprises and Stereotypes after 20 Years of Independence.* New York: Continuum, 2012.

Blackmon, Pamela. *In the Shadow of Russia: Reform in Kazakhstan and Uzbekistan.* East Lansing, MI: Michigan State University Press, 2011.

Bonora, Gian Luca. *Guide to Kazakhstan: Sites of Faith, Sites of History.* Torino: Umberto Allemandi, 2010.

Dilip, Hiro. *Inside Central Asia.* New York: Overlook Duckworth, 2009.

Kassymova, Didar, Zhanat Kundakbeyeva, and Ustina Markus. *Historical Dictionary of Kazakhstan.* Lanham, MD: Scarecrow Press, 2012.

Olcott, Martha Brill. *Kazakhstan: Unfulfilled Promise?* Washington, DC: Carnegie Endowment for International Peace, 2010.

Salhani, Claude. *Islam without a Veil: Kazakhstan's Path of Modernization.* Washington, DC: Potomac Books, 2011.

Stark, Soren, et al., eds. *Nomads and Networks: The Ancient Art and Culture of Kazakhstan.* Princeton, NJ: Princeton University Press, 2012.

Tredinnick, Jeremy. *An Illustrated History of Kazakhstan.* Hong Kong: Odyssey, 2014.

Works Cited

"Kazakhstan." *Alliance for International Women's Rights.* http://www.aiwr.org/kazakhstan

Amnesty International. Kazakhstan: Summary of Concerns on Torture and Ill-Treatment." November 2008. http://www.amnesty.org/en/library/asset/EUR57/001/2008/en/1b06381e-8bd5-11dd-8e5e-43ea85d15a69/eur570012008en.html

"Country Profile: Kazakhstan". 7 August 2008. *BBC News.* <http://news.bbc.co.uk/2/hi/asia-pacific/country_profiles/1298071.stm>.

"Foreign Policy". 17 October 2008. *Embassy of Kazakhstan.* <http://kazakhembus.com/index.php?page=foreign-policy>.

"Profile: Kazakhstan." *Kwintessential.* http://www.kwintessential.co.uk/resources/global-etiquette/kazakhstan.html

Loy, Lily. *Countries of the World: Kazakhstan.* Milwaukee: Gareth Stevens, 2005.

Mayhew, Bradly, Greg Bloom, John Noble, and Dean Starnes. *Central Asia.* Oakland, CA: Lonely Planet, 2007.

Pang, Guek-Cheng. *Cultures of the World: Kazakhstan.* New York: Marshall Cavendish, 2001

Reporters Without Borders. "Profile: Kazakhstan." http://www.rsf.org/print.php3?id_article=25492

U.S. Department of State. "Country Reports on Human Rights Practices: Kazakhstan." 23 February 2001. http://www.state.gov/g/drl/rls/hrrpt/2000/eur/798.htm

U.S. Department of State. "Country Reports on Human Rights Practices: Kazakhstan." 8 March 2006. <http://www.state.gov/g/drl/rls/hrrpt/2005/61656.htm>.

Ancient pictograms discovered in Kyrgyzstan/Stock photo © MisoKnitl

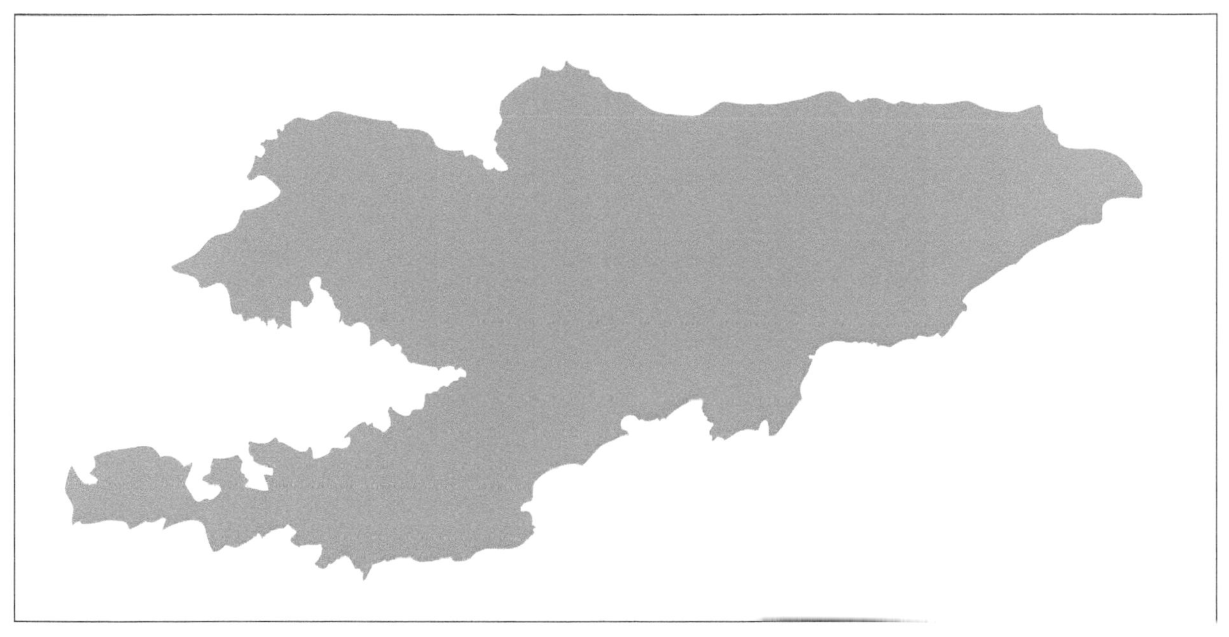

Kyrgyzstan

Introduction

Kyrgyzstan, officially the Kyrgyz Republic, is a small Central Asian republic bordered by China, Kazakhstan, Tajikistan, and Uzbekistan. Long dominated by Russia, the country gained independence from the Soviet Union in 1991. Kyrgyzstan faces numerous challenges related to political reform and economic development. In early 2005, a popular movement ousted the country's authoritarian president. A return to civil unrest in April 2010 led to another change in leadership. Since then, the country has seen its first peaceful transfer of power with the election of Almazbek Atambaev in 2011; however, systemic corruption, sectarian violence, and rampant human rights abuses have all cast a shadow of uncertainty on Kyrgyzstan's democratic future.

GENERAL INFORMATION

Official Language: Kyrgyz and Russian
Population: 5,604,212 (2014 estimate)
Currency: Kyrgyzstani som
Coins: Subdivided into 100 tyiyn, the som is available in coin denominations of 10 and 50 tyiyn and 1, 3, and 5 som; coin denominations of 1 tyiyn and 10 som are minted, but rarely used.
Land Area: 191,801 square kilometers (74,054 square miles)
Water Area: 8,150 square kilometers (3,146 square miles)
National Anthem: "National Anthem of the Kyrgyz Republic"
Capital: Bishkek
Time Zone: GMT +6
Flag Description: The flag of Kyrgyzstan features a red field, or background, with a golden, 40-rayed sun in the middle. Centered in the sun is a red ring with two sets of three red lines crossing within it, intersecting just above center. The design represents the crown, or roof, of a yurt, the traditional tent-like structure of the country's nomadic population. The flag and its colors are symbolic of various ideals, namely valor, peace, and prosperity, while the sun's 40 rays represent the 40 tribes that were united, according to legend, to form the historic Kyrgyz nation.

Population

Kyrgyzstan has a young, growing population; approximately 28 percent of the population is below the age of fifteen (2014 estimate). Life expectancy at birth is seventy-four years for females and sixty-five years for males (2014

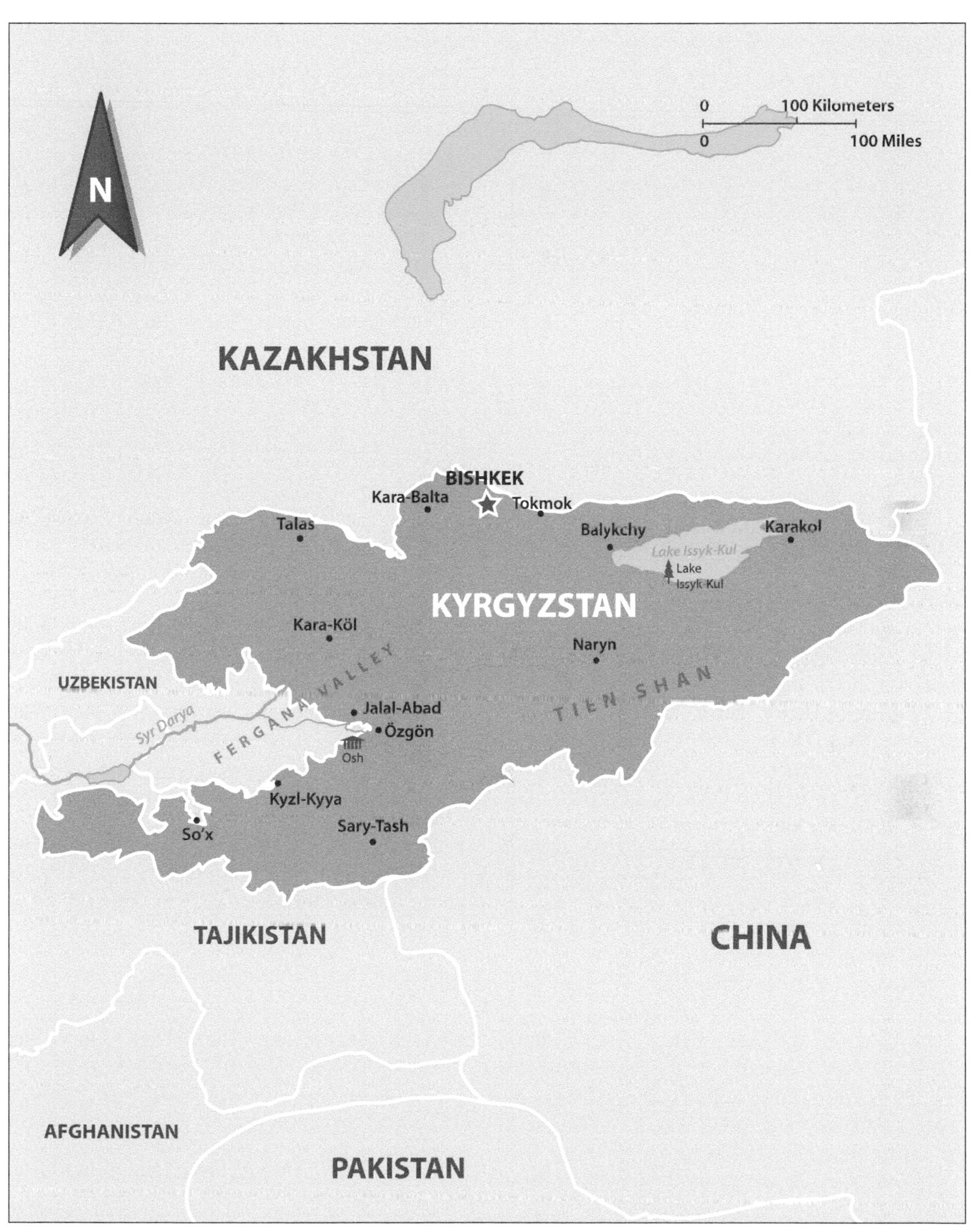
N
0 100 Kilometers
0 100 Miles
KAZAKHSTAN
BISHKEK
Kara-Balta
Tokmok
Talas
Balykchy
Karakol
Lake Issyk-Kul
Lake Issyk-Kul
KYRGYZSTAN
Kara-Köl
Naryn
UZBEKISTAN
FERGANA VALLEY
TIEN SHAN
Syr Darya
Jalal-Abad
Özgön
Osh
Kyzl-Kyya
So'x
Sary-Tash
TAJIKISTAN
CHINA
AFGHANISTAN
PAKISTAN

Principal Cities by Population (2012 estimate unless otherwise noted):

- Bishkek (977,204)
- Osh (246,881)
- Celalabat (81,280)
- Karakol (68,562)
- Tokmok (59,352)
- Kara-Balta (53,573)
- Uzgen (49,400) (2009 estimate)
- Balykchy (42,200) (2009 estimate)

estimate). The population, with an average density of roughly 27 persons per square kilometer (71 persons per square mile), is densest in the northern Chu Valley and the southwestern Fergana Valley. Roughly 65 percent of the population lives in rural areas.

Bishkek, the largest city, is home to 977,204 people (2012 estimate); unofficial numbers for the metropolitan area place the population at over 1 million, however. Bishkek is famous for being one of the greenest cities in the world, let alone Central Asia, due to the cityscape's numerous parks, gardens, and tree-lined boulevards.

The population of Bishkek has increased steadily through the late 20th and early 21st centuries. However, the political instability following the Tulip Rebellion of 2005, in which the government and president were overthrown, resulted in many residents fleeing the capital. In addition, ethnic tensions between Kyrgyzs, Russians, Koreans, and other smaller European populations caused many Russians and Koreans to leave the city in 2005.

The country's ethnic composite changed in the post-independence period, as many Russians and Germans emigrated. Kyrgyzs account for 70 percent of the population. Identification with a specific clan is still important in Kyrgyz society. There are three broad clan groups, which are in turn divided into sub-clans.

Uzbeks and Russians are the largest minorities, accounting for 14 percent and 7.7 percent of the population, respectively. Uzbeks are concentrated in the Fergana Valley, while Russians generally live in urban areas. Other minorities include Dungans, Ukrainians, and Uygurs.

Languages

Kyrgyz and Russian are the two official languages of Kyrgyzstan, the latter being the language of inter-ethnic communication. Kyrgyz is a Turkic language of the Altaic family. During the Soviet era, it lost many native speakers. Since independence, there has been a concerted effort among ethnic Kyrgyz to re-establish their language. It is now written in the Cyrillic alphabet, which will eventually yield to the Latin alphabet.

Native People & Ethnic Groups

The Kyrgyz settled the region in the 16th century. Only with the downfall of the Soviet Union have they been able to promote their interests and fully protect their culture. The encroachment of the Russians, beginning in the 19th century, disrupted their traditional nomadic lifestyle and distanced them from their religion, language, and history.

Some ethnic tensions exist between the majority Kyrgyz and other minorities, particularly the Uzbeks, who are concentrated in and around the western city of Osh in the Fergana Valley. Following independence, these tensions erupted in incidences of bloody conflict between local Uzbeks and Kyrgyz over housing and land.

As of the 2009 census, Kyrgyz account for over two-thirds of the population. Uzbeks and Russians are the largest minorities, accounting for roughly 14 percent and 7.7 percent of the population, respectively.

Religions

Sunni Islam has been the dominant religion of the Kyrgyz majority since the 19th century, though religion was suppressed, sometimes brutally, during the Soviet era. There has been a revival of religious sentiment throughout the country, but only in the more traditional south has it become extreme; the government has intervened militarily in the region, in response to attacks by radical Muslim groups. In some northern areas, the people incorporate elements of totemism and shamanism into their religious practices. The country's Russians are most often Russian Orthodox.

Climate

Landlocked Kyrgyzstan has a continental climate. Outside of the steep valleys, the country is generally sunny. It has two main climatic regions: the mountains and the lowlands. The lower mountains are temperate, whereas at the highest elevation, a polar climate allows for glaciers and year-round snow-capped peaks.

The upper elevations receive the most precipitation, ranging from 180 to 1,000 millimeters (seven to 40 inches) annually. Here, the average temperature is –28° Celsius (–18° Fahrenheit) in January, and 5° Celsius (41° Fahrenheit) in July. The lowlands of the Fergana and Chu valleys have a subtropical climate and considerably less precipitation. The January average is –4° Celsius (25° Fahrenheit), and the average July temperature is 27° Celsius (81° Fahrenheit).

Kyrgyzstan is prone to strong earthquakes, particularly in the Naryn Basin. An earthquake could in turn cause flooding if one of the river's dams were damaged. Mudslides have increased as more topsoil becomes eroded.

Bishkek has a continental climate; temperatures vary greatly between the seasons. Summer temperatures are often above 37° Celsius (100° Fahrenheit), and winters can be as cold as –28° Celsius (–20° Fahrenheit); the average annual temperature is –1° Celsius (30° Fahrenheit). The rainy season lasts from March through June.

ENVIRONMENT & GEOGRAPHY

Topography

Kyrgyzstan has a mountainous terrain and generally high elevation, with over 90 percent of the country surpassing 1,500 meters (4,921 feet) above sea level. The two main mountain systems which dominate Kyrgyzstan are the Tian Shan and Pamir ranges, extending east to west. From these two respective ranges extend the Alai and the Trans-Alai Mountains. Victory Peak, known in Kyrgyz as Jenish Chokosu, is the highest point in the country and in the entire Tian Shan range. It rises 7,439 meters (24,406 feet) in the northeast near the border with China. Characteristic of geographically young mountains, Kyrgyzstan's ranges have many sharp peaks.

Kyrgyzstan has more than 2,000 lakes, many of them small and most of them at high elevations. The shrinking, saline Ysyk-Kol is the largest lake, located in the northeast at 1,607 meters (5,273 feet) above sea level; it is 170 kilometers (105 miles) long and 70 kilometers (43 miles) wide. Other large lakes include Song-Kol and Chatyr-Kol, in the Naryn Basin.

Numerous streams and rivers run from the mountains and down through deep valleys into the lowlands. None of the rivers are navigable, since they are generally short and fast. Most of them are tributaries of the Naryn River, which has its source in the Tian Shan Mountains and crosses Kyrgyzstan, eventually converging with another river in Uzbekistan and forming the Syr Darya. The other large river of Kyrgyzstan is the Chu, which flows through the capital.

There are two fertile lowlands in Kyrgyzstan: the Fergana Valley in the west and the Chu Valley in the north. Supported by the country's major rivers, they have been extensively cultivated.

Bishkek, the capital, is located in the central-northern part of the country of Kyrgyzstan, over 90 percent of which is covered by the Tian Shan mountain range. Bishkek is located in the Chui Valley, at the base of the Ala-Too Mountains, a western range of the Tian Shan. The city sits at the intersection of the Chu River with the Bolshoy Chuysky Canal (or the Great Canal) and the Alamedin and Alaarcha rivers, both tributaries of the Chu. The city lies at an altitude of roughly 750 meters (2,460 feet).

Plants & Animals

Approximately 5 percent of Kyrgyzstan's territory is covered by forest. Among the species of trees are pine, juniper, birch, and spruce. The country is also home to the largest natural growth walnut forest in the world. In the mountains, high altitude meadows ideal for grazing are common.

Marco Polo sheep, common to Kyrgyzstan

The forests and mountains provide habitats for a wide array of animals, including wild boar, lynx, ibex, badger, muskrat, gopher, fox, antelope, Marco Polo sheep, brown bear, and Siberian deer. Migratory birds settle around the country's many lakes, which contain large populations of fish. Endangered animals include the elusive snow leopard and the tiger. Though the animals are protected by law, poaching and smuggling is still a problem.

CUSTOMS & COURTESIES

Greetings

One common greeting in Kyrgyz is the Muslim phrase "As-salamu alaykum" ("Peace be upon you"). Young people sometimes greet each other with "Kandai" ("How are you?"). Handshakes are customary, and women may kiss each other on the cheek. However, it is a good idea to let the woman initiate the greeting, since different Kyrgyz women may have different preferences depending on their religious beliefs. (Islam is the dominant religion in Kyrgyzstan.) When greeting, one should generally make eye contact. It is also considered polite to inquire about a person's health, family, work, or studies.

When addressing someone of the same age or younger, it is acceptable to use only the person's first name. When speaking to elders or those in a more senior position, it is common to use their first name, plus their patronymic name in the Russian style. In Russian, this would be "Asan Bolotovich" (which means "Asan, son of Bolot") or "Ainura Maratovna" (which means "Ainura, daughter of Marat"). Last names are used on very formal occasions, when addressing one's superior, or when meeting someone for the first time. When addressing older colleagues, it is also not unusual for Kyrgyzstanis to add "baike" or "ake" ("older brother") to the ends of the names of male colleagues, and "edje" ("older sister") for those of female colleagues.

Gestures & Etiquette

As in many Muslim countries, eating or offering food with the left hand is technically considered impolite, although many Kyrgyz do not pay strict attention to this rule. At the beginning or end of meals, and when passing mosques or mausoleums, it is common to make a gesture asking for God's blessing, called omin. This involves lifting the hands in front of the face with the palms facing inward and then drawing the hands straight down. Many Kyrgyz will make this gesture whenever they pass a mosque, even while driving.

Pointing at someone is considered impolite in Kyrgyz culture. Rather, to indicate something, one should gesture with the palm up and all fingers extended. To beckon someone, one should extend the hand palm up and curl all fingers inward. Making a fist at someone or showing one's middle finger are considered offensive gestures. Humor is appreciated in Kyrgyz culture, but sarcasm should be avoided. It is also considered a friendly gesture for visitors to try to learn a few words of Kyrgyz. Strong public displays of emotion are not very common, although Kyrgyzstanis will be very warm and loving toward family members. Kyrgyzstanis tend to dress very neatly and formally on all occasions.

Eating/Meals

Kyrgyz people typically eat four or five times a day, with most of the meals composed of small snacks like tea and bread, and one being the large main meal. In the south, meals are often served on a long embroidered cloth laid on the floor, called a dastarkon. Guests sit cross-legged around the cloth on embroidered cushions called tushaks. The dastarkon is treated like a table and never stepped on.

Kyrgyz families are very friendly and will often extend invitations to visitors to eat with them. Before eating, the host will customarily pour warm water over the guests' hands and give them a towel. The guest of honor sits at the place farthest from the door, called tyor, and is traditionally served first. Men usually sit on the right-hand side and women on the left. The host sits by the door, and pours tea and passes food to the guests. Due to Kyrgyzstan's Muslim culture, meals usually end with an omin, a way of giving thanks for the meal.

Visiting

It is not polite to visit before noon, but after that all hours are considered open for visiting, and visitors generally do not need to inform their hosts when they are coming. When visiting, it is polite to bring a small gift such as a cake, a bottle of wine, or fruit, as well as a present for the children if there are any. People usually remove their shoes, although it is best to check with the host first. Often guests are given a pair of slippers to wear, called tapochki.

During visits, guests will be offered food and drink, such as bread and tea, and it is considered polite to accept. Visitors may be encouraged to eat and drink a great deal.

At meals, guests will often be asked to give a toast. It is common to offer toasts to the host, the other guests, and world peace. At special dinners and celebrations, visitors may be given heavy embroidered mats to sit on called tushaks. Since tushaks are relatively expensive, the number of tushaks a family owns is an indicator of their wealth and status.

LIFESTYLE

Family

Traditionally, Kyrgyzstanis have a very broad view of family, with aunts, uncles, cousins and grandparents in addition to the nuclear family all playing a role in daily life. More recently, however, due to urbanization and economic issues, nuclear families are becoming more common. In 2007, an estimated 60.8 percent of families were composed of either one or two parents with children or of a childless couple, while only 26.2 percent of families were extended. Although both parents usually work to support the family, Kyrgyzstan experienced a resurgence of interest in traditional gender roles after Soviet rule ended, and so most domestic labor and childcare is performed by women. Daycare institutions are few, and children are often left alone or in the care of older siblings.

Housing

Most modern housing in urban areas is in the Soviet architectural style, featuring long rows of apartment blocks in which each family has a two- or three-room apartment. Some people also live in houses, usually consisting of a single story with a peaked roof extending over the walls. Houses are encircled by fences, and might also include an animal pen, an outdoor kitchen, a storage shed, gardens, and fruit trees. Houses can be very large and feature an entire extended family. Many houses include a separate room for gatherings with two alcoves on the sides, in which are decorated bureaus displaying the family's embroidered pillows and sleeping mats.

In Kyrgyz homes, the banya is the sauna room where people bathe. Many homes do not have hot running water. In the banya, there is one tub of hot water and a smaller tub of cool water; when bathing one mixes a little of the cool water and hot water together in a separate basin to use for washing and rinsing. Water is typically heated for baths once a week.

In the north, which has been influenced by Russian culture, furniture such as tables, chairs, beds, and sofas are used. In the south, where Uzbek influences are more prominent, homes do not include much furniture. Families eat around a tablecloth spread on the floor, called a dastarkon, and sit on mats called tushaks. They may sleep on several tushaks stacked together, which are then folded and put away during the day.

Food

Kyrgyz food has been influenced by the culinary traditions of Russian, Dungan (Muslims of Chinese origin), Uzbek, and even Korean culture, as well as by the necessities of a nomadic lifestyle. Animal products like meat and yogurt play a central role, and tea is a staple. To serve tea, the host holds the teacup in the right hand while supporting the right elbow with the left hand, a gesture that signifies respect. Bread, such as fried bread called borsok, is common and symbolically important. Bread is never set on the ground or thrown away; instead, leftover bread is given as fodder to animals. Since Kyrgyzstan is a predominantly Muslim country, eating pork is taboo, and mutton (domestic sheep), goat, and horse are more common. Vodka is often served with meals.

One national dish of Uzbek origin is plov, which is fried rice mixed with onions, carrots, red pepper, caraway seeds, and meat. In the north, noodles mixed with onions, tomatoes, and cabbage in a spicy broth (called lagman) and dumplings filled with onion, meat, or pumpkin (called manti) are common. Kumyss is a traditional, mildly alcoholic drink made of fermented mare's milk, available only in summertime when the mares are nursing their young. Bozo is a carbonated drink made from fermented millet, which is drunk in the winter.

A special national dish with its own ritual is besh barmak, which means "five fingers" because the dish is eaten with the hands. It is made with sheep or horsemeat and eaten on holidays such as Ramadan (the Islamic month of fasting). The preparation of besh barmak is very elaborate. The animal is slaughtered and its blood drained, and then the meat and innards are prepared and the intestines are braided. First, guests drink a soup made from boiling the meat and organs with vegetables and pieces of fat in an iron pot called a kazan. Then the sheep's head is roasted and served to the most honored guests, such as elders, teachers, and other respected figures. Next, chunks of meat, fat, liver, and organs are distributed among the guests according to their status. The rest of the meat is then tossed with noodles and a little broth and served out of a communal bowl, out of which guests eat with their hands.

Life's Milestones

Traditional Kyrgyz weddings are music-filled, and can last as long as three days. In the weeks before the ceremony, the bride and her family spend many hours cooking food for the wedding feasts. On the day of the ceremony, the groom and guests feast in a special yurt while the bride and bridesmaids wait upstairs. After much singing, the groom is finally allowed into the house, where the bride and groom exchange vows and prayers. The groom then haggles with the bride's family over the price of a slaughtered sheep and other food the groom must buy. This is followed by more feasting and dancing. It is also common for the wedding party to drive to the site of a local monument, where all the guests take pictures with the bride and groom.

To celebrate a birth, the parents of the newborn will give their friends and neighbors a kind of yellow butter called sary mai, which is kept in the stomach of a slaughtered lamb, sheep, or calf. Sary mai is given first to the baby, and next to the oldest guest as a sign of respect. Funerals traditionally last 40 days and members of the deceased's family often stay to mourn for the entire period. Once a week during this time, family and friends will gather to show appreciation for the deceased at the family's house.

CULTURAL HISTORY

Art

As a nomadic community, traditional Kyrgyz people did not have room to carry things that were not necessary or functional. Because of this, artistic expression in traditional society was focused on decorating and beautifying items of daily life. One of the best examples of this is Kyrgyz felt making.

To make felt—traditionally from sheep, goats, or even camels—wool is washed, dried, and then laid out flat on a large piece of animal hide, where it is whipped with willow sticks. Next, the felt is laid on top of a reed mat, sprinkled with hot water, and rolled up in the mat to form a long cylinder. This cylinder is attached to the back of a horse and dragged overland for as long as an hour; as it is dragged people step on it continuously to further flatten it. Then the wool is unrolled, sprinkled with more water, and rolled up again. This process is repeated until the wool is sufficiently compressed.

Kyrgyz rugs, called shyrdaks, are fine examples of such felt craftsmanship. These rugs are made of colorful felt from sheep or goat's wool. They are decorated with symbolic designs of birds, plants, animals, and cosmological, religious, or historical icons. Many symbols have been passed down through generations. Shyrdaks are often hung on the inner walls of the yurt to beautify it and keep it warm.

In addition to felt making, Kyrgyz weaving and embroidery are also sophisticated forms of traditional Kyrgyz artistry. Embroidery, called sayma, uses woolen or cotton threads and features complex designs of animals and other symbols. Kyrgyz families are very proud of their embroidered wall hangings. Weaving is done outside on a wooden loom, usually by two women working together. Three of the most common types of woven cloth are terme, kadjary, and besh keshte, which vary in their color, intricacy, and labor-intensiveness. Felt making, weaving, and embroidery are all activities usually performed by women.

Architecture

The traditional Kyrgyz dwelling is the yurt, called boz-ui, made of a willow frame covered by decorated wool felt. The yurt can be easily folded up and transported. The top of the yurt surrounding the hole where the smoke escapes is called the tunduk. The tunduk has become a symbol of Kyrgyz culture and family, and is featured in the center of the Kyrgyz flag. Traditionally, the right side of the yurt is considered the women's side, and the left is the men's. The yurt is now used mostly for celebrations and by shepherds during the summer.

Drama

Kyrgyz cinema began late but has gradually become a strong presence in the country's contemporary arts. In 1955, the Russian-made feature film *Salanat* was produced, and the first Kyrgyz-made film, *My Mistake*, came out in 1958. A leading director of this early period was Tolomush Okeyev (1935–2001), whose minimalist films such as *The Fierce One* (1963) are centered on landscapes and focus on environmental and political themes. One of the most widely known films from contemporary Kyrgyzstan is *Beshkempir* (The Adopted Son, 1998), about an abandoned child raised by five women. It was directed by Aktan Abdykalykov (1957–) and won the Locarno Film Festival's Silver Leopard Prize in 1998. Recent notable films include *My Brother, Silk Road* (2001), directed by Marat Sarulu (1957–), which explores themes of innocence and civilization, and traditional Kyrgyz culture and Soviet influence.

Music

The komuz (which means "instrument"), a three-stringed lute, is the most widely used traditional musical instrument in the country. Many of the famous epics of Kyrgyz culture, traditionally told at holidays, ceremonies, and important social gatherings, are often accompanied by the komuz. Other common instruments include the kyl kiak (bowed string instrument held upright on the lap) and the timur komuz (mouth harp). Two musical traditions are predominant in Kyrgyz culture: instrumental music called kyy, and vocal music called yr. Yr is characterized by the ability of the singers to hold a note for an extended period of time. One of the best-known contemporary singers in this traditional style is Salamat Sadikova.

One of Kyrgyzstan's most famous akyns, or traveling storytellers, was Toktogul Satylganov (1864–1933). Growing up under the Russian czarist government, Toktogul (as he is most commonly called) wrote of the hardships and suffering by Kyrgyz peasants under czarist rule. Due to his songs praising freedom and criticizing the government, he was exiled to Siberia, returning to Kyrgyzstan in 1903. Many of his songs after his return are nationalistic, and he was lauded as a social hero by the Soviet government because of his portrayal of and empathy with class struggles. Toktogul is also credited with the inception of Kyrgyz Soviet literature.

Literature

In Kyrgyz culture, the telling of epic poems is considered the epitome of skill and creativity, and epic poetry from Kyrgyzstan is considered one of the greatest examples of this genre worldwide. Traditionally, poems, ballads, and stories were told by traveling minstrels, called akyns, or Kyrgyz epic tellers. Akyns memorized epic tales and sang them to their audiences, along with their own personal poetic innovations. They also tailored their stories to fit their audience. For example, the akyn would expand the sections that discuss Islam for a more religious audience. Akyns were also competitive, and often competed against each other in contests of spontaneous composition, some of which could last for hours. In 2003, the United Nations Educational, Scientific and Cultural Organization (UNESCO) recognized the "Art of the Akyns" as one of the Masterpieces of the Oral and Intangible Heritage of Humanity.

One of the most culturally important and historically significant epic poems of Kyrgyzstan is the *Manas* trilogy. Named for the legendary father of the Kyrgyz people, it is told in a cycle of three legends, which together are 20 times longer than Homer's famous *Odyssey*. Storytellers who chant the *Manas* are called manaschi. The first section of the tale celebrates the bravery and deeds of Manas, a great khan thought to have lived in the eighth century who united and defended the Kyrgyz people. The second section celebrates the exploits of his son, and the third tells the tale of his grandson. The *Manas* epic has remained entrenched in Kyrgyz culture and serves as a rallying point for Kyrgyz nationalism. Contemporary Kyrgyzstani writers continue to explore it in their writing, and the figure of Manas is commonly featured in public works of art. UNESCO declared 1995 "The Year of the Manas" in celebration of the millennial birthday of this epic poem. In addition to the tale of Manas, more than 40 other well-known epics exist in Kyrgyz culture.

One of Kyrgyzstan's most famous storytellers was Toktogul Satylganov, who wrote of the hardships and suffering by Kyrgyz peasants under czarist rule. Due to his songs praising freedom and criticizing the government, he was exiled to Siberia, returning to Kyrgyzstan in 1903. Many of his songs after his return are nationalistic, and he was lauded as a social hero by the Soviet government because of his portrayal of and empathy with class struggles. Toktogul is also credited with the inception of Kyrgyz Soviet literature.

Most arts were subsidized by the government under Soviet rule. During this period, writers like Chinghiz Aitmatov (1928–2008) rose to prominence. Aitmatov is considered the dominant figure in contemporary Kyrgyzstani literature. His many novels fuse elements of folklore with contemporary settings, and the relationship between animals and the human protagonists often feature prominently. He wrote in both Russian and Kyrgyz, and his most popular works include *Jamila* (1958) and *The Day Lasts More Than a Hundred Years* (1980). During the late 1980s he served as an advisor to Soviet leader Mikhail Gorbachev (1931–). He also served as a diplomatic envoy to various nations and international organizations, such as the North Atlantic Treaty Organization (NATO) and UNESCO, under both the Soviet and independent Kyrgyzstan governments.

CULTURE

Arts & Entertainment

Most arts were subsidized by the government under Soviet rule. After independence, a lack of funding caused many art institutions in Kyrgyzstan to close. Artists could not depend on the government for their living, and the production of, and respect for, art declined. One example of this general decline was that many of the bronze statues from Bishkek's outdoor sculpture museum were stolen, presumably to be sold for scrap metal. Kyrgyzstan's art scene gradually revived in the early 21st century. Kyrgyzstani artists often focus on the many diverse layers that make up contemporary Kyrgyzstani culture—a mix of Uzbek, Kazahk, and Kyrgyz traditions, nomadic and shamanic roots, recent history under Soviet rule, and present-day struggles with independence and building a democratic and capitalist society. Kyrgyzstan's place in Central Asia, as well as broader questions of the purpose and identity of the region in the modern world, also figure prominently.

The visual art scene in Kyrgyzstan has also begun to develop in recent years. The Bishkek International Exhibition of Contemporary Art is held biannually in the capital, in the tunnels under Ala-Too Central Square, which in Soviet times served as the headquarters of the local KGB (the Soviet secret police force). Past themes include ideas which express the state of flux and disorientation in contemporary Central Asian society. Among Kyrgyzstani artists, video installation art has become especially popular. Gulnara Kasmalieva (1960–) and Muratbek Djumaliev (1965–), an artist duo based in Bishkek, create video performance pieces with minimal narrative, focusing instead on imagery to evoke both poetry and politics. Their latest work, *A New Silk Road: Algorithm of Survival and Hope* (2006), debuted at the Art Institute of Chicago in February 2007 and explores the "new Silk Road" between Kyrgyzstan and China.

Although Western and Russian music are popular among Kyrgyzstani youth, traditional music still has many fans. Under Soviet rule, the folk music of the various Soviet republics was adapted to fulfill a political agenda. As a result, traditional Kyrgyz music was infused with Soviet themes. Many traditional practices fell out of use, such as solo performances and the oral teaching tradition between master and disciple. In recent years many Kyrgyzstani musicians have worked to revive these traditional forms. The music ensemble Tengir-Too plays traditional mountain music of Kyrgyzstan, called küü, which tells a story through instrumental musical performance and gestures. The group also performs traditional solo pieces of storytelling accompanied by music, which are performed by akyns.

Kyrgyz play many games that revolve around horsemanship. Ulak Tartysh is the local form of buzkashi, a rough sport involving two teams of horse riders who compete to make a goal with a salt-filled goat carcass. Horse races, archery, and wrestling are also common sports.

Another tradition which is very much alive in Kyrgyzstan is staying at a jailoo during the summer months. Families journey into the mountains with their herds, which they put to pasture, and live in portable nomadic tents called boz ui. Games and festivities are central to this annual occasion.

Cultural Sites & Landmarks

Osh, Kyrgyzstan's second-largest city, is one of the oldest cities in Central Asia. Due to its proximity to the border of Uzbekistan, many ethnically Uzbek people live in Osh, and the city's culture has been influenced accordingly. The city's enormous market is the largest, and considered one of the best, bazaars in Central Asia. One of the few surviving statues of Vladimir Lenin (1870–1924) also stands in a city square in Osh. The mountain in the center of the city is called Suleiman-Too (Solomon's Mountain), as the 10th-century Muslim prophet Suleyman is said to be buried there. After Mecca and Medina, Solomon's Mountain is the third most revered holy site for Central Asian Muslims.

Karakol is a small town with many fascinating cultural sights. Tucked between Lake Issyk-Kul and the Tian Shan and Terskey Alatau Mountains, Karakol is a gateway to Kyrgyzstan's many natural wonders or recreations. The architecture of Karakol reflects many of Kyrgyzstan's different cultural influences. One example is the Chinese-style mosque, distinctive for its red walls and sloping turquoise roof and minaret. It was built in the first decade of the 20th century, and is held together without the use of metal nails. The town is also home to the ornate Russian Orthodox Holy Trinity Cathedral, which was used as a club during Soviet rule, but which now functions once again as a church. The town also has many Russian-style wooden cottages painted with brightly colored trim. Karakol is also the site of the weekly Mal Bazaar, or animal market.

Close to Karakol is Lake Issyk-Kul, called "the pearl of Kyrgyzstan" for its beauty. Issyk-Kul is the second-highest navigable lake and the ninth largest lake in the world. Due in part to the many hot springs which feed it, the lake never freezes (the name Issyk-Kul translates as "hot water"). The dark blue water, red rocks, and snowcapped peaks of the lake make it one of the most scenic places in Central Asia. Historically, the lake was a central stopping point on the Silk Road. The remains of a 14th-century Armenian monastery and other historical artifacts, such as the world's oldest extant coins, have been discovered in the lake's vicinity. Additionally, in 2007, Kyrgyz and Russian archaeologists announced that they had discovered a 2,500-year old city whose foundations lie at the bottom of the lake. Evidence of bronze work and other recovered artifacts from the city indicate that the civilization which built it was highly advanced.

Bishkek is considered one of the world's most attractive capitals, famous for its parks and gardens. Dubovy Park, in particular, is located in the city center, and contains numerous cafés, sculptures and an outdoor gallery. The famous Erkindik Statue, or Statue of Freedom, which commemorates Kyrgyz independence, is also found near the park. At the city center, in Victory Square, is a World War II monument built in 1984; the monument features a marble statue of a woman ever vigilant over an eternal flame.

Another famous landmark in Bishkek is the White House, a white marble palace that serves as the seat of Kyrgyzstan's government offices. The president's office is located in the White House, and it is where the Parliament of the Republic meets. The palace lies west of City Square, where the changing of the National Guard occurs.

Bishkek is also known for its many bazaars or open markets. They include the Osh Bazaar, located over a mile from the city center; the Ortosay Bazaar, located just south of the city center; and the Alamedin Bazaar, located in northeastern Bishkek. Dordoy Bazaar is the city's largest market and is open on weekends. It is located north of the center of the city.

Libraries & Museums

The capital is also home to various museums, including the Museum of Fine Arts, which is also located close to Dubovy Park. Constructed in 1974, the museum contains over 17,500 works of art. The collection represents ancient Greek civilization through the period of Soviet rule. In the Ala-Too Square, formerly known as Lenin Square after Russian leader Vladimir Lenin, is the Historical Museum, formerly the Lenin Museum. The museum features various symbols of Kyrgyz culture and customs, as well as a display dedicated to Lenin and the Russian Revolution of 1917, which led to the establishment of the Soviet Union. This museum provides a fascinating window into Kyrgyzstan's history under the Soviet Union. Murals on the museum walls abound with Soviet themes, and among the notable exhibits is a shrine to Lenin and the Bolshevik Revolution of 1917. In addition, the Frunze-House Museum and Log House is a traditional Russian-style home that is also a museum.

The National Library of the Kyrgyz Republic is located in the capital, Bishkek, and serves as the nation's legal depository. It dates back to the early 20th century, and now consists of roughly 6 million resources.

Holidays

Secular holidays include Victory Day (May 9), commemorating Soviet victories in War World II, and Independence Day (August 31), commemorating the end of Soviet rule. In addition, there are special ceremonies for weddings and the birth of children.

The most important religious holidays are Ramadan, Kurman-Ait (Eid al-Fitr), the feast which marks the end of fasting, and Nowruz, an Islamic new year's celebration that welcomes spring. Taking place in the third week of March, it involves the wearing of new clothes, gift-giving, elaborate feasts, and sporting and music events.

Youth Culture

Both rural and urban youth in Kyrgyzstan interact primarily with their peers. For rural Kyrgyzstani, this means that they are more embedded in Kyrgyz traditions than their urban counterparts. In traditional Kyrgyz nomadic culture, children learn to ride horses from the time they are very young, and horseback riding remains a practical skill in rural areas. As such, games involving horses are popular amongst rural Kyrgyzstani youth. Ulak is considered the national game and is similar to rugby. It is played on horseback and traditionally uses a goat carcass instead of a ball. Teams compete to get the goat carcass into the other team's goal. Horse-related games are often played on holidays and chabana (cowboy) festivals.

Since most urban teenagers socialize with peers from a variety of cultural backgrounds, Russian is the common language used in schools and social interaction. As such, urban Kyrgyzstani youth are heavily oriented toward Russian culture and trends. Western culture is also growing in popularity, particularly in terms of fashion, such as clothing and hairstyles. Tattoos, formerly considered vulgar, are also increasing in popularity. Hip-hop and rap are popular musical influences, and rock is often considered the music of choice among the ethnic Russian community. Similar to their Western counterparts, Kyrgyz youth consider cell phones and cars to be status symbols.

Discussing sex is taboo in Kyrgyz culture, and parents and schools typically offer little sex education to Kyrgyzstani youth. Due to various factors, such as decreased parental oversight and an influx of Western cultural influences, sexual activity among Kyrgyz youth is on the rise. This has led to a corresponding increase in teen pregnancies and the spread of sexually transmitted diseases in the early 21st century. It is also estimated that one in ten Kyrgyzstani women has had an abortion.

SOCIETY

Transportation

Marshrutkas, or mini-buses, are a common way to travel short distances. Peddlers may board the bus at the station to sell their goods, such as fruit, herbs, or newspapers; imams (Muslim religious leaders) may also collect donations to bless the bus. Agrarian modes of transportation, such as by horse and donkey, also remain common and most children learn to ride when they are quite young. Traffic moves on the right-hand side of the street. Traffic rules are not strictly enforced or followed, and so driving can be dangerous, especially at night and during the winter.

Transportation Infrastructure

Kyrgyzstan is not very well connected by air to other countries. Manas International Airport at Bishkek was renovated in 2007, and can now be reached by flights from Moscow, Kiev, Istanbul, and St. Petersburg. Many travelers choose to fly into Almaty, Kazakhstan, instead, and take the bus or shuttle from there to Bishkek. The trip takes approximately three hours, but border checks may make the process more time-consuming.

The two highways running through Kyrgyzstan both cross Bishkek. One leads to the country's second largest city, Osh, in the southwest, and the other to Lake Issyk-Kul in the northeast. Roads in Kyrgyzstan are generally poorly maintained. Additionally, because much of Kyrgyzstan's infrastructure was built during the Soviet era, roads may pass through Kazakhstan or Uzbekistan, which makes traveling with visas necessary. The nation's railway system is comprised of two non-connected rail lines, one connecting to Uzbekistan and Turkmenistan, the other continuing to Russia and Kazakhstan.

Media & Communications

As of 2008, there were more than 50 regular newspapers, with eight being government-owned. One of the largest daily newspapers in Kyrgyzstan is the privately owned, government-leaning *Vecherniy Bishkek*, published daily in Russian. *ResPublika* is a privately owned, Kyrgyz-language daily paper, and *Slovo Kyrgyzstana* is a government-owned, Russian-language paper published three times a week. The Kyrgyz National News Agency, Kabar, offers online news sources in Kyrgyz, Russian, Turkish, and English. Privately owned television channels include Piramida and NTS (in Bishkek), Ecological Youth (Issyk-kul), and Osh TV (Osh). The government runs the Kyrgyz National TV and Radio Broadcasting Corporation, which offers programming in Russian and Kyrgyz.

In 2002, Kyrgyzstan had 7.7 telephone lines per every 100 inhabitants. In 2012, there were over 6.8 million cell phones in use in the country (with a population of around 5.6 million). As of 2012, an estimated 21.7 percent of Kyrgyzstanis were considered Internet users, and the Internet was not censored by the government.

Kyrgyzstan has come under criticism for its freedom of press and handling of the media in recent years. Reasons for this include widespread intimidation of journalists, uneven legal protections, and attempts by the government to impose media censorship. International monitoring agencies have also maintained that police and official responses to journalist intimidation are lukewarm and not sufficiently focused on bringing the perpetrators to justice. The organization, Reporters Without Borders, reports that in some cases, police and other official forces have worked to prevent journalists from covering politically sensitive stories.

SOCIAL DEVELOPMENT

Standard of Living

Kyrgyzstan ranked 125th out of 187 countries on the 2014 United Nations Human Development Index, which measures quality of life and standard of living indicators.

Water Consumption

According to 2012 statistics published by the World Health Organization and United Nations Office for the Coordination of Humanitarian Affairs, approximately 97 percent of the population has access to improved sources of drinking water, while an estimated 91.9 percent of the population has access to improved sanitation.

Education

Education for children between the ages of six and seventeen is free and compulsory.. Qualified students may then finish secondary school and continue on to higher education free of charge. Teaching materials, the number of teachers, and facilities are generally limited. The average literacy rate stands at 99.3 percent of the adult population (2010 estimate). As of 2006, education enrollment rates were at 93 percent. Net enrollment and attendance for primary education in 2010 was published as 92 percent.

Higher education is concentrated in Bishkek. Institutions include Kyrgyz State University, the Kyrgyz-American University, and the Kyrgyz-Slavonic University, as well as numerous institutes and vocational programs.

Reforming the curriculum has proven a difficult issue in Kyrgyzstan. Since independence, it has undergone changes to reflect Kyrgyz language, history and culture in addition to the standard subjects. The Russian minority has protested against its reduced influence in the area of education and the lack of opportunities in its native tongue.

Women's Rights

Discrimination against women in Kyrgyzstan is a significant problem. According to a 2008 poll by the UN Development Fund for Women (UNIFEM), 80 percent of respondents reported physical abuse in their home. Domestic and spousal abuse is prohibited by law, but apathy and inaction on the part of authorities prevents many women from reporting cases of domestic abuse or rape. Sexual harassment is also widespread and, in some instances, considered normal, while rape, including spousal rape, is illegal. Several local NGOs provide services for victims of domestic abuse. According to the interior ministry, 235 of the 259 cases of rape reported resulted in conviction in 2007. However, according to one local NGO, the actual number of rapes is ten times the reported amount. Bribery in rape investigations is also not uncommon.

The wage gap between men and women has been increasing; in 1999, the average income of women was 72 percent that of male counterparts and in 2006 it was only 65.8 percent. Domestic tasks such as housework and childrearing are still performed predominately by women. After the 2007 elections, 23 women from three different political parties held seats in parliament, and several high-level government posts such as the minister of finance and minister of science and education were held by women. In August 2007, the president signed a national action plan concerning gender equality for 2007–2010, which, according to the World Economic Forum's 2013 Global Gender Gap Report, increased the total number of women representatives in government up to 23 percent. During the political upheavals of 2011, Roza Otunbaeva served as transitional president, effectively becoming the country's first woman president.

Bride kidnapping (ala kachuu) is one of the most serious threats to women's rights in Kyrgyzstan. In traditional Kyrgyz culture, a man would arrange with a woman's parents to undergo a "bride-catching" ritual to determine if they would marry. As part of the traditional ritual, a woman would be chased by her suitor, seated on horseback, and must defend herself from his pursuit, typically with a strong whip. If she could successfully defend herself, it was thought that the man was not good enough for marriage; but if he caught her, they were married.

Today this practice has resurfaced, and is considered by some a part of Kyrgyz identity and manhood. However, the specifics have changed to include kidnapping, forcible detainment, and the placement of a scarf, called a jooluk, on the woman's head. In some cases where the woman resists, rape is used as a means of subjugating the woman and consummating the marriage. It is also not uncommon for women who escape to experience rejection, since it is seen as a mark of honor to be chosen to be kidnapped. This increase in forced marriages is particularly common in rural areas. In 2007, there were 35 reported cases of forced marriage, though the actual number is suspected to be much higher.

Health Care

Kyrgyzstan's health care system is in transition. During most of the Soviet era, decent medical services and supplies were available in the form of socialized medicine. This system went into decline during the 1980s, and deteriorated further in the immediate post-independence period.

Government reforms and international donors have brought about improvements, particularly in pre-natal and post-natal care, but further changes and funds are needed in order to provide the vaccines, medicines, treatment and training necessary to maintain the health of the population. The government's attempt to implement a health insurance program has had mixed results, with many patients paying out-of-pocket for their care.

According to 2010-published statistics, there are approximately 251 doctors per 100,000 people in Kyrgyzstan, with 51 hospital beds per 10,000 people.

GOVERNMENT

Structure

In early 2005, frustrated with corruption, cronyism, increasing authoritarianism, and a lack of political accountability, a popular movement ousted the president who had governed since the downfall of the Soviet Union. An interim government held power until elections in July, and the new president was sworn in the following month. Further protest and violence followed until new elections were held in 2011.

Kyrgyzstan is a republic. The president is elected by popular vote and serves as the head of state for a five-year term, with a two-term limit. He or she is responsible for appointing a prime minister as well as the 12 cabinet ministers.

The unicameral legislative branch is the Supreme Council. The council is made up of 120 members, elected to five-year terms by party-list proportional vote. Plans to combine the two houses into a single body with 75 members are expected to be carried out under the new government.

Political Parties

With the Tulip Revolution of 2005, Kyrgyzstan now has a multiparty political system. To prevent political parties from wielding too much power, parties are limited to only sixty-five seats in the Supreme Council. As of the 2010 parliamentary election, the Ata-Zhurt held the most seats, with 28, followed by the Social Democratic Party of Kyrgyzstan, with 26 seats; the Ar-Namys political party, with 25 seats; Kyrgyzstani political party Respublika, with 23 seats; and the Ata-Meken (Fatherland) Socialist Party, which totaled 18 seats. No other political parties are represented. As of 2006, there were 42 recognized and operating political parties.

Local Government

For administrative purposes, Kyrgyzstan is divided into seven provinces and one city, the capital Bishkek. The president is responsible for appointing a governor for each province, which are further divided into districts. Overall, there are three tiers of local government: the oblast (district) level; the raion (department) level; and the village or rural level.

Judicial System

The judicial branch consists of a Supreme Court and a Constitutional Court as well as local courts and special courts for economic and military matters. Under the previous government, the Higher Court of Arbitration was abolished; it is uncertain whether it will be reformed. Reforms to make the judiciary independent are expected to be undertaken by the new government. The country's legal system blends together elements of both the legal systems of Russia and the France.

Taxation

Tax rates in Kyrgyzstan are relatively low, and both the personal income and corporate tax rates are levied at a flat rate of 10 percent. Other taxes include a value-added tax (VAT, similar to a consumption tax), levied at 12 percent, as well as an excise tax, land tax, road tax, and real property tax.

Armed Forces

Kyrgyzstan's armed forces consist of several service branches, including both air and land forces, as well as a border guard contingent. Conscription exists, with eighteen years of age the minimum age for a one-year compulsory term. In fact, a large number of military personnel—numbering approximately between 12,000 and 13,000 troops in 2007—are estimated to be conscripts, a number reported as 3,000 by the Kyrgyz Defense Ministry in 2009. In 2010, reservists under the age of 50 were called up by the government to aid in stabilizing an outbreak of riots in southern Kyrgyzstan.

Foreign Policy

Since achieving independence, Kyrgyzstan's foreign relations have focused on strengthening relations with former Soviet republics, particularly through the Commonwealth of Independent States (CIS), while fostering Western support (though anti-West sentiments have been charged). Kyrgyzstan has also shown pro-China sentimentalities in recent years. Although relations with Russia remain good, Kyrgyzstan's leaders have become increasingly concerned about Russia's growing conflict with Ukraine. Kyrgyzstan joined the United Nations (UN) in 1992, and in 1998 became the first former Soviet republic to join the World Trade Organization (WTO). Kyrgyzstan is a member of the Shanghai Cooperation Organization (SCO), which also includes members China, Russia, Kazakhstan,

Tajikistan, and Uzbekistan, and observers India, Iran, Pakistan, and Mongolia.

Kyrgyzstan's relations with China have been particularly friendly in recent years, in part because Kyrgyzstan hopes to benefit from trade to boost its economy, which lags behind neighboring Kazakhstan and Uzbekistan. Kyrgyzstan is also a trading hub for exporting substantial goods from China into Central Asia. This influx of goods has been accompanied by an increase in the number of Chinese living in Kyrgyzstan, a number which increased to 100,000 in 2008. In 2002, China and Kyrgyzstan signed a Treaty on Good-Neighborliness, Friendship and Cooperation. China has also funded construction and infrastructure development projects in Kyrgyzstan. This is in exchange for Kyrgyzstan's support in the SCO and the UN on issues such as fighting separatism and terrorism, particularly in China's predominantly Muslim province of Xinjiang.

In recent years, Kyrgyzstan's "multi-vector" foreign policy has been aimed at maintaining a balance between its powerful neighbors, China and Russia, and the United States. On February 4, 2009, however, Bishkek refused to continue to allow the U.S. and its allies to use the Manas Air Base, a key transit point for the U.S. military engaged in operations in Afghanistan, citing discontent with the financial remuneration provided. Kyrgyzstan had hosted the Manas Air Base, considered an important international link for the country, since 2001. Foreign policy experts voiced concern that this decision was influenced by a $2 billion (USD) aid package from Russia, as well as pressure from China. Total yearly U.S. aid to Kyrgyzstan has been $150 million (USD), including $63 million (USD) for the use of the base. A new pact was signed in June 2009, with the U.S. shelling out $60 million annually for continued use of the air base, however tensions with Russia, which has two bases in Kyrgyzstan, led to a U.S. withdrawal from the country in 2014.

Kyrgyzstan's relations with its Central Asian neighbors Uzbekistan and Kazakhstan are generally good. In 1993, Kyrgyzstan suddenly withdrew from the ruble zone, a currency union among post-Soviet countries, and began to use its own currency, the som. This sparked initial panic among its neighbors regarding trade issues and inflation. However, tensions soon decreased and the countries signed an economic agreement in 1994. Kyrgyzstan has invested effort in regional cooperation with Uzbekistan and Kazakhstan, such as joint military exercises. Regarding the country's relations with Russia, in 2008 the Kyrgyzstani government awarded Russian gas conglomerate Gazprom exploration rights for two oil and natural gas fields, in which Gazprom planned into invest $300 million. In 2012, Kyrgyzstan signed an agreement with Russia and Kazakhstan to build a hydroelectric plant within its territory.

Human Rights Profile

International human rights law insists that states respect civil and political rights, and also promote an individual's economic, social and cultural rights. The United Nations Universal Declaration on Human Rights (UDHR) is recognized as the standard for international human rights. Its authors sought the counsel of the world's great thinkers, philosophers, and religious leaders, and were careful to create a document that reflects the core values shared by every world culture. (To read this document or view the articles relating to cultural human rights, visit: http://www.udhr.org/UDHR/default.htm.)

The human rights situation in Kyrgyzstan has improved steadily in the early 21st century, particularly since the installation of Kurmanbek Bakiyev (1949–) in 2005. However, the country continues to face numerous human rights challenges, with more recent developments including proposed legislation that would allow more government oversight of non-governmental organizations (NGOs) and the barring of a leading human rights activist from entering the country.

According to the U.S. State Department's 2007 report, minorities in Kyrgyzstan suffered discrimination in hiring, promotion, and housing. Homosexual men were also significantly discriminated against in society (and faced further discrimination in the prison system). Although Kyrgyz is the state language, with Russian a designated official language, Russian-speaking citizens alleged discriminatory practices in obtaining government jobs on the basis of language ability. In order to revive the use of Kyrgyz, the government has been calling for increased study and official use of the Kyrgyz language.

The death penalty was abolished in Kyrgyzstan in 2007. Although torture and cruel and degrading punishment are prohibited by law, the U.S. Department of State reported that in 2007 such methods were employed on several occasions by the police and State Committee on National Security (GKNB) forces, particularly in order to force confessions to close unsolved cases. Rape and physical abuse of detainees was also reported. Additionally, although arbitrary arrest and detention are prohibited by law, police occasionally arrest people on false charges in order to solicit bribes.

Kyrgyzstani law provides for asylum and refugee status in accordance with the 1951 UN Convention Relating to the Status of Refugees and its 1967 protocol. According to Amnesty International (AI), however, the government habitually denies asylum to Uzbeks and Uighurs, who are occasionally extradited or deported. The first refugee center in Central Asia was opened in Kyrgyzstan in 2006. Freedom of religion is generally respected in Kyrgyzstan and is protected under the law, although the government does employ restrictions against groups it suspects of being militantly Islamist. Religion and the state are separate according to the constitution, and all religious groups must register with the Ministry of Justice, a process which can be burdensome. In March 2009, headscarves were banned from schools.

Kyrgyzstan, now an electoral democracy, still struggles with widespread corruption. According to Transparency International's (TI) 2014 Corruption Perception Index (CPI), Kyrgyzstan was rated 136 out of 175 countries surveyed.

Child abuse, abandonment, child labor, and trafficking in children for labor and sexual exploitation are a problem. As of 2008, 5,388 children were living in orphanages, although many had living parents.

ECONOMY

Overview of the Economy

In the 1980s, the economy of the Soviet Union went into a decline from which it would never recover. The impact of this decline and subsequent breakup of the union had serious effects on Kyrgyzstan, which had to cope with the disappearance of economic support and its severely restricted prospects of generating revenue. Solid economic reforms and international donations have stabilized the economy and reduced inflation, but prosperity is still far off. In 2014, the estimated gross domestic product (GDP) per capita was $3,400 USD.

While Bishkek is Kyrgyzstan's economic center, it has few natural resources, and imports most of its useable products. Agricultural regions in the rural outskirts of Bishkek produce potatoes, vegetables, and fruits for trade, as well as tobacco, cotton, wool, and meat for export, with tobacco and cotton being the primary agricultural exports. Bishkek also exports gas, oil, coal, and gold; the Bishkek economy relies heavily on the export of the latter. A decline in gold exports in 2002 and 2005 threatened the economy, but levels grew again in 2007 because of higher gold prices and demand.

Industry

Most industry is based in or around Bishkek. It accounts for 31 percent of the GDP and employs 12.5 percent of the labor force. These figures show a decline from the Soviet era, when Kyrgyzstan supplied the Soviet Union with defense equipment and raw materials. The need for these products, along with an energy crisis and the emigration of Russians and Germans, who accounted for a large percentage of skilled workers, contributed to the economic slump of the early 1990s.

The situation has since improved. The country produces small machinery, building materials, textiles, and furniture, and is an important provider of hydroelectricity. Industry relies on agricultural production for raw materials, many of which are now processed within the country. These include meat, wool, and leather.

Heavy industry in Bishkek includes the manufacture of machinery such as electric motors, textiles, foodstuffs, and other metal products. When Kyrgyzstan was part of the Soviet Union, the meatpacking and machinery plants in Bishkek were some of the largest in that socialist state.

Labor

The labor force numbers 2.6 million (2014 estimate), with eight percent unemployed (2011 estimate). Nearly half of the population lives below the poverty line. The majority of the workforce—an estimated 48 percent in 2005—is employed in agriculture. The services sector and industry employed 39.5 and 12.5 percent of the work force, respectively.

Energy/Power/Natural Resources

Gold is the most valuable natural resource found in Kyrgyzstan. Like the country's other mineral resources, which include oil, natural gas, coal, lead, zinc, copper, iron ore, nepheline, mercury, and bismuth, it has not yet been exploited to its fullest potential. During the Soviet era, Kyrgyzstan was an important supplier of uranium, but it is no longer mined.

Kyrgyzstan's fast-flowing rivers present great potential for generating hydroelectric power, but programs to further harness this potential have been slow to develop. Nonetheless, through its hydroelectric stations on the Naryn and other rivers, the country is an important provider of electricity for its own needs and for the region. In 2009, however, the country's largest hydroelectric plant experienced the lowest water level in the past 50 years.

Though the environmental record in Kyrgyzstan is not as poor as that of other former Soviet republics, it still has serious problems that are made worse by lack of funding for cleanup. Poor agricultural practices have led to salinization and erosion of the soil, inefficient use of water, and livestock overgrazing. Moreover, the use of fertilizers and pesticides has polluted the soil and water. The incidence of waterborne diseases is high in Kyrgyzstan, particularly in heavily populated regions, because of inefficient sewage treatment. The land and water near mines and metallurgy plants has also been degraded by toxic waste.

Fishing

Aquaculture (particularly cage farms) is the primary means of fish production in the country; however, the fishing industry of Kyrgyzstan is unable to meet domestic demand. An estimated 140 tons of fish are produced annually. Poaching remains a concern.

Forestry

An estimated five percent of Kyrgyzstan is forested, and the country has worked to improve its forest cover in recent years. In a fifteen year period, in fact, between 1990 and 2005, the country improved its forest cover by four percent. However, Kyrgyzstan still lacks a commercially significant logging industry. Illegal logging remains a concern, with domestic fuel the primary driver for illegal harvesting.

Mining/Metals

The mining sector has attracted foreign investment and contributes significantly to the GDP. Many minerals are mined and processed in Kyrgyzstan, gold being the most important. Other important commodities include industrial minerals such as cement and kaolin, and mercury. The country has minor reserves of coal, oil, and gas. In 2007, mining accounted for just over 10 percent of the country's gross domestic product (GDP).

Agriculture

Agriculture accounts for 19 percent of the GDP and employs 48 percent of the labor force. Only seven percent of the land is arable, mostly in the fertile valleys of the Fergana and Chu Rivers and the Ysyk Kol basin; approximately 70 percent of this land requires irrigation. Agriculture yields fruits, vegetables, tobacco, cotton, sugar beets, and various grains.

Animal Husbandry

The country's ancient livestock tradition is still central to the economy. Sheep, goats, and cattle are the most commonly raised animals, as are horses and poultry. Animal husbandry is concentrated in the central and eastern mountains, where there is ample though reduced land for grazing.

Tourism

Kyrgyzstan's tourist infrastructure is basic. The industry is seen as a means to boost the economy, however, and large-scale efforts are being undertaken to broaden the sector. Approximately 500,000 tourists were visiting each year, generating an estimated $15 million (USD) annually. In 2007, tourism revenue accounted for approximately four percent of the gross domestic product (GDP), and tourism revenue grew from a reported $70.5 million in 2005 to $341.7 million in 2007. The recent political upheavals in the country have limited tourism, however.

Kyrgyzstan is promoting itself as an adventure destination, stressing the country's natural beauty and the hospitality of its people. Activities include jailoo homestays, horseback riding, mountain trekking, and skiing. In Bishkek, the country's art and culture are on display at the State Museum of Fine Art and the State Historical Museum. In 2009, Lonely Planet, a global travel guide and information publisher, listed Kyrgyzstan as one of the top ten destinations to visit.

Evelyn Atkinson, Michael Aliprandini, Anne Whittaker

DO YOU KNOW?

- The word "Kyrgyz" means "forty clans" in the Kyrgyz language.
- There are an estimated 6,500 glaciers in the mountains of Kyrgyzstan.

Bibliography

Dilip, Hiro. *Inside Central Asia.* New York: Overlook Duckworth, 2009.

Ingmen, Ali F. *Speaking Soviet with an Accent: Culture and Power in Kyrgyzstan.* Pittsburgh: University of Pittsburgh Press, 2012.

Lonely Planet and Bradley Mayhew. *Central Asia.* Oakland, CA: Lonely Planet, 2014.

Marat, Erica. *The Tulip Revolution: Kyrgyzstan One Year After.* Jamestown Foundation, 2006.

McMann, Kelly. *Economic Autonomy and Democracy: Hybrid Regimes in Russia and Kyrgyzstan.* England: Cambridge University Press, 2006.

Meyer, Karl E. and Shareen Blair Brysac. *Tournament of Shadows: The Great Game and the Race for Empire in Central Asia.* New York: Basic Books, 2006.

Mitchell, Laurence. *Kyrgyzstan (Bradt Travel Guide).* Bucks, England: Bradt, 2015.

Thubron, Colin. *Shadow of the Silk Road.* New York: Harper Perennial, 2008.

Works Cited

Abikeeva, Gulnara. "Review: My Brother Silk Road." *KinoKultura: New Russian Cinema.* 2003. http://www.kinokultura.com/CA/reviews/silkroad.html.

"About the Artists." Past Exhibitions. Philadelphia Museum of Art. 2008. http://www.philamuseum.org/exhibitions/2008/296.html?page=2.

Ahmady, Leeza. "Central Asia Dream." *Nafas Art Magazine.* Institute for Foreign Cultural Relations of Germany. May 2004. http://universes-in-universe.org/eng/nafas/articles/2004/contemporaneity/central_asia_dream.

Allen, Daniel. "China Strengthens Its Role in Kyrgyzstan." *Asia Times Online.* 1 August 2008. http://www.atimes.com/atimes/China/JH01Ad01.html.

"Archaeologists discover remains of 2500-year-old advanced civilization in Russia." Yahoo! *News India.* 28 December 2007. http://web.archive.org/web/20080101111204/http://in.news.yahoo.com/071228/139/6oy8j.htmlArnett, Jeffrey Jensen.

"Kyrgyzstan." *International Encyclopedia of Adolescence.* Routledge Press. New York: 2007.

Beehner, Lionel and Preeti Bhattacharji. "The Shanghai Cooperation Organization." *CFR.org.* 8 April 2008. http://www.cfr.org/publication/10883/.

"Cell Phone Usage Worldwide by Country." *InfoPlease.* 2007. http://www.infoplease.com/ipa/A0933605.html.

Claytor, Ian. "The Manas Epos." *Kyrgyzstan Hotels, Tourism, and Travel Information.* 2009. http://www.kyrgyzstan.org/the_manas_epos.

Cohen, Ariel. "Don't Push the Reset Button Yet." *International Herald Tribune.* 25 February 2009. http://www.iht.com/articles/2009/02/25/opinion/edarielcohen.php.

"Culture." Plants Genetic Resources in Central Asia and Caucasus. 2003. http://www.cac-biodiversity.org/kgz/kgz_culture.htm.

Dorin, Lisa. "From the Silk Road Into the Future." *Nafas Art Magazine.* Institute for Foreign Cultural Relations of Germany. November 2007. http://universes-in-universe.org/eng/nafas/articles/2007/djumaliev_kasmalieva.

Garrard, Robyn. "Where the Heck is Kyrgyzstan?!" *Peace Corps Journals.* 2006. http://www.robyngarrard.blogspot.com/.

Gleason, Gregory. "Kyrgyzstan's Multivector Foreign Policy Unravels." *Radio Free Europe Radio Liberty.* http://www.rferl.org/Content/Kyrgyzstans_Multivector_Foreign_Policy_Unravels/1491581.html. 12 March 2009.

Handrahan, L.M. "International Human Rights Law and Bride Kidnapping in Kyrgyzstan." *Eurasianet.org.* 28 January 2000. http://www.eurasianet.org/departments/insight/articles/eav012400.shtml.

Humphrey, Mark. "Briefing from Bishkek." *Kyrgyz Music.* June 1999. http://www.kyrgyzmusic.com/.

"In the Shadow of 'Heroes': 2nd Bishkek Internat. Exhibition of Contemporary Art." *Nafas Art Magazine.* Institute for Foreign Cultural Relations of Germany. November 2005. http://universes-in-universe.org/eng/nafas/articles/2005/in_the_shadow_of_heroes.

"Issyk-kul Lake." *FantasticAsia.* 2008. http://www fantasticasia.net/?p=136.

Johnson, Justine. "Justine in Kyrgyz." *Peace Corps Journals.* 2009. http://justinepc.blogspot.com.

Kasymalieva, Aida. "Kyrgyzstan: Rising Teen Pregnancy Blamed on Ignorance." *Institute for War and Peace Reporting.* 3 November 2005. http://www.iwpr.net/index.php?apc_state=hen&s=o&o=p=wpr&l=EN&s=f&o=258121. 23 March 2009.

Kasmalieva, Gulnara and Muratbek Djuamliev 'A New Silk Road'." *NY Art Beat.* 2008. http://www.nyartbeat.com/event/2008/0051.

Köçümkulkïzï, Elmira. "The Kyrgyz Epic *Manas.*" Ph.D. *Dissertation, Near and Middle Eastern Studies. University of Washington (Seattle).* 2005. http://www.silk-road.com/folklore/manas/manasintro.html.

Kutueva, Aizada. "Child abandonment is on increase in Kyrgyzstan." *24 News Agency.* 25 March 2008. http://eng.24.kg/community/2008/03/25/4957.html.

"Kyrgyz Culture Overview." *Bukhara-Carpets.com.* 2009. http://www.bukhara-carpets.com/making/kyrgyz.html "Kyrgyz President Reiterates One-China Policy." *Xinhua.* 6 March 2009. http://news.xinhuanet.com/english/2009-03/06/content_10957060.htm.

"Kyrgyz Music." 2002. http://www.kyrgyzmusic.com.

"Kyrgyz Republic." *Bureau of Democracy, Human Rights, and Labor. U.S. Department of State.* 11 March 2008. http://www.state.gov/g/drl/rls/hrrpt/2007/100616.htm.

"Kyrgyz Republic." *Country Insights. Centre for Intercultural Learning.* 14 June 2006. http://www.intercultures.ca/cil-cai/country_overview-en.asp?lvl=8&ISO=kg.

"Kyrgyz Republic: Country Specific Information." *U.S. Department of State.* 29 August 2008. http://travel.state.gov/travel/cis_pa_tw/cis/cis_945.html.

"Kyrgyz writer, Perestroika Ally Aitmatov dies." *Reuters UK.* 10 June 2008. http://uk.reuters.com/article/stageNews/idUKL1059845020080612.

"Kyrgyzstan." *City Population.*13 July 2008. http://www.citypopulation.de/Kyrgyzstan.html.

"Kyrgyzstan." *Eurasianet.org.* 2009. http://www.eurasianet.org/resource/kyrgyzstan/index.shtml.

"Kyrgyzstan." *Stylus Magazine.* 31 October 2007. http://www.stylusmagazine.com/articles/weekly_article/almaty-or-bust-central-asian-music-in-words-and-pictures.htm#kyrgyzstan.

"Kyrgyzstan (2008)." Map of Press Freedom. *Freedom House.* 2008. http://www.freedomhouse.org/template.cfm?page=251&country=7427&year=2008.

"Kyrgyzstan – Amnesty International Report 2008." *Amnesty International.* 2008. http://www.amnesty.org/en/region/kyrgyzstan/report-2008.

"Kyrgyzstan – Annual Report 2008." *Reporters Without Borders.* 2008. http://www.rsf.org/article.php3?id_article=25486&Valider=OK.

"Kyrgyzstan Bans Head Scarves from Schools." *Radio Free Europe Radio Liberty.* 3 March 2009. http://www.rferl.org/content/Kyrgyzstan_Bans_Head_Scarves_From_Schools/1503459.html.

"Kyrgyzstan Closes Airbase to US Allies Too." *Radio Netherlands.* 6 March 2009. http://www.radionetherlands.nl/news/international/6204048/Kyrgyzstan-closes-airbase-to-US-allies-too.

"Kyrgyzstan Culture." *Oriental Express Central Asia.* 2009. http://www.kyrgyzstan.orexca.com/culture_kyrgyzstan.shtml.

"Kyrgyzstan: New Independent Printing House Opens in Bishkek." *IRIN Humanitarian News and Analysis.* UN Office for the Coordination of Humanitarian Affairs.

14 November 2003. http://www.irinnews.org/report.aspx?reportid=21351.

"Kyrgyzstan News." 17 January 2005. http://friendsofkyrgyzstan.org/links/news.htm.

"Let's go to... Kyrgyzstan!" *The Lutheran Church – Missouri Synod*. 2009. www.lcms.org/graphics/assets/media/World%20Mission/MF_Kyrgyzstan.pdf.

Lukashov, Nikolai. "Remains of ancient civilization discovered on the bottom of a lake." *RIA Novosti*. 27 December 2007. http://en.rian.ru/analysis/20071227/94372640.html.

Mamatov, Arslan. "Kyrgyzstan: NGOs Assail Proposed Legal Changes as 'Threat to Democracy.'" 10 March 2009. http://www.eurasianet.org/departments/insightb/articles/eav031009a.shtml.

Mitchell, Laurence. *Kyrgyzstan*. Bradt Travel Guides. England: 2008

"Osh, Kyrgyzstan." *Advantour*. 2009. http://www.advantour.com/kyrgyzstan/osh.htm.

Peyrouse, Sébastien. "The Growing Stakes of the China-Kyrgyz-Uzbek Railway Project." Central Asia-Caucasus Institute Analyst. 11 March 2009. http://www.cacianalyst.org/?q=node/5058.

Rozen, Laura. "Trouble in Kyrgyzstan." *The Cable*. 9 February 2009. http://thecable.foreignpolicy.com/posts/2009/02/09/trouble_in_kyrgyzstan.

"Russia's Gazprom gets Kyrgyz gas field licenses." *Reuters*. 20 February 2008. http://www.reuters.com/article/rbssEnergyNews/idUSL2046013920080220.

"Safeguarding of the Art of Akyns, Kyrgyz Epic Tellers." *Intangible Heritage Section/UNESCO*. July 2008. http://www.unesco.org/culture/ich/doc/src/00554-EN.doc.

Scott, Audrey, and Daniel Noll. "Kyrgyzstan Reflections: A Well-Rounded Visit." *Uncornered Market*. 2009. http://www.uncorneredmarket.com/2007/12/kyrgyzstan-well-rounded-visit/.

"Switzerland of the Stans." *Peace Corps Journals*. 2009. http://switzerlandofthestans.blogspot.com.

Synovitz, Ron. "Kyrgyz Eviction Warnings Intensify Over U.S. Air Base." *Radio Free Europe Radio Liberty*. 4 February 2009. http://www.rferl.org/content/Kyrgyz_President_Threatens_To_Kick_US_Troops_Out_Of_Air_Base/1379212.html "Parker-stan… Kyrgyzstan that is!" *Peace Corps Journals*. 2009. http://www.parkerkyrgyz.blogspot.com/.

"The Golden Road to Samarqand." 2006. http://amiralace.blogspot.com/2006/05/roads-in-kyrgyzstan.html.

"The Story: Synopsis of 'The Kidnapped Bride.'" *Frontline World*. 2009. http://www.pbs.org/frontlineworld/stories/kyrgyzstan/thestory.html.

"Tengir-Too: Mountain music of Kyrgyzstan." *Aga Khan Trust for Culture*. 2008. http://www.akdn.org/aktc_music_tengir_too.asp.

"The Voice of Kyrgyzstan." *Artists Direct*. 2009. http://www.artistdirect.com/nad/store/artist/album/0,,1629339,00.html.

"Timeline: Kyrgyzstan." *BBC News*. 4 February 2009. http://news.bbc.co.uk/1/hi/world/asia-pacific/country_profiles/1296570.stm.

"Today is Toktogul Satylganov's memorial day." *Kyrgyz National News Agency*. 17 February 2009. http://eng.kabar.kg/2009/02/17/today-is-toktogul-satylganov%E2%80%99s-memorial-day/.

"Toktogul Satylganov." *Fantasia*. 2008. http://www.fantasticasia.net/?p=151.

"Turk Telekom excluded from Kyrgyztelecom tender." *Hurriyet Daily News*. 2008. http://www.hurriyet.com.tr/english/finance/9813863.asp?gid=236&sz=377. 12 March 2009.

"27 Months in Kyrgyzstan." *Peace Corps Journals*. 2009. http://marthapcadventure.blogspot.com.

Weisman, Steven R. and Thom Shanker. "Uzbeks Order U.S. from Base in Refugee Rift." *The New York Times*. 31 July 2005. http://www.nytimes.com/2005/07/31/international/31uzbek.html.

"Welcome to CBT Arslanbob." *Kyrgyz Community Based Tourism Association*. 2009. http://www.cbt-arslanbob.com/.

Winkleman, Edward. "Zone of Risk – Transition: 3rd Bishkek Exhibition of Contemporary Art." *Nafas Art Magazine*. Institute for Foreign Cultural Relations of Germany. November 2006. http://universes-in-universe.org/eng/nafas/articles/2006/zone_of_risk_transition.

"Work and Family: the Republic of Kyrgyzstan." *Publications, International Labor Organization*. Moscow. 2008. www.ilo.org/public/english/region/eurpro/moscow/info/publ/wfd_kyrguz_en.pdf.

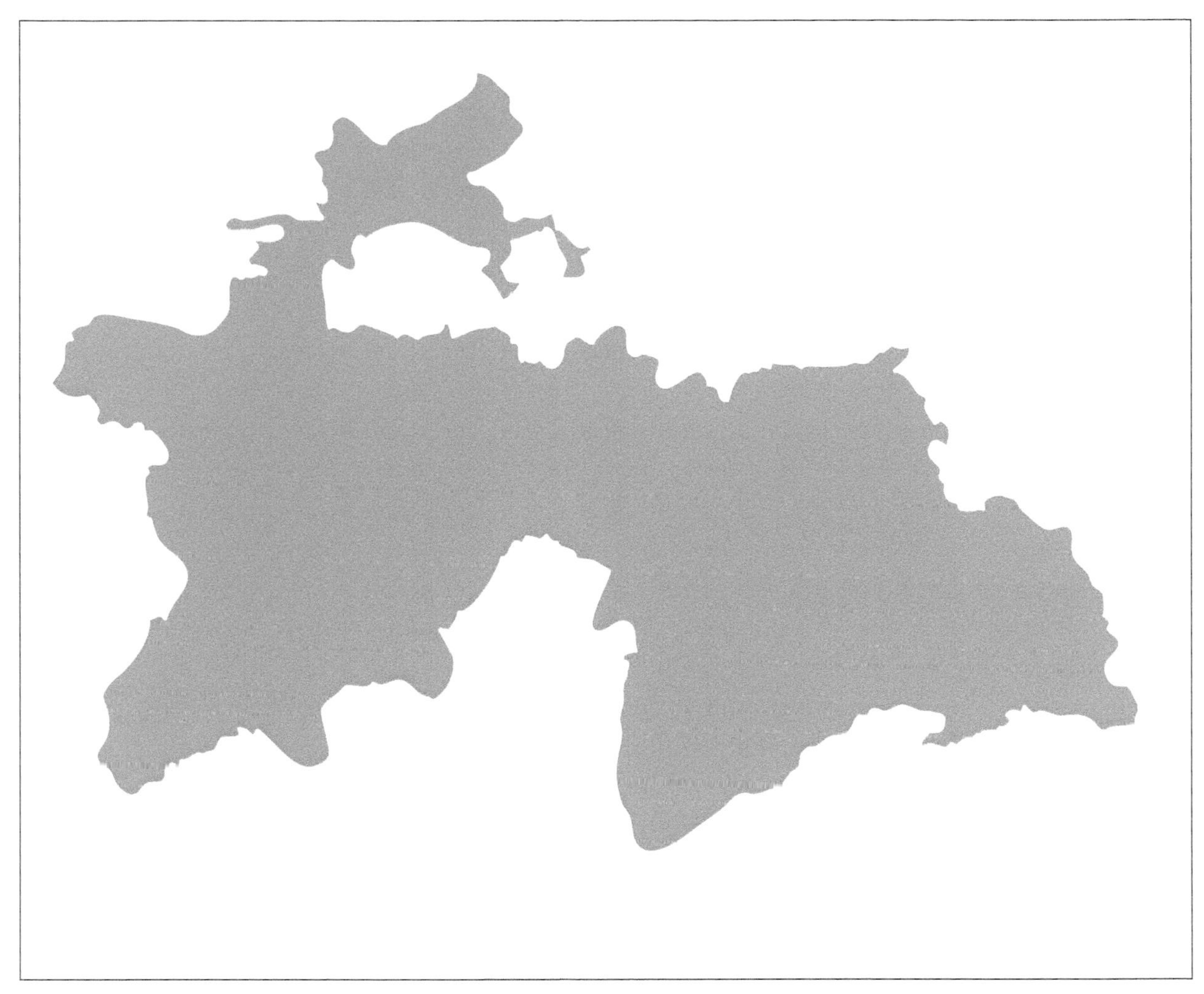

Tajikistan

Introduction

The Republic of Tajikistan is a small country in Central Asia bordering Afghanistan, Uzbekistan, Kyrgyzstan, and China. It is home to the awe-inspiring Pamir mountain range in the east. In fact, over 90 percent of Tajikistan is mountainous, and nearly half of the country's territory lies above 3,000 meters (9,843 feet).

Visitors to this beautifully rugged, mountainous region are able to experience one of the last wild places in Central Asia. They retrace sections of the famous Silk Road, the important trade route that connected China to Europe from ancient times. Through the centuries, countless travelers have made the trek across the Pamirs, including ancient Chinese explorers, Buddhist pilgrims, Christian missionaries, Persian traders, and even the legendary merchant and explorer Marco Polo.

Formerly a Soviet republic, Tajikistan emerged as an independent nation in 1991, for the first time in its history. After a crippling civil war, the government has slowly started to make modest economic reforms and forge a post-Soviet, multi-ethnic identity.

GENERAL INFORMATION

Official Language: Tajik
Population: 8,051,512 (2014 estimate)
Currency: Somoni
Coins: The Somoni is subdivided into 100 diram, and coins are circulated in denominations of 5, 10, 20, 25, and 50 dirams, and 1, 3, and 5 Somoni.

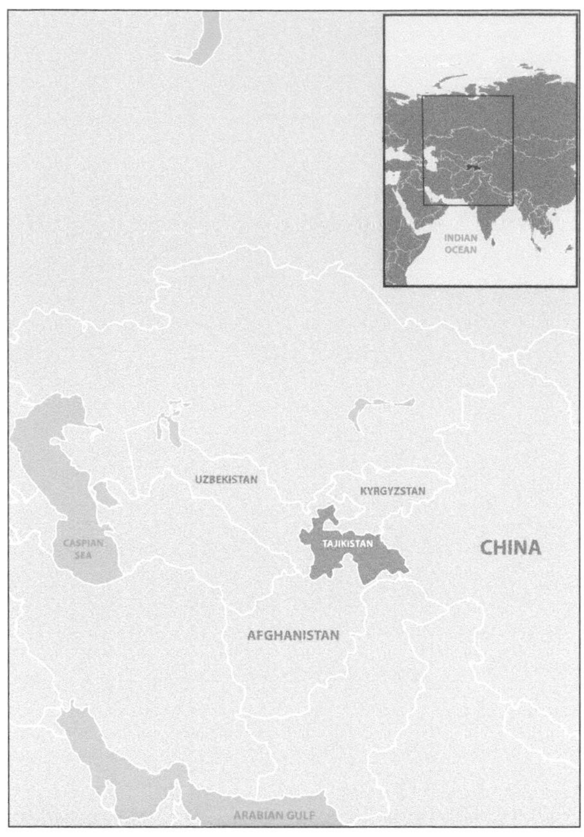

Land Area: 141,510 square kilometers (54,637 square miles)
Water Area: 2,590 square kilometers (1,000 square miles)
National Anthem: "National Anthem of the Republic of Tajikistan"
Capital: Dushanbe
Time Zone: GMT +5
Flag Description: The flag of Tajikistan features three horizontal bands of red (top), white (center), and green (bottom), with the top and bottom stripes of equal proportion. The colors symbolize agriculture (green), the cotton crop or purity (white), and the land or independence from Russia (red). Centered in the larger middle band is a golden crown topped by an arc of seven stars. (The use of the numeral seven is representative of both Tajik and Islamic symbolism.)

Population

Tajikistan is a mountainous country with lowlands in the north and west. The vast majority of

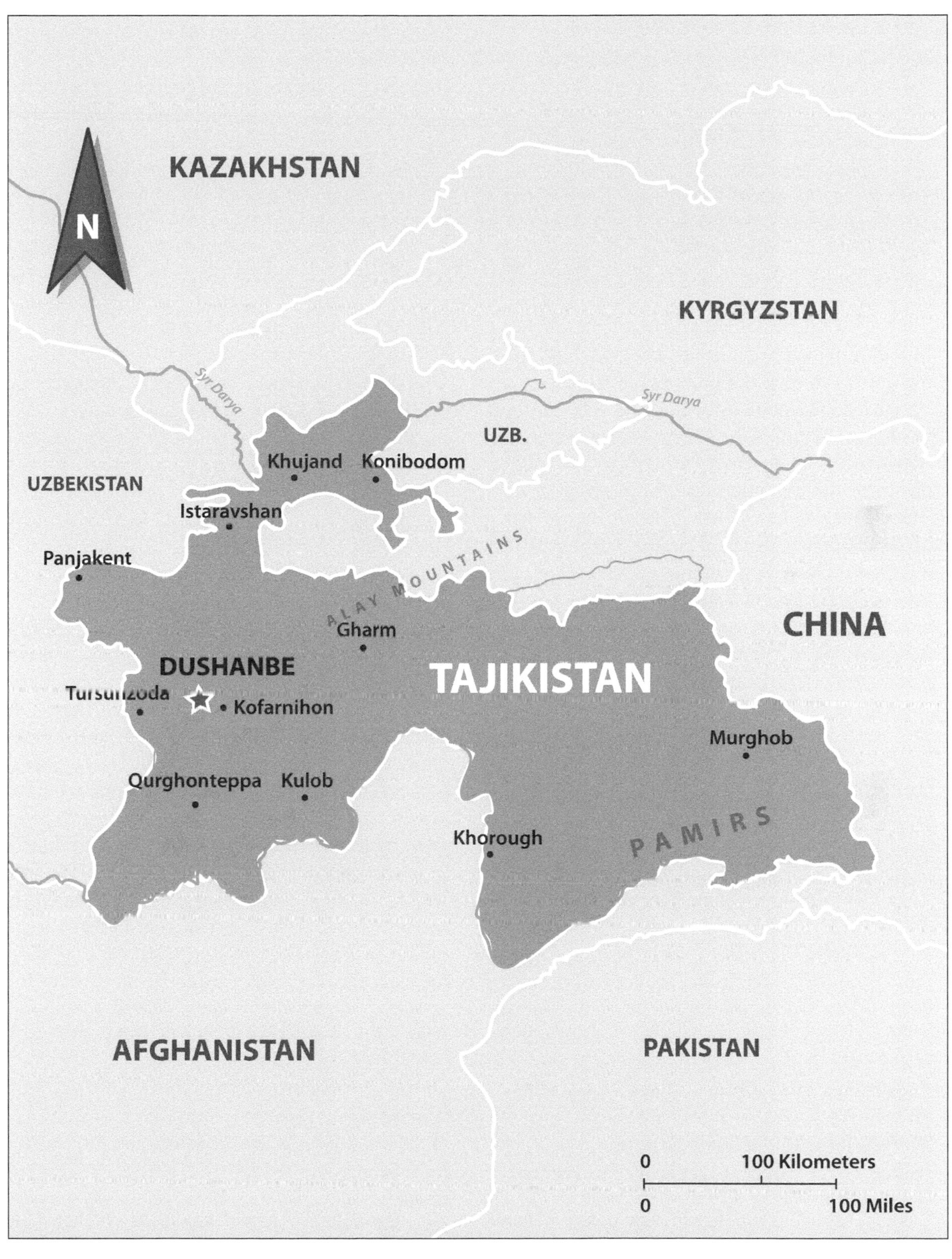
N
KAZAKHSTAN
KYRGYZSTAN
Syr Darya
Syr Darya
UZB.
UZBEKISTAN
Khujand
Konibodom
Istaravshan
Panjakent
ALAY MOUNTAINS
Gharm
CHINA
DUSHANBE
TAJIKISTAN
Tursunzoda
Kofarnihon
Murghob
Qurghonteppa
Kulob
Khorough
PAMIRS
AFGHANISTAN
PAKISTAN
0
100 Kilometers
0
100 Miles

Principal Cities by Population (2014 estimate):

- Dushanbe (778,500)
- Khujand (169,700)
- Kurgonteppa (101,600)
- Kulob (100,000)
- Istaravshan (56,600)
- Tursunzoda (50,900)
- Konibodom (48,900)
- Isfara (45,900)

the population lives in the lowlands and in the river valleys near the mountains. Nearly 75 percent of the population is rural, and small villages, built around collections of families, are common. Dushanbe, in western Tajikistan, has a population of nearly 800,000. The northern city of Khujand (also known as Chucand, or Leninabad until 1991) is the second largest in the country.

Tajikistan has a young, growing population (33 percent of its people are aged 14 or younger) and a high birth rate—25 births per 1,000 population (2014). The population growth rate was estimated at 1.75 percent in 2014. Large families are culturally favored. Life expectancy is 64 years for men and 70 years for women (2014 estimate).

Languages

Tajik is the most commonly spoken language in Tajikistan. Belonging to the Indo-Iranian language family, it is currently written in the Cyrillic alphabet, a legacy of Soviet rule. However, efforts are being made to return to the Arabic script. Uzbek, a Turkic language, is spoken by approximately onc-quarter of the population. Russian is the language of the Russian minority and is still frequently used in government and business. Minorities living in the Pamir Mountains speak distinct Iranian languages.

Native People & Ethnic Groups

Tajiks are the largest ethnic group, accounting for nearly 80 percent of the total population. The earliest written records for the region indicate that they have lived there for at least 2,500 years, having descended from Eastern Iranian tribes such as the Sogdians and Bactrians. Culturally they are similar to Uzbeks, who make up approximately 15 percent of the population and from whom they have long been undifferentiated. As of the last official Tajik census, in 2000, other ethnic groups and minorities include Russian, at 1.1 percent of the population, and Kyrgyz, also at 1.1 percent.

There are also small indigenous ethnic groups, such as the Pamiri, living in the eastern autonomous region of Gorno-Badakhshan. Historically, this area has had little political clout, and so separatists have declared it an autonomous region of Tajikistan. Non-indigenous populations such as the Russians and Germans have been in decline since Tajikistan's independence, a decline which sped up during the civil war years.

Religions

Islam has been the dominant religion since its introduction to the region in the eighth century. Under Soviet rule, religion was officially considered regressive and its practice was discouraged. Since independence, Tajiks have enjoyed greater freedom of worship, and Islam has resurged. Some Tajikistanis, while not adhering to the faith, recognize it as an important part of their culture.

Sunni Muslims account for approximately 85 percent of the population. An estimated 5 percent is Shia, which includes the Pamiri people who belong to a persecuted Shia sect called Ismailism. (The name of this Shia branch derives from Isma'il ibn Ja'far, an 8th-century imam.) Christianity, usually Russian Orthodoxy or Catholicism, is practiced by small minority groups. There is also a small Jewish community which diminished considerably following an airlift of thousands to Israel in 1992.

Climate

Tajikistan has a wide range of climates, mirroring its range of elevations. The Pamir Mountain region is the coldest, and can reach temperatures of –60° Celsius (–76° Fahrenheit) in winter. The average temperature, however, is 5° to 10°

Celsius (41° to 50° Fahrenheit) in July and -15° to -20° Celsius (5° to -4° Fahrenheit) in January.

In contrast, a continental climate prevails in the lowlands. Hot summers and cold winters are the rule. In Khujand, for example, 27° Celsius (81° Fahrenheit) is the average temperature for July, and -1° Celsius (30° Fahrenheit) is the average temperature for January.

Rainfall is not heavy in Tajikistan. The annual average for the entire country is between 70 and 160 centimeters (28 and 63 inches), but the Pamirs receive far less than the average. When it does rain, the valleys are prone to landslides.

Earthquakes, some of them severe, are common throughout the country. In the lowlands, summer dust storms often occur. In spring and summer, the river levels rise as the glacial waters leave the mountains. The springtime flow, heavier than the summer's, can cause flooding.

ENVIRONMENT & GEOGRAPHY

Topography

Over 90 percent of Tajikistan is mountainous, and nearly half of the country's territory lies above 3,000 meters (9,843 feet). In the lower elevations of the north, northwest and southwest, where the population is concentrated, steppe land and foothills predominate. The capital of Dushanbe lies at an elevation of 785 meters (2,575 feet) in the west central part of the country.

Part of the Fergana Valley is in the far north of Tajikistan. Rivers flowing from higher elevations bring water and fertile soil deposits to this valley, making it a rich agricultural center. The Turkestan, Zarafshon, and Hisor Mountains (the western end of the Tian Shan mountain system) traverse these lower elevations and divide the north from the south.

The other two principal mountain ranges are the Pamir and the Alay, in eastern Tajikistan. The Pamir Mountains, called the "roof of the world," contain several peaks that rise above 7,000 meters (22,965 feet). The highest, at an elevation of 7,495 meters (24,590 feet), is called Ismail Samani Peak (formerly Mount Communism). From these mountains descend many streams and rivers. They also contain numerous glaciers and the majority of the country's lakes. The largest lake is the dead, salty Lake Karakul.

The Syr Darya and the Zeravshan are the major rivers of northern Tajikistan, the Syr Darya feeding the Fergana Valley. The Amu Derya is the largest river in Central Asia. The Vakhsh and the Kofarnihon are its major tributaries. Most of the country's southern border with Afghanistan is formed by the Amu Darya and the Panj Darya, its tributary.

Plants & Animals

The vegetation of Tajikistan is variously polar, alpine, arid and tropical. There are approximately 5,000 species of plants, the majority of them growing in the foothills and mountains. These include wildflowers such as poppies, tulips, iris and edelweiss, and trees such as the spruce, juniper, and walnut. These middle and higher elevations, where they are not covered by forest, have meadows that are used as pastures during summer and winter months. Wild plants are gathered as sources of medicine, dye, and oil. Hearty grasses and shrubs cover the steppe land.

The country's abundant animal life also varies according to elevation. In the higher mountains, goat and sheep are plentiful. This is also the habitat of three of the country's endangered animals: the snow leopard, the tiger, and the markhor, a type of horned goat. In the lower mountains, wolves, boar, and bear are found. Deer and fox commonly occupy the lowlands.

CUSTOMS & COURTESIES

Greetings

When people meet in Tajikistan, it is customary for one person to say "Salom aleikum" ("Peace be with you"), and for the other person to then say the same as a response. After making an initial greeting, it is typical for the two people to ask one another apparently personal questions, even if they are strangers. Inquiring about the health of one's family is considered polite. People also enjoy exchanging stories, especially humorous ones, as a way of breaking the ice after making initial greetings. Older people are afforded much respect in Tajikistan, and are allowed to guide conversations. It is considered rude to directly contradict an elder. Among more conservative people, especially in rural areas, it is deemed improper for a man to address a woman he does not know.

It is typical for people to refer to one another by their first name, followed by their father's first name. Sometimes people add the suffix "-jon" to a person's first name instead, which is also considered a polite gesture. Since social hierarchy is important to Tajik culture, it is also common to use titles that reflect relative ages. Older people often refer to younger people with the title "uko," while younger people use the term "ako" to address elders.

Gestures & Etiquette

Tajiks are generally considered very welcoming people, and cherish visitors. However, they are also known for being inquisitive. Even upon first meeting, they often ask questions that Westerners would find quite personal. Etiquette involving eating traditions is also important. Meals are traditionally eaten while sitting on the floor, around a table cloth called a dastarkhan. It is important to avoid stepping on this cloth, as the feet are considered unclean. It is also rude to point one's feet at another person while seated for a meal. Eating and passing dishes is conducted only with the right hand, as the left hand is used for cleansing the body, and is thus considered impure. Washing hands before a meal is also required, since there are many dishes that are shared. The traditional bread, non, is considered a gift from Allah, and is never to be placed on the ground or thrown away. Meals end with a prayer called the amin, and it is impolite to eat after the prayer is said.

There are also several points of protocol to obey that stem from the fact that Tajikistan is a Muslim country. Dress should be modest and not revealing. This is particularly important for women, and female travelers should also remember to cover their heads when entering a place of religious significance. Additionally, some women in Tajikistan will completely refrain from interacting with strangers out of this sense of modesty. Elders are also afforded the utmost respect, and are allowed to lead most conversations. They are expected to entertain guests with stories, and it is not polite to talk over or ignore them.

Eating/Meals

Breakfast, which is eaten early in the morning, generally consists of tea and the ubiquitous flat bread, called non, often accompanied by fruit and nuts. In the middle of the day, people traditionally take a long break to have an unhurried lunch with their family members. Lunch usually starts out the same as breakfast, with tea, bread and nuts. Several dishes, such as soup, pilov and lamb, are also shared at this meal. Dinner, which begins in the early evening and can last for several hours, is usually a more elaborate version of lunch, and sometimes finishes with sweets and alcohol.

People in Tajikistan traditionally gather at mealtime by sitting on the floor around a cloth called a dastarkhan, which is used as a table would be in Western cultures. Per tradition, meals commence with the washing of the hands, which is usually done with water offered by the host. In addition, a short prayer is traditionally said before eating. Since the left hand is associated with the cleansing of the body—a common custom throughout the Muslim world—it is proper to eat and pass communal dishes with the right hand. All meals traditionally end with a final and more important prayer, called an amin, which is a signal to the group that they are dismissed from the gathering.

Visiting

The people of Tajikistan pride themselves on their bountiful hospitality, and it is common for travelers to be invited to a private home by local people. However, visits in Tajik culture are traditionally not short, and hosts often go to great lengths to provide the very best to visitors. Traditionally, this may have even included the slaughter of one of their prized livestock for the occasion.

When invited to a person's home in Tajikistan, it is considered proper to bring presents such as flowers or chocolates. As Tajikistan is a relatively poor nation, it is also appropriate to give gifts of money to help offset the cost of the elaborate meal that the hosts are sure to provide. While hosts may initially refuse to take payment, it is not rude to insist, or to give the monetary gift to another member of the household. A guest should also try all the foods offered, even if they are not to his or her personal liking. Unlike many Muslims, people in Tajikistan are fond of drinking alcohol, and often offer vodka or other strong drinks to guests. However, it is not impolite to refuse alcohol, and those who choose to partake should keep in mind that one toast is likely to lead to many more.

LIFESTYLE

Family

Family is extremely important to the people of Tajikistan. The social bonds created by overlapping family ties are fundamental to the wider community. Because of the central role that family plays in social life, it is considered proper for an individual to know the names and birth dates of all his or her extended relations. It is also normal for several generations to live in the same household. Newly married couples sometimes seek permission to move out of their family home, but traditionally remain in the same town or neighborhood as their relatives.

Families tend to be quite large in Tajikistan, and it is common for a couple to have five to 10 children. In the past, wealthier men sometimes had multiple wives. As was once the case throughout much of the Muslim world, men in Tajikistan were allowed to take up to four wives if they could support them. The Soviet government banned this custom, and it is now rarely practiced.

Housing

Most people in Tajikistan live in rural areas, and there are several types of simple dwellings utilized throughout the countryside. One simple form of housing, traditional in the most remote areas, is the yurt. A circular tent made of animal hides stretched over a wooden frame, the yurt is both extremely resistant to the weather and can be easily transported. More permanent houses are also built, using bricks, stones, mortar, and thatched roofs. Most rural homes lack indoor plumbing.

Traditional Tajikistan yurt

There is a difference between urban and rural housing in Tajikistan. In bigger cities, people tend to live in apartments. However, due to Tajikistan's rapidly expanding population, there has often been a shortage of housing in urban centers. Urban apartments usually have modern plumbing and electricity, but power shortages are common.

Food

People in Tajikistan eat many different foods. In part, this is because of Tajikistan's varied topography, as specific crops thrive in the nation's different regions. As a result, typical dishes vary considerably throughout the country. Tajikistan's culinary diversity is also a product of the nation's place in the world. As a crossroads between Europe and Asia, Tajikistan has been influenced by many cultures throughout history. The many foods eaten in Tajikistan reflect these multiple influences.

In some parts of the country, the primary starch is rice, usually served as a spicy casserole called pilov. Wheat is also an important staple, cooked into a kind of flat bread called non. A huge range of produce is grown in Tajikistan, including carrots, apricots, raisins, melons, apples and pears. People in Tajikistan also consume quite a bit of meat. The most common meat is lamb, often served in grilled kebabs. As a majority Muslim country, pork is not consumed in Tajikistan. Unlike most Muslims, however, people in Tajikistan often consume alcohol. Rural people make their own vodka and sweet wine. Tea, particularly green tea, is the favorite nonalcoholic beverage. It is sometimes served with flavorings such as nuts or dried fruit.

Life's Milestones

The idea of family and kinship is central to the people of Tajikistan, and they vigorously celebrate the significant events in the lives of family members. The birth of a first child, the circumcision of an eldest son, and marriages are accompanied by family celebrations called tois. Tois are large parties, often involving more than 100 people, thrown for the extended family and neighbors and typically feature music, dancing and food and drink. Hosting impressive tois is a sign of the family's wealth, and is a way of achieving social influence in the wider community.

Marriage is an important milestone in Tajik culture, both for the individual and the family. For the individual, it marks the end of childhood and the beginning of adulthood; for the family, marriage holds the promise of healthy growth. While the prospective bride and groom have ultimate say over the matter, families hold considerable influence over the marriage process. Typically, the search for potential mates is conducted by an extended network of relatives, who pride themselves on their ability to pick the best partner for the young people in question. The groom's family pays a bride price called a kalym, often a considerable sum of money, which can only be raised through cooperation with a network of relatives.

CULTURAL HISTORY

Art

Historically, Tajikistan was located along the ancient Silk Road, an important network of overland trade routes that profoundly impacted development in the region. Beginning in the second century BCE, the Silk Road connected Europe with China, providing a major artery for transporting material goods and people. Tajikistan's artistic traditions were therefore influenced by the ancient Chinese, Persian, Indian and Hellenistic (Greece) cultures for thousands of years. Early traditional crafts included ceramics, metalwork and jewelry, and decorative carving. Tajikistan's weavers, in particular, had a reputation for excellent craftsmanship. They used locally available silk and wool to make warm, durable, geometrically patterned rugs to outfit the people who traveled across their land. Early Tajik art was also largely religious in nature. For example, due to the influence of Islamic art, early painting was mostly found on manuscripts, such as the Koran (Islam's holy book).

Architecture

Its location along the Silk Road also endowed Tajikistan with a history of impressive architecture. In order to defend positions along the profitable trade route, large citadels were constructed throughout Tajikistan since ancient times. These featured massive walls made from heavy stones, fortified gates, and dome-topped towers. One remaining example of this type of building is the Mugh Tappa, located in Istaravshan, which was captured by Alexander the Great (356–323 BCE) in 329 BCE. Since the 14th century, Islam has also been a major influence on the architecture of Tajikistan. Tajik mosques feature grand blue or golden domes, colorful mosaics, and tall towers called minarets from which the faithful are summoned to prayer. Mosques are often large complexes, containing religious schools called madrassas.

Drama

Historically, the most popular form of dramatic performance in Tajikistan has been storytelling. Traditionally performed by respected elder members of society, called aksakals, stories were told at family events, and at teahouses called chaikhanas. Storytelling tended to cover themes such as historical battles, journeys to distant lands, morality tales, and the adventures of Tajik heroes. Many stories had to do with the comical exploits of a 13th-century hero named Afandi. Religious stories were also popular, recounting the lives of Islamic figures. Music was often performed along with storytelling to enhance the effect of the spoken dramas.

Dance

Dance has been a favorite form of expression in Tajik culture, especially at festivals. A good example is the festival called Nowruz, which is of Persian origin, held to mark the first day of spring. Communities across Tajikistan traditionally celebrated Nowruz by gathering to be entertained by troupes of musicians and dancers. Tajik dancers tended to follow the strong rhythm of their folk music, taking exaggerated steps back and forth while they swayed their arms above their heads. Dancing during festivals was one time that the genders could mingle, and has long been associated with courtship.

Music

Music has historically been a very important part of Tajik culture. It served as a form of everyday entertainment, as well as a way to mark significant events within the local community. Music was also part of the Silk Road experience, as musicians were often attached to the caravans that traveled through Tajikistan. Though a number of traditional instruments were commonly played throughout the country, Tajik music tends to be very percussive, and uses a variety of drums. These included the goblet-shaped tablak and the kettle-shaped nagora. These were often accompanied by a horn called a karnai and a stringed instrument called a dutor, as well as vocal arrangements.

There are several different folk music traditions in Tajikistan which reflect the country's long and varied cultural history. One form of folk music is falak, popular throughout Tajikistan's mountainous Pamir region, which is distinctive for its mournful singing. Associated with Sufism (a mystical branch of Islam), falak came from Persia through Afghanistan, and many of its songs are often credited to the 13th-century Persian poet Rumi (1207–1273). Another style of music is garibi, known for its lyrics about missing home and family. Though garibi has been performed by travelers since medieval times, it became especially popular throughout Tajikistan in the early 20th century, as patterns of migration caused by modern agriculture reshaped traditional Tajik life.

Literature

The people of Tajikistan are justifiably proud of their nation's long and prestigious literary tradition. Strictly speaking, the earliest literature in Tajikistan dates back to before recorded history. Petroglyphs (stylized images carved into rock) dating back at least 10,000 years are found throughout the Pamir mountain range. These represent an early form of human writing. Poetic verses, often composed as part of the venerable tradition of storytelling, are part of a Central Asian oral tradition that also goes back to ancient times. These may be considered part of Tajikistan's literary history as well, since they served as a source of inspiration to later masters of the written word.

Tajik people trace their literary heritage back to the ninth century CE, when the legendary Persian poet Rudaki (858–c. 941) created poems filled with humor and praise, called ghazals. In the 11th century CE, a poet named Omar Khayyam (1048–1122) pioneered a new form of poetry called rubiayyat. Distinctive for its quatrain format, meaning that verses consisted of four lines, rubiayyat greatly influenced the literature of Persia and south Asia. Rumi, the great Sufi poet, brought a mystical influence to Tajikistan's literature in the 13th century CE. In the 15th century, literature spread in popularity throughout all areas of society. One author who stands out as responsible for this popularizing of written poetry in the 15th century was Jami (1414–1492), a Sufi poet who gained fame throughout the Persian Empire.

CULTURE

Arts & Entertainment

The people of Tajikistan endured a century of external rule. By the end of 1991, the Soviet Union had collapsed, and Tajikistan was left to determine its own future. There was a meltdown of political power, and a bloody civil war ensued. After nearly a decade of bloodshed, a peace accord was drafted that stopped the fighting. However, the various political factions that fought in the civil war have found it an ongoing struggle to unite as a modern nation state. The revival of the traditional Tajik arts has accompanied that struggle, and reflects a growing sense of national pride. Through renewed interest in their traditional forms of expression, the people of Tajikistan are developing connections to their venerable cultural history, and a sense of national unity.

Tajik culture was deeply impacted by the Soviet Union. Under Moscow's control for most of the 20th century, Tajikistan developed in ways that were both helpful and detrimental to the traditional arts. During this period, all citizens were offered free university education, which enabled many people, who would otherwise not be able to afford it, to study the arts. The arts also received ample funding, and museums and galleries displaying Tajik art were established throughout the country. However, these positive developments were motivated by the Soviet desire to use the arts as a way of shaping public opinion. Specifically, they were employed as a means of giving the country's ethnically diverse population a united national identity.

Many Tajik art students went to Russia during this period and returned to Tajikistan with new artistic sensibilities. This change was especially apparent in music. In the first half of the 20th century, opera and classical music came to Tajikistan, and towards the end of the century, Western-style genres such as rock, jazz and hip-hop began to influence Tajik music. At the beginning of the 21st century, pop music in Tajikistan combined traditional sounds and themes with standard rock sensibilities, often acting as a complement to the traditional music played at social events.

Literature was also changed by the Soviet experience. This period produced a plethora of notable writers who took a non-traditional approach to literature. As young writing students came back from universities in Russia, they brought a new tone to the national literary scene. Unlike the rather flamboyant, poetic traditional Tajik style, the Russian-influenced Tajik literature of the late 20th century was much more realistic in tone. One author who stands out as pioneering this new style of Tajik literature is Sadriddin Aini (1878–1954), who used his writing ability to portray the contemporary Central Asian experience, and call for solutions to the region's unique problems.

Soviet rule also impacted drama and dance traditions by encouraging new kinds of performance art. Ballet and Western-style theater were introduced to Tajikistan during the Soviet period. However, Soviet control suppressed traditional forms of drama and dance. Because those folk traditions were associated with religious festivals, and religious expression was suppressed by the Soviets, traditional storytelling and dance became less central to public life in the 20th century than in previous centuries.

Since Tajikistan gained independence in 1991, the national arts have experienced further important changes. The end of Soviet rule meant that the ample state funding of the arts stopped. Education is no longer provided by the government, and aspiring artists could no longer count on the arts as a career path. However, traditional crafts reemerged as important trade goods. Since tourism grew significantly in the post-Soviet period, and tourists were eager to pay good money for items such as traditional textiles and jewelry, artists became able to make a living through manufacturing and selling traditional craft products.

The end of Soviet rule also meant that the prohibition on religious expression ceased in the early 1990s. Festivals that had been suppressed throughout the 20th century were again able to take place without any government interference, and were renewed with great exuberance. The arts that have traditionally accompanied festivals, especially dancing and storytelling, have been revived and are now extremely popular within Tajikistan, both as casual entertainment, and to reassert traditional social ties.

Cultural Sites & Landmarks

Tajikistan's cultural and political capital is Dushanbe. However, in contrast to its current status, it has not always been a city of particular cultural importance. Before the Soviet era, Dushanbe was a fairly average village, notable because it hosted a market every Monday. (In fact, its name comes from the Tajik word for "Monday," which reflects the rather mundane nature of the village throughout history.) Despite its relative obscurity in the past, there are some places of cultural significance in Dushanbe. The Writers' Union Building, an impressive structure built like a cathedral, houses statues of some of the Persian Empire's most celebrated authors. Friendship Square is a park in the center of the city with a lovely flower garden. It is watched over by an enormous statue of an ancient king named Ismoil, who is regarded as a folk hero by the people of Tajikistan. The Haji Yakoub mosque, with its golden dome, is an important center of Muslim worship in Dushanbe.

Dushanbe is also home to Tajikistan's museums. The Museum of Musical Instruments provides great insight into this aspect of Tajik culture, while the Bekhzod Museum gives a broader overview of Tajikistan, through exhibits about the country's natural history, as well as ethnographic and archaeological artifacts. The Museum of Antiquities mostly displays objects relating to the country's ancient history. It also houses an impressive reclining Buddha, dating back to the sixth century CE, which was unearthed in 1966. It is the largest statue of Buddha in Central Asia.

The northern city Istaravshan, which is reputed to date back to 500 BCE, is also an important cultural center in Tajikistan. There are several historically significant sites within this ancient city. One of the most impressive is the Kok Gumbaz, or Blue Dome, which has served as a mosque and religious school since the 15th century. This mosque is distinctive for its ornate façade (exterior) and grand blue-domed top. Another important destination is the Mugh Tappa, an ancient fortress that was taken by Alexander the Great in 329 BCE, Genghis Khan in 1220 CE, and then the Russian army in 1866.

Tajikistan is also home to the awe-inspiring Pamir mountain range in the east. Visitors to this beautifully rugged, mountainous region are able to experience one of the last wild places in Central Asia. They retrace sections of the famous Silk Road, the important trade route that connected China to Europe from ancient times. Through the centuries, countless travelers have made the trek across the Pamirs, including ancient Chinese explorers, Buddhist pilgrims, Christian missionaries, Persian traders, and even the legendary merchant and explorer Marco Polo.

Libraries & Museums

The National Museum of Antiquities of Tajikistan is located in the capital of Dushanbe. Many of its exhibits and artifacts are related to the historic Silk Road that connected India with Central Asia, including a reclining Buddha statue excavated in southern Tajikistan, considered the largest Buddha statue in the Central Asian region. Also located in Dushanbe is the National History Museum and the National Kamoliddin Behzod Fine Arts Museum, which has over 50,000 exhibits ranging from fine art to archeology and ethnography. As of 2007, Tajikistan was home to forty-two museums overall.

Tajikistan's key repositories include the National Library of Tajikistan, the Central Scientific Library of Tajikistan, and the National Archives of Tajikistan, all located in the capital of Dushanbe. The National Library contains over three million volumes, including approximately 10,000 rare books.

Holidays

Independence from the Soviet Union is commemorated on September 9 each year. Outside the major Islamic holidays, which are no longer repressed, Tajikistanis celebrate Nowruz on March 21 and 22. It is an Islamic new year's celebration with pre-Islamic Persian roots, welcoming spring. The festivities, which are preceded by elaborate preparation rituals such as spring cleaning, include a purification rite in which people jump over fire, the buying of new clothes, trips to the countryside, and feasting. People also play buzkashi, a game similar to polo, and stage horse races.

Youth Culture

In general, Tajikistan has a young population, and an estimated one-third of the population is between the ages of ten and twenty-four in the early 21st century. Youth in Tajikistan tend to have a different cultural outlook than their parents and grandparents. In many ways, young people gravitate more toward Western trends than do their elders. This is certainly reflected in their musical tastes, as hip-hop, rock and jazz are popular among younger people.

In other ways, young people are also more connected to their historical culture than most of their elders. Since Tajikistan achieved independence in 1991, there has been a revival of national pride and interest in traditional forms of expression. Many young people have embraced this return to the older traditions, which were largely suppressed during the Soviet period. This rapid return to traditionalism is a cause for concern as well. For example, the majority of Tajik youth are Muslim, and many are being recruited by Muslim extremist groups linked to terrorism.

SOCIETY

Transportation

Public and private buses are the most reliable means of transportation in the country. Taxi services also operate along regular routes, and it is common to travel between cities by shared taxis. International flights to Tajikistan arrive at Dushanbe, the capital. There are regular flights from Russia, Turkey, United Arab Emirates (UAE) and Iran. It is also possible to enter the country by land from Afghanistan, Kyrgyzstan, Uzbekistan, and China, though border crossings are sometimes closed due to diplomatic disputes. Domestic flights connect Dushanbe with several smaller cities within the country, but the availability varies, and is often curtailed due to bad weather. Traffic moves on the right-hand side in Tajikistan.

Transportation Infrastructure

The transportation infrastructure in Tajikistan is in poor condition and still developing. Outside of primary roads and main towns, rural roads are poorly maintained and interior roads are open seasonally depending on weather. (As the country is mostly mountainous, accumulation of snow often separates northern and southern Tajikistan during winter months.) Recognizing the need to improve its transportation infrastructure, the government of Tajikistan launched several projects in the early 21st century, including the Anzab Tunnel, which connects Dushanbe to Khujand, the second largest Tajik city. (However, the tunnel, even after its inaugural opening in 2006, remained unpaved.) As a landlocked nation, Tajikistan's continued development of a road transport system remains a priority. There is less than 450 miles of railroad tracks in the entire country.

Media & Communications

Modern media in Tajikistan were mostly developed during the period of Soviet occupation. On the one hand, media outlets received funding from the central government in Moscow, allowing them to distribute their products without considering costs, thus, the people of Tajikistan became avid consumers of media. On the other hand, the Soviet government strictly censored media outlets, and prohibited foreign media within the country. Since Tajikistan gained independence in 1991, the situation has changed, and the new government has ceased direct censorship.

However, media outlets still practice self-censorship, and are sometimes less than assertive in their reporting. Additionally, they are now run for profit, and are dependent on advertisers.

Tajikistan has a large number of media outlets considering the relatively small size of the country. Some are state-run, while others are entirely private. State controlled newspapers include the Tajik-language *Jumhuriyat*, the Uzbek-language *Khalq Ovozi*, and the Russian language *Narodnaya Gazeta*. Private newspapers, such as *Neru-i Sukhan* and *Tojikiston*, are also popular. Radio stations transmit throughout the country, and government-owned stations such as Tajik Radio and Radio Sado-i Dushanbe are the best established. Several private radio stations have emerged in recent years, including Asia-Plus and Radio Vatan. State-run television is also the most watched, including channels such as Tajik TV, Soghd TV, and Khatlon TV. There are also new private stations, including the popular TV Safina. Internet usage in Tajikistan remains low, with an estimated 700,000 users—representing just over nine percent of the population—in late 2010, partially due to cost and reliability issues.

SOCIAL DEVELOPMENT

Standard of Living

Tajikistan ranked 133rd on the 2013 Human Development Index (HDI), which measures standards of life indicators from the previous year, out of the 187 countries surveyed. As of 2013, an estimated 35.6 percent of the population lives below the poverty line. Tajikistan is considered the poorest country in Central Asia, with the exception of war torn Afghanistan.

Water Consumption

Tajikistan has abundant water resources, but deteriorating, or lack of, infrastructure, consumption, and water quality remain issues. As of 2012, approximately 64 percent of the rural population has access to safe drinking water, and only about one-quarter of rural regions are connected to the country's centralized water system. The government planned to provide the entire population with safe drinking water by 2010, and now keeps moving the goal further into the future each year. Furthermore, the water supply and sanitation systems in the capital of Dushanbe cannot serve the needs of the population. As a result, outbreaks of typhoid and other water-borne illnesses are not uncommon, especially in the city's poorer quarters. International observers rate the risk of contracting infectious diseases as high.

Education

The Soviet system left a tradition of free and universal education and a high literacy rate. After independence, the six-year civil war seriously interrupted the educational system, driving out skilled teachers and resulting in deteriorated infrastructure (one out of five schools were destroyed). While the system is functioning better in the early 21st century, it is still not adequately funded by the state. Furthermore, a lack of qualified professionals entering into the educational field and declining standards are other factors affecting the education system in Tajikistan, which is seen by many as failing and in need of a major overhaul. In fact, many outside observers have questioned the state-reported literacy rate of 99.7 percent as dubious.

It is compulsory for children to attend primary and secondary school (years six through 15). The government has announced that beginning in 2016, 12 years of schooling will be compulsory. However, it has been estimated that less than 10 percent actually completes the full nine years. In addition, estimates of school-aged children who remain outside of the educational system range from five to 20 percent, and are contrary to state-reported enrollment estimates.

Most institutions of higher education are located in Dushanbe. These include Tajik State University, Tajik Technical University, the Tajik Academy of Sciences, and the Tajik Agricultural University. As of 2012, there were thirty institutions of higher education in Tajikistan. As with the lower levels of education, the provision and compensation of a specialized or trained teaching staff remains a concern.

Women's Rights

Despite the fact that they are officially considered equal according to the nation's constitution and legal code, women in Tajikistan face many significant obstacles. These problems stem from a variety of causes, including poverty, uneven enforcement of laws, and traditional attitudes toward women. The government of Tajikistan has taken some measures to improve the lives of women. There are also a number of non-governmental organizations (NGOs) working to ensure that women in Tajikistan are afforded the rights spelled out in the country's laws.

One cause for concern among the women of Tajikistan is the lack of equal economic opportunities. Tajikistan is a relatively poor country, and women often cannot find stable employment since it became independent from the Soviet Union. Factories which used to be large employers of women, such as textile manufacturers, have declined in recent decades. Women are also less likely than men to receive the vocational training required to pursue more lucrative professions, and work mainly in agriculture, informal jobs, or other lower-paying careers.

Domestic violence against women is a problem throughout Tajikistan. While technically illegal, it is considered a normal part of married life, and people are generally discouraged from intervening in the abuse. Husbands are the most common perpetrators of domestic violence against women, but other relatives may also be abusive. Tajik men often travel abroad for extended periods of time as migrant laborers, and their wives—usually left to live with their absent husbands' families—commonly face abuse if their husbands do not return for long periods of time, or do not send home enough money.

Ultimately, the problems faced by women in Tajikistan are influenced by traditional gender attitudes. Historically, women were considered to be in charge of the household and child rearing, while men dealt with the public sphere. In the past, it was even considered inappropriate for women to go out in public without male escorts, and they were not encouraged to participate in community affairs and government. During the Soviet period, this changed, and women were officially considered to be equal to men. Since Tajikistan gained its independence, there has been a backlash against the externally imposed ideas about gender equality, and a trend toward renewing old practices of gender segregation.

Despite this backlash against the gender equality forced on Tajikistan by the Soviet Union, there are reasons to be optimistic about the development of Tajik women's rights. The government seems to be sincerely interested in helping the country's female citizens achieve lasting equality. This is evidenced by the establishment of the Committee on Women's Affairs, a governmental agency to oversee the creation of a legal framework that protects women's rights. In the past decade, a number of NGOs have started operating throughout the country, proving shelter for victims of domestic abuse and other forms of gender violence.

Health Care

Tajikistan's health care system is underdeveloped. There is a shortage of medical facilities, equipment and supplies, and access to even the most basic health care and medicine is difficult for much of the rural population. The number of health care professionals also decreased dramatically during the civil war, since many were non-indigenous and had the opportunity to immigrate.

Ecological mismanagement has further compromised the public health of Tajikistan. The food and water supply is polluted with bacteria and toxic levels of pesticides and chemical fertilizers.

GOVERNMENT

Structure

Tajikistan was unprepared for independence in 1991. After decades of domination by the Soviet Union, the lack of experience with reform and the desire of the local ruling elite to maintain the status quo led to extreme social instability and sparked a violent civil war that lasted until 1997. Those who opposed communist forces had various visions for the future of Tajikistan: some were fighting for a secular parliamentary democracy, others for an Islamic republic. The secular forces were prevailing and a brief period of power sharing was put in place with elections to follow. The Communist Party and its allies which had been winning the civil war and won the elections and now dominate the country, often through elections that are considered neither free nor fair.

The Republic of Tajikistan is divided into two provinces and the autonomous region of Gorno-Badakhshan, which are further divided into districts. Dushanbe is considered a capital district. In early 2015, the president announced that a new capital, Saihun, would be constructed in the desert near the city of Khujand. Local councils administer the regions, though power is concentrated at the national level.

The head of state in Tajikistan is a president. The president nominates the prime minister, as well as the council of ministers and the Supreme Court judges for the approval of the legislature. He or she can serve a maximum of two consecutive seven-year terms. The current president was elected to his second term in 2013. The bicameral legislature is made up of the Assembly of Representatives and the National Assembly. Members are appointed and elected, both by direct and indirect vote.

Political Parties

The People's Democratic Party of Tajikistan currently dominates the political life of Tajikistan; in the February, 2010, elections, with 55 of the 63 seats in the National Assembly. In the interests of national reconciliation, opposition parties which were once banned now have the right to operate. These include the Islamic Rebirth Party, the nationalist Rastokhez party, and Lali Badakhshon, the party working towards broader rights for the Autonomous Region of Gorno-Badakhsan. The other eight seats were split among four parties. In March, 2015, elections were held with the People's Democratic Party obtaining more than 62 percent of the vote, winning 51 of the 63 seats, while for the first time the party representing those who had fought on the losing side of the civil war did not win any seats.

Local Government

There are three levels of local government in Tajikistan: the community level, which consists of town and village governments in rural regions; the district level, which includes the governance of cities and raions (administrative unit similar to a district); and the oblast (territorial divisions) level, which includes the oblasts of the Gorno-Badakhshan Autonomous Region (GBAR) and Khatlon. Raions, or districts, are subdivided into jamoats (similar to municipalities, of which there are approximately 406), and then into villages. Tajikistan has 58 districts. All tiers of local government are headed by elected councils.

Judicial System

The independent judicial branch is composed of the Supreme Court and several subsidiary courts such as the Supreme Economic Court and the Constitutional Court. Judges are appointed for 10-year terms. The country's legal system has its origins in the Romano-Germanic legal system.

Taxation

With a top income tax rate of 13 percent, and a top corporate tax rate of 25 percent, Tajikistan is considered competitive in terms of taxation. Other taxes include a value-added tax (VAT), levied at 20 percent, and a property tax.

Armed Forces

The armed forces of Tajikistan consist of land and mobile forces, air and air defense forces, as well as a national guard and security forces, including border personnel. Both the compulsory and voluntary recruitment age is eighteen. As of 2015, military personnel numbered an estimated 6,000. Russia also maintains a military base in Tajikistan that is considered the largest in the region, with over 7,000 personnel.

Foreign Policy

Tajikistan is a relatively young country, formed after the dissolution of the Soviet Union in 1991. However, after achieving independence Tajikistan fell into a devastating civil war, which lasted throughout the 1990s. The first stable central government emerged in 2000, when the conflicting factions settled on a power sharing agreement. Because of its short and turbulent history as a modern state, Tajikistan has not had the chance to fully develop a systematic foreign policy. However, the central government is beginning to take steps toward establishing normalized diplomatic relations with other countries and multilateral organizations. However, with Russian troops near the capital, some international military agreements depend upon the Russian government also agreeing to the accord. Thus while Tajikistan and India signed an agreement to allow the Indian air force to establish a base in Tajikistan in 2012, the Russian military has prevented any military planes from flying to the new base.

Tajikistan shares borders with Uzbekistan to the west and Kyrgyzstan to the north. The three countries also have many cultural and historical commonalities. They were formed from the collapse of the Soviet Union, and are struggling to define themselves as sovereign nation states. There have been occasional disputes among these three young countries, and conflicts of interest have come to light as they develop as separate nations. The precise locations of borders are often challenged, and armed skirmishes occasionally break out over this issue. Tajikistan's development of hydroelectric power facilities has also been a source of concern for Uzbekistan and Kyrgyzstan, which view such projects as potentially disruptive to water sources needed for crop irrigation. (Approximately 80 percent of Central Asia's water originates in Kyrgyzstan and Tajikistan.) This escalated into an early 2010 feud with Uzbekistan, which maintained an economic blockade against Tajikistan. After five years, the feud continues limiting economic interaction and with each side taking symbolic steps against the other.

Tajikistan also borders China. In the early years of Tajikistan's existence as an independent nation, it had occasional moments of tension with this giant neighbor. During the Soviet period, the border between what is now Tajikistan and China was hotly contested, as it represented the frontier between two superpowers. Disagreement over the exact border continued after Tajikistan's independence. The two countries have sought to normalize relations in recent years. As well as coming to an agreement over the location of the border, they have become trading partners, creating an important economic relationship.

Tajikistan's neighbor to the south, Afghanistan, has created problems and opportunities for the young nation. When the Taliban were in power in Afghanistan, Tajikistan provided a safe haven for opposition fighters, many of whom were of Tajik origin. Since the overthrow of the Taliban in 2001, relations between the two neighboring countries have thawed considerably. However, the huge increase in heroin production in Afghanistan since the fall of the Taliban has greatly impacted Tajikistan. Tajikistan is now a major transit point for heroin destined for Russia and the rest of Europe, with an estimated 1,000 tons of the illicit substance passing through the small country each year. As of 2015, a new military base was being constructed on the border to restrict cross-border traffic.

Tajikistan's proximity to Afghanistan, and the drug trafficking across Tajikistan's southern border, has brought increased international attention to the small country. The United States leads a multilateral effort to provide political and economic assistance to Tajikistan. This assistance is largely aimed at curbing the flow of narcotics, and also at preventing Tajikistan from becoming a safe haven for extremists seeking refuge from the new government in Afghanistan. Attention from powerful countries outside the region is helping Tajikistan's efforts to become a full member of important global institutions, such as the World Trade Organization (WTO). Tajikistan has been a member of the UN since 1992, and is also a member of the World Bank, the International Monetary Fund ((IMF) and the Asian Development Bank (ADB).

Human Rights Profile

International human rights law insists that states respect civil and political rights, and also promote an individual's economic, social and cultural rights. The United Nations Universal Declaration on Human Rights (UDHR) is recognized as the standard for international human rights. Its authors sought the counsel of the world's great thinkers, philosophers, and religious leaders, and were careful to create a document that reflects the core values shared by every world culture. (To read this document or view the articles relating to cultural human rights, visit: http://www.udhr.org/UDHR/default.htm.)

Many human rights abuses occur in Tajikistan. These are often compounded by the country's political instability and government corruption. Tajikistan, which came into being as a modern nation in 1991 when the Soviet Union collapsed, fell into a bloody civil war in the 1990s. Though warring factions eventually agreed to put aside their differences for the sake of the country, divisions still remain, leading to an uneven implementation of policy. Elections have mostly been free of violence, but marred by unfair practices and tampering.

The narcotics trafficking that plagues Tajikistan is also a factor in the country's human rights record. Tajikistan shares a substantial border with Afghanistan, considered the world's foremost producer of opium, and has become a major transit point for heroin en route to Russia. In fact, it is estimated that as much heroin is transported through Tajikistan as is imported to Europe and North America put together. Additionally, a number of Tajik government officials have been suspected of being involved with drug trafficking.

Law enforcement has been severely compromised by the chaotic atmosphere created by these factors, and abuses of power happen on a regular basis. Police officers commonly extort bribes from the public, and are known to buy their way to higher ranks. False arrests and arbitrary detentions are commonplace, and sometimes have political motivations, with officers targeting members of rival parties or media critics. Torture is also widespread, and victims of violence while in government custody have very little legal recourse. Additionally, the right to a fair trial and hearing, as stated in Article 10 of the UDHR, remains a question. Judges are highly susceptible to bribery and political influence in Tajikistan's legal system, allowing innocent people to be sent to prison on weak or fabricated evidence.

Overall, the situation in Tajikistan contradicts several important principles of the UDHR. The corrupt nature of Tajik politics is a form of citizen disenfranchisement, and is therefore a violation of Article 21, which articulates that the will of the people should be the basis of government. Since those able to pay bribes are allowed to get away with crimes in Tajikistan—and those unable to pay are targeted for arrest—the government fails to provide equal protection under the law as stated in Article 7. The arbitrary arrests which routinely occur within the country are specifically forbidden by Article 9. People in custody are commonly victims of torture, which is in violation of the ban on inhumane treatment in Article 5.

Migration

The migration of Afghan refugees into Tajikistan has become an issue in the early 21st century. According to the UN's refugee agency, the United Nations High Commissioner for Refugees (or UNHCR), Tajikistan is not set up to handle an influx of refugees. Tajikistan also has a large number of labor migrants working in Russia.

ECONOMY

Overview of the Economy

During the Soviet era, Tajikistan was primarily forced to produce cotton, process aluminum, and mine certain minerals. The economy was further restricted by the post-independence civil war, which was estimated to have caused $12 billion USD in damage to industry. At the same time, production levels plummeted.

Since the peace accords, the economy has made progress. The per capita gross domestic product (GDP) was estimated at $2,300 USD in 2013. The total labor force is approximately 2.2 million people. Officially, the 2013 unemployment rate was 2.5 percent, how observers estimate that unemployment really runs between 20 and 40 percent, particularly among the young of working age. Europe, Russia and Uzbekistan are its main trading partners.

Industry

Only about 10.7 percent of the work force is engaged in industry. Aluminum processing is the most important industrial sector, and aluminum is one of the country's largest exports. The main processing plant, west of the capital, was built by the Soviets. It now produces approximately a quarter of its capacity, largely because it depends on importing raw material.

The majority of Tajikistan's industries are centered in or near the capital of Dushanbe. Factories produce industrial machinery for oil drilling, textile production, and agriculture. Foods that are processed include fruit, vegetables, and meat. Textiles produced from local raw materials are generally made of silk and cotton. Near Dushanbe are located several hydroelectric stations, responsible for supplying local chemical and metal plants.

Labor

In 2013, the labor force was estimated at 2.2 million, with approximately 46 percent working in the agricultural sector, and nearly 43 percent working in services industries. As of 2013, the official unemployment rate was 2.5 percent, though that number is believed to be higher. Unofficially, an estimated 40 percent of the workforce is considered underemployed.

Energy/Power/Natural Resources

The country's mountainous terrain restricts agricultural activity to about 7 percent of its total land area. The mountains, however, yield a variety of mineral deposits. These include iron, tin, lead, gold, silver, and mercury. Other deposits, such as uranium, have been exhausted.

The extensive network of rivers gives landlocked Tajikistan great potential for generating hydroelectricity, but only a few rivers, such as the Vakhsh, have been harnessed for this purpose. In fact, a project to construct a hydroelectric dam has caused friction between Uzbekistan and Tajikistan, with the Uzbek government in Tashkent stating that the dam will hurt agriculture, particularly the cotton industry. The World Bank's decision, in 2014, to fund a new dam has increased Tajik-Uzbek stress. Deposits of alternative fuel sources, such as coal, natural gas, and petroleum, do exist, but they have not yet been exploited.

Tajikistan has severe environmental problems that stem from the Soviet legacy of poor land management and pressure to increase yield. Soil and water are both polluted from chemical fertilizers and pesticides, and the soil has also suffered from excessive irrigation, increasing saline levels. Tapped so heavily for irrigation, the levels of the Amu Darya and the Syr Darya have decreased drastically, affecting in turn the water level of the threatened Aral Sea.

Fishing

While Tajikistan has an abundance of water resources, and is home to numerous types of freshwater fish such as trout and carp, commercial fishing has yet to be fully developed in the Central Asian nation.

Mining/Metals

Despite large mineral resources, Tajikistan is not a major provider of metals or minerals. Mined resources and metals in Tajikistan include antimony, uranium, brown coal, zinc, lead, tungsten, gold, and silver. The country's mining industry has also attracted foreign interest in the early 21st century. In 2008, a Chinese mining corporation announced an investment of $100 million (USD) to extract copper, silver, and gold in Tajikistan.

Agriculture

Agricultural production has also rebounded since the end of the civil war. Just under 50 percent of the labor force is engaged in farming. Fruit, vegetables, wheat, and silk are major crops, but cotton is still the leader, primarily as an export crop in unprocessed form. As a result of this lack of diversification, not enough food is grown to meet domestic needs.

Animal Husbandry

Livestock remain an important part of the Tajik economy. Animal husbandry extends to cattle, sheep, and goats. In particular, Tajikistan is a regional leader of the breeding of wool-angora goats.

Tourism

Since the end of the civil war, tourism has increased in Tajikistan, though infrastructure remains largely undeveloped. Since the cities are generally modern or ancient but not well-preserved, the country's tourist highlights are mostly natural. Mountain treks and eco-tourism are the most popular visitor activities. The festivities of Nawruz also attract some tourists.

Adam Berger, Michael Aliprandi

DO YOU KNOW?

- Tajikistan is home to the largest glacier in the world outside the Polar Regions. Called Fedchenko, it is located in the Pamirs and measures over 700 square kilometers (270 square miles). It is estimated that the glacier is retreating at a rate of 16–20 meters annually.
- Dushanbe means "Monday" in Farsi, probably in reference to a weekly market.
- One of the highest dams in the world lies east of Dushanbe at Norek, on the Vakhsh River.

Bibliography

Abazov, Rafis. *Cultures of the World: Tajikistan.* New York: Marshall Cavendish Benchmark, 2006.

"Background Note: Tajikistan." U.S. Department of State. October 2008. <http://www.state.gov/r/pa/ei/bgn/5775.htm>.

"Country Profile: Tajikistan." *BBC News.* July 20, 2008. <http://news.bbc.co.uk/2/hi/asia-pacific/country_profiles/1296639.stm>.

Hiro, Dilip. *Inside Central Asia.* New York: Overlook Press, 2011.

Lonley Planet and Bradly Mayhes. *Central Asia.* Oakland, CA: Lonely Planet, 2014.

Middleton, Robert and Huw Thomas. *Tajikistan and the High Pamirs.* New York: W.W. Norton, 2008.

Nourzhanov, Kirill and Christian Bleuer. *Tajikistan: A Political and Social History.* Canberra: ANU Press, 2013.

Olcott, Martha Brill. *Tajikistan's Difficult Development Path.* Washington, D.C.: Carnegie Endowment for International Peace, 2012.

Rodgers, Mary, Tom Streissguth and Colleen Sexton. *Tajikistan.* Minneapolis: Lerner, 1993.

"Tajikistan Profile–Timeline." *BBC News.* 30 March, 2015. <http://www.bbc.com/news/world-asia-16201087>

Works Cited

"2003 Country Report on Human Rights Practices in Tajikistan." *U.S. Department of State.* 25 February 2004 http://www.state.gov/g/drl/rls/hrrpt/2003/27868.htm

"2005 Country Report on Human Rights Practices in Tajikistan." *U.S. Department of State.* 8 March 2006 http://www.state.gov/g/drl/rls/hrrpt/2005/61679.htm

"2006 Country Report on Human Rights Practices in Tajikistan." *U.S. Department of State.* 6 March 2007 http://www.state.gov/g/drl/rls/hrrpt/2006/78843.htm

"China-Tajik Border Opened." *BBC News.* 25 May 2004 http://news.bbc.co.uk/2/hi/asia-pacific/3745921.stm

"International Religious Freedom Report: Tajikistan." *U.S. Department of State.* 19 September 2008. http://www.state.gov/g/drl/rls/irf/2008/108507.htm

"On Edge: Afghanistan's Neighbors." *BBC News.* 19 September 2001 http://news.bbc.co.uk/2/hi/south_asia/1548452.stm

Shahriari, Shahriar. "Rubaiyat of Omar Khayyam." 2 June 2004 http://www.okonlife.com/

"Tajik Songs of Sky and Destiny at Fest." *Moscow Times.* 12 November 2008 http://www.themoscowtimes.com/article/1013/42/372292.htm

Spinetti, Federico. "Sonic Practices and Concepts in Tajik Popular Music." August 2007 http://www.mcm.asso.fr/site02/music-w-islam/articles/Spinetti-2007.pdf

"UN Special Rapporteur On Violence Against Women Concludes Visit to Tajikistan." *United Nations.* 23 May 2008 http://www.unhchr.ch/huricane/huricane.nsf/view01/03E589518A1B6415C125745200742F4F?opendocument

"UN Urges Close Central Asian Ties." *BBC News.* 7 December 2005 http://news.bbc.co.uk/2/hi/business/4506466.stm

"Voyage: ABC of Tadjikistan." *Discovery Central Asia.* Winter 2005 http://www.discovery-central-asia.com/archive/2005/win7.php

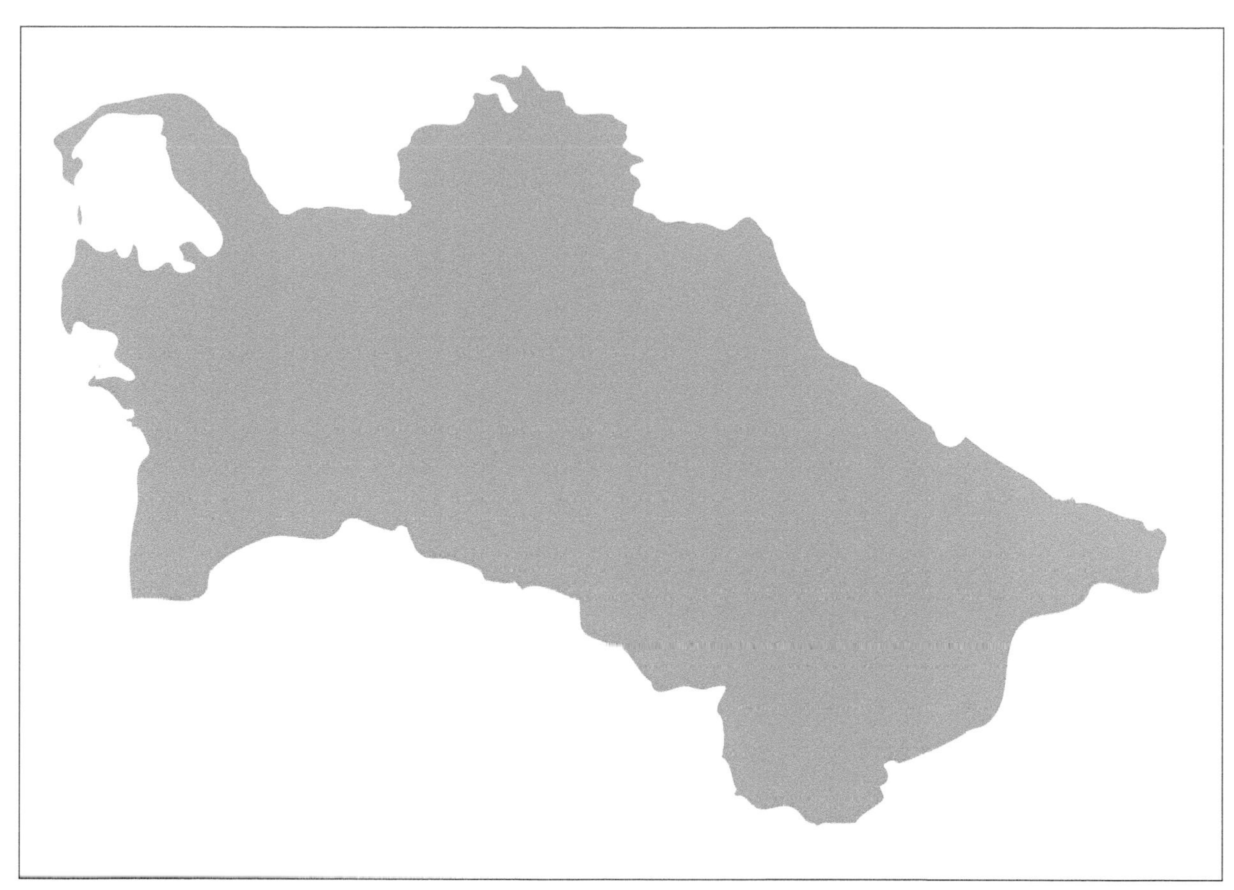

TURKMENISTAN

Introduction

Turkmenistan is located in Central Asia. A Soviet republic for much of the 20th century, it became an independent nation in 1991 following the dissolution of the Soviet Union. Turkmenistan has evolved a rich, distinctive culture based on various folk traditions. The applied arts, including jewelry, embroidered clothing, and carpets, are widespread. Turkmen carpets are known the world over for their dense weave and traditional patterns. The Turkmen are also great horse enthusiasts, and they are famous for the akhal teke breed. The animal's preservation has attained the status of an art form in the country.

GENERAL INFORMATION

Official Language: Turkmen
Population: 5,171,943 (2014)
Currency: Turkmen manat
Coins: Following independence, coins were minted in denominations of 1, 5, 10, 20 and 50 tennesi (100 tennesi is equivalent to 1 manat). In January 2009, coins were redenominated and reminted as 1 tenge (50 old manta), 2 tenge (100 old manta), 5 tenge (250 old manta), 10 tenge (500 old manta), 20 tenge (1,000 old manta), and 50 tenge (2,500 old manta), following inflation.
Land Area: 469,930 square kilometers (181,440 square miles)
Water Area: 18,170 square kilometers (7,015 square miles)
National Anthem: "Garassyz, Bitarap, Turkmenistanyn Dowlet Gimni" ("Independent, Neutral, Turkmenistan State Anthem")
Capital: Ashkhabad (Ashgabat)
Time Zone: GMT+5
Flag Description: The Turkmen flag consists of a green field with a red vertical band on the right (hoist) side. The band itself consists of five traditional tribal guls (carpet design element), which highlight Turkmenistan's proud heritage of handwoven, ethnic carpets; two olive branches are depicted at the bottom of the red stripe. Directly to the stripe's right is a white waxing crescent moon with five white stars, each with five points (representing Islam), partially encircled in the upper corner.

Population

Turkmenistan has a young, growing population. While recent statistics place the overall

N
0
200 Kilometers
0
200 Miles
Aral Sea
KAZAKHSTAN
KAZAKHSTAN
Amu Darya
Saygamysh Koh
Dasoguz
UZBEKISTAN
Garbogazkol Aylagy
Türkmenbasy
TURKMENISTAN
Balkanabat
Gyzylarbat
Turkmenabat
CASPIAN SEA
ASHGABAT
Silk Route Oasis of Merv
Tolkuchka Bazaar
Tejen
Mary
Bayramaly
IRAN
Serhetabat
AFGHANISTAN

Principal Cities by Population (2011 estimates):

- Ashgabat (683,000)
- Turkmenabat (279,765)
- Dashogus (245,872)
- Mary (126,141)
- Serdar (93,692)
- Baýramaly (91,713)
- Balkanabat (90,149)
- Tejen (79,324)
- Turkmenbashi (73,803)
- Abadan (Buzmeyin) (42,868)

population figure at just over 5 million, some government statistics have revealed a larger number, including 6.7 million in 2006. In April, 2014, the president requested that a national census be undertaken, if completed, it will be the first official census since independence. Turkmenistan has a population density of 11 people per square kilometer (28 per square mile), but large tracts of the central desert are uninhabited. Life expectancy is 61 years for men and 70 for women (2012).

Over 50 percent of the population lives in rural areas and carries on traditional pastoral lifestyles. Most large urban centers are located near a major source of water. The central desert area and western region are the least populated areas of the country, with the population in the central desert region estimated at one person per several square kilometers.

Languages

Turkmen is the official national language, spoken by 72 percent of the population. Russian is often spoken as a second language, and English is becoming more widely spoken. Turkmen, like Uzbek and Kazakh, belongs to the Oghuz family of Southern Turkic languages. It was originally written in Arabic script. Cyrillic was then adopted under the forced system of Russification. Within a decade of independence, the native population had adopted a modified Latin alphabet.

Native People & Ethnic Groups

An estimated 85 percent of the population is Turkmen, an ethnic group divisible into many tribes. The Yomud, who occupy the west, the Ersary, who occupy the southeast, and the Tekke, who occupy the central portion of the country, are the three largest. Minority groups include Uzbeks (five percent of the population), Russians (four percent), and Kazakhs (two percent). The Russian population decreased dramatically after Turkmenistan's declaration of independence, and then again once dual citizenship was abolished in 2003. Smaller ethnic minorities include Azeris, Armenians, Koreans, Tatars, and Ukrainians.

In truth, national identity is somewhat new to the people of Turkmenistan, who had never been organized along such lines before independence in 1991. Instead, people identified with family and tribe. The region had been inhabited for centuries by various nomadic tribes and ethnic groups before Russia began annexing territory. Those social principles are still significant in Turkmen society. Conflict, which has been kept to a minimum in the post-communist period, is most often inter-tribal rather than inter-ethnic.

Religions

About 89 percent of the population identifies themselves as Muslims, mainly the Sunni branch of Islam, but many are not active practitioners and view religion only as an important cultural trait. Small groups also practice Sufism, a mystical form of Islam, and Shia Islam. During the Soviet era, religious practices were officially repressed by the atheistic state; since independence there has been renewed interest in Islam, though not as strongly as in some other Central Asian republics. Approximately nine percent of the population adheres to the Eastern Orthodox faith.

Climate

Turkmenistan has a subtropical climate. Winters are dry and cool; summers are dry, hot and long. Temperatures average between –6° and 5° Celsius (21° and 41° Fahrenheit) in January and between 27° and 32° Celsius (81° and 90° Fahrenheit) in

July. Desert areas are much hotter. Precipitation, which falls between January and May, averages 22 centimeters (9 inches). Amounts are lower in the desert, higher in the Kopet Dag Mountains. Winds are nearly constant.

The country is prone to violent earthquakes, most acutely in the Kopet Dag mountain range. Ashgabat was destroyed by one such earthquake in 1948. Sandstorms from the Karakum (Garagum) Desert are also common.

ENVIRONMENT & GEOGRAPHY

Topography

Turkmenistan is bordered by Iran, Kazakhstan, Uzbekistan and Afghanistan. Its western border is formed by the Caspian Sea. The country's capital, Ashkhabad, is located in the southwestern region of the country, just north of the Iranian border.

The Karakum Desert occupies roughly 80 percent of Turkmenistan, or 350,000 square kilometers (135,136 square miles). Most of it is characterized by shifting sands, though hard clay deposits also occur. Marshy salt flats have formed in some of the depressions. The desert falls within the Turan Depression. The rest of the terrain is steppe and mountain.

The Kopet Dag Mountains rise in the east of Turkmenistan, along the border with Iran. Mount Shahshah is the highest point of the range, which is characterized by foothills, plateaus and ravines. Stream-fed oases are found in the foothills. Mount Ayrybaby, measuring 3,137 meters (10,292 feet), is the country's highest point. It rises in the far east in the Kugitang Range, which is part of the extensive Pamir-Alay chain.

Ashkhabad lies in a prime location between the southern point of the desert and the mountain range. Due to this location, the city is considered an oasis. However, the city also lies in a fault zone, leaving it at risk for earthquakes. In fact, a devastating earthquake in 1948 killed nearly two-thirds of the population.

Turkmenistan has scant water resources. Few rivers flow permanently; they originate in other countries and are concentrated in the south and east. The most important is the Amu Darya, the longest river in Central Asia. Other rivers are the Tejen, the Murgap, and the Atrek. The Caspian Sea, a landlocked salt lake, forms the country's western border. Its most prominent characteristic is the Garabogazkol Gulf, in the northwest.

Plants & Animals

Only tough shrubs and grasses grow across the vast desert regions and steppe of Turkmenistan, except along river banks, which support dense shrubs and a variety of wildlife. Desert animals include foxes, gazelles, rodents, and reptiles such as the Central Asian cobra, vipers, tortoise, and monitor lizards. The shore of the Caspian Sea is home to migratory birds during the winter months.

The mountains support a greater variety of both plant and animal life. Wild walnut, pistachio, and almond trees as well as juniper grow on the mountain slopes. Many herbaceous plants found in the country are harvested by Turkmen for traditional medicines and for dyes. Lynx, wild goats, cheetahs, porcupines, and snow leopards inhabit the forests and foothills. Among the country's endangered species are the markhor and the tiger.

CUSTOMS & COURTESIES

Greetings

Greetings in Turkmenistan vary depending on gender and the relationship between the people involved. When men meet other men, they generally shake hands and say "Asalaam aleikum" ("Peace be with you"). If the men greeting one another are close friends or family members, it is common for them to embrace. Some people also engage in the Russian-influenced custom of kissing close friends and relatives on the cheeks as a form of greeting. It is also common for male friends to touch one another lightly on the arm when conversing. This gesture is considered to be a sign of paying close attention to what the other person is saying.

Greetings between women tend to be similar. Women, however, also tend to bow their heads slightly when greeting. When greeting family or friends, women might also embrace one another or kiss on the cheek. Since many people in Turkmenistan are rather conservative Muslims, it is often considered inappropriate for women to interact with men they do not know. In general, a man should wait to see if a woman is comfortable shaking hands before initiating the gesture, as some women will prefer to simply bow their heads when uttering the greeting phrase.

Gestures & Etiquette

As is the case throughout Central Asia, the people of Turkmenistan are very welcoming of guests. However, there are several points of etiquette that are considered important throughout the region. First and foremost, many people in Turkmenistan are devout and rather conservative Muslims. Therefore, it is important to respect local sensibilities regarding religious places. Although Turkmen people often travel great distances to visit the country's historically significant mosques, these are often closed to non-Muslims.

Part of respecting the beliefs of Turkmen Muslims is accepting their ideas about gender. Although women are often active in economic and community life, many people feel that it is their duty as Muslims to maintain a sense of modesty. This means that some women are uncomfortable interacting with men they do not know. In addition, people in Turkmenistan are usually uncomfortable with men and women publicly displaying affection. Another aspect of Turkmen religious culture is respect for elders, who are considered to possess great wisdom. Visitors should treat older people with the utmost courtesy, as failure to do so could be interpreted as an insult to Turkmen culture in general.

There are also several points of etiquette to bear in mind when eating in Turkmenistan. First of all, eating is always conducted with the right hand. This is because the left hand is used for the cleansing of the body, and is thus considered impure or unclean. The feet are also considered unclean, and it is rude to point the bottom of the feet at other people when eating. Bread is considered to be a divine gift in Central Asia. It is therefore always treated with respect and reverence, never placed upside down, and certainly never wasted.

Eating/Meals

Meals in Uzbekistan are traditionally eaten at home with the entire family. Typically, these meals are highly social events and provide an opportunity to discuss daily news. Breakfast is usually quite simple, sometimes only consisting of bread, tea, and a fermented milk drink called chal. Lunch and dinner are larger meals, during which the assembled family shares the ubiquitous flat bread and an assortment of communal dishes spread out on a low table or table cloth. Lunch and dinner dishes typically include a rice and vegetable casserole called plov, meat, and vegetable pastries called samosas, dumplings called manty, and a lamb and vegetable soup called chorba. Tea and mineral water are generally the preferred drinks at lunch, but at dinner people may linger to share alcoholic beverages, most commonly vodka.

Eating is also an important part of traditional Turkmen festival culture. Sharing food with the extended family and wider community is considered to be a way to achieve social harmony and honor. Wealthier families would traditionally slaughter a lamb to mark special occasions, and share it with those who are less fortunate. Being able to provide an ample feast to assembled guests on days of special cultural significance is believed to attract good luck. This is particularly true on New Year's Eve, when Turkmen people believe that serving the best possible assortment of delicacies will bring fortune in the year to come.

Visiting

As is the case throughout Central Asia, the people of Turkmenistan are extremely gracious hosts. In fact, they consider it a religious duty to treat guests as generously as possible and will often give beyond their means to make visitors feel welcome. It is typical for women in a Turkmen home to keep water boiling in a special kettle all day long, so that they can serve tea to visitors. After serving tea to guests, the women of the household will immediately busy themselves with preparing a gracious meal, believing that it is inappropriate for a guest to ever leave the house without eating.

When visiting, it is considered polite to bring gifts for the family. This may include fruit or candy for the children. Since the people of Turkmenistan tend to be quite poor, it is appropriate to leave some money to help offset the family's expenses in preparing food. Adults may feel embarrassed at the offer of money, in which case it is best to give a small cash tribute to the oldest son or daughter.

LIFESTYLE

Family

Family is extremely important to the people of Turkmenistan. This is because the extended family is the basic economic unit in Turkmen society. People have traditionally depended on relatives for support in the region's harsh desert climate. Family is also divided along gender, a division that is most apparent when labor and family responsibilities are involved. For example, male family members traditionally handle all agricultural and commercial activity at market, while the women are responsible for domestic duties and child rearing.

Typically, people in Turkmenistan marry at an early age. The extended family of the groom is responsible for providing a gift for the bride's family, usually money or livestock. After marriage, a woman generally goes to live with her husband's family, where the young couple will usually reside for several years. Around the age of 30, the couple may move out and establish their own household, with money and livestock gifted to them by the husband's parents. Only then is the couple considered to be fully mature, and able to participate in the community as adults.

Housing

In urban areas, most people live in very modest housing units, a reminder of Turkmenistan's Soviet past. Luxurious single-family homes are reminiscent of traditional Turkmen palaces. In smaller towns, people also live in modest single-family detached homes. These houses are typically made of bricks and dried mud. In rural areas, many people also live in the type of home used for centuries by Turkmen nomads. These circular dwellings, called yurts, are a form of transportable tent. Constructed with wooden frames lined with felted wool walls, yurts are both portable and extremely resistant to the elements. Reminiscent of Turkmenistan's nomadic heritage, these dwellings are an ideal structure for herdsmen who shepherd their livestock to find grazing land.

In recent years, the government has made efforts to improve the living conditions of its citizens, especially in urban areas where there has been a housing shortage. In 2008, an initiative was launched to construct 35 four-story apartment buildings, each containing 40 apartments, in the cities of Ashgabat and Abadan. The apartments will feature increased living space and the program will target low income residents. The initiative is slated to branch out to other cities in subsequent years. Private and energy efficient construction has also increased since the turn of the century. Since 2008, there has been a construction boom financed by the government in selected cities of Turkmenistan, with a goal of transforming most by 2020.

Food

The cuisine of Turkmenistan is similar to other Central Asian cuisines, and is characterized by simplicity. Due to the impoverished nature of most citizens and the arid climate, much is made from simple ingredients. One constant is the heavy use of cereals, mainly hearty strains of wheat, rice, and corn. Grains are mainly used to produce the common flat bread served at most meals. People also depend on other starchy foods, such as rice casseroles, noodles, and porridge. In addition, since refrigeration is often uncommon in most areas, food tends to be produced locally. Thus, there is significant variation in diet within the different parts of Turkmenistan.

There are a number of other crops grown throughout the country, varying from place to place due to environmental factors. These include a number of vegetables, especially onions, carrots, pumpkins and beans. Fruits such as melons and pomegranates are also enjoyed. People also enjoy eating meat, though it is considered a luxury and is used sparingly in daily cooking. The most common meats are lamb, mutton (mature sheep), poultry and beef. Goat is also served in many areas.

There are several typical Turkmen dishes. Plov, a rice casserole made from lamb and root vegetables such as carrots and onions, is considered the national dish. Hearty soups are often served, such as chorba, made with mutton and vegetables. A form of grilled meat on a stick called shashlyk is enjoyed in some areas. Meat and vegetable pastries called samosas are commonly eaten. Steamed dumplings called manty are often available at meals, and are usually smothered in sour cream. Tea is the typical beverage, but a sour milk drink called chal is also enjoyed. Although most people are Muslim, alcoholic beverages such as vodka are often served with the evening meal.

Life's Milestones

Turkmenistan's former leader, Saparmurat Niyazov, officially codified the ages that people pass through. The ages he established as official Turkmen milestones are childhood, adolescence, youth, maturity, prophetic age, age of inspiration, age of wisdom, and old age. While this might be considered an act of hubris by the eccentric leader, it also reflects traditional Turkmen values about age and social hierarchy.

The birth of a child, especially a son, is a time of celebration for a Turkmen family. If the child survives the first two stages of life, and becomes old enough to marry, the family rallies around the youth. They work together to provide sons with enough wealth to pay the family of a potential bride. Weddings are also times of great celebration, usually marked by the men of the extended family preparing a feast of plov (ceremonial rice), meat and vegetable casserole. The young couple lives in the household of the husband's parents until they reach the age of maturity and have several children of their own. At that point they move out, and establish their own household, marking their acceptance as full adults by the community.

CULTURAL HISTORY

Art

The first inhabitants of what is now Turkmenistan were nomadic herdsmen who depended on their livestock to survive in the arid desert climate. In 600 BCE, the region became part of the vast Persian Empire and was later conquered by the Greeks in 350 BCE. In the second century BCE, this region in Central Asia developed as part of the Silk Road, a series of overland trade routes that connected Europe to India and the Far East. Trade caravans carrying precious textiles, gems and spices passed through Turkmenistan in the centuries that followed. Arabs began to assert control over Central Asia in the seventh century CE, lending their cultural influence to the area. This was followed by Mongol and Russian invasions in the 13th and 18th centuries, respectively, both of which would leave a cultural imprint on Turkmen culture.

The arts of Turkmenistan reflect this rich history. The country is best known for its textile art, especially rugs, which are known for their density and high knot count. Weaving has been practiced in the region since ancient times, when the area was first settled by nomadic tribes. Traditionally, women practiced the craft, using wool from the family's sheep. A skilled weaver could typically weave two rugs from wool harvested from an average flock of sheep.

Turkmen rugs represented a significant portion of the family's wealth. Another artisan craft valued highly in Turkmenistan was ornate jewelry. Typically, jewelry was made from silver and adorned with gold and precious stones. Some jewelry held religious significance. For example, a tamar bracelet often contained written prayers or talismans.

Architecture

Turkmenistan's architectural heritage also reflects its diverse history and the importance of the Silk Road to the region. Architectural styles range from medieval Persian architecture to Islamic architecture to traditional and residential architecture. Examples of Turkmenistan's medieval architecture are the grand fortresses, many of which can be found in the city of Merv, that were built to protect the lucrative Silk Road trade. Turkmen fortresses were designed for defense with massive walls, huge gates, and tall ramparts for surveying the surrounding desert landscape. Examples of Islamic architecture include the country's numerous palaces, mosques and medreses (theological schools). Characteristics of this type of architecture include symmetrical ornate patterns, radiant domes and tall minarets (spires). Traditional and residential Turkmen architecture was mostly influenced by the local climate and made from native materials that included wood and clay.

During the era of Soviet influence in the 20th century, when Turkmenistan was known as the Turkmen Soviet Socialist Republic (SSR), a massive effort was made to modernize many urban areas. The dominant architecture of this period was socialist classicism, or Stalinist architecture—derived from Joseph Stalin (1878–1953), the authoritarian ruler of the Soviet Union from 1922 until 1953. This style was functional in nature and combined traditional Turkmen motifs and ornamentation with monumentalism. It is mostly reflected in apartment blocks and state buildings within larger cities. More modern aesthetics, including the use of glass and marble, were adapted in the late 20th and early 21st century. In the post-1991 building programs, white marble has been the material of choice for new buildings in the central area of the capital, Ashgabat.

Music

Music has always been an important part of life in Turkmenistan. Historically, musicians entertained traders along the Silk Road, sometimes accompanying caravans as they traversed the trade routes. Music was also central to traditional festivals and family celebrations, especially weddings. Traditional Turkmen instruments include a stringed instrument called the dutar, a banjo-like instrument called the gyjakand, and a form of mouth harp called the gopuz.

Music in Turkmenistan is poetic and is often used as a form of storytelling. Turkmen music has been used to recount legends and describe important events in epic or narrative songs called destans. One of the oldest and best-loved Turkmen destans, called the story of Koroglu, is about a magical river that gives everlasting health and life. Similarly, the historical roots of Turkmen literature and drama come from the region's rich history of performance art. Destans, which are usually accompanied by music, are in fact sophisticated epic poems. Public musical and poetic performances are traditionally conducted by specially trained bards called bakshis. The repertoire of a skilled bakshi incorporates modes of expression that would be considered music, poetry and drama by Westerners.

Dance

Dance is an important part of Turkmen culture, and is especially popular at weddings, festivals and other social events. Several folk dances are performed in Turkmenistan. One style of dance is called ekhembel. This graceful dance style is performed by a group of women, and emphasizes head and shoulder movements. Another dance tradition is zekr khanjar, performed by men in a semi-circle wielding daggers or sabers, and accompanied only by vocal music. Koshtibidi is a similar men's dance, and is performed to clapping rhythms, and the strumming of the dutar.

Literature

The people of Turkmenistan also have a long history of non-musical poems called epos. These were passed on orally until they were first transcribed in the 16th century. Beginning in the 11th and 12th centuries, many of these epic poems began to reveal a distinct Islamic influence. One of the most important poets in Turkmen history was Makhtumkuli (1733–1783), a Sufi philosopher. Makhtumkuli used his art to record and criticize the chaos and warfare that marked life in Turkmenistan during his time. He also presented a poetic vision of a united Turkmenistan that would someday be strong enough to resist external conquest. Makhtumkuli is still revered as a national hero, and there is an annual holiday to remember his contributions to Turkmen literary culture.

CULTURE

Arts & Entertainment

The contemporary arts of Turkmenistan have been deeply impacted by the period of Soviet control that ended in 1991 and the subsequent totalitarian rule of Saparmurat Niyazov (1940–2006), who exercised his repressive control through a cult of personality. Both eras had mixed effects for the arts in Turkmenistan. For example, the Soviets demanded that carpet makers change from the traditional geometric designs to portraits of communist figures. (Since independence, carpet makers have returned to more traditional designs.) The Soviets also discouraged Turkmen jewelry makers from pursuing their craft, one of the main reasons being that they considered the use of precious metals for decorative purposes to be contrary to the spirit of communism. Similarly, Western-style theaters fell into disuse after independence due to Niyazov's disapproval of foreign forms of dramatic expression.

The Soviet experience also introduced outside ideas about literature to Turkmenistan. Young writers often returned from studying abroad in Russia with new literary approaches. Novels and short stories became as important as the traditional epic poetry that dominated Turkmen literature for centuries. Since independence, writers have been strictly scrutinized by the government. Some authors have met with official approval, while others have been forcefully discouraged. For example, novelist Rakhim Esenov (c. 1926–)—whose work *Ventsenosny Skitalets* (*The Crowned Wanderer*) was banned nationally—endured torture and imprisonment for his unflattering portrayal of the history of Turkmenistan.

Music in Turkmenistan has undergone important changes in recent decades. Since the country became independent from Soviet control in 1991, traditional music has enjoyed a resurgence in popularity, and has been encouraged as a way of asserting national pride. Traditional sounds have also blended with Western musical sensibilities, creating a distinctive new sound. Turkmen musician Atabal Tshaykuliev exemplifies this recent musical transformation. Imprisoned in the 1970s for performing music that Soviet officials deemed too religious, he was freed in 1985 and put together the popular band Ashkabad. Using traditional Turkmen and Western instruments, this band pioneered a new form of musical expression by combining traditional elements with outside influences such as jazz and rock and roll.

Perhaps the most noticeable change to Turkmen arts in recent decades is the development of official architecture and monuments. Saparmura Niyazov created a cult of personality that abounds in the form of impressive palaces, most notably the golden-domed Palace of Turkmenbashi in Ashgabat. Perhaps the most dramatic is the statue atop the Arch of Neutrality in the capital, wrought from gold and designed to turn to follow the sun throughout the day. While his successor has moved toward more freedom for the arts, and dismantled some of Niyazov's eccentric creations, Turkmenistan is still far from a country which allows total freedom of expression.

The Turkmen are great lovers of horses, and they take pride in the akhal teke breed for which they are famous. A strong and graceful animal, the breed's preservation has attained the status of an art form in the country. The breed is celebrated in a festival every April.

Cultural Sites & Landmarks

Visitors to Turkmenistan usually begin their travels in the capital, Ashgabat. Though the city was almost entirely destroyed by an earthquake in 1948, many culturally important sites remain. Several of these, located right in the downtown area, are monuments to the current political establishment. The Palace of Turkmenbashi, the official home of the country's leader, is an impressive example of Central Asian architecture, complete with a gleaming golden dome. The Arch of Neutrality, constructed to pay tribute to the policy of neutrality adopted in 1998, is another important landmark. It is topped with a golden statue of the first leader of Turkmenistan after independence from the Soviet Union. Visitors can go to the top of the arch, which offers panoramic views of the surrounding city.

South of downtown is a part of the city known as Berzengi. This area houses several important monuments and cultural attractions. One is the Monument to the Independence of Turkmenistan, a white gilded tower that locals compare to an enormous plunger. The Museum of Turkmen Values is directly beneath the monument, and the National Museum is located nearby.

One of the most interesting places in Central Asia for outsiders is the Tolkuchka Bazaar, an amazingly diverse market, just north of the city. The Bazaar presents an opportunity for visitors to experience an aspect of Turkmen life that has changed very little since the glory days of the Silk Road. Traders offer livestock, produce, and an array of traditional craft goods in the same manner that they have for centuries. Haggling is expected, and the people of Turkmenistan have a reputation as shrewd bargainers. However, it is possible to find jewelry, textiles, and headdresses at very good prices at this huge market.

In order to fully appreciate the long, rich history of Turkmenistan, visitors travel outside of the capital. The country's Silk Road heritage is evident in the eastern city of Merv. It is possible to explore the ruins of some of Central Asia's oldest fortresses in this small but ancient city. One of the most interesting and intact of these fortresses is the Shahriyar Ark, with its massive stone walls rising out of the surrounding desert. Merv is also a city of historically important mausoleums. Among the most important of these are the mausoleums of two askhab, or companions of the Prophet Mohammed. These are important pilgrimage sites for Central Asian Muslims, who come here to gain spiritual merit.

Libraries & Museums

The National Museum of Turkmenistan, located in the capital of Ashgabat, was founded in 1998 to celebrate the cultural heritage of the Turkmen people. Among its thousands of artifacts are rare Turkmen carpets, traditional bridal costumes and fabrics, Neolithic ceramics, and Parthian-era ivory rythons (drinking vessels). The museum consists of the Hall of Independence, the Hall of Middle Ages, the Hall of Ancient History, and the Hall of Antiquity, as well as two halls dedicated to ethnography. The museum also provides an overview of native flora and fauna. Other museums in Turkmenistan include the Turkmen Museum of Fine Arts, founded in 1927, and the Turkmen Carpet Museum.

Turkmenistan's National Library is located in the National Cultural Center in the capital of Ashgabat. In 2009, the library opened up an "Internet Center," granting Internet access to the public via 18 linked computers. The library, which opened over a century ago, moved to its present location in 2006.

Holidays

Secular holidays include Remembrance Day (January 12), which commemorates the earthquake of 1948; National Flag Day (February 19), and Independence Day (October 27).

Eid al-Fitr, ending the holy month of Ramadan, and Eid al-Adha, commemorating Abraham's obedience to God, are the most important Islamic holidays. Turkmen also celebrate Nowruz, an Islamic new year's festival with pre-Islamic roots. It is celebrated around March 21st to welcome spring.

Youth Culture

More than 45 percent of Turkmenistan's population is made up of youth under the age of 24, whose attitudes have the potential to significantly impact the wider culture. Former president Niyazov recognized this potential disruption of traditional beliefs when he embarked on a conscious and articulated policy to prevent young people from becoming influenced by Western cultural influence.

While the current government has reversed past youth policies, they have had damaging effects. A lack of government funding for education funding that drastically limited the amount and quality of schooling that Turkmen youth could receive. Additionally, as the industrial infrastructure built during Soviet rule became obsolete, unskilled laborers found it increasingly difficult to get jobs. As a result, most members of the present youth generation are not well educated, and they face many economic and social problems. Limited opportunities to pursue careers that require higher degrees have increased unemployment, especially among young men in urban areas. Alcohol and drug abuse has become an epidemic among this demographic.

SOCIETY

Transportation

There are several options for travel within Turkmenistan. Domestic flights are reasonably priced because they are subsidized by the government. Travel by rail can be slow and uncomfortable, while buses are crowded and unkempt, but typically reliable. Both popular modes of public transportation are relatively inexpensive. Minibuses called marshrutkas operate in most urban areas, and are more comfortable than regular buses. There are also taxi services, some official and some simply run by private citizens. Both types of taxi are convenient and reasonably priced, though using unofficial and unmarked private taxis, called "gypsy" taxis, typically requires bargaining for the fare. Traffic moves on the right-hand side of the road. Cell phone usage is also prohibited while driving.

Transportation Infrastructure

Like most former Soviet republics, the transportation of Turkmenistan was aging or in deteriorating quality heading into the 21st century. In recent years, particularly with the emergence of a national gas and oil industry, the improvement of existing infrastructure and the development of new infrastructure has become a government priority. A project to improve transportation infrastructure in the capital of Ashgabat commenced in 2009 (including new roads, modern lighting, and elevated bridges), and in 2010, the Asian Development Bank allocated an estimated $225 million (USD) to help build a new railway line to help accelerate the north-south transportation corridor. In 2009, the Islamic Development Bank provided funding to help construct the southern part of the Iran-Turkmenistan-Kazakhstan railway. Foreign investment has also come from Russia and China, among other nations. Transportation infrastructure in rural areas remains underdeveloped and underfunded.

Media & Communications

There is no freedom of speech in Turkmenistan and all press outlets are directly controlled by the state. Dissidents are routinely jailed for expressing opinions contrary to the official government line. There are several state-run newspapers. These include Turkmen language publications such as *Adalat, Galkynys, Turkmenistan*, and *Watan*. There is also a Russian language daily paper called *Neytralnyy Turkmenistan*. Broadcast media is limited; as of 2015, all radio and television broadcasts were from government run Turkmen radio and Turkmen TV. Television broadcasts from Russia can be watched in some areas of the country, but are heavily censored by the Turkmen government. Internet is becoming more available, and the state-run Turkmen Telecom is increasing the areas where it can be accessed. As of 2015, there were an estimated 125,000 Internet users, representing about two percent of the total population. Although the Internet became legal in 2008, current fees make it impossible for the average wage earner to afford to use it.

SOCIAL DEVELOPMENT

Standard of Living

In 2013, Turkmenistan ranked 103rd of 187 countries on the Human Development Index (HDI), which measures quality of life indicators. In 2014, life expectancy at birth was estimated at 69.5 years. In comparison, the highest ranked country was Japan, at 84.5 years.

Water Consumption

Because of Turkmenistan's arid desert climate—desert areas occupy more than 80 percent of the territory—water consumption and supply is a significant issue in the Central Asian country. The situation has been particularly exacerbated due to the severe desertification of the Aral Sea basin, which has seen its volume decrease by up to 90 percent in recent decades. Surface waters, mainly in the form of rivers, constitute much of the country's water resources—an estimated 99 percent—but most rivers flow heavily outside of Turkmenistan's boundaries, and their water-bearing capacity within the country itself has been a concern, especially regarding their use as a primary source for irrigation.

According to early 21st-century reports, it was estimated that less than 50 percent of the Turkmen population had access to a centralized water supplying system, with that number as low as 14 percent in rural areas, where access to clean drinking water is limited. However, the official government figures, in 2012, are that overall 71 percent of the population has access to improved water supplies and 29 percent sanitation facilities. Nonetheless, as of 2008, per-capita water consumption rates in Turkmenistan were believed to be among the highest in the world. However, the government increased water charges, resulting in a decline in water use. Water supply system maintenance also continues to be a concern. According to official government statistics, as of 2010, Turkmenistan had 15 water reserves, holding a total capacity of 3,017 billion cubic meters (over 106 trillion cubic feet). Since that time most efforts have concentrated on the efficient use of this water, since a 2013 report estimated that 50 percent of the water was lost due to inefficient systems.

Billed as a "hydraulic facility of the third millennium," Lake Turkmen (formerly the Golden Age Lake of Turkmen) constructed in the Karakum Desert will eventually be capable of holding more than 130 billion cubic meters (4,600 billion cubic feet) of water. The man-made lake, with the first phase opened in 2009, is designed to help conserve water resources and to promote sustainable agricultural practices. However, the project also has raised some environmental concerns, such as its effect on the Amu Darya River, a major Central Asian river, and pollution from pesticides.

Education

Primary education in Turkmenistan is free, universal and compulsory. In 2013, a 12-year system of education was implemented, with eighth grade students taking a national exam that determines the type of secondary education they will receive. Institutes of higher education are largely centered in Ashkhabad, with Turkmenistan University the largest. There are also institutes that specialize in teacher training, agriculture, economics, art, medicine, sport, and tourism.

Since independence, the educational system has undergone several reforms, particularly in the curriculum, which now stresses Turkmen culture and history. At the primary level, Turkmen schools emphasize three levels of development: grammar, reading, and cultural discourse. However, Turkmen teaching philosophy and methodologies have been criticized for minimizing independent thought, particularly through the promotion of the cult of personality associated with the former president, Saparmurat Niyazov. Overall, the state-funded educational system requires more funding, modernization, and a greater number of qualified teachers if it is to provide the foundation for an educated, competitive work force. At least 99 percent of the population is literate.

Women's Rights

Women face many problems in Turkmenistan. They have always been very important to maintaining household wealth, performing such economically important tasks as weaving textiles, milking livestock, and helping to harvest crops. Nonetheless, women have traditionally been considered less important than men in Turkmen society, and unable to participate in political decision making. During the period of Soviet rule, the genders were officially considered to be equal, though many Turkmen people resented this new arrangement. Since independence, there has been something of a backlash against this forced equality, and women are once more considered to be subservient to men in most matters.

Despite the fact that women are considered equal under the law, they face many hurdles because of their gender. Domestic abuse is a major problem in the country. While it is banned by law, there is a cultural stigma against speaking out about it, as well as a general fear of going to the authorities. Women also face workplace discrimination, which is again officially illegal, but widespread. Moreover, traditional attitudes toward the proper place of females prevent many women from pursuing higher education or careers outside the home. Women legally have the same inheritance and property rights as men. However, in practice, inheritance and property disputes are generally settled by Muslim religious authorities, who almost always favor men.

Women in Turkmenistan are also vulnerable to sexual exploitation because of social attitudes and the refusal of the government to address these problems. Rape is illegal, and the government does enforce laws against it. However, many women are uncomfortable going to the authorities to report rape. This is partially due to the social stigma attached to being a victim of this crime. It also reflects the mistrust that the population has for the government. Sexual harassment is not illegal and is ignored by the government. The absence of legal protection against this form of abuse has serious economic consequences for female citizens. Women are often discouraged by their families from pursuing careers because they may be sexually harassed. With limited economic opportunities, women may resort to prostitution. Prostitution is illegal, but laws are not strictly enforced. So, it has become a growing problem that is now also linked to human trafficking.

In other sectors, women are beginning to gain more control over public life in Turkmenistan. Female citizens now fill several prominent government offices, including those that oversee such important aspects of society as the media, technology and human rights. Although the executive branch dominates politics in the country, the parliament theoretically has significant power to shape the law and government policy. As of early 2008, eight of 50 parliamentary seats were filled by women, marking a gradual increase in the number of female representatives. In December 2007, parliament passed a new law designed to protect the rights of women. While gender discrimination and violence certainly continue to exist in Turkmenistan, the increasing participation of women in national decisions gives female citizens reason to hope for a more equitable future.

Health Care

Turkmenistan extends free, universal health care to its citizens. Even in urban centers, however, the quality is quite low, and in rural areas the poor conditions are only exacerbated. The system suffers from lack of funds, modern equipment, basic supplies, and well trained medical personnel. Thus many sectors of the population are vulnerable to serious health problems brought on by environmental degradation, improper or nonexistent medical care, and poor education.

GOVERNMENT

Structure

Turkmenistan is a secular republic, with power strongly vested in a president as chief of state, head of government, and chief of the armed forces. According to the 1992 constitution, with major revisions in 2008, he or she is directly elected to a five-year term, with a two term limit. Approved candidates are not allowed to run in elections. The president is also responsible for appointing the judiciary and the Cabinet of Ministers. His selections are not subject to legislative approval. In the 2012 election the incumbent won with 97.1 percent of the vote.

The legislature is comprised the National Assembly (Mejlis), which is presided over by the president. Prior to 2008, there had been a People's Council with 2,500 members. The National Assembly has 65 members serving five-year terms.

Political Parties

The Democratic Party of Turkmenistan (DPT) was the country's only legal party for most of the first two decades of independence, and still the dominant party. Opposition parties, approved by the government, were allowed for the 2013 parliamentary elections. However, the approved parties had no major differences in political philosophy, as they were created by the government or by members of the ruling party. Gundogar and Erkin are two political parties in exile.

Local Government

The administrative unit of Turkmenistan is the region, of which there are five. These are further divided into fifty districts, which are governed by hekims, or district heads. Each region is presided over by a governor, who is appointed by the president. Local governance also includes provincial and local councils. The capital of Ashgabat has provincial status.

Judicial System

The judicial branch is similarly dependent on the president. The highest court is the Supreme Court. The Supreme Economic Court deals with business disputes. There are also five provincial courts, and a court for the capital of Ashgabat, with district and city courts below them.

Taxation

Turkmenistan's tax code was adopted in 2004, and was changed in 2005, 2006, and 2007. Taxation includes a 15 percent value-added tax (VAT), an income tax of eight percent—20 percent on foreign-owned and state-owned enterprises—and a personal income tax rate of 10 percent. In addition, dividends are taxed at a 15 percent rate. There is no tax on land.

Armed Forces

The armed forces of Turkmenistan were created in 1992, and consist of an Army, Air Force (including air defense forces), a relatively small Navy, as well as Border Troops and a National Guard. As of 2015, the armed forces had an estimated 30,000 personnel, not including the air force (4,300) and navy (2,000). Because of tensions in the region, in early 2015, Turkmenistan began increased training of its reserves. The armed forces have a policy of constant neutrality. Since the early 21st century, Turkmenistan has maintained bilateral military ties with China.

Foreign Policy

Since gaining independence from the Soviet Union in 1991, Turkmenistan has had an official policy of neutrality. The position also proved to be an impossible ideal. In reality, Turkmenistan has a very complex foreign policy, and has mixed relations with various countries. It also suffers from a poor reputation for government corruption and illegitimacy. Although the government claims to derive its power from the will of the people, elections are widely considered to be flawed, and real political power resides with the executive. Until his death in 2006, Saparmurat Niyazov ruled the country with absolute power and often eccentric mandates. His successor, Gurbanguly Berdimuhammedow (1957–), appeared to be following the dictatorial lead of his predecessor, while pursuing a much more realistic foreign policy.

Turkmenistan's location makes the simple policy of neutrality impossible. In reality, it faces complex problems and varied relationships with neighboring countries. As a Central Asian country that was a former republic of the Soviet Union, it shares a set of concerns with Kazakhstan, Kyrgyzstan, Tajikistan, and Uzbekistan. The Aral Sea was massively polluted during the Soviet period. It has also been overused for irrigation. Central Asia is increasingly arid, and competition for water is becoming a major economic problem. Turkmenistan is also facing many foreign relations problems over the Caspian Sea, which it shares with Azerbaijan, Iran, Kazakhstan and Russia.

Turkmenistan has important and complicated economic relationships with three regional giants: China, Iran and Russia. As a major exporter of oil and natural gas, Turkmenistan is quite valuable to these powerful countries. China is a major trade partner, and a significant buyer of oil and natural gas. Sales of energy products to the West are more tenuous. Since energy is mainly exported to Europe via Russian pipelines, the trade is grossly in Russia's favor, and the two countries have come into frequent conflict over this issue. Relations with Iran are somewhat smoother, but having open trade ties with Iran has put them in conflict with the global community, especially the United States.

Turkmenistan was a key player in the U.S. Caspian Basin Energy Initiative, and began to build energy pipelines that favored the U.S. rather than Russia. However, this initially positive relationship was compromised by the fact that Turkmenistan had good bilateral relations with Afghanistan under Taliban rule. When the Taliban was removed from power in 2001, relations between the U.S. and Turkmenistan suffered considerably. Relations are starting to become more stable, however. After the eccentric dictator Niyazov died in 2006, the U.S. made diplomatic overtures to the new leader, Berdimuhamedov. In 2007, the countries declared that they intended to pursue better diplomatic and economic ties. As a sign of the closer cooperation, in 2014, the U.S. gave just under $6 million (USD) in aid to Turkmenistan, although still criticizing the human rights record of the country.

Human Rights Profile

International human rights law insists that states respect civil and political rights, and also promote an individual's economic, social and cultural rights. The United Nations Universal Declaration on Human Rights (UDHR) is recognized as the standard for international human rights. Its authors sought the counsel of the world's great thinkers, philosophers, and religious leaders, and were careful to create a document that reflects the core values shared by every world culture. (To read this document or view the articles relating to cultural human rights, visit: http://www.udhr.org/UDHR/default.htm.)

Under the repressive rule of Saparmurat Niyazov, Turkmenistan was considered to have one of the worst human rights records in the world. Although the government theoretically has multiple branches, real power was held by a permanent leader. Niyazov exiled or jailed all of his political opponents, effectively dismantling anything that resembled a representative government.

Conditions for political prisoners remain notoriously bad, and fear of punishment has stifled political debate within the country. Despite expressed interest in improving human rights standards, political plurality is still absent under the current government. While elections are now being held, the will of the people has never been the real basis of power in Turkmenistan, contradicting Article 21 of the Universal Declaration of Human Rights (UDHR).

Although Turkmenistan's government has stated that it intends to bring the country's human rights situation up to international standards, many people are still imprisoned for expressing political beliefs. However, there is still no transparency within the judicial system, hindering adequate legal protection from arbitrary imprisonment. Arbitrary arrests are common, violating Article 9 of the UDHR. Torture, which is specifically banned in Article 5, is common among prisoners. Arbitrary execution of prisoners, contrary to the right to life explained in Article 3, has been common in the past but is now officially stopped.

The government signed on to an international moratorium on execution in 2008.

ECONOMY

Overview of the Economy

The economy of Turkmenistan is still state-controlled, and the government has lagged on market reforms. It also guards most statistics about the country's economic performance, and thus does not attract many investors or international loans. In 2013, the per capita gross domestic product (GDP) was estimated at $9,700 (USD). The Turkmen economy showed a strong 12.2 percent growth in GDP in 2013.

Industry

The industrial sector occupies 14 percent of the labor force and accounts for 24 percent of the GDP in 2013. Except for the oil and gas industries, this sector is underdeveloped, and only since independence have there been efforts to expand the base. Other industries include the production of building materials, fertilizer, some machines, and textiles as well as food processing. Traditional crafts, mainly carpets, are an important cottage industry.

Oil and gas production, the mainstay of the economy, is vulnerable to international demand, export problems, and strong regional competition. Nonetheless, since the late 1990s, the industry has been steadily growing with an improvement in export routes. The plenitude of natural gas has also enabled the government to supply it free of charge to the populace.

Labor

The labor force is estimated at 2.3 million people. Approximately 30 percent of the population lives below the poverty line. According to the U.S. Department of State, underemployment and unemployment rates are about 60 percent.

Energy/Power/Natural Resources

Turkmenistan has vast natural resources, particularly oil, natural gas and coal. Their exploitation has been somewhat hindered by a developing industrial sector and transportation difficulties. Significant deposits of sulfur, salt, magnesium, limestone, and gypsum are also present. It has been estimated that as much as 99 percent of the country's territory might yield these or other natural resources.

Fishing

The fishing industry, which is state-owned, has experienced a decline in recent years. Nonetheless, the government views the industry as one of the more promising sectors of the country's economy. In the early 21st century, the Azov Sea sprat was considered the primary industrial fish crop.

Mining/Metals

As of the early 21st century, the mineral industry of Turkmenistan was still growing, and required foreign investment. The Central Asian nation contains a variety of resources, including bromine, salt, sodium sulfate, and sulfur, as well as lead and zinc.

Agriculture

Approximately 48 percent of the population is engaged in agriculture, which accounts for 25 percent of the GDP. Arable land, however, is limited to four percent of the total area, and most of it has to be heavily irrigated.

The principle crop is cotton, a legacy from the Soviet era, when Turkmenistan was forced to produce it despite the region's scant water supplies. Crop diversification plans have been implemented with good results, though the country still has to import a lot of its food to meet domestic needs. Other crops include wheat, nuts cereals, vegetables and fruits such as melons, olives and pomegranates.

During the Soviet era, little attention was paid to the adverse environmental effects of poor agricultural practices, including heavy and improper use of fertilizers and pesticides. Since independence, there have been few changes in soil and water management. Desertification thus continues at an alarming rate.

As a result of over-saturation of the soil, salinization is common. Over one million hectares (2,471,054 acres) have been damaged in this manner. Overgrazing is also leading to soil erosion. Without adequate breaks, frequent winds cause further damage.

Finally, Turkmenistan contributes to the ecological disaster of the disappearing Aral Sea by diverting the Amu Darya. This in turn has led to serious health problems among the populace, especially in the northern province of Dashowuz.

Animal Husbandry

Karakul sheep, which are used for wool and meat, are the most important livestock. Horses, camels, cattle, and silkworms are also raised.

Tourism

The tourism industry is developing slowly in Turkmenistan, hindered by a basic infrastructure, the poor reputation of its government abroad, and some travel restrictions on foreign nationals. According to the Turkmenistan government's statistical report, tourist arrivals in 2011 were 8,697 decreasing from 9,631 the previous year, with the largest number from Iran.

Turkmenistan has several interesting archaeological sites at Merv, Keneurgench, and Nisa. Other attractions include the Turkmen State Museum of Fine Arts and the National Museum of History and Ethnography of Turkmenistan in Ashkhabad, and the country's national parks and reserves. Camel treks in the Karakum Desert are becoming a popular way to see one of the largest sand deserts in the world. In 2007, Turkmenistan introduced a National Tourism Zone (NTZ) to promote tourism on the coast of the Caspian Sea.

Adam Berger, Michael Aliprandi,
Anne Whittaker

DO YOU KNOW?

- Ashkhabad (Ashgabat) means "City of Love."
- The Karakum Canal, dug during the Soviet era, measures 1,100 kilometers (684 miles) and diverts water from the Amu Darya into the desert. It is the largest irrigation canal in the world.
- A popular Turkmen proverb states, "Water is a Turkmen's life, a horse his wings, a carpet his soul."

Bibliography

BBC News. "Country Profile: Turkmenistan." November, 2014. 2 April 2015. <www.bbc.com/news/world-asia-16094646>.

BBC News. "Turkmenistan profile – Timeline" November, 2014. 2 April 2015. <www.bbc.com/news/world-asia-16098048>.

Golden, Peter B. *Central Asia in World History.* (New Oxford World History) Oxford: Oxford University Press, 2011.

Knowlton, MaryLee. *Cultures of the World: Turkmenistan.* New York: Marshall Cavendish, 2006

Lonely Planet, Bradley Mayhew, Mark Elliot Tom Masters, and John Noble. *Central Asia.* Oakland, CA: Lonely Planet, 2014.

Rodgers, Mary, Tom Streissguth, Colleen Sexton. *Turkmenistan.* Minneapolis: Lerner, 1993.

U.S. Department of State. "Background Note: Turkmenistan." January, 2012. 2 April 2015. < http://www.state.gov/outofdate/bgn/turkmenistan/>.

U.S. Department of State. "Turkmenistan" 2 April 2015. <http://www.state.gov/p/sca/ci/tx/>.

U.S. Department of State Country Reports on Human Rights Practices. 11 March 2008. http://www.state.gov/g/drl/rls/hrrpt/2007/100622.htm.

U.S. Department of State County Reports on Human Rights Practices. "Uzbekistan" 2013. April 2015. <http://www.state.gov/j/drl/rls/hrrpt/humanrightsreport/index.htm?year=2013&dlid=220410>.

Works Cited

"Country Reports on Human Rights Practices." *U.S. Department of State.* 11 March 2008 www.state.gov/g/drl/rls/hrrpt/2007/100622.htm

"Growing Calls for End to Executions at UN." *Amnesty International.* 18 December 2008 http://www.amnesty.org/en/news-and-updates/good-news/growing-calls-end-executions-un-20081218

"Human Rights Reform in Turkmenistan: Rhetoric or Reality." *Human Rights Watch.* November 2007

"Turkmen Dance and Festivity Music." *H&S Media.* 2003

"Turkmenistan: Culture, Customs, and Etiquette." *Culture Crossing.* http://www.culturecrossing.net/basics_business_student.php?id=209

"Turkmenistan: Human Rights Update." *Human Rights Watch.* 14 May 2004 http://www.hrw.org/legacy/english/docs/2004/05/14/turkme8964 txt.htm

Marjani, Farzad. "Turkmen International Homepage." www.turkmens.com/

www.hrw.org/legacy/backgrounder/eca/turkmenistan1107/turkmenistan1107web.pdf

Coins of Uzbekistan/Stock photo © wrangel

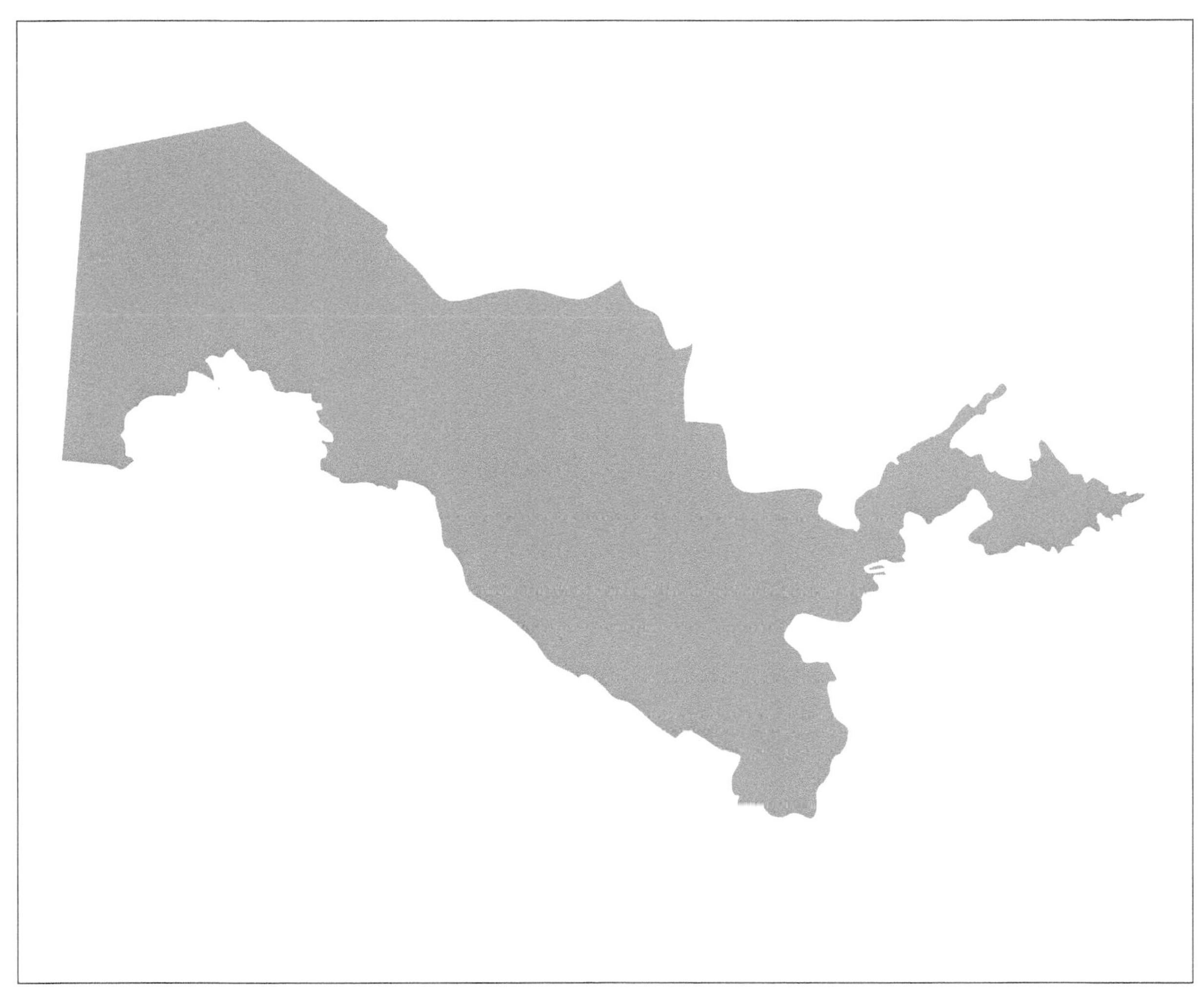

Uzbekistan

Introduction

Uzbekistan's artistic heritage is rooted in the historical Silk Road, a series of trade routes that existed between Europe, North Africa and Asia for centuries. Because of this long-term commercial activity, the area was influenced by multiple cultures. These included the historic cultures of Greece, Italy, Persia, India, Mongolia and China.

Though it possesses the most advanced infrastructure of all the Central Asian republics, Uzbekistan's political and economic development has been limited. Uzbekistan declared independence from the former Soviet Union in 1991, and its government exerts strong authoritarian control, which threatens basic human rights and political freedoms.

GENERAL INFORMATION

Official Language: Uzbek
Population: 28,929,716 (2014 estimate)
Currency: Uzbekistani som
Coins: Coins are available in denominations of 1, 3, 5, 10, 20, and 50 tiyn (100 tiyn is equal to one som). Several commemorative coins have also been minted. A second series of coins was minted with the value of 1, 5, 10, 25, 50, and 100 som.
Land Area: 447,400 square kilometers (172,742 square miles)
Water Area: 22,000 square kilometers (8,494 square miles)
National Anthem: "O'zbekiston Respublikasining Davlat Madhiyasi" ("National Anthem of the Republic of Uzbekistan")

Capital: Tashkent
Time Zone: GMT +5
Flag Description: The Uzbekistani flag features three equal, horizontal bands separated by two small, thin red stripes; the top band is light blue (sky and water), the middle is white (peace and purity), and the bottom band is green (nature). A white crescent moon and twelve white stars—arranged in a descending order of three, four, and five—are located in the upper right corner of the flag (upper hoist-side quadrant).

Population

The population of Uzbekistan, the largest in Central Asia, is growing at 0.9 percent annually, having slowed in the last decade. Life expectancy at birth is 70 for men and 76 years for women (2014 estimate).

As of 2014, Uzbekistan has an average population density of 64.6 people per square kilometer of land. The Fergana Valley in the northeast is the most densely settled area. At the turn of

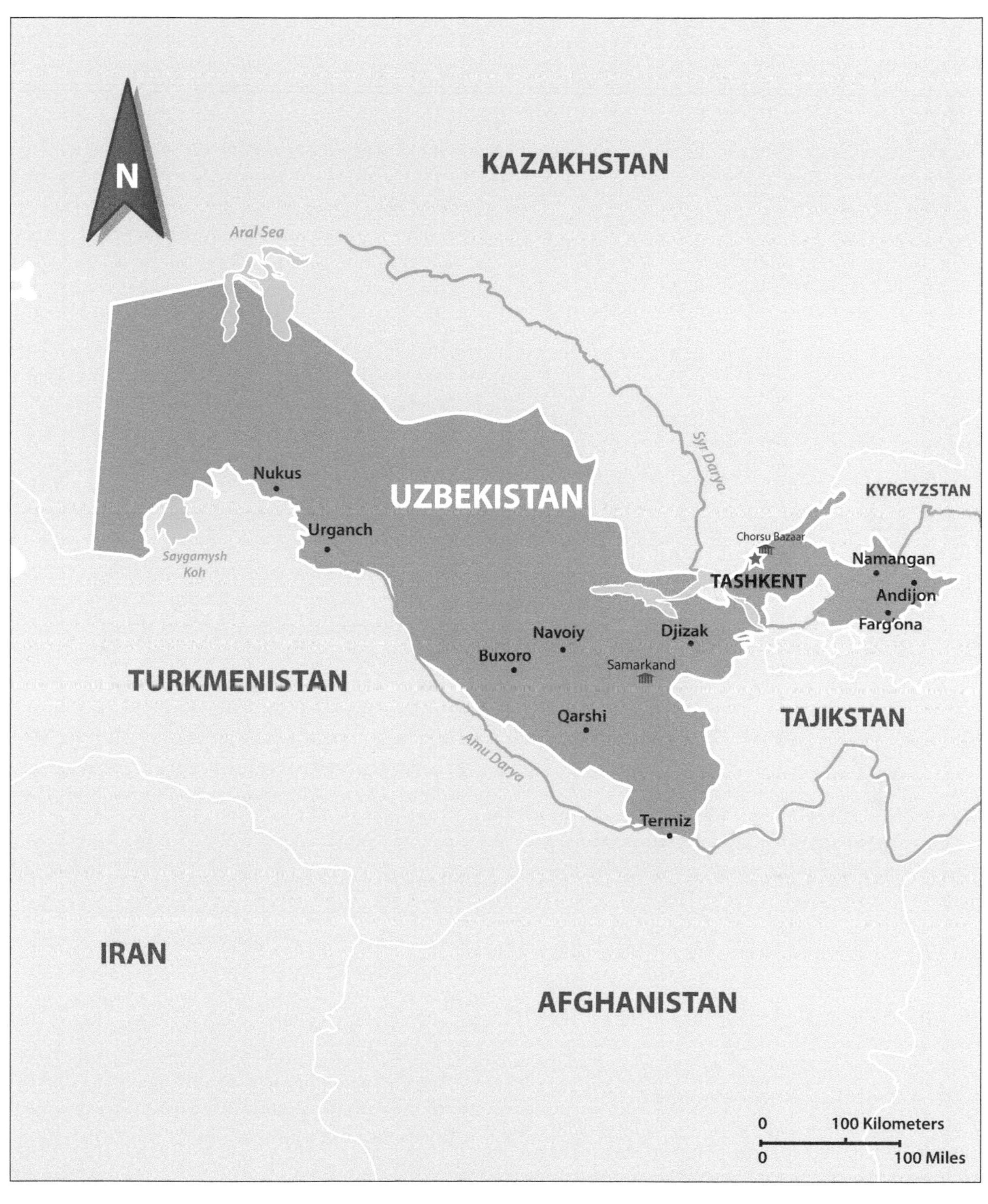
N
KAZAKHSTAN
Aral Sea
Syr Darya
UZBEKISTAN
Nukus
Urganch
Saygamysh Koh
KYRGYZSTAN
Chorsu Bazaar
TASHKENT
Namangan
Andijon
Farg'ona
Navoiy
Djizak
Buxoro
Samarkand
TURKMENISTAN
Qarshi
TAJIKSTAN
Amu Darya
Termiz
IRAN
AFGHANISTAN
0 100 Kilometers
0 100 Miles

Principal Cities by Population (2014 World Population Review estimates):

- Tashkent (2,227,000)
- Namangan (432,456)
- Samarkand (319,366)
- Andijon (318,419)
- Buxoro (247,644)
- Nukus (230,006)
- Qarshi (222,898)
- Kogon (187,477)
- Chirchiq (167,842)
- Farg'ona (164,322)

the century, approximately two million people officially lived in Tashkent, the largest city, with more recent numbers placing the unofficial population at closer to four million. (It is also considered the largest city in Central Asia.) About 64 percent of the nation's population lives in small rural settlements; according to United Nations' statistics, the urban population in 2011 was approximately 36 percent. In addition, the population growth rate between 2005 and 2010 was estimated at 1.4 percent.

Languages

Uzbek, a Turkic language belonging to the Altaic family, is the native language of 74 percent of the population. It includes several dialects, but the Tashkent dialect predominates in Uzbekistan. Russian speakers make up an estimated 14 percent of the population, followed by Tajik at four percent.

Efforts are under way to change from the Cyrillic alphabet to an adapted Latin alphabet. Minorities gencrally speak their own languages, and Russian is still widely used in official business.

Native People & Ethnic Groups

Uzbeks comprise the largest ethnic group, at between 74 and 80 percent of the total population, with the official number at 80 percent. According to 2014 estimates, Russians are the largest minority at just under six percent, though many are leaving to return to Russia. They are followed by Tajiks (4.5 percent) and Kazakhs (2.5 percent), and to lesser extents, Karakalpaks (Turkic speaking people mainly concentrated in the Autonomous Republic of Karakalpakstan), Tatars, Kyrgyz, Ukrainians, and Turkmens. The country officially recognizes some 130 different nationalities and ethnicities residing within thc country.

The territory of modern-day Uzbekistan has been settled and conquered by a succession of ethnic groups, Persians being the earliest. Uzbeks came to dominate the region in the 1500s. The country came under Russian control in the late 1800s, then under Soviet control in the early 20th century. It was during this period that the borders of the republic were defined, regardless of ethnic realities.

During the Second World War, many ethnic groups were deported to the region, Volga Germans, Koreans, and Meskhetian Turks (from modern-day Georgia) among them. With independence, many minorities chose to leave Uzbekistan, fearing a curtailment of their rights. A departure of skilled professionals within these groups followed, depleting the country's wealth of technological expertise.

The Russian minority, which has not been granted dual-citizenship, has made claims of government discrimination against it. The Meskhetians were the focus of violence perpetrated by the Uzbek majority, and have all fled the country.

Religions

Islam has been the dominant religion in the region since the eighth century. During the Soviet period, religion was officially proscribed and many mosques throughout Central Asia were closed. Since independence, religious practice has been less restricted, though there have been some tensions between the secular government and Islamic fundamentalists who practice Wahhabism. For the most part, Islam has been articulated throughout the region in a moderate Sunni form. The Russian minority is Orthodox Christian, and the majority of the Jewish population has immigrated to Israel.

According to 2012 figures from the government, about 93 percent of the population identifies as Muslim (particularly Sunni), while approximately 4 percent identifies as Eastern Orthodox, with three percent of the population adhering to various other faiths.

Climate

Uzbekistan's continental climate dictates hot summers and cold winters. Average January temperatures fall between -6° and 2° Celsius (21° to 36° Fahrenheit); average July temperatures fall between 26° to 32° Celsius (79° to 90° Fahrenheit).

The country does not receive much rain, but spring is the wettest season. Precipitation in the Fergana Valley, the least arid region, measures only 100 to 300 millimeters (4 to 12 inches) annually. Though snowfall is common, snow generally melts within a few days.

Earthquakes are a threat throughout the country, particularly in the eastern mountain ranges. The last major earthquake, in 1966, devastated Tashkent. Sandstorms are another natural hazard, and have been exacerbated by environmental degradation.

ENVIRONMENT & GEOGRAPHY

Topography

Uzbekistan is a landlocked republic bordered by Afghanistan, Kazakhstan, Kyrgyzstan, Tajikistan, and Turkmenistan. The country's terrain is varied, but generally flat. Desert and steppe dominate the western autonomous region of Karakalpakstan, which comprises 37 percent of the country's total territory. Geographic features in this region include the Turan Plain, the Ustyurt Plateau, the Karakum Desert and, in the northwest, the Aral Sea.

One of the largest deserts in the world, the Kizilkum, lies east of the Karakalpakstan and occupies the north central lowlands of the country. Further east, and shared with neighboring Tajikistan and Kyrgyzstan, is the fertile Fergana Valley. Occupying 21,440 square kilometers (8,278 square miles), it is bounded on three sides by the massive Tian Shan, Pamir and Alay mountain ranges. Adelunga Toghi, measuring 4,301 meters (14,111 feet), is the highest peak.

The western edge of the Fergana Valley is formed by the Syr Darya River, which crosses from Kazakhstan and flows into the Aral Sea. Uzbekistan's largest river, the Amu Darya, runs along the country's southern border before it flows north to Karakalpakstan and into the Aral Sea. Like the Zeravshan, once a tributary of the Amu Darya, many of the smaller water courses have been significantly reduced by irrigation projects. Uzbekistan has few lakes, the largest being Lake Aydarkul in the northeast.

Since the 1930s, the Aral Sea has been diverted to feed irrigation projects. As a result, the volume of water has been reduced by two-thirds, and vast areas of seabed have been exposed. Before this catastrophe, it was the fourth largest inland sea in the world. The capital of Tashkent is situated in the Chirchiq River valley at an elevation of approximately 480 meters (1,575 feet) above sea level, in the northeastern region of Uzbekistan. The Chirchiq River is the source of many canals, several of which run through Tashkent. To the east of the city lie the Chatkal Mountains.

Plants & Animals

Each of Uzbekistan's natural zones has distinctive animal life. Desert regions are home to gazelles, a large type of monitor lizard, and rodents. Deer, fox, and badger inhabit the steppe. River basins attract deer and jackal. In the eastern mountains, boar, brown bear, and ibex are found. The markhor, the snow leopard, the antelope and the tiger are listed as endangered, while the Turan tiger is now extinct.

Plant life has several distribution patterns as well. Walnut, juniper, larch and spruce trees grow in mountain regions. Along river courses, poplar and elm trees grow as well as shrubs, but in general the steppe only supports hearty shrubs and grasses.

CUSTOMS & COURTESIES

Greetings

In Uzbekistan, the normal greeting is to say "Asalomaleikum" ("Peace be upon you"), which is a blessing of peace. The proper response is "Waleikum-assalom," which returns the blessing. Men usually shake hands, often with their hands over their hearts to underscore the sincerity of their blessings. Handshakes among men tend to be lighter than in Western culture, and it is common for men who know one another to interlace their fingers slightly when shaking hands. Younger men may bow slightly when greeting older men, reflecting the respect that Uzbeks have for their elders. When meeting a number of men, it is polite to go around the room greeting and shaking hands with each person.

Women will often touch each other's shoulders with the right hand when greeting other women. While women may sometimes shake hands with men, they are more likely to be modest with men they do not know well. Men should wait for a woman to extend her hand before starting this greeting gesture. Close friends and relatives often kiss one another on the cheek. Typically, a younger person will kiss an elder on the cheek first, which is considered a sign of family love, as well as deference to social hierarchy.

Gestures & Etiquette

People throughout Central Asia are known for their unending selflessness toward guests, as generosity as a host is considered a religious imperative. Guests should be gracious, but understand that Uzbek hosts might give more than they can afford, and be sensitive to the fact that many people throughout the country live in conditions of extreme poverty.

Etiquette and social graces in Uzbek culture are largely based on the country's Muslim heritage. For example, the right hand is only used during meals and when shaking some one's hand because the left hand is used for cleansing the body, and is thus considered impure. The feet are also considered unclean, and it is usually appropriate to remove shoes when entering a household. People should be avoid stepping on anything that is associated with eating, such as the cloth food is set upon, called the dastarkhan, or pointing the bottom of their feet at anyone else. Additionally, when visiting a mosque, generally considered off limits to non-Muslims, it is important to avoid stepping in front of anyone praying. However, people in Uzbekistan allow some behaviors that other Muslims do not, such as drinking alcohol and depicting living things in art. Lastly, gender segregation is still practiced in more conservative households, and honoring elders, called aksakals, is considered a religious duty.

Eating/Meals

People in Uzbekistan consider meals to be very social events. They gather with their friends and family for a simple breakfast early in the morning, a large and leisurely lunch in the middle of the day, and for a smaller dinner at night. Meals are usually taken in the home, but are sometimes eaten in a chaykana, or public tea house. In both contexts, it is fairly common for the sexes to eat separately. Traditionally, women are responsible for the cooking. However, the men of the community customarily gather early in the morning on before special events, such as a circumcision, wedding or funeral, to make a special pilov (rice casserole).

Meals usually begin with a short prayer, and green tea is then served in a ritual manner. The host pours himself or herself a cup, then pours it back into the pot three times, which serves to strengthen the tea. The server then pours each person a half-filled cup of the tea, so that it cools quickly. The traditional flat bread (non) is set out on the dastarkhan in a ritualized manner. Bread is always treated carefully, never wasted, and placed so it is facing upward. Nuts and fruits are served next, and this usually is all that is eaten for breakfast. For lunch and dinner, many common dishes are placed on the dastarkhan, which people share, always using their right hands. After everyone is done eating, a prayer called the amin is traditionally spoken, which marks the end of the meal.

Visiting

The people of Uzbekistan are famous for their hospitality and consider it a religious imperative to treat guests with honor. Often, they will give well beyond their means to make a visitor content. It is considered polite to arrive with a small gift, such as fruit, sweets, or treats for the children of the family. Since people in Uzbekistan tend to be rather poor, it is proper to offer money to help cover the host family's expenses.

When entering an Uzbek home, a guest is expected to remove his or her shoes. The host will tell visitors where to sit, and seating is often segregated by gender. Guests will be expected to wash their hands, and the host will go around the room with a basin of water. A towel will be provided, and it is considered rude to shake the water off the hands. Guests will then be served tea. If one's tea is too hot, it is considered proper to swirl the cup to cool it, as blowing on it is considered rude. When served non (the traditional bread), it is important to treat it with respect, and not set it down upside down, or waste it. During the meal, it is polite to eat with gusto, taking from each common dish as one pleases. After the meal, a prayer called the amin will be spoken, and it is rude to eat after the amin.

LIFESTYLE

Family

Family is extremely important to the people of Uzbekistan. This is because the extended family network is the basis of economic activity. Family identity is also central to the Uzbek sense of self, and some families wear specific colors at public events as a badge of honor. Elders, called aksakals (or white beards), are the center of the extended family. They are consulted in all significant matters, and are often the respected leaders of local communities. In general, men are considered to have more authority over family decisions than women, and in more conservative households, the sexes are keep separate during many daily activities, including meals.

Housing

The larger cities in Uzbekistan are filled with sprawling blocks of Soviet-style apartments, many of which have fallen into disrepair. In the countryside, most people live in simple houses made from sun baked bricks, as they have for many centuries. Made with a simple mud mortar, these structures are largely permanent because of Uzbekistan's extremely arid climate. Access to clean water is also a problem in rural areas. The simple outdoor plumbing that people have used for centuries now only produces polluted water.

In 2008, under the government's "Year of Youth" state program, funding was provided for the construction of housing to help support young families. In 2009, dubbed the "Year of Development and Improvement of Countryside," the housing focus transitioned to improving rural infrastructure and constructing new houses in the Uzbek countryside. Since that time the government's goal has been the construction of 11,000 new houses in rural areas each year.

Food

Uzbekistan has a highly diverse and developed Central Asian cuisine, largely because Uzbek culture was historically not as nomadic as neighboring cultures. This culinary diversity is also a product of the multiple cultures that have passed through the region. It also reflects the fact that Uzbekistan has some of the most fertile land in Central Asia. Grains such as rice and wheat are abundant. Vegetables such as onions, cucumbers, tomatoes, eggplant, and carrots are popular, and there are a number of different types of fruit grown in Uzbekistan, including apricots, apples, cherries, melons, and grapes. Lamb, mutton (made from the fat-tailed sheep), beef, chicken, and horse are regularly eaten.

The national dish of Uzbekistan is pilov, a rice casserole made with stewed meat (mostly mutton or lamb) and vegetables, fruits and nuts. This dish also has ceremonial importance, and is often made by a gathering of men on the morning of special events, such as weddings or funerals. Other common dishes include grilled meat and onions on a stick, called schaslik; steamed ravioli filled with minced meat and herbs, called manti; and shurpa, a soup made mostly from mutton broth with vegetables and herbs.

The most common beverage, served at nearly all meals and social events, is green tea (chay). It is served in a ritually prescribed manner, with the host pouring the tea into a cup and then back into the pot three times to enhance the strength of the brew. A thin yogurt drink called katyk is also popular. Unlike most Muslims throughout the world, Uzbeks are also very fond of alcoholic beverages. Beer is available in most places, and vodka is also often served.

Life's Milestones

As is the case throughout the region, the people of Uzbekistan consider personal rites of passage to be highly social events, an opportunity to show family solidarity and pride. The birth of a new child, circumcision, weddings, and funerals are all attended by entire families and even neighborhoods. For each event, the family traditionally hosts a celebration called a toi, which is a festive party complete with bountiful foods, music, and dancing. On the morning of a significant event, it is customary for the men of the community to gather and cook the traditional rice casserole, called pilov. It is fairly common for people to wear colors identifying their family group at tois, especially those involving marriage.

CULTURAL HISTORY

Art

Uzbekistan's artistic heritage is rooted in the historic Silk Road, a series of trade routes that existed between Europe, North Africa and Asia for centuries. Because of this long-term commercial activity, the area was influenced by multiple cultures. These included the historic cultures of Greece, Italy, Persia, India, Mongolia and China. Thus, the region of modern-day Uzbekistan was historically an important crossroads. This resulted in a particularly rich and diverse cultural history that is reflected in Uzbekistan's proud traditions of artistic expression.

The architecture of Uzbekistan is particularly reflective of the country's Islamic heritage. Many historical buildings in the country are gracefully designed and ornately decorated, especially mosques and mazars (mausoleums). These feature characteristic prayer towers called minarets and colorful domes. Architecture in Uzbekistan was also influenced by both Persian and Russian architecture. Uzbek art and architecture is also well known for its impressive tile mosaics and mural paintings. The sort of tile work done in Uzbekistan is distinctive, both for its fine quality and unusual subject matter. While Islam normally forbids the depiction of living beings in religious art, Uzbek tile mosaics on sacred buildings are often stylized representations of flowers, birds, animals, and sometimes even people. Much of Uzbek art is also characterized as arabesque, which is a geometric style of Islamic art.

While traditional Uzbek arts have included metalwork, ceramics and carpet weaving, Uzbekistan is also particularly renowned for its textiles and jewelry making. For centuries, artisans have spun locally produced silk and cotton into ornately decorated fabrics to outfit the caravans that passed along the Silk Road. Suzanis, embroidered cloths featuring floral or geometric designs, are the most distinctively Uzbek form of textile. They are used to make clothing, tapestries and bedspreads. Weaving, using local wool colored with natural dyes, has also been an important textile tradition. Woven rugs, bags and blankets were historically sold along the Silk Road. Uzbek jewelry has also been prized for its ornate detail and complex designs. Jewelers, called zargars, have created beautiful pieces of jewelry for centuries, working with various metals and exotic stones. Historically, jewelry was a way that families could store their wealth and pass it along to future generations. The most distinctive form of Uzbek jewelry is the tumar, a jeweled container used to store written prayers or other charms. These are worn to ward off bad luck and achieve spiritual purity.

The Uzbek tendency toward creating elaborate works of art is also evident in the traditional woodwork that is found throughout the country.

Combining expert carpentry with detailed carving and painting, highly skilled Uzbek artisans have long produced sturdy and ornately detailed pieces. Since the Middle Ages, wood carvers have used locally available woods such as juniper, walnut, mulberry and elm to craft a range of decorative and practical items, including furniture, pillars and musical instruments. The city of Khiva is traditionally associated with woodworking. It remains one of the most important sources of this type of art in Central Asia.

Architecture

Uzbekistan has venerable artistic traditions, many of them influenced by Islam. This is perhaps most evident in the field of architecture. Ancient Silk Road cities such as Samarkand, Bukhara, and Khiva each have mosques, minarets, and mausoleums that rank among the foremost expressions of Islamic architecture.

Music

Music was always an important part of life along the Silk Road. Local minstrels entertained traveling merchants and musicians and sometimes accompanied caravans. Uzbekistan therefore has a rich and textured musical history, with several distinctive traditions. Classical Uzbek music, called shashmaqam, developed in the 16th century in Central Asia has distinct Jewish and Persian influences. Shashmaqam songs are distinctive for their slow beginnings, increasing tempo, and frenzied culminations. Instruments used in this tradition include a stringed instrument called a dutor, a flute called a nai, and a drum called a doira. There is also a popular folk tradition, called sozanda, which is performed at festivals. Sozanda is made using percussive instruments, castanets (vibrating instrument) and bells, and is usually accompanied by female vocalists.

Female vocalist in traditional Uzbekistan costume

Literature

Uzbekistan also has a rich oratory tradition. Historically, Uzbek authors created poems and stories to be performed rather than written. These orations often accompanied musical performances, and may be thought of as a form of theater as much as literature. The spoken word has remained an important form of art in Uzbekistan, and is traditionally associated with festivals.

As the region was known for its scholars throughout history, written literature also has flourished through the centuries. Uzbek literature traces its roots to the poet Rudaki (858–c. 941), who pioneered Persian literature in the 10th century. The most famous Uzbek author was Ali-Shir Nava'i (1441–1501), who produced poetry in the late 15th century that celebrated the folk heroes and natural beauty of Central Asia. Nava'i is considered to have started a form of literature which is distinctly Uzbek. Another notable Uzbek writer was Shermuhammad Munis (1778–1829), who wrote in the early 19th century and penned an epic poem (known as a devan) that recounted the history of the region.

In the 19th century, literature in Uzbekistan was dominated by poetry. Typically consisting of highly lyrical descriptions of natural beauty, these poems reflected a longstanding Uzbek tradition of performance poetry that can be set to music. However, in the 20th century, the Soviet influence inspired a new generation of authors, including Sharof Boshbekov (1951–) and Shukur Holmirzaev (1940–). They turned to a new form of writing, the realistic novel, which became popular throughout the country. Even after independence, literature remains under fairly strict government control.

CULTURE

Arts & Entertainment

One of the country's most popular sports is Kurash, a form of wrestling in which participants must remain on their feet while attempting to grapple their opponent to the ground. The game buzkashi is popular in winter and is usually played at important ceremonies. Riders on horseback compete in a style that inspired the game of polo. Holding a kind of stick or mallet, they strike a salt-filled goat carcass, moving it to score a goal.

The arts in Uzbekistan experienced significant changes in the 20th century. Soviet policies provided ample funding for the study of the arts and culture, but strictly controlled artistic expression. Consequently, several key Uzbek artistic traditions were suppressed. However, the arts are flourishing in the early 21st century, and are once again a central part of life within the country. Since Uzbekistan gained independence in 1991, the arts have emerged as an important way to express Uzbek pride and national solidarity.

Uzbekistan has always been known for producing high quality textiles and jewelry. Since Uzbekistan achieved independence, there has been something of a revival of the traditional textile arts and jewelry making. Traditional handicrafts have become a valuable source of income for the artisans who have kept these traditions alive. Carpets, embroidered textiles, and brightly glazed earthenware ceramics are some of the products produced. Uzbek jewelers have been relearning the skills that were used in the past to craft distinctive, and often spiritually inspired, pieces.

The performance arts are a good example of how the Soviet experience impacted Uzbek culture. Performance in Uzbekistan has traditionally been associated with festivals. During the Soviet period, new ideas about the performance arts began to emerge. Opera, ballet and Western-style theater emerged as popular forms of entertainment in the 20th century. Soviet investment also helped to establish theaters and concert halls. After independence, the government of Uzbekistan continued to fund these new forms of performance art. However, the themes and content have changed in recent decades. There is now a strong emphasis on performances that highlight the country's traditional forms of drama and venerable folk legends.

Music in Uzbekistan has also gone through significant changes in recent decades. Since independence, traditional music has become even more popular. Religious festivals that were discouraged by the Soviet state are now allowed to be freely celebrated. The music that has traditionally been played at these festivals is therefore enjoyed by a far wider audience than it was during the years of Soviet control. At the same time, young musicians have mixed traditional Uzbek sounds with Western music, creating a new genre of pop music. Popular artists producing this new kind of music include singer Yulduz Usmanova (1963–), who emigrated to Turkey in 2008.

Cultural Sites & Landmarks

Tashkent, the capital, is one of the most important cultural cities in Central Asia. Despite its recent urban sprawl, Tashkent contains several significant cultural sites and landmarks. Much of the city is new, having been reconstructed after a devastating earthquake in 1966.The Chorsu Bazaar, a grand covered market, forms the living center of the city. Filled with a variety of merchants, the bazaar provides insight into the importance of the public market to traditional Uzbek life. Overlooking the Bazaar are the 16th-century Kulkedash Medressa (religious school) and accompanying Juma mosque. The Barakhon Medressa, which also dates to the 16th century, is the headquarters of the Muslim Board of

Uzbekistan, a group of elders that governs religion within the country. Tashkent also has many impressive mausoleums, such as the 15th-century Yanus Khan Mausoleum.

The United Nations Educational, Scientific and Cultural Organization (UNESCO) recognizes four sites in Uzbekistan as requiring international recognition and preservation efforts, with another 31 under consideration. The recognized sites include the historic centers of the cities of Bukhara and Shahrisabz, Itchan Kala, the walled inner city of Khiva, and the picturesque city of Samarkand, which ranks among the most ancient settlements in Central Asia. Dating back to at least the fourth century BCE, Samarkand was an important stop along the Silk Road. The ancient central plaza, called the Registan, is surrounded by three of the oldest and most graceful medressas in the world. A fourth-century mosque, the Bibi-Khanym Mosque, is also located nearby. Samarkand also boasts some of the country's most beautiful mausoleums, several of which can be seen along an avenue of mausoleums called the Shah-I-Linda, considered one of the most dramatic sights in Central Asia.

In 2001, UNESCO also proclaimed the Boysun District in southeastern Uzbekistan an intangible cultural heritage (ICH). Officially listed as the Cultural Space of the Boysun District, the region was added to UNESCO's list of Masterpieces of the Oral and Intangible Heritage of Humanity. Now an isolated region, the Boysun is considered to be one of the oldest inhabited places in the world. It was recognized for its prevailing practices of ancient tradition and arts, many of which are rooted in shamanism, Zoroastrianism and Buddhism.

Libraries & Museums

Tashkent is home to the country's most important museums, including the Museum of History, the Fine Arts Museum of Uzbekistan, and the Amir Timur Museum, known for its distinctive blue dome. On display in the Museum of History is one of the famous Twelve Keys. These gold keys were hand-delivered to Russian invaders during the 1865 assault on Tashkent, signifying Tashkent's surrender to the invading force.

Holidays

Important secular holidays in Uzbekistan are Victory Day, commemorating Soviet victories in War World II (May 9); Children's Day (June 1); Independence Day (September 1); and Constitution Day (December 8).

The other important holidays are Islamic. Eid al-Fitr commemorates the end of the holy month of Ramadan, and Eid al-Adha commemorates Abraham's obedience to God. Uzbeks also celebrate Nowruz, an Islamic new year's festival that welcomes spring. The festivities are preceded by elaborate rituals such as spring cleaning, and include feasting and the wearing of new clothes.

Youth Culture

In many ways, life is rapidly changing for the youth of Uzbekistan in the early 21st century. Since the end of the Soviet period, there has been a shortage of jobs and an increase in poverty. As a result, many young people have been forced to emigrate to find work, with nations such as Russia, Korea, and Kazakhstan popular work destinations. However, this has led to an increase of illegal foreign workers who are afforded little protection. Some young migrants who have had their passports seized have been forced into virtual slavery to earn their release.

Exposure to foreign cultures, whether as migrant workers or through increasing globalization, has deeply impacted youth culture in Uzbekistan. This is apparent in the new forms of music that have begun to dominate Uzbek radio, such as hip-hop and hard rock. However, Uzbek youth are also a part of the cultural revival movement that has spread across Uzbekistan since the end of the Soviet period. The coexistence of the new and the old is reflected in the increasing number of pop musicians blending Western and traditional Uzbek sounds. This has created a form of music that is both avant-garde and rooted in Uzbekistan's cultural past.

SOCIETY

Transportation

There are several ways to travel within Uzbekistan. Domestic flights through Uzbekistan Airways (HY) connect Tashkent to other main cities and trains connect most of the larger cities. Bus service connects all major towns and urban areas, and other modes of popular transportation are large vans called marshrutkas, though their schedules can be rather haphazard.

Many Uzbeks travel between cities in shared taxis, which usually collect passengers at bus stations and run fairly fixed routes. The capital of Tashkent is also home to a metro system, the only one in Central Asia.

Vehicles travel on the left side of the road in Uzbekistan. In general, a large number of secondary roads, especially those outside of the capital of Tashkent, may be in relatively poor condition. In 2007, the country banned the use of cell phones while driving.

Transportation Infrastructure

Uzbekistan is believed to have the highest density of highways and railways in Central Asia. As of 2009, there were approximately 183,000 kilometers (113,710 miles) of developed roads in the nation, of which an estimated 80 percent have hard surfaces. In 2006, an estimated 85 percent of shipped goods traveled by truck. As of 2010, the national airlines, Uzbekistan Airways, operate a network of 12 airports. It is the largest national airline in Central Asia.

Due to its landscape, Tashkent is prone to earthquakes. As a precaution, the city's subway tunnels are padded with rubber to protect the trains. Completed in 1977, it is the first public transit system in Central Asia, and in 2014 comprises approximately 37.5 km (23.3 miles) of track, which is still expanding. Extending and improving railway infrastructure has been a government priority in the early 21st century.

Media & Communications

There are several private and state-run media outlets in Uzbekistan, and the government claims it does not censor its media. In reality, these media outlets are closely monitored by the government and often practice self-censorship. As such, the Russian press, international radio broadcasts, and the Internet have all become popular outlets for news. Government-owned newspapers include *Khalq Sozi*, which publishes in Uzbek, and *Pravda Vostoka*, which publishes in Russian.

The National Television and Radio Company is the main broadcast media source, and several private broadcasters have also emerged in recent years. Private television stations include MTRK and Orbita. Private radio, including Oriat FM and Radio Grand, are popular in the larger cities. As of 2014, there were an estimated 11,051,000 Internet users, representing just over 38 percent of the population, a percentage which has been increasing rapidly in recent years.

SOCIAL DEVELOPMENT

Standard of Living

In 2013, Uzbekistan ranked 116th of 187 nations on the United Nation's Human Development Index.

Water Consumption

Uzbekistan has limited water resources, and its primary freshwater sources are its rivers (in the form of surface runoff). Since the mid-20th century, unsustainable practices regarding water resources, such as the channeling and damming of rivers for irrigation purposes, have resulted in environmental degradation and water quality concerns throughout Uzbekistan—to the extent that some damage is considered irreversible. (The Aral Sea ecosystem, in particular, has been devastated.) This, coupled with droughts and the growing demand for water, has made water supply and quality an urgent issue for Uzbekistan in the 21st century.

As of 2013, irrigated agriculture accounts for about 90 percent of the water resources used (and about 19 percent of the country's gross domestic product). The quality of drinking water remains a concern and many waterways in the country are polluted. According to the United Nations Development Programme, only approximately 2 percent of the Uzbekistani population has access to good water quality, and as much as half the population accesses water with poor or very bad quality, even though a 2012 government report stated that over 87 percent had access to an improved water supply. According to 2009 prosperity reports, an estimated 96 percent of the population has access to good sanitation, with the government claiming 100 percent in 2012.

Education

The Ministry of Education oversees schooling at the primary, secondary, and vocational levels. Education is free and compulsory for children between the ages of six and 15. Since independence, the government has made concerted efforts to reform the educational system, yet it has experienced setbacks. State funds are inadequate, and there is no system to ensure that all school-age students attend; this is particularly a problem in rural areas. Despite these problems, the literacy rate is nearly universal among both males and females; as of 2011, the adult literacy rate was estimated at about 99.4 percent, and was slightly higher for youth (ages 15 through 24).

Uzbekistan has numerous technical schools, institutes, and teacher colleges. Its four universities, named for the cities in which they are found, are Tashkent State University, Tashkent Islamic University, Nukus State University, and Samarkand State University. However, some estimates suggest that only a fraction—about 10 percent—of the population pursues higher education. According to the UNESCO Institute for Statistics, in 2008 virtually 100 percent of boys and girls were enrolled in primary school, while 94 percent of boys and 92 percent of girls were enrolled in secondary education.

Women's Rights

Women do not enjoy the same legal protections as men in Uzbekistan. Part of the reason for this is a cultural value that places more importance on the male gender and the traditional belief that women should only wield influence in the domestic rather than public sphere, all of which reflects the country's Muslim heritage. There is a social stigma against women participating in government, despite the fact that women are technically allowed equal access to civic jobs. As a result, many women do not feel that the government reflects their opinions or is able to give them equal and adequate legal protection.

Domestic abuse remains a significant social issue for women throughout Uzbekistan, because it is not clearly illegal. In fact, domestic violence is largely considered an internal matter and a normal part of marriage, and most people are reluctant to discuss the problem with outsiders. There is also no real legal protection for wives against marital rape. It is often difficult for abused women to escape this cycle of violence as divorce is socially stigmatized and legally complicated. This forces many abused women to remain in a violent situation or marriage for lack of a realistic alternative. Furthermore, while rape is prohibited, many rapists go unpunished due to lax enforcement and a cultural hesitation to report it.

Sexual intimidation and violence are also major problems, and there is no legal consequence for sexual harassment. There is also social pressure to avoid speaking out about harassment. Hence, women are commonly victimized and have no meaningful mode of recourse. While prostitution is illegal, many women are also ensnared by the sex trade and the trafficking of women remains a major problem. Part of the difficulty with enforcing laws against prostitution and human trafficking is the corruption of law enforcement and the dependence on extortion. As a result, Uzbekistan is a major source country for coerced prostitutes, who often end up working in Europe, India or the Middle East.

Recently, a number of organizations have managed to operate within the country, bringing attention to the gender problems that plague Uzbek society. However, these groups are often subjected to government monitoring and harassment. The government has particularly cracked down on Muslim women's organizations and has targeted women who choose to wear the traditional Muslim head scarves. As a result, many women who would otherwise not be involved with public life are becoming politicized, and are starting to demand an equal voice in establishing government policy.

Health Care

Uzbekistan has a national health care system. The quality of the care has declined since independence from a lack of adequate funding, supply shortages, and poorly trained caregivers. The situation has been worsened by moderate to extreme environmental degradation. There is also a disparity between the urban and rural populations. The latter not only suffers shortages more acutely, but has less access to proper sanitation and potable water.

GOVERNMENT

Structure

Like other former Soviet republics, Uzbekistan was unprepared for independence in 1991, and the party which has ruled the country since has shown little desire to change the strong central government. Opposition parties are frequently banned, and power is maintained through state-backed violence and elections which have been deemed neither free nor fair by the international community. The ruling party has argued that only through harsh measures has it avoided a civil war similar to the one that plagued neighboring Tajikistan for much of the 1990s.

According to all the constitutions, since the first one in 1992, Uzbekistan is a secular, democratic republic. Power is vested in a president who is elected by direct vote and can serve two consecutive five-year terms, under the 2011 constitution. The president is responsible for nominating the prime minister, the cabinet of ministers, and the Supreme Court justices. He or she appoints the lower court justices as well as provincial governors, and can dissolve the legislature. With over 90 percent of the vote, Islam Karimov was elected to his fourth term as president in 2015, as the election commission ruled that only terms under the current constitution count toward the two term limit.

Legislative powers are concentrated in the bicameral Supreme Assembly. The lower house consists of 135 members directly elected to five-year terms, with an additional 15 from the Ecological Movement of Uzbekistan. The upper house is comprised of 84 local council members and 16 presidential nominees.

Uzbekistan is divided into 12 regions, one autonomous republic, and one city government, Tashkent. The Karakalpakstan Autonomous Republic has its own government and courts, but is nonetheless under the control of the central government.

Political Parties

The Liberal Democratic Party of Uzbekistan dominates the political life of the country, wining 52 seats in the lower house in the 2014–2015 election. Opposition parties are frequently banned, as are religious parties. Only those parties which pose no real threat to the Liberal Democratic Party's monopoly on power are allowed to function. These other "sanctioned" parties include the Uzbekistan National Revival Democratic Party (36 seats), the People's Democratic Party (27 seats), and the Justice Social Democratic Party (20 seats). In 2007 and 2015, all four registered parties nominated the incumbent president as their official presidential candidate. In the 2014–2015 legislative elections the results were similar to the previous election.

Local Government

Local governance in Uzbekistan is subdivided into regional, district, and city administrations or governments. (There are also some instances of community self-governance, and they act separately from the country's centralized government.) Khokims, or governors and mayors, are the acting administrative heads, and exercise legislative and executive power at the regional, district, and city level. Councils of people's deputies, called kengashes, also form the basis of local government on the regional, district, and city level. Regional khokims are based on recommendations by the president, and, in turn, district and city khokims are based on recommendations by the regional khokim.

Judicial System

The judiciary has little independence from the executive branch. The Supreme Court, the Constitutional Court, and the High Economic Court are the highest judicial bodies. Other judiciary bodies include civil and criminal regional courts, civil and criminal district or city courts, and martial courts. In addition, Karakalpakstan maintains its own supreme civil and criminal courts, and there are economic courts for that autonomous republic and Tashkent.

Taxation

Uzbekistan has a unified tax system, and taxes, which also include duties, are levied at both the state and local level. Personal taxation rates were set at 22 percent for 2015, and there is no capital acquisition or inheritance tax. The value-added tax (VAT) has a standard rate of 20 percent, and a corporate income tax is generally levied at a rate of nine percent. Other taxes include land and property tax, water use tax, ecology tax, and infrastructure tax.

Armed Forces

Uzbekistan maintains the largest armed forces in Central Asia, and consists of the Army, Air and Air Defense Forces, and National Guard. The US State Department reports place the number of personnel in the Uzbekistani armed forces at around 65,000. Since its formation after Uzbekistani independence, the armed forces have relied on conscription. In 2010, Uzbekistan instituted sweeping new reforms regarding military service in an attempt to professionalize their armed forces. For example, statutory military service now occurs one time per year; awards, orders, and medals were instituted; and military schools and colleges are being improved. In response to the move toward a professional military, in 2013, more people tried to enlist in the military than it had the capacity to absorb. From 2001 to 2005, the country and military allowed the United States to base troops in Uzbekistan for use in Afghanistan.

Foreign Policy

Uzbekistan achieved independence in 1991, following the dissolution of the Soviet Union. Although relations with Russia were originally tense, they have improved significantly in recent decades. In 2005, Uzbekistan signed a mutual defense agreement with Russia, marking an important step in cooperation between the two nations. Uzbekistan has recently pursued closer ties with another regional superpower, China. This has led to fears, especially among the Russian establishment, that China may gain influence in the region. However, Uzbekistan has so far managed to strike a delicate balance in maintaining good formal relations with both larger countries.

Uzbekistan also enjoys a fairly good relationship with the United States, which has offered financial and political support since 1991. Uzbekistan has also received ample military aid from the U.S., allowing it to maintain the largest military in Central Asia. Uzbekistan proved to be a close ally when the U.S. invaded Afghanistan in 2001. However, some tensions have emerged between the two countries in recent years. In particular, the U.S. remains concerned about the lack of political opposition within Uzbekistan, and has repeatedly condemned the human rights violations that have become commonplace in the country.

Despite its internal problems, Uzbekistan is a leader in the region, and has helped to establish a uniform foreign policy among the states of Central Asia. It is an active member of the Commonwealth of Independent States (CIS), a political, military and economic association of countries that were once former Soviet republics. It also helped found the Central Asian Union and is an active member of the Organization of Central Asian Cooperation (OCAC), reinforcing its commitment to regional diplomacy. In 2006, Uzbekistan became involved with the Eurasian Economic Community (EAEC), an organization founded to bolster trade within the region. In its first two-and-a-half decades of independence, Uzbekistan's strength within the region has allowed it to be somewhat more independent in its foreign policy than is the case for many other former Soviet republics.

Uzbekistan is a participant in a number of multilateral organizations that have influence beyond the region, including the United Nations (UN), which it joined in 1992. Uzbekistan is a part of the North Atlantic Treaty Organization's (NATO) global security network, and joined NATO's Partnership for Peace in 1994. Since most of the population is Muslim, Uzbekistan is also active in the global Islamic community, and has been a member of the Organization of the Islamic Conference (OIC) since 1996.

Human Rights Profile

International human rights law insists that states respect civil and political rights, and also promote an individual's economic, social and cultural rights. The United Nations Universal Declaration on Human Rights (UDHR) is recognized as the standard for international human rights. Its authors sought the counsel of the world's great thinkers, philosophers, and religious leaders, and were careful to create a document that reflects the core values shared by every world culture. (To read this document or view the articles relating to cultural human rights, visit: http://www.udhr.org/UDHR/default.htm.)

Human rights abuses routinely occur within Uzbekistan and are largely a result of the dictatorial political system. Since gaining independence from the Soviet Union in 1991, Uzbekistan has been ruled by Islam Karimov (1938–). Under his rule, political opposition has been almost entirely abolished. According to the constitution of Uzbekistan, the government is bound to elections. However, international monitoring agencies contend that the government is strictly controlled by Karimov, and most observers allege that elections are neither free nor fair.

Freedom of speech is largely compromised in Uzbekistan, especially pertaining to open criticism of the government. Self-censorship is practiced amongst the media and government critics are subjected to legal sanctions. Intimidation, denial of a fair trial, and arbitrary arrest is also widespread and people are often jailed for peaceful political activities. Forced labor, particularly child labor, in the government-run cotton industry is also a pressing concern.

The government has officially banned a number of Islamist political organizations, accusing them of having ties with terrorism. Uzbekistan has also been criticized for its poor prison and labor camp conditions, especially for those incarcerated for political reasons. In addition, reports of torture are rampant among political prisoners, with some cases of torture fatal. The situation has become worse since 2001, when the U.S. invaded Afghanistan. Since Uzbekistan has become a reliable ally in the "war on terror," the government has increased its oppression of Islamist political parties. Despite promises to stop the practice in 2008, execution of political dissidents continues to occur on a regular basis.

ECONOMY

Overview of the Economy

Uzbekistan has made little progress towards a market economy. Though the government has reduced post-independence inflation and diversified its trading partners, it has not relinquished control of the dominant industries. Nonetheless, the country as shown an average gross domestic product (GDP) growth of about eight percent between 2004 and 2012, slowing slightly to seven percent in 2013. Manufacturing and agriculture combined account for slightly more than one half of the country's GDP.

Industry

Industry occupies 13 percent of the labor force and accounts for approximately 32 percent of the GDP. This sector is most developed in and around Tashkent. Heavy industry includes the production of agricultural machinery, automobiles, aircraft, and fertilizer as well as the processing of minerals, metals, natural gas, and oil. Light industry is centered on textile production and food processing.

Tashkent is also a major player in the silk industry (being on the Great Silk Road) and is known as a center for silkworms.

Labor

The labor force is estimated at 17 million people. In 2013, the estimated gross domestic product (GDP) per capita was $3,800 (USD). Unemployment officially stands at approximately five percent (2013 estimate), however at least another 20 percent are underemployed.

Energy/Power/Natural Resources

Uzbekistan has abundant natural resources. Large deposits of gold are the most valuable, but tungsten, fluorspar, zinc, uranium, lead, copper, and molybdenum are also mined. The country's energy resources include natural gas and deposits of coal and oil, though the oil reserves have so far only been exploited for domestic consumption.

Uzbekistan has one of the most serious environmental situations of any former Soviet republic. The depletion of the Aral Sea has caused an array of serious health problems among the populace of Karakalpakstan in particular. This has also led to widespread salinization of the soil throughout the already arid region, as the wind carries the sand of the exposed seabed for hundreds of miles.

Furthermore, the use of pesticides and fertilizers in the agricultural sector has raised the toxicity of soil and water to critical levels. Untreated wastewater, lack of clean drinking water, and air pollution from heavy industry are also pressing concerns. Since independence, the government has accomplished little towards minimizing further environmental degradation.

Fishing

The Aral Sea, once considered the main fishing body within the country, has been declared an environmental crisis, and the southern section has decreased by more than 90 percent. Aquaculture is now the primary sector of the local fishing industry, and provides between 60 and 80 percent of Uzbekistan's total fish production. Farmed fish include silver, common, grass, and bighead carp.

Forestry

Forests make up less than eight percent of the land of Uzbekistan, with some estimates placing that number as low as 5 percent. Most of these forest ecosystems are considered to be fragile (only two percent are primary forests), and commercial forestry is not an important industry, nor does it figure significantly into the country's GDP. Illegal logging continues to be a concern.

Mining/Metals

The Uzbekistani mining industry is overseen by the State Committee for Geology and Mineral Resources. Gold remains perhaps the most important export of the national mining industry—the third overall after energy products and cotton—and the country is considered the seventh-largest gold producer in the world, as well as having the fourth-largest reserves. Other significant metals include silver, copper, lead, tungsten, zinc, and uranium. Uzbekistan, in fact, is the fifth largest producer of global uranium. The country also has a large reserve of natural gas.

Agriculture

According a 2012 estimate, 26 percent of the labor force works in agriculture, which accounts for 19 percent of the GDP. During the Soviet era, Uzbekistan was forced to produce cotton, and it remains Uzbekistan's primary industry. In fact, the country is often considered the second highest cotton exporter in the world. (Over irrigation and salinity, however, have resulted in severe economic degradation and the loss of the country's commercial fishing industry.) Crops now include rice, tobacco, fruits, vegetables, wheat and barley, but the republic relies heavily on food imports. Large state-run farms are still common, and the entire cotton industry is government-run. Large numbers of people are forced by the government to leave their regular jobs during the cotton harvest, to pick cotton. Under international pressure, in 2013 Uzbekistan stopped closing all the schools and using school children to pick cotton. However, the government still drafted all their teachers.

Animal Husbandry

Animal husbandry is concentrated on sheep, cattle, goats and pigs.

Tourism

With its historic, Silk Road cities and vibrant modern culture, Uzbekistan has great but largely unrealized tourism potential. An underdeveloped infrastructure combined with bureaucratic hassles for foreign visitors has held the industry back, though some progress has been made in recent years. Having grown rapidly in the first decade of the 21st century, the number of tourists has stabilized around 1,000,000 tourists annually in the second decade.

The main attractions of Uzbekistan are the ancient cities of Samarkand, Bukhara and Khiva, with their unique and well preserved examples of early Islamic architecture. Tashkent is home to numerous museums, and the eastern mountains attract hikers in the summer and skiers in the winter.

Adam Berger, Michael Aliprandi, Alex K. Rich

DO YOU KNOW?

- The Silk Road was a series of trade routes between China and Europe that began during the Roman Empire. It was of great importance to the development of Uzbek culture.
- The Muruntau gold mine, located in the Kizilkum Desert, is thought to be the largest in the world.
- The name Tashkent is translated as "stone village," or "stone fortress," and the capital is often referred to as the most beautiful city in Central Asia.
- In 2007, Tashkent was appointed as the cultural capital to the Islamic World by the Islamic Educational, Scientific and Cultural Organization (ISESCO).

Bibliography

Amnesty International. "Uzbekistan: Amnesty International Report." 2015.
<https://www.amnesty.org/en/countries/europe-and-central-asia/uzbekistan/>.

BBC News. "Country Profile: Uzbekistan." 2 April 2015.
<http://www.bbc.com/news/world-asia-16218112>.

Golden, Peter B. *Central Asia in World History.* (New Oxford World History) Oxford: Oxford University Press, 2011.

Knowlton, MaryLee. *Cultures of the World: Uzbekistan.* New York: Marshall Cavendish, 2006.

Lonely Planet, Bradley Mayhew, Mark Elliot Tom Masters, and John Noble. *Central Asia.* Oakland, CA: Lonely Planet, 2014.

Rodgers, Mary, Tom Streissguth and Colleen Sexton. *Uzbekistan.* Minneapolis: Lerner, 1993.

Spatz, John E., Corina A. Malavez (ed.), James L. Frederick (ed.), and Maria A. Colpano (ed.). *Uzbekistan: Profiles, Foreign Relations, and Human Rights.* Hauppauge, NY: Nova Science Publishers, Inc., 2013.

U.S. Department of State. "2004 Country Report on Human Rights Practices in Uzbekistan." 28 February 2005 <http://www.state.gov/g/drl/rls/hrrpt/2004/41717.htm>.

U.S. Department of State. "Background Notes: Uzbekistan." January, 2012. 2 April 2015. <http://www.state.gov/outofdate/bgn/uzbekistan/196027.htm >.

U.S. Department of State. "Uzbekistan" January, 2015. 2 April 2015. < http://www.state.gov/p/sca/ci/uz/>.

Works Cited

"About Commonwealth of Independent States." *Commonwealth of Independent States.* http://www.cisstat.com/eng/cis.htm

"Euro-Atlantic Partnership Council." *NATO.* 12 December 2008 http://www.nato.int/issues/eapc/index.html

"In Pictures: Uzbek Women's Rights." *BBC News.* 19 January 2001 http://news.bbc.co.uk/2/hi/asia-pacific/1125985.stm

"Member States." *Organization of the Islamic Conference.* 2008 http://www.oic-oci.org/oicnew/member_states.asp

"The Partnership for Peace." *NATO.* 1 October 2008 http://www.nato.int/issues/pfp/index.html

"United Nations Member States." *United Nations.* 3 October 2006 http://www.un.org/members/list.shtml

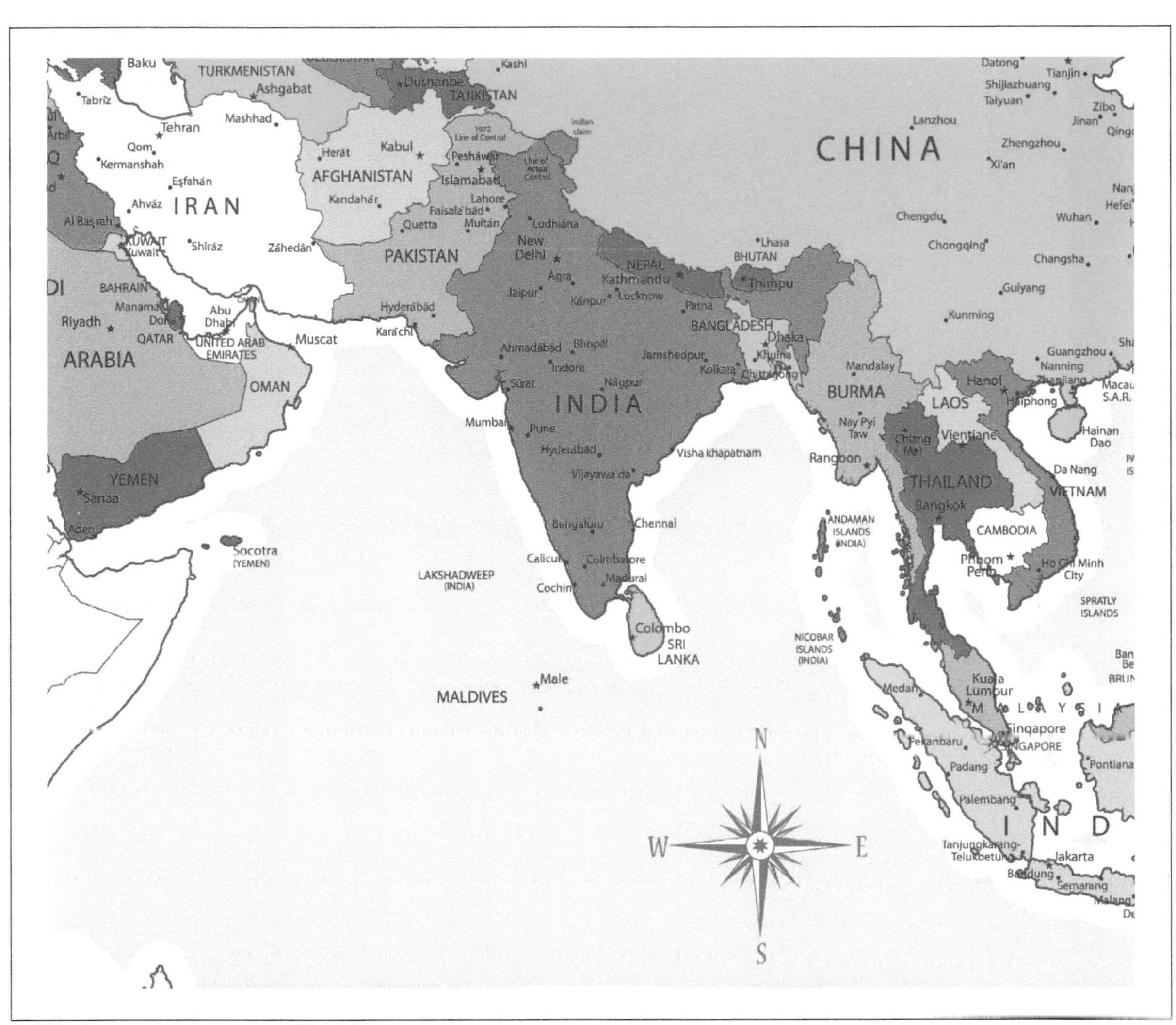

Baku
TURKMENISTAN
Ashgabat
Kashi
Dushanbe
TAJIKISTAN
Datong
Tianjin
Shijiazhuang
Taiyuan
Tabrīz
Tehran
Mashhad
Lanzhou
Zibo
Jinan
Qom
Kermanshah
Herāt
Kabul
Peshāwar
CHINA
Zhengzhou
Xi'an
AFGHANISTAN
Islamabad
Eşfahān
IRAN
Ahvāz
Kandahār
Lahore
Faisalābād
Multān
Ludhiāna
Quetta
Al Başrah
Chengdu
Wuhan
Hefei
KUWAIT
Kuwait
Shīrāz
Zāhedān
PAKISTAN
New Delhi
Lhasa
BHUTAN
Chongqing
Changsha
NEPAL
Kathmandu
Thimpu
BAHRAIN
Manama
Doha
QATAR
Riyadh
Abu Dhabi
UNITED ARAB EMIRATES
ARABIA
Muscat
OMAN
Karāchi
Hyderābād
Jaipur
Āgra
Kānpur
Lucknow
Patna
BANGLADESH
Dhaka
Khulna
Chittagong
Guiyang
Kunming
Guangzhou
Nanning
Zhanjiang
Macau S.A.R.
Ahmadābād
Bhopāl
Indore
Sūrat
Jamshedpur
Kolkata
Nāgpur
INDIA
Mandalay
BURMA
Hanoi
Haiphong
LAOS
Hainan Dao
Mumbai
Pune
Hyderābād
Vishakhapatnam
Nay Pyi Taw
Vientiane
Rangoon
THAILAND
Bangkok
Da Nang
VIETNAM
YEMEN
Sanaa
Aden
Socotra (YEMEN)
Bengaluru
Chennai
ANDAMAN ISLANDS (INDIA)
CAMBODIA
Phnom Penh
Ho Chi Minh City
LAKSHADWEEP (INDIA)
Calicut
Coimbatore
Cochin
Madurai
SPRATLY ISLANDS
Colombo
SRI LANKA
NICOBAR ISLANDS (INDIA)
MALDIVES
Male
Medan
Kuala Lumpur
Singapore
SINGAPORE
Pekanbaru
Padang
Pontianak
Palembang
Tanjungkarang-Telukbetung
Jakarta
Bandung
Semarang
Malang
N
W
E
S

SOUTH ASIA

Afghan man feeding doves at the Blue Mosque in Mazar/Stock photo © MivPiv

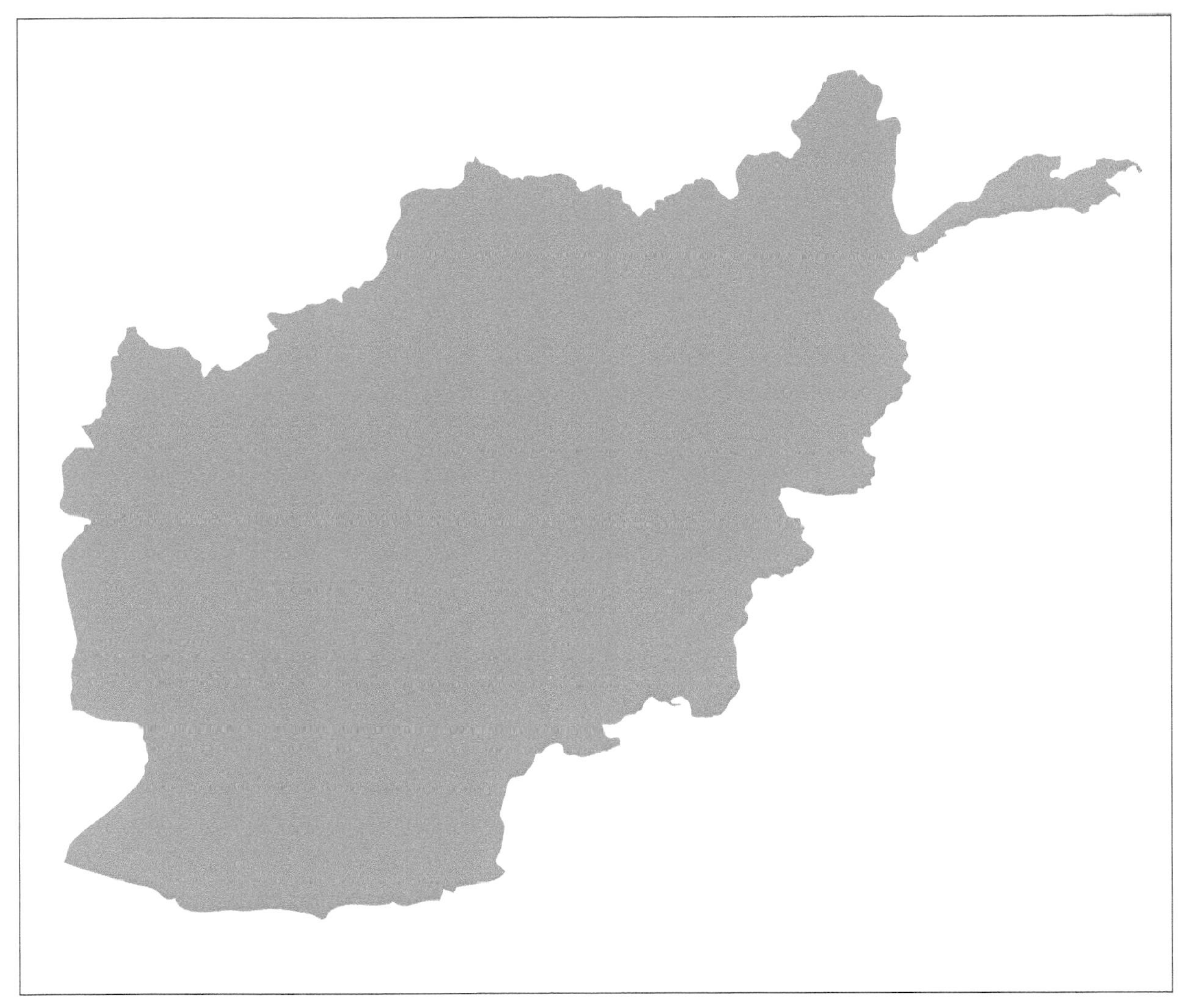

Afghanistan

Introduction

Afghanistan is located in Central Asia, and borders Iran, Pakistan, Tajikistan, Uzbekistan, and Turkmenistan. For millennia, it was a crossroads along ancient trade routes, and as a result, Afghanistan's governance, art, and culture have been influenced by various Asian and Middle Eastern traditions.

By the beginning of the 21st century, Afghanistan had been devastated by nearly three decades of warfare and political upheaval, which culminated in the 2001 U.S.-led toppling of the Taliban government and the bombing of various Al-Qaeda encampments throughout the country. Although it has since held democratic elections, much of Afghanistan remains beyond control of a central government widely viewed as corrupt. A resurgent Taliban poses a serious challenge to national stability.

The capital of Afghanistan, Kabul, has experienced little peace or prosperity over the last several decades. Beginning with the Soviet invasion of Afghanistan in 1979, and continuing through civil war and the rise and fall of the Taliban, the city has been the focal point in the struggle to rule the country, and has suffered extensive destruction as a result.

GENERAL INFORMATION

Official Language: Pashtu
Population: 31,822,848 (2014 estimate)
Currency: Afghani

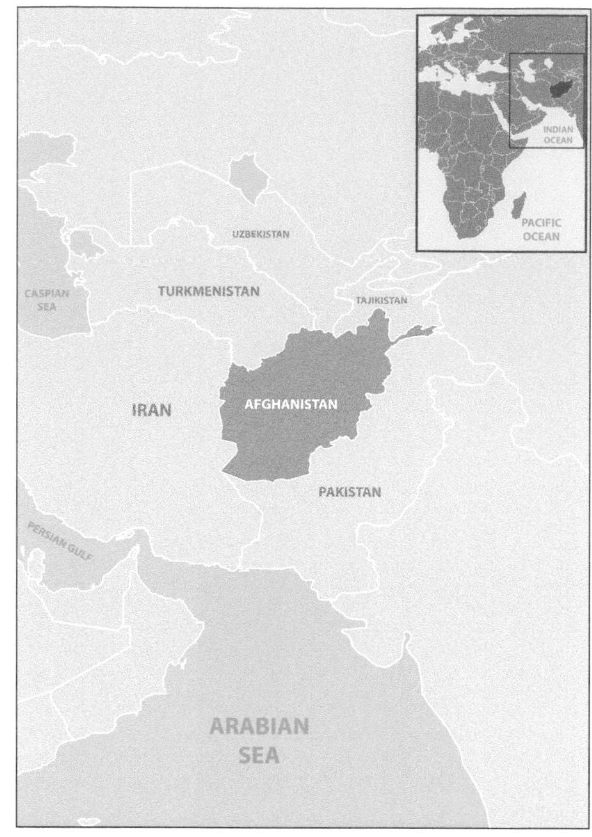

Coins: There have been numerous coins minted throughout the history of Afghanistan. As of 2005, the Afghani was available in coin denominations of 1, 2 and 5.
Area: 647,497 square kilometers (249,935 square miles)
National Anthem: "Sououd-e-Melli"
Capital: Kabul
Time Zone: GMT +4.5
Flag Description: The Afghan flag consists of three horizontal bands, one black, one red, and one green. In the center is an image of a white mosque surrounded by wheat sheaves.

Population

Decades of civil unrest have severely affected the Afghan population. Life expectancy is forty-nine years for men and only fractionally higher for women. The country has one of the highest infant mortality rates in the world, with approximately 117 deaths per 1,000 live births. Before the downfall of the Taliban,

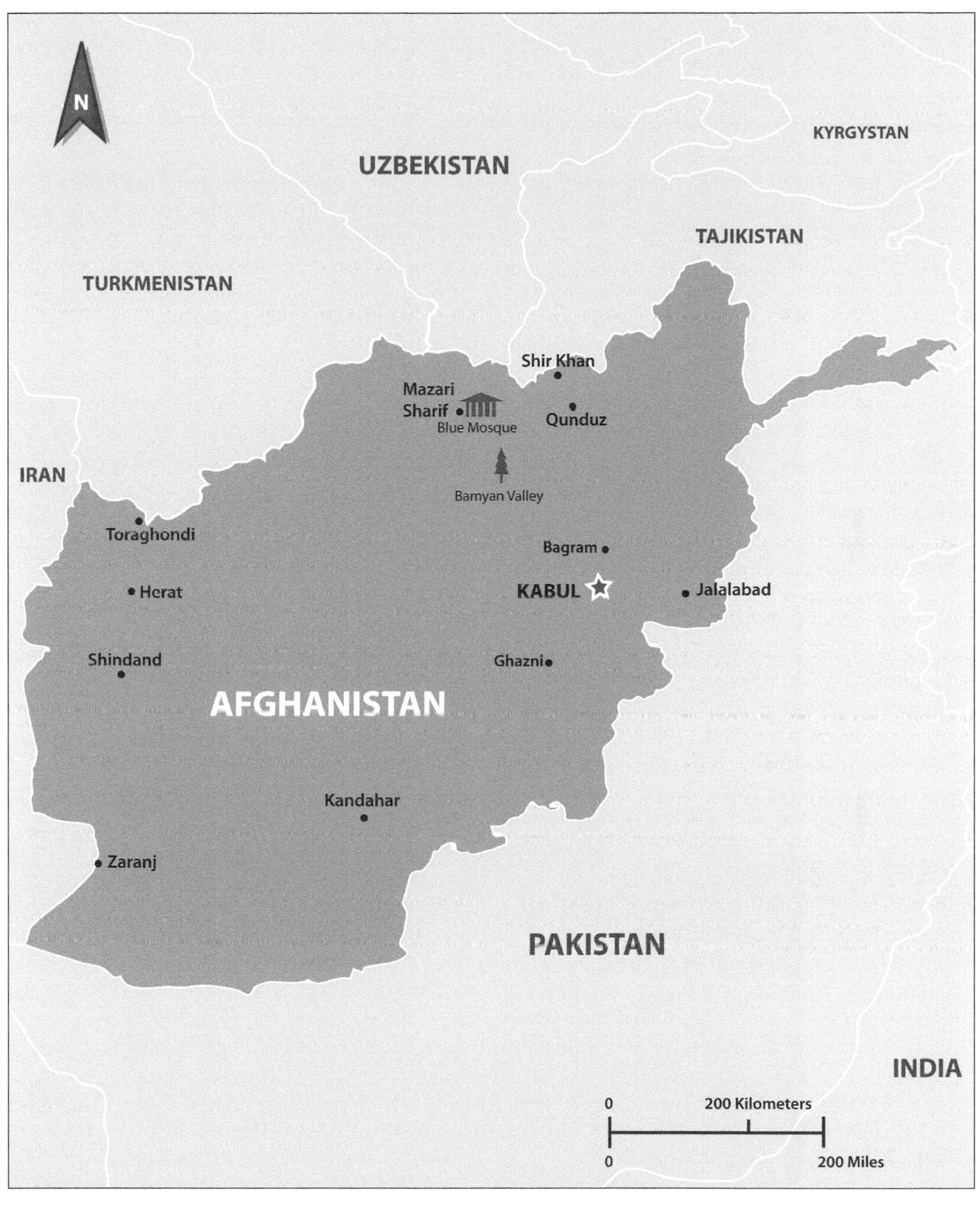

N
UZBEKISTAN
KYRGYSTAN
TAJIKISTAN
TURKMENISTAN
Shir Khan
Mazari Sharif
Blue Mosque
Qunduz
IRAN
Bamyan Valley
Toraghondi
Bagram
Herat
KABUL
Jalalabad
Shindand
Ghazni
AFGHANISTAN
Kandahar
Zaranj
PAKISTAN
INDIA
0
200 Kilometers
0
200 Miles

Principal Cities by Population (2012, unless noted):

- Kabul (3,289,000)
- Kandahar (368,099)
- Herat (308,203)
- Mazari Sharif (267,147)
- Jalalabad (151,010)
- Qunduz (124,567)
- Balkh (87,052)
- Baglan (83,117)

approximately four million refugees lived outside of Afghanistan; 2.7 million are thought to have returned. The country ranks 169th out of 187 countries on the Human Development Index.

An estimated 77 percent of the population lives in small rural communities, and perhaps 2.5 million people lead a nomadic lifestyle. Kabul, with 3.2 million, is the most populous city. Other major urban centers are Kandahar, Herat, and Mazar-e Sharif.

Languages

Many Afghans are bilingual, and Pashtu and Dari are the most widely spoken languages. Pashtu is the language of the Pashtuns, the largest ethnic group in the country. Afghanistan's ethnic-Iranian Tajiks speak Dari. Both Pashtu and Dari are Indo-European languages, but are written in a modified Arabic script.

Native People & Ethnic Groups

The Afghan population is a complex ethnic composite. It has evolved after millennia of migrations from surrounding regions. Rather than conflicts between indigenous and non-indigenous people, tensions have arisen instead between tribes or between sub-groups within tribes. The struggles have been over access to natural resources as well as over power.

Pashtuns account for 42 percent of the population. Tajiks, accounting for 27 percent, are the largest minority, followed by Hazaras, Uzbeks, and many other smaller groups. The Pashtuns have been the dominant group for several centuries and have often persecuted minorities, such as the Shia Hazaras. Pashtuns live throughout the country, but the other ethnic groups generally live in specific regions.

Religions

One of the few characteristics, which unite the disparate groups in Afghanistan, is conservative Islam. Eighty percent of the population is Sunni Muslim, and 19 percent is Shia Muslim. Hazaras and some Tajiks practice Shia Islam, comprising a religious minority.

Sunni Islam is the primary religion of those living in Kabul. Shia Muslims comprise a significant minority. Strong adherence to Islamic traditions and the Islamic calendar, with its cycle of religious holidays, remain a daily part of life. Other religions are practiced by only small fractions of the populace.

Climate

Afghanistan's climate varies as extremely as its terrain. In the mountains of the northeast, a subarctic climate prevails. The summers are dry and the winters cold; glaciers and year-round snow are common. January temperatures can fall to –15° Celsius (5° Fahrenheit) at the highest elevations, whereas summer temperatures usually range between 0° and 26° Celsius (32° and 78° Fahrenheit).

Precipitation, mostly in the form of snow, measures more than 1,000 millimeters (40 inches) each year. Farther south, along the border with Pakistan, summer winds from the Indian Ocean moderate the temperature in the mountain valleys.

These same warm winds can reach the central and southern steppe, bringing rain and humidity to the arid region. It is otherwise hot during the day and cold at night, especially in the western deserts. Less than 100 millimeters (4 inches) of rain falls annually in the driest areas.

Seasonal winds sometimes bring severe dust storms to the steppe, and long droughts are common. Moreover, sudden rainstorms can cause the flooding of streams and riverbeds. In the mountains, particularly in the Hindu Kush, frequent seismic activity occurs.

ENVIRONMENT & GEOGRAPHY

The mountains of the Hindu Kush cross Afghanistan from the northeast to the southwest. Smaller ranges branch out from this range, which is the western portion of the Pamir Mountains and the Himalayas. Crossing the mountains is made possible by the passes that transect them, most famously the Salang Pass linking the north and the south, and the Khyber Pass leading into Pakistan.

Afghanistan is landlocked but has several river systems as well as a few lakes and marshes. The Amu Darya, the Hilmand, the Harirud, and the Kabul are the four major rivers. With its tributary, the Panj, the Amu Darya forms the country's northern border. The largest lakes are Lake Zarkol and Lake Shiveh in the northeast.

Topography

Afghanistan has mountainous terrain, roughly half above 2,000 meters (6,600 feet). Only in the northwest, west and southwest border areas do desert and rocky plains predominate. The Rigestan Desert and the Turkistan Plains are two such areas. The terrain rises in a northeasterly direction, towards the country's highest mountains, found in a strip of land called the Wakhan Corridor. There, Nowshak is the highest peak at 7,485 meters (24,557 feet).

Plants & Animals

Plant life in Afghanistan ranges from the sparse to the verdant. The western deserts support little vegetation. The northern steppe is dry and treeless, and only hardy shrubs such as the camel thorn, mimosa, sagebrush, and wormwood thrive.

As the elevation increases, so does the vegetation. This is particularly true in areas affected by the rain patterns and warm weather from the Indian Ocean. Above 3,048 meters (10,000 feet), conifer forests are common, with fir and pine trees being prevalent. Lower down, cedar trees grow; and lower yet alder, ash, juniper, oak, pistachio, and walnut trees are common.

Animal distribution is similar. The foothills and mountains are home to large mammals such as bears, wolves, hyenas, gazelles, ibex, and wild sheep. Smaller mammals include hedgehogs and mongooses.

Populations of many animals are in decline, and 11 percent of the total number of species in Afghanistan is threatened. Endangered species include the markhor and the snow leopard, and the Asiatic black bear and a variety of bats are threatened. Among the common birds are vultures, pheasant, ducks, and flamingoes.

CUSTOMS & COURTESIES

Greetings

It is customary for friends and strangers to meet by exchanging the Arabic greeting "As-salamu alaykum." This phrase is prevalent throughout the Muslim world, and it means "Peace be upon you." The proper response to this greeting is "Wa alaykum as-Salaam," which is translated as "And upon you be peace." In more informal greetings, the shorter "Salaam," meaning simply "Peace," may be used instead.

A number of other greetings, such as "Welcome," "May you stay alive," "May you not be tired," or "May you not be poor," often accompanies the "Salaam alaykum" greetings. These greetings may typically be followed by a series of inquiries about family and health. One may also inquire about the well-being of specific family members. However, female family members should not be asked about family members except those who are very close friends or relatives.

Male friends and relatives greet each other by embracing and shaking hands, while women kiss each other's cheeks two or three times alternately. The protocols around male-female meetings also depend on region. In cities, women and men may shake hands, but in rural settings, they do not.

Gestures & Etiquette

In Afghan culture, polite social behavior is an important indicator of one's reputation and that of one's immediate and extended family. The rules for proper social behavior are not uniform. They vary from region to region and family to family, and parents teach these manners in their home. In addition, Islam, the predominant religion in Afghanistan, also influences social behavior and etiquette.

In rural settings, standards remain strict while in large cities, increased social equality has brought about a simplification and relaxation of codes among educated elites. Afghanistan's civil war since the late 1970s has also affected the rules of social decorum. Life in exile, either in refugee camps or in border countries, brought about new strictness in polite behavior as Afghan families struggled to maintain their identities and status while living far from home and in foreign cultures.

Some general rules are always followed: One should stand when a new person enters the room and properly greet him or her. Boisterous behavior, such as loud laughter or speech, is considered impolite. Showing respect to elders is mandatory. Women should also dress humbly and cover their hair before strangers. Generally, not following these rules brings embarrassment to the offender's family.

Names are often replaced by titles as a sign of respect. For example, a doctor or engineer may be referred to as "Doctor" or "Engineer," rather than by name. Children address elders as aunts and uncles. Women may be addressed as the mother of their oldest child. Husbands and wives may call each other by the name of their first child or first male child.

Eating/Meals

The center of every meal is traditionally a large thin tablecloth spread on the floor. Everyone typically sits on flat cushions laid out around the cloth. An Afghan feast usually has numerous dishes. These dishes are not served in any particular order but are instead set on the cloth spread, and each person eats what he or she would like. Generally, large platters of rice are supplied for three or four people to share communally along with the dishes. Desserts are served after the meal, often with tea.

Although cutlery is not altogether uncommon, eating is traditionally done with the right hand by scooping food into a ball at the tip of the fingers. Often a young child of the host family will bring a pitcher and bowl around to each guest. The child pours water over the guest's hands, which are held over the bowl catching the used water. Spoons are supplied for desserts such as rice pudding.

Visiting

Hospitality is an important part of Afghan culture. Guests are typically offered the best seat at the head of the room as well as the best food, even at the expense of the host's family. Hosts will always welcome even the most unexpected guests into their home and immediately provide tea. Often, guests are not asked the reason for their visit or how long they plan to stay. Whether a casual visit or a special occasion, guests should accept multiple helpings of food lest they offend their hosts.

Polite behavior traditionally reflects the reputation of oneself and of one's family. Status in a community is dependent upon maintaining proper decorum. Women will often cover their hair with a chador, an outer garment, when guests are present. Etiquette forbids loud laughing, joking, and singing, interrupting others, sitting with one's legs outstretched, smoking before elders, and being unhelpful. Shoes worn outdoors are not typically worn in an Afghan home; guests should remove their shoes at the door.

LIFESTYLE

Family

The extended family is considered the sacred pillar of Afghan culture. Families are made up of several generations and are led by a patriarch, or the eldest male, who is the primary decision-maker. Women are responsible for maintaining the household and raising children, while men are the financial providers. As with other forms of social etiquette, the strict roles of gender in the family may be more relaxed in urban areas. Generally, family is very private and personal, and it is considered rude to ask about another's household, especially about a man's wives, mothers, and daughters.

The Afghan family structure underwent immense pressure in the course of the 20th century, and especially in its last few decades. Modernization efforts from 1929 to 1978 sought to bring women out of the home and into the public sphere. After 1960, families increasingly accepted roles that are more public for their female members. This trend was largely limited to educated urban families, but lower middle class families eventually began to follow. When the Taliban came to power in 1996, this trend was inhospitably reversed. Women were barred altogether from the public sphere, except if accompanied by a male relative. In the 21st century, ongoing security problems posed by armed insurgents continue to make it difficult for women to leave the private sphere.

Housing

Afghanistan has a range of housing types based on variations in ethnic cultures, population density, and climate. The country is home to hot deserts, high-altitude cold mountains, and fertile, subtropical valleys. Nomadic populations in the north use yurts (portable and often framed housing with felt covering), while those in the south rely on tents. Settled populations also create homes that are regionally distinct. In the north and west, homes are constructed from stone and mud-bricks. Housing if typically constructed of wood in the north and east. In cities, families often live in walled compounds. For the many millions of Afghans that fled the Soviet invasion, civil war and the Taliban regime, and live in refugee camps, housing usually involved tents provided by foreign assistance.

After decades of civil war, the government began reconstructing the country's housing infrastructure. With many Afghans returning home after the 2001 fall of the Taliban regime, Kabul's population skyrocketed from 800,000 to 4 million people in 2007. Nearly half of this population lived in illegally occupied abandoned buildings. With aid from the World Bank, the Ministry of Urban Development began a $28.2 million (USD) project to improve housing, water access, sanitation, and infrastructure in Kabul.

Food

Afghan cuisine is largely multicultural, and influenced by Pakistani, Indian, Persian, Mongolian, and Arabic cultures. Culinary variety is also facilitated by Afghanistan's ethnic diversity and extreme climatic variations, which allows for many different locally grown crops. Common ingredients for meals across the country include yogurt, coriander, garlic, onions, mint, cumin, cloves, cinnamon, nutmeg, cardamom, and nuts. Fresh and dried fruit, especially apricots and pomegranates, are also popular. Main dish staples include bread, rice, lamb, and chicken. Afghan naan, similar to Indian breads, has a long, flat shape and is sprinkled with nigella seeds. Another bread, lavash, is thinner and is more similar to the bread of Iran.

Rice is prepared in many forms in Afghanistan. Chalau, made of basmati white rice, is first drained, parboiled briefly, and then baked with oil and salt. Like chalau, palau involves baked rice, but it contains meat and vegetables that are added before baking. Palau also comes in many variations. Kabuli palau is an especially popular rice dish containing meat (chicken or lamb), raisins, carrots, and pistachios. The process of making Kabuli palau involves baking parboiled rice with onions, meat, spices, carrots, and raisins that are fried in ghee (clarified butter) or oil. Another typical dish is kadu bouranee, a dish of pumpkin in yogurt sauce. Noodle and dumpling dishes, often attributed to Mongolian culture, include mantu, aush, and aushak. The preparation of these dishes varies greatly across region and family.

Desserts include pastries, fresh fruit, and firni, a sweet rice pudding. A popular pastry is gosh-e feel, literally "elephant's ears," which is made of fried dough shaped like an elephant ear and topped with the spice cardamom, ground pistachios, and sugar. In addition, green or black tea, or chai, is served throughout the day and at the end of meals. The partaking of food and tea has a ceremonial aspect among Afghan people.

Life's Milestones

Engagements are celebrated with a party called shirini-khori, or the "eating of sweets" ceremony. The marriage typically follows a few months later. Although wedding details vary across region and ethnicity, they generally take place in two parts. First, there is a religious swearing ceremony called the nikah. For this event, the bride wears green, the color of Islam. Afterward, a reception called the arusi takes place, and it can last well into the morning hours. Long after all the guests have arrived, the bride arrives during the playing of a song that recites "Walk slowly, my moon, walk slowly." As the bride walks, the Qur'an (Koran), the holy book of Islam, is held over her head.

In modern weddings, the bride and groom enter and walk together. After this procession, the bride and groom sit together on a stage or throne with a veil thrown over their heads. A mirror is placed before them so that the two may gaze at each other in privacy. In arranged marriages, this might be the first time that the newlyweds see each other's faces.

In Afghan culture, the birth of a child is cause for a large celebration and feast that may last for several days. Typically, large varieties of specialty Afghan dishes are prepared. A local Muslim leader, called a mullah, will also come to bless the child. The child's name is chosen during this celebration.

CULTURAL HISTORY

Art

Historically, Afghanistan has rested at the crossroads of Asia and the Middle East, and its art and culture have largely been influenced by various traditions and ethnicities. While traces of many religions exist in Afghanistan—such as the monumental Buddhas of Bamyan statues—Islam has largely influenced its culture. However, one of the earliest known arts practiced in Afghanistan is Gandhara art, which mixes Buddhism with classical Greek culture. The origins of this art are traced to Afghanistan, where it flourished between the first and seventh centuries CE. It wasn't until the 1900s that art in Afghanistan incorporated Western styles and techniques. In addition, traditional Afghan arts include carpet-weaving, calligraphy (which has its roots in Islam) and sculpture.

Music

Music and poetry remain two of Afghanistan's most well-preserved and rich artistic traditions.

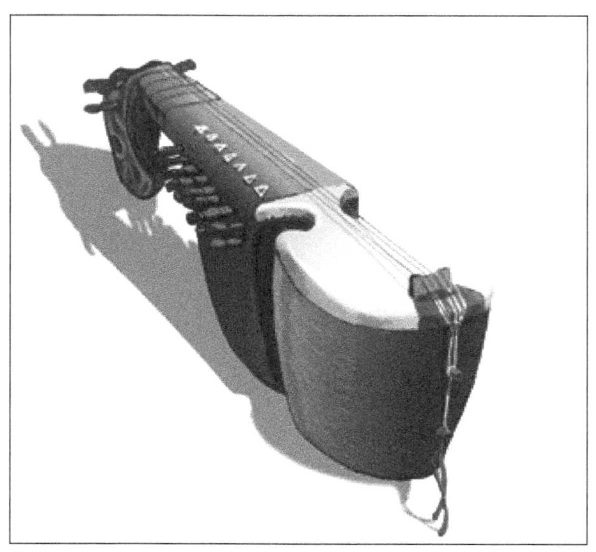

The rubab is indigenous to Afghanistan

Classical instrumental music is called naghma-ye-kashal. Performed with the rubab, a six-stringed lute, this instrumental music is indigenous to Afghanistan. In the 1860s, naghma-ye-kashal developed a new ghazal form when Punjabi musicians began performing regularly in Kabul. Ghazal refers to sung poetry constructed from rhyming couplets. In the 20th century, instruments from India, such as the sitar (stringed instrument) and tabla (percussion instrument) were introduced to classic music compositions. Prominent musicians during this time include Ustad Ghulam Hussein (1887–1967) and Ustad Qasim Afghan (1878–1957), often called the "Father of Afghan Music."

Influenced by Indian and Iranian music, popular music emerged in the 1940s. In the 1970s, Ahmed Zahir (1946–1979), the son of a prime minister, was the foremost popular singer in Afghan history. His music continues to be heard throughout the world in Afghan communities today.

Following the Soviet invasion of 1979, music was suppressed under Soviet rule and remained alive only through underground channels. In 1996, the Taliban, who administered an Islamic fundamentalist government, outlawed music. Even the most traditional musical practices such as making and playing instruments and singing at weddings were illegal. Since the US-led invasion of Afghanistan in 2001, musicians have begun to come out of hiding and stores have begun selling music again, ranging from traditional to popular genres.

Literature

Afghanistan's strong storytelling tradition began to transform into written form in the medieval period. Literature at this time was written in Persian, Arabic, Turkish, and Pashto, an Iranian language spoken by the Pashtun people, indigenous to southern and eastern Afghanistan. The most well-known work from this time is the *Shahnameh*, or the *Book of Kings*, an epic poem consisting of 60,000 rhyming couplets, It was written by the Persian poet Ferdowsi (935–1020) around 1,000 CE, and is considered a national epic of Persia, which modern Afghanistan was then a part of.

In the 13th century, Jalāl ad-Dīn Muhammad Rūmī (1207–1273), a Persian Sufi poet known simply as Rumi, made a significant contribution to literary history with his mystical meditations on spirituality. His work remains immensely popular in the Persian-speaking world and has been translated into English. Khushal Khan Khatak (1613–1689), a 17th century poet writing in Pashtu, is considered the national poet. Both a warrior and a tribal chief, Khatak wrote of the need for national unity.

In the early-19th century, modern literature emerged with a focus on modernizing and democratizing Afghanistan. In 1911, Mahmud Tarzi (1865–1933) began publishing *Seraj ul-Akhbar*, or *Lamp of the News*, a newspaper that aimed to modernize Afghan society through education. He is often referred to as the "father of Afghan journalism." Throughout the 1950s, numerous other newspapers were established with similar goals, but turned toward reaching a wider segment of the population. They supported and published literary work, especially short stories and poetry.

Afghanistan's most renowned modern poet is Khalilullah Khalili (1907–1987). Khalili was the national poet laureate as well as a historian, parliamentarian, philosopher and professor. His work bridged traditional and modern themes within classical poetic form. After the Soviet invasion in 1979, Khalili and many other literary figures were forced to flee the country for their safety.

Film

Though film was introduced to Afghanistan in the early 20th century, Afghan cinema emerged in the 1960s. Before this time, film in Afghanistan was limited to Indian imports. In 1951, the first Afghan film was released, *Eshq-o-Dusti* (*Love and Friendship*), directed by Ustad Rashid Latif. Though the film was popularly received, the government of Afghanistan was unwilling to fund a film industry. However, filmmaking continued, and rising nationalism inspired many artists to make works about Afghan identity. Other early films included *Like Eagles, Ages, Village Tunes,* and *Difficult Days*. During this period, the first university film department was established, along with the Afghan Film Organization (AFO), which produced documentaries about the government.

By the 1970s, the capital of Kabul was the site of a flourishing filmmaking industry with eighteen theatres and significant funding from Hollywood. Afghan filmmaking collapsed, however, with the invasion of the Soviets in 1979. Filmmakers were unable to express their beliefs or their heritage, and many had to leave the country with other artists. Filmmaking all but ceased during this time. In 1996, the new Taliban government outlawed cinema altogether.

After the fall of the Taliban regime in 2001, film began reemerging. Kabul Film was the first film company to be established after the U.S.-led invasion. Upon opening in 2002, Kabul Film began working with the Afghan Visual Communication Institute, a project of the French-based non-governmental organization (NGO) AINA. The project created independent media and brought educational films to remote areas of the country. Subjects of their films include women's health, landmine awareness, and Afghanistan's cultural and political histories.

CULTURE

Arts & Entertainment

Afghanistan has a rich history of music, literature, and art, but it has been severely impacted by decades of conflict. When the Soviet Union invaded the country in 1979, the new Ministry for Information and Culture sought to silence resistance to its occupation by curtailing artists' free expression. This forced poets like Afghanistan's poet laureate Khalilullah Khalili into exile in Peshawar, Pakistan. With so many educated Afghans leaving their home country, Peshawar became a center for Afghan intellectuals, artists, and musicians. One Peshawar block called "Khallil House" became the home of more than two dozen musical groups exiled from Afghanistan.

Censorship worsened when the Taliban took control of Afghanistan in 1996. Its fundamentalist Islamist government founded the Ministry for the Promotion of Virtue and Suppression of Vice (also known as the "religious police"). This government ministry banned a large number of activities that defined Afghan cultural identity, including music, film, dancing, television, and kite flying. During Taliban rule, many artists and musicians had to bury their work and their tools to save them from destruction, and poets memorized their poems for fear of carrying them in their pocket.

Furthermore, the Taliban regime destroyed the archive of Afghan folk music housed at Kabul Radio, reels of stock footage owned by Afghan Films, and much of what was left of the National Museum's collection. In 2001, the world was outraged when the Taliban dynamited two monumental Buddha carvings, long considered world treasures. The Buddhas were carved within a cliff in the Bamiyan Valley.

After the fall of the Taliban in 2001, the National Museum of Kabul and the Artists' Union quickly reopened. The Artists' Union of Afghanistan has 3,000 members working in the fields of painting, music, theatre, sculpture, and film. The cultural ministry has brought back television with a special emphasis on programs featuring Afghan history, art, music, and film in order to counteract years of suppression. During nearly three decades of war and conflict, the National Museum lost more than one-quarter of its collection. However, in 2004, a collection of Afghan artifacts, dating from 2200 BCE to 200 CE, was discovered in a presidential palace vault where it had been protected from the violence. The items had been secretly stored there in 1988 by the National Museum director Omar Khan Massoudi.

In 2008, the National Museum of Kabul curated a traveling exhibit titled "Hidden Afghanistan" that includes items from the secret vault. The exhibit demonstrates Afghanistan's rich cultural history, including its central location on the Silk Road, an ancient trading route that reached across China to the Mediterranean Sea. This exhibit was brought to the United States for a tour that included the National Gallery of Art in Washington, DC.

Because so many Afghans fled their country between 1978 and 2001, there is a large diasporic community living around the world. A diaspora is a population of people dispersed from their homeland but still united by their shared culture and identity. More than one-half of Afghanistan's 26 million inhabitants were forced to flee their homes—millions to border countries and thousands to Western countries. The best-known work coming from the Afghan diaspora is Khaled Hosseini's internationally bestselling novel *The*

Kite Runner, published in 2003. The novel told the story of a friendship between two Afghan boys born in Kabul.

In 2003, Siddiq Barmak directed the first feature film made in Afghanistan since the Taliban's 1996 takeover. The film, titled *Osama,* is the story of a 12-year-old girl in Kabul who must pose as a boy in order to find work to support her mother and grandmother. Because women were forbidden to work by the Taliban, many families without males were destitute. *Osama* has won numerous international film awards.

Afghanistan's rich classical music tradition has been influenced by other Asian countries. No longer forbidden as it was under the Taliban, music is once again a part of daily life and important ceremonies. Each region is known for its unique musical traditions, though regional differences have faded over time. Ustad M.H. Sarahang and Ustad Naim Nazary are two respected modern singers in the classical tradition.

The national instrument of Afghanistan is the rebab. Its four main strings are plucked, and the instrument can be played solo or in vocal and instrumental ensembles. Another popular string instrument is the dutar, which is often accompanied with different hand-played drums.

In a country with low literacy rates, oral narratives are important. Many of these have ancient roots, but others have been modernized according to contemporary developments in Afghanistan. Of any single book, the Koran is the most important, but it is studied in the original Arabic rather than in one of the country's indigenous languages. The national poet of Afghanistan, who wrote in Pashto, is Khushal Khan Khattak.

Afghans have several sporting traditions, including soccer and *buzkashi*. Buzkashi is a gamed played throughout Central Asia. In the spirit of polo, it involves teams of horse riders who attempt to score a goal by moving a salt-filled goat carcass along the field. Kite flying is also popular. Small or large and very colorful, the kites generally have two children to handle them. The object of the game is to cut the opponent's kite string with one's own.

Afghan artisans excel in creating durable, beautiful handcrafts. Flat or piled wool carpets made with natural fibers and dyes on a hand-loom are the most famous. Other important crafts include pottery and tile making, metal and leatherwork, and embroidery.

Cultural Sites & Landmarks

Two of Afghanistan's most famous historical sites include the Minaret and Archaeological Remains of Jam and the Cultural Landscape and Archeological Remains of the Bamiyan Valley. The United Nations Educational, Scientific, and Cultural Organization (UNESCO) designate both as World Heritage Sites. Constructed in the 12th century, the Minaret of Jam is a work of Islamic architecture created by the Ghurids, a Persian Sunni Muslim dynasty that spread over all of Afghanistan, as well as parts of Iran, India, and Pakistan. In the Bamiyan Valley of Afghanistan is a historical monument of ancient Bakhtria life, which dates from the first to the thirteenth centuries. The site includes ancient Buddhist sanctuaries, statues and cave paintings, and the religious and artistic works represent the origins of Gandhara art.

However, military and political unrest in Afghanistan has threatened the longevity of the Cultural Landscape and Archaeological Remains of the Bamiyan Valley. In 2001, the Taliban destroyed two monumental Bamiyan Buddhas at this site, claiming that they were idolatrous and promoted un-Islamic values. These statues reached 53 and 38 meters (173 and 124 feet), respectively. In 2003, UNESCO placed the historical site on its list of World Heritage Sites in danger. Because of military activity and bomb detonations, the site has been weakened. In addition, its subsequent abandonment has allowed looting to take place. This situation was worsened by the inability of experts to access the site because of the widespread dissemination of landmines by the Soviet military in the 1980s.

A top tourist destination before war broke out in Afghanistan was Bagh-e Babur, or the Babur Gardens. Located just west of Kabul, the gardens date back to the 16th century and cover

11 hectares (27 acres) of the Sher-e Darwaza Mountain. Bagh-e Babur contains the tomb of Muhammed Zahir al-Din Babur (1483–1530), founder of the Moghul Dynasty and descendant of both Timur and Genghis Khan. Many believe that Bagh-e Babur was the first Moghul garden and served as a model for many imperial gardens throughout South Asia. From 2003 to 2005, the Aga Khan Trust for Culture restored the gardens to their original splendor with assistance from the German Archaeological Institute.

One of Afghan's most well-known landmarks is the Blue Mosque of Mazar-e Sharif, the fourth largest city in the country. The Blue Mosque is also known as the Shrine of Hazrat Ali and is believed to be the burial site of Ali ibn Abu Talib (c. 600–661), the cousin, and son-in-law of the Prophet Muhammed.

Afghanistan also established its first national park in April 2009, called Band-e Amir. The area is known for its natural beauty, including sapphire lakes. The park was to be initially established in the 1960s, and has been recommended as a World Heritage Site.

Kabul's ancient history is not generally evident, as it has undergone modernization and extensive destruction, particularly during the civil war (1992–1996). Some of the city's most famous monuments are targeted for restoration, while others remain in a state of ruin. The presence of landmines limits access to some sites in the city.

Several large mosques serve the Muslims of Kabul. These include the Pul-e Khisti mosque, the Sha-Do-Shamshira mosque, and the Sherpur mosque. The Id Gah mosque is the largest in the city.

The Mausoleum of Timur Shah, dating from 1816, houses the tomb of the ruler who moved the Afghan capital to Kabul. The Abdur Rahman Mausoleum memorializes the ruler who reigned until the beginning of the 20th century and was responsible for unifying and modernizing Afghanistan.

Other notable structures in Afghanistan's capital include Bala Hissar, an old fortress that overlooks Kabul, the old city walls, and the ruined Darulaman Palace. Kabul University, founded in 1931, is recovering from the decades of conflict and the persecution of its academic staff and students. It has reopened, but lacks many essential resources. Ghazi Stadium, damaged in the civil conflicts, was also notorious during Taliban rule as a site of public punishments and executions.

In the city's bazaars, clustered in the old town, all types of goods are sold, from regional handicrafts and pets to imports both cheap and costly. Chicken Street is one well-known shopping area.

Libraries & Museums

The Kabul Museum, once the repository for artifacts from Central Asia's ancient history, was destroyed and looted during the civil conflicts. Moreover, the Taliban were responsible for destroying artifacts that they considered an affront to Islam. Though the museum has been restored and reopened, an estimated three-quarters of its collections have been lost.

Holidays

The most important Afghan holidays relate to its Islamic religious traditions. The end of the holy month of fasting, Ramadan, is marked by Eid Al-Fatr. Eid Al-Adha commemorates Abraham's subservience to God and marks the beginning of the Haj, the pilgrimage of the faithful to Mecca. Ashura commemorates the martyrdom of Hussein, Mohammed's grandson, and Mawleed Al-Nabi marks Mohammed's birthday. Additionally, the pre-Islamic festival of Nawruz, celebrated on March 21, welcomes spring and the New Year. On these holidays, people visit their family and friends, hold feasts, attend prayers, and often exchange gifts.

Other national holidays include Afghan Independence Day (August 19), marking the day that the country regained control of its foreign policy from Britain; and Remembrance Day for Martyrs and Disabled (May 4).

Youth Culture

Afghanistan's civil war created a very young population. In 2008, more than half of the national population was under the age of eighteen. In addition to not knowing peace, most youth have grown up with little or no education. During Taliban rule (1996–2001), fewer than one million boys were enrolled in schools. By 2007, that number has jumped to seven million girls and boys. However, there are still millions of children, especially girls, not attending school.

Despite these immense obstacles, à youth culture has begun to emerge, especially in cities like Kabul. Standing up to conservatives, young people have been vocal proponents of women's rights, the arts and entertainment, and freedom in the media. For example, performer DJ Besho has emerged as a rapper who sings empowering lyrics of unity for the country. As communications systems are modernized and updated, many young Afghans have taken to the Internet to communicate with the world about their country. As a result, blogging has been a common means for youth communication. In 2008, the Association of Afghan Blog Writers held the first public blogging workshop.

SOCIETY

Transportation

Transportation in Afghanistan ranges from the most traditional means, such as camels and donkeys in rural areas, to public transportation and international air travel in the cities. Public city transportation includes buses and trucks. Individuals also use personal automobiles and bicycles. Afghanistan drivers travel on the right hand side of the road.

Transportation Infrastructure

There are 34,782 kilometers (21,600 miles) of roads in Afghanistan. However, most are not paved. Many of these roads were built in the 1960s, but are now in poor condition after decades of war and neglect. Since 2001, the government has worked to rebuild this infrastructure. For example, the Salang Tunnel, once the most efficient passageway between Kabul and northern Afghanistan, was unusable after it was bombed in fighting between the Taliban and Northern Alliance in 1998. In 2002, the tunnel was repaired through $1.6 million USD in aid provided by the United States Agency for International Development (USAID).

Afghanistan has 46 airports. Twelve of these have paved runways and 34 have unpaved runways. The national airline is Ariana Afghan Airlines. International airports operate in Kabul and Kandahar. Kabul International Airport is the largest airport and is the primary means of civilian air travel.

In 2007, a U.S.-funded bridge was completed over the Pyanj River, providing travel between Tajikistan and Afghanistan. The bridge is intended to strengthen trade between the countries. The U.S. contributed $37 million to the project with assistance from Japan, the European Union (EU), and Norway.

Media & Communications

From 1996 to 2001, Afghanistan's media were under the strict control of the Taliban. As such, the state-controlled media reflected the regime's fundamentalist interpretation of Islam. Television was banned for spreading moral decay, and Radio Afghanistan was transformed into Radio Voice of Shariah. Shariah is the Arabic term for the body of Islamic laws that govern every aspect of life.

After the Taliban were toppled in 2001, the media landscape of Afghanistan transformed dramatically. For the first time in the nation's history, electronic and print media were able to operate independently of the government. As a result, numerous newspapers and television and radio stations emerged. By 2005, Afghanistan had more than 300 newspapers, over 50 radio stations and five televisions stations. However, all media remains subject to censorship if their programs are deemed to be un-Islamic. The government is also under pressure from conservative religious leaders to curb immoral content.

Radio is an especially popular medium because Afghanistan has a high illiteracy rate and strong oral tradition. The government uses radio to broadcast educational programs aimed at children in order to reach youth unable to attend school during Taliban rule and the civil war beforehand. Afghan radio also broadcasts many news programs, including the British Broadcasting Corporation (BBC), Radio France Internationale (RFI), and Deutsche Welle, Germany's international broadcaster.

Television programs often broadcast shows produced in India or programs modeled on American or European shows. Indian "Bollywood" films have caused some controversy for their portrayal of relationships between men and women. In 2003, the minister of information and culture temporarily interrupted cable broadcasting in order to deal with complaints from conservatives.

SOCIAL DEVELOPMENT

Standard of Living

The discrepancy between rich and poor, especially refugees and migrant workers, is pronounced in Kabul. Wealthy Afghanis and foreigners tend to live in gated communities such as Sharak-i-Sabz, a new residential and business district in northeast Kabul. The poorest, in contrast, depend on food aid and live in tenement-like conditions or on the street. The government has encouraged development outside of the center of Kabul as a means to relieve overcrowding in the city.

Water Consumption

Afghanistan's water infrastructure has been severely damaged by decades of war. In some areas, plumbing systems have been destroyed or have ceased operation due to neglect. The Supreme Council of Water Affairs Management of Afghanistan oversees the country's water resource management. Through a diplomatic agreement, Afghanistan draws some of its water supply from Russia. The availability of clean water in the country is limited and much of it is supplied by aid organizations.

Education

It will take decades for the educational system to be further developed. During the civil war, 70 percent of the facilities were destroyed, and many educated Afghans fled the country.

Education is once again free and compulsory for both males and females, and the system is one of the major focuses for the current Afghan government. A recent report estimated that 61 percent of children are not attending school. The current estimate for literacy is 51 percent for males and 21 percent for females.

Institutes of higher education include Kabul University, the University of Nangarhar in Jalalabad, and the University of Herat. Technical and pedagogical institutes have also reopened.

Women's Rights

Conditions for women have improved slightly since the fall of the Taliban government in 2001. Afghan women have formed NGOs and community-based groups in order to improve the conditions of women's lives in the reconstruction of the country and culture.

In 2003, the Afghan government accepted the terms of the Convention on the Elimination of Discrimination Against Women (CEDAW). Since 2004, women voted in presidential elections. Yet, a great number of women in Afghanistan are often denied basic rights protected by the UN Universal Declaration on Human Rights (UDHR). These include the rights to movement, employment, health, and education as outlined in Articles 13, 23, 25 and 26. Women's rights took a major step back in 2013, when Afghanistan's religious advisory body, the Ulema Council, reiterated many of the edicts concerning women espoused by the Taliban, including dress, avoidance of men, and exclusion from education and commerce. To the shock of many Western observers, then President Karzai welcomed the document.

Women's freedom of movement is impeded by Afghanistan's security problems. Human rights organizations routinely accuse the Afghan government of failing to protect women from dangers they face when they venture outdoors, such as rape, kidnapping, assault, and robbery. Although women enjoy more freedom in Kabul, this sense of relative security does not exist elsewhere. For example, in 2006 Safiye Amajan, Kandahar Women's Affairs Department director, and Zakia Zami, a vocal critic of warlords, were both murdered.

Women's access to education remains limited. Eighty percent of women are illiterate. Decades of war have also forced women to head their households financially. This responsibility is very difficult when women have not had access to education. In 2004, only 34 percent of children in school were girls. In the provinces of Zabul and Badghis, only 10 percent of girls between the ages of seven and twelve attend school. Girls and women seeking education also face threats from armed conservatives like the Taliban. Amnesty International reported 172 attacks on girls' schools in the first half of 2006 and 4,154 cases of violence against women in 2014.

Access to health care, especially reproductive health care, has improved for women. In 2010, Afghanistan's maternal mortality rate was 460 per 100,000 live births—down from 1,600 in 2008. In Badakshan's eastern province this rate has been recorded at 6,500 deaths per 100,000 live births, the highest ever recorded in world history. Furthermore, it is estimated that only 28 percent of married women under age 50 are aware of pregnancy prevention methods.

Although the Afghanistan government has made some strides in regards to women's rights, much ground is left to be covered to address and prevent domestic violence against women. There are no institutional resources for women enduring domestic violence, and police are unaware of how to deal with complaints even if they are taken seriously. Child marriage also prevents girls from going to school and contributes to the country's high maternal mortality rates. Fifty-seven percent of females are married before the age of 16, and forced marriages and are not uncommon.

Outside Kabul, women are generally unable to leave home without wearing a burqa, a garment that covers the entirety of a woman's body, including the face. The burqa is sewn with a small mesh-like screen that covers the face, and through which the wearer views the world. For many women, this covering limits mobility, but provides a modicum of security against harassment, violence, and armed insurgents.

Although most women remain in the private sphere, managing their homes and performing reproductive labor, some have begun to take part in civil society yet again. In 2003, the loya jirga, a legislative body of the new Afghan government, convened to ratify the proposed constitution, and 20 percent of the delegates were women.

Health Care

Even before the decades of conflict, Afghanistan was one of the world's least developed countries. The health care situation is worse now, though it has improved since the end of major hostilities.

Non-governmental agencies and the country's decrepit infrastructure cannot cope with the massive health problems of the population, including many preventable illnesses. Trachoma, tuberculosis, dysentery, and malnutrition are a few of the most common. Among other health problems are war-related injuries, inadequate obstetric care, a dearth of supplies and equipment, and a severe shortage of qualified medical personnel.

GOVERNMENT

Afghanistan was subject to several forms of rule in the 20th century. The Taliban took control of Kabul in 1996, instituting a strict Islamic fundamentalist style of rule. They remained in power until 2001. In the wake of the September 2001 terrorist attacks, the U.S. supported Taliban opposition forces with massive air strikes against Taliban positions. U.S. forces and United Nations forces have remained present in the country since 2001, when President Hamid Karzai took power.

Structure

The 2004 constitution declares Afghanistan an Islamic Republic, but also safeguards freedom of worship as well as minority languages and gender equality. Power is vested in a president. The president is elected by popular vote to a five-year term, with a two-term limit; two vice-presidents are similarly elected. The country's first presidential election was held in late 2004. The most recent presidential election, in 2014, was close enough to force a runoff, which was won by Ashraf Ghani. His opponent, Abdullah Abdullah, claimed that the voting was flawed. After a standoff, a power-sharing arrangement was agreed to whereby Abdullah would serve as the president's chief executive officer.

The most recent elections for the bicameral legislature, called the National Assembly, took place in September 2010. The 249 seats of the Wolesi Jirga (House of People) are filled for five-year terms by popular vote. The Meshrano Jirga (House of Elders) has 102 seats. These seats are filled by several methods, and the elders serve various term lengths. As needed, the Loya Jirga can convene to discuss constitutional issues. A traditional council consisting of 1,050 seats, it is composed of members from the National Assembly and local councils.

Political Parties

Among the numerous political parties in Afghanistan, each of which adheres to some version of Islam and Islam's political tenets. These parties include the Islamic Party, the Republic Party of Afghanistan, the Islamic Society, and the Islamic Movement of Afghanistan. Several other minor parties exist in the country.

Local Government

Afghanistan has 34 provinces that are divided into districts and sub-districts. The central government appoints a governor to each province. During the years of Soviet control, many mujahidin groups assumed the role of local government. When Afghanistan was under the control of the Taliban, the group appointed local tribal leaders to enact its code of strict Islamist law. Following the U.S.-led toppling of the Taliban, efforts began to recreate the country's government, beginning at a local level. These consist of shura councils, which select electors for municipal elections. However, warlords continue to maintain local control of many regions of Afghanistan. Some of these militia groups are sympathetic to the Western-led rebuilding efforts in the country, but others are not.

Throughout Afghanistan, a sense of cultural and territorial loyalty often results in groups of citizens having more reverence for local tribal political systems than any that might attempt to be imposed on them by the central government established in Kabul. Communal groups such as these are known as the local "qwam."

Judicial System

The Afghan judiciary is composed of a Supreme Court with nine justices., Pending the approval of the National Assembly, they are appointed by the president to 10-year terms. There are also High Courts and Appeal Courts below this level.

Taxation

Like much of the country's government, Afghanistan's tax collection system has been impacted by decades of warfare. During its years in power, the Taliban taxed humanitarian goods imported into the country. Since the establishment of a new government in recent years, an annual income tax has been introduced. However, efforts to implement a taxation system in Afghanistan's rural areas have yet to take hold.

Armed Forces

Afghanistan's armed forces consist of the Afghan National Army and the Afghan National Army Air Corps. The country has no navy. The Afghan Army and the Afghan National Police have received a substantial amount of funding and training from U.S. and allied forces since the toppling of the Taliban government.

Foreign Policy

Since the 2001 invasion, Afghanistan has been saddled with the task of rebuilding its society while trying to maintain political stability within its borders. Foreign assistance, in the form of military and monetary aid, is a decisive factor in this process. During the Taliban regime, the Central Bank of Afghanistan (Da Afghanistan Bank, or DAB) became bankrupt. As a result, Afghanistan relies on foreign aid to reconstruct its economy and become an active player in the world economy. Elected in 2004, President Hamid Karzai encouraged Afghans living abroad to return home to aid in the rebuilding of the country. He traveled around the world urging other nations to invest in the country's growth.

In 2008, Oxfam International, a British-based NGO, reported that little more than half of the $25 billion (USD) in aid pledged by Western countries between 2002 and 2008 has reached Afghanistan. The U.S. and other nations were hesitant to send this money because of concerns that it would not be used properly due to corruption.

In 2008, the U.S., Europe and 60 other countries pledged that they would contribute $20 billion (USD) in aid, including $10.2 billion from the U.S., $1.2 billion from the UK, $165 million from France, $550 million from Japan, and $600 million from Germany. The World Bank also pledged $1.1 billion (USD) and the Asian Development Bank (ADB) $1.3 billion (USD), to be disbursed over five years. Each contributing nation sought assurance that the money would go directly into rebuilding Afghan society and not into the hands of local officials and warlords, who many fear must be bribed to maintain stability. Further pledges from donor countries came to a total of $67 billion by 2010. In 2012, countries meeting in Tokyo pledged a further $16 billion in civilian aid.

In 2008, 6 million of an estimated 32 million Afghans were receiving food assistance from foreign sources. In the same year, soaring food prices around the globe brought the government to ask the UN World Food Programme (WFP) for more assistance, and $75 million (USD) was granted for six months of assistance. The WFP called for international investment in Afghanistan's agricultural programs as the only way to prevent the country's long-term dependence on food aid.

Afghanistan also relies on foreign assistance to maintain security and peace. After the US-led invasion in 2001, the UN Security Council authorized the deployment of an International Security Assistance Force (ISAF) led by the North Atlantic Treaty Organization (NATO). ISAF began with 32,000 troops from thirty-four different countries in 2001. By 2008, the numbers reached 47,000 troops from forty different nations. By 2014, this number surged to 86,000. However, after a U.S.-led withdrawal of the bulk of its forces in 2014, and the scheduled end of the NATO mandate by the end of 2015, the stability of Afghanistan in the years to come remains in doubt.

Initially, ISAF limited its responsibilities to securing Kabul. However, in 2003, it expanded its range to the entire country, sometimes in combat operations. In 2003, US Special Forces began training Afghan National Army soldiers. Five years later, Afghan troops numbered 76,000. Defense Minister Abdul Rahim Wardak reported that the number of troops would have to be doubled in order for the army to be able to combat threats to national security without international assistance. The United States has pledged to remain committed to Afghanistan and the training of the Afghan army beyond 2015.

Human Rights Profile

International human rights law insists that states respect civil and political rights, and promote an individual's economic, social, and cultural rights. The United Nations Universal Declaration on Human Rights (UDHR) is recognized as the standard for international human rights. Its authors sought the counsel of the world's great thinkers, philosophers, and religious leaders, and were careful to create a document that reflects the core values shared by every world culture. (To read this document or view the articles relating to cultural human rights, visit: http://www.udhr.org/UDHR/default.htm.)

Obstacles to establishing peace and security have created a poor human rights profile in Afghanistan. In 2008, Human Rights Watch reported that instability has resulted in most Afghans failing to have their most basic rights fulfilled. In 2014, Amnesty International reported that 4,853 noncombatants had been killed in the past year in conflicts involving the Afghan National Army, the International Security Assistance Force (ISAF), or Taliban insurgents. The Taliban and other armed insurgent groups specifically target civilians believed to be cooperating with the ISAF or Afghan government.

Article 5 of the UDHR protects individuals from torture and inhuman punishment, yet ISAF transfers suspected terrorists and criminals to Afghanistan's intelligence agency, the National Directorate of Security (NDS). This agency has been accused of torturing and mistreating detainees accused of undermining national security. The NDS routinely disallows its inmates fair trials in violation of Article 11 of the UDHR, which calls for the accused to have public trials and to be treated as innocent into proven guilty. In 2008, Human Rights Watch warned that the country's judicial system was ill-equipped to provide fair trials for the 100 prisoners on death row and that their executions would be in violation of Articles 5 and 11. In 2014, Amnesty international reported that the death penalty had continued to be widely applied, often after unfair trials.

The freedom of expression upheld by Article 19 is severely restricted in Afghanistan. Journalists who hold critical views of the government, regional warlords, drug lords, or Taliban insurgents continue to face violence and death threats and receive little protection from police. In 2007, the Journalists' Independent Union of Afghanistan identified both the government and the Taliban as the perpetrators of 53 violent crimes against journalists. In 2008, journalist Pawwiz Kambakhsh was sentenced to death for circulating information on women's rights within Islam. In the years since, violence against journalists has only increased. In 2014, 20 journalists were attacked and seven killed.

Human rights groups have also warned that corruption and impunity are widespread in Afghanistan's justice system as powerful government officials and warlords routinely escape persecution for crimes. The Afghan Independent Human Rights Commission reported that 94 percent of Afghans believed it important to bring war criminals and perpetrators of crimes against humanity to justice. The failure to do so has created widespread distrust of the current government.

Migration

In recent years, a large number of Afghanis from rural areas have moved to Kabul and other cities in the country seeking employment. Young people make up the majority of this migrating group.

ECONOMY

Overview of the Economy

Statistics regarding the Afghan economy are unreliable, but by all estimates, the country's economic situation has improved each year since 2001, largely because of the $6 billion (USD) in international aid that has been pledged by donor countries through 2015. Afghanistan's per capita gross domestic product (GDP) now stands at $1,100, though this figure does not account for two of the most significant sources of revenue: the illicit cultivation of opium and gunrunning. The largely uneducated labor force is thought to number 11.7 million people, and unemployment is high.

Industry

Industry accounts for 25.6 percent of the GDP and occupies 10 percent of the labor force. Much of the industrial sector was devastated by the decades of conflict, and the parts of it currently operating are small in scale. Furniture, fertilizer, cement, and handcrafts, most importantly carpets, are all produced in Afghanistan. The exploitation of natural resources is also increasing.

Labor

The vast majority of Afghanistan's labor force works in agriculture. Another important source of employment is the textile industry. Many of the country's agricultural jobs are part of an informal economy that exists without labor laws or tax regulations. In addition, a large portion of agricultural activity is related to the illegal opium trade.

Energy/Power/Natural Resources

Afghanistan is rich in natural resources, but the country's upheavals have impeded their large-scale, regular exploitation. Afghanistan is the most heavily mined country in the world, with an estimated 6 million landmines and 750,000 pieces of ordnance littering the landscape.

Afghans generate a large amount of energy from firewood. This pattern has had serious effects on the environment, which is increasingly prone to erosion and salinization. Overgrazing and deforestation are also problems.

Fishing

Fishing is not a contributor to Afghanistan's economy.

Forestry

Overgrazing and deforestation are serious problems in Afghanistan.

Mining/Metals

The most valuable are precious and semi-precious stones like lapis lazuli, natural gas, oil, and gold. The country also has significant deposits of coal, copper, lead, zinc, iron, sulfur, and salt. Some of the rivers have been harnessed for hydroelectric power, but many stations and dams were damaged during the war years.

Agriculture

Agriculture occupies 78.6 percent of the Afghan labor force and accounts for 20 percent of the GDP. The amount of arable land is small, and irrigation is necessary for much of it. Crops include wheat, corn, cotton, nuts, and various fruits and vegetables. The most valuable crop grown in Afghanistan is opium. In 2004, Afghanistan was the world's prime supplier of heroin, earning an estimated $2.8 billion (USD) in total, $600 million of which went to the farmers. Hashish is also a valuable crop. U.S.-led coalition forces have attempted to curb opium production in Afghanistan, because the proceeds of the nation's drug trade are known to support the Taliban and other anti-government militias. However, these efforts have been largely unsuccessful, especially because local farmers cannot equal their profits in opium by growing crops for food.

Animal Husbandry

Many Afghans depend on a combination of farming and animal husbandry for survival. A semi-nomadic lifestyle is common among some Afghans, with large flocks seasonally transferred between lowland and highland pastures. Sheep are the most common animal, followed by goats. The animals are important sources of meat, wool, and hides. Camels and horses are used for transportation of people and goods.

Tourism

In the 1960s and early 1970s, Afghanistan was a major stop for tourists traveling overland between Europe and India. Today, with ongoing U.S. military operations, banditry, unexploded landmines, a devastated infrastructure, and a population in crisis, tourism is virtually nonexistent and will probably remain so for the near future.

Many of the country's major attractions have been devastated as well, some by warfare, others by the Taliban. The Kabul Museum was damaged by rocket fire and then looted, reducing its once important collection of Asian antiquities by two-thirds. Then in 2001, the Taliban blew up the ancient, world-renowned Buddhist statues in the town of Bamiyan, which had been carved into a Cliffside. A few mosques, such as the Friday Mosque of Herat, and some archaeological sites have survived.

C. Nadir, Michael Aliprandini

DO YOU KNOW?

- Around the year 320 BCE, Alexander the Great invaded the land now known as Afghanistan on his way to conquer India.
- The Kharka Sharif shrine in Kandahar holds a cloak that some believe was worn by the Prophet Mohammed.
- In an effort to raise awareness of the presence and danger of landmines in the country, the OMAR Mine Museum in displays the various types of landmines that have been used in Afghanistan as well as the types of bombs that the US dropped on the country during the bombardment in 2002. OMAR is the Organization for Mine Clearance & Afghan Rehabilitation.

Bibliography

Ansary, Mir Tamim. *Games without Rules: The Often Interrupted History of Afghanistan.* New York: PublicAffairs, 2012.

Ball, Warwick. *The Monuments of Afghanistan: History, Archaeology and Architecture.* London: I.B. Tauris, 2008.

Barfield, Thomas J. *Afghanistan: A Cultural and Political History.* Princeton, NJ: Princeton University Press, 2012.

Collins, Joseph J. *Understanding the War in Afghanistan: A Guide to the Land, the People, and the Conflict.* New York: Skyhorse Publishing, 2013.

Crews, Robert D., and Amin Tarzi.. *The Taliban and the Crisis of Afghanistan.* Cambridge, MA: Harvard University Press, 2008.

Dupree, Louis. "Afghanistan." Oxford: Oxford University Press, 2012.

Human Rights Watch. Homepage. <http://www.hrw.org/>.

Gunaratna, Rohan, and Douglas Woodall, eds. *Afghanistan after the Western Drawdown.* Lanham, MD: Rowman and Littlefield, 2015.

Heath, Jennifer, and Ashraf Zahedi, eds. *Children of Afghanistan: The Path to Peace.* Austin: University of Texas Press, 2014.

Hosseini, Khaled. *The Kite Runner.* New York: Riverhead Books, 2004.

Kabul Museum National Gallery. Homepage. <http://www.fehe.org/index.php?id=561>.

Revolutionary Association of the Women of Afghanistan (RAWA). Homepage. <http://www.rawa.org/>.

Simpson, St. John. *Afghanistan: A Cultural History.* Northampton, MA: Interlink Books, 2012.

Works Cited

"Afghanistan: World News About Afghanistan." *The New York Times.* <http://topics.nytimes.com/top/news/international/countriesandterritories/afghanistan/>.

"Afghanistan: Hidden Treasures from the National Museum of Kabul." *National Gallery of Art.* 23 Jun. 2008 <http://www.nga.gov/exhibitions/afghanistaninfo.shtm>.

"Afghanistan: Cultural Profile." *Visiting Arts Cultural Profiles Project.* 23 Jun. 2008 <http://www.culturalprofiles.org.uk/>.

Amnesty International. "Afghanistan." *Amnesty International Report 2008: State of the World's Human Rights.* 2008. 23 Jun. 2008 <http://thereport.amnesty.org/eng/regions/asia-pacific/afghanistan>.

_______. "Afghanistan: Women Human Rights Defenders Continue to Struggle for Women's Rights." *Public Statement.* 07 Mar. 2008. 23 Jun. 2008 <http://www.amnestyusa.org/document.php?id=ENGASA110032008>.

_______. "Afghanistan: No-One Listens to Us and No-One Treats Us as Human Beings: Justice Denied to Women." 6 Oct. 2003. 23 Jun. 2008 <http://archive.amnesty.org/library/Index/ENGASA110232003?open&of=ENG-AFG>.

_______. "Afghanistan: Women's Human Rights Defenders Continue to Struggle for Women's Rights." *Public Statement.* 7 Mar. 2008. 23 Jun. 2008 <http://www.amnesty.org/en/library/asset/ASA11/003/2008/en/ASA110032008en.html>.

_______. "Afghanistan: Constitution Fails Women." *Press Release.* 26 Nov. 2003. 23 Jun. 2008 <http://asiapacific.amnesty.org/library/Index/ENGASA110272003?open&of=ENG-AFG>.

_______. "Bagh-e Babur Restoration: Gardens." *ArchNet: Islamic Architecture Community.* 23 Jun. 2008 <http://archnet.org/library/sites/one-site.jsp?site_id=12541>.

Central Intelligence Agency. "Afghanistan." *The World Factbook.* 23 Jun. 2008. <https://www.cia.gov/library/publications/the-world-factbook/geos/af.html>.

Central Statistics Office of Afghanistan. Population census. 2006.

Comiteau, Lauren. "Saving Afghanistan's Art." *Time.* 8 Jan. 2008. 23 Jun. 2008. <http://www.time.com/time/arts/article/0,8599,1701306,00.html>.

"Bush Praises NATO Afghan Pledges." *BBC News.* 2 Apr. 2008. 23 Jun. 2008. <http://news.bbc.co.uk/2/hi/europe/7325632.stm>.

Chopra, Anuj. "Afghanistan Faced with Severe Housing Shortage." *World Politics Review: A Foreign Policy and National Security Daily.* 18 Oct. 2007. 23 Jun. 2008 <http://www.worldpoliticsreview.com/article.aspx?id=1255>.

Cooper, Helene. "Donors Press Karzai on Corruption." *The New York Times.* 13 Jun. 2008. <http://www.nytimes.com/2008/06/13/world/europe/13afghan.html>.

"Defence Minister Says Afghan Army Must Be 5 Times Larger." *The Associated Press.* 12 Jul. 2006. 23 Jun. 2008 <http://www.cbc.ca/world/story/2006/07/12/afganistan12072006.html#skip300x250>.

Emadi, Hafizullah. *Repression, Resistance, and Women in Afghanistan.* Westport, CT: Praeger Publishers, 2002.

Dupree, Nancy H. "Etiquette in Afghanistan." *Encyclopedia Iranica.* Vol. IX, Fasc.1, 1998: 50–54. 23 Jun. 2008 <http://www.iranica.com/newsite/>.

———. "The Family during Crisis in Afghanistan." *Journal of Comparative Family Studies* 35.2 (Spring 2004): 311-31.

Gall, Carlotta "Afghans Lack $10 Billion in Aid, Report Says." *The New York Times.* 26 Mar. 2008. 23 Jun. 2008 <http://www.nytimes.com/2008/03/26/world/asia/26afghan.html>.

Greenblatt-Harrison, Andrew. "Strengthening Afghan Women's Civil Society to Secure Afghanistan's Future: An Analysis of New U.S. Assistance Programs." *Women's Edge Coalition.* 2005.

"Hazrat Ali Shrine Complex." *ArchNet: Islamic Architecture Community.* 23 Jun. 2008 <http://archnet.org/library/sites/one-site.jsp?site_id=10561>.

Human Rights Watch. "The Status of Women in Afghanistan." Oct. 2004. 23 Jun. 2008 <http://www.hrw.org/campaigns/afghanistan/facts.htm>.

———. "Open Letter from Human Rights Watch to the International Afghanistan Support Conference on June 12, 2008." 10 Jun. 2008. 23 Jun. 2008 <http://hrw.org/english/docs/2008/06/10/afghan19086.htm>.

Kabul Museum National Gallery. *Homepage.* <http://www.fehe.org/index.php?id=561>.

Labi, Nadya. "Rhythmless Nation: The Taliban Believes Music Is Wrong. Musicians Are Paying the Price." *Time* 158.14. 15 Sept. 2001. 23 Jun. 2008 <http://www.time.com/time/musicgoesglobal/asia/mtaliban.html>.

Meo, Nick. "How the new voice of Afghan youth has made conservatives hopping mad." *The Independent.* 27 Apr. 2005.

Mills, Margaret A., and Abdul Ali Ahrary.. "Folklore of Afghanistan." *Encyclopedia Iranica.* 23 Jun. 2008 <http://www.iranica.com/newsite/articles/unicode/v10f1/v10f116b.html>.

Saikal, Amin. *Modern Afghanistan: A History of Struggle and Survival.* London: I.B. Tauris, 2006.

Shalizi, Hamid. "Afghanistan Army to Reach Targeted Strength by March." *Reuters.* 2 Dec. 2007. 23 Jun. 2008 <http://www.reuters.com/article/worldNews/idUSISL5175520071202>.

Siddiqi, Shirazuddin. "Afghanistan's Post-Taleban Media." *BBC News.* 12 Sept. 2005. 23 Jun. 2008 <http://news.bbc.co.uk/2/hi/south_asia/4222082.stm>.

Solomon, Andrew. "An Awakening from the Nightmare of the Taliban." *The New York Times.* 10 Mar. 2002. 23 Jun. 2008 <http://query.nytimes.com/gst/fullpage.html?res=9806E0DF1330F933A25750C0A9649C8B63>.

"Revolutionary Association of the Women of Afghanistan." *Homepage.* 23 Jun. 2008 <http://www.rawa.org/>.

"Tajikistan/Afghanistan: Road Bridge Opens With Aim Of Strengthening Trade." *Radio Free Europe / Radio Liberty.* 23 Jun. 2008 <http://www.rferl.org/featuresarticle/2007/08/c2469723-5de7-4c33-992b-d5df4bfcdb42.html>.

"World Heritage List." World Heritage Centre.. *Homepage.* 23 Jun. 2008 <http://whc.unesco.org/en/list>.

A Bangladeshi woman in traditional dress and adornment/Stock photo © steve-goacher

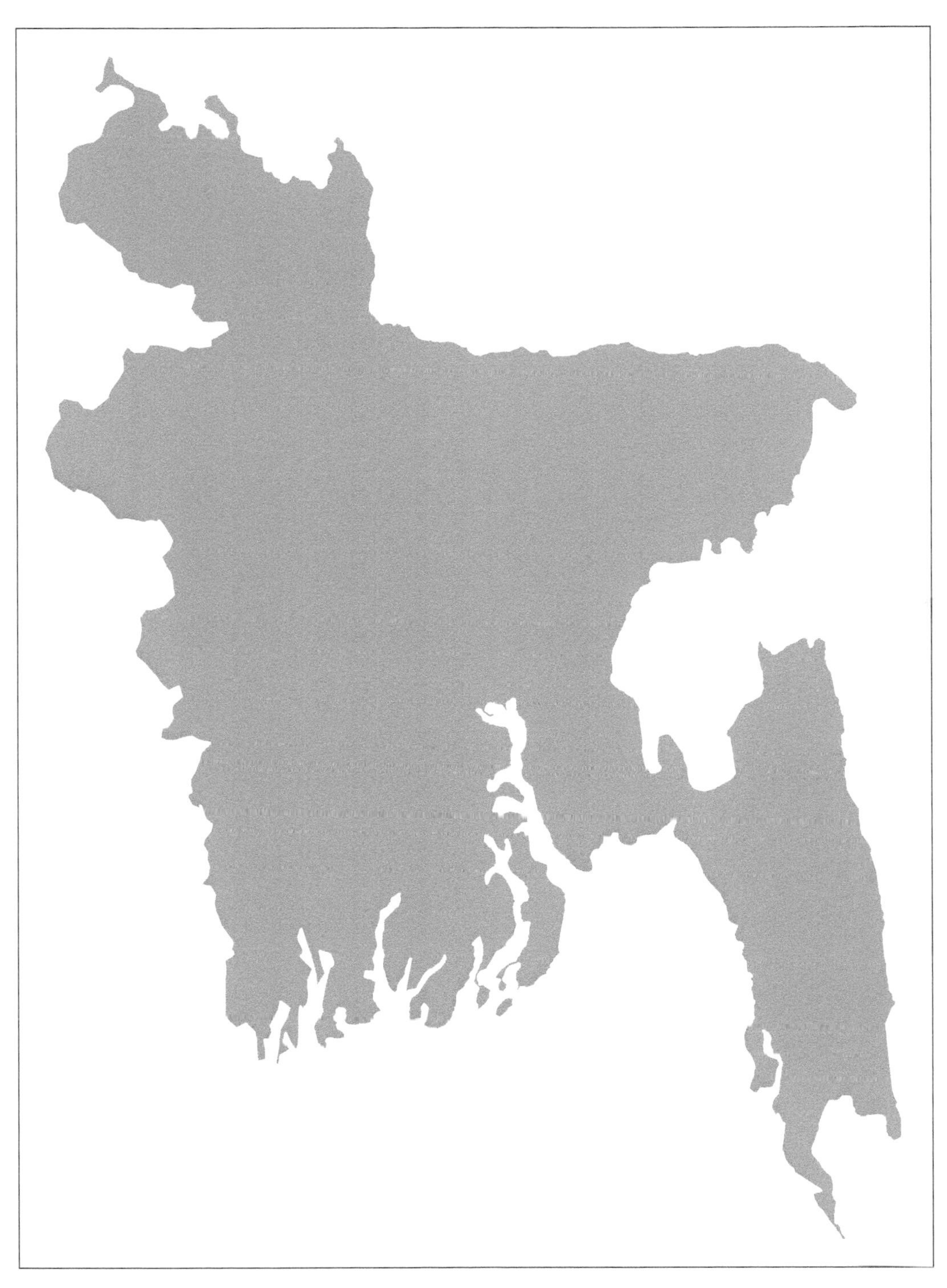

BANGLADESH

Introduction

The People' Republic of Bangladesh, located in Southeast Asia, is bordered by Myanmar and India; the Bay of Bengal forms its southern border. It shares the wider ancient culture of the vast Indian subcontinent, but is a young nation.

In 1947, following the end of the British colonial period, the subcontinent was partitioned along religious lines into West and East Pakistan (now Bangladesh) and India. In 1971, East Pakistan ceded from West Pakistan and won its independence after a short, violent war; East Pakistan declared its independence in 1971, becoming Bangladesh. The decades since have been marked by political turmoil, human rights abuses, government corruption, and a series of devastating natural disasters to which the low-lying country is prone.

GENERAL INFORMATION

Official Language: Bangla (Bengali)
Population: 166,280,712 (2014 estimate)
Currency: Bangladeshi taka
Coins: The taka is divided into 100 paisa or poisha. Coins are available in denominations of 1, 2, and 5 taka, which are frequently used, and 1, 5, 10, 25, and 50 poisha, which are rarely used.
Land Area: 130,168 square kilometers (50,244 square miles)
Water Area: 13,830 square kilometers (5,338 square miles)
National Anthem: "Amar Shona Bangla" ("My Golden Bengal")

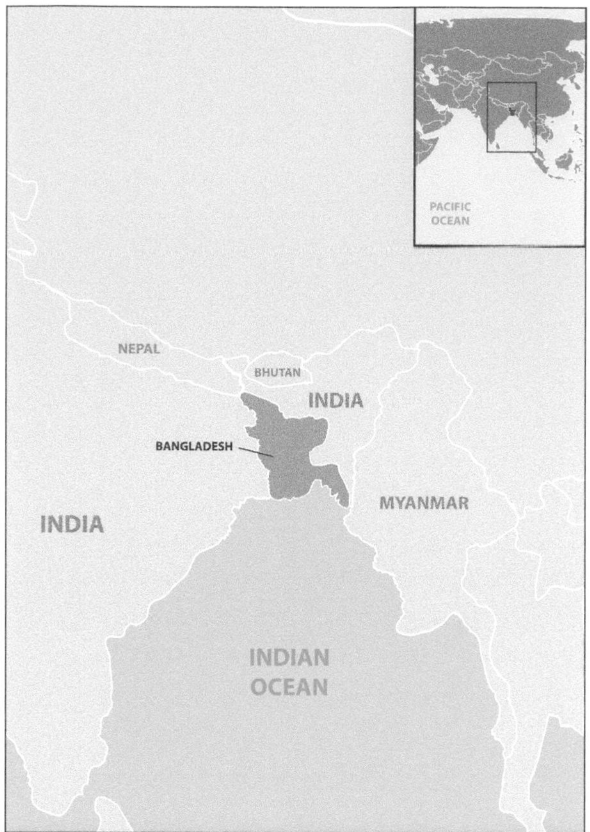

Capital: Dhaka
Time Zone: GMT +6
Flag Description: The flag of Bangladesh is characterized by a solid dark green flag with a large red circle placed slightly to the left of center.

Population

The population of Bangladesh is largely homogenous, 98 percent being ethnic Bengali, who are of Indo-Aryan descent. Minority groups include the Biharis and various indigenous tribes. The Biharis, who today number around 500,000, settled in Bangladesh after the partition; many were forced to resettle in Pakistan after Bangladesh's secession.

The tribal groups generally live in rural border regions and are of Sino-Tibetan or Sino-Burman descent. The Chakmas are the largest tribal group. Others are the Marma, the Tripura, the Mrus, and the Santals.

Bangladesh has a young, growing population; in 2014, 32 percent of the population was younger

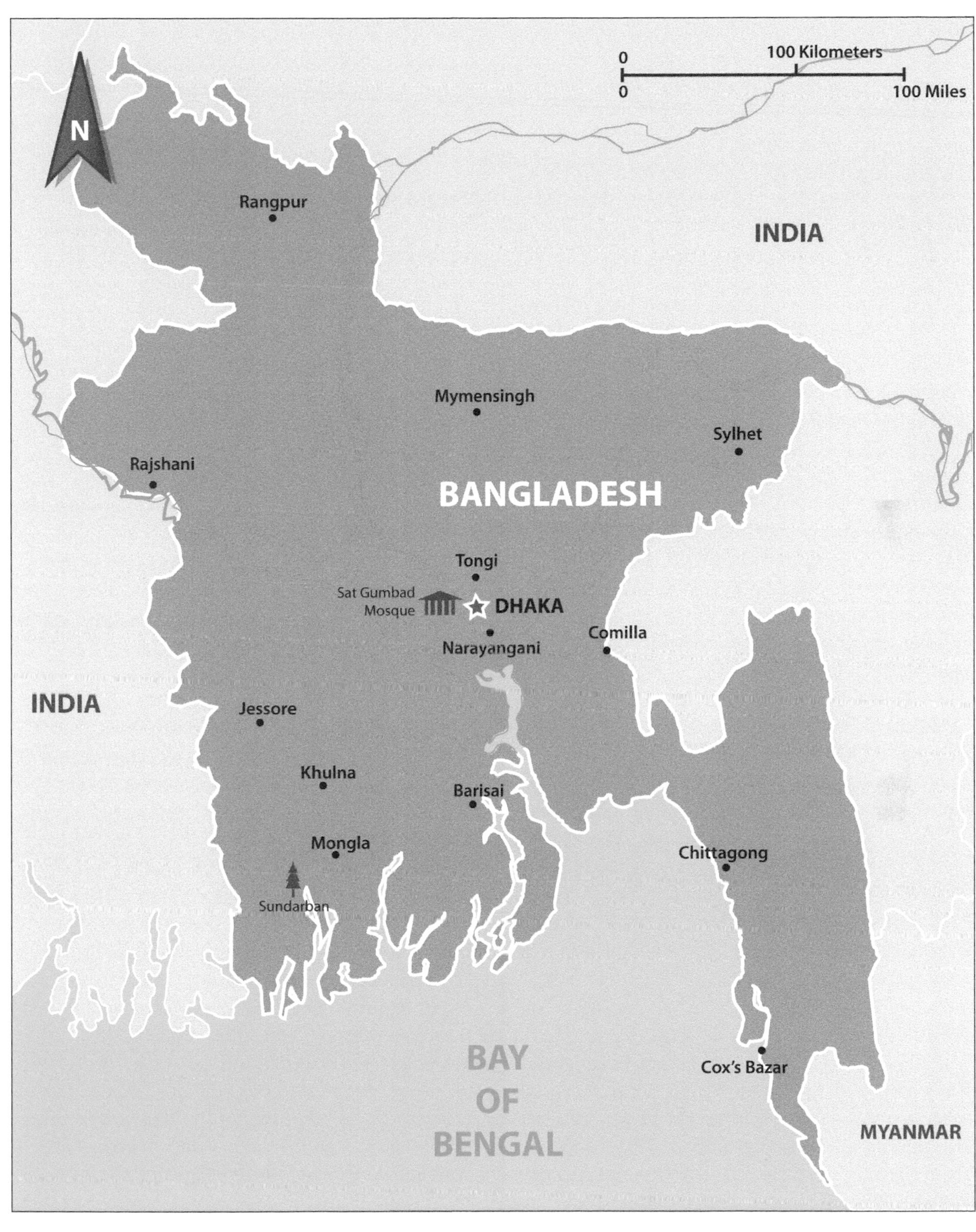
N
0
100 Kilometers
0
100 Miles
Rangpur
INDIA
Mymensingh
Sylhet
Rajshani
BANGLADESH
Tongi
Sat Gumbad
Mosque
DHAKA
Narayangani
Comilla
INDIA
Jessore
Khulna
Barisai
Mongla
Chittagong
Sundarban
Cox's Bazar
BAY
OF
BENGAL
MYANMAR

Principal Cities by Population (2012 unless otherwise noted):

- Dhaka (11,700,000)
- Chittagong (4,100,000)
- Khulna (1,600,000)
- Gazipur (1,300,000)
- Rajshani (842,701)
- Tungi (478,982)
- Mymensingh (407,798)

than 14 years old. Government efforts to encourage family planning have successfully slowed the population growth rate. Life expectancy averages almost 71 years, with women at 72 years and men at almost 69 years (2014 estimate).

Population density is 1,014 persons per square kilometer. Three-quarters of the population lives in small rural settlements. The Bengali population saw a sharp increase in population, from 50 million people to 90 million, in the 1960s and 1970s and now has surpassed 116 million. Dhaka, the capital, is by far the largest urban center, with a population of just under 12 million people (2012).

Languages

Bangla, the dominant language of the country, belongs to the Indo-European language family. It is written in a script related to Sanskrit, and has 57 letters in its alphabet. The Biharis speak Urdu, and the tribal groups speak Sino-Tibetan and Sino-Burman languages. English is an important second language and in the capital, Dhaka, English is primarily used for business transactions.

Native People & Ethnic Groups

The Bengalis, the Biharis, and some tribal groups have been settled on the Indian subcontinent since ancient times. Indo-Aryans began migrating into the region now known as Bangladesh from the north around 3,500 years ago. It is not certain whether they displaced or intermingled with indigenous groups already living in the region.

Over 35 ethnic groups call Bangladesh home. The Mandi and Hajong have settled in the north; the Manipuri and Khasia populate the northeast; the Santal and Rajbangshi are found in the west; and the Chakma, Tripura, Marma, Rakhain, Mru, Tanchyanga, and Murong peoples are situated in the east and southeast.

Religions

About 90 percent of the Bangladeshi population practices Islam and most predominantly Sunni Islam; there is, however, a small group of Shia Muslims. Hindus make up the largest minority religion, at over nine percent of the population. Small groups of Christians, Buddhists, and animists also live in Bangladesh.

Climate

Bangladesh has a subtropical climate. Warm temperatures and high humidity occur throughout the year, with only minor variations in temperature between seasons and regions. In May, temperatures average between 32° and 38° Celsius (90° and 100° Fahrenheit); in January, the average is around 19° Celsius (66° Fahrenheit).

Three seasons prevail in Bangladesh. From March to June, the weather is hot and humid. A cooler monsoon season lasts from June to October. From October to March, the weather is cool and dry. During the monsoon season, when 80 percent of the annual rainfall occurs, approximately one-third of the country is flooded. The northeastern region of Sylhet receives the most rainfall, averaging 5,080 millimeters (200 inches) annually. In most of the country, however, rainfall measuring 2,000 millimeters (79 inches) annually is typical.

In addition to the flooding of the rivers during the monsoons, several types of natural disasters can affect Bangladesh. Tidal waves, tropical cyclones, and tornadoes generally strike between April and May, and again between September and November. They can bring widespread destruction of land, property, and human life. During the 20th century alone, Bangladesh has been the center of some of the world's worst natural disasters.

ENVIRONMENT & GEOGRAPHY

Topography

Bangladesh has two basic topographic regions: the flat, broad low-lying alluvial plain criss-crossed with rivers, and the hilly terrain in the southeast and north. The alluvial plain accounts for approximately 80 percent of the country's total area. Its elevation does not generally exceed 10 meters (33 feet), though it is higher in the north and reaches sea level along the southern coast. More than 10 percent of the plain is regularly covered with water; during the monsoons, flooding is extensive.

In the southeast of Bangladesh, the Chittagong Hills rise above the plain to elevations between 600 and 900 meters (2,953 feet), generally extending from north to south. The country's highest point, Keokradong, rises to 1,046 meters (3,432 feet) above sea level in these hills. There are also highlands in the north, and the low Sylhet Hills in the northeast.

Approximately 700 rivers drain the plain of Bangladesh, most of them flowing south into the Bay of Bengal from their origins in the Himalayan Mountains. The three major river systems are the Ganges, the Brahmaputra, and the Meghna. The Ganges and the Brahmaputra join to form the Padma, which in turn joins the Meghna. The rivers have formed estuaries in the coastline, which measures 580 kilometers (360 miles).

Plants & Animals

Animal life in Bangladesh is extensive. Among the mammals are monkeys, apes, tigers, boar, elephants, deer, and leopards. There are also many fish, reptiles, and birds, including kingfishers, myna birds, crocodiles, and woodpeckers. Approximately 24 percent of the species are threatened. The Asian elephant, the tiger, and several primates are listed as endangered, whereas the clouded leopard and the Asiatic black bear are listed as vulnerable. Wildlife poaching remains a problem despite government efforts to curb it.

With humans inhabiting 81 percent of the land, Bangladesh has few uninterrupted forests. Exceptions are the Sundarbans, an area bordering the Bay of Bengal that has a large mangrove swamp, and the country's hilly regions, where evergreens grow. In the lowlands, bamboo, banyan, palm, acacia, and fruit trees grow.

CUSTOMS & COURTESIES

Greetings

Greetings vary somewhat throughout Bangladesh, depending on the religious background of those involved. For the majority Muslims, the traditional greeting is "As-salamu alaykum" ("Peace be upon you"). The response to this greeting is "Walekum asalam" ("Peace also be upon you"). Traditionally, members of the Hindu minority greet by saying "Namashkar," a variation of "Namasté" ("I bow to you"), while pressing their palms together in a gesture of prayer. Urban Bangladeshis are also increasingly shaking hands when greeting, though this is normally done with a gentler grip than Western handshakes.

Bangladeshi society is very hierarchical. Men are considered to be higher status than women, and older people are given more respect than younger people. This sense of social hierarchy informs the ways in which people greet one another. According to the Islamic principle of purdah, men and women are assumed to inhabit separate social spheres. This means that a person is not permitted to touch or even look directly at a member of the opposite gender in public. The elderly are traditionally allowed to speak first in a mixed age group, and are expected to be treated with greater respect than younger people. It is also customary to refer to older people as bahadur (sir) or begum (madam).

Gestures & Etiquette

Since Bangladesh is a predominantly Muslim country, there are several important points of etiquette that stem from Islamic religious beliefs. According to the Muslim concept of purdah, males and females are supposed to stay separate in most activities, which is particularly important in public. It is considered inappropriate for unmarried men and women to have any sort of physical contact, or even to stand too close to one another. It is also important to obey local standards of behavior when visiting mosques. These standards include taking off shoes before entering, wearing clean and modest clothing (especially women), abstaining from walking in front of someone who is praying, and talking in a respectfully soft voice.

Elders are held in the highest regard in Bangladesh. They are allowed to go first in social activities, such as eating or conversing. It is considered rude to look an elder person directly in the eye or contradict what an elder says. The decisions of the senior male in a situation or group are generally considered to be proper and should be heeded. Respect for elders is also shown through maturity of action. This sometimes means refraining from unwarranted laughing or other such behavior in the presence of elders. However, this custom is often attributed to the incomplete impression that Bangladeshis rarely smile.

Eating/Meals

Meals are very social activities in Bangladesh, and people prefer to eat at home with their families. Breakfast is eaten quite early in the morning, right after sunrise and the first prayers of the day. Most people start their day with cha (sweet tea with milk), rice, and some fruit. Lunch, which is the most substantial meal, is eaten at the middle of the work day. It typically consists of rice or flat bread with a creamy curry called korma or a lentil stew called daal. People like to drink a refreshing yogurt drink called lassi or a spiced milk-based drink called sandesh, at lunch. Dinner is eaten late in the night, and is similar to lunch, but usually smaller in size.

Meals are typically eaten on the floor, with people sitting on straw mats called patis. Food is served on plates or, more often, banana leaves. People eat with their right hand, as the left hand is considered impure since it is associated with the cleansing of the body according to Muslim belief. Since texture is an important part of the appeal of food, people tend to handle their food to a degree that outsiders can find somewhat surprising. It is considered a sign of appreciation to eat vigorously and noisily. Thus, smacking the lips and handling the food is considered a sign of appreciation, and burping after eating is a normal way to express satisfaction.

Visiting

Although many people are relatively poor in Bangladesh, the Bangladeshi have a tradition of being gracious hosts. People are eager to share what they have with visitors. They also enjoy being entertained, and will look upon the opportunity to chat with a guest as a welcome diversion. A visitor will often be invited to a person's home to share a cup of cha and conversation. It is considered unfriendly to turn down an invitation, and people prefer to give noncommittal promises to visit in the future instead of rejections.

When visiting someone's house, it is polite to bring along a small gift, such as chocolates or other sweets. Flowers may also be given as a gift, though it is important to keep in mind that white flowers are associated with mourning and should be avoided. It is normally inappropriate to bring gifts of alcohol, since most people in the country refrain from drinking for religious reasons. Gifts should be presented to the host with both hands.

LIFESTYLE

Family

Family is extremely important to Bangladeshi people. The extended family network, or poribar, is the basic unit of society. The poribar is headed by the oldest living male, who is afforded the utmost respect. Elders of the family are allowed to speak first in all circumstances, and younger members are expected to pay close attention to the advice they give. Women are considered to be subservient to their male relatives. Men participate in public activities such as business and community decisions, and women are expected to stay at home and maintain the household. Bangladeshis tend to have many children so that there will always be someone to look after the elder relatives in their old age.

In the latter half of the 20th century, families became more segmented. This was due to globalization, deteriorating and shifting economic conditions, and the migration of the population from villages to cities. Additionally, single-parent families became more commonplace.

Housing

Most people in Bangladesh live in very simple homes. In rural areas, they are commonly built with bamboo walls and thatched roofs. In cities, most houses are built from scraps of wood or tin. Urban houses built of more durable materials such as brick or concrete often signify wealth.

In general, houses usually consist of one or two rooms. Indoor plumbing and electricity is not common, and kitchens are usually very basic, often consisting of little more than a clay stove dug into the dirt floor. It is common for several houses to be clustered around a courtyard that neighbors share. The courtyard is typically used for food preparation and cooking. Many houses also have a garden area in back, where produce is grown for the family.

Food

Bangladeshi cuisine is primarily based on rice, which is the main starch crop in the country. Rice is a symbol of prosperity and plenty, so it is considered appropriate to serve rice with every large meal. Wheat is also produced, especially in the south. There are two main kinds of flat bread produced from wheat: naan, baked in clay ovens, and a fried bread called chappati. A range of other vegetables crops are grown, including green beans, squash, onions, and lentils. Potatoes are a popular crop as well, and feature in a variety of Bangladeshi meals. Bangladesh also enjoys a great bounty of fruits, such as bananas, guavas, papayas, mangoes, and watermelons.

Meat is highly prized by Bangladeshis, many of whom are unable to afford it on a regular basis. Goat, beef, and chicken are the most common meats. Bangladesh is a predominantly Muslim country, so pork is not eaten. Fish and seafood from rivers and the ocean is also an important source of protein in the Bangladeshi diet.

Traditional Bangladeshi dishes include biryani, a fried rice casserole made with meat and spices, or pulao, similar to biryani but made without the meat (it is a more everyday meal). Korma, a mildly spiced curry made with yogurt, vegetables, and meat, is also eaten throughout the country. Daal, a lentil stew with vegetables, is a common staple. Kebabs, pieces of spicy grilled meat, are enjoyed by those who can afford them. Fish, such as a favorite variety of sea bass called bhetki, is usually served baked or fried.

Life's Milestones

In Bangladesh, children are usually born at home. A room is set aside for the birthing process, and the new child and mother are confined to it after birth. It is common for the baby to be smudged with ash on its forehead and feet to ward off evil spirits. Nine days after birth, the baby and mother are given a ritual bath. After another month, the mother and baby leave the birthing room.

Families traditionally arrange most marriages in Bangladesh. There are a series of rituals associated with weddings. For example, a common custom involves showering the bride and groom with gifts in two ceremonies that together are called gae halud. A ritual called akht follows, where the couple exchange vows and eat a date (the fruit of the date palm tree) to symbolize their new unity. The bride and groom then exchange garlands and drink a special yogurt drink in a ritual called mala badol. The last ritual is bou bhat, a party where the couple receives well-wishers.

In contrast, funerals are typically simple affairs. When a person dies, family members traditionally wash the body and wrap it in a clean, white cloth. It is promptly buried, usually no more than a few days after death. The household of the mourning family is often decorated with white flowers, particularly a type called frangipanis. Visitors bring white flowers as a sign of sympathy.

CULTURAL HISTORY

Art

Bangladesh's artistic heritage begins with the artistry of the region's ancient ceramics and terracotta pottery. The region is also famous for its long tradition of weaving. Bangladeshi textiles have been renowned throughout Europe since the Middle Ages for their delicate beauty. Influenced by Persian craftsmen, weavers from this region used complex looms to produce very fine silks for royalty. Weaving became a way of recording history in Bengal, with textile pieces woven to depict events and mythical stories.

Historically, religious art—ranging from Buddhist to Islamic styles—was the first dominant style of art in the region, and painting did not fully emerge until the 20th century. Modern painting was pioneered by several artists, most notably Zainul Ahedin (1914–1976) and Quamrul Hassan (1921–1988). Ahedin became famous for his depiction of the Bengal Famine in 1943 (in which an estimated four million people perished). Hassan's legacy centers on themes of political history and rural life. Both painters are celebrated for their role in establishing Bengali (Bangladeshi) identity through art.

Architecture

Although Bangladesh did not become a modern nation until 1971, the Bengal region has a long cultural history, which can be seen in Bangladesh's rich architecture. Dating back to 300 BCE, simple bamboo structures with curved roofs can still be found scattered throughout rural Bangladesh. In 300 CE, Buddhist culture from northern India began to influence the architecture of the region. Brick temples and monasteries with square bases and bulbous domes exemplify the architecture of this period. The construction of Hindu temples, with characteristic square bases and ornately sculpted pyramid-shaped towers, began in 1100 CE. From 1200 CE onward, Muslim mosques were built throughout the area. Strongly influenced by architecture of the Islamic Mughal Empire (1526–1858), which combines Persian, Indian, and Islamic styles, these mosques were distinctive for their wide square bases and smaller domed tops.

Dance

Historically, the inhabitants of the Bengal region had very low rates of literacy. This made performance art an important form of communication. Dance performances have always been popular, and were historically the highlight of festivals in rural areas. Among the most traditional forms of dance is the jatra style. Demonstrating techniques that go back for centuries and showing an influence from classical Indian dance, jatra performers recreate legends and religious myths with exaggerated dramatic flair.

Manipuri dance also has a long history in the area that is now Bangladesh. Originating in the hilly northeastern Indian state Manipur, this dance tradition goes back to at least 1500 CE. Manipuri dances use soft, gentle movements and commonly depict religious stories, often about the Hindu hero Krishna. Clad in colorful costumes, dancers play small hand cymbals called kartals, helping create the rhythm that guides their steps. A cylindrical drum called a pung is also used. The popularity of Manipuri dance in Bangladesh was enhanced in the 1920s, when celebrated poet Rabindranath Tagore became interested in the tradition.

Drama

Live theater is an extremely popular form of entertainment in Bangladesh. Less than half of the population is literate, so it has also been an important vehicle for educating people about social issues. The nation's foremost playwright, Munier Chowdhury (1925–1971), produced several plays (controversial at the time) advocating national liberation. He was killed just before Bangladesh gained its freedom, and is revered as a martyr. Many Bangladeshi playwrights have followed his lead, using live theater as a means of social and political commentary. One theater group that has followed this tradition is the Centre for Asian Theatre (CAT), founded in 1994. This organization sponsors street theater productions to deal with issues such as political corruption, violence, and human rights.

While live drama is still popular within Bangladesh, a new form of performance art has gained influence. Cinema has become a major form of artistic expression. Influenced by the Bollywood films of India (Hindu-language film industry), Bangladeshi filmmakers have developed their own genre. This new industry, known locally as Dhallywood, produces hundreds of movies per year. Many of these Dhallywood films challenge conservative ideas about love and sexuality, inspiring the younger generation to question the religious fundamentalism that has spread throughout the country.

Music

In ancient times, music in Bangladesh was strongly influenced by religion. The earliest known music came from religious chants called charya songs. Though these were originally Buddhist chants, they also came to reflect Hindu themes. One legendary artist was the 12th-century poet Jaydeb, who composed charya songs with lyrics about Hindu myths, such as the love story of Krishna and Radha. The tradition was further influenced by north Indian courtly music, which introduced orchestral instruments to the region. Instruments introduced from India included the complex stringed sitar, flutes made from bamboo, and a pair of small and large drums which are together called the tabla.

Bangladeshi men playing musical instruments from India.

While music has long been a way to express traditional religious beliefs, it has also been a means to express freedom from orthodox beliefs. For centuries, musicians called Bauls have wandered throughout the region, entertaining locals with their distinctive musical performances. Named for the word for wind, Bauls borrow beliefs from Hinduism and Islam and practice a form of mysticism which emphasizes individual enlightenment, personal freedom, and a lack of personal possessions. Baul instruments include a small drum called a dugi, ankle bells called gungar, a single-stringed harp called the extara, and a multiple-stringed instrument called the dotara. In 2005, the music of the Bauls was named an intangible cultural heritage (ICH) by the United Nations Educational, Scientific and Cultural Organization (UNESCO).

Literature

Literature in the historic Bengal region dates back thousands of years, but did not fully emerge until the medieval period, when it was fostered under Muslim rule. Poetry was the predominant literary form, and also flourished outside of royal patronage. However, Bangladeshi literature entered into a renaissance era in the 19th century, largely through the work of several esteemed poets.

Though Rabindranath Tagore (1861–1941) was born in the Indian city Calcutta, and died before Bangladesh achieved independence, he is considered a national hero. His picture is commonly displayed throughout the country, and he wrote and composed the Bangladeshi national anthem. His deeply philosophical poetry has profoundly shaped Bangladeshi literature. Tagore's belief that Hindus and Muslims should learn to coexist in order to improve the lives of people throughout Bengal held much appeal. When he won the Nobel Prize in Literature in 1913, Tagore brought the world's attention to Bengal. His poetic descriptions of the area's natural and cultural beauty helped create a sense of pride that is still apparent in the modern nation of Bangladesh.

Another celebrated Bengali writer is Kazi Nazrul Islam (1899–1976). Dubbed the rebel poet, he used his craft to speak out about the need to correct social injustices. This message found a receptive audience during the colonial period, when the people of the Bengal region started to call for independence from Britain. His poetry, prose, and plays helped define Bangladeshi identity, and continue to be a source of national pride.

CULTURE

Arts & Entertainment

Though many Bangladeshi citizens are materially poor, they are extremely proud of their country's rich artistic traditions. While Bangladesh is a relatively new nation, this pride has been a characteristic of the culture of Bengal throughout recorded history. As a modern nation, Bangladesh has faced many hardships, including natural disasters, social strife, and political instability. Their creative wealth has always been a source of inspiration to the people of Bangladesh. Therefore, it is not surprising that they have turned to the arts as a means of dealing with social issues.

Despite its limited financial resources, the government of Bangladesh has made significant efforts to support the traditional arts. One example of this commitment is the Shilpakala Academy, which has been an important institution since it was founded in 1974. Its stated goals include preserving Bangladesh's artistic heritage, conducting research into the regions artistic culture, and promoting Bangladeshi arts to a global audience. It also assists monetarily poor artists, making it possible for people with talent to contribute to the traditional arts regardless of their financial status.

Although institutions such as the Shilpakala Academy do important work preserving traditional forms of expression, most art in Bangladesh is created and experienced in an informal manner. An excellent example of how basic a part of life art is in Bangladeshi culture is the common practice of painting vehicles. Trucks and rickshaws are often emblazoned with elaborately painted decorations and scenes. This practice started in the 1960s with portraits of movie stars. In the early 1970s, as Bangladesh moved toward independence from Pakistan, these paintings began to take on a more political tone, depicting nationalist heroes and atrocities committed by the Pakistani army. Vehicle painting has continued to develop as an important, and commonplace, genre of art within Bangladesh. Today, truck and rickshaw paintings often portray movie stars, political figures, rural and natural scenes, myths, and historical events.

Art has sometimes caused a great deal of controversy in Bangladesh. Writer Taslima Nasrin (1962–) uses her craft to speak out about the status of women in the country. She has also criticized the Muslim fundamentalism that has spread within Bangladesh. This has made her a target for religious conservatives, who staged large rallies directed against her. Rather than protecting her right to free speech, the government turned against Nasrin, forcing her to flee the country. She has lived in exile in India and Europe since 1994, but continues to use her writing to further gender equality and religious tolerance within Bangladesh.

Among Western sports, football (soccer), cricket, and badminton are the most popular in Bangladesh. They are widely played, and both football and cricket have a devoted following. Local sports include kabaddi, a type of wrestling between two teams of six players, and river races with vessels that resemble canoes.

Cultural Sites & Landmarks

The capital of Dhaka offers perhaps the best insight into the country's unique culture. Bangladesh is a nation of rivers and water. Spending time on the Buriganga River, the main artery of transportation and commerce in Dhaka, allows one to appreciate the important role water plays in Bangladeshi life. There is an amazing variety of activities occurring along the river, including bathing, the washing of clothing, and cooking. The river also features many floating restaurants that serve Dhaka's citizens.

Dhaka is also home to many important examples of Bangladeshi architecture. There are several mosques that attract large numbers of visitors. Perhaps the finest is the Sat Gumbad Mosque (the "Seven Dome" mosque), which dates back to 1680 CE. With seven onion-shaped domes and a massive prayer hall, it is a testament to the influence of the Mughals on Bangladeshi culture. The Lalbagh Fort, completed in 1684 CE, is another impressive example of Muslim architecture. With its imposing red walls, enormous arched doorways, and pointed minarets, the Lalbagh Fort has become a popular tourist destination in Dhaka.

Less than an hour away from Dhaka by bus is Mograpara, a bustling rural village that offers glimpses into a way of life that has changed little for hundreds of years. Mograpara also houses the ruined site of Sonargaon (Hindi for golden town), which was the capital of the East Bengal region from the 13th to the 16th centuries. In 1985, UNESCO inscribed the Mosque city of Bagerhat as a World Heritage Site—one of three such sites within Bangladesh. The city was founded in the early 15th century and contains a large number of mosques and Islamic monuments. The ruins of the Buddhist Vihara at Paharpur, an important archeological site that houses a large Buddhist monastery, was also named a World Heritage Site in 1985.

In 1997, Bangladesh added its third World Heritage Site, the Sundarbans. Occupying more than 9,583 square kilometers (3,700 square miles) between India and Bangladesh, it is the largest mangrove swamp in the world. The forest is home to a thriving population of Royal Bengal tigers, which are a symbol of pride for the people of Bangladesh. The Sundarbans area also has an interesting history as a place of refuge for people fleeing religious oppression, the extremely poor and starving, pirates, and other socially marginalized populations. As such, the Sundarbans swamp is more than a wilderness, and occupies an important place in the Bangladeshi national identity.

Libraries & Museums

The Bangladesh National Museum is located in Dhaka, and was established in 1983. The museum has more than forty galleries and is considered one of the largest cultural institutions in Southeast Asia. Other museums in Dhaka include the Mukti Juddha Museum, the National Art Gallery, and the Bangabandhu Memorial Museum, housed in the former house of Bangabandhu Sheikh Mujibur Rahmanm, considered to be the father of Bangladesh and a leader in the independence movement against Pakistan. He also served as the prime minister and president of Bangladesh.

The capital is also home to the Liberation War Museum. Its collection focuses on the 1971 war for independence from Pakistan through artifacts, newspaper articles, and photographic evidence of the bloody struggle.

The National Archives and the National Library of Bangladesh are both located in Dhaka. The archives contain documents dating back to the 18th century, while the national library serves as Bangladesh's legal depository.

Holidays

The main religious celebrations in Bangladesh are Islamic. These include Ramadan, the month of dusk-to-dawn fasting; Eid al-Fitr, which ends Ramadan; and Eid al-Adha, a day which commemorates Abraham's willingness to sacrifice his son to God. These latter two holidays entail visits to family and friends, large feasts, the donning of new clothes, visits to the mosque, and the exchange of small gifts.

The country's Hindu population holds a religious festival called Durga Puja. It entails the building of a clay statue of the fertility goddess Durga, days of prayers and feasting, and, at the holiday's end, the dissolving of the statue in sacral waters.

New Year's Day, known as Pohela Boisakh, falls in mid-April. At this time, festivals are held across the country. Families and friends gather for feasts, and traditional musical and theatrical entertainments are performed.

Important secular holidays focus on Bangladesh's struggle to become a nation. Martyrs' Day (February 21) commemorates a 1952 pro-independence demonstration which ended in bloodshed. Independence Day (March 26) marks the day on which Bangladesh proclaimed its independence from Pakistan. Nine months of civil war followed, and the end of the war is marked on Victory Day (December 16).

Youth Culture

Bangladesh has a far larger youth population than other countries, with over a third of its population under fourteen years of age as of 2014. This high percentage of youth is starting to have an effect on Bangladeshi culture, particularly as they become more Internet-savvy and are increasingly introduced to Western influences. One sign of the youth population's influence is the nation's changing musical taste. Rock singer Maqsoodul Haque (also known as Mac) has gained widespread celebrity for putting the words of celebrated traditional poet Rabindranath Tagore to a new style of jazz fusion music, thus making it more accessible to younger generations.

Another sign of the emerging youth culture is the reemergence of the Bangladeshi film industry, known as Dhallywood. Popular with Bangladesh's youth, Dhallywood films reflect the changing youth culture by challenging traditional values about fashion and dating. In recent years, largely as a response to the increasing popularity of better quality films released by Hollywood and the cinema of India, particularly Bollywood, Dhallywood films have become more racy and graphic in nature.

SOCIETY

Transportation

Very few people in Bangladesh—less than two in a thousand—own private vehicles. Public transportation is, therefore, very important to Bangladeshi society, and there are a number of travel options within the country. There is a wide range of choices for local transportation. Common vehicles for shorter distances include buses, taxis, rickshaws, three-wheelers called tempos, and river ferries. In rural areas, bicycles are common, and traditional means such as ox or horse-drawn carts can still be found.

Traveling longer distances is usually accomplished by bus or train, and there are public and private bus and rail companies that operate throughout the country. In Bangladesh, traffic passes on the left-hand side of the road.

Transportation Infrastructure

There are three international airports in Bangladesh. These are Zia International Airport, near the capital; Osmani International Airport, in Sylhet; and Patenga International Airport, in Chittagong. These three airports serve regular flights from Asian countries such as Bhutan, India, Myanmar, Malaysia, Nepal, Pakistan, and Thailand. There are also flights to Bangladesh from European countries, such as Britain, France, and Russia. Bangladesh has two domestic airlines, Biman and GMG, which fly within the country.

Since Bangladesh has over 7,885 kilometers (4,900 miles) of navigable rivers, boats provide important transportation options.

Media & Communications

There are many media outlets in Bangladesh. Media freedom, however, is somewhat limited, and political commentary tends to follow the official government line. Nonetheless, certain journalists and newspapers have become known for their outspoken reporting, largely because newspapers are all privately owned. English language papers, which are mostly read in urban centers, include the *Bangladesh Observer, Daily Star*, *Holiday*, and *New Age*. There are also several Bengali papers, such as *Daily Prothom Alo, Dainik Jugantor*, and *Dainik Ittefaq*.

Broadcast media is far more popular than print in Bangladesh, which is to be expected, since only 48 percent of the population is literate. However, broadcast media are also far more prone to government censorship. In fact, the main television and radio stations are run by the government. The state radio station is Radio Bangladesh. The only terrestrial television station is Bangladesh Television (BTV). In addition to BTV, there are several popular satellite stations, including ATN, Channel I, Channel One, BanglaVision, NTV, and RTV. Internet usage in Bangladesh remains low, and in 2012 there were an estimated 10.2 million Internet users, representing 6.2 percent of the population.

SOCIAL DEVELOPMENT

Standard of Living

Bangladesh ranked 142nd out of 187 countries on the 2014 United Nations Human Development Index, which measures quality of life and standard of living indicators.

Water Consumption

According to UNICEF (United Nations Children's Fund), 80 percent of residents in Bangladesh have access to improved drinking water; in urban areas, access measures 85 percent while 84 percent of the rural population has improved access. Although improved in recent years, access to improved sanitary facilities falls far behind water access, with the country average measuring 57 percent—55 percent in urban areas and 57 percent in rural areas.

Education

Education is free and compulsory for eight years, beginning at the age of six. There is a general shortage of facilities and materials at government institutions; private schools are better equipped and cater to the wealthier classes.

Enrollment tapers off considerably at the secondary school level, when tuition fees are charged. Though education is encouraged for both sexes, girls in rural areas are at more of a disadvantage than boys. This is reflected in the country's literacy rate, which is 62 percent among males and 53 percent among females. In addition to its efforts to improve primary and secondary education, the government sponsors adult literacy programs.

Alternative educational systems include the Madrasah system, which has an Islamic curriculum and teaches Arabic; these schools also educate homeless children. Cadet colleges are military secondary schools that create a path for future military leaders. Their curriculum is based on the British public school system and military training is mandatory.

The largest universities in Bangladesh are the University of Dhaka and the University of Engineering and Technology, also in Dhaka. There are also universities in Mymensingh, Chittagong, and Rajshahi.

Women's Rights

Bangladeshi women continue to face numerous human rights abuses and issues in the early 21st century. These result from a range of social ills, such as corruption of government to increasing Islamic conservatism. Poverty also plays a significant role in women's rights, as the economic desperation affecting much of the country means that women are often exploited for financial gain. Furthermore, laws designed to protect women from abuse and gender-based violence is often incomplete and weakly enforced. As a result, and also largely due to the instability of the government, people naturally turn to religious laws for guidance. However, religious principles have commonly been used to justify heinous attacks on women accused of transgressing gender norms.

The laws protecting women are not regularly enforced. Domestic abuse is widespread throughout Bangladesh, despite the fact that it is illegal. People are often opposed to involving the authorities in domestic issues, however, so instances of abuse are considered to be grossly underreported. Additionally, spousal rape is not considered a crime. Though there are stringent legal penalties for other forms of rape, they are largely unenforced, and sexual assault continues to be a major problem in the country. As with cases of domestic abuse, victims are often reluctant to report assaults, as there is a strong social stigma associated with being the victim of a sexual crime. Even when rape is reported, prosecution is considered uneven at best. According to a women's right organization, Bangladesh Mahila Parishad, there were 423 acts of violence against women and girls, including murder and rape in October 2014 alone.

The problems facing women in Bangladesh often stem from issues of poverty, and many women are exploited for financial gain in a number of ways. Impoverished young women are often coerced or sold into sexual slavery, and many are sent to India, where they are forced to work as prostitutes. Women also continue to face exploitation and abuse through the traditional dowry practice, in which a bride's family commonly pays a groom's family at the time of marriage. Violence toward women often surrounds this practice, and grooms sometimes beat and torture new brides if their families fail to pay the full dowry. There have also been disturbing instances of men marrying women just for the dowry, and killing their new wives, though these incidents are most likely isolated.

Because of the political instability in their country, many Bangladeshis turn to religious authorities to settle disputes. This promotes dangerous forms of vigilantism that victimize women throughout the country. The judgments of these religious authorities are often uneven, biased against females, and sometimes shockingly harsh. Women accused of offenses such as extramarital sex are sometimes whipped in public, burned with acid, or exiled from their home villages.

Nonetheless, there is hope for the future development of women's rights in Bangladesh. In the last few decades, a number of organizations have formed to advocate for the advancement of women. One important group is the Bangladesh National Women Lawyers' Association (BNWLA), a group that provides legal assistance to women facing abuse or discrimination. Another organization, called Naripokkho, deals with rights issues that impact women's health, including contraception and violence against women. A third group, the Bangladesh Nari Progati Sangha (BNPS), trains women to assume leadership positions within unions and the government.

Health Care

Though it has improved over the last several decades, Bangladesh's health care system is still inadequate and struggles to cope with the needs of its large population. There are too few hospitals and health care workers, and many rural areas lack medical services. The country relies on nongovernmental organizations (NGOs) and foreign aid for many of the services and supplies that are available; in rural areas, many people follow traditional medical practices.

Natural disasters and general poverty have combined to create a situation in which many treatable illnesses, including cholera, bacterial diarrhea, hepatitis, typhoid fever, malaria, and dengue fever, are prevalent. Malnutrition among children is also a serious problem.

GOVERNMENT

Structure

Independent since 1971, Bangladesh is a young nation. According to the constitution that was enacted the following year and reaffirmed by referendum in 1991, the country is a parliamentary democracy.

Executive power is vested in a prime minister, who serves as head of government. A president, elected by the parliament to a five-year term, serves in the largely ceremonial role of head of state. He or she is responsible for appointing the prime minister based on a majority nomination of the parliament; it is usually the head of the political party which wins a legislative majority. The executive cabinet is also composed of parliament members.

The legislature is a unicameral body called the Jatiya Sangsad. It consists of 300 directly-elected members holding five-year terms; according to legislation passed in 2004, 45 of the 300 members must be women.

Political Parties

The Bangladesh Nationalist Party (BNP), the Awami League, Jatiya Party, and the Jamaat-e-Islami Party are the main political parties in Bangladesh. The Awami League is a center-left, secular party. In the 2014 general election, the Awami Party garnered secured 234 seats in the parliament. The Jatiya Party, which gained 34 seats in the parliament. The Worker's Party received six seats, while other smaller parties received an additional seventeen seats. The BNP gained only one seat after leading a boycott of the elections.

Local Government

Bangladesh has seven administrative divisions which are further divided into districts, sub-districts, and unions (groups of villages). There is a popularly elected government at the district level and a popularly elected council at the union level.

Judicial System

The Supreme Court, the country's highest court, is divided into the High Court and the Appellate Court. The president is responsible for appointing the justices. Lower courts include district, thana, administrative, family, labor, land, commercial, municipal, and marine courts.

Taxation

The government of Bangladesh levies income, corporate, and value-added taxes (VAT). Corporate taxes are high, while income taxes are moderate. The top income tax rate is 25 percent, while the highest corporate tax is 45 percent. A tax on interest is also levied.

Armed Forces

The Bangladesh Armed Forces has numerous service branches, including an army, navy, air force, and coast guard, as well as border guards. As of September 2010, the armed forces have nearly 11,000 military personnel deployed as part of UN missions; active personnel overall totals more than 250,000.

Foreign Policy

Bangladesh was formed in 1971, when the region formerly known as East Pakistan split off from Pakistan. Pakistan sent troops to stop the Bangladeshi revolution, but failed, in part because of the intervention of India. After the uprising that resulted in an independent Bangladesh, actions were taken to heal the wounds of war. In 1973, Bangladesh released over 90,000 Pakistani prisoners of war. In the years that followed, over 250,000 people moved between Bangladesh and Pakistan, with the assistance of the UN. Despite the initial bitterness between the two countries, Bangladesh now enjoys fairly good bilateral relations with Pakistan. As Muslim South Asian nations, they share many religious, historical, and cultural commonalities.

Bangladesh's ties with India are extremely important, as the two countries share strong cultural, historical, and trade connections. Bangladesh shares especially close ties to the Indian state of West Bengal. Without India backing their cause in 1971, Bangladeshi separatists would probably not have been able to establish an independent nation. However, the relationship is not perfect, and the two countries have occasional diplomatic conflicts. Sporadic tensions arise from border disputes, questions about the citizenship of people living in tribal areas, access to water, and illegal immigration of Bangladeshis to India.

Bangladesh's relationship with its other neighbor, Myanmar, is generally positive. However, the two countries have faced occasional diplomatic problems, most notably concerning the exact location of the border. There is also an ongoing refugee crisis; over 270,000 Muslim refugees from Myanmar have flooded into Bangladesh, seeking religious freedom. With the assistance of the UN, most of these Myanmar Muslims have now returned home. In recent years, however, other Myanmar citizens have come to Bangladesh, fleeing the oppressive military junta in their own country. These new immigrants are not officially recognized as refugees, and are considered illegal aliens by the government of Bangladesh.

Relations with the United States were fairly tense in the early years of Bangladesh's independence. Since the U.S. considered Pakistan to be a strategically valuable ally, it was wary of the Bangladeshi separatists. However, the two countries developed stronger diplomatic ties in the decades to follow, and financial and humanitarian assistance from the U.S. has become an important source of revenue for Bangladesh. In turn, Bangladesh has been a loyal diplomatic ally, supporting the U.S. in the first Gulf War in 1990 and the 2001 "war on terror."

Bangladesh is also a participant in several multilateral organizations. It joined the UN in 1974, and served on the United Nations Security Council (UNSC) twice. Bangladesh is a driving force behind the Group of 48 as well, advocating for the world's poorer countries. Officially, Bangladesh has a diplomatic policy of non-alignment, and is an active member of the Non-Aligned Movement (NAM). It enjoys close ties with fellow Muslim nations, and is part of the Organization of the Islamic Conference (OIC). Bangladesh is also very active in development issues affecting the region, and is part of the South Asian Association for Regional Cooperation (SAARC), among other regional organizations.

Human Rights Profile

International human rights laws insist that states respect civil and political rights, and also promote an individual's economic, social and cultural rights. The United Nations Universal Declaration on Human Rights (UDHR) is recognized as the standard for international human rights. Its authors sought the counsel of the world's great thinkers, philosophers, and religious leaders, and were careful to create a document that reflects the core values of every world culture. (To read this document or view the articles relating to cultural human rights, visit http://www.udhr.org/UDHR/default.htm.)

Bangladesh faces many human rights problems. Most result from the political instability caused by government corruption. Military dictators and democratically-elected governments, dating back to 1971, have failed to solve this systemic problem. In January 2007, a military-backed caretaker government came into power. The caretaker government arrested the prominent members of the two main political parties, disbanded trade unions, and curbed press freedom. The new government declared a state of emergency, and made arbitrary arrests in the name of rooting out corruption. Tens of thousands of people were arrested in this sweep, and individuals were not given proper legal recourse to dispute the charges of corruption. As a result, many of these prisoners faced torture, while others were executed.

The government of Bangladesh continues to violate several core principles of the UDHR. Banning important forms of political discourse and limiting the freedom of the media is a clear violation of the freedom of expression outlined in Article 19. Persecuting individuals for their political affiliation and banning trade unions is contrary to the freedom of peaceful assembly stated in Article 20. By imprisoning citizens without any due process, the government of Bangladesh is contrary to the promise of liberty stated in Article 3, the ban on arbitrary arrest outlined in Article 9, and the guarantee of a fair trial described in Articles 10 and 11. The rampant use of torture on prisoners goes against the ban on inhumane treatment stipulated by Article 5. The fact that prisoners are sometimes killed in custody is a serious violation of the right to life stipulated by Article 3.

In June 2008, the government strengthened its power through laws passed in the name of preventing terrorism. This legislation gave the government broad powers of arrest. For example, anyone suspected of financing, associating with, or speaking out about terrorist groups became subject to arrest and execution. Under this counter-terrorism ordinance, the government is not required to present proof of guilt, and it now arrests people for all forms of dissident behavior. As of October 2008, reports of torture and arbitrary execution in custody continued to emerge.

In 2014, the Bangladesh Nationalist Party led a boycott of the general election in protest of the Awami League's many constitutional violations. Violence was widespread, resulting in the death of at least 21 people. Human Rights Watch reported numerous government and military abuses, warning that unless steps were taken to repair the situation things were likely to worsen.

ECONOMY

Overview of the Economy

Bangladesh has one of the least developed economies in the world, and around 31 percent of the population lives below the poverty line. Though international aid has been high, foreign investment is low compared to the amounts received by other Asian countries. Moreover, corruption is widespread in the country's upper echelons.

Approximately 40 percent of the labor force, which numbers 65.5 million, is either unemployed or underemployed (working less than a full work week); money earned by laborers working abroad in low-paying jobs (remittances) remains important to the economy. The GDP of Bangladesh is $140.2 billion USD (2013). The country's per capita gross domestic product (GDP) in 2013 was an estimated $2,100 USD.

Industry

Industry accounts for approximately 29 percent of the GDP and employs 13 percent of the labor force. Unlike other Asian countries, Bangladesh does not have a large-scale manufacturing sector. Textiles, garments, chemical fertilizers, beverages, steel, and cement are produced, and tea, sugar, jute, and tobacco are processed. Dhaka is a major hub for the production and export of textiles, such as muslin, jute, and cotton. The city is also home to Bangladesh's Export Processing Zone, a section of the city where over eighty textile factories and export operations are centered.

Labor

The labor force in Bangladesh numbered more than 78 million people in 2013, 40 percent of whom were underemployed. Of those holding jobs, 47 percent work in agriculture, 13 percent in industry, and 40 percent in services. The unemployment rate measured five percent in 2013.

Energy/Power/Natural Resources

Bangladesh's most important natural resources are natural gas and rich alluvial land. Timber, peat, limestone, clay, and coal are present in small quantities. Bangladesh produces energy through thermal and hydroelectric plants. Natural gas reserves in the Bay of Bengal, as well as onshore, are being developed. It is hoped that these reserves will help foster substantial economic growth. Bangladesh's energy consumption, per capita, is the lowest on the Indian subcontinent.

Bangladesh has several major environmental problems which are naturally occurring. Flooding, which brings rich silt to the plains of the country, can also cause widespread death and destruction. Arsenic, found in the soil, contaminates the ground water and makes much of it unsafe for drinking.

Man-made problems threatening the environment include the pollution of water and soil from pesticides, soil erosion, deforestation, and overpopulation. Scientists have predicted that Bangladesh will be one of the countries most adversely affected by global warming.

Fishing

Bangladesh's fishing industry has developed since independence. Three sectors contribute to industry: inland capture, inland culture, and marine capture. Species of note in the industry include carp, catfish, snakehead, hilsha, and finfish and shrimp. In the years 2005 to 2006, the fisheries GDP measured $236.48 million USD.

Forestry

The forestry industry in Bangladesh contributes about five percent to the nation's GDP and about 2 percent of the population is employed in this industry. Wood for fuel is the industry's major contribution. Rubber trees are cultivated for rubber, and hardwoods such as teak as well as bamboo are central to the small timber industry.

Mining/Metals

Bangladesh has few mineral resources. There is coal in the north, but there are potential natural gas reserves which are largely undeveloped.

Agriculture

Agriculture accounts for approximately 17 percent of the GDP and employs 47 percent of the labor force. Subsistence farming is the norm. Rice is the most widely cultivated crop, and jute is the biggest earner in the export market. Wheat, pulses, oilseeds, sugarcane, fruits, tobacco, tea, and potatoes are also important crops.

Animal Husbandry

Cattle and buffalo are the most common livestock. They are used for work and as sources of meat, leather, and dung. Freshwater fish are commonly raised in ponds.

Tourism

Bangladesh's undeveloped infrastructure has hindered the growth of a tourism sector that could potentially rival that of other Asian countries. However, tourism in Bangladesh is growing, particularly in regards to ecotourism. The country receives approximately 392,000 tourists each year.

Cultural attractions include mosques and Hindu and Buddhist temples. Collections of historical artifacts from all three religious traditions are displayed at the National Museum in Dhaka. Many visitors come for river trips through the lush natural landscapes and to see the flora and fauna, especially in the Surma River Valley and the coastal area known as the Sundarbans. Cox's Bazar, a beach resort, is one of the country's most visited places.

Adam Berger, Michael Aliprandini,
Amanda Wilding

DO YOU KNOW?

- Bangladesh's national flower is the lily. Bangladesh is also home to several species of giant lilies.
- Bangladesh is the world's leading producer of jute, a fiber that can be processed into twine and rope.

Bibliography

BBC News. "Country Profile: Bangladesh. February 2008. <http://news.bbc.co.uk/2/hi/south_asia/country_profiles/1160598.stm>.

Central Intelligence Agency. "The World Factbook: Bangladesh." 2014-15. <https://www.cia.gov/library/publications/the-world-factbook/geos/bg.html>.

Lonely Planet and Daniel McCrohan. *Bangladesh.* Oakland, CA: Lonely Planet, 2012.

Guhathakurta, Meghna, and Willem van Schendel, eds. *A Bangladesh Reader: History, Culture, Politics.* Durham, NC: Duke University Press, 2013.

Lewis, David. *Bangladesh: Politics, Economy and Civil Society.* New York: Cambridge University Press, 2011.

Phillips, Douglas & Charles Gritzner. *Bangladesh.* New York: Chelsea House, 2007.

Saikia, Yasmin. *Women, War, and the Making of Bangladesh: Remembering 1971.* Durham, NC: Duke University Press, 2011.

U.S. Department of State. "Background Note: Bangladesh." 2015. <http://www.state.gov/r/pa/ei/bgn/3452.htm>.

van Schendel, Willem. *A History of Bangladesh.* New York: Cambridge University Press, 2009.

Works Cited

Asiatic Society of Bangladesh. "Banglapedia: Chowdhury, Munier." http://banglapedia.search.com.bd/HT/C_0250.htm

BBC News. "Bangladesh Election Talks Begin." 22 May 2008. http://news.bbc.co.uk/2/hi/south_asia/7414519.stm

BBC News. "Bangladesh Singer Rocks Traditionalists." 2 March 2000. http://news.bbc.co.uk/2/hi/south_asia/663489.stm

BBC News. "Profile: Khaleda Zia." 3 September 2007. http://news.bbc.co.uk/2/hi/south_asia/6975798.stm

Bangladesh Nari Progati Sangha. "BNPS." http://www.bnps.org

Bangladesh Shilpakala Academy. "National Academy of Fine & Performing Arts." http://www.bdska.org

Capwell, Charles. "The Esoteric Belief of the Bauls of Bengal February." *Journal of Asian Studies* 33 (1974)

Centre for Asian Theatre. "About Us." 2014. http://www.catbd.org/about.html

Independent. "Inside the Slave Trade." 15 March 2008. http://www.independent.co.uk/news/world/asia/inside-the-slave-trade-795307.html

Islam, Rafiqul. "Kazi Nazrul Islam: A Biographical Sketch." 1994. http://www.nazrul.org/main_page/main.htm

Kirkpatrick, Joanna. "Bangladeshi Arts of the Ricksha." 5 December 1997. http://www.asianart.com/articles/ricksha/

Kwintessential. "Bangladesh: Culture, Customs, Language, and Etiquette." http://www.kwintessential.co.uk/resources/global-etiquette/bangladesh.html

Muktadhara. "Bangla Music." 9 May 2001. http://www.muktadhara.net/page16.html

Naripokkho. "Naripokkho." http://www.naripokkho.com/index_home.php

Nasrin, Taslima. "Official Home Page of Taslima Nasrin." http://taslimanasrin.com

Singha, Ashim. "Manipuri Dance: Both Ritualistic and Recreational." 1 July 2008. http://www.manipuri.20m.com/

Costumed dancers performing at a traditional festival in Bhutan/Stock photo © Leezsnow

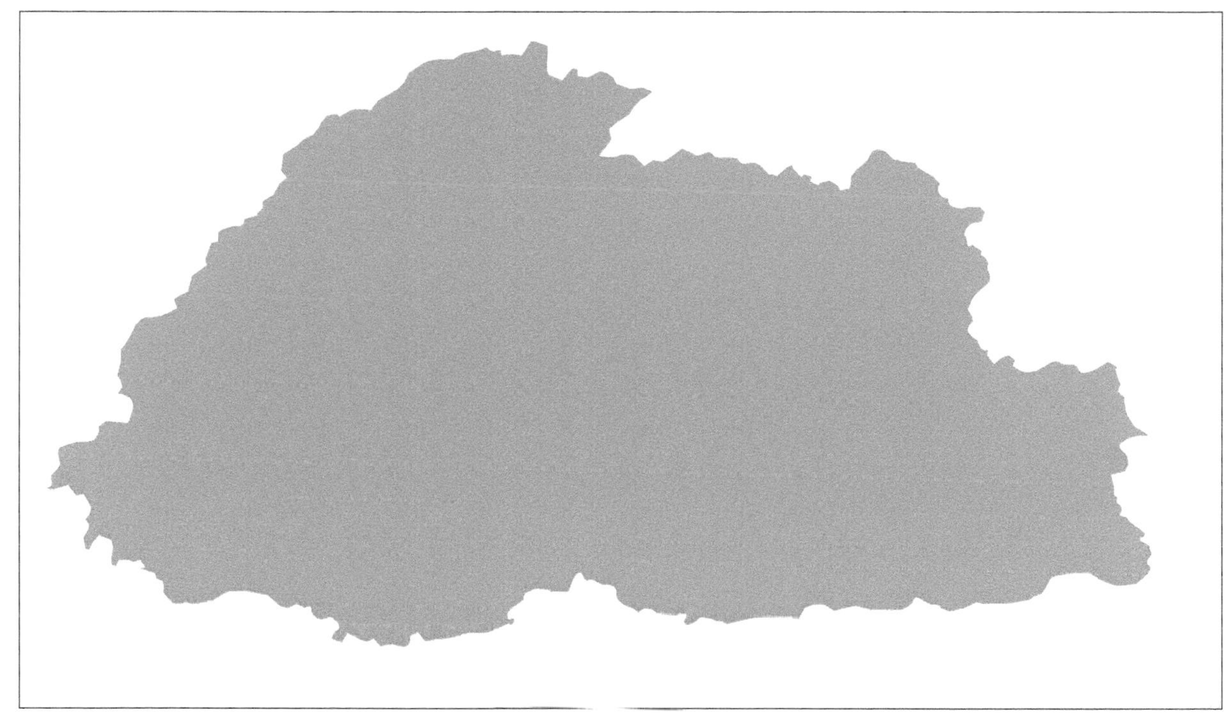

Bhutan

Introduction

The Kingdom of Bhutan is a landlocked, mountainous country in the eastern Himalayas. Located between India and China on the Asian continent, Bhutan also borders Tibet. The country's name means "land of the thunder dragon" a reference to the often brutal Himalayan storms experienced there. People who live in Bhutan are known as Bhutanese.

Bhutanese culture is strongly influenced by Buddhism and the agrarian lifestyle of its founding population. In Thimphu, the capital of Bhutan, the government requires that all new buildings follow a traditional design style and also maintains laws requiring citizens to wear native dress. Though Bhutan's urban areas continue to develop, much of Bhutanese life is still closely linked to the nation's cultural heritage.

GENERAL INFORMATION

Official Language: Dzongkha
Population: 733,643 (2014 census)
Currency: Bhutanese ngultrum
Coins: Coin denominations of the ngultrum are known as chetrums. 100 chetrums are equal to 1 ngultrum. The most commonly used coins are 20, 25, and 50 chetrums and the 1 ngultrum coin. Chetrum coins in denominations of 5 and 10 exist, but are rarely used.
Land Area: 38,394 square kilometers (14,824 square miles)

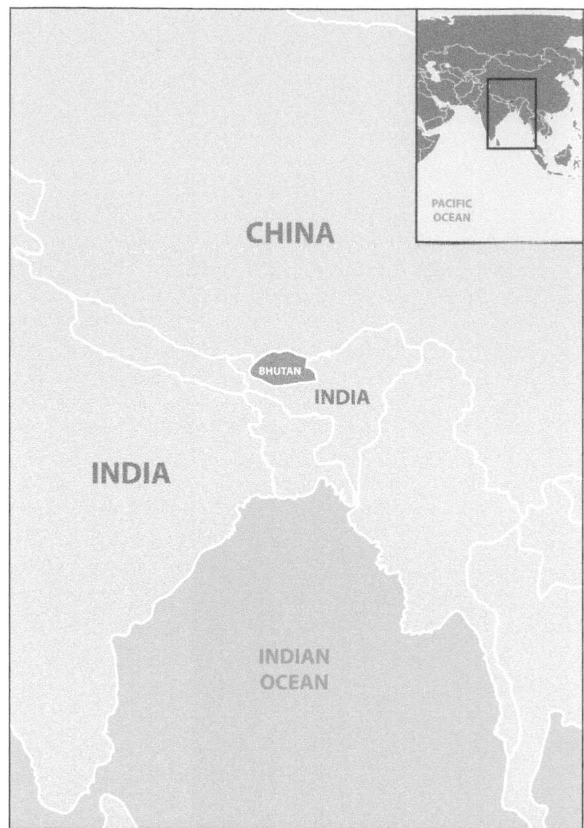

National Anthem: "Druk tsendhen" ("The Thunder Dragon Kingdom")
Capital: Thimphu
Time Zone: GMT +6
Flag Description: The flag of Bhutan features to opposing triangular color fields of yellow and orange. The color fields divide the flag diagonally. In the center of the flag is a large black and white drawing of a dragon. The yellow symbolizes Bhutan's civic traditions while the orange represents the country's roots in Buddhism. The dragon, or "druk," is the official symbol of the Kingdom of Bhutan.

Population

The primary ethnic group in Bhutan is the Bhotiya, an indigenous trans-Himalayan ethnic group, which accounts for 50 percent of the population. Most of the remaining Bhutanese (35 percent) are descended from Nepalese ethnic groups. Bhutan also has a small population

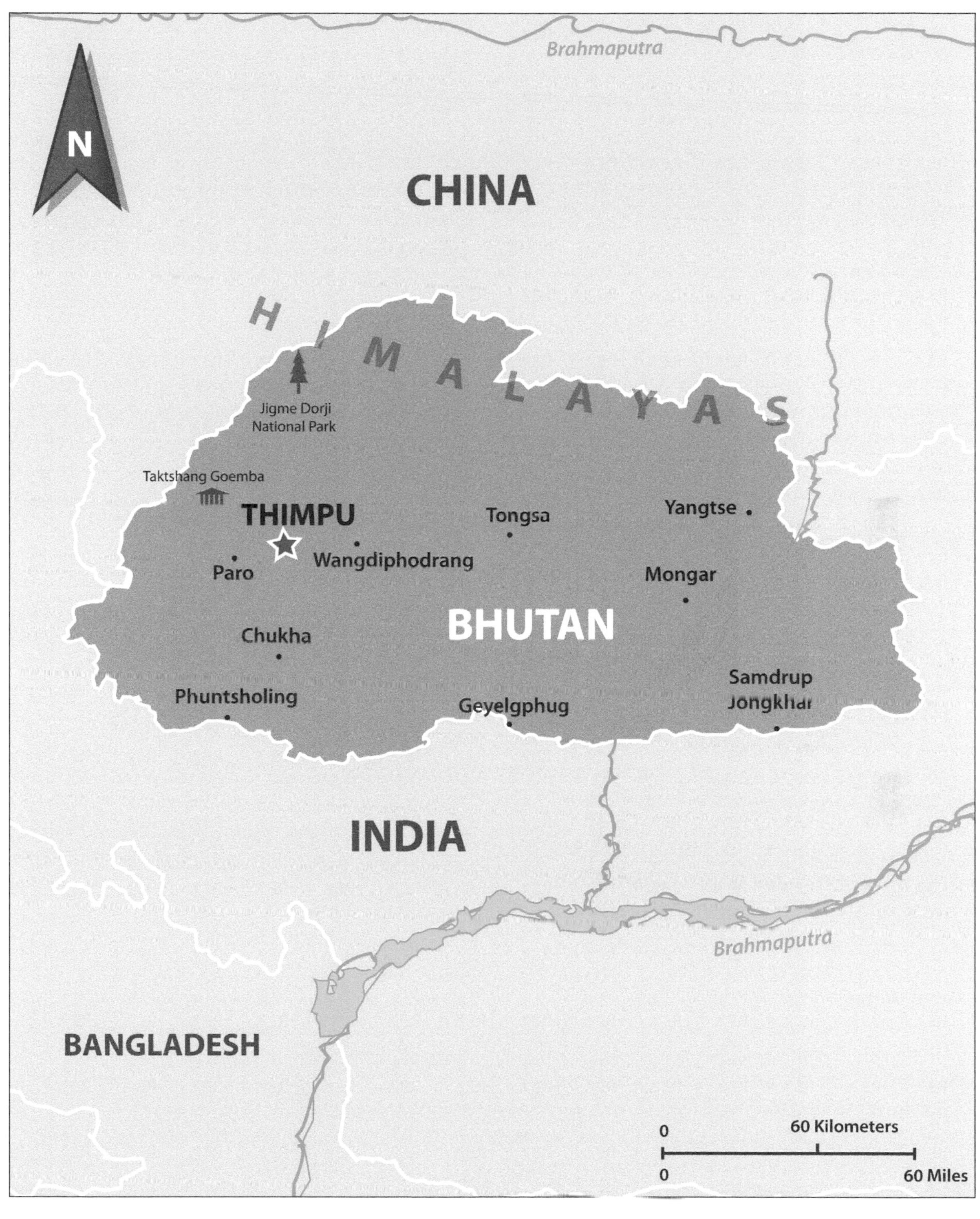
Brahmaputra
N
CHINA
HIMALAYAS
Jigme Dorji
National Park
Taktshang Goemba
THIMPU
Tongsa
Yangtse
Wangdiphodrang
Paro
Mongar
BHUTAN
Chukha
Samdrup
Jongkhar
Phuntsholing
Geyelgphug
INDIA
Brahmaputra
BANGLADESH
0
60 Kilometers
0
60 Miles

Principal Cities by Population (2012 estimates unless noted):

- Thimphu (99,021)
- Phuntsholing (23,915)
- Gelaphu (10,416)
- Wangdue (7,507)
- Samdrup Jongkhar (6,709)
- Samtse (5,201) (2008 estimate)

(15 percent) of indigenous, tribal groups. The Bhotiya reside mainly in the eastern and northern regions of the country, where the Nepalese are forbidden from settling by the Bhutanese government. Nepalese are banned from this region because the Bhutan government feels that an influx of immigrants will threaten Bhutanese traditions and culture. Indigenous populations are more common in rural areas.

Bhutan is a sparsely populated country. Roads are difficult to build in the mountainous terrain, and some communities can only be reached on foot. The population of Thimphu is estimated to be over 99,021 in 2012, constituting just over 15 percent of the total population. Over 35 percent of Bhutan's population lives in one of the nation's urban areas.

The population density of Thimphu is significantly greater than the rest of the country, with a density of 54 persons per square kilometer. Bhutan as a whole has a density of 18 persons per square kilometer. The growth rate for the population was estimated in 2010 at approximately 1.3 percent, of which natural birth constitutes the most significant vector of expansion.

Languages

The official language is Dzongkha, but other Tibetan and Nepalese dialects are spoken. English is used in schools, as well as on some road signs and government documents. In all, there are twenty-four living languages spoken in Bhutan, including Adap, Brokkat, Brokpake, Chalikha, Tshangla, and Nepali. Most of the Bhotiya speak Tibetan dialects, while most of the nation's Nepalese residents speak Nepalese dialects.

Native People & Ethnic Groups

Archaeologists speculate that the original inhabitants of Bhutan first settled there in 2,000 BCE. During the ninth century, the Bhotiya moved to Bhutan from Tibet, and came into contact with the native Tephu tribe.

In modern Bhutan, the ethnic group known as the Sharchops, who live in eastern Bhutan, are considered the indigenous population of the region. The Ngalongs live in the western part of the country and originate from Tibet. The Nepalis are primarily settled in the south.

The Nepalis are the most recent inhabitants of Bhutan and the largest minority group. Although the "Nepali Bhutanese" became citizens of Bhutan in 1958, many were suddenly cast out of society as illegal immigrants when anti-Nepalese immigration laws began being established in the late 1950s. More than 100,000 Nepalis were forced out of the country by the Bhutanese government in 1990. They eventually settled in refugee camps in Nepal. This aggressive action caused anger among Nepalese living in and outside of Bhutan and resulted in widespread pro-Nepali political activism. The Bhutan People's Party, operating out of Nepal, has become an important public voice in these matters.

Religions

Religion is a major part of life in Bhutan. Religion also significantly influences the shaping of government policy. The primary religion practiced in Bhutan is Lamaistic Buddhism. Approximately 75 percent of Bhutanese are adherents of Lamaistic Buddhism. There are an estimated 5,000 Buddhist monks in Bhutan. Monasteries, shrines, and prayer flags can be seen throughout the country. An estimated 25 percent of Bhutanese practice Indian and Nepalese-influenced Hinduism.

The form of Buddhism officially practiced in Bhutan is Drukpa Kagyupa, which stems from Mahayana Buddhism. Hindu forms practiced in Bhutan include the Shaivite, Vaishnavaite, Shakta, Ghanapr, Paurinic, and Vedic schools. Religious freedom is minimal, and the law forbids religious conversions.

Climate

The climate in Bhutan varies from tropical in the south to temperate in the north and west. In the mountainous areas of northern Bhutan, conditions are very cold and wet. With snow in the winter and rain in the summer, there is also considerable danger of landslides. In these areas, travel becomes impossible during the winter when the numerous mountain passes are blocked by snow.

In the central regions, conditions can vary depending on the elevation, but essentially it is cold in the winter and hot in the summer. In the south, at the foothills of the Himalayas, the climate is semi-tropical.

The winter season is from December through February and is marked by low humidity and temperatures falling below zero. The summer occurs between June and August and is marked by heavy rainfall and temperatures ranging from 8° to 21° Celsius (46° to 70° Fahrenheit). In mid-June, Bhutan experiences its monsoon season, which often results in flooding.

ENVIRONMENT & GEOGRAPHY

Topography

Bhutan is a completely landlocked and extremely mountainous. The Great Himalayan range features some of the tallest mountains in the world. The highest point in Bhutan is Mt. Kula Kangri (7,553 meters/24,780 feet), on the border with Tibet. The country's lowest point is at the Drangme Chhu basin (97 meters/318 feet).

Bhutan consists of three major regions: the sparsely-populated north, which features the Tibetan border region and the Great Himalayan range; the middle Himalayan zone, which has more fertile valleys and is more temperate; and the southern portion of the country, which is semi-tropical.

Major rivers in Bhutan include the Brahmaputra, Ama, Raidak, Sankosh, Ai, Tongsa, Bumtang, Kuru, and Dangma. Most rivers flow into the Brahmaputra River in India.

Thimphu, the capital, is located in a river valley with a maximum elevation of 2,350 meters (7,656 feet). The urban area occupies approximately 26 square kilometers (10 square miles). A major expansion and redevelopment, known as the Thimphu Structural Plan, was approved in 2003 and is designed to double the size of the city by 2027. Part of the plan includes the relocation of most of the city's industries to the suburbs in order to increase the residential capacity of the valley. In addition, military and police offices will eventually be relocated to strategic locations at the periphery of the residential and administrative districts.

Plants & Animals

Bhutan has gone to great lengths to conserve its wildlife. The country ranks as one of the top ten "global biodiversity hot-spots," with 770 species of birds and abundant plant life.

The golden langur monkey is one of the rare mammals living in Bhutan.

National policy regarding conservation is in accordance with Buddhist teachings. The Bhutanese believe that all forms of life should be treated as sacred. Some have attributed the successful survival of many rare wild animals and the increased protection of important habitats to this policy. The Bhutanese Duar Plains, in the southern portion of the country, are known for the diversity of wildlife found there.

There are many rare and exotic mammals in Bhutan. Some of these include the takin, snow leopard, cheetah, goral, sambar, rhinoceros, golden langur, blue sheep, water buffalo and elephant. Different species of deer, including the barking deer, are found at higher elevations.

Some of the trees commonly found in Bhutan include the beech, ash, birch, maple, cypress, and yew. There are also oak, rhododendron, firs, and pines at higher elevations. Plants, such as priumlas, poppies, magnolias, and orchids are also common.

Bhutan is home to many species of endangered mammals, including many birds. It is also home to many endangered plants and reptiles.

CUSTOMS & COURTESIES

Greetings

Bhutanese people are remarkably tolerant toward others, and enjoy a high level of political equality. However, they adhere to a strict code of etiquette, enforced by both tradition and law. This code is called driglam namzha. It controls many areas of social life, including dress, gestures, and the way that individuals of different social ranks address one another. Driglam namzha also represents the Bhutanese government's efforts to preserve traditional respect for elders and superiors. As such, it is taught to all students. According to the principal of driglam namzha, people of different ranks wear differently colored scarves. Most people wear white scarves, but government officials wear blue, red, orange, or yellow scarves. Thus, social rank can be quickly established based on scarf color, age, and gender.

Upon meeting a person of a higher social rank, as dictated by the driglam namzha code, a person will bow forward slightly and say "Kuzu zangpola," and the person of higher rank will say "Kuzu zangpo." Both are common greetings, loosely translated as "Hello." It is also important to use the appropriate title before a person's name. Those given ceremonial rank by the king are addressed with the title dasho (male) or ashi (female) before their first name. Elder monks, nuns, or teachers will be referred to as lopon (male) or anim (female). Formal modes of address are also used for people of the regular class. Children will be called busu (male) or bum (female), and adults are given the title aap (male) or am (female).

Gestures & Etiquette

The Bhutanese code of etiquette, driglam namzha, also establishes legally binding public requirements for wearing traditional modes of dress and interacting with people of different social class. Despite this apparently rigid social hierarchy, the Bhutanese are actually very tolerant people, especially where foreigners are concerned. However, there are a number of points of etiquette to keep in mind in order to appreciate the Bhutanese way of life.

Bhutan takes its unique form of Buddhism very seriously. Religion informs all aspects of Bhutanese life, often to an extent that outsiders find difficult to fully comprehend. Visiting a religious center such as a temple or monastery requires particular attention to etiquette. In Bhutan, people remove shoes and hats before entering a temple. They also take care to step over—and not on—the doorstep of a religious building. When inside a temple, Bhutanese people always move in a clockwise manner. They also speak as quietly as possible. In addition, photography is not permitted in temples. It is also customary to leave a small monetary offering on the altar.

There are also points of etiquette when visiting family homes. A house in Bhutan is not just a place to live. It is considered the center of the family's economic strength and identity. Therefore, visiting family homes requires attention to traditional values. For example, many homes in Bhutan feature painted or sculpted phalluses on their walls, doorways or roof. These represent the celebrated Bhutanese saint Lama Drukpa Kunley (also known as the Divine Madman). This saint was believed to be responsible with blessing young families with fertility. To that extent, fertility is the key to a family's wealth in Bhutan. As such, this mark of blessing should be treated as a religious symbol.

Furthermore, visitors should only enter a family's houschold shrine if invited. These shrines are treated with the same respect as a public temple. Clockwise movement is important here as well, and it is polite to make a small cash offering on the family altar.

Eating/Meals

The Bhutanese typically eat three meals a day: at morning, midday, and late evening. Meals are always very social events, and families typically eat all meals together. Meals are also commonly eaten while sitting together on the floor of the household kitchen. Each individual is given a personal bowl for rice, and takes meats and vegetables from several shared dishes. People in Bhutan eat with their right hands. As such, individual utensils may not always be available outside of restaurants. Tea (either salty butter tea or sweet milk tea) or domestic beer is freely served during meals.

Meals in Bhutan are considered a time to relax and enjoy both food and company. The length of a given meal is as much a product of how much there is to discuss with the assembled group as the quantity of food served. After eating in the evening, it is common for adults to chew doma, which is a mixture of areca nut, lime powder, and betel leaf. Doma is classified as a mild intoxicant, or stimulant. It is also considered a digestive aid which stains the teeth a characteristic red color. At the end of an extended meal, it is polite for guests to depart immediately so that the host family can take care of necessary cleaning and household chores. While women are usually considered to be in charge of household tasks, men and children are also expected to participate in the work involved with meals.

Visiting

The Bhutanese put a high priority on being hospitable to visitors. They take pleasure in sharing whatever they can with household guests. Doma is traditionally presented to guests when they arrive at a host's home, though tea, spirits, and domestic beer are now more commonly offered instead. It is considered polite for a guest to refuse when first offered food or drink. However, a good host will persist in his or her offer until the guest agrees to partake of food or beverage. Once a guest agrees to tea, spirits, or beer, it may be taken as impolite to have less than two glasses during the visit.

The Bhutanese enjoy exchanging presents, and it is always a good idea to bring a small gift, such as a box of candy or a bottle of wine or alcohol, when invited into a person's home. However, the recipient will probably not open the gift in public, as doing so is considered socially awkward. If visiting a family with a new child, it is customary to bring gifts such as nutritious foods for the nursing mother or practical items for the baby. However, visiting a household with a newborn child should only be done with clear permission. Guests to a houschold in mourning are also expected to bring certain types of presents. On the solemn occasion of a death in the family, presenting the grieving household with a white scarf and money, food, or bottle of expensive alcohol is considered an appropriate sign of sympathy.

LIFESTYLE

Family

Family is extremely important in Bhutan. This is due to the fact that the family unit is the basic economic unit. The vast majority of Bhutanese are subsistence farmers, and growing crops and raising livestock in this mountainous country is extremely labor intensive. Nonetheless, Bhutanese families are self-sufficient to a remarkable degree. They will normally produce and process their own food, clothing and other items needed for daily life. Having a large, cohesive family is therefore an important economic asset. The value of keeping families together in Bhutanese culture is evidenced in the fact that the Bhutanese have historically allowed multiple forms of marriage and cohabitation. This includes polygamous marriages.

Housing

Since families are mostly self-sufficient and reliant on domestic production, houses in Bhutan are more than just dwellings. They are important centers of economic activity. Houses are usually three-floored structures made of wood and stone, though in the southern region it is more common to see houses constructed of bamboo and mud. Bhutan houses typically have two separate walled yards for livestock and crops. Housing in Thimphu, the capital, is more consistent with other international urban centers, and consists of apartments and modern amenities.

Often, the first level of such a home has a dirt floor where livestock can shelter in times of bad weather. It also serves as storage for the equipment used to produce food and clothing. The second floor provides a place to store the appropriate food supplies for both the family and their livestock. Typically, the family lives on the top floor. In addition, the kitchen is commonly located on the third floor. In Bhutan the kitchen is a multi-purpose room which also serves as a bedroom and family hearth. Most houses also have a worship room on the top floor as well. This room contains the family shrine and serves as a guest bedroom for visitors.

Food

Food production in Bhutan is extremely small-scale and local. What grows well in one part of the country may not in another. Hence, Bhutanese cuisine involves a large variety of different ingredients that vary regionally. Staple starches include red and white varieties of rice, potatoes, barley, and buckwheat. A huge range of vegetables, both cultivated and wild, are also used in Bhutanese cuisine. These include radishes, asparagus, spinach, garlic, fern fronds, mushrooms, and chili peppers. Meat such as yak, beef, chicken, and pork is common in Bhutanese cuisine. Cow or yak cheeses are also enjoyed, both in fresh and dried forms. Preparation tends to be fairly simple, with basic noodle dishes, potato stews, rice-based soups, and momos (dumplings) making up much of the diet. Locally produced wheat beer (chang) and butter tea are the most common beverages.

While Bhutanese dishes might be characterized as simple or lacking in their complexity of palate, or sense of taste, this is often made up for by their sheer heat. No single ingredient is as important to cooking in Bhutan as the chili pepper, and Bhutanese people have great affection for the extremely hot chili peppers that grow in their country. In fact, a tolerance for spicy food is considered an important part of being Bhutanese. Even babies are encouraged to eat chili peppers. If one dish were chosen to represent the national cuisine, most people agree that it would be ema datse, a simple yet fiery cheese and chili pepper concoction. The dish is sometimes eaten for every meal of the day.

Most Buddhists around the world do not eat meat because of their religious respect for all sentient beings. Bhutanese, on the other hand, eat a great deal of it. This is particularly notable since they are quite familiar with Buddhism's restrictions against it. Technically, Buddhism permits eating meat for strictly nutritious purposes, but only from animals that died of natural causes. The Bhutanese seem to take this one step further, and simply try to avoid meat from animals specifically killed on their behalf. This helps to explain Bhutan's massive beef imports from India.

Life's Milestones

Having a large family is the key to material stability in traditional Bhutanese culture. In a tradition that dates back to an important fifteenth-century Buddhist saint known as the Divine Madman, fertility is encouraged by paintings and sculptures of phalluses placed on the outside walls and doorways of houses. Young couples also seek the Divine Madman's blessing at a special temple, the Chimi Lhakhang. Here, resident monks ritually bless visitors with a large wooden phallus. When a woman becomes pregnant with the family's first child, a ritual called the tsangman is performed by an astrologer. The tsangman ritual is a marriage of the young couple, a purification of the new baby, and an occasion to try to understand the child's past lives and future.

The Bhutanese, as Buddhists, also believe in rebirth. Thus, death represents an occasion to consult an astrologer. When a person dies, he or she is placed in the family's household shrine room. An astrologer then performs a reading to tell the family when, where, and by whom the deceased should be cremated. Bhutanese believe that when a person dies their soul enters an otherworldly state called the bardo. The soul remains in the bardo for 49 days, and is then reborn. In order to encourage a favorable rebirth, ritual blessings are performed on the seventh, 14th, 21st, and 49th days after a person dies. After that, families hold rituals on the anniversary of the death for three years.

CULTURAL HISTORY

Art

Bhutan has had a remarkably stable culture since the eighth century. During this period Buddhism was first introduced to this remote and isolated Himalayan country. Since that time, Buddhism has informed nearly every aspect of Bhutanese cultural life. This Buddhist influence has resulted in a flourishing artistic tradition, since patronage of the arts is considered an important way to gain spiritual merit. Bhutan's often martial, or combative, foreign relations have also influenced its culture. For example, since the Chinese invasion of Tibet in the 20th century, Bhutan has maintained a tense peace with China.

The Bhutanese themselves identify 13 traditional arts. These include sculpture, painting, woodworking, wood-turning, stone-carving, basketry, clay work, metal-casting, metal-forging, jewelry, paper-making, weaving and embroidery. Together, these traditional arts are known as zorig chusum. While zorig chusum clearly encompasses what would be considered symbolic religious art, they also include practical trades and crafts. This connection between high religious artistic traditions and the practical trades is significant. It speaks to the central place of Buddhism in all aspects of daily culture. The Bhutanese material arts reflect the Buddhist ideal that there is no separation between the sacred and profane, or the holy and the worldly. Overall, painting and architecture are Bhutan's most visible artistic traditions.

The Bhutanese have long produced spectacular paintings. These are always religious in nature, and are anonymous rather than attributed to individual artists. Historically, paints were created from mineral and vegetable pigments, though synthetic paint came into use in the twentieth century. Brushes are traditionally made with small sticks and animal hair.

All Bhutanese paintings fall into one of three categories: thankas, wall paintings, and statues. Thankas are a form of religious tapestry that is painted on canvas. They depict religious figures or scenes framed by colorful geometric patterns and complex natural backgrounds. Thankas are designed to be rolled up for storage, and are used for special events. Wall paintings, similar in theme and creation to thankas, are painted on thin pieces of fabric. This fabric is permanently affixed to the inside walls of public buildings. The Bhutanese have also historically produced wonderfully colorful painted statues. Made of clay or, less commonly, bronze, these statues depict the Buddha or important Buddhist saints. These are painted with gold colors, particularly on the face. The paint is used to add lifelike details. Painted statues are often found in dzongs and are usually present in lhakhangs.

Architecture

The influences of Buddhism and warfare are particularly apparent in Bhutanese architecture. The two most important types of public buildings in Bhutan are dzongs (fortified monasteries) and lhakhangs (temples/monasteries). Dzongs are large, whitewashed complexes made of compacted earth or stone, with square or rectangular frames made of large timber beams. Built on the side of mountains and near rivers for strategic advantage, dzongs have traditionally served as administrative buildings, monasteries, and forts that offer protection in times of war. The dzong form comes from Tibet's influence on Bhutanese culture. Lhakhangs are more specifically religious buildings. They are typically topped by a rounded cupola, or domelike structure, and are surrounded by paved paths for ritual use. Typically, they have Buddhist prayer wheels on their outside walls. Inside, they have large halls, often decorated with colorful murals depicting the life of the Buddha. An altar is usually present, often featuring a huge gilded statue of the Buddha or an important Buddhist saint.

Dance

Bhutanese dance further blurs the distinction between the sacred and the profane. It is considered extremely theatrical, with colorful wood or paper masks and bright costumes. This makes it a popular form of entertainment, especially at folk festivals. It is also highly ritualized and expresses religious ideas. Specific dances are all considered sacred but to varying degrees, in a spectrum from more mystical to more lifelike. Bhutanese dance is often performed by monks, who practice for months to execute the dance performance in perfect traditional form.

The masks of dancers usually depict religious personages, such as Himalayan Buddhist demons and protective deities, legendary sages, and other mystical beings. The most clearly mystical masked dances are traditionally credited to three legendary authors: Padmasambhava (also known as Guru Rinpoche) in the eighth-century; Pema Lingpa, who is said to have seen the dances in visions in the fifteenth-century; and Zhabdrung Ngawang Namgyel, who unified Bhutan in the 17th century.

Music

Bhutan also has a rich and diverse musical history. Buddhist chants, led by monks often dressed as gods and demons, have always been an important part of folk festivals. These chants are usually accompanied by cymbals and huge alpine horns. Two types of folk singing are also important to Bhutanese musical culture. Zhungdra, which emerged in the seventeenth century, is considered a purely Bhutanese invention. Boedra, which is considered a form of Tibetan folk music, also has a long history of popularity in Bhutan.

Bhutanese music is traditionally played on four instruments: the draymen (a form of lute), the pchewang (a two-string guitar), the lyem (bamboo flute), and the yanchcn (a stringed harp, with 72 strings, played with bamboo sticks). Musical compositions are dominated by themes of Buddhism and daily life. As such, it is difficult to distinguish between folk and religious music.

Literature

Bhutanese literature also reflects the important role Buddhism plays in the culture. Most literature was historically produced through woodblock printing in monasteries. Almost entirely produced by monks, this historical literature is dominated by Buddhist themes. Much of it is translations of Buddhist sacred texts from Sanskrit and religious philosophy. In modern times, Bhutanese literature has reflected the country's deeply Buddhist culture and tumultuous past. The most popular modern works published in the local Dzongkha language are stories based on religious themes and images, and histories of Bhutan.

CULTURE

Arts & Entertainment

Art in Bhutan has remained remarkably stable for hundreds of years. This is due to the country's extreme cultural isolation. The contemporary arts in Bhutan still reflect ancient Buddhist religious ideas and traditional craft techniques. However, since the 1950s Bhutan has been slowly opening to outside cultural influences. These influences include television, which came to the country in 1999. While they realize that they cannot remain isolated forever, the Bhutanese are wary of the effects that the outside world may have on their proud culture. The changes that have happened to Bhutanese art as the country has come out of its isolation are subtle, but worth noting. In the context of Bhutan's new connection to the outer world, the arts have emerged as a gentle defense against what is considered the cultural ravages of globalization.

Masked dances have become more popular in recent decades. They are a uniting force within modern Bhutanese culture. Dances from various regions have come together into a single tradition. Dance is now considered an important medium for communicating a unified national identity and set of values. They are highly public events, bringing area people together in an atmosphere of celebration. This contrasts with new kinds of entertainment, particularly television, which tends to isolate individuals.

Similar developments have taken place in Bhutanese literature. Bhutan's literary wealth, in the form of wood-block printing, was historically scattered across thousands of temples and monasteries throughout the country. The National Library of Bhutan has recently collected these treasures through an extensive national literary survey project. This has led the people of Bhutan to gain a new appreciation of their literary traditions. Popular books produced with modern printing techniques, both in Dzongkha and English, reflect this reverence for traditional Bhutanese literature. This new writing covers such traditional themes as religion, morality, folktales, and rural life.

Music in Bhutan has also undergone changes in the late twentieth and early twenty-first centuries. The two varieties of traditional folk music—boedra and zhungdra—are being supplanted by a new kind of popular music, called rigsar. This new music combines the sounds of traditional Bhutanese and outside instruments, including the electric piano and synthesizer. Stylistically, it blends Bhutanese folk songs with popular music from Tibet and India. These latter sounds came to Bhutan through radio. Rigsar lyrics typically speak about issues of life in present-day Bhutan. The style developed in urban areas and is now spreading among rural youth. Some Bhutanese musical scholars criticize the increasing popularity of rigsar. They perceive this style of music as being devoid of religious themes and traditional values, qualities which made folk music so important to the wider Bhutanese culture.

Perhaps the most important change to the arts in modern Bhutan is the awareness that they represent something unique, powerful, and worth preserving at any cost. This sentiment is what has led many Bhutanese to perceive the outside world as potentially disruptive to traditional culture. However, the Bhutanese are committed to transitioning to a modern nation state. The key to doing this, they understand, lies in their artistic tradition. This is evidenced by the fact that two arts schools have recently opened in Thimphu. The establishment of a national arts and culture museum in the city of Paro is also proof that the Bhutanese seek a renewed sense of unification and national pride through their arts.

The two new arts schools are the National Institute for Zorig Chusum which opened in 1999, and the Choki Traditional Art School (CTAS) that also opened in 1999. These two schools teach the thirteen traditional Bhutanese arts (sculpture, painting, woodworking, woodturning, stone-carving, working in clay, casting and metalwork, metal-forging, jewelry-making, basketry, paper-making, embroidery and weaving) to a new generation. These schools are a notable way in which the Bhutanese are turning to their artistic traditions as a source of national strength. They are very much vocational schools, teaching male and female students the crafts they will need to help keep up the traditional infrastructure of Bhutan. Interestingly, they are also charitable schools, designed to help those who are having difficulty keeping up with the transition to a modern nation.

Cultural Sites & Landmarks

Visitors have only been allowed into Bhutan since 1974, and tourism remains highly restricted by the Bhutanese government. However, the country is a popular destination for those interested in the ecology and the culture of the Himalayan region. Over 26 percent of the country is protected land, and Bhutan boasts a rich biological diversity. The country's vast wildernesses are home to rare mammals such as tigers, red pandas, Asiatic elephants, one-horned rhinos and snow leopards. There are also over 770 known bird species, and 5,400 different kinds of plants in Bhutan.

Because of this diversity, Bhutan is gaining a reputation as an eco-tourism destination. Eco-tourism is primarily active around Bhutan's national parks and wildlife sanctuaries. These include Bomdeling Wildlife Sanctuary in the northeast, Jigme Dorji National Park in the northwest, Jigme Singye Wangchuck National Park in the central-west, Khaling Wildlife Sanctuary in the southeast, Phibsoo Wildlife Sanctuary in the south, Royal Manas National Park also in the south, Satken Wildlife Sanctuary in the east, and Thrumshing La National Park in the central-east.

The nation's natural habitats are themselves national landmarks. They are living demonstrations of Bhutan's unique Buddhist heritage, which holds a great reverence for nature. Buddhism particularly teaches respect for all sentient beings. It also echoes ancient pre-Buddhist beliefs in the existence of powerful nature deities.

Bhutan is also home to numerous manmade landmarks. In the Trashi Chhoe Dzong precinct of the capital of Thimphu are many of Bhutan's famous dzongs. Here on display are huge prayer wheels, lively murals and sculptures, including a statue of Sakyamuni, the historical Buddha. To the west of Thimphu, near the small city of Paro, is the temple Kyichu Lhakhang. Built in 659 by the Tibetan king Songsten Gampo, Kyichu Lhakhang is one of Bhutan's oldest remaining temples. Legend has it that the king built this temple in order to pin down an ogress who sought to prevent the spread of Buddhism into Tibet.

Not far from there is the celebrated Taktshang Goemba, also known as the Tiger's Nest Monastery. Perched on a cliff face, this monastery is said to be the place where Buddhism first came to Bhutan. According to myth, Guru Rinpoche flew up the cliff on the back of a tigress, defeated a demon, and then spent three months in meditation on this spot.

Libraries & Museums

Thimphu has one of the nation's largest libraries, the National Library, which was established in 1964 to preserve the national collections of Tibetan and Dzongha texts. The library building is constructed in a traditional Bhutanese style and contains a large collection of books related to Bhutanese history and culture. In addition, the National Library has a collection of international and foreign language books.

The National Museum of Bhutan first opened in 1968, and has since expanded into a world-class institution. Its holdings are centered on the uniquely Bhutanese themes of Buddhism and national unification by Zhabdrung Ngawang Namgyel in the seventeenth century. It also houses various military artifacts. Temporary exhibits also have nationalistic themes, such as the display of 105 photographs celebrating a century of stable rule by the present monarchy. These exhibits are designed to promote a sense of national identity in the face of modernization, especially among young Bhutanese people.

Holidays

Public holidays in *Bhutan* are almost all religious in nature, with prayers offered to bless the day. Holidays include the winter solstice (around January 1), the lunar New Year (January or February), the birthday and the anniversary of the coronation of the Druk Gyalpo (the king), the beginning of monsoon season (September 22), National Day (December 17), and other Buddhist and Hindu celebrations.

Youth Culture

Youth in Bhutan in the early 21st century is coming of age at a time of unprecedented cultural change for the country. Long isolated from the outside world, the Bhutanese are now embracing modernization. However, many Bhutanese are concerned about the negative effects of rapid cultural change. To many Bhutanese, youth culture reflects a series of problems that demonstrate the difficulty of this transition. The worst fear of concerned Bhutanese people is that their youth will turn away from their traditional Buddhist lifestyle, a trend which some believe is already occurring.

One cause for worry is the realization that the modernized educational system alienates some young people. For a myriad of reasons, including family crisis, poverty, medical emergencies, and behavioral problems, some students are unable to finish their basic education. Often these youth lack traditional support networks and move to urban areas, where they have difficulty finding employment. In addition, youth in urban areas are increasingly turning away from traditional music in favor of the new pop style called rigsar, which is criticized as undermining Buddhist values. Television, which came to the country in 1999, is also blamed for corrupting traditional morality as it increases in popularity with young people. Another cause for worry among older Bhutanese is the fact that youth culture increasingly glamorizes the smoking of marijuana, a plant that grows wild throughout Bhutan, but has traditionally only been used as a feed for livestock.

SOCIETY

Transportation

Most internal travel is by road, and the government provides some bus services through the postal department. Vehicle traffic in Bhutan travels on the left-hand side of the road. Roads in each district have check posts and route permits are required. Private bus lines flourish in Bhutan. However, inclement weather, land slides, and rock falls routinely disrupt road travel. Remote rural areas of Bhutan are accessible only by foot. Hitchhiking is also common in Bhutan's rural areas.

Transportation Infrastructure

Because of Bhutan's extremely mountainous landscape and remote location, road transportation is difficult. Bhutan's inaccessibility is the primary cause of the country's unique isolation from the outside world. Travel within the country remains challenging and restricts the internal flow of goods and services.

Travel difficulties have stalled economic development in Bhutan, and the government has made efforts to improve the country's transportation infrastructure. Recent developments have done much to improve Bhutan's links to the outside world and unify the country internally. This includes the Road Act of 2004, which outlines the Bhutanese government's commitment to maintaining and improving Bhutan's vital transportation network

Since 1983, Bhutan has had a national airline called Druk Air. It connects the only airport in Bhutan, located in the small city of Paro, with other international airports in India, Nepal, Bangladesh, and Thailand. This has been a major development for the Bhutanese tourist industry. Previously, the only other way to enter the country was overland from the Indian state of West Bengal.

Media & Communications

Major innovations in media and communications infrastructure have occurred in Bhutan since the country made the decision to open up to the outside world. Bhutan now has three regularly published newspapers. All three of these papers are printed in English and the local Dzongkha language. The oldest of these is *Kuensel*, which started as a government paper in 1974, but became independent in 1998. Two other independent newspapers opened in 2006. These are the *Bhutan Observer* and the *Bhutan Times*. The Bhutan Broadcasting Service (BBS) has aired radio programming since 1973, and became independent from the government in 1992. The BBS has also aired TV programming since the government legalized television in 1999. Internet and digital telephone service also came to Bhutan in 1999. Bhutan Telecom now provides fixed line and mobile telephone service in most areas of the country. Internet is also available through Bhutan Telecom, using the country's own DrukNet server.

SOCIAL DEVELOPMENT

Standard of Living

Bhutan ranked 136th on the 2014 Human Development Index. However, some argue that this ranking underestimates the individual quality of life in Bhutan. In 2006, for example, Bhutan was rated as the "happiest country in Asia" by *Business Week* magazine, based on a global survey by a British university and as the eighth happiest country overall on the globe.

Water Consumption

Bhutan is a completely landlocked country with extremely high elevations. There are no major bodies of water in the country, which makes access to potable water problematic. Approximately 99 percent of people living in cities and 97 percent of those living in rural communities have access to improved drinking water.

However, many households are without water and many families in rural areas still travel long distances to access water supplies. In 2008, the health ministry estimated that approximately 65 percent of Bhutan's rural water infrastructure is in need of repair. Critics have stated that the Bhutanese government may have misstated recent statistics related to the availability of fresh water in the country.

Education

Schools in Bhutan were originally run by Buddhist monasteries. Since the 1950s, secular and government-funded schools have become more widespread.

Bhutan spends an estimated five percent of its gross domestic product (nearly 13 percent of all government expenditures) on education. Schooling is publicly funded for the first 10 years of a student's formal education. Primary school lasts for five years, followed by three years of lower secondary school, and two years of upper secondary school. However, only about a quarter of the Bhutanese population attends school.

Schools must adhere to a national core curriculum which includes English, mathematics, and Dzongkha. Literature, social studies, history, geography, general science, biology, chemistry, physics, and religion are some of the other subjects studied. Agricultural and animal husbandry courses are also taught where such instruction is practical.

The Royal University of Bhutan, which is the national university system, is headquartered in Thimphu and is composed of eight separate institutions. The university center in Thimphu currently accommodates approximately 500 students, though the department of education has plans to expand the student capacity.

The literacy rate in Bhutan is 38 percent among women, 65 percent among men, and 52 percent overall. Approximately 90 percent of the Bhutanese population completes an education up to the fifth grade.

Women's Rights

Women have traditionally enjoyed a good deal of respect and equality in Bhutan. However, women have faced new challenges as the country continues to develop and more Western influences have been introduced to Bhutanese culture.

Bhutanese Buddhism grants inheritance to daughters, meaning that the majority of landowners in rural areas are women. Bhutan has a matriarchal kinship system. In addition, Bhutanese culture has always been open to multiple forms of marriage, including polygamy, in which the husband has multiple wives, and polyandry, in which the wife has multiple husbands, all with the spouse's permission. Most importantly, women have historically been considered responsible for teaching or transmitting traditional Bhutanese culture to the next generation. This important role endowed women with a high degree of respect in Bhutanese society.

However, women traditionally did not venture into the wider world, because it potentially poses dangers. For example, families are often very protective of their daughters. Though schools in modern Bhutan are free and open to both genders, attendance is not mandatory and often females are not allowed to attend. This is because families worry that their daughters will come to harm if sent to school. Although sexual violence is extremely rare in Bhutan, they are often concerned that older daughters will be raped or sexually harassed. The effect of this is that attendance of school is lower for girls than boys in the higher grades. Hence, the status of women within the government has been limited. In fact, women only account for 2.5 percent of representation at the district level, far worse than other south Asian countries that do not have the same traditions of gender equality.

The Bhutanese government is aware of growing inequality, and has made efforts to ensure that the country's development occurs through gender-neutral policies. For example, Bhutan is one of the numerous countries to sign the Convention of Elimination of All Forms of Discrimination against Women (CEDAW). In addition, several organizations have been created in Bhutan to ensure and protect women's rights. They include RENEW (Respect, Educate, Nurture, and Empower Women) and the National Women's Association of Bhutan (NWAB).

Health Care

Bhutanese receive free but rudimentary medical care, primarily dispensed from the general hospital in the capital, Thimphu. The health care system is supported by domestic funds as well as foreign donors (India is a major contributor).

Efforts have been made to improve access to important drugs and vaccines in the more remote villages of the country. Currently, 83 percent of Bhutanese one-year olds have been vaccinated against tuberculosis, and 78 percent against the measles. Up to 95 percent of people have access to essential drugs and medicines.

GOVERNMENT

Structure

Bhutan is officially a monarchy, but executive power lies with a Council of Ministers and a National Assembly (or "Tshogdu") whose members can take power away from the king with a two-thirds vote.

The members of the Council of Ministers (or "Lhengye Shungtsog") are nominated by the king and serve five-year terms. Members of the Royal Advisory Council (of "Lodoi Tsokde") are also nominated by the monarch.

The National Assembly consists of 150 seats. Of these, 105 are elected locally, ten represent religious bodies, and 35 are appointed by the king. Members of the National Assembly serve three-year terms. There are no national elections in Bhutan, but local elections are held every three years.

Political Parties

Bhutan began making the transition from an absolute monarchy to a constitutional monarchy in 1999. The two major political parties in Bhutan are the People's Democratic Party and the Bhutan Peace and Prosperity Party. The party known as the Druk National Congress, which represents exiled Nepalese people, operates in Kathmandu. Other exiled parties include the Bhutan Peoples' Party, the Bhutan Communist Party, the Bhutan National Congress, and the Bhutan Democratic Socialist Party. In 2013, Bhutan experienced a peaceful turnover of power when parliamentary elections ousted the incumbent party.

Local Government

Bhutan is separated into twenty different administrative divisions ("dzongkhas"). These are run by commissioners ("dzongdas") who are responsible for upholding the law in their territory. There are also smaller divisions of land (blocks, or "gewog") in Bhutan, around which community development or other localized projects are organized.

Judicial System

Historically, the Bhutanese judicial system was based on a seventeenth-century Tibetan system. The law code known as Tsa Yig resolved domestic issues related to marriage, divorce, civil disputes, and adoption based on a local leader's interpretation of Buddhist or Hindu beliefs. Today, village leaders continue to resolve such disputes in rural areas of Bhutan.

Judges in Bhutan are appointed by the head of state (Druk Gyalpo). Lawyers have been introduced to the Bhutanese judicial system only during recent decades. Outside of petty crime incidents, Bhutan has a low crime rate.

Taxation

After first introducing an income tax in 1999, Bhutan's system of taxation continues to develop. Taxes are overseen by the Ministry of Finance. A business income tax and corporate income tax is charged, but exports are not taxed. Other taxes include a land tax, house tax, and cattle tax. Foreign travel taxes, motor vehicle taxes, and foreign travel taxes are also collected.

Armed Forces

The armed forces of Bhutan consist of the Royal Bhutan Army, Militia, Royal Bodyguards, and Royal Bhutan Police. The Bhutan Air Arm is a recent addition to Bhutan's military. The armed forces of Bhutan maintain a training relationship with the Indian Armed Forces. The army participated in their first offensive in 2003 when they engaged Indian separatist rebels. Bhutan's military expenditures represent approximately 2 percent of the country's GDP.

Foreign Policy

Since the mid-to-late 20th century, Bhutan has increasingly opened to the outside world, breaking a tradition of isolationism that has made it a remarkably insular country. Over this period, Bhutan has pursued diplomatic relationships with neighboring countries. While Bhutan has been especially careful to develop systematic foreign policies towards other nations in the region, it has also entered the global community as a modern state. China's invasion of Tibet in 1950 remains the most significant reason for Bhutan's sense of connection to the rest of the world. The invasion made Bhutan wary of the potential threat China poses to its continued independence. Ongoing border disputes with China have kept Bhutan active in building relationships with other nations, particularly those who support Tibetan independence.

Bhutan's closest ally is India, which borders Bhutan to the west, south, and east. From Bhutan's standpoint, India's large size and global importance make it an ideal counterweight to China, which now borders Bhutan to the north. For its part, India has sought to maintain the strategic advantage of having an independent Bhutan as a buffer between it and China. In fact, it was India which first sought diplomatic relations with Bhutan. In 1958, Indian Prime Minister Jawaharlal Nehru convinced the Bhutanese king of the importance of forming an alliance. In the decades that followed, the two countries developed vital economic ties. In fact, Indian aid largely financed the initial stages of Bhutan's modernization program. Nearly all aspects of Bhutan's modern infrastructure are a result of ongoing economic cooperation with India. For example, Bhutan's hydroelectric projects, the nation's only airport, the new highway system, and the BBS were all made possible by this relationship with India.

On the other hand, Bhutan has had less-than-friendly relations with another one of its neighbors, Nepal. This stems from the crisis created when Bhutan expelled nearly 100,000 Nepali-speaking Bhutanese citizens in the late 1980s and early 1990s. A large number of the refugees created from this controversial act remain in camps administered by the United Nations (UN) in eastern Nepal. Despite good faith efforts to negotiate a settlement with Bhutan about these refugees, Nepal has had little success brokering a meaningful resolution to the refugee problem. Bhutan's reluctance to cooperate on this issue has hindered relations with Nepal. In addition, this reluctance has tarnished Bhutan's otherwise positive international reputation.

Aside from this refugee crisis, Bhutan has managed to build friendly relationships around the world. It joined the UN in 1971, which allows the small country to effectively assert its diplomatic interests. Bhutan also enjoys the diplomatic and economic support of another multinational organization, called the Friends of Bhutan. This coalition consists of Austria, Denmark, Japan, the Netherlands, Norway, Sweden, and Switzerland. This organization works to promote goodwill and a better understanding of Bhutanese people and culture.

Human Rights Profile

International human rights laws insist that states respect civil and political rights, and also promote an individual's economic, social and cultural rights. The United Nations Universal Declaration on Human Rights is recognized as the standard for international human rights. Its authors sought the counsel of the world's great thinkers, philosophers, and religious leaders, and were careful to create a document that reflects the core values of every world culture. (To read this document or view the articles relating to cultural human rights, visit: http://www.udhr.org/UDHR/default.htm.)

The human rights situation in Bhutan in the early 21st century is complicated and contradictory. On the one hand, the Bhutanese government is explicitly committed to the well-being of its citizens. This commitment is based on Buddhist ideas about the importance of personal development, and reflects the degree to which Buddhism informs all aspects of Bhutanese life. For example, in the 1980s, King Jigme Singye Wangchuck stated that the encouragement of "gross national happiness" (GNH) would be the guiding principle for national development.

On the other hand, the Bhutanese government has deprived nearly one in six Bhutanese of several basic human rights. In the late 1980s and early 1990s, nearly 100,000 Nepali-speaking Bhutanese from the south regions of Bhutan were forced into exile. More than a decade later, they remain in seven UN administered refugee camps in eastern Nepal. While the Bhutanese government claims those who left the country did so voluntarily, refugees describe being coerced into leaving by violence, or threats of violence, and ongoing harassment by Bhutanese security forces.

In this regard, Bhutan is in clear violation of the UN's Universal Declaration on Human Rights, specifically Articles 2, 9, 13, 15, and 23. For instance, Article 2 states that no one may be denied human rights because of the language they speak. The approximately 100,000 Nepali-speaking Bhutanese refugees living in UN camps were systematically selected for exile on the basis of their linguistic identity. Further, Article 9 states that no one shall be subjected to arbitrary, or unreasonable, arrest, detention or exile. Nepali-speakers were clearly coerced into leaving Bhutan, despite government claims that they left the country voluntarily. The Bhutanese government's actions also breach Article 13, which states the right to both leave and return to one's country. These refugees are not allowed to return home even a decade after their forced departure, as they were stripped of their citizenship by the Bhutanese government. This violates Article 15, which declares that no one may be deprived of his or her nationality without due cause.

The Bhutanese government's exile of Nepali-speaking southerners complicates its stated commitment to the well-being of all its citizens. It also contradicts the stated principle of development for the goal of maximizing gross domestic happiness. In the long term, the exile of Nepali-speaking Bhutanese may also jeopardize the human rights of the majority Dzongkha language group. Several insurgent groups have been linked to the refugee camps in Nepal. These groups are suspected of being behind a series of bombings in 2008, which injured Dzongkha speaking citizens in Thimphu. The cycle of violence created by the refugee situation threatens to undermine Bhutan's Buddhist ideals regarding national development.

Migration

Bhutan has two major urban centers, the capital of Thimphu and the city of Phuntsholing. Although both cities remain underdeveloped in comparison to Western standards, significant numbers of Bhutanese are moving to them from rural areas. It has been estimated that the populations of Thimphu and Phuntsholing are growing at 10 percent annually.

ECONOMY

Overview of the Economy

Bhutan has close economic ties to India. Trade with India accounts for over 69 percent of Bhutan's export revenues and 75 percent of its imports. Bhutan's economy also relies on economic aid, most of which is distributed from India. The nation's other chief export partners are Japan and Germany. Over 90 percent of the population is employed in small, subsistence farming. Commercial farms produce rice, wheat, and a variety of vegetables. Spices, including cardamom, are among the nation's chief export commodities. Agriculture and forestry contribute the greatest portion of the GDP. The country's gross domestic product (GDP) in 2013 was $5.2 billion USD ($7,000 USD per capita).

Industry
In Bhutan, industry is limited and out of the technological mainstream. 12 percent of the labor force works in industry. Major industries include cement, wood products, processed fruits, alcoholic beverages, and calcium carbide. The industrial production growth rate is 7 percent.

Industrial manufacturing is more common in the areas surrounding the larger cities. Manufacturing plants in and around Thimphu produce concrete and other mineral products. In addition, Thimphu has a number of timber mills that produce wood products and furniture.

Labor
According to recent statistics, Bhutan's labor force was about 336,400, though the country lacked skilled workers. Two-thirds of the workforce was employed in the agricultural sector. As of 2012, the unemployment rate in the country was estimated at 2 percent.

Energy/Power/Natural Resources
One of Bhutan's major potential resources is hydropower. That industry has recently expanded with the construction of hydropower plants and the development of closer ties to the Indian market.

Thanks to Bhutan's widespread forests, wood-fuel is the major source of energy used for cooking and heating, but may also cause pollution. Plant and soil erosion is one of the most difficult environmental problems in Bhutan. The country's mountainous terrain makes it prone to landslides, which contribute to the erosion problem.

Fishing
Fishing has long had a minimal impact in Bhutan, despite the fact that many mountainous rivers and streams are believed to be teeming with cold water fish species. Most attribute the large number of fish such as trout—not native, but introduced by British colonists—to Buddhists principles, as the mostly Buddhist population refrains from killing any species.

Forestry
The country's forests remain an important natural resource, and ply wood products, laminated boards, and ready-to-assemble furniture represent major forest-based industries in Bhutan. Much of the forested areas in Bhutan are protected and logging is strictly controlled. As recently as the early 21st century, Bhutan had an estimated forest cover of over 64 percent.

Mining
Mining is not a significant contributor to Bhutan's economy. However, the country is a leading producer of the alloy known as ferrosilicon. Bhutan Ferro Alloys Ltd. exports the alloy to India and Japan. There are also Japanese companies that mine ferrosilicon in Bhutan. However, the country's weather and terrain make mining in Bhutan difficult.

Agriculture
Agriculture is the major economic activity in Bhutan. More than 90 percent of Bhutanese people are engaged in farming-related occupations, primarily subsistence farming and animal husbandry.

There are 160,000 hectares (395,369 acres) of arable land in Bhutan. This represents only three percent of the country's total area. Due to the mountainous terrain, most land cannot be farmed. Nonetheless, Bhutanese farmers provide practically all of the country's food supply. Major crops include rice, corn, root crops, citrus, grains, dairy products, and eggs. Rice and corn are the most abundant crops.

Animal Husbandry

Yaks and sheep in Bhutan migrate from higher to lower altitudes seasonally. Rural herders depend on these animals for food, fur, and manure for farming. Other livestock in the country include pig, cattle, and buffalo. Although poultry is not a traditional livestock staple in Bhutan, the herding of poultry eggs has increased in recent decades.

Tourism

Isolated from much of the outside world for many years, Bhutan only recently opened its borders to tourists in the 1970s. Tourists (particularly eco tourists) are drawn to Bhutan to for the abundant wildlife and extensive trekking terrain offered by the country's pristine landscape. The elaborate religious festivals are another major attraction.

The government still has strict policies regarding the entrance of tourists, and in 1998 only permitted 5,000 tourists into the country (though that number increased to over 105,000 in 2012). Tourism is controlled by the government through officially designated tour groups, and visitors must arrange their travel through these agencies in order to enter Bhutan.

To boost tourism revenue, the country has improved infrastructure and hosted the 16th South Asian Association for Regional Cooperation (SAARC) summit in 2010.

Adam Berger, Kim Nagy & Micah Issitt

DO YOU KNOW?

- Bhutan is the only nation in the world that attempts to create a measure for the happiness of its citizens. The Gross National Happiness index uses surveys to measure the average satisfaction of the populace on issues ranging from the performance of the monarch to the effect of Internet access.
- Bhutan is the only national capital that does not use traffic lights. The nation's lack of traffic signals did not become an issue until recently as population expansion and growth in the automotive industry have combined to increase road traffic. Bhutan's police monitor and direct traffic in busy intersections, however, as the population of Bhutan remains relatively small, only one police officer is needed even in the busiest traffic areas.

Bibliography

ACCU. "Bhutan: Country Profile." 2007. Asia-Pacific Database on Intangible Cultural Heritage. Asia/Pacific Cultural Centre for UNESCO. <http://www.accu.or.jp/ich/en/policies/C_BTN.html>.

Bartholomew, Terese Tse, and John Johnston. *The Dragon's Gift: The Sacred Arts of Bhutan.* Chicago: Serindia Publications, 2008.

BBC News. "Country Profile: Bhutan." <http://news.bbc.co.uk/2/hi/south_asia/country_profiles/1166513.stm>.

Bhutan Portal. "National Portal of Bhutan"." <http://www.bhutan.gov.bt/government/index_new.php>

Centre for Bhutan Studies. "Home." <http://www.bhutanstudies.org.bt/main/index.php>

Frontline. "Bhutan—The Last Place." May 2002. PBS. <http://www.pbs.org/frontlineworld/stories/bhutan/thestory.html>.

Grange, Kevin. *Beneath Blossom Rain: Discovering Bhutan on the Toughest Trek in the World.* Lincoln, NE: University of Nebraska Press, 2011.

Jigs-med-qe-sar-mam … King of Bhutan. *Bhutan: Through the Lens of the King.* New Delhi: Lustre Press, 2012.

Lonely Planet and Lindsay Brown. *Bhutan.* Oakland, CA: Lonely Planet, 2014.

National Museum of Bhutan. "About the National Museum." <http://www.nationalmuseum.gov.bt/about-national-museum.html>.

Wangchuck, Ashi Dorji Wangmo. *Treasures of the Thunder Dragon: A Portrait of Bhutan.* New York: Penguin, 2006.

Zeppa, Jaime. *Beyond the Sky and Earth: A Journey into Bhutan.* Boston: Riverhead Books, 2000.

Works Cited

ACCU. "Bhutan: Country Profile." Asia-Pacific Database on Intangible Cultural Heritage. Asia/Pacific Cultural

Centre for UNESCO. <http://www.accu.or.jp/ich/en/policies/C_BTN.html>.

Ahsan, Syede Aziz-al and Bhumitra Chakma. "Bhutan's Foreign Policy: Cautious Self-Assertion?" *Asian Survey*. 33.11(1993): 1043-1054.

Amnesty International. "Bhutan: Ten Years Later and Still Waiting to Go Home". *AI Index*: ASA14/001/2002 (2002): 1-13.

BBC News. "Country Profile: Bhutan." 12 April 2008. 19 June 2008 <http://news.bbc.co.uk/2/hi/south_asia/country_profiles/1166513.stm>.

Brown, Lindsay, et al. "Bhutan". Oakland CA: Lonely Planet, 2007

Bhutanese Broadcasting Service. "History of BBS." 2007. <www.bbs.com.bt/BBS-history.htm>.

Bhutan News Online. "Bhutan-China Relations." 5 July 2004. <http://www.bhutannewsonline.com/bhutan_china.html>.

Bhutan News Online. "Festivals (Tsechus) of Bhutan." 21 January 2005. <http://www.bhutannewsonline.com/festival.html>.

Bhutan Observer. "About Us." 2008. <http://www.bhutanobserver.bt/about>.

Bhutan Observer. "The Magic of the Wooden Phallus." <http://www.bhutanobserver.bt/2008/citizen-news/05/the-magic-of-the-wooden-phallus.html>.

Bhutan Portal. "News in Detail: A Promise of Hope." 19 March 2008. 18 June 2008 <http://www.bhutan.gov.bt/government/newsDetail.php?id=475%20&%20cat=2>.

Bhutan Portal. "News in Detail: Photo exhibition to celebrate 100 years of Monarchy opens." 2 June 2008. Government of Bhutan. 18 June 2008 <http://www.bhutan.gov.bt/government/newsDetail.php?id=645>.

Bowman, John S. "Columbia Chronologies of Asian History and Culture." New York: Columbia University Press, 2000.

Choki Traditional Art School. "CTAS: Background (How it Started)." 2004. 16 June 2008 <http://www.chokischool.com/background.htm>.

Conserve Nature. "Family Life." <http://www.conservenature.org/bhutan/family_life.htm>.

Craft Revival Trust. "National Institute for Zorig Chusum (Traditional Arts and Crafts)." 18 June 2008 <http://www.craftrevival.org/detailsNgos.asp?CountryCode=Bhutan&NgosCode=002197>.

Frontline. "Bhutan--The Last Place." May 2002. *PBS*. <http://www.pbs.org/frontlineworld/stories/bhutan/thestory.html>.

Helliwell, B.O., and Kim Smith "View from Bhutan: In Bhutan, Life and Architecture Have Changed Little for the Last Four Centuries." The *Architectural Review* 214 (2003)

Kinga, Sonam. "The Attributes and Values of Folk and Popular Songs." *Journal of Bhutan Studies*. 3 (2001) 16 June 2008 <http://www.digitalhimalaya.com/collections/journals/jbs/pdf/JBS_03_01_05.pdf>.

Kingdom of Bhutan. "Convention on the Elimination of All Forms of Discrimination against Women." 2003. <http://www.pc.gov.bt/publications/rep/ceafdawr.pdf>.

Kuensel Newspaper. "Kuensel Online." <http://www.kuenselonline.com/index.php>.

Lawson, Alastair. "Bhutan's Growing Cannabis Problem." *BBC News* 30 May 2002. 17 June 2008 <http://news.bbc.co.uk/2/hi/south_asia/2016895.stm>.

Lhundup, Shera. "The Genesis of Environmental Ethics and Sustaining its Heritage in the Kingdom of Bhutan." *Georgetown International Environmental Law Review* 14.4 (2002): 693-739.

McDonald, Ross. "Television, Materialism and Culture: An Exploration of Imported Media and its Implications for GNH." *Journal of Bhutan Studies*. 11 (2004) 18 June 2008 <http://www.bhutanstudies.org.bt/admin/pubFiles/v11-4.pdf>.

Ministry of Foreign Affairs. "Multilateral Relations." Royal Government of Bhutan. 17 June 2008 <http://www.mfa.gov.bt/index.php?categoryid=83>.

National Library of Bhutan. "National Literary Survey." 2008. 15 June 2008 <http://www.library.gov.bt/IT/survey.html>.

National Museum of Bhutan. "About the National Museum." 18 June 2008 <http://www.nationalmuseum.gov.bt/about-national-museum.html>.

Nestroy, Harald. "Bhutan: The Himalayan Buddhist Kingdom." *Asian Affairs*. 35.3 (2004):

Nock, David. "The Architecture of Bhutan." *Architectural Review* 198 (1995): 78.

NWAB. "National Women's Association of Bhutan." 2006. 16 June 2008 <http://www.nwabbhutan.org.bt>.

Osiro, Joleen. "Bhutan's Sacred Treasures." *Star Bulletin* 13.53. 22 February 2008. 16 June 2008 <http://starbulletin.com/2008/02/22/features/story02.html>.

Pelden, Sonam. "Is Eating Meat Un-Buddhist"?" *Kuensel Newspaper* 16 August 2007. 21 June 2008

Pommaret, Françoise. "Dances in Bhutan: A Traditional Medium of Information." *Journal of Bhutan Studies*. 17 (2006) <http://www.bhutanstudies.org.bt/admin/pubFiles/14-4.pdf>.

RENEW. "RENEW- Respect, Educate, Nurture, and Empower Women." 17 June 2008. <www.renew.org.bt>.

Rinpoche, Jangtrul. "Q&A with HH Jangtrul Y Rinpoche." *Kuensel*. 16 June 2008. 17 June 2008 <http://www.kuenselonline.com/modules.php?name=News&file=article&sid=10579>.

Sharma, Chandra Shekhar. "Echoes of Folksongs in Bhutanese Literature in English." *Journal of Bhutan Studies*. 15 (2006). <http://www.bhutanstudies.org.bt/admin/pubFiles/15-5.pdf>.

Smithsonian Folklife Festival. "Zorig Chusum." Bhutan: Land of the Thunder Dragon. 2008. 15 June 2008

<http://www.folklife.si.edu/festival/2008/Bhutan/Zorig_Chusum.html>.

Sociology Index. "Social Customs and Traditions in Bhutan." 2008. <http://sociologyindex.com/social_customs_and_traditions_bhutan.htm>.

Tiwara, Chitra. "Bhutan Refugees Remain in Limbo; Thimphu Halts Talks with Nepal on Repatriation." *Washington Times*. 16 August 2003

UNDP Bhutan. "Supporting Women in Bhutan by Mainstreaming Gender." September 2007. 18 June 2008 <http://www.undp.org.bt/gender/msgender_fs.pdf>.

U.S. Department of State. "Country Reports on Human Rights Practiccs." March 6 2007. <http://www.state.gov/g/drl/rls/hrrpt/2006/78870.htm>.

U.S. Department of State. "Background Note: Bhutan." March 2008. <http://www.state.gov/r/pa/ei/bgn/35839.htm>.

U.S. Library of Congress. "Marriage and Family Life." Bhutan: A Country Study. 1991. 19 June 2008 <http://countrystudies.us/bhutan/22.htm>.

World Bank, "Conserving Bhutan's Natural Heritage through a Trust Fund." 2008. <http://web.worldbank.org/WBSITE/EXTERNAL/COUNTRIES/SOUTHASIAEXT/BHUTANEXTN/0,,contentMDK:20208772~pagePK:141137~piPK:141127~theSitePK:306149,00.html>.

WWF Bhutan. "Introduction & Background to WWF Bhutan." <http://www.wwfbhutan.org.bt/wwfbhutanbackground.htm>.

Young, Lincoln. "Agricultural Changes in Bhutan: Some Environmental Questions". *The Geographic Journal* 157.2 (1991)

Zurick, David. "National Happiness and Environmental Status in Bhutan". *The Geographical Revue* 96.4 (2007): 657-681.

Amritsar, India/Stock photo © MasterLu

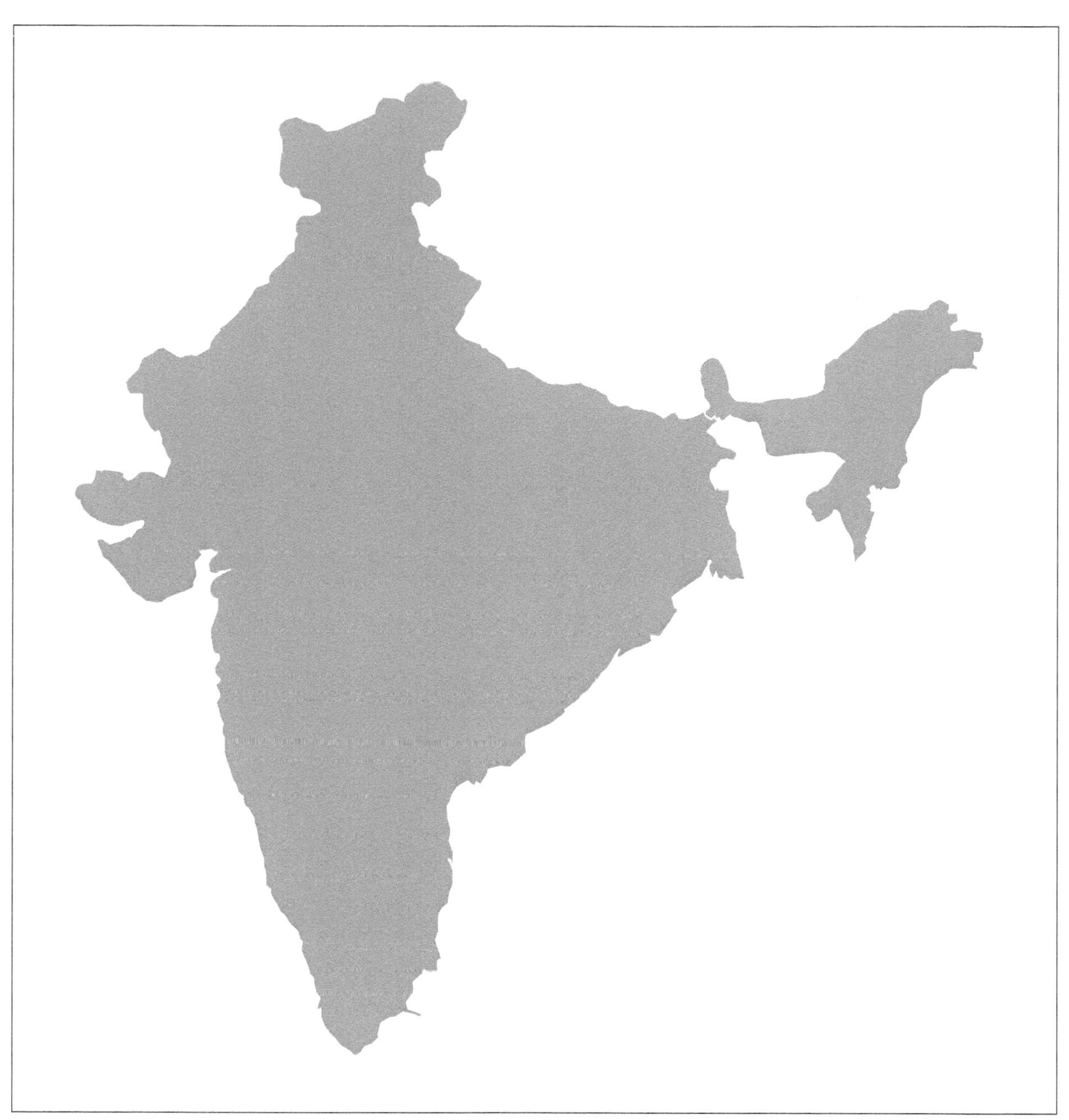

India

Introduction

India dominates the South Asian subcontinent both in geographical size and population density. With the second largest population in the world, India is home to over one billion people. India borders several other Asian countries including Bangladesh, Bhutan, Burma, China, Nepal, and Pakistan. India also ranks as the second-fastest growing economy in the world.

India is well known for its rich, vibrant culture, especially its music and dance. Indian classical music can be divided into two different groups: the Carnatic form, originating in southern India, and the Hindustani form from the north. There are also many different styles of Indian dance, many of which follow the storyline of Indian epics, such as the *Mahabharata*, one of the primary texts of Hinduism (and considered one of the longest literary works in the world), and the Hindu epic the *Ramayana*, written circa 250 BCE. These epics are derived from the oral tradition, which has greatly influenced Indian literature. India also produces more motion pictures each year than anywhere else in the world.

GENERAL INFORMATION

Official Language(s): Hindi, English, and twenty-two other recognized national languages
Population: 1.23 billion (2014 estimate)
Currency: Indian rupee
Coins: The Indian rupee is subdivided into 100 paise, and coin denominations include 1, 2, 5, 10, 20, 25, and 50 paise, and 1, 2, 5, and 10 rupees; however, only 1, 2, and 5 rupees are frequently used.
Land Area: 2,973,193 square kilometers (1,147,956 square miles)
Water Area: 314,070 square kilometers (121,263 square miles)
National Motto: "Satyameva Jayate" ("Truth Alone Triumphs")
National Anthem: "Jan Gana Mana" ("Thou Art the Ruler of the Minds of All People")
Capital: New Delhi
Time Zone: GMT +5:30
Flag Description: The flag of India features three horizontal bands of color: saffron (top), which represents sacrifice and courage; white (middle), which represents purity; and green (bottom), which represents faith. In the center of the white band is a blue chakra, a wheel with twenty-four spokes that is meant to symbolize the wheel of life and death.

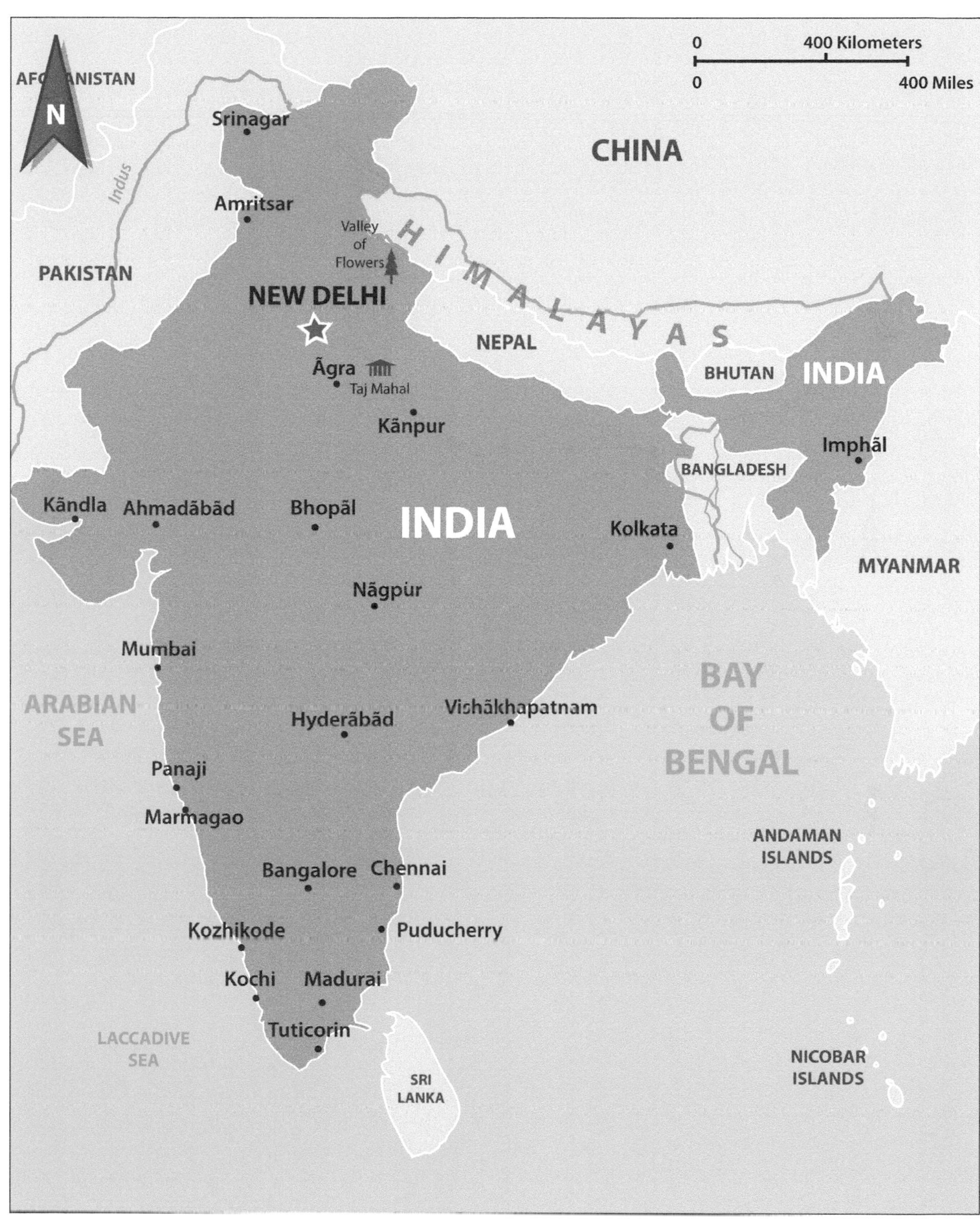

0 400 Kilometers
0 400 Miles
AFGHANISTAN
N
Srinagar
CHINA
Indus
Amritsar
Valley of Flowers
HIMALAYAS
PAKISTAN
NEW DELHI
NEPAL
Āgra
Taj Mahal
BHUTAN
INDIA
Kānpur
Imphāl
BANGLADESH
Kāndla
Ahmadābād
Bhopāl
INDIA
Kolkata
MYANMAR
Nāgpur
Mumbai
BAY OF BENGAL
ARABIAN SEA
Hyderābād
Vishākhapatnam
Panaji
Marmagao
ANDAMAN ISLANDS
Bangalore
Chennai
Kozhikode
Puducherry
Kochi
Madurai
Tuticorin
LACCADIVE SEA
SRI LANKA
NICOBAR ISLANDS

Principal Cities by Population (2012):

- Greater Mumbai (14,300,000)
- Delhi (11,300,000)
- Bangalore (6,400,000)
- Hyderabad (5,742,036)
- Chennai (4,700,000)
- Kolkata (4,500,000)
- Hyderabad (3,900,000)
- Pune (3,700,000)
- Jaipur (3,400,000)
- Kanpur (3,200,000)

Population

The majority of Indian people live outside of large cities. About 70 percent of the population resides in rural areas, while 31 percent lives in urban areas (2011). As of 2014, the country's population growth rate was 1.25 percent. The majority of the population—an estimated 72 percent—is of the Indo-Aryan ethnicity, while those of Dravidian descent account for a quarter of the population.

According to a 2010 report from the McKinsey Global Institute, an economics research group, at least 68 Indian cities will have a population exceeding one million by 2030, with six cities having a population of more than 10 million. Greater Mumbai had a population total of 14.3 million per the 2012 census, and had an unofficial population total of nearly 20 million in 2010. Additionally, the population of the Delhi metropolitan area is estimated at more than 17 million (2010); with a population density of 11,200 persons per square kilometer (29,000 per square mile), it is among the most crowded cities in the world. Other cities, such as Chennai, have shown tremendous population growth since the 2001 census.

Approximately 45 percent of the total population of India lives in the following five states: Bihar, Orissa, Madhya Pradesh, Rajasthan, and Uttar Pradesh. The state with the highest population density is West Bengal. Other states with high population densities include Haryana, Kerala, Bihar, Punjab, and Tamil Nadu.

Languages

There are as many as 1,652 languages and dialects spoken in India. The official language in India is Hindi (in the Devanagari script). However, other tongues are approved by the central government as co-official languages.

Hindi is the primary language for about 18 percent of Indian people, though it is spoken and understood by a much larger percentage of the population. Individual states are allowed to designate their own regional languages. The most prevalent of the official languages are Bengali, Telugu, Marathi, Tamil, Urdu, Gujarati, Malayalam, Kannada, Oriya, Punjabi, Assamese, Kashmiri, and Sindhi.

English is also an important language in the country and, along with Hindi, is the official language of communication for the national government. It is also important in commercial correspondence. Though there have been efforts to decrease the use of English for official business, this has been unpopular in regions with small Hindi-speaking populations.

Native People & Ethnic Groups

The original population of India can be traced back 9,000 years to settlements in the Indus Valley. The Indus people developed a sophisticated culture with a complex language, as well as systems of trade and architecture. Their civilization reached its pinnacle between 2600 and 1900 BCE.

The Aryans invaded India around 1500 BCE, and it is believed by some scholars that Aryans introduced Sanskrit and the caste system to the region, before eventually moving to Northern India. Today, nearly three-quarters of the population of India are of Indo-Aryan descent.

Religions

Religion is very important in India, and the various religions practiced throughout the country add to its diversity. Hinduism is the most popular, and is practiced by nearly 81 percent of the population. However, the religion itself can take many different regional forms. It is speculated that Hinduism is the oldest of the major religions, and that it is the result of interaction between Vedic (or Early Aryan) culture and non-Aryan cultures in the Indus region thousands of years ago. India also has the world's second-largest populations of Muslims, who make up 13.4 percent of the population (2001). Other religious groups include Christians, Sikhs, and Buddhists.

Climate

India has three major seasons. Lasting from March to June, summers in India are very hot in every region of the country. Winter lasts from November to February. Most of the rainfall occurs during the monsoon season between July and October. Natural hazards in India include flash floods, severe thunderstorms, and earthquakes.

New Delhi's climate is notable for its oppressively hot summers. Temperatures in May, June, and July regularly climb as high as 45° Celsius (113° Fahrenheit). The heat does not significantly subside until October. The spring and summer also subject the city to violent dust storms and hot, dry winds called loo. The monsoon brings some relief when it arrives at the beginning of July. The rainy season lasts through September, bringing with it most of Delhi's annual rainfall.

ENVIRONMENT & GEOGRAPHY

Topography

India is the seventh largest country in the world. With a total area of 3,287,590 square kilometers (1,269,346 square miles), India has 2,973,193 square kilometers (1,147,956 square miles) of land. India can be divided into three major geographical regions: the mountains of the Himalayas in the north, the Indo-Gangetic Plain, and the southern peninsula of the Deccan Plateau.

The Himalayas, the highest mountain range in the world, are in the northern part of India. In the south, there are plateaus, tropical rain forests, and deserts. The most fertile soil is found in the Indo-Gangetic Plain, where the three main rivers of India (the Ganges, Brahmaputra, and the Indus) form basins. Other important rivers are the Godavari, Krishna, and Mahanadi. The Arabian Sea, the Indian Ocean, and the Bay of Bengal all lie off the coast of India.

The highest point in India is Kanchenjunga ("five treasures of the snow"), on the border with Nepal, at 8,598 meters (28,209 feet). It is the third highest mountain in the world. New Delhi, the capital, is strategically situated on the plains of northern India, where the Ganges and Indus river valleys meet. The Delhi urban area sits on both banks of the Yamuna River and covers about 1,500 square kilometers (585 square miles). The division of New Delhi and historical Old Delhi reflects the era of British imperial rule in India. In 1912, the British moved the capital from Calcutta (anglicized name for Kolkata) to Delhi, building the section of the city that would become New Delhi, just south of the existing Old City.

Plants & Animals

Animal life in India is exotic and varied; in fact, the country accounts for over 7 percent of the world's total fauna. The national animal is the Bengali tiger, which is increasingly threatened by local hunters and encroachments upon its habitat. Other common wild animals in India include the single-horned rhino, Asian elephant, lion, and wild buffalo, as well as small cats, deer, monkeys, and wild goats.

More than 1,200 species of birds are found in India, including purple herons, stork-billed kingfishers, gray-headed fish-eagles, crested hawk-eagles, and jungle fowl. There are also hundreds of species of reptiles, including the king cobra, and 30,000 different species of insects.

In terms of plant life, there are 45,000 different species of plants and shrubs in India. Some native flowers include orchids, rhododendrons, musk rose (Rosa moschata), begonia, balsam (Impatiens balsamina), and globe amaranth (Gomphrena globosa).

CUSTOMS & COURTESIES

Greetings

The traditional Indian greeting, largely practiced by Hindus, is "Namaste." During this traditional greeting, the palms are placed facing each other and the head is bowed slightly. The literal meaning of the word in Sanskrit is "I see the Self in you." Physical contact between unrelated men and women is a social taboo, and shaking hands, especially among older people, is rare. However, in urban areas exposed to Western business culture, a handshake is considered appropriate, even between the sexes. Socially, younger people are commonly greeting each other with a casual "Hello."

In rural areas and in more traditional urban families in the north, young people greet older family members by touching their feet, signifying that they are asking for their blessings. In the south, young people touch the feet of elders when bidding goodbye.

Among Muslims, the traditional greeting is the phrase "As-salamu alaykum" ("Peace to you"), to which the answer is "Alaykum salaam" ("And on you be peace"). Traditionally, Sikhs greet each other with the words "Sat sri akaal" ("Be blessed who speaks truth to God"), though this is gradually being replaced by a casual "Hello" among urban youth.

Gestures & Etiquette

Subtle body language signals are reflective of the Indian custom of public modesty. In addition, etiquette in Indian culture strongly emphasizes an aversion to aggressive gestures in social situations. For example, it is considered impolite to say "No" outright, and people will spend considerable time trying to convey a refusal in indirect ways. Indians also have a unique movement whereby the head is rotated from side to side. Depending on the situation, this gesture could have several meanings. Also, it is considered rude to point fingers, and directions are noted by motioning with the chin. Beckoning is done by laying the palm downward and moving the fingers inward.

The concept of "personal space" is not given much weight in Indian society. Strangers will think nothing of playfully pinching a baby's cheek, which could be seen as intrusive in some other cultures. Similarly, Indians will ask questions that others might consider overly personal. However, this is commonly done in order to situate a foreigner or stranger within a socioeconomic construct and it is best to answer such questions lightly and in good humor.

Certain body parts are commonly considered unclean in Indian culture. For example, it is considered rude to have the soles of one's feet facing another person. Similarly, touching a book or paper with one's feet is seen as denigrating learning and knowledge. It is unacceptable to use the left hand to eat, as it is considered unclean. This is consistent with Muslim culture, in which the left hand is designated as the hand used to cleanse the body.

Hospitality is a cherished element of Indian culture. Often, this is expressed through food. Foreigners, in particular, are often the recipients of warmth and hospitality that can seem overwhelming at times. Even on the briefest of visits, guests will be pressed to have something to drink, commonly tea. While it is considered acceptable to refuse the first offer of food or drink, it should be accepted on the second or third offer. Hospitality is almost a religious tenet, as demonstrated by the saying "Athithi devo bhavo," meaning "The guest is God."

Additionally, modesty in dress is well received, especially in places of worship. Age is also given much respect and deference. It is rare to address an older person by their first name. A respectful honorific or title is always used in all regions of the country, and in all situations. In business circles, it is polite to refer to an older acquaintance using the titles "Mr." or "Mrs." unless specifically asked not to do so by the person concerned.

Eating/Meals

The main meal of the day is dinner, which can be served as late as eight o'clock in the evening, or even later. The whole family typically sits together for dinner, which can consist of six or seven dishes standard to the regional cuisine. However, with greater exposure to international cuisines, many urban families cook international foods at home. Generally, freshly cooked food is still the norm in the majority of households in the country, though ready-to-eat processed foods are making inroads with busy urban professionals.

Assimilation of foreign culinary influences is a significant part of the Indian diet. "Indian Chinese" is a type of Chinese food that incorporates ingredients such as paneer (cottage cheese) and chili powder into traditional Chinese cuisine. In addition, as more women begin to work outside the home, the concept of "eating out" has gained popularity. People are willing to experiment with other cuisines so long as it conforms to their religious dietary restrictions. For example, since beef is taboo among Hindus, India is the only country in the world where McDonald's restaurants use lamb rather than beef.

India is also the world's largest producer of chai (tea), and it is commonly consumed throughout the day. Sweets are a nationwide favorite. They are usually milk-based, with a wide variety of flavorings including saffron, cardamom, cashew, pistachios, and nutmeg.

Visiting

Indians do not customarily give gifts when visiting each other. When invited for dinner, it is normal to arrive fifteen or thirty minutes later than expected. People customarily remove their shoes at the entrance to the home. However, many urban households would not expect a visitor to remove his or her shoes. It is customary that all children in the house, regardless of age, be introduced to the visitor and bid farewell at the end of the visit.

A guest specifically invited for a meal would be served at least six or seven dishes. It is preferable to inform the host of any dietary preferences (such as non-spicy food, for instance) rather than refuse food while at their table. Food that is refused or left uneaten signifies that the guest is unsatisfied, an important issue for a culture that places an almost ritual value on food and hospitality. Furthermore, even if the host family is eating with their fingers, a non–Indian visitor will be offered a fork or spoon. It is not impolite to accept the offer. Indians appreciate others trying to partake of their cultural mores, but not if it causes discomfort to the guest.

LIFESTYLE

Family

Until a few decades ago, family life in India was characterized by the joint family system, wherein the sons, unmarried daughters, and widowed relatives of the oldest male member of the family lived under the same roof. The different generations shared a kitchen, religious practices, and finances. This centuries-old social system also ensured a built-in support system for elderly members of the family. However, with younger generations moving to the cities in search of job opportunities, the joint family system is disintegrating and being replaced by nuclear families (typically a mother, father, and two children) in the urban areas. Despite this trend, it is still generally expected that the oldest son will be responsible for supporting elderly parents.

Housing

With economic growth and the rise of urbanization, India's metro areas are witnessing a growth in high-rise apartment complexes, typically constructed using steel and cement. Independent single-family homes are also being replaced by apartment buildings at a rapid pace. At the same time, migrant populations in the large cities often live in slums consisting of flimsy structures made from plastic and other waste materials.

Rural housing in India has historically made use of environmentally friendly and locally available materials, including stone, mud, and brick. However, with the modernizing influence of the cities, more people are opting to use cement and steel in rural areas as well. Many poorer rural inhabitants live in houses that use cheaper materials like straw or grass for thatched roofs and mud for the walls.

Food

Indian food consists of numerous regional cuisines and hundreds of variations unique to different ethnic communities. It can, however, be broadly categorized into two main culinary traditions: North Indian and South Indian.

North Indian food centers on wheat, which is the main crop grown in that part of the country. The staple food is the roti, which is unleavened whole wheat flat bread cooked on an iron griddle. A typical meal consists of rotis accompanied by a daal (lentil curry), one or two vegetables, yogurt, and a salad consisting of onions, tomatoes, and green chilies. More elaborate North Indian fare such as tandoori meats (a tandoor is a clay oven) and naans (leavened breads) are usually found in restaurants rather than in homes, and are reflective of the region's Mughal heritage.

South Indian food is dominated by rice, the principal crop in that tropical region. The distinctive foods of this cuisine are idli (rice pancakes made from a fermented batter of rice and split peas) and masala dosa (thin crepes made from a variation of the same batter, with a spicy potato filling).

All Indian food, however, is characterized by the liberal use of spices, herbs, and condiments as flavoring agents. These include turmeric, chilies, coriander, cumin, ginger, garlic and mustard seeds. These spices are used in most Indian kitchens. In addition, relishes (known as chutneys) and spicy pickles are an integral part of both cuisines. The meats most widely eaten are chicken or lamb and goat, while fish is popular in the coastal areas in the east and south.

Life's Milestones

Different ethnic communities in India place varying importance on ceremonial rituals. Generally, a naming ceremony is held for the newborn soon after birth. Shortly after that, the child's first solid food (usually rice) is celebrated.

Weddings are usually three-or-four day extravaganzas, full of color and ceremony. Celebrating a daughter's wedding in grand style is one of the last things a father will do for his daughter before she moves away to her husband's family. Often, parents will opt to accumulate debt rather than scale down marriage festivities.

In the seventh month of pregnancy, a small ceremony is held for the well-being of the child and mother. Unlike at baby showers in other cultures, no presents are given to the expectant mother at this time, except the gift of a sari and jewelry by the pregnant woman's mother-in-law.

Given the country's historically low life expectancy, the occasion of a sixtieth birthday was celebrated in temples with special pujas (services). However, that practice has been declining as many Indians are living longer. The Hindus cremate their dead often with elaborate ceremonies that traditionally involve wooden pyres. Muslims and Christians in India bury their dead.

CULTURAL HISTORY

Art

The arts have flourished in India throughout its history, dating back to the ancient cave paintings, rock carvings, and excavated painted ceramics of the Indus Valley Civilization (3000–1500 BCE). In particular, India has a rich tradition of hand-woven and embroidered textiles. The temple town of Kanchipuram is famous for its silk saris (a garment worn by Indian women consisting of 6 yards of unstitched fabric) woven with pure gold thread. Varanasi in the north is famous for its silk brocade work. Other traditional Indian arts include sculpture, heavily influenced by Hinduism and Buddhism, and rangoli, a decorative form of sandpainting.

Painting in India has historically been associated with murals and miniatures. The latter were introduced to India by the Mughal Empire (1526–1858), and were often painted on cloth and manuscripts. Many different schools and styles of painting have developed, often varying by region or kingdoms. These different schools of painting are characterized by their themes (commonly, depictions of love, religion symbolism or pastoral life), their use of colors (many styles featured striking primary colors such as red, green, and yellow) and the depiction of facial features. One of the most important styles was the Mughal school of painting, introduced by the Mughals and heavily influenced by Islamic art. Other well-known schools of painting in India include the Deccan, Kangra, and Rajput schools, all known for their miniature paintings and vivid, sophisticated styles.

Modern art began to fully emerge in India during the 20th century with the Bengal school of painting. This style of painting was heavily influenced by European painters and is often associated with Indian nationalism. Renowned painters from this school include Raja Ravi Verma (1848–1906), known for his realistic depictions of mythology and his blending of modern and classic Indian traditions. Rabindranath Tagore (1861–1941) is often considered the father of modern Indian art. Tagore was also an esteemed poet and writer, and received the Nobel Prize in Literature in 1913.

Architecture

Like Indian painting, Indian architecture can be classified into various schools and styles based on region and kingdom. The first prevailing styles were the religious architecture of Buddhism, Jainism, and Hinduism, still preserved in India's ancient shrines and temples. These styles soon gave way to the influence of Islamic and Mughal architecture, which included the elaborate designs of mosques, the incorporation of courtyards, and the use of domes and arches. Under colonial rule, Indian architecture developed distinct European influences. These can be seen in the tree-lined streets and British colonial architecture of New Delhi.

A unique element of traditional Indian architecture is the concept of vaastu—a term that refers to the codification of scientific and aesthetic principles used while designing a building. It was believed that adhering to these principles would ensure the harmony of the physical and spiritual environment, and bring peace, health, and prosperity to the inhabitants of the building. Vaastu is particularly popular among the middle class in India, and is equivalent to the ancient Chinese discipline of feng shui.

Different regions have their own unique architectural features. The havelis, or houses, of rich Rajasthani (typically, indigenous to Rajasthan, India's largest state) merchants in the 19th and 20th centuries featured intricate wooden balconies. Many Hindu houses across India had a central courtyard. Often, these courtyards featured a sacred tulsi (basil) plant, which was a focal point for daily worship. However, with single-family houses being replaced by apartment buildings, many of these features are rapidly vanishing from the Indian landscape

Drama

Cinema has a special place in culture of India, and an estimated 14 million people attend the movies everyday. Post-independence India saw the release of several critically acclaimed and commercially successful films that tackled controversial social themes. Some significant films are *Devdas* (which was released in several versions), which deals with arranged marriage; *Achut Kanya* (1936), which addresses the caste system, and *Do Bigha Zamin* (1953), which dealt with themes of rural poverty, oppression, and socialism. The well-known directors of this genre include V. Shantaram (1901–1990), Guru Dutt (1925–1964), and Satyajit Ray (1921–1992).

The 1960s saw a trend toward making populist films that revolved around spectacular song and dance sequences. Even today, Bollywood (the Hindi film industry) is known for its big budget musical extravaganzas. These films have an audience in India and throughout the Indian diaspora, including the United Kingdom, the United States and South Africa. Prominent figures of contemporary Indian cinema include Amitabh Bachchan (1942–) and Aishwarya Rai (1973–). In addition, popular Indian music is overwhelmingly associated with songs from popular cinema. For example, Lata Mangeshkar (1929) and her sister, Asha Bhonsle (1933–), launched their highly successful, decades-spanning careers as playback singers, singing prerecorded cinematic music.

Music & Dance

The classical origins of Indian music can be dated back to 1500 BCE with the chanting of Vedic hymns. Music in India would evolve into strong traditions of spiritually inspired folk music, pioneered by wandering poet-saints in medieval times such as Mirabai (1487–1547) and Tulsidas (1532–1623). These compositions, which have become mainstays of contemporary popular worship, were composed in vernacular languages in order to appeal to a wider audience.

With the establishment of Mughal rule in the north, Indian classical music diverged into the North Indian (Hindustani) and South Indian (Carnatic) systems. The Mughals were generous patrons of the arts, and brought with them the Persian and Islamic influences that characterize Hindustani music. Carnatic music also absorbed outside influences, such as the violin, which was introduced to India by the British.

The *Natyashastra* ("Treatise on Dramatic Arts") is considered the world's oldest surviving text on the dramatic arts. It is the basis of traditional Indian artistic expression. Historically, classical dance in India was associated with Hindu temples, as both the themes (such as divine love) and performance spaces (the temple) were religious in nature. The oldest dance form is called Bharatanatyam, which was performed by Hindu women known as devadasis, who were charged with the care of the temple.

With the influence of Victorian morality during British colonial rule, middle class families did not take up Bharatanatyam. This was because the devadasis were considered prostitutes, as they depended on male patrons for their livelihood. Dance revivalist Rukmini Devi Arundale (1904–1986), a famous dancer born into an upper class family of Madras, was largely responsible for restoring respectability to this classical dance.

The predominant dance in North India is Kathak. The advent of Mughal culture and patronage in the 16th century meant that Kathak absorbed Persian influences. It became a more secular dance—performed in royal courts and small gatherings—with an emphasis on rhythmic footwork. In addition, the traditional Indian dance of Kathakali is an ancient dance form known for its dramatic facial makeup, costumes, and stylized eye movements. Other major dances that are rooted in an ancient classical regional tradition include Odissi, Kuchipudi, and Manipuri.

Literature

India has a rich history of literature spanning both classical Sanskrit—one of the two classical Indian languages, the other being Tamil—and other vernacular languages. India's early literature can be traced to the oral tradition of Vedic chanting, dating from 1500 BCE. (The Vedas are Hindu religious texts written by Aryan migrants dating from that time.) Famous literary works of ancient India include the epics *Ramayana*, composed by Sage Valmiki circa 400 BCE, and Vyaasa's *Mahabharata*, attributed to Vyasa, a revered figure in Hindu tradition. The most famous Sanskrit poet/playwright is Kālidāsa, the equivalent of Shakespeare in Sanskrit. He wrote the epics *Shakuntala* and *Meghadutta* during the golden age of the Gupta Dynasty (320–550 CE). The *Kamasutra* ("Manual on Love") was also written during this period.

The latter half of the 20th century saw the growth of Indian authors writing in English and reaching a wide international audience. The Indian-born author Salman Rushdie (1947–) helped pioneer the genre of magic realism in his acclaimed second novel *Midnight's Children*. The setting, themes, and characters were Indian, and Indian words were used liberally throughout the text. Other notable modern authors of Indian origin include Arundhati Roy (1961–), Kiran Desai (1971–), and V. S. Naipaul (1932–), who won the Nobel Prize in Literature in 2001.

CULTURE

Arts & Entertainment

Historically, the arts in India were an anonymous endeavor carried out for royal patrons. In fact, few historical works can be ascribed to individual artists. Unlike the celebrated artists of the Italian Renaissance, little is known about the miniaturists of the Mughal or Kangra schools of painting or the bronze sculptors of the Chola Dynasty. This tradition continued until the 20th century, when individualism began to be celebrated.

The opening up of the Indian economy in the 1990s has been the single greatest influence on the trajectory of the arts in the country. The loosening of currency restrictions and import laws has facilitated international commercial dealings in art. Moreover, the influx of foreign media channels has meant greater exposure to global trends. As such, artists are no longer dependent on government support as there is a vast and easily accessible private market for art.

One by-product of economic liberalization has been the rise of contemporary Indian art. Driven by more financial resources and prominent and numerous buyer networks, Indian art has gained an increasingly higher profile both domestically and internationally. As a result, collecting traditional Indian art has become a status symbol or a sound financial investment. In fact, several prominent auction houses established a presence in India in the 1990s, and Indian painters have even achieved celebrity.

However, censorship remains a grey area, and is applied on a case-by-case basis by government. Usually, a work is censored because it offends the sentiments of a particular community. One high profile example is the banning of Salman Rushdie's book *Midnight's Children*, on the grounds that it might be offensive to the Muslim minority. Similarly, there was an outcry from Hindu groups when leading painter M. F. Hussein (1915–2011) depicted Hindu goddesses in what were termed vulgar and insulting images.

The multi-billion-dollar Hindi and regional language film industries have had the most pervasive influence on contemporary Indian society and popular culture. Indians have always been keen followers of film and cinematic music. It was the cheapest and most accessible form of mass entertainment for generations, and had an outsized role in the landscape of popular culture. That influence is now magnified by the newly open Indian economy and the changing economic and social demographic it has created.

A newly prosperous, confident, and numerically significant youth population takes its cultural cues from the movies. These films don't just mirror society and trends—in many cases, they initiate these trends. This includes the influence on popular music, fashion, and dance. Even the storylines have become progressively bolder, and have made Western ideas such as dating and love marriages (as opposed to arranged intra-caste marriages) more commonplace and acceptable.

Similar to movies, the privatization of television channels and the influx of foreign channels such as MTV have also contributed to the Westernization of urban culture in the 21st century. This assimilation in the arts is taking place almost exclusively at the level of popular youth culture.

India's national sport is field hockey. Other popular sports are cricket and football (soccer). Some games that originated in India include the team sport Kabaddi, and gilli-danda, which involves hitting a small piece of wood with a stick.

Cultural Sites & Landmarks

With its rich heritage and multitude of ethnicities, India has a wealth of cultural sites and landmarks. In fact, the country is home to twenty-eight World Heritage Sites as designated by United Nations Educational, Scientific and Cultural Organization (UNESCO), a specialized agency of the UN promoting international culture. Some of the most famous of these protected sites include ancient rock-cut caves, Buddhist monuments, ancient temples, and several national parks and wildlife sanctuaries.

Perhaps the most famous monument in India is the Taj Mahal. This marble mausoleum, built by the Mughal Emperor Shah Jahan (1592–1666) in memory of his wife, is considered one of the wonders of the world. It took 20,000 workers over 22 years to build. Popular Indian lore even states that the emperor cut off the chief mason's hand so he could not replicate this building anywhere else. The beauty of the Taj Mahal is accentuated as its white marble takes on different hues throughout the day and night.

The construction of large-scale monuments in India dates back to the reign of Emperor Ashoka in the second century BCE. The sanctuary at Sanchi was a major center of Buddhist life in India. It features the Great Stupa, a ceremonial structure containing the relics of Buddha. Another significant Buddhist landmark is the Ajanta caves built during the Gupta Age. These man-made caves feature stunning rock-cut architecture. Inside, the walls are covered with magnificent murals depicting scenes from the life of the Buddha.

The 8th to the 12th centuries CE saw the flowering of Hindu temple architecture in South India under a series of powerful dynasties. The Pallava kings, who rose to power between the 6th and 9th centuries, built temples cut from a single block of granite along the shore at Mahabalipuram. The towering Brihadeeswara temple at Thanjavur was the center of a vibrant cultural life during the Chola Dynasty. The temples at Belur and Halebid, built during the Hoysala Empire (1026–1343), feature complex floor plans and sculpted exteriors. The monumental temple complexes built during the reign of the Vijayanagara Empire (1336–1646) mark the pinnacle of South Indian temple architecture, the best examples being at Vellore and modern Hampi.

Two other important temples were built during this time. The Sun Temple in Konarak was dedicated to Surya, the sun god, who rode a chariot. The entire temple was designed as a giant chariot. The base of the temple has twelve wheels which are each three meters (nine feet) high, though it is now in ruins. In contrast, the Jagannath Temple in Puri is a living temple. It is known for its annual procession, wherein thousands of impassioned devotees pull a chariot through the city streets.

Some of the most impressive monuments in India are those built by the Muslim Mughals at the height of their power in the 16th and 17th centuries. The harmonious fusion of Indian and Islamic styles is a testament to cultural assimilation, and the huge scale of their projects is symbolic of their political confidence. The massive Red Fort in Delhi takes its name from the red sandstone used in its construction. In addition, the forts of Jodhpur and Jaisalmer of the Rajput kingdoms of the eighth through 11th centuries are popular tourist attractions.

India's many natural cultural sites include the Valley of Flowers National Park, in West Himalaya, and the Nanda Devi National Park, a vast wilderness area encircled by peaks. Both sites are designated as World Heritage Sites. Of the several national wildlife reserves, Kaziranga is famous for its population of great one-horned rhinoceroses, Ranthambore National Park is known for its tiger population and conservation efforts, and Mudhumalai in the south has a large elephant population.

Libraries & Museums

New Delhi is home to many museums dedicated to preserving India's ancient history and culture. Some of the most notable include the National Museum, which features artifacts from the full spectrum of Indian civilization dating to the prehistoric era; the National Gallery of Modern Art, which displays paintings from the mid-19th century to the present day; the Rail Transport Museum, which traces the 140-year-old history of the Indian railways; the Gandhi Memorial Museum, which is dedicated to the life of Mahatma Gandhi; the Museum of Archeology, whose collections focus on the Mughal era in Delhi's history; and the Museum of Arms and Weapons, which traces the development of weaponry from the Mughal era through the First World War.

The National Library of India is located in Kolkata, and is the largest library in the country. Other premier libraries in the country include the National Institute of Science Communication and Information Resources (NISCAIR), located at New Delhi, and the National Science Library of India, also located in the capital. The history of the national library dates back to the first half of the 19th century.

Holidays

There are many public holidays in India, though there are many regional differences in the observation and celebration of certain holidays. Festivals such as Dussera (September/October) and Diwali (October/November) may be celebrated with parades, fireworks, and other festivities. Indian Muslims, Hindus, and Christians all celebrate the major holidays of their faith. The birthdays of Sikh religious leaders Guru Nanak and Guru Gobind Singh are also widely celebrated.The secular holidays of Independence Day (August 15), Mahatma Gandhi's birthday (October 2) and Republic Day (January 26) are observed throughout India.

Youth Culture

India has one of the youngest populations in the world, with 25 as a median age. Young people are generally technologically proficient and knowledgeable consumers. With the rise of the outsourcing industry, many young people find themselves with high salaries and strong purchasing power. They in turn are driving the consumption patterns and economy of the country. Many traditional cultural systems, such as marriage and joint families, are still prevalent, despite a generational shift toward a more Western attitude.

With Hollywood movies and foreign channels easily available, Indian youth are exposed to global influences that are reflected in their changing tastes in entertainment, choice of careers, and other aspects of life. However, the local film industry—particularly the Hindi-language industry known as Bollywood (a combination of Bombay and Hollywood)—still holds sway over youth attitudes and culture. Even the pop music scene is dominated by film soundtracks. The younger generation of movie stars, such as Rani Mukherjee and Hrithik Roshan, are national idols.

SOCIETY

Transportation

All the major cities have cheap and extensive bus systems. In addition, all Indian cities have the autorickshaw, a three-wheeled vehicle unique to the country. This mode of transportation is an inexpensive alternative to taxis. Meanwhile, a rapidly growing middle class is trading up from scooters to automobiles, though this leads to more congestion on the roads. Traffic problems in larger cities such as Bengaluru have reached serious proportions. Minivans and buses remain the popular modes of travel in rural and remote areas. Automobile traffic travels on the left side of the road in India, and drivers sit on the right-hand side of the car.

Transportation Infrastructure

With the population surging over 1.1 billion in recent years, transportation issues have become paramount in India. The country's overburdened urban infrastructure often strains to keep pace with the demands of the growing economy. The major cities like Delhi, Kolkata, Chennai, and Mumbai have well utilized rail networks (the Mumbai system carries six million commuters per day). In addition, India has one of the largest rail networks in the world, carrying 14 million passengers and over one million tons of freight daily. It is heavily subsidized and a relatively reasonable means of transport for those living in rural areas.

The government opened the skies to private carriers in the late 1980s. Today, the deeply competitive airline industry is leading to cheaper fares and reaching out to an expanding market of newly prosperous middle class Indians. There are over 20 international airports located in the country.

Media & Communications

The government monopoly over television and radio was dismantled in 1992. Since then, there has been a proliferation of private cable and satellite channels and radio stations. International media companies have a large presence in India, with channels in English, Hindi, and other languages. In addition, India has one of the world's biggest cable markets, with 60 million subscribers. The government's premier channel DD1, which stretches into the rural interior, reaches 400 million viewers. India also has one of the largest radio networks in the world, All India Radio (AIR).

The print media continues to maintain an active and significant presence. There are over 5,600 daily newspapers published in over 100 languages, and the daily circulation of newspapers and periodicals is roughly 60 million. Both vernacular and English-language dailies continue to remain influential within India's rapidly expanding middle class. The largest daily is the *Dainik Jagran*, a Hindi-language newspaper read by over 55 million people. *The Times of India* (TOI) is India's leading English-language daily.

Internet usage has seen rapid growth in India in recent years, despite the fact that it is restricted to only a small part of the population. In 2008, with a population of over 1.1 billion, India had an estimated 4.38 million broadband subscribers. This is largely due to India's vast population and rural interior. There were an estimated 81 million users in 2010, up from an estimated 42 million in 2007. The country also has one of the fastest growing telecom markets in the world. It grew tenfold between 2001 and 2005, reaching 60 million subscribers. In addition, India's Internet and technology industry is growing in the 21st century, largely due to outsourcing, further revamping Internet access in the country.

SOCIAL DEVELOPMENT

Standard of Living

India ranked 135th out of 187 countries on the 2014 United Nations Human Development Index, which measures quality of life and standard of living indicators.

Water Consumption

Water resources in India include rainwater, groundwater (which is used largely for irrigation), and surface water, which includes fourteen major rivers. Access to sanitation and clean water is lower among rural and poor urban populations. In rural areas, over 80 percent of the water supply comes from groundwater; in some rural areas, women are forced to travel long distances to access water.

According to the World Health Organization, 92 percent of the population has access to improved drinking water sources and 36 percent had access to improved sanitation. According to India's 2001 Census, 190 million households had some access to water sources, with 74 million of those households having a water source such as tap water and/or wells within their premises; however, 32 million households did not have access to water sources either within or near their premises.

Education

Although education in India is free and compulsory for children up to the age of fourteen, only an estimated 50 to 55 percent of six-to-14 year olds attend school. Many children work at home or in family-operated businesses and other cottage industries. School attendance also depends a great deal on the resources available in rural communities.

India has done much to address illiteracy, and the country's average literacy rate has improved dramatically. In 2006, the literacy rate was an estimated 62 percent (75 percent for men and 50 percent for women).

There are several different types of colleges and universities in India, including government colleges, private colleges, university colleges, and professional colleges. The primary type of university is the teaching university. Unitary universities are situated on a single campus, while the more common affiliating universities have central campuses that work in conjunction with many other colleges and can span several districts. The largest of these are in Delhi, Calcutta, Mumbai, and Bangalore.

There are also technical schools at the college level, such as the Indian Institute of Technology, the Birla Institute of Technology, the All India Institute of Medical Sciences, the Indian Forest Research Institute, and the Indian Veterinary Research Institute.

Gender inequities in education are blatant. According to the 2001 census, of the 228 million people attending educational institutions, 129 million were men and 99 million were women; of the 37 million people in higher secondary schools (or senior secondary), 24 million were men and 13 million were women; and, additionally, of the 37 million with graduate-level educations, 25 million were men and 12 million were female.

Women's Rights

Gender discrimination is prohibited by law and the government has passed significant legislation over the years to strengthen women's rights. However, these laws have been difficult to enforce, especially in rural areas. Economic prosperity and job opportunities in urban areas have brought about a positive change in the status of women since the 1990s. The majority of Indian women still have to struggle for their rights in a traditionally male-dominated, patriarchal society.

One of the biggest issues is that of domestic violence arising from dowry harassment (a dowry is any payment or gift traditionally offered by the bride's family, often criticized as a bribe). The Dowry Prohibition Act of 1961 makes it illegal to accept a dowry, but the practice remains entrenched and widespread. Often, women are subjected to mental abuse, violence, and even death when the dowry demands of a husband and his family are not met. In a celebrated case in 2003, Nisha Sharma reported the exorbitant dowry demands of her groom and his family to the police minutes before her wedding. Her inspiring story is now part of the social studies curriculum in Delhi schools.

Partly related to the problem of dowry is the incidence of female infanticide (the intentional killing of baby girls due to a family's preference for a male child). This is because girls are regarded as a financial drain and hardship. While it is now illegal to determine the sex of a child through the use of sonograms and other medical procedures, enforcing the law has been difficult given the scale of the problem. While the normal female/male ratio is around 952 girls for every 1,000 boys, it has dipped to 793 in the state of Punjab.

Sexual exploitation of women also remains a significant issue in modern-day India. Often, poor women are sold into either the sex trade or forms of domestic slavery overseas. Criminal networks in neighboring countries also use India as a transit point for trafficking in women. The Prevention of Immoral Traffic Act was passed in 1956 to curb these practices, but the law's enforcement has been patchy and inefficient given the scale of the problem.

India has elected several women to high political office. Indira Gandhi (1917–1984) was elected prime minister in 1966, and Pratibha Patil (1934–) was elected to the presidency in 2007. In addition, several states have elected women as chief ministers (executive heads). Successive governments in independent India have tried to improve the situation of women in the political arena. For example, a constitutional amendment in 1993 stipulated that one-third of all seats in local panchayats (councils) were to be reserved for women. However, repeated efforts to pass legislation reserving seats in the central and state legislatures have been unsuccessful.

The state of Tamil Nadu was the first to set up police stations staffed entirely by women. This occurred when the state was governed by a woman chief minister. This act was undertaken to assist and influence women to come forward with complaints, which they might have been reluctant to do when faced with a male police force.

Most state governments now actively promote micro credit loans, which allow women to borrow small amounts in order to set up a business and become financially independent. One of the pioneers in this field is the Self Employed Women's Association (SEWA), a non-governmental organization (NGO) set up in 1972. As of 2008, SEWA had 700,000 women members and average loan amounts of just $293 (USD).

However, the most potent change in the status of Indian women is being brought about by economic and market forces. A greater number of women in the twenty-first century are joining the workforce and becoming financial contributors to the family. In 2007, women formed 30 percent of the workforce in the Indian information technology industry, a figure that is expected to rise to 45 percent by 2010. Furthermore, more middle class families are willing to invest in their daughters' education. This planned act of economic independence is slowly transforming societal attitudes, particularly in urban areas.

Health Care

Health care in India is dispensed primarily through Primary Health Centers (PHC), run by the federal Ministry of Health and Family welfare. Individual states also contribute substantial amounts to health services as well as public health education. In rural areas especially, most routine medical care is conducted by paramedics and other health care professionals. Serious medical cases are usually referred to larger urban hospitals. India has approximately 22,400 primary health centers, 11,200 hospitals, and 27,400 dispensaries.

During the mid-1990s, health care spending accounted for about six percent of India's gross domestic product (GDP). State governments spend about 15.2 percent, the central government contributes 5.2 percent, and third-party insurance and employers spend 3.3 percent of the total costs. Municipal government and foreign donors provide about 1.3 percent of the total spent. Most of the expenditure is for primary health care, including curative and preventative costs.

Medical care in India is based both on Western medicine and traditional practices. Ayurveda, which means "life science," is a practice that aims to treat every part of human wellbeing, including mental, physical, and spiritual components. Practitioners of ayurveda are called vaidya. Unaani is an herbal medical practice the practitioners of which are referred to as hakims (or Muslim physicians).

GOVERNMENT

Structure

India achieved independence from the United Kingdom in 1947 and is now the largest democracy in the world. The legal system is structured on English common law. The president and vice president are elected by an electoral college and serve five-year terms. The prime minister, who holds more executive power than the president, appoints the Council of Ministers (or cabinet).

There are two houses in India's parliament: the Council of States (Rajya Sabha) and the House of the People (Lok Sabha). The dominant political party in India is the Indian National Congress Party, though the Bharatiya Janata Party has also had some success.

Political Parties

National political parties in India include the Bharatiya Janata Party, which won 31 percent of the vote in the 2014 elections and has 282 seats in the Lok Sabha. The Indian National Congress won 19 percent of the vote in the 2014 elections and has 44 seats in the Lok Sabha. All India Anna Dravida Munnetra Kazhagam won three percent of the vote and holds 37 Lok Sabha seats. Biju Janata Dal won nearly two percent of the vote, or 20 seats. Shiv Sena won nearly two percent of the vote, or 18 seats. Other parties, including Telangana Rashtra Samithi, Communist Party of India and the YSR Congress, all received small portions of the vote and several seats in the Lok Sabha each.

Local Government

There are 25 states and seven union territories in India. A governor is appointed to each state by the president. Generally, union territories are subject to greater control by the central government. Local governments oversee water supply, road maintenance, primary schools, and public hospitals.

Judicial System

The highest court in India is the Supreme Court, and most states have High Courts, each of which is led by a Chief Justice appointed by the president. There are 18 High Courts, with three of those courts having jurisdiction over multiple states. Union territories fall under the jurisdiction of other states' High Courts.

Taxation

The top corporate tax rate and top income tax rate were each, as of 2010, 33.99 percent. Other taxes levied include a value-added tax (VAT) and a dividend distribution tax.

Armed Forces

The armed forces of India, or Indian Armed Forces, consist of an army, navy, and air force, as well as paramilitary forces and the Indian Strategic Forces Command (SFC), which administers the country's nuclear weapons. India also maintains an armed forces branch that oversees the security of its space-based systems. There is no conscription, and 16 is the minimum age for service. Active personnel in 2006 numbered more than 1.3 million (not including reserve and paramilitary troops, which account for roughly an additional 2.4 million).

Foreign Policy

The foreign policy of India has undergone a significant shift since the late 20th century. In 1961, India was one of the founding members of the Non-Aligned Movement (NAM). This movement was comprised of developing countries that chose to maintain independent, or non-aligned, with any major powers or alliances during the Cold War (a state of conflict existing between the Soviet Union and the U.S. between the 1940s–1990s). However, India has gradually become the most populous democracy in the world and, with a rising economic and military strength, a more assertive player on the world stage.

Economic considerations, in particular, are playing an increasingly significant role in India's foreign policy formulation. Its gross domestic product (GDP) is growing at a rapid pace per year (7.4 percent in 2009). As such, India requires large investments of foreign capital to continue this growth. This has been one of the driving forces behind warmer relations with the US and other developed countries. The need for energy security has also led to greater engagement and bilateral agreements with oil-producing countries in the Middle East and elsewhere. For example, India signed a bilateral agreement with the U.S. in 2007 involving civilian nuclear cooperation. The deal greatly expanded nuclear trade between U.S. and India and opened up cooperation on satellite and energy technology. India has also recently strengthened its relations with the European Union (EU).

Within Asia, India is engaged with numerous multilateral organizations, most notably the South Asian Free Trade Agreement (SAFTA), the Association of South East Asian Nations (ASEAN), and the South Asian Association for Regional Cooperation (SAARC). As a leading member of the Group of 77 (G77), it also negotiates on behalf of developing countries at various summits held by the World Trade Organization (WTO). In addition, India has recently undertaken assertive efforts to assume a global strategic leadership role. At the turn of the 21st century, India was regarded as one of the largest troop contributors to UN peacekeeping efforts, and it continues to press its goal of becoming a permanent member of the UN Security Council (UNSC).

India has been considered a regional power since achieving independence in 1947, but has frequently had difficult relations with neighboring countries. For example, India has engaged in three separate wars with Pakistan. India also dealt with a major Pakistani incursion into Indian territory in 1999. Further heightening the tension between India and Pakistan is the disputed territory of Kashmir. India controls approximately half of this northwestern region, with Pakistan and China each also controlling territory. In fact, India also engaged in war with China in 1962 over a border dispute.

In addition, both Pakistan and China are considered nuclear powers. This prompted India to conduct successful nuclear tests in 1998 in order to establish a "credible deterrent" to its neighbors. Though it has been criticized for not being a signatory to the Nuclear Non-Proliferation Treaty, India has said that it will conform to the terms of the treaty even while being outside the system. It has also consistently declared that it will follow a "no first use" policy.

India has improved its relations with China in recent years. Both countries have young populations, vibrant economies, and global geo-political ambitions, which have led to tensions in their bilateral relations. Regardless, India and China are working toward developing a parallel relationship that sidesteps these political and border conflicts, and focuses on promoting mutual economic interests. Relations, although still tense, have also improved in recent years with Pakistan. In 2011, then Prime Minister Manmohan Singh and Pakistani Prime Minister Yousuf Raza Gilani watched the cricket World Cup together, pledging to normalize relations between the two nations. Relations with its other immediate neighbors, Bangladesh, Sri Lanka, and Nepal, are also characterized by tensions. Many of the issues with these neighboring countries range from the sheltering of militants and civil war strife, to the sharing of resources and border disputes.

Human Rights Profile

International human rights law insists that states respect civil and political rights, and also promote an individual's economic, social and cultural rights. The United Nations Universal Declaration of Human Rights (UDHR) is recognized as the standard for international human rights. Its authors sought the counsel of the world's great thinkers, philosophers, and religious leaders, and were careful to create a document that reflects the core values shared by every world culture. (To read this document or view the articles relating to cultural human rights, visit: http://www.udhr.org/UDHR/default.htm.)

In keeping with Article 2 of the Universal Declaration of Human Rights, India's constitution forbids discrimination based on religion, gender or race. While the law is seemingly unambiguous, true social equality for women, children, tribal groups and Dalits (the so-called "untouchables" of the lowest castes) is still lacking. Only recently has India elected a Dalit, K. R. Narayanan in 1997, and a woman, Pratibha Patil, in 2007, to the office of the presidency. The government has established a system of reservations for underprivileged castes and communities (akin to affirmative action) in colleges and government jobs since 1947. The percentage of reserved seats can reach as high as 69 percent in certain states. Social equality, particularly in rural areas, remains a significant issue.

This social complexity means that the law has to tread a fine line between ensuring equality based on universal rights and being sensitive to the particular traditions and religious laws of minority religious groups. For example, with regard to Article 16 of the declaration, which relates to marriage, India allows Muslim law to govern marriage within the Muslim community, thereby allowing divorce by triple talaq (whereby a man can divorce his wife by uttering the word "talaq" three times).

In accordance with Article 18 of the UDHR, freedom of religion is one of the cornerstones of the constitution and it allows for complete freedom of thought and conscience. However, violence between Hindus and Muslims has been a recurrent feature of post-independent India, with the riots in the state of Gujarat in 2002 being one of the worst episodes in recent history. Caste violence continues to be a prevalent issue, with the government unable to prevent continuing conflicts.

The constitution also protects freedom of opinion and expression, as per Article 19 of the UDHR. Human Rights Watch describes India as having a "vibrant media and civil society." However, there have been occasional efforts to censor the media. In the late 1980s, the press was involved in a flurry of investigative reports into government corruption and incompetence. The government attempted to censor the media with a defamation bill that included imprisonment for offending journalists. The bill was quickly withdrawn after protests from the media and opposition parties.

The most controversial aspect of India's human rights record relates to the militant political movements in various parts of the country, particularly Kashmir. India's armed forces have been accused of extra-judicial killings in staged "encounters" when dealing with separatist forces during the Kashmir conflict, as well as when dealing with insurgents in the northeastern states and armed left-wing extremists of the Naxalite movement (an armed communist movement). In fact, the government signed a UN treaty in February 2007 to deal with "forced disappearances." The prime minister at the time, Dr. Manmohan Singh, declared there would be "zero tolerance" for human rights violations. However, both the armed forces and the militants continue to be responsible for serious human rights abuses of the civilian populations in these troubled areas. After the 2014 elections and the victory of the Bharatiya Janata Party, Prime Minister Narendra Modi reaffirmed India's commitment to human rights. However, abuses against women and minorities continue.

ECONOMY

Overview of the Economy

The Indian economy is one of the fastest growing in the world. In 2013, India's gross domestic product (GDP) was estimated at $4.99 trillion USD. The economy's annual growth rate is estimated at around 3.2 percent. The service industry dominates the economy, composing 56.9 percent of the GDP. Industry and agriculture follow with 25.8 percent and 17.4 percent of the GDP, respectively.

Indian exports in 2013 amounted to $313.2 billion (USD), and included precious stones, chemicals, vehicles, apparel, and petroleum products. The United States, China, the United Kingdom, and the United Arab Emirates (UAE) are India's major export trading partners.

New Delhi, one of the nine districts of Delhi, is one of India's commercial epicenters. The corporate headquarters of most leading Indian firms are located in the capital, as are the offices of many multinational companies. The nation's key government, financial, medical, and educational institutions are also concentrated in New Delhi.

Industry

India's major industries include textiles, chemicals, food processing, steel, transportation equipment, cement, mining, petroleum, machinery, and software. The capital features a significant manufacturing base, which turns out consumer products including automobiles, pharmaceuticals, sporting goods, razors, textiles, electronic components, and clothing.

The Indian government has in recent years taken steps to develop New Delhi as a hub of nanotechnology and biotechnology. In 2005, authorities inaugurated the capital's first Information Technology (IT) Park. Its launch was one of several steps by the government to place New Delhi on a competitive footing with the information technology-intensive economies found in Indian cities such as Bangalore and Hyderabad.

Labor

Forty nine percent of India's labor force works in agriculture. Roughly one-third of the work force is employed in service industries, with the remainder working in manufacturing and other industry. Many of India's highly skilled workers speak English, and work in the high-technology sector. As a result, India has become a major exporter of software services and workers. As of 2013, the labor force numbered approximately 487.3 million, with an unemployment rate of 8.8 percent.

Energy/Power/Natural Resources

Coal is a particularly important natural resource in India, and the country possesses the fourth-largest coal reserves in the world. Other valuable natural resources include iron ore, manganese, mica, bauxite, titanium ore, chromite, natural gas, diamonds, petroleum, limestone, and farmland. However, India faces many pressing environmental issues, including deforestation, soil erosion, overgrazing, air and water pollution, and population growth.

Fishing

The fishing industry is an important aspect of India's economy; in fact, India is one of the largest fish producers in the world. Common species include pomfret, shrimp, ghol, lobsters, mackerel, and catfish. In the early 21st century, overfishing is a significant issue affecting the industry.

Forestry

Forestry is a significant industry in early 21st century India. According to the State of Forest

Report, India's forest cover is increasing, and, as of 2012, 23 percent of the country is forested. Common wood products produced in India include lumber, wood panels, paper, paperboard, and pulp.

Mining/Metals

In 2009, the mining industry contributed fewer than two percent to India's GDP. It has significant reserves of coal, iron ore, and bauxite. Commonly mined materials include aluminum, copper, gold, zinc, lead, iron, feldspar, gypsum, and steel.

Agriculture

Agriculture is a dominant force in the Indian economy, employing more than half of the work force. More than 50 percent of the land in India is capable of supporting agriculture. Key crops include rice, wheat, oilseed, cotton, jute, tea, sugarcane, and potatoes.

Animal Husbandry

The livestock industry accounts for approximately 8 percent of the India's GDP. Cattle, water buffalo, sheep, goats, and poultry are raised as livestock. Eggs and dairy products are two of the most economically significant aspects of the livestock industry.

Tourism

India has many diverse tourist destinations, and is one of the most popular places to visit in Asia. The Taj Mahal, a gigantic monument built during the 17th century in Agra, is among the most-visited sites in India. The frequently visited tourist circuit known as the "Golden Triangle" includes the cities of Delhi, Agra, and Japur. In addition, India has many wildlife sanctuaries, including sites in Corbett, Kanha, Sariska, Periyar, Ranthambhor, and Bharatpur.

India declared 2002 the "year of ecotourism" in. India receives more than one million visitors each year, and tourism supplies approximately six percent of all jobs in the country. The tourism industry is growing in the early 21st century; in fact, it is estimated that the sector will, by 2019, employ over 40 million workers.

Achala Punja, Kim Nagy, Beverly Ballaro

DO YOU KNOW?

- After the United States, India has the largest number of English speakers in the world, though the version of English spoken in India is based on British English.
- The British designed New Delhi to accommodate 70,000 people; today the total population of the Delhi urban area exceeds 10 million.
- Every January 29, at Vijay Chowk in the heart of New Delhi, the capital hosts a ritual known as the Beating Retreat ceremony. The ceremony marks the official end of Republic Day celebrations. Historically, it reflects an ancient battlefield custom that dictated that all fighting cease at sunset. When troops on both sides heard bugles announcing the sunset, they would lay down their arms for the night.

Bibliography

Basham, A.L. *A Cultural History of India*. New Delhi: Oxford University Press, 1975.

Boo, Katherine. *Behind the Beautiful Forevers: Life, Death, and Hope in a Mumbai Undercity.* New York: Random House, 2014.

Dalrymple, William. *City of Djinns: A Year in Delhi.* London: Harper Collins, 1993.

Das, Gurcharan. *India Unbound: The Social and Economic Revolution from Independence to the Global Information Age.* New Delhi: Viking, 2000.

Grihault, Nicki. *India - Culture Smart! A Quick Guide to Customs and Etiquette*. London: Kuperard, 2003.

Guha, Ramachandra. *India after Gandhi: The History of the World's Largest Democracy*. New York: Harper Collins, 2007.

Kapur, Akash. *India Becoming: A Portrait of Life in Modern India.* Boston: Riverhead Books, 2013.

Keay, John. *India: A History.* New York: Grove Press, 2011.

Lonely Planet and Sarina Singh. *India.* Oakland, CA: Lonely Planet, 2013.

Luce, Edward. *Despite the Gods: The Rise of Modern India*. Anchor, 2008.

Rough Guides. *Rough Guide to India.* London: Rough Guides, 2013.

Roy, Srirupa. *Beyond Belief: India and the Politics of Postcolonial Nationalism.* Durham, NC: Duke University Press, 2007.

Trautmann, Thomas R. *India: Brief History of a Civilization.* New York: Oxford University Press, 2015.

Wolport, Stanley. *India.* Berkeley: University of California Press, 2009.

Wood, Michael. *India.* New York: Basic Books, 2007.

Works Cited

"Country Profile: India." *BBC News*. http://news.bbc.co.uk/2/hi/south_asia/7069922.stm

"Census of India." *Office of the Registrar General and Census Commissioner, India.* 2001." http://www.censusindia.gov.in/Census_And_You/area_and_population.aspx

Davies, Philip. *The Penguin Guide to the Monuments of India, Vol. II*. London: Viking, 1989.

Dormandy, Xenia. "India's Foreign Policy." Conference Paper. November 5, 2007. http://belfercenter.ksg.harvard.edu/publication/17778/indias_foreign_policy.html

Government of India website. http://rural.nic.in/book00-01/ch-4.pdf

"India: Internet Usage Stats and Telecommunications Market Report." http://www.internetworldstats.com/asia/in.htm

Jaffrey, Madhur. "A Taste of India." London: Pan Books, 1987.

Library of Congress Country Studies: India. http://lcweb2.loc.gov/cgi-bin/query/r?frd/cstdy:@field(DOCID+in0165)

National Association of Software and Services Companies (Nasscom) website. Nasscom Newsline. "Bridging the Gender Divide. The Indian IT-BPO Industry Aims for more "Inclusive" People Policy." January 2007.

National Human Rights Commission website. http://www.nhrc.nic.in/

U.S. Department of State. "Country Reports on Human Rights Practices – 2004." *Released by the Bureau of Democracy, Human Rights, and Labor*." February 28, 2005. http://www.state.gov/g/drl/rls/hrrpt/2004/41740.htm

http://www.nasscom.in/Nasscom/templates/NormalPage.aspx?id=50996

"U.S. Department of State, Bureau of South and Central Asian Affairs." *Background Note: India*. June 2008. http://www.state.gov/r/pa/ei/bgn/3454.htm

"Website of the Ministry of Railways, Government of India."http://www.indianrail.gov.in/abir.html

"Website of the Self Employed Women's Association." www.sewa.org

"Website of the Government of Tamil Nadu." http://www.tn.gov.in/policynotes/bcmbc.htm

India – SEWA Bank. *Women's World Banking website.* http://www.swwb.org/node/223

"World Report 2007 - India." *Human Rights Watch website*. http://hrw.org/englishwr2k7/docs/2007/01/11/india14868.htm

Beach at Maldives/Stock photo © PhotoTalk

MALDIVES

Introduction

The Republic of Maldives is a small island nation in the Indian Ocean, located southwest of India and Sri Lanka. The archipelago, or chain of islands, is composed of 26 atolls, which consist of approximately 2,000 coral islands. No part of the archipelago rises more than 2.3 meters (7.5 feet) above sea level, and the islands are protected by natural reefs, or faros, that encircle them. Fewer than 200 islands are inhabited, and there is only one prominent urban center, the national capital.

In general, the local culture of the Maldives has evolved hand-in-hand with its history, and is a reflection of its location in the Indian Ocean. Because of its long-standing contact and economic ties with India and Sri Lanka, Maldivian culture reflects a strong Indian and Sri Lankan influence. With the establishment of Islam in the 12th century, Arabic, East African, and Malay traditions were introduced to the archipelago, producing what was to become a uniquely Maldivian culture.

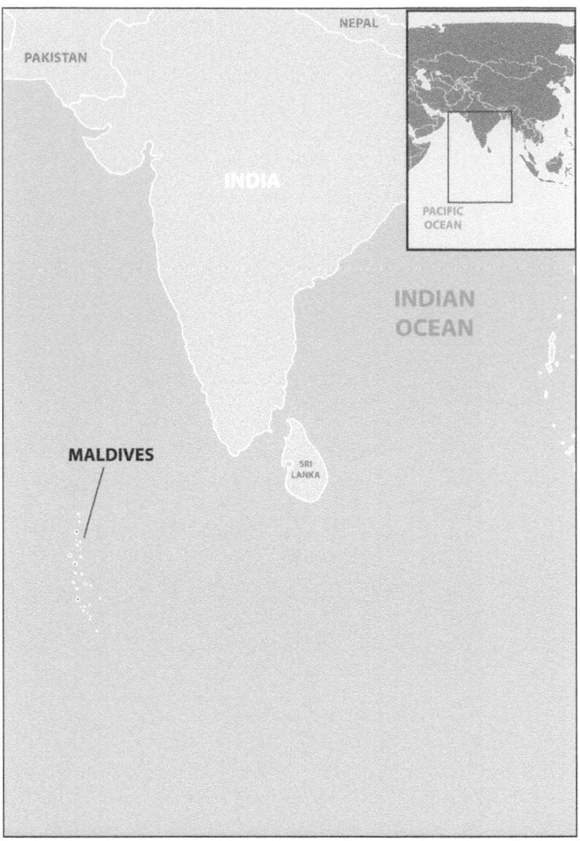

GENERAL INFORMATION

Official Language: Maldivian Dhivehi
Population: 393,595 (2014 estimate)
Currency: Maldivian rufiyaa
Coins: The Maldivian rufiyaa is divided into 100 laari. Coins are available in denominations of 1, 2, 5, 10, and 50 laari, which are rarely used, and 50 laari and 1 and 2 rufiyaa.
Land Area: 298 square kilometers (115 square miles)
National Anthem: "Qaumii salaam" ("National Salute")
Capital: Malé
Time Zone: GMT +5
Flag Description: The Maldivian flag features a centered green rectangle over a red field, or background. Centered inside the green rectangle, which takes up two-thirds of the flag, is a vertical white crescent symbol, facing away from the hoist (left) side. Red represents the sacrificial blood of those who fought for independence and the nation's sovereignty; the green represents prosperity and progress; and the white crescent stands for the archipelagic nation's Islamic faith.

Population

The Maldives has a young population, with roughly 21 percent under age fourteen and another 73 percent between the ages of fifteen and sixty-four (2014 estimates). Life expectancy

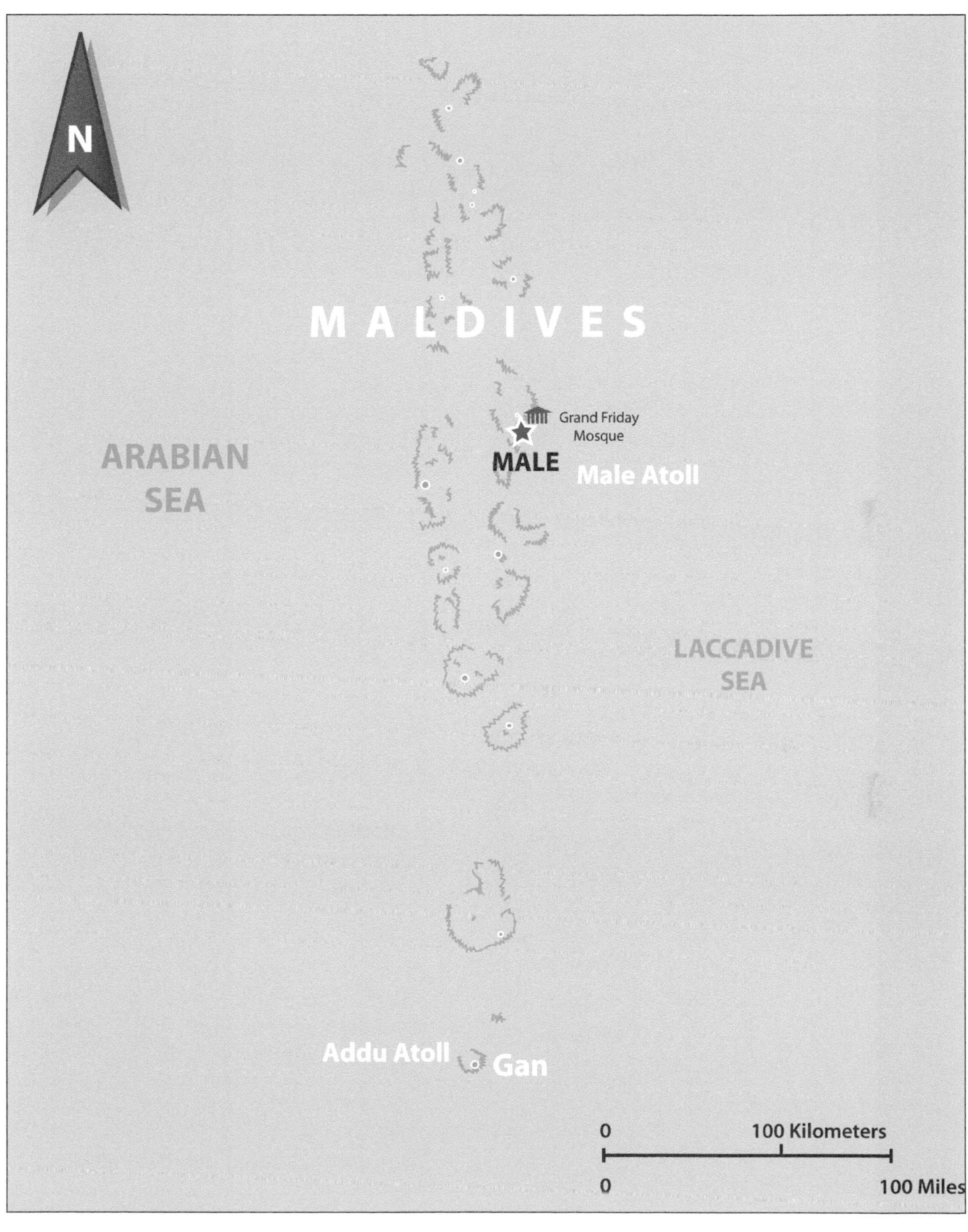
N
MALDIVES
Grand Friday Mosque
MALE
Male Atoll
ARABIAN SEA
LACCADIVE SEA
Addu Atoll
Gan
0
100 Kilometers
0
100 Miles

Principal Localities by Population (2012 estimate unless otherwise noted):

- Malé (134,232)
- Hithadhoo (9,394)
- Fuvahmulah (7,674)
- Kulhudhuffushi (6,434)
- Villingili (6,956) (2006 estimatc)
- Thinadhoo (4,442) (2006 estimate)
- Naifaru (3,687) (2006 estimate)
- Hinavaru (3,017) (2006 estimate)
- Un'goofaaru (2,988) (2006 estimate)
- Hulhumale' (2,866) (2006 estimate)

at birth is seventy-seven years for women and seventy-two years for men (2014 estimate). Since the islands are small (no single island is larger than 13 square kilometers/5 square miles), population density is high, at 1,105 persons per square kilometer (2,862 per square mile).

The capital Malé is the most populous area of the Maldives. The next most populous area in the islands is Seenu, on the southern Addu Atoll. As of 2008, approximately 44 percent of the population resides in urban areas.

There are concerns about population growth overwhelming the islands' national resources. With only a small amount of arable land and fresh water, the country may be reaching the limit of the amount of people it can support. The population growth rate was reported as –0.09 percent in 2014.

The people of the Maldives are a mix of Sinhalese, Dravidian, Arab, and African ethnicities. Arab sailors and later the Portuguese made stops at Malé. The rate of migration has been nil for decades.

Languages

The official language, Dhivehi, is a Sinhalese dialect written in Arabic script. English is also widely spoken, and is often used in government business.

Native People & Ethnic Groups

It is thought that the Maldives were settled by Dravidian people from India about 2,500 years ago. Other archipelagos in the Indian Ocean, such as the Seychelles, were settled only in recent times and have a strong African influence. The Maldives were settled much earlier by migrants from India, and so the islands' culture has a more Asian flavor. More recently, immigrants from Arab countries and from Africa have added to the country's ethnic composition.

Religions

People from Sri Lanka or India brought Buddhism to the area. In the 12th century, the king converted to Islam and set up an Islamic sultanate. This was the form of government until 1968, when the country became a republic. The Arabs brought African slaves who eventually became part of the population.

The modern Maldivian population reflects the blend of these cultures. Sunni Islam is practiced by nearly the entire population; it is the official state religion, and adherence is required by law. Belief in spirits, both good and bad, also persists in the Maldives. Known as jinni, these spirits occupy the trees, the sea, and the sky, and can cause disease and hardship or bring prosperity.

Climate

The Maldives lie across the equator, so the climate is tropical, with typically hot and humid weather. The daytime temperatures range from 24° to 33° Celsius (75° to 91° Fahrenheit). The ocean temperature is a constant 27° Celsius (81° Fahrenheit).

The Maldives is affected by two monsoon seasons. The northeast monsoon lasts from November to April, and is mostly dry with gentle winds. The southwest monsoon appears from May to October, and features heavy rains and higher seas. Average annual rainfall is approximately 1,900 millimeters (74 inches).

The tsunami of December 2004 killed 82 people in the Maldives and damaged countless homes and businesses. Almost 30,000 people lost their homes. Total losses were estimated to be $472 million (USD), equivalent to more than 60 percent of the country's gross domestic product.

ENVIRONMENT & GEOGRAPHY

Topography

The atolls that form the Maldives are actually the tops of the Laccadive-Chagos Ridge. (The word "atoll" comes from a Dhivehi word "atholhu.") The Maldives is situated at a very low elevation, averaging 1.2 meters (3.9 feet). The highest point is on Wilingili Island in the Addu Atoll at an elevation of 2.4 meters (7.9 feet) above sea level. The highest point in Maldives is the lowest high point of any country in the world.

The warm water surrounding the Maldives is perfect for the quick growth of coral, and over 200 different species of hard coral are found in the reef surrounding the islands. Hard coral is formed from the skeletons of tiny creatures called polyps. As the coral piles up and recedes into the sea, it leaves C-shaped atolls and lagoons behind. The reef provides a habitat for a myriad of marine life. There are no rivers; the islands' supply of fresh water comes from underground wells.

Plants & Animals

A wide variety of marine life, including clownfish, damselfish, surgeonfish, triggerfish, and whitetip sharks, thrive in the lagoons throughout the Maldives. Outside the lagoons, an amazing number of marine species can be found. Over 1,000 have been counted, making Maldives one of the richest marine environments in the world. Species include the manta ray, the whale shark, reef fish, angelfish, groupers and many others. Sharks, turtles and dolphins are commonly found in the waters surrounding the Maldives.

The wildlife found on land is not nearly as diverse; the land animals of the Maldives are similar to those found in Sri Lanka and India. The exception is the fruit bat, which is native to the Maldives. Most other species have been brought to the islands either intentionally or accidentally. The black rat and house mouse probably arrived on the islands aboard ships from foreign ports. Geckos and nonpoisonous snakes may be found on some of the islands.

Approximately 70 species of butterflies and over 100 of birds have been sighted in the Maldives. Most of these are migratory species that stop over on the islands. The most common birds are the house crow, the koel, and the gray heron. In recent years, the crow population has been approaching pest proportions. Sea birds such as the tern and white-tailed tropic bird are also common.

Plants native to the Maldives include hau (used for making mats), bamboo, mango and breadfruit trees, and the coconut palm. The vegetation on most of the islands consists of scrub brush.

CUSTOMS & COURTESIES

Greetings

As the state religion of the Maldives is Islam, Islamic principles influence every aspect of life in the islands. Thus, the formal greetings are Muslim in nature. Upon meeting someone, the common greeting is "Assalam-o-Alaiqum" ("May the peace and blessings of Allah be upon you"). The greeting is returned by saying "Wa-alaiqum-us-Salam." When saying goodbye, "Allah Hafiz" or "Khuda Hafiz" ("May Allah be your guardian"). Youngsters usually use the informal greeting of "Kihineh" ("Hello") among themselves, as do those who enjoy a certain degree of familiarity. It is interesting to note that there are no Dhivehi words for "hello" or "good-bye," largely because the islanders are so accustomed to frequent traveling that these concepts are somewhat meaningless.

When a stranger visits an island, it is customary for the visitor to introduce himself to the island chief, and the gazi, who is the island judge and religious leader. If the island is an atoll capital, he is supposed to introduce himself to the atoll chief as well. The Maldivians address each other using either first or last names, as some of their names are very common. The use of nicknames is also common. When meeting someone for the first time, a handshake is the gesture most commonly used.

Gestures & Etiquette

While Maldivians may appear to be a shy, timid, and reserved group of people, they are, in fact, considered to be a friendly people. The strenuous island life has made them independent and hardworking. Traditionally, a lazy Maldivian was considered to be one who didn't eat. This work ethic and these qualities are reflected in their gestures and social etiquette.

The Maldivians follow the Islamic code of conduct in their behavior. Thus, they are very respectful of each other, and especially of elders. Youngsters are supposed to greet their elders with an attitude of respect, and the elderly are particularly cared for. In addition to elders, educated people are also particularly revered. Furthermore, when in a social setting, people are expected to display perfect manners and etiquette.

In general, the people of the archipelago are very polite and patient, and dress neatly and conservatively when in public places. The men usually wear long trousers, a shirt, slip-on shoes and sometimes a tie, in contrast to their traditional dress of a sarong and a loose shirt. The women typically wear long skirts and shirts. They have a reputation for acting in a generous and kind manner amongst themselves, as well as with their foreign visitors, and are generally willing to offer prompt and eager assistance to others.

When conversing, the Maldivians rarely use exaggerated hand gestures and are generally a soft-spoken people. Even though the traditional caste system (a social system based on inherited social status) no longer officially exists, remnants of this code of social conduct which once dictated the terms of interaction between the social castes are still practiced to a certain degree. This is evident in even simple affairs such as address and seating arrangements. In general, the lower classes are respectful of the upper classes.

Eating/Meals

In Malé, mainly because of the large influx of tourists, traditional patterns of life are quickly disappearing and being replaced by modern or Western trends. In the outlying atolls, however, the lifestyle has remained largely unaltered, and more traditional patterns of life are still observed. This is particularly true of the eating patterns of the Maldivians.

Maldivians typically eat two main meals in a day, called long eats. Traditionally, these meals are prepared by women (in ancient culture, men who cooked were considered to be effeminate). There are no fixed meal times, and men and women typically do not dine together. In fact, it often happens that the husband is not aware of whether his wife takes her meals, or what she eats. In addition, men belonging to different social classes do not eat together.

Generally, a meal is taken sitting cross-legged on a mat on the floor, according to the preferred Islamic way of eating. The Maldivians eat with their fingers, also an Islamic concept, and use only their right hand for handling food (the left, because it is associated with the cleansing of the body, is considered impure in Muslim culture). During the meal, one is typically not permitted to cough or spit, and the meal is usually taken in silence.

Traditionally, the food was served on banana leaves. However, in recent times, dishes are more commonly used. These dishes may be made locally, of lacquered wood, and are covered to protect the food from ants and other insects. Imported vessels are also used; these include earthenware as well as porcelain. Beverages are commonly served in covered copper cups.

Visiting

The Maldivians are considered a very hospitable people and welcome their guests warmly. Traditionally, when a newcomer visits an island, it is a common custom for the chief of the island to present the visitor with a gift. This is typically something representative of the local cuisine or culture such as a cold coconut drink and a snack consisting of seafood. The host usually provides all the meals for his guest, along with other amenities and comforts.

Since Maldivians generally retire early at night, most people do not visit late in the evening. Before visiting, people often take into consideration their religious duties, for these take precedence over business and pleasurable activities. For example, social visits are not conducted during prayer times. In addition, if a guest happens to visit at a mealtime, they are usually urged to stay and partake of the food.

It is customary for a visitor to remove his or her shoes before entering someone's house. Likewise, visitors to a mosque should also remove any footwear, as it is customary in Islamic culture to reserve the highest respect for religious or holy sites. If the visitor is a male stranger, he is typically not allowed to enter the main house, and will be entertained in the anteroom—an outer room often used as a waiting room. If he stays for a meal, he will not be expected to eat with the family. This practice is typically in keeping with the Islamic tradition of restricting social interaction between unrelated men and women.

LIFESTYLE

Family

Maldivian society is strongly family-oriented. Family structures form the basic unit of society, and family bonds and loyalties are strong. The Islamic tradition of polygamy is practiced in the archipelago, with one variation: the Maldivian law does not allow more than three wives at one time, provided that the man is able to provide them all with equal financial and emotional support. Marriages between first cousins are acceptable, also in concordance with Islamic tradition.

However, while the Maldivian society closely follows Islamic precepts in every aspect of life, it also interprets some of these commandments in a uniquely Maldivian way. For example, divorce is more prevalent on the islands than in any other Islamic country. In fact, the Maldives have one of the largest divorce rates in the world, and in the 1970s, it was estimated that almost 85 percent of the marriages on the islands ended in divorce. The Maldivians also have a unique law that allows a set of partners to marry each other up to three times, before they have to marry other partners. If these marriages are not successful, they can marry each other another three times. They can do this three times, or in other words, they can marry each other nine times.

A typical Maldivian household, in contrast to typical Muslim households, often consists of the nuclear family model—typically a father, mother, and their children—with the father as the head of the family. Unmarried adults typically live with their families. The island communities themselves are close-knit and self-contained, and often function like a large extended family. In some cases, the majority of the community members are related through generations of interfamilial marriages. These extended families assist each other in the trials of everyday life, and family connections are important as nepotism (favoritism based upon familial relationships) is widespread.

Housing

The division between the increasingly urban lifestyle of Malé and the rural lifestyle of the atolls is reflected in their respective housing patterns. Many of the houses recently constructed in Malé reflect modern architectural styles. The houses in the atolls, however, follow the traditional Maldivian architectural style. Land is predominantly government-owned, and each family is allotted an area called goathi, which typically measures 15 meters (49 feet) by 30 meters (98 feet). Most of the traditional houses have one or two stories.

Historically, these traditional houses were built with palm-thatched roofs, and later with Mangalore tiles imported from India. In the 20th century, corrugated iron sheets became a common material for the building of roofs. Even though these caused the houses to become warmer, they were durable and needed to be replaced less frequently. The poorer houses were constructed out of split-bamboo matting, woven coconut fronds (large leaf or palm) tied on timber frames or of washed canvas. The more upscale houses were traditionally constructed out of worked coral stone and held together by lime mortar, or a cement made from ash, lime, charcoal and a syrup made from coconut sap. Typically, there was a platform constructed out of coral-stone in order to elevate the building to protect it from flooding. Often, the superstructure of the house was made of wood. Since the Maldivians are skilled boat makers, they typically build their houses with tight joints without the use of nails.

Traditionally, Maldivian houses did not have windows. This was largely due to the belief in "jinns," or evil spirits. In addition, many older homes had a low barrier in the front to ward off these spirits. However, windows are now a common feature of modern residential construction in the Maldives. Furthermore, newer houses are typically constructed around a hall, which opens up into an anteroom known as the maalem (where male guests are received). The maalem is usually connected to the main house by a back door. The main house has several rooms and is used for sleeping purposes, and there is a separate coral house, called the bhadige, which functions as a kitchen. This structure typically has a thatched roof, no windows and several hollows for stoves.

Generally, the furniture in Maldivian houses is very basic. Flat, wooden benches are commonly used as beds at night and as seats during the day. The family usually stores its valuables in a wooden chest hidden under these beds. Divans (backless sofas) are common, and are usually covered with woven mats. Two distinctively Maldivian pieces of furniture are the undholi and joli chairs. The former consists of a wooden platform or a netted seat, which is usually hung from either a tree or a triangular frame; the latter is a net seat slung on a rectangular frame, and is made in sets of three or four.

Food

Fish forms a large part of the Maldivian diet, and along with rice, is the archipelago's staple food and most important source of protein. Meat, with the exception of pork since it is forbidden to Muslims, is eaten only on special occasions, and the Maldivians eat very few vegetables. The Maldivian cuisine reflects a strong Indian and Sri Lankan influence, especially in the types of spices used. Various types of curry, including prawn curry and mas riha (fish curry), are preferred by the Maldivians, and these are at times flavored with curry powder or curry leaves.

A common Maldivian dish is called garudiya, which is essentially a soup made of tuna. The tuna is cut in the traditional manner after having its gills and innards removed, and is boiled with salt to make the clear broth. Garudiya is usually eaten with rice, roti (flatbread), taro (alocassia) or breadfruit, and can be flavored with chilies, onions, and curry leaves. Rihaakuru is another common dish, and is made by letting the garudiya cook until all the water evaporates, leaving a thick brown paste. The rihaakuru could be flavored with chilies or coconut milk, and is typically eaten with rice.

The Maldive fish, which is a cured tuna fish, is not only a staple food, but a significant export as well. It is made by gutting and skinning the fish, cutting it into longitudinal pieces called ari, and then boiling it, smoking it and drying it in the sun until it acquires a wood-like appearance and texture. Other staple dishes include mas huni, a popular breakfast dish, which is a mixture of tuna, onion, coconut, and chilies, often consumed cold with roshi or unleavened bread; and kavaabi, which is a deep-fried snack made from tuna, rice, coconut and lentils.

Hedtukaa is the name given to a selection of finger foods and snacks, which are also known as "short eats." The snacks include filhuni mas (pieces of fish with a coating of chilies), gulha (fried dough balls filled with fish and various spices), keemia, (fish rolls fried in batter), kuli boakiba (spicy fish cakes), and zilaybee (colored coils of sugared batter). Bondi bai is a rice pudding, and may also be served as a snack.

The Maldivians usually take a cup of sweetened black tea with their meals. The local brew is called raa, and this is a sweet drink made from the crown of the coconut palm. A popular after-dinner mint is called areca nut, which are thin slices of oval nuts added to cloves and lime paste and wrapped up in an areca leaf. Some elderly people may smoke gudugudu, which is an elongated pipe that goes through a water trough. Alcohol is not consumed in any form by the Maldivians, as it is forbidden to Muslims.

Life's Milestones

Birthdays are not traditionally celebrated in the Maldives. The most important celebration in a young boy's life is his circumcision ceremony. This usually occurs when the boy is six or seven years of age. The celebrations are typically elaborate, and may take up to a week, which is usually the time that it takes the boy to heal from the procedure. Young girls also have a ceremony to mark the onset of puberty, but the celebrations are not as elaborate as the boys' circumcision ceremony.

Although marriage is a significant event in the life of a Maldivian, it is not typically celebrated elaborately. The reason for this is perhaps the large number of marriages that a single Maldivian is likely to enter into, or perhaps the great frequency with which a Maldivian marriage ends. There is sometimes a small reception given, and this is called a kaiveni sai. At this reception, tea and snacks may be served and dancing is often common. However, a recent trend of large, elaborate receptions seems to be emerging among the wealthy classes. There may be as many as two hundred guests at such a reception, and the guests will include local dignitaries. Maldivian funerals are conducted in the Islamic tradition, and are typically quiet affairs.

CULTURAL HISTORY

Art

Due to the strenuous nature of island life—in which survival is often the first priority—and the long absence of communication with the outside world, there has been little development of the arts in the Maldives. For example, there has been no tradition of the visual arts in the Maldives, and the indigenous art forms that have flourished have a practical rather than aesthetic history. These include architecture and a variety of traditional and local crafts still thriving today, including mat-weaving, lacquering and lace-making. Many other handicrafts were developed initially out of necessity and catered to the demands of island life. These crafts included carpentry, stone-work, masonry, cloth-weaving, net-making, sail-weaving, boat-building, coir-work, rope-making, and fish-hook making. Often, these crafts are all specific to the various islands that specialize in them.

One traditional craft that did not develop from necessity was jewelry making. The island of Ribudhoo in Dhaalu (South Nilandhoo Atoll), in particular, is famous for its gold jewelry. Huludeli Island, in the same atoll, is also famous for silver jewelry. According to ancient legends, a royal jeweler was exiled to Ribudhoo, where he introduced metalworking, specifically with gold, to the island. Another legend claims after the islanders plundered a shipwreck in the 17th century, they redesigned the recovered gold from the shipwreck to disguise it, thus discovering the art of metalworking.

Architecture

As Malé is the only significant urban center, there are very few public buildings in the Maldives. With the exception of a few government buildings and former royal palaces, the majority of these are mosques and shrines (there are thirty-three mosques in Malé). The public architecture reveals a strong influence of the traditional Islamic design combined with a uniquely Maldivian style. In addition, coral stone is the most common material used in the construction of buildings, and even the streets in Malé are paved with coral. The buildings are usually plastered with lime mortar and then whitewashed (to coat or gloss, typically with paint).

The basic structure of a Maldivian mosque has remained largely unchanged since the 17th century. The mosque is either a coral-stone or wooden building raised on a rectangular platform. It has thick walls and is well-bonded, and the roof is typically supported by cross-beams. The mosque, usually square, stands in the middle of a walled courtyard. It has an entrance at the east end and a rectangular recess at the west. Maldivian mosques do not generally have mihrabs (a niche design in the wall that points to Mecca, the holy city of Islam) and minarets are also rare. Instead, all mosques themselves are oriented toward Mecca, and there is a square recess at the end of the mosque directly pointed to the holy city

Drama

The Maldivian film industry is only 30 years old, and produces fewer than 10 movies a year. It is mostly influenced by Indian cinema. These movies are typically screened in the only cinema in the archipelago, the Olympus Cinema in Malé. Traditionally, because of strict state-imposed censorship as well as the nation's conservative Islamic ideology, local filmmakers have not had much freedom to explore certain taboo subjects, such as impotency, violence against women and loveless marriages. However, these trends are now changing, and the government is attempting to support local filmmakers.

Music & Dance

There is a long tradition of music and dance in the Maldives. It is believed that these traditions of music and dance developed out of a need to alleviate boredom in the islands. Usually, the music and dance are performed together by groups of people. A traditional form of music is bodu beru, which is believed to date back to the pre-Islamic era and has East African origins. It is typically performed by a group of fifteen people, which includes a singer and three drummers. Bodu beru means "big drum," and the dance is accompanied by three or four drums made from hollowed coconut wood, as well as other accompanying percussion instruments. The performance also includes an instrument called onugandu, which is a grooved percussion instrument made of bamboo. The bodu beru begins slowly, and as the rhythm gradually quickens, the dancers keep up the beat. It is believed that this style of music, as the volume gradually increases, can induce a trance-like state. In this way, it is considered a tribal dance and is usually performed on celebratory occasions.

Another traditional song form is called thaara, which is also the Dhivehi word for tambourine. It was introduced by the Arabs in the 17th century. The thaara is sung by two lines of 22 people, who are typically seated facing each other. Like bodu beru, the thaara also begins slowly and builds up to a crescendo. In addition, the instrument that the dance is named after exists in three forms. The largest form is octagonal and nearly 40 centimeters (15 inches) long, with a deep frame and supporting three pairs of cymbals on each side. Another form is circular, nearly 23 centimeters (9 inches) in diameter, and has no cymbals. The third form is 25 centimeters (10 inches) long, covered with the skin of a ray, and supports cymbals.

In the thaara dance, these last two forms of the instrument are usually used. The song, at times semi-religious in nature, has been traditionally performed to celebrate the fulfillment of vows. It is also believed to have a soothing effect on the listener. Traditionally, the performers wear white sarongs (a loose sheet of fabric, typically wrapped around the body) and white shirts, with green scarves tied around the neck.

Contrary to Islamic custom, Maldivian women take part in traditional music and dancing as well. Some dances, such as the maafathi neshun, are performed exclusively by women. This is typically performed by two lines of women dressed in traditional clothes. Another such dance is the bandiyaa jehun, which is a variation of the Indian pot dance, a folk dance in which a pot is usually balanced on the dancer's head. The dancing women keep the beat by drumming her finger rings on a metal. A harmonica or drums may also accompany the dance. There is no specific dress for this dance, but the dancers typically dress alike, usually wearing a long skirt and blouse called dhigu hedhun.

Other traditional and folk dances in Maldivian culture include the bolimalaafath neshun dance, a reenactment of an ancient tradition in which women offered gifts to the sultan on festive occasions; the kadhaa maali, a dance typically performed by thirty men and in accompaniment to a copper percussive instrument called the kadha; the dhandi jehun, a dance also performed by 30 men that is believed to have originated in the Minicoy Islands, the only inhabited island of the Maliku Atoll; and the gaa odi lava folk music dance, typically performed in celebration of a difficult task having been completed to satisfaction. Many of these traditional dances are performed specifically at local festivals, and some are spiritual in nature, and thus have specific functions such as warding off evil.

Literature

Historically, a rich tradition of literature has not been developed in the Maldivian archipelago. The tradition of Maldivian oral literature, on the other hand, goes back to ancient times. Consisting largely of myths and legends, it has been passed down orally from generation to generation, and has thrived because of the Maldives' isolated position in the Indian Ocean. Because the ocean plays such a significant role in the daily lives of the Maldivians, images and symbols of sea-life and sailors figure prominently in these myths. Another recurring motif is that of the supernatural. In fact, many Maldivians still believe strongly in witchcraft and evil spirits and. One form of this oral literature is the traditional raivaru poetry, which is recited in a certain manner so that the lines of poetry are melodic.

Important myths of oral literature of the island include the Koimala story, which is the islands' creation myth and exists in various forms. Another important myth is that about the archipelago's conversion to Islam. This latter describes the arrival of Moroccan Arab Abul Barkat ul Barbari el Moghrebi in Malé, who rescues the nation from a genie, or "jinn," called Rannamari by reciting from the Koran. Impressed and grateful, the sultan accepted Islam, as did his people.

The national language, Dhivehi, also has a long history. It developed initially out of Elu, an archaic form of Sinhala (spoken by the Sinhalese, the largest ethnic group of Sri Lanka), and later integrated elements of Arabic and Persian. It is written in a script called Thaana, which is derived from the Arabic-Persian script. Dhivehi uses forms that are based on Arabic numerals for consonants, and following the Arabic pattern, it is written from right to left. Before the introduction of the printing press in the archipelago in the 20th century, Dhivehi texts were largely handwritten and then duplicated. This prevented the mass distribution of Dhivehi literature and traditional forms of poetry, and hence, hindered its development. The archaic form of Dhivehi has all but disappeared today.

The advent of the printing press, in addition to increasing the potential audience of Dhivehi literature, also saw developments in the local literary tradition. The Dhivehi novel, with Dhivehi prose using imagery for the first time, and a formal style of poetry called Ihen were developed. Most of the predominant Dhivehi writers and scholars date from this era. One of the most prominent and prolific writers of Maldivian literature was Husain Salaahuddin (1881–1947). He published several novels and poetic anthologies and his *Biography of the Prophet* remains one of the most influential Dhivehi books. Muhammad Jameel Didi (1915–1989) was another influential writer and statesman, and he wrote the lyrics of the Maldivian national anthem.

CULTURE

Arts & Entertainment

Historically, the visual arts did not have a healthy development in the Maldives. Much of this stems from a general lack of art education and few exhibition opportunities. Nevertheless, craftsmanship has a long tradition in the Maldivian archipelago. Initially, these artistic traditions had a utilitarian purpose, serving daily island life in Maldives. In the late 20th century, however, a boom in tourism transformed traditional crafts from a source of local income, to a reflection Maldivian cultural identity.

The National Art Gallery of Maldives was founded in 2005, and with it, the government has made a concerted effort to develop and promote the visual arts. In addition to exhibitions, the gallery also hosts artistic workshops, exhibits of traditional crafts, and features the work of nearly thirty native artists. Tourist resorts also promote the traditional arts.

Lace making is one of these crafts. The lace is typically handmade by women; delicate fingers are best suited to the intricate task. Maldivian lace is often made with silver and gold thread imported from India.

Mat weaving is another traditional skill dominated chiefly by craftswomen. The industry thrives largely in the Huwadu, Suvadiva, and Gaaf Dhaal Atolls, where a natural abundance of rush (grasslike plant) offers ready raw materials. The work of gathering rush and weaving may take several weeks. Designs reveal a heavy Arabic and Persian influence, and colors that are most favored are black, yellowish-brown and white. Mats range in size from that of an ordinary prayer mat, to larger sizes suitable for sleeping.

Lacquer work, or laa jehun, is another important art form. Historically, objects such as boats, vases, lances, tools, dishes and other daily items were decorated with lacquer details, particularly if they were to be given as gifts. Objects were constructed from various kinds of wood, and then decorated with multiple layers of richly colored lacquer. Vivid combinations are common, such as yellow, with red trim, applied to a black background. After the lacquer hardens, artists incise designs on object, such as a box or bowl, using sharp tools. This technique exposes the brightly colored layers. Floral motifs are a common lacquer design. The island of Tuladu/Thulhaadhoo and the Baa Atoll are famous for this craft.

The advent of the Internet and the archipelago's flourishing tourism industry exposed the Maldives to a broad global audience. As a result, an increasing number of Maldivian writers are choosing to write in languages other than Dhivehi, such as English and Arabic. Some traditional linguists worry that Dhivehi, confined to the Maldives, is becoming an endangered language. The Maldivian government has made attempts to preserve the national language, setting up centers for the study of Dhivehi, as well as establishing a scholarly Dhivehi journal titled *Fat-tuva*.

Cultural Sites & Landmarks

With the exception of the secluded tourist resorts, which are generally located on the uninhabited islands of the archipelago, all other cultural sites and landmarks are located on the island of Malé. There are several popular markets, including the Fish Market, the Majeedhee Magu market and the Chaandanee Magu, formerly known as Singapore Bazaar.

Among the most prominent of Malé's cultural landmarks are its mosques. The Grand Friday Mosque, the largest mosque in Malé, dominates the city skyline. The exterior features a large golden dome and a slender minaret, or tower decorated with intricate coral engravings. In addition, the mosque's adjoining cemetery holds the tombs of several national heroes and members of the royal family.

Another important mosque is the mosque known as Hukuru Miskit. It was initially constructed in the 12th century, and has been restored several times since, most notably in the 14th and 17th centuries. The mosque's towering minaret features unusual architecture. Added to the mosque in 1674, the main tower is cylindrical, and stands about 50 meters (164 feet) high. A smaller cylindrical tower tops the minaret, inscribed with Koranic verses in blue script. The mosque's interior boasts columns lacquered in red and black, and cross-beams intricately carved with Koranic inscriptions. Elaborate carvings adorn the wooden door posts and screens. Ornate details carry outside as well, to the decorated coral-stone tombstones in the adjacent cemetery. Shrines of noted Muslim saints surround the mosque.

A third mosque, Idu Miskit, represents another example of fine local artisanship. The mosque's foundation, or plinth, is finely carved coral limestone, now blackened by prolonged exposure to the elements. Traditionally, the nation's sultan would attend this mosque to offer his Eid prayers. Eid is the Muslim holiday marking the end of Ramadan, the holy month of fasting.

Malé also is home to the Mulee Aage Palace, constructed in 1906 by Sultan Muhammad

Shamsuddeen III for his son. The beautiful colonial style palace, with elaborate white carvings, was re-named the Presidential Palace. Today it serves as the office of the president.

The Maldivian resorts, however, are what have made the archipelago an international tourist haven. Mostly located on secluded islands, the resorts themselves are constructed in a range of eclectic architectural styles, combining local styles, such as wooden structures built on stilts with conical thatched roofs, with luxurious modern amenities. In fact, many islands were developed specifically for tourism, and tourists are often specifically confined to these areas, and discouraged from visiting certain inhabited islands. In some cases, a specific invitation from an island resident, in addition to a travel permit, is required to visit certain atolls or islands in the Maldives.

Libraries & Museums

The National Museum in the Sultan Park was a popular tourist site. Converted into a museum from an old palace building, it housed a valuable collection of archeological artifacts recovered from the archipelago, as well as objects depicting and celebrating the rich cultural history of the islands. Many of the museum's artifacts are prehistoric in nature, and the cultural items included royal ornaments and as well as ancient paper and cloth manuscripts. It was opened to the public in 1952.

On July 26, 2010, a new national museum opened. Exhibits at the new museum include the full skeleton of a rare tropical bottlenose whale; centuries-old copies of the Quran (or Koran); Buddha sculptures made from coral; and artifacts related to the nation's royalty, such as ceremonial robes, jewelry, and thrones.

Holidays

Maldivians celebrate their Independence Day on July 26; the country obtained its independence from Great Britain on this date in 1965. Republic Day, celebrated on November 11, commemorates the establishment of the republic in 1968. Victory Day (November 3) commemorates a 1988 incident in which a group of Tamil mercenaries tried to take over the government. The coup was put down with the help of troops from India.

Youth Culture

Historically, there has been a strong tradition of sports among Maldivian youth. Soccer (football) is the most popular sport and is played year-round. On some islands, a mid-afternoon match between the local youth has become a daily ritual. There are organized soccer clubs in Malé, which occasionally hold national and international tournaments. Other popular sports include cricket and volleyball. Traditional games are also popular, including bai bala, in which one team tags another inside a circle; wadhemun, a form of tug-of-war; bashi, a variation of tennis; and thin magoali, a variation of baseball that has been played in the islands for over 400 years.

Even though most of the islands now have television and radio, there is little to do in the atolls besides attending services at the local mosque, which is a social as well as religious activity. Most children, therefore, go to boarding school on larger islands such as Malé. In these urban areas, the advent of the Internet has brought a new level of awareness, as well as discontent, to the youth population of Maldives. In addition, drug use has increased in recent years among the island nation's youth, a trend that has become worrisome for local authorities and parents alike.

SOCIETY

Transportation

As the Maldives archipelago consists of coral islands, the most common and effective method of transportation is by water. However, there is no regular ferry service between the islands, and getting from one atoll to another may take several days. Some common types of boats that may be used are motorboats, fishing, cargo, and sail boats. Another common mode of inter-island travel is by seaplane. Traffic moves on the left-hand side of the road.

As the Maldivians have been expert sailors for centuries, they have developed a number of uniquely Maldivian sailing crafts. The dhoni is the most common type of fishing craft. It has a tall, curved prow and a flat stern, and the rudder is attached with a neat rope lashing. Dhonis are usually built on the Raa Atoll, a center for boat building. Typically, 12 workers—six working on each side—can build a 14-meter (45 feet) long hull in about 45 days. In addition, dhonis can be sail powered or motorized. Other common sailing crafts include the wooden buggalow, or bagala, a wooden boat that resembles an Arab dhow; the odi, a boat with a thatched roof astern; the bokura, a small boat that resembles half a walnut shell; and the masodi, a large fishing boat.

In the construction of their boats, the Maldivians typically only use wooden pegs. There are many reasons for this, including the high cost of iron nails, the durability of wooden nails, the fact that wooden nails cause less damage than iron nails, and long-held superstitious beliefs concerning the magnetic properties of iron.

Transportation Infrastructure

There is only one international airport in the archipelago, which is on Hulhule Island and has only two paved runways. There is another airport on Gan Island with a paved runway, but it does not cater to international flights. The total length of paved roads in the island nation is 88 kilometers (54 miles), of which 60 kilometers (37 miles) are in Malé alone.

Media & Communications

Malé and the numerous tourist resorts have had access to various modes of modern communication, including cellular phone service and Internet, for some time. In 2012, there were over 23,000 main telephone lines operating in the archipelago, and an estimated 560,000 mobile cellular phones (up from 20,000 in 2005). Every inhabited island has a telephone and fax, as well as radio access, and inter-atoll communication takes places through microwave links and HF trans-receivers. On several islands, VHF and UHF telephones are also used.

The Maldivian media is typically subjected to a state-imposed censorship. In 1993, the government established a national press council, which was aimed at monitoring, reviewing and developing the journalism of the archipelago. There are a number of daily newspapers, such as the *Haveeru Daily* and the *Jazeeru Daily*, as well as some weekly publications. These daily newspapers are published in both Dhivehi and English, with the majority of the publications being in Dhivehi. The state-run radio and television are also subjected to strict censorship.

SOCIAL DEVELOPMENT

Standard of Living

The Maldives ranked 103rd out of 187 countries on the 2014 United Nations Human Development Index, which measures quality of life and standard of living indicators.

Water Consumption

The drinking water of the Maldives is supplied by underground wells. According to 2012 statistics from the World Health Organization (WHO), approximately 99 percent of the country has access to clean or improved sources of drinking water, while an estimated 97 percent of the population has access to improved sanitation.

Education

Traditionally, education in the Maldives has consisted of studying the Qur'an (or Koran), reading and writing Dhivehi, and learning basic arithmetic skills. In 1961, the educational system was overhauled to more closely resemble the British model. Primary schooling is compulsory and most students continue on to secondary school. The country does suffer from a shortage of qualified teachers, however. The Maldives College of Higher Education was established in 1998, offering citizens the chance to receive a postsecondary education on the islands.

Due to the island's archipelagic nature and remoteness, it is estimated that up to 80 percent of teacher and education-associated costs are related to transportation. In 2007, the island nation implemented broadband-enabled learning centers across the islands, which has helped teachers to enhance their training and skills, and to cut down transportation costs—as well as the dangers inherent in students traveling between islands for schooling. As of 2010, the country also launched its first digitized-structured learning institution.

The average adult literacy rate in the Maldives is 98 percent, the highest rate in the South Asia and Indian Ocean region. The country has reached universal access to primary education—one of the goals of the UN Millennium Development Goals (MDGs)—in the 21st century. As of 2010, a high incidence of dropouts in the secondary level of education remains a concern.

Women's Rights

The women of the Maldives have historically enjoyed a degree of equality with their male counterparts that women belonging to Islamic or Hindu societies rarely experience. As early as the 14th century CE, women were ruling the archipelago. The Maldives had three famous queens, the most significant one being Sultana Khadija, who reigned for 33 years from 1347 until 1379 CE. However, when the archipelago abolished monarchy and became a constitutional republic, a clause in the new constitution barred women from holding the position of president. Despite this, women continue to hold important political, economic and social positions in the archipelago.

The domestic roles of men and women, especially in the more rural outlying atolls, are divided along traditional lines, with men being the primary breadwinners and decision-makers. As such, men typically wield greater power, and the women are responsible for the domestic duties of household chores and taking care of the children. However, because of the particular nature of island life, women perform additional duties such as tending to the crops while the men are away on fishing trips, which is often for long periods of time. They also produce general handicraft items, such as coir rope and woven coconut palm leaves, for domestic use as well to sell in order to supplement the family income. The overall division of labor between the genders is thus more or less equal as women make significant contributions to family life.

Women are also increasingly being formally employed, thus making contributions to the economic and political sectors as well. The economic sectors where they are predominantly employed include the education, health and welfare, transport and communications and the services sectors. They are also employed in the burgeoning tourism industry, but to a lesser degree as the government seeks to minimize the influence of the tourist industry on the conservative Islamic lifestyle of the people. Because of this, women are generally discouraged from working at the tourist resorts. In the political arena, women hold many important positions, including those of atolu verin, or atoll chief, as well as that of island chief.

Maldivian women have enjoyed a more relaxed social ethos, or accustomed place in society. Even though marriage is considered necessary for a woman, and most women are married by the age of 15 (the legal age is 18), marriages are hardly ever arranged. Moreover, even though divorce is more difficult for a woman to obtain than it is for a man, it is less of a social stigma than it is in other South Asian societies, and women easily remarry. After marriage, a Maldivian woman usually keeps her maiden name, and can lawfully own and keep property, giving her economic independence. Also unlike South Asian tradition, the dowry, called the bride-price, is paid by the groom in accordance with Islamic tradition.

Domestic and sexual violence against women is also far less frequent than other South Asian societies. The social status and respect for a woman remains unaffected by her marital status. However, Maldivian women's rights came under increased international scrutiny when in

2013 a 15-year-old rape victim was sentenced to 100 lashes for fornication. Even though the state religion of the Maldivian archipelago is Islam, and is strictly enforced by the government, women were never forced to cover themselves in public. This has allowed women a freedom of movement and association hardly ever experienced by Muslim women.

Health Care

In recent decades, public health in the Maldives has improved in most categories. The government's extensive immunization program has almost eliminated such diseases as polio, whooping cough, diphtheria, and tetanus. However, maternal and infant death rates are still high. Malaria is a problem throughout the islands, due in part to the humid climate. Also, there is concern about the country's rapid population growth.

There is a high incidence of the blood disease thalassemia among Maldivians. The disease can be controlled with medication, and the Maldivian Society for Health Education has been working to provide education and testing for the disease.

GOVERNMENT

Structure

The Maldives gained independence from Great Britain in 1965 and became a republic in 1968. A new constitution was adopted in January 1998. The country is divided into 19 atolls, for administrative purposes.

The executive branch consists of a president, who is both chief of state and head of the government and serves for a five-year term. The president is nominated by the Majlis (People's Council) and then ratified by a national election requiring 51 percent approval. The Cabinet of Ministers is appointed by the president, with parliamentary approval.

The legislature, the Majlis, contains 77 seats, all elected by the people. The term of office is five years. After riots in Malé in 2004, the government instituted a program of democratic reforms, including broader political representation. In May 2005, the Majlis endorsed a proposal to begin a multiparty political system.

Political Parties

A multiparty system was implemented in the Maldives in 2005. The creation of a multiparty system followed decades of authoritarian rule. Following the first multiparty parliamentary elections in 2009, the liberal Maldivian Democratic Party became the ruling party, winning 26 seats in parliament, and the most number of votes. However, this result was decisively overturned in 2014 when after a series of political upheavals the Progressive Party of Maldives, the former opposition party, came to dominate the parliament. Other parties of note include The Dhivehi Rayyithunge Party, the second party registered in the country's history, the Dhivehi Qaumee Party and the Republican Party.

Local Government

The Maldives has 20 administrative units, broken down as atolls. The heads of the administrative units are known as atoll chiefs, and are appointed by the president. Atoll and municipal administrations are overseen by the Ministry of Home Affairs.

Judicial System

The legal system of the Maldives is based on Islamic law, with English common law used in commercial fields. The court system includes a High Court, both a civil and criminal court, and lower courts on each atoll (or island).

Taxation

There is no corporate, personal income, or broad sales tax on in the Maldives. Taxes levied include customs duties, tourism taxes, and a profit tax for financial institutions. In 2008, the government discussed instituting a climate tax for tourists; the country is at high risk due to climate change, and the revenue would fund projects related to renewable energy. In 2010, a global survey on business taxes by the World Bank ranked the

Maldives as the best location for "ease of paying business taxes."

Armed Forces

The armed forces of the Maldives, officially the Maldives National Defence Force (MNDF), consist of several service branches, namely a coast guard, marine corps, special forces, and service corps. Conscription does not exist, and the minimum age of voluntary service is 18. In 2009, the Maldives and India signed a defense pact.

Foreign Policy

The foreign policy of the Maldives has historically been influenced by four important factors: the domestic needs of the archipelago, its potential and untapped resource base, its highly strategic location in the Indian Ocean and international power alliances. The geographic position of the Maldives, in particular, is a constant and significant factor in shaping the nation's foreign policy. In particular, the Maldives have recently sought assistance concerning environmental issues, especially concerning the scientific prediction that if global warming and sea levels continue to rise at the current rate, the Maldives will gradually be completely submerged under water.

For a large part of its early history, the Maldives had strong economic links with India and Sri Lanka, traditionally the island nation's only two contacts with the outside world. It gradually developed economic ties with the Malabaris from western Africa and the Arabs and the Moors from the Middle East, and later with the European colonial powers. From the nineteenth century until 1965, the archipelago was a British protectorate, and hence, unable to dictate its own foreign policy.

The Maldives joined the United Nations (UN) in 1965 for several reasons. It recognized the need for international protection of its vulnerable and isolated geophysical position, and saw also the necessity of acquiring technical assistance and development of trade relations with the world. Its foreign policy thus was determined by its need to end its isolation from the world.

From the beginning of its tenure in the UN, the archipelago has always remained constant to its policy of peaceful coexistence and nonalignment. Along with the majority of South Asian nations, it has favored disarmament, nuclear nonproliferation, banning of nuclear weapons, and the declaration of the Indian Ocean as a zone of peace. It became a member of the Colombo Plan, the Inter-Governmental Maritime Consultative Organization (IMCO), the Universal Postal Union (UPU), the United Nations Development Programme (UNDP) and the World Health Organization (WHO). In 1976, the island nation joined the club of nonalignment and opened a permanent mission in the UN. The Maldives also maintain membership in the South Asian Alliance for Regional Co-operation (SAARC).

Following its policy of furthering its own development while remaining unequivocal on most of the important global issues, the Maldives played an increasingly active role in international and regional bodies on issues of global significance. In 1982, it was accorded a special membership to the Commonwealth of Nations, a voluntary association of 53 independent states, most of which are former British protectorates or colonies. By 1985, five countries have resident missions in the Maldives: Pakistan, India, Libya, Sri Lanka and Iraq.

Human Rights Profile

International human rights law insists that states respect civil and political rights, and also promote an individual's economic, social and cultural rights. The United Nations Universal Declaration on Human Rights (UDHR) is recognized as the standard for international human rights. Its authors sought the counsel of the world's great thinkers, philosophers, and religious leaders, and were careful to create a document that reflects the core values shared by every world culture. (To read this document or view the articles relating to cultural human rights, visit: http://www.udhr.org/UDHR/default.htm.)

Overall, the Republic of Maldives has a passable human rights record. In theory, the government strives to protect the rights of its citizens, which are protected by the Maldivian constitution. In 2003, the president of Maldives established by decree an independent statutory body called the Human Rights Commission of Maldives. This commission is an autonomous legal entity, and has the capacity to sue and be sued and enter transactions in its own name. The aim of the commission is to protect and promote the human rights of the Maldivian citizens under the Maldives Constitution, Islamic Shari'a law, and the international Human Rights Conventions ratified by the republic. As such, it has been given the right to visit any authority, jail or organization in the archipelago.

In practice, however, the human rights record of the Maldives has been less than perfect. The contemporary Maldivian society is no longer based on a strict hierarchy of social castes, as it was for most of its history. This transition preserved the fundamental rights of the citizens, such as the right to life, freedom and equality as decreed by Articles 1, 2 and 3 of the UDHR. However, there is an occasional impingement of other rights by the government. Articles 9 and 19 are frequently violated, often in conjunction. Article 9 forbids arbitrary detention or exile and Article 19 guarantees the right to opinion and freedom of expression. In the Maldives, there is a strict measure of state-imposed censorship on all forms of media, including journalism, and many political parties and independent media companies have been banned by the government.

There have also been numerous cases in recent years of journalists, satirists, and critics being arbitrarily arrested and imprisoned because of their political beliefs. For example, in 2001, Abdulla Shakir, a member of parliament for the Malé Atoll, was arrested for exercising his right to free speech, and subsequently reported as missing. In addition, political activist Jennifer Latheef was sentenced to a 10-year prison term in 2005 on charges of terrorism after protesting against deaths in prison and political repression. There are also numerous prisoners of conscience in the Maldives—typically journalists and critics of the government—arrested and detained for unnecessarily prolonged periods of time for exercising their rights to speech. In jail, there have been reports of torture and inhumane treatment, a violation of Article 5 of the UDHR.

Article 20, which ensures the right to peaceful assembly, is also violated frequently by the government, as many protesters face arbitrarily arrest. Such prisoners of conscience do not always receive a full and fair trial, and many often do not even have access to a lawyer or an impartial method of appeal when tried in court, a clear violation of Article 10. The Maldivian criminal justice system has been declared by international watchdogs to have certain fundamental flaws in its system, which the government has taken some steps to remedy. However, it is still far from being completely fair and just.

The Maldivian constitution itself violates Article 18 of the UDHR, which ensures the right to religion, and the freedom to publicly observe any religion. The Maldivian constitution is interpreted to mean that citizens must be Muslim, and converts from Islam lose their Maldivian citizenship. It considers the public practice of a religion other than Islam illegal, although visiting non-Muslims are allowed to practice their religion in private. In fact, as of 2008, a revision of the constitution states that a non-Muslim is denied citizenship.

ECONOMY

Overview of the Economy

The economy of the Maldives depends heavily on tourism and fishing. In 2014, the gross domestic product (GDP) per capita was estimated at $12,400 (USD). Tourism accounts for 47.8 percent of the GDP. Industry accounts for 23 percent, with service industries accounting for the remainder. The economic effects of the 2004 tsunami are still being felt.

The main export products of Malé, the capital and commercial center of the country, are fish and agricultural products. These include bonito and tuna fish, shells, coconut, breadfruit and hand-woven palm mats. Canned tuna fish from other islands is sold in the markets in Malé. In addition, Malé is home to one of the two major ports in the Maldives. Its size and central location make it the main area for import and export, and help facilitate trade with Arabia, China, and India.

Industry

Fishing and related activities comprise the largest industry in the Maldives.

Tourism is an expanding industry in the Maldives. Some 500,000 or more tourists visit the Maldives each year. Annual revenues from the tourist trade continue to rise. The islands' resorts and scuba diving tours attract visitors from around the world.

Labor

The Maldivian labor force was estimated at 159,700 in 2012. Manufacturing and tourism employ 15 and 11 percent of the workforce, respectively; the largest concentration of workers is in the services sector, which employs approximately 70 percent of the Maldivian work force (2010 estimate). The unemployment rate was reported as roughly 11 percent in 2002.

Energy/Power/Natural Resources

The Maldives' only real natural resources are the abundance of fish, and the natural beauty of the surrounding waters and coral reef.

Environmental challenges faced by the Maldives include the depletion of fresh groundwater combined with population growth, and rising sea levels due to global warming. The islands also sustained extensive damage during the tsunami caused by an earthquake in the Indian Ocean in December 2004.

In 2009, the president of the Maldives announced plans for the country to become carbon-neutral within one decade. The low-lying country is at high risk due to climate change, and would become the first country to adopt a carbon-neutrality plan.

Fishing

Fishing and related activities comprise the largest industry in the Maldives. Dried, frozen, and canned fish is exported, mostly to Sri Lanka. About two-thirds of the country's exports are fish, including tuna, corals and shells; the most important commercial catch is skipjack tuna, which constitutes more than half of the industry's total catch. The Maldives have been involved in the cowrie trade since the ninth century. Cowrie shells were used as currency in Africa until the 1900s. The shells are still exported today. Environmental concerns include overfishing and marine pollution.

Agriculture

Agricultural exports include coir (coconut fiber) and dried coconut. The unique composition of the coral islands makes only 13 percent of the land useful for crops. The soil that is cultivated is poor in plant nutrients.

Most food is imported, especially rice. The most important crops grown in the Maldives include millet, yams, breadfruit, watermelons, and a green vegetable called murunga. On some islands, pineapple and citrus fruits are grown.

Tourism

Over 1 million visitors come to the Maldives each year. Most of these tourists come from Germany, Italy, Japan, and Great Britain. Tourists generally stay in resort areas isolated from the general populace. There are resorts on eighty of the islands. Scuba diving among the islands' extensive coral reef is a popular tourist activity.

The Islamic Center in Malé is the most famous landmark in the Maldives. The gold-domed building houses a library, conference hall and the Grand Mosque. Woodcarvings and calligraphy by Maldivian artists decorate the prayer hall.

Izza Tahir, Roberta Baxter, Anne Whittaker

DO YOU KNOW?

- Huvadhoo Atoll is the largest atoll in the world. It has a lagoon that measures 112 kilometers (70 miles) in diameter.
- There are more than 40 known shipwrecks in the waters around the Maldives, ranging from ancient vessels to a ship sunk in 1981. Divers can visit many of these shipwrecks.
- An undersea restaurant has opened at a resort in the Maldives. Diners can view marine life and the coral reef through clear walls.

Bibliography

Ahmed, Rizwan A. "The State and National Foundation in the Maldives," in Kamala Visweswaran, ed., *Perspectives on Modern South Asia.* Malden, MA: Wiley-Blackwell, 2011.

Hockly, T.W. *The Two Thousand Isles: A Short Account of the People, History and Customs of the Maldive Archipelago*. New Delhi: Asian Education Services, 2003.

Lonely Planet and Tom Masters. *Maldives.* Oakland, CA: Lonely Planet, 2012.

Maloney, Clarence. *People of the Maldive Islands.* Telangana, India: Orient Blackswan, 2013.

Romero-Frias, Xavier. *Folk Tales of the Maldives.* Copenhagen: Nordic Institute of Asian Studies, 2012.

Works Cited

"Human Rights Commission of the Maldives." < http://www.hrcm.org.mv/aboutus.aspx>

Lyon, James. Maldives. Singapore: *Lonely Planet Publications*, 2003.

"Maldives". *Central Intelligence Agency: The World Factbook.* <https://www.cia.gov/library/publications/the-world-factbook/geos/mv.html#Govt>

"Maldives." *Tourism-Sri Lanka.* < http://maldives.tourism-srilanka.com/arts-and-crafts.html>

"Maldives you could look it up." *Sports Illustrated.* 88.7 (1998): 130.

Masters, Tom and James Lyon. Maldives: Country Guide. Oakland (CA): *Lonely Planet Publications*, 2006.

"People of Maldives." *Hello Maldives.* <http://www.hellomaldives.com/maldives/people/index.htm>

Phadnis, Urmila. "Maldives: The Land of Wonders and Woes." *Encyclopedia of SAARC Nations.* Vol. Verinder Grover (ed.). New Delhi: Deep and Deep Publications, 1997. 22–25.

Poché, Christian. "Ṭār." Grove Music Online. *Oxford Music Online.* <http://www.oxfordmusiconline.com.myaccess.library.utoronto.ca/subscriber/article/grove/music/27503>.

Sathuendrakumar, Rajasundrum. "Culture of Maldives." *Countries and Their Cultures.* <http://www.everyculture.com/Ja-Ma/Maldives.html>

"The Maldives." *Europa World online.* <http://www.europaworld.com.myaccess.library.utoronto.ca/entry/mv.dir.1.SOC-AND-MEDIA

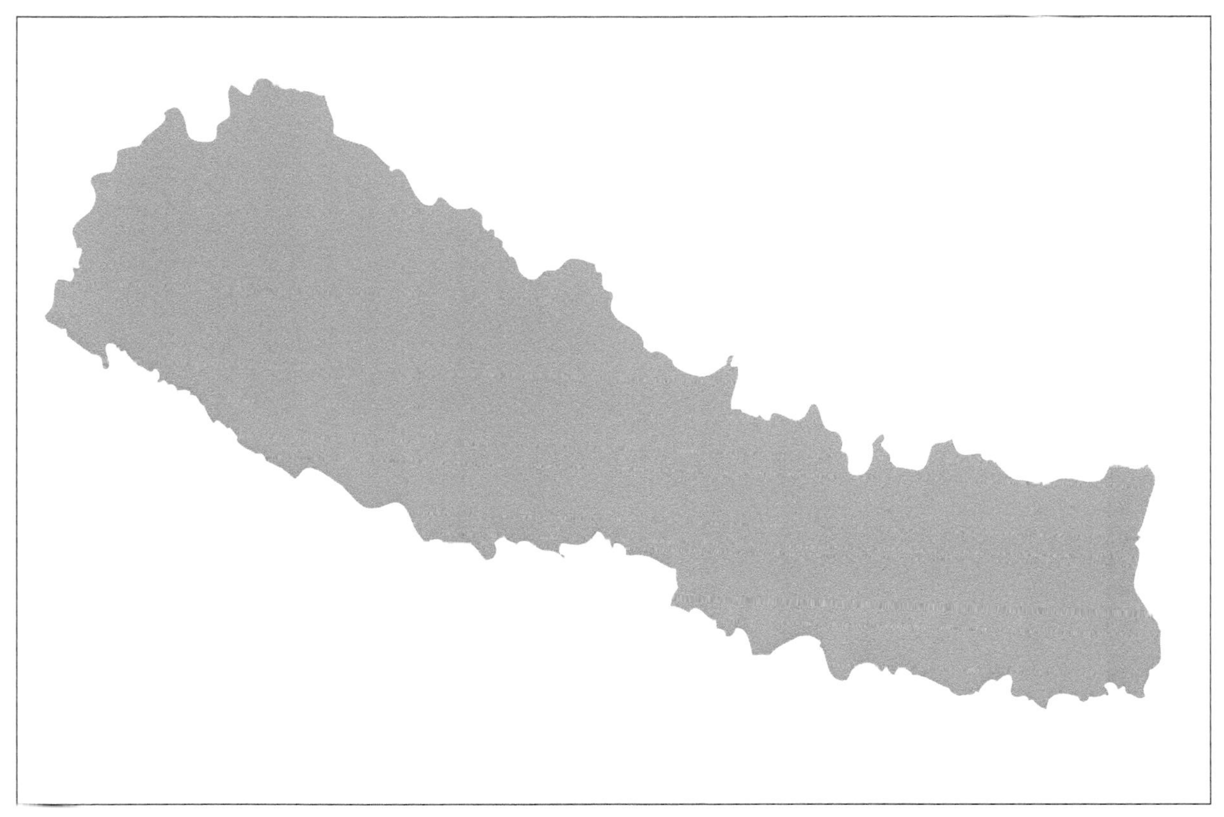

NEPAL

Introduction

The Federal Democratic of Nepal is perhaps best known as the home of Sagarmatha, known in the West as Mount Everest, the highest mountain in the world. The landlocked country lies along the Himalaya mountain range, between Tibet and India.

Nepal is the only Hindu kingdom in the world. The cultural heritage of the area is illustrated by its numerous Buddhist and Hindu monuments and shrines. It is to this region that mountain trekkers and climbers travel, and experience the beauty of a land that sits on the rooftop of the world.

GENERAL INFORMATION

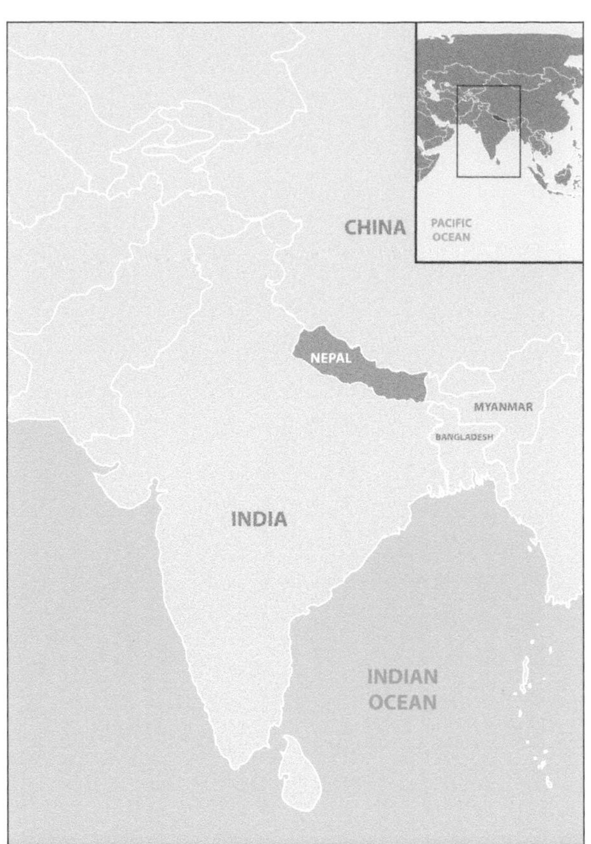

Official Language: Nepali
Population: 30,986,975 (2014 estimate)
Currency: Nepalese rupee
Coins: One hundred paisa equal one rupee. Coins are issued in denominations of 1, 5, 10, 25, 50 paisa and 1, 2, 5 and 10 rupaiya.
Land Area: 143,351 square kilometers (55,348 square miles)
Water Area: 3,830 square kilometers (1,479 square miles)
National Motto: "Janani Janmabhumishcha Swargadapi Gariyasi" ("Mother and Motherland are Dearer than Heaven")
National Anthem: "Sayaun Thunga Phool Ka" ("Made of Hundreds of Flowers")
Capital: Kathmandu (Katmandu)
Time Zone: GMT +5:45
Flag Description: Nepal's flag differs from other nations in that it does not have four sides. Instead, the flag of Nepal is the shape of two merged pennants, one atop the other. The flag is solid red with the smaller pennant on top emblazoned with a sun resting in a crescent moon; the lower pennant, which is slightly larger, features a sun. A blue border surrounds the flag, symbolizing peace and harmony. The red signifies bravery.

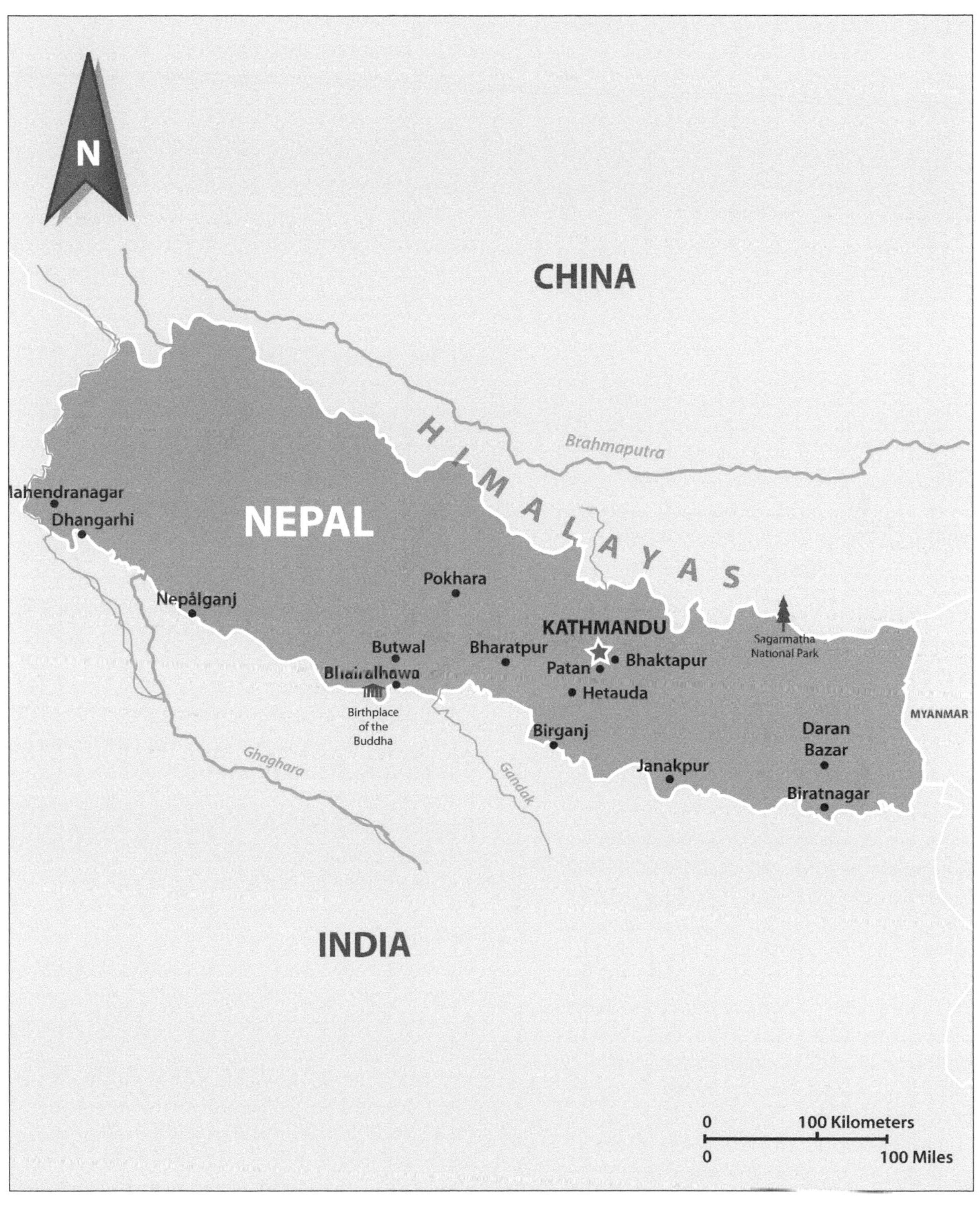
N
CHINA
HIMALAYAS
Brahmaputra
NEPAL
lahendranagar
Dhangarhi
Nepålganj
Pokhara
KATHMANDU
Sagarmatha National Park
Butwal
Bharatpur
Patan
Bhaktapur
Bhairalhawa
Hetauda
Birthplace of the Buddha
Birganj
Daran Bazar
MYANMAR
Janakpur
Biratnagar
Ghaghara
Gandak
INDIA
0
100 Kilometers
0
100 Miles

Principal Cities by Population (2011, except where noted):

- Kathmandu (1,142,000, 2014)
- Pokhara (264,999)
- Biratnagar (261,125)
- Bharatpur (239,867)
- Lalitpur (220,802)
- Itahari (140,517)
- Birgunj (135,904)
- Butwal (118,462)
- Dharan (116,181)
- Bhim Datta (104,599)

Population

Approximately 45 percent of Nepal's population lives along the border with India. Another 10 percent lives on farmland in the mountains. The overwhelming majority of the population is rural, living in small villages. About 18 percent of Nepal's people live in cities and towns. Although the population statistics for Kathmandu in 2001 showed an estimated population of less than 700,000, by 2014 it grew significantly, with a population exceeding one million. The metropolitan area, which lies in the Kathmandu Valley of the Himalayas, is even greater, measuring over 2.5 million people. The city experiences an estimated population growth rate of four percent a year.

The country's population makeup is highly diverse, as many people have migrated to Nepal from neighboring regions, including India, Tibet, China, and Burma. Nepal's largest ethnic group is the Chhettri (or Kshetri), an Indo-Aryan people comprising over 16 percent of the population. The Brahman-Hill, a Brahmin caste of people, comprise over 12 percent, the Magar (an indigenous population) seven percent, Tharu (an indigenous Asian population from the foothills of Nepal and India) over six percent, Tamang (from Tibet) over five percent, and the Newar (another Indo-Aryan people) at five percent. Other ethnic groups include Muslims (four percent), Kami (almost four percent), and Yadav (almost four percent). The largest segment of the population (almost 33 percent) falls under the category "other."

Nepal's mountainous terrain and deep river gorges isolate its people from each other and hamper development. Though castes are officially outlawed, discrimination based on caste persists and also prevents real economic progress.

Languages

Nepali, the official language, is spoken by roughly half of the population, and is a second language for most others. It is related to the languages of northern India. Other major languages spoken in Nepal include Malthir and Bhojpuri. Nepal has more than fifty languages and dialects.

Native People & Ethnic Groups

Throughout Nepal's long history, groups of nomads, refugees, and conquerors entered the country from India, Tibet and Central Asia. These peoples became the ancestors of the modern Nepalese.

Today, Nepal's many ethnic groups are separated by the rugged terrain. The Nepalese are closely related to the northern Indian peoples. Many others are Tibetan and a variety of Tibeto-Burman and Indo-Aryan groups, including, the Newar, Limbu, Rai, Magar, Tharu, Sherpa, Tamang and Gurung, as well as the Bahun and Chhetri, who claim the highest castes (a type of social class division) in the Hindu caste system. The Sherpas, both men and women, are an ethnic group, but are perhaps best known to Westerners because of their work as guides for mountain climbers. Another group, the Gurkhas, often serve with distinction in the British and Indian armies.

Religions

Hinduism is the state religion and the religion of more than 80 percent of the population. Nepal is the only Hindu kingdom in the world. Nowhere is the influence of Hinduism more apparent in Nepal than Kathmandu. The city is home to hundreds of Hindu temples, shrines and public artwork. Religious tolerance permits Hindus and Buddhists to pray at the same temples, celebrate the same festivals and even worship the same deities. Hindu beliefs in Nepal are often combined with Buddhism. Shrines and temples of both religions are sacred. A little more than 10 percent of Nepalese are Buddhist. Other religions include Islam, Bahai, Jainism, Sikhism, Christianity, and Kirat, a local traditional belief.

Climate

Nepal's climate varies according to altitude. The higher peaks have a permanent snow cover while Kathmandu, in the central valley, experiences humid, warm and sunny summer weather. The Terai lowland area has a tropical climate. Kathmandu's temperature ranges from 2° Celsius (35° Fahrenheit) in winter to 30° Celsius (86° Fahrenheit) in summer. Average temperatures in the Terai vary from 19° Celsius (66° Fahrenheit) in winter to 28° Celsius (82° Fahrenheit) in the summer.

The Terai also experiences the tropical monsoon. Rainfall in the western lowlands ranges from 760 millimeters (30 inches) to 1,000 millimeters (39 inches) annually. In the east, annual rainfall of 1,800 millimeters (70 inches) to 4,000 millimeters (157 inches) is normal.

ENVIRONMENT & GEOGRAPHY

Topography

Nepal is a small, landlocked country in the Himalayas. It shares a border with China (Tibet) on the north and with India on the east, south and west.

The highest elevation is Sagarmatha, or Mount Everest, rising 8,850 meters (29,035 feet) above sea level. The lowest point is Kanchan Kalan, 70 meters (229 feet) above sea level.

Nepal has three topographical regions: the Himalayas, the central hills and valleys, and the Terai lowlands. The first two regions account for 80 percent of the country's area. The Himalayas cross the northern part of the country from east to west. They are characterized by steep, river-cut valleys, glaciers and snow. Forests cover the mountain slopes. Mountain people herd sheep and yaks (long-haired oxen).

South of the mountains stretch the hills and valleys, again from east to west. Many crops are grown in this area. Farmers also herd goats, sheep and cattle. The Terai, along Nepal's southern border with India, is a lowland area of rainforests, swamps and fertile farmland.

Nepal's most prominent river is the Karnal, 180 kilometers (111 miles) long. It rises in Tibet and flows through western Nepal into the Terai and finally joins the Ganges River and the Bay of Bengal.

The Marsayangdi ("raging river") is a favorite among expert whitewater rafters. The river rises in the northern Annapurna Himalayas, and then flows east and south, joining the Trisuli River at Muingling. Another good rafting and kayaking river is the Sun Kosi ("river of gold"), the watershed for eastern Nepal. The Sun Kosi rises in Tibet and runs east, joining the Ganges in India.

These rivers exist in sharp contrast with the three heavily polluted rivers that run through the capital city Kathmandu: the Bishnumati, the Bagmati, and Dhobi Khola. As the only metropolitan city in Nepal, Kathmandu has the most educational and employment opportunities, the most financial institutions and the best infrastructure. However, poor urban planning has led to severe environmental degradation. The nearby rivers are examples of this

With an area of 50.67 square kilometers (19.56 square miles), Kathmandu is the largest city in Nepal. It is situated at an elevation of approximately 1,360 meters (4,462 feet) in Kathmandu Valley, a basin in the mid-hill region of Nepal that was once a lake. To the north is the Himalaya mountain range and to the south is the Mahabharat mountain range.

Air quality in the city is extremely poor—valley topography coupled with winter temperature inversions prevent wind from dispersing the large amounts of automobile and factory emissions that accumulate in the atmosphere. The number of days with high visibility between November and February has dropped considerably since the 1970s.

Plants & Animals

Nepal boasts surprising biodiversity for such a small country. Wildlife in the Himalaya area includes mountain sheep, snow leopards, musk deer, kyangs (wild horses), tahrs (mountain goat-antelopes), Danfe pheasants (the national bird), blood pheasants, ravens, Tibetan snowcocks, protected Tibetan black-necked cranes, bearded vultures and Himalayan griffons (eagles).

The Terai is home to numerous species including royal Bengal tigers, hog and spotted deer, tigers, leopards, wild elephants, fresh-water dolphins, wild boars, blue bulls, and a variety of snakes. Endangered animals in this region include gharials (crocodiles), native one-horned rhinoceroses, and the last surviving population of arn, or wild buffalo.

More than 400 species of birds are also found, especially in parks and reserves, including ibises, storks, egrets, herons, endangered swamp partridges, Bengal floricans, many migratory birds and more than twenty species of ducks.

Nepal is home to more than 10,000 plant species, 5 percent of which are endemic (growing naturally only in Nepal). Of these, roughly 1,600 species are medicinal or aromatic plants, which are used frequently in Nepal. The country also boasts forty-seven species of orchids, thirty species of rhododendrons, fifteen species of oaks, and forty-eight species of primroses. Many plants are protected in national parks and conservation areas.

The Terai is home to such trees as teak and sal (shorea robusta). Savanna (grasslands) and khair-sissoo (scrub forest) are also common in this area. Higher elevations host forests of rhododendron, pine, fir, birch and bamboo. Grasses, juniper and herbs grow in mountain pastures.

CUSTOMS & COURTESIES

Greetings

The traditional Nepali greeting is "Namasté" ("I bow to you"), which is typically said while pressing the palms of one's hands together. When two people meet, the person of younger age or lower social status will initiate the greeting while bowing their head as a sign of respect; the older or higher ranking person then responds in kind. When there is a significant difference in age or rank, the response may be a simple acknowledgment of the greeting. Namaste is also used as a way of saying goodbye. In instances where a person is greeting someone of very high social standing, it is customary to use the more formal greeting of "Namaskar" (loosely, "I bow to the divinity in you") instead. When saying hello or goodbye to a group of people, it is polite to speak to the older people first. It is also important to note that the depth of these two phrases—"Namasté" and "Namaskar"—extends beyond salutation, and the two phrases are also associated with the affirmation of one's faith.

There are also several less formal greetings. It is common to greet a friend by asking if they have eaten rice today. When greeting someone who one knows, it is respectful to add the suffix "-ji" to the end of their name. While traveling, it is polite to ask where a person is going to or coming from. In addition, Nepalis sometimes use kinship names to address strangers. For example, the elderly are called grandfather (baje) and grandmother (baji), and somewhat older people are referred to as elder brother (daai) and elder sister (didi). Younger people are called younger brother (bhaai) and younger sister (bahini).

Gestures & Etiquette

Nepalese are generally considered very welcoming people who cherish visitors. However, there are several points of etiquette that are very important and highly characteristic of Nepal's unique culture. Nepalese can be very inquisitive, and often ask questions about very personal issues, including income or a woman's fertility. Despite this openness, Nepalese—and travelers alike—are careful not to raise certain topics. For example, it may be considered rude to comment on the poverty of the country, caste inequality or the status of women. Additionally, it is also wise to be careful about discussing the nation's current political situation.

Because religion plays such an important role in Nepali culture, consideration of people's religious beliefs is taken very seriously. Nepalese participate in a wide range of religious ceremonies, and some of these are meant to be very private. As such, it is important for one to ask permission to view a religious event, let alone photograph it. Nepalese are also very respectful when visiting a Hindu or Buddhist temple, and remove their shoes before visiting. (Visiting a Hindu holy place may also require removing any items made of leather, as cows are considered sacred.) In addition, when visiting a place sacred to Nepali Buddhists, it is necessary to always move in a clockwise manner.

Nepalese have a culture of physical gestures and beliefs that should be politely considered and appreciated. For example, the gesture indicating an affirmative answer is not a nod, but involves leaning the head from side to side. In addition, the gesture to beckon someone is to point the palm outward, while the gesture to go is to point the palm inward. It is considered polite to exchange money with another person with the right hand, while holding the right elbow with the left hand. Nepalese consider the feet to be the dirtiest part of the body, and the head the cleanest. As such, it is considered rude to point at anything with the feet. It is also considered impolite to step over someone, as this could accidentally result in touching the person with one's feet.

Eating/Meals

Nepalese generally eat only two main meals per day. Immediately after waking, Nepalese traditionally start their day with a cup of milky sweet tea called chiya. This is sometimes accompanied by pieces of fried dough. The large meal is eaten at mid-morning. This meal is usually dhal baat, the staple rice and lentil dish. The second significant meal is eaten in the late evening. This meal also consists of dhal baat, often with pickled and spiced vegetables. Snacks are typically eaten between large meals, and may include spicy potatoes, popped rice, dried peas and steamed dumplings called momos. Milky sweet tea is also commonly consumed throughout the day.

Nepalese typically eat with their fingers. Traditionally, Nepalese only eat with the right hand because the left hand is used to cleanse oneself. The left hand is considered impure, and is never used to pass food to another person. Similarly, food left on a plate after eating is also considered impure, so it is impolite for a person to take excessively large portions. Metal spoons are rarely used, as they are believed to make food taste bad and cause unwanted weight loss. Nepali Hindus also follow additional standards of food purity. For example, a Hindu person of the Brahmin caste must never eat food made by someone of a lower caste.

Visiting

Nepalese are generally considered very welcoming people. It is common to be invited to enjoy food and drink at a Nepali home, even by strangers. Rather than turning down an invitation outright, it is polite to agree to visit at some unspecific point in the future. While not required, hosts will be pleased to receive a small gift, such as flowers or chocolate. People of certain ethnic backgrounds may invite guests to their house, but then serve them on the porch. This is because there are caste restrictions on who can actually enter the home. When invited into a house, it is necessary to remove one's shoes. In addition, because the kitchen often contains a shrine and the hearth is considered holy, outsiders should be respectful when entering a Nepali kitchen.

It is common for a guest to be served food first. A good host will only begin eating once a guest is clearly enjoying the meal. In turn, a good guest will make his or her enjoyment apparent. It is completely acceptable to eat with enthusiasm, even to the point of making noise, as this is a sign of appreciation. To that extent, burping at the end of the meal is considered good manners.

It is also considered polite to ask for a second helping. Asking for more is not always necessary, however, as an attentive host will refill a guest's plate when it is empty. A guest should leave a small (not large) amount of food on the plate to indicate that he or she is done with the meal. Nepalese tend to not talk very much at mealtimes, which are reserved for eating and not socializing, and there are other opportunities for conversation.

LIFESTYLE

Family

Family is the most important component of Nepali society, and generally defines all aspects of life. It is normal for extended families to live together in a house since extended families provide the individual with a support network. The extended family network is also organized into a hierarchy of respect. Younger family members are expected to obey older relatives, particularly the family patriarch. In addition, an adult son is required to care for his elderly parents and is obligated to perform the cremation rituals after death. Since this ritual is believed to allow them to be reborn in the next life, Nepali Hindus and Buddhists consider it a religious duty to have children. Traditionally, marriages are arranged by one's older relatives, and a new wife is expected to move in with her husband and his family.

Housing

Houses vary considerably throughout Nepal. This is due to several factors, most notably ethnic traditions, economic class, climate and access to building materials. Homes range from simple bamboo structures, mud huts and impermanent driftwood shelters, to multi-floor thatched clay buildings and walled mansions. Despite this diversity, there are common forms to the Nepali house.

The basic design is typically rectangular, with two or three rooms connected by a hallway or external walkway. Houses almost always contain a household shrine, either in a dedicated room or in the kitchen. Kitchens tend to be very simple rooms with a fireplace or kerosene cooking stove. Generally, running water is not common in kitchens. In fact, most houses do not have any indoor plumbing. As such, bathroom facilities are usually simple outhouses, and are often shared among several households. In addition, bathing is normally conducted at outdoor water taps or public pumps.

Food

In general, the national cuisine of Nepal has been heavily influenced by the culinary traditions of India, as well as by Nepal's climate. A largely steep country, Nepal's mostly rugged terrain often yields few and distinct crops, thus giving the Nepali cuisine a bland and simple reputation. Other foreign influences on Nepali cuisine include the food traditions of China and Tibet. Traditionally, many of the Nepal's typical meals consist of rice, lentils, and curried and pickled vegetables, in addition to curried meat dishes.

There are a number of grains grown throughout Nepal, with crops varying by elevation. Rice is grown in lower areas, while wheat, corn and millet are cultivated at middle elevations. Barley, potatoes, and buckwheat are more common in higher areas. A boiled rice and lentil dish, known as dhal baat, is the most common meal in Nepal, and is eaten twice each day by most Nepalis. In the higher zones where rice does not grow, it is considered a rare delicacy. Boiled potatoes and roasted flour (called tsampa) are dietary staples in these highland areas. Other vegetable crops include eggplants, peas, peppers, spinach, tomatoes and squash. These are often pickled and spiced, adding flavor to dhal baat.

Dairy products also form an important part of the Nepali diet. Yogurt, butter and cheese are commonly made from the milk of cows, water buffaloes and yaks. Juju dhau, or yogurt, often serves as dessert.

Spices that are commonly used in Nepali dishes include ginger, garlic, coriander, pepper, cumin, and turmeric. Due to Nepal's diverse religious beliefs, ethnic traditions and income levels, patterns of meat consumption vary. Since most people are Hindu, beef, particularly from the cow, is rarely consumed. Hindus of the Brahman caste favor vegetarianism and do not eat chicken, pork, or water buffalo. However, these meats may be enjoyed on occasion by other ethnicities. Goat meat, on the other hand, is widely consumed, though for some, it is reserved for special occasions. A popular way to prepare meat is by steaming it, and steamed, meat-filled dumplings, called momos, are common.

Other traditional Nepali dishes include gundrook-dheedo, which is typically made of wheat, maize, and vegetables, and is known for its nutritional value; alu tama, a curried dish typically featuring bamboo shoots and potatoes; vegetable pulao, or Nepali fried rice, a rice and vegetable dish often flavored with spices such as coriander, cinnamon, ginger, garlic, cumin and turmeric; masu, a curried or spiced meat dish, typically served with rice and gravy; and chatamari, which is Nepali flat bread that is commonly served with a topping such as meat, vegetables, eggs, or even sugar. Other popular dishes include sukula (spicy, dried meat), sanya khuna (jellied fish soup), baji samay (flattened rice), and palu (sliced ginger).

Nepalese enjoy a variety of traditional beverages. The most common beverage aside from water is a sweet milky tea called chiya. A sweet or salty yogurt beverage called lassi is commonly sold in cities. Tibetan butter tea is enjoyed in the highlands. Several alcoholic beverages are brewed from grains. A Tibetan form of beer called chang is made from barley in the highlands. At lower elevations, a form of beer called tongba is made from millet. Distilled grain liquor called rakshi is produced, and is generally the most widely consumed hard alcoholic beverage in Nepal.

Food is usually eaten with the fingers (using the right hand only). Nepalese do not eat from a common pot. In fact, if someone eats from another person's plate, the plate is considered unclean.

Tourism has introduced international cuisine to Nepal, including Chinese, Japanese, Indian and other foreign foods.

Life's Milestones

When a child is born, it is often taken from the mother by the paternal grandmother, who cleans it and inspects it for good health. Though Nepalese revere children, birth is considered to bring ritual impurity onto a household. Family members traditionally participate in rituals such as special diets and prayer after birth. Among some ethnic groups, there is a special ceremony to name the child. This is ceremony is typically attended by priests and astrologers. When a child is six months old, most Nepalese hold a ceremony in which the child eats rice for the first time.

Marriages are usually arranged by families, and wedding ceremonies are very elaborate parties, and largely considered a time for celebration, feasting, and good cheer. Often, wedding celebrations can last for several days. They are also commonly held on ritually auspicious dates, as determined by astrologers. In addition, weddings are also considered a sacred time. In contrast, death is considered to be the most impure time. At a time of an individual's death, the deceased person is typically wrapped in white. The body is then carried to a riverside, and cremated. This ritual is considered extremely important, as it allows the person's spirit to be reborn. Traditionally, the ritual is conducted by the person's eldest son, and the anniversary of the death is often observed for several years.

CULTURAL HISTORY

Art

Nepal's rich cultural history has its origins in the Kathmandu Valley, located in the central part of the country. Historically, the valley was an important stop on the ancient trade routes between India and China. The cultural heritage of the Kathmandu Valley is further illustrated by its numerous Buddhist and Hindu monuments and shrines. In fact, Indian Hindu and Buddhist artistic techniques left lasting influences on Nepal, resulting in a national art and culture that is predominantly religious in nature. As a result, the styles, techniques and symbolism inherent in Nepali art have been traditionally conservative, and there is no real distinction between decorative and religious art.

In addition to religion, art and culture in Nepal was also influenced by geography. Because the Kathmandu Valley was very fertile, agriculture and trade were the two primary occupations, and those that did not become farmers typically became skilled craftsman. Traditionally, the role of the craftsman or artist in Nepali society was defined and preserved by a guild structure. In this manner, handicrafts and techniques were directly passed down, often from father to son, and outsiders rarely become artists. In addition, many artistic traditions were associated with lower castes. Some of the earliest forms of art and crafts that flourished in Nepal were metalworking, sculpture and painting.

Metalworkers made items out of precious metals using methods perfected in the 15th-century. Traditionally, metalwork was done through two main techniques: items such as bells, reliefs on temples and lamps were made by hammering, while an elaborate technique using wax statues and clay molds was used to produce detailed figurines, typically of gods and goddesses. This style of sculpture, particularly made with bronze and cooper, is representative of one of the earliest art forms of metalwork found in the Nepali valley, with some figurines dating from the fifth to eighth century BCE. Pottery was also an important handicraft in Nepal's cultural history, with terra cotta oil lamps one of the most common forms.

The oldest known paintings in Nepal are highly decorative religious manuscripts from the 11th century. Nepali visual artists also produced iconic pauba paintings, or scroll paintings, called thangkas by people of Tibetan ethnicity. Largely displayed in monasteries or carried as educational tools, these scroll or cloth paintings typically depicted richly religious scenes, such as the life of the Buddha and other religious figures. By the 15th century, thangkas became more decorative in manner and more influenced by Hinduism, often displaying Hindu deities.

Architecture

Nepal's architectural tradition is also influenced by religion. There are two main styles of temples prominent in Nepali culture. The first, influenced by Indian Hindu traditions, is the shikhara style. These have a long, pyramid shape, often said to resemble the mountains. The second is built in the tiered-roof pagoda style, and typically features detailed brickwork and carving, elaborate gilding, and colorful painting.

Music

Nepal has a wide range of musical traditions. These can generally be broken down into classical and folk music. Traditionally, classical music was performed by men. One popular style of classical music, called bhajan, consists of singing religious hymns to an accompanying instrument, most notably the tabla hand drum. Bhajan is generally performed at night, and outside of temples. Buddhist chants are also a popular form of classical music in Nepal. Most Nepalis, even those who are not Buddhist, know the words to Om Mani Padme Hum, the most famous mantra, or prayer, in Buddhism.

There are many more folk music traditions associated with Nepal's various ethnic groups, reflecting the cultural diversity of the country. These various ethnic folk music traditions are all very different in terms of sounds, techniques and styles. However, most traditions use relatively few instruments—mainly vocals and percussion, sometimes accompanied by the flute or stringed harp. These folk music traditions have some cultural similarities as well. One common feature is that folk performances are very social events and usually performed at night, typically as neighborhood entertainment. In addition, songs are often improvised, and musicians try to outperform one another with clever lyrics. Singing folk songs is also an important aspect of the courtship process among many of Nepal's ethnic groups.

Dance

Historically, conventional theater was mostly attended by Nepal's wealthy classes. However, Nepal enjoyed other traditional forms of dramatic expression, and there are many dance traditions in Nepal that reflect the country's ethnic diversity. For example, the Sherpa people are famous for their line dancing, the Tharu people performed distinctive stick dances, and Tibetans were known for their masked cham dances. Dance also became a common form of expression in a variety of situations, and Nepali people continue to dance at home and in public, at both secular and religious events.

Certain dance traditions in Nepal are considered forms of worship. These dances substitute movement for words as prayer. For example, there is an elaborate Buddhist ritual dance called charya nritya, which largely originated in seventh-century India. It has been passed down through history as a secret form of tantric meditation. (Typically, tantric meditation is a spiritual practice, prevalent in Buddhism, in which results are visualized and interconnectedness is emphasized.)

In addition, many Hindu temples host performances in which masked dancers act out religious legends and Indian epic poetry, also referred to as Sanskrit epics. Similar performances are often part of the many festivals which continue to take place throughout the country. Many of these festival dances feature wild costumes, face paint and masks, dramatically transforming participants into Hindu gods and demons. Festival dances often take the form of torch-lit nighttime processions, which wind through the streets of Nepal's cities and villages.

Literature

Nepal has a long literary tradition that is also clearly religious in nature. However, Nepal is not particularly well known for its historical literature. This is due in part to the fact that the country has always had a very low rate of literacy. The illuminated manuscripts first produced in the 11th century could be considered an early kind of literature. These were typically written on palm leaves, and used a form of Sanskrit script adopted from India (Sanskrit is one of the two classical languages of ancient India). Translations of Sanskrit and Urdu language religious texts from the 13th century also exist. Paper first came to Nepal in the 15th century, and volumes of hand-lettered religious texts were produced during this period.

Nepali literature began to fully flourish in the 19th century. One of the first popular literary works in Nepal was an adaptation of the Ramayana epic of ancient India, translated by Nepali poet Bhanubhakta Acharya (1814–1868). In the 20th-century, Nepali writers moved beyond merely translating Indian texts. In the first part of that century, writers mostly wrote in styles popular in India and the West. In contrast, truly unique Nepali literature flourished in the second half of the 20th-century, inspired in part by the groundbreaking author Lakshmi Prasad Devkota (1909–1959).

CULTURE

Arts & Entertainment

Nepalese music often employs the saringhi, a four-stringed instrument, or the flute. Traditional folk musicians, called gaines, often provide entertainment for evening social gatherings. Modern musical ensembles, known as damai, are present at virtually every wedding. Jazz is becoming popular, and aficionados hold an annual jazz festival in Kathmandu.

The most popular sports in Nepal are football (soccer) and cricket. However, it was the national taekwondo team who won Nepal's first-ever gold medals in the 1999 South Asia Federation Games.

Cultural Sites & Landmarks

Nepal's Kathmandu Valley itself is perhaps the country's most significant cultural site. The valley is home to nearly 130 historical and religious monuments and its townscapes are renowned for their architectural heritage. Furthermore, the valley holds great importance for followers of both Hinduism and Buddhism. In fact, many worshippers of both religions refer to the area's many religious sites as "living monuments," and worthy of pilgrimage. In 1979, the United Nations (UN) recognized the cultural heritage of the historic valley, and inscribed it as a World Heritage Site protected by the United Nations Educational, Scientific and Cultural Organization (UNESCO). In particular, UNESCO recognizes seven distinct groupings of ancient monuments and buildings: the Buddhist stupas (holy monument or temple) of Swayambhu and Bauddhanath, the Hindu temples of Pashupati and Changu Narayan, and the Durbar Square (three royal plazas) of the cities of Kathmandu, Patan and Bhaktapur.

The Swayambhunath temple, located across the Vishnumati River from Kathmandu, is often referred to as the Monkey Temple, due to the large population of monkeys that inhabit the surrounding woods. Considered one of the most important Buddhist shrines in the country, the Swayambhunath temple is said to have been built to house a sacred lotus that blossomed on the legendary lake that once dominated the Kathmandu valley. The temple's gilded spire is an important landmark that can be seen from Kathmandu. Buddhist worshipers and other visitors come here to walk in a clockwise direction around the temple's base, which is decorated with elaborate carvings. People also like to climb the 365 stairs to the top of the temple, where they are met with Swayambhunath's famous painted eyes and gilded thunderbolt.

Kathmandu's Durbar Square is the traditional center of the Nepali monarchy. It houses, many of Nepal's most historic buildings, and an extensive array of traditional Hindu temples and shrines. One of the most notable of these is the Kasthamandap, a 13th-century temple dedicated to the famous Hindu holy man Gorakhnath, who lived in the 11th and 12th centuries. Kathmandu is, in fact, named after this ancient temple. The square is home to several significant temples and shrines, including the gilded Maru Ganesh shrine, which celebrates the popular Hindu elephant god Ganesh, the Maju Deval, a temple dedicated to the Hindu god Shiva, and the Shiva-Parvati Temple, celebrating Shiva and his divine consort (spouse) Parvati.

The city of Pokhara is second only to Kathmandu in terms of popularity with tourists. Some of the city's famous landmarks include the World Peace Pagoda, a strikingly white monument donated by Buddhist monks from Japan. The Karma Dubgyu Chokhorling Monastery, overlooking the city, offers a glimpse into Nepali Buddhist monastic life. It also features some interesting Buddhist statuary. The city also has a museum dedicated to the famed Gurkhas, elite Nepalese soldiers historically known for their bravery and who continue to serve in the British Army.

The city of Pokhara is another important cultural site within Nepal, largely because it serves as a starting point for treks into the Himalayas. Specifically, the city is considered a gateway to the picturesque Annapurna range—a series of peaks in the Himalayas considered to be among the most dangerous to climb in the world. The Annapurna Sanctuary, located near Pokhara, is considered to offer some of the most majestic mountain views in the Himalayas.

In addition to the Kathmandu Valley, Nepal is also home to three other World Heritage Sites, most notably the Buddhist pilgrimage site of Lumbini. This particular site is believed to be the birthplace of Siddhārtha Buddha (c. 563–483 BCE), the founder of Buddhism. The site, designated as a World Heritage site in 1997, features the ruins of several ancient monasteries, as well as the sacred Bodhi Tree, underneath which Siddhārtha was believed to have achieved enlightenment. The remaining World Heritage Sites are the Chitwan National Park, the oldest national park in the country, and Sagarmatha National Park, which includes a portion of the famed Mount Everest, the world's highest mountain.

Libraries & Museums

Nepal is a popular destination for mountaineers and trekkers. Fittingly, the recently built International Mountain Museum in Pokhara presents visitors with information about the mountains of Nepal and the people from around the world who have climbed them. The National Museum features a collection of bronze sculptures as well as scroll paintings. Nepal's National Library houses over 70,000 books, mostly in English, but also holds several 17th-century Sanskrit and English texts, as well as a small collection of texts in Sanskrit, Nepali, Hindi and Nepalbhasa.

Holidays

Official holidays include National Unity Day (January 11), Martyrs' Day (January), National Democracy Day (February 19), King Gayanendra's Birthday (July 7), Constitution Day (November 9), and King Birendra's Birthday (December 28).

Since Nepal uses several different calendars, including the lunar calendar, the dates or religious holidays vary from year to year. All major Buddhist and Hindu holidays are celebrated, including the birthdays of Buddha and Krishna.

Youth Culture

Young people are highly revered in Nepalese culture. As such, it is extremely rare for a young couple to choose to not have children. However, young people in Nepal live rather difficult lives. Nepal's poverty heavily impacts its youth, who often suffer from hunger and lack of medical care. In addition, children are expected to work, resulting in the prevalence of child labor. In some cases, children, particularly girls, are sold as slaves. The violence created by the Maoist insurgency that lasted until 2006 also affected children. Both government soldiers and Maoist rebels are accused of killing children during the civil war, and the Maoists also had many child soldiers in their ranks.

Many changes to Nepali youth culture have taken place in the present generation. Westernization is occurring at a rapid pace, especially within large cities such as Kathmandu. For example, Western fashion, such as wearing jeans, is catching on among urban youth in these cities. Young people's musical tastes also reflect this outside influence, and contemporary genres such as rock, jazz, reggae and hip-hop have recently become popular among Nepali youth. Young people are also starting to demand more control over their own lives. Young Nepalis increasingly reject the tradition of arranged marriages, and marriage for the sake of love is becoming more common.

SOCIETY

Transportation

There are several options for ground transportation within Nepal. Buses can be uncomfortable, crowed beyond capacity, and slow. However, they remain the most important form of mass transportation since rail service in Nepal is very limited. For local trips within cities, taxis, rickshaws and three-wheeled buses called tempos are some of the most popular and common modes of transportation.

Several airlines offer flights to and from Nepal. These fly to Nepal's only international airport, Tribhuvan Airport, located in Kathmandu. Operating since 1958, Nepal Airlines Corporation (which used to be called Royal Nepal Airlines) is the largest and oldest in the country. It offers international flights to major Asian air hubs such as Bangkok, Dubai, New Delhi, Hong Kong, Mumbai and Singapore. It also offers domestic flights, linking Kathmandu to Nepal's smaller cities. Several smaller airlines opened in 1997 to provide domestic travel. This may be due in part to Nepal Airlines Corporation's rather poor reputation for customer satisfaction. However, most of these smaller airlines found the market difficult and closed down. The best known of the smaller airlines that still operates is Buddha Air. Drivers in Nepal travel on the left side of the road and the driver's seat is in the right side of the car.

Transportation Infrastructure

There is only one railroad in Nepal, with steam-driven trains that only travel short distances along the border with India. Buses operate along the highways, which span almost 12,800 kilometers (8,000 miles) throughout the country. Transportation in rural areas is far more difficult, and many destinations are still accessible only by the approximately 19,300 kilometers (12,000 miles) of footpaths within the country.

Media & Communications

Since only 40 percent of the population is literate, broadcast media are particularly important to the people of Nepal. Broadcasting since 1951, Radio Nepal has historically been the country's primary source of news and entertainment. Television came to Nepal in 1985, when the government-controlled Nepal Television began broadcasting. A number of private radio and television stations have emerged since the democratic reforms of 1990. These include Kantipur FM, Hits FM, Kantipur TV and Channel Nepal.

Despite the relatively small percentage of literate citizens, Nepal has a wide range of newspapers. However, newspapers are available only in urban areas. The most popular daily papers are the government owned *Gorkhapatra* and the independent *Kantipur*. There are also weekly papers such as the government affiliated *Deshantar* and the more independent *Budhabar*.

All forms of Nepali media entered a period of heavy censorship when King Gyanendra (b. 1947–) took control of the country in 2005. Restrictions were eased somewhat in 2006. However, pressure on the media from the king continued until he left office in 2008. Despite these restrictions on the media, the Internet has also flourished in Nepal in recent years. In fact, citizens have embraced Internet as a way to communicate with the outside world, and most towns and cities now have Internet cafés. This is particularly important since most Nepali households do not have telephone service. In 2013, Internet usage in Nepal was estimated to be just over 13 percent of the population; mobile and fixed line telephone penetration was measured at about 15 percent of the population in 2008.

SOCIAL DEVELOPMENT

Standard of Living

In 2013 Nepal ranked 145th out of 185 countries on the United Nations Human Development Index, which measures quality of life and standard of living indicators.

Water Consumption

According to UNICEF (the United Nations International Children's Emergency Fund), about 88 percent of the Nepalese population enjoys improved access to water sources, with urban dwellers (90 percent) having the advantage over rural populations (88 percent). Improved sanitation does not score as highly, with a national average of 37 percent having improved access to sanitation. Again, urban populations have an advantage, with 51 percent having access compared to 34 percent of rural populations. Threats to the water supply include pollution and arsenic in wells. Nepal's government has set a target of universal coverage by 2017.

Education

School attendance is compulsory for children between the ages of six and 11, but more than 41 percent of adult Nepalese have had no formal schooling. Education in state schools is free. Secondary education is provided in three cycles over the course of seven years.

Tribhuvan University was for a long time the only university in the country. Now, other state universities include Mahendra Sanskrit Viswavidyalaya, Purbanchal University and Pokhara University. There is also a private university in Banepa.

According to UNICEF, Nepal's adult literacy rate was estimated at 57 percent in 2011; women fall far behind men in literacy rates, with only 47 percent of the female population literate. For the same time period, primary school enrollment measured 84 percent. In the capital city of Kathmandu, literacy rates are indicative of societal gender inequality—90 percent of males are literate, yet only 66 percent of females are literate.

Women's Rights

The status of women in Nepal has historically varied among the different ethnic groups that populate the country. Overall, however, women have not enjoyed the same social rights as men. When married, a Nepali woman typically leaves her own family and becomes part of her husband's family. She generally enters the new family at a very low status, and has to obey her in-laws. A woman's worth has traditionally been tied to her ability to produce sons. In part, this is because sons perform the funeral rights for their parents. A man is allowed to take a second wife if his first wife remains childless for 10 years. Until the practice was outlawed in the 1920s, a widow was expected to throw herself on her husband's funeral pyre in an act of self-sacrifice called seti. In many cases, a widow is still expected to marry her deceased husband's brother, and allow her sons to take control of all financial property.

Women in modern Nepal face many difficulties. Poverty has a greater impact on women than men. They usually work more hours, but for less pay. In addition, girls are half as likely to attend school as boys, leading to widespread female illiteracy. Due to tradition and a gender-biased legal system, most women are also unable to participate in the national economy. Because of this poverty and lack of education, Nepali women are vulnerable to human trafficking and sexual exploitation. Human Rights Watch reports that over 100,000 Nepali women have been trafficked across the border to India, where they are forced into unlawful employment as sex workers.

Nepali women have made some gains in recent decades. Unmarried women over 35 now enjoy the right to inherit property upon the death of their parents. In 2005, women under 35 also gained the right to apply for a passport without permission of husbands or parents. Abortion became legal in 2002. Prior to this, abortion was punishable by long jail sentences and was physically very dangerous. Efforts have been launched to give women more of a voice in the government. In 2006, the government passed a resolution setting a goal of 30 percent female representation in parliament. While this goal has yet to be realized, the resolution was an important first step in achieving gender equality.

The Maoist revolution depended on the significant participation of women. It is estimated that up to 50 percent of those who participated in the struggle were female. They saw the rebellion as a way to assert the importance of women's rights. Further, there were many important female leaders in the Maoist insurgency. The best-known woman Maoist is Comrade Parvati (Hisila Yami), who is regarded as a hero by many Nepalis. There is some hope that the feminist rhetoric voiced during the insurgency will translate into a new respect for women's rights.

Health Care

Generally, Nepalese believe that some illness is caused by spirits. People tend to treat themselves with home remedies, or turn to traditional healers, known as dhami or jhankri.

The number of doctors in Nepal has increased in the 2000s, as the country moved from having only 0.4 doctors per 1,000 people in 1998 to .21 doctors per 1,000 people in 2004. However, hygiene and sanitation are still poor. Diseases such as cholera, leprosy and tuberculosis are common. Malnutrition is also prevalent. Major causes of death include infectious and parasitic diseases, respiratory diseases, and diseases of the nervous system. Life expectancy is 67 years—66 years for men and 69 years for women (2014 estimate). Annual health expenditure is 5.5 percent of the Gross Domestic Product, which ranks 125th among the 191 nations tracked.

In 2011, the government initiated a new campaign called New Nepal: Healthy Nepal, which aims to improve health care, especially in rural areas. To that end, all government-sponsored health medical students are now required to spend at least two years serving in rural areas.

GOVERNMENT

Structure

In 1996, the Communist Party of Nepal (Maoist) attempted to overthrow the government and install a socialist system in its place. In 2001, as the Maoist insurgents became increasingly violent, the government was thrown into chaos when most of the royal family was shot to death. The official explanation is that the crown prince killed his parents and several siblings, and then shot himself, over a dispute about his chosen bride. This sparked a civil war (or "Nepalese People's War") that lasted into 2005.

Nepal was briefly a constitutional monarchy, with the king as head of state and the prime minister as head of government. However, Nepal's fragile hold on democracy was broken in February 2005, when the new King Gayanendra dissolved the multi-party system and made himself the executive head of government, creating an absolute monarchy. The king's stated purpose was to put an end to the Maoist insurgency.

In 2005, Nepal's government became an absolute monarchy, ruled by the king. The

European Union (EU) expressed concern over political and civil repression in the country. This changed in 2006, when the king agreed to relinquish absolute power and a representative government was again formed, with the Maoists in control. In 2007, a federal republic was formed and the monarch was abolished in 2008. The republic established a Constituent Assembly with a total of 601 seats: 240 directly elected members by popular vote, 335 members elected by proportional representation, and 26 appointed positions, led by a prime minister as head of government.

The first Maoist government following reorganization dissolved in 2009. The succeeding government also failed to succeed. In June 2010, Prime Minister Madhav Kumar Nepal also resigned under pressure from the Maoists. As of September 2010, the position of prime minister remained vacant as the Constituent Assembly failed in its attempts to find a head of government. The Maoists and Nepali Congress are at a standstill, with the Maoists seeking to form a coalition government. Concerns have been raised that Nepal could see increased disruption should the government fail to coalesce.

Political Parties

As of 2010, two parties were engaged in a political stand-off in Nepal, the Maoists and the Nepali Congress. The Maoists (also known as the Unified Communist Party of Nepal [Maoist] or CPN-M) is the strongest party in the nation, gaining 220 seats and 30 percent of the vote in the 2008 election. The Nepali Congress, which gained 110 seats in the 2008 election and over 22 percent of the vote, is considered a centrist, reform party. The Communist Party of Nepal (Unified Marxist-Leninist) is considered a moderate-leftist party and received 21 percent of the vote and gained 103 seats. There are numerous other political parties.

Local Government

Nepal is divided into fourteen zones, 75 districts, and five development regions. Decentralization efforts that had begun in the early part of the 21st century came to a standstill in the latter part of the first decade due to the inability to form a government. Non-government agencies such as the UN are working with other agencies to get local government up and running. As of 2009, politicians at the national level were trying to work out their differences in order to fill administrative positions at the local level.

Judicial System

The Supreme Court of Nepal is the highest court in the country. District courts are the court of first instance, hearing criminal and civil matters. The Court of Appeal is the second tier. The Supreme Court has a total of fourteen appointed justices who may hold that position until the age of 65.

Taxation

Taxation in Nepal includes a tax on employment income, investments, and business profits.

Armed Forces

The volunteer Nepal Army consists of an army and an air force.

Foreign Policy

Geographically situated between the two giants of China and India, Nepal has long been conscious of the need for a careful foreign policy. Officially, Nepal's foreign policy is one of nonalignment (not affiliated with any major power blocs). This approach was established to keep Nepal out of any conflict between its large neighbors. As such, relations with China and India have generally been good. As a predominantly Hindu country, Nepal has always had close cultural, economic and diplomatic connections with India. Since Nepal established official relations with China in 1956, the two countries have been on fairly friendly terms. However, India expressed its concern at this close relationship between Nepal and China by temporarily halting trade with Nepal. In 1990, India agreed to restore its traditionally close ties with Nepal.

Nepal's diplomatic relationship with its tiny neighbor Bhutan has suffered significantly in recent decades. The Bhutan government expelled many of its Nepali-speaking citizens in the early

1990s. A decade later, an estimated 110,000 of these Bhutanese refugees continued to live in UN-administered camps inside Nepal. Nepal patiently pursued a diplomatic solution to this crisis, but the government of Bhutan remained firm in its position that these refugees cannot return to their country of birth. As of 2008, the United States and New Zealand began taking in these refugees, providing an unorthodox solution to Nepal's unusual diplomatic problem with Bhutan.

Nepal is a member of several multilateral organizations. It became part of the UN in 1955, has been an active member since. For example, tens of thousands of Nepali troops have served around the world in UN peacekeeping missions. Nepal joined the World Trade Organization (WTO) in 2004, and also works closely with the World Bank and International Monetary Fund (IMF) to manage its small economy. In addition, the country is founding member of the South Asian Association for Regional Cooperation (SAARC), and is part of the South Asian Free Trade Area (SAFTA). As one of the world's poorest nations, Nepal depends on foreign aid from these organizations and their individual member states.

Maoist rebels launched an insurgency in 1995. The insurgency gained traction in 2001, when Crown Prince Dipendra killed King Birendra, Queen Aishwarya and himself, allegedly while intoxicated. This led to general instability in the country. Following the massacre, King Gyanendra, who was third in line to the throne, took power, but proved to be an unpopular monarch, and the Maoists took advantage of this social disruption. In 2006 they gave up arms, and in 2007 began to participate in the parliamentary government of Nepal. In April 2008, the Maoists unexpectedly won national elections, and former rebel leader Prachanda (b. 1954–) became prime minister that August. He resigned over the firing of the head of the army. His successor resigned the following year. As of 2010, Nepal is facing a political standoff between the Maoists and the Nepali Congress parties.

Human Rights Profile

International human rights law insists that states respect civil and political rights, and also promote an individual's economic, social and cultural rights. The United Nations Universal Declaration on Human Rights (UDHR) is recognized as the standard for international human rights. Its authors sought the counsel of the world's great thinkers, philosophers, and religious leaders, and were careful to create a document that reflects the core values shared by every world culture. (To read this document or view the articles relating to cultural human rights, visit: http://www.udhr.org/UDHR/default.htm.)

Maoist rebels began waging an armed struggle against the constitutional monarchist government in 1996. The government cracked down on the population as a result of this rebellion. The fighting killed an estimated 12,000, and left 100,000 homeless. As a result of the rebellion, the monarchy temporarily dissolved the elected government, imposed severe restrictions on the media, and jailed peaceful protesters, a severe violation of several articles of the UDHR. Arbitrary arrests and disappearances were also commonplace during this period, which violated Articles 9 and 10, and people in police custody were routinely subjected to beatings, torture and other forms of violence, a gross violation of Article 5. Furthermore, some prisoners died from this torture, and thousands of civilians were killed by government and Maoist forces.

The economic disruption caused by the fighting was also devastating, especially to poor rural farmers. Worse, the Maoists intentionally brutalized rural villagers in an attempt to get them to join their struggle. Many rural people left their traditional home areas, with some migrating to the already crowded cities. Others left Nepal altogether, and attempted to find work abroad. In addition, a study by Anti-Slavery International on the economic impact of the insurgency found that slavery was tolerated and widespread in Nepal, with over 40,000 living as slaves.

The conditions Nepalese lived under during the insurgency clearly contradicted several provisions of the UDHR. People were targeted for participating in peaceful protests. This violated the principle of freedom of political opinion outlined in Article 2 and Article 19, as well as the freedom of assembly stated in Article 20. Arbitrary arrests and killings contradicted the right to life and liberty described in Article 3. Further, these arrests were in violation of the ban on arbitrary arrest outlined in Article 9, and Article 11 which states that punishment must be based on actual crimes. The tolerance of slavery in Nepal was a clear breach of Article 4, which prohibits slavery. When the king dissolved the elected government, this was a violation of Article 21, which states the right to a representative government.

The human rights situation in Nepal is at an important crossroads. The Maoists gave up their armed struggle in 2006. After winning a surprise landslide in the 2008 elections, former Maoist leader Prachanda was sworn in as prime minister. This new political situation may bring an end to the human rights abuses that have recently plagued Nepal. However, there is no guarantee of this. In early 2008, Tibetan refugees living in Nepal held peaceful protests against China. They were violently arrested by police on orders of the outgoing government. How the new Maoist government treats pro-Tibet activists will be an important test of their commitment to human rights.

Migration

As of 2014, Nepal's migration rate stands at -3.71 migrants per 1,000 people.

ECONOMY

Overview of the Economy

Nepal is one of the poorest countries in the world. The economy has been adversely affected by the civil war that has been fought in the country since 1996. Economic growth is further inhibited by environmental degradation and poor management of utilities, which discourage foreign investment. For example, Kathmandu's burgeoning information technology (IT) industry must contend with an unreliable power supply, while importing and exporting firms are at the mercy of disintegrating roads.

The per capita gross domestic product (GDP) was an estimated $2,400 (USD in 2014. The unemployment rate is a staggering 46 percent (2008). Approximately 76 percent of the people make their living by subsistence farming. The salaries and pensions of Gurkha soldiers, amounting to more than $32 million (USD) annually, are important to the national economy.

Industry

Industrial products include textiles (particularly rugs), cigarettes, jute (for rope), steel rods, cement, clothing and food products. Traditional cottage industries involving the production of baskets, cooking oils and cotton fabrics are also important.

The main products exported include food and live animals, carpets, clothing (such as pashminas, a kind of scarf or wrap), chemicals and pharmaceuticals, animal and vegetable oils and fats (ghee).

Labor

Nepal's labor force numbers 15 million people; as of 2014, the unemployment rate was 46 percent. The labor force is most heavily concentrated in the agricultural industry, accounting for 75 percent of the population, while 18 percent of the population works in the service industry and 7 percent works in the manufacturing sector.

Energy/Power/Natural Resources

Nepal's natural resources include its extensive forests and its swift rivers, which produce hydroelectricity.

Forestry

Deforestation is a problem, particularly in the lowlands, where land clearance and overgrazing have destroyed most of the tropical forests that used to cover the area. Mountain forests remain, but they have suffered degradation. Villagers collect large amounts of leaf fodder for animal feed and gather wood for fuel, increasing the damage.

Mining/Metals

Mica is mined, as are small deposits of copper, talc, lignite, iron ore, cobalt, and limestone.

Agriculture

Most farming in Nepal is on the subsistence level, and some farms are too small even for that. Many farms are less than 1 hectare (2.4 acres) in size. Roughly 10 percent of the people own more than 60 percent of the farms. Many people are landless.

Principal crops grown in Nepal include rice, corn, millet, wheat, sugar cane, oilseeds, potatoes, melons and vegetables.

Animal Husbandry

Livestock products include buffalo's milk, cow's milk, buffalo meat, goat's milk and meat, and eggs.

Tourism

The Himalayas are Nepal's greatest draw for tourists. Climbers, trekkers (hikers), kayakers and rafters visit the country in great numbers. More than 360,000 adventurous tourists generated receipts of $145 million (USD) in 2014. Other tourist attractions include mountain scenery, wildlife parks, religious sites, historical sites, and, in Kathmandu, even gambling casinos. Violence against travelers rarely occurs.

Tourism is the backbone of Kathmandu's economy. The tourist and services industries employ a sizeable portion of the workforce and generate the most foreign income of any industry. Tourism has declined in recent years, however, because of the civil war. In 2005, the increasingly brutal Maoist insurgency and the king's seizure of absolute power sharply curtailed the number of tourists visiting Nepal.

Adam Berger, Ellen Bailey

DO YOU KNOW?

- The British Army defeated the Gurkhas in Nepal in 1817. Even in defeat, the Gurkhas so impressed the British with their fighting ability, that the British Army recruited Gurkha soldiers to a special regimental force that remains to this day.
- It is believed that spiritual leader Lord Gautama Buddha was born on Nepal in 563 BCE.
- The Kumari Devi, or "living goddess," resides in Kathmandu, in the form of a pre-pubescent girl. She is worshipped until her first menstrual cycle, when she returns to mortal status.
- The original layout of Kathmandu resembled the sword of Manjushri, a bodhisattva (a Buddhist practitioner who has achieved enlightenment) who, according to legend, drained the lake that once filled Kathmandu Valley.

Bibliography

Adhikari, Aditya. *The Bullet and the Ballot Box: The Story of Nepal's Maoist Revolution.* New York: Verso, 2014.

Feller, Tessa. *Culture Smart!: Nepal.* New York: Random House, 2008.

Jha, Sunil Kumar. *Customs and Etiquette of Nepal.* London: Global Books, 2007.

Jha, Prashant. *Battles of the New Republic: A Contemporary History of Nepal.* London: Hurst & Co., 2014.

Mayhew, Bradley, Joe Bindloss, & Stan Armington. *Nepal.* Oakland, CA: Lonely Planet, 2015.

McConniche, James, and Shafik Meghji. *Nepal.* London: Rough Guides, 2012.

Moran, Kerry. *Nepal.* Emeryville, CA: Moon Handbooks, 2004.

Rosenthal, Chuck. *Are We Not There Yet? Travels in Nepal, North India, and Bhutan.* Los Angeles: What Books Press, 2009.

Works Cited

Feller, Tessa "Culture Smart!: Nepal" New York: Random House, 2008.

Greene, Paul "Mixed Messages: Unsettled Cosmopolitanisms in Nepali Pop" *Popular Music* Vol 20:2 2001.

Human Rights Watch "Appeasing China: Restricting the Rights of Tibetans in Nepal" July 2008 http://hrw.org/reports/2008/tibetnepal0708/

Human Rights Watch "Rape for Profit: Trafficking of Nepali Girls and Women to India's Brothels" June 1995 http://www.hrw.org/reports/pdfs/c/crd/india957.pdf

Jha, Sunil Kumar "Customs and Etiquette of Nepal" London: *Global Books*, 2007.

Mayhew, Bradley, Joe Bindloss, & Stan Armington "Nepal" Oakland, CA: Lonely Planet, 2015.

Moran, Kerry "Nepal" *Moon Handbooks*. Emeryville, CA: 2004.

"Nepal at a Crossroads: Urgent Need for Delivery on Mechanisms of Truth, Justice, Inclusion and Security" *Amnesty International*. 20 November 2007 https://www.amnesty.org/en/documents/ASA31/011/2007/en

"Nepalese Women Suffer from Ill Health, Poverty, Legal Discrimination Women's Anti-Discrimination Committee Told." *United Nations* 15 June 1999 http://www.un.org/News/Press/docs/1999/19990615.WOM1136.html

Samson, Karl "Frommer's: Nepal" New York: *Simon & Schuster,* 1999.

Xaykaothao, Doualy "Nepal Maoist Leader: Women Driving Movement" National Public Radio 8 September 2008 http://www.npr.org/templates/story/story.php?storyId=5387419

U.S. Relations with Nepal. U.S. Department of State. February 2015. <http://www.state.gov/r/pa/ei/bgn/5283.htm>.

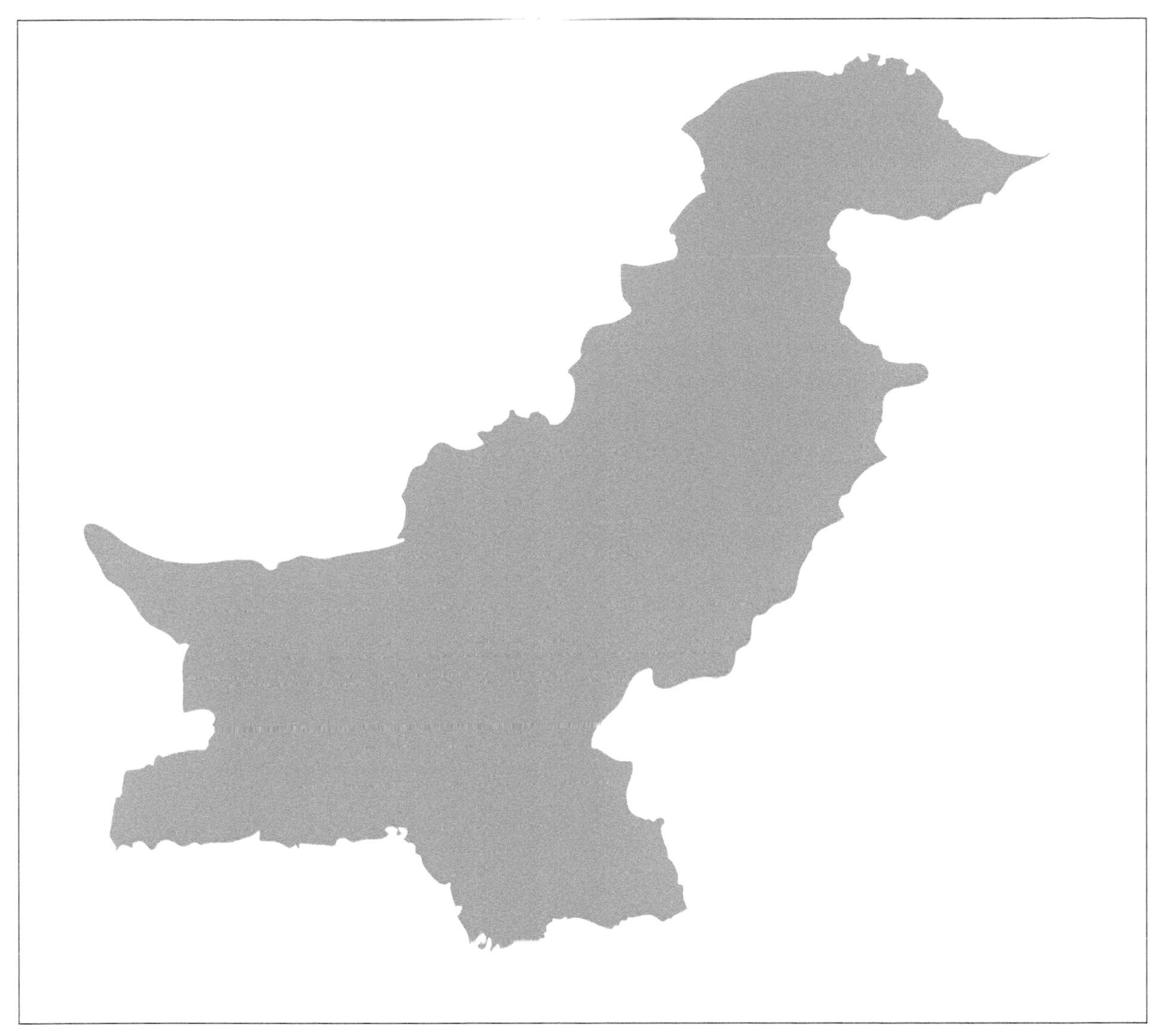

Pakistan

Introduction

The Islamic Republic of Pakistan, bordered by Afghanistan, China, India, and Iran, is considered one of the cradles of human civilization. Following independence from British colonial rule, it was partitioned from India as a home for Muslim peoples.

The last several decades of Pakistani history have been marked by ethnic and sectarian violence, allegations of corrupt leadership, and tensions with India over the disputed territory of Kashmir. With both countries possessing nuclear capabilities, the situation between India and Pakistan has approached disaster several times. Some degree of reconciliation has occurred in recent years, but tensions returned to fever pitch following the 2008 terrorist attacks in Mumbai.

The only country to have recognized the Taliban's rule in Afghanistan, Pakistan nevertheless became an ally in the United States-led fight against global terrorism in the wake of the September 11, 2001 attacks.

Calligraphy is a popular art form in Pakistan, and is viewed as a foundation of Muslim art. In fact, it is but one example of the influence Islam has brought to some of Pakistan's highest expressions of culture. In architecture, this influence can be seen in the country's mosques, gardens, palaces, and tombs. Islamic-inspired geometric patterns figure heavily in building, carpet, and textile design.

GENERAL INFORMATION

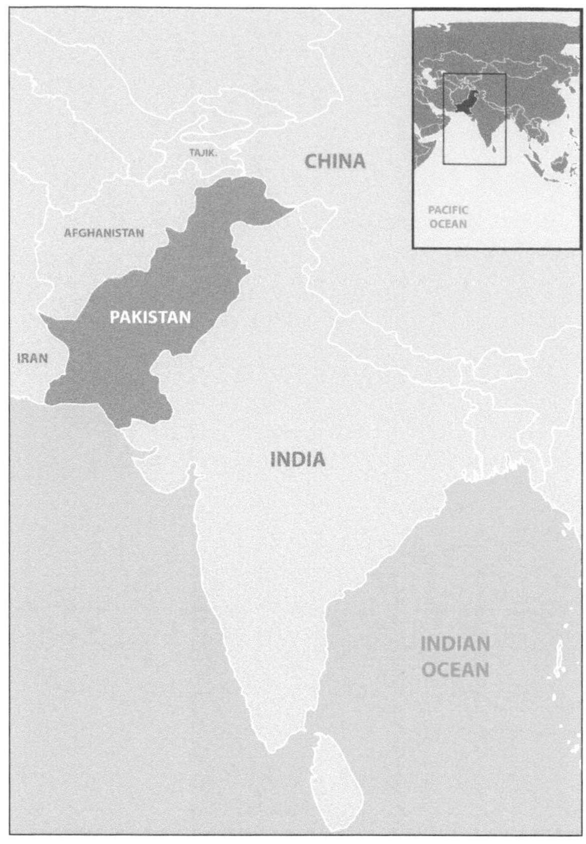

Official Language: Urdu
Population: 196,174,380 (2014 estimate)
Currency: Pakistani rupee
Coins: Coins come in denominations of 1, 2, and 5 rupees.
Land Area: 803,940 square kilometers (340,403 square miles)
Water Area: 25,220 square kilometers (9,738 square miles)
National Motto: "Iman, Aktad, Nizam" ("Faith, Unity, Discipline")
National Anthem: "Pak sarzamin shad bad" ("Blessed Be the Sacred Land")
Capital: Islamabad
Time Zone: GMT +5
Flag Description: The flag of Pakistan features a white vertical band on its hoist (left) side; the remaining three quarters of the flag is green. Centered in the green section is a white crescent moon and star, which are symbols of Islam.

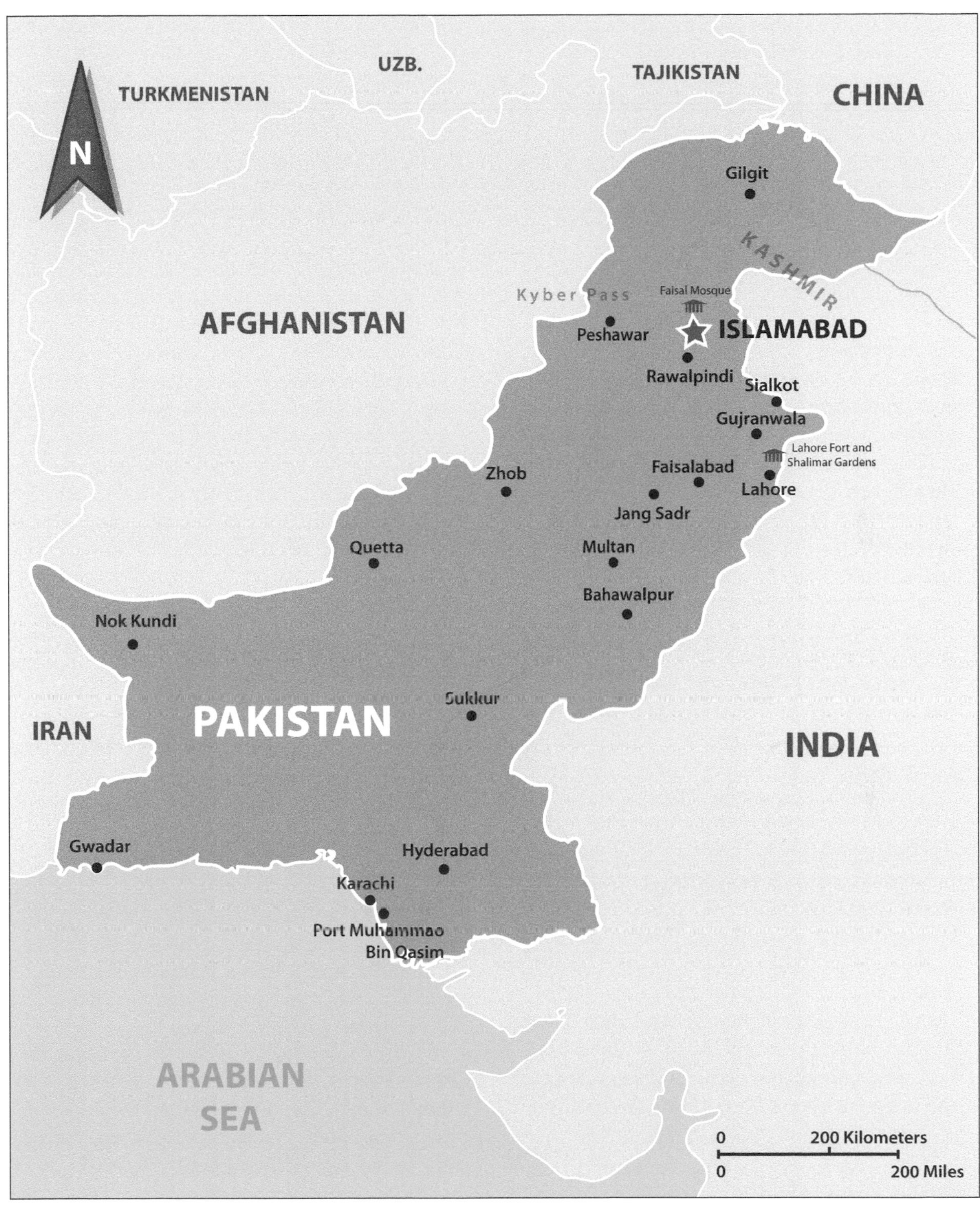

N
UZB.
TURKMENISTAN
TAJIKISTAN
CHINA
Gilgit
KASHMIR
Kyber Pass
Faisal Mosque
AFGHANISTAN
Peshawar
ISLAMABAD
Rawalpindi
Sialkot
Gujranwala
Lahore Fort and Shalimar Gardens
Zhob
Faisalabad
Lahore
Jang Sadr
Quetta
Multan
Bahawalpur
Nok Kundi
Sukkur
IRAN
PAKISTAN
INDIA
Gwadar
Hyderabad
Karachi
Port Muhammad Bin Qasim
ARABIAN SEA
0 200 Kilometers
0 200 Miles

Principal Cities by Population (2015):

- Karachi (31,500,625)
- Lahore (14,218,745)
- Faisalabad (7,347,446)
- Rawalpindi (5,829,471)
- Hyderabad (5,607,798)
- Multan (5,339,550)
- Gujranwala (4,899,766)
- Sargodha (4,557,514)
- Peshawar (4,133,252)
- Islamabad (2,706,481)

Population

Pakistan's young and growing population is the ninth largest in the world. Life expectancy at birth is 65 years for males and 69 years for females (2014 estimate). The average population density is 236 persons per square kilometer (611 persons per square mile), but the population is concentrated in the east and southeast, in the Indus River valley.

Roughly 38 percent of the population lives in urban centers (2014). Karachi is the largest with 31.5 million people, followed by Lahore, Faisalabad, and Rawalpindi. In 2014, the population growth rate of Pakistan was 1.5 percent.

Languages

Urdu, a language related to Hindi with many loan words from Arabic, was designated as the official language in 1978. It is the native language of only the Muhajirs people, who are Muslims who fled to Pakistan from India after the partition of territory, and was chosen as a means to unite the country's diverse population. Most people in Pakistan speak at least two languages: their own, which is tied to their ethnicity, and Urdu. Punjabi, Pashto, Sindhi, and Balochi, plus numerous dialects and several minority languages, complete the linguistic picture. English is commonly used in government and is also widely spoken.

Native People & Ethnic Groups

Centuries of invasion and migration have given Pakistan an extremely complex ethnic composite. The four major classifications are the Punjabis (45 percent of the population), the Pashtuns/Pathans (15 percent), the Sindhi (14 percent), and the Balochis (four percent). These groups are further divided according to classifications such as caste, occupation, and tribe. Each group is concentrated in one of the country's four provinces. Minority groups include the Siraikis, the Muhajirs, and the Brahuis.

Except for Pashtun refugees, who fled Afghanistan, and the Muhajirs, who settled in Pakistan after the partition, the country's ethnic groups have long histories in the region. Some ethnic groups have been traditionally underrepresented in the power structure, while others exercise influence out of proportion to their size. This is one factor which has led to violence in Pakistan. Another source of the conflict with the country has been religious differences, with fighting breaking out between Sunni and Shia Muslims. Sindh, Balochistan, and Punjab are the provinces most beset by strife.

Religions

Pakistan is an Islamic republic, and the vast majority of the population is Muslim. 70 percent are Sunni and 20 percent Shia. Hinduism and Christianity are the largest minority religions. The country's constitution guarantees freedom of worship.

Climate

Pakistan experiences four distinct seasons: dry and cool between December and March, hot and humid between April and June, wet between July and September, and dry and hot in October and November. The higher elevations are colder in winter, cooler in summer, in contrast to the lower elevations of the Indus plains.

In the lowlands, temperatures average 13° Celsius (55° Fahrenheit) in winter, and fall between 32° and 49° Celsius (about 90° and 120° Fahrenheit) in summer. Temperatures in the mountains fall well below freezing during the winter; some peaks remain snow-capped throughout the year and numerous glaciers are present.

Pakistan receives less than 25 centimeters (10 inches) of precipitation annually. In the mountains, it falls in the form of snow; on the plains, monsoon winds bring torrential rains that cause rivers to flood and measure 500 millimeters (20 inches) annually. The more arid southwest and southeast receive a quarter of that amount.

In addition to the floods in July and August, Pakistan is susceptible to frequent earthquakes. The worst occur in the north and west of the country.

ENVIRONMENT & GEOGRAPHY

Topography

Pakistan is part of the Indian subcontinent, which also includes the countries of India, Nepal, Bhutan, and Bangladesh (formerly East Pakistan). The Himalayas, the Karakoram Range, and the Hindu Kush mountain range define much of Pakistan's extreme-northern and southwestern landscapes, including the provinces of Baluchistan and the North-West Frontier. To the east and southeast, the Indus River and its tributaries mold the landscape in the provinces of Punjab and Sindh.

Islamabad is the national capital, and is located in northern Pakistan. It is roughly the size of Texas and Oklahoma combined.

Pakistan has nine ecological zones, but its terrain is largely comprised of mountains, a broad river plain, and an arid western plateau. Mountains predominate in the north and the northwest. The northern ranges, which include portions of the Hindu Kush and the Himalayas, contain thirteen of the world's highest peaks. The highest in Pakistan, and the second highest in the world, is K2, which rises in the Karakoram Range of the Himalayas to an elevation of 8,611 meters (28,251 feet). Numerous glaciers and glacial lakes are found in these ranges. Two of the most historically significant mountain passes which link Pakistan to its neighbors are the Khyber Pass on the border with Afghanistan, and the Karakoram Pass on the border with China.

The Indus River rises in the Chinese Himalayas and courses along the length of Pakistan for 2,900 kilometers (1,800 miles). The river branches into five major tributaries, creating a fertile plain from which the country draws its sustenance, and then empties into the Arabian Sea. The southern coastline is dominated by the broad Indus River delta and the Makran Mountains, which stretch for three-quarters of the 1,046-kilometer (650-mile) coastline.

Plants & Animals

Pakistan's natural zones support a variety of plant and animal life. In the northern mountains, trees such as pine, polar, cedar, and spruce are found. In the west, only grass, hearty plants, and scattered trees survive the arid climate except in the hills, where juniper and cedar trees are also found. The Indus Valley plain, also arid outside of the monsoon season, is covered with grass and thorn trees. Forests grow along the banks of the Indus River, and stands of mangrove grow along the coast.

Mammals commonly found in Pakistan include wild sheep, wolves, hyena, bear, boar, and deer. The wetlands are particularly rich in animal life and provide habitats for otters, dolphins, and crocodiles as well as numerous migrating birds. Reptiles include the python, the cobra, the horned viper and the Afghan tortoise. The Indus River and the Arabian Sea support numerous species of fish.

Hunting and stress on their habitats threaten several species, among which are the snow leopard, the ibex, the Marco Polo sheep, the Asiatic black bear, the wild goat, and the Eurasian otter.

CUSTOMS & COURTESIES

Greetings

The greetings used in Pakistan are typically Islamic. To greet someone, one would say "Assalam-o-Alaiqum," meaning "May the peace and blessings of Allah be upon you." A typical reply to this would be "Wa alaiqum-us-salam," which returns the greeting. To bid farewell, one would say "Allah Hafiz," meaning "May Allah be your guardian."

Except in upper-class urban areas, men and women do not normally greet each other. This is because they hardly ever come into social contact, as physical proximity between unmarried members of the opposite sex is considered a social taboo. Men also shake hands when greeting each other for the first time, while women may kiss and embrace. In addition, men may also embrace if they have known each other for some time. Youngsters are encouraged to greet their elders first, and show their respect by standing up.

Greetings are usually elaborate, with both parties expected to inquire about each other's health, family and general well-being. Introductions take place after the greetings have been exchanged, and both names of a person are used, with the surname revealing the person's social caste or religious affiliation. Afterwards, in the absence of a close relationship, only the last name accompanied by the appropriate salutation is used.

Gestures & Etiquette

Respect for elders is an old Pakistani tradition. Thus, elders are served first at meal times, and given the first choice of the food. They also have their drinks prepared for them. Children are expected to stand up when conversing with elders, and to address them respectfully. In addition, children are expected to offer their elders a seat and to perform other required courtesies. When addressing an unrelated elder, one is expected to address him or her as "Uncle" or "Auntie" as a sign of respect. The wisdom of the elders is valued so much that they are given the right to make certain important decisions on behalf of the group.

Pakistani women in particular are expected to be gentle and modest in their speech and mannerisms. Both genders are also expected to exhibit good manners in all social settings. Postures such as standing with one's hands on the hips are considered indecent. There is no concept of personal space or privacy in Pakistani culture, and people are likely to stand in close proximity and ask personal questions in an effort to develop a relationship. Relationships are deeply valued and much time and effort are devoted to them. It is also common for Pakistanis to converse in an indirect manner, using exaggerated gestures and mannerisms.

Eating/Meals

Pakistanis eat three meals a day, and usually take an elaborate tea in the late afternoon. An indigenous tradition that is still observed in rural areas is that of sitting on the floor and eating from a thick mat, or from a knee-high round table. Many people still do not use eating utensils, harking back to an ancient Islamic tradition, though this is more common in rural settings.

Food is typically served first to the guests, and then to the family in descending order of age and gender. Men are traditionally served first. Nobody is expected to begin eating until the eldest member of the family at the table has done so. This applies to leaving the table as well. Second and third helpings are common, and guests will be urged to eat their fill. Typically, refusals to eat further are initially accepted as mere politeness, and not to be taken seriously. Most importantly, all meals and drinks are taken with the right hand, as the left hand is primary used for cleansing purposes in Muslim cultures, and thus considered impure.

Visiting

Pakistanis are generally very sociable people and live in close-knit families. There is a very strong tradition of visiting and hospitality in Pakistan, especially among women. Visiting is almost always unannounced and usually informal. Even on an informal visit, the guest will typically be offered food and drink. Tea, in particular, plays a central role in almost all social visits. If a guest happens to be visiting close to a meal time, he or she will commonly be invited to partake of that meal with the family.

Formal dinner parties are also very common in Pakistan. At such social gatherings, the guests are expected to arrive as late as an hour after the stipulated time, and are expected to bring the hostess a small gift, such as flowers or something sweet. Men do not give flowers or gifts to women not related to them, unless such a gift is from a female relative. Gifts are given and received with both hands, and are not opened until after the guest has left.

LIFESTYLE

Family

Pakistani society is strongly family-oriented. As a whole, Pakistan families tend to be quite large. This is partly because Islam allows polygamy and permits a man to have four wives at one time, and partly because contraception is frowned upon by religious authorities and in society as a whole. Furthermore, contraception has not been actively promoted by the government.

The basic structural unit of Pakistani society is the extended family, based on strong patriarchal precepts. A typical Pakistani family may include the nuclear family—a father, mother and typically two children—as well as near and distant relatives. In rural areas, the extended family may include tribe members as well. In recent years, a trend toward strictly nuclear family systems has emerged in urban centers. However, the majority of the populace continues to live in the joint family system.

Even after marriage, which is almost always arranged by the elders of each family, a man is expected to live with his parents. Thus, Pakistani children often grow up surrounded by their grandparents, and aunts and uncles. Because the family is a very important institution in Pakistan, loyalty to the family is highly valued. Nepotism, the showing of favoritism toward relatives and friends, is not only acceptable, but encouraged. Families are typically very private and close, and usually, interfamilial marriages, such as between first cousins, are encouraged as a means of keeping the family together. In addition, female members of the family are very sheltered and protected from outside influence by their male relatives.

There is also the widespread tradition in Pakistan of hiring live-in domestic help. This tradition is so prevalent that even lower middle-class families are rarely without maids, cook, drivers, gardeners and watchmen. Typically, these domestic and service workers belong to the lowest social strata.

Housing

Housing in Pakistan is typically limited to bungalows and houses. This is largely because most Pakistani families in one household include extended family members. It is only in Karachi, the most populous city, that some people have adopted apartment living. However, the number of apartment-dwellers is still quite small. Thus, there are hardly any high-rise residential buildings in Pakistan.

Housing trends in Pakistan are also influenced by climate. For example, many houses are open and spacious partly due to the weather, which, for the most of the year, remains hot, with varying conditions of humidity and dryness. The architectural style of the houses, with their large windows, open verandas and spacious lawns, reflect this climate. It is also for this reason that almost every room in every house is equipped with a fan and an air conditioner. Central air conditioning has not yet been fully introduced in Pakistan.

Food

Pakistani cuisine is largely influenced by Turkish, Persian, Arabic, and Indian elements. The latter is particularly influential in terms of the large variety of spices used. Since Muslim tradition forbids the consumption of pork, Pakistani cuisine focuses predominantly on beef, chicken and mutton (domestic sheep) for its meat. Grilled meats, in the form of kebabs—a Middle Eastern staple—are popular. Common vegetables used in Pakistani cuisine include cauliflower, eggplant, okra, cabbage, potatoes, rutabaga and spinach.

A typical Pakistani meal usually consists of rice, either boiled or made into pilaf such as biryan, or roti, a traditional Indian bread. Naan, a flat, round bread made in a clay oven, and paratha are some other common types of bread. Meals are also often accompanied by a stew of vegetables, meat or lentil curry, or a salad. Popular desserts include kheer, a rich rice pudding, and mithai, or sweetmeats. Tea, in a variety of forms, is a very popular drink. Other favored drinks include lassi, which is made from milk and yogurt, and fresh juices, especially sugar cane juice. Alcohol is forbidden in Islam and is not consumed in any form. Fruit, particularly abundant in Pakistan, is often eaten after meals in place of dessert.

Life's Milestones

Pakistani people enjoy lavish celebrations. When a baby is born, there is traditionally an 'Aqiqa ceremony on the seventh day after birth. In this tradition, the baby is given a name and has its hair shaved off. Alms and food are also given to the poor and an animal can be sacrificed in the name of Allah.

Most Pakistani households also celebrate birthdays and anniversaries, even though these are secular traditions, and not Islamic. In addition, when a child finishes reading the Qur'an for the first time, usually around the age of seven or eight, there is a small ceremony to celebrate this event, usually consisting of presenting a gift to the teacher. Weddings, however, are the most lavishly celebrated affairs in Pakistan. Consisting of a three- or four-day extravaganza, they are typically filled with dancing, music and feasting, as well as the traditional wedding rituals.

CULTURAL HISTORY

Art

Even though Pakistan is a relatively young nation, having gained independence from the British in 1947, it boasts a rich cultural heritage that can be traced back several millennia to the Indus Valley Civilization (2800–1800 BCE). While Pakistan has been largely influenced by neighboring cultures such as India, Turkey, Persia and Afghanistan, it is considered one of the first areas in which Islam was fully embraced. As such, religion has historically played a prominent role in all aspects of life in Pakistan, especially shaping the arts and culture.

Islam forbids any depiction of the human form. For this reason, abstract forms of painting have become more developed than portraiture and nudist painting. Following Pakistan's independence, Pakistani artists began to adopt modern styles, using abstract styles as a metaphor for economic and political change. Several influential artists of this period included Abdur Rahman Chughtai (1899–1975), Allah Bux (1895–1978), Ahmed Parvez (1926–1979) and Moyene Najmi (1928–1997).

In the decades following independence, Pakistani artists began to incorporate Western trends into their art. Zubeida Agha (1922–1997) introduced abstract "idea" art in 1949, Shakir Ali (1914–1975) introduced cubism (which remained popular for decades) in the 1950s, and Ismail Gulgee (1926–2007), who also painted portraits, introduced non-objective art. Other popular art movements included abstract expressionism and the Lahore landscape movement of the 1980s. However, these Western-inspired painting trends were usually short-lived, and often outside the mainstream.

One art form that has been consistently popular in Pakistan is calligraphy, which upholds and celebrates Islamic precepts. In fact, calligraphy is considered one of the foundations of Muslim art, and the preservation of the Qur'an, the primary sacred text of Islam, has been due in large part to calligraphy. Historically, calligraphy evolved and increased in popularity as a response to Islamic restrictions on art.

In Pakistan, in particular, calligraphic murals have long been a fixture of government buildings and other public spaces. Pakistan also witnessed a calligraphic revival during the 1950s. During this period, calligraphic art assumed a variety of forms, including traditional, abstract, creative and non-objective. Many artists, including Sadequain (1930–1987), popularized this genre. Sadequain famously painted Qur'anic and poetic verses on surfaces ranging from public and private buildings—including the Punjab Public Library—to leather, stone, canvas and paper.

Although sculpture of the human form has historically not been developed in Pakistan, other forms of sculpture have emerged in recent decades, including geometric, abstract and calligraphic. Such sculptures are usually rendered in wood, steel, stone or bronze, and range from small objects to corporate or state commissioned works. They often draw heavily on both local culture as well as Islamic ideology.

Architecture

Pakistani architecture can be broadly classified into four historical periods: the pre-Mughal era, the Mughal era, the British era, and the post-colonial era. Of the pre-Mughal era, most of the buildings which still remain date from the Sultanate period (1200–1600 CE), and are found mostly in the city of Multan and in eastern Punjab province. The main building materials were brick and timber. Common characteristics of this architectural style were flat roofs of brick and timber, battered walls and wooden and glazed tile work. Some of the oldest buildings from this era include the Ghaznavid Mosque in Swat, the 12th-century mosque of Khalid Walid and the shrine of Shah Yusuf Gardizi in Multan.

The Mughal Dynasty, which ruled the Indian subcontinent from the 16th until the 19th centuries CE, developed a majestic and distinctive architectural style. This style was considered an integration of Islamic, Persian and indigenous Indian styles. Mughal architecture is characterized by large courtyards and terraced gardens designed in the Persian quadrilateral style, complete with fountains. Other features include majestic domes and minarets, elevated, dome-shaped pavilions, intricate overhanging balconies (jharokas), and perforated stone or latticed screens. The Mughal Dynasty was also known for its magnificent forts, mosques and funerary architecture. Common building materials included red sandstone and marble.

In the 16th century, the prevalent style in Punjab was the use of blue-and-white square tiles. In the 17th century, a new style emerged in which the façade, or building exterior, was divided into depressed quadrilateral panels. These panels were in turn covered with glazed mosaics. Common designs included flowering plants and floral geometric designs and patterns, called arabesques. The latter were commonly found on framed arches which were at times inscribed with verses. The color scheme was limited to seven colors: cobalt blue, turquoise, green, orange, cadmium yellow, purple, and white. An example of this style is the Wazir Khan Mosque in Lahore, which was built in 1634. This mosque is also famous for its extensive tile decorations and glazed tile work, which was a prevalent feature of architectural design during this period.

The architecture of the British era, lasting from the early 19th century until 1947, was mainly civic. The British constructed government buildings, railway stations and other public monuments. The prevalent architectural styles were classical, gothic and Victorian, consistent with popular architectural styles in Europe during the 19th and 20th centuries. Some significant buildings in Lahore dating from this period include the High Court, the Government College University, the National College of Arts, Montgomery Hall, the famous Tollinton Market and the Provincial Assembly.

The post-colonial era, dating from 1947 onward, reflects contemporary Pakistani architecture. This architecture is not considered particularly unique, and involves relatively few locally trained architects. Mostly foreign-qualified architects were commissioned for public projects and they applied European concepts, leading to indigenous trends becoming obsolete. The first professional program in architecture was offered in 1958 at the National College of Arts in Lahore, though residency for this program was typically low.

Drama

Traditionally, cinema and drama have not been popular in Pakistan. There is a film industry operating in the country, based largely in Lahore and Peshawar. However, it produces only a handful of films every year. The Pakistani film industry experienced its golden age in the 1960s and 1970s, but, as a result of the policy of Islamization imposed by General Muhammad Zia-ul-Haq (1924–1988), who ruled in Pakistan from 1977 until his death, the industry and accompanying theatres all but disappeared. Recently, there have been attempts aimed at the revival of cinema, and Pakistan's first Western-style multiplex opened in 2007 in Lahore.

Theatre, because of its potential to be politically and religiously subversive, did not develop in Pakistan until the 1980s. Prior to this, there did exist some indigenous forms of theatre, such as the swang, or folk theatre, in western Punjab, and the Parsi Theatre in Karachi. However, these were not integrated into mainstream society because of the prevalent Islamic bias against art forms such as theatre and dance, which were thought to be related to Hinduism. Despite this bias, a commercial theatre emerged in Pakistan, developing out of a local form of folk theatre called lok. This theatre consisted of travelling actors who presented popular epics and ballads at local fairs around harvest time.

During the military regime of General Zia, many of these plays were political satires, and "street," or protest theatre, was committed to criticizing human rights violations. In the late 20th century, however, commercial theatre took on the character of lewd, slapstick comedy, and began to attract predominantly middle class audiences. Commercial theatre and stage plays have long been considered in decline.

Music

Music in Pakistan has historically not received much institutional support, which has hindered its development. The Islamic tradition of Qur'anic recitation, however, has given rise to various distinct genres of music in Pakistan. One popular genre is religious chant, which is usually not accompanied by instruments and relies solely on rhythmic beats. There are various kinds, including the hamd, which commemorates God, the na'at, which commemorates the Prophet Muhammad, and the soz, marsiya, and ma'atam, which are Shi'ite lamentations commemorating the tragic death of Muhammad's family. Another genre that has emerged is that of qawwali, or Sufi devotional music. Often accompanied by drums and hand clapping, this genre has recently become popular in the international arena, largely through the work of Ustad Nusrat Fateh Ali Khan (1948–1997). The chanting of Urdu poetry, called trannum, also developed out of this tradition.

The romantic ghazal, a semi-classical, lyrically-rich song, is also quite popular. Prominent singers of this genre include Farida Khanum, Iqbal Bano, Malika Pukhraj (1912–2004), Mehdi Hassan and Ghulam Ali. Local film music was popularized mainly by the famous singer Noor Jehan (1926–2000). The most commonly used musical instruments in Pakistan are the harmonium, the tabla and the dholak (types of drums), and traditional string instruments such as the sitar, the saragi and the rubab.

Dance

There are two forms of dance in Pakistan: classical and folk. The former was used within the courts and priesthood while the latter was used by the majority of the population to celebrate certain occasions, such as the birth of a child or a marriage. During the regime of General Zia, which lasted from 1977 through 1988, dancing was in large part banned, including the classical Kathak dance. The general term for dance in Pakistan is "attan." Attan usually involves its participants dancing in a circle or curving line and may be accompanied by sung poetry, known as "attan songs."

Literature

Pakistan has a strong literary tradition that dates back several centuries. Perhaps as a result of Islamic influence, a stronger emphasis has always been placed on the poetic tradition as compared to the other literary arts. Poetry was being written in the Indian subcontinent well before most of the area's major languages evolved. Punjabi poetry, in particular, was prolific. This poetry was strongly influenced by Sufism, a mystical sect or tradition of Islam. The area that constitutes present-day Pakistan produced many great poets, including Baba Bulleh Shah (1680–1757) and Waris Shah (1706–1798), who composed the famous work *Heer Ranjha*. More recent Pakistani poets such as Mohammad Iqbal (1877–1938) and Faiz Ahmed Faiz (1911–1984) have carried on this poetic tradition.

Pakistan also has an established tradition of Urdu (a language spoken in Pakistan and India) and English prose literature. During the post-partition era of the early 19th century (the partition of India and Pakistan occurred in 1947, with Pakistan's independence), prose literature, especially children's literature, played an important role in creating a sense of national pride and identity. As such, it was encouraged by the state. During subsequent years, Pakistan's literary tradition was firmly established, producing internationally renowned contemporary writers such as Bapsi Sidhwa.

CULTURE

Arts & Entertainment

Over the centuries, Islam has fostered some of Pakistan's highest expressions of culture. In architecture, this influence can be seen in the country's mosques, gardens, palaces, and tombs. Intricate geometric designs and Qur'anic inscriptions written in calligraphy figure heavily in religious buildings. These designs also carry over into Pakistan's traditional arts and crafts. They include carpet and textile weaving, basketry, pottery-making and ceramics, metal, leather, stone and wood work, and jewelry-making.

Carpet weaving goes back to the Mughal period, when weavers drew on Islamic and Persian motifs and developed the Mughal style. It is now a major industry in Pakistan, producing knotted woolen carpets, embroidered felted rugs, woven cotton floor coverings (called daris), and colorful rugs woven from wool, goat hair and mixed yarns called kilims.

The textile weaving industry is also quite active. Some of Pakistan's most prized textiles are embroidered bedcovers and woolen shawls. Balochistan, a region in southwestern Pakistan, is famous for its unique mirror-work embroidery and rillis, which is an integration of the techniques of painting, printing, appliqué; and embroidery. Kashmiri shawls, with their distinctive paisley and floral designs, are famous the world over.

Pottery has also developed into a large industry in Pakistan, and is centered in the cities of Hala, Multan and Peshawar. At Hala, glazed pottery is produced for domestic use and is inscribed with floral and geometric designs, often in browns, yellows and greens. Glazed Multani pottery is characterized by a blue and white floral pattern. Bahawalpur produces the famous paper-thin unglazed pottery. In Gujrat, hand-made pottery is produced with embossed decoration, and in the northern regions, pottery designs are bold and geometric.

Another distinctively Pakistani tradition is that of truck decoration. Truck owners typically decorate their vehicles with bright and colorful poetic inscriptions, figural images, repetitive geometric patterns, epigraphic formulae and, most importantly, religious inscriptions. At times, ornaments such as woven ribbons of colorful thread and mirrors are also applied to the vehicles. This practice has developed into an indigenous art form. Often, the decorations reveal much about the background of the truck owner.

Traditional music is another widely practiced art and is one of the most common vehicles for the country's beloved poetry. The two dominant, lyrically rich types are the romantic ghazal and qawwali, the traditional music of Sufi poets. Among the many Pakistani musicians, few are as revered in his native country and abroad as the singer Nursat Fateh Ali Khan (1948–1997), who specialized in qawwali yet frequently collaborated with Western musicians in the latter part of his career to create a more modern sound. In Islamabad, the Folk Heritage Center, the Pakistan Arts Council, and the National Council of the Arts cultural events such as plays, literary readings, storytelling performances, and concerts, which often feature secular and non-secular qawwali.

Regarding contemporary architecture, music and cinema or theatre, each has slowly developed in Pakistan since the mid-20th century. Many local architects have emerged since the National College of Arts in Lahore established an architectural program in 1958. Many have successfully adapted European styles to indigenous materials and local environmental constraints, thereby creating a distinctive style of their own. One of the most prominent of these is Nayyer Ali Dada, who created an eclectic form of modernism, and designed many famous public buildings, including the Alhamra Arts Council and the Open Air Theatres in Lahore.

In recent years, contemporary Western styles of music, especially rock, have become popular in Pakistan. Young musicians have been successfully integrating Western styles with indigenous musical styles. This music is often characterized by rich lyrical poetry and melodious beats, which creates a distinct sound. Contemporary bands such as Fuzon and Strings have gained international renown for their music. In Pakistan, this music typically appeals to the urban upper classes.

Alternative forms of theatre have also emerged in Pakistan in recent years, partly as a result of collegiate efforts and dramatic societies. These societies are often frequented by an English-speaking upper class. The Rafi Peer Group has done much work to promote this particular genre, organizing performances, puppet shows and local and international theatre festivals. However, there is still a strict measure of censorship imposed on all public performances.

The British colonial years left behind them a passion for several sports in Pakistan, including squash, polo, and cricket. Football (soccer) is popular as well, but cricket is considered the preeminent national sport.

Cultural Sites & Landmarks

Pakistan can trace its history back to the Indus Valley Civilization, an advanced, urban civilization boasting large, well-planned cities and extensive irrigation systems. This civilization flourished on the plains of the Indus River from 2500 to 2000 BCE. The two principal Indus Valley cities that have been excavated are Mohenjo-daro and Harappa. Considered two of the most significant historical sites in Pakistan, these are two of the best-preserved Bronze Age (3000–1200 BCE in India) archaeological sites in the world. Mohenjo-daro is a United Nations Educational, Scientific and Cultural Organization (UNESCO) World Heritage Site, one of seven such sites in Pakistan.

Mohenjo-Daro is located in the province of Sindh, and literally means "Mound of the Dead." The ancient city is most famous for its grid plan, perhaps the earliest known in history, as well as its excavated public and private wells and bathing platforms. Harappa lies approximately 644 kilometers (400 miles) northeast of Mohenjo-Daro, in Punjab. Ancient mounds, cemeteries and granaries have been excavated there. Artifacts that have been recovered include square stamp seals, black-on-red painted pottery, carnelian beads (gemstone jewelry) and terracotta figurines. All of these artifacts are preserved at the Harappa Museum located near the ruins.

The ruins of another ancient civilization have been uncovered at Taxila, located about 40 kilometers (25 miles) from Islamabad. The ancient city is believed to be the capital of the Kingdom of Gandhara, which lasted from the sixth to the 11th centuries BCE, and later became an important center of Buddhist culture. The ruins at Taxila reveal traces of Buddhist influence in the preserved art, stupas (mound-like structures), and monasteries. In 1980, Taxila, was designated as a UNESCO World Heritage Site.

Many of the architectural monuments created by the Mughal Dynasty are in modern-day Pakistan. Lahore, an important center of the Mughal Empire, is home to many of these monuments, and is considered the cultural capital of Pakistan. Monuments include the mausoleum of Jehangir (1569–1627), an ancient ruler of the Mughal Empire, and a monument he had built for his pet antelope, the Hiran Minar; the tomb of Anarkali, a legendary slave girl, built by Jehangir in 1616; the Shalimar Gardens built by Shah Jehan (1592–1666) in 1641; and the famous Badshahi Mosque, built by Aurangzeb (1618–1707) in 1673, which can accommodate 55,000 worshippers.

Another Mughal architectural feat is the Lahore Fort. The construction of the fort began during the reign of Akbar (1542–1605). It consists of public and private audience rooms, the impressive Moti Masjid Mosque, the Sheesh Mahal courtyard, and the Naulakha Pavilion. In particular, the tile mosaics are unique due to their figurative motifs. Lahore is also home to the tomb of the Sikh Emperor Ranjit Singh (1780–1839) and the shrine of Sikh Guru Arjan Dev (1563–1606).

During the Mughal era, Lahore was fortified by a circular wall, and access to the city was gained by thirteen gates. Although the wall itself was destroyed by the British in 1849, much of the original city, as well as some of its gates, remains intact. Inside the city, there are havelis, or mansions, which are still preserved. These mansions, as well as the city's old bazaars such as the Anarkali Bazaar, pay tribute to the artisanship of Mughal and Sikh architects. Lahore also houses the shrine of the Sufi saint Hazrat Syed Al-Hajweri, considered by many to be the patron saint of Lahore, where thousands of people are provided free meals every day.

Some other important cultural sites date from the twentieth century, and are associated with Pakistan's fight for sovereignty. These sites are a particular source of pride for the Pakistani people. The Minar-e-Pakistan at Lahore is a tall minaret that commemorates Pakistan's independence. Other important landmarks include the mausoleums of Mohammad Iqbal (1877–1938) in Lahore, and that of Mohammad Ali Jinnah (1876–1948), Pakistan's founding father, in Karachi. Pakistan is also home to one of the largest and most magnificent mosques in the world, the Faisal Mosque, in Islamabad.

Libraries & Museums

The National Library of Pakistan, inaugurated in 1993 as Pakistan's official legal depository, contained approximately 130,000 volumes of books, over 500 manuscripts, and 40,100 Pakistani publications at the turn of the 21st century. In 2008, the country initiated the Pakistan Libraries Program, a national program focused on developing community-driven libraries. Prior to the program, an estimated 7 percent or fewer of schools maintained a book collection or library.

The National Museum of Pakistan, inaugurated in 1950 in Karachi, contains over 300 copies of the Koran, as well as a wide range of cultural and historical artifacts and items. Other museums in Pakistan include the National History Museum, also in Karachi; the Museum of Science and Technology, in Lahore; and the Zoological Museum, also in Lahore. There are also numerous regional history, religious, and archaeological museums throughout Pakistan.

Holidays

Islamic holidays predominate in Pakistan. Among the most significant are Ramadan, the month of dusk-to-dawn fasting, Eid-al-Fitr, which concludes Ramadan, and Eid-al-Adha which commemorates Abraham's willingness to sacrifice his son to God. These holidays are celebrated with feasts, visits to family and friends, the wearing of new clothes, gift-giving, and the distribution of food and alms to the poor.

Secular holidays center on Pakistan's nationhood. These include Republic Day (March 23), Independence Day (August 14, marking the country's independence from Britain), and the anniversary of the death of Pakistan's founder, Mohamed Ali Jinnah (September 11).

Youth Culture

Sports and other activities such as physical training are very popular among the urban youth of Pakistan. Introduced into the sub-continent by the British, sports such as cricket, squash, tennis and polo are quite popular. Even though the official national sport of Pakistan is field hockey, cricket is by far the most popular sport. Matches are typically attended in large numbers by enthusiastic crowds. Football (soccer) is also gaining popularity among young Pakistanis.

The Internet has also become quite popular with the youth of Pakistan, and an increasing number of young people spend their free time online, especially on social networking sites (SNS) such as Orkut and Facebook. Other electronic media such as cell phones and iPods have also become a part of the local youth culture.

SOCIETY

Transportation

Generally, public transport in Pakistan is inefficient and not commonly used. Although public transportation is inexpensive, it is considered uncomfortable and overcrowded. However, there is an ongoing effort to improve Pakistan's public transportation system and to make local transit more efficient.

The preferred mode of travel amongst the majority of Pakistanis is by car. In fact, because the number vehicles in Pakistan are drastically increasing, there has also been an increase in severe traffic problems in the major cities. For personal domestic and international travel, most Pakistanis prefer to travel by air. There are 139 airports in Pakistan.

Personal transportation by sea is virtually non-existent, and this mode of transport is used primarily for commercial transport. Pakistan has ports on the Arabian Sea, including the Karachi, Mohammad Bin Qasim and Gawadar Ports, and these allow foreign imports to be easily transported into the country. From there, goods are moved by the extensive river systems.

Traffic in Pakistan moves on the left-hand side of the road.

Transportation Infrastructure

The road system extends over 258,340 kilometers (160,525 miles), of which 711 kilometers (441 miles) are expressways. The road system is also commonly used to transport commercial goods across the country.

The railway system, although inexpensive, is characterized by inefficiency and low comfort levels. As such, railways are used mostly for the transportation of industrial goods and raw materials. The network extends over 8,000 kilometers (4,900 miles).

Media & Communications

In Pakistan, a strict censorship is imposed on all media, including newspapers, television, radio and films. Overt political criticism of the government and any material likely to offend Islamic sensibilities, as well as sexually explicit materials, are all heavily censored. For this reason, most foreign films in Pakistan are censored, if not banned. Because of the long-standing enmity with India, Indian films have been officially banned until very recently.

Newspapers are usually published in Urdu and English, although some small presses also publish in other local languages. English-language newspapers are read by only a very small percentage of the population. However, in academic, political and corporate circles their influence is significant. There are four main national press houses in Pakistan. These are Jang Publications, which publishes *The Daily Jang*, *The News*, and *The Daily News*; the Dawn or Herald Group, which publishes *The Dawn*; the Khabrain Group, which publishes *The Daily Khabrain* and *The Post*; and the Nawa-i-Waqt Group, which publishes *The Nawa-i-Waqt* and *The Nation*.

Other forms of media, such as telephone and Internet, have also experienced a steady increase in the number of users, as well as improvement in the infrastructure. In 2006, there were over 12 million Internet users in Pakistan. There was also a corresponding increase in the number of broadband users. However, it is the telecommunications industry that has experienced the largest boost in Pakistan, probably as a result of the legislation passed by the government in 2004, allowing for competition in the industry. In 2006, there were 34.5 million cellular phone users in Pakistan. The significant progress in the industry has led also to the advent of international telecommunications firms in Pakistan, such as Telenor and Warid.

SOCIAL DEVELOPMENT

Standard of Living

Pakistan ranked 146th out of 185 countries on the 2013 Human Development Index, which measures quality of life and standard of living indicators.

Water Consumption

Approximately 96 percent of Pakistan's urban population and 89 percent of its rural population have access to improved water sources. An estimated 72 percent of its urban population and 34 percent of its rural have access to improved sanitation systems.

Education

Even at the most basic levels, Pakistan is struggling to provide an adequate education for its young, rapidly growing population. Less than half of the total population above fifteen years of age is literate, and the literacy rate is significantly higher for men than for women. Both government-funded schools and private schools operate in Pakistan, and both stress the tenets of Islam as well as basic academic subjects.

Government-funded schools provide free education, but attendance is not compulsory and many children work to help support their family instead of studying. Primary and secondary school lasts for twelve years. Male students outnumber female students by far, with fewer than half of school-age girls in attendance.

Only a small percentage of college-age Pakistanis obtain a higher education. In addition to numerous vocational schools and professional schools, there are many public and private universities. Prestigious public universities include Quaid-e-Azam University in the capital, and the University of Peshawar. The Agha Khan University Medical College in Karachi and the National University of Sciences and Technology in Rawalpindi are major private universities.

Women's access to education and employment are significantly lower than men's, particularly in rural areas of the country. In some areas of the country, particularly the north, women's access to education is blocked on religious grounds. The 2014 Nobel Peace Prize winner Yousafzai Malala was granted the award on the basis of her advocacy for women's education.

Women's Rights

Women have never enjoyed complete equality in Pakistan, but conditions have improved somewhat in recent years. For example, an increasing number of women in urban centers are now working, and seats are reserved for women in government bodies. However, the literacy rate for women is half of that for men, with the former obtaining on average 0.7 years of formal education as compared to the average of 2.9 years for men. Consequently, women have far fewer employment opportunities, and a large number still remain economically dependent on their male counterparts.

Partly as a result of the lack of education on the part of the women themselves, and partly due to official neglect, there has not been sufficient attention paid to the improvement of reproductive and post-natal health. This leads to an inordinately high birth rate, and contributes to the deaths of thousands of women during childbirth every year. This lack of attention paid to female healthcare is also the result of rigid religious and cultural beliefs.

Violence against women remains a serious problem in Pakistan. It has been estimated that approximately 50 to 90 percent of women experience some form of violence, including rape, honor killings, forced marriages and murder, every year. As there is very little recognition of equal rights for women, there is no proper treatment of gender-based violence by the authorities. Furthermore, there is an absence of adequate laws to punish the perpetrators. The government has also done very little to eliminate the oppressive Hudood Ordinances, which are laws that do not recognize marital rape and punish non-marital consensual sex. These laws cause many victims of sexual violence to be punished instead for non-marital sexual relations.

Health Care

The health care system of Pakistan is inadequate to meet the needs of the population, and suffers from a shortage of medical practitioners, facilities, and funds. Despite these problems, some progress has been made in primary health care to reduce infant mortality, improve pre- and post-natal care, and carry out immunization campaigns.

Prevalent illnesses, many of them derived from poor sanitation practices, include gastroenteritis, hepatitis A and E, typhoid fever, malaria, tuberculosis, and dengue fever; childhood malnutrition is also a serious problem.

GOVERNMENT

Structure

Pakistan was partitioned from India and gained its independence from Britain in 1947. In 1971, the eastern wing of Pakistan seceded and became Bangladesh. Internally, Pakistan has undergone major political upheavals, including periods of martial law and several coups, most recently in 1999, when the military seized control of the government. The general who organized the takeover won a controversial referendum on his presidency in 2002, extending his rule until 2007.

Officially, Pakistan is a federal republic. According to its 1973 constitution, executive power is vested in a president, who is elected to a five-year term by the legislature. The president in turn appoints a prime minister from the majority party or coalition. The government cabinet is appointed by the prime minister. Amendments made to the constitution in 2002 grant the president wide-ranging powers, including dismissal of the legislature and the prime minister.

Pakistan's legislative branch is bicameral. The Senate consists of eighty-seven seats, which are filled for six-year terms by vote of the national and provincial legislatures. The National Assembly consists of 342 seats. Members are elected by direct vote to five-year terms, and women and minorities are allotted set numbers of seats.

The Supreme Court presides over the judicial branch; its justices are appointed by the president. At the federal level, there is also a court based on Sharia, or Islamic law. High courts hear cases at the provincial level. Both secular and religious laws are binding.

Pakistan is divided into four provinces, two federally administered areas, and a Capital Territory. The president is responsible for appointing a governor to each province. Power at the provincial level has been sharply curtailed since the 1999 coup. Pakistan also administers portions of the disputed Kashmir territory.

Political Parties

Major political parties include the Pakistan People's Party and the Pakistan Muslim League. There are, in addition, numerous parties representing ethnic groups. It is common for parties to splinter and for new coalitions to be formed.

In the 2013 general elections, the Pakistan Muslim League earned 33 percent of the vote, giving them 126 seats in parliament, while the Pakistan People's Party earned 15 percent of the vote, giving them 33 seats. In March 2008, Nawaz Sharif became the country's prime minister, and in September 2013, Mamnoon Hussain was appointed president.

Local Government

Pakistan is divided into four provinces, two territories, and one capital territory. The provinces are governed by elected provincial assemblies, each of which is overseen by a chief minister. Each province is divided into zillas, or districts, which are then further subdivided into tehsils, or boroughs.

Judicial System

The Pakistani judiciary comprises a Supreme Court, several High Courts, and a Federal Shariat Court.

Taxation

The top corporate tax levied is 35 percent, while the top income tax is 25 percent. A property tax and general sales tax (GST) are also levied.

Armed Forces

The Pakistani Armed Forces comprises an army, air force, navy, and coast guard, as well as a paramilitary force. In 2007, the country had approximately 600,000 active military personnel.

Foreign Policy

Pakistan's foreign policy has always been oriented toward the preservation of its national integrity and security, while also focusing on its economic interests. Pakistan is a member state of the British Commonwealth of Nations as well as the South Asian Association for Regional Cooperation (SAARC), which focuses on the economic and political issues in Southeast Asia. Pakistan is also a member of the Organization of the Islamic Conference (OIC), which includes fifty-seven member states, and the Economic Cooperation Organization (EOC), which promotes trade and investment in Asia. Pakistan joined the United Nations (UN) in 1947.

Historically, Pakistan has always sought to make alliances, especially with Western nations. For example, Pakistan has always been eager to sign anti-communist and other such treaties in accordance with Western interests. After the September 11, 2001 terrorist attacks in the United States, its relations with the US improved as it became an ally in the US-led "War on Terror." As part of its allegiance, Pakistan pledged to combat any terrorist activity on its soil. This also brought Pakistan a drastic increase in military aid from the US, totaling more than $4 billion (USD) since 2001.

Pakistan has sought to make bilateral alliances with other nations as well. This is particularly evident in Pakistan's foreign relations with other Muslim states. It thus has significant security and economic interests in the Middle East and the Persian Gulf. Its relations with its neighbor China have always been good, and it has repeatedly stressed that the stability of Afghanistan is in its interests.

Relations with India, however, remain strained. From the time both nations simultaneously gained independence from Britain, Pakistan has been involved in a number of conflicts with India, most notably in 1965 and 1971. Often at the root of Pakistan's conflict with India is the territorial dispute over Kashmir, a northwestern region bordering both countries that has been the site of frequent terrorist activity. In addition, animosity has continued to build concerning both countries' respective nuclear programs.

Human Rights Profile

International human rights law insists that states respect civil and political rights, and also promote an individual's economic, social and cultural rights. The United Nations Universal Declaration on Human Rights (UDHR) is recognized as the standard for international human rights. Its authors sought the counsel of the world's great thinkers, philosophers, and religious leaders, and were careful to create a document that reflects the core values shared by every world culture. (To read this document or view the articles relating to cultural human rights, visit: http://www.udhr.org/UDHR/default.htm.)

Although Pakistan officially accepts the Universal Declaration of Human Rights, its human rights record has been less than impressive, and some significant human rights concerns are still present. These have been especially alarming in the wake of political turmoil in the early 21st century. In contradiction of Article 9 of the declaration, there have more cases of arbitrary detention for indefinite periods of time, especially those of protesters, human rights activists and lawyers. This also includes the mistreatment, torture and forced "disappearances" of suspected terrorists, prisoners, journalists and political opponents. The right to peaceful assembly and protest, protected in Article 20, has also been repeatedly breached.

In defiance of Article 10, there has been a lack of fair trials in Pakistan. Articles 18 and 19, allowing the freedom of speech, thought and belief, have also been violated. For example, the national media has been placed under a program of strict censorship, and the Pakistani government has repeatedly disrupted the democratic processes since its emergence as a sovereign nation.

In contradiction of Article 2, occurrences of discrimination and violence against religious and other social minorities are not uncommon. Religious communities, such as the Ahmedi community for instance, are discriminated against. In addition, homosexuality is not tolerated under any circumstance. Child and bonded labor has also been a cause for concern. However, Pakistan has pledged to abolish the death penalty.

ECONOMY

Overview of the Economy

Recent market reforms have benefited Pakistan's economy, and international investment has increased since the government began cooperating with Western countries to clamp down on terrorists. Nonetheless, widespread poverty and lack of economic opportunity still afflict huge portions of the population; an estimated 32 percent of the population is living below the poverty line.

The gross domestic product (GDP) was $884 billion in 2014, and its GDP per capita was estimated at $4,700 USD that same year. These figures do not include the underground economy, which is thought to constitute 30 percent of the total economy.

Industry

Industry accounts for 21 percent of the GDP and employs 20 percent of the labor force. Much of the industrial sector depends on the agricultural sector for raw materials. Refined petroleum, cigarettes, construction materials, chemicals, pharmaceuticals, and paper products are all manufactured in Pakistan. Traditional craftwork, especially handmade carpets and pottery, is also important.

Currently, Pakistan does not produce enough energy to satisfy its needs. Potential increases in hydropower, nuclear power and thermal power, however, could help the country reduce its dependence on petroleum imports.

Labor

The labor force is 62 million, with an estimated 6.8 percent unemployment rate in 2014, as well as significant underemployment.

Energy/Power/Natural Resources

Pakistan's most valuable natural resources are arable land and wetlands. Though many minerals are present, most of them are either difficult to access, of poor quality, or occur in small quantities. The country also has significant reserves of natural gas and potential reserves of oil.

Pakistan suffers from a host of environmental problems that it has done relatively little to counteract. Poor conservation practices are the most problematic. The country has one of the fastest rates of deforestation in the world. This in turn has led to soil erosion. Poor agricultural practices have caused groundwater degradation and a decrease in available water sources, and also threaten the country's fragile wetlands. Air pollution in major cities is also a problem.

Fishing

Pakistan's fishing sector is quite developed and still growing. It is currently focused mostly in the Indian Ocean and employs over 1 million workers, overall.

Forestry

Deforestation is a huge issue in Pakistan. In 2010, it was estimated that Pakistan had the lowest forest coverage in South Asia (5.2 percent). The Pakistan government has set a goal to increase its forest coverage to 6 percent by 2014.

Mining/Metals

The mining industry of Pakistan is relatively small, as the materials can be difficult to mine. Chromite is the most widely exploited; other minerals include coal, copper, iron ore, gypsum, limestone, marble, silica sand, anhydrite, dolomite, and onyx.

Agriculture

Agriculture accounts for only 20 percent of the GDP but employs 43 percent of the labor force. Approximately 28 percent of the land is under cultivation, and much of it is irrigated with water from the Indus River.

Cotton, rice, sugarcane, wheat, rice, corn, fruit and vegetables are the country's major crops.

Animal Husbandry

Livestock is also important for milk, meat, and eggs; sheep, cattle, water buffalo, goats, and poultry are all raised in Pakistan.

Tourism

Pakistan's tourism sector has untapped potential. A basic but developing infrastructure combined with fears of terrorism has contributed to the industry's slow growth. Approximately 400,000 tourists visit annually, generating around $110 million USD in revenue.

Pakistan boasts both extensive natural beauty and cultural riches. The rugged northern terrain, which includes several of the highest mountain peaks in the world, attracts climbers and hikers. Several national parks protect the natural scenery as well as rare wildlife. Culturally, Pakistan offers architecture from three major religions: Buddhism, Hinduism, and Islam. In addition, there are ancient archaeological sites, bazaars, and well-preserved examples of British colonial architecture.

Izza Tahir, Michael Aliprandi

DO YOU KNOW?

- After several attempts by climbers of various nationalities, Italian climbers Lino Lacedelli and Achille Compagnoni became the first to reach the summit of mountain known as K2, in 1954. K2 is the second-highest mountain in the world.
- Pakistan is home to the two largest mosques in the world: the Badshahi Mosque in Lahore and the Faisal Mosque in Islamabad.
- Islamabad, or "City of Islam," was named the capital of Pakistan in 1960, after the original capital, Karachi, was deemed unsuitable.

Bibliography

Akbar, M.J. *Tenderbox: The Past and Future of Pakistan.* New York: Harper Perennial, 2012.

Belokrenitski, V. I. *A Political History of Pakistan, 1947–2007.* Karachi: Oxford University Press, 2013.

Chak, Farhan Mujahid. *Islam and Pakistan's Political Culture.* New York: Routledge, 2015.

Cohen, Stephen P. *The Idea of Pakistan.* Washington, DC: Brookings Institution Press, 2006.

Dilip, Hiro. *The Longest August: The Unflinching Rivalry between India and Pakistan.* New York: Nation Books, 2015.

Haleem, Safia. *Pakistan—Culture Smart! The Essential Guide to Customs and Culture.* London: Kuperard, 2013.

Hay, Stephen, ed. *Sources of Indian Tradition, Volume 2: Modern India and Pakistan.* New York: Columbia University Press, 1988.

Jalal, Ayesha. *The Struggle for Pakistan: A Muslim Homeland and Global Politics.* Cambridge, MA: Belknap Press, 2014.

Lieven, Anatol. *Pakistan: A Hard Country.* New York: Public Affairs, 2011.

Malik, Iftihkar Haider. *Culture and Customs of Pakistan.* Westport, CT: Greenwood Press, 2006.

Mouiuddin, Yasmeen Niaz. *Pakistan: A Global Studies Handbook.* Santa Barbara, CA: ABC-CLIO, 2007.

Ramzi, Shanaz. *Food Prints: An Epicurean Journey through Pakistan.* New York: Oxford University Press, 2013.

Zakaria, Rafia. *The Upstairs Wife: An Intimate History of Pakistan.* Boston: Beacon Press, 2015.

Works Cited

Losty, J.P. et al. "Indian Subcontinent." *Grove Art Online. Oxford Art Online.* 30 July 2008.

"Lahore." *World Encyclopedia.* 2008. *Oxford Reference Online.* Oxford University Press.

Nesom-Sirhandi, Marcella, et al. "Pakistan." *Grove Art Online. Oxford Art Online.* 30 July 2008.

"Pakistan." *Europa World.* Routledge. 19 July 2008.

"Pakistan: Foreign Policy." *Country Studies*. 19 July 2008. <http://countrystudies.us/pakistan/82.htm>

"Pakistan." *The World Factbook*. Central Intelligence Agency. 10 April 2015. <https://www.cia.gov/library/publications/the-world-factbook/geos/pk.html>

Possehl, Gregory L. "Harappa." *The Oxford Companion to Archaeology*. Brian M. Fagan, ed., Oxford University Press 1996. *Oxford Reference Online*. Oxford University Press.

Qureshi, Regula. "Pakistan." *Grove Music Online. Oxford Music Online*. 30 Jul. 2008

Shayma Saiyid "Pakistan." *The International Encyclopedia of Dance*. Ed. Selma Jeanne Cohen and the Dance Perspectives Foundation. Oxford University Press, 2003.

Svetich, Kella. "Asian American Literature." *The Oxford Encyclopedia of American Literature*. Jay Parini, ed. *Oxford University Press*, 2004.

"U.S. Relations with Pakistan." *U.S. Department of State*. September 2014. <http://www.state.gov/r/pa/ei/bgn/3453.htm>

"Universal Periodic Review of Pakistan." *Human Rights Watch*. 6 May 2008. <http://hrw.org/english/docs/2008/04/11/global18516.htm>

Possehl, Gregory L. "Mohenjo-Daro." *The Oxford Companion to Archaeology*. Brian M. Fagan, ed., Oxford University Press 1996. *Oxford Reference Online*. Oxford University Press.

Wescoat Jr., James L. "Lahore." *Grove Art Online. Oxford Art Online*.

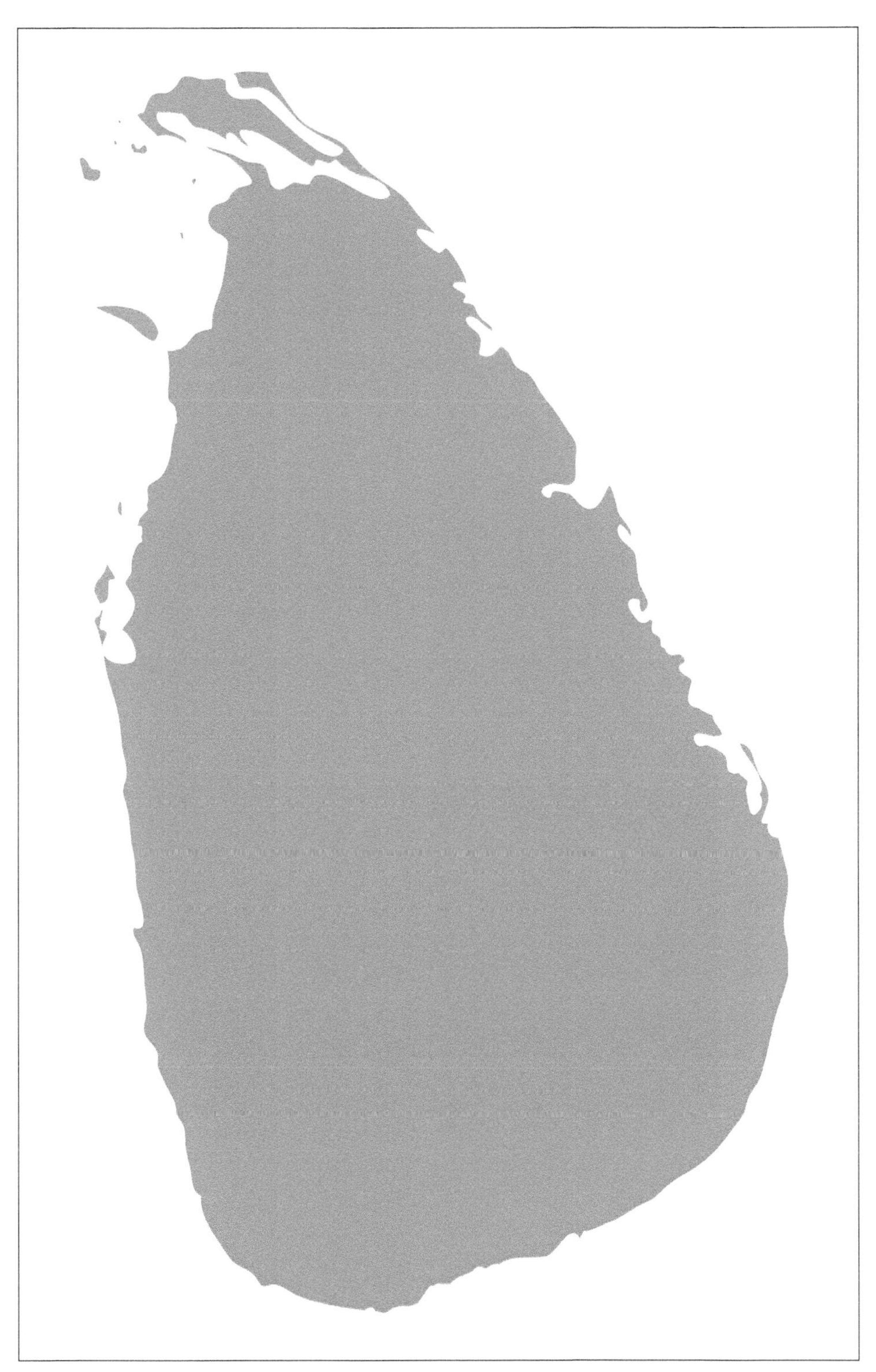

Sri Lanka

Introduction

The Democratic Socialist Republic of Sri Lanka, formerly known as Ceylon, is a small island nation in the Indian Ocean. The island lies southeast of India, from which it is separated by the Palk Strait and the Gulf of Mannar. The Maldives lie to the west of Sri Lanka, the Bay of Bengal lies to the east, and a chain of islands called Adam's Bridge lies to the north. Sri Lanka, which is widely known for its tea, has formerly been a colony of the Netherlands, Portugal, and Great Britain.

The Sinhalese people live in a caste system. This system establishes accepted societal divisions based on economic class and profession. Marriages are typically arranged by families, and are usually determined by caste. Professions are usually chosen by family members as well, and it is rare that a Sinhalese person will gain employment in a position outside of his or her caste.

Sri Lanka's caste system includes a separate caste for artists, and the majority of Sri Lankan art has historically been produced by this caste. (However, the national government now allows any citizen, regardless of caste, to work in the arts professionally.) Traditional crafts include jewelry, pottery, baskets, mats, and wooden masks. Dance is an important aspect of Sri Lanka's art culture, and most festivals and religious ceremonies incorporate dance in some way. Architecture is also considered one of Sri Lanka's noteworthy art forms. Places of worship and religious significance, such as Buddhist dagobas and Hindu kovils, feature some of the nation's most revered architecture and sculptures.

GENERAL INFORMATION

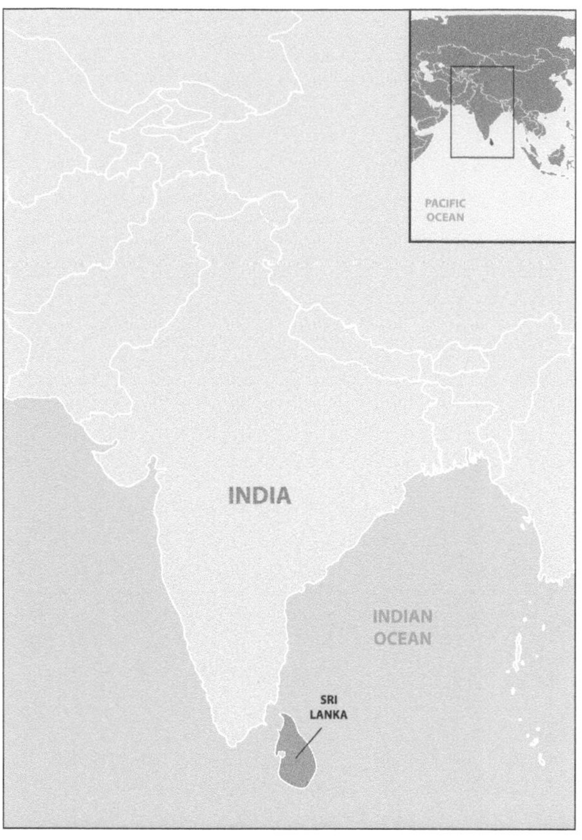

Official Language: Sinhala, Tamil
Population: 21,866,445 (2014 estimate)
Currency: Sri Lankan rupee
Coins: The Sri Lankan rupee is subdivided into 100 cents. Coins are available in denominations of 25 and 50 cents, and 1, 2, 5, and 10 rupees; rarely circulated coins include the 1-, 2-, 5-, and 10-cent coins.
Land Area: 64,630 square kilometers (24,953 square miles)
Water Area: 980 square kilometers (378 square miles)
National Anthem: "Sri Lanka Matha" (Sinhala, "Sri Lanka, Motherland")
Capital: Colombo (Sri Jayewardenepura Kotte is the legislative capital)
Time Zone: GMT +5.5
Flag Description: The flag of Sri Lanka is also known as the "Lion Flag." It depicts a golden lion with a sword in its right front paw. The lion is featured on a crimson background and bordered in

0 60 Kilometers
0 60Miles
N
INDIA
Jaffna
Palk Bay
BAY OF BENGAL
Mannar
Gulf of Mannar
Trincomalee
Anuradhapura
Mihintale
Puttalam
SRI LANKA
Polonnaruwa
Batticaloa
Matale
Kalmunai
Kandy
Negombo
Temple of the Tooth
Badulla
COLOMBO
Sri Jayawardenepura Kotte
Moratuwa
Ratnapura
Beruwala
Galle
INDIAN OCEAN

Principal Cities by Population (2012):

- Colombo (752,993)
- Dehiwala-Mount Lavinia (245,974)
- Moratuwa (207,755)
- Sri Jayawardenepura (Kotte) (135,806)
- Kandy (125,351)
- Kalmunai (106,783)
- Galle (99,478)
- Batticaloa (92,332)
- Matara (47,420)
- Negombo (127,754)

gold and by four fig leaves or "bo" leaves. The left section of the flag features two horizontal stripes of color; one green and one orange. The orange represents the Sri Lankan Tamils and the green represents Sri Lankan Moors.

Population

The Sinhalese are the largest ethnicity in Sri Lanka, representing approximately 73.8 percent of the population as of the 2001 census. The largest minority group is the Tamil people, comprised of Sri Lankan Tamils and Indian Tamils. Other minorities include the Moors, a Muslim group descended from Arabs; the Berghers, who are descended from European inhabitants of Sri Lanka; the Malays, from modern Malaysia; and the Veddahs, who are descended from the Wanniyala-Aettos, the earliest inhabitants of the island. The majority of the country's Moors live on the east coast, while most native Tamils occupy Sri Lanka's northern coast.

Colombo is the cultural and commercial capital of Sri Lanka, and the country's largest city; as of 2012, the Colombo Metropolitan Region (which includes three districts) had an unofficial population count of 5,851,130. The legislative capital is Sri Jayewardenepura Kotte. The majority of the population (roughly three-quarters) lives in rural areas. Most urban Sri Lankans live in or around Colombo. Other major cities are Dehiwala-Mount Lavinia, Maratuwa (an industrial center), Jaffna (a seaport), Kandy, and Galle.

Most Sri Lankans are farmers, many of whom live on farms with their extended families. Approximately 15 percent of the population resides in urban areas. As of 2014, the population growth rate was 0.86 percent.

Languages

The languages of the Sinhalese and Tamil people, Sinhala and Tamil, are the official languages of Sri Lanka. Approximately 75 percent of the population speaks Sinha as a primary language. About 10 percent of the population speaks English as well. Hindi is also common in urban areas. A Malaysian-Creole language is spoken in some parts of Sri Lanka and is occasionally encountered in the cities.

Native People & Ethnic Groups

The earliest inhabitants of the island occupied by Sri Lanka were the Wanniyala-Aettos. These people remain in Sri Lanka today, but are known as Veddahs. Traditionally forest dwellers, the Veddahs have lived in Sri Lanka for nearly 18,000 years. However, in 1983, the government of Sri Lanka established a national park on the Veddahs' ancestral lands and forced the natives to leave the area. The group faces the threat of extinction due to the loss of their land.

The Sinhalese have inhabited Sri Lanka since the fifth century BCE. In the first century BCE, the Tamil people invaded Sri Lanka from India. Arabs first came to Sri Lanka as traders in the eighth century. After a period of invasions from China, Malaysia, and India, Sri Lanka was invaded by Portugal and the Netherlands in the 16th and 17th centuries. Finally, Great Britain invaded Sri Lanka in 1795, and a long period of British rule followed until the island became independent in 1948. The effects of European colonialism have since dominated the politics and culture of Sri Lanka.

Today, Sri Lanka's population is comprised of several ethnic groups, the largest of which is the Sinhalese. The largest minority group is the Tamil people, comprised of Sri Lankan Tamils and Indian Tamils. Long-standing ethnic tension exists between the Sinhalese and the Tamils. The

Sinhalese are in control of Sri Lanka's government. Tamils feel that they are not represented by the government and want to create an independent Tamil nation, or Eelam, within the borders of Sri Lanka. Some Tamil separatist groups, such as the Liberation Tigers of Tamil Eelam (LTTE), use military force to fight for their cause. Because of the conflict between the Sinhalese government and the Tamil separatists, Sri Lanka was in a state of civil war from 1983 to 2009, with a victory by the government's forces. Although the fighting ended, the relationship between the Tamils and the central government has continued to be very tense.

Religions

Sri Lanka has a diverse religious heritage, as centuries of immigration from Asia and India brought religious traditions to the nation. Buddhism is the most popular religion and accounts for approximately 69 percent of the population. Some estimates indicate that around six percent of the population practices some form of Christianity, which is mainly in urban areas. Most members of the Tamil ethnic group practice Hinduism, while Sri Lankan Moors are typically Muslim.

Climate

The climate of Sri Lanka is equatorial and tropical. Temperatures are generally high, averaging 32° Celsius (90° Fahrenheit) in the lowlands and 21° Celsius (70° Fahrenheit) in the mountains.

The weather is humid, and Sri Lanka receives an enormous amount of rainfall. The average annual rainfall in the northeast plains is 127 centimeters (50 inches), while the average in the southwest rainforest is upwards of 508 centimeters (200 inches).

The months between May and November constitute the monsoon season, during which Sri Lanka receives most of its rain. However, due to shifts in the prevailing winds, the northeast gets most of its rain from December to February. Occasional cyclones and tornadoes are significant natural hazards. In 2004, a tsunami in the Indian Ocean killed almost 40,000 Sri Lankans. An additional 500,000 Sri Lankans lost their homes.

ENVIRONMENT & GEOGRAPHY

Topography

The northern areas of Sri Lanka are mostly covered with low plains. The southwest region contains a tropical rainforest, while the southern central region is a large mountain range. Among these mountains is Pidurutalagala, which at 2,524 meters (8,281feet) is the highest point in Sri Lanka. The uplands region contains two large plateaus, Nuwara Eliya and Horton Plains. North of the mountain region is a vast, dry plain.

There are several rivers running through Sri Lanka. The largest of these is the Mahaweli Ganga. Others include the Kelani, the Kalu, and the Aruvi. The coastline has several natural harbors, such as the Trincomalee Harbor in the northeast, and several artificial harbors, such as the ones at Colombo and Galle.

Plants & Animals

Palm trees such as coconut palms, arecas and palmyras grow in the lowlands and along the coast. Large amounts of mangroves and screw pines are also found in coastal areas. Flowers such as hyacinths, acacias, and cypresses are found throughout Sri Lanka. The rainforest is home to several other varieties of orchid, bougainvillea, poinsettia, and 3,000 species of fern.

Wildlife in Sri Lanka includes bears, cheetahs, leopards, monkeys, elephants, crocodiles, and snakes. Sri Lanka is home to about 2,500 Asian elephants, which are endangered due to poaching. The Pinnawela Elephant Orphanage, which contains about 60 elephants, is a habitat dedicated to preserving the Asian elephant.

Inland water habitats are home to fish such as red scissortail barb and paradise fish. Ceylon blue magpies, golden orioles, and bee-eaters are some of the bird species native to Sri Lanka.

CUSTOMS & COURTESIES

Greetings

There are several differences between the greetings used by Sinhalese and Tamil people.

However, there are a few practices that bridge this cultural divide. Older Sri Lankans will often greet one another by saying "Namaste" ("I bow to you"), and pressing the palms together in a gesture of prayer. Younger people tend to use the less formal phrase "Kuhomadu" ("How do you do?"). The younger generation also commonly uses Western-style handshaking as a common gesture of greeting. Sri Lankans tend to use formal titles and surnames. Even in less formal settings, typically among younger people, a woman will often refrain from shaking hands because it could be considered impolite to have contact with a man to whom she is not related.

Sinhalese people have complicated rules for greeting one another. For example, there are over 20 ways to say the word "you" in the Sinhala language, depending on the relative status of the people in the conversation. It is common for Sinhalese people to address one another by their surnames. Typically, surnames are followed by the appropriate gender title: "Mahaththeya" for a man or "Nohna" for a woman. Both Sinhalese and Tamils greet people with a blessing for long life. In the Sinhala language the word is "Ayubowan," while the equivalent greeting in Tamil is "Vanakkam."

Gestures & Etiquette

There are several gestures that are distinctively Sri Lankan. One is the head motion signifying agreement, which consists of a short back and forth shaking, and a slight up and down movement, similar to the Western gesture for "no." The gesture to summon someone consists of extending the arm, pointing the back of the hand outward, and wagging the fingers. This gesture means the opposite in Western cultures, where it is typically construed as "go away."

In terms of etiquette, Sri Lankans treat places of religious significance with great respect and reverence, and expect the same treatment from foreigners as well. When visiting a Buddhist temple, for example, it is considered very impolite to wear shoes or hats. It is also rude to wear clothing that is too revealing. In addition, foreign women are expected to refrain from interacting directly with Buddhist monks.

Eating/Meals

Meals are very social events for Sri Lankans, and most people prefer to take all three meals of the day at home, surrounded by family. Meals are also quite leisurely, and it is not uncommon for dinner to go on for quite a long time, with people chatting at length before the meal is actually served. It is traditional for men and guests to be served first, with the women of the household waiting until they are certain that everyone else is satisfied. As slowly as they can begin, meals are usually finished quickly, and are usually adjourned when everyone has eaten their fill.

Rice typically dominates almost every meal in Sri Lanka. Breakfast usually consists of a sweetened rice and coconut milk porridge called congee, rice and coconut milk squares called kiribath, or rice pancakes called hoppers. Lunch and dinner incorporate starches such as hoppers, a shredded variety of hoppers known as string hoppers, a rice flour and coconut mixture called pittu, or yellow rice. Starch dishes are commonly accompanied by several different sauces, gravies and curries. Common sauces include an oil and onion gravy called sambol, a vegetable and lentil curry called sambar, and chili water gravy called rasam.

While dishes are used in some households, many people prefer the traditional method of serving food on warmed banana leaves. This is done to enhance the aroma of the food and stimulate the appetite. Utensils are not generally used, and eating is done with the tips of the fingers. Additionally, it is deemed proper to only eat with the right hand, a custom similar to Muslim cultures where the left hand is considered impure because it is associated with the cleansing of the body. Eating without utensils and feeling the food with the fingers is considered an important part of appreciating good food.

Visiting

Sri Lankans tend to be extremely social. Generally, they are considered gracious hosts and openly receptive to receiving visitors. Visiting is usually not formal, as formality implies a level of distance that is considered contrary to friendship. People often drop by for visits without making arrangements in advance. In addition, dress when attending a host's house typically reflects a level of comfort associated with friendship and relaxation, unless specifically stated otherwise in the invitation. Gifts are not required, but will be appreciated. It is appropriate to give flowers, chocolate or alcoholic beverages, the latter only if the hosts drink. More importantly, gifts should be given with the right hand.

People in Sri Lanka are generally very relaxed about time. When attending a dinner party, it is not uncommon for the meal to be served late, as Sri Lankans tend to chat and socialize at length before the actual meal. Beverages may be served during this time, and nonalcoholic beverages such as sweet tea and fruit juices are common. This leisurely time is considered the most important part of the meal, as establishing social harmony is a primary goal of hosting a dinner party. However, it is normal to depart as soon as everyone has finished eating, as lingering after eating is considered impolite.

LIFESTYLE

Family

Family is extremely important to Sri Lankans. In part, this is because the village, or gamma, is traditionally the basic economic unit. Each gamma is comprised of a few extended families. Historically, having a large extended family was the way to attain influence and power within the gamma. Therefore, children have always been highly prized, while not having children was traditionally considered abnormal. While children are still revered, younger couples now consciously plan how many children they can afford to have.

Even though modern conditions have somewhat altered the role that the gamma plays in the economy, the extended family is still extremely important to Sri Lankans. When a child is born, the infant is normally cared for by grandmothers (especially the maternal grandmother), aunts and other female relatives almost as much as by its own mother. In addition, Sri Lankan people maintain a high level of respect for their relatives throughout their entire lives, especially for their elders. Family advice is sought and heeded when making major decisions, and families still assert much control over Sri Lankan people's lives. This is evidenced by the fact that arranged marriages are still quite common.

Housing

Sri Lankans live in several different kinds of houses that largely reflect differences between rural and urban life and household income. Residents of rural villages tend to live in very simple homes, built on wood frames and covered with thatched palm leaves. These simple, small houses usually consist of one or two living rooms, and a basic kitchen. Roofs are usually thatched, but may be made of ceramic or metal. Many rural homes lack electricity and indoor plumbing. Housing in urban areas reflects variations in economic class. Houses range from simple shanties to spacious townhouses with walled gardens and modern amenities such as central air conditioning.

Food

Sri Lankan cuisine is extremely diverse and flavorful. It is rooted in the culinary traditions of India and Malaysia, and later influenced through foreign trade with Arab cultures. Additionally, due to Sri Lanka's colonial history, Sri Lankan cuisine has some distinct Portuguese, Dutch, and British influences as well. Generally, rice is the primary grain—Sri Lankans eat several types of rice, including basmati, jasmine and red rice—and coconut milk is widely used. The country's cuisine is also heavily dependent on fish, fruit and curries.

The island of Sri Lanka provides a rich variety of cooking ingredients. Vegetables such as long beans, okra, cassava root and bitter gourds are grown throughout the country. Many different fruits are produced in abundance, including coconuts, pineapples, papayas and bananas. Sri Lankans typically make good use of seafood, and staple fish commonly consumed include tuna, shark, swordfish and mackerel. Additionally, prawns, crab and squid are also found in many recipes. Chicken is the most common meat in Sri Lankan food, and some ethnic groups also eat beef or pork. Furthermore, Sri Lanka has historically been the center of a very lucrative spice trade, and its cuisine is richly flavored with black pepper, mustard powder, tamarind, dill, fennel, cinnamon, cardamom and a huge range of hot chilies.

Sri Lankan curry dishes are usually eaten with rice. Curry is also eaten with hoppers, a kind of pancake made from rice flour. String hoppers, which are more like noodles, are also enjoyed as a base for curry dishes. Sri Lankans make many kinds of desserts, which incorporate the sweetness of the coconut, pineapple, dates and other fruits. Tea—the country is famous for Sri Lankan tea, which is also known as Ceylon tea—all kinds of fruit juices, coconut water and locally produced ginger beer are common soft drinks. Alcoholic beverages include locally brewed beer, a palm sap wine called toddy, and a distilled version of toddy called arrack.

Life's Milestones

The birth of a child is a joyful event in a Sri Lankan family. It is customary for friends and family to visit and bring gifts as soon as possible, either a toy for the child or jewelry if it is a girl. An astrologer may also be consulted soon after the birth to determine the child's future. When the child is ready, the family holds a celebration to feed the child his or her first solid food, typically a small amount of rice, sometimes with curry.

Marriage, which is traditionally arranged by the family, is also a joyful ceremony. Among the Buddhist majority, it is customary for the young couple to stand on a raised structure called a poruwa, which represents the household, and exchange rings while people recite religious chants. A Hindu wedding traditionally consists of the couple and their families spending several hours chanting and performing a series of religious rituals, such as the bridegroom walking around a holy fire seven times.

Additionally, death and aging are treated as a natural part of life by Sri Lankans, and the elderly are afforded the utmost respect. When a person is seriously ill, it is expected that his or her family and friends will visit on a regular basis, bringing food and gifts. When a person dies, their body is laid out in their house, and people come to pay their last respects. Buddhists and Hindus typically cremate their dead, while members of the Christian and Muslim minorities adhere to religious or modern burial practices.

CULTURAL HISTORY

Art & Architecture

Sri Lankan art and architecture represents the assimilation and subsequent evolution of two different cultural groups: the Sinhalese and the Tamils. Both groups arrived on the island from mainland India—the Sinhalese came from northern India while the Tamils came from southern India. Generally, the Sinhalese people tend to be Buddhist, and Buddhism had a major influence on the architectural and artistic styles associated with this cultural group. This influence is particularly evident in Sir Lankan monasteries. Other architectural structures associated with the Sinhalese people are dagobas (also called stupas), made of brick and smooth plaster, and shaped like giant bells, and vatadages, which are open, ornately sculpted and circular buildings. Both buildings are traditionally used to house Buddhist relics and treasures. The Tamils, who are mainly Hindu, have created impressive religious buildings as well, often devoted to the god Shiva. Hindu temples, called kovils, usually feature large, sculpted towers over a central prayer room.

Sri Lankan Sinhalese Buddhism traditionally discouraged painting, but there are a few historical examples. The most famous are the fourth-century frescoes within the huge rocky outcropping called Sigiriya, or the Lion Rock, in the center of Sri Lanka. These paintings are very detailed and colorful depictions of beautiful women. They are thought to depict the incarnations of Tara Devi, the divine consort, or companion, of the bodhisattva (enlightened being) Avalokiteshvara, sometimes known as the Buddha of Compassion. However, the Sinhalese are better known for their masterful sculptures. Sinhalese giant Buddhas, crafted from variety of stones and metals, are found throughout the country. Tamils, on the other hand, have a rich tradition of painting. However, the vast majority of Tamil paintings are impermanent kolams, a form of sand painting. Traditionally created every sunrise by women as a household blessing, kolams are made from colorful rice flour, which is then eaten by small creatures. They are offerings to nature as much as they are art.

In the 18th and 19th centuries, Sri Lankan art became more stylized. This is evident in the expressive and colorful sculptures and wall paintings of the era. Buddhist murals and other artwork of the 20th century show the influences of European colonialism (1517–1948), as well as nationalism and a return to traditionalism. Sri Lankan artist George Keyt (1901–1993) is considered the country's foremost modern painter, and his works show influences from such modern styles as cubism, an avant-garde art movement popularized by Pablo Picasso (1881–1973). Other well-known Sri Lankan artists of the early 20th century include Solias Mendis, known for his historic depictions and revivalist murals or temple paintings, and M. Sarlis, also famous for his Buddhist murals.

Drama

Sri Lankan theater has four distinct styles. Sokari theater focuses on rituals related to the harvest. Nadagam and kavi nadagam theater styles incorporate story-telling and masked actors. Kolam theater involves a performance that lasts all night and into the next morning. Theater is performed in urban areas at venues such as the Tower Hall theater in Colombo.

Cinema is a popular form of entertainment as well. Director Lester James Peiris (1919–) has emerged from Sri Lanka as a noteworthy filmmaker. His films have focused on rural life in the country, with *Rekava* (1956), a film based on Sri Lankan village life, nominated for a coveted Palme d'Or.

Sri Lankan folk songs known as bailas are often sung accompanied by drumming or guitar music.

Music & Dance

Sri Lankan music is a product of the island's complicated history. Sinhalese music reflects a northern Indian and Buddhist influence, and traditionally consists of poems sung over the beats of drums. Sinhalese songs are typically about the life of the Buddha or tell the Buddhist Jataka tales, a collection of fables and other stories that belong to the canon of revered Buddhist literature. Tamil music, derived from the traditions of southern India, is much more orchestral, often involving string and wind instruments. Tamil tunes are often ragas, or Hindu devotional songs. Sri Lanka's colonization by Portugal in the 16th century also left a lasting impression. The Portuguese brought slaves with them, blending African drumming techniques with Sri Lankan musical traditions. Additionally, folk songs known as bailas are popular in Sri Lanka. This type of music, which incorporates drumming or clapping with a guitar, largely derive their name and style from the Portuguese colonial experience.

Generally, many different instruments are used in Sri Lankan music. Hand drums are the most common, and include traditional percussion instruments such as the yak beraya, geta bera and udakki. There is also a flat, one-sided hand drum called the raban, which is played like a tambourine, and was traditionally made with goat skin. Other drums are played with sticks, and include the barrel-shaped dawula, important in Buddhist ceremonies, and the bongo-like thammettama, which includes twin drums. Several wind instruments are played in Sri Lankan music, especially by Tamil musicians. Among these are the horanewa, similar to a clarinet and traditionally made with the teeth and horns of animals, and a flute called the bata nalawa, traditionally made of bamboo. There are also plucked string instruments, such as the south Indian sitar, which features a gourd-like base.

Dance is one of the most beloved forms of expression in Sri Lanka. One style, known as devil dancing, dates back to the pre-Sinhalese animists who originally inhabited the island, and is a form of ritual healing. Traditionally performed at night by torchlight, a devil dancer dons a mask of the demon presumed to be causing a sick person's illness. The dancer's movements are typically dramatic and whirling, accompanied by the frantic beat of a large beraya drum. Another popular form of dance is kandyan dancing. This style originated among the royal courts in the city of Kandy. It often features acrobatic dancing, performed to the complex beats of the tambourine-like raban, and larger geta bera and udakki hand drums.

The other important form of dancing, referred to as masked dance, is actually a kind of performance art or theater. Performers traditionally wear ornate and grotesque masks, often carved from a light wood, representing different characters. They then act out various long traditional stories and danced dramas, the themes of which typically consist of Buddhist legends, tragic love tales and supernatural adventures. The best-known masked dance performance takes place over several nights in late April, for the Sri Lankan New Year.

Literature

Sri Lanka has a long history of literature, largely consisting of distinct Sinhalese and Tamil literary traditions. Sinhalese literature was first written on palm leaves, and was created by Buddhist monks, since they were the only members of the community who learned how to write. Two early works, from the 10th century, form the basis of the Sinhalese tradition. These are the *Mahavamsa* (*Great Chronicle*) and *Culavamsa* (*Lesser Chronicle*), both of which are mythologized accounts of Sri Lankan history. The early Sinhalese also produced poetry, often recounting the popular Buddhist Jataka tales and pondering Buddhist philosophy.

The Tamils also have a venerable literary tradition. Around the first century CE, there was a major literary movement in southern India called the Sangam period (300 BCE to 400 CE). Eelattu Poothanthevanar, regarded as the first Tamil Sri Lankan author, is perhaps the most renowned poet from this period, though much of the work associated with this movement was lost. He is best known for two classic epics, *Manimekhalai* (*The Dancer with the Magic Bowl*) and *Silappadhikaram*. The celebrated Tamil poet Tiruvalluvar, who wrote the famous poetic work called the *Thirukkural*, is also considered to have been writing at this time, though his specific dates are disputed. His famous work consists of a series of kurals, a traditional form of poetic verse written in couplets. Tamil writing during this period expressed a wide range of themes, including morality, medical theory, astrology and history. This diversity of topics continued through the centuries within Tamil literature, resulting in a very complex tradition.

CULTURE

Arts & Entertainment

Modern developments in the arts reflect the political turbulence that has marked Sri Lanka's recent history. Ethnic conflict between different groups, namely the Sinhalese and Tamils, left the island in a violent civil war. Armed Tamil groups, especially the Liberation Tigers of Tamil Eelam (LTTE), commonly known as the Tamil Tigers, engaged in a long-term struggle with the central government and paramilitaries associated with the Sinhalese majority. With this conflict as a backdrop, art has been used as a way of expressing ethnic identity and pride. Art has also given ordinary people, those not directly involved with the fighting, a way to escape the violence. Some artists have even created works encouraging a unified Sri Lankan identity that transcends ethnic boundaries.

Sri Lankan literature has developed as a way of expressing ethnic identity. In particular, Tamil literature has flourished. A minority ethnic group in conflict with a majority that speaks another language, Tamils naturally turned to the written word to make sense of their social and political conditions. Tamil authors were so prolific that a grand library was built in the northern city of Jaffna—where most residents are Sri Lankan Tamils—to house their works. However, in 1981, a Sinhalese mob burned down the library. This act radicalized Tamil authors, who consciously turned to the written word as a way of defending their identity. In addition, some contemporary authors have used writing as a way of healing the cultural wounds of this ethnic conflict. Author Romesh Gunesekera (1954–), for instance, has written many short stories describing the ethnic conflict from a variety of perspectives.

Performance art in Sri Lanka has been transformed by the influence of Indian movies and television, though a local film industry has developed over the past generation. The first Sri Lankan film, *Kadavuna Poronduwa* (*Broken Promise*), was screened in 1947. Many other Sri Lankan films followed, either made locally in Sri Lanka, or produced in Indian studios. Recently, Sri Lankan movies have attempted to deal with the ethnic fighting that has divided the country. An example of this genre is the film *Purahanda Kaluwara* (*Darkness on a Full Moon Day*), directed by notable Sri Lankan filmmaker Prasanna Vithanage (1962–). In addition, the Sri Lankan film industry is almost entirely dominated by members of the Sinhalese ethnic majority, and nearly all movies are in the Sinhala language.

Contemporary and popular Sri Lankan music has also been influenced by outside cultures. Baila music, which reflects the island's Portuguese colonial past, has been a favorite genre for centuries, and Bollywood film music dominated popular taste in the late 1980s and early 1990s. (Bollywood refers to the Hindu-language cinema based in India.) However, baila music using electric guitar experienced a major resurgence in the late 1990s. Even more recently, a new Sri Lankan pop music has emerged. It incorporates the sounds of baila, Indian film songs, hip-hop and other popular Western styles. A uniquely Tamil form of pop music is also gaining popularity among youth of that ethnic group. It incorporates the sounds of Indian film music, hip-hop and Sri Lankan drumming, and tends to feature very political lyrics.

The visual arts have been used in recent decades to express the challenges and dilemmas of Sri Lankan society. For example, painters in the northern city of Jaffna have used their work to witness the violent reality of life for Sri Lanka's Tamil population. Painting has also been used to give a visual account of the devastating tsunami that hit the island in late 2004. An exhibit of children's paintings of the tsunami traveled throughout the world, earning relief money for the villages affected by the disaster.

A new generation of architects has brought in a new era of creativity to the island. Members of this new generation were largely inspired by the pioneering work of British-trained Sri Lankan architect Geoffrey Bawa (1919–2003). Bawa's style incorporated traditional South Asian cultural sensibilities and appreciation of the natural environment. He is best known for designing the Sri Lankan parliament building. In many ways, architecture in Sri Lanka has remained very traditional. Rural housing, in particular, has changed very little, and still features typical wood framed and thatched houses.

Cricket is Sri Lanka's national sport. Other popular sports are tennis, field hockey, soccer, and golf. Cricketer Muttiah Muralitharan (1972–), who retired in 2010, and sprinter Susanthika Jayasinghe (1975–) are Sri Lanka's most famous athletes.

Cultural Sites & Landmarks

Sri Lanka is home to eight World Heritage Sites, as designated by the United Nations Educational, Scientific and Cultural Organization (UNESCO). These sites were recognized for their cultural and scientific significance to Sri Lanka, and mankind in general, and include the Golden Temple of Dambulla, a temple consisting of a complex series of caves which contain religious sculptures and murals; the Sinharaja Forest Reserve (also known as Kingdom of the Lion), a national park that is home to rare flora and fauna; the ancient city of Polonnaruwa, inscribed as a World Heritage Site in 1982; the sacred cities of Anuradhapura and Kandy, both considered sacred Buddhist sites; and the Old Town of Galle and its Fortifications, a fortified European city founded by the Portuguese in the 16th century.

Many of Sri Lanka's cultural sites originated as natural formations. One of the most impressive is Sigiriya, a massive volcanic outcropping that juts out of the surrounding plains. According to legend, Kashyapa I (also known as King Kassapa), who ruled Sri Lanka from 473 to 495 CE, converted Sigiriya into a palace. In fact, it was probably the site of a Buddhist monastery from the third century BCE until the 14th century CE. The Lion Rock, as Sigiriya is also known, is surrounded by impressive gardens, and contains a hidden gallery with famous frescoes of beautiful women thought to be manifestations of Tara Devi, the Buddha Avalokiteshvara's divine consort. The site was recognized as a World Heritage Site in 1982.

One of the most symbolically important sites in Sri Lanka is Sri Dalada Maligawa, the Temple of the Sacred Tooth Relic. Located in the royal city of Kandy, this temple was built in the 18th century, and is now considered a pilgrimage site because it is believed to contain a tooth from the Buddha. According to legend, a tooth was taken from the Buddha's funeral pyre, and was secretly brought to the island hidden in the hair of a princess. It was moved around the country for centuries, until it was permanently housed in the temple. The relic has withstood several incidents in which it was stolen or nearly destroyed. It was taken by Indian invaders in the 13th century and the Portuguese in the 16th century, and it was bombed by Tamil separatists in 1998.

Another site of great significance in Sri Lankan culture is Mihintale, a mountain peak featuring the ruins of a monastery and stupa, the latter dating to the first century BCE. The site is considered the cradle of Buddhism in the country. In the third century BCE, the Indian Buddhist King Ashoka the Great (304–232 BCE) sent his son Mahinda, a Buddhist monk, to Sri Lanka, where he met Sri Lankan king Devanampiyatissa (c. 247–207 BCE) while the king was out hunting. Prince Mahinda gave a powerful sermon to the king, who then converted to Buddhism (70 percent of the country is now Buddhist). The site is eight miles from the sacred city of Anuradhapura, renowned for its ancient architecture.

The northern city of Jaffna is particularly important for its Tamil culture. Jaffna has historically been the Hindu religious center of Sri Lankan Tamil society. The city is dotted with significant Hindu kovil temples, with the most famous of these the Nallur Kandaswamy Kovil. Originally built in the 16th century, the temple was destroyed by the Portuguese a hundred years later, and then rebuilt in the 18th century. The Nallur Kandaswamy Kovil is an important pilgrimage site for Sri Lankan Hindus, who flock to the temple for a 25 day festival of worship in July and August.

Libraries & Museums

The Kotte Museum (or E.W. Perera Memorial Kotte Archaeological Museum), which is located between Sri Jayawardenapura and Colombo, provides examples of the stone, metal, and pottery work found in the ancient city of Kotte. Primarily an archaeological museum, the museum is open for public tours and admission is free. The museum's notable collection includes a number of metal and clay coins, which are examples of the earliest currency systems used in Sri Lanka. The largest museum in Sri Lanka is the National Museum of Colombo, founded in 1877. Other museums in the country include the National Museum of Natural History; the Maritime Museum, the Dutch Museum; the Independence Memorial Museum; and the Ratnapura National Museum.

The National Library of Sri Lanka (called the National Library and Documentation Centre) is located in Colombo, and was established in 1990. There are approximately 1,185 public libraries throughout the country, and 6,000 school libraries.

Holidays

Sri Lanka celebrates Independence Day on February 4, the day the nation obtained its status as an independent republic. May Day (May 1) is celebrated as a public holiday as well. On May Day, political parties stage rallies and parades in city streets.

Most holidays in Sri Lanka are religious observations. Buddhist holidays include Perahera, a festival that involves dancing and a parade of elephants, and Poya, a monthly celebration of the full moon. Hindus celebrate holidays such as Thai Pongal, the holiday of the harvest, and Deepavali, the festival of lights. One of the most significant Muslim celebrations is Milad-un-Nabi, the birthday of the prophet Muhammed.

Youth Culture

Throughout Sri Lanka's modern history, children have been considered important to the country's future development. Education has always been encouraged for both genders, and literacy rates are 92 percent for males and 90 percent for females, which is quite high for the region. However, the ongoing civil war has had many negative effects on Sri Lanka's youth culture. Children living in the areas of heavy fighting, especially the north of the island, are most impacted. Those forced to flee their homes to avoid fighting between Tamil insurgents and government forces are often unable to access adequate educational facilities. Additionally, many of the children are forced to fight in the conflict or are put in danger of sex trafficking because of the chaos and conditions civil war has caused.

Youth culture throughout the island reflects the social disruption caused by the civil war. Many older people consider this generation of young people to be dangerously uninterested in Sri Lankan traditions. For example, young people are more likely to enjoy Indian or Western pop than traditional Sri Lankan music, and this change in musical taste is reinforced by the large number of radio stations that play popular music. Young people have also adopted more Western forms and styles of dress. At the same time, new social problems have emerged. Levels of unemployment, alcohol and drug use, and incidents of crime are quite high among young people. This adds to the national concern that young Sri Lankans are turning their backs on traditional social norms.

SOCIETY

Transportation

There are many options for travel within Sri Lanka. Domestic flights connect Colombo with the northern city of Jaffna, and rail service is available in select areas. Trains are reliable, though they can be very slow and crowded. Bus lines connect more towns and cities than trains, and for shorter distances, there are city bus lines. It is also possible to hire a taxi or three-wheeler. Bicycles are commonly used for getting around, and are available for rent in most cities. Traffic moves on the left side of the road in Sri Lanka.

Transportation Infrastructure

The urban areas of Sri Jayawardenapura are still undergoing a process of development including improvements to public transportation and services. Sri Jayawardenapura has a public bus system and a train system that travels to Colombo,

Kandy, and many of the nation's other cities. In 2005, the city began construction on a passenger boat service that will transport residents between Sri Jayawardenapura and Colombo, which, a decade later, has begun some operations.

Bandaranaike International Airport, located near the capital of Colombo, links the country to the outside world. There are direct flights to Sri Lanka from India, Thailand, Singapore, Britain, Canada, Australia, France, and Germany. It is also possible to travel by sea from India, and regular ferry service is in place to and from the Sri Lankan port city of Manna.

Media & Communications

Sri Lanka has a large number of newspapers, published in English, Sinhala and Tamil. Though government papers are sometimes accused of being mouthpieces for the state, private papers in Sri Lanka are well known for their honest and accurate journalism in a country ravaged by civil war. The *Daily News* is Sri Lanka's state-owned English paper, and there are also two influential private English papers, *Daily Mirror* and *The Island*. Papers in the majority Sinhala language include the government owned *Dinamina*, and the private papers *Lakbima* and *Lankadeepa*. There are two main private Tamil papers, *Virakesari* and *Uthayan*.

There are numerous broadcast media sources on the island, reflecting the small country's ethnic and class diversity. The two state-controlled television stations are Sri Lanka Broadcasting Corporation (SLBC) and Independent Television Network (ITN). Private stations include the English language Maharaj TV (MTV), the Sinhala language Swarnavahini and the Tamil Shakthi TV. Radio is dominated by the state-controlled Sri Lanka Broadcasting Corporation (SLBC). There several popular English radio stations, including YES FM and TNL Rocks. Sinhala stations include Sirasa FM and Shree FM. Tamil stations also broadcast throughout the country, such as Shakthi FM and Sooriyan FM. The Tamil Tigers operated a radio station called Voice of the Tigers during the civil war. In addition, Internet usage in Sri Lanka continues to steadily increase, an estimated 24 percent of the adult population being Internet users in 2013.

SOCIAL DEVELOPMENT

Standard of Living

Sri Lanka ranked 73rd out of 187 countries on the 2013 United Nations Human Development Index, which measures quality of life and standard of living indicators.

Water Consumption

According to statistics released by the World Health Organization in 2012, approximately 94 percent of the Sri Lankan population has access to improved drinking water, while an estimated 92 percent of the population had access to improved sanitation. Other international agencies, such as UNICEF, reported in 2012 that about 15 percent of households in Sri Lanka lack access to any sanitation. Water and sanitation infrastructure in the country was also affected by the 2004 tsunami.

Education

At 92 percent, Sri Lanka's literacy rate is one of the highest in all of Asia. Education is compulsory and provided by the government for all students between ages five and fifteen. Most students attend school through the secondary level, and many continue at the university level.

Sri Lanka has 10 universities. The most popular curricula among students are engineering, medicine and computer science. During the course of their university studies, many Sri Lankan students visit the United States through the Fulbright exchange program.

The University of Sri Jayawardenapura is one of the nation's leading universities and was founded in 1873 as a center for Buddhist studies. The university was rebuilt in the 1950s as a public university. It was renamed the University of Sri Jayawardenapura in 1978 when the city was designated as the administrative capital. The university receives thousands of students each year from across Sri Lanka, as well as international students from India and other Asian nations. Sri Lanka's literacy rate was estimated at 92 percent in 2010.

Women's Rights

While women in Sri Lanka are generally considered equal, they do not receive equal protection under the law. They have the same rights as men according to criminal and civil law, but matters of family law are often left to ethnic customs. Issues of inheritance, marriage, divorce and child custody are therefore not clearly defined by the legal code. For example, the legal age for marriage is 18, but some ethnic groups follow different customs, such as Sri Lankan Muslim women, who traditionally marry at 15 years old. Additionally, laws prohibiting violence against women within the family are typically not enforced. As a result, domestic abuse is a significant issue in Sri Lanka.

Female workers do not have the same rights as men. Gender discrimination in hiring is banned in the public sector, but not in the private sector. Even in the public sector, there are subtle forms of discrimination and gender inequality, and women participate in the government in fewer numbers than men do. Though women make up half of the Sri Lankan workforce, the lack of equal protection laws in the private sector results in rampant economic inequality, and it is more difficult for women to advance in their careers. Hence, women tend to have nonsupervisory jobs and lower wages when they hold similar positions as their male counterparts. Additionally, women do not enjoy legal protection against sexual harassment in the private sector.

Violence against women is a problem throughout Sri Lanka, worsened by unenforced or inadequate laws, poverty and the social disruption caused by the Tamil insurgency. Gender-based crimes such as sexual assault and rape are rarely prosecuted, limiting the degree to which the law protects women. Prostitution is illegal, but prostitution rings often bribe police to ignore illegal activities. Sex trafficking is also a major problem in the country, and sometimes involves children. In addition, refugees, forced from their homes by fighting between government forces and Tamil insurgents, were at particular risk of gender-based violence, rape, and other forms of sexual violence common in refugee camps.

In spite of the many problems they face, women in Sri Lanka enjoy a high degree of social equality, particularly for the region. Sri Lankans consider education important for both genders, and female literacy is high in the country. Though career advancement is unduly difficult for females, some Sri Lankan women have reached the highest levels of professional society. For example, in 1960, Sirimavo Bandaranaike (1916–2000) became Sri Lanka's prime minister, the first democratically elected female leader of a modern country.

There is a strong feminist movement in Sri Lanka, and many organizations exist to improve the lives of women in various sectors of society. Some groups, such as the Women's Liberation Movement of Sri Lanka, lobby for the improvement of women's status as urban workers. Others, including the Hatton Women's Committee, advocate for the rights of rural women. Several groups, including one called Kantha Handa, seek to protect female refugees displaced by the civil war.

Health Care

Sri Lanka has an effective health care system. Residents receive free, government-provided health services. In addition to public hospitals, there are private hospitals and clinics. The life expectancy in Sri Lanka is high, at almost 80 years for women and 73 years for men (2014 estimate). Although Western medicine is the standard at public hospitals and clinics, there are a number of facilities that practice traditional healing techniques as well.

GOVERNMENT

Structure

Sri Lanka is a democratic socialist republic. The executive branch consists of a president and prime minister. The president is the chief executive and the head of state.

The president serves a term of up to six years, and holds the power of appointing cabinet members. Sri Lanka's legislative branch is a unicameral parliament with 225 members. The judicial branch is made up of a Court of Appeals and a Supreme Court. The president appoints the members of the courts. The president has the power to dismiss members of the parliament. The prime minister is elected when his party is elected.

Eighteen is the age of suffrage in Sri Lanka. Like the president, parliament members are elected by popular vote. The highest law in Sri Lanka is the constitution, which was adopted on August 16, 1978.

Political Parties

Prominent political parties include the United People's Freedom Party, United National Party, Democratic National Alliance, and the Tamil National Alliance, which hold seats in the 2010–2016 parliament. Other parties participate in the political process. A former political party, the Tamil United Liberation Front, LTTE, which the United States government had listed as a terrorist organization, is the party that instigated the 1983 uprising against the Sinhalese government, which over the course of many years resulted in over 40,000 deaths. They were defeated by the government in May 2009.

Local Government

Local government in Sri Lanka is organized into urban councils, municipals councils and "pradeshiya sabhas" in the countries rural regions. There are forty-two urban councils and eighteen municipal councils. Colombo is administered by its own municipal council. The term pradeshiya sabha means "divisional council." There are 270 pradeshiya sabhas in Sri Lanka.

Judicial System

Sri Lanka's system of criminal law is based on that of the United Kingdom. The Supreme Court is the country's highest judicial entity, followed by a Court of Appeal and a High Court. Several subordinate courts adjudicate at the municipal level. Supreme Court judges are appointed by the president. Three Supreme Court judges, including the Chief Justice, appoint judges to the lower courts.

Taxation

Income taxes have been collected in Sri Lanka since 1932. The individual income tax in the country varies depending on salary. Both resident and non-resident business in Sri Lanka pays a flat income tax of 28 percent. Other taxes paid by residents include a national security levy, a Save the Nation contribution, and a goods and services tax.

Armed Forces

The Sri Lanka Armed forces consists of three service branches, the Sri Lanka Army, the Sri Lanka Navy, and the Sri Lanka Air Force. There is no conscription; 18 is the minimum age for voluntary military service. Members of the military are obligated to serve a five-year term of service. The largest service branch, the Sri Lanka Army, concluded a nearly 30-year military campaign on home soil against the Tamil Tigers (or Liberation Tigers of Tamil Eelam) with the 2009 defeat of the separatist organization. The Sri Lanka Army has also provided insurgency and guerilla warfare training to the United States Army.

Foreign Policy

Sri Lanka has had a foreign policy of non-alignment for most of its history as an independent nation, and was an original member of the Non-Aligned Movement (NAM). Sri Lanka belongs to several other global multilateral organizations, including the UN, which it joined in 1955. It is also part of the major global economic organizations, such as the International Monetary Fund (IMF), World Bank and Asian Development Bank (ADB). Sri Lanka also has diplomatic connections to its regional neighbors through the South Asian Association for Regional Cooperation (SAARC), in which it is an active member.

Sri Lanka's relationship with its closest neighbor, India, is somewhat complicated, particularly considering that the nations share strong cultural and religious ties. This is particularly true of Tamils in Sri Lanka, who are originally from the Indian state of Tamil Nadu. India is also Sri Lanka's most significant trading partner. However, Sri Lanka's relationship with India has been tense because of the position of Tamils within Sri Lankan society. In 1983, the Tamil Tigers killed 13 government soldiers. The Sri Lankan government's brutal crackdown on its Tamil population after that incident resulted in over 100,000 Sri Lankan Tamils fleeing to India. The Indian government responded to the situation by sending humanitarian aid to Sri Lankan Tamil cities, including Jaffna. The Sri Lankan government did not approve of this interference in its domestic affairs.

Sri Lanka and China have had important trade connections for many centuries. Official diplomatic ties between the two countries were established in 1950, and since that time, Sri Lanka has repeatedly asserted its respect for the "One China Policy," meaning that it defends China's assertion that Taiwan, or the Republic of China (ROC), should not be a separate country or government. Maintaining good relations with China has proved profitable for Sri Lanka, which has benefited from substantial Chinese investment capital.

Great Britain, the last country to occupy Sri Lanka, is now a strong diplomatic and economic ally. The two countries share a good deal in common, since the colonial period brought English language and culture to Sri Lanka. Britain has been vocal in its opposition to the Tamil Tigers, deriding the separatist movement as a terrorist organization. In addition, Britain extends a good deal of credit to Sri Lanka, which allows the smaller island nation to develop and improve its infrastructure.

Sri Lanka also has cordial relations with the U.S. Since 2001, the Sri Lankan government has sought to strengthen these ties. From Sri Lanka's standpoint, this relationship is a guarantee of its continued sovereignty, which is important considering the connection between India and Sri Lanka's Tamil separatists. The U.S. also provides financial aid to Sri Lanka, and has given Sri Lanka more than $1.63 billion (USD) in assistance, with more than $6 million is basic aid requested for 2015. After the devastating tsunami that hit the island in 2004, the U.S. sent $135 million (USD) in relief funds.

Human Rights Profile

International human rights laws insist that states respect civil and political rights, and also promote an individual's economic, social and cultural rights. The United Nations Universal Declaration on Human Rights (UDHR) is recognized as the standard for international human rights. Its authors sought the counsel of the world's great thinkers, philosophers, and religious leaders, and were careful to create a document that reflects the core values of every world culture. (To read this document or view the articles relating to cultural human rights, visit: http://www.udhr.org/UDHR/default.htm.)

The ongoing Tamil insurgency has created a human rights crisis in Sri Lanka. Over 80,000 people have been killed in the civil war, which has lasted more than two decades. Fighting between Tamil groups such as the Tamil Tigers and government forces endangered Sri Lankan civilians. Bystanders are often caught in the crossfire, creating an unstable situation for many citizens. Both sides in the struggle were also guilty of directly inflicting violence on noncombatants.

Citizens living in the north have been especially affected by fighting between insurgents and government forces. More than 150,000 people in this region fled their homes to escape government shelling of presumed Tamil Tiger positions. These displaced people have found it very difficult to travel to safety. Fearing that the population will leave the area for good, the Tamil Tigers continue to prevent movement out of the areas they control. Those citizens that do manage to exit the war zone are often forced into detention camps by government troops, who want to be sure that no insurgents slip away from the fighting.

Both insurgents and government forces have committed intentional acts of violence against unarmed civilians. Tamil Tiger fighters, for instance, carry out deadly attacks in the capital of Colombo. These often involve bombing or shooting at civilian buses. The government's treatment of Tamil civilians has been brutal as well. Tamil citizens suspected of collaboration with the insurgents, or participating in pro-Tamil independence politics, typically face arbitrary detention and torture. More importantly, tens of thousands of Tamil people have permanently disappeared after being detained by government forces, and it is presumed the government executed them for association with separatists.

The government of Sri Lanka was clearly in violation of several articles of the UDHR. Civilians were not allowed to flee war zones, which contradicts the freedom of movement described in Article 13. The government routinely detained subjects without legal cause, which violates the ban on arbitrary arrest stipulated by Article 9 and the presumption of innocence outlined in Article 11. People were targeted for suspected sympathies for Tamil separatists, which is contrary to the freedom of thought and expression outlined in Articles 18 and 19, and the right to peaceful association asserted in Article 20. Government troops tortured prisoners, which was a breach of the ban on torture and cruel treatment outlined in Article 5. By executing suspects without any legal process, the Sri Lankan government was violating Article 10, which guarantees the right to a fair trial.

ECONOMY

Overview of the Economy

Sri Lanka has a developing economy that has faced many crises. The civil war and the tsunami have forced the government to take on large amounts of foreign debt. Increased economic aid is vital to Sri Lanka's economic future. The economy is in the process of moving away from government-controlled socialism and allowing free enterprise and privatization. In 2013, the per capita gross domestic product (GDP) of Sri Lanka was estimated at $6,500 USD.

The agricultural industry contributes approximately 10 percent to the nation's gross domestic product (GDP), with the primary products being fruits and vegetables and plantation products such as rubber, tea, and coconuts.

Industry

Over one-third of the Sri Lankan work force is employed in the service sector. The service sector is primarily concentrated in wholesale and retail sales, but also includes communications, government, and transportation. The manufacturing sector involves the processing of agricultural goods and textiles and contributes over 30 percent to the gross domestic product (GDP). Primary manufacturing exports include textiles and clothing, chemicals, and petroleum products

Sri Lanka's major trading partners are India, Singapore, China, Hong Kong, Malaysia, and Japan. Imports include textile fabrics, mineral products, petroleum, food, machinery, and transportation equipment. Sri Lanka's main exports are textiles and clothing, which together account for almost half of the total exports. Other leading exports are tea (the largest single export), spices, precious stones, and agricultural goods.

Labor

Sri Lanka has an estimated work force of approximately 8.53 million (2013 estimate). More than 42 percent of Sri Lanka's total workforce is employed in the service sector, while roughly 25 percent of workers are employed in manufacturing. Agriculture accounts for about 32 percent of the labor force. The unemployment rate is about five percent (2013 estimate).

Energy/Power/Natural Resources

Sri Lanka's primary natural resources are timber, minerals, and hydropower. Timber trees include mahogany, fruit trees, ebony, and satinwood. Rubber trees provide a significant resource as well. Due to deforestation concerns, the exploitation of tree resources is limited.

Sri Lanka has the largest concentration of gems in the world. Among the 50 varieties of gems found on the island are sapphires, rubies, and amethysts. Sri Lanka's mines also produce graphite, zircon, limestone, and salt.

Fishing

Agriculture, which includes fishing, represents an estimated 10.6 percent of Sri Lanka's overall GDP. However, the country's fishing industry sustained significant damage following the 2004 tsunami, which destroyed approximately 80 percent of the country's fishing boats. Since then, the government's Reconstruction and Development Agency (RADA), with the help of nearly $100 million foreign donations, have worked to resuscitate the industry. Although many small fishing vessels have been donated to artisanal fisherman, larger fishing operations continue to lack appropriately sized vessels. Tuna and seer fish are included among the species of fish harvest in waters off Sri Lanka.

Forestry

Sri Lanka's forestry industry contributes an estimated one percent to the country's overall economy. Most of the country's trees and wood products, particularly those made of timber, are used for domestic consumption. Forest products represent less than one percent of total exports. However, both domestic demand and demand for exports has been increasing. Sri Lankan wood products include furniture, flooring and wood paneling.

Mining/Metals

Sri Lanka has a profitable mining industry, which accounts for approximately 1 percent of the gross domestic product (GDP). The mining industry produces mica, feldspar, and precious stones. Sri Lanka, in fact, is one of the world's top producers of gemstones, most of which are mined near the city of Ratnapura, which translates as "city of gems." The main gems found in pits near Ratnapura are rubies, cat eyes, and sapphires, while a variety of other semiprecious stones are also mined in nearby regions.

Agriculture

Over 30 percent of Sri Lanka's workforce is employed in agriculture. Major tea plantations are on the plateaus at Nuwara Eliya and Horton Plains. Tea accounts for over 13 percent of Sri Lanka's total exports. Sri Lanka mostly farms rice, sugarcane, grains, spices, tea, and oilseed. Rubber, coconuts, and dairy products are also produced.

Animal Husbandry

There are many cattle raised on Sri Lanka's farms, though livestock is not a significant part of the country's agricultural sector. Most dairy and beef cattle are raised for domestic consumption. In addition, an increasing amount of dairy and beef is being imported. Most of Sri Lanka's domestic demand for poultry is raised domestically. Other livestock animals include goats and buffalo. Regulations and development initiatives related to animal husbandry are overseen by the Ministry of Livestock and Rural Community Development.

Tourism

Many Sri Lankans employed in service jobs work in the tourism sector. However, revenues from tourism declined due to the nation's civil war, and tourism has been greatly affected by the tsunami of 2004. Much of the island was destroyed by the tsunami, which made Sri Lanka an undesirable tourist destination. However, with both events receding into history, the number of tourists reached an all-time high in 2013.

The island's tourist attractions include natural parks and animal sanctuaries, such as the Pinnawela Elephant Orphanage. Many tourists visit Sri Lanka's ancient capital city, Anuradhapura. The city features the nation's former palace, which lies in ruins. Also in Anuradhapura is one of the world's oldest trees. The sacred bo tree, worshipped by Buddhists, is believed to have been brought from India while it was a sapling. It is now over 2,000 years old.

Adam Berger, Richard Means,
Micah Issitt

DO YOU KNOW?

- English speakers in Sri Lanka use a unique dialect known as "Sri Lankan English," that is based partially in English from Great Britain but also uses words and structure from Malaysian dialects. Though the government officially discourages Sri Lankan English and encourages citizens to speak the dialects most commonly accepted in Great Britain or the United States, some linguists and sociologists have been studying the development and evolution of Sri Lankan English.
- The Bodhi Tree, located in the city of Anuradhapura, is the oldest documented human-planted tree in existence, having been planted from a cutting of the Bodhi tree in India, which is famous as the site where Buddha gained enlightenment. The tree has been dated at over 2,000 years, and receives thousands of visitors each year to celebrate Buddhist holidays.
- The first female head of government in the world was Sirimavo Ratwatte Dias Bandaranaike, who became prime minister of Sri Lanka in 1960.

Bibliography

BBC News. "Country Profile: Sri Lanka." 19 June 2008. <http://news.bbc.co.uk/2/hi/south_asia/country_profiles/1168427.stm>.

Barlas, Robert and Nanda Wanasundera. *Culture Shock: Sri Lanka*. Tarrytown, NY: Marshall Cavendish, 2006.

Bowman, John. *Columbia Chronologies of Asian History and Culture*. New York: Columbia University, 2000.

"CIA World Factbook: Sri Lanka." *Central Intelligence Agency*. <https://www.cia.gov/library/publications/the-world-factbook/geos/th.html>

Holt, John Clifford, Robin Kirk and Orin Stam. eds. *The Sri Lanka Reader: History, Culture, Politics*. Durham, NC: Duke University Press, 2010.

Seneviratne, Suharshini. *Exotic Tastes of Sri Lanka*. New York: Hippocrene, 2003.

U.S. Department of State. "Background Note: Sri Lanka." September 2008. <http://www.state.gov/r/pa/ei/bgn/5249.htm>.

U.S. Department of State. "Sri Lanka: Country Reports on Human Rights Practices." 6 March 2007. <http://www.state.gov/g/drl/rls/hrrpt/2006/78875.htm>.

Ver Berkmoes, Ryan, Stuart Butler and Iain Stewart. *Lonely Planet Sri Lanka*. Oakland, CA: Lonely Planet, 2015.

Wickramasinghe, Nira. *Sri Lanka in the Modern Age: A History*. Oxford: Oxford University Press, 2015.

Works Cited

"Background Note: Sri Lanka." *U.S. Department of State.* September 2008 <http://www.state.gov/r/pa/ei/bgn/5249.htm>

Barlas, Robert & Nanda Wanasundera. "Culture Shock: Sri Lanka." Tarrytown NY: *Marshall Cavendish*, 2006

BBC News "Children's Tsunami Art in Wales." 9 June 2005 <http://news.bbc.co.uk/2/hi/uk_news/wales/mid_/4073258.stm>

BBC News "Country Profile: Sri Lanka."19 June 2008 <http://news.bbc.co.uk/2/hi/south_asia/country_profiles/1168427.stm>

Bowman, John "Columbia Chronologies of Asian History and Culture." New York: Columbia University, 2000

"Bridges of Friendship from Britain." *Government of Sri Lanka.* 16 November 2007 <http://www.priu.gov.lk/news_update/Current_Affairs/ca200711/20071116bridges_of_friendship_from_britain.htm>

"CIA World Factbook: Sri Lanka." *Central Intelligence Agency.* <https://www.cia.gov/library/publications/the-world-factbook/geos/ce.html>

Cummings, Joe, Teresa Cannon, Mark Elliot, and Ryan Ver Berkmoes. "Sri Lanka." Oakland CA: *Lonely Planet.* 2006.

"Speeches of Chandrika Bandaranaike Kumaratunga." *Government of Sri Lanka.* 17 May 2001 <http://www.priu.gov.lk/execpres/speeches/2001/20010517Zhu_Rongji_PM_China.html>

Kwintessential Cross Cultural Solutions <http://www.kwintessential.co.uk/resources/global-etiquette/srilanka.html>

Laade, Wolfgang "The Influence of Buddhism on the Singhalese Music of Sri Lanka." Asian Music Vol 25 No. ½ 1993-1994

"List of Member States." *United Nations.* 3 October 2006 <http://www.un.org/members/list.shtml>

"More Women Become National Leaders; When Will the U.S. Follow?" *Voice of America* 19 November 2005

<http://www.voanews.com/specialenglish/archive/2005-11/2005-11-19-voa1.cfm?CFID=53877936&CFTOKEN=75920200>

Pate, Alan "Devil Dance Masks of Sri Lanka" 2005 <http://www.antiquejapanesedolls.com/pub_masks/masks.html>

"Remember Geoffrey Bawa, 1919-2003." *Architecture Week*. 4 June 2003 <http://www.architectureweek.com/2003/0604/news_1-1.html>

Savage, Polly. "Serendipity: New Art from Sri Lanka" February 2004 <http://www.artsrilanka.org/artgallery/index.html>

Seneviratne, Suharshini "Exotic Tastes of Sri Lanka." New York: *Hippocrene* 2003

"Sri Lanka: Language, Culture, Customs, and Business Etiquette. Sri Lanka Youth Parliament." *Bandaranaike Centre for International Studies*. 2006 <http://www.bcis.edu.lk/slyp/slypissues/issues.htm#youthculture>

"Sri Lanka Travel Guide and Reference for Travelers." 2004. *Sri Lanka Travel and Tourism Development*. <http://www.srilankareference.org>

Switala, Kristin. "Feminism in Sri Lanka." 1999 <http://www.cddc.vt.edu/feminism/sri.html>

"Tamil Music Rising" *Toronto Star* 4 September 2008 <http://www.thestar.com/DesiLife/article/489935>

"Sri Lanka: Country Reports on Human Rights Practices." *U.S. Department of State*. 6 March 2007 <http://www.state.gov/g/drl/rls/hrrpt/2006/78875.htm>

Virtual Library of Sri Lanka. 2005. <http://www.lankalibrary.com>

Sigiriya, Sri Lanka/Stock photo © aleskramer

Southeast Asia

Sultan Omar Ali Saiduddin Mosque in Brunei with a ceremonial barge in front/Stock photo © TheDoe

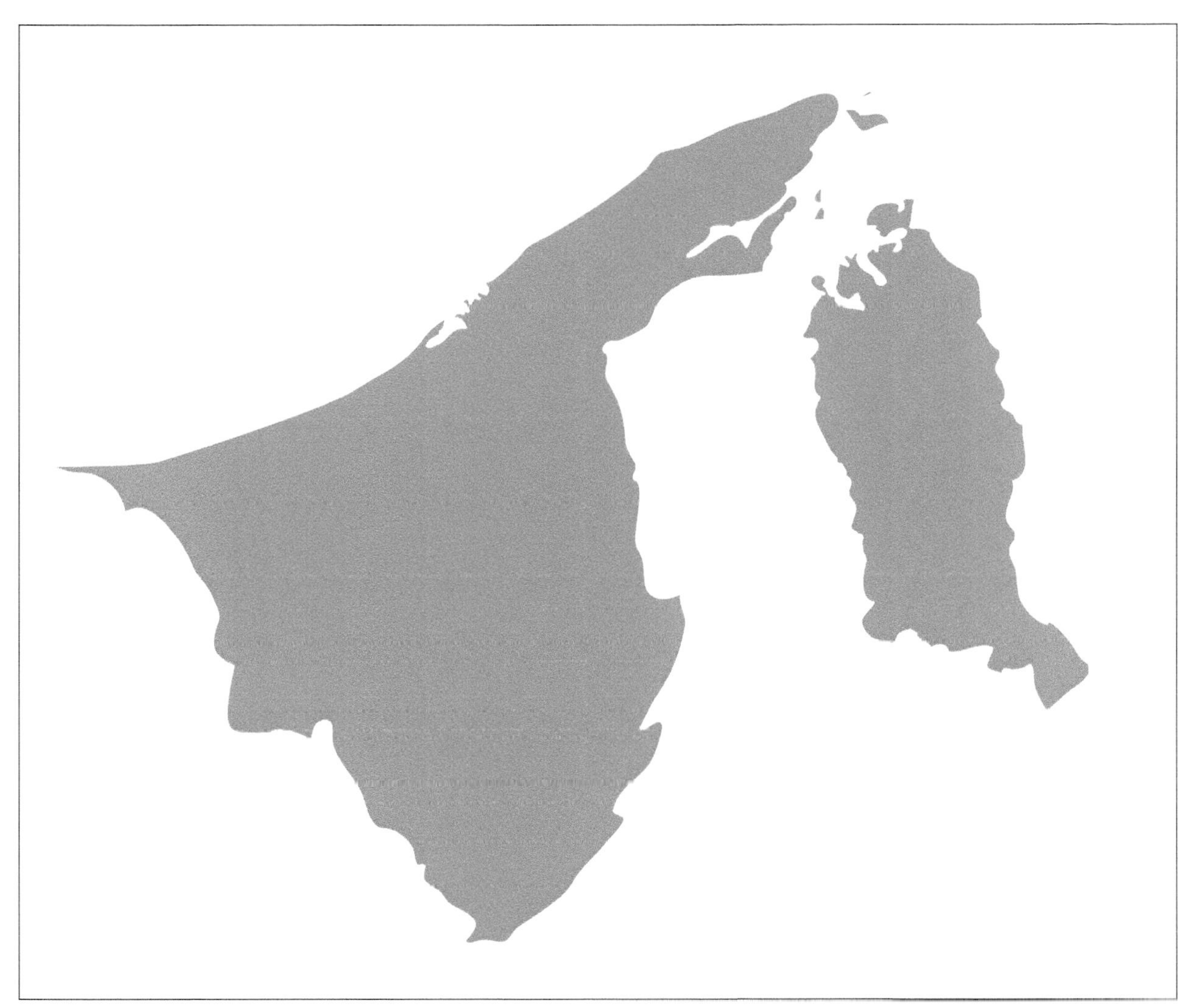

BRUNEI

Introduction

The State of Brunei Darussalam (or the Nation of Brunei, the Abode of Peace), more commonly known as Brunei, is an independent Islamic state located in Southeast Asia. It is situated on the northern coast of Borneo, an island whose land area is divided between the countries of Brunei, Malaysia, and Indonesia. It is bordered by East Malaysia and the South China Sea.

From the fifteenth to the 17th century, Brunei controlled virtually all of Borneo and the southern Philippines to Manila. European colonialism and conflict over the royal succession weakened the state, and for a time, Brunei was a haven for pirates. In the late 19th century, Brunei became a British protectorate. It declared its independence in 1984. Today, Brunei enjoys a high standard of living thanks to the economic returns from offshore deposits of oil and natural gas. Recently, however, things have become somewhat uncertain politically, as the country's ruler, Sultan Hassanal Bolkiah imposed Sharia (Muslim law).

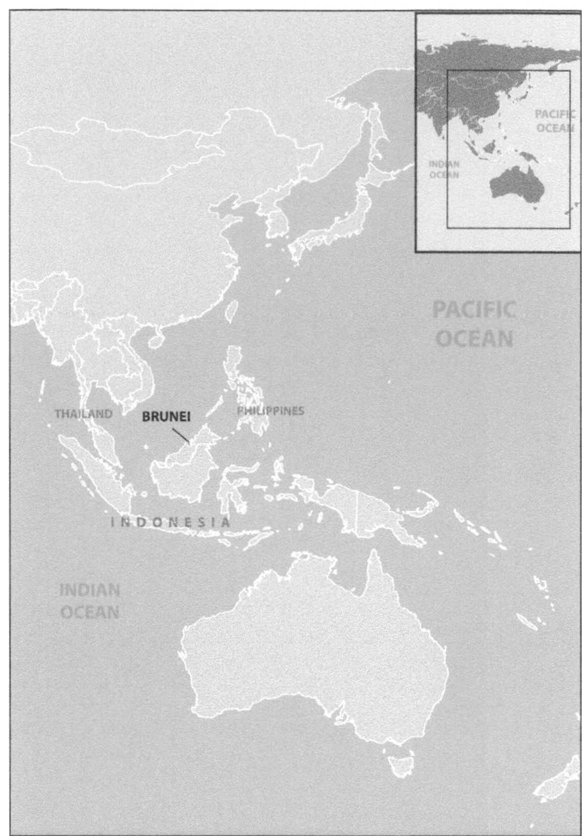

GENERAL INFORMATION

Official Language: Malay
Population: 422,675 (2014 estimate)
Currency: Brunei dollar
Coins: Coins are available in denominations of 1, 5, 10, 20, and 50 cents, or sen (Malay).
Land Area: 5,265 square kilometers (2,032 square miles)
Water Area: 500 square kilometers (193 square miles)
National Motto: "Always in Service with God's Guidance"
National Anthem: "Allah Peliharakan Sultan" ("God Bless the Sultan")
Capital: Bandar Seri Begawan
Time Zone: GMT +8
Flag Description: The flag of Brunei is yellow and features two bands of white and black that run diagonally across from left to right. In the center of the flag is the coat of arms of Brunei, featured in red. The coat of arms features an Islamic crescent and a parasol and gloves, representing the country's monarchy. It also features two inscriptions written in Arabic: "Always in service with God's guidance" and "State of Brueni, Abode of Peace."

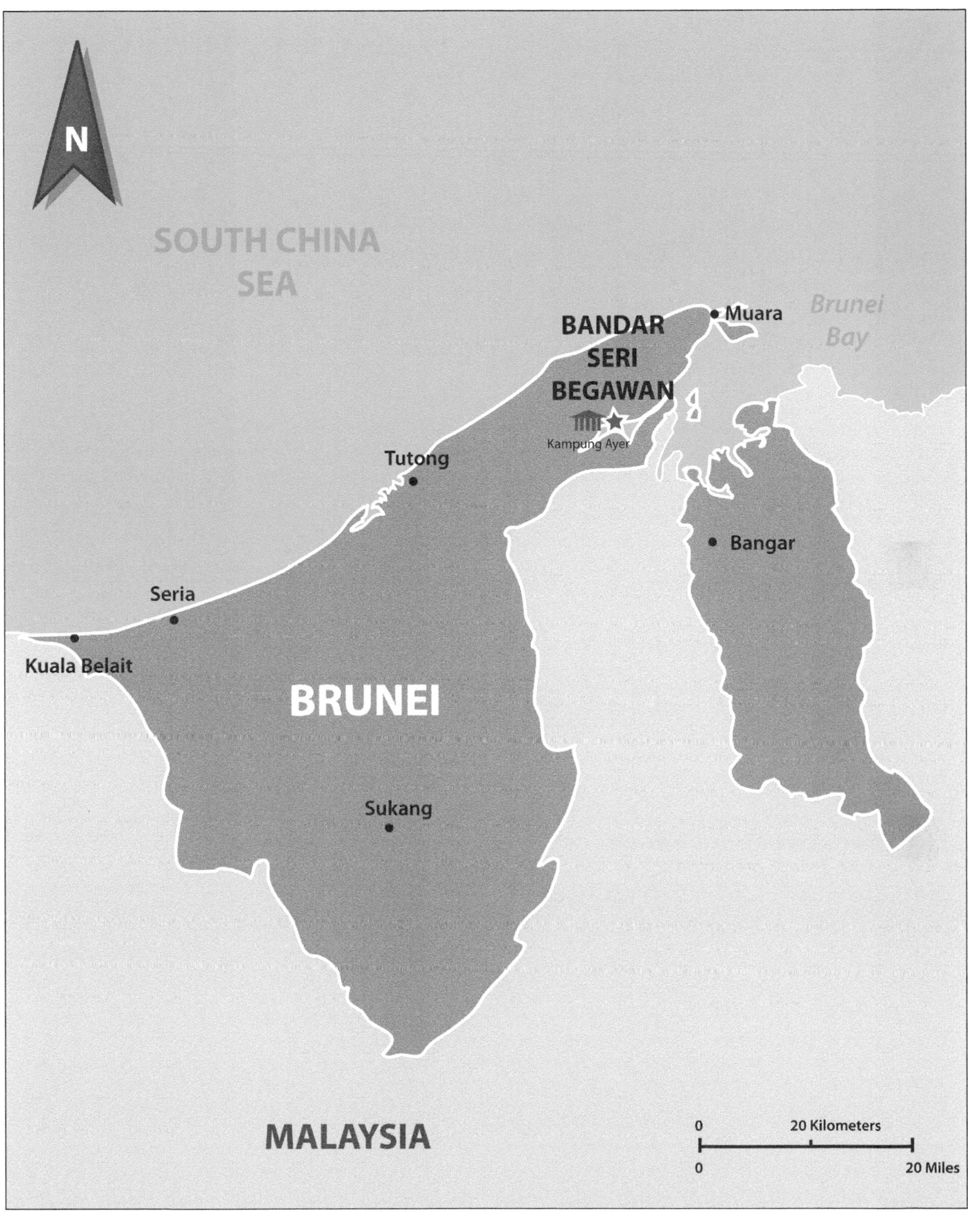
N
SOUTH CHINA SEA
BANDAR SERI BEGAWAN
Muara
Brunei Bay
Kampung Ayer
Tutong
Bangar
Seria
Kuala Belait
BRUNEI
Sukang
MALAYSIA
0 20 Kilometers
0 20 Miles

Principal Cities by Population (2012 estimate, unless noted):

- Bandar Seri Begawan (241,000; 2011)
- Ayer (44,687)
- Kuala Belait (29,682)
- Seria (29,569)
- Tutong (22,532)

Population

More than 70 percent of Brunei's people live in urban areas. The largest city is Bandar Seri Begawan, the capital, which had its boundaries greatly expanded in 2007, and experienced a major population boom in 2011, resulting in approximately 241,000 residents. Other large cities include Kuala Belait (population 30,000), Seria (population 29,000), and Tutong (population 22,000).

More than 65 percent of the population is of Malay ethnicity. The largest minority group is Chinese, accounting for 10 percent of the population. Indigenous groups, including the Iban, Dayak, and Kelabit peoples, make up three percent of the population.

Languages

Although Malay is Brunei's official language, Chinese is spoken by many Bruneians and English is also widely used, especially in business. Official documents are published in English as well as Malay. English is taught in schools and spoken widely in Bandar, the capital, along with several Chinese and indigenous dialects.

Native People & Ethnic Groups

Brunei has been inhabited since the seventh century, and it is mentioned in Chinese history as early as the ninth century. Much of Brunei's culture is based on ancient Malay civilization.

Indigenous groups include the Dayaks, Iban, Murut, Tutong, Kedayan, and Dusun. The Dayaks and Iban traditionally live in longhouses built on stilts in the rainforest. The Iban were also warriors, and they are still known for their distinctive ilang, a type of machete.

The largest ethnic group in Brunei today is Malay (65 percent). Minority ethnic groups include Chinese and indigenous Bruneian groups.

Religions

The official religion of Brunei is Islam. Roughly 79 percent of Brunei's population is Muslim, grown quickly following the 2014 imposition of Sharia (Muslim law). Another 7.8 percent are Buddhist, 8.7 percent are Christian (mostly Roman Catholic and Anglican), and almost five percent hold some indigenous beliefs.

Climate

There is little variation in Brunei's hot tropical climate. The average temperature ranges from 24° to 32° Celsius (75° to 90° Fahrenheit). Humidity levels are always high.

Rainfall varies from 2,500 millimeters (100 inches) along the coast to 7,500 millimeters (295 inches) in the interior rainforest. Few natural hazards plague Brunei, although the rare typhoon, earthquake, or flood does occur.

ENVIRONMENT & GEOGRAPHY

Topography

Brunei is a tiny country on the northwest coast of the island of Borneo, in the South China Sea. The rest of the island is occupied by Kalimantan, a province of Indonesia, and by Sabah and Sarawak, provinces of Malaysia.

Sarawak surrounds Brunei and cuts it in two at the Bay of Brunei, an inlet of the South China Sea 26 kilometers (16 miles) long and 19 kilometers (12 miles) wide. Brunei is close to important shipping lanes linking the Pacific and Indian Oceans.

The country's flat coastal areas have been cleared for agriculture, residential area, and commerce. The interior is dominated by dense rainforest. The ground is mostly sandstone, shale, and clay, rising to mountains in the east. The highest point is Bukit Pagon, 1,841 meters (6,040 feet) above sea level, in the extreme southeast tip of the country.

The Baram River is 402 kilometers (249 miles) long, rising in the Iran Mountains in northern Sarawak, flowing through Brunei and emptying into the sea at Baram Point, just to the west of the Brunei-Sarawak border. The Limbang River, 196 kilometers (121 miles) long, rises in northwest Borneo, flows through Brunei and empties into Brunei Bay. The Brunei River flows through the capital.

Tasek (Lake) Merimbun is the largest lake in the country and an important conservation and tourist area. The lake is part of the 7,800-hectare (19,274-acre) Tasek Merimbun Heritage Park, an ASEAN (Association of South East Asian Nations) National Heritage Site. The park includes wetlands surrounding the lake, peat swamp forest, and lowland rainforest.

Bandar is located on Brunei Bay, not far from where the mouth of the Brunei River opens into the South China Sea. The downtown area of the city is surrounded by water, with rivers running by its eastern, western, and southern borders. One of its most noteworthy features is the fact that some areas of the city are not located on dry land, but consist of buildings (houses, schools, mosques, and health centers) built on stilts over the water.

Plants & Animals

Brunei's biodiversity includes more than 580 endemic species of plants, such as the Manggachapui tree, used for shipbuilding and other construction. The country also has 107 endangered species, such as the Manggachapui and the Panau gracilis tree.

Mangrove swamps line the coasts of Brunei. Rubber trees and many palms, including rattan palms, grow in the rainforests. Many tree species have edible parts or fruits, such as bamboo, banana, coconut, assam aur aur (related to the mangosteen), gnetum, and durian. The durian alone appears in 27 species in Brunei, seven of which bear edible fruit. There are approximately 400 species of fern found in Brunei.

The seaweed agar-agar is used both as a culture medium in scientific experiments and as a gelling agent in foods such as ice cream. Trepang, a kind of sea cucumber also called sea-slug and beche-de-mer, is valued in Chinese cooking.

The endangered orangutan is endemic to northern Borneo and the Indonesian island of Sumatra. Other land animals found in Brunei include the arboreal tarsier, several species of fruit bats (also called flying foxes), gibbons, languors, pig-tailed macaques, clouded leopards, sun bears, wild boars, Malay weasels, and giant squirrels.

Brunei's birds include raptors, the Argus pheasant, hornbills, barbets, terns, cuckoos, woodpeckers, and kingfishers. The rainforest is also home to crocodiles, monitor lizards, skinks, and geckos, snakes such as the paradise tree snake, yellow-throated king cobras, pit vipers and pythons, and water, ground, and tree frogs.

CUSTOMS & COURTESIES

Greetings

The Malay population in Brunei accounts for approximately two-thirds of the country's ethnic makeup—an estimated 66 percent in 2011. The national language of the country is Malay. For speakers of Malay, greetings usually depend on the time of day, such as "Selamat pagi" ("Good morning"), "Selamat tengah hari" ("Good afternoon"), and "Selamat malam" ("Good night"). When welcoming a guest, the phrase "Selamat datang" ("Welcome") is common, as is "Apa khabar" ("How are you?").

Customarily, greetings in Malay are accompanied by the name and honorific title of the person being greeted. It is considered impolite to address a person without a formal title, such as "Ms." or "Mr." "Encik" ("Mister") and "Puan" ("Madam") are also used, especially when greeting an elder. When addressing someone who is, or was, a teacher, the title "Cikgu" is appropriate.

Men do not traditionally shake women's hands, and vice versa. When greeting a member of the opposite sex, it is considered courteous to wait for the other person to offer his or her hand first. When Bruneians shake hands, they do so with a light touch; after gently shaking the other person's hand they will bring their own right hand to the center of their chest. Embracing and kissing another person in public is not customary in Brunei.

Gestures & Etiquette

Practicing proper etiquette in Brunei often involves taking a person's ethnicity and cultural origins into account. For example, when conducting business with members of the Brunei Chinese community, it is common to receive a business card or a gift item with both hands. The etiquette involved in exchanging business cards is considered fundamental for the Brunei Chinese community, and carelessly placing the card in a pants pocket is interpreted as impolite. For members of the Brunei Malay community, it is courteous to receive and give items with the right hand when offering a gift or passing a dish during a meal. This is because the left hand is associated with the cleansing of the body, and using the left hand in such situations would be deemed offensive. In addition, it is considered disrespectful to show the bottoms of one's feet to another person and to cross one's legs.

If someone needs to point in Brunei Malay culture, that individual will customarily do so with the thumb of the right hand, while the other fingers remain clenched together in a fist. In general, it is considered improper etiquette to touch or point in Malay and Chinese culture. Additionally, the Western gesture of bending a finger in the air toward oneself is considered obscene. Instead, people will signal to someone by holding their hand flat with their palm facing downward, with their fingers simultaneously contracting toward the ground.

Most people in Brunei dress modestly, which reflects the country's relatively conservative nature. Visitors to Brunei are expected to comply with the local dress code and refrain from wearing revealing outfits, particularly when attending places of worship. When visiting a mosque, a woman is expected to cover her head, arms, and knees. Many Muslim women wear clothing that conceals everything except their face and hands.

Eating/Meals

Table manners and eating habits in Brunei can differ significantly due to the range of cultural traditions represented in the country. Since Brunei has a considerable Muslim population, respecting Bruneian conventions often involves understanding Muslim customs. The Muslim community in Brunei adheres to the principles set in the Koran (Islam's holy book), which prohibits eating pork and shellfish or drinking alcohol. Prohibition, or the law establishing the sale of alcoholic beverages as illegal, began in the early 1990s. Due to the establishment of prohibition, all bars and nightclubs were closed. Non-Muslims are still allowed to drink alcohol in private, but must import it. (Tourists and non-Muslims are allowed two bottles of alcohol and twelve cans of beer per entry into Brunei.)

For Muslims, the left hand is not to be used for eating, since it is considered unclean (it is traditionally associated with the cleansing of the body). Additionally, feet should remain under the table. During Ramadan, the most holy month of the Islamic calendar, Muslims will fast (abstain from eating anything) until sunset. It is considered respectful not to eat in the presence of a Muslim during the daytime while they are celebrating Ramadan.

For the Brunei Chinese population, meals are eaten family-style, traditionally with chopsticks. Everyone shares from communal plates. During these meals, seniority traditionally dictates how everything is eaten; the most senior people determine when the meal begins, and can decide who gets the best parts of a dish.

Visiting

In general, events that include Muslim guests are not held on Thursday evenings. Thursday night is usually reserved for religious activities in preparation of Friday, which is considered the holiest day of the week. It is customary that visitors to a Brunei Malay or Chinese home remove their shoes before entering the house, and leave the shoes outside or by the door until they leave the premises. Gifts are only passed to a host using the right hand, but it is acceptable to clasp someone's right wrist with the left hand for support. Guests should wait for the host to request that the guests sit before they take a seat and begin eating.

If a host presents a guest with a particular food or type of beverage during the meal, it is considered polite for the guest to always accept a little of the food or drink offered. If a guest really must decline whatever is offered, it is courteous for him to gently touch his plate or the plate being offered with his right hand, rather than verbally rejecting the offer. A well-mannered guest will also try to be as discreet as possible when using a toothpick after a meal. This is accomplished by covering one's mouth with one hand while using the toothpick with the other hand.

LIFESTYLE

Family

Gender roles in rural longhouse communities are clearly defined. Women historically are accountable for domestic duties, such as child rearing. They are also responsible for any agricultural responsibilities, especially those related to cultivating the rice. Men were traditionally given tasks related to hunting and combat. These typical male roles continued until the early 20th century, but men are now mainly responsible for hunting animals for sustenance. It is common for parents to have their other young children help raise their newborn siblings, as it is considered a good opportunity for the children to learn responsibility and the workings of a household. This is especially common in rural areas.

The definition of family in Brunei is often flexible; it encompasses either a nuclear family (parents and their children) or an extended family. Traditionally, a newly married couple will initially live with the bride's parents after marriage. After some time has passed, the married couple can make the decision to separate from the bride's family and begin their own household. Kinship terms are used based on a person's generational relationship toward another person. In this way, an aunt and uncle would become a parent, and a cousin would be considered a sibling. Kinship networks vary depending on the ethnic background of the person. For example, the indigenous Kedayan, a traditionally closed community of people, will regard a relative obtained through marriage as equal to a blood relative, while the ethnic Barunay give priority to blood relatives.

Housing

The government of Brunei has modernized many of the urban centers, replacing traditional houses with contemporary buildings and apartments equipped with modern appliances. Nevertheless, there are still a large number of longhouses made out of wooden logs and bamboo that have been preserved. They serve as traditional, affordable housing for many citizens. In the capital of Bandar Seri Begawan, the majority of people living in longhouses reside in communities situated on stilts in the Brunei River. Since Brunei is located a few degrees from the equator, longhouses are typically designed with an outer porch that extends the length of the house and provides a reprieve from the heat. The structure of the longhouse is designed to contain a large kin network, with many families separated by walls, but living under the same roof. The size of these networks can reach up to around 80 people.

Food

Urban areas contain a range of restaurant options, similar to what Malaysia and Singapore offer. Most meals draw from the country's local wildlife, and a common dish will involve rice combined with a curry made from indigenous vegetables, fruits, fish, and shellfish. On special occasions, the curries will incorporate poultry or the meat from a larger animal, such as water buffalo or cows. In rural areas, the people make use of the protein and animals unique to the surrounding forests. Mouse deer, barking deer, and sambar (a large deer with a reddish coat) are eaten, in addition to game birds. Fish is often made into ampap, which involves flavoring the fish with salt, chili, and tamarind (a tropical spice with a sour taste). The fish is then dried so that it retains all of the seasoning. Pegaga is a popular vegetable. It is a plant with small leaves that is thought to have medicinal value. The plant leaves are often chopped into tiny pieces and then mixed into rice. Brunei Malays believe that this culinary practice will extend their lives and improve their health.

Although much of the nation's cuisine is comparable to the food of its Southeast Asian neighbors, ambuyat is a dish that is uniquely Bruneian. It is made from the center of a sago palm, which is extracted from the tree and ground into a fine powder. It is then mixed with water, which makes it thick and gelatinous. It is always eaten with a series of spices, like sambal, which is a mix of shrimp and hot chilies. The spices reduce the bland, gummy consistency. After it is served, it must be eaten quickly, since the dish continues to thicken and harden.

Other common dishes include bak kut teh, a spicy consommé made from mutton spareribs; murtaba, or meat crepes; and beriani, chicken cooked with cinnamon, cashews, coconut milk, and curry and served with rice. Another popular dish is kurma, which consists of chicken cooked in coconut cream and spiced with cardamom, anise, cinnamon, chilies, garlic, and ginger. Spicy satay (skewers of mutton, chicken or beef) is a favorite for both holiday and daily meals. Other holiday dishes may include ketupat or lontong, which is rice cakes in coconut or banana leaves; and rendan, a spicy dish of marinated beef. Fish dishes include gulai daun singkong tumbuk or grilled fish with greens; malu abulthiyal, fish with curry and other spices; and Sri Lankan cutlets, made with tuna, potatoes, and spices.

Life's Milestones

Arranged marriages are no longer the norm in Brunei, but performing the rituals of a traditional marriage remains important to both the bride and groom and their families. There are many elaborate engagement customs leading up to a wedding that are still maintained by Malay Bruneians. The berjarum-jarum is a ceremony during which the parents of both the bride and groom first meet. The parents of the man proposing will then confirm that the woman is available for marriage. After receiving confirmation from the woman's parents, both sets of parents will make arrangements to formalize the couple's engagement.

Another official meeting between the bride and groom's parents is the menghantar tanda pertunangan. During this time, an entourage that was arranged by the parents during the berjarum-jarum comes to the bride and the details of the wedding are finalized. Details include the date of the wedding and the hantaran (or a list of wedding gifts requested by the bride). During this time the groom will offer two rings: one is the pembuka mulut, which signifies the man's interest in proposing, and the other is the real engagement ring.

Menghantar berian is the ceremony when the gifts discussed in the hantaran are delivered to the bride. There may also be additional gifts given by the groom's side and the bride's side. The presentation of gifts is usually extravagant; it often involves a series of men and women presenting the gifts to the couple on silver trays that have been covered with ornate cloths. This ceremony signifies the end of the engagement period, which can last between a few weeks to more than a few years.

CULTURAL HISTORY

Art

Brunei's loyalty to its traditional culture shows in its relationship to the arts. Conventional approaches to art and craftsmanship are lauded or praised, whereas newer forms of art tend to be overlooked. The government created the Brunei Arts and Handicrafts Training Center (BAHTC) in 1975 to preserve long-established methods of art, such as weaving, silversmithing, and making songkok (a traditional Muslim hat). Additionally, committees and local communities often finance programs and contests at schools to uphold traditional practices, such as the recitation of Islamic poetry.

The tradition of weaving intricate designs into cloth was first recorded during Sultan Bolkiah's reign between 1485 and 1524. The

15th-century Italian chronicler Antonio Pigafetta, an assistant for the explorer Ferdinand Magellan (1480–1521) recorded his observations on the technique of the traditionally feminine art. At the time of Pigafetta's observations, the art of weaving was already a well-established industry.

Before the weaver can attach the thread to her loom, she must first decide on the pattern, the colors involved, and the size and number of pieces being made. The number of strands of thread to use is determined from this information, and can range from 1,200 to 1,500 strands. Methods of loom weaving differ according to the pattern of the cloth, but weavers must be highly coordinated with their legs, feet, arms, and hands, as they all must work together in order to create the intricate designs. An average finished product will take around 10 to 15 days to complete, while an especially complicated design may take a weaver months to finish.

The most recognized pattern is the jong sarat, an elaborate design that involves the use of gold or silver thread. It is considered the pattern that best reflects the skill of the weavers and the beauty of the weaving tradition. Jong sarat designs are used at royal and government-related events, and are also worn at marriages by both the bride and groom.

Architecture

Brunei's architectural heritage is largely defined by classical Islamic architecture, with an influence from cultures that the country relies on for trade, both historically and present-day. Perhaps best representative of Brunei's architectural heritage is the capital's Omar Ali Saifuddien Mosque. The building was the vision of an Italian architect, and contains a number of Italian and Renaissance-inspired architectural elements, including Italian ceramic details and marble walls. The most impressive of these features is the main minaret, a tall spire with a dome-shaped crown. It is the tallest section of the mosque and made of pure gold. Although it reflects a classic Islamic design, the interior of the building is almost completely imported from other countries, including mosaic-stained glass from England, granite from China, and carpets from Saudi Arabia and Belgium. It was named after Omar Ali Saifuddien III (1914–1986), the twenty-eighth sultan who is considered the founder of modern Brunei.

Music & Dance

Many of the traditional performances practiced in Brunei are drawn from Malay culture. The Kedayans, an indigenous ethnic group, have their own unique customs and dances that differ from those of Malay Bruneians, but still include elements of Malay culture. Aduk-aduk is a dance that the Kedayan people perform at times of celebration, such as the end of the harvest season. The dancers are traditionally accompanied by percussion-based music that involves drums and coconut shells. The performance entails silat, a Malay form of martial arts. It turns into a folk dance when complemented with the beat of a kendang, a traditional drum with two sides, or a similar instrument. Dancers participating in the aduk-aduk are adorned in a customary warrior outfit that includes a tengkolok, which is an elaborate headdress.

A traditional dance that remains important for Malay Bruneians is the jipin or zapin dance. Accompanying the dance is an arrangement of vocal melodies, which are layered over a number of native instruments. These include the gambus dan biola (a large lute), the dombak (a drum in the shape of a goblet), gongs such as duck gongs (small gongs with especially thick discs), and kulintangan (a series of small gongs placed together on a wooden frame). Although the dance originated in the Middle East, it has been altered by Malay culture over the years. It is traditionally performed on special occasions by a troupe composed of six men and women. There is also an interactive element to the piece whereby dancers pair up to tease and challenge each other.

Singing is a vital part of Bruneian weddings. "Alus Jua Dindang" is a song that grooms traditionally sing to their brides. During the song, the groom compliments his bride and articulates his affection and loyalty toward her. Guests will sometimes participate by singing the dondang and yadan songs, which are designed to be interactive. There is usually a standard phrase that is sung, and then other lyrics are improvised onto the end of the phrase. The song has a light mocking tone, and singers try to emulate a jovial attitude.

Literature

The literary tradition in Brunei mirrors the country's devotion to convention. The work of Bruneian authors is known for similarities in structure and in style; books are generally straightforward, succinct, and unpretentious. Themes in literary works generally concern religion, and do not overstep societal boundaries. A few poets and authors stand out for their provocative content and themes. Mussidi is considered a pioneer of modern literature in Brunei, having written quirky short stories filled with caricatures of life in Brunei. He won the SEA (South East Asia) writer award in 1994. Pengiran Metassan is another contemporary writer. His work was deemed inflammatory by the government and Bruneian literary critics alike. The critics disapproved of Metassan's literature because they believed that it reflected poorly on Brunei's virtuous nature. Metassan is known for writing stories with racy content by Brunei standards, including stories with Bruneian characters engaged in extramarital affairs.

Asterawani, also known as the Brunei Darussalam association of writers, began the Titian Puisi in 2008. Titian Puisi is an event meant to revive Brunei's literary traditions and elevate Brunei's quality of writing. Hj Ahmad Hj Abdul Rahman served as Brunei's deputy permanent secretary of the Ministry of Culture, Youth, and Sports. He criticized Brunei's literature in 2007 for having an increase of "viruses" that sought to disgrace Brunei's pure literary heritage. Titian Puisi is an answer to the deputy secretary's critique. Asterawani is composed of the nation's lead writers and scholars, and was most active in the 1960s and 1970s. Titian Puisi provides a forum where authors can share their work, receive comments for improvement, and brainstorm ways to encourage the literary arts in Brunei.

Syair is a Malay form of poetry that is unique to Southeast Asia, including Brunei. Its name comes from the Arabic term "sha'ir," which means "poet, one with keen senses." The syair is constructed with a sequence of quatrains, or four-line stanzas. There are generally 13 to 15 quatrains per poem, but the length of a syair can also range from 10 to 20 quatrains. Writing a syair and then reciting it in front of an audience is considered a traditional form of communication and entertainment. In the past, the syair has been an important method of historical documentation, and one of the limited means of artistically expressing sarcasm.

Syair Awang Semaun is considered the best-known work of literature in Brunei. The foundation myth serves as the country's national poem and chronicles the history of the sultanate in an epic fashion. According to the syair, the first sultan, Dewa Emas Kayangan, was born out of a heavenly egg that fell to earth. He fathered children with the native women of Brunei, and one of his children chose to convert to the Muslim faith. This child went on to become Brunei's first Muslim ruler.

CULTURE

Arts & Entertainment

Developing a contemporary art scene in Brunei has been a challenge. Most Bruneians do not collect fine art, and the art industry remains aimed at tourists in order to generate profits. Bruneian society does not generally see art as a viable profession. Instead, making art is considered a hobby and families do not usually encourage children to develop any artistic talents. Nevertheless, a small, dedicated art community has continued to grow since the 1960s.

While the culture of Brunei has not always promoted artistic innovation, the number of expatriates or foreigners living in the country has encouraged a new wave of experimentation. The Brunei Art Forum (BAF) was introduced in November 2002. It presented a unique opportunity for artists to exchange ideas and present their concepts in one place. Although, it was originally launched as an expatriate project, BAF is now a place for both foreign and Brunei-born artists to collaborate and develop their art. In 2008, BAF commenced its first international exhibition, which featured 59 art pieces from 15 Brunei artists. The exhibit took place in Penang, a small state in Malaysia.

The arrival of more art programs, competitions, and award ceremonies has helped spotlight the burgeoning modern art community. The Philip Morris Group of Companies held the inaugural Brunei Art Awards in 1994. The competition involves a jury choosing five artists from Brunei, who go on to compete against the jury choices from other countries that are part of the Association of Southeast Asian Nations (ASEAN). The countries that participate in the annual competition include Indonesia, Malaysia, the Philippines, Singapore, Thailand, and Vietnam.

The most popular sport in Brunei is soccer. The national soccer team won the Malaysia Cup in 1999. Silat is a form of Malay martial arts. Brunei won three gold medals in silat at the 1999 SEA (South East Asia) Games. Other sports include sepaktakraw, which is played with a rattan ball, and gasing, played with polished giant tops. From 1998 to 2000, Brunei hosted the Baiduri World Grand Prix Badminton Finals.

Cultural Sites & Landmarks

Bandar Seri Begawan (or BSB), the capital of Brunei, holds the famous Sultan Omar Ali Saifuddien Mosque, recognized as one of the most impressive mosques in Asia. Completed in 1958, this mosque serves as one of the main places of public prayer for followers of Islam and is the largest structure in the capital. Bandar is also the location of the Brunei History Center, which houses information about the royal family and many original documents pertaining to the country's history, and the Royal Ceremonial Hall, where the sultan is crowned and other royal affairs take place. Another interesting place to see in Bandar is the Mausoleum of Brunei's fifth sultan, Sultan Bolkiah, who ruled from 1485 until 1521. He is remembered for expanding Brunei's rule to the entirety of Borneo Island, as well as some of the Philippine Islands.

Kampung Ayer is a town composed of twenty-eight longhouse communities. The area houses around 30,000 people, who live a traditional way of life. Although many of these homes contain modern facilities such as electricity, color televisions, and plumbing systems, the local people still maintain the customs of a close-knit longhouse society. The more remote parts of Kampung Ayer can only be reached by water taxi. These tend to be more traditional than the areas closer to the urban center, which are connected to land by wooden walkways. Everything in these communities is on stilts above water, or floating directly on the water. Wooden planks connect villagers to their neighbors and act as roads between the houses, schools, and other facilities.

The Ulu Temburong National Park is considered one of the best-conserved rainforests on the island of Borneo, which Brunei occupies along with Malaysia and Indonesia. It is only accessible by boat and takes up approximately 40 percent of Brunei's Temburong district, the nation's eastern-most district. The terrain is mountainous and filled with steep, hilly climbs. The environment of the park ranges from low-growing plant areas—known as secondary vegetation—to concentrated jungle areas. It is a habitat for a number of endangered species, including the proboscis monkey, known for its bulbous nose and its distinctive call. Other endemic species include the temple viper, the painted tree frog, the rhinoceros hornbill, and the Bornean gibbon.

Libraries & Museums

Museums in Brunei include the Arts and Handicraft Centre, with examples of the traditional crafts of boat-making, silver-smithing, bronze tooling, cloth weaving, and basket and mat weaving. The Brunei Historical Centre display relics of Malay weaponry, wood carvings, and traditional musical instruments. In Bandar, the Brunei Museum exhibits Malay and Islamic art, as well as natural history, archaeological, and cultural artifacts, and the Malay Technology Museum is a showcase for the traditional technologies used in water villages.

The Dewan Bahasa Pustaka Library, located in Bandar, serves as the nation's legal depository and national library. The library system contains more than 385,000 volumes of books. Brunei's largest public library is the academic library of the University of Brunei Darussalam.

Holidays

Many of Brunei's holidays are religious, and follow the Islamic lunar calendar. Chinese New Year is also widely celebrated in the country.

Secular holidays include National Day, celebrating Brunei's independence from British protection (February 23); Royal Brunei Armed Forces Day, commemorating the formation of the armed forces (May 31); Teachers' Day, recognizing the accomplishments of teachers (September 23); and Public Service Day, to encourage efficient and honest public service (September 29).

Youth Culture

As Muslims account for approximately 79 percent of the total population, conservative Islamic laws (Sharia) and values play an important role in the lives of Brunei's youth. Islamic beliefs promote a sense of collectivism, and building and maintaining a community is important to young Bruneians. Many young people create community through group activities. Teenagers enjoy going to the cinema together and participating in group sports, including football (soccer), badminton, and sepak takraw, a sport that involves kicking a rattan ball.

It is estimated that nearly half of Brunei's population is comprised of people under the age of 24 in the first decade of the 21st century. The government considers it a priority to encourage youth to participate in local mosque activities. Family members further emphasize the importance of attending mosque. Due to efforts by government agencies and local councils, taking an active role in one's religious community is an increasingly popular activity for young people.

SOCIETY

Transportation

In Brunei, there is a lack of public transportation in most towns outside of Bandar Seri Begawan. Instead, many Bruneians own cars for their daily transportation needs. There is approximately one car for every 2.09 people, making the country's rate of car ownership one of the highest in the world. Automobile traffic in Brunei travels on the left side of the road.

Transportation Infrastructure

Brunei's transportation infrastructure is considered convenient and efficient. An estimated total of 3,650 kilometers (2,268 miles) of roads, the majority of which are paved, connect the major villages (known as kampongs), while rivers provide access to remote jungle areas. The international airport in the capital accounts for around 32,000 flights annually. Royal Brunei Airlines is the country's international airlines. It flies to over twenty cities outside of Brunei, including destinations in Europe and the Middle East.

Media & Communications

The sultanate government controls much of the media in Brunei. It manages two television channels, with one focusing on international events and the other covering local events. The local channel also regularly shows religious programs, government-related shows, and documentaries. The government also passed a law stating that all films broadcast on television must first pass a rigorous screening process by a censoring committee and must show Malay subtitles before being broadcast. Most wealthy citizens subscribe to a satellite television service and have access to international television programming. The government also owns and operates three radio stations through Radio Television Brunei (RTB).

Other media coverage of events is mainly restricted to a singular perspective that sides with the government and reports on uncontroversial community events. Both Reporters without Borders and Freedom House, two non-governmental organizations (NGOs) advocating for international political liberties, have reported on the Brunei media's lack of freedom.

There are four main newspapers in Brunei. The *Borneo Bulletin* is the first English-language daily newspaper that was originally published to serve expatriates working for the Brunei Shell Petroleum Company. The other three newspapers are *The Brunei Times*, *Media Permata*, and *Pelita Brunei*. The latter is a free bi-weekly newspaper mainly concerning government policies. It is published in Malay by the prime minister's information department.

In terms of Internet penetration and telecommunications infrastructure, Brunei has a higher ranking than most Asian countries. According to 2010 estimates, there were 318,900 Internet users in Brunei, representing approximately 80 percent of the population.

SOCIAL DEVELOPMENT

Standard of Living

Brunei ranked 30th out of 187 countries on the 2014 United Nations Human Development Index, which measures quality of life and standard of living indicators.

Water Consumption

Clean water is widely available in Brunei, which is supplied by the basins of regional rivers, including the Belait and the Temburong Rivers. The country has some of the world's highest water use rates per capita. Water is imported to urban reservoirs over a pipeline system that is approximately 50 miles long. Brunei's Department of Water Services and Ministry of Health oversees the safety of the country's water supply.

Education

Schooling in Brunei is free at all levels. Attendance is compulsory for children between the ages of five and seventeen. In 2008, UNICEF estimated the country's overall literacy rate to be 95 percent among both males and females.

Islamic studies are part of the curriculum in Bruneian schools, which are classified by language of instruction (Malay, English, or Mandarin Chinese). The government offers free lodging and free transportation or an allowance to Brunei citizens who live more than 8 kilometers (5 miles) from a school. The University of Brunei Darussalam was established in 1985. Many students also study abroad on government scholarships.

Women's Rights

Brunei's religiously conservative culture has been encouraged and maintained through strict adherence to the Muslim faith and Sharia as interpreted by the sultan. In the context of Brunei's traditional society, women have limited legal rights. The judicial system favors men over women, especially in familial matters such as inheritance, divorce, and child custody. There are some exceptions: women can own their own property (as well as business properties) and they can decide whether their child should be the same nationality as them, but only if they have a different citizenship.

Many women work for the Brunei government and experience the inequalities inherent in the government's hiring system. Men may be considered for permanent jobs working for the state regardless of their higher education backgrounds. Women, on the other hand, are expected to hold a university degree if they wish to be hired on a permanent basis. Otherwise, women are only qualified to work on a month-to-month basis. This temporary status means that women receive lower salaries, fewer benefits, and more restricted annual vacations than if they held a permanent position. Despite these inequalities, women are making strides in the workplace and in universities. In 2007, an estimated 40 percent of workers in human resource departments were women. Female students are also surpassing their male counterparts with regard to higher enrollment ratios in universities. According to a 2007 UN study, the total number of women enrolled in higher education programs exceeds the number of men by over seven percent.

The status of female domestic servants is an overlooked issue in Brunei society. The majority of domestic helpers are overseas workers. They face the challenge of contending with discrimination on a number of levels: as a foreigner, a servant, and a woman. Employers will sometimes beat a servant or prevent the servant from leaving the house, even on their days off. These incidents are more common than other forms of domestic abuse. Few women who experience this kind of abuse report it due to their reliance on the financial support that domestic servitude brings.

For many Bruneian women, following Islam entails wearing conservative clothes. Religious and government officials promote the practice of wearing the tudong, a traditional Muslim garment that covers a woman's head. Most women choose to follow the custom of wearing a tudong. For others, it is a mandatory tradition, and most departments of government service have dress codes that include the required wearing of the tudong for both Muslims and non-Muslims. Furthermore, some educational institutions, including all the state schools, insist that non-Muslim students wear the tudong as part of the school uniform. In recent years, punishments for failure to adhere to the conservative dress code have become increasingly harsh.

Health Care

The World Health Organization (WHO) reported in 2014 that Bruneians had a life expectancy of seventy-six—seventy-four years for men and seventy-nine years for women. The most common cause of death among Bruneians is cardiovascular disease, followed by cancer and respiratory disease.

The government pays for medical care, but there is a shortage of doctors and hospital beds in the country. The infant mortality rate is 10 deaths per 1,000 live births, about twice that of the United States. Annual per capita health expenditure is $638 (USD).

GOVERNMENT

Structure

Brunei is a constitutional sultanate. The sultan is head of state and head of government. He is chosen for life by the Council of Succession. The sultan's power has remained within the same dynasty for more than five centuries. The sultan appoints, is advised by, and presides over the Cabinet of Ministers. The sultan also appoints the Council of Succession and the advisory Religious Council and Privy Council.

In 2004, the 21-member Legislative Council met for the first time in 20 years. The sultan appoints the council members. There is only one political party, the Brunei Solidarity National Party, and there are no elections.

Political Parties

Brunei is an absolute monarchy and political parties are not officially permitted. Political parties have been banned from participating in elections since the 1962, but many still operate in secret or in other countries. These include the National Development Party and the Brunei Peoples Party.

Local Government

The country is divided into four administrative districts, each with a district council appointed by the sultan. As an absolute monarchy, political power in Brunei is centralized.

Judicial System

Law in Brunei is based on Indian penal code and English common law. In some areas, Islamic Sharia law overrides civil law for Muslims. Courts are overseen by judges, as there is no jury system in any court in Brueni. The country's high court consists of three judges, as does the Court of Appeal. Intermediate courts and ten magistrates administer judicial proceedings at the municipal level.

Taxation

Bruneians do not pay individual income taxes. Corporations operating in Brunei pay an income tax of 23.5 percent as of 2010. There is no capital gains tax, sales tax, or payroll tax in Brunei. Individuals do contribute five percent of annual earnings to a provident fund that is managed by the Ministry of Finance. Social security is not collected from individual earnings.

Armed Forces

The Royal Brunei Armed Forces consists of an army, navy, and air force. Service is restricted to citizens of Malay ethnicity, and the minimum age of service is 18. The armed forces have mostly been deployed for humanitarian purposes.

Foreign Policy

Brunei's foreign policies are based on the constitution and the traditions of the Malay Islamic Monarchy, specifically known as the concept of Melaya Islam Beraja (MIB). The fundamental elements behind MIB are adhering to Malay culture, the religion of Islam, and the political traditions of a monarchy. Under the constitution, the sultan has absolute executive authority. He not only serves as the monarch, but also acts as the prime minister, finance minister, and defense minister.

Although Brunei is one of the smallest countries in the world—in 2008, Brunei had an estimated population of around 398,000—it is also one of the richest in natural resources. Its oil supply has helped the nation maintain itself as a self-sufficient, self-contained wealthy state. Nonetheless, Brunei realized that strategic allies and alliances were essential for maintaining political and economic freedom. As a result, Brunei has maintained a close relationship with the United Kingdom (UK). The countries held a joint-commission in 2003 regarding the willingness of both countries to increase their defense relationship.

In the past, Brunei has been embroiled in land disputes with both Malaysia and Indonesia. Relations between the nations have improved since 1980 when the sultan visited Malaysia for the first time in seventeen years. Brunei and Malaysia subsequently agreed to manufacture defense equipment together in 1987, and Sultan Hassanal Bolkiah proposed an interest-free $100 million (USD) loan to Indonesia for the purpose of developing that country's infrastructure. Brunei's wealth has also helped it gain good stead with more powerful countries. For example, Brunei sent $10 million (USD) to the Nicaraguan Contras after a request from the United States.

Brunei has advanced in the political arena over the years, and is working toward becoming a more international presence. It joined both the United Nations (UN) and the Association of South East Asian Nations (ASEAN) in 1984 after it regained a status of full independence from Britain. The country places its relationship with its neighboring states, and its participation in ASEAN, as the cornerstone of its foreign policy agenda. Besides its membership with the UN and ASEAN, the nation has contributed to international conferences, including the World Trade Organization (WTO), the Asia Pacific Economic Conference (APEC), and the East Asian Growth Area (EAGA). It also hosted the 20th South East Asian Games (SEA) and APEC in 2000.

In addition to maintaining relations with ASEAN states, Brunei considers it a priority to preserve close relations with Islamic countries. The nation holds membership in the Organization of the Islamic Conference (OIC). Due to their geographical proximity to each other, as well as their cultural and political connections, Singapore and Brunei also maintain close relations. This includes close military relations and the establishment of an interchangeable currency. Additionally, Brunei has continued to uphold a number of diplomatic missions abroad, including missions in Britain, India, Australia, and Switzerland.

Human Rights Profile

International human rights law insists that states respect civil and political rights, and also promote an individual's economic, social and cultural rights. The United Nations Universal Declaration on Human Rights (UDHR) is recognized as the standard for international human rights. Its authors sought the counsel of the world's great thinkers, philosophers, and religious leaders, and were careful to create a document that reflects the core values shared by every world culture. (To read this document or view the articles relating to cultural human rights, visit: http://www.udhr.org/UDHR/default.htm.)

In recent history, the government of Brunei generally adhered to the principles set forth in the UDHR. The Bruneian sultanate and the country's religious ideology are fundamental reasons why the nation has achieved complete freedom of the press or freedom of religion. However, there are some human rights violations that have been detected within the country's social and political structure, including a limited freedom of the press, constraints on labor rights, and a lack of religious freedom. The 2014 adoption of Sharia (Islamic law) has produced a series of ever harsher laws, focused especially on women and homosexuals.

The Brunei government is known for limiting the religious freedoms of people who do not practice the Shafi'i sect of Sunni Islam, which is considered the national religion as determined by the sultan. The government is responsible for organizing the weekly sermons given by mosques every Friday and has prevented the practice of other religions by forbidding other religious groups from proselytizing, or attempting to spread their teachings. The government also forbids certain religious clergy members from entering the country, and prevented any religious manuscripts that did not pertain to the Shafi'i Islamic faith from being imported into Brunei. In addition, schools are forbidden from teaching comparative religious studies or teaching other religions, and the Ministry of Education has established mandatory classes on the national Islamic ideology. Muslims who decide to convert to another faith deal with considerable societal pressure from their community and the government. In order to change their religion, they must first gain consent from the Ministry of Religious Affairs, and there are usually long-term delays before permission is granted.

Privacy continues to be an issue in Brunei, relating to both national and religious law. For example, Brunei's legal system allows for officials to enter homes and monitor the private data of individuals that they consider potentially subversive. In addition, Islamic law allows for the implementation of khalwat, which makes it illegal for a Muslim to remain in close proximity to a non-spousal or non-familial person of the opposite sex. Khalwat cases also give officers the authority to raid homes, and regular reports have been made of khalwat being implemented to intrude on private property without prior consent.

In terms of freedom of the press and speech, Brunei's efforts to preserve the sultan and the royal family's reputations have severely restricted the media. Certain statutes adopted in the constitutional amendments of 2004 allow for the persecution of any author, editor, or media outlet that publishes content that is deemed subversive or disloyal toward the sultan. Punishments include being blacklisted from working in media, having printing equipment seized, paying heavy fines of over $3,000 (USD), and imprisonment of up to three years.

In May 2014, a new penal code was introduced in Brunei that imposed the punishment of death, by stoning, for offenses such as extramarital sexual relations, rape, theft, and consensual sex between people of the same gender. Although groups such as Amnesty International have warned that this might lead to violations of human rights, the death penalty has as yet not been enforced.

ECONOMY

Overview of the Economy

Brunei's oil and natural gas industries account for half of the country's gross domestic product (GDP). As a result, Brunei has a relatively high per capita GDP of $54,800 (USD). It is Southeast Asia's wealthiest nation and third largest producer of oil. The government provides free medical care, education, and other benefits to Bruneians, and there is no personal income tax. Brunei has a central currency board but no central bank, and instead pegs its currency to the Singapore dollar, its largest trading partner.

Bandar, the capital and commercial center, is also almost entirely driven by the fuel industry. Because of its intense focus on one highly profitable industry, however, Bandar is forced to import a large percentage of its food and virtually all its manufactured goods. Bandar does produce a small amount of furniture, traditional textiles, and handicrafts. Since the city's petroleum and natural gas earnings still far exceed its spending on imports, most of the trade surplus is directed into investments abroad.

Industry

Because Brunei's oil and gas deposits are expected to be depleted by mid-century, the government is encouraging the development of diverse industries. Textile production has become the most important industry behind oil and gas. Other industries include cement, mineral water, canned food, silica sands, leather products, printed circuits, and publishing and printing.

Exports generated approximately $12.75 billion (USD) in 2011, consisting mostly of oil, both crude and partly refined, and natural gas. The government has taken steps to encourage the diversification of industry in the early 21st century, and has focused much of its efforts on agriculture and fishery in order to make Brunei less dependent on imported food.

Labor

In 2011, the unemployment rate was estimated to be 2.6 percent. The government is the largest employer, accounting for about one-quarter of the work force. More than one-third of the labor force is made up of foreign workers.

Energy/Power/Natural Resources

Brunei's two main natural resources are offshore oil and natural gas. The country also has a considerable amount of hardwood and rubber trees in the rainforest.

Brunei's environmental concerns are few. Although the air is usually clear, smoke from seasonal forest fires in Indonesia causes some problems, especially among people with respiratory disease.

Fishing

Some aquaculture is also practiced in Brunei; prawns, fish, and shrimp are raised. The coastal waters are also fished, though the catch is primarily for domestic consumption. The country is estimated to have one of the highest per capita fish consumption rates in the region. The estimated fish catch in 2005 was approximately 3,000 metric tons.

Forestry

Forestry in Brunei accounts for approximately 0.25 percent of overall GDP. Brunei's domestic forests have provided large amounts of timber for its construction industry, but this has also caused concerns related to the viability of the country's forest resources. The country imports plywood, wood furniture, and paper. The Department of Forestry has taken significant steps in recent years to assure the sustainability of the country's forest resources, though challenges related to over harvesting remain. In addition, the Department of Forestry has proposed new efforts to establish Brunei's forests as ecotourism attractions.

Mining/Metals

Brunei's oil and gas resources are the mainstay of the country's economy. In addition, approximately twenty privately-operated companies produce sand and gravel. The country's major cement producer is the Butra Heidelberg Cement Sendirian Berhad. An estimated 15 percent of those employed in the country's mining industry have jobs in the non-petroleum sector. In 2005, Indonesia, Korea and Australia were the main importers of Bruneian crude oil.

Agriculture

Less than one percent of the land in Brunei is arable. Major crops include cassava, coconuts, pineapples, bananas, vegetables, and sweet potatoes. Most farmers are engaged in subsistence agriculture. Because of the poor soil and small size of the country, about 80 percent of Brunei's food is imported.

Animal Husbandry

Livestock in Brunei includes cattle, water buffaloes, goats, and chickens. Livestock represents approximately 20 percent of the country's agricultural trade.

Tourism

In recent years, the government of Brunei has begun actively promoting tourism. Approximately one million travelers visit the country annually. Singapore is one of Brunei's key targets in terms of tourism marketing. However, despite its bright shopping plazas and opulent hotels, Bandar, the capital and largest city, does not see a lot of tourist traffic. The lack of tourism to Bandar has been blamed on the city's notoriously high prices.

Popular tourist attractions include the rainforest, the coastal areas, the national parks, museums, and Kampong Ayer, a residential quarter of homes built on stilts. Tasek Merimbun Heritage Park is another favorite site as ecotourism increases in popularity. Pula Tiga Marine National Park was the site of the first season of the television show "Survivor."

Danielle Chu, Ellen Bailey, M. Lee

DO YOU KNOW?

- English writer Anthony Burgess, author of *A Clockwork Orange*, took up a teaching post at the Sultan Omar Ali Saifuddin College in Bandar Seri Begawan when Brunei was a British protectorate.
- The Iban and Dusun peoples have been particularly helpful to scientists in identifying medicinal plants in the rainforest.

Bibliography

Bhagowati, Surajit Kumar. *Women in Southeast Asia.* New Delhi: New Century Publications, 2014.

Garbutt, Nick (Cede Prudente). *Wild Borneo: The Wildlife and Scenery of Sabah, Sarawak, Brunei, and Kalimantan.* Cambridge: The MIT Press, 2006.

Gunn, Geoffrey C. *Language Power & Ideology in Brunei Darussalam.* Athens: Ohio University Press, 1997.

Harrisson, Barbara. *Pusaka: Heirloom Jars of Borneo.* New York: Oxford University Press, 1986.

Hutchison, C.S. *Geology of North-West Borneo: Sarawak, Brunei and Sabah.* Amsterdam: Elsevier B.V., 2005.

Kimball, Linda Amy. *Alam Brunei: The World of Traditional Brunei Malay Culture.* Bellingham: Western Washington University, 1991.

Leffman, David, and Richard Lim. *Malaysia, Singapore, and Brunei.* London: Rough Guides, 2012.

Lonely Planet and Simon Richard. *Malaysia, Singapore, and Brunei.* Oakland, CA: Lonely Planet, 2013.

Majid, Harun Abdul. *Rebellion in Brunei: The 1962 Revolt, Imperialism, Confrontation and Oil* New York: I.B. Tauris & Co. Ltd, 2007.

Park, Stanley. *Fifa 192: The True Story behind the Legend of the Brunei Darussalam National Football Team.* Boca Raton: Universal Publishers, 2004.

Saunders, G. *History of Brunei.* Kuala Lumpur: Oxford University Press, 2004.

Works Cited

Arnett, Jeffrey Jensen. *International Encyclopedia of Adolescence: A Historical and Cultural Survey of Young People around the World.* Boca Raton: CRC Press, 2007.

Bruckner, D.J.R. "The Riches of Brunei." *The New York Times.* Online.

Brunei Art Forum. Online. http://bruneiartforum.com/

Brunei Press. "About Brunei" Online. http://www.bruneipress.com.bn/brunei/brunei.html

Brunei Tourism. "Visitor Info: Do's and Don'ts" Online. http://www.tourismbrunei.com/info/do.html

Daery, Viddy Ad. "Brunei's classic literary world at crossroads." *The Brunei Times.* Online.

Freedom House. "Freedom of the Press – Brunei (2006)" Online. http://www.freedomhouse.org/inc/content/pubs/pfs/inc_country_detail.cfm?country=6929&year=2007&pf

Filmer, Andrea. "Displaying the arty side of Brunei." *The Star Online.* Online.

Gapar, Wani. "Brunei's Theatre Art Needs Support." *Brunei Direct.* Online.

Goh, Jeani. "Brunei artists honoured." *BruneiDirect.com.* Online.

Han, Shareen. "Be sensitive to women's rights, urges minister." *The Brunei Times.* Online.

Han, Shareen. "Syair-writing contest." *The Brunei Times.* Online.

Hizam, Nasroul. "'Titian puisi' to revive local literary activities" *The Brunei Times*. Online.

Katti, Anand Madhura. "Brunei Beckons." *The Hindu Business Line*. Online. Accessed January 29, 2009.

Lonely Planet. "Introducing Brunei Darussalam" Online. http://www.lonelyplanet.com/brunei-darussalam

Ministry of Foreign Affairs and Trade–Brunei Darussalam. "Brunei Darussalam's Missions Abroad" Online. http://www.mfa.gov.bn/overseas_missions/missionsabroad.htm

Renard, John. *Seven Doors to Islam: Spirituality and the Religious Life of Muslims*. Berkeley: University of California Press, 1996.

Salam, Nurkhayrul. "Efforts needed to promote local literature." *The Brunei Times*. Online.

The Brunei Times. "Art: A medium to promote versatile Bruneians." Online. http://www.bt.com.bn/en/home_news/2008/09/29/art_a_medium_to_promote_versatile_bruneians

The Brunei Times. "Belait mosque programmes attract more young people." Online.

The Brunei Times. "Contest preserves traditional art of Syair Asli." Online.

The UN Refugee Agency (UNHCR). "Freedom in the World–Brunei (2004)" Online. http://www.unhcr.org/refworld/docid/473c547b23.html

U.S. Department of State. "Brunei: Country Reports on Human Rights Practices 2002" Online. http://www.state.gov/g/drl/rls/hrrpt/2001/eap/8255.htm

U.S. Department of State. "Brunei: Country Reports on Human Rights Practices 2006" Online. http://www.state.gov/g/drl/rls/hrrpt/2005/61602.htm

U.S. Department of State. "Brunei: Country Reports on Human Rights Practices 2007" Online. http://www.state.gov/g/drl/rls/hrrpt/2006/78767.htm

Cambodian children are comfortable in traditional boats/Stock photo © Bartosz Hadyniak

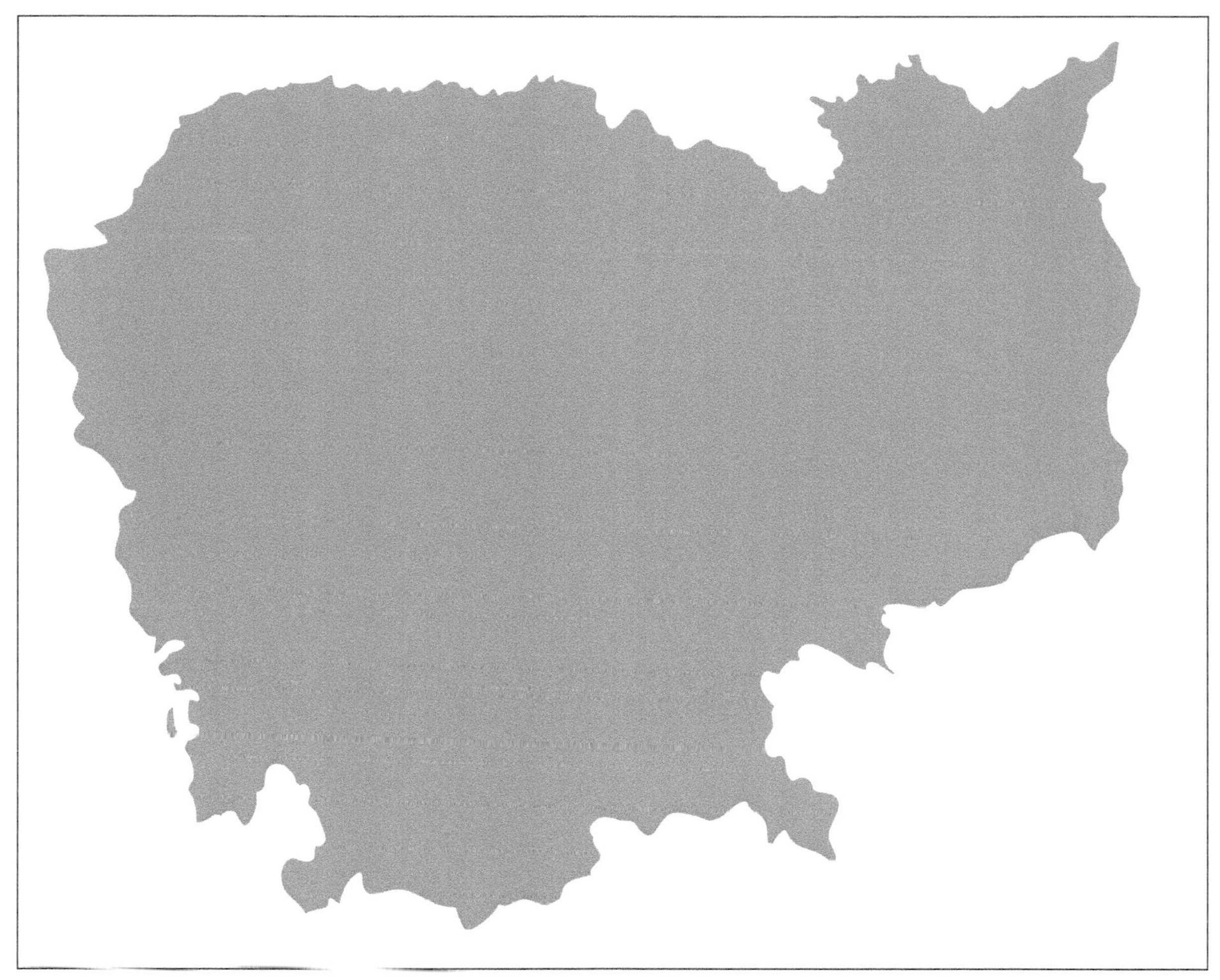

CAMBODIA

Introduction

Bordered by Thailand, Laos, Vietnam, and the Gulf of Thailand, the Kingdom of Cambodia is a small, developing country in Southeast Asia. Once the center of a kingdom which ruled much of the region for six centuries, Cambodia became part of French Indochina until 1953. Its history in the latter half of the twentieth century was marked by the ravages of war that engulfed the region, including the brutal dictatorship of Pol Pot and his Khmer Rouge. Around 2 million people died during this period of genocide (1975–1979), and a half million more became refugees before the Khmer Rouge was overthrown.

Peace accords signed in 1991 brought a greater measure of stability to the country and renewed regional cooperation. While the prospects for Cambodia look better than they have for several decades, recovery and further progress will require massive international assistance and greater economic and political transparency.

Cambodia's cultural history has been influenced by the neighboring countries of India and China. Historically, Cambodia has been at the center of ancient trade routes, both by land and river, linking its larger neighbors. However, Cambodia and the Khmer people, the country's largest ethnic group, have forged their own unique culture over several thousand years. Cambodia is also often cited as the ancient source of Buddhism, and Buddhist traditions provide the basis for the highest forms of cultural expression in Cambodia.

GENERAL INFORMATION

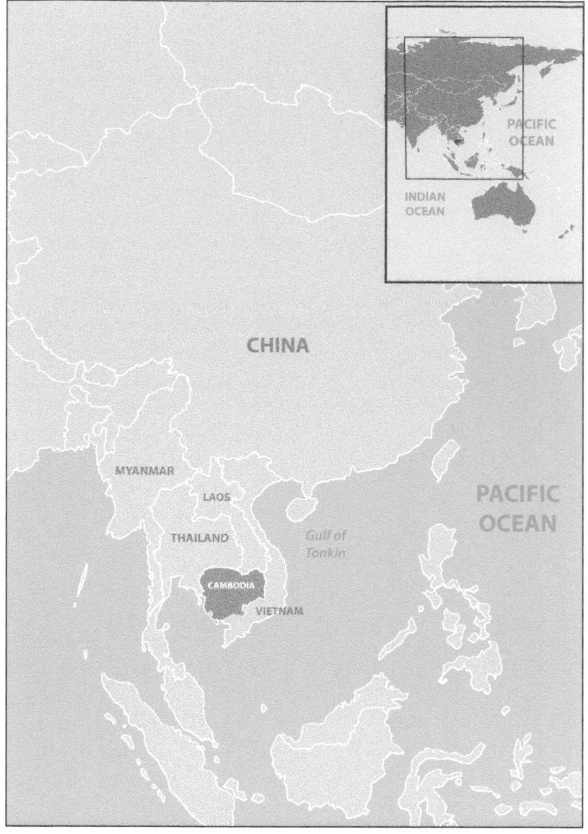

Official Language: Khmer
Population: 15,458,332 (2014 estimate)
Currency: Cambodian riel
Coins: Coins in denominations of 50, 100, 200, and 500 were issued in 1994, but rarely used. The Unites States dollar has recently become an unofficial second currency, though US coins are not in circulation.
Land Area: 176,515 square kilometers (68,152 square miles)
Water Area: 4,520 square kilometers (1,745 square miles)
National Motto: "Nation, Religion, King"
National Anthem: "Nokoreach" ("Royal Family")
Capital: Phnom Penh
Time Zone: GMT +7
Flag Description: The flag of Cambodia features two horizontal bands of blue on the top and bottom and one horizontal band of red across the middle. Red and blue are the national colors of Cambodia. In the center, a white image of Angkor Wat, a 12th-century Hindu Temple in Angkor, Cambodia, is featured.

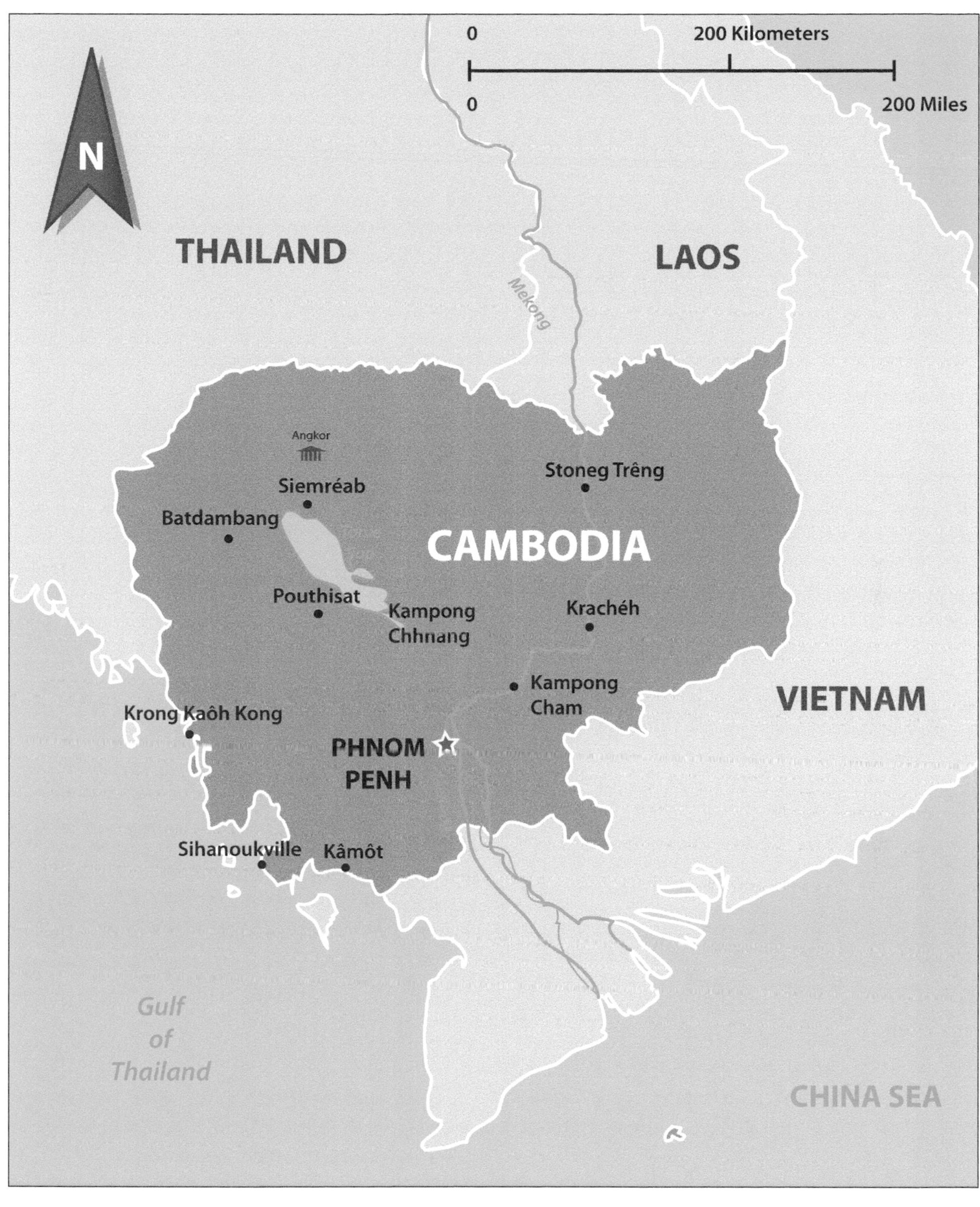
0
200 Kilometers
0
200 Miles
N
THAILAND
LAOS
Mekong
Angkor
Siemréab
Stoneg Trêng
Batdambang
CAMBODIA
Pouthisat
Kampong
Chhnang
Kracheh
Kampong
Cham
VIETNAM
Krong Kaôh Kong
PHNOM
PENH
Sihanoukville
Kâmôt
Gulf
of
Thailand
CHINA SEA

Principal Cities by Population (2012):

- Phnom Penh (1,400,000)
- Ta Khmau (205,756)
- Battambang (196,709)
- Sisophon (190,349)
- Siem Reap (189,292)
- Kampong Thom (118,699)
- Preah Sihanouk (110,856)
- Kratie (79,123) (2009 estimate)
- Pursat (57,000) (2009 estimate)
- Prey Veng (55,000) (2009 estimate)
- Kampong Cham (46,000) (2009 estimate)

Population

Cambodia's population is young and growing quickly. It is estimated that over 50 percent of Cambodians are under the age of twenty-four. However, this imbalance in Cambodia's age demographics is a growing concern. The country's large youth population continues to challenge 'Cambodia's already-strained education infrastructure. In addition, employment opportunities in urban areas remain scarce. The country's population density is approximately 82 persons per square kilometer (212 per square mile), but most of the population is concentrated in the fertile central lowlands. Roughly 85 percent of Cambodians live in rural areas, generally in small villages. Phnom Penh, with an unofficial population totaling about 1.4 million in 2012, is Cambodia's largest city.

Languages

Khmer, an Austro-Asiatic language related to Vietnamese, Thai, and Lao, is spoken by 96 percent of the population. Unlike these languages, however, Khmer's semantics do not depend on vocal tone. Khmer is written in an alphabet related to Sanskrit. It is common for the older generations to speak French, but in recent years English has become Cambodia's most common second language.

Native People & Ethnic Groups

During the period that the Khmer Rouge ruled Cambodia, ethnic minorities and educated ethnic Khmer were targets of genocide. The Khmer Rouge regime sought to expunge Western influences and religious beliefs and return Cambodia to an agrarian society based on Maoist, or communist, principles. Those who were not killed or forced into labor in the countryside fled the country. Mistreatment of ethnic Vietnamese, combined with incursions across Cambodia's and Vietnam's shared border, led Vietnam to invade Cambodia and help topple the regime.

In the early 21st century, the Khmer, or ethnic Cambodians, make up 90 percent of the population. Vietnamese is the single largest ethnic minority group, followed by Chinese. Smaller minority groups include the Cham, Khmer Loeu, and European.

Religions

Approximately 96 percent of Cambodians are practitioners of Theravada Buddhism, which has been a vital force in Cambodia since its arrival thousands of years ago. In addition, Roman Catholicism, Islam, Animism, and Mahayana Buddhism are practiced by small numbers of Cambodians.

Climate

Cambodia has a tropical climate with two distinct monsoon seasons. The rainy season occurs in the summer, brought by winds from the southwest. This season lasts from May to October and accounts for approximately 80 percent of the country's annual rainfall, which averages between 100 and 150 centimeters (39 and 59 inches). The southwest receives a considerably higher amount of precipitation, and the average can fluctuate from year to year. The dry monsoon season, lasting from November to April, comes from the northeast. Humidity can be high throughout the year, but is particularly high in the rainy season, usually averaging 60 percent each day.

The warmest temperatures occur in March and April, the coolest in December and January. The average annual temperature ranges from 21° to 35° Celsius (70° to 95° Fahrenheit). Unlike in neighboring Vietnam, typhoons rarely affect the

Cambodian coastline. The country is, however, prone to floods in the rainy season and, occasionally, droughts when the summer monsoon fails.

ENVIRONMENT & GEOGRAPHY

Topography

Cambodia's terrain consists of a central alluvial plain encircled by mountains. Along the border with Thailand rise the Dangrek Mountains. The Cardamon Mountains, which contain Phnom Aural—the country's highest point (1,813 meters/5,948 feet)—are located in the southwest, as are the Elephant Mountains. Cambodia's coastline along the Gulf of Thailand is 443 kilometers (275 miles) long.

The lowlands of the Mekong River Valley and the Tonle Sap Basin comprise approximately 75 percent of the country's total area. These areas are the agricultural heart of the country and support the majority of the population.

Two bodies of water dominate the central plains: the Mekong River, which crosses Cambodia for almost 500 kilometers (311 miles), and the shallow Tonle Sap Lake, which drains into the Mekong along the Tonle Sap River. During the rainy season, however, when the Mekong River floods, the Tonle Sap River is forced to reverse its course and the lake increases to four times its size. At its largest, the Tonle Sap Lake measures 10,000 square kilometers (4,000 square miles). The alluvial soils left by the receding waters are vital to local agricultural production.

Plants & Animals

Rapid deforestation and wildlife poaching have diminished the variety and number of plants, trees, animals, and their habitats. Prevalent trees include palm, coconut, banana, kapok, rubber, mahogany, and teak. Among Cambodia's large mammals are elephants, bears, wild boars, tigers, and leopards. There are also populations of birds, reptiles, and fish.

The Javan and Sumatran rhinoceroses, the Asian elephant, the tiger, the Asiatic black bear, and several types of monkeys are a few of the country's endangered animal species. Efforts to place more natural areas under government protection are underway.

CUSTOMS & COURTESIES

Greetings

The common greeting among most Cambodians is the sompiah. The sompiah involves placing the hands together as if praying and then bowing. To show respect—especially to elders, people with official titles and those of a higher social standing—Cambodians lift their hands higher and bow lower. It is traditional that younger people offer the sompiah first.

The Western-style handshake is now common in Cambodia. However, handshakes are usually performed by men, and Cambodian women greet people of both genders with the traditional sompiah. It is customary to respond with the greeting one is given. In addition, Cambodians use the honorific title "Lok" when addressing men, and "Lok srey" when speaking to a woman. This is typically followed by the person's first name, with the surname also often used. A common spoken greeting among Cambodians is "Sok sebai" ("How are you?").

Gestures & Etiquette

Communication in Cambodia can often be indirect and body language and nonverbal behavior is important. Many Cambodians are very modest and showing emotions such as anger, impatience or frustration is considered poor manners. Such behavior can be viewed as a sign of weakness. In addition, loud and boastful language and expressive gestures are considered inappropriate. Traditionally, social interactions among Cambodians are rooted in the concepts of honor, reputation, and dignity. These values are attributed to a person largely through their social status and behavior. A person can cause offense or dishonor by exhibiting improper behavior or by criticizing or embarrassing another.

There are several commonly accepted gestures or social norms in Western cultures that are considered rude or inappropriate in Cambodian society. For example, kissing and hugging are not commonly seen public gestures in Cambodia, even among family members. Also, smiling can have many meanings among Cambodians. For example, it can be a sign of irritation, nervousness or a lack of understanding, as well as happiness. In addition, prolonged direct eye contact is considered disrespectful among Cambodians, especially between men and women.

Additionally, much of Cambodian etiquette derives from the Theravada Buddhist faith, followed by close to 95 percent of Cambodians. For example, Cambodians, as well as many people throughout Asia, view a person's head as sacred. Touching someone's face or head, including stroking the head of an infant or toddler, is considered inappropriate. Hats are always removed when in the presence of an older or esteemed person, as well as when entering any sacred building. In addition, Cambodians consider feet to be impure, especially the soles of the feet. As such, Cambodians avoiding showing the bottoms of their feet to other people or towards sacred items or places.

Eating/Meals

Cambodians typically eat three main meals each day. Most Cambodians eat a breakfast consisting of either kyteow (rice-noodle soup) or bobor (rice porridge). The French influence in Cambodia is evident in the popularity of baguettes (French bread) as a breakfast food. Lunch is typically eaten at midday, with a staple lunch item being sour soup, called samlor machou. For rural Cambodians, lunch is often brought to them as they work in the fields. Dinner for most Cambodians is a time for families to come together. Dinners traditionally include rice and fish. In addition, most meals are eaten communal-style, with everyone sitting around centrally placed bowls of food from which they serve themselves.

Common eating utensils in Cambodia are chopsticks, forks, knives and spoons. Many Cambodians prefer to eat rice in balls using their right hands, and most place settings include a small bowl that is used to hold dipping sauces. When chopsticks are not being used, it is customary to place them on a rest or across the top of the bowl and never sticking straight up or in a V-shape, as these images are typically associated with death.

Social and familial hierarchies also are important when Cambodians eat together. Traditionally, the oldest or most senior person is seated first. This person is also the first diner to begin eating.

Visiting

Cambodians are generally very sociable, and visits among relatives and friends are common and often unannounced. It is also common for Cambodians to remove their footwear upon entering a home. Hosts usually offer drinks and refreshments to visitors and, in some cases, invite guests to stay for a meal. In such situations, guests are usually offered the best seating. When invited for a visit, guests usually present a small token of gratitude to their hosts. Traditional gifts for such occasions include fruit, candy, pastries or flowers. Customarily, gifts are not opened when they are first received.

LIFESTYLE

Family

The extended family is important in Cambodian society. Traditionally, multiple generations and extended family members live together in one house or in close proximity. In addition, daily life for most Cambodians revolves around family and the running of the household. For example, because 80 percent of Cambodians live in rural areas, family life is often dictated by farming and the cycles of planting and harvesting.

Urban families share similar traditional bonds. For example, the elderly are often cared for by their adult children. However, Cambodians living in urban areas, with greater access to outside media and other cultures, and many younger Cambodians who have matured in the post-Khmer Rouge era are pushing the boundaries of the traditional family. In addition, the deaths of so many men during the Khmer Rouge rule has created a situation in which an estimated one-fifth of households in Cambodia are headed by women. It is common for single women who have not remarried to gather in small clans of women and children to share resources and to seek companionship.

Housing

The rural villages and hamlets of Cambodia are home to 80 percent of the country's population. More than half of all homes in these areas are built of local or available materials such as bamboo, reeds, thatch and grass. Additionally, most rural homes in Cambodia are built on wood pilings, or stilts, elevating the living space above the ground and protecting it against annual floods. Homeowners often use the areas beneath their homes for storage and for shade. Kitchens are usually separate from the house but nearby, as are toilets, which can be as simple as pits in the ground.

From 1975 to 1979, Phnom Penh and other cities in Cambodia were evacuated, leaving homes and other structures abandoned. With the fall of the Khmer Rouge regime, Cambodians returned to urban areas and were faced with overcrowding and a lack of habitable housing. These problems still affect the country today. The Cambodian government and a variety of international aid groups are working to construct safe, affordable housing throughout the country. For example, Habitat for Humanity is working to build over 300 homes for families living in Phnom Penh, with plans to eventually serve 5,000 families in five provinces. Urban homes are now built using standard construction materials such as wood, reinforced concrete, brick, stone, sheet metals and tiles.

Improving the sanitation conditions of communities throughout Cambodia is a major effort of the government and international aid organizations. According to 2004 statistics from the Cambodian government, 70 percent of households had access to safe water in the wet season and 48 percent in the dry season. In addition, 75 percent of households did not have any modern sanitation facilities.

Food

Cambodian cuisine, like much of Cambodian culture, has been greatly influenced by neighboring India and China. In addition, Cambodian cuisine has similarities to Thai, Laotian and Vietnamese cooking. As a whole, this blend of flavors and styles has created a unique national cuisine. At the heart of the Cambodian diet are rice, noodles and fish. Almost all Cambodian meals include a samlor (traditional soup) that is served with the main course and not before. Samlor machou banle is a popular hot and sour soup that is made with fish flavored with pineapple and spices. Ginger, lemongrass, garlic, mint and fermented fish sauces and pastes are all important elements to Cambodian cooking.

Most of the fish that Cambodians eat are freshwater fish caught in the Tonlé Sap Lake or the Mekong River. Amoc, one of the most popular Cambodian dishes, is a baked fish wrapped in a banana leaf and flavored with coconut, lemongrass, and chilies. Prawns, Mekong catfish and whitebait are other seafood commonly eaten in Cambodia. In addition, teuk kalohk (fruit shakes) are very popular in Cambodia. Vendors sell teuk kalohk from stalls or pushcarts set up on street corners or near night markets. Locally grown bananas, mangoes, papayas, rambutan, and palm fruit are also widely eaten. Tea, coffee, fruit juices, coconut water, and fermented palm juice are all popular drinks.

Life's Milestones

Many Cambodian rites of passage are derived from Theravada Buddhism, the official religion of Cambodia. The birth of a baby is a joyous event in the lives of Cambodian families. Traditionally, Buddhist monks were called upon to officiate at baby naming celebrations. However, Cambodians do not consider subsequent birthdays to be special, and therefore do not celebrate them. Instead, parents customarily remember the season in which their children were born.

Almost all Buddhist males in Cambodia are expected to become a monk at some point in their lives. Most males are initiated once they leave school and before marrying or starting careers. The initiation ceremony involves the young male shaving his head and putting on the robes of the monk before petitioning a senior monk for admittance. Time served as a monk can range from one week to a lifetime of devotion.

Marriage is, for most Cambodians, the most important milestone in life. Men typically marry between the ages of 19 and 25, and women between the ages of 16 and 22 years. Rural and urban courtship patterns differ, with rural Cambodians generally following a more traditional path of arranged marriages. Arranged marriages are still quite common throughout Cambodia, but more men and women are opting to choose their own spouses.

Parents of the bride and groom customarily play important roles in all marriages, from the initial approval of the marriage to the exchange of presents and the organizing of the wedding itself. Traditionally, Cambodian weddings lasted three days. However, most weddings in contemporary Cambodian society take place in a single day. Important aspects of the ceremony include ritual hair cutting, tying cotton threads soaked in holy water around the bride's and groom's wrists, and passing a candle around a circle of happily married and respected couples to bless the union. After the wedding, a banquet is typically held. In urban areas, a dinner is usually held at a restaurant, while rural wedding banquets are often held in temporary shelters constructed by the two families.

CULTURAL HISTORY

Art

Traditional Cambodian crafts include pottery and weaving. Carbon-dated pottery shards found in Cambodia indicate that people inhabited the region as early as 4000 BCE. Pottery pieces ranged from practical items to intricately designed works in the images of animals and gods. In fact, the Chinese-style ceramics made by Khmer potters in the twelfth century are praised today for their quality and unique glazing techniques. Ancient Khmer potters produced a translucent glaze that resembled jade, utilizing kilns fired at temperatures between 982° to 1,093° Celsius (1,800° to 2,000° Fahrenheit). However, until recently, these ancient firing techniques had been lost due to political upheaval in Cambodian society.

Cambodia has an ancient and renowned weaving culture, dating back to the Angkorian period (9th to 12th century CE), if not before. Silk weaving, in particular, has played an integral artistic role in Cambodian society for centuries. Silk weaving is used to create sampot, which is Cambodia's traditional and national garment. A variation is sampot hol, a twill weave with a traditional ikat design. Ikat refers to a particular style of weaving in which patterns are created using resist dyeing, or the prevention of the dye from reaching the entire cloth. Traditional Cambodian weavers typically created these ikat designs by tying vegetable or synthetic fibers on sections of the threads before dyeing. Sampot hol designs are often floral or geometric, and are usually more sophisticated and intricate than other weaving styles, making them highly prized and expensive.

Traditional colors for sampot hol are red, yellow, green, blue and black. Items made from hol cloth include garments such as the sampot hol and pidan hol, which is a ceremonial hanging used for religious or sacred purposes. In addition, other traditional textiles in Cambodian culture include pamung, which are fabrics made of solid-color silk twills. Another traditional weaving style involves the making of a simpler cloth of cotton, silk, or a cotton-silk blend. This has been used to weave sarongs or the traditional scarf called a krama.

Beginning in the 1990s, private organizations and the United Nations Educational, Scientific and Cultural Organization (UNESCO) have been working to revive weaving in Cambodia. Research and educational programs were created, and the reintroduction of sericulture (the raising of silkworms) has contributed to the revitalization of this culturally significant craft. Other traditional arts that were largely practiced in Cambodian culture include mural painting—largely confined to wats (monasteries or temples)—as well as non-textile weaving (such as baskets and mats), lacquerware and kite-making.

Traditional Cambodian, or Khmer, sculpture is influenced by Indian sculpture. From the sixth to the sixteenth centuries CE, Khmer sculptors typically worked in wood, stone and bronze to create works that many experts consider some of the finest in human history. Unlike ancient Indian sculpture, which presents a wide variety of subjects, the ancient Cambodian work is much narrower thematically. Buddha and the main Hindu deities of Shiva, Vishnu and the elephant god Ganesha are the primary subjects. However, Cambodian sculpture is highly refined and rich in detail, and what it lacks in subject variety it makes up in style and execution. The Banteay Srei style of the late tenth century, which features unique coloration and wall carvings, is often considered the peak of Khmer art.

Because of the political and social upheaval in Cambodia over the past six centuries, much of the great ancient sculpture of the Khmer people has been lost. Also, most Cambodian sculpture was used as decoration for temples, many of which were destroyed, looted or lost to jungle overgrowth. With increasing political stability, archaeologists and art experts are learning more about the ancient sculptures. Visitors to Cambodia and art collectors throughout the world have created a market for reproductions of ancient Cambodian sculpture. Modern-day artisans are rediscovering the skills and techniques of their ancestors to once again express this important aspect of Cambodian culture.

Architecture

The ancient Hindu temple Prasat Angkor Wat was built in the 12th century in Angkor, Cambodia. It is arguably the most widely known example of Khmer architecture and remains Cambodia's most popular tourist destination. The temple is adorned with numerous examples of low relief sculpture and sculptural decorations. The Angkor region is also home to other 12th-century temples, including Banteay Srei and Ta Prohm.

Modern-day Phnom Penh features numerous examples of French colonial architecture. The city's post office is a former colonial villa. In addition, the city features more modern buildings whose design reflects influences from early Khmer culture. Several modern office towers have also been constructed in Phnom Penh and urban development in the city continues.

Drama

Cambodian theater has its roots in the sixth century. Examples of folk theater, featuring masks and shadow play, continue to be performed throughout the county. These works often retell folk legends and ancient Indian stories pertaining to Hinduism and Buddhism. The Cambodian Royal Theater continues to perform renditions of the *Ramayana*, an Indian epic poem about the adventures of Prince Rama. The Cambodian version of the *Ramayana* is known as the *Reamker*.

Music & Dance

Cambodia's rich cultural traditions of music and dance were almost lost during the Khmer Rouge period (1975–1979), during which an estimated 1.5 million people were killed and culture was repressed. As such, musicians, dancers and teachers were targeted by the Khmer Rouge and very few survived. Even traditional Cambodian instruments were destroyed in the attempt to eradicate anything that was a reminder of the past. The early years of the twenty-first century are witnessing a revival of this important cultural heritage. The Royal Ballet of Cambodian continues to perform acclaimed productions of Khmer classical dance.

Music played a significant role in traditional Cambodian culture. Ancient sculpture and decorations often depict musicians playing similar-looking Khmer instruments. In addition to being a significant aspect of cultural and religious celebrations and festivals throughout Cambodia, music was also an everyday indulgence practiced by everyone. Traditional Cambodian music can be grouped into several forms that were used for different purposes.

The most traditional type of music is the areak ka, which is an ensemble that typically performs at weddings. The members of the areak ka use instruments such as the tro khmae (three-stringed fiddle), a khsae muoy (single-stringed bowed instrument), and skor areak (drums). In many of the traditional forms, the musicians follow a lead instrument, often a xylophone-type instrument, and then improvise using conventional rhythms. Chapaye is a uniquely Cambodian form of music sung to the accompaniment of a two-stringed wooden instrument similar to an unamplified bass guitar. Chapaye has often been compared to blues music.

Traditional Cambodian dance, or royal ballet, is considered one of the greatest cultural traditions of Cambodia. Dating to the Angkor era, Cambodian royal dance was influenced by Indian culture, sharing very intricate and stylized hand movements, as well as special costumes and headwear. The royal ballet specialized in apsara dances (classic Khmer dances with similarities to the traditional dances of Thailand and Laos) and dance-dramas that retold epic tales. The royal ballet traditionally was performed exclusively by females except for a few specific roles. Contemporary dances in the royal ballet style, however, feature more male dancers.

Khmer classical dance is now also part of the world's shared cultural heritage. In 2003, UNESCO designated the royal ballet of Cambodia a Masterpiece of Oral and Intangible Heritage of Humanity. This distinction honors the most remarkable examples of oral traditions and forms of cultural expression in all regions of the world.

Literature

Ancient Khmer literature consists mainly of written works commissioned by monarchies or monasteries. In addition, early Khmer literature often captures Buddhist and Hindu folklore which was often transmitted by storytellers and religious figures. One popular Khmer legend is the story of Vorong and Sorvong, which tells the tale of two Khmer princes.

More modern words of Cambodian literature reflect the influence of the years during which the country was a French colony. Nonetheless works by the novelist Som, including *Dik ram phka ram* (*The Dancing Water and the Dancing Flower*, 1911) and *Tum Teav* (1915) retain elements of early Khmer storytelling.

During the years of the Khmer Rouge, writers and others who were considered "intellectuals" were openly enslaved, imprisoned, or killed. The Khmer Rouge also undertook rigorous actions to erase the early Khmer folklore and Buddhist traditions from Cambodian culture.

The Cambodian writer and human rights activist, Somali Mam, published *The Road of Lost Innocence* in 2007. The work recounts the author's own experience in Asia's human trafficking underworld.

CULTURE

Arts & Entertainment

It is estimated that as much as 90 percent of Cambodia's artists, dancers, musicians, actors, playwrights and poets were killed during the Khmer Rouge period. As a result, many traditional cultural dances and theater forms were lost. More than two decades following that era, the arts in contemporary Cambodia are reemerging and helping to revitalize Cambodian culture; traditional crafts such as textile-making, woodcarving, and metalwork have been enjoying a revival, and the country has received international donations necessary to restore and maintain its architectural wonders. These efforts are being lead by the Cambodian governments Ministry of Culture and Fine Arts, foreign countries, and non-governmental organizations (NGOs), and local and expatriate artists.

The Cambodian government created the Ministry of Culture and Fine Arts in 1997. The ministry is responsible for protecting and developing the culture and fine arts in Cambodia, primarily by nurturing creativity and innovation and promoting the diverse Cambodian cultural heritage. Funded by the government, the Royal University of Fine Arts is an important driving force in revitalizing the fine arts in Cambodia. The university reopened in 1980 following the Khmer Rouge era and soon attracted many surviving artists. The school has two key units: one focused on archaeology, architecture, urbanism and plastic arts, and the other specializing in choreographic arts and music.

Cambodian Living Arts (CLA) is an educational organization that is working to revive the disappearing system of masters and apprentices in Cambodia. The CLA typically funds sixteen classes in Phnom Penh and seven other provinces, and supports around 300 students nationwide. The CLA also provides instruments, costumes and classroom space, as well as wages and healthcare. Projects enacted by the CLA include the Masters Teaching program, in which musicians and performance artists who were performing before 1975 are financially supported in order to teach their crafts to students. (This is crucial because traditional Khmer performing arts were passed down orally from teacher to student.) The organization recently began to produce audio-visual documentaries to preserve dance, shadow puppetry and other uniquely Cambodian performing arts.

Many artists who fled Cambodia when the country was in turmoil returned in the 1990s. These artists are creating what many call modern Khmer art. This style combines subject matter from Khmer culture with forms borrowed from modern Western styles. Prom Sam An is a sculptor who evokes rural Khmer culture to create modern works. The work of Leang Seckon (1972–) incorporates sewing, painting, metalwork, collage and the plastic arts to reflect Cambodian traditions such as apsara dancing and fortune telling, to comment on modern culture, society and politics. Phy Chan Than (1962–) and Soeung Vannara (1962–) are two of the leading painters in this contemporary movement.

Common recreational activities in Cambodia include football (soccer), volleyball, swimming, and dancing, in both traditional and modern forms.

Cultural Sites & Landmarks

Though much of Cambodia's cultural history was destroyed or compromised during the repressive reign of the Khmer Rouge, the country still boasts numerous cultural sites and landmarks, as well as two World Heritage Sites designated by UNESCO. Perhaps no other site symbolizes Cambodian culture as strongly as Angkor. Angkor was the capital of the Khmer empire from the ninth to the fifteen century CE, a period that is considered the height of Cambodian culture. Angkor's most famous landmarks are Angkor Wat, a temple complex built in the twelfth century by King Suryavarman II (reigned 1113–c. 1150), Angkor Thom, a temple complex built in late twelfth and early thirteenth centuries by King Jayavarman VII (reigned 1181–1219) and the Bayon Temple.

Angkor Archaeological Park covers about 154 square miles (400 square kilometers), including forested areas. As one of the most important archaeological sites in Southeast Asia, UNESCO designated Angkor a World Heritage Site, and added it to the list of World Heritage Sites in danger in 1992. The Angkor Wat temple complex is believed to be the largest religious structure in the world. Inscriptions in the sandstone walls indicate that its construction required the labor of 300,000 workers and 6,000 elephants. Experts now believe that Angkor Wat was built as both a temple and a mausoleum, or tomb, for Suryavarman II. Additionally, carved into the walls of Angkor Wat are more than 3,000 distinct apsaras (heavenly nymphs).

Designated a World Heritage Site in 2008, the Temple of Preah Vihear is situated near the Cambodian border with Thailand. The temple was built in the first half of the 11th century CE as a dedication to the Hindu god Shiva. The Preah Vihear complex consists of several sanctuaries linked by a network of staircases and pavements. In the late 12th and early 13th centuries, the temple became a place of Mahayana Buddhist worship by Jayavarman VII. The temple is also renowned as an excellent of Khmer architecture.

The capital, Phnom Penh, is home to numerous landmarks, including the Royal Palace of the Kingdom of Cambodia, constructed in 1866. The palace grounds include the family residence and numerous other structures and gardens. The Independence Monument in the center of Phnom Penh was created by renowned Cambodian architect Vann Molyvann to commemorate the country's independence. The monument, which also serves as a memorial to Cambodia's war dead, was dedicated on November 9, 1962. Celebrations for Independence Day and Constitution Day are held around the lotus-shaped monument.

Phnom Penh's oldest and largest temple, Wat Phnom, marks the legendary founding point of the city and is a popular destination for tourists. The stupa, a dome-shaped Buddhist monument used to house statues of the Buddha, within Wat Phnom contains the remains of Cambodian king Ponhea Yat, who named Phnom Penh the capital of Cambodia.

Libraries & Museums

Cambodia offers two culturally important museums, the Cambodian National Museum and the Tuol Sleng Museum. The National Museum is housed in a ninety-year-old red sandstone building located next to the Cambodian Royal Palace in Phnom Penh. The museum contains the world's largest exhibit of ancient Khmer artifacts. The museum is divided into several categories, including prehistoric items, stone, bronze and wood sculptures, ceramics and ethnographic objects from the prehistoric, pre-Angkor, Angkor, and post-Angkor periods. The stone and bronze sculpture collections are considered among the finest in the world.

Located in a residential neighborhood in suburban Phnom Penh, the Tuol Sleng Museum, (also known as the museum of genocide) memorializes the atrocities of the Khmer Rouge regime. The museum is located in the former Tuol Svay Prey High School, which became a prison and execution center in 1976. Officially called Security Prison 21 (S-21) by the Khmer Rouge, it became the largest center of detention and torture in Cambodia. On display at the museum are black and white photographs of the majority of the 17,000 detainees who were held at the prison and eventually taken to the killing fields of Choeung Ek. Formerly an orchard and graveyard, Choeung Ek is now a memorial to those who were killed and buried there, and features a Buddhist stupa (commemorative structure) that contains an estimated 5,000 human skulls unearthed in the field.

The National Library of Cambodia is also located in the capital of Phnom Penh. Inaugurated in 1924, the library housed a collection of over 103,000 books as of 2005. Library infrastructure in the country is lacking.

Holidays

Cambodia's most important holidays pertain to the agricultural seasons and to Buddhist traditions. The Khmer New Year, a three-day celebration in the middle of April, coincides with the end of the harvest. Families visit each other, exchange gifts, and offer food and flowers to their local Buddhist temple and its monks. The end of the rainy season, falling in either October or November, is another three-day festival. Its main components are fireworks and a boat race on the Mekong River, intended to appease the god of the river and guarantee an abundance of rice and fish.

Buddha's birth, death, and enlightenment are celebrated on May 15. People go to temple and bring food and flowers. Similar traditions are followed on the Day of Souls (September 22), when deceased family and friends are remembered.

Among the secular holidays celebrated in Cambodia are occasions related to the dictatorship of the Khmer Rouge. These include National Day (January 7), marking the overthrow of the regime, and the Day of Hatred (May 20), marking its atrocities. Constitution Day is marked on September 24, and Independence Day is observed on November 9.

Youth Culture

As Cambodia entered the 21st century, more than half its population was under the age of 18. This demographic imbalance has particularly strained the county's educational system and labor markets. A significant number of youth in Cambodia deal with poverty, unstable home lives and substance abuse problems, as well as other factors that lead many to a life on the streets. Many young Cambodians earn a living by working in the private retail sector (restaurants and shops) or by selling newspapers or other street jobs. Others turn to the commercial sex industry or criminal activities.

Cambodian youth are increasingly being exposed to telecommunications and computer technologies that have become a significant part of their lives. Mobile phone usage and text messaging are both popular forms of communication. In addition, blogging on the Internet is also increasing. Although only a small percentage of Cambodians have Internet access, young Cambodians see blogging as an effective way to communicate with other Cambodians and others around the world.

Music is also an important part of the Cambodian youth culture. The Khmer Rouge regime targeted traditional Cambodian musicians, songwriters and performers during its rule. Consequently, many young Cambodians are unfamiliar with traditional Cambodian music and have thus embraced pop music. In addition, Cambodians who relocated to the West during the country's turbulent years have returned, bringing the contemporary sounds of rock, pop, and hip-hop music with them. Cambodian musical artists that exhibit distinct Western influences include Lisha, Cambodia's first female rapper, and Klap ya Handz, a hip-hop group.

SOCIETY

Transportation

The steady growth of the middle class has increased automobile ownership in Cambodia. As of 2004, there were an estimated 126,446 registered car owners in Cambodia, which is a 171 percent increase from 1990. Bicycles, motorbikes, walking and buffalo-drawn carts are often the primary forms of transportation for many rural Cambodians. Traffic in Cambodia travels on the right-hand side of the road.

Transportation Infrastructure

After years of neglect and destruction during the reign of the Khmer Rouge and the civil war that followed, Cambodia's transportation system is being rebuilt with aid from the UN and other countries, particularly Japan. Generally, road systems and inland waterways form the basis of Cambodia's main transportation routes. According to the Cambodian Ministry of Public Works and Transport, road transportation accounts for about 65 percent of all passenger transport and 70 percent of goods transport. Six major highways originate from Phnom Penh and fan out into the country. Only a small portion of the road system is paved, however. Annual rains and flooding, along with the poor conditions of secondary roads, often make these routes impassable for parts of the year.

Cambodia has more than 2,400 kilometers (1,490 miles) of navigable waterways, primarily on the Mekong River and Tonle Sap systems. However, maritime commerce is carried out almost exclusively by foreign vessels. In addition, shallow waters and frequent flooding restrict shipping on the country's water routes. The government is working to provide funding to dredge rivers and improve navigation capabilities. Kampong Saom (Sihanoukville) is Cambodia's only maritime seaport. Phnom Penh, on the Mekong River, also handles international shipping. In addition, international air traffic now has access to airports in Siemreab and Pochentong, which is near Phnom Penh.

Media & Communications

There are roughly 25 radio stations operating in Cambodia, 17 of which broadcast from Phnom Penh. Only three television stations broadcast national coverage in Cambodia: National Television Kampuchea (TVK), Bayon (owned by the ruling Cambodian People's Party), and the privately owned Cambodia Television Network (CTN). Smaller, private stations serve local communities by broadcasting a variety of content in several languages. Around 10 percent of Cambodians now have access to outside television broadcasts through satellite services. The

British Broadcasting Corporation (BBC), Cable News Network (CNN), Star TV (Hong Kong) and UBC (Thailand), in particular, are viewed by a significant portion of the Cambodian population. Overall, the broadcast media in Cambodia tends to be politically affiliated, and access for opposition parties is extremely limited and monitored.

Although estimates put the total number of Cambodian newspapers at more than 100, only a few have the distribution capacity and networks to reach a wide audience. The *Rasmei Kampuchea* (*Light of Kampuchea*) and the *Kampuchea Thmei Daily* are two of the more popular publications. In addition, low literacy rates outside urban centers limits readership numbers. The Cambodian government enacted the 1995 Press Law to constitutionally guarantee freedom of the press. However, because the Cambodian People's Party (CCP) holds such dominance within the country, journalists are often very careful about expressing dissenting opinions. Corruption does exist in the press corps and within the business and political communities, and the exchange of money for favorable coverage is not uncommon.

Cellular phones far outnumber traditional fixed-line telephones in Cambodia. In fact, according to 2005 statistics, Cambodia was the first country in the world in which mobile phones outnumbered land lines. Internet penetration in Cambodia remains among the lowest in the world. As of 2007, Cambodia had 10 Internet Service Providers offering full Internet access throughout the country. An estimated 78,500 Cambodians use the Internet, with the vast majority of them located in the Phnom Penh and Siem Reap areas. Inadequate infrastructure, a lack of qualified computer workers, and the problems of adapting the Khmer script to electronic communications have hindered Cambodia's attempts to increase Internet usage. However, there is no official policy regarding Internet censorship, which has led to the increasing popularity of blogging within the country in recent years.

SOCIAL DEVELOPMENT

Standard of Living

One of the poorest countries in the world, Cambodia is ranked 136th on the 2014 United Nations Human Development Index, which measures quality of life indicators. (The 2014 index is based on 2013 data.) Life expectancy is 61 years for men and 66 years for women (2014 estimate); the infant mortality rate is, however, high.

Water Consumption

While Cambodia has an ample supply of fresh water sources, oftentimes the drinking water is also used for other purposes, such as bathing and waste disposal. The Mekong and Tonlé Sap Rivers serve as two primary sources of fresh water in the country. According to estimates at the turn of the 21st century, only 36 percent of the population had improved sanitation coverage, while 71 percent of the population had improved drinking water coverage.

Education

Educated people were one of the primary targets of the Khmer Rouge's genocide. Many were killed, many others fled the country, and schools were closed. The effect that this had on the educational life of the country still resonates today. Though the situation has improved in the last decade, the country still lacks adequate funds, teachers, facilities, and educational materials. The current literacy rate is higher for males than for females: 82 percent versus 65 percent.

Education is free and compulsory for six years of primary school. It is followed by three years of middle school and three years of secondary school. The number of students enrolled in the upper levels drops significantly and only a fraction of university-age students receive a higher education. Among the country's post-secondary institutes are the University of Phnom Penh, the University of Agricultural Sciences, and the University of Fine Arts.

Women's Rights

The role of women in Cambodian society is changing. As the younger generation of women mature, they are challenging the traditional position of women as primarily homebound. Cambodia's constitution protects equal rights for women, equal pay for equal work, and equal status in marriage. In theory, women have equal rights to property, the same legal rights as men to initiate divorce proceedings and equal access to education, as well as equal access to certain jobs. In reality, traditional and cultural attitudes toward gender roles still work against the full and free exercise of women's rights in Cambodia.

Women play an indispensable role in the Cambodian economy due to their slightly higher population. At the turn of the 21st century, women made up 60 percent of all agricultural workers, 85 percent of the business work force, 70 percent of the industrial work force, and 60 percent of all service sector workers. However, most women continue to occupy lower-paying jobs, and are still underrepresented in the managerial workforce. Recently, the government has addressed this issue with the Neary Ratanak (Women as Precious Gems) initiative, created by the Ministry of Women's Affairs to offer and ensure the protection of women's rights and to promote gender equality in society. In addition, Cambodian labor law has provisions against sexual harassment in the workplace. Although the International Labor Organization (ILO) has reported that sexual harassment against women in the workplace was rare, other organizations report that violations are widespread.

Women in Cambodia have also seen their representation in politics increase in recent years. Heading into the 2008 elections, women held just under 11 percent of legislative seats in the Cambodian parliament, while comprising 56 percent of Cambodian voters. Things did not improve in the 2013 elections, where only 25 women were elected to the legislature. However, local elections in 2007 saw women's representation at the communal level double, from 8 percent in 2002 to about 15 percent.

Cambodian law outlaws rape and assault. However, domestic violence is quite widespread, and because of the fear and shame often associated with such incidents, it's not known exactly how serious a problem it is. The Cambodian domestic violence law criminalizes domestic violence, but does not specifically set out penalties. The Ministry of Women's Affairs has created programs to help handle these issues, and NGOs offer assistance and shelter for women in crisis.

In 2005, the National Assembly passed a domestic violence law to help prevent domestic violence and protect victims. The law breaks from the cultural tradition of noninvolvement in domestic life, allowing citizens and government authorities to intervene. However, NGOs report that local Cambodian officials often follow the traditional practice of not interfering in domestic issues. In addition, prostitution and trafficking remain persistent problems within Cambodia.

Health Care

The reign of the Khmer Rouge also had a devastating impact on the country's health care system. Many doctors were murdered by the regime, while others fled the country. In addition, most of Cambodia's hospitals were destroyed.

Some progress has been made in the last decade, but the system is still unable to provide adequately for the health care needs of the majority of Cambodians. There is a lack of trained medical personnel, facilities, and medical supplies, and as a result, many illnesses which could be treated are prevalent. These include diarrhea, hepatitis, and typhoid fever all of which are contracted from unclean drinking water. In addition, incidents of dengue fever, malaria, tuberculosis, trachoma, leprosy, and encephalitis also occur. The rate of HIV infection in Cambodia is one of the highest in the world, and malnutrition is a major problem, particularly among children.

GOVERNMENT

Structure

For many centuries, Cambodia was governed by a monarchy. Though it became part of French Indochina in 1863 and did not gain independence until 1953, the French did not depose the monarchy.

In 1970, Cambodia became a republic. This period lasted only five years before the communist Khmer Rouge seized power. The ensuing dictatorship devastated the country. Neighboring Vietnam was brought into the conflict and helped overthrow the Khmer Rouge in 1979. Years of civil war followed between government forces and the remaining members of the Khmer Rouge, who surrendered only in 1999. The monarchy was restored in 1993, though the king serves primarily as a figurehead, and the country has embarked on political and economic reforms designed to help it recover from decades of conflict.

Cambodia is a constitutional monarchy with multi-party democracy. The king, limited to an advisory role, serves as the chief of state while a prime minister is head of government. The prime minister is chosen from the majority party after legislative elections. The executive cabinet, appointed by the prime minister pending legislative approval, is called the Council of Ministers.

The legislative branch is bicameral. The lower house, the National Assembly, has 122 members who are elected by popular vote to five-year terms. The upper house, the Senate, has 61 members. The king is responsible for appointing two of these members; a further two are chosen by the National Assembly, and the remaining members are elected by popular vote to six-year terms. The Senate serves in an advisory capacity to the more powerful lower house.

Political Parties

Although it is officially a parliamentary representative democracy, Cambodia is essentially a one-party state. The country's most powerful political party is the Cambodian People's Party (CPP). A major opposition party is the Cambodian National Rescue Party, which in 2014 reached an agreement with the CPP following a year-long electoral boycott. Other parties include the Sam Rainsy Party and Funcinpec (United National Front for an Independent, Neutral, Peaceful and Cooperative Cambodia). Minor political parties are numerous and include the Khmer Front Party, the Khmer Republican Party, the Rice Party, United People of Cambodia, and the Indra Buddra City Party.

Local Government

Cambodia is divided into twenty provinces and three municipalities. A governor presides over each provincial division, which is subdivided into districts, communes and villages. Each of Cambodia's municipalities are subdivided into sectors and wards. A mayor oversees each municipality. Aside from governors and mayors, local governments consist of elected People's Committees that oversee the civil bureaucracy.

Judicial System

Cambodia's judicial branch is developing. The 1993 constitution makes provision for a Supreme Court, a Supreme Council of the Magistracy to appoint and oversee judges, an appeals court, and lower courts. In addition, the Constitutional Council is responsible for interpreting the legality of laws. An important temporary tribunal, intended to try those who committed atrocities during the reign of the Khmer Rouge, has received significant international funding.

Taxation

In Cambodia, trafficking of non-taxed goods remains widespread and much of the country's poor population does not pay taxes. In addition, corruption and lack of government transparency makes it difficult to tell what monies are collected or appropriated illegally and by whom. The Cambodian government collects an income tax, but does not collect real estate taxes, social security taxes, unemployment taxes or inheritance taxes. Foreign investors are subject to taxes on their earnings and the tax rate is dependent upon industry. Oil, gas, and mineral operations pay a higher profit tax. In order to encourage new development in the economy, the government can grant a tax holiday for new business operations of up to eight years.

Armed Forces

The Royal Cambodian Armed Forces (RCAF) consists of an army, navy, and air force, as well as the Royal Gendarmerie of Cambodia, or military police. Since 2006, a small contingent of Cambodian forces has assisted in UN peacekeeping missions in Sudan. In 2010, Cambodian peacekeeping forces were also dispatched to Chad and the Central African Republic. Also in 2010, to help support Cambodian troops, the government announced the corporate sponsorship of the armed forces.

Foreign Policy

The foreign policy of the Cambodian government places priority on the development of relations with regional neighbors, as well as the strengthening and development of foreign relations with donor countries throughout the world. These foreign relations have become crucial as Cambodia continues to face massive recovery issues following the devastating social, economic, and political effects of the Khmer Rouge rule. As one of the world's least developed countries, Cambodia largely relies on foreign investment to spur these redevelopment efforts.

Cambodia is an active member of the Association of Southeast Asian Nations (ASEAN), through which it seeks to maintain stable and friendly relations with countries in the region, including Brunei, Indonesia, Malaysia, Myanmar, Laos, the Philippines, Singapore, Thailand and Vietnam. The Cambodian government has also worked with ASEAN and the UN to settle disputes within the region. In addition, Cambodia joined the World Trade Organization (WTO) in 2004. Membership in the WTO and ASEAN required Cambodia to enact reciprocal tariff reductions and trade legislation that present national budgetary issues for the government. Cambodia is also a member of the Asian Development Bank (ADB), which serves as the country's largest lending agency. The tourism industry remains Cambodia's largest economic and foreign exchange activity.

Cambodia's foreign relations have also been influenced by the country's location between Thailand and Vietnam. The Cambodian government has worked to integrate its economic interests with Thailand. However, the two countries continue to have territorial disputes; there are claims of Thai encroachments into Cambodia. In July 2008, Thai and Cambodian armed forces engaged in a months-long standoff over the ancient Hindu temple, Preah Vihear, on the Thailand-Cambodian border that resulted in the death of two Cambodian soldiers. This border has never been fully defined, in part because it is littered with landmines left from decades of war. In addition, Cambodia and Vietnam continue to dispute the large part of southern Vietnam, called Kampuchea Krom, which Cambodia claims as its own. In recent years, disputes with Laos have developed over proposed dam construction.

Relationships with China and Japan play integral roles in Cambodian foreign policy. Cambodia receives substantial bilateral aid from both countries, with Japan providing the largest amount of support. China also maintains strong ties to the government and former king, Norodom Sihanouk (1922–), who abdicated in 2004. In addition, at the end of July 2008, a Japan-Cambodia investment agreement went into effect, further strengthening the economic relations between those two countries.

Human Rights Profile

International human rights law insists that states respect civil and political rights, and also promote an individual's economic, social and cultural rights. The United Nations (UN) Universal Declaration of Human Rights (UDHR) is recognized as the standard for international human rights. Its authors sought the counsel of the world's great thinkers, philosophers, and religious leaders, and were careful to create a document that reflects the core values shared by every world culture. (To read this document or view the articles relating to cultural human rights, visit: http://www.udhr.org/UDHR/default.htm.)

The Cambodian constitution of 1993 provides for a wide range of internationally recognized human rights. The document contains a chapter on "The Rights and Obligations of Khmer Citizens." Since the adoption of the constitution, the UN appointed a special representative of the secretary-general for human rights in Cambodia, and the UN high commissioner for human rights opened a Cambodian office. These institutions, along with local and international human rights groups, have documented a wide range of human rights violations.

Cambodia's constitution is generally in line with Article 18 of the UDHR, which outlines freedom of religion. The constitution prohibits discrimination based on religion. However, Buddhism is the state religion and receives preferential treatment. The government promotes national Buddhist holidays, provides Buddhist training and education to monks and others, and supports groups that research and publish materials on Khmer culture and Buddhist teachings.

Article 19 of the UDHR protects the universal rights to freedom of opinion and expression. These rights can be difficult for citizens to exercise fully in Cambodia, particularly as they apply to political expression. The government and the major political parties have in the past carried out successful lawsuits against political opponents and those who have criticized state policies, such as the October 2005 arrest of critics of Cambodia's border treaties with Vietnam. In addition, the constitution limits free speech by requiring that it not adversely affect public security. Recently the Ministry of Information reinforced this decree by issuing a directive that limits and prohibits publishers and editors from running articles that insult or defame government leaders and institutions.

Child labor in Cambodia is rampant and in many cases ignored. This issue has become particularly challenging in the early 21st century, as a construction boom has increased the need for cheap labor. Many of these workers are children—some as young as six—who either quit or are forced to leave school to sign on for hazardous work in factories or at construction sites. A 2006 study conducted by the World Bank, ILO and UNICEF estimated that there were 1.5 million children involved in illegal labor in Cambodia.

In addition, human trafficking has become a serious problem in Cambodia. Although the constitution outlaws trafficking in persons, Cambodia is a source, destination and transit country for men, women and children trafficked for sexual exploitation and labor. However, Cambodia is a signatory to the Coordinated Mekong Ministerial Initiative against Trafficking (COMMIT). This organization works to ensure the legal, social and community protection of victims of trafficking, as well as to provide law enforcement agencies with the capacities to prevent trafficking.

Other human rights violations in Cambodia include the torture of prisoners by law enforcement agencies and the use of forced confessions as legal evidence during trials, despite both being outlawed under Cambodian law. In addition, there have been reports of police, prosecutors and investigating and presiding judges accepting bribes. Many outside agencies have largely attributed prevalence of prostitution and trafficking, and lax law enforcement, to this corruption.

ECONOMY

Overview of the Economy

Decades of conflict destroyed Cambodia's economy. In recent years, some progress has been made in rebuilding and expanding the economy, but major problems remain, such as massive corruption and low levels of technical training. Approximately 40 percent of the population lives below the poverty line. In 2013, the country's gross domestic product (GDP) was estimated at $15.64 billion. The per capita GDP is $2,600 (USD).

In the capital of Phnom Penh, the two most successful industries are the garment industry and the tourism industry. In 1999, the United States and Cambodia signed a Bilateral Textiles Agreement, which guaranteed Cambodia a quota of U.S. textile imports and encouraged improvements in Cambodian working conditions.

Industry

The Cambodian industrial sector does not have a large base. It accounts for 24 percent of the GDP and employs almost 17 percent of the labor force. Mining, oil drilling, rubber processing, and the manufacture of building materials, furniture, and clothing are the main components of the sector.

Labor

According to the CIA World Factbook, the labor force of Cambodia numbered approximately eight million in 2011. As of 2013, the unemployment rate was estimated at 0.3 percent, an increase of 0.10 percent from 2012.

Energy/Power/Natural Resources

Cambodia's natural resources include oil, natural gas, gemstones (sapphires, rubies, and zircons), phosphates, limestone, clay, salt, iron ore, and arable land. There are also prospects for hydropower and greater oil production. The country once had extensive timber reserves, but these have been seriously depleted over the last decade. Oil, mining, and natural gas are all being explored as future industry options for Cambodia.

Cambodia's environmental record is poor. Logging has taken its toll on the forests, and reforestation programs have not been adequately implemented. In addition, strip mining has destroyed the land in some areas, soil erosion is becoming more common, and the coastal waters have been over-fished. The presence of landmines remains a pressing problem which will not soon be resolved. An estimated four to six million mines and unexploded ordnance have yet to be cleared, and numerous deaths and injuries have resulted from them.

Fishing

Fishing is essential to the lives of Cambodians. Freshwater fish is widely caught and fish is a crucial element of the everyday diet. Freshwater fish species include the giant salmon carp, goby, catfish, perch, and eel. In 2008, it was estimated that Cambodia had the highest per-person fish catch total in the world. Although an estimated three million tons of fish are caught each year in Cambodia, increasing population pressures and the impact of overfishing threatens this cultural lifeline.

The government has made efforts to establish more rigorous fishing season schedules in order to protect the country's fish resources. In addition, regulations related to fish size and species have been recommended by the UN Food and Agriculture Organization and the World Fish Centre. However, illegal fishing practices continue. Increasing industrialization in Cambodia and an increase in dam construction has also impacted the availability of fish resources.

The challenges related to Cambodia's fishing industry are complex. Rural fishermen looking to feed the country's growing population are decreasing regional fish stocks, which in turn negatively impacts the country's overall economy. Cambodia's poor rural population has few alternative food sources, given the lack of available and viable land. The survival of Cambodia's freshwater fishing culture will depend upon finding a balance between a variety of needs and necessities, none of which are mutually exclusive.

Forestry

Since the 1970s, Cambodia has lost over 70 percent of its primary forest cover to deforestation. Deforestation has occurred as a result of illegal logging and as new construction occurs throughout the country. The International Monetary Fund and the World Bank suspended economic aid to Cambodia in the 1990s until the government moved to take more significant steps to combat illegal logging. However, much of the deforestation has also occurred because Cambodia's poor rural population has used wood for fuel and cleared land for agriculture.

Although environmental regulations are in place, corruption and disorganization have allowed illegal foresting to continue. The significant decrease in primary forest cover has jeopardized a variety of Cambodia's native animal species, including bird, mammals, and reptiles. The total annual value of the country's forest products is an estimated $22 million (USD).

Mining/Metals

Cambodia has significant mineral resources, although the country's mineral industry remains undeveloped. Available mineral resources include copper, gold, and gemstones in addition to offshore resources of oil and gas. Mineral operations in Cambodian are overseen by the Ministry of Industry, Mines and Energy (MIME). The contribution of mining to the Cambodian GDP was less than one half of a percent in 2005. Numerous foreign countries have signaled to Cambodia their interest in assisting in the development of the country's mineral industry, including China, South Korea, Thailand, Australia, and the United States. It is likely that mining will be an increasingly significant contributor to the Cambodian economy in the future.

Agriculture

Agriculture accounts for nearly 40 percent of Cambodia's GDP and employs 75 percent of its labor force. Rice is the largest cash crop, and is essential for domestic consumption. Rubber, soybeans, fruits and vegetables are other important crops.

Animal Husbandry

The most commonly domesticated animals in Cambodia are chicken, pigs, water buffalo, and cattle. Livestock animals are used in agricultural production and used for fertilizer. Animal disease control and animal health services remain problematic. Animal feed is generally low quality and not monitored.

Tourism

Cambodia's tourism industry is developing and has been targeted by the government as an integral sector for sustained economic growth. Approximately 100,000 employees are supported by the industry. Tourism in Cambodia centers particularly on Phnom Penh; in 2005, it was estimated that more than one million people visit Phnom Penh annually. In 2010 over 2.5 million people visited Cambodia overall.

By far the most significant tourist draw is the Angkor temple complex, the ancient seat of the Khmer empire. The country's beaches, national parks, and the French colonial architecture are also popular with visitors.

Michael Carpenter, Michael Aliprandini, Lynn-nore Chittom

DO YOU KNOW?

- The Mekong River is the tenth-longest river in the world.
- Rural Cambodians typically live in small houses built on stilts so as to avoid seasonal flooding.

Bibliography

Brinkley, Joel. *Cambodia's Curse: The Modern History of a Troubled Land.* New York: PublicAffairs, 2012.

Chandler, David. *A History of Cambodia*. New York: Westview Press, 2007.

Coates, Karen J. *Cambodia Now: Life in the Wake of War*. Jefferson, North Carolina: McFarland & Company, 2005.

Derks, Annuska. *Khmer Women on the Move: Exploring Work and Life in Urban Cambodia*. Honolulu: University of Hawaii Press, 2008.

Gottesman, Evan R. *Cambodia after the Khmer Rouge: Inside the Politics of Nation Building*. New Haven, Conn: Yale University Press, 2004.

Lonely Planet and Nick Ray. *Cambodia.* Oakland, CA: Lonely Planet, 2014.

Riviere, Joannes. *Cambodian Cooking: A Humanitarian Project in Collaboration with Act for Cambodia*. North Clarendon, VT: Periplus, 2008.

Rooney, Dawn, and Peter Danford. *Angkor: Cambodia's Wondrous Khmer Temples*. Hong Kong: Odyssey, 2005.

Rough Guides. *Rough Guide to Cambodia.* London: Rough Guides, 2014.
Saunders, Graham. *Cambodia—Culture Smart: A Quick Guide to Customs and Etiquette.* London: Kuperard, 2008.
Sheehan, Sean, and Barbara Cooke. *Cambodia.* Tarrytown, NY: Benchmark Books, 2007.
Strangio, Sebastian. *Hun Sen's Cambodia.* New Haven, CT: Yale University Press, 2014.
Zhou, Daguan. *A Record of Cambodia: The Land and Its People.* Seattle: University of Washington Press, 2007.

Works Cited

"Buddhism." *Encyclopedia Britannica Online.* http://www.britannica.com/EBchecked/topic/83184/Buddhism/68762/Rites-of-passage-and-protective-rites
"Cambodia." *CIA World Factbook.* Online. https://www.cia.gov/library/publications/the-world-factbook/geos/cb.html "Cambodia: Buddhism." U.S. Library of Congress website. http://countrystudies.us/cambodia/48.htm
"Cambodia Country Brief." *Australian Government Department of Foreign Affairs and Trade.* August 2008. http://www.dfat.gov.au/geo/cambodia/cambodia_brief.html
"Cambodia Country Report." *UN Economic and Social Commission for Asia and the Pacific website.* http://www.unescap.org/icstd/events/Info-Society-Stats-Workshop-2007/Cambodia.pdf
"Cambodia: Cultural Profile." *Visiting Arts: Cultural Profiles Project website.* http://www.culturalprofiles.net/cambodia/Directories/Cambodia_Cultural_Profile/-1792.html "Cambodia." Culture Grams website. http://www.cseas.niu.edu/outreach/KMcKee/Justice/Handout1B.pdf
"Cambodia." *Encyclopedia Britannica Online.* http://www.britannica.com/EBchecked/topic/90520/Cambodia.
"Cambodia: Families." U.S. Library of Congress website. http://www.country-data.com/cgi-bin/query/r-2124.html
"Cambodia: Language, Culture, Customs and Etiquette." *Kwintessential website.* http://www.kwintessential.co.uk/resources/global-etiquette/cambodia.html
"Cambodia." London: *Lonely Planet*, 2008. Science Daily website. http://www.sciencedaily.com/releases/2005/03/050326101411.htm
Cambodian Ministry of Public Works and Transport website. http://www.mpwt.gov.kh/
"Cambodia Socio-Economic Survey, 2004." *Cambodian National Institute of Statistics website.* http://statsnis.org/SURVEYS/CSES2003-04/summary.htm
"Cambodia." UNESCO website. http://portal.unesco.org/geography/en/ev.php-URL_ID=2395&URL_DO=DO_TOPIC&URL_SECTION=201.html
Cambodian Living Arts website. http://www.cambodianlivingarts.org/about
"Cambodia: Child Labour Surges with Building Boom." *Child Rights Information Network website.* June 17, 2008. http://www.crin.org/resources/infodetail.asp?id=17543
Cowden, Michael, and Pin Sisovann. "Auto Sales Driven by Burgeoning Middle Class." *The Cambodian Daily*, July 19, 2005. http://www.camnet.com.kh/cambodia.daily/selected_features/cd-19-7-05.htm
"CLT: The Royal Ballet of Cambodia." *UNESCO website* http://portal.unesco.org/en/ev.php-URL_ID=17902&URL_DO=DO_TOPIC&URL_SECTION=201.html
Crossette, Barbara. "An Ancient Silk Trade Is Reborn." *The New York Times.* April 20, 1997. http://web.ebscohost.com/src/detail?vid=4&hid=12&sid=7f2b4391-274b-4598-b6fb-a33470e6233f@SRCSM1&bdata=JnNpdGU9c3JjLWxpdmU db=ulh&AN=16492913
Embassy of Japan in Cambodia website. Online. *The Transport Trust website.* http://www.kh.emb-japan.go.jp/political/nikokukan/invest-e.htm
Habitat for Humanity Cambodia website. http://www.habitat.org/intl/ap/35.aspx
Hughes, Robert. "Ancient, Frozen Smiles." *Time.* August 18, 1997. http://www.time.com/time/printout/0,8816,986862,00.html#
King, Charles C. "The National Museum of Cambodia." *Mekong Network website.* http://www.mekong.net/cambodia/museum.htm
Lesley University Center for Special Education website. http://www.ldldproject.net/cultures/cambodia/differences/nonverbal.html
McGivering, Jill. "Cambodia's Ambitious Youth." *BBC News Channel.* August 7, 2003. http://news.bbc.co.uk/2/hi/asia-pacific/3132931.stm
Munthit, Ker. "Blogs Open Communication in Cambodia." *USA Today website.* September 21, 2007. http://www.usatoday.com/tech/world/2007-09-21-cambodia-bloggers_N.htm
Mydans, Seth. "Cambodia Asks U.N. for Help in Dispute With Thailand." *The New York Times*, July 23, 2008. http://www.nytimes.com/2008/07/23/world/asia/23cambo.html?_r=3&rcf=world&oref=slogin&oref=slogin
Ray, Nick, and Daniel Robinson. "Cambodia." London: Lonely Planet, 2008.
Travel Etiquette website. http://www.traveletiquette.co.uk/etiquette-in-cambodia.html
UNESCO World Heritage website. http://whc.unesco.org/en/list/374
United Nations Development Fund for Women website. June 2007. http://www.unifem.org/news_events/currents/issue200706.php#cambodia
U.S. Department of State. "Country Reports: Cambodia—2008, released by the Bureau of East Asian and Pacific Affairs. June 2008. http://www.state.gov/r/pa/ei/bgn/2732.htm

U.S. Department of State. "Cambodia: International Religious Freedom Report 2007." http://www.state.gov/g/drl/rls/irf/2007/90132.htm

U.S. Department of State. "Country Reports on Human Rights Practices—2007." Released by the *Bureau of Democracy, Human Rights, and Labor*. March 11, 2008. http://www.state.gov/g/drl/rls/hrrpt/2007/100516.htm

U.S. Department of State. "Country Reports on Human Rights Practices—2005," released by the *Bureau of Democracy, Human Rights, and Labor*." March 8, 2006. http://www.state.gov/g/drl/rls/hrrpt/2005/61604.htm

World Education, Inc. website. http://www.worlded.org/WEIInternet/projects/ListProjects.cfm?Select=Country&ID=38

Worldwide Traveler website.

http://www.theworldwidetraveler.com/destinations/asia/cambodia/

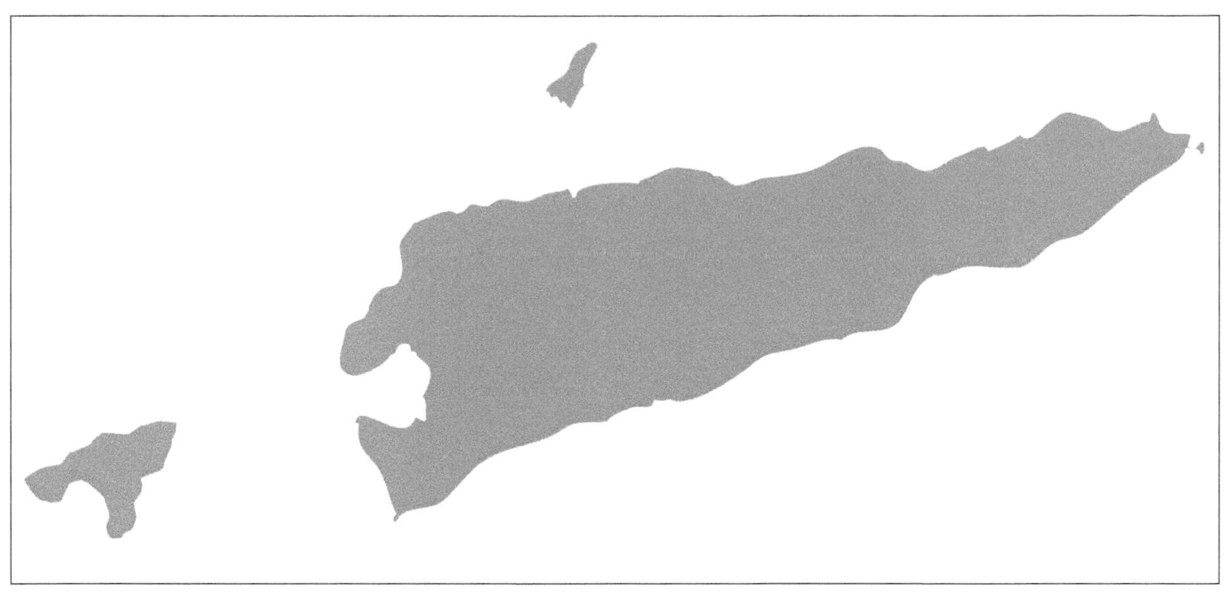

East Timor

(Timor-Leste)

Introduction

East Timor, also known as Timor-Leste, is a small nation in Southeast Asia. The country gained independence from Indonesia in 1999 and its independence was formalized in May 2002. Officially known as the Democratic Republic of Timor-Leste, it is one of the poorest nations in Asia and has a long history of violence and civil war. Portuguese, Malay, and Pacific Islander culture and language are strong influences in the country; the Catholic Church has also been an important political and cultural power.

Between 1975 and 1999, Indonesian occupation forces upheld a repressive government, and human rights violations such as torture, kidnapping, and mass murder were common. Prior to the 1975 occupation, East Timor was a colonial territory of Portugal. It was a valuable colony due to its natural resources such as sandalwood and spices.

The culture of East Timor reflects the population's mixed ethnic heritage. Much of Timorese mythology and history exists in an oral tradition and in poetry, while the music of East Timor reflects both Portuguese and Indonesian influences. Traditional Timorese arts include textile arts, basket weaving, woodcarving, and ceramics.

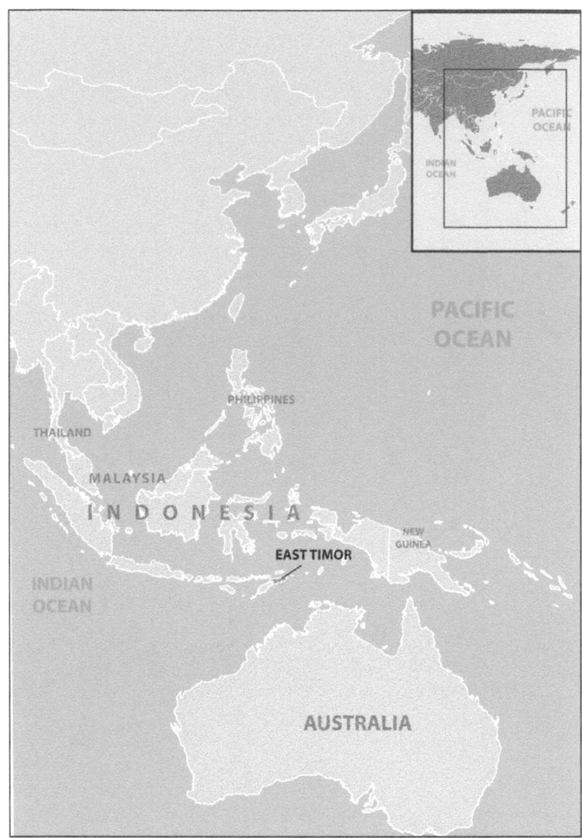

GENERAL INFORMATION

Official Language: Portuguese, Tetum
Population: 1,201,542 (2014 estimate)
Currency: United States dollar
Coins: The US dollar is divided into 100 cents. Coins are available in denominations of 1, 5, 10, and 25 cents, with a 50 cent and 1 dollar coin both rarely used.
Land Area: 14,874 square kilometers (5,742 square miles)
National Motto: "Unidade, Acção, Progresso" (Portuguese, "Unity, Action, Progress")
National Anthem: "Pátria" ("Fatherland")
Capital: Dili
Time Zone: GMT +9
Flag Description: The flag of East Timor is red. The left side or "hoist" side of the flag features a black triangle in front of a yellow triangle. The two triangles represent the country's move from colonialism to independence while the color red represents the struggle to achieve independence. In the center of the black triangle is a white star, representing peace.

Population

The Timorese people have forged their cultural and ethnic identity out of a variety of different cultures and races. Much of the country's

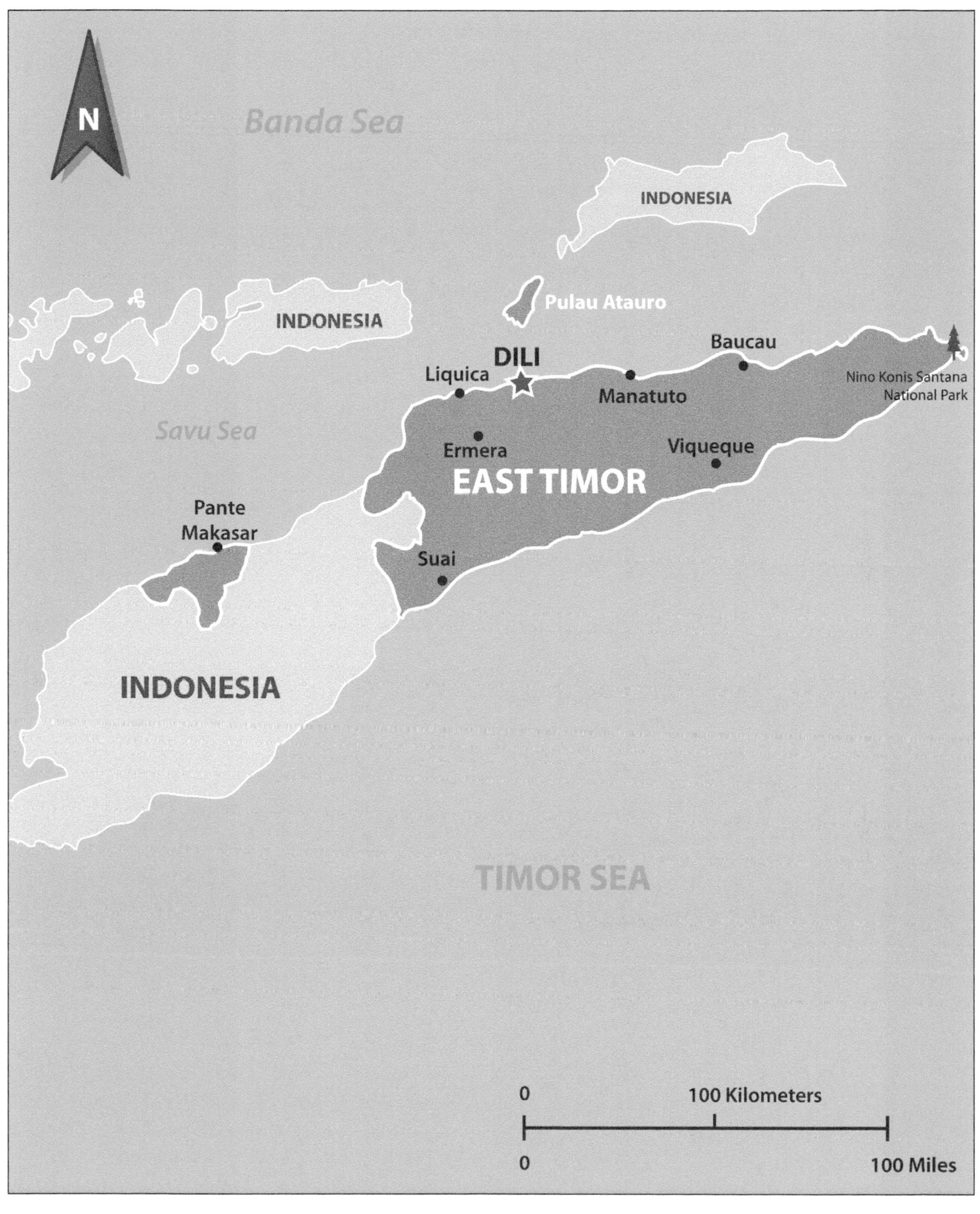
N
Banda Sea
INDONESIA
Pulau Atauro
INDONESIA
Baucau
DILI
Liquica
Manatuto
Nino Konis Santana
National Park
Savu Sea
Ermera
Viqueque
EAST TIMOR
Pante
Makasar
Suai
INDONESIA
TIMOR SEA
0
100 Kilometers
0
100 Miles

Principal City by Population (2014):

- Dili (228,000)

population is of mixed ethnic heritage, including the Afro-Timorese, the Goan-Timorese, the Portuguese-Timorese, and the Sino-Timorese. Cultures from Africa, Polynesia, Malaysia, and Portugal have played a part in forming the Timorese national identity. (East Timorese are sometimes referred to as Maubere.)

The population of East Timor has undergone radical changes since 1975, the year that the Indonesian military invaded. During the occupation, an estimated 200,000 Timorese (roughly a third of the island's population) were killed. Indonesians from other islands were also relocated to East Timor from 1980 onward, with the goal of diluting the island's distinctive culture and quelling the separatist movement.

Dili, the capital, is the largest and principal city of East Timor. Tetum comprise the majority in Dili, but there are also small populations of Eurasians and Arabs. As of 2014, over 30 percent of the population resided in urban areas. The population growth rate was estimated at 2.4 percent in 2014.

Languages

While Portuguese is the one of the official languages of East Timor, it is only spoken by roughly 16 percent of the population. The most widely spoken language is Tetum, the country's second official language. A large number of people also speak Bahasa Indonesia, and many also speak English. Other languages spoken there include Fataluku, Kemak, and Mambae. Portuguese colonization also contributed to the development of Tetum Prasa, a pidgin version of the main language which incorporates numerous loan words from Portuguese, and is generally only spoken in the capital and its environs.

Native People & Ethnic Groups

Timor has experienced migrations of different ethnic groups throughout its history. One of these groups, the Melanesian Atoni people, may have been the first to settle there. The Balu people were another group of early settlers. Some of the island's indigenous people resemble the native populations of New Guinea and Melanesia, while others are similar to the Malay people.

The people of Timor have had a long history of involvement in trade, which brought about interaction between different cultures and peoples. China was a long-time trading partner of the island. The first Europeans reached East Timor in the 16th century from Portugal. Other early European settlers came from Holland; the Dutch eventually came to control West Timor. Today, the largest ethnic group in East Timor is Austronesian. There is also a small Papuan and Chinese population.

Religions

Most citizens of East Timor belong to the Roman Catholic Church, which became involved with social justice issues during the time of the country's occupation and civil war. However, some Timorese still uphold pre-Christian animist beliefs. Catholicism was first introduced to East Timor by Portuguese settlers, and has become the country's leading religious institution. The country is also home to Muslims, Protestants, and Hindu.

Climate

Timor is the most arid island of the Indonesian archipelago. It has a savannah climate that is desert-like in dry areas and tropical in wet regions. East Timor experiences a dry season and a rainy season. The dry season occurs from July to November. The rainy season lasts from December to March, and corresponds with the monsoon.

The weather is often hot and humid, although the mountains tend to experience cooler temperatures and higher humidity. July is the coolest month, while November is the hottest. The temperature ranges from highs of 30° to 34° Celsius (86° to 93° Fahrenheit) to lows of 20° to 23° Celsius (68° to 73° Fahrenheit).

ENVIRONMENT & GEOGRAPHY

Topography

East Timor is located in the far south of the Indonesian archipelago, occupying the eastern half of Timor Island, which is 470 kilometers (292 miles) long and 110 kilometers (68 miles) wide. The country has a mixture of tropical rainforests, such as those found throughout Indonesia, and arid ecosystems that are similar to those found in northern Australia.

The Timor Sea separates the island from Australia, to the southeast. The Wetar Strait lies to the north of the island, and the Ombai Strait is located to the northwest. East Timor's territory also includes the Oecussi enclave in Indonesian West Timor, and the islands of Atauro and Jaco.

East Timor is a mountainous country with many rocky outcroppings known as fatus. A range of mountains stretches across the middle of the island. The highest peak is Mount Tatamailau, which measures 2,963 meters (9,721 feet) high. A large plateau covers most of the eastern part of the island, and a number of rivers run through the mountains.

The capital of Dili is positioned on the northern coast of the island of Timor, one of the Lesser Sunda Islands, along the Ombai Strait, which connects the Savu and Banda seas. The coastal plain along the city's northern edge and west and east of the city is dominated by beaches. Dili is also the country's largest settlement.

Plants & Animals

East Timor has both arid and tropical regions, and a wide variety of flora and fauna. Eucalyptus and acacia are commonly found in the forests; the island is also home to rainforests. One of the most valuable trees found in Timor is the sandalwood, which grows in upland areas. Grasses and shrubs are common in low-lying savannah areas.

There are a number of animals found on the island, including a marsupial known as the cuscus, and a variety of monkeys, deer, civet cats, snakes, and crocodiles. Buffalo are also common there. The kuda is a breed of pony native to the country; other domestic animals include pigs, goats, and dogs.

A marsupial known as the cuscus lives on the island of East Timore.

Among the birds found in East Timor include the Timor black pigeon (Turacoena modesta), the yellow-crested cockatoo (Cacatua sulphurea), the Timor sparrow (Padda fuscata), and the Wetar ground-dove (Gallicolumba hoedtii). Many birds living in East Timor are listed as endangered or vulnerable species.

CUSTOMS & COURTESIES

Greetings

When men greet each other in East Timor, they normally shake hands. Women often greet each other with a kiss on the cheek, even when meeting for the first time. When a man and woman are introduced, they will usually shake hands. If they are well acquainted, they will usually kiss on the cheek.

Some Tetum greeting phrases show the influence of the Portuguese language. Timorese greet each other with a simple "Elo" ("Hello"), or with a more time-specific phrase such as "Bon dia" ("Good morning"), "Botarde" ("Good afternoon"), or "Bonoite ("Goodnight"). The Timorese phrases of "Hau ba lai" or "Adeus" are commonly used when saying farewell. "Diak ka lai?" is a common phrase to ask how someone is doing, with a common reply being "Diak, obrigadu" as a male, or "Diak, obrigada" for females.

Gestures & Etiquette

Timorese people generally abide by the Far Eastern cultural value of "face." Face is a combination of honor, public reputation, and dignity that is attributed to a person. Timorese people are thus characterized by outward humility; it is more important to be polite than to be truthful, as it maintains agreeable relations. Communication tends to be of an indirect style, though direct eye contact is usually acceptable. Conflicts are often dealt with through a third party.

Physical contact during conversation is more common in Timor-Leste than in the West, as Timorese are accustomed to interacting within a large family. Male friends often hold hands in friendship, though women and men do not hold hands in public. Most public displays of affection are frowned upon. Touching other people's heads is also seen as disrespectful.

Eating/Meals

Chronic food shortages and poverty have resulted in limited resources for the majority of East Timorese. As a result, the East Timorese lifestyle is one of subsistence, and locally available produce, meat, and grains are the standard. Imported food and Western style dishes are available in urban restaurants. Timorese coffee is very popular, as is tea. Many rural households and eateries serve fermented palm wine. Restaurants in the city have imported Portuguese wines and beer from Mozambique (a former Portuguese colony).

Visiting

Despite any hardships, hospitality remains important to the East Timorese. When invited to someone's home, it is appropriate to bring a gift such as red wine or chocolate. Money will only be accepted if it is said to be for the children. Punctuality is not highly valued in Timor-Leste, and it is expected that people will arrive late to most events. However, when invited to dine at someone's home, it is considered respectful to arrive on time.

LIFESTYLE

Family

Most East Timorese live a rural lifestyle that has often been characterized as feudal in nature. As a result, the family unit and the institution of marriage remain strong, and most families are close. Children are usually responsible for taking care of their parents when they grow older, and they often help out financially as well. Many families also have relatives who have emigrated, and the money they send provides a substantial portion of income for many families.

The birth rate in Timor-Leste is among the highest in the world, at approximately 7.8 births per woman. Families are large, though many families now have fewer children due to economic strain. Maternal death remains a problem in the early 21st century, as approximately 300 women die from complications for every 100,000 babies born. Infant mortality is also high, estimated at 39 deaths per 1,000 live births in 2014.

Traditional Roman Catholic values are strong in Timor-Leste, where about 97 percent of the population is Roman Catholic. Although only 33 percent are practicing, the church has a broad influence stemming from its role as a source of national identity during the occupation of the Muslim Indonesians. A tradition of animist spiritualism also remains strong, and there is a heightened sense of fear and worship for ancestors for those that adhere to animism as their main religion.

Housing

Traditional Timorese houses often have thatched roofs, earth or bamboo floors, and walls made of bamboo. There is usually a veranda (roofed open area attached to a house), with woven screens hanging to create privacy. Urban houses often mix the traditional and contemporary styles by adding brick walls or cement floors, or even corrugated iron roofs. Rural houses are usually built in aldeias, which are hamlets up in the hills. This style of grouping was encouraged by the government to highlight sustainable means of development. Since the majority of Timorese live in rural areas, it is imperative to monitor sustainable development in the countryside rather than only in urban areas.

The post-election violence and destruction in 1999 demolished approximately 70 percent of housing in Timor-Leste, forcing over 200,000 people to emigrate into the safety of Indonesian West Timor. The refugees returned once the violence calmed down, but they returned to an enormous housing shortage and property disputes.

Food

The cuisine of East Timor is similar to other East Asian cuisines, with distinct Indonesian and Portuguese influences modified with uniquely Timorese spices. Rice is the staple food of East Timor, and typical local meals include rice with satay or pen bose, an Indonesian corn stew. Grilled sardines, a traditionally Portuguese dish, are also popular in Timorese cuisine. Timorese cook with chicken, pork, and goat meat, as those are the animals normally raised for food. Meat is usually grilled or fried, and the meat selection depends on what is locally available.

Other main crops include maize, cassava, taro, and sweet potatoes. The vegetables most commonly grown and used are beans, cabbage, spinach, onions, and cowpeas. Timorese fruits include coconuts, mangos, bananas, watermelons, and papayas. Fish is another source of protein in their diet. Meals are generally cooked with a variety of spices.

It is important to note the widespread food insecurity in Timor-Leste, a result of low incomes, drought, low crop yields, and civil instability. Regular food shortages are a reality for one-third of Timorese people, meaning that malnutrition is a significant issue.

Life's Milestones

Timor-Leste is a predominantly Roman Catholic nation—one of only two in Asia—and many milestones are rooted in the Catholic faith. This includes baptism, first communion, and marriage. First birthdays are often a cause for great celebration in Timor-Leste. This is possibly due to the high infant mortality rate, which means a child reaching the first birthday provides some relief to the parents.

One of the most unique observances of the East Timorese is their funerary ceremonies, particularly among the Atsabe Kemak peoples. The elaborate series of funerary ceremonies, called tau tana mate, include animal sacrifice, and are considered metama no, or "black rituals." The second phase of the funerary rites, called leko-cici lia, is a complex process of digging up the bones of ancestors to clean and rebury them. During this process, the gase ubu, which is the sacred man of the clan, guides the ancestors' souls through ritual chants. As the chants follow an in-depth history of the clan, this ritual can take more than fourteen hours.

These funeral rites carry a high economic cost, particularly due to the large numbers of animal sacrifice. The first stage of the ceremonies, huku bou, calls for at least five water buffaloes to be sacrificed alongside the sacrifice of pigs and goats. These funerary traditions are an important means of maintaining strong bonds across generations and between the living and dead. The Kemak people value the power of these ceremonies to restructure and renew social relations.

CULTURAL HISTORY

Art

Timor-Leste culture is largely influenced by Catholicism and Austronesian (referring to the islands of the central and South Pacific) legends, with numerous Malay and Portuguese influences. The main decorative arts in East Timor are weaving, pottery, and carving. Examples of traditional tribal artwork can still be seen today, and include masks carved from bone and wood, jewelry made from silver, and baskets weaved from the betel plant. Some of the masks represent ancestors, and were used as a medium for the living to contact their dead relatives. The masks were also used to tell stories and evoke memories of the ancestors. They also carved animal skulls, engraving them with decorative designs.

The trademark craft of Timor-Leste is perhaps the weaving of tais, woven cotton cloths used in religious ceremonies, special rituals, and dances. Women wear feto tais, shaped like tubes, as a type of dress, while men wear mane tais around their waists. Scarves made from tai cloth, called selendang, are worn by both men and women on special occasions. Tais are often used as gifts, for welcoming important figures, and for covering dead bodies. The number of tais laid on a dead body—and the higher their quality—represent the social status of the deceased. These textiles are highly valued as an expression of local culture and knowledge, and different designs, passed down matrilineal lines, show folklore and historical stories. During the Indonesian occupation (1975–1999), tais even served as a sort of passive resistance for women who asserted their identity through design. Tais were also traded for goods to support the resistance.

Textile arts in East Timor also range from bags and tablecloths to bookmarks. The process of making the textile is a highly respected cultural tradition, principally done by women. Traditionally, the process begins with turning cotton wool into thread. Spinning the cotton takes one month, followed by one week to boil and dry the cotton, followed by four days of rolling the cotton. Finally, it takes two months to make the design with the thread. Because this is a long process, many women now make tais using modern threads imported from Indonesia.

Woodcarving, on the other hand, is primarily done by men. They use local woods, such as teak, palm, eucalyptus, and cedar, to carve a myriad of objects. These range from masks, statues, jewelry, and furniture, to instruments, boxes, looms, and toys. Boxes to hold betel nuts are a very common craft, carved from bone, wood, coconut shells, bamboo, or horns. (Timorese often chew betel nut, a habit similar to chewing tobacco.) These boxes are called kalau or tempar kapur.

Architecture

Portugal ruled Timor-Leste for over 400 years; Portuguese Timor (1702–1975) was established at the turn of the 18th century. The Portuguese left a significant legacy of colonial architecture. The capital of Dili and the old city of Baucau both have examples of Portuguese-style architecture, including a Portuguese fort in Dili that dates back to 1627. Urban buildings are usually in the Portuguese style of architecture, though traditional elements are often blended in. The colonial style traditionally included a concrete or brick building with high ceilings and a ceramic tiled roof. Many of these buildings have front gardens as well, and they are often situated right on the street. A mixed-style house may be concrete with a front garden and a thatched roof.

Traditional houses, called uma lulik, were particularly common in the eastern region of the country. In general, houses are traditionally built on stilts (due to flooding) and are constructed using a variety of local materials. These include grass, palm and palm thatch, local wood, bamboo, and Ylang-Ylang thatch. The use of local wood has brought certain species, including sandalwood and ironwood, close to extinction. Seven different types of residential architecture have been named, corresponding to different regions and different migration patterns: Maubisse, Bobonaro, Viqueque, Baucau, Lautem, Suai, and Oecusse. The styles differ in the shape of their thatched roofs, the height of their stilts, and the layout of the entrance and interior.

Drama

One of the best known theater troupes in East Timor is the Bibi Bulak Performance Arts and Music Troupe. The group tours throughout the country to perform live and also performs on the radio. Its work aims to entertain, while also educating the public on such social issues as domestic violence, gender quality, and reproductive health. Bibi Bulak is connected with the free, non-profit art school known as Arte Moris, which was founded by Swiss artists Luca and Gabriela Gansser.

Music & Dance

Both Portuguese and Indonesian musical traditions have strongly influenced Timorese music, creating a uniquely blended style. Portuguese influence on Timor-Leste's music is very clear in the popularity of fado music, a type of melancholy singing with guitar accompaniment. The Indonesian influence brought gamelan music, performed with a set of percussion instruments such as drums, marimba (similar to a xylophone), and gongs. This musical ensemble, of Javanese origin, also combines the sounds of bamboo flutes, wind chimes, and stringed instruments. (The term gamelan can also refer to the set of instruments used in performing this style of music.) The combination of fado with gamelan accompaniment has created a distinctly Timorese music style.

Much of modern Timorese music stems from the independence movement, and it has been a strong force in supporting Timorese identity. The guitar, as well as several native string instruments, plays an important part in Timorese music.

A longstanding tradition of folk music is the likurai, a dance with a small drum that women performed to welcome men back from war. Women now perform contemporary versions of the dance as courtship. The bidu hena mutin dance is more formal, and it is performed to welcome visitors to ceremonies. It is contemporarily performed as a casual, social dance on nights where there is a full moon.

Literature

Before the arrival of the Portuguese, Timorese stories were not written down, but rather passed along as oral folklore. Often, these stories were didactic in nature, and included various proverbs, jokes or creation myths. One popular Timorese myth attributes the creation of the island of Timor to the death of a crocodile (the island of Timor, of which East Timor comprises half, is shaped like a crocodile). Poetry was also a prominent oral tradition, and remains a strong tradition in modern times. When the Portuguese arrived, they introduced writing as a means of enabling the Timorese to evangelize. The practice of writing increased once the Portuguese colonized Timor-Leste.

The tradition of literature developed slowly, in part due to the low numbers of people who could read and write. Through the beginning of the 20th century, few literary works were produced. Political changes in Portugal in the early 1970s sparked large shifts in literary output in Timor-Leste. Many young authors began to publish work in Tetum, the ethnic language, and Portuguese, despite an Indonesian ban on the Portuguese language.

Literature in Timor-Leste traditionally focuses on poetry. Prime Minister Xanana Gusmão (1946–) is a renowned writer of prose and poetry. He is particularly known for the books he wrote as leader of the Revolutionary Front for an Independent East Timor (Frente Revolucionária de Timor-Leste Independente, or FRETILIN), a resistance organization during the country's fight for independence. His poetry and paintings depict Timorese culture and values. Francisco Borja da Costa (1946–1975), who wrote the text of the national anthem, was a poet who wrote primarily in Tetum, the indigenous language. He was killed on the first day of the Indonesian invasion of East Timor in December 1975. Other notable writers include Fernando Sylvan (1917–1993), a poet and folklore writer who wrote in Portuguese, as well as a whole litany of poets whose works explore national liberation, loss, and struggle.

CULTURE

Arts & Entertainment

Timor-Leste has aimed to use art as a force for rebuilding the country's psychological and social identity. Art is seen as a viable means of therapy for the people who have suffered trauma. To this end, the non-profit arts school Arte Moris, the country's first fine arts school, was established in 2003, after the country gained independence. The school was established with the help of a Swiss painter.

In 2008, a group of young Timorese artists created an art collective called Gembel. (Gembel is a derogatory Indonesian word meaning "homeless person" or "bum.") This art collective works on projects in music, visual arts, and theatre, operating without studios, official structure, or government support. These artists aim to show a different image of Timorese youth, one apart from the gang violence portrayed in international media. The artwork of Gembel focuses on themes of cooperation, relationships, and discussions, while bringing in traditional cultural themes and ideas.

Because they have limited access to materials and equipment, printmaking has been a feasible art form for Gembel. In October 2008, Australian and Indonesian art groups joined Gembel to produce collaborative art projects that would be shown in Indonesia and Australia. This represented a significant step of modern Timorese art being exhibited outside the country.

Since the turn of the 21st century, Timorese music has been strongly tied to the independence movement. The group Lahane was commissioned by the United Nations (UN) to write a song inspiring people to participate in the referendum. In addition, the band Dili All Stars had a popular song that was played as an anthem leading up to the referendum. Much of the music popular in Timor-Leste today is mixed with different international styles, as a result of the high number of East Timorese who emigrated to Portugal, Australia, and other countries. Teo Batiste Ximenes, a Timorese man raised in Australia, became a popular musician incorporating the folk rhythms of Timor-Leste into his songs. At refugee camps in Portugal, traditional Timor-Lesteese styles were blended with music from other Portuguese colonies such as Angola and Mozambique. Other modern musicians are influenced by hip-hop, reggae, and rock music.

Popular sports in East Timor include cycling, badminton, weightlifting, and table tennis. The country belongs to the International Olympic Committee.

CULTURAL SITES & LANDMARKS

Timor-Leste has a wealth of built cultural heritage, ranging from its traditional architecture to structures built during the country's colonial period. The capital of Dili boasts a Portuguese castle built in 1627, along with many examples of colonial architecture such as Portuguese churches. (However, many buildings were damaged following the ensuing violence of the 1999 independence vote and remain in need of restoration.) The city of Baucau also has many buildings remaining from Portuguese colonialism, as well as caves that the Japanese used during their World War II occupation. There are also numerous Portuguese fortresses built in East Timor, including the 17th-century fort in Maubara, which once served as a prison, and an old Portuguese garrison in Fatsuba, overlooking the town of Pantemakassar.

Evidence of East Timor's Catholicism is abundant in Dili, as the city is home to numerous churches, including one on the waterfront, which served as a focal point for resistance during the occupation. Built during the Portuguese era, it is known as the San Antonio or Motael Church. A massive statue of Christ also overlooks Dili from atop a nearby headland. One major landmark that speaks to the city's grim history of violence and repression is the Santa Cruz Cemetery. It was there in 1991 that Indonesian troops fired on a peaceful protest, killing an uncertain number of people (thought to be several hundred).

Timor-Leste also boasts a wide diversity of landscapes. The Lautém area is characterized by savannah plains and expansive rice paddies. The Manatuto coastal areas have dramatic cliffs hovering above the ocean. Maubisse, Baucau, and Viqueque are all mountainous areas, in contrast with the flat Oecussi enclave and the rice and coffee fields of Bobonaro. There are even rainforests (Lore) and islands (Ataúro and Jaco) to complete the diverse offerings of Timor-Leste. In 2007, the country declared its first national park, Nino Konis Santana National Park, which is home to numerous endemic bird species and other significant biodiversity. The park is named after Nino

Konis Santana (1959–1998), an important East Timorese guerilla liberation fighter.

Libraries & Museums

The United Nations Educational, Scientific and Cultural Organization (UNESCO) has worked with East Timor in recent decades to help preserve and protect the country's historical architecture, works of art, and cultural heritage. UNESCO helped found The Museum and Cultural Centre of Timor-Leste, which features antique tribal works, including statuary and bowls. Plans are in place to construct the country's first National Library building and National Archives building.

Holidays

Because the majority of East Timorese belong to the Catholic Church, many public holidays in East Timor are Christian holidays. The country also celebrates its independence on May 20. November 12 is set aside to honor those killed in the Santa Cruz massacre, a mass murder of East Timorese student protestors that occurred on November 12, 1991.

Youth Culture

Timor-Leste's extremely high fertility rate has resulted in a population with more than 50 percent under the age of seventeen. Although there has been a sharp increase in youth gang involvement in recent years, there have been several positive examples of youth pushing for progress.

Radio is a popular media source, due to the high illiteracy rate in Timor-Leste. When community radio stations began opening, many people were impressed by the number of young people who signed up to volunteer. These volunteers have learned broadcasting skills, and are a continuous source of information and news for the many communities that tune in. The radio stations have also attracted young female volunteers, whose options for work are often limited by protective families.

Timorese youth came into the spotlight in 2006 when there was an eruption of gang-related violence. A high number of male youth are members of martial arts groups, and these groups have showed behavior increasingly similar to gang behavior, becoming involved in a growing number of violent incidents. Other volatile conditions include the tens of thousands of displaced people who have fled from unrest, and are now living in haphazard housing. The unemployment rate, which is estimated at up to 40 percent for young males in urban areas, is a symptom—and cause—of the widespread poverty.

SOCIETY

Transportation

Buses are the most common mode of transportation in East Timor, and run to most parts of the country. The most popular variety of bus is the mikrolet, a minibus that functions as a bus within and between cities. Mikrolets are usually very crowded, but offer daily routes to other towns. Another Indonesian-style vehicle is a bemos, a van that runs from cities to nearby hamlets and villages. Affordable taxi service is also available in some parts of the country. Traffic moves on the left-hand side of the road.

Transportation Infrastructure

Dili's Comoro Airport has limited options. There are daily flights to Darwin, Australia, but for all other destinations, a connection must be made in Bali. Timor-Leste has no railway. Ferry service connects Dili and the Oecusse enclave (in West Timor). The country's poor and lacking infrastructure, coupled with the nation's often difficult topography, results in some rural areas becoming inaccessible during certain parts of the year, or if impacted by natural disasters such as floods.

Media & Communications

Media in Timor-Leste is still in the development stage. After more than 400 years under Portuguese rule, freedom of the press was virtually nonexistent and censorship was widespread. Independence for Timor-Leste was not addressed in the media until the Portuguese rule was nearly over, around 1975. The socialist revolution in

Lisbon brought discussion of Timorese independence to the media for the first time.

However, the end of Portuguese rule was overshadowed by the quick succession of Indonesian occupation. The Indonesian ruling restricted media access to carefully constructed government propaganda. An underground media sector emerged, in efforts to counter this extreme censorship. One example of this underground media was the group Radio Mubere that illegally broadcasted news from guerilla independence fighters to the people.

During the violent aftermath of the Timor-Lesteese vote for independence in 1999, the Indonesian Military and Militia left an enormous path of destruction. This included the destruction of the country's printing facilities and TV and radio broadcasting facilities. The violence spurred Timor-Lesteese journalists into action after the Indonesian troops withdrew. Together, these journalists founded the Timor Loro Sa'e Journalists Association (TLJA) to seek to maintain integrity in the media.

Several new daily newspapers and weekly magazines were founded in 1999, and five of them are still being printed today. The weekly *Lalenok* was the first regularly published media source to be printed in Tetum, the Timorese dialect, which was traditionally recognized as only a spoken language. *Lalenok* aimed to legitimize Tetum as a standard language, in addition to exploring its possibilities in writing.

Several community radio stations also arose after independence was won, including Radio Falintil, founded by the members of the former underground group Radio Mubere. Because of the low literacy rate in Timor-Leste, radio is a popular medium. However, media in Timor-Leste has not maintained the momentum it had in 1999, as many people moved on to other sectors because they could not afford to be journalists for little or no pay.

As of the early 21st century, public Internet access was only in the capital, Dili. As of 2010, only an estimated 0.2 percent of the population—representing roughly 2,100 people—are Internet users.

SOCIAL DEVELOPMENT

Standard of Living

East Timor ranked 138th out of 207 countries and territories on the 2014 United Nations Human Development Index, which measures quality of life and standard of living indicators.

Water Consumption

According to 2012 statistics, approximately 70 percent of the population of Timor-Leste has access to improved drinking water, while only an estimated 39 percent of the population has access to improved sanitation. Students and faculty from the University of Western Australia (UWA) have assisted with water quality and sanitation improvement initiatives in East Timor in recent years. The Australian government has provided over $1 billion in aid in development assistance to East Timor.

Education

Education in East Timor is managed by the Ministry of Education, Youth, Culture, and Sports. Prior to independence, education followed Indonesian models and standards. Since gaining independence, the country has had to build up a national system of education. The education redevelopment project involves training teachers and rebuilding schools, and has been supported by the World Bank and the United Nations Children's Fund.

Schools were reopened after the violence ended in 1999, with the Catholic Church playing a large role in reorganization. Because students often suffer from malnutrition and poor hygiene, schools play an important role in nourishing them and providing them with the support they need in their daily lives. The country's schools provide primary and some secondary education.

The country's only tertiary educational institution, Universitas Timor Timur, was destroyed during the violence in the late 1990s. After East Timor gained independence, the National University of East Timor was constructed and opened in 2000. University education is supported by scholarships for some students. Some students also travel to Australia to pursue higher education. In 2010, the national literacy rate of East Timor was estimated at 58.6 percent.

Women's Rights

Gender equality is assured under the Timorese constitution, and the National Development Plan (NDP) has promised to work toward mainstreaming gender. Timor-Leste signed the Convention on the Elimination of All Forms of Discrimination Against Women (CEDAW), and the Office for the Promotion of Equality was created to consult with the government departments and ministries on promoting gender equality. An increasing number of women have been voted into parliament and selected as village elders. However, the Timorese society continues to be strongly patriarchal and there are many barriers for women seeking leadership positions, or even women seeking to make decisions in their families and communities.

The number of women in the work force has also increased since independence, though only 48.1 percent of women take part in labor, as opposed to 69.3 percent for men. Women continue to be hindered by a high rate of illiteracy and face limited access to education. More women are also bringing cases of gender-based violence to court, including cases of domestic violence. Domestic violence seems to be more widespread than it previously was, though an increased exposure of it in the legal system has also affected numbers.

Many women suffer mental health problems due to traumatic gender-based violence under the Indonesian occupation. Rape, sterilization programs, and other types of sexual abuse were systematically used. Another health issue is the maternal mortality rate, which was 300 deaths per 100,000 live births in 2014, a number somewhat higher than most rates in the region. Early pregnancies are common, and the fertility rate is nearly eight, one of the highest in the world. Hair removal is a noteworthy cultural practice, as women aged 15 and older are expected to remove all hair on their bodies, except for the hair on their head.

Health Care

Political and economic problems have made it very difficult for East Timor to establish a working health care system. During the Indonesian occupation, health services improved, as the Indonesian government attempted to gain the support of the Timorese citizens by providing medical care. Indonesia constructed a number of hospitals and health clinics, and supplied the country with doctors and nurses. However, growing violence in the late 1990s forced many health professionals to leave East Timor.

The country's Division of Health Services has been instrumental in the process of transition from a state of health emergency to a more stable health system. Emergency services were provided by the International Committee of the Red Cross. Religious groups and non-governmental organizations also help to distribute health services in the country, and private health providers are beginning to operate there as well. The largest hospitals are Dili Hospital and Baucau Hospital.

GOVERNMENT

Structure

On November 28, 1975, East Timor achieved independence from Portugal. The Portuguese government had administered East Timor since the early 17th century. The only interruption of Portuguese rule occurred during World War II, when the Japanese took control of the country. After the war, Portugal resumed control of East Timor until the early 1970s, when it began to grant its colonies independence.

The tensions of decolonization and the concern that Indonesia might take control of the country resulted in a coup d'état in April 1975. Begun by the Timorese Democratic Union Party, the coup turned into a civil war when the Revolutionary Front for an Independent East Timor, or FRETILIN, fought back and took over the country. FRETILIN declared East Timor an independent state.

In response, Indonesia invaded. Although it was ordered out of the country by the United Nations, Indonesia maintained that it was protecting East Timor from the FRETILIN government. Guerrilla warfare between supporters of Timorese independence and the Indonesian occupation forces followed, lasting through the 1990s.

During the occupation, civil rights such as freedom of speech, freedom of assembly, and freedom of the press were rigidly suppressed. A number of human rights violations occurred during the occupation, including false arrests and imprisonment, torture, kidnapping, rape, and mass murder. The most notorious large-scale murder occurred in 1991 at Santa Cruz. Overall, the death total resulting from the occupation is thought to have reached 300,000 people.

The worst of the violence and destruction occurred in September 1999, when militia groups burned buildings and destroyed most of the country's infrastructure in retaliation after voters overwhelmingly supported independence. The conflict was contained in 1999 by United Nations peacekeeping forces. With the end of the violence, many refugees returned to East Timor from exile. The country finally gained independence in May 2002.

Today, East Timor is a parliamentary democracy with three separate branches of government: the executive, the legislative, and the judicial. The executive branch consists of a president, who is the head of state, and a prime minister, who is the head of government. East Timor's parliament is made up of one house with 29 elected members, and elections have been supervised by the United Nations.

Political Parties

East Timor's largest political party is the Revolutionary Front of Independent East Timor (FRETILIN). Other parties include the Democratic Party, the National Congress for Timorese Reconstruction, and the Frenti-Mudanca.

Local Government

East Timor is organized into thirteen administrative districts, which are further divided into subdistricts. Subdistricts are divided into sucos or villages. There are 65 subdistricts, and over 440 sucos. Local government operations are overseen by the Ministry for State and Internal Administration.

Judicial System

As a former Indonesia territory, East Timor's system of law is based on that of Indonesia. The country's judicial system is one of the youngest in the world, having been established in 2000. The Supreme Court of Justice is the country's highest court. The head of the Supreme Court of Justice is appointed by the president and serves a four-year term. The other members of the court are selected by the Superior Council for the Judiciary and the National Parliament. There are also four district courts in Baucau, Oecussi, Dili, and Suai. There is also a Court of Appeal in Dili. Following independence, a UN-controlled Ad Hoc Human Rights Court was established in Jakarta to try Indonesian military officials on charges of crimes against humanity.

Taxation

In 2008, the government passed the Taxes and Duties Act. Under the act, both the tax rate for citizens and the wage income tax decreased from 30 to 10 percent. Other taxes levied include import duties and a sales tax rate, which decreased from six to 2.5 percent.

Armed Forces

Timor-Leste's armed forces, officially the Falintil-Forças de Defesa de Timor-Leste (Timor-Leste Defence Force, or FALINTIL-FDTL), consists of an army and small navy. The armed forces' priorities consist mostly to protect against external threats. As of 2010, the defense force maintains just over 1,200 personnel, with plans to develop a force of 3,000 active military personnel by 2020. The United Nations Integrated Mission in Timor-Leste (formerly the UN Office in Timor-Leste, or UNOTIL) left the country at the end of 2012. Significant military training and support comes from Australia, New Zealand, Brazil, Portugal, China, and Malaysia.

Foreign Policy

Timor-Leste prioritizes its foreign relations with countries in the immediate region and countries that serve as donors. The country has been a member of the UN since 2002, and it is currently seeking to join the Association of Southeast Asian Nations (ASEAN). In 2005, it became a member of the ASEAN Regional Forum.

Timor-Leste and Indonesia have full diplomatic relations that are constantly improving. In 2004, Timor-Leste sent humanitarian aid to Indonesian victims of the Indian Ocean tsunami, while Indonesia offered humanitarian assistance for internally displaced people during the Dili unrest in 2006. The two nations formed a bilateral Truth and Friendship Commission (TFC) to determine what actually happened before and immediately following the 1999 independence vote, and to promote reconciliation. The TFC is criticized by many international human rights groups, however, for having made no visible progress and for failing to provide for accountability and prosecutions.

Timor-Leste also maintains good relations with donor countries, including the United States, Australia, and Japan. The U.S., in particular, has a large development assistance program for Timor-Leste, and donated $20.6 million in 2007. (East Timor's currency is the U.S. dollar.) Timor-Leste also maintains solid ties with the European Union (EU), particularly with its former colonizer, Portugal. EU efforts have aimed to increase stability and humanitarian support in Timor-Leste, while also working to decrease poverty. The ultimate goal of this cooperation is to allow Timor-Leste to develop self-sustenance and economic independence. Since 1999, half of all aid donated to Timor-Leste has come from the EU.

Human Rights Profile

International human rights law insists that states respect civil and political rights, and also promote an individual's economic, social and cultural rights. The United Nations (UN) Universal Declaration of Human Rights (UDHR) is recognized as the standard for international human rights. Its authors sought the counsel of the world's great thinkers, philosophers, and religious leaders, and were careful to create a document that reflects the core values shared by every world culture. (To read this document or view the articles relating to cultural human rights, visit: http://www.udhr.org/UDHR/default.htm.)

It is estimated that between 100,000 and 200,000 Timorese people died as a result of the Indonesian occupation, which lasted from 1975 to 1999. The deaths have been attributed to widespread murders, as well as rampant starvation and disease as a consequence of the living conditions imposed by the Indonesian army. The 24-year period was sandwiched by extreme bouts of violence in 1974, the year leading to the Indonesian occupation, and 1999, when militias backed by the Indonesian army massacred over 1,000 people who had voted for Timorese independence.

In 2008, Indonesia accepted guilt for the human rights abuses committed in 1999 after the Timorese vote for independence, but did not offer a formal apology or prosecution of the perpetrators. These abuses clearly violate Article 2 of the UDHR, which states that everyone is entitled to the rights and freedoms of the declaration, regardless of race, sex, national origin, or other distinguishing factors. The Indonesian occupation targeted native Timorese with a brutal campaign of murder and forced relocation. Additionally, Article 5 states that no one should be subjected to torture, a right that was blatantly ignored during the Indonesian occupation. Police abuse has become a problem again in recent years, as Human Rights Watch documented in a 2006 report detailing torture and ill treatment committed by Timor-Leste's national police.

Under the more than 400 years of Portuguese rule and 24 years of Indonesian rule, media in Timor-Leste was highly censored and manipulated as government propaganda. Timor-Leste's 2002 constitution, drafted when independence was officially gained, protects freedom of expression and media, but it also declares that the right to freedom of speech and information will be regulated by the law. In 2005, parliament gave the prime minister the power to enact a new penal code outlining strong penalties for defamation. This law, which denies freedom of expression, was strongly protested by journalists and legal experts, but passed nonetheless.

Although the security situation in Timor-Leste has improved significantly since 1999, stability is still lacking. International security officers and Australian peacekeepers were brought in to heighten security against a backdrop of violent discontent, resulting from economic hardship and unemployment, and weak government institutions. For example, an explosion of violence in 2006 left 37 dead and over 150,000 people displaced from their homes. Furthermore, in 2008, the attempted assassination of President José Ramos-Horta (1949–) was evidence of the high tension between the government and insurgents. This ongoing instability does not allow for the manifestation of Article 28, which entitles everyone to a social order conducive to realizing the rights and freedoms of the declaration.

ECONOMY

Overview of the Economy

East Timor is one of the poorest nations in Asia. Economic problems stem from a lack of jobs and an infrastructure that was extensively damaged during the Indonesian occupation. Rural areas tend to be poorer than urban areas, and lack services such as electricity and a safe water supply. The country's economic future may be based on its supplies of offshore petroleum and natural gas, although it will take a great deal of time and investment to exploit these resources.

Australia, the United States, and the United Nations have given financial support to East Timor. The United States is also one of the country's largest trading partners, along with Australia, Europe, and Japan. East Timor exports coffee, oil, and natural gas to these markets. The country also belongs to the International Monetary Fund, the World Bank, and the Asian Development Bank. East Timor's estimated gross domestic product (GDP) for 2014 was estimated at $8.4 billion USD. The GDP per capita was an estimated $6,800 (USD).

Industry

Manufacturing industries account for nearly one-fifth of East Timor's GDP, while the service industries bring more than half of GDP. The coffee industry is very important to the country's economy. The oil and natural gas industries have the potential to grow into a vital sector. Products that are manufactured in East Timor include soap, perfume, processed food, and chemicals.

Labor

The labor force was estimated at 247,500 in 2012, with the majority of the population—an estimated 64 percent in 2010—employed in the agricultural sector. The unemployment rate was reported as 18.4 percent in 2010.

Energy/Power/Natural Resources

East Timor has significant oil and natural gas reserves located offshore. However, because of the country's past political instability and economic devastation, it has been unable to develop these resources. Turning the oil and gas into a viable industry will require investment and extensive reconstruction of the country's infrastructure.

Fishing

Fishing is a major source of employment in East Timor, particularly on the island of Atauro. Pearl cultivation is an important sector within the fishing industry. The fishing sector, however, remains underdeveloped, and illegal fishing has become a concern at times. Most fishing occurs along the nation's southern and northern coasts, and most of the catch is used for domestic consumption.

Forestry

Sandalwood is a valuable hardwood tree that produces fragrant oil, which can be used to make perfume and other products. The trees are also used as a source of lumber. The country is also home to some of the best bamboo in the world. However, East Timor does face problems related to deforestation, including landslides and decreasing soil fertility. Efforts to better protect and sustainably cultivate the country's forest resources are underway.

Mining/Metals

East Timor has reserves of natural gas and oil. Australian and Japanese country have arranged deals with the country's government to explore and exploit these reserves. Although East Timor's current natural gas and oil infrastructure provides the government with revenue, critics have said that foreign companies are taking advantage of the country's resources for their own gain. Maritime boundaries in the region that would determine the rightful owner of oil fields and gas resources remain in dispute. Nonetheless, the government has established a Petroleum Fund that provides over 95 percent of its revenue.

Agriculture

Agriculture employs the majority of the working population of East Timor, and accounts for approximately 25 percent of its GDP and 90 percent of exports. However, this sector remains underdeveloped and subject to weather conditions such as droughts and flooding. The most important crops are coffee, rice, a coconut byproduct known as copra, and cotton. Other crops that are grown in the country include wheat, tobacco, and potatoes. Livestock yields hides and wool.

Animal Husbandry

Cattle are an important livestock, and some cattle from East Timor are exported to Indonesia. Poultry, pigs, and goats are also increasing in rural areas. However, the lack of knowledge regarding modern livestock farming on East Timor has prevented animal husbandry from become a significant source of revenue or employment.

Tourism

Due to the years of violence and upheaval, East Timor's tourist industry has suffered. However, the government is working to develop this sector. The country has joined the World Tourism Organization and has been trying to promote itself as a new tourist destination, including appearing at the 2010 Shanghai Expo in China. Tourist attractions in East Timor include scuba diving, hiking through the rainforests, and visiting the country's beaches.

The Tourism Directorate of Timor-Leste, which is part of the Ministry of Commerce and Industry, is working to better promote the country as a tourist destination. Portugal and Macau have assisted the country in developing its tourism infrastructure. In 2010, the country's tourism budget was approximately $4 million. Most foreign visitors to East Timor are Australian.

Zoë Westhof, Christina Healey, Michael Aliprandini

DO YOU KNOW?

- The pre-Christian animist religion in East Timor honors the spirits of the dead within ancestral objects called "luliks."

Bibliography

Cocks, Rodney. *Timor-Leste.* Oakland, CA: Lonely Planet, 2011.

Cristalis, Irena. *East Timor: A Nation's Bitter Dawn.* New York: Verso, 2009.

Gunn, Geoffrey C. *Historical Dictionary of East Timor.* Lanham, MD: Scarecrow Press, 2011.

Hamilton, Roy W., and Joanna Barrkman, eds. *Textiles of East Timor.* Los Angeles: Fowler Museum, 2014.

Hicks, David. *Tetum Ghosts and Kin: Fertility and Gender in East Timor.* New York: Waveland Press, 2003.

Joseph, Abraham, and Takako Hamaguchi. *Timor-Lest: The History and Development of Asia's Newest Nation.* Lanham, MD: Lexington Books, 2014.

Kingsbury, Damien, and Michael Leach, eds. *East Timor: Beyond Independence.* New York: Monash UP, 2007.

Leach, Michael, and Damien Kingsbury, eds. *The Politics of Timor-Lest.* Ithaca, NY: Cornell University Press, 2013.

Molnar, Andrea Katalin. *Timor Lest: Politics, History, Culture.* New York: Routledge, 2010.

Tanter, Richard, Gerry Van Klinken, and Desmond Ball, eds. *Masters of Terror: Indonesia's Military and Violence in East Timor.* New York: Rowman & Littlefield, 2006.

Works Cited

"Coders Bare Invasion Death Count." http://www.wired.com/science/discoveries/news/2006/02/70196?currentPage=all

"Culture of East Timor." http://www.spiritus-temporis.com/east-timor/culture.html

Arte Moris: http://www.artemoris.org/

"Defamation a Criminal Offence under New Penal Code." http://www.ifex.org/fr/content/view/full/71410/

"Drawing on Tolerance: Indonesians and Timorese Collaborate in Art Projects." http://www.etan.org/et2008/11november/23/22drawin.htm

"East Timor Art." http://www.mapsofworld.com/timor-leste/culture/art.html

"East Timor: City Population." http://www.citypopulation.de/EastTimor.html

"East Timor Food." http://www.mapsofworld.com/timor-leste/culture/east-timor-food.html

"East Timor: Torture and Mistreatment by Police." http://www.hrw.org/en/news/2006/04/18/east-timor-torture-and-mistreatment-police

"East Timor – Transportation." http://www.nationsencyclopedia.com/Asia-and-Oceania/East-Timor-TRANSPORTATION.html

"East Timor Media." http://mail.sarai.net/pipermail/cr-india/2002–May/005315.html

"Indonesia and Timor-Leste Strengthen Cooperation." http://www.indonesia-oslo.no/political-affairs/410-indonesia-and-timor-leste-strengthen-cooperation.html

"East Timorese Youth Make a Success of Radio." http://mail.sarai.net/pipermail/cr-india/2004-February/006187.html "East Timor Declares Emergency after Attack on Leaders." http://www.nytimes.com/2008/02/12/world/asia/12timor.html?_r=1&scp=3&sq=timor&st=cse "Indonesia accepts guilt over East Timor human rights abuses." http://www.guardian.co.uk/world/2008/jul/15/indonesia.easttimor

"Music of East Timor." http://www.spiritus-temporis.com/music-of-east-timor/

"Renova Timor: Timorese Literature Abstract." http://renovatimor.blogspot.com/2009/01/timorese-literature-abstract.html

"The Buka-Hatene Community Learning Centre: Community Building in Timor-Leste." http://www.scribd.com/doc/7688269/The-BukaHatene-Community-Learning-Centre-Community-Building-in-Timor-Leste

"Timor-Leste – Culture, Customs & Etiquette." http://www.culturecrossing.net/basics_business_student.php?id=236

"Timor-Leste Gender Brief." http://web.worldbank.org/WBSITE/EXTERNAL/COUNTRIES/EASTASIAPACIFICEXT/TIMORLESTEEXTN/0,,contentMDK:20873682~pagePK:141137~piPK:141127~theSitePK:294022,00.html

"Timor-Leste: Youth Brief." http://web.worldbank.org/WBSITE/EXTERNAL/COUNTRIES/EASTASIAPACIFICEXT/TIMORLESTEEXTN/0,,contentMDK:20877757~pagePK:141137~piPK:141127~theSitePK:294022,00.html

"Timor-Leste's Youth in Crisis." http://web.worldbank.org/WBSITE/EXTERNAL/COUNTRIES/EASTASIAPACIFICEXT/TIMORLESTEEXTN/0,,contentMDK:21653749~pagePK:1497618~piPK:217854~theSitePK:294022,00.html

"UK Launch of Timor Justice Report." http://www.hrw.org/en/news/2006/11/27/timor-leste-uk-launch-timor-justice-report "U.S. Department of State: Timor-Leste." http://www.state.gov/r/pa/ei/bgn/35878.htm

"World InfoZone" – *East Timor Information.* http://www.worldinfozone.com/country.php?country=EastTimor

"World Food Programme – Timor-Leste." http://www.wfp.org/country_brief/indexcountry.asp?country=626

"Women's Issues in East Timor." http://www.peacewomen.org/un/sc/et.html

Indonesia

Introduction

Indonesia is located in the Malay Archipelago that separates the Indian Ocean from the Pacific in Southeast Asia. Consisting of thousands of islands, Indonesia is also an impressive array of more than 250 distinct cultures and ethnic groups that have settled on the islands over the course of centuries, each with different languages, dialects, and histories. Following the region's emergence from Dutch colonization in the mid-20th century, the effort to meld all of these cultural groups into a cohesive and stable nation has proved to be Indonesia's greatest challenge.

With such diversity, Indonesia is known for an array of traditional arts and crafts. The country is particularly famous for its batik fabrics, produced especially in Yogyakarta. The Balinese have developed fabric, woodcarving, and furniture styles that are now marketed throughout the world, while the people of Java cherish a centuries-old tradition of puppet theatre known as wayang kulit. The musical style known as gamelan, practiced in Java and Bali, weaves together patterns created by drums and other percussion instruments. Traditional Indonesian crafts also include kris, a form of artwork that often includes jewels, and a woven silk cloth called songket.

GENERAL INFORMATION

Official Language: Indonesian
Population: 253,609,643 (2014 estimate)

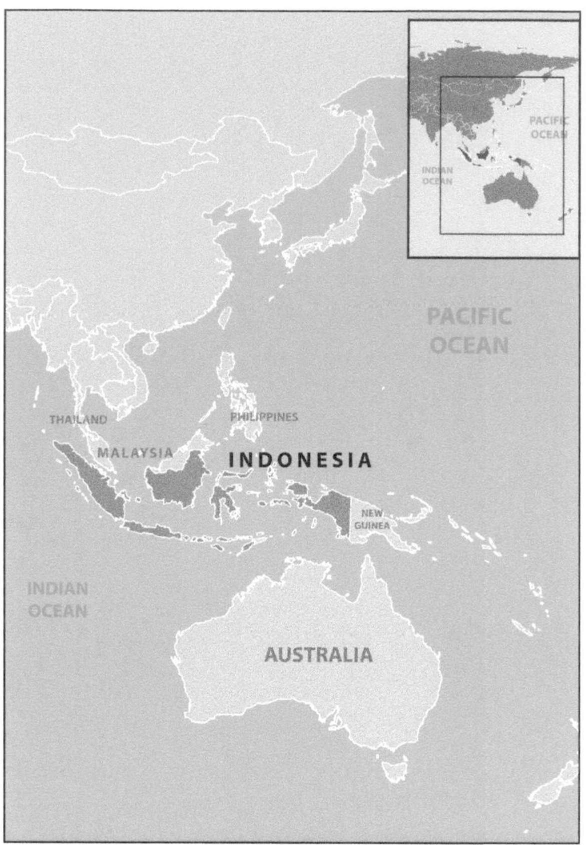

Currency: Indonesian rupiah
Coins: The Indonesian rupiah is divided into 100 sen, and coins are available in denominations of 100, 200, and 500 rupiah, which are frequently used, and 50 and 1000 rupiah, which are rarely used.
Land Area: 1,811,569 square kilometers (699,540 square miles)
Water Area: 93,000 square kilometers (35,907 square miles)
National Motto: "Bhinneka Tunggal" ("Unity in Diversity")
National Anthem: "Indonesia Raya" ("Great Indonesia")
Capital: Jakarta
Time Zone: Indonesia has three Standard Time zones, GMT +7, GMT +8, and GMT +9.
Flag Description: Indonesia's flag consists of two equal and horizontal stripes of red (top) and white (bottom). It is commonly called the Sang Saka Merah Putih or "The Red and White." The red represents courage and the white, purity.

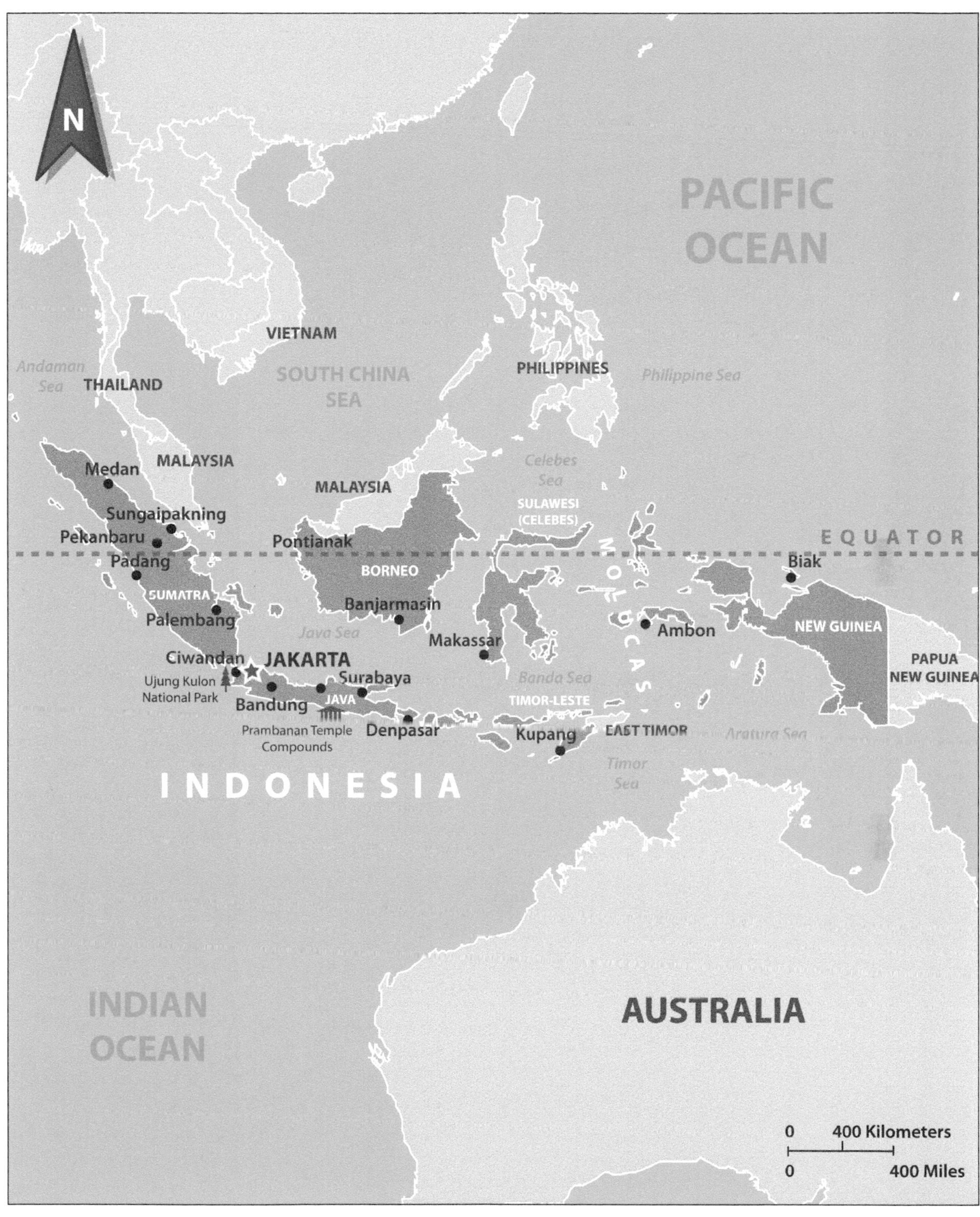
N
PACIFIC OCEAN
VIETNAM
Andaman Sea
THAILAND
SOUTH CHINA SEA
PHILIPPINES
Philippine Sea
MALAYSIA
Medan
MALAYSIA
Celebes Sea
SULAWESI (CELEBES)
Sungaipakning
Pekanbaru
Pontianak
EQUATOR
Padang
BORNEO
MOLUCCAS
Biak
SUMATRA
Banjarmasin
Palembang
Java Sea
Ambon
NEW GUINEA
Makassar
Ciwandan
JAKARTA
PAPUA NEW GUINEA
Ujung Kulon National Park
Surabaya
Banda Sea
Bandung
JAVA
TIMOR-LESTE
Prambanan Temple Compounds
Denpasar
Kupang
EAST TIMOR
Arafura Sea
Timor Sea
INDONESIA
INDIAN OCEAN
AUSTRALIA
0 400 Kilometers
0 400 Miles

Principal Cities by Population (2012):

- Jakarta (9,800,000)
- Surabaya (2,800,000)
- Bekasi (2,600,000)
- Bandung (2,500,000)
- Medan (2,200,000)
- Depok (1,900,000)
- Tangerang (1,900,000)
- Semarang (1,600,000)
- Palembang (1,500,000)
- Makassar (1,400,000)

Population

Javanese descendents make up the largest ethnic group in Indonesia, accounting for about 40 percent of the total population. Another 15 percent of the population is ethnic Sundanese, three percent Madurese, and about 7.5 percent coastal Malay. The remaining 34.5 percent is made up of hundreds of different ethnic groups descending from people who came from all over the South Pacific region.

West Java is the most populous province, with a 2010 population of 43,021,826, followed by East Java (37,476,011) and Central Java (32,380,687). As of 2014, just over half of the population lived in urban areas. Jakarta is the largest Indonesian city and also one of the most densely populated cities in the world, with an estimated 13,000 people per square kilometer (2008). In 2010, estimates placed its total population at around 9.6 million. The population is a melting-pot of national and ethnic backgrounds, including Chinese, Arabs, Indians, Europeans, and ethnic Indonesians, such as Balinese and Sumatrans, who have migrated to the city from other islands. The population growth rate for 2014 was .95 percent.

Languages

Bahasa Indonesian, a modified form of Malay, is the official language, and English and Dutch are also spoken by many Indonesians. Local dialects, especially Javanese, Sundanese, Malay, Madurese, Minangkabau, Balinese, Bugisnese, Acehnese, Toba Batak, Makassarese, Banjarese, Sasak, Lampung, Dairi Batak, and Rejang, are also commonly spoken. A total of 669 languages and dialects are spoken in the 6,000 inhabited islands of Indonesia.

Native People & Ethnic Groups

The long history of habitation in Indonesia (dating back before the existence of Homo sapiens), and the complex movement of cultures into and across Indonesia make identifying a native culture impossible. However, Indonesians recognize the cultural impact of its largest ethnic groups on the national culture.

The ethnic Javanese descend from Malay people and live on the island of Java. Their influence in Indonesia dates back to the 9th through the 14th centuries when Hindu and Buddhist empires expanded across the region.

Also descended from Malay people, but culturally distinct, the present-day Madura live on Madura Island and in the eastern portions of neighboring Java. Unlike the Javanese, the Madura are a maritime people who subsist by fishing.

The Sundanese, also located on Java, trace their roots back to the Sunda Empire of Pajajaran, which thrived in the mountains of Java prior to the 16th century. The Sundanese now inhabit the mountainous region of western Java, including the capital, Jakarta. Once an agrarian culture, the Sundanese are assimilating into Jakarta's modern urban culture except in more rural areas. The Sundanese are also known for following a more orthodox form of Islam than their other Muslim neighbors.

The islands of Bali and Lombok and the western half of Sumbawa are home to 2.5 million Balinese. Unlike the Javanese, the Balinese resisted the spread of Islam in the 12th century and afterward, developing their own form of Hindu worship. Like the ethnic Javanese, they tend to maintain a caste system, though with more flexibly than their counterparts in India. Building on their long history, ornate arts and rituals, and stunning tropical environment, the Balinese have successfully made their island and their culture a central part of Indonesian tourism from the West.

Sumatra lies on the Strait of Malacca, one of the world's most important shipping lanes. Perhaps for this reason, several of Sumatra's cultural groups have incorporated a tradition of going abroad to seek wealth. Amongst the people of the Special Region of Aceh, women are responsible for domestic chores and for agricultural production of rice and other food sources, while men are expected to leave the home in source of fortune according to the practice of merantau. Like the Acehnese, the Minangkabau of the Sumatran mainland incorporate merantau as a means for young men to gain wealth and power. However, Indonesia's 3.5 million Minangkabau people prioritize maternal lineage, and women hold elevated property and social rights.

The Batak, Sumatra's other large ethnic group, include three million members of the Angkola, Karo, Mandailing, Pakpak, Simelungen, Toba, and other cultural groups who inhabit the Utara Province to the south of Aceh. The Batak are agricultural peoples who are organized into marga, familial landowning groups based on paternal descent. While immigration to urban areas and the decline of forested land in Sumatra have threatened some Batak traditions, the Batak have successfully translated marga ties into an urban lifestyle.

In spite of their differences, Indonesia's people are increasingly united at a national level by the spread of the Bahasa Indonesian language; by adat, a form of Indonesian traditional law; and by a rapidly urbanizing culture that encourages tolerance, if not assimilation among different religious and cultural groups.

Religions

Approximately 87 percent of Indonesians are Muslim. Indonesia is home to the world's largest Muslim population. Protestants and Roman Catholics account for about seven percent and three percent of the population, respectively. The remainder of the population adheres to Hinduism (two percent), Buddhism (one percent), or other faiths.

Indonesia's many minority native groups are generally characterized by their adherence to a religion other than those recognized by the state: Islam, Christianity, Hinduism, Buddhism, and Confucianism. Groups like the Toraja of central Sulawesi, the Dayak of southern Kalimantan, and the Weyewa of Nusa Tenggara Timur Province often practice a local form of animism. In part because some, though not all of Indonesia's minority groups, have been associated with practices like headhunting or slavery in the past, Indonesian governments have worked to convert these populations to one of the recognized world religions.

Climate

Indonesia has a tropical climate, but temperatures are more moderate at higher elevations. The average temperature year-round is approximately 27° Celsius (80° Fahrenheit). The weather is typically humid, except in mountain regions, where the air tends to be cooler and drier.

Western Indonesia has a tropical climate, with a defined dry season between June and September, and a season of heavy rains between December and March. Average annual rainfall in this region is roughly 2,000 millimeters (80 inches).

ENVIRONMENT & GEOGRAPHY

Topography

Indonesia's five main islands (Sumatra, Java, Kalimantan, Sulawesi, and Irian Jaya) combined with the two primary archipelagos (Nusa Tenggara and Maluku Islands), sixty smaller archipelagos, and more than 13,000 smaller islands form a long curving barrier between the Indian Ocean and the Pacific.

Indonesia's lands masses are volcanic in origin, and about 100 of the nation's roughly 400 volcanoes are still active as the tectonic plates beneath Indonesia continue to shift.

Because of their volcanic origins, Indonesia's islands and archipelagos are mountainous. In the western islands, elevations reach about 3,800 meters (almost 12,500 feet) above sea level, but the highest elevations are found in Irian Jaya, which reaches 5,039 meters (16,532 feet) above sea level at Puncak Jaya.

The city of Jakarta, located on the northwestern coast of the island of Java, developed along the mouth of the Ciliwung River, which runs into Jakarta Bay. About a dozen other rivers run through the city toward the Java Sea. Northern Jakarta is built on a floodplain just 8 meters (about 26 feet) above sea level. This low elevation, coupled with the city's extremely wet climate—annual rainfall can exceed 1.7 meters (about 5.5. feet)—leads to frequent flooding during the rainy season (between October and May), when monsoons can be expected.

Plants & Animals

Indonesia's tropical plants include thousands of species of orchids, palms, and hardwood trees like teak and mahogany. Mangrove and nipa palm trees, as well as bamboo and rattan plants, are also common. The tough grass known as alang-alang is common throughout the islands.

Orangutans, tigers, elephants, deer, and rhinoceros find habitats in its rainforests. Domesticated water buffalos, known as kerbau, are used extensively by Indonesian farmers. Lizards and snakes are common throughout Indonesia. One of the country's best known reptiles is the Komodo dragon, which can grow as large as three meters (nearly 10 feet) in length.

CUSTOMS & COURTESIES

Greetings

The traditional Indonesian greeting begins with "Selamat" ("Safe"), and typically precedes the time of day at which the greeting is spoken. For example, "Selamat pagi" ("Safe morning") is used in the morning, "Selamat siang" is used for the afternoon, and "Selamat sore" or "Selamat malam" is used in the evening and nighttime. Additionally, the comment "Apa bakar?" ("What's news?"), is often informally used between friends in the place of a greeting.

In general, Indonesian greetings, as well as the language itself, are influenced by the Muslim beliefs and customs of the Indonesian majority. When Muslim Indonesians greet one another, they will often use the traditional Islamic greeting of "As salamu alaykum" ("Peace be with you") instead of a general greeting. The appropriate response is then "Wa alaikum assalaam" ("And upon you be peace").

It is customary to shake hands upon meeting and leaving. The handshake is typically weaker than what is expected in Western cultures, and more similar to the light touching of the palms. The handshake often lasts 10 to 15 seconds, and is sometimes followed by the touching of the hand to the heart. Men and women may shake hands; however, if one of the parties is a Muslim woman, she must initiate the handshake.

People generally address one another using their title and full name when first meeting. The concept of authority is also very important. However, this may differ on some islands. For example, there is a custom in Java that locals address one another by first names only. In addition, the phrases of "Selamat tinggal" ("Good stay") and "Selamat jalan" ("Have a safe journey") are both equivalent to saying farewell.

Gestures & Etiquette

There is a complex system of etiquette in Indonesian culture that has developed over the centuries, and is a reflection of indigenous, Islamic, Hindu, and Chinese heritages. The use of the left hand is particularly important; in Islam, the left hand is traditionally associated with the cleansing of the body, and is thus considered impure. As such, the left hand is typically never used in social settings, including handshakes, the passing of an object to another person, or eating. It is also considered improper etiquette to walk in front of people. Additionally, there should be no physical contact between genders in public, with handshakes being the only exception (with the right hand).

In Indonesian culture, the soles of the feet are typically not shown and especially not used to touch anything. In particular, Indonesians refrain from putting their feet up when sitting down. Other practiced forms of etiquette include refraining from turning one's back to an elderly person or a high-ranking official, and refraining from placing the hands in the pocket when conversing. In general, heeding these rules is considered good manners for foreigners, though Indonesians, for the most part, have an easygoing attitude and manner when dealing with visitors.

Modesty is culturally important in Indonesian society. As such, Indonesians find it very difficult to say no, and typically refrain from raising their voices, whether in anger or happiness. Proper and conservative dress is also very important. As the vast majority of Indonesians are Muslim, Islamic expectations of proper dress are imposed on the general population. Women in particular must dress modestly, including covering their arms at all times, and wearing, at the most, a knee-length skirt with hosiery. Muted or dark-colored clothing, as opposed to anything bright and colorful, is also generally expected. Men and women refrain from wearing shorts, and shirts are generally collared. Given the humid weather, it is common for people to change their clothes throughout the day, but they will not dress more informally than custom requires.

Eating/Meals

Traditionally, the main meal in Indonesia is typically served in the mid-afternoon or midday, with the morning often used as preparation time. This meal largely consists of rice (or sometimes noodles), generally with some combination of chicken, fish, egg, vegetables, and tofu. Families do not necessarily eat together, and the meal is often left out for people to reheat throughout the day. Often, a later meal may consist of lighter fare or the reheated main meal from earlier, sometimes with additions. Breakfast is also served, with popular meals consisting of bubur nasi, a rice porridge with toppings, and nasi uduk, slightly sweet rice cooked with coconut milk, eaten with an omelet and fried chicken.

Throughout the day, eating from a street vendor and other various food stalls is popular, particularly in urban areas. Such stalls include kaki lima, mobile stalls by the side of the road. At night some vendors may provide bamboo mats for customers to sit on and chat. The warung is slightly less mobile, but offers much the same food, often with the some basic comforts of seats and shelter. Indonesian restaurants or eating-houses, called rumah makan, are typically very simple. More Western-style restaurants, typically featuring amenities such as air conditioning and table service, are called restoran. In some circumstances, customers are only required to pay for what they eat, no matter what has been placed before them.

Eating with the right hand, instead of using utensils, is very common. Utensils are still used to serve the food from communal dishes, using the left hand. Indonesians traditionally do not have tables in their home and eat sitting in a circle on the floor, with the food served communal style from the middle.

Visiting

In Indonesian culture, it is polite to remove one's shoes when visiting someone's home. Gifts for the host are customary, and small gifts are given frequently (although never opened at the time, just graciously received). Visitors must also be mindful of a host's religious or cultural background, as there are many cultural and social restrictions associated with Muslim, Hindu or Chinese culture that a host may practice. For example, alcohol and pork are not appropriate for Muslims; Hindus refrain from eating beef; and there are various items that are considered "bad luck" to Chinese Indonesians, such as knives or umbrellas. In addition, due to culture of modesty in Indonesia, it is not uncommon for a visitor or host to refuse something three times before accepting.

If a visitor is invited to share a meal with the host, it is important to refrain from talking unless the host initiates conversation. This is because Indonesians customarily reserve conversation for before and after mealtime, and eating does not usually have social connotations. Typically, when a visitor finishes their drink, it is indicative that they would like more. Visitors are also expected to eat all the food on plate, as not doing so is considered impolite. Guests, and all present, will also rise when the host or hostess enters the room.

LIFESTYLE

Family

Family is strongly valued in Indonesia, as the culture emphasizes community and family over individualism. As the government provides little social security, including support for the unemployed and the elderly, the family unit is also particularly vital in providing care and financial support. In general, the nuclear family of husband, wife, and children is the most common family unit in Indonesia, although the emphasis on extended family should be noted. Elders and unmarried siblings may live in the same house as the immediate family at various times, and supporting extended family is considered a large part of traditional familial responsibility.

Typically, there is a strong social pressure for marriage in Indonesian culture, in particular because full adult status in Indonesian society is usually reserved for married adults. Thus, marrying young is still a prevalent practice, and unmarried adults are not common. The same may be said about the social pressure to produce children–it would be unusual for a couple to not have children simply because they did not want them. More recently, with the high cost of living and low wages—particularly in urban areas—living independently is becoming less common, and more young adults are preferring to stay at home and save money. Newly married couples are also usually expected to live with the parents of one spouse, especially before the birth of their first child. The husband may be required to serve the wife's parents during this period, as well.

Marriages between people of different religions and ethnic groups remain relatively uncommon. However, this is becoming less so, particularly in the larger cities and urban areas. Arranged marriages (where love may be considered, but other factors are also taken into account) are very common, especially among clans with lineal descent and high status families. Divorce is legal, although it is relatively uncommon.

Housing

Village houses are generally one or two-room buildings, typically constructed of bamboo or wood. In urban areas, a wider variety of housing styles exist, including new suburban housing developments and modern high-rise apartments. Often, these urban centers are surrounded by crowded urban villages called kampungs (or kampongs). Shantytowns, which are informal settlements often built with discarded materials, have recently become more common in larger cities.

A lack of adequate housing has been a major political issue in Indonesia in recent years. According to national statistics, a significant portion (41.2 percent) of the population did not have access to improved sanitation in 2012, a situation which is worse in rural areas. In addition, it is estimated that over 1 million people are either displaced or homeless. This situation has been worsened by numerous natural disasters, including floods and earthquakes, and because of local conflicts. The Asian Tsunami of December 2006, in particular, had a severe impact on housing, causing widespread devastation in the Aceh province of western Sumatra.

Food

The cuisine of Indonesia has been influenced by the culinary traditions of India, the Middle East and China. European influences were brought through Spanish, English and Portuguese traders, and a distinct Dutch influence was established after the Netherlands colonized much of the country. More importantly, there is a vast array of regional cuisines that have their own unique foreign and cultural influences. For example, regional cuisines of eastern Indonesia have distinct Polynesian influences, and the Minangkabau culture of western Sumatra is known for their Padang-style cuisine, which is traditionally spicy. Other regional cuisines include Javanese, Balinese, Manado and Indonesian Chinese.

Rice is the most important ingredient in the Indonesian diet, and is eaten at almost every meal. Other important ingredients include corn, cassava, coconut milk, and sweet potatoes. Seafood is a significant part of the daily diet of Indonesians, and includes lobsters, oysters, prawns, shrimp, and squid. While chicken and beef are commonly consumed meats, pork is traditionally only used in Balinese cuisine, as Muslims are forbidden to consume it by Islamic law (Indonesia is roughly 87 percent Muslim).

Traditional Indonesian meals include gado-gado, a salad of boiled vegetables covered in peanut sauce; ayam taliwang, which is chicken cooked in various spices; opor ayam, which is chicken cooked in coconut milk, and traditionally eaten with herbs and seasoning; and sambal, a spicy sauce made from chili peppers that is traditionally prepared with a variety of flavors. Other popular sauces include sambal ulek, which is chili peppers, oil and lime juice; sambal pecel, with peanut; and sambal terasi, with shrimp paste. The national dish is called nasi goreng, and consists of fried rice with chopped meat, vegetables, and egg.

Fresh fruit is also very important to the Indonesian diet. Mango, banana, papaya, and guava are all popular. Fruits unique to Indonesia are also eaten, including the scaly-skinned "snake fruit," salak, and the durian, a light-green melon-like fruit with a very strong odor. A traditional snack is called kerupuk (or keropok), and is a type of cracker. It is made from any grain, fruit, vegetable or seed, and can be eaten with almost every meal. At street stalls, barbecued lamb or chicken on skewers is common, featuring a variety of sauces made from coconut milk, soy beans or peanuts.

Life's Milestones

As the vast majority of Indonesians are Muslim, Islamic traditions concerning marriage, birth, and death are primarily practiced. Special Islamic birth rites include whispering into a newborn baby's ear, which symbolizes the welcoming of the child into the world. On the seventh day after the birth, males are typically circumcised and the heads of newborns, both male and female, are shaved, and a sacrifice is offered. In addition, more of these traditions are being practiced in an orthodox Islamic fashion.

In Bali, where the majority of the population is Hindu, the celebrations of certain milestones incorporate traditions of Hinduism. For example, there are complex rituals surrounding birth, including a celebration that occurs when a woman is six months pregnant, and another celebration at birth involving the burial of the placenta. In addition, three more celebrations are held over the first 42 days. At three months, the largest celebration is held, and the baby is dressed in traditional Balinese clothing for the first time. The child is also formally named, and given bracelets and amulets to ward off evil spirits. At the onset of puberty, girls are typically given a ceremony, and their six front teeth are filed in an attempt to eliminate unwanted feelings, such as lust and jealousy. Balinese Hindu weddings are also becoming quite similar to Western-style ceremonies.

Additionally, some Hindu and indigenous rituals have blended with Muslim traditions, making them more distinctly Indonesian. For example, marriage ceremonies with some Hindu-derived and indigenous rituals are common, especially in Java. There, the marriage ceremonies are held at the bride's house over six-to-eight days and involve several traditional aspects. One such tradition is based on the belief that a spirit called "dunken manten" enters the bride's body on the eve of her wedding. Because of this belief, the bride-to-be must sit secluded and motionless until midnight to allow the spirit to enter her body. Afterward, both the spirit and Allah are recognized in prayers at the end of the marriage ceremony.

CULTURAL HISTORY

Art

Art was an integral part of Indonesian culture, and continues to flourish in contemporary society. Early art in Indonesia was influenced by tribal beliefs, and later incorporated Hindu, Buddhist, Chinese, and Islamic motifs and characteristics. Some of the famous arts and handicrafts associated with Indonesia include ritualistic jewelry, ornamental textiles, and stone and woodcarvings, including figurines, ceremonial masks, and furniture. It was also common for everyday items to feature intricate designs. Traditional Batik designs in particular—which characteristically feature intricate geometric patterns and nature motifs—are often highly prized by foreigners and have become synonymous with Indonesia.

The visual arts in Indonesia, in particular, originated from the cave paintings of ancient civilizations, and developed through the decoration of traditional clothing and manuscripts. Bali has a particularly strong artistic heritage. Traditionally, every person had to develop skills in a particular art form—visual arts, dance or music. In the early 20th century, this rich cultural community attracted many Western artists, who visited and settled there. These artists, such as Walter Spies (1895–1942) and Rudolf Bonnet (1895–1978), not only painted their own works, but were also instrumental in the development of local art.

One of Indonesia's most famous artists from this period is Gusti Nyoman Lempad (1862–1978), who incorporated narrative elements and traditional designs in his work. Other famous Indonesian artists include Affandi (1907–1990), whose distinctive style consisted of using his hands as a paintbrush and squeezing the paint directly out of the tube, and Raden Saleh Sjarif Boestaman (1807–1880), considered a pioneer of modern Indonesian art.

Architecture

Indonesia has a strong history of vernacular architecture, in which buildings are designed and built according to specific and unique environmental and cultural needs. In this way, each ethnic group developed its own distinctive architectural style. This traditional architecture, prevalent in rural villages, is often referred to as rumah adat. While distinct, each share a number of characteristics, including timber construction, varied and elaborate roofs, non-load bearing bamboo walls, and pile or beam structuring.

Foreign influences are also prevalent in Indonesian architecture. In particular, traditional Indonesian architecture is most strongly influenced by Indian designs. The influence of Chinese, Arabic, and European styles—the latter from the nation's colonial period—is also prominent. As Indonesia has become more urbanized and developed, further modern and Western designs have been particularly influential, as is seen in the design of modern apartment and commercial buildings.

Religious architecture in Indonesia is also noteworthy for its distinctive style. For example, multi-tiered roofs and timber structures are characteristic of Hindu, Buddhist, and Islamic architecture. This is significant because Islamic mosques have traditionally been built as dome-like structures. However, when they were built in Indonesia they adopted the square, timber design of the earlier Balinese Hindu temples. Many of the earliest Hindu temples, built between the eighth and 14th centuries, and Islamic mosques, from the 15th century, still remain.

Drama

Indonesia has a long tradition of dance and drama, and both have played a central role in the country's cultural history. Wayang Theater, ancient plays featuring puppets, is perhaps the best-known theater tradition in Indonesia, and has existed as a court art for centuries. Closely associated with both Bali and Java, it is considered the largest theater tradition in Southeast Asia, and several thousand puppeteers still continue this storied tradition today. There are several variations of this traditional puppet theater, most notably wayang kulit, which uses shadow puppets, and wayang golek, which features rod puppets.

Many of the stories featured in these puppet plays derive from Indonesian folklore or ancient epics such as the *Ramayana* and *Mahabharata*, the two major epics of ancient India. In addition, many performances are based on a "play cycle" of roughly 100 plays about the Pandawa brothers, two brothers who are consistently placed in different situations. Other plays concern indigenous spirituality, Islamic and Christian religious stories (wayang sadat and wayang wahyu, respectively), and dramatize the revolutionary struggle against the Dutch (wayang sulu). Wayang kulit remains the most famous of these traditions, and in recognition of this artistic heritage, the United Nations Educational, Scientific and Cultural Organization (UNESCO) designated wayang kulit as an Intangible Cultural Heritage in 2003.

Cinema in Indonesia first developed during the late colonial period—during the early 20th century—but has struggled in recent years. In fact, during the Sukarno administration, foreign films were banished and local films were only produced for nationalistic or political purposes. However, independent filmmaking emerged in the late 20th century, and 2005 witnessed the international release of Indonesia's first animated film, *Beauty and Warrior* (2002). In addition, Indonesia is home to two prominent film festivals, the Jakarta International Film Festival and the Indonesian Film Festival.

Music & Dance

There are hundreds of different forms of music which have developed in Indonesia, often to accompany drama and dance. Perhaps the most popular and famous form of traditional Indonesian music is gamelan, which typically features an ensemble of instruments. These include metallophones (tuned metal bars struck with a mallet), drums, gongs, spike fiddles (an Arabic stringed instrument with a spike which rests on the ground, played with a bow), and bamboo flutes. Gamelan differs between regions, but generally the tune is played on metallophones, accompanied by the percussion. Some forms are considered "high-class" entertainment in their own right, while others, such as galeman salendro from West Java, are considered only to be musical accompaniment.

Traditional dance in Indonesia first began as a form of religious worship, beginning in the prehistoric era. Gradually, dance in Indonesia was influenced by Hinduism and Buddhism, and native dance styles were paired with the adopted stories of these religions, much in the same way theater evolved in Indonesia. Then, as Islam spread throughout the islands, Islamic traditions and stories were gradually incorporated. In addition, many of these dance and theater traditions developed in the courts, particularly during Dutch colonization when the royal courts had minimal power. While there are over 700 different ethnicities in Indonesia, each with their own traditions in the performing arts, the traditional and folk dances of Bali and Java are perhaps the most famous.

In general, many of the dance styles and traditions of Java, particularly central Java, have been divided into three categories: beksan wayang, which incorporates narrative elements; beksan putri, which is typically a non-narrative style of dance; and beksan putra, which are described as warrior dances reserved for men, often as practice or a showcasing of technical combat skills. In addition, jaipongon is a popular dance tradition associated with the working class. It typically incorporates the martial arts and Islamic influences. Wayang orang is a popular form of traditional dance-drama in Javanese culture. It involves an all-female dance group, which imitates and acts out the gestures and actions of the puppets featured in Wayang Theater. Similar forms of dance theater include wayang topeng, in which the performers wear masks.

Dance is often considered the essence of Balinese culture, and many of its dance traditions are known the world over. Some of Bali's most notable and classic dance traditions include the barong dance, which is also an exorcism ritual to cleanse evil spirits; legong keratin, which is associated with femininity and considered the dance of nymphs; sang hyang, which originated as religious worship and typically involves two young girls dancing with spiritual influences; and ketjak, the famous "monkey dance" which is accompanied by chanting rather than music.

Literature

The early literature of Indonesia is very closely related to Malay, which is the written language of the Malay-speaking Muslims of ancient Southeast Asia. Thus, this early literature emerged with the introduction of Islam in the 15th century. Prior to this, the early cultures of Indonesia relied on oral traditions for storytelling and learning. Traditional literature included a number of forms, including syair (traditional narrative poetry), hikayat (fairy-stories and fables), and babad (histories or chronicles). A number of the earliest works include *Hikayat Bayan Budiman,* a Malay work based on the *Shuka Saptati* (*Seventy Tales of the Parrot*) of ancient India, and *Hikayat Hang Tuah*, about the legendary Muslim warrior Hang Tuah, who lived during the 15th century.

During Indonesia's colonial period (1600–1942), in which it was a colony of the Netherlands, its literary traditions were largely influenced by other cultures, namely Western Europe, India, and the Middle East. In the late 19th century, translated Western novels became popular, and by the 1930s, contemporary Indonesian literature had emerged, featuring fiction written in the Indonesian language. The Bureau for Popular Literature was also established during the 20th century, and functioned as a government-controlled publisher. Western-style literature, such as fiction, drama, and poetry, remained prevalent, with influences from Dutch poetry and Asian literature.

Literature also changed in the 1940s, transitioning from predominantly romantic and idealistic content to focusing more on political and social issues and realism. It thus played an important part in the formation and development of the independence movement. The works of Indonesian author Pramoedya Ananta Toer (1925–2006) are particularly significant because of their strong themes of national identity. His works include *The Earth of Mankind* (1980), written while the author was imprisoned under the oppressive administration of President Sukarno (1901–1970), Indonesia's first president.

Famous poets during this period include Chairil Anwar (1922–1949) and Muhammad Yamin (1903–1962), both considered pioneers of modern poetry in Indonesia. In addition, a group of writers known as Angkatan '45, or Generation 45, and which included Anwar, were active in Indonesia's independence movement of the mid-20th century. Other well-known writers include Goenawan Mohamad (b. 1941–), a poet and editor of Indonesia's controversial *Tempo* (*Time*) magazine; Sapardi Djoko Damono (b. 1940–), a poet renowned for his lyrical poems; and Ayu Utami (b. 1968–), whose novel *Saman* (1998) has broken many records in terms of sales and success. More recently, the works of many authors have ignited political feelings about the state of the country through their descriptions of the nation. While such books are often banned in the country, the Internet has helped increase the influence of and access to this type of material.

CULTURE

Arts & Entertainment

Traditional forms of drama and dance continue to focus on Indonesian mythology and indigenous stories and history. In recent years, literature has also ensured that a permanent record of many of the oral stories passed down for generations still exists. The development of Indonesian art has helped create a sense of nationhood. Being such a diverse nation—with over 17,000 islands and hundreds of different languages and distinct ethnicities—this has been and continues to be an important challenge.

In a country where free speech has often been limited for most of its history, the arts have been very important politically. The independence movement in the 1940s used the arts in many ways, both reflecting on and encouraging the movement as it grew. For example, from the 1940s onward, the kroncong style of music—a sentimental and popular style of music that has long-standing Portuguese and other European influences—became associated with the struggle for independence. Perhaps the most famous song in the kroncong style is "Bengawan Solo," written by Gesang Martohartono (1917–2010). Kroncong has since become a generic term used to describe popular and romanticized music in Indonesia.

The arts continued to flourish during Sukarno's tenure as president, despite widespread censorship and political oppression. For example, while the use of foreign instruments and Western styles of music such as rock and roll were banned, a variety of distinctively Indonesian musical forms were created and revived using only Indonesian instruments so that music could continue.

Indonesian pop music is referred to as pop daerah (regional pop). It uses local languages and a mix of western and regional music styles and instruments, and includes many sub-forms, including, for example, pop sundra, pop minag, and pop batak. Other forms of Indonesian music include dangdut, a form of dance music distinctive to Indonesia.

Cultural Sites & Landmarks

Indonesia is home to an array of cultural and historic sites, from the "living traditions" of the country's diverse dance and theater traditions and tribal communities, to the natural landmarks and national parks that dot the landscape. In particular, Indonesia is home to seven World Heritage Sites, recognized by the United Nations Educational, Scientific and Cultural Organization (UNESCO) for their cultural significance. They include the Borobudur and Prambanan Temple Compounds, the Sangiran archaeological site, the tropical rainforests of Sumatra, and several national parks.

The Borobudur Temple Compound, in central Java, is a famous Buddhist monument originating in the eighth century. The compound is comprised of a pyramid base, and contains over 500 Buddha statues. Restored in the 1970s, the site is considered Indonesia's most popular tourist destination. The Prambanan Temple, also in central Java, is a famous Hindu temple built in the 10th century. It is considered to be the largest temple compound in the world dedicated to the Hindu god Shiva, and is famous for its Hindu temple architecture. It is made up of three concentric squares. In the last square, there are three temples decorated with images from the epic *Ramayana*, dedicated to the three Hindu gods of Shiva, Vishnu, and Brahma, along with three temples dedicated to the animals that serve them.

The Sangiran Early Man site, in central Java, is the location of some of the most significant discoveries of early hominid fossils. In fact, half of the world's hominid fossils were excavated at the site. The archaeological site remains an important cultural link for the understanding of human evolution. It was recognized as a World Heritage Site in 1996. Other buildings of cultural or historical significance in Indonesia include the Kratons, or royal palaces, of the sultans, most notably in Surakarta and the Yogyakarta region; the Maimun Palace of Medan, built by the Sultanate of Deli in 1888; Kerta Gosa, or the Hall of Justice, in Bali, constructed in the middle of an artificial lake; and the many buildings of architectural heritage and war monuments from the Dutch colonial era.

There are a substantial number of national parks and natural attractions in Indonesia, four of which were designated as World Heritage Sites for their ecological importance. Ujung Kulon national park in West Java is one of the most famous. It contains the natural reserve of Krakatowa, some of the most significant inland volcanoes, and the largest remaining area of lowland rainforest in Java. Several species of endangered animals and plants are based there, including the Javan rhinoceros. It was inscribed as a World Heritage Site in 1991.

The largest protected area in Southeast Asia, Lorentz National Park in Papua, encompasses 25,056 square kilometers (9,674 square miles). It is also the only protected area in the world that includes snowcapped mountains, tropical coral reefs, and lowland wetlands. In addition, it contains the highest level of biodiversity in the region, and is of great geological and historical interest for its mountain and glacial formations and fossil sites.

Komodo National Park includes a series of volcanic islands, white sandy beaches, and coral reefs, as well as some of the most diverse marine environments in the world. The park is home to the Komodo dragon, a large species of lizard unique to the area. The park was established in 1980 to help protect the animal, the population of which is estimated at 5,700. The park is also a popular scuba diving destination due to the diversity of marine life. It was inscribed as a World Heritage Site in 1991.

The Tropical Rainforest Heritage of Sumatra was recognized as a World Heritage Site in 2004, both for its ecological and biological significance. The area, which encompasses three national parks, is home to numerous endangered species, including the Sumatran orangutan. Overall, the rainforest contains an impressive biodiversity of 10,000 plant species, 200 mammal species, and 580 bird species. It is also of particular importance because the lowland forests within the site are becoming increasingly scarce in the region due to deforestation. The total area of the park is roughly 25,000 square kilometers (9,652 square miles).

Libraries & Museums

Of Jakarta's many museums, the most prominent is the National Museum, where archeological exhibits detailing the history of Indonesia are displayed. The museum is also home to a commemorative stone pillar, called a padrao, which signified the treaty between the Portuguese and the Pajajarans; it is the only surviving remnant of early Jakarta prior to its destruction by the Dutch in 1619. Jakarta is also the home of the Shadow Puppet Museum, which showcases the traditional Indonesian art of wayang kulit, and the Fine Art and Ceramic Museum, originally built by the Dutch in 1870 to serve as a judiciary building.

Indonesia's National Library boasts photo, video, painting, and manuscript collections. A special collection of paintings by Johannes Rach (1720–1783) has been shared with the Rijksmuseum in Amsterdam.

Holidays

Because many of Indonesia's holidays are determined by lunar calendars, public days vary from year to year. January holidays in Indonesia include New Years Day and the Eid-ul-Adha, the Muslim Festival of Sacrifice. In February, the country celebrates both the Chinese New Year and the Islamic New Year.

Nyepi takes place in March, and is celebrated by Balinese who fast, turn out all lights, and maintain a period of silence to mark the Balinese New Year. About two weeks later, Christian Indonesians celebrate Good Friday in preparation for Easter. Muslim Indonesians mark the Maulid (birthday) of the Prophet Muhammad in April with festivities, acts of charity, and meditation. The Christian Feast of the Ascension is celebrated in May, along with Vesak, a celebration of feasting and meditation to mark the birthday of Buddha. August 17 is Indonesian Independence Day.

The Isra Mi'raj of the Prophet Muhammad falls in late August or early September, and marks Mohammed's journey by night from Mecca to Jerusalem, where he briefly ascended to heaven. The two-day celebration of Idul Fitri usually takes place in November, and marks the end of Ramadan with feasts and public celebrations. Christmas and Boxing Day are celebrated by Christians on December 25 and 26, respectively.

Youth Culture

Traditionally, young people in Indonesia lived in rural communities, and their parents and community elders were the role models for their behavior and culture. However, with the increasing urbanization of the country and the spread of technology, a distinctive youth culture has emerged. Jakarta is in many ways the center of youth culture, largely because most of the nation's entertainment industries, such as television, film, and fashion, are based there. These emerging industries—most notably television, which now features MTV-style programming, and the increasing popularity of the Internet—are creating a new style for youth to follow that is a mix of Indonesian, Asian, Islamic, and Western tastes.

However, the widespread influence of this youth culture largely depends on access to technology and money. In Indonesia, only 16 percent of youth have access to the Internet, and 27 percent use mobile phones (early 21st century estimates). Many young people continue to live in rural villages and urban areas that are generally very poor. In fact, over half of the population lives on less than $2 (USD) per day. For these young people, daily life and routine is much more about survival than cultural dislikes and image.

SOCIETY

Transportation

Outside of main islands, maritime transportation is important, and ferries and motorized boats are primary modes of transportation. Within the main islands, buses operate as the main mode of public transportation, while taxis are more common in major cities such as Jakarta. Traveling by car is also common; however, private car ownership remains low and is common only in larger cities. Car ownership among Jakartans is steadily increasing. Traffic moves on the left-hand side of the road.

In major cities, traffic congestion and the failure to obey road rules—including traffic lights, lanes, and traffic islands—often make for hazardous trips. In addition, traffic congestion is a major problem in Jakarta, partly because the public transportation system—which consists mainly of buses and taxis, plus a new river boat service that travels along the Ciliwung—is very much underused by residents.

Traditional forms of transportation are still common for traveling within cities and for small distances within residential areas. These may include the becak (a tricycle pedi-cab), and various motorized scooters and three-wheeled carts—similar to an auto rickshaw (a motorized three-wheeled vehicle for hire, common in parts of Asia). For example, motorcycles with side-cars, known as bentor, are common in certain provinces, while motorcycle taxis, called ojeks, are widely available. Indonesians frequently ride bicycles and motorbikes rather than cars.

Transportation Infrastructure

Indonesia is considered the world's largest archipelagic state, and is made up of 17,508 islands. As such, maritime transportation is important, and common modes of travel include ferries, sailing ships, and various motorized boats. In certain areas, ferry service is available twenty-four hours a day, and passenger ships are often used for longer and more remote connections. Within the major islands, established rail networks connect the larger cities. Outside major cities, road maintenance is generally poor. The quickest mode of transportation throughout Indonesia is by plane. Many domestic and international carriers exist, although the safety record of some of the small local companies is questionable.

Jakarta is the home of Indonesia's busiest trading harbor, Tanjungpriok, and its largest international airport is located about 20 kilometers (about 12 miles) to the west of the city. Numerous railway lines and roadways connect the city to the rest of the country.

Media & Communications

A wide variety of national and regional printed media is available, with *Kompas* and *Media Indonesia* two of the most popular dailies based on circulation and readership; the *Jakarta Post* is Indonesia's largest daily English language newspaper. Radio Republik Indonesia (RRI) is the national radio network of Indonesia, covering a wide array of frequencies and radio formats. The previously state-controlled Televisi Republik Indonesia (TVRI) is the longest running television station, and the first private TV stations were established in the late 20th century. In addition, the Indonesian mobile phone market is highly competitive and mobile phone use is widespread. There is a preference for mobile phones over fixed lines, with 37.9 million land lines, and over 281.9 million mobile phone users as of 2012. In recent years, the Internet has gradually made strides in terms of access, but the costs remain high; as of 2010, an estimated 12 percent of the population was measured as Internet users.

The media is largely controlled by the government's Ministry of Communications. There has been a strong history of censorship, harassment, and closure of media outlets, particularly over politically sensitive issues and criticisms of the government. Additionally, human rights groups have long expressed concern over detained and intimidated journalists. In fact, thousands of newspapers, magazines, and radio stations have been closed down or banned for political reasons, and arrests and jailing still occur. Recently, censorship has been relaxed somewhat, especially with the advent of the Internet and the establishment of foreign press. In addition, the underground press has made use of the Internet to deliver its message to a wider audience.

SOCIAL DEVELOPMENT

Standard of Living

Indonesia ranked 108th out of 187 countries on the 2014 United Nations Human Development Index, which measures quality of life and standard of living indicators.

Average life expectancy in Indonesia is 69 years for men and seventy-four years for women (2014 estimate). The infant mortality rate was an estimated twenty-five deaths per 1,000 live births in 2014. Indonesia's quality of life indicators changed somewhat as a result of a 2004 tsunami in the Indian Ocean, which affected northwestern areas of the country. According to estimates, the death toll from the tsunami in Aceh Province and in Northern Sumatra exceeded 200,000, and more than 400,000 people were displaced.

Water Consumption

According to 2012 statistics from the CIA World Factbook, approximately 84 percent of the population has access to an improved source of drinking water, while an estimated 58 percent have access to improved sanitation. In addition, many sources of water are under constant threat of pollution, and access to sanitation or sewerage in urban areas ranks among the lowest in the world. Aside from its poor health implications, lack of sufficient sanitation and clean water also has a major economic impact. In 2006, Indonesia lost roughly 6.3 billion (USD) due to poor hygiene and sanitation.

Education

Nine years of education is compulsory in Indonesia. The nation's literacy rate was measured at 90 percent in 2011, with men at 95 percent and women at almost 90 percent. Education spending accounted for 2.8 percent of GDP in 2011.

About 85 percent of Indonesia's primary and secondary school students are enrolled in public schools under the supervision of the Department of Education and Culture. The public schools are non-religious. The remaining 15 percent of Indonesian school students attend private, religiously oriented schools under the Department of Religious Affairs. Most private schools include Islamic teachings. Public school curricula include Indonesia's Pancasila, a set of five principles related to nationalism, diversity, Indonesian sovereignty, social justice, and non-denominational religious belief.

Indonesia has about 900 institutions of higher education, including two major universities: the University of Indonesia in Jakarta and Gadjah Mada University in Yogyakarta.

Women's Rights

Indonesia has been slower than many other countries in recognizing the rights of women. However, Indonesia recently passed domestic violence and anti-trafficking legislation, in 2004 and 2007, respectively. It is also a member of the Convention on the Elimination of All Forms of Discrimination against Women (CEDAW), and has long recognized, at least in principle, the right of women to equality. Nonetheless, women still suffer from systemic discrimination and lack of opportunity compared to men. Women and girls working in domestic services are often the most vulnerable to exploitation and abuses.

Discrimination in the workplace is very common, and women generally only get work in female-dominated industries. These industries also offer less pay and worse conditions than the jobs taken on by men. For example, over 90 percent of textile workers are women, and work in some of the worst conditions in all of Indonesia. Often, these women laborers work over 12 hours a day, typically for less than $2 (USD) a day. Additionally, many women, particularly in rural areas, quit school to start work at the age of 12 or 13, and therefore do not receive a full education. They also do not get adequate information on sexual and reproductive rights.

There are no legal restrictions on women in politics. In fact, a woman, Megawati Sukarnoputri, was elected president in 2001, serving until 2004. As of 2007, women represented only two of the 32 cabinet ministers, 44 of the 500 DPR members, and eight of the 45 justices of Indonesia's Supreme Court. However this issue of underrepresentation was dramatically improved when in the 2014 general elections women's representation increased by a staggering 22 percent within provincial and district parliaments. This was the result of a 2013 law making it mandatory for political parties to field at least 30 percent women in elections. Unfortunately, while more women entered politics overall, women's numbers decreased at the national level.

Health Care

Indonesia's health care system has undergone substantial changes in recent decades. With little government funding or involvement during Dutch colonization, the nation began creating government health policies and the first community-based health clinics during the mid-20th century. This system included community health centers, mother and childcare clinics, government-run hospitals, and disease prevention programs like immunizations, sanitization of water supplies, and family planning.

In 1987, many local health care resources and responsibilities were shifted to the provincial governments. In 1992, an overhaul of laws and regulations related to national health included a requirement that employers provide health benefits to their employees. Few Indonesians who are not covered under the employer health benefit law have any sort of health insurance, and most services provided in public clinics and hospitals must be paid for by the patient. The government has been considering a law to mandate universal health insurance, funded primarily by an additional tax on employers.

A high birth rate throughout the 20th century caused concern about overpopulation, which would, in turn, have significantly worsened poverty. Indonesia, therefore, has ongoing family planning programs, educational programs, and policy initiatives designed to lower birth rates.

The 2004 tsunami overwhelmed health care resources in Indonesia, particularly in the Aceh region where the tsunami hit hardest. As a result, the Indonesian government has allowed aid workers from a number of non-governmental organizations and foreign military personnel into the country to help meet health care needs.

GOVERNMENT

Structure

Indonesia is a republic with thirty provinces, two special regions (Aceh and Yogyakarta), and one special capital city district (Jakarta). The executive branch of government is run by a president and vice president with a cabinet appointed by the president. Citizens elect the president and vice president by direct vote.

The legislative branch of government consists of a House of Representatives called the Dewan Perwakilan Rakyat (DPR), and a House of Regional Representatives called the Dewan Perwakilan Daerah (DPD). The DPR has 560 seats; the DPD has 132 seats. Its members are elected by the public to serve five-year terms. The DPD provides legislative input to the DPR on issues affecting different regions.

The Indonesian constitution also provides for a People's Consultative Assembly (Majelis Permusyawaratan Rakyat or MPR), which participates in the inaugurations or impeachments of presidents and in constitutional amendments, but does not help to form national policy. MPR members are elected by popular vote from within the DPR and DPD.

Political Parties

In the 2014, presidential and legislative elections, 12 political parties were represented. Of those, three parties succeeded in gaining more than 10 percent of the vote. The Indonesian Democratic Party – Struggle, the former party of the country's first president, Sukarno and founded on the Indonesian idea of pancasila (or the five principles of one God, humanity, unity, democracy, and social justice), garnered 19.46 percent of the vote in the legislative race, securing 109 seats in the DPR. The Party of the Functional Groups (Sekber Golkar), the party of former President Suharto, and which is largely supported by senior military officials, took 16 percent of the vote and 91 seats. The Democratic Party, the former ruling party, is also a party that advocates pancasila. It gained 10.89 percent of the vote and secured 61 seats in the 2014 election.

The presidential election of 2014 was characterized by coalitions. In that election, the Indonesian Democratic Party–Struggle coalition, which included the Indonesian Democratic Party–Struggle party, was victorious. Their candidates, Joko Widodo and his running mate, Jusuf Kalla, were elected president and vice president, respectively. The former vice president, Prabowo Subianto, challenged the victory of Widodo, charging election fraud. However, a month later Indonesia's Constitutional Court rejected the allegations and confirmed the results.

Local Government

Indonesia is divided into 33 provinces, five which have special status. Local government in Indonesia has five levels: the chief executive and his or her deputies, a House of Representatives, the secretariat, administrative or operational units, and a planning division. The House of Representatives elects the chief executive. The secretariat is responsible for the administration of the province, under the authority of the chief executive. Local government is responsible for monitoring adherence to government regulations in terms of agriculture, housing, education, social welfare, and other responsibilities.

Judicial System

Indonesia's judicial system is characterized by several legal traditions, including adat law (traditional village law), Sharia law (Islamic law), and Dutch colonial law. The Supreme Court is the highest court in the country. Lower courts include state, commercial, state administrative, and constitutional courts. Religious courts deal with Sharia law concerns.

Taxation

The government of Indonesia levies personal and corporate income, value-added, sales, property, road, transfer, excise, and stamp taxes. The highest personal income tax rate is 30 percent, while the highest corporate tax rate is 28 percent.

Armed Forces

Indonesia's armed forces, officially the Indonesian National Armed Forces, consist of three service branches—army, navy, and air force. Conscription is selective, and the minimum age for service is eighteen. As of 2010, the government has been pushing for a reserve component to the military, a ratification that critics claim will fully implement conscription. The country has also come under international criticism for the military's economic activities (the government permits military ownership of the armed forces' businesses).

Foreign Policy

Indonesia classifies its foreign policy as an "Independent and Active Foreign Policy," which it first articulated in 1948. In particular, neutrality is one of its key principles, and it has not aligned itself with any particular superpowers or major blocs. In fact, Indonesia is one of founding members of the Non-Aligned Movement (NAM), an international organization established in 1955. However, despite Indonesia's policy of refraining from establishing defensive and military pacts, it maintains strong relations with nations in the interest of economic and regional development, and supports international cooperation efforts through the UN, Association of Southeast Asian Nations (ASEAN), and the Organization of the Islamic Conference (OIC). It also plays an important role in groups for developing countries, including the G-77 and G-15.

Generally, Indonesia has established strong diplomatic relations with the neighboring countries in its region, most notably Singapore, the Philippines, and Thailand, as well as the Pacific Islands to the east, and Australia to the south. Indonesia also focuses on maintaining good relations with its Asian neighbors such as Japan, China, and South Korea. In addition, Indonesia considers the United States and the European Union (EU) major economic partners, and it has received significant developmental and humanitarian aid from the US, Europe, Japan, and Australia.

However, despite Indonesia's policy of avoiding international conflict, the country has been involved in its share of international disputes. In particular, tensions increased between Indonesia and Australia, Portugal, and the US over East Timor (Indonesia occupied East Timor, a country in Southeast Asia, from 1975 to 1999). In 1999, Indonesia relinquished control of East Timor, but only after violence swept the country, and Australia deployed troops in a peacekeeping effort. In addition, the US threatened to withdraw economic aid. In all, 17 nations were represented in the peacekeeping force that intervened.

More importantly, Indonesia has consistently been the focus of human rights abuses, and its strict policy of capital punishment, particularly involving foreigners, has strained relations with other nations, most notably Australia. Other significant disputes include the problem of piracy in Indonesian waters and surrounding international waters such as the Strait of Malacca, and illegal fishing in the waters of Australia and the Philippines.

Human Rights Profile

International human rights law insists that states respect civil and political rights, and also promote an individual's economic, social and cultural rights. The United Nations Universal Declaration on Human Rights (UDHR) is recognized as the standard for international human rights. Its authors sought the counsel of the world's great thinkers, philosophers, and religious leaders, and were careful to create a document that reflects the core values shared by every world culture. (To read this document or view the articles relating to cultural human rights, visit: http://www.udhr.org/UDHR/default.htm.)

Indonesia has been criticized for violating basic human rights principles in a number of areas. In particular, vast human rights abuses occurred during the administration of President Suharto (1967–1998). After seizing power in a bloody coup, Suharto's regime was responsible for genocide, war crimes, torture, attacks on the rights of minorities, and tight restrictions on the media and freedom of movement and assembly. These acts violate almost all of the articles of the UDHR. In the wake of Surharto's oppressive regime, human rights groups continue to criticize Indonesia for continuing to fail to prosecute those responsible. The Indonesian government is also widely suspected of supporting and even encouraging military and subversive actions in areas of Indonesia with a strong movement toward independence, such as West Papua and Aceh, where many of Suharto's most notorious crimes were committed.

Other human rights abuses continue to take place in the country. Numerous laws infringe on the rights to freedom of expression, assembly and religious freedom, as articulated in Articles 18, 19 and 20. The mistreatment of journalists, most notably their unlawful detainment and arrest for peacefully expressing their opinions, continues to be widely practiced. Media censorship in general is also criticized. There are also accounts of ill treatment and torture in detention facilities and prisons, which violate Article 5. In addition, an unreliable, government-influenced judiciary is also a concern, as it potentially violates Article 10. Indonesia's strict enforcement of the death penalty is also in contradiction of Article 3 of the UDHR.

Indonesia has recently ratified the International Covenant on Civil and Political Rights and the International Covenant on Economic, Social and Cultural Rights, but has not passed legislation to make it binding. Controversially, it was given membership of the Human Rights Council and UN Security Council in 2006, despite being listed as a major offender of human rights by all international monitoring agencies.

ECONOMY

Overview of the Economy

Historically, Indonesia's economy has relied on agriculture; today, nearly half of the country's workforce is employed in this sector. Since the 1970s, the country's petroleum supplies have diminished, but the potential of the natural gas industry has grown. The gross domestic product (GDP) was estimated at $856.1 billion USD in 2014, with a per capita GDP of $10,200 (USD).

Although Indonesia's economy has been on the upswing in recent years, the revenue generated by the increase in prices of food and mineral exports has generally not trickled down to local residents, many of whom struggle with unemployment and poverty. Economists estimate that more than two-thirds of the country's citizens work in the informal sector, meaning that they do not receive benefits and are not protected by employment legislation.

Industry

Indonesia's most significant industries include petroleum and natural gas production, mining, and tourism. Important manufactured products include textiles, apparel, footwear, cement, chemical fertilizers, and plywood. Some of the country's key exports include rubber, food products, and electrical appliances. The country trades mostly with other large Asian nations, including Japan and China, and with Western nations such as the United States and Australia.

Because Jakarta serves as Indonesia's economic center, it is where the majority of the nation's banking and financial activity occurs. The manufacturing industry also has a major presence in Jakarta in the form of soap, glassware, paper, and automotive parts factories. In addition, the city produces textiles, iron, aluminum, asbestos, and leather. Indonesia's small local film industry is centered in Jakarta as well. Recently, Jakarta's telecommunications sector has seen particularly strong growth, largely due to the increasing demand for cell phones among residents; earnings due to telecommunications are now close to those associated with manufacturing.

Labor

In 2014, Indonesia had an estimated unemployment rate of 5.7 percent of a workforce of more than 124.3 million. The majority of the labor force—an estimated 38.9 percent in 2012—is concentrated in agriculture. Service accounts for approximately 47.9 percent of the labor force, followed by the industrial sector at just over 13.2 percent.

Energy/Power/Natural Resources

Indonesia's greatest natural resource may be its location at the junction of some of the world's most important shipping zones. Indonesian waters host trade routes between Asia, Europe, the Middle East, and Africa.

The island nation also has reserves of petroleum, coal, and natural gas, tin, nickel, bauxite, copper, gold, and silver. Heavily forested islands like Sumatra provide ready supplies of timber, and the rich, volcanic soil and tropical climate provide an agricultural base for Indonesia's famous spices, tropical fruits, and hardwoods.

Fishing

As the world's largest archipelagic nation, Indonesia enjoys access to a large and diverse supply of marine resources and environments, and has the fifth largest exclusive economic zone in the world. Fishing production grew exponentially for the country from the mid-20th century until the early 21st century. Important commercial catches include anchovy, mackerel, tuna, and sardines, while prawns are an important cultivated resource. Indonesia is also the largest shark producer in the world. Much of Indonesia's fishing industry is artisanal, and the country has worked to modernize the industry. In 2010, Indonesia's Minister for Maritime Affairs and Fisheries stressed the need for Indonesia to have the world's largest fishing industry by 2015. Foreign trawlers and illegal fishing, as well as overfishing, continue to be concerns for the Indonesia fishing industry.

Forestry

Two-thirds of the country's area is forested; most of this land consists of rainforests. Like most of the world's tropical rainforests, those in Indonesia are increasingly threatened by farming, pollution, and human encroachment.

Illegal logging poses a threat to the timber industry, which finds itself unable to compete with illegal logging concerns who offer lower prices. With the forestry industry contributing almost $7 billion in state income, this could have a detrimental effect on the economy and employment.

Mining/Metals

Indonesia's mining sector focuses on the extraction of coal, copper, gold, nickel, and tin. It is among five countries who lead in the production of copper and nickel and is among the ten highest producers of gold and natural gas. Mining accounts for almost nine percent of the country's GDP.

Agriculture

Straddling the equator, Indonesia maintains a consistent, tropical climate throughout the year. Approximately 12 percent of the land is used for farming, although this is only one-third of the arable land available. Most of this land is located in Java, which produces the bulk of Indonesia's rice and soybeans.

The temperatures and volcanic-enriched soil produce rice, cassava, peanuts, rubber, cocoa, coffee, palm oil, and copra, as well as spices. Indonesians also raise poultry, beef, and pork. After Malaysia, Indonesia is the world's largest producer of palm oil. Likewise, Indonesia is the second-largest exporter of rubber in the world, after Thailand.

Animal Husbandry

Livestock is largely raised in small farms, where they provide draft power, manure, and meat. Goats and sheep dominate, followed by cattle, water buffalo, and poultry.

Tourism

With its wealth of tropical islands and dramatic volcanic landscapes, Indonesia has a well-established tourist industry. Political instability, violent conflict in some regions, and a slowing economy has had a great impact on Indonesia's tourism revenues in recent years. The 2004 tsunami that hit northern Sumatra and Aceh caused extensive damage to the area's tourist infrastructure. Tourism is accountable for 9.2 percent (or $68.7 billion USD) of the nation's GDP, providing more than 9.2 million jobs.

Bali is the nation's greatest attraction, drawing more than 2.5 million tourists.

Alice Ashbolt, Amy Witherbee, M. Lee

DO YOU KNOW?

- When the capital was destroyed by fighting in 1619, the Dutch renamed it Batavia—a name which stuck for more than 300 years until the Japanese renamed it Jakarta during their occupation of Indonesia in the Second World War.
- Pramoedya Ananta Toer, a renowned figure in modern Indonesian literature and the author of a series of novels exploring the country's history, was considered for the Nobel Prize in Literature.
- Many ethnic groups in Indonesia do not follow the tradition of having surnames.

Bibliography

Berkmoes, Ryan ver. *Indonesia.* Oakland, CA: Lonely Planet, 2013.

Bhagowati, Surajit Kuma. *Women in Southeast Asia.* New Delhi: New Century, 2014.

Frederick, William H., and Robert L. Worden. *Indonesia: A Country Study.* Washington, DC: Library of Congress, 2011.

Hellwig, Tineke, and Eric Tagliacozzo, eds. *The Indonesia Reader: Culture, History, Politics.* Durham, NC: Duke University Press, 2009.

Parry, Richard Lloyd. *In the Time of Madness: Indonesia on the Edge of Chaos.* London: Richard Lloyd Parry Grove Press, 2005.

Pisani, Elizabeth. *Indonesia, etc.: Exploring the Improbable Nation.* New York: W.W. Norton, 2014.

Saunders, Graham. *Indonesia - Culture Smart!* London: Kuperard, 2007.

Sen, Krishna and Hill, David Media. *Culture and Politics in Indonesia.* Perth: Equinox Publishing, 2006.

Solomon, Charmaine. *Food of Indonesia, Malaysia, Singapore, and the Philippines.* Melbourne, Australia: Hardie Grant Books, 2014.

Taylor, Jean Gelman. *Indonesia: Peoples and Histories.* New Haven and London: Yale University Press, 2003.

Vickers, Adrian A. *History of Modern Indonesia.* England: Cambridge University Press, 2013.

Works Cited

"Amnesty International." *Indonesia profile.* http://www.amnesty.org/en/region/asia-and-pacific/south-east-asia/indonesia

"Amnesty International." *Report on Human Rights in Indonesia*, 2007 http://thereport.amnesty.org/eng/Regions/Asia-Pacific/Indonesia

Andreas Harsono, '"Indonesia: From Mainstream to Alternative Media'", *First Monday*, July 15, 1996, http://www.firstmonday.org/issues/issue3/harsono/

Badan Pusat Statistik." *Republik Indonesia.*

Bev, Jennie S. '"A Struggling Nation: Indonesia in Food, Fuel and Compassion Crises'" 24 July 2008

Bev, Jennie S. '"Growing up a Minority Female in Indonesia'", 26 June, 2000, http://www.suite101.com/article.cfm/human_rights/42410/1

Bronwyn Powell and Susan Austin, "Fighting for Women's Rights in Indonesia" http://en.wikipedia.org/wiki/Indonesian_literature#Notes

Cohen, David, ed. *The Circle of Life*

http://family.jrank.org/pages/868/Indonesia.html

http://hrsbstaff.ednet.ns.ca/waymac/Sociology/A%20Term%201/2.%20Culture/Rituals.htm

http://whc.unesco.org/en/list

http://www.bps.go.id/sector/population/pop2000.htm

http://www.embassyofindonesia.org/foreign/foreignpolicy.htm

http://www.indonesia-tourism.com

http://www.loc.gov/rr/international/asian/indonesia/resources/indonesia-language.html

http://www.mongabay.com/igapo/Indonesia.htm

http://www.onlinewomeninpolitics.org/indon/jinx.sistm.unsw.edu.au-~greenlft-2000-395-395asp3.htm

http://www.thewip.net/contributors/2008/07/a_struggling_nation_indonesia.html

"Indonesia profile." *Human Rights Watch.* http://hrw.org/doc/?t=asia&c=indone

"Indonesia."- *Marriage and Parenthood, Family and Gender, Inheritance.*

"Indonesia." http://www.cyborlink.com/besite/indonesia.htm

"Indonesia." *Global Education.* http://www.globaleducation.edna.edu.au/globaled/go/cache/offonce/pid/645

"Indonesia: Suharto's Death a Chance for Victims to Find Justice, *Human Rights Watch*, http://hrw.org/english/docs/2008/01/27/indone17892.htm

"Indonesian architecture." http://www.asiarooms.com/travel-guide/indonesia/culture-of-indonesia/architecture-of-indonesia.html

"Indonesian Arts and Crafts." *Living in Indonesia*, http://www.expat.or.id/info/art.html

"Indonesia's Foreign Policy." *Embassy of the Republic of Indonesia*, Washington D.C.,

"Language and Literature: Indonesia." U.S. Congress.

"Network Indonesia." http://users.skynet.be/network.indonesia/ni3001.htm

"Official Tourism Site of Indonesia." http://www.my-indonesia.info/

"Promoting Indonesia through Literature and Culture." *Lontar Foundation* http://www.lontar.org/home/index.php

Butler, Rhett. "Cities and urban areas in Indonesia with a population over 100 000." (extract from *The World Gazetter*)

"Rites of Passage." http://blog.baliwww.com/religion/151/

Saxby, David "Youth Indonesian." *Inside Indonesia* http://insideindonesia.org/content/view/108/29/

"The Indonesian Language." http://home.mira.net/~wreid/bali_lng.html

"Traditional Performing Arts of Indonesia." http://users.skynet.be/network.indonesia/ni3001b6.htm

"Urban Youth Culture: Forging a New Identity." http://www.unfpa.org/swp/2007/youth/english/story/angelo_youth.html

Vickers, Adrian "A History of Modern Indonesia" extract. http://www.cambridge.org/catalogue/catalogue.asp?isbn=9780521542623&ss=exc

Williamson, Lucy "Indonesian clerics growing force" BBC News, 7 July 2008 http://news.bbc.co.uk/2/hi/asia-pacific/7493829.stm

"Women and girl domestic workers." *Briefing to the UN Committee on the Elimination of Discrimination against Women*. http://www.amnesty.org/en/library/asset/ASA21/007/2007/en/dom-ASA210072007en.html

A cave in Laos filled with statues of Buddha/Stock photo © Enrico01

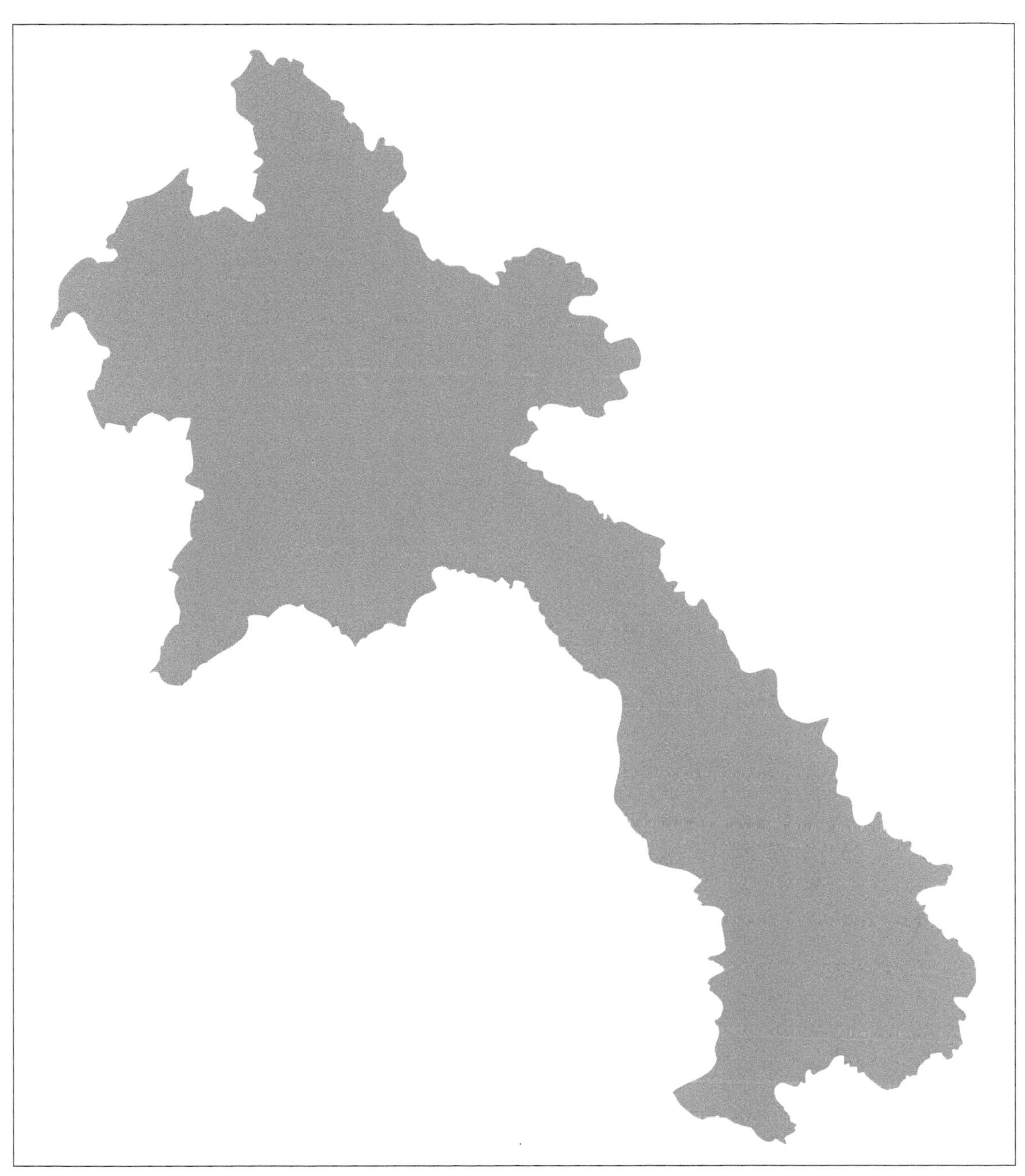

Laos

Introduction

The Lao People's Democratic Republic is a Southeast Asian country bordered by China, Vietnam, Cambodia, Thailand, and Myanmar. For centuries a monarchy, Laos became part of the French colony of Indochina and gained its independence only in 1953.

Communist forces overthrew the government in 1975, after years of internal fighting which became part of the larger conflict engulfing Vietnam and Cambodia. As an important supply route to troops in Northern Vietnam, and with a communist movement of its own, Laos was devastated by secret United States bombing campaigns (1964–1973).

The post-war years were marked by a slow, difficult recovery and the emigration of many Laotian people. Though Laos remains a communist country, the unraveling of the Soviet Union and subsequent loss of its support caused the government to undertake market reforms which have bolstered the economy and led to improved relations with the international community.

Eastern religions have widely influenced the arts in Laos. Such influence is immediately obvious in the Buddhist temples and monasteries throughout the country, and the sculptures and decorations that are part of these structures. Buddha is also a central figure in the epics, proverbs, parables, poems, and lyrics of Laotian literature. Laotians also excel at traditional arts, and woven and embroidered cloth, silk, ceramics, jewelry, and carvings are all commonly produced.

GENERAL INFORMATION

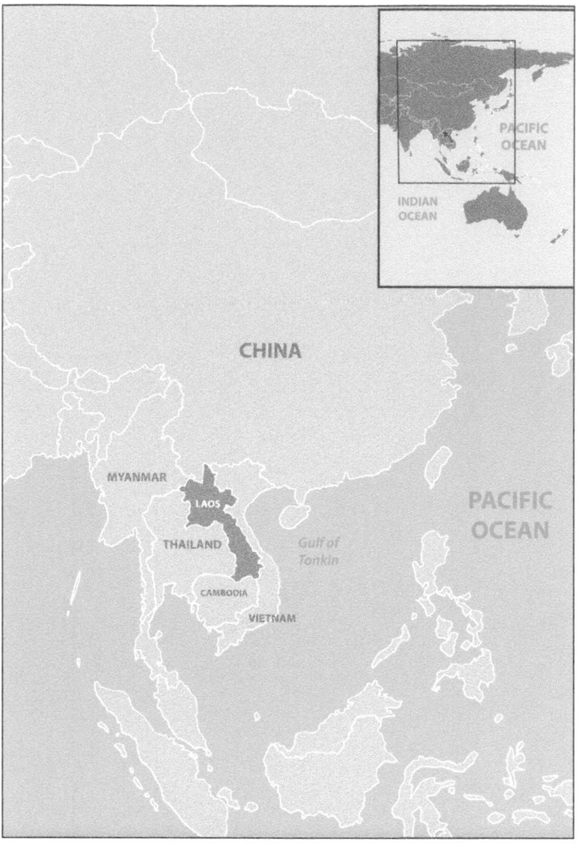

Official Language: Lao
Population: 6,803,699 (2014 estimate)
Currency: Lao kip
Coins: The Lao kip is subdivided into 100 att. Coins, in denominations of 10, 20, and 50 att, are rarely used. They were only issued in 1952, with no further minting.
Land Area: 230,800 square kilometers (89,112 square miles)
Water Area: 6,000 square kilometers (2,317 square miles)
National Motto: "Peace, Independence, Democracy, Unity and Prosperity"
National Anthem: "Pheng Xat Lao" (Hymn of the Lao People")
Capital: Vientiane
Time Zone: GMT +7
Flag Description: The flag of Laos features three horizontal bands of color, with a blue stripe between two stripes of red. A white disc is located in the center of the flag on the blue stripe, symbolizing the unity of the Laotian people.

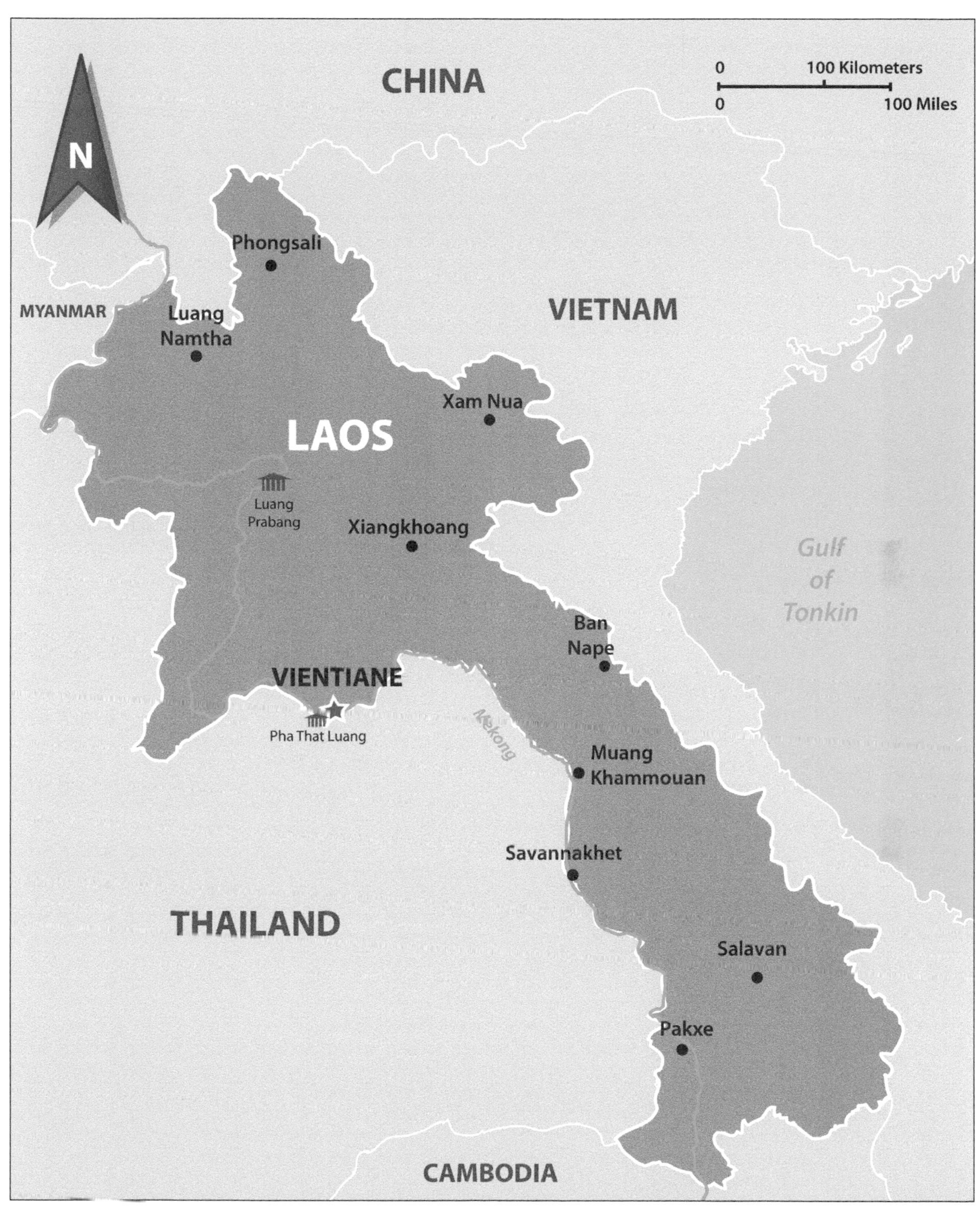
N
CHINA
0 100 Kilometers
0 100 Miles
Phongsali
MYANMAR
Luang Namtha
VIETNAM
Xam Nua
LAOS
Luang Prabang
Xiangkhoang
Gulf of Tonkin
Ban Nape
VIENTIANE
Pha That Luang
Mekong
Muang Khammouan
Savannakhet
THAILAND
Salavan
Pakxe
CAMBODIA

Principal Cities by Population (2012 estimate):

- Vientiane (248,692)
- Pakxe (108,079)
- Savannakhet (79,908)
- Luang Prabang (53,792)
- Xam Nua (40.931)
- Thakek (31,129)

Population

The largest portion of the Laotian population is concentrated on the alluvial plains of the Mekong River Valley, but the overall population density is 27 people per square kilometer (70 people per square mile). With only roughly 38 percent (2014 estimate) of Laotians living in cities, the population is overwhelmingly rural. The population growth rate was estimated at 1.59 percent in 2014.

Migration to urban centers has become a trend in the early 21st century. Vientiane, with an unofficial population of 730,000 residents, is the largest urban center. The central urban area's population is around 248,692, while the remaining population lives in residential areas on the periphery of the city.

Ethnic Laotians, who can be divided into numerous sub-groups, make up approximately 99 percent of the population. Vietnamese, Chinese, and Indians are the only minority groups of note. Approximately 200,000 Hmong live in the United States. Many Hmong are still leaving Laos because, having backed the United States during the Second Indochina War, they are experiencing persecution in their native country.

Languages

Lao is the country's official language and belongs to the Austro-Asiatic family. It is spoken by over 98 percent of the population, and is written in an alphabet related to Sanskrit and depends on the tone of the voice for meaning. There are numerous dialects of Lao spoken throughout the country, some by only small groups of people. Each of the major Laotian ethnic groups speaks one of four major branches: the Tai-Kadai languages are spoken by the lowland populations, the Mon-Khmer languages by the upland populations, and Tibeto-Burman and Hmong-Mien languages by the mountain populations. A majority of Laotians are bilingual; French and English are common in the major cities.

Native People & Ethnic Groups

Laos' many ethnic sub-groups have been categorized into three major groups: the Lao Loum, who occupy the lowlands and account for 68 percent of the population; the Lao Theung, who occupy upland valleys and account for 22 percent of the population; and the Lao Soung (or Hmong), who occupy the mountains and account for nine percent of the population.

The Lao Loum and the Lao Theung have long been in the region, whereas the Lao Soung are thought to have migrated there in the 19th century. In addition to being divisible by language and custom, each group undertakes specific work. The Lao Loum specialize in wet rice farming, while the other two groups use slash-and-burn techniques to clear the hillsides and plateaus for their crops.

The Lao Loum ("lowland Lao") represent the largest ethnic group in Laos today, representing approximately 68 percent of the population. The Lao Theung ("upland Lao") represent an estimated 22 percent. Ethnic minorities include Hmong, Vietnamese, and Yao.

Religions

Although Laos is a communist country, the government does not repress religious expression. An estimated 60 percent of the population adheres to Theravada Buddhism, which is most widespread among the lowlanders. Some Laotians who live in the uplands and the mountains have converted to Buddhism, but many practice phi worship, which is a form of animism. A majority of Laotians respect both Buddhist and animist traditions and mixed temples and prayer areas are common in rural areas. There are also small groups of Christians and Muslims; Christianity is more common in Vientiane and other cities, but accounts for only 1 percent of religious participants nationwide.

Climate
Monsoons dictate Laos' distinct tropical seasons: the rainy period from May to October, the cool, dry period from November to February, and the hot, dry period of March and April. Temperature and average annual rainfall vary according to elevation.

The highest temperatures occur in the lowlands, which average 40° Celsius (104° Fahrenheit) in April. The lowest temperatures occur in the mountains, which average 5° Celsius (41° Fahrenheit) in January. Average annual rainfall is 178 centimeters (about 70 inches), but is significantly higher in the southern lowland areas.

The rainy season usually commences at the same time throughout the country, but it can be delayed. In some years, regional droughts affect the harvest. In other years, high levels of precipitation cause the Mekong River to flood.

ENVIRONMENT & GEOGRAPHY

Topography
Laos is a landlocked country. Mountains and plateaus account for 70 percent of its terrain. The primary range extends across much of the country's north and along half of the border between Laos and Vietnam. Known as the Annam Highlands (Truong Son), these mountains average between 1,500 and 3,000 meters (4,921 and 9,843 feet) in height, and reach the country's highest point at Phou Bia (2,819 meters/9,249 feet). The southeastern portion of the country is also mountainous. Three high plateaus rise in Laos: the Plain of Jars in the north, the Vientiane Plain in the center, and the Bolaven Plateau in the south.

The heavily cultivated alluvial plains of the Mekong River Valley account for approximately 20 percent of the country's terrain. This region is dominated by the Mekong River, which originates in China and flows along the length of Laos. The river forms the western border with Thailand and Burma and is vital for agriculture, fishing, and transportation. Small tributaries flow from the mountains in northern and eastern Laos and join the Mekong in its course towards the South China Sea.

Vientiane, the capital, is located in the north-central part of Laos, in the Mekong River Valley near the border of Thailand. The average elevation in the river valley is 150 meters (492 feet) above sea level. Many of the city's buildings are located along the Mekong River or one of its tributary streams. Most of Laos is composed of mountainous terrain with the exception of the lowlands found near the river valleys.

Plants & Animals
Laos is rich in plant and animal life, and the government has established twenty Biodiversity Conservation Areas designed to protect their populations. Primary forest covers approximately 54 percent of the terrain while secondary forest covers about 30 percent. Tree species include ironwood, teak, pine, mahogany, rosewood, and bamboo.

Elephants, monkeys, leopards, pandas, rhinoceroses, anteaters, venomous snakes, leopards, black bears, wild pigs, and tigers are found in Laos. There are also numerous bird and rodent species. The Javan and Sumatran rhinoceroses are listed as critically endangered, while the Asian elephant, the red panda, the tiger, and several monkey species are listed as endangered.

CUSTOMS & COURTESIES

Greetings
Courtesy in Lao culture is dictated by social hierarchies. Wealth, age, and education grant superiority, and therefore a greater display of respect. The traditional greeting in Laos is the nop, where the palms are placed together in prayer position and held in front of the chest. The higher a person's hands are held, the higher the level of respect displayed. Although the nop was not encouraged after the communist revolution, it is now quite common in society. The nop is used as

a gesture of greeting, of farewell, of thanks, and of apology. In exchanges with Westerners, handshakes are acceptable. The most common greeting is "Sa bai dee" (loosely meaning "Hello"), which is normally accompanied by a nop.

The social hierarchy is reflected in pronoun usage, as Laotians address their male elders with "ai" preceding their name, and female elders are addressed with the prefix "ew." Young people's names are preceded with "bak" for boys and "i" for girls. During informal conversation, pronouns may be omitted completely, while more formal exchanges may call for special pronouns.

Gestures & Etiquette

In Lao culture, it is severely frowned upon to touch someone else's head or use one's feet for pointing. The top of the body (the head) is deemed sacred, and the bottom (feet) is considered to be low and indecent. Women and men should not show public displays of affection, such as kissing or hugging. In addition, Lao people dress modestly, especially outside of the bigger cities.

In general, Lao cultural behavior traditionally takes into account the feelings of others before speaking, seeking to avoid conflict and confrontation. As such, Lao culture strongly values the concept of "saving face." Losing one's temper or raising one's voice is seen as a "loss of face," and is therefore embarrassing for all parties involved. As Buddhism plays a strong role in social interactions, a gentle and patient manner is favored.

Etiquette is particularly important when entering temples. Clothing should cover shoulders and extend below the knees, and shoes must be removed before entering the temple. Additionally, women are forbidden from touching a monk, and monks are only allowed to converse with women within a temple.

Eating/Meals

In households, meals are often taken at low tables with people sitting on cushions on the floor. In light of the Lao attitude toward feet, legs should be crossed (for men), or folded to the side with feet tucked in (for women). Traditional Lao meals are communal, with diners seated on mats surrounding a ka toke table, or rattan platform. (Rattan refers to a species of palm largely used in furniture making).

Each meal generally has sticky rice, which is the standard staple of Lao cuisine, and the various dishes are placed on the ka toke. There is normally no particular order in which dishes must be eaten, and all dishes, including soup, are sampled throughout the meal. Spoons and forks are used with most dishes, though sticky rice is eaten with the hands. Chopsticks are typically used for noodle dishes. Though this traditional style of eating may not be strictly adhered to in contemporary times, the basic idea of family-style meals persists.

Lao cities typically have French-style cafés and several offerings of foreign cuisine. Roadside restaurants are common throughout the country, serving standard dishes such as feu, a noodle soup derived from Vietnamese cuisine.

Visiting

When entering a Lao household, it is normally expected that visitors remove their shoes before crossing the threshold. Guests are welcome to offer sweets, fruit, or alcohol as gifts to their hosts. Even if not hungry or thirsty, guests should accept a small bit of food or drink to show their gratitude to their host. Even simply tasting a dish is an appreciated gesture.

LIFESTYLE

Family

Lao families are traditionally large and close-knit. Women typically have many children, as birth control was banned until recent years, and access remains limited. Even married sons and daughters will often continue to live with the wife's family, creating an even more extended household. This family network is considered crucial to the children's upbringing, as it implicitly teaches them how to function in society. After the young couple's first child is born, the couple will usually move closer to the family of the groom.

Traditionally, dating is not a common practice. However, young men will often spend evenings visiting all the houses of the village and courting young women while chatting with their families. After young Laotians choose their spouse (arranged marriages are not common), a dowry is paid before the couple weds. After the older daughters have wed and moved into their own households, the youngest daughter is expected to stay and care for the aging parents. Eventually, the youngest daughter will inherit the family's home and land.

Housing

The rural and agricultural lifestyle largely dictates the traditional Lao housing, as at least 80 percent of the population relies on agriculture for their survival. Houses in the countryside are typically constructed of bamboo or wood, with thatch or corrugated tin roofs. These houses are built on stilts to account for flooding, and furniture is extremely modest or non-existent. Mats are often used as seats, tables, and beds, and walls may be bamboo matting as well. The Hmong and other ethnic minorities in northern Laos often build large houses on the ground, instead of on stilts. In addition, rural houses usually have no electricity or running water, as Laos does not have a national power grid. Electricity is brought in from Thailand, and normally reserved for the cities.

Urban housing is more diverse, comprising influences from several countries. French colonial architecture is evident in urban structures, alongside wooden houses on stilts, large Thai-style houses, and even houses built in the American style during the 1950s and 1960s. Cities in Laos are not highly populated, so rural housing is more representative of the traditional Lao style.

Food

Sticky rice, pa daek (fermented fish paste), and chili paste are the traditional staples of Lao cuisine, though the Hmong, Chinese, and certain other ethnic groups use regular white rice as a staple. Sticky rice is eaten by hand and dipped in various sauces, while white rice is eaten with spoons or chopsticks. Soup, such as the Vietnamese-derived feu or the bamboo shoot soup, keng noh mai som, is also a traditional part of Lao cuisine.

Rural Lao cuisine often incorporates raw meat and plants easily found in the forest. For example, laab, often considered the national dish, is minced meat prepared with spices, a popular dish that is made both raw and cooked. The meat can be anything from pork, duck, chicken, and beef, to venison and buffalo. Sai oua (sausage) and ping sin (dried, grilled beef) are also popular cooked meat dishes. However, raw meat is less common in the cities, where hygiene concerns have prompted more cooks to avoid it. Interestingly, urban cuisine has also adopted the practice of cooking dog meat, which men usually enjoy with a strong alcoholic drink. Coffee and bread, culinary legacies of the French, are typically found in urban eateries.

Lowland Lao cuisine centers on fish, though beef, chicken, and buffalo meat are popular as well. Som pa (pickled fish) and tom padek (a padek fish stew) are two popular dishes, while Tam mak houng, made with shredded green papaya and plenty of spice, is another popular dish. Typical ingredients used to prepare meat, salads, and soups include lemongrass, kaffir lime, chili, ginger, bamboo shoot, tamarind, and garlic, among many others.

Life's Milestones

The strongest rite of passage in Lao culture is a man's ordination as a Buddhist monk. Although the practice is not as prevalent as it once was, it is still an honorable tradition that many men seek to uphold. Ordination can be done for any amount of time, though the minimum was three months in the past to coincide with Buddhist Lent. For the ordination ritual, the Lao man must perform the life of Prince Gautama, famous for becoming the enlightened Buddha. The man's eyebrows and head are then shaved before he puts on a simple robe and takes his vows. During the period as a monk, men will practice meditation and Pali chanting, as well as study religion.

CULTURAL HISTORY

Art

Aside from crafts, most Lao visual or fine art is heavily influenced by Theravada Buddhism, as well as by Hinduism. For example, the traditional Indian epic, the *Ramayana*, is the subject of many religious murals and decorations in its Lao form, the *Pharak Pharam*. Murals were mostly painted on temple walls and hanging cloths, and often display a simple style with no shading or perspective. (Western-style painting would emerge during the French colonial period.) Geography was also a significant influence on Lao culture. Northern Laos shows a clear artistic influence from the Thai and Burmese styles, while the influence of the Khmer people—the predominant ethnicity in Cambodia—is strong in southern Laos.

Buddhist sculpture was another distinct Lao fine art, with bronze sculptures of the Buddha the most common. These large bronze sculptures were typically cast in separate parts, and later assembled to create an impressive religious image, many of which survive today. Additionally, while precious metals such as gold and silver were used for sculpture, they were usually reserved for smaller images. The sculpting or carving of wooden small objects was also typical, and wooden carvings adorn temple doors, roofs, and pillars. Other media for sculpture included brick-and-mortar and jade. A modern spin on Buddhist sculpture is found in the Buddha Park outside Vientiane, a sculpture park where over 200 contemporary Buddha and Hindu sculptures reside in a garden setting.

Traditional crafts in Laos include textile arts such as weaving and embroidery, wood and ivory carving, silver and goldsmithing, and basket making. Weaving and embroidery are the most prevalent crafts, reflecting the geographic and ethnic diversity of the Lao people. Lao traditional clothing exhibits silk and cotton weaving, with the wrap skirts, shawls, and bags, all with intricately embroidered hems. Certain styles and designs are found throughout Laos, such as dragon and naga (the mythical cobra) images, as well as star- and diamond-shaped patterns.

Silver and goldsmithing date back to the 9th century in Laos, though they not become a significant cultural crafts until the 16th century. At this time, jewelry, urns, and intricately designed ceremonial boxes were created for the royalty and upper class. Ceramics date back even further, as pottery from as early as the second century has been discovered outside Vientiane. Though pottery remains a popular craft in Laos, production is now mostly industrial, with few ceramic villages surviving.

Architecture

Lao architecture is known for its intriguing combination of Asian and religious influences—particularly Buddhism—and French colonial architecture. Some of the more famous religious architecture in Laos includes the wat (temple) as well as the stupa, a high peaked-roof structure traditionally used to hold both holy and royal relics. The traditional style of the Lao stupa is a four-cornered structure whose roof curves into a peak. The 16th-century Pha That Luang (Grand Stupa) in the capital of Vientiane is emblematic of Lao religious architecture. King Setthathirat (1534–1572) had the structure erected when he moved the capital from Luang Prabang to Vientiane. Several invasions by Thailand (then the Kingdom of Siam), Burma, and China largely destroyed That Luang, but it was reconstructed in the 1930s. The site has since become a symbol of nationalism, and its image appears on the Lao national crest.

Luang Prabang is also admired for its temples and architecture, including the 14th-century Wat Manorom. While many maintain it was actually founded in the 15th century, most experts agree that it was built at one of the area's first Khmer Buddhist missions. Also in Luang

Prabang is Wat Wisunalat, an early 16th-century temple that reflects an earlier Lao style of architecture. This style includes a two-tiered, simple roof and ornate wooden carvings. In 1995, Luang Prabang was listed as a World Heritage Site—one of two in the country—for its blend of traditional, colonial, and urban architecture. World Heritage Sites are designated by the United Nations Educational, Scientific and Cultural Organization (UNESCO).

Traditional and religious Lao architecture, including bamboo and wooden houses, often built on stilts, and Buddhist temple architecture, exists alongside French colonial architecture. This is particularly evident in Luang Prabang, where the Royal Palace (Haw Kham), built in 1901, mixes the French colonial style with traditional Lao elements. Additionally, Vientiane's Patuxai, or Victory Monument, strongly recalls the Arc de Triomphe in Paris, and the wide boulevards lined with trees are also reminiscent of the French style.

Drama

Beginning with the revolution in 1975, the Laotian film industry became solely devoted to communist propaganda. All film production was created under the Cinema Department of the Ministry of Culture, pushing out any remnants of the private sector film production. State documentaries were released annually, as well as two feature films that flopped in the box office. The Cinema Department was replaced in 1988 with the State Cinematographic Company, which did not produce any films itself, but rather distributed foreign films in Laos.

As the economy has slowly recovered somewhat since 1986, some documentaries have been created. However, it was not until 2008 that the first privately funded film was released in Laos, *Good Morning, Luang Prabang*. The government has actually supported the film's release, despite the plotline's lack of communist propaganda. The government seems hopeful that a budding film industry could be a new source of revenue for Laos. However, private production does not ensure freedom of expression, as demonstrated by the government official who was on the *Good Morning, Luang Prabang* set daily to make sure that every scene was appropriate. The plot is a light love story, which allowed the film to be more easily approved by the government.

Music & Dance

The history of music in Laos is often subdivided into classical and folk traditions. Classical music in Laos was largely developed in the royal courts, favoring instruments such as the lanat (xylophone), pi kaeo (a wind instrument), and the khong vong (a set of gongs). This form of music was banned when the Lao People's Democratic Republic was established in 1975, as it was seen to be at conflict with the communist values of the new regime. It was not until later in the 20th century that classical music was reintroduced to Lao society.

The folk music of Laos is largely associated with the khaen, a free-reed bamboo mouth organ that is a key feature of Lao music in general. The khaen is often used to accompany a maw-lam, a solo singer who sings a brisk melody that is mostly improvisation. The khaen is also used as a solo and ensemble instrument. Different regions of Laos have adapted various styles of this genre, which is also popular in areas of northeast Thailand. One folk style in particular, the lam (often used as an umbrella term for Laos folk music as a whole, and called khap in northern Laos), involves a call-and-response style that most likely originated form the storytelling traditions that predated the spread of Buddhism in the country.

Traditional Lao folk dance, called fon phun muang, often depicts and celebrates scenes of nature. Royal court dance performances gave rise to a number of other dance traditions, including the fon uay phone (welcome dance), the fon sithone manora tale of a half-human, half-bird woman, and the fon sang sinxay (the portrayal of the Sinxay epic). In addition, the lam vong (circle dance) is a popular social dance that inspired several variations across the different regions of Laos.

Literature

Early Lao literature arose from the oral tradition of storytelling, which featured a rich collection of myths, legends, and proverbs associated with the various ethnicities. (Among the rural villages and populations, several ethnic minority groups maintain this oral tradition to this day.) Following the emergence of Buddhism, Buddhist monks used these storytelling traditions to spread Buddhist teachings. Eventually, these teachings would become transcribed onto texts, the earliest medium being palm leaves.

The emergence of Lao literature is usually dated under the reign of King Wisunarath (also spelled Visunarat) in the 16th century, when he commissioned the compilation of various stories under the title *Tamnan Khun Burom* (*Legend of Khun Burom*). Subsequent kings enjoyed strong relationships with the Lanna Kingdom (in present-day Thailand), which led to the recording of the traditional jataka tales (about previous Buddha incarnations) and panchatantra fables. The *Pharak Pharam* was also developed during this time. The canonical poems of Lao literature, such as *Kalaket, Nang Phom Hom*, and *Champasiton*, were written in the 17th century, considered a golden age for Lao culture.

Under French colonial rule, Laos was introduced to printing—but not until the 1920s. High illiteracy rates led to a low interest in developing print quality, as oral traditions still prevailed. The 1960s brought a veritable wave of publications, ranging from traditional literature to promote the royal government's message, to revolutionary poetry and short stories published by the Pathet Lao resistance. Though high costs and low readership made publishing limited during much of the 20th century, the past few decades have seen a revival of contemporary literature. Bounthanong Somsaiphon (1953–) is one of the best-known modern authors, having published poetry, novels and short stories addressing current political and cultural issues in Laos. Another important contemporary writer was Outhine Bouyavong (1942–2000), whose work also offered social commentary, and often celebrated rural life and traditions in Laos.

CULTURE

Arts & Entertainment

The visual arts in Laos are dominated by Buddhist sculpture, murals, and carvings. Though Western styles of painting such as watercolor and oil were introduced during the period of French colonization, a unique Laotian tradition has not emerged. Contemporary Laotian artists normally gain popularity by painting idyllic rural landscapes or precise portrayals of national monuments. The lack of a market for innovative endeavors discourages even those artists who have participated in international workshops and exhibitions from exploring these novel ideas in Laos. Further, the government does not encourage individual expression.

Another barrier for Laotian artists is the limited range of options in art education. There are only a few established art institutes, and reading material on the arts is usually published in English or French. The first Western art school was opened in 1940 in the Champasak Province by French painter Marc Leguay (1910–2001). After he was briefly imprisoned by the Japanese in 1945, he reopened the school in Vientiane before finally closing it in 1949 due to insufficient funding. Leguay was also associated with what is now called the National Faculty of Fine Arts in Vientiane, which offers secondary level art programs. A sister school offering music and dance instruction was opened simultaneously. These art schools teach fine arts and craft techniques, but originality is not generally encouraged.

The Lao artist Kongphat Luangrath (1950–), who became a teacher at the National Faculty of Fine Arts, has gained international recognition for his oil paintings. He is also known for assembling a small group of artists in Vientiane who seek to create an artistic space separate from politics. Though these artists have yet to produce work that significantly deviates from the Laotian mainstream, small innovations in composition and subject matter have shown promise.

Contemporary music in Laos ranges from rock music to hip-hop and rap. Thai pop music also flows heavily into Laos, though Lao pop stars such as Ting, Alexandra Bounxouei, and Cream have a thriving fan base. There have been recent waves of rock bands becoming popular with Laotian youth. These rock bands include Smile Black Dog, Khem Tid, Aluna, and The Cell. Laotian contemporary music is also springing up in the United States, Canada, and France, and Lao-American pop stars such as Phone Phoummithone and Birdie are establishing themselves by blending modern pop styles and traditional country music from Laos.

Football (soccer), volleyball, and track and field are popular Western sports in Laos, but Laotians also play games typical to the country and region. These include Thai kickboxing and sepak takraw, a game involving two teams who must pass a ball over a net without using the hands. Dancing is also popular among Laotians.

Cultural Sites & Landmarks

Despite being known as one of the most bombed nations in history, Laos is renowned for its cultural heritage, often in the form of architecture and monuments, and its rugged and heavily forested geography. In addition, many ethnicities still adhere to traditional means and culture in the rural villages that dot the country's jungles. Many distinct geographical places—such as the Kuang Si Falls, the Pak Ou Caves, famous for their ancient sculptures, and the Mekong River—have become tourist destinations in recent years. Laos is also home to two UNESCO World Heritage Sites: the town of Luang Prabang and Vat Phou and its surrounding ancient settlements.

Luang Prabang, former capital of the kingdom, earned its title because of its elegant blend of traditional Lao architecture and French colonial style. The 18th- and 19th-century Wat Mai Suwannaphumaham is one of Luang Prabang's best-known temples. It is featured on postcards and situated conveniently near the local night market. Besides it striking appearance, Wat Mai earned its fame as the royal family's temple, and as the home of the highest Laotian Buddhist dignitary. Luang Prabang is also home to the Royal Palace, which was built in the beginning of the 20th century, and now houses a cultural museum.

Officially designated as Vat Phou and Associated Ancient Settlements within the Champasak Cultural Landscape, the Vat Phou (also spelled Wat Phou) World Heritage Site is a ruined temple complex built by the Khmer people. The temple complex and the various ancient settlements of the province of Champasak date back more than 1,000 years. The cultural landscape of Champasak was created to reflect the Hindu notion of relations between humans and nature, using a geometric pattern of structures and waterways that has been artfully preserved. This complex is largely associated with the Khmer Empire.

In Vientiane, Ho Phra Kaeo (Altar of the Emerald Buddha) was constructed in 1565 as a temple to house the revered Emerald Buddha. When the statue was captured by the Thais in 1778, the name of the structure was changed to Ho Phra Kaeo (instead of Wat Phra Kaeo) to reflect that the Buddha image no longer resides there. Another notable temple in Vientiane is Wat Ong Teu, originally constructed in the 16th century and later restored after the 1828 Siamese invasion. Wat Sisaket, built in 1818, is the oldest temple in Vientiane that survived the destructive invasions of the Siamese armies.

One of the city's most famous landmarks is the Pha That Luang, a Buddhist stupa (mound-shaped monument) that was built in the 16th century, among the ruins of an ancient Khmer building. The stupa was destroyed by the Siamese army in 1828, but was rebuilt by the French in the late 19th century. Since 1991, the Pha That Luang has been designated as the national symbol of Laos and has therefore been elevated in cultural significance. The central tower in the center of the stupa is 45 meters (148 feet) tall.

Libraries & Museums

Vientiane contains a majority of the nation's museums and cultural centers. The Lao National

Museum contains relics and historical artifacts related to the nation's history. The museum's collection includes artifacts and photographs related to the extensive damage suffered in Laos during the Vietnam conflict. The museum also contains a collection of items related to the history of the Mekong Delta and the various tribes that have inhabited the region. The Wat Sisaket Temple and Museum contains a collection of paintings and sculpture documenting Buddhist history in Laos. The connected temple was built between 1819 and 1824 and is one of the oldest surviving religious structures in Laos.

The National Library of Laos was established in 1956. The building that houses the library was originally constructed in 1923. Since then, it has undergone several renovations and expansions. The library includes a facility for children and the Lao Ancient Manuscript Preservation Project. However, the library continues to struggle with issues related to funding.

Holidays

Laos' major holidays and festivals are religious in nature, inspired mainly by Buddhism but also by pre-Buddhist practices meant to invite rain and a good harvest. The week-long Laotian New Year is celebrated in April. Families clean house in preparation for the holiday, during which they gather together for feasts, sing and dance, and visit local temples for prayers and ceremonies.

Buddha's birth, enlightenment, and death are celebrated on Visakha Puja in May. The faithful visit local temples for prayers and to offer food. Boon Bang Fai, the rocket festival, takes place at the same time. Laotians build rockets and enter them into a competition. The holiday is intended to bring rain.

Haw Khao Padap Din is a festival of remembrance for the dead involving visits to temple, special prayers, and cremations. The end of the harvest is marked with the week-long That Luang festival at the Great Stupa in Vientiane. It involves a candlelit procession around the stupa and offerings of food and flowers to the monks.

Youth Culture

Laotian youth culture was long dominated by Thai influence, largely due to the influx of Thai pop music and television programming available in Laos. The influence of Western—particularly American—youth culture has also been significant. In recent years, however, urban youth have increasingly turned to hip-hop, especially Laotian hip-hop groups. Although hip-hop was not initially accepted when it was introduced to Laotian radio, it has now become one of the main genres of modern Lao youth music, and one of the main avenues of youth expression in Laotian youth culture. However, the lyrics must be deemed appropriate by Laotian authorities, which eliminates some of the offensive or controversial content that can be pervasive in American hip-hop.

Hip-hop culture, in general, has also risen in popularity among Laotian youth, especially hip-hop fashion. For example, one of the most common trends among urban teenagers, most notably males, is the enormous t-shirt and baggy pants, fashion trends that are often emblematic of the hip-hop lifestyle. Many Laotian teenagers also see hip-hop as a means of spreading modern Laotian culture worldwide. By taking a foreign influence and making it distinctly their own, these youth hope to create a cultural movement that will entice youth in other countries.

SOCIETY

Transportation

Roads in Laos are largely underdeveloped, with over half of the highways unpaved. The principal road, Route 13, runs from the south to the north of the country, with variable conditions throughout. Driving through Laos offers a broad view of the countryside, however, and all hired cars include a driver. Transport between Vientiane, Luang Prabang, Vang Vieng, and Savannakhet—the four major hubs in Laos—is accessible via minibus, bus, and converted pickup truck. Within cities, jumbos (motorized three-wheel vehicles) are common, and function as taxis. Bicycles and motorcycles are the primary modes of transportation in the capital, though automobiles are increasingly common. Traffic moves on the right-hand side of the road in Laos.

Transportation Infrastructure

The road network of Laos is underdeveloped, and paved roads are few and far between in certain regions. Over half of the Mekong River runs through Laos, making boat travel a viable option. However, river travel becomes less practical during the dry season, when navigation can be nearly impossible. Slow boats and speedboats are the main forms of river transportation. Additionally, Lao Airlines is the only airline that runs domestic flights, operating in Vientiane, Luang Prabang, and Pakse, among others. Only few airports in Laos have paved runways—less than 10 in the early 21st century—while roughly 43 are unpaved. Laos has no railway.

Vientiane is the site of the nation's only international airport, located approximately three kilometers (1.8 miles) from the city. In addition to providing a means of transportation throughout the entire country, the Mekong River and its tributaries are major routes for transportation to and from the capital. A variety of boats, including water taxis, frequent the Vientiane portion of the Mekong. The infrastructure of the city includes a minimal telecommunications network and few paved roads to connect the nation's cities. Vientiane is the most developed of Laos' principle cities, but is relatively underdeveloped when compared to major cities in Cambodia, Thailand, or Vietnam.

Media & Communications

The government has used mass media as a propaganda tool since 1975, mainly through television, radio, and print media. Almost all Laotian media is run by the government. In recent years, the government has increased its focus on entertainment programming, largely as a means of competing with the Thai media that is widespread in Laos. Lao National Radio (LNR) enjoys popularity throughout the country, while Lao National Television (LNTV) still struggles to compete with Thai television programming.

Printing was not introduced to Laos until the 1920s, but it did not produce significant publications within the country until the early 1940s. The *Lao Nhay* (*Great Laos*) newspaper was launched by the French colonial government to encourage Lao national pride. This newspaper published historical and cultural features, as well as poetry and short stories about Laotian culture.

The pre-revolution Khaosan Pathet Lao (KPL) News Agency was created to collect and supply news to revolutionary publications. After the 1975 revolution, the KPL News Agency became the national news agency. Only one pre-revolution newspaper, the *Vientiane Post*, continued publication by the Vientiane Prefectural Government after the revolution, albeit under a new name (*Vientiane Mai*). All other publications were changed and taken over by the new communist government.

In the past two decades, a number of regional newspapers have emerged in the Lao language, as well as English and French. The main Lao language daily newspapers are *Sieng Pasaxon* (*Voice of the People*) and the *Pathet Lao Daily Newspaper*. Major English language newspapers include the *Vientiane Times* and the *KPL News*.

SOCIAL DEVELOPMENT

Standard of Living

Laos ranked 139th out of 187 countries on the 2014 United Nations Human Development Index, which measures quality of life and standard of living indicators

The population of Laos is growing rapidly. Though it has a high birth rate, infant mortality is also high. Life expectancy is 61 years for males and 65 years for females (2014 estimate).

Water Consumption

Drinking water is widely available in Laos and is of relatively good quality. However, access remains an issue in some areas of the country. An estimated 60 percent of the country's urban population and 50 percent of the country's rural population has access to water. Rainwater serves as an ample water source for the country's agricultural sector. According to 2012 statistics from the World Health Organization, 64.6 percent of the population has access to improved sanitation.

Education

The Laotian government has long emphasized the need for universal education, but it lacks the resources to realize this goal, especially in rural areas. In theory, a compulsory five years of primary school is followed by six years of secondary school. In practice, primary school attendance is high among the Lao Lum but secondary school attendance is much lower. Among other ethnic groups, it is low for both levels, and many children do not receive any formal education.

There are several institutes of higher education in Laos. They include the National University of Laos, the National Polytechnic Institute, the Medical Sciences University, and smaller technical colleges located outside of the capital. In 2005, the country's literacy rate was estimated at 73 percent (83 percent among males and 63 percent among females).

Women's Rights

The Laos constitution calls for gender equality, and the Lao Women's Union, founded in 1955, has a strong foothold in promoting women's roles in Laotian society. Three years after the founding of the Lao Women's Union, women were granted the right to vote and run for public office. Additionally, women comprise 25 percent of the Lao National Assembly and are active in private business, often earning higher incomes than men in urban areas do. However, women represent only two percent of government leaders at the local level, which indicates a significant discrepancy.

Discrimination against women is prevalent in traditional communities, with rural and ethnic minority women particularly affected. In addition to suffering severe poverty, these women are often uneducated and illiterate. This is due, in large part, to government initiatives to eradicate opium cultivation, which forces ethnic minority groups from their homes. Oftentimes they settle in new villages whose resources are inadequate. One such group forced to live in the jungle—the Lao Hmong—were victim to an attack in 2006 that killed at least 26 people, the majority of whom were women and children. The attack, launched by Laotian government troops, represents another incident in the long list of assaults and arbitrary detention of women and children and other members of the Hmong community. Women then suffer in the face of no education, no job, and no access to healthcare. In addition, maternal and infant mortality rates are very high for these rural and ethnic minority women, mostly due to the lack of access to both healthcare facilities and contraception.

Although it is against the law, human trafficking is a recognized problem in Laos. The number of Laotians trafficked annually out of the country is unknown, but data show that the most common destination is Thailand. Children and women are trafficked to other countries often from lowland Laos, and they are usually forced into the sex industry. Ethnic minorities are particularly vulnerable due to lower socioeconomic positions and the inability to speak Lao, which is similar to the Thai language.

In 2004, the Law on Women was passed, criminalizing human trafficking and domestic violence. This law is closely modeled on the UN Convention on the Elimination of Discrimination against Women and the Convention on the Rights of the Child. However, marital rape is not criminalized, and though spousal abuse is illegal, it is unknown how much domestic abuse goes unreported. It is believed that domestic violence is not widespread, and may only be prevalent in more traditional communities.

Health Care

Though Laos has a system of socialized medicine, it cannot adequately cope with the health needs of the population because of shortages of medical supplies, facilities, and health care practitioners. The situation is even worse in rural areas, and many people have recourse only to traditional medicines. As a result, many easily-remedied illnesses adversely affect the Laotian population. These include typhoid, malaria, bilharzias, chickenpox, diarrhea, and intestinal parasites. Malnutrition, especially among children, is also a significant problem.

GOVERNMENT

Structure

Though there have been significant reforms over the last decades, they have been concentrated in the economic and not the political sphere. The Lao People's Democratic Republic remains a communist country, governed by the Lao People's Revolutionary Party (LPRP), despite parliamentary elections and a new constitution. The government controls the country's media outlets, and dissent from the official line is not allowed.

According to the 1991 constitution, the executive branch consists of a president, a vice president, a prime minister, and a cabinet called the Council of Ministers. The president is elected by the legislature to a five-year term. The prime minister and the Council of Ministers are appointed to five-year terms pending legislative approval. The president has the power to dismiss the prime minister and the cabinet.

The National Assembly controls the legislative branch. It normally meets twice a year and consists of 109 members who are elected to five-year terms. In addition to approving the executive branch and making judicial appointments, its responsibilities include making constitutional amendments, approving the budget and international treaties, and setting taxes.

Political Parties

Laos is a single-party state. The Lao People's Revolutionary Party (LPRP) is the sole legal party in Laos. All non-communist parties are forbidden, and some opposition leaders and supporters have been imprisoned for political reasons.

Local Government

Laos consists of 16 provinces, the capital city of Vientiane, and one special zone, known as the Saysomboune Special Zone. Saysomboune is administered by the Laotian army. People's Committees are responsible for overseeing the provinces as well as districts and villages. Districts and villages are overseen by chiefs. However, both are closely overseen by the central government. Vientiane is overseen by a provincial governor.

Judicial System

Judicial power is concentrated in the Supreme People's Court. In addition, there are People's Provincial Courts, Municipal Courts, People's District Courts, and Military Courts. The Laotian legal system is still developing. In 2010, it consisted of an estimated 100 lawyers. The country's criminal justice system and legal system is lacking in manpower and infrastructure. Generally, law enforcement and the dispensation of punishments for those who break the law remains the domain of the government.

Taxation

The Laotian tax system consists of indirect and direct taxes. Indirect taxes include a turnover tax and an excise tax. Direct taxes include a profit tax, income tax, and minimum tax. Excise taxes are applied to gasoline, tobacco, and alcoholic drinks. Although income taxes are collected from the formal economy, income generated by peasants working in agricultural production is exempt.

Armed Forces

The armed forces of Laos, officially known as the Lao People's Army, are small, and typically under-funded, though the country has improved its bilateral military relations with numerous countries in recent years, including India. As of 2006, 15 was the minimum age for conscription, which consisted of an 18 month service obligation. In 2010, Laos and China pledged to strengthen military ties. That same year, the armed forces participated in a joint military operation with Vietnam to hunt down both Hmong and Laotian groups in the country's mountainous and jungle regions, groups that, according to some reports, were facing government-forced eviction or avoiding government persecution.

Foreign Policy

Laotian foreign policy has changed dramatically since the 1980s, particularly after the dissolution of the Soviet Union. Laos had long received substantial international aid, including from France, Germany, Australia, and Sweden. Laos also received aid from the United Nations Development Programme (UNDP), the International Monetary Fund (IMF), and other UN agencies.

Laos is a member of the Association of Southeast Asian Nations (ASEAN). Thailand is its principal trading partner of the group, though past relations between the two countries have been rocky. Border conflicts in the late 1980s and disputes regarding Lao refugees in Thailand caused rifts, but Thailand has grown closer to Laos as Vietnam has pulled back. Vietnam removed its troops from Laos in 1989, which significantly reduced its physical and influential connection to Laos. Additionally, for landlocked Laos, Thailand serves as its principal means of accessing the sea.

Japan became the primary bilateral donor of foreign aid to Laos after the Soviet Union's collapse, and relations with Thailand and China grew stronger. China offered an economic model that Laos was eager to follow—a single-party government enacting market reforms and allowing private ownership. Moving beyond the Vietnamese model of economics has allowed Laos to enjoy a greater range of trading partners, donors, and investors. In 2014 Laos signed seven economic co-operative agreements with China.

Although Laos and the United States have never broken diplomatic relations, ties were minimized for a period until ambassadorial relations were restored in 1992. The U.S. imposed a full diplomatic and economic embargo on Vietnam and Cambodia in 1975. However, relations with Laos were maintained as the only open link to this group of states that had been at odds with the U.S. Trade relations between Laos and the U.S. were normalized in 2004. Laos formally became a member of the World Trade Organization in 2013.

Human Rights Profile

International human rights law insists that states respect civil and political rights, and also promote an individual's economic, social and cultural rights. The United Nations (UN) Universal Declaration of Human Rights (UDHR) is recognized as the standard for international human rights. Its authors sought the counsel of the world's great thinkers, philosophers, and religious leaders, and were careful to create a document that reflects the core values shared by every world culture. (To read this document or view the articles relating to cultural human rights, visit: http://www.udhr.org/UDHR/default.htm.)

The Laos constitution, adopted in 1991, clearly specifies the existence of equal rights for all ethnic groups, as well as gender equality, freedom of speech, press, and assembly, and freedom of religion. However, the Lao government has been criticized for its treatment of ethnic minorities, particularly members of the Hmong group. Independent human rights monitors have not been allowed to observe conditions within Laos, creating difficulties in assessing the extent of human rights violations. The grave accusations of persecution of the ethnic Hmong demonstrate a disregard for Article 2 of the UDHR, which states that all citizens must receive equal rights.

Since agreements of cooperation were made between the Laotian and Thai governments, pressure has increased for the forced return of thousands of Lao refugees in Thailand, mostly made up of Lao Hmong. Hundreds of asylum seekers from a camp in the northern Phetchabun Province were forcibly returned, with independent monitoring of the situation prohibited. Their refugee claims were not assessed before the forcible return, in violation of human rights law, as well as international refugee law.

Another case that has provoked international disapproval involves groups comprised mostly of ethnic Hmong forced to live in the jungle to avoid persecution. These groups were once part of a faction that fought with the U.S. against the communist Laotian troops in the Vietnam War. Once Pathet Lao, the communist party, was victorious in Laos in 1975, these opposition groups remained in the jungle and defended themselves from the ruling Pathet Lao party. Today, these groups do not organize any armed resistance, yet they are confined to the jungles under the threat of regular attacks by the Laotian military. Their standard of living in the jungle is notably lacking in regards to health and medical care, food, shelter, and clothing. Of those who have sought asylum in Thailand, many have been forced to return to Laos, where their fates are unknown.

In the 2014 World Press Freedom Index, released by Reporters Without Borders, Laos was ranked 171 out of 180 countries—an extremely critical rating of freedom of the press in Laos. International media are barred from covering many issues, particularly alleged human rights abuses inflicted on the ethnic minorities. Two Hmong men, Thao Moua and Pa Phue Khang, helped visiting European journalists access Hmong groups to document the attacks by the Laotian military in 2003. The journalists and the Hmong men were all jailed, but while the journalists were subsequently pardoned, the Hmong guides were kept imprisoned. This reflects clear violation of Article 19 of the UDHR, which demands freedom of media, expression, and opinion.

ECONOMY

Overview of the Economy

Laos' economy has improved since the government began implementing market reforms and allowing international investment. Though it still relies on foreign aid and experienced the setbacks that struck the region in the late 1990s, it has made significant improvement from a very low base. The estimated gross domestic product (GDP) per capita in 2014 was $5,000 (USD). Some 40 percent of the population lives below the poverty line.

Subsistence agriculture is the major industry in Laos, accounting for over 50 percent of the gross national product (GDP). The primary export crops are sweet potatoes, corn, coffee, rice, tea, peanuts, and various meat products.

Thailand is the nation's chief export partner; Vientiane and Thailand are directly connected by busy trade routes. Over 60 percent of products imported into Laos come from Thailand by way of Vientiane. China, Vietnam, and Malaysia are the nation's other significant trading partners.

Industry

Industry accounts for 32 percent of the GDP and employs six percent of the labor force. The sector is small but developing. Major products include building materials, clothing, drinks, matches, and cigarettes. The country also has the capacity to mill timber and rice.

The manufacturing and services industries are more common around the nation's major cities, including Vientiane, which serves as the nation's economic headquarters. Industry accounts for approximately 30 percent of the GDP, and includes tourism, garment and textile production, agricultural processing, and mining. Primary products include gypsum, tin, copper, and wood products.

The potential for mining minerals and gems has not yet been fully explored, while hydroelectricity is one of its most valuable exports. Should more dams be built on the Mekong River, this sector will expand further.

Labor

The labor force was estimated at 3.44 million in 2014, with an estimated 1.3 percent unemployed or underemployed, especially in rural areas. The majority of the work force is employed in agriculture, while the services and industry sectors account for 26 percent of the work force (2014 estimate). An estimated 40 percent of Laotians live below the poverty line.

Energy/Power/Natural Resources

Mineral deposits found in Laos include iron ore, limestone, tin, gypsum, potash, coal, lead, zinc, gold, silver, and precious gems. Timber is, however, the most widely exploited resource, though there have been efforts to curtail the rapid deforestation that is occurring by concentrating on other economic targets. One target is to increase hydropower production by expanding the number of dams on the Mekong River.

Laos' developing economy and growing population are placing stress on plant and animal populations. Illegal logging and poor agricultural management, including slash-and-burn methods, have reduced the forests considerably and led to soil erosion. In addition to losing their habitats, wild animals are hunted for food, medicine, and labor.

Another major environmental problem is the vast amount of unexploded ordnance from aerial bombardments which took place during the Second Indochina War. The ordnance has been responsible for numerous deaths and injuries, and the government has not yet effectively dealt with the problem. It has been estimated that between 1964 and 1973, the United States military bombarded Laos with more than 2 million tons of ordnance.

Fishing

The country lacks a large-scale fishing industry, and traditional or artisanal methods are still employed by a large percentage of the population. Dam projects financed by the government are projected to further decrease fisheries resources in the country. Aquaculture is an important industry in Luang Prabang.

Forestry

An estimated 40 percent of Laos is forested. The country's forests are used for domestic fuel and exports of wood products, particularly timber. However, mismanagement of the country's forest resources continues to be a problem. Both the World Bank and the government of Finland have worked to develop the infrastructure of the country's forest industry and to establish more sustainable forestry models.

Mining/Metals

Laos is home to a wide variety of mineral resources, including coal, copper, gold, limestone, and silver. However, these resources are mostly undeveloped. Several Australian mining outfits are active in Laos. These companies and the government's Department of Geology and the Department of Mines continue to study the country's mineral resources. An estimated 600,000 metric tons of coal was mined in Laos in 2008.

Agriculture

Agriculture, long the main occupation of Laotians, accounts for 50 percent of the GDP and employs 80 percent of the population. Major crops include rice, sweet potatoes, corn, coffee, sugarcane, cotton, tea, peanuts, and various vegetables. The rivers are widely exploited for fish, but the catch is consumed domestically.

Animal Husbandry

Water buffalo, cattle, pigs, and poultry are also raised by Laotian farmers. Buffalo and oxen are used for agricultural labor. Laos is domestically self-sufficient in terms of livestock. The livestock industry is largely based in the northern provinces of Houaphanh, Luang Prabang, and Xayabury.

Tourism

Laos is noteworthy for its natural beauty, its Buddhist architecture, and the largely undisturbed customs of its people. Vientiane is known for its French colonial architecture and That Luang, the country's most important Buddhist stupa (a religious monument), dating from the 16th century. Luang Prabang is a small city known for its ancient temples and the Royal Palace Museum. The Plain of Jars is an important archaeological site boasting large stone jars of unknown purpose and origin.

Since Laos became open to tourists, the industry has grown quickly and the infrastructure is developing. Tourism is now the country's single most important industry for earning foreign currency. In 2009, approximately 1.23 million tourists came to Laos, generating over $235 million (USD).

Zoë Westhof, Michael Aliprandini, Micah Issitt

DO YOU KNOW?

- The name "Vientiane" is derived from an ancient Buddhist language known as Pali, and is generally translated to mean "City of Sandalwood." Similarities between the spoken Lao language and the Pali language mean that the name of the city, when spoken, can also be taken to mean "City of the Moon."
- During the Lao civil war from 1962 to 1976, thousands of men from the Hmong ethnic group were recruited to fight communists in Laos and Vietnam. When the war ended and communist forces took control of Laos, the Hmong were forced to evacuate and thousands were relocated to the United States.

Bibliography

Bhagowati, Surajit Kumar. *Women in Southeast Asia.* Delhi: New Century, 2014.

Cooper, Robert Grange. *Culture Shock! Laos* Tarrytown, NY: Marshall Cavendish, 2011.

Evans, Grant and Milton Osborne. *A Short History of Laos: The Land in Between.* Crows Nest NSW, Australia: Allen & Unwin, 2002.

Pholsena, Vatthana. *Postwar Laos: The Politics of Culture, History, and Identity.* Ithaca, NY: Cornell University Press, 2006.

Ray, Nick, et al. *Laos.* Oakland, CA: Lonely Planet, 2014.

Simmala, Buasawan and Benjawan Poomsan Becker. *Lao for Beginners.* Grand Rapids: Paiboon, 2003.

Solomon, Charmaine. *Food of Thailand, Burma, Cambodia, Laos, and Vietnam.* Melbourne: Hardie Grant Books, 2014.

Stuart-Fox, Martin. *A History of Laos.* New York: Cambridge UP, 1997.

Vickers, Steve, and Edward Aves. *Rough Guide to Laos.* London: Rough Guides, 2014.

Works Cited

Adler, Christopher. "The Music of Laos." *The Classical Free-Reed, Inc.* <http://www.ksanti.net/free-reed/reviews/laos.html

Amnesty International USA. "Laos: Massacre of Unarmed Hmong Women and Children." 4 May 2006. <http://www.amnestyusa.org/document.php?lang=e&id=ENGASA260022006>

Amnesty International. "Hiding in the Jungle – Hmong under Threat." <http://www.amnesty.org/en/library/asset/ASA26/003/2007/en/dom-ASA260032007en.html>

Amnesty International. "Report 2008: Laos." 2008. <http://thereport.amnesty.org/eng/regions/asia-pacific/laos>

Asia-Planet. "Laos Information" provided by *Laos National Tourism Authority.* 2002. <http://www.asia-planet.net/laos/people.htm>

AsiaRecipe.com. "Laos culture and recipes from Asia." <http://asiarecipe.com/laoculture.html>

Astaman, Margareta. "Laos Youth Hip-Hop to a Local Beat." 13 December 2007. <http://www.worldhiphopmarket.com/blog/?p=27>

Bulatlat. "Reporting the ASEAN: Repression of the ASEAN Media Continues." 2007. <http://www.bulatlat.com/2008/09/reporting-asean-repression-asean-media-continues>

Buncombe, Andrew. "Good Morning, Luang Prabang – and Hello to Laos's Film Industry." *The Independent.* <http://www.independent.co.uk/news/world/asia/good-morning-luang-prabang-ndash-and-hello-to-laoss-film-industry-843557.html>

CIA. "The World Factbook – Laos." 20 November 2008. <https://www.cia.gov/library/publications/the-world-factbook/geos/la.html#Geo>

Encyclopaedia Britannica. "Laos." http://www.britannica.com/EBchecked/topic/330219/Laos

FIDH.org. "A UN Body Expresses Concern Regarding Women Rights in Laos." 15 February 2005. <http://www.fidh.org/spip.php?article2223>

Google Laos. "Fashion over Necessity." <http://www.googlelaos.com/mobilephone.html>

Guide for Laos: Tourist Places in Vientiane Province http://www.guideforlaos.com/vientiane.html

Gunther, Michael D. "Art of Southeast Asia: Laos." 2004. <http://www.art-and-archaeology.com/seasia/seasia.html#laos>

In Asia. "From Laos: Women Unite to Protect Rights." 5 March 2008. <http://asiafoundation.org/in-asia/2008/03/05/from-laos-women-unite-to-protect-rights/>

Lao Press. "Lao Pop Music Artists." <http://www.laopress.com/images/artists/type/pop/index.htm>

Laos Cultural Profile. 13 March 2008. <http://www.culturalprofiles.net/laos/>

NYTimes.com, by Frommer's. "Etiquette: Laos." <http://travel.nytimes.com/frommers/travel/guides/asia/laos/frm_laos_2411026691.html>

Radio Free Asia. "Interactive Chart: Press Freedom in Radio Free Asia's Target Countries." 24 October 2008.

Reporters Without Borders. "Laos" <http://www.rsf.org/article.php3?id_article=7430>

St John, Ronald Bruce. "Laos: Power Trumps Reform." *Foreign Policy in Focus*. 28 December 2006. <http://www.fpif.org/fpiftxt/3831>

Tageo. "Laos City and Town Populations." http://www.tageo.com/index-e-la-cities-LA.htm

U.S. Library of Congress. "Laos – Foreign Policy." <http://countrystudies.us/laos/96.htm>

U.S. Library of Congress. "Laos- U.S." <http://countrystudies.us/laos/101.htm>

U.S. State Department. "Laos." 2004. <http://www.state.gov/g/drl/rls/hrrpt/2004/41648.htm>

UNESCO World Heritage Centre. "Town of Luang Prabang." <http://whc.unesco.org/en/list/479>

UNESCO World Heritage Centre. "Vat Phou and Associated Ancient Settlements within the Champasak Cultural Landscape." <http://whc.unesco.org/en/list/481>

Wikipedia. "Lao language." <http://en.wikipedia.org/wiki/Lao_language>

Wikipedia. "Laos Buddhist sculpture" <http://en.wikipedia.org/wiki/Lao_Buddhist_sculpture>

Wikipedia. "Laotian Cuisine." <http://en.wikipedia.org/wiki/Cuisine_of_Laos#Eating_customs>

World Cultures. "Laos." <http://www.everyculture.com/wc/Japan-to-Mali/Lao.html>

World Heritage Site. "Laos." <http://www.worldheritagesite.org/countries/laos.html>

Asia King Travel. "Laos Transport." <http://www.asiakingtravel.com/Laos/laos_transport.htm>

MALAYSIA

Introduction

The Federation of Malaysia is a collection of land areas spread over a peninsula that juts into the South China Sea from Thailand, and along the northern coast of Indonesia in southeastern Asia.

After an armed uprising, Malaysia gained its independence from the British government on August 31, 1957. Originally consisting of Peninsular Malaysia only, the future state formed a federation with Sabah, Sarawak, and Singapore on July 9, 1963. Singapore left the Federation on August 9, 1965, leaving Malaysia's current territory.

Malaysia began as a federation of former British colonies, and its history is evident in the ethnic and linguistic diversity of its people. The population is roughly 50 percent Malay, 33 percent Chinese, and 9 percent Indian. Like its population, Malaysia's traditional art is diverse, influenced by Chinese, Indian, and Malay popular forms. The work of Batik artisans, Chinese potters, and Malay bead workers from Sabah and Sarawak and silver artisans can be found throughout Malaysia.

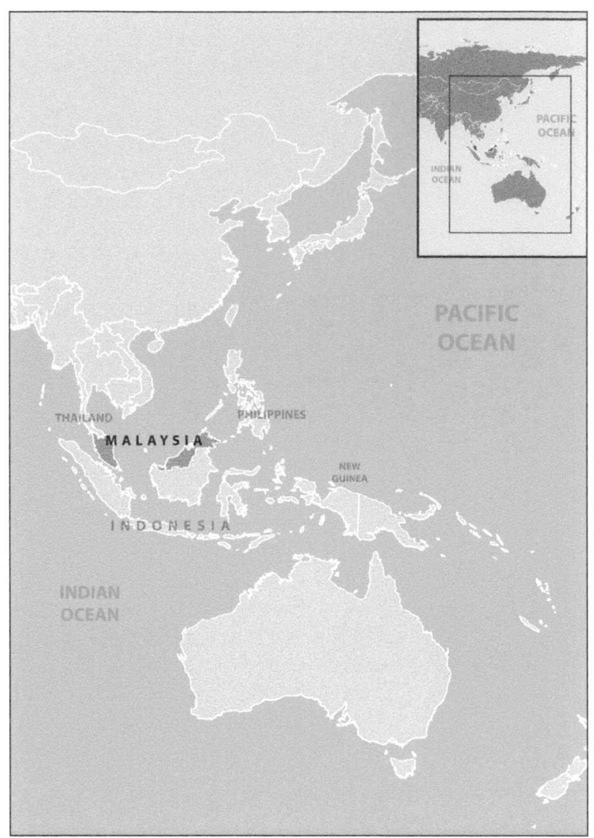

GENERAL INFORMATION

Official Language: Malay (Bahasa Melayu)
Population: 30,073,353 (2014 estimate)
Currency: Malaysian ringgit
Coins: The Malaysian ringgit is subdivided into 100 sen, and coins are circulated in denominations of 5, 10, 20, and 50 sen.
Land Area: 328,657 square kilometers (126,895 square miles)
Water Area: 1,190 square kilometers (459 square miles)
National Motto: "Unity is Strength"
National Anthem: "My Country" ("Negaraku")
Capital: Kuala Lumpur (however, Putrajaya serves as the administrative center)
Time Zone: GMT + 8
Flag Description: The flag of Malaysia consists of a dark blue canton (upper left quarter) with a field, or background, composed of fourteen alternating and equal red and white horizontal stripes (seven each). Within the blue canton are a golden crescent and a fourteen-point golden star. Concepts represented by the flag include unity, Islam, and Malay royalty.

Population

Malaysia began as a federation of former British colonies, and its history is evident in the ethnic and linguistic diversity of its people. The population is roughly 50 percent Malay, 33 percent

N
0
400 Kilometers
0
400 Miles
LAOS
CAMBODIA
VIETNAM
SOUTH CHINA SEA
Gulf of Thailand
THAILAND
PHILIPPINES
Kudat
Kota Baharu
Kota Kinabula
Sandakan
George Town
Kuala Terengganu
MALAYSIA
BRUNEI
Taiping
Lahad Datu
Ipoh
Strait of Malacca
Tawau
Lumut
Miri
Kuantan
KUALA LUMPUR
Gunung Mulu National Park
Celebes Sea
Klang
Tugu Negara
Kepulauan Natuna (INDONESIA)
Bintulu
Seremban
Port Dickson
Sibu
Melaka
Kuching
Johor Bahru
SINGAPORE
EQUATOR
SUMATRA (INDONESIA)
BORNEO (INDONESIA)
INDONESIA
Java Sea
INDIAN OCEAN
Banda Sea

Principal Cities by Population (2012):

- Kuala Lumpur (1,634,996)
- Ipoh (441,628)
- Johor Baharu (441,239)
- Kuantan (356,153)
- Seremban (317,813)
- Klang (254,919)
- Taiping (220,364)
- Kota Kinbalu (208,779)
- Kuching (138,306)

Chinese, and 9 percent Indian. The remainder of the population is comprised of various indigenous tribes, such as the Orang Asli and Iban, and people of European descent.

Two-thirds of the country's population lives in Peninsular Malaysia, on the western side of the South China Sea. The states of Sabah and Sarawak in the eastern half of the country are less developed overall. Malaysia's urban areas are becoming increasingly cosmopolitan, with international business interests and tourism creating a thorough mix of cultures and people.

Approximately 74 percent of the population resides in urban areas (2014 estimate). The population growth rate is 1.47 percent.

Languages

Although Bahasa Melayu is the official language, Malaysians commonly speak Chinese, English, Tamil, and an assortment of other Asian languages and dialects. Most residents of Kuala Lumpur speak Bahasa Melayu, which the government has promoted as the official national language to promote cultural unity. Many of the capital's residents also speak English.

Native People & Ethnic Groups

Archeologists believe that Malaysia's first inhabitants, the Orang Asli, migrated to the Malaysian Peninsula about 10,000 years ago from southwestern China. Over the millennia, the region became part of a number of empires and dynasties, such as the Funan in Cambodia, the Srivijaya of Sumatra, and the Majapahit of Java. The Chinese empire and Islam both arrived in Malaysia in the early 15th century, further changing Malaysia's pre-modern culture.

As a result, Malaysia became a unique mix of early Asian cultures. Bumiputera, the term for indigenous people in Malaysia, means "sons of the soil" and Orang Asli actually refers to several distinct peoples who are native to the Malaysian Peninsula. The Orang Laut, Orang Seletar and Mah Meri live close to the coast on Peninsula Malaysia where their livelihood depends on local fishing industries. The Temuan, Jakun and Semai manage farms and plantations specializing in rubber and cocoa. The Temiar, Che Wong, Jah Hut, Semelai and Semoq Beri generally live in forested areas, where they grow rice and trade in petai, durian, rattan and resins. Still others, like the Jahai and Lanoh, are semi-nomadic hunters and gatherers in Malaysia's forested regions. Many Orang Asli now live in urban areas, having adopted urban Malaysian jobs and lifestyles.

Though they do not claim as long a history in Malaysia as the Orang Asli, the Malay people also have the constitutional protections that come with indigenous status in the Federation. The Malay are originally from a group of Malayo-Polynesian peoples who emigrated from Yunnan, China circa 2000 BCE. Today, the Malay account for about half of Malaysia's population, and are characterized by their adherence to a form of Islam whose ceremonies are influenced by Hindu and animist practices.

In Sarawak, Malays form a quarter of the state's population. These Malays originally migrated from Sumatra and speak a different dialect from the Malays of the Peninsula. Most of Sarawak's Malays still live along the coast in kampungs (unplanned, low-income housing areas) and make their living from the sea.

Sarawak claims several other groups of non-Malay, indigenous people, including the Bidayu, who were forced into the mountains of Sarawak centuries ago and are also known as "Land Dayaks." The Iban, who make up one-third of Sarawak's population, migrated in large numbers from Borneo between the 16th and 19th centuries. Other groups include the Melanu, Kayan, Kelabit, Kenyah, Orang Ulu, Penan, and Punan.

In Sabah, the Kadazandusun are the largest indigenous group. Other groups include the Rungus, Bajau, and Murut. In all cases, these names refer to a collective assortment of peoples who often speak distinct languages and dialects. Like the indigenous groups of Sarawak, those of Sabah have found different ways of adapting to their Malaysian landscape. Many, like the Kadazandusun, are farmers, while the Bajau have become famous for their horsemanship.

Religions

Malaysia is religiously tolerant and diverse. Approximately 52 percent of its citizens are Muslim, 17 percent are Buddhist, 12 percent are Taoist, 8 percent are Christian, 8 percent are Hindu, and 2 percent practice traditionally-based shamanism.

Climate

Malaysia lies only seven degrees north of the equator, giving the country a tropical climate throughout. Temperatures range from 21° to 32° Celsius (70° to 90° Fahrenheit) year-round. Malaysia has an average annual rainfall of 2,000 to 2,500 millimeters (79 to 99 inches). The humidity in Malaysia hovers around 80 percent throughout the year.

Monsoons frequently blow in from the northeast between the months of November and March, and from the southeast between May and September. Between monsoons, rainfall increases.

Kuala Lumpur lies just 348 kilometers (216 miles) north of the equator and its tropical climate produces hot, sticky conditions year round. Daytime temperatures average between 22° and 32° Celsius (70° and 90° Fahrenheit) and the humidity often hovers around 80 percent. Occasional forest fires in the country of Sumatra, which lies west of Kuala Lumpur, sometimes envelop the capital in a thick, dusty haze.

ENVIRONMENT & GEOGRAPHY

Topography

In Peninsular and Eastern Malaysia, coastal areas are broad, flat lowlands that gradually climb in elevation near the mountainous interiors. The difference in altitude can be striking. Malaysia contains two of Southeast Asia's highest peaks: Gunung Tahan in Peninsula Malaysia's Titiwangsa Mountain range, and Gunung Kinbalu, a 4,100-meter (13,452-foot)-high peak in Sabah.

The capital, Kuala Lumpur, lies in a valley at the junction of the Klang and Gombak Rivers; the city's name literally translates as "muddy estuary" in the Malay language. It is located about 40 kilometers (25 miles) inland from the midpoint of the Malaysian peninsula's western coast.

Plants & Animals

Tropical rainforests cover about four-fifths of Malaysia. The government has already set aside approximately 1.5 million hectares (3,706,580 acres) of this land for preservation.

Scientists estimate that Malaysia's rainforests sustain over 200 species of mammals, 600 species of birds, and about 15,000 species of flowering trees and plants. Many of these species are now endangered, including the Orangutan, the Malayan Sun Bear, and the Gharial, a fish-eating crocodile. Ecologists are also concerned about the country's rapidly disappearing rainforests and tropical hardwood trees

CUSTOMS & COURTESIES

Greetings

In Malaysia, most greetings begin with the word "Selamat." This is equivalent to the English word "Good." "Selamat" loosely means "Wishing you a safe…" For example, "Selamat Pagi" is similar to "Good morning" in English.

Muslim Malays greet each other with a gesture called a "salaam." This is similar to a handshake. The younger person initiates the salam by using clasping the hands of the older person. The younger person will then say, "Assalamualaikum," meaning "Peace be upon you." If the greeting is between a younger and highly respected elder, such as a parent, it is often customary for the younger person to kiss the elder as a sign of respect. Oftentimes, after a salam or handshake between men, the hand holding will continue as the men walk, especially if one is leading the other. It is not uncommon for men to hold hands in Malaysia.

Additionally, all Muslims greet with the salam, but only Malays follow the salam by touching the left side of their chest. This placing of the hand over the heart symbolizes sincerity. Also, since physical contact between the opposite sexes is traditionally discouraged in Islam, if a non-Muslim offers a handshake to a member of the opposite sex, it will commonly be refused.

Gestures & Etiquette

The right hand and left hand have very different functions and importance in Malaysia. The left hand is to be used to clean oneself, while the right hand is used for everything else, specifically eating, shaking hands, and most importantly, for picking up the Qur'an (or Koran). This custom is consistent with the cultural customs of Islamic countries. In addition, hands are typically not to be placed in pockets, as this signifies anger. More importantly, hand gestures are not used to beckon to adults, as this is considered to be rude. Moreover, making a fist and hitting it into the palm of the other hand is generally perceived as an obscene gesture.

Public displays of affection are offensive to most people in Malaysia, even between married couples. Long embraces are thus avoided, and contact between the opposite sexcs is forbidden in public. Even hugging or holding hands are considered "makruh," or disliked, although not forbidden. Furthermore, public displays of anger are also considered offensive. As in many other Asian countries, Malays do not often show anger in public.

When addressing elders, it is common to refer to them as "pakcik," or "uncle," and "makcik," or "aunty." It is also common to bow one's head as a sign of respect when passing an elder. A slight bow when passing someone means "Excuse me."

The top of the head is considered to be the home of the soul, and as such, it is never touched, even with children.

Eating/Meals

Indian and Malay communities in Malaysia commonly use the fingers of the right hand, rather than utensils, to eat foods such as rice. The left hand is not used, as that hand is traditionally considered unclean. Chinese Malaysians do not typically follow this custom of eating with the fingers. Generally, Malays wash their hands before meals. Oftentimes a kettle or pot filled with water is placed on the table for the guests to wash their hands. In traditional Malay homes, meals are often eating while sitting on the floor. As such, guests are commonly seated on cushions placed around a long, low table.

Most other eating customs in Malaysia depend on religion. For example, Malaysian Muslims are forbidden by the Quran (or Koran) to eat pork or drink alcohol. Similarly, Malaysian Hindus do not eat beef, as the cow is sacred to them, and many Buddhists do not eat meat at all. For these reasons, most hosts in Malaysia check with their guests in advance before planning a meal. It is considered to be highly impolite if the host does not take a guest's dietary restrictions into consideration before inviting them to dinner. Also, guests should never complain about the food, or eat to excess, as both of these can be perceived as rude.

Visiting

It is customary in Malaysia, as in many other Asian countries, to remove footwear before entering someone's house, unless the host specifies otherwise. This traditional practice derives from the simple fact that Malays traditionally ate and prayed on the floor; shoes are likely to bring dirt inside the house and onto the floor. Many common areas in a Muslim home are also used for group worship and prayers. In addition, footwear is commonly removed when visiting a place of worship.

When invited to someone's house, it is considered polite to bring a gift. The right hand is used to give and accept the gift, since the left hand is associated with impurity. This practice is known as carrying "buah tangan," which means, "fruit of the hands." Wine or other alcohol is typically not an appropriate gift. Fruits, sweets, perfumes, or crafts, on the other hand, are considered appropriate. It is also considered rude to smoke around the elderly or in someone's home without asking permission. Most notably, it is forbidden to smoke around royal family members.

LIFESTYLE

Family

Malays, Chinese Malaysians, and Indian Malaysians are the three dominant ethnic groups in Malaysia. Each has a slightly different family unit, although there are some similar trends across all ethnic groups. One of these trends is that Malaysians are choosing to marry at an older age than in the past. Another common thread is the predominance of the nuclear family (consisting of a mother, father and, commonly, two children) and the rarity of divorce.

Extended families living together in the same household are most commonly found among the Chinese Malaysians, and least likely among the Malays. Indian Malaysians, like the Chinese, have a strong cultural tradition that emphasizes care for elders.

Housing

Housing in urban areas of Malaysia predominantly consists of modern, high-rise apartment buildings with a definite Western influence in appearance and design. Also interspersed throughout the cities and countryside are colonial-style houses. These dwellings are usually connected by stone terraces.

Very rural villages still contain many traditional Malay houses, or "kampongs," which are built on stilts and contain large windows throughout. The stilts protect the house from flooding during the monsoon, or rainy, season, and the windows help to keep the house cool. These houses are detached and do not usually have fences around them.

Indigenous groups in Sabah and Sarawak live in longhouses. These are long, narrow houses, similar to kampongs, which are shared by a large, extended family, or by more than one family. They are also built on stilts. There are many superstitions, mainly indigenous, still surrounding longhouses, including the fact that one should never walk under a longhouse, nor enter one without being invited.

Food

Malaysia does not have a national dish. However, one common dish commonly found throughout the country, whether on street corners or in restaurants, is nasi lemak, which is simply rice cooked in coconut milk. The coconut milk gives the rice a sweet, rich flavor. It can be cooked to a creamy texture, or to a crisp. The dish is typically eaten anytime and can be served in a great number of ways. One popular presentation of the dish is to serve it with fried anchovies, peanuts, cucumber slices, eggs, and sambal (chili paste).

Another favorite food in Malaysia is banana leaf rice, or BLR as it is often called. Of south Indian origin, BLR is popular all over the country, but served mainly in Indian restaurants. The dish consists of rice eaten off a banana leaf and accompanied by meats, vegetables and curry. Portions are typically large.

Satay is another popular food in Malaysia, and the town of Kajang is famous for it. In fact, many original inhabitants of Kajang have migrated to other parts of the country, making a living selling the town's satay recipe. Satay consists of pieces of meat—usually chicken—skewered and grilled over charcoal, then dipped in a spicy peanut sauce.

Life's Milestones

Many popular and widespread customs and milestones in Malaysia are dependent upon religion. For example, an extremely meaningful ceremony in Malaysia is the Khat am al-Qur'an. This is a celebration of the completion of a course in the reading of the Qur'an (or Koran), which is the holy book of Islam. This ceremony, for boys only, is usually held when the child is around nine or ten years old.

The Khat am al-Qur'an, is often held before a boy's circumcision, or it can be held as a separate ceremony. During the celebration, the boy is seated at a dais, or pelamin (platform), and is required to read verses from the thirtieth section of the Qur'an to his teacher and guests. Afterward, the boy kisses the hands of his Qur'an teacher, parents, and guests, and is then finally able to join the feast. As a parting gift, guests are presented with a bunga telor, which is a boiled egg attached to the tip of a stick, usually decorated with flowers.

In addition, it is compulsory for all Muslim boys to be circumcised. Bersunat, or circumcision, is also a very important ceremony for Malays in general. Historically, this ceremony was festive, lasting two days, with large groups of people attending. Often, many boys were circumcised at the same. Typically, the parents choose a date for the circumcision, which would occur between the ages of six and 10 years old, and send out invitations.

Traditionally, on the first day of the ceremony, the boy's hair is cut short, and he is taken in a procession around the village. Afterward, the child is then placed on a pelamin. The circumcision takes place on the second day, and a specialist called "tok mudin" performs it, with much ritual and prayer. Although circumcisions are still performed this way in many traditional and rural Malay villages, more and more parents in urban areas are choosing to send their children to hospitals for the procedure.

CULTURAL HISTORY

Art

Traditional Malaysian handicrafts have been heavily influenced by Islam, as most artists are Muslims. Islam forbids the depiction of the human form in art. For this reason, most Malaysian artwork contains organic, or natural, designs that feature elements such as leaves, flowers, and animals. Overall, the arts of painting and sculpture are poorly developed in Malaysia's history. Malaysia is covered with forests, and as such, is known for its woodcrafts. Each cultural group in Malaysia has contributed to the country's rich tradition of wood handicrafts, ranging from elaborate Chinese containers and Malay-style engraved panels to the intricate walking sticks of many indigenous groups.

Malaysia is also known for its traditional textiles. In particular, the Malays, an ethnic group that has historically inhabited the Malay Peninsula, have played a major role in the development of Malaysian textile art. Traditionally, the Malays used gold thread to signify elite social status and decorate traditional formal clothing. Songket cloth, for example, was created by weaving gold thread in between the lengthwise silk threads of a background cloth. This creates a rich and luxurious fabric still popular today. Tekat was the art of embroidering golden thread onto velvet, and was traditionally used to decorate Malay wedding clothing.

Batik is another well-known Malaysian art form. Originating in India, it is still performed today in the traditional manner by many Malays. The technique consists of applying melted wax to cloth. Traditionally, this is done with a wooden-handled tool with a tiny metal cup tipped with a tiny spout, out of which the wax dribbles. Then, the fabric is dipped in dye, often more than once. After drying, the fabric is dipped in a chemical to dissolve the wax, or irons are used to melt the wax.

Architecture

Architecture in Malaysia is reflective of the many cultures and religions that make up the country. While representing a fusion of the modern and the traditional, Malaysian architecture is largely influenced by the religious architecture associated with Hinduism and Islam, as well as the architecture of China and Europe. The assimilation of these various influences has resulted in an architectural style that is still uniquely Malaysian.

Generally, traditional Malay structures were designed and built for life in a tropical environment. Homes were often built on stilts to sit above floodwaters, and high-pitched roofs and large windows allowed for cross-ventilating breezes. These homes were often carved with intricate designs inspired by those found in nature. A famous example of this type of architecture is the Istana Kenangan in the royal town of Kuala Kangsar. It was built in 1926 and is the only Malay palace built with bamboo walls.

As Malaysia's entered into its colonial period, its architecture became largely influenced by the influx of Chinese and European immigrants. Chinese architecture in Malaysia is either traditional in nature or inspired by the Baba-Nyonya heritage, also known as Peranakan culture. This culture developed when Chinese cultural elements, brought by immigrants, blended with Malay customs, predominantly through the marriage of male Chinese immigrants to local females. Houses built in the latter style are built with indoor courtyards and beautiful, colorfully hand-painted tiles.

Between 1511 and 1957, architecture was heavily influenced by British, Dutch, and Portuguese colonies. For example, British architecture is popular in the northwest Malaysian state of Penang. Other types of architecture found in Malaysia include Hindu temples, stilted, thatched-roofed longhouses, and water villages of the indigenous peoples of Sabah and Sarawak, or East Malaysia.

Drama & Dance

As with other art forms in Malaysia, Islam has had a heavy influence on Malaysia's drama and dance. The dance form known as zapin combines Islamic chanting with body movements. Traditionally, only men performed the dance, though this has changed over time. The dance, believed to have been brought by Muslim missionaries in the 14th or 15th centuries, is typically accompanied by the traditional instruments such as the lute, violin, and percussions. The zapin is also accepted as a secular, or non-religious, form of dancing. The exact performance of the dance usually varies depending on tradition and region.

Another dance, the kuda kepang, is regularly performed in ceremonies such as state celebrations and cultural shows. It features dancers sitting astride mock horses. The dancers then reenact battles to the beat of a percussion ensemble. This dance is believed to have traditional links to the spirit world, but this belief is not encouraged in contemporary Malaysia.

Also unique to Malaysia is the performance art wayang kulit, which is part puppet show and part shadow play or puppetry. The art consists of the use of carved and painted flat, two-dimensional puppets, typically of exaggerated human form. Each puppet is unique and distinctive, and often has jointed arms. One master storyteller called a tok dalang performs the show, which usually features ancient Indian epics. Wayang kulit is believed to have a documented existence dating back over 800 years.

Music

Malaysian traditional music is based largely on percussion instruments, including the kompang, or hand drum, and is heavily influenced by Chinese and Islamic traditions. The kompang is still widely used today in many social situations and celebrations, including parades, football matches, and even weddings. The sape is another traditional Malaysian (Sarawak) musical instrument that is becoming more and more popular around the world. There is even an electrical version that is popular with Malaysian youth. The traditional sape is a lute, or stringed instrument, carved from white wood, featuring between three and five strings held by wood frets.

Islam has not only been an influence on Malaysian traditional music, but is popular today in pop music as well. Muslim singer Siti Nurhaliza (1979–) is a singing sensation in Malaysia. Her albums feature Malay pop, rhythm & blues, and Malay traditional music. Western music is also popular in Malaysia, along with underground Malaysian punk rock. In addition, Malaysia is home to two types of orchestras, the Gamelan and the Nobat. The Gamelan originated in Indonesia and uses percussion and stringed instruments to play light, lilting melodies. The Nobat is a royal orchestra that features wind instruments; this music is much more solemn.

Literature

Identifying literature as uniquely Malaysian is a difficult process at best, due to the different cultures and religions that have formed and influenced the country's historical culture. The *Sejarah Melayu* ("Malay Annals"), written in the 16th century, tells the history of the Malacca sultanate, a Malay dynasty. It is widely considered to be the most important Malaysian literary work. It is also one of the oldest works in the Malay language.

In eastern Malaysia, Western influences have made little impact on the arts, and the indigenous cultural heritage includes no written history or literature. In contemporary Malaysia, however, there is not an agreed-upon national culture that is accurately reflected in literary works. Authors from each major ethnic group in Malaysia tend to write in a style that is unique to their own cultural heritage. For example, a Chinese-Malaysian author might write a book in English or Chinese, with a Chinese main character.

Generally, it is difficult to find literature in Malaysia that is uniquely Malaysian. There are few popular fictional titles and only a few books written about Malaysian history or culture by non-Malaysians, although they are not considered classics. However, Malaysia formed the backdrop to the bestselling novel *The Soul of Malaya* (1930), by French author Henri Fauconnier (1879–1973), who lived in Malaysia. Recent Malaysian author Rani Manicka also brought Malaysian culture to the forefront in her debut novel *The Rice Mother* (2003).

CULTURE

Arts & Entertainment

Malaysia has historically been home to a variety of different religious and ethnic groups, Malay art is multicultural, and a source of national pride. In addition, traditional Malaysian textiles and intricately carved wooden pieces are highly sought after by collectors throughout the world. The work of Batik artisans, Chinese potters, and Malay bead workers from Sabah and Sarawak and silver artisans can be found throughout Malaysia.

Despite its diversity, though, Malaysia's artistic expression and identity narrowed in the 1970s with the rise of Islam. Since that time, conservative political religious groups have been working to diminish Indian and Chinese influences in art, and create a new Malaysian identity that is more heavily influenced by Islam. This new identity is gradually eroding the importance of traditional cultural activities in the Malaysian's public life and replacing them with puritan and modest expectations of behavior. For example, traditional ceremonial dances are often regulated and their music is typically performed only at cultural centers or during state events. Furthermore, this new national identity also rejects and censors Western fashions, music, and films.

As a result, many young artists in Malaysia, including filmmakers and other artists such as painters and visual artists, are turning to figurative styles of artistic expression. Through figurative expressions, these contemporary artists are able to insert angst into their modern designs as an expression of rebellion. This backlash against conservatism can also be seen in the popularity of Malaysia's underground punk music scene.

Cultural Sites & Landmarks

The island of Borneo, in which the nation of Malaysia is one of three divisions (the nations of Brunei and Indonesia form the other two regions) is known for its beautiful beaches. Malaysia is also home to the renowned Gunung Mulu National Park. Encompassing roughly 52,000 hectares (128,494 acres), the park, known as "Mulu" to the locals, is considered the most studied tropical karst area in the world (karst topography is formed by the dissolution of soluble rocks by groundwater). The site also contains the Sarawak Chamber, the world's largest underground chamber.

Recently added to the park is a 480-meter (1,574 feet) long skywalk, called the Canopy Skywalk. It is considered to be the world's longest tree-based skywalk, and access requires a guided tour of the park. It takes about an hour to complete the skywalk, which spans the tops of fifteen trees and over the Paku River. The park as a whole was designated as a United Nations Educational, Scientific and Cultural Organization (UNESCO) World Heritage Site.

Malaysia is also home to the Tugu Negara, or National Monument. Located within the Lake Gardens near the Parliament House in Kuala Lumpur, Malaysia's largest city and capital, the National Monument site consists of a long, rectangular reflecting pool with a fountain, pavilion, and gardens. The monument itself sits at the center of the reflection pool. Over 15 meters high (49 feet), the monument was built to honor those who courageously gave up their lives to preserve freedom for Malaysia. It is made of bronze and consists of seven human figures each standing for one of seven qualities: courage, leadership, sacrifice, strength, suffering, unity, and vigilance.

The city of Kuala Lumpur is also home to the 88-story Petronas Twin Towers, known also as KLCC. Considered the world's tallest twin structures, this mega structure contains office buildings, conference halls, a shopping complex, and a large park. Geometric shapes found in Islamic architecture inspired the towers" beautiful and distinctive design. The twin towers are connected by a sky bridge, which is open to visitors.

North of Kuala Lumpur, in Penang, lies the most popular beach in Malaysia, Batu Feringgi. The beach is famously lined with four and five star international resorts and restaurants. Windsurfing, canoeing, parasailing, and other water sports are prevalent. The beach also features a renowned open-air bazaar, dubbed the Feringgi Walk by locals and tourists.

Across the country from Kuala Lumpur lies the tiny island of Sipadan. Divers around the world have voted this small island as one of the top five dive sites in the world. Although small (it can be circled in roughly 30 minutes on foot), this island supports a large variety of tropical birds and marine life, including sea turtles, barracudas, and many different species of parrots. The coral composition of the island and the crystal-clear water surrounding it offer divers stunning and clear glimpses of underwater life.

Libraries & Museums

Kuala Lumpur's most notable museums include the National Museum, which is dedicated to different aspects of Malaysian history and culture; the Natural Rubber Museum, which traces the history and development of the rubber industry in Malaysia; and the National Art Gallery, which features the works of contemporary artists. The highly modern National Mosque, completed in 1965, features a rooftop built in the shape of an eighteen-point star. The Kuala Lumpur's Islamic Centre, which sits opposite the highly modern National Mosque (known for its rooftop built in the shape of an eighteen-point star), hosts both local and international exhibits designed to showcase Islamic learning, art, design, and culture.

The National Library of Malaysia serves as the county's legal depository and is located in Kuala Lumpur. The library's architecture was inspired by the tengkolok, traditional Malay headwear. There are an estimated 1,392 public libraries throughout the country.

Holidays

Malaysia celebrates 11 federal holidays and 26 state holidays. Christmas Day is the major Christian holiday, but Malaysia celebrates a number of Hindu, Buddhist, or Muslim holidays, including Ramadan in October, the Prophet Mohammed's Birthday (Maulidur Rasul) in May, and Chinese New Year and Deepavali in January and November.

Like other followers of Islam throughout the world, Malaysia's Muslims celebrate the month of Ramadan with fasting from sunset to sundown, until the first new moon signals the beginning of the celebration of Eid ul-Fitr. Other religious observances are more unusual. During Thaipusam, it is common for followers of Lord Subramaniam to pierce their bodies with metal hooks and spikes to prove their devotion. The less grisly Deepavali is a festival of lights during which Hindu people tempt the goddess of wealth (Lakshmi) into their homes with small oil lamps hung by the doors.

Malaysia also has a number of secular holidays. The Flora Fest in July brings flower exhibits and an international flower procession to the streets of Kuala Lumpur. On August 31, cities and villages all over the country host celebrations in honor of Malaysia's independence. Events like the Harvest Festival in May and the Dayak Festival in June showcase Malaysia's ancient cultural heritage.

Youth Culture

Malaysian youth are caught between religious principles of Islam, and the appeal of a Western way of life. As Malaysia's economy has begun to prosper, Western culture has become more popular. This includes the introduction and increasing popularity of reality TV shows, Internet and mobile communication technology, and American fashions, all of which influence the way the Melauyu, or Malaysian teenagers, live their lives. This shift away from Muslim values, and toward a "Mat Saleh," or Western copycat look, has been an issue of contention between the youth and older generations.

Generally, social contact between the opposite sexes is frowned upon in Malaysian society. For this reason, many young Malaysians rely on cell phone and Internet technology to connect with their peers. However, recent surveys show that 43 percent of youth do not have Internet access in their homes.

Education is mandatory only through primary school, but most Malaysian youth attend school throughout their teenage years. Common after school activities commonly include sports, musical lessons, and attending tutoring centers.

SOCIETY

Transportation

Traveling by car is the preferred mode of transportation in Malaysia. In fact, Malaysians are very proud of their expressway network, as it is often considered to be the best in Southeast Asia. Malaysian expressways are found at all major cities. Major cities in Malaysia also feature the Light Rail Transit (LRT), typically used by commuters to avoid crowded city streets. Traffic in Malaysia moves on the left-hand side of the road.

Transportation Infrastructure

Malaysia's expressway network is often considered to be the best in Southeast Asia. Malaysian expressways are found at all major cities, and roads in Malaysia cover about 63,445 kilometers (39,422 miles). Malaysia also has six international airports, and a state-run train system that only covers western Malaysia. It is possible to take a train or drive to Malaysia from Thailand or Singapore. Malaysia also has regular ferry services to its most popular island destinations, including Pangkor and Tioman.

Media & Communications

Malaysia publishes several newspapers in various languages, including Malay, Tamil, Chinese, and English. There are two state-run television networks: Radio Television Malaysia (RTM) operates TV1 and TV2 networks, as well as some 30 radio stations across the country. In addition, there are two private FM radio stations, one in Kuala Lumpur, and three commercial television networks: TV3, NTV7, and 8TV. Authorities exert substantial control over radio and print content and newspapers must obtain permission annually to renew their publication licenses.

Mobile telephone service is available in Malaysia through some international companies, although coverage can be sporadic. Internet access is generally available almost anywhere, including at Internet cafés and hotels. Malaysia has pledged not to censor the Internet in the hopes that this will spur the growth of information technology industries. However, the state does monitor the contents of websites. Many independent news websites, such as Malaysiakini.com, claim to have been the subject of police investigations. Although almost 50 percent of Malaysians have access to the Internet, most use dial-up modems.

Malaysia has strict censorship laws. Restrictions are often imposed in the name of national security, or with the explanation that the government is striving to shield Malaysians from harmful foreign influences. All media are subject to censorship, including television, films, and print. Commonly censored materials include programs that show kissing or swearing.

SOCIAL DEVELOPMENT

Standard of Living

Malaysia ranked 62nd out of 187 countries on the 2014 United Nations Human Development Index, which measures quality of life and standard of living indicators.

Water Consumption

According to 2012 statistics from the World Health Organization, Malaysia's population has near universal access to improved sources of drinking water—an estimated 100 percent—while approximately 96 percent of the population has access to improved sanitation. An estimated 98 percent of the country's water is sourced from surface water. While wastewater treatment in the country has improved dramatically recently, including the construction of four treatment plants in 2008, solid waste management continues to be a pressing issue in the country.

Education

By putting the largest segment of its annual budget toward its National Education System, the Malaysian government guarantees a free primary and secondary education for all citizens. Experts believe that primary education will soon be made mandatory in the Federation, though presently, more than 97 percent of seven-year-olds are enrolled in a primary school.

Students may begin pre-school at age five. At age seven, a child enrolls in primary school for five-to-seven years. At age 13, students progress to lower secondary schools for three years, and at the age of 17 or 18, finish with upper secondary education

Students who fare well on the series of compulsory exams that finish each level of primary and lower education may enroll in post-secondary education, or Sixth Form, for up to one-and-a-half years. Undergraduate and postgraduate studies are provided at Malaysia's higher education institutions, which enroll about 271,000 students, including international scholars.

While the government provides almost all primary and lower school education in the country, private institutions dominate higher education. English is a compulsory subject throughout the Federation. Most instruction occurs in the Malay language, but the government permits teaching in other languages in regions where another tribal language dominates.

In 2004, there were fewer female students than male enrolled in the country's primary education system, which includes preschool through year six, as well as special education, and in lower secondary education; however, female students outnumbered male students in post secondary education.

Women's Rights

Although the Malaysian constitution was amended in 2001 to specifically prohibit discrimination on the basis of gender, women in Malaysia still face several inequalities and discrimination in contemporary society, culture and the political arena.

In Malaysia, women in the workplace are generally not afforded the same benefits and salary as men. Their rights are not protected in marriage laws as well. Married Muslim women, in particular, especially face hardships relating to divorce, polygamy, custody battles and division of property. While a man can easily obtain a divorce, it is much more difficult for a Muslim woman to do so.

Violence against women in Malaysia has continued to rise due to ineffective laws relating to rape, domestic violence and sexual harassment. Violence against women also continues to rise due to deeply held attitudes and beliefs about the unequal role of women in society. Often, stereotypical gender roles are reinforced in religious and educational curriculum. The same is true in media images, which continue to portray women as homemakers and perpetuate patriarchal attitudes. After marriage, many women are expected to remain in the home, giving up their jobs in order to do so if necessary.

As a way to help reduce the rate of violence against women, the Malay government launched an initiative in 2010 to provide women-only transportation in most urban centers. This includes women only train cars, buses, and taxis.

Undeniably, the different religious cultures of Malaysia have positive effects in the lives of women. However, several religions in Malaysia—including Islam, Catholicism, Buddhism, and Hinduism—deny women access to their sacred texts and places, rituals, and leadership positions within the religion. These practices perpetuate demeaning and disrespectful attitudes towards women.

Malaysian children who are born outside of the country to a father who is not a Malaysian citizen cannot become citizens themselves, regardless of whether the mother is Malaysian. A foreign man who marries a Malaysian woman cannot become a citizen either, unlike foreign women married to Malaysian men.

The All Women's Action Society, or AWAM, is the biggest independent feminist organization in Malaysia, and is committed to improving the lives of Malaysian women. The group has been successful in campaigning against violence to women, and passing amendments to improve rape, sexual harassment, and domestic violence laws. They continue to work on issues such as workplace and marriage rights, and reducing violence against women.

Health Care

Malaysia's national health care system provides medical care at little or no cost depending on the income level of the patient. Government-subsidized health stations throughout the country provide general treatment, emergency care, and educational programs. The government also funds more than 100 public hospitals throughout the country.

For those who can afford them, Malaysia's more populated areas have private physicians and practices, and a total of 197 private hospitals that are generally better equipped and better staffed than those provided by the government. In the most remote areas, people often depend on Chinese medicine therapies or other traditional remedies.

An estimated eight percent of Malaysia's population lives below the poverty line, and the infant mortality rate 13.69 deaths for every 1,000 births. Malaysia's population has a long average life span, however, at approximately 74 years (2014 estimate).

GOVERNMENT

Structure

Malaysia is composed of 13 states, called negeri: Johor, Kedah, Kelantan, Melaka, Negeri Sembilan, Pahang, Perak, Perlis, Pulau Pinang, Sabah, Sarawak, Selangor, and Terengganu. The country also has one federal territory, called a wilayah persekutuan, which is composed of the three cities of Kuala Lumpur, Labuan, and Putrajaya.

Malaysia has a unique form of constitutional monarchy. Each state, except Sabah, Sarawak, Melaka, and Penang, is run by a hereditary ruler who is subject to federal law. In the remaining four states, a governor is appointed to run the local government. At the federal level, Malaysia has two houses of Parliament, one elected (the lower house) and one appointed (the upper house); the non-elected Senate comprises 69 members, while the elected members of the House of Representatives, who serve five-year terms, number 193. A Paramount Ruler, elected from among the hereditary heads of state, leads the Federation within the powers outlined in the country's federal constitution.

Political Parties

Malaysia's political system is often generally characterized as a dominant-party system, with that party being the Alliance Party, the ruling party in some form or fashion since 1955. Its successor party, the Barisan Nasional (National Front), a coalition party, is the ruling party as of 2010. A loose coalition of opposition political parties, Pakatan Rakyat, has continued to make headway in the 2008 and 2013 elections. The voting age is 21 in Malaysia.

Local Government

In terms of governance, Malaysia consists of thirteen states and three federal territories (including the capital area of Kuala Lumpur), with local government operating at the city, municipal, and district levels through councils. Councils are state-appointed, with terms lasting three years. Peninsular states maintain hereditary rulers, while four states—Malacca, Pulau Pinang, Sabah, and Sarawak—have state-appointed governors.

Judicial System

Malaysia's judiciary system is based upon British common law, with some Islamic influence. Superior courts include the Federal Court, which is the highest court, the Court of Appeal, and two High Courts. Lower, or subordinate, courts include magistrates' courts and sessions courts, both of which have jurisdiction in civil and criminal issues. Other, lower courts, such as those at the village level which hear civil matters, or those courts dealing with juveniles, are also established. Syariah Courts hear matters pertaining to Sharia (Islamic law).

Taxation

Tax rates in Malaysia are characterized as relatively fair and moderate, with a top corporate tax rate of 25 percent, and a personal income tax rate that peaks at 27 percent. Other taxes levied include a vehicle tax, and indirect taxes such as excise duty, service tax, and sales tax.

Armed Forces

The Malaysian Armed Forces are made up of three service branches, the Malaysian Army, the Royal Malaysian Navy, and the Royal Malaysian Air Force. There is no conscription, and the minimum age for voluntary service is eighteen. Non-Malays make up a very small percentage of the country's armed forces. The Malaysian Armed Forces celebrated its 80th anniversary in 2011.

Foreign Policy

Historically, Malaysia's foreign policy has centered on The Commonwealth of Nations, an association of 53 sovereign states. These nations, most formerly British colonies, assisted Malaysia in its bid for independence in 1957. At that time, there were no formal regional organizations in Southeast Asia that could help Malaysia develop as a country. With the formation and rise of the Association of South-East Asian Nations (ASEAN), Organization of the Islamic Conference (OIC) and other organizations, Malaysia's dependence on the Commonwealth has diminished.

Today, Malaysia plays a quiet role in supporting the Commonwealth. Malaysia is also active in the Non-Aligned Movement (NAM), an organization of nations not formally aligned with major powers, and the United Nations (UN). Malaysia is also a founding member of ASEAN. Furthermore, the country is active in promoting reform on issues such as environmental degradation, terrorism, the reform of the UN Security Council and human rights issues, even amidst accusations that its own citizens suffer from human rights violations.

In particular, Malaysia has a strong relationship with the United States. The U.S. is Malaysia's largest trading partner and the largest foreign investor in the country. The two countries cooperate closely in security matters, including regional stability in Malaysia and counter-terrorism activities and training. The U.S. and Malaysia signed a Mutual Legal Assistance Treaty (MLAT) in July 2006.

Generally, Malaysia strives to cooperate with its neighbors, establishing separate joint commissions between Malaysia and Brunei, the Philippines, Thailand, Indonesia, Laos and Vietnam. Malaysia has hosted several summits in recent years. This has helped strengthen ties with other nations such as Japan and South Korea, and even with traditional opponents Indonesia and Singapore. However, a dispute still exists with Indonesia over oil-rich territories off the Sulawesi Sea. Malaysia also maintains close economic ties with Singapore, but international disputes have recently arisen over water rights, airspace and border crossings.

In 2014, the loss of Malaysian Airlines Flight 370 somewhere in the Pacific Ocean, led to a general outpouring of sympathy and aid for the Asian nation. The loss of Malaysian Airlines Flight 17 over the Ukraine only a few months later, once again refocused attention on Malaysia and greatly soured relations with Russia, thought to be ultimately responsible for arming the separatist groups blamed for the attack.

Human Rights Profile

International human rights law insists that states respect civil and political rights, and also promote an individual's economic, social and cultural rights. The United Nations Universal Declaration on Human Rights (UDHR) is recognized as the standard for international human rights. Its authors sought the counsel of the world's great thinkers, philosophers, and religious leaders, and were careful to create a document that reflects the core values shared by every world culture. (To read this document or view the articles relating to cultural human rights, visit: http://www.udhr.org/UDHR/default.htm.)

Malaysia adopted its constitution, called the Merdeka, or Freedom Constitution, after the country became independent in 1957. These laws were written to reflect the fundamental human rights as defined in the UDHR. Malaysia's Freedom Constitution agrees with Article 2, declaring all citizens as equals before the law regardless of race, religion or gender. Qualifying clauses within the constitution, however, empower the Malaysian parliament to legislate restrictions to many of the freedoms listed in the UDHR, especially those of expression, association and assembly. The clauses allow these freedoms to be restricted if the government deems to be a threat to the security of the country, or to keep public order and morality.

Articles 6 through 11 of the UDHR outline the rights of a person as pertaining to arrest, trial, and the presumption of innocence. However, a series of Malaysian laws and regulations, namely the Internal Security Act (ISA) and Emergency Ordinance, undermine these basic due process rights. The ISA gives the government permanent, arbitrary powers to detain without trial, and has, over time, stripped away judicial safeguards used to protect against abuse of human rights law. These include the rights to freedom from arbitrary arrest, the right to be informed of the reasons for arrest, and a fair trial in a court of law.

Article 18 of the declaration outlines freedom of religion. Although Islam is the official state religion, the Malaysian constitution protects freedom of religion for non-Muslims. Still, discussions continue as to whether Malaysia is an Islamic or secular state, and Muslims who convert from the religion are widely discriminated against.

The rights to freedom of speech and expression in Malaysia, as outlined in Article 19 of the UDHR, are subject to autocratic, unwarranted restrictions and censorship. The Printing Presses Ordinance of 1948, which was revised as the Printed Presses Act in 1971, requires all newspapers and printing presses to obtain a license that must be approved and renewed each year. In addition, newspapers that are critical of the government or "national sensitivities" can have their licenses revoked at any time. Today, authorities continue to monitor writers and publishing companies, encouraging them to self-censor. Authorities also caution private medial outlets against abusing their privileges and warning webmasters and bloggers to use their power "cautiously" in order to avoid being sued for defamation.

The right to assemble, outlined in Article 20, is also supported in the constitution, but not in practice. Two large (over 30,000 protesters) demonstrations in 2007 were met with the use of water cannons, tear gas and excessive force, with police arbitrarily arresting and detaining large numbers of protestors.

In addition, the existence of a body of "emergency" laws based on constitutional clauses in

Malaysia has allowed the government to circumvent important human rights safeguards within the constitution and UDHR. These laws have facilitated unjustified and arbitrary violations of human rights, including the ability to forbid meetings, ban print publications, and deprive a person of his or her liberty indefinitely without trial.

ECONOMY

Overview of the Economy

The past several decades have witnessed dramatic changes in Malaysia's economy. Once dependent on exports of natural resources and agricultural products, Malaysia is now a manufacturing power. In 2014, more than a third of Malaysia's gross domestic product (GDP) came from manufacturing, particularly in electronic goods that are exported.

Malaysia still depends on the processing and export of certain natural resources: palm oil, hardwoods, petroleum, chemicals, and textiles. The Federation's most important trading partners are, in order, the United States, Singapore, Japan, China, Hong Kong, and Thailand. As a result of its dependence on Asian markets, Malaysia's economy suffered significantly with the Asian economic crisis of 1997. Since then, however, Malaysia's economy has recovered its rate of growth.

Industry

The capital, Kuala Lumpur, is Malaysia's premier center for exports, banking and financial services, information technology, tourism, industry, and transportation. Kuala Lumpur controls the lion's share of the country's economy. Its manufacturing sector turns out machinery, textiles, steel, and electronics. Major exports include automotive parts, machinery, and electronics.

Labor

The country's labor force was estimated at 14 million in 2014, with an unemployment rate of 2.9 percent. As of 2012 estimates, just over half of the work force is employed in the services sector, while the agriculture and industry sectors account for 11 and 36 percent of the work force, respectively.

Energy/Power/Natural Resources

Malaysia's ancient rainforests have provided much of the world's supply of mature hardwoods over the past five centuries. However, Malaysia also has natural gas and oil reserves, and the world's largest deposits of tin.

Fishing

Between 2006 and 2010, the Malaysian government aimed to increase fisheries production under the Ninth Fie Year Malaysia Plan with particular focus on tuna fishing and production. As of 2008, fisheries output amounted to roughly $1.5 billion (USD). Other primary commercial species caught include mackerel, squid, scad, and bream. The fishing industry is also important in meeting local demand. According to a 2010 report, the Malaysian fishing industry suffers from substantial annual losses due to foreign encroachment in Malaysian waters.

Forestry

According to recent figures, Malaysia's total forest cover amounted to just over 20,000,000 hectares (49,421,076 acres), covering approximately 63 percent of the country's land area. Primary forest cover (or pristine forest), however, amounts to only 18 percent of total forest area (largely concentrated on Borneo). Agriculture and urbanization have contributed to declining forest cover and degradation. Despite extensive rainforest protection laws, illegal logging remains a problem. Wood for fuel is a primary cause of deforestation.

Mining/Metals

The mineral and mining industry of Malaysia accounted for less than 20 percent of the gross domestic product (GDP) in 2008. A major tin producing country, Malaysia also produces industrial minerals such as feldspar and silica sand, metals such as bauxite, gold, and iron ore, and fuels such as natural gas and petroleum, though production of many resources is trending toward decline or depletion.

Agriculture

The agricultural industry still accounts for a little more than seven percent of the country's gross domestic product. While economic centers on Peninsular Malaysia are increasingly dependent on industry, agriculture, and even subsistence farming, are important in many of the communities in Sabah and Sarawak.

Peninsular Malaysia exports rubber, palm oil, cocoa, rice. In Sabah, the agriculture focus is on subsistence crops, rubber, timber, coconuts, and rice. Sarawak exports rubber, pepper, and timber.

Animal Husbandry

The livestock sector in Malaysia accounts for only approximately two percent of land use. A majority of the sector is poultry and pig farming, distantly followed by cattle, goat, and sheep. The government has announced plans, such as the construction of feed mills, to develop the beef industry, including upping the supply to meet domestic consumption.

Tourism

Malaysia has yet to develop a strong tourism industry. With more government plans to protect Malaysia's natural resources and to diversify its manufacturing and export-based economy, the country is aggressively pursuing tourists from within and outside of Southeast Asia. In 2013, tourist arrivals numbered over 25.7 million, a 700,000 increase over the previous year. The tourism sector has been boosted by an increase in air connections in recent years, but it is unclear what affect the loss of two Malaysian Airlines flights within months of each other will have on the sector.

April Sanders, Amy Witherbee, Beverly Ballaro

DO YOU KNOW?

- Joseph Conrad, one of English literature's most renowned authors, set three of his novels in Malaysia: *Lord Jim* (1900), *Victory* (1915), and *The Rescue* (1920).
- Archeologists found a skull from the Niah Caves in Sarawak that dates to 35000 BCE.

Bibliography

Baker, Jim. *Crossroads: A Popular History of Malaysia and Singapore.* Tarrytown, NY: Marshall Cavendish, 2014.

Joseph, Cynthia. *Growing Up Female in Multi-Ethnic Malaysia.* New York: Routledge, 2014.

Frisk, Sylva. *Submitting to God: Women and Islam in Urban Malaysia.* Seattle: University of Washington Press, 2009.

King, Victor. *Malaysia—Culture Smart! A Quick Guide to Customs and Etiquette.* London: Kuperard, 2008.

Koh, Jaime. *Culture and Customs of Singapore and Malaysia.* Santa Barbara, CA: Greenwood Press, 2009.

Lonely Planet and Simon Richmond. *Malaysia, Singapore, and Brunei.* Oakland, CA: Lonely Planet, 2013.

Ooi, Keat Gin. *The A to Z of Malaysia.* Lanham, MD: Scarecrow Press, 2010.

Solomon, Charmaine. *Food of Indonesia, Malaysia, Singapore, and the Philippines.* Melbourne: Hardie Grant Books, 2014.

Stivens, M. *"Family Values" and Islamic Revival: Gender, Rights and State Moral Projects in Malaysia.* New York: Elsevier, 2006.

Vadaketh, Sudhir Thomas. *Floating on a Malayan Breeze: Travels in Malaysia and Singapore.* Hong Kong: Hong Kong University Press, 2012.

Weiss, Meredith L, ed. *Routledge Handbook of Contemporary Malaysia.* New York: Routledge, 2015.

Works Cited

"2005 Population Estimates for Cities in Malaysia." *Mongabay.com.* <http://www.mongabay.com/igapo/2005_world_city_populations/Malaysia.html >.

"About Malaysia." Tourism.gov.my. *Tourism Asia.* <http://www.tourism.gov.my/>.

Ahmad, Nik Nazmi. "The Coming of Age of Malaysia's Youth." *Opinionasia.org.* 06 June 2008. < http://www.opinionasia.org/TheComingofAgeofMalaysiasYouth>.

Hazri, Herizal. "In Malaysia: Empowered or Disempowered Youth?" Asiafoundation.org. 05 December 2007. 26 July 2008 < http://asiafoundation.org/in-asia/2007/12/05/in-malaysia-empowered-or-disempowered-youth/>.

"Malaysia." *Ediplomat.com.* <http://www.ediplomat.com/np/cultural_etiquette/ce_my.htm>.

"Malaysia." *Britannica.com.* <http://www.britannica.com/EBchecked/topic/359754/Malaysia>.

"Malaysia: Government failing to respect the right to freedom of assembly." Amnestyusa.org. *Amnesty International USA*. 31 July 2008 < http://www.amnestyusa.org/document.php?lang=e&id=ENGASA280082007>.

"Malaysia." *Opennet.net.* < http://opennet.net/research/profiles/Malaysia>.

"Malaysia: Events of 2007." Hwr.org. *Human Rights Watch World Report 2008*. < http://hrw.org/englishwr2k8/docs/2008/01/31/malays17608.htm>.

"World Heritage List." *UNESCO.org*. <http://whc.unesco.org/en/list>.

A woman from Long Neck Karen Tribe, Mayanmar/Stock photo © Bartosz Hadyniak

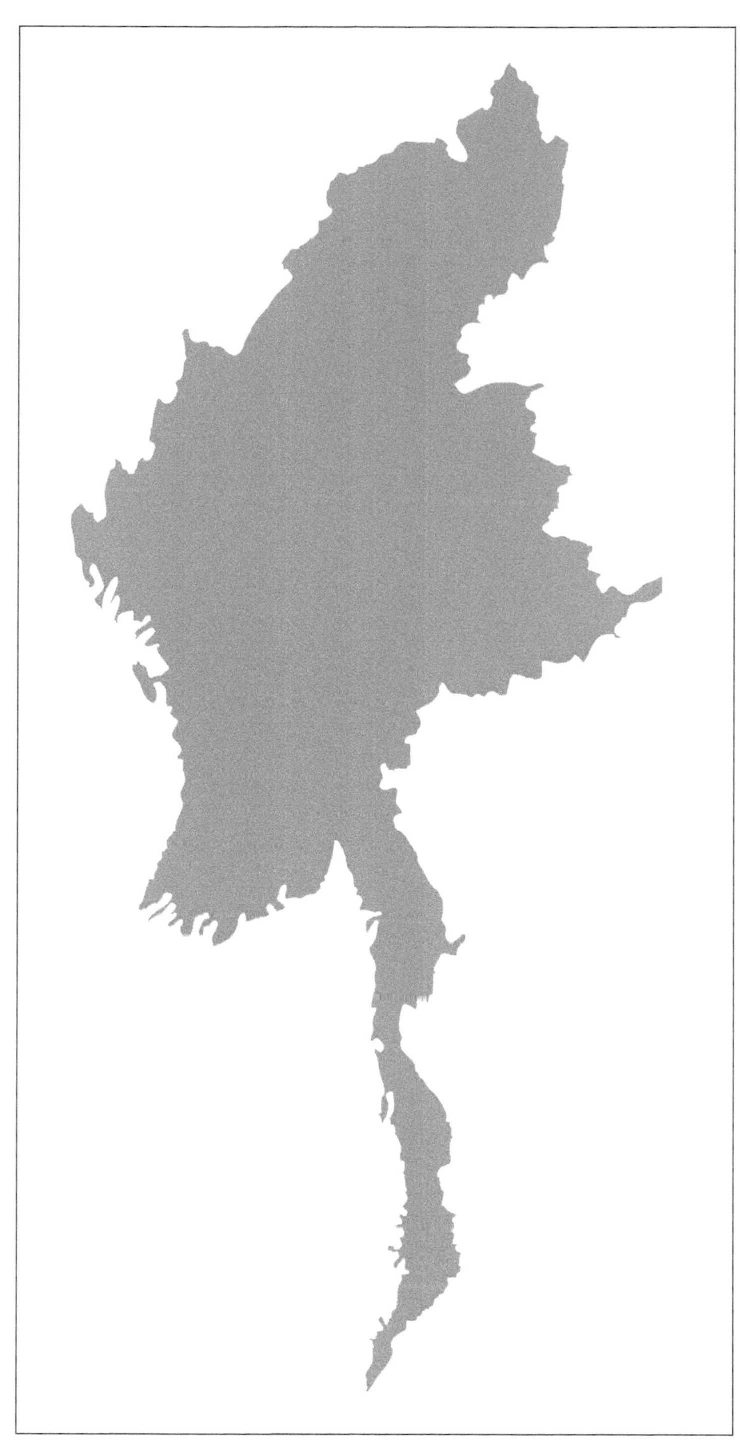

Myanmar
(Burma)

Introduction

The Republic of the Union of Myanmar, the nation formerly known as Burma, is a Southeast Asian country that was ruled by a military dictatorship from 1988 until 2011, when the military junta was dissolved and democratic reforms were enacted. The name Myanmar is not recognized by Britain, the nation's former colonial ruler, or the United States, although the name has received official recognition by the United Nations. Myanmar was an independent kingdom in ancient times, and then a British colony from the late 19th century, until regaining independence in 1948.

Naypyidaw is the administrative capital of Myanmar. It is one of the world's youngest capitals, having been formed in 2005 and opened to the public in 2006, when the government relocated its capital from the city of Yangon (formerly Rangoon). The city's name translates as "abode of kings."

Burmese culture is dominated by Buddhist ceremonies and rituals, and has evolved to include characteristics from native Chinese, Indian, and Thai culture. Open-air markets are common and provide a social center where residents gather to purchase food and engage in recreational activities. Visitors enjoy the country's beautiful landscapes and ancient Buddhist temples.

Myanmar has a rich artistic history. There are ten traditional arts, sometimes called the Ten Flowers. The arts in Myanmar changed dramatically because of restrictions imposed by the ruling military junta. Controlling the arts was a conscious government strategy for controlling the population, and although change is progressing at a rapid pace, contemporary art in Myanmar is still largely defined by the underground art movement that government censorship created.

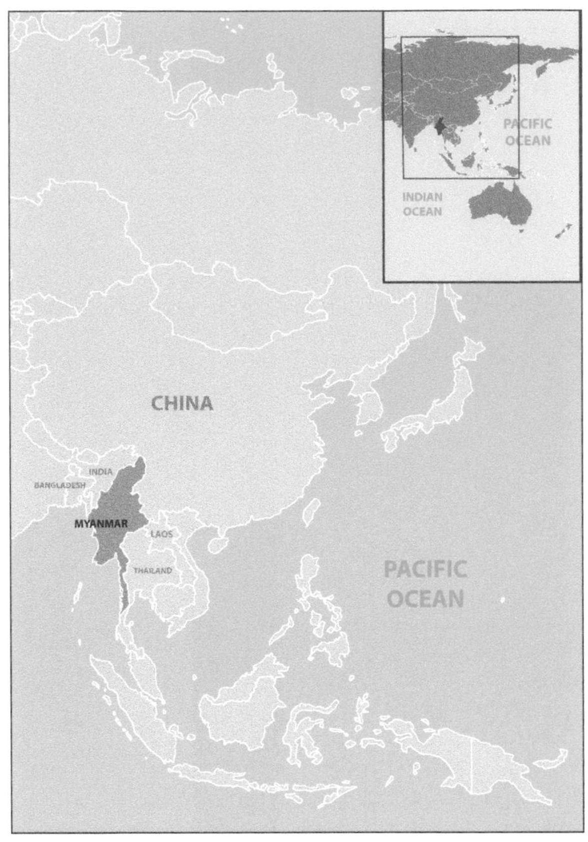

GENERAL INFORMATION

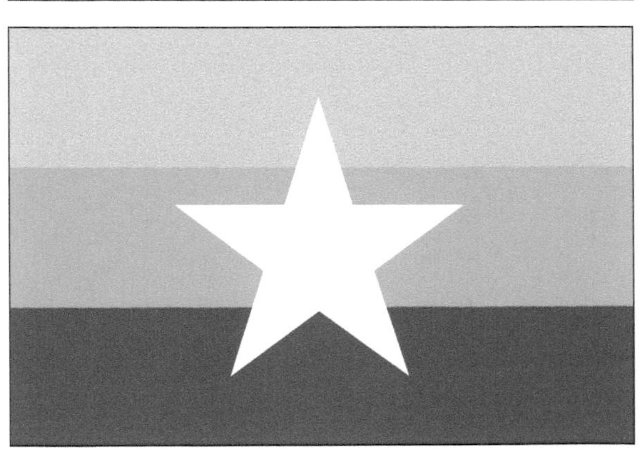

Official Language: Burmese
Population: 50,020,000 (2009 estimate)
Currency: Myanmar kyat
Coins: The Myanmar kyat is subdivided into 100 pya. Coins are available in denominations of 1, 5, 10, 25, and 50 pyas, and 1, 5, 10, 50, and 100 kyat.
Land Area: 653,508 square kilometers (252,320 square miles)
Water Area: 23,070 square kilometers (8,907 square miles)
National Anthem: "Kaba Ma Kyei" (Burmese, "Till the End of the World")
Capital: Yangon is the official capital, Naypyidaw is the administrative capital.

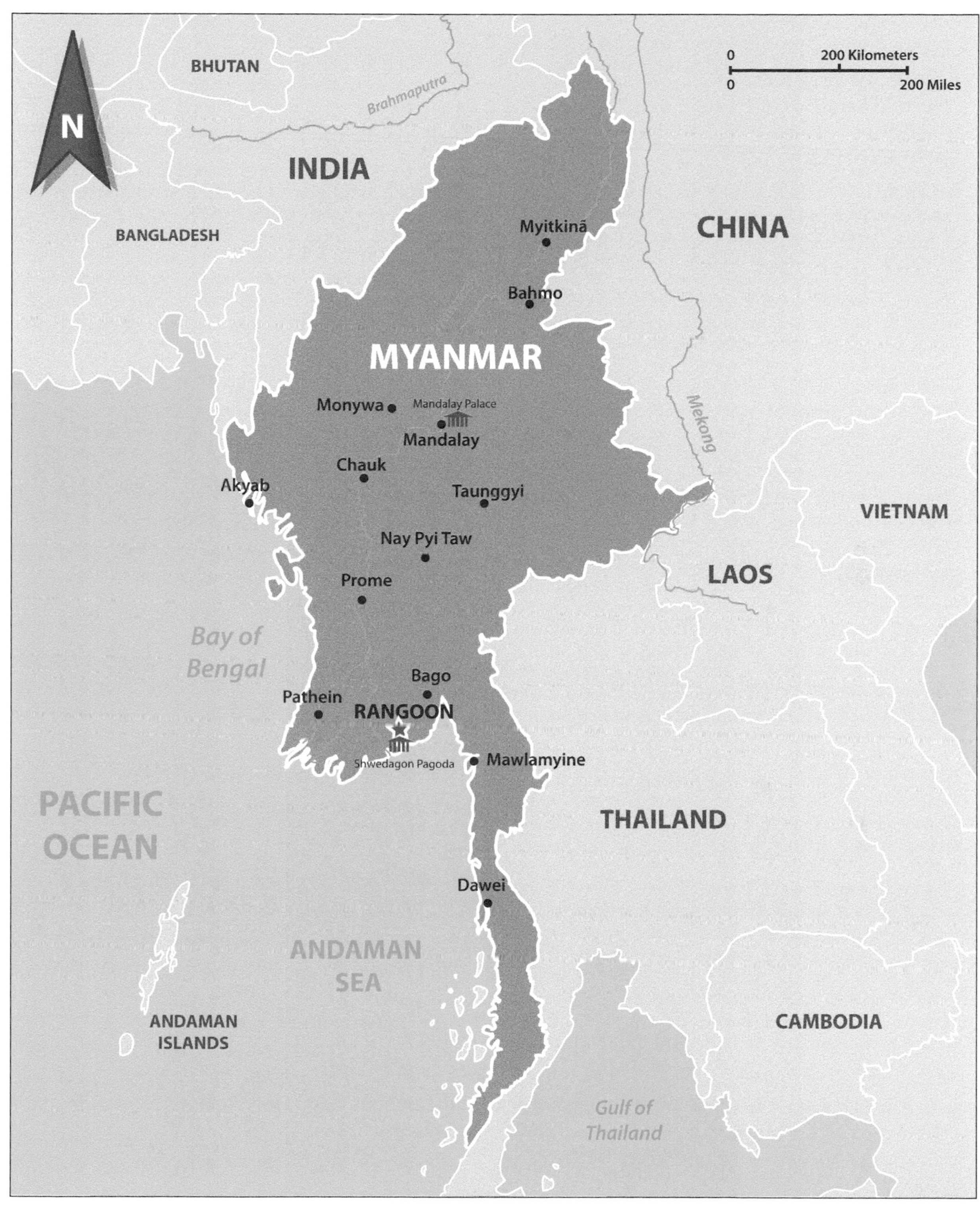
N
BHUTAN
Brahmaputra
0 200 Kilometers
0 200 Miles
INDIA
CHINA
BANGLADESH
Myitkinā
Bahmo
MYANMAR
Mekong
Monywa
Mandalay Palace
Mandalay
Chauk
Akyab
Taunggyi
VIETNAM
Nay Pyi Taw
LAOS
Prome
Bay of Bengal
Bago
Pathein
RANGOON
Shwedagon Pagoda
Mawlamyine
PACIFIC OCEAN
THAILAND
Dawei
ANDAMAN SEA
ANDAMAN ISLANDS
CAMBODIA
Gulf of Thailand

Principal Cities by Population (2014):

- Yangon (5,209,541)
- Mandalay (1,225,133)
- Naypyidaw (1,158,367)
- Mawlamyine (491,130)
- Bago (288,120)
- Pathein (286,684)
- Pyay (251,145)
- Monywa (371,963)
- Meiktila (309,465)
- Sittwe (149,348)

Time Zone: GMT +6:30

Flag Description: The flag of Myanmar (formerly Burma) features a tricolor design of three equal horizontal bands of yellow (top), green (middle), and red (bottom). Centered in the flag is a large, five-pointed white star. The colors are said to symbolize solidarity, tranquility, and courage and decisiveness.

Population

The population of Myanmar is very young, with a median age of around 28 years. Roughly 26 percent of the population is under the age of 15. Disease, particularly HIV/AIDS, has taken a heavy toll on the population. As of 2014, the population growth rate was estimate at 1.03 percent. Most of the population is concentrated in the central flood plain, dominated by the Ayeyarwady (or Irrawaddy) River.

The last official census was taken in 2014. According to recent statistics, Yangon, the capital, is the largest city, while Mandalay, Burma's last royal capital, is the second largest city. The government estimates the current population of the administrative capital of Naypyidaw to be over 1 million people

The majority of the population belongs to the Burman ethnic group, who speak the Burmese language. Together, the Shan, Karen, and Rakhine ethnic groups account for 20 percent of the population—the Shan (nine percent of the population), the Karen (seven percent), and the Rakhine (four percent of the population). Small numbers of Chinese (three percent), Mon (two percent), and Indian (two percent) round out the country's total population.

Languages

Burmese is the national language of Myanmar and is used in all official, governmental, and educational functions. It is a tonal language, and the first language of about half the population. Some ethnic groups speak regional dialects, though most also speak Burmese.

Part of the Tibeto-Burman language group, it is distantly related to other Asian languages such as Chinese. Burmese is written using the distinctive script, based on the Mon script. There are two many types of Burmese language: the formal, literary variety, and the informal, used in casual speech.

English is widely spoken as a second language, owing especially to the legacy of British colonial rule. Recognized regional languages include Jingpho, a Tibeto-Burman language; Kayah and Karen languages, spoken by the Karen ethnicity; Kiki-Chin, another Tibeto-Burman language; the Austro-Asiatic Mon language; Rakhine; and the Shan language (spoken in Myanmar's Shan State.)

Native People & Ethnic Groups

Burman (Bamar) is the most populous ethnic group in Myanmar and accounts for close to 68 percent of the population. This group first settled in Myanmar in the ninth century. Additionally, the Shan, Karen, and Rakhine ethnic groups, together account for 20 percent of the population. (Some estimates place the various ethnic groups in Myanmar as comprising upwards of 35 to 40 percent of the total population.) Myanmar also has small populations of ethnic Chinese and Indians, which together account for approximately five percent of the population.

Most of Myanmar's indigenous ethnic groups are believe to be descended from native Tibetan ethnic groups that migrated into the nation. The Mon people, related to the Vietnamese and

Cambodians, were among the earliest groups to establish a civilization in what is now Myanmar, probably settling in the region around 1500 BCE. Though once the dominant group, they now represent only about two percent of the population. The Pyu people were another early group to settle the region.

The central government's wars against ethnic insurgents have produced hundreds of thousands of refugees and internally displaced persons (IDPs). The insurgencies are motivated in part to environmental concerns, to protest such projects as the government's development of hydroelectric dams.

Religions

The religious composition of Myanmar is highly homogenous with over 89 percent of the population practicing some form of Buddhism. Christianity accounts for approximately 4 percent of the population and is more common in the larger cities where churches and other religious institutions are located. Another four percent of the population is Muslim. Roughly one to two percent of the remaining population follows some form of animistic or tribal religion.

Climate

Myanmar experiences three seasons: winter, summer, and the rainy season. Summers, which generally last from March to May, are hot and humid. Summer temperatures may climb as high as 38° Celsius (100° Fahrenheit). Winters are milder, with little rain, and last from November to February.

Like other parts of Southeast Asia, Myanmar receives most of its rain from the fierce tropical winds known as monsoons. The rainy season lasts from May to October, and can bring as much as 5,000 millimeters (approximately 200 inches) of rain to parts of the country. The winds also regularly produce cyclones.

Despite the regular rain during the rainy season, Myanmar often suffers from droughts. The central plains region of the country, known as the "dry zone," typically receives around 760 millimeters (30 inches) of rain each year.

ENVIRONMENT & GEOGRAPHY

Topography

Much of Myanmar is covered by mountains and high hills, particularly along the borders. Southeast Asia's highest peak and Myanmar's highest point is Hkakabo Razi, which rises (5,881 meters/19,294 feet) above sea level, on the border with Tibet.

Myanmar's water borders include the Bay of Bengal to the west and the Andaman Sea to the south. On land, the country is bordered by Bangladesh and India to the west, by Thailand and Laos to the east, and by China to the north.

The Ayeyarwady is the longest river in Myanmar, stretching over 1,000 miles. It is formed from the Mali and Nmai Rivers in Northern Myanmar. The Ayeyarwady is Myanmar's most commercially important river and is widely used for fishing. The other major rivers are the Salween, along the eastern border, and the Sittang, located between the Salween and the Ayeyarwaddy. Around half of the country is forested.

The administrative capital city of Naypyidaw is located in Myanmar's geographic center, in what was once a dense cluster of tropical forest. The city sits at an average elevation of 92 meters (302 feet) and is surrounded by tropical scrubland and forest.

Naypyidaw is located approximately 460 kilometers (285 miles) from the official capital of Yangon (formerly Rangoon). It is near the town of Pyinmana, which is an important location in terms of the nation's military history.

The administrative capital region is the axis of the nation's newly expanded transportation system, but is restricted to tourists without direct permission from the government. The city is organized according to strict zoning ordinances that dictate which locations can be used for residential, commercial, and governmental buildings.

Plants & Animals

Myanmar is heavily forested, though deforestation is an ongoing concern. The northern parts of the country, in the foothills of the mountains, are covered with pine trees. However, deforestation has sharply reduced the number of bird and mammal species found in Myanmar. Large mammals such as the Asiatic black bear and the barking deer that were once plentiful are no longer found there.

The central flood plain of the Irrawaddy Delta has large rainforests as well as freshwater swamps. Typical tree species found in this area include evergreens and mangroves. Human encroachment and hunting have almost eliminated the large mammals of the flood plain, including elephants, leopards, and tigers.

Small mammals such as tapirs and wild boars still exist in fairly sizeable numbers in the forests. Many water birds, including several varieties of plover and heron, live in the rainforests and mangrove forests.

CUSTOMS & COURTESIES

Greetings

According to Burmese culture, a greeting should reflect social relationship and standing. This is reflected in the formal use of pronouns. In the Myanmar (Burmese) language, the pronouns "I" and "you" indicate relative social rank. When addressing someone of higher rank, the word for "you" would be akin to "master," and the word for "I" would be akin to "servant." In addition, it is traditional to greet someone by inquiring about their well-being. It is also common for people to use the term "mingala-ba," which is a blessing of auspiciousness, or fortune. Interestingly enough, the English phrase "Hello" is commonly used when communicating on the telephone.

Among friends and family, people use a more casual mode of address. A speaker will commonly address another person by the most fitting familial term. For example, a younger male will be called "Nyi" (younger brother), and a younger female will typically be called "Nyi ma" (younger sister). An older male may be referred to as "Ah ko" (elder brother), while an older female may be addressed as "Ma ma" (elder sister). When addressing elders or people of high social rank, it is considered respectful to use "U" (uncle) for men and "Daw" (aunt) for women. In urban areas, however, it is polite to refer to professional women of high rank as "Ma ma" (elder sister), because "Daw" (aunt) has a potentially offensive connotation of old age.

Gestures & Etiquette

Much of Burmese culture is still recovering from decades of repressive military rule. Under the rule of the military junta, in which perceived dissidents were subjected to incarceration, torture, and sometimes death, it was important for citizens and travelers alike to be aware of how they conduct themselves. Though many people in Myanmar disliked the government, as evidenced by the institution of reforms in 2011–2013, these reservations were to be expressed privately. Talking about politics was never done in public, as it was likely to make people nervous and could lead to real danger. Care was even taken with such mundane activities as reading the foreign press, as these could be considered signs of political dissent. In addition, though many in Myanmar considered the democratically elected leader and Burmese activist Aung San Suu Kyi to be a hero, it was inadvisable to seek out or ask the location of the home where she was under house arrest. (Following a 2009 trespassing incident involving an American man, for example, the uninvited trespasser was sentenced to prison—it was later commuted—and Suu Kyi was faced with further confinement.) Suu Kyi was released from house arrest in November 2010, and in 2012, she won a seat in Parliament for the minority National League for Democracy (NLD), becoming the leader of the opposition in the People's Assembly.

Most people in Myanmar are devout Buddhists. As such, proper etiquette requires respecting religious values. People are expected to be particularly respectful when entering a temple or monastery. Conservative dress is mandatory, as wearing shorts, short skirts, or other revealing clothing could be perceived as disrespectful. It is also necessary to remove shoes and socks when entering a religious building. Images of the Buddha are treated with reverence, and not casually touched or sat upon. Also, women in Myanmar, both citizens and visitors alike, are expected not to touch a monk or his clothes. Before leaving a temple, it is customary to leave a small cash offering in an envelope with a monk or temple attendant.

Personal cleanliness is also an important aspect of social etiquette in Burmese culture. People in Myanmar consider the head to be the cleanest part of the body, and the feet to be the least clean. This belief results in several points of etiquette. For example, it is considered rude or disrespectful to point using one's feet. It is also considered improper to step over someone, as this poses a risk of touching that individual with the feet. Shoes and sandals are also considered dirty. In addition, it is considered culturally and socially unacceptable for a person to ask someone older to assist with putting on or taking off footwear, though older people may ask their juniors for this kind of help. It is also considered impolite to touch a person on the head for any reason.

Eating/Meals

People in Myanmar typically have three meals a day. Breakfast is generally a simple meal, often made from leftover rice fried up with vegetables and eggs. Lunch is more elaborate, consisting of rice, salads, soups and various kinds of curry (typically a dish flavored with curry powder). Dinner is similar to lunch, but is commonly followed by fresh fruit. Generally, meals are very social events in Myanmar. Lunch and dinner in Myanmar usually consist of several different dishes to be shared among those joining in the meal, and food is typically served on a single round table. People sit around the table floor mats. Eating is commonly done with the tips of fingers, and there are normally finger bowls and towels at the table for washing hands.

In urban areas, it is common to purchase breakfast from food stalls. People also like to go to a teahouse for the morning meal in urban areas, where they enjoy a warm coffee or tea accompanied by naan (oven-baked flat bread). Restaurants are fairly popular for lunch and dinner in cities. In addition to restaurants serving local Burmese cuisine, there are also many that specialize in Chinese and Indian food. It is not common to serve alcohol in the home. However, there are establishments known as beer stations in urban areas that sell draft beer to commuters at the end of the workday.

Visiting

In Myanmar, casual visits are often common; making appointments to visit friends is considered pretentious. Visitors are expected to remove their shoes when entering a home, and offering to help out with any work that needs to be done is considered polite. Since sons and daughters are highly revered in Myanmar, guests often focus on paying attention to the host family's children. In addition, guests from other countries should always remember that the ruling military junta enforces strict laws dictating overnight visits by foreigners. Failure to get prior authorization from the government could endanger one's hosts.

Since the feet are considered the dirtiest part of the body and the head the cleanest, it is proper for guests to sleep with their heads pointing toward the family shrine. Furthermore, feet are commonly washed in designated water bowls before getting into bed.

LIFESTYLE

Family

Family is extremely important in Burmese culture and the extended family—including aunts, uncles, and cousins—is an important part of day-to-day life for people in Myanmar. It is also considered proper for multiple generations to live together in the same home. Traditionally, the female relatives are in charge of maintaining the household.

Children are highly prized and treated with great indulgence, or favor. Parents are expected to do everything possible to guide and nurture their sons and daughters, even into adulthood.

In turn, children are taught to have a deep gratitude for elders and their parents, especially their mothers. In particular, respect and obedience of parents is expected.

Sons and daughters are considered an important blessing to the family, and nearly all couples have children as soon as possible after marriage. Parents are also very protective of their children. One demonstration of this is the tradition of never commenting on a child's good health. Traditionally, this is considered bad luck because it could attract harmful evil spirits.

Housing

In traditional villages, there are two main kinds of housing. Most people live in thatch and bamboo huts, while others live in wooden houses, some built with metal roofs. Most homes in villages are typically raised up from the ground to protect against floods. In urban areas, houses are also raised off the ground. However, these are mostly built with concrete and plywood.

Houses normally have one main room, which is a living room typically containing the household shrine where the family worships. A household shrine normally consists of a statue of Buddha, flower, candles, and small offerings of rice and fruit. Generally, all beds in the house are situated with the head towards the household shrine. Kitchens are normally quite small, and contain a stove that consists of a small electric or kerosene-fueled pot on a table or concrete block. Drinking water is often stored in the kitchen in clay vases. Indoor bathrooms are the norm in urban areas, but in rural villages bathrooms are situated away from houses.

Food

Burmese cuisine reflects the county's geography as well as its Buddhist values. It is largely influenced by Chinese and Indian cuisine, and features the unique tastes of the tribes that historically inhabited the country. As Buddhists, most people in Myanmar have religious beliefs about eating meat, since killing and eating four-legged animals is considered a sin in Buddhism. As such, people are more comfortable eating poultry and seafood. Chicken and duck are common meats. Popular fish include tuna, snapper, and mackerel. Generally, sea creatures of all kinds are eaten, including eel, squid, and shrimp. Poultry and seafood are often flavored with the dried shrimp paste known as ngapi.

Common dishes include curries, noodle dishes, soups and salads. Curries are slow-cooked, oily and fairly mild compared to curries from neighboring India, and are almost always eaten with rice, which is considered central to any meal. Noodle dishes are primarily considered a breakfast staple, and are usually made from rice noodles and simple ingredients. Soups are served with meals, and are considered a form of sweet, bitter or peppery beverage. Salads are made from a wide range of fresh vegetables, tossed with flavoring ingredients such as lime juice and chilies. A favorite Burmese salad is made from tea leaves, which provide a traditional flavor as well as a dose of caffeine.

Many of Myanmar's dishes are considered spicy. Curry, lemongrass, bamboo shoots, and coconut milk are common ingredients in many dishes. Mohinga, considered one of the country's "national dishes," is a soup of rice noodles and fish.

Life's Milestones

The union of a young couple is a cause for great celebration for Burmese families. People usually hold a small engagement party to announce a couple's plan to marry. Traditionally, male guests of high social standing make speeches praising the future groom, who then formally asks for the bride to marry him in the near future. The wedding itself is a larger event. It is conducted by an older married couple of high social standing, not a monk. The older couple gives the newlyweds a blessing to have many children. When a child is born, it is customary to give the mother small practical gifts. Perhaps due to high infant mortality, a child is typically not named until 100 days after birth. This happens at a morning feast attended by friends, family, and local monks.

When a family member is dying, people are obligated to visit and bring small food gifts.

When a person dies, the body is washed, clothed in the person's finest outfit, and laid on a decorated bed. A monk is then typically invited to the home for a meal and to administer a blessing. The extended family attends a burial a few days later. Following a death, the surviving family members traditionally cook and receive mourners for one week. It is also believed that the spirit of the deceased lingers in the house for one week. On the seventh day after death, a larger feast is given to local monks. This is believed to help the deceased person's spirit be reborn in a new body.

CULTURAL HISTORY

Art

Myanmar has a rich artistic history. There are 10 traditional arts, sometimes called the Ten Flowers: sculpting with stone, sculpting in wood or ivory, painting, lacquer, building masonry, making floral designs with masonry, blacksmithing, working with precious metals, bronze casting, and making designs with a lathe (a machine tool used in metalworking). These traditional arts developed from diverse cultural influences, but are considered to have come together in the 11th century when Buddhism arrived from India.

Myanmar is famous for its sculpture. Statues usually depict religious motifs. The Buddha, typically a representation of the founder of Buddhism, is the most common subject, often portrayed in giant size. There are many examples of this form of sculpture. The Shwethalyaung Buddha in Bago is particularly popular among the people of Myanmar. This sculpture, believed to be commissioned by King Migadepa II in 994, has a length of over 55 meters (180 feet), and is considered the second largest Buddha in the world. Another statue of this kind is the enormous quadruple Buddha, or Kyaik Pun Paya, also in Bago. It was constructed in 1476 by King Dhammazedi, and consists of four Buddhas nearly 30 meters (100 feet) tall each.

Painting in Myanmar has also been traditionally dominated by Buddhist themes. Caves, pagodas, temples, and monasteries throughout the country typically contain colorful wall murals. The most well preserved wall paintings date back to the 17th century. An excellent example of this traditional style of mural painting can be found at the Taungbi monastic library, located in the city of Bagan. Stylistically, these mural paintings are influenced by the art of ancient India. Vibrant colors and fine detail make them very lifelike, and elements are arranged to tell a story. Common themes are the life of the Buddha and acts of worship by royalty.

Parabeik (parchment) painting also developed as a traditional art in Burmese history, and was used to record the history of the country's royal courts. The art reached its highest height of development during the Konbaung Dynasty (1752–1885), an expansionist period in Burmese history. During colonialism (1885–1945), watercolors became an important medium, and more Western styles of painting began to predominate (many Burmese artists were sent to England to study). It was during this period that impressionism, which dominates contemporary art in Myanmar, was introduced to the country.

In the contemporary era, Myanmar's most famous painter is U Lun Gywe (1930–), often considered a master of Burmese painting. An impressionist, much of U Lun Gywe's work focuses on the female figure, particularly his impressions of feminine beauty in such simple acts as dancing and bathing. His work also portrays the Buddhist heritage of the country, including the artist's impressions of the Shwedagon Pagoda and the ancient temples of Bagan. Exhibitions of his work have spanned the globe, from the United States and Australia to Japan and the People's Republic of China, and his works are housed in the national collections of various Western nations, including England, Germany, and Canada.

Architecture

Myanmar's artistic history is especially apparent in its architecture. Thousands of payas or pagodas (tiered structures or temples common in the Far East) dot the landscape, giving Myanmar its distinctive look. Pagodas are also closely connected to the nation's Buddhist heritage. In the Myanmar, or Burmese, language, paya is literally translated as "holy one." Pagodas are typically constructed in two main shapes. One is the squared shape, called pahto, built to contain a shrine. The most famous of these is the Ananda Pahto, located in Bagan. It is believed to have been constructed by King Kyanzittha, who reigned from 1084 to 1113.

Another style of pagoda is the rounded zedi, or stupa. Zedis were often built to house important Buddhist relics. The most famous zedi is the Shwedagon Paya in Yangon, which has been continuously constructed and reconstructed since the 15th century.

Drama & Dance

The oldest form of Burmese dance is a ritual called the nat pwe. In this ancient dance, performers and even members of the audience experience possession by spirits. However, the dance and drama tradition associated with classical music is considered more definitive of Burmese culture. Like the music that accompanies it, this tradition was brought from Thailand after King Hsinbyushin forced Thai performers to come to Myanmar. Dances are typically characterized as lively, and feature distinctive kicks and movements of the head, arms, and torso. Dancers often act out stories from the legend of the Buddha or scenes from the Ramayana drama, an ancient epic of India.

Marionette Theater is also a popular form of drama. It traditionally features twenty-eight puppets, which typically stand several feet tall. These are decorated to represent various traditional characters, including gods, several members of the royal court, monsters, and animals. Highly skilled puppeteers manipulate these colorful puppets to entertain the audience with detailed movements. Like classical music and dance, traditional marionette theater developed after the conquest of Thailand in 1767.

Music

Folk singing is the oldest form of music in Myanmar. Work songs, often sung without instruments, define this style of music. Agricultural workers in rural areas of the Ayeyarwady (or Irrawaddy) River delta particularly keep this ancient tradition alive. However, Myanmar is better known for its classical music. This genre of music is thought to have originally derived from ancient Indian ensemble music traditions, which spread throughout the region. It came to Myanmar when King Hsinbyushin (1736–1776) conquered Thailand in 1767. Classical music in Myanmar is considered a percussive style of music, and is typically performed by seven to ten musicians. Instruments usually include the distinctive circle of drums, brass gongs, a bass drum, an oboe-like instrument, cymbals, a lute, and a form of xylophone, a musical instrument in which wooden bars are struck to produce sound. A gem-encrusted, boat-shaped harp often accompanies the percussive ensemble, though this harp is sometimes played alone as well.

Literature

Historically, Burmese literature has mostly consisted of decorative lacquered Buddhist scriptures. These were first created in the 12th century, just after Buddhism came to Myanmar. In the 15th century, books celebrating the life of the Buddha were also created. Often, these books were painted on dried palm leaves. Royal court poets began a tradition of writing plays in the 16th century. These were based on the life of the Buddha and Indian dramas such as the epic Ramayana. The last royal court, which ruled in the 19th century at Mandalay, brought together the nation's great poets. They crafted a form of colorfully illuminated texts on thick, folded paper.

The British annexed Burma in 1886, and Burmese literature changed significantly in the colonial period that followed. The development of a Western form of education brought a new awareness of foreign literature to Myanmar. Modern printing presses were also built during this time. Authors began experimenting with a form of literature popular in the outside world: the novel. In fact, the first two Burmese novels appeared in 1904: *Maung Yin Maung—Ma Me*

Ma, by U Hla Gyaw (1866–1920) and *Maung Hmaing*, by U Kyee (1848–1908). The former is a Burmese adaptation of the classic *The Count of Monte Cristo* by Alexandre Dumas, written in 1844. Several authors gained fame as pioneers of the Burmese novel, including P Moe Nin (1883–1940), who is also considered a pioneer in Burmese short story writing. In time, writers started to use literature as a way to criticize colonial rule and argue for independence. One of the most famous political writers was Thakin Kodaw Hmaing (1876–1964), who maintains a strong legacy among pro-democracy activists in Myanmar.

CULTURE

Arts & Entertainment

The arts in Myanmar changed dramatically because of restrictions imposed by the ruling military junta. In 1988, the government banned all art that did not serve its interests, designating such art as selfish. The government's attempt to control the arts must be understood in a historical context. The arts have clearly influenced the county's politics over the last century. Controlling the arts was therefore a conscious strategy for controlling the population. However, the Burmese people have always been extremely artistic. Contemporary art in Myanmar is thus defined by the underground art movement censorship created.

Writing played an important role in the movement to end British and Japanese colonial occupation. Authors such as Thakin Kodaw Hmaing used literature to build a cultural resistance to foreign rule in the 1920s through the 1940s. He also inspired a new generation of activists who are resisting the current military junta. The most famous of this next generation of writers is the elected president of Myanmar, Aung San Suu Kyi (1945–), who lives under house arrest. Her books, which are about the political situation and how it relates to Buddhism, generated a new wave of resistance to the military government. Other new writers have gained fame for their political statements. In 2008, poet Saw Wai was arrested after publishing a nondescript love poem about Valentine's Day. It was actually a creative and bold public statement. When the first letters of the words were read, they spelled out the words "Power Crazy than Shwe." (Saw Wai was released in 2010.)

Despite severe government restrictions, Burmese painters continued to do socially relevant work. Portraits of pro-democracy leaders such as Suu Kyi were created and sold in secret. Some painters used their talents to depict the grim reality of life in Myanmar under the rule of the junta. One example of this is an artist by the name of Maung Maung Tinn (1969–), a refugee living near the border of Burma and Thailand. He paints images from his native home in the tribal highlands of Myanmar, including subjects such as child soldiers and emaciated elderly people. These paintings are a way to bring world attention to the brutal situation in the tribal highlands. Even jailed artists continued to work. During his six-year sentence, artist Htein Lin (1966–) worked with items such as dinner plates, cigarette lighters, and prison uniforms, along with smuggled paint. He produced significant works depicting symbols of the pro-democracy resistance and his prison experience.

Performance artists also turned their craft to the service of the pro-democracy movement. The three performers known as the Moustache Brothers Troupe are arguably the most famous artists in Myanmar. The three members are U Maw, U Par Par Lay, and U Lu Zaw. (The latter two were imprisoned in 1996 for their comedy routine, which focused on the government, and were released in 2000 and banned from performing in front of the public.) The classically trained Moustache Brothers were a major tourist draw in the city of Mandalay. They used a mixture of silly comedy, classical dance, and clever skits to satirize the military junta. Their bravery and talent became a major source of inspiration to the pro-democracy movement. In October and November of 2010, a time of public celebration in the country, the military government banned all stage performances and performing troupes due to what the government call security issues related to elections.

New forms of music have emerged in recent decades. Most notably, a Burmese form of rap or hip-hop music came into popularity in the late 1990s. This new kind of music was influenced by rappers and performance artists outside Myanmar. One Burmese rap pioneer is Myo Kyawt Myaing, who learned about this kind of music while living in Singapore. Many Burmese rappers have used the new form of music to speak out against the military government, and several have been jailed for voicing their pro-democracy sentiments, including the popular rappers Yan Yan Chan and Zayar Thaw. Other rappers, realizing that they would be targeted by the military junta for their political lyrics, released their music on the Internet, including a group known as Myanmar Future Generations.

In fact, the advent of the Internet in Myanmar opened up many new possibilities for the pro-democracy movement, leading to political pressure on the military junta that some argue contributed to its dissolution. A variety of activists went online as a way of using art to resist the junta. One way the Internet was used during the junta was to publish photographs of the reality of life in Myanmar. In 2007, monks engaged in nonviolent marches were brutally attacked by government forces. Images of this violence were distributed and posted online, providing outsiders a rare glimpse of life under the military junta. Web publishing also gave dissident groups operating inside the country a chance to report news to the world. One notable example of this was websites maintained by groups such as the Free Burma Rangers, a medical and humanitarian charity operating in the heavily repressed tribal areas of Myanmar. These websites provided glimpses into otherwise isolated areas of the country.

Cultural Sites & Landmarks

One landmark stands out as the most famous destination in Myanmar. The Shwedagon Pagoda defines the skyline of the capital, Yangon (formerly known as Rangoon). Standing over 98 meters (320 feet) tall, the main pagoda is gilded with gold donated by 15th-century royalty. Its base is surrounded by seven sets of smaller pagodas which represent the days of the week. There are also intricate statues around this base, depicting the Buddha, ogres, goddesses, and other mystical beings. Believed to have been built to house eight hairs from the Buddha himself, the Shwedagon Pagoda is still an important pilgrimage destination for Burmese Buddhists. Monks and lay worshipers come to walk around the massive pagoda in a clockwise manner in order to gain religious merit.

The Shwedagon Paya in Bago is another famous pagoda in Myanmar. Often known as the Golden God Temple, it is the largest pagoda in Myanmar at 114 meters (375 feet).

Another important destination is the ancient city of Bagan. This city was officially named the Bagan Archaeological Zone due to its wealth of significant ruins. Founded in the ninth century, Bagan was once the center of a great Burmese empire that extended into modern India to the west and Cambodia to the east. Burmese kings have always competed with one another to build spectacular Buddhist temples in this city. Despite an earthquake in 1975 that destroyed thousands of these temples, over 2,000 still exist. One of the most famous of these is the Shewsandaw Temple, believed to house a hair from the Buddha's head.

Myanmar's former royal capital, Mandalay, is also a popular destination. Of particular note is the Mandalay Palace. This massive fort is surrounded by a wide moat and walls that are over 7.6 meters (25 feet) tall. Inside this fortress are several interesting attractions, including an inner building known as the Glass Palace, once home to kings; the tomb of King Mindon (1808–1878), who built the Mandalay Palace; and a famous watchtower, called the Nan Myint Saung, which affords spectacular views of the former capital. In addition, there are also reminders of more recent Burmese history. An unusual Culture Museum, featuring full-sized statues of former cabinet members, is located within the Mandalay Palace compound. The area is now used to house soldiers.

Myanmar is also famous for its giant statues of the Buddha. Among the most visited of these is the Shwethalyaung Buddha, located in the city of Bago. The Shwethalyaung Buddha is approximately 55 meters (180 feet) long and 16 meters (52 feet) tall. The Buddha's face itself is nearly seven meters (22.5 feet) long, and the palm of his outstretched hand roughly measuring the same size. The Shwethalyaung Buddha is also unusual for its reclining pose. Its size and rare resting posture make it a famous destination for people in Myanmar, including artists.

Libraries & Museums

Myanmar's national repository is the National Museum of Myanmar, located in the capital of Yangon. Established in 1952 (along with the Ministry of Culture), the five-story structure consists of fourteen galleries of exhibits, ranging from natural history and models of the thrones of ancient kings to traditional folk art and images of the Buddha. Burmese art displayed at the museum ranges from prehistoric cave art to 20th-century paintings. The country is also home to a network of regional cultural and archaeological site museums (such as the Bagan Archaeological Museum), including cultural museums for the country's major ethnic groups. The Myanmar Gems Museum, also located in Yangon, displays Burmese gems and precious stones.

Myanmar's legal depository is the National Library of Myanmar, also originally established in Yangon in 1952. The library and its contents were moved to the new administrative capital, Naypyidaw, in 2008. The library is home to over 200,000 volumes of books, as well as ancient palm-leaf texts and parabeik (folding manuscripts). Plans to digitize the new library were reported underway in 2010.

Many libraries (roughly 2,000) in Myanmar were destroyed as a result of the devastation of Cyclone Nargis in 2008, the worst natural disaster recorded in the country's history. The Nargis Library Recovery project has worked to rebuild these libraries, and has included a donation of more than 1 million books by one corporate sponsor alone in 2009. The first libraries were rebuilt in 2010.

Holidays

Myanmar's main holiday is Independence Day (January 4), celebrating the country's independence from Great Britain. Another holiday is Union Day (February 12), celebrating the 1947 alliance of nationalist leader Aung San with ethnic leaders to overthrow British rule.

Most of the population is Buddhist, so Buddhist holidays are an important part of the calendar. Among the most important holidays is the Thingyan Water Festival, held in mid-April to celebrate the Buddhist New Year. Other festivals, such as the Kason Festival, celebrate events in the life of Buddha.

Youth Culture

Childhood in Myanmar is an important time in a religious sense. According to the customs of Burmese Buddhism, all boys and some girls spend part of their childhood as monks or nuns. Boys are actually expected to live as monks twice in their lives, at around 10 years of age and then again in their early twenties. There are two main results of this tradition of monastic service. One is that most lay people have a great sympathy for Buddhist monks and nuns. The other is that there are more than 500,000 monks in Myanmar.

Childhood in Myanmar changed dramatically with the rise of the military junta in 1962. Children have been particularly impacted by military rule. The quality of education diminished due to the lack of government investment in education. It was also more difficult to travel to and from school as the country's transportation infrastructure deteriorated. More importantly, children faced other risks while traveling to school; boys were often stolen away by military recruiters and sold into the army, while girls were at risk of rape and being sold into sexual slavery by the military.

Because of required monastic service, Burmese youth culture has traditionally been tied to the Buddhist monastic experience. The Burmese religious community emerged as a source of resistance to military rule. Monks provided important forms of social welfare for people left in poverty by government policies. They also engaged in direct activism to overcome the government. For example, monks and nuns staged coordinated protests in September 2007 to bring world attention to the plight of Burmese citizens. As a result, many were subjected to arrest and murder at the hands of the military for their participation in these protests. Youth culture is now defined by the aftermath of this activism, and more young people in Myanmar are participating in, and even leading, an important social revolution.

SOCIETY

Transportation

A variety of travel options are available in Myanmar. Local buses are commonly available for shorter distances. People also travel short to medium distances by private pick-up trucks, which are outfitted with bench seats and packed with passengers. Taxi service is available in more urban areas, and ox or horse carts are common in more rural areas. Bicycles are very popular in Myanmar, and are favored by locals traveling short distances. Bicycle rickshaws (typically, two-wheeled carriages carried by a person) are also available in more populated places. Buses are also popular for traveling between cities, and there are both private and government bus lines. Train travel is also common. Traffic moves on the right-hand side of the road.

Air travel is available, but the relatively high cost makes this a limited option for most people. Myanmar is served by three private airlines—Air Bagan, Air Mandalay, and Yangon Airways—and one government-run airline, Myanmar Airways International.

Transportation Infrastructure

Myanmar has over 1,770 kilometers (1,100 miles) of coastline and over 7,885 kilometers (4,900 miles) of navigable rivers. Therefore, boat travel is an important means of long distance transportation. Private and government-operated riverboats, cargo ships, and ferries are among the most commonly used vehicles for moving people and goods throughout Myanmar.

Most trains in Myanmar are run by the government rail company, Myanma Railways, which controls over 4,667 kilometers (2,900 miles) of track. Rural infrastructure was critically damaged in the country's southern region following the impact of Cyclone Nargis in 2008, Asia's deadliest cyclone since the early 1990s.

Media & Communications

The Myanmar government restricted all media within the country until the end of the junta. There are two main newspapers with national circulation that are printed in both English and Myanmar (Burmese), and both are state owned. During 1965–2012, all newspapers were government owned and all content was subjected to censorship by the Press Scrutiny and Registration Division of the Ministry of Information. In August 2012 the censorship laws were lifted sixteen new daily newspapers were granted licenses to publish beginning in April 2013. The largest newspaper is still the *New Light of Myanmar*, which is largely regarded as a vehicle for government news propaganda. The *Myanmar Times*, which focuses on travel, entertainment and lighter subjects. Four privately-owned newspapers, *Golden Fresh Land*, *The Standard Time Daily*, *The Union Daily*, and *The Voice Daily*, began publication in April 2013. The two main radio stations are Radio Myanmar, run by the national government, and City FM, broadcast by the Rangoon City Development Committee, or the Yangoon City Development Committee (YCDC). There are four main television stations, with the primary channel being TV Myanmar, operated by the Myanmar TV and Radio Department. MRTV-3 and Myawady TV are also entirely run by the state. TV5 is a paid subscription entertainment service that is partially owned by the state and private investors.

The government's tight control of the media made it difficult for the people of Myanmar to let the outside world know about conditions in the country. However, new media technologies gave Myanmar citizens a chance to work around the state controlled media. Pro-democracy activists outside the country made good use of the Internet. For example, Mizzima News Agency, maintained by Burmese journalists in exile in India, runs a website reporting the news that was otherwise censored by the military junta.

Furthermore, activists inside Myanmar also gained access to the Internet. Interestingly, this new access was the unexpected result of the devastating cyclone that hit Myanmar in 2008. The military junta decided to allow outside charity groups to shoulder the burden of providing assistance to those impacted by the cyclone. In order to communicate with their home offices, many of these charity groups immediately set to work establishing emergency telecommunication links. This resulted in important digital links to the outside world. As of 2010, there were only an estimated 400,000 Internet users, representing approximately 0.8 percent of Myanmar's total population.

SOCIAL DEVELOPMENT

Standard of Living

Myanmar ranked 150 out of 185 countries on the 2013 Human Development Index, which measures quality of life and standard of living indicators.

Water Consumption

According to 2012 statistics from the World Health Organization, an estimated 77 percent of the population had access to improved sanitation, while 86 percent of the total population had access to an improved source of drinking water. Following the devastating cyclone that hit the country in 2008, the disaster-stricken Ayeyarwady (or Irrawaddy) delta region faced severe drinking water shortages. Regions of the country were also affected by arsenic contamination in the drinking water supply in 2010. According to many observes, the consumption of bottled water has become a way of life in urban areas of the country.

Education

Myanmar's educational system is relatively weak, particularly in primary education. The literacy rate is estimated is at 93 percent of the total population, but the actual number may be much lower, particularly in rural areas. (According to the UNESCO Institute of Statistics, the literacy rate for the country was approximately 89 percent in 2005—93.7 percent for males and 86.2 percent for females—though some international observers have pegged the rate as much lower, particularly in rural areas.) Semi-literacy is also a problem, because many children drop out of school even before completing the primary grades. Buddhist monasteries, which are found in villages throughout the country, play an important rule in continuing education, or lifetime learning.

Education is largely administered by the state Ministry of Education, in support of the military government's social objectives, which include national morale, patriotism, and support of the nation's cultural heritage and character. Schooling is only compulsory until the completion of elementary levels. Entrance into secondary schools is based upon an examination of basic subjects. English is often commonly taught as a second language during the secondary level. The country's main university is the University of Yangon (formerly Rangoon University), founded in 1878 by the British colonial rulers as Rangoon College. The government has instituted strict censorship of academic research.

Women's Rights

Burmese women have traditionally been considered equal to men in most regards. For example, they have equal rights to inheritance and property ownership, and education is just as important for girls as boys. In fact, there are more women than men in the Burmese university system. Women are also able to enter almost any profession they choose. However, women are not allowed equal participation in some religious activities and are not allowed to enter the most sacred religious buildings. While almost all boys become monks for some period of their lives, it is somewhat less common for girls to become nuns. Moreover, nuns do not have the same central importance to Burmese culture as monks.

Despite the relative gender equality, girls and women endured unique suffering during the military junta's rule. The military used the systematic rape of women and girls as a way to terrorize the population, especially in areas inhabited by ethnic minorities. Human trafficking became a major problem in Myanmar during the junta's rule, and women and girls were in constant danger of being sold into prostitution. The U.S. Department of State repeatedly criticized Myanmar's junta for failing to address this problem, but as of 2013 noted that the situation was improving rapidly with the reforms that began in 2011. Several women's rights organizations formed in order to address the gender-based dangers in Myanmar. One of the largest is the Women's League of Burma, which was formed in neighboring Thailand in 1999. This organization is an umbrella group seeking to give an international voice to women in Myanmar, especially those in the minority areas most impacted by gender-based violence.

Health Care

Myanmar suffers from severe health problems. Epidemic diseases, like human immunodeficiency virus (HIV) and acquired immune deficiency syndrome (AIDS), pose a serious threat to the Burmese population. An estimated 190,000 people in Myanmar are infected with HIV/AIDS (2013 estimate). Other deadly diseases include tuberculosis, malaria, and dengue fever.

The life expectancy at birth is low, estimated at 65 years for the total population (63 years for men and 67 years for women). Infant mortality is also high, registering 45 deaths per 1,000 live births. Public health is poor, especially in rural areas.

GOVERNMENT

Structure

After political and economic instability during the early years of independence, Burma eventually came under the control of General Ne Win. He ruled the country in one form or another from 1962 until 1988, when he was overthrown by a military coup. The coup ushered in an area of political contradiction and repression. The military junta leaders established the current government, initially known as the State Law and Order Council (SLORC). The Council officially changed the country's name to Myanmar. In 1997, the government was renamed the State Peace and Development Council (SPDC).

A new constitution had been drafted in 2008 established a civilian government that included a new Parliament. Under the constitution, 25 seats in Parliament remained in the hands of the military, and the ruling head of state retained full authoritative control by assuming all legislative, judicial, and executive powers. In addition, constitutional amendments would require a 75 percent majority vote in Parliament. The junta ruled Myanmar until its dissolution in March 2011, at which time Myanmar established a parliamentary democracy. The Parliament quickly instituted sweeping democratic reforms of the 2008 constitution, ending many vestiges of military rule.

Myanmar's bicameral Parliament consists of the 224-seat House of Nationalities and the 440-seat People's Assembly. The Supreme Court of the Union consists of a chief justice and between seven and 11 associate justices, who are appointed by the president and approved by the House of Nationalities. Judges serve until the age of 70, at which time they retire.

Myanmar's first post constitution election, held in 2010, resulted in the election of three vice presidents (one each nominated by the House of Nationalities, the People's Assembly, and the military), and the Parliament then chose the president from among the vice presidents. The president serves a five-year term.

Political Parties

With an authoritarian regime in power, many parties were unrecognized by the military government while others, such as the National League for Democracy (founded by Aung San Suu Kyi), were considered defunct. Heading into the 2010 general elections, 40 parties were approved for participation. The government-sanctioned party, Union Solidarity and Development Party (USDP), was one of six political parties tied to the military government, and claimed a membership that encompassed half of the country's population.

With the 2011 revisions to the constitution, Burmese politics have opened up considerably, with 11 political parties having sizable representation in Parliament after the 2012 elections. The USDP still maintains a sizable majority, with 124 members in the House of Nationalities and 212 in the People's Assembly. The military still maintains a presence, with 56 members in the House of Nationalities and 110 in the People's Assembly.

Local Government

Myanmar is subdivided into seven divisions and seven states, which reflect, in part, the country's ethnic groupings. The divisions include the cities of Mandalay and Yangon; the states are Chin, Kachin, Kayin, Kayah, Mon, Rakhine, and Shan. Traditionally, further local governance was subdivided into townships, village tracts, and wards (which subdivide towns).

Judicial System

Historically, Myanmar's legal system has been partially influenced by British common law. The judicial system is technically independent of the executive branch, but reports in 2012 stated that both corruption and the power of the military have prevented the judiciary from keeping pace with the democratic reforms impacting the rest of the country. The country also rejects jurisdiction of the International Court of Justice. The Supreme Court is the highest court. Lower courts remain under the supervision of the Supreme Court, and include state and township courts.

Taxation

Tax rates in Myanmar are high; both the highest corporate and income rates are levied at 30 percent. Non-resident foreigners are subject to a higher flat rate of 35 percent. Other taxes include commercial, profit, and lottery taxes, and a stamp duty.

Armed Forces

The Tatmadaw is the official name of the armed forces of Myanmar, which consists of an army, navy, and air force. In terms of military manpower, Myanmar's global ranking is high, and the Myanmar Police Force, operated as a junior branch of the armed forces, works in conjunction with the military. China is a primary arms supplier of Myanmar. Ranging from forced conscription of children to the government destruction of crops, the armed forces have consistently been targeted by human rights organizations for abuses.

Foreign Policy

Overall, Myanmar has had a poor reputation in the world community, which has gradually changed since the dissolution of the junta. The United States first imposed trade sanctions against Myanmar in 1997, and the sanctions were progressively tightened through further legislation in 2003, 2007 and 2008. The European Union imposed similar trade sanctions against Myanmar in 2007. The easing of these sanctions has allowed the economy and relationships with foreign nations to improve, with U.S. President Barack Obama even embarking on a state visit in November 2014.

Due to its geography, Myanmar is considered a strategically important ally to some countries. This is because it provides a buffer zone between the two regional powers, India and China. As of 2009, these two countries have established and maintained good diplomatic relations with Myanmar. In fact, China was a strong ally to the Myanmar military junta, largely because Myanmar allowed China military and economic access to the Indian Ocean. (In August 2009, China was the recipient of 30,000 refugees after violent skirmishes broke out in Myanmar's Kokang Special Region between military junta forces and ethnic minorities.) For its part, India supported the pro-democracy opposition within

Myanmar until the early 1990s. However, it later developed a working relationship with the junta in an effort to counter growing Chinese influence in Myanmar.

Myanmar also shares borders with Laos and Thailand. The border area between these three countries forms the Golden Triangle, notorious for the large-scale production of opium. Thailand has repeatedly criticized Myanmar for its role in the production of drugs, but has had little success stopping the flow of narcotics from the country. In 2001, Myanmar and Thai troops engaged in combat along the border over this particular issue. However, subsequent fears that these border skirmishes would lead to larger conflict faded, and as of 2008, the countries enjoy fairly close relations. Myanmar and Laos have had a friendly relationship for decades. The two countries have held annual meetings of a Joint Commission for Bilateral Cooperation since 1997. These meetings are intended to increase economic trade between the two countries.

Myanmar, Thailand, and Laos are also all members of the Association of Southeast Asian Nations (ASEAN), a multilateral group seeking to encourage economic growth in the region. Myanmar became a full member of ASEAN in 1997. However, its membership was controversial while the junta ruled the country. It has been claimed that Myanmar was let into the group because other member nations wanted access to its natural gas reserves. The move has brought international criticism of ASEAN, and continues to be a point of controversy within the group. ASEAN later took a stronger position against the military junta's actions. In 2008, ASEAN strongly criticized Myanmar for the continued detention of pro-democracy activist and elected leader Aung San Suu Kyi.

Human Rights Profile

International human rights law insists that states respect civil and political rights, and also promote an individual's economic, social and cultural rights. The United Nations Universal Declaration on Human Rights (UDHR) is recognized as the standard for international human rights. Its authors sought the counsel of the world's great thinkers, philosophers, and religious leaders, and were careful to create a document that reflects the core values shared by every world culture. To read this document or view the articles relating to cultural human rights, click here: http://www.udhr.org/UDHR/default.htm.

The human rights situation in Myanmar was among the worst in the world. The military junta was largely criticized for controlling the diverse population through fear and repression, and the people of Myanmar suffered widespread human rights abuses under military rule. The junta was also accused of mismanaging public funds—creating an upper class that supports the military—at the expense of essential social programs. It also exploited natural resources (including gemstones, natural gas, and oil) in ways that have not benefited average citizens. Kidnapping and forced labor, or slavery, was common, especially in areas inhabited by ethnic minorities. This included forced conscription into the military, which even extended to children. In addition, the ruling junta systematically used forced relocation, rape and extrajudicial execution as ways to control the population.

The U.S. State Department noted that as of 2013 the government's human rights record continued to improve since the end of the junta, with notable decreases in torture, kidnappings, and forced conscriptions. Ethnic minority areas, which were most heavily oppressed during the junta, saw particular improvement. In February 2012, President Thein Sein formed a committee to identify and release political prisoners, and by the end of the year the committee had released some 330 prisoners, in addition to the over 700 that had been released since the end of the junta. The Parliament passed anticorruption laws, but the reform of the military has been gradual. Armed forces faced charges of killings, rape, and torture, especially in ethnic minority areas.

The conditions in prisons have improved since the UN issued a scathing report in 2008, but they are still considered to be poor, with massive overcrowding and food, clothing, and water being in short supply and poor quality.

The spread of personal freedoms has been uneven. Though freedom of speech was and assembly was far greater than under the junta, many Burmese remain wary of publically discussing politics, and there have been reports that the press and opposition politicians are still routinely monitored by the police and other government bodies. The government is also still in control of Internet service and has the legal authority to intercept electronic communications. In many universities, academic freedom has led to a greater discussion of ideas that might have previously been considered dangerous.

Of course, most important is the political freedom of the people to elect governments of their own choice. Though the 2012 by-elections were largely considered by international observers to be free and fair, the military is still guaranteed 25 percent of all seats in Parliament, which effectively gives them veto power over constitutional revision, as it takes a 75 percent vote to effect such changes.

ECONOMY

Overview of the Economy

Myanmar's economy is generally poor, despite rich natural resources and growing amounts of foreign investment in the country's tourism industry. However, since the end of the junta and the easing of economic sanctions, growth has been rapid. The gross domestic product (GDP) was estimated at $65 billion (USD) in 2014, but was increasing at a rate of 8.5 percent. The per capita GDP was estimated at $4,800 (USD) (2014 estimate). The United Nations still rates Myanmar as one of the world's poorest nations.

Approximately one-third of the population lives below the poverty line. But since the end of the junta, the nation has attempted to attract foreign investment and trade.

Industry

Myanmar's major manufactures include clothing, wood and wood products, industrial meters, and pharmaceuticals. As of 2014, industry represented just 21 percent of the country's GDP, and services accounted for 42 percent. Myanmar has generally good trading relations with its neighbors, including Bangladesh, China, and Thailand, and trade with the United States has grown rapidly since 2011.

There is a sizeable black market in Myanmar, which makes its difficult to gauge the actual size of the country's economy. Some estimates place the black market at twice the size of the official economy. The opium trade is one of the largest industries; Myanmar is the world's second-largest producer of the illegal narcotic. Although international law enforcement efforts have sharply reduced production by approximately 40 percent, estimated production in 2004 was still 292 metric tons.

Labor

As of 2014, the labor force in Myanmar numbered 35.23 million people. Of that number, 70 percent were working in the agricultural sector, seven percent in manufacturing, and 23 percent in the service industry. In 2009, unemployment was measured at about five percent.

Energy/Power/Natural Resources

Myanmar has rich energy resources, particularly petroleum, coal, and natural gas. The government is working to develop hydropower by building dams. Important minerals include tin, antimony, zinc, copper, and tungsten. The rapid industrialization has caused many environmental problems, including deforestation, erosion, and pollution.

Fishing

Historically, the fishing industry has played both a vital economic and cultural role in Myanmar, and the consumption of fish is relatively high among the population. The government reports an annual yield of 1.05 million metric tons from marine fishery resources. Commercially viable freshwater fish include carp, tilapia, and catfish, while prawn and shrimp are important exports. Due to a lack of processing facilities, much of the resources provided by the industry are consumed domestically. The fishing industry is still reeling from the devastation of Cyclone Nargis in 2008, which resulted in the loss of nearly 30,000 fishermen and the destruction of industry infrastructure such as boats and processing plants.

Forestry

Forest resources in Myanmar are under threat from development, population expansion, and rising demands for wood products. In 1989, more than 50 percent of the country was forested. Since that time, Myanmar has lost almost 18 percent of its forest cover, and deforestation continues at a rate of 0.3 percent per year. Myanmar has the world's largest teak forests, which count among the country's largest exports. The U.S. CIA reports that Myanmar's export estimates are underestimated because of the large black market trade with Thailand, China, and Bangladesh.

Mining/Metals

Historically known for its precious stones and gems—estimates have placed nearly 90 percent of global ruby production in the country—Myanmar is home to substantial mineral resources, and the mining sector is one of few economic sectors in the country that has attracted foreign investment, particularly from China. However, mineral production remains limited and the industry is responsible for widespread environmental degradation due to unsustainable practices. Valuable commodities include copper, tungsten, iron, jade, and construction materials such as cement and gypsum.

Agriculture

Despite efforts at industrialization, Myanmar's economy is still heavily agricultural. Farming represents over a third of Myanmar's GDP. Because of the mountains and heavy forestation, only about 15 percent of the land is cultivated. Myanmar's vital rice-growing region along the southern coast, known as the Rice Bowl, was devastated after the 2008 landing of Cyclone Nargis.

The major food crop is rice, but beans are also grown. Fishing and timbering are also important activities. A major cash crop is opium; Myanmar is one of the world's largest producers of the drug.

Animal Husbandry

Common livestock include cattle, buffalo, sheep, goat, pigs, and poultry, most of which are raised and bred for local consumption. Dairy breeding of cattle remains a fledgling sector, and the domestic consumption of meat remains relatively low.

Tourism

Myanmar has become more open to tourism in recent years, accelerating after the transition to civilian rule. Cruises to Myanmar have become particularly popular. Tourism is under the authority of the Ministry of Hotels and Tourism, and foreign visitors' activities were strictly controlled, but this has eased with the transition to democracy.

Adam Berger, Eric Badertscher, Micah Issitt

DO YOU KNOW?

- Mandalay, the last royal capital of Myanmar, was immortalized in Rudyard Kipling's poem "The Road to Mandalay."
- The Burmese cat is a cat breed native to Myanmar, which is also widely bred in the United States and Europe. Burmese cats have been bred in the United States since the 1930s.
- Maha Thray Sithu U Thant, one of the first people to serve as United Nations Secretary General, was a native of Myanmar.
- Myanmar was once known as the "Rice Bowl of Asia," because it was the primary exporter of rice in Asia, accounting for over 90 percent of the nation's exports.

Bibliography

Bhagowati, Surajit Kumar. *Women in Southeast Asia.* New Delhi: New Century, 2014.

Bowman, John S. *Columbia Chronologies of Asian History and Culture.* New York: Columbia University, 2000

Chan, Susan. *Flavors of Burma.* New York: Hippocrene Books, 2003.

Gravers, Mikael, and Flemming Ytzen, eds. *Burma/Myanmar: Where Now?* Copenhagen: NIAS Press, 2014.

Reid, Robert & Michael Grosberg. *Burma (Myanmar).* Oakland, CA: Lonely Planet, 2014.

Rieffel, Lex, ed. *Myanmar/Burma: Inside Challenges, Outside Interests.* Washington, DC: Brookings Institution Press, 2010.

Seekins, Donald M. *The A to Z of Burma (Myanmar).* Lanham, MD: Scarecrow Press, 2010.

Steinberg, David I. *Burma/Myanmar: What Everyone Needs to Know.* New York: Oxford University Press, 2013.

Topich, William J., and Keith A. Leitich. *The History of Myanmar.* Santa Barbara, CA: Greenwood Press, 2013.

Yin, Saw Myat. *Culture Shock! Burma.* White Plains, NY: Marshall Cavendish, 2007.

Works Cited

"Annual Report: Myanmar 2013." *Amnesty International.* 23 May 2013. http://www.amnestyusa.org/research/reports/annual-report-myanmar-2013.

Baily, Jane Terry. "Some Burmese Paintings of the Seventeenth Century and Later. Part II: The Return to Pagán." *Artibus Asiae.* 40.1 (1978): 41–61.

Baynham, Jacob. "Burma Artists Hide in Shadow Their Sad Work." *San Francisco Chronicle* (9 April 2008). <http://www.sfgate.com/news/article/Burma-artists-hide-in-shadow-their-sad-work-3219141.php>

Bowman, John S. "Columbia Chronologies of Asian History and Culture." New York: *Columbia University*, 2000.

Brinkhoff, Thomas. "Myanmar." October 8 2007. <http://www.citypopulation.de/Myanmar.html>

"Burmese Artist Shows Prison Era Creations in London." *VOA News.* 29 August 2007. <http://www.voanews.com/content/a-13-2007-08-29-voa45-66579287/555440.html>

Central Intelligence Agency. *World Factbook: Burma.* 10 April 2014. <https://www.cia.gov/library/publications/the-world-factbook/geos/bm.html>

Chan, Susan. "Flavors of Burma." New York: *Hippocrene Books*, 2003.

"Free Burma Rangers." *Free Burma Rangers.* 2015. <http://www.freeburmarangers.org>

"Human Rights Issues in Burma." Human Rights Watch. *12* March 2015. <http://www.hrw.org/asia/burma >.

McCrum, Mark. "Burma Special: Rangoon Rappers Who Have to Be Careful How They Hip Hop." *New Statesman* (14 August 2006). <http://www.newstatesman.com/node/153977>

McNern, Ethan. "Love Poem's Hidden Insult Lands Poet in a Burmese Jail." *Scotsman* (25 January 2008) <http://news.scotsman.com/world/Love-poem39s-hidden-insult-lands.3710621.jp>

"Myanmar: Eighteen Years of Persecution." *Amnesty International.* 24 October 2007. <http://www.amnesty.org/en/news-and-updates/feature-stories/myanmar-eighteen-years-persecution-20071024>

Pe, U. "On Modern Burmese Literature." *The Atlantic Monthly* (February 1958). <http://www.theatlantic.com/doc/195802/burma-literature>

Reid, Robert & Michael Grosberg. "Burma (Myanmar)." Oakland, CA: *Lonely Planet*, 2014.

Ross, James. "Burma's push for freedom is held back by its institutionally corrupt courts." *The Guardian*, March 20, 2012.

Smith, David Gordon. "A Double Game: India Suffering Fallout from Burma Crisis." *Spiegel Online* (28 September 2007). <http://www.spiegel.de/international/world/0,1518,508491,00.html>

"Sold to Be Soldiers: The Recruitment and Use of Child Soldiers in Burma." *Human Rights Watch.* 15 October 2007. <http://www.hrw.org/reports/2007/burma1007/>

Staker, Brian. On The Border: A Story of Forced Migration from Burma. *Salt Lake City Weekly* (December 23, 2013) <http://www.cityweekly.net/utah/on-the-border-a-story-of-forced-migration-from-burma/Content?oid=2305976>

"Time to Release Aung San Suu Kyi." *Amnesty International.* 25 March 2008. <http://www.amnesty.org/en/appeals-for-action/time-release-aung-san-suu-kyi>

"Women's League of Burma." Women's League of Burma. <http://www.womenofburma.org/>

Yin, Saw Myat. "Culture Shock." White Plains, NY: *Marshall Cavendish*, 2007.

Philippine Tarsier/Stock photo © Holger Mette

PHILIPPINES

Introduction

The Republic of the Philippines is an Asian island nation with a democratic government and close ties to the United States. In spite of modern industrial development, it remains a poor country. While the country features magnificent biodiversity and beautiful scenery, industrialization, population growth and development have created pollution and destroyed natural habitats. The country also suffers from extreme weather, terrorism, and the loss of skilled medical personnel who leave the country for work abroad.

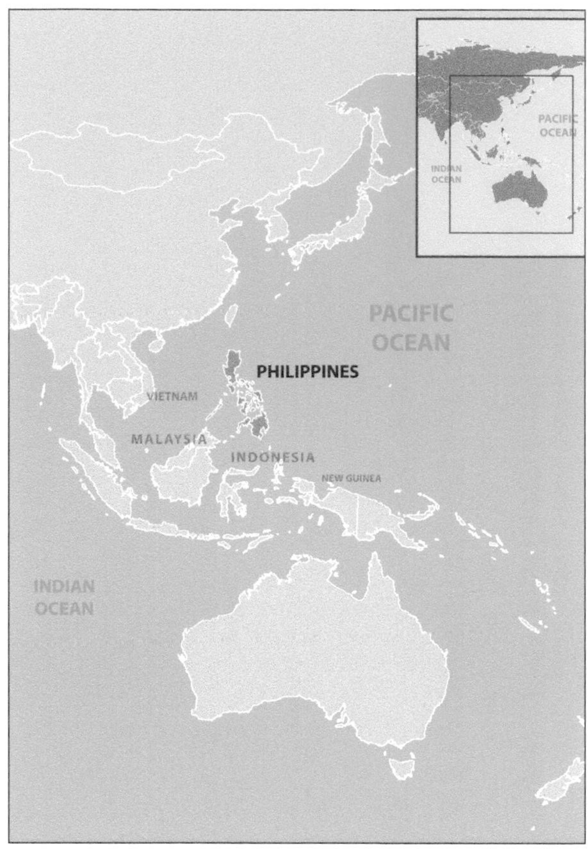

GENERAL INFORMATION

Official Language: Filipino, English
Population: 107,668,231 (2014 estimate)
Currency: Philippine peso
Coins: The seven coins in circulation are the 1, 5, 10, and 25 sentimo, and the more-frequently-used 1, 5, and 10 peso. The peso is subdivided into 100 sentimo.
Land Area: 298,170 square kilometers (115,124 square miles)
Water Area: 1,830 square kilometers (706 square kilometers)
National Motto: "Maka-Diyos, Maka-Tao, Makakalikasan at Makabansa" (Filipino, "For Love of God, People, Nature and Country")
National Anthem: "Lupang Hinirang" ("Beloved Land")
Capital: Manila
Time Zone: GMT +8
Flag Description: The flag of the Philippines features a horizontal bicolor design, with equal bands of blue over red, and a white equilateral triangle on the hoist (left) side. Centered in the triangle is a golden sun emitting eight rays, surrounded by three five-pointed golden stars in each corner, representing the major island groups of Luzon, the Visayas, and Mindanao. The sun itself represents liberty, or the "dawning" of a new era, while the blue and red stripe are supposed to represent courage and noble ideals, respectively.

Population

The Philippines has a dense population, with 313 persons per square kilometers (810 persons per square mile). The majority of the people, (45 percent), live in urban areas, while the remainder of the population lives in rural areas. As of 2010, approximately 53 percent of the population is below the age of 24; the fastest growing segment of the population is 60 years of age and above.

The major cities are Manila, with a population of 1.6 million; Quezon City, which is

N
0
200 Kilometers
0
200 Miles
Babuyan Islands
Aparri
Baguio
Luzon
Philippine Sea
SOUTH CHINA SEA
Angeles
Intramuros
Quezon City
PHILIPPINES
MANILA
Batarigos
Mindoro
Legaspi
Samar
Panay
Iloilo
Bacolod
Leyte City
Palawan
Cebu
Surigapo
Puerto Princesa
Tubbataha Reef Marine Park
Negros
Butuan
Ligan
Cagayan de Oro
Sulu Sea
Mindanao
Davao
Zamboanga
Jojo
Basilian
MALAYSIA
Celebes Sea

Principal Cities by Population (2010):

- Quezon City (2,761,720)
- Manila (1,652,171)
- Calookan (1,489,040)
- Davao City (1,449,296)
- Cebu City (866,171)
- Zamboanga City (807,129)
- Antipolo (677,741)
- Pasig (669,773)
- Taguig (644,473)
- Cagayan de Oro (602,088)

actually part of Metro Manila, with 2.7 million people; Caloocan City, also part of Metro Manila, with 1.5 million; and Davao City, with 1.4 million.

Languages

Of the more than 101 languages spoken and used throughout the Philippines, Tagalog (Ta-GAH-log) is most often used. Nearly 30 percent of the population speaks Tagalog, and the Filipino language takes its origins from it. Other major languages include Cebuano, Ilocano, Hiligaynon (Ilongo), and Bicol. Nearly 75 percent of Filipinos speak English. Some communities are Spanish-speaking.

Native People & Ethnic Groups

Archaeologists believe that the islands of the Philippines have been inhabited for thousands of years. The ancestors of modern-day Filipinos arrived in the islands from Indonesia and Malaysia.

Aboriginal tribes in the Philippines include the Ati, the Aeta, the Maranao, and roughly 20 others. As of the 2000 census, the three largest ethnicities are the Tagalog, Cebuano, and Ilocano peoples. Collectively, these peoples are sometimes known as "Negritos." This name, now considered derogatory, was given by Spanish explorers who incorrectly assumed that the people of the Philippines were from Africa.

After Filipino, the largest ethnic group is Chinese. Americans, Europeans, Indians and Japanese also contribute to a culture that blends Asian and Western features.

Religions

Approximately 94 percent of the country's population is Christian, more than any other Asian country. The majority (about 83 percent) are Roman Catholic. Other denominations include the Philippine Independent Church (Agilpayan) and Protestants. About five percent of the population is Muslim. The national constitution guarantees freedom of religion, and there is no state church.

Climate

Except for the mountainous areas, the Philippines has a maritime tropical climate, making for consistently hot and humid weather.

The hottest season comes in March through May, with temperatures that reach 39° Celsius (102° Fahrenheit). The rainy season is slightly cooler, but temperatures usually remain above 21° Celsius (70° Fahrenheit). Manila's average temperature in January is 24° Celsius (75° Fahrenheit); in May the average is 28° Celsius (82° Fahrenheit).

Rainfall is heavy, up to 250 centimeters (100 inches) annually; some areas receive as much as 475 centimeters (180 inches). The highlands get more rain than the coastal areas.

The Philippines lies along the circum-Pacific seismic belt, also known as the "Ring of Fire." This Pacific Ocean zone is prone to earthquakes and volcanic eruptions. Typhoons also strike the islands often.

ENVIRONMENT & GEOGRAPHY

Topography

The Philippines is a Southeast Asian archipelago in the Western Pacific Ocean. It is situated between the Philippine Sea and the South China Sea, east of Vietnam, northeast of Borneo and northwest of New Guinea.

The country consists of three groups the islands. Together, the northern islands of Luzon and Mindoro account for 66 percent of the 'country's area. The middle group, the Visayans, consists of 7,000 islands. The southern group is made up of Mindinao and the 400 islands of the Sulu Archipelago.

The highest point in the Philippines is at the top of Mount Apo (2,954 meters/9,691 feet). Off the northeast coast of Mindinao lies the Philippine Trench, one of the deepest spots in the ocean at 10,539 meters (34,577 feet).

The Philippines features lowland coasts with many good bays and harbors, inland plains, and active volcanoes. There are several large lakes. The largest is Laguna de Bay on Luzon, which, with a surface area of 949 square kilometers (336 square miles) is nearly as big as all the other Filipino lakes combined. The lake contains three bays and nine islands. Lake Sultan Alonto (Lake Lanao) on Mindinao is the second-largest lake, with 355 square kilometers (137 square miles) of surface area.

Most rivers are dry except during the rainy season (June to February). Earthquakes are frequent, as is volcanic activity.

Plants & Animals

The Philippines has an abundant variety of flora and fauna, but much of it is in trouble as a result of development and population growth.

The islands are home to 3,000 species of giant trees and 9,000 species of flowering plants. Nearly one-quarter of the islands is covered with forests of palm and banyan trees. Groves of bamboo flourish along with coconut palms, rubber trees, and mahogany. Indigenous trees include mayapis, apitong, lauan, camagon, and narra, the national tree. The fruit of the durian tree, known for its offensive odor, tends to be either loved or hated by those who taste it.

The sampaguita, a kind of orchid, is the national flower. The roughly 900 other species of orchids found in the Philippines include the giant waling-waling, or insect-eating pitcher plant. Abac, or Manila hemp, is used to make textiles, hats and rope. Other common plants include pepper plants, clove and cinnamon.

Among the wildlife typically found in the Philippines are snakes, crocodiles, mongoose, monkeys, deer, and tarsiers, which are endemic on to the Philippines and the East Indies. There are more than 700 species of tropical birds, including several types of parrots. The carabao, a kind of water buffalo, is a common domestic animal, used for such heavy work as pulling plows.

However, the plant and animal life of the Philippines is being destroyed faster than in any other country. Most of the forests have been cut down. Mangrove swamps are important sites for breeding and spawning of fish and shellfish, but they also are being cut down.

The country has an estimated 680 endangered or threatened species, a large portion of which are plants. Among the endangered animal species are the Mindoro crocodile, the three-striped box turtle, the tarsier, the cockatoo, the dugong (sea cow), Subic fruit bats, the white spotted deer, and the Philippine eagle.

CUSTOMS & COURTESIES

Greetings

Protocol for greetings in the Philippines typically depends on the age and the relationship between the people. Handshakes are a friendly and informal form of interaction. A handshake—utilizing a limp grip as opposed to a firm shake—with an accompanying warm smile is often used instead of a verbal greeting. Familiar female friends may exchange a hug and a kiss when they see each other.

The customary greeting between Filipinos is "Kumusta" ("How are you?"). The response to this is commonly "Mabuti" ("Fine"). The expression "Mabuhay" is also used to greet guests, as a way of showing hospitality, or at toasts during various festivities. Comparable to the Spanish word "Viva," "Mabuhay" encompasses "Welcome," "Hello" and "Greetings" in one expression. Close friends of the younger generation will commonly greet each other with a casual "Hi" or "Hello" in English rather than in Filipino (the national language of the Philippines).

Filipino has polite and informal forms of address, and using the formal mode with friends or younger people sounds affected and awkward. Likewise, misuse of the informal mode of address can lead to uncomfortable social situations. Greeting adults that one is unfamiliar with always requires a formal form of address. The formal form is especially important when expressing respect toward elders and superiors. Creating a formal grammatical structure in Filipino requires the use of the particle "po" or "ho." Formal variations of the common greeting "Kumusta" can turn into "Kumusta na po kayo" or "Kumusta na po sila" depending on the situation. Since seniority is important in Filipino society, the oldest or most senior authority figure is always greeted first at social events. Young people often greet the older generation through the act of pagmano whereby the young person will take an elder's right hand and place it on their forehead before releasing it.

Gestures & Etiquette

While Filipino culture often appears carefree in nature, Filipinos also maintain a deep understanding of familial obligation and honor. This balance between a relaxed, yet serious, society has largely informed social etiquette in the Philippines.

Hiya is the Filipino concept of shame, which is instilled in Filipinos at a young age. Hiya is a motivating factor in conforming to accepted standards of behavior. Filipinos take great care to prevent themselves and others from losing face, which can be caused by a public criticism, an embarrassing situation, or a disappointment. A Filipino who fails to live up to societal norms not only brings shame upon him or herself, but also to his or her family. This sometimes leads to Filipinos spending more than they can afford in social situations, rather than experience shame in light of their financial situation. It can also cause Filipinos to avoid disagreements, and prevent them from asking questions that might potentially make them look foolish.

Communication between Filipinos is peppered with gestures, and oftentimes a specific gesture can be used in place of a verbal phrase. For example, a "Yes" response is indicated by an upward jerk of the head, while "No" is a downward jerk of the head. While Filipinos rarely say no, they sometimes use a combination of verbally agreeing or saying "Yes" to a request while non-verbally jerking their head down in a "No" response. In doing so, Filipinos can express a "No" answer, without stating "No" in an outright manner.

Filipinos tend to refrain from using a lot of eye contact when speaking to others, and staring is deemed impolite. Similarly, pointing at another person is considered rude. Certain gestures and body stances are utilized to express emotion. For instance, when Filipinos stand with their hands on their hips, it indicates that they are irritated. Preserving certain formalities, especially in business settings, is a way of showing respect to others. It is customary to ask Filipinos which name they prefer to be addressed by, since most Filipinos have multiple names. It is also considered polite to use honorific titles plus the person's surname when addressing him or her until they give permission to use their first name or nickname.

Eating/Meals

Meals play a fundamental role in the social lives of Filipinos. Food is usually served buffet-style on a table on communal plates. All the food is shared, and everyone can select what he or she wants to eat. The Filipino day consists of up to five meals; there is breakfast, a morning meryenda (snack), lunch, an afternoon meryenda, and dinner. Even though meryenda means "snack" in Filipino, the dishes served during afternoon meryenda are not necessarily light, such as bihon (fried rice sticks) and goto (Filipino congee, or rice porridge). The typical eating utensils in a Philippine household are a fork and spoon. Traditionally, the fork is held in a person's left hand and is used to shovel food onto the spoon in the person's right hand.

Guests invited to dinner follow specific behavioral guidelines, taking care to follow the host's lead. A Filipino at a formal dinner waits until the host has designated a specific seat at the table for him to sit, and will only begin eating after the host invites guests to begin the meal. It is considered proper protocol for guests to decline a host's first offer to sit, drink, or eat. Instead, they should accept the host's second offer in a courteous manner. Filipino guests indicate that they are satisfied with the food and hospitality of the host by leaving some food on their plate at the end of the meal.

Visiting

Visitors to a Filipino home generally bring candies, flowers, or some small gift to give their hosts. Bringing large food items or alcohol can offend the host, as it may give the impression that the guest is dissatisfied with the host's hospitality. Presents play a large role in maintaining and strengthening social relationships, as they are a way of demonstrating respect, trust and friendship. Gifts are typically not opened when they are received, and many guests take care in wrapping their gifts. Presentation is considered incredibly important.

In the Philippines, it is customary to leave one's shoes outside when entering a Filipino house. When arriving at a Filipino party, it is also common to arrive 15–30-minutes later than the suggested time of arrival. Thus, it is common to see the most important guests arriving the latest to a social function. Emphasis is placed on appearance and guests will take care to dress well, and will also judge others based on their appearance. In the Philippines, guests should not refer to the host's wife as the "hostess," since in Philippine English a hostess may refer to a waitress at a beerhouse, who may also serve as a prostitute. Guests are expected to compliment the host and hostess on their house. Sending flowers or a handwritten letter following the visit is a common gesture of thanks.

LIFESTYLE

Family

Family is the focal point of life in the Philippines. Filipinos generally think of family in a broad sense. They extend their familial support network far beyond the traditional nuclear family to encompass grandparents, aunts, uncles, cousins, nieces, nephews, and kin acquired through marriage. Often, extended family members will live under the same roof and assume important roles in the household. Care of and respect toward elders is also a fundamental aspect of the Filipino household. The younger generation is always expected to address elders in a reverential manner, and value the authority of the older generation.

Additionally, the concept of compadrazgo, or co-parenthood, relates to the bond between godparents and their godchildren, which is considered as strong as blood relations. A custom instituted by Spanish-influenced Catholicism, the system of "compadres," or godfathers, may also provide a sense of stability to families, since godparents can be called on in times of need. Beyond socializing with the family, responsibilities of a godparent may include supervising the child's religious education, supporting him or her in times of financial need, assisting in the cost of the child's education, and helping the godchild find employment. The family network can extend even further to include landlords and employers, ultimately creating a wide network of kinship relationships within the community.

Within the family sphere, there is an implicit sense of equality between genders, and women wield considerable authority. An ancient Malay tradition that has endured over the years is a system of bilateral kinship. This social structure gives equal importance to families of both the mother and the father. It is thus common for a mother's maiden name to be given to a child as his or her middle name, and names, in general, may be inherited from the father's or mother's side, or both.

Housing

The diversity of housing in the Philippines is an indication of the climate, the country's access to natural construction materials, and the varied financial situations of citizens. Bamboo, straw and wooden boards are the basic building blocks of traditional houses found in more rural and remote areas. Houses in mountainous regions commonly feature bamboo walls, which allow for a comfortable circulation of air. The Ifugao people, in particular, are known for their unique houses with pyramid-shaped roofs made from long straw.

In urban areas, housing varies from upscale apartment buildings to huts in shantytowns (informal settlements) or slums that are assembled out of cardboard and plastic or tin. Large migrations of rural inhabitants to cities have contributed to overpopulation resulting in a housing shortage and adding to the sprawl of slum neighborhoods. This influx of people into the nation's urban environments has exacerbated traffic congestion, and heightened the unemployment problem. It is estimated that the Philippines has one of the highest rates of urbanization in the world—the rate was recorded at 52 percent in the year 2001.

Food

Similar to many elements of Philippine life, Filipino cooking is a mixture of cultural influences that have impressed themselves on the country over the course of history, and have been appropriated to fit Filipino tastes. Local food is thus a combination of Spanish, Malay, Chinese and American cuisines. Meals become uniquely Filipino because they are cooked in the Filipino spirit, characterized by a sense of creativity and a lighthearted attitude. An example of a large celebratory meal in the Philippines might include noodles, dumplings, sinigang (a sour soup incorporating tamarind, onions, tomatoes, green peppers and meat), grilled fish, paella, adobo, pizza and ice cream.

The staple of Filipino food is steamed rice. Most traditional meals revolve around eating whatever meat is readily available—usually chicken or pork—with rice. Dishes tend to emphasize simplicity with little attention paid to spices. Adobo is a beloved Filipino dish, representative of Filipino home cooking. It is a basic dish of chicken, pork, or both, cooked slowly in soy sauce and vinegar. Another favorite Filipino dish is lechon, a pig stuffed with screwpine leaves (from a tropical local tree) and then roasted until the skin becomes crispy. One of the rare spicy dishes in the Philippine kitchen is bicol express, which is pork ribs cooked with coconut milk, vinegar, soy sauce and hot chilies.

Philippine cuisine reflects the Filipino sweet tooth, and dessert is a significant part of the Filipino dining experience. Popular desserts include halo-halo, which is a mixture of fruit and cooked sweet beans combined with shaved ice and milk. Filipinos also enjoy sampling the many local ice cream flavors, ranging from purple yam and corn, to avocado and jackfruit (fruit from a tropical tree native to the Philippines).

Life's Milestones

The Filipino summer ritual of pagtutuli (circumcision) is a Filipino rite of passage representing a pubescent boy's entrance into manhood. The custom involves the removal of the foreskin from the male genitalia, and is traditionally performed during the Christian season of Lent (a season of prayer and fasting prior to Easter). While there is speculation over whether the ceremony was initiated by Christians or Muslim settlers, it is clear that pagtutuli is a fundamental element of Philippine society. The term supŏt is used for uncircumcised men, and is considered a derogatory term. Circumcision is also used as a basic standard of male personal hygiene. Several Filipino myths relate to circumcision, including the belief that circumcision will lead to improved fertility and virility.

Among the upper class in the Philippines, cotillions (formal balls) and debutante balls (often known as "debuts") are popular celebrations held on a young woman's 18th birthday as a symbol of her formal entrance into society. A cultural remnant of Spanish colonial rule, debuts also traditionally symbolized the woman's eligibility for marriage. At the start of a debut, a priest traditionally gives his blessing, and 18 candles are given to the debutante by 18 of her girlfriends and family. The candles are then traditionally arranged on a cake for the debutante to blow out. Eighteen male friends and family members then present 18 roses to the debutante. Another feature of the debut is when the debutante, her escort, and her court of 18 people (or nine couples) perform the cotillion de honor together. The dance traditionally involves a waltz or the Filipino aristocratic dance known as the "rigodon."

CULTURAL HISTORY

Art

A most distinctly Filipino form of art, known as bulol, was never originally intended to serve as art alone. Bulol are sacred statues carved by the Ifugao people, an indigenous tribe of the Philippines. The bulol traditionally serve as guardians of the Ifugao rice fields located in the Cordillera Administrative Region (CAR). These statues typically require approximately six days to produce, and are made from local narra trees (red sandalwood trees), which are believed to have medicinal properties. The wood obtained from narra trees signifies wealth, happiness, and good fortune to the Ifugao.

Creating a bulol involves a number of ceremonies in order to ensure its effectiveness in the rice fields. There is a ceremony regarding narra tree selection, a ceremony for when the bulol is presented to its owner, as well as ceremonies requiring the blood of a sacrificed animal and smoke rituals. When they are not used in harvest ceremonies, the bulol are placed in granaries to protect the rice and enhance harvests in the future. Although the sculptors' identities generally go unrecorded, some elderly members of the Ifugao community can trace a sculptor's identity to a particular bulol based on its style.

Architecture

The development of architecture in the Philippines is a testament to the country's ability to adapt to other cultures while maintaining its own traditions. Prior to Spanish colonialism, buildings in the Philippines were temporary dwellings made out of native materials, including bamboo, wood, palm fronds, and rattan (a tropical palm tree native to Asia). These one-room structures still exist in rural areas and are known as "Nipa huts." The huts are raised on stilts to avoid flooding from monsoons and increase air circulation.

Augustinian friars (a Roman Catholic missionary order) from Spain changed the landscape of the Philippines when the first Spaniards settled permanently in 1565. Besides converting the majority of the population to Roman Catholicism, the friars headed the construction of numerous churches throughout the country. In this way, the country was introduced to baroque and classical styles of architecture, which were popular in Spain.

When the Spanish-American War ended in 1898, the United States took the Philippines from Spain and became a new cultural authority. During this time, American architect Daniel H. Burnham (1846–1912) was commissioned to create a novel architectural plan for the capital of Manila. The plan concentrated on building civic and government buildings along wide avenues lined with trees. Filipino architects also began studying in the U.S. One of these U.S.-trained architects was Juan F. Nakpil (1899–1986). He is considered the father of modern architecture in the Philippines, creating art deco designs like the Capitol Theater in Manila.

Drama

Drama in the Philippines originated in the epic chanting sessions and oral legends passed down generation to generation by indigenous tribes. One example of this is the Ifugao tradition of hudhud, a series of chants used to pass the time while planting and harvesting the rice fields. The hudhud serves as an oral record of the Ifugao's history and customs, and comprises more than 200 chants. One chant can take up to four days to recite.

In 2001, the hudhud chants of the Ifugao were proclaimed an Intangible Cultural Heritage (ICH). These are living cultural and social traditions, typically passed down orally, that have been recognized by the World Heritage program administered by the United Nations Educational, Scientific and Cultural Organization (UNESCO). In 2005, the Philippines was recognized with another ICH, the "Darangen Epic of the Maranao

People of Lake Lanao," an epic song sung by the indigenous Maranao people which celebrates their history and myths.

The Spanish colonists introduced their own form of theater with stages, costumes, and scripted dramatic roles in the 16th century. Sinakulos was the particular type of theater that the Spanish established. The plays portrayed the life and death of Jesus Christ, since they were meant solely as teaching tools to convert locals to Christianity.

Although Philippine theater originally served the purpose of colonialists beginning in the 16th century, Filipinos managed to create a uniquely Filipino sense of drama beginning in the 20th century. The theater environment provided a rare opportunity for Filipinos to express their indignation regarding political and social matters beyond their control. For example, sarsuela is a playful type of musical that was originally brought to the Philippines by the Spanish, but was used at the beginning of the 20th century as a way to protest the American occupation.

Music

Most music in the Philippines is a fusion of native, Malay, Muslim, Spanish, and Western influences, reflecting the nation's diverse population and history. In general, performance is an essential part of Filipino culture, and reveals the lively and social nature of the Filipino people. Indigenous dance and music serve as important aspects of community life for many ethnic groups. For these groups, traditional song and dance complement every aspect of life. There are appropriate performances for birth, childhood, adolescence, courtship, marriage, work, sickness, and death. Songs are often sung unrehearsed, and the audience judges each performer based on his or her ability to create new song lyrics, rather than his or her singing ability.

Music was an important tool for the missionaries from Spain in the late 16th century, who used songs to teach the native Filipinos about the Roman Catholic Church's beliefs. Spanish colonialism also paved the way for European secular music and dance.

Kundiman, the style of song used by the Tagalog (the country's principle ethnic group), is possibly the best-known indigenous Filipino musical form. Kundiman is distinct for linking expressive lyrics with the tranquil rhythms of a serenade. This kind of love song has also been applied at key political moments. One example of this is when the patriotic poem "Bayan Ko" ("My Country") by José Corazón de Jesús (1896–1932) became the unofficial anthem for nationalist students in the 1960s. Later, in 1986, hundreds of thousands of citizens challenged the corrupt rule of President Ferdinand Marcos by singing "Bayan Ko" while blocking government tanks with their bodies.

Original Pilipino Music (OPM) is a genre that emerged in the late 1980s. It defines a type of music characterized by a distinctively Filipino sound, rather than replicated American beats. Folk musician Grace Nono is considered one of the pioneers of this movement. In 1989, at an arts festival in Baguio, she performed songs she had learned from the native tribes of the Mindanao region. She also created her own label, Tao Music, so that she would have complete creative license with her songs. Her music frequently incorporates tribal chanting and indigenous instruments, such as a runo (a reed flute). Nono also employed Freddie Aguilar as a model for her tribal-pop sound, often featuring a socially conscious message within her lyrics. An example of this is "Batang Lansangan," which was originally an Ibaloi tribe's children's rhyme that Nono modified to raise awareness of the issue of street children in the Philippines.

Dance

Non-religious music soon became embedded in Philippine culture thanks to its association with dance parties. Before electricity, Filipinos traditionally held a baile (dance party) when there was no other source of entertainment. Such parties served as good socializing opportunities for the young men and women of the villages.

Tinikling is the national folk dance, and is named after a local bird known as the tikling. The motion of the dance is supposed to resemble tikling birds darting around the rice fields as they avoid bamboo traps. During the dance, one or more dancers hop between two bamboo poles, which are held slightly above the ground and struck together and on the floor to the beat of music. As the dance develops, the pace with which the poles hit each other increases, and the dancers must quicken their dance steps in order to avoid getting their feet caught between the bamboo traps.

Literature

American cultural influence in the 20th century helped pave the way for a new generation of writers, who began to explore and establish their own definition of Filipino literature. This brand of writing utilized the English language and American writing techniques, which focused on a clean and forthright storytelling style. One prolific writer of this new generation is Francisco Sionil José (1924–), who has criticized the Spanish, the Americans, and the Marcos regime through his writing. José's work commonly ridicules the pretentious nature of the elite while portraying the struggles of everyday Filipinos in a sympathetic manner.

CULTURE

Arts & Entertainment

The development of the arts in the Philippines reflects much of the country's struggle to maintain a unique identity in the face of Western influences and trends. The music community in the Philippines is known for its performers' ability to mimic famous Western singers and entertainers. Mimicry is the nation's specialty, and shows the Filipino aptitude at incorporating other cultures into its own in a seamless fashion. The nation's musical culture, in general, has been largely informed by American culture. Beginning with Elvis, the Philippines found itself drawn to everything that emerged from the U.S. onto its own shores. From the mid-20th to the early 21st centuries, the nation has modeled its own music icons on Western names and styles. This has resulted in cover bands that emulate, among others, renowned artists such as James Brown, Carl Perkins and the Rolling Stones.

The Philippines has produced many painters and writers. Artist Fabian de la Rosa painted scenes of everyday life during the 19th century. Fernando Amorsolo, on the other hand, painted portraits and rural landscapes of the 1900s. Literature, especially in the novels of Jose Rizal and essays of Renato Constantino, played a large part in the independence movement.

When it comes to sports, basketball is at the top of the list for Filipinos. The national team has placed third in the World Basketball Championship. Professional teams draw big crowds, and pickup games are common in school gyms and on the streets. The Philippines has produced top competitors in both boxing and chess. Mansuetto Onyok Velasco won the silver medal in flyweight boxing in the 1996 Olympic Games. Chess grandmasters Eugenio Torre and Rosendo Balinas Jr. are both Filipino. In 1992, the Philippines hosted the World Chess Olympics. The indigenous martial art of kali originally used wavy-edged swords. Legend says that explorer Ferdinand Magellan was killed in a kali contest in 1524. Modern kali experts use sticks and knives.

Cockfighting, often called "sabong," is another popular sport, and often described as the "national pastime." On weekends and holidays, men swarm to the cockpits in nearly every town to bet on the fights.

CULTURAL SITES & LANDMARKS

Intramuros is one of the most compelling and significant landmarks of the Philippines. This fortress was a transplant of European urban ideals on Asian soil, and the vision of Spanish conquistador Miguel López de Legazpi (1502–1572). It serves as a symbol of Legazpi's reign over Manila in 1571, when he established the fortress as the capital of the Spanish East Indies. It sits at the mouth of the Pasig River on the remains of the Muslim settlement that preceded it, and has remained a resilient part of Philippine history.

At its height, Intramuros represented to the Western world the strength of Spanish colonial rule. Its pure scale intimidated rivals, and the walls surrounded an area of 64 hectares (158 acres). It housed government buildings, residences, schools, hospitals, churches, monasteries, and plazas. Drawbridges offered the only access to the rest of the world. The fortress has withstood attacks by Chinese pirates, a Dutch invasion, and occupations by the British, Americans and Japanese. It was finally razed by U.S. bombing during the last days of World War II at the Battle of Manila, an attack that left only its walls and some basic structures intact.

The San Agustin Church (built in 1587–1606) is the oldest church in the country, and a model of the baroque style of architecture unique to churches in the Philippines. The nation's Baroque churches are significant because they embody a synthesis of European aesthetics and indigenous construction methods. Notable features that separate these churches from a classical European design include their separate bell towers and their fortified buttresses (or structures built specifically to provide extra support to a building). Such characteristics give it protection against earthquakes, which are common in the area. Collectively, the churches were designated as a World Heritage Site by UNESCO in 1993.

The rice terraces of the Philippine Cordilleras have served as a geographical representation and reminder of indigenous cultural life, which has prevailed in the face of colonialism and modernization. For around 2,000 years the terraces have remained a consistent feat of agricultural engineering. Using their natural mountainous landscape, the Ifugao people have carved out a sustainable farming system without the use of machinery. The system includes a complex irrigation system, an understanding of soil conservation, and an intricate use of herbs to control pests. The area's rice production is also part of an important cultural structure that involves religious customs and revolves around the Ifugao's interpretation of the lunar calendar. In 1995, these terraces were designated as a collective UNESCO World Heritage Site, nevertheless, the site was listed as endangered in 2001.

The Philippines is also home to several other World Heritage Sites, recognized for their cultural and scientific importance to mankind. They include the Puerto Princesa Subterranean River National Park, designated for its underground landscapes and biodiversity; the Tubbataha Reef Marine Park, named a World Heritage Site for its coral geography and surrounding ecology (the site was also nominated as a "New Seven Wonders of Nature"); and the Historic City of Vigan, selected for its Spanish colonial heritage.

Libraries & Museums

The National Library of the Philippines, inaugurated in 1891, is located in Manila. As of 2007, its collection consists of more than 210,000 books and more than 880,000 manuscripts, and amounts to more than 1,678,000 items overall. The national library acts as the central body of the country's public library system, and a network of public libraries operates throughout the Philippines under the patronage of the national library. As of 2007, there are 861 public libraries in the Philippines. The country is also home to eight library associations, encompassing medical libraries, law libraries, and agricultural libraries. The first academic library in the country, established in 1611, was the Library of the Colegio de St. Tomas.

The National Museum of the Philippines acts as the national repository for the cultural and natural heritage of the Philippines. It dates back to 1901 and is comprised of nineteen branches nationwide. Several significant collections include ancient and cultural artifacts of the various ethnicities and communities of the ancient Filipino peoples; a 17th-century galleon, the *San Diego*; and *Spoilarium* (1884), a gold-medal painting by Filipino painter Juan Luna (1857–1899), one of the first internationally recognized Filipino artists.

Other museums include the Ayala Museum, an art and history museum in Makati City; the Cathedral Museum of Cebu; a regional museum concentrating on religious artifacts; and Museo Sugbo, or Cebu Provincial Museum.

Holidays

Many holidays observed in the Philippines are linked to the country's turbulent history. Araw ng Kagitingan (Bataan Day, or Day of Valor), celebrated on April 9, pays homage to those who fought for Bataan and those who died on the Bataan Death March during World War II. National Heroes' Day, observed on the last Sunday of August, marks the defeat of revolutionary Andres Bonifacio by the Spanish at the Battle of Pinaglabanan. Bonifacio Day (November 30) honors the leader of the 1896 revolution against Spain.

Other official holidays include Labor Day (May 1), Independence Day (June 12), and All Saints' Day (November 1). The Philippines does not celebrate its independence on July 4, the day the United States granted independence in 1946. Instead, Filipinos celebrate their independence on June 12, in honor of the 1898 declaration of independence from Spain.

Youth Culture

Filipino youth are technologically savvy, and accessories such as cellular phones are a dominant part of Filipino youth culture. In fact, a person's cellular phone is commonly a reflection of their socioeconomic status. Aside from using a cell phone to stay connected to their social network at all times of the day, most youth also use the gadget for other functions as well, such as listening to music.

The emphasis placed on feminine beauty in Filipino society has influenced the country's youth culture. Beauty pageants are held in high esteem, and have become so common that most small towns will feature their own beauty pageant. Fair skin is a physical trait that is especially revered by women. A woman's light skin reflects her high social status and desirability. For this reason, most young Filipinas will buy skin care products that promise to lighten their natural skin tone.

A 2007 study by the Philippine National Statistical Coordination Board (NSCB) concluded that many Filipino youth are sacrificing their studies to pursue work in call centers and low-skilled jobs. The study also pointed to UNESCO's World Education Indicators program, which showed that Filipinos completed their primary education at a rate of 88 percent to 91 percent, while neighboring countries such as Thailand, Malaysia, and Indonesia had higher graduation rates of 92 percent to 99 percent. Education advocates identify the low amount of money allocated to public schools as the primary problem with the current Philippine educational system.

SOCIETY

Transportation

The variety of transportation options in the Philippines lends itself to the archipelago's unique geographical landscape, which encompasses more than 7,000 islands. Ferries and bancas are necessary to navigate between islands. Bancas are wooden outrigger boats, characterized by a beam projecting from each side of the vessel. Large bancas can hold approximately 50 passengers. Safety regulations for sea transport have seen little improvement over the years, and ferry accidents are frequent. To date, no ferry company has been forced to shut down its services due to accidents leading to passenger deaths. However, ferries are often packed with passengers, and most of the larger ships are old and have been bought in used condition from Japan or Europe.

Jeepneys are an icon of Philippine culture and the most popular form of public transport in the country. Originally a hybrid of military jeeps abandoned by Americans after World War II, the jeepney has developed into a vibrant, flexible mode of transport that fits with the Filipino way of life. Jeepneys are able to function on roads that are too narrow for buses, and millions of Filipinos use jeepneys in their daily lives to get to school, work, or to the market. Gaudy decorations adorn jeepneys, and are proudly referred to as bongga; oftentimes, this is meant to be a symbol of the driver's machismo. Bongga often come in the form of blinking lights, oversized speakers, and flamboyant velour seats. In addition, many jeepneys feature stallion figurines attached to their hood, which is supposed to signify how many mistresses a driver has. Traffic moves on the right-hand side of the road.

Transportation Infrastructure

The road network of the Philippines, which consists of approximately 202,000 kilometers (125,516 miles) of roads, supports an estimated 50 percent of freight service and an estimated 90 percent of passenger service in the archipelagic nation. An estimated 60 percent of nationwide roads are rural, such as farm-to-market roads, with a large majority unpaved.

Heavy rail infrastructure is operated by the Philippine National Railways, a government-owned entity. Within metropolitan Manila, there are three light rail transit lines. As of the early 21st century, there are approximately 2,456 ports in the Philippines, the majority of which are small, and approximately 85 registered airports.

Media & Communications

Following 20 years (1965–1986) of censorship under the reign of Ferdinand Marcos, independent, outspoken, and often sensationalist newspapers and magazines immediately flourished due to the more politically liberated environment. The free press in the Philippines continues to be lively and opinionated, with over 500 newspapers and magazines since 2000. Publications are printed in a number of languages, from English and Chinese to Filipino and Taglish. (Taglish is a form of Tagalog—the language that Filipino is based on—combined with American English terms.)

However, the continuous uncensored nature of the press is, in many ways, surprising, especially since journalists in the Philippines have continuously been targeted and killed for their candid political and social commentaries. Besides Iraq, the Philippines has the highest homicide rate for journalists than any other country. As of December 2008, a total of 62 journalists had been murdered under the Arroyo administration, with the majority of victims being radio commentators. There has been no formal government intervention to prevent the attacks against journalists, even though freedom of the press and freedom of speech are preserved by the 1987 constitution. Furthermore, even though there have been nearly 100 reported murders of press members since the 1990s, only four suspects have been convicted, and only a handful of investigations remain active.

Cellular phone usage is popular and many Filipinos frequently use a short message service (SMS) to send text messages to each other. In 2014, it was estimated that the 50 million Filipinos with cellular phones sent 400 million text messages per day. In 2013, Internet penetration was estimated at 37 percent.

SOCIAL DEVELOPMENT

Standard of Living

The Philippines is ranked 117th out of 185 nations on the 2013 United Nations Human Development Index, which measures quality of life indicators.

Water Consumption

Clean and potable water distribution and adequate sanitation remain significant issues to the Filipino population. In many areas, drinking water must be purchased, while even a large percentage of urban households in metropolitan Manila lack heated water. According to 2012 estimates, approximately 74 percent of the population had access to improved sanitation services, while 92 percent of the total population had access to improved drinking water.

The National Water Resources Board is charged with overseeing policymaking and regulation of the Filipino water sector.

Education

Education is compulsory and free for children between the ages of seven and 12. Secondary school lasts from age 13 to 16. The first two years of secondary school consist of a general curriculum. During the third and fourth years, students have a choice of vocational or college preparatory courses.

Private schools generally teach in English. In the public schools, local dialects are the language of instruction for the first two years; then English and Filipino are used. Most high schools and universities teach in English.

Numerous universities, mostly private and religious, are located in the Philippines. The University of the East in Manila, a private Catholic institution, is the largest university in the country. The oldest school in the Philippines is the University of Santo Tomas, also Catholic, founded in 1611 in Manila. The literacy rate in the Philippines is 95 percent (2008).

Women's Rights

Women in the Philippines enjoy comparatively more social and political autonomy than their counterparts in other Asian countries. Since the country's 1899 constitution was ratified, two out of the 14 presidents have been women, including President Gloria Macapagal-Arroyo (1947–), who served from 2001 until 2010.

Nevertheless, culture in the Philippines is still characterized by machismo, and women are expected to behave within certain social perimeters. Women who cannot afford household help must take responsibility for the household, cooking and child-rearing duties. There are also double standards for extramarital affairs. While men are allowed and even encouraged to have a querida (mistress), women who commit infidelities are ostracized by their community and may even be physically abused or abandoned by their husbands. As a Catholic nation, abortion in the Philippines is illegal, and there is no exception included in the law for cases where the pregnant woman's life is endangered by the birth. Further, if women choose to undergo an illegal abortion, they, and anyone who assists them, face imprisonment.

Several laws acknowledge the equality of men and women in Filipino society. The Philippine Constitution of 1987 established a basic notion of gender equality, and the New Family Code of 1987 acknowledged the right of women to basic autonomy without their husbands' consent. The law formally established the right of women to own property and obtain a job without needing the written approval of their husbands. In 2004, President Macapagal-Arroyo signed the Violence against Women and Children Act (VAWC), which established more severe penalties for verbal, psychological, economic and physical abuse toward a woman or child.

The PNP released statistics stating that reported abuse cases grew in 2007 to 2,387. When the law was first passed in 2004, the number of reported cases numbered 218. This significant increase in reported cases can be attributed to an increased awareness of the law. Still, it is believed that the large majority of domestic abuse incidents go unreported. Despite the existence of laws protecting women's rights, patterns of domestic abuse and societal inequalities continue. This is mainly due to a lack of awareness by the public of laws that might protect them, and difficulties in enforcing and monitoring such laws in Filipino society.

Health Care

The Philippines Health Sector Reform Agenda works to provide equitable and efficient health care. The program has been partly successful. Life expectancy is 72 years; 70 for men and 76 for women (2014 estimate).

But obstacles remain, including an insufficient number of health-care professionals, low incomes, an ever-increasing population, hard-to-reach isolated populations, and a lack of government funding and support. Each year, the Philippines spends roughly $122 (USD) per capita on health care (2013).

In the 1970s, large numbers of nurses and doctors began leaving the Philippines for the United States. These doctors were welcomed there, because the Philippines is an English-speaking country, and medical training is based on the American model. The Philippines exports more nurses than any other country, and more doctors than any other country except India.

Many times, if recovery from illness is slow, some Filipino people turn to traditional medicine, which teaches that illness is a punishment for breaking taboos.

Illnesses with a high degree of risk include diseases borne by food or water, such as hepatitis A, typhoid fever and bacterial diarrhea. Malaria, dengue fever, and rabies are also prevalent.

GOVERNMENT

Structure

The Philippines became a colony of Spain in the 16th century. On June 12, 1898, General Emilio Aguinaldo, supported by the United States, declared independence from Spain. Later that same year, during the Spanish-American War, the United States forced Spain to cede the islands.

In 1935, the Philippines became a self-governing commonwealth, with full independence scheduled for 1945. During World War II, the nation was occupied by the Japanese. On July 4, 1946, the United States granted independence to the Philippines.

The constitution and economic system is similar to that of the United States. The Philippines is a unitary republic with universal adult suffrage at age 18. Baragays (citizens' councils) govern locally.

The president, who is head of state, head of government and commander-in-chief, is elected directly by the people for a single term of six years, and cannot be re-elected. The president appoints the cabinet with the approval of the Commission on Appointments (commissioners represent both chambers of Congress). The vice president is also directly elected and may serve two consecutive terms of six years.

The Kongreso (Congress) is bicameral, with a Senate and a House of Representatives. The 24 members of the Senado (Senate) are elected directly by voters to six-year terms. One-half of the senators are elected every three years.

The Kapulungan Ng Mga Kinatawan (House of Representatives) may have no more than 250 members. Most of the house members, who serve three-year terms, are elected by the people. An additional 50 members are elected from lists drawn up by the parties to ensure representation by ethnic minorities, women and certain economic and occupational groups.

Political Parties

The Philippines has a multiparty political system consisting of major partics and minor parties or organizations that use the party-list system, or a system of proportional representation, to win congressional seats. Often, government is ruled by coalitions of two or more parties that unite to form a majority coalition, and party-switching prior to elections can be common.

As of 2013, the United Nationalist Alliance, a socially conservative political party, is the country's minority party, while the Liberal Party of the Philippines is the ruling party. Other parties with congressional representation include the Nationalist People's Coalition, the neoliberal Nacionalista Party, the leftist New Patriotic Alliance (Bagong Alyansang Makabayan), and the populist Force of the Filipino Masses (Pwersa ng Masang Pilipino), among several others.

Local Government

Local governance in the Philippines consists of administrative divisions designated as local government units, or LGUs. These units are subdivided into autonomous regions; provinces and independent cities; component cities (part of a province) and municipalities; and barangays, which are small administrative units equal to villages. Local government is also divided into three branches consisting of the judiciary, executive (governor or mayor), and legislative, which is composed of assemblies at various levels, such as the regional, provincial, or municipal levels. All elected officials within local governance serve three-year terms.

Judicial System

The main judiciary body is the Supreme Court, which consists of a chief justice and fourteen associate judges. Underneath the Supreme Court are three tiers of lower-level courts, including trial courts such as regional and municipal trial courts, which act as the lowest level of the Philippines four-tiered judiciary system. Special courts include Muslim courts, or Sharia Courts, and courts of tax appeals.

Taxation

For corporate taxes, the highest rate is 30 percent, and for personal income taxes, the highest rate is 32 percent. Other taxes levied include a value-added tax (VAT), inheritance tax, and property tax.

Armed Forces

The Armed Forces of the Philippines (AFP) consists of an army, navy, and air force. The AFP, which is a voluntary force, marked 75 years of service in 2010. Recent estimates place the armed forces at approximately 153,000 strong.

Foreign Policy

Much of the Philippines's foreign relations is shaped by the U.S. This is principally due to the country's long historical relationship with the US as a former American territory and commonwealth. The Philippine government has remained a loyal supporter of U.S. decisions on international matters, acting as an ally in the 2001 war on terror and the U.S.-led Iraq War in 2003. The U.Ss mildly reproved the Philippine's decision to withdraw its peacekeeping troops from Iraq in July 2004 as part of a negotiation to release a Filipino hostage. In May 2004, the Philippines signed an agreement excusing U.S. military personnel in the Philippines from any trials conducted by the International Criminal Court (ICC). The Philippines is also a founding member of the United Nations (UN), and has served as an elected member of the United Nations Security Council (UNSC).

China and the Philippines have preserved a tenuous, but civil relationship. Although the two countries established diplomatic relations on June 9, 1975, with the signing of a Joint Communiqué, it was President Macapagal-Arroyo's visit to China in 2001 that signaled a shift in policy toward China. Since 2001, the Philippines have sought more economic and political cooperation from China. However, the relationship continues to be strained due to a number of factors. China is wary of the Philippines's connection to the U.S., and the Philippines remains cautious in light of China's emergence as an economic and military force. As of 1999, Philippine naval ships have arrested Chinese fishermen for catching fish in the Philippines. Moreover, territorial disputes have discouraged any notable improvements in the relationship between the two countries. China and the Philippines are still in disagreement over a number of territories (and their natural resources) in the South China Sea. Theses include the Malampaya and Camago gas fields, the Scarborough Shoal and the Spratly Islands.

The relationship between Japan and the Philippines saw a vast improvement following World War II. Besides the U.S., Japan is the Philippines's key trade partner and the country's main source of international investment. In 2006, Japan relieved the Philippines from a debt worth $8 billion (USD). Moreover, Japan has invested in much of Manila's infrastructure plans, aiding in the construction of bridges, highways and tunnels.

In recent years, the country has seen a pattern of Filipinos moving abroad to send supplementary income back to their families. The government census estimated the number of overseas Filipino workers at around 1.75 million in 2007. This accounted for a 15.3 percent increase in the number of Filipinos working abroad in 2006. The nation has thus designed its foreign policy with these overseas workers in mind. Diplomacy with Middle East countries has become especially important, since the majority of Filipino workers are employed by Saudi Arabia (19.8 percent) and the United Arab Emirates (12.1 percent).

Human Rights Profile

International human rights law insists that states respect civil and political rights, and also promote an individual's economic, social and cultural rights. The United Nations Universal Declaration on Human Rights (UDHR) is recognized as the standard for international human rights. Its authors sought the counsel of the world's great thinkers, philosophers, and religious leaders, and were careful to create a document that reflects the core values shared by every world culture. (To read this document or view the articles relating to cultural human rights, visit: http://www.udhr.org/UDHR/default.htm.)

Human rights in the Philippines are a controversial and complex topic. While the government's constitution is largely consistent with the rights outlined in Article 2 of the UDHR, the government itself has also been accused of committing grievous human rights violations. The Philippine National Police (PNP) has been particularly singled out as a governmental body that has engaged in human rights abuses. These include extrajudicial killings (where the victims did not have a trial proving them guilty or not guilty), forced disappearances and torture.

It has been estimated that there have been over 800 victims of extrajudicial killings during President Macapagal-Arroyo's term, with both the U.S. State Department and the United Nations issuing reports on the subject. Identified victims have included indigenous minority community members, religious minorities, lawyers, journalists and political activists. Furthermore, homosexuality is still met with discrimination due to the country's macho culture. Some schools incorporate "masculinity tests" or similar testing methods into their admissions process in order to weed out potential gay or lesbian students. This kind of discrimination is largely considered a result of the country's predominantly Roman Catholic society (roughly 80 percent of Filipinos identify as Catholic). Since the Roman Catholic Church explicitly objects to homosexuality, gay marriage and civil unions are also prohibited.

Two significant problems marring the government's attempt to uphold an equal, democratic society are human trafficking and child prostitution. In 2003, the Philippines passed the Anti-Trafficking of Persons Act, but implementing the law has been difficult, and the nation has seen little improvement. Many of the pedophiles involved in the child prostitution industry are foreigners, and economic incentives from tourism are enough to make most officials overlook the problem.

Article 18 of the declaration involves freedom of religion, which is assured through the Philippine constitution. Nevertheless, discrimination against Muslim minority groups still occurs. Christian groups in the Philippines have been the main source of discrimination against Muslims, with most prejudice occurring in the workplace and through the media.

The right to freedom of opinion and expression, as it is understood in Article 19, is generally respected by the Philippine government and outlined in the nation's constitution. However, certain media are subject to censorship, such as cinema. Films must pass a strict censor system, and government film censors have the ability to cut any scenes that they deem inappropriate. The movie *The Da Vinci Code* (2006), for example, garnered an "adults only" rating (due to its implication that Jesus Christ and Mary Magdalene may have produced a child together), allowing only audience members aged eighteen or over to watch the film. Additionally, sexual content will either earn a film a high rating or, in the most extreme instances, cause it to be banned. President Macapagal-Arroyo has publicly advocated for a more modest and pious entertainment industry.

ECONOMY

Overview of the Economy

In recent years, the effects of heavy debt and the Asian economic crisis have slowed the growth of the Philippines' economy. In 2014, the gross domestic product (GDP) was estimated at $695 billion USD, with a per capita GDP of $7,000 (USD). Unemployment was 7.2 percent during the same period. Roughly 27 percent of the population lives below the poverty line.

Industry

The most important economic activity in the Philippines is manufacturing. Products include fuel oils, paper and cardboard, jet fuels, cement, gas and raw sugar. Many city-dwellers work in factories.

Major exports include food and live animals; animal and vegetable oils, fats and waxes; basic manufactures; and machinery and transport equipment. Exports account for roughly $53 million (USD) annually. The Philippines' main trading partners are Japan and the United States.

Labor

According to an April 2012 Labor Force Survey, the labor force of the Philippines is approximately 41.7 million, with a labor force participation rate of 63.6 percent. The unemployment rate is 7.2 percent while the underemployment rate is 17.8 percent.

Energy/Power/Natural Resources

The Philippines' natural resources include gold, cobalt, silver, salt, timber, and petroleum. The country is rich in mineral resources, especially chromite, copper, and nickel, though the full potential of the mining industry has not been realized. Offshore deposits of natural gas have also been discovered.

Environmental concerns facing the Philippines include soil erosion, degradation of coral reefs, air and water pollution in urban areas, and increasing pollution of coastal mangrove swamps. More than 50 percent of the coral reefs, sea grass beds and mangroves have already been destroyed, to the detriment of commercial fish and shellfish populations.

Fishing

The commercial fishing industry in the Philippines is an estimated $1.1 billion (USD) industry, contributing nearly 5 percent of the country's gross national product and providing an annual haul of 4.7 million metric tons (including fishery products such as seaweed). Fish with high commercial value include tuna (with skipjack making up the majority of the tuna catch), sardines, tilapia, and anchovies, as well as shrimp and prawns. Rising fuel costs, fishing bans, and declining stock have negatively affected the tuna industry in recent years, while aquaculture has helped to improve fishery production, particularly marine fisheries, since 2002.

Forestry

It is estimated that over a 15-year period, between 1990 and 2005, approximately one-third of the Philippines' forest cover was lost, a figure that increases to approximately two-thirds lost dating back five decades. As a result, logging bans were implemented in certain parts of the country.

According to official Philippine forestry statistics, the top 10 forestry-based exports in 2008 include wood-based manufactured products, paper products and paperboard, and forest-made furniture. That same year, an estimated 43,609 hectares (107,760 acres) were reforested.

Mining/Metals

Historically one of the most mineralized countries in the world, the Philippines contains large deposits of chromate, copper, nickel, and gold with other significant minerals including coal, silver, and gypsum. Deposits of clay, marble, silica, limestone are also significant. In 2010, the Philippine government took an aggressive and proactive investment stance on mining, opening up undeveloped land and brining in an estimated $2 billion in foreign investments. According to recent government estimates, the Philippines' mineral ore deposits stand at more than 83 billion tonnes.

Agriculture

Filipino farmers rarely own their own land. Approximately 35 percent of the land is owned by large estates; laborers are employed by the estates and live on the land they work. These farm workers constitute 40 percent of the labor force. Principal crops include rice, sugar cane, coconuts, bananas, and corn.

Animal Husbandry

Filipino farmers raise chickens, ducks, pigs and goats. Important animal products include pork, poultry, eggs, beef, and veal.

Tourism

The Philippines' 2.3 million yearly visitors (the largest number from the United States, closely followed by Korea) generate $1.7 billion (USD) in revenue.

Tourists are drawn to the islands' abundant scenery, flora, and fauna. Popular tourist sites include the 400-year-old Manila Cathedral; and Lucban, at the foot of Mount Banahaw in Quezon, which features cool mountain air and springs.

The world-famous Ifuago Rice Terraces in Banawe are listed as a World Heritage Site by the United Nations Educational, Scientific and Cultural Organization (UNESCO). Eco-tourism is being developed in the Philippines in an effort to counteract the ecological problems caused by other forms of tourism.

Danielle Chu, Ellen Bailey, Jamie Aronson

DO YOU KNOW?

- By law, the Philippine National Anthem may be sung only in Filipino.
- For the 1998 Philippine Centennial celebration of independence, the Central Bank produced commemorative bills, measuring 8 1/2 inches wide and 14 inches long, the world's largest money.
- The oldest and tallest tree in the Philippines is a 500-year-old bita-og tree at the entrance gate of Magallanes town, east of Butuan City. Its diameter measures 305.585 centimeters (120.3 inches).

Bibliography

Abinales, P.N. *State and Society in the Philippines.* Lanham, MD: Rowman and Littlefield, 2005.

Bloom, Greg, and Adam Karlin. *Philippines.* Oakland, CA: Lonely Planet, 2012.

Burns, Lucy Mae San Pablo. *Puro Arte: Filipinos on the Stages of Empire.* New York: New York University Press, 2013.

Capino, Jose B. *Dream Factories of a Former Colony: American Fantasies, Philippine Cinema.* Minneapolis: University of Minnesota Press, 2010.

Francia, Luis H. *A History of the Philippines.* New York: Overlook, 2013.

Hamilton-Patterson, James. *America's Boy: A Century of United States Colonialism in the Philippines.* New York: Henry Holt, 1999.

Keeling, Stephen, and Simon Foster. *Rough Guide to the Philippines.* London: Rough Guides, 2014.

Reid, Robert H. *Corazon Aquino and the Brushfire Revolution.* Baton Rouge: Louisiana State University Press, 1995.

Roces, Alredo R., and Grace Roces. *Culture Shock! Philippines.* Singapore: Marshall Cavendish, 2013.

Solomon, Charmaine. *Food of Indonesia, Malaysia, Singapore, and the Philippines.* Melbourne: Hardie Grant Books, 2014.

Works Cited

"12 Years' Jail for Attempted Murder of Philippine Journalist." *Pinoy Press.* April 2, 2008. Online. Accessed April 15, 2015. http://www.pinoypress.net/2008/04/02/12-years-jail-for-attempted-murder-of-philippine-journalist/

"40 Die in Philippines Ferry Accident." November 5, 2008. *New York Times.* Online. Accessed April 15, 2015. http://www.nytimes.com/2008/11/06/world/asia/06phils.html?_r=0

"Amnesty International Launches Global Campaign to Press Passage of LGBT Anti-Discrimination Law in the Philippines." May 16, 2006. *The Guardian UK.* Online. Accessed December 8, 2008.

Arnett, Jeffrey Jensen. *International Encylopedia of Adolescence: A Historical and Cultural Survey of Young People around the World.* Boca Raton: CRC Press, 2007.

Cavendish, Marshall. *World and Its Peoples: Eastern and Southern Asia.* Tarrytown, NY: *Marshall Cavendish*, 2007.

"Deadly dirty work in the Philippines." February 13, 2007. *Asia Times.* Online. Accessed April 15, 2015. http://www.atimes.com/atimes/Southeast_Asia/IB13Ae01.html

"Food and Agricultural Organization of the United Nations Report, 1995." Online. Accessed April 15, 2015. http://www.fao.org/docrep/V9095e/v9095e04.html

Hans Brandeis. "Music and Dance of the Bukidnon of Mindanao – A Short Introduction" *Filipino Association of Berlin*. Online. Accessed April 15, 2015. http://aedv.cs.tu-berlin.de/~brandeis/bukid_music.html
Hicap, Jonathan M. "Neighbors outstrip Pinoys in primary education rate." January 11, 2007. *Manila Times*.
"Intervention of Hon. Rodolfo G. Biazon." June 7, 2001. *United Nations Report*. Online. Accessed April 15, 2015. http://www.un.org/ga/habitat/statements/docs/philE.html
"Manila's Jeepney Pioneer Fears the End of the Road." November 20, 2007. *Reuters*. Online. Accessed April 15, 2015. http://www.reuters.com/article/2007/11/20/us-philippines-jeepney-idUSMAN1276320071120
"Philippine Government Census 2010." Online. Accessed April 15, 2015. http://web0.psa.gov.ph/
"Philippines 2013 Human Rights Report." *U.S. Department of State*. Online. Accessed April 15, 2015. http://www.state.gov/documents/organization/220436.pdf
"Philippines: Law fails to stem domestic violence." *UN Office for the Coordination of Humanitarian Affairs* Online. Accessed April 15, 2015. http://www.irinnews.org/report/81668/philippines-law-fails-to-stem-domestic-violence.
"Philippines: UN Probes Extra-Judicial Killings." February 12, 2007. *Inter-press Service News Agency*. Online. Accessed April 15, 2015.
Rodell, Paul A. "Culture and Customs of the Philippines." Westport, CT: *Greenwood Publishing Group*, 2001.
Santos, Ramon. "Tunugan: Four Essays on Filipino Music." Manila: University of the Philippines Press, 2007.
"Two-thirds of Pinoys use Cellphones." *GMA News and Public Affairs* August 18, 2008. Online. Accessed April 15, 2015. http://www.gmanetwork.com/news/story/114433/economy/two-thirds-of-pinoys-use-cellphones
Zaide, Gregorio F. *Philippine History and Government*. Manila: National Bookstore Printing Press, 1984.

Temples of dieties are common in Singapore/Stock photo © Dhoxax

SINGAPORE

Introduction

Singapore is a city-state, a state in which a city has sovereignty over a particular region. Singapore rose to prominence as a major trading port in Southeast Asia and a British colony. It declared its independence in 1965, and since that time, has developed into an international finance center, a hub for electronics manufacturing, and one of thc world's busiest ports in terms of total shipping tonnage. It is one of only three city-states in the world (the other two being Vatican City and Monaco). The entire island shares a single urban and commercial center, and operates as a single administrative region.

Singapore's territories also include more than sixty neighboring islands and islets, none of which are larger than roughly 24 square kilometers (9.5 square miles). These islets are largely uninhabited, though some have been turned into resort locations, most notably the island of Sentosa.

Singapore is overwhelmingly urban, with the modern amenities, superb health care, and long life spans typical of a fully-developed industrialized nation. The city-state is now one of the fastest-growing economic powers in Southeast Asia, as well-developed and modern as Taiwan and Japan. Its diverse population is reflected in the city's art and culture, where music, drama, and painting are strongly influenced by Chinese, Indian, and Malay traditions.

GENERAL INFORMATION

Official Language: English, Mandarin Chinese, Malay, Tamil
Population: 5,469,724 (2014)
Currency: Singapore dollar

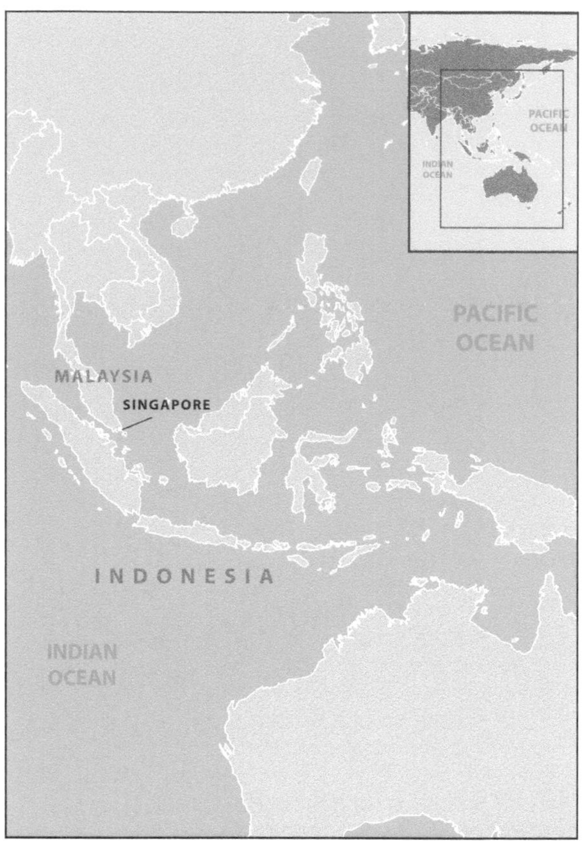

Coins: One hundred cents equal one Singapore dollar. Coins in Singapore are issued in denominations of 1, 5, 10, 20, and 50 cents, as well as 1 dollar.
Land Area: 687 square kilometers (265 square miles)
Water Area: 10 square kilometers (3 square miles)
National Motto: "Majulah Singapura" (Malay, "Onward, Singapore")
National Anthem: "Majulah Singapura" (Malay, "Onward, Singapore")
Capital: Singapore
Time Zone: GMT +8
Flag Description: Singapore's flag is a horizontal bi-color featuring a white band on the bottom and a red band on the top. Featured on the left (hoist side) of the red band is a white crescent with five white stars in a pentagram formation. The red of the flag represents brotherhood and equality; the white represents purity and virtue;

N
0
10 Kilometers
0
10 Miles
MALAYSIA
MALAYSIA
Kuala Johort
Johore Strait
Johore Strait
Yishun
New Town
Pulau Ubin
Pulau
Tekong
Ang Mo Kio
New Town
SINGAPORE
Tuas
Bedok
The Merlion
Queens-town
SINGAPORE
Raffles Hotel
Singapore Strait
Main Strait
INDONESIA

Principal City by Population (2014):

- Singapore 4.469 million

and the crescent symbolizes the country's youthful rise, while the stars stand for principles of democracy, peace, progress, justice, and equality.

Population

Due to Singapore's history as a busy port, its population has grown through immigration. According to Statistics Singapore, in 2014, 76 percent of the population is Chinese, Malays made up 15 percent, and Indians accounted for 7.42 percent of the population, with less than 2 percent from other parts of the world.

Many of the country's ethnic groups have their own dialects. Most of Singapore's Chinese population hails from the Fukien province and speaks the Amoy dialect, while the Malay population is more uniform with fewer dialects, mainly Javanese and Boyanese. The Indian population is the country's most diverse, and includes Tamils, Malayahis, and Sikhs.

Languages

Four official languages reflect Singapore's diverse population. Mandarin Chinese is the primary language spoken by 35 percent of the population, English by approximately 23 percent, Malay by 14 percent, and Tamil by just over 3 percent. Other non-official languages spoken in Singapore include Hokkien, Cantonese, and Teochew, all Chinese dialects.

English is the language of education, commerce, and government administration. The official inclusion of Malay helps maintain relations with Malaysia, Singapore's northern neighbor.

Native People & Ethnic Groups

Singapore's indigenous people were Malays. Yet with the arrival of Sir Stamford Raffles and the British East India Company, the population quickly grew with immigrants from Southeast Asia and across the world. In 2013, the United Nations (UN) estimated that among the world's nations, Singapore had the ninth highest percentage of international migrants in its population (and the highest percentage in Asia, except for the Middle East).

Religions

According to a 2013 survey, Singapore's majority Chinese population, religion was primarily a mixture of Buddhism, Confucianism, and Taoism, with substantial numbers of Christians and non-religious individuals. 41 percent of the population adheres to Buddhism or Taoism. The Malay population is virtually all Muslim, with many Indians also Muslim. This represented about 15 percent of the population. About 21 percent of the people (mostly Chinese) are Christian. There is also a small Hindu population in Singapore, accounting for about 7 percent of the population. Almost 15 percent of the population claims no religious affiliation at all.

Climate

Singapore has a tropical climate. The country lies within the Southeast Asian equatorial monsoon region, meaning that the weather is consistently hot and humid, and rain normally falls most days.

The official wet season coincides with the northeast monsoon, and lasts from November to March. The rainy season peaks in December, with an average rainfall of 250 millimeters (10 inches). The "dry" season lasts from May to September, with a low average of 180 millimeters (seven inches) in July. The country's total precipitation is around 2,400 millimeters (95 inches) annually.

Temperatures range from 27° Celsius (81° Fahrenheit) in June to 25° Celsius (77° Fahrenheit) in January. The highest temperature ever recorded in Singapore was 36° Celsius (97° Fahrenheit).

ENVIRONMENT & GEOGRAPHY

Topography

Singapore is a small, low-lying island. The country's highest peak is at Bukit Timah (Malay, "tin hill"), 162 meters (531 feet) above sea level. In fact, only two-thirds of the country's area is higher than 15 meters (50 feet) above sea level. The center of the island is comprised of rugged granite rocks. The eastern part of the island is a low plateau with eroded hills and valleys of sand and gravel. To the west and south lie lower areas of sedimentary rock.

The main island makes up the majority (more than 90 percent) of Singapore's area. Some of the largest islands among the fifty that make up the rest of the country's area include Pulau Ubin, Jurong Island, and Pulau Tekong. Singapore is connected to the Malaysian mainland by a causeway and a road bridge. There is also a water pipeline across the Johor Strait.

The country's total coastline measures 193 kilometers (120 miles). The country's longest river is the 14.5-kilometer (9-mile) Seletar River. Most inland water is found in small streams.

Plants & Animals

Because of exploitation, deforestation, and the fact that Singapore is overwhelmingly urban, few plants and animals remain. At one point, the island was covered by jungle. There are some mangrove forests left in the northwest Kranji area, as well as some preserved evergreen rainforests. Coral reefs may be found off some of the smaller outlying islands.

Exotic animals found in Singapore include the scaly anteater, the long-tailed macaque (a local monkey), the slow loris lemur, and the Indian mynah bird. Lizards and snakes, especially cobras, are common.

CUSTOMS & COURTESIES

Greetings

The common greeting among most Singaporeans can consist of a nod, smile or a handshake. Handshakes among Singaporeans tend to be less firm and last slightly longer than handshakes in Western cultures. Greetings are also influenced by tradition and religion. For example, some Malay men and women may be uncomfortable shaking hands with each other. This may be due to the traditional taboo against physical contact between unrelated members of the opposite sex. One simple, elegant Malay greeting consists of both parties reaching out to lightly touch each other's hands and then bringing them back to touch their own hearts.

In addition, older Hindus in Singapore often greet each other with the "namasté," a gesture in which the palms of the hands are placed together as if in prayer, and the head is slightly bowed. Conservative Hindu women may also greet elder family members or those of higher status by briefly bending to touch the feet of the person they are greeting. Casual verbal greetings in Singapore range from the familiar ("Hello" or "Hi") to the inquisitive. Typical greetings include "Ni hao?" which is "How are you?" in Chinese, and "Apa macam?" which is "What's happening?" in Malay.

Gestures & Etiquette

Singaporeans typically do not use large, expressive hand or arm gestures to accompany their speech. Standing with hands on one's hips is often considered a rude and angry posture. This is especially true when interacting with an older person or someone in authority such as a boss or a teacher. However, other habits that are typically considered impolite in Western cultures are common practice in Singapore. These include eating with one's elbows on the table or pushing gently against other people in order to get out of a crowded train or elevator car. Another uniquely Singaporean practice is the habit of "reserving" a seat in a food court by placing a small item on it such as a packet of tissue paper. This is not considered rude and the signal will be understood and respected by other patrons.

Among Indian Singaporeans, a shake of the head from side to side, instead of a nod up and down, indicates assent. Across all ethnic groups in Singapore, expressing strong disagreement in social or business situations is uncommon, since all parties concerned are largely committed to preserving each other's dignity.

When Singaporeans are speaking to older persons to whom they are not related, it is common practice to politely address them as "Auntie" and "Uncle" instead of by their first names or with the honorifics "Mr." and "Mrs." This rather intimate form of address indicates both respect and familiarity. It is also used when conducting certain types of public transactions. For instance, small business owners such as the proprietors of small news and food stands and taxi-drivers are often addressed in this way by their customers, no matter their age.

Eating/Meals

In Singapore, most dishes are eaten family-style, with everyone at the table serving themselves from large central bowls and platters. Depending on the household and the dishes being served at that particular meal, chopsticks are the most common utensil. When chopsticks are not being used, however, they must be placed either on a rest or across the top of the bowl. The image of chopsticks sticking straight up is associated with funerals in Chinese culture.

It is not uncommon for Indians and Malays to eat with their right hands, neatly scooping food into the cupped tips of the fingers with the thumb. In addition, keeping to a vegetarian diet for religious reasons is more common in Singapore than is vegetarianism inspired by political or philosophical beliefs.

Visiting

It is common for Singaporeans to remove their footwear while they are at home. Visitors are typically expected to also remove their shoes or slippers outside the door before they enter the house. Guests are inevitably offered an assortment of snacks and drinks, and will often be invited to join the family for a meal if the visit occurs around lunch or dinner time.

It is not considered impolite to decline refreshments, which guests are commonly offered. A visitor may find that a refusal has to be given more than once before it is accepted. It is customary to call ahead before dropping in on someone's house. Gifts are not generally expected unless one is visiting during a holiday such as Chinese New Year or Deepavali.

LIFESTYLE

Family

Grown children in Singapore commonly continue living with their families until they are married, instead of moving out of their homes after they enter the working world. This is due in part to a rule under which single people (including single parents) are not eligible to purchase property in public housing except under special circumstances. In Singapore, several generations often live together under the same roof, with grandparents taking on some of the responsibility of raising grandchildren while parents work. In many other families, childcare is a role that has been transferred, either partially or entirely, to female live-in domestic workers. These workers are usually from the Philippines, Sri Lanka, or Indonesia.

The state has been closely involved in shaping family planning through its population growth policies. These were designed to limit births in the 1960s (driven by concern about Singapore's limited space and resources). Beginning in the 1990s, the government changed its position due to Singapore's aging population. Now, financial incentives are used to encourage families—especially those with highly educated parents—to have more children.

In addition, there is an increasing language gap between the younger, Mandarin-speaking generation, and an older generation that is more comfortable speaking dialects such as Hokkien or Teochew. This is a result of the longstanding Singaporean campaign to promote the use of Mandarin over other Chinese dialects.

Housing

More than 80 percent of Singapore's population lives in public housing. This typically consists of one to five-room apartments, or flats, located in high-rise tower blocks usually clustered together. These buildings, as well as surrounding parking lots and playgrounds, are constructed and managed by the Housing Development Board (HDB). Individual flats, however, are owned by residents. The towers, most of which are made out of reinforced concrete, are simply designed and relatively homogeneous.

Building upwards is one practical solution to the problem of land scarcity in densely-populated Singapore. As a result, residents who rely on HDB housing are used to living in close proximity to one another. Corridors between apartments are considered common areas. Many residents set out plants, shoe-racks, or decorations in these areas while remaining considerate of the space belonging to their neighbors.

Food

Singapore's cuisine comprises an eclectic mixture of Chinese, Malay, and Indian dishes. Many dishes come from the Peranakan, or Nyonya, tradition. This group traces its heritage back to the intermarriages between Chinese and Malays in the 16th century. One such dish is otak-otak, which is ground fish mixed with chili paste, coconut milk, and other spices wrapped in a banana leaf before being grilled. Popular snacks and street food include curry puffs, which are baked pastries filled with spiced chicken, sardines, or eggs. Another popular snack is yu char kway, deep-fried fingers of dough.

In fact, there are few things as culturally and socially significant in Singapore as food. If they are not actively eating, Singaporeans are usually talking about where to go for their next meal. Popular dishes include laksa, a spicy coconut noodle soup that contains seafood and eggs. Chili crab consists of hard-shelled crab served in a thick tomato-chili gravy, mopped up with deep-fried Chinese buns. Rojak is a sweet, spicy salad made from shredded turnip, pineapple, cucumber, fried tofu, and bean sprouts.

In addition, Singapore is home to the annual Singapore Food Festival, which lasts nearly a full month every July. The festival celebrates local cuisine through a series of fairs, classes, and other food-related events. Besides the abundance of local eating houses and food stalls around the country, Singapore is also home to an impressive variety of restaurants serving international cuisines.

Life's Milestones

Among Chinese Singaporeans, the first public celebration of the arrival of a newborn baby occurs one month after the birth. This event is known as the "man yue." Parents distribute sweet cakes and red dumplings to family and friends, who offer "ang pow" (cash contained in a red envelope) and gold jewelry for the baby. Muslim babies in Singapore celebrate their seventh day of life by having their hair cut or shaved. It is also traditional for an animal to be ritually slaughtered on the same day. Hindu children undergo a similar shaving ceremony, but this occurs when they are slightly older, between one and three years of age. Since Christians make up a significant religious minority in Singapore, some families choose to observe these cultural rituals as well as holding baptism or christening ceremonies.

CULTURAL HISTORY

Art

Although Singapore is a relatively young country, it has a rich cultural history. This is due in large part to the variety of traditional art forms that have their roots in the ancient cultures from which Singapore's diverse population is descended. Within the Chinese community, for example, ink and brush painting, as well as calligraphy, or the art of writing, are important forms of expression.

Realism also played an important role in Singaporean Chinese paintings. Classical Chinese brush painting is not intended to capture the specific details of a scene. Instead, it aims to evoke a particular mood or atmosphere through somewhat broad, abstract strokes. Therefore, the "Nanyang School" of artists chose local scenes, such as the Singapore River and Singaporean houses, as subjects, and depicted them in a more naturalistic style beginning in the 1960s.

The traditional Indian dance form Bharatanatiyam and the musical sounds of the angklung, a bamboo instrument that originated in Indonesia, are two other traditional arts that have been preserved in Singapore through several generations.

Architecture

In the pre-colonial period, Singapore was a community made up mostly of Malay and Chinese fishing villages. Its architecture was characterized by structures known as "kampongs." These houses by the sea were built on stilts (in order to raise them above the level of the water) and made out of wood, leaves, and other natural materials. The typical layout of a kampong dwelling included a large, open porch at the front of the house. This was used for social gatherings, while work took place in a room at the back of the house.

The architectural design of the kampong strengthened the social connections between families, creating a sense of community. Today, the design of a typical public housing apartment in Singapore evokes the original kampong houses of the island's history. The ground level of a modern block of flats usually serves as a common social space where weddings or other gatherings can take place. This area, which is called a "void deck," is also left open to allow for the movement of cool air in Singapore's tropical climate.

Drama

In the early years of Singapore's history, a small but thriving film industry existed on the island. This was largely driven by the work of two major film production studios known as Shaw Organization and Cathay Organization. The first locally produced film, *Xin Ke*, was made in 1926. It chronicled the experiences of Chinese immigrants ("xin ke" means "immigrant"), and was produced by Liu Peh Jing. Other films followed, many produced in languages such as Malay, Hokkien, Cantonese, and Teochew.

During the 1970s, the Singaporean producer Sunny Lim made a series of low-budget action films. One of these, 1977's *Cleopatra Wong*, later became a cult favorite. In the late 1980s, the Singapore government began actively investing in the local film industry. The first full-length feature film in English, *Medium Rare*, was produced in 1991.

The 1990s saw serious efforts to make realistic films that captured the spirit and character of life in Singapore. The most notable of these was 1995's *Mee Pok Man*, and 1997's *12 Storeys*, both by renowned director Eric Khoo. Both these films take as their subject the ordinary, and yet often unpleasant, lives of lower and middle-class Singaporeans. The latter was selected for inclusion in the Cannes International Film Festival in the year it was produced.

In the late 1990s and the early 21st century, filmmaker Jack Neo (1960–) rose to prominence, having got his start in Eric Khoo's film *12 Storeys*. Neo's first comedic film as a writer and actor, *Money No Enough* (1998), tells the story of three financially-strapped men who start a car wash. To date, the film still holds the title for the country's highest grossing film. Since that time, Neo has produced cultural satires almost every year, and directed seven of the ten highest grossing films made in Singapore.

In 1998, the Singapore Film Commission was established. The organization funds and subsidizes films, which is becoming less expensive as digital technology improves. In the early 21st century, the Singapore film industry is gaining international recognition. Filmmakers like Royston Tan (1976–) are challenging censorship boards and making waves with films such as *881* (2007), his film about two girls rising to the top of the Getai scene in Singapore. The film received both popular and critical acclaim. The government sponsored Media Development Corporation has enticed North American production companies to use Singapore resources, with the Oscar winning film *Rango*, mostly animated in the Singapore studios.

Music

Singapore's vibrant and diverse music scene is fueled by its cultural diversity and its strong economy. Folk, rock, and nationalistic music are the three existing formats still seen today.

Peranakan folk music is sung in English to traditional Malay tunes. Other folk music traditions from China and Malaysia are common.

Singapore's contemporary music scene is populated by both Western pop and rock music, as well as active and popular local talent. Fueled by the British pop music scene in the 1960s, Singapore developed its own music scene prompted by the success of groups such as Sweet Charity in the 1970s. Since then, rock, punk, heavy metal, and indie rock groups have gained a local following.

In an effort to promote national pride and patriotism, the government annually commissions local musicians to compose songs that celebrate the country's accomplishments, called National Day Songs. These songs are usually performed at the National Day Parade, but some have found fame outside of this process, becoming part of Singapore's popular culture.

Literature

Some Singaporean writings had been published in both English and other languages during the first half of the 20th century. However, the Singaporean literary tradition began in earnest after the country gained its independence in 1965. Singapore might be considered to have four independent literary sub-genres: its Chinese, Malay, Tamil, and English writings each belong to separate schools with separate influences. Nevertheless, the themes explored by novelists, short story writers, and poets in the year's immediately following independence often focused on Singapore's struggle to define its unique national and cultural identity.

The poet Edwin Thumboo (1933–) is perhaps the most renowned Singaporean writer working in English. His poem *Ulysses on the Merlion* (1979) makes use of an extended reference to the ancient Greek hero Ulysses to explore the dual themes of wandering and home in the Singaporean context. Other literary pioneers include Goh Poh Seng (1936–2010), who is considered to have produced the first true Singaporean novel, *If We Dream Too Long*, in 1972. Catherine Lim's (1942–) short story collection Little *Ironies: Stories of Singapore* (1978) is studied in Singapore's high schools.

CULTURE

Arts & Entertainment

Popular culture in Singapore is dominated by cinema, with the country's most popular films coming from Hong Kong, Taiwan, and the United States. Among the country's Hindi- and Tamil-speaking populations, musical films have been a great success.

On the sports front, soccer is the most popular sport in Singapore. In 2004, 2007, and 2012, the country's national team won the regional AFF (Tiger Cup) tournament.

The diversity of Singapore's population is reflected in its art and culture. Music, drama, and painting in Singapore are strongly influenced by Chinese and Indian traditions, and Singapore's Malay music is played by Western-style orchestras.

The place of the arts in contemporary Singapore is a complex one. The state has become increasingly invested in recent years in crafting an internationally recognized arts and performance hub in Singapore. One sign of this interest is the massive Esplanade-Theaters on the Bay. This space opened in 2002 and houses a 2,000-seat theater and a 1,600-seat concert hall. Another is the Singapore Biennale, a huge international visual arts festival established in 2006, and held every two years.

The arts, and the creativity associated with their practice, have also received more of an emphasis in Singapore's schools. This is due in part to the long-standing criticism that the country's education system places excellent test results at too high a premium, and neglects the teaching of critical and innovative thinking.

The role of the government in sponsoring and promoting the development of the arts in Singapore has also strengthened the state's ability to control the nature of the art its citizens produce. All theater performances, for example, must have their scripts read and approved by a government body before they can be staged. In fact, performance art, which typically takes place without a script, was banned in Singapore for almost ten years. This was due to a performance by artist Joseph Ng, whose work was largely seen as an act of protest against the government rather than a form of theater.

Nonetheless, this atmosphere has tended to produce two divergent streams of art in Singapore. The small body of "mainstream" visual and performance art is housed in impressive state-sponsored spaces. An even smaller body of subversive art engages in critical or satirical commentary on social and political issues. These performances are hosted by a tiny number of independent art spaces that often focus on experimental theater.

Cultural Sites & Landmarks

Among Singapore's most significant landmarks is the 1887 Raffles Hotel, named after the country's British founder, Sir Thomas Stamford Raffles. The hotel was designed in the grand style of early colonial buildings. Declared a national monument in 1987, the hotel contains the Jubilee Theater, an elegant Victorian-style performance space. It has also hosted a series of literary guests, including Somerset Maugham, Rudyard Kipling, and Joseph Conrad.

Many of Singapore's public and administrative buildings have become historic or cultural attractions, most notably the official residence of the country's president. Known as the Istana, which is Malay for "palace," the main building is characterized by tall white columns and spacious porches and surrounded by large, well-kept gardens. The Istana is located in the heart of Singapore's commercial district, and is open to the public only five times a year.

Singapore's Parliament House, which was built as a private mansion during colonial times, is another major landmark. Outside the building is a bronze statue of an elephant, presented to the government of Singapore by King Chulalongkorn of Siam (now Thailand) after his 1871 visit. Since the construction of the new Parliament House a few streets away, the building has been transformed into a popular space for music, theater, and dance.

One of the most recognizable icons on the Singaporean landscape is the 8.6-meter (28-foot)-tall statue of a creature with a lion's head and a fish's tail that stands along the Singapore River. Known as a merlion, the animal is a symbol Singapore has adopted to represent itself. The country's name means "lion city," and legend has it that a lion was sighted when the island was first discovered.

Singapore's oldest and largest museum is the National Museum, originally built in a neoclassical style. It was later renovated to include the addition of a modern wing constructed out of glass and metal. The Singapore Art Museum, housed in a building that was once a Catholic school, contains the world's largest public collection of 20th century Southeast Asian art. Other museums include the MINT: Museum of Toys, which holds more than 50,000 vintage toys dating back to the 19th century.

Libraries & Museums

The National Library of Singapore is overseen by the National Library Board Singapore. The National Library is a repository of cultural and literary artifacts, and serves as both a reference and lending library in its new facility. The lending library has over 200,000 books in circulation, and the reference library boasts a collection of more than 530,000. A national Drama Centre is also housed in the National Library and is managed by the National Arts Council.

The Singapore National Museum was established in 1887 and is the country's oldest museum. It houses the 11 National Treasures, which includes the Singapore Stone, the Gold Ornaments of the Sacred Hill, and other defining artifacts of this small city-state. Recently renovated, it contains both past and present national treasures. Other national museums include the Asian Civilisations Museum (ACM), the Peranakan Museum, the Singapore Art Museum, and 8Q SAM. Private museums and public heritage sites also provide further cultural preservation and development.

Holidays

The citizens of Singapore follow the lunar calendar, and the multiple Hindu, Chinese, and Muslim festivals fall on different days each year. Important festivals include the Chinese New Year in January or February, the Dragon Boat Festival in May or June, and the Chinese Hungry Ghost Festival in autumn. The Muslim holy month of Ramadan is also observed in the fall. Singapore celebrates the anniversary of its 1965 independence on National Day (August 9).

Youth Culture

The youth culture in Singapore in the early 21st century is largely a product of the information age. Most young people are extremely adept at communicating with each other through electronic media such as cell phones, which are known as "hand phones" or "mobile phones," most notably through text messaging. An Internet-savvy group, fully half of all Singaporeans between the ages of fifteen and nineteen also post regularly to a personal blog or podcast, according to a 2006 study by the Media Development Authority (MDA). Similar estimates during that time period indicate that only about 19 percent of American teenagers were actively blogging. In 2011, 97 percent of individuals from the age 15 to 19 used the internet, almost twice the average for Southeast Asia.

Music is a tremendously diverse and important part of youth culture in Singapore. A local teenager is as likely to follow a popular act from Japan or Norway as one from the U.S. or England. The Taiwanese R&B singer Jay Chou, for example, played to a sold-out crowd of over 10,000 in January 2008. The American rock band Linkin Park performed in the massive Singapore Indoor Stadium for the second time in November 2007.

Singapore also has a small but active independent music scene. Popular genres such as pop, punk and rock have tended to be the most successful at gaining a following. The band Plain Sunset, a local indie rock band, has been playing punk rock shows for enthusiastic audiences since the mid-90s.

SOCIETY

Transportation

Congestion is a persistent problem on Singapore's busy roads. To combat this, the government has put in place a wide-ranging system of policies intended to encourage the use of public transportation while discouraging private automobile ownership. These policies include levying high tariffs on the purchase of new cars and tolls for entering the central business district during rush hours. Nevertheless, vehicle ownership remains high among the country's large middle class. Automobiles tend to be quickly replaced by their owners, thanks to regulations which make the value of a car drop sharply after five years. Cars are often perceived as status symbols by the middle class, as well.

Driving on the left side of the road is consistent with Singapore's British past and cell phone use while driving is prohibited.

Transportation Infrastructure

The public transportation system in Singapore is considered one of the most efficient and reliable systems in the world. The country has an extensive bus and passenger train network, and taxis with standardized fares. The result is a simplified transportation system that has made remote areas more accessible. In addition, public transportation in Singapore is more likely a comfortable and cheap alternative to driving. Every train and train station, and most buses, are air-conditioned.

Media & Communications

The media in Singapore operates under strict regulations designed to limit or prohibit the dissemination of material that the state considers undesirable (which applies to sexual content) or inflammatory (which applies to overtly racial, political, or religious commentary). These regulations govern both locally produced media and media imported from other countries. Foreign films, for example, may be subject to numerous edits and scene deletions by the Board of Film Censors before being released in Singapore. The American magazine *Cosmopolitan* was banned in the country for more than two decades because of its sexual content. Local films that are overtly political are banned entirely.

Two corporations own and operate virtually all media in Singapore, including newspapers, television stations, and radio stations: Singapore Press Holdings and MediaCorp. The former is a private company, but local law stipulates that its management shareholders must be approved by the government. The latter is owned by Temasek Holdings, the investment house that manages the government's portfolio. These circumstances result in news reporting and editorials that tend to speak with a single voice—one that is very much aligned with current government policies and positions.

Singapore's major English-language newspaper is *The Straits Times* and the leading Chinese daily is *Lianhe Zaobao*. As of 2014, Singapore's economically developed status, resulted in the statistic of household internet penetration of over 100 percent, obviously reflecting the fact that some households had multiple sources. Combining traditional Internet connections and smart phone connections, at least 93 percent of all households in Singapore had access to the Internet, an increasingly popular outlet for alternative political commentary and discussion. The country's mobile phone usage in 2014 was down slightly from the three previous years, with 1,480 phones per 1,000 people, meaning that many citizens own more than one mobile phone.

SOCIAL DEVELOPMENT

Standard of Living

The country ranked 9th out of 187 countries on the 2013 United Nations Human Development Index.

Water Consumption

Singapore, for all its wealth, is water poor. It has no natural lakes, gets almost half (47 percent) of its water from reservoirs and the country's rainfall catchment infrastructure, and imports the rest from desalinization plants in Malaysia. Further reservoir and catchment development, currently at 67 percent of the country's land surface, is planned, with a goal of collecting water from 90 percent of its territory. Having ended one agreement with Malaysia for water, water conservation and water from reclamation (up to 30 percent) and desalinization (up to 25 percent) are all part of the country's water resource development plan.

Education

Education is extremely important in Singapore. Primary education is free for children between the ages six to 18. Students are taught in English, though they are required to learn at least one additional official language. There are three separate educational tracks: academic, vocational, and commercial. The academic track is comprised of four to five years of courses.

Further access to higher education is determined by a student's performance in primary school. There is a two- to three-year preparation course for university or technical study. The country's largest university is the National University of Singapore, which was formed by the merger of the University of Singapore and the Nanyang University in 1980.

The average literacy rate in Singapore is nearly 95.9 percent (98 percent among men and 93.8 percent among women).

Women's Rights

In Singapore, many women's rights are protected by legislation designed to prevent gender discrimination and expand opportunities for women in society. For example, universal suffrage has been practiced since Singapore gained independence (indeed, voting is not only a right but also a legally mandated responsibility that is compulsory for all citizens above the age of twenty-one). As a result, women have not had to fight for the right to vote.

The Women's Charter of 1961 prohibits polygamy for all non-Muslims and protects the rights of both married and divorced women. In 1962, the government adopted an official policy of equal pay for male and female civil servants doing the same work. However, a significant gap—roughly 30 percent—remains in the average monthly salary of men and women outside the civil service sector, however due to the large numbers of government positions, in 2014 Singapore ranked 10th best in the world for pay equity.

More than 58 percent of women of working age are employed, as of 2013, while over 75 percent of men were in the workforce. A 2005 survey found that the salaries of wives with degrees made up an average of 46 percent of their total household incomes. Because higher income positions have had the highest percentage wage increase in the decade since then, this disparity has not decreased. However, fewer than half of all married couples in the country are both in the workforce, and culturally, men are still seen as the primary breadwinners.

Men are also more likely to be found in high-profile professional careers such as medicine, business, and law. In fact, it was only in 2003 that a controversial limit on the number of female medical students was lifted. The quota had previously prevented qualified female applicants from gaining entry into the country's medical school. In contrast, women continue to be overrepresented in traditionally female careers such as teaching.

There have been female members of the legislature in Singapore since 1959, and the number of female members of parliament has steadily increased since the latter part of the 20th century. However, women remain somewhat underrepresented in the government and political life of Singapore. In 2015, 25 of the 99 serving parliamentary members were women.

While the Singapore government has promoted the cause of equal rights for men and women, traditional attitudes toward gender roles still serve to work against the full and free exercise of women's rights in the country. For example, most women are under more pressure than men are to marry and have children. This pressure may come from a woman's family, society as a whole, or even the government—especially in light of the country's declining birth rate in recent years and government incentives to start a family. The expectation that childcare is primarily a woman's responsibility is reinforced by the fact that, while most working women are eligible to receive between eight to twelve weeks of maternity leave, paternity leave is generally confined to a few days.

Singapore law also safeguards certain cultural practices that undermine the autonomy of women. For example, Muslim women, by law, are required to gain the consent of a male guardian before entering into marriage. In addition, Muslim men are allowed to practice polygamy under certain conditions.

In general, the opportunities available to women in Singapore, the rights they can expect to exercise, and the prevailing attitude toward their roles in society are comparable to those of other developed countries. According to a 2013 UN report, Singapore ranked ninth best, out of 187 countries on the Gender Inequality Index. This takes into consideration women's economic power and political participation in a given country (in comparison, the United Kingdom ranked 14th and the U.S. ranked fifth).

Health Care

The quality of health care in Singapore is comparable to that found in other developed countries. The island is filled with both private and government-run hospitals, outpatient clinics, and mobile medical units. According to the World Health Organization, the country has one of the world's best health care systems, ranking sixth out of 191 countries.

Universal healthcare is available to all Singapore's citizens, with a "mixed financing system." The government subsidizes up to 80 percent of medical expenditures in public facilities, and the remaining costs are covered by Medisave, a compulsory medical savings plan that employees pay through their employers. According to the Ministry of Health, the average Singaporean in 2012 had about $14,000 (USD) in this account. Further protections such as MediShield, ElderShield, and Medifund are available.

Social welfare programs that care for the elderly, sick, or unemployed are overseen by the Council of Social Service, and enacted by a combination of government and volunteer organizations.

The infant mortality rate in Singapore is very low, at less than three deaths per every 1,000 live births. Average life expectancy is over 84 years; 81 years for men and 87 years for women (2014 estimate).

GOVERNMENT

Structure

Singapore became a British colony in 1867. During World War II, it was invaded by Japan. After a brief membership in the Federation of Malaysia (with Malaysia, Sarawak, and Sabah), Singapore became an independent nation in 1965.

Today, Singapore is a parliamentary republic with a president that serves as the head of state. The presidency was a mostly ceremonial position until 1991, when a constitutional amendment that year expanded presidential powers, and made it a popularly-elected position.

The legislative branch consists of a unicameral 87, or more, member parliament. The members serve five-year terms. Eighteen additional members may be appointed, up to nine by the president to make the parliament more diverse, and up to nine who were almost elected, as selected by the election commission. The parliament selects the prime minister and the cabinet. Singapore's legal system is based on English Common Law, with a Supreme Court and lower district and magistrate courts.

Voting is compulsory for Singaporeans 21 years of age and older. Singapore also has an active military, supported by conscription of males 18 and over.

The dominant political party, the People's Action Party (PAP), has been in control of the country since 1959. There is a strict sense of public morality in Singapore, with an emphasis on appearance, hygiene, and political loyalty. This loyalty is enforced by local laws that allow political dissidents to be held indefinitely and without a trial.

In 1994, Singapore caned an American teenager, Michael Fay, for vandalizing cars. The incident brought international attention to Singapore's strict sense of public decency and use of flogging as punishment. In a gesture of good will, Singapore government reduced Fay's sentence from six lashes to four.

Political Parties

Singapore politics have been dominated by the People's Action Party (PAP) since 1959. The socially and fiscally conservative party won 81 of the 87 contested seats in the 2011 parliamentary election. Other political parties in the parliament include the Worker's Party, a center-left party which won the other six seats, and then gained a seat in a by-election, and was granted two seats by the electoral commission. The Singapore People's Party was granted one seat by the electoral commission. There are ten other parties active, but with no representatives in the national government.

Local Government

As a city-state, Singapore's local administration is handled by the central government. A People's Association Board appoints Community Development Councils in each of Singapore's five districts. They are largely responsible for human services, and are not responsible for infrastructure, tax and revenue collection, or urban planning concerns often seen in traditional local governments.

Judicial System

Singapore has a common law system and cases are heard by a judge, not a jury. The Supreme Court is the highest court in the state; it consists of an Appeal Court and a High Court. A Constitutional Tribunal, which is a division of the Supreme Court, hears constitutional matters referred by the president. Subordinate courts are comprised of district and magistrate courts, small claims, and family courts.

Taxation

The government of Singapore levies taxes on individual income, corporate profits, goods and services, and property. Additional assessments include withholding, excise and customs, betting, and stamp taxes.

Armed Forces

Singapore's armed forces include an army, navy, and air force. Two years of compulsory military service is required of all male citizens between the ages of 18 and 21.

Foreign Policy

Singapore's foreign policy is shaped by two factors: its small size, and its position as a largely ethnically Chinese nation that has achieved tremendous economic success in comparison with the larger, predominantly Malay-Muslim countries that surround it. As such, the principles that govern Singapore's foreign relations are influenced by the need to overcome what its leaders see as its inherent vulnerability.

For example, Singapore has used a conscription, or mandatory service, policy to build and maintain a military force. This consists of a relatively small cadre of active professional soldiers and several hundred thousand trained reservists. The country's three military branches—army, air force and navy, all three of which are substantial in relation to Singapore's size—have never been employed either for threat or defense. However, Singapore has sent international peacekeeping forces to other nations, such as East Timor in 1999. Instead they serve as a powerful deterrent to indicate the nation's ability to defend itself against aggression.

This sense of vulnerability has its roots in the circumstances surrounding the country's road to independence. After spending two years as part of a federation with its neighbor to the north, Malaysia, Singapore separated in 1965 to become an independent republic. This declaration occurred during a period of racial tension within Malaysia. Nonetheless, the two nations enjoy a generally positive and interdependent relationship in the early-21st century. A significant number of Malaysians live and work in Singapore, and Singapore imports much of its fresh produce from Malaysia. However, a few areas of conflict remain. Among these is the issue of fresh water delivery from Malaysia to Singapore, the details of which have engendered numerous historical disputes between the two countries. However, this has lessened with the expiration of one water treaty in 2011, with the other treaty running until 2061.

Singapore also has good relations with neighboring Indonesia, although tension exists over a permanent Indonesian ban on the export of sand and granite. Singapore has recently embarked on the construction of a massive casino and resort complex, and uses Indonesian sand not only for building purposes but also for land reclamation. Singapore has expressed dissatisfaction with the Indonesian government's decision.

In addition, Singapore is an active member of the Association of Southeast Asian Nations (ASEAN), through which it seeks to maintain stable and friendly relations with countries in the region, including Brunei, Cambodia, Indonesia, Malaysia, Myanmar, Laos, the Philippines, Thailand, and Vietnam.

Singapore is also a member of the Non-Aligned Movement (NAM), an international organization of countries that have agreed to abide by a set of principles advocating—among other things—national independence and the right of any nation to defend itself. The movement largely consists of developing countries. Singapore has also maintained formal diplomatic relations with the U.S. since 1965. The two have been partners in a bilateral free trade agreement since 2003. Singaporean and American citizens can each visit each other's countries without a visa.

Human Rights Profile

International human rights law insists that states respect civil and political rights, and also promote an individual's economic, social and cultural rights. The United Nations Universal Declaration on Human Rights (UDHR) is recognized as the standard for international human rights. Its authors sought the counsel of the world's great thinkers, philosophers, and religious leaders, and were careful to create a document that reflects the core values shared by every world culture. (To read this document or view the articles relating to cultural human rights, visit: http://www.udhr.org/UDHR/default.htm.)

Overall, Singapore's human rights profile is a positive one. In some cases, though, the effort to preserve peace, prosperity and the efficient functioning of the country results in the sacrifice of individual rights and freedoms.

For example, Singapore's constitution is generally in line with Article 2 of the Universal Declaration of Human Rights. It enshrines the equality of all its citizens before the law, regardless of race, religion, or gender. Singaporeans of all races and religions receive equal benefits from the government. However, women are not required to serve in the army and divorced men are not permitted to seek alimony from their wives.

Although freedom of religion, outlined in Article 18 of the declaration, is generally protected in Singapore, a few religious organizations are prohibited from holding public meetings. They include Jehovah's Witnesses, whose members refuse to perform national service or swear allegiance to the nation's flag.

Article 19 of the declaration protects the universal rights to freedom of opinion and expression. These rights can be difficult for citizens to exercise fully in Singapore, particularly as they apply to politics. The government has in the past carried out several successful suits against political opponents and those who have criticized the state. These individuals have been charged with both slander and libel.

Freedom of assembly and association, outlined in Article 20, are restricted in other ways. Public gatherings involving five or more persons require advance official permission and all political activities are banned. The exception is gatherings conducted by organizations that are officially registered with the government, are banned.

Migration

Singapore's migration rate is estimated at 4.79 per 1,000 people in 2010. As a central point between India and China, Singapore is seeing a consistent flow of immigrants and has made efforts to open its doors to entrepreneurs and start-up businesses. The PAP government has been characterized as liberal in its immigration policy, which they view as critical to economic growth.

ECONOMY

Overview of the Economy

Singapore has been a tremendous economic success since it was colonized by the British in the early 19th century. Its strength comes from its function as an international trading post, as well as its healthy financial and industrial sectors.

The economy has seen tremendous growth since 1960. At the start of the 21st century, Singapore's economy was affected by global recession as well as an outbreak of Severe Acute Respiratory Syndrome (SARS), but it has since begun to recover.

In 2013, Singapore's per capita gross domestic product (GDP) was estimated at \$62,400 (USD). The country's estimated GDP was \$295.7 billion, among the highest in the world.

Industry

Since the mid-20th century, the primary focus of Singapore's economy has been on exports and industrialization. The government has created free trade zones as well as incentives for investment from foreign corporations. The country's most important exports include textiles, electronic components, and refined petroleum. Most of Singapore's industrial activity takes place in Jurong and on Jurong Island.

Modern Singapore functions as an intermediate point for the assembly or processing of goods. For instance, Singapore imports crude petroleum and exports it after refining it. The same process is applied to imported machinery, rubber, and lumber. The country's largest trading partners are the United States, Malaysia, and Japan.

Labor

The 2013 unemployment rate in Singapore was just under 2 percent of a labor force of 3.44 million. More than 80 percent of the labor force finds employment in the services sector, with fewer than 19 percent work in manufacturing, and 1 percent in agriculture/aquaculture.

Energy/Power/Natural Resources

Since it lacks mineral resources, and the country is mostly urban, Singapore's greatest resource is its strategic location and its large natural deep-water harbor, necessary for its lucrative trade activity. There are few forests and little fertile farmland left in Singapore, and the local fishing industry is economically insignificant.

Because of its small size and relatively large urban population, Singapore faces several environmental challenges, including a lack of fresh water resources and industrial pollution. Waste disposal also poses a problem for the small island nation.

Fishing

Prawns and sea bass are raised for export, and the country is also known for producing aquarium fish.

Agriculture

Because of massive urbanization and two centuries of deforestation, there is little agriculture to speak of in Singapore. Almost all of the country's agricultural products are imported from other Southeast Asian countries.

In general, the country's land is infertile, due to poor soil and drainage, and over-exploitation. However Singapore is known for the cultivation of orchids. Singaporean farmers produce fruits, vegetables, and poultry for domestic consumption.

Tourism

Tourism is another vital component in Singapore's economy. Visitors are attracted to its beaches, its diverse cultural makeup, and its modern urban landscape. As a regional business center, the country features many opportunities for shopping and dining, and boasts many fine hotels and other amenities.

Singapore's tourist industry is complimented by its excellent transportation infrastructure, including a modern highway system, light monorail service, and an international airport.

M. Lee, Barrett Hathcock

DO YOU KNOW?

- Some of Singapore's more unusual laws include a ban on chewing gum and fines for spitting, littering, and failure to flush public toilets.
- Singapore is the smallest Southeast Asian nation.
- While Singapore is one of the world's smallest countries, it boasts 3,500 kilometers of roads and one of the world's most dense populations.
- Singapore's is the world's greatest exporter of ornamental fish.

Bibliography

Barber, Nicola. *Singapore.* Milwaukee, WI: World Almanac Library, 2005.

Leifer, Michael. *Singapore's Foreign Policy: Coping with Vulnerability*. London: Routledge, 2000.

Liu, Gretchen. *Singapore: A Pictorial History*. Singapore: Routledge, 2001.

Lonely Planet and Cristian Bonetto. *Lonely Planet Singapore (Travel Guide).* London: Lonely Planet, 2015.

Milligan, Angela. *Singapore—Culture Smart!: A Quick Guide to Customs and Etiquette*. London: Kuperard, 2004.

Plate, Tom. *Conversations with Lee Kuan Yew Citizen of Singapore: How to Build a Nation.* 2nd ed. Singapore: Marshall Cavendish International (Asia) Pte Ltd, 2013.

Singapore. *Government of Singapore.* Singapore: Government of Singapore, 2015. Web. 30 March 2015.

Tsang, Susan. *Discover Singapore: The City's History and Culture Redefined.* Tarrytown, NY: Marshall Cavendish, 2007.

Vasil, Raj. *Governing Singapore: A History of National Development and Democracy.* Australia: Allen & Unwin, 2000.

Wong, Kokkeong. *Media and Culture in Singapore: A Theory of Controlled Commodification.* Cresskill, NJ: Hampton Press, 2001.

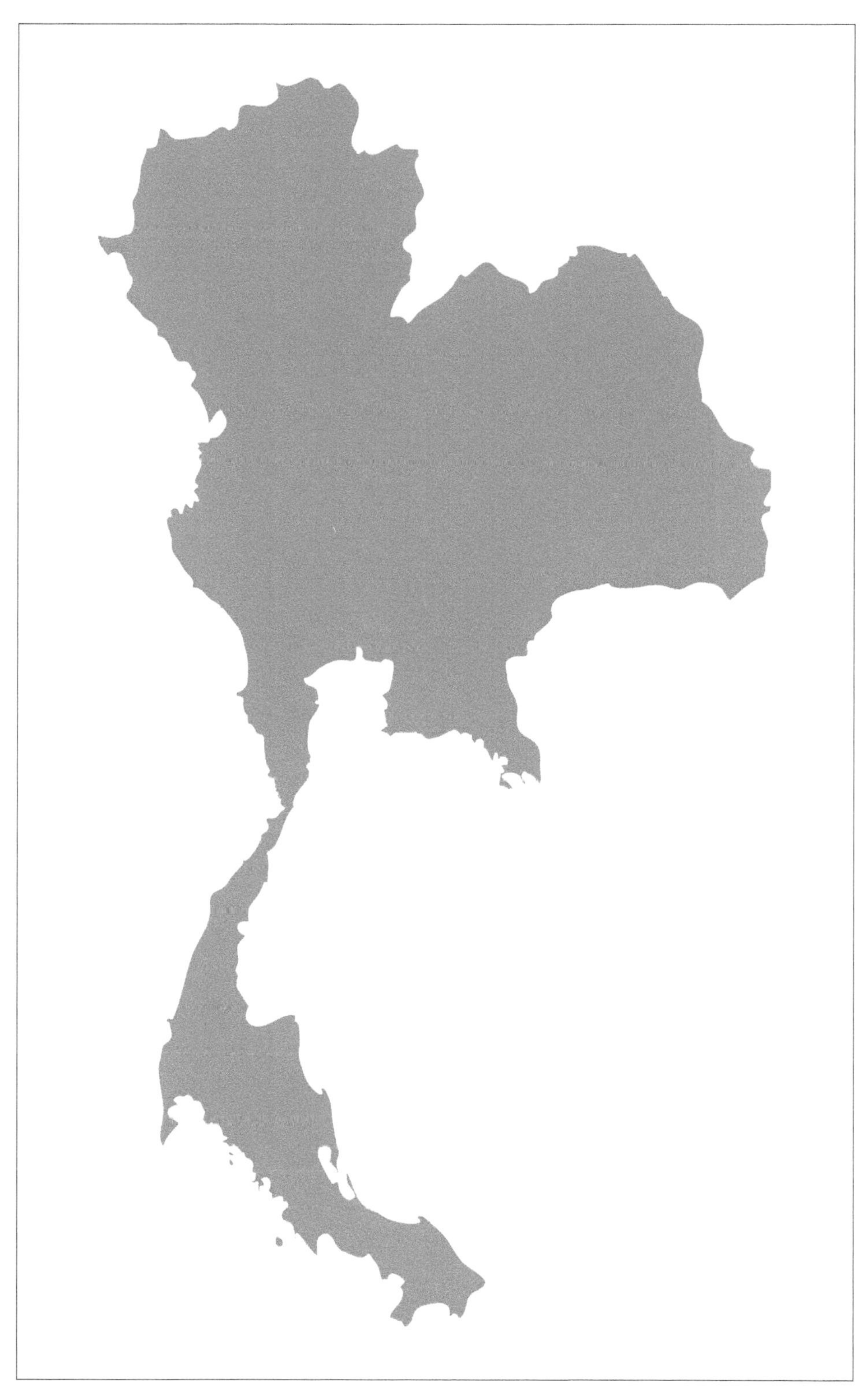

THAILAND

Introduction

The Kingdom of Thailand (Prathet Thai) is located in Southeast Asia. The country's name means "land of freedom" in the Thai language. Thailand has a diverse population that mixes Chinese, Vietnamese, and Indian cultures with the indigenous Thai culture.

The country has been unified as a kingdom since the 14th century, though thc namc "Thai" has been used to describe its people only since the 20th century. In fact, the kingdom was known as Siam until 1939.

Thailand's renowned cultural attractions in are its temples, known in the native language as wats. There are over 30,000, and they epitomize stunning architecture and religious veneration.

Bangkok is the capital of Thailand and the country's political, commercial, and cultural center. Bangkok's thriving business and consumer culture exists alongside an ancient spiritual heritage that is reflected in the city's many Buddhist temples. This heritage is also evident in the city's traditional name, Krung Thep, which means "City of Angels."

GENERAL INFORMATION

Official Language: Thai
Population: 67,741,401 (2014 estimate)
Currency: Baht
Coins: Thai coins come in denominations of 1 satang, 5 satang, 10 satang, 25 satang, and 50 satang, as well as in denominations of 1 baht, 2 baht, 5 baht, and 10 baht.

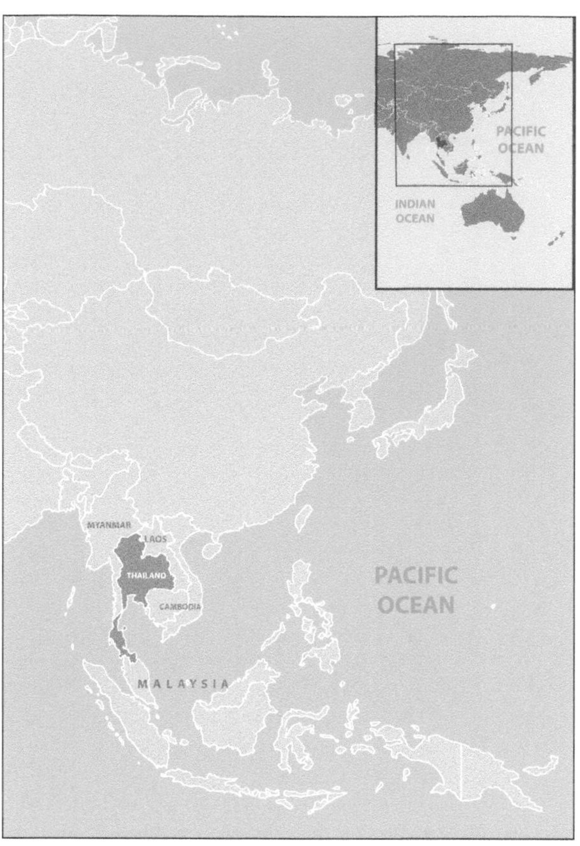

Land Area: 513,115 square kilometers (198,115 square miles)
Water Area: 2,230 square kilometers (861 square miles)
National Anthem: "Phleng Chat"
Capital: Bangkok
Time Zone: GMT +7
Flag Description: The flag of Thailand consists of five horizontal bands, with the center blue band being the largest, and flanked with white bands below and above it. Above and below the white bands are bands of red. (The white and red bands are of equal size, with each being roughly one-half of the width of the blue band.)

Population

Since ancient times, Thailand has functioned as a crossroads for the rest of Southeast Asia. Not surprisingly, then, the population of Thailand is a diverse mixture of regions, dialects, and cultures, the result of generations of migration southward through the Thai mainland to the peninsula.

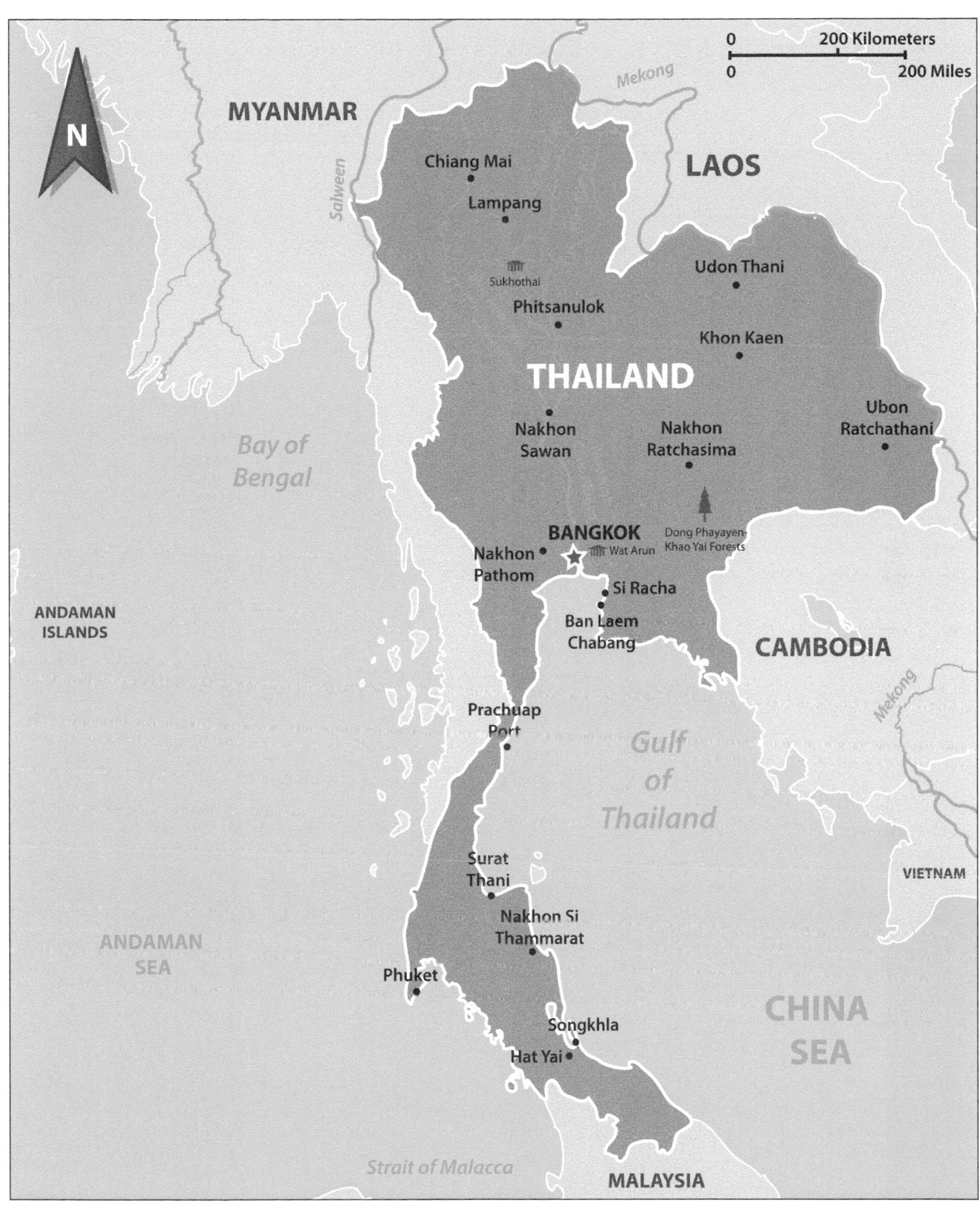
N
0
200 Kilometers
0
200 Miles
Mekong
MYANMAR
LAOS
Salween
Chiang Mai
Lampang
Sukhothai
Udon Thani
Phitsanulok
Khon Kaen
THAILAND
Ubon
Ratchathani
Nakhon
Sawan
Nakhon
Ratchasima
Bay of
Bengal
BANGKOK
Dong Phayayen-
Khao Yai Forests
Nakhon
Pathom
Wat Arun
Si Racha
ANDAMAN
ISLANDS
Ban Laem
Chabang
CAMBODIA
Mekong
Prachuap
Port
Gulf
of
Thailand
Surat
Thani
VIETNAM
Nakhon Si
Thammarat
ANDAMAN
SEA
Phuket
CHINA
SEA
Songkhla
Hat Yai
Strait of Malacca
MALAYSIA

Principal Cities by Population (followed by Date of Estimate):

- Bangkok (8,280,925) 2010
- Nonthaburi (291,555) 2010
- Udon Thani (247,231) 2011
- Nakhon Ratchasiama (208,781) 2011
- Chiang Mai (200,952) 2011
- Pak Kret (182,926) 2011
- Hat Yai (158,218) 2012
- Khon Kaen (145,579) 2011
- Surat Thani (128,179) 2009
- Nakhon Si Thammarat (120,836) 2011

In 2014, the population was just over 67 million, with a population growth rate of 035 percent. The median age is thirty-seven years old, while the life expectancy was seventy-four. In 2011, it was estimated that 34 percent of the population lives in urban areas. According to data from the 2010 census, around 19 million people live in the country's northeast region, 18.2 million live in the central region, 11.7 million people live in the northern, mountainous region, 8.9 million live in the southern region, and 8.3 million in the Bangkok region.

Languages

Different dialects of the Thai language are spoken throughout the country, but are concentrated mostly in the Chao Phraya River region. Thai serves as the official language of the country, dominating the schools and the press. (In 2010 census, it was reported that 89 percent of the country spoke only Thai at home, while an additional 8 percent spoke Thai and one other language.) Thai speakers can also be found in the surrounding countries of Laos, Vietnam and China.

Native People & Ethnic Groups

Recent archaeological evidence suggests that what is now northeastern Thailand has been inhabited for more than 5,000 years, and that the area's early people were among the first in the region to cultivate rice and work in bronze. The area's early Bronze and Iron Age civilizations were eventually supplanted by the Mon, Malay, and Khmer people. The ethnic Thai arrived during the first millennium.

The Thai Kingdom was established in 1238, and had become the dominant regional power by the 14th century. Although the Thai had contact with European traders in the ensuing centuries, their land was never colonized.

Depending upon how the ethnic group is defined, at least 75 percent of the population is ethnic Thai, formerly known as Siamese. The country's next largest ethnic group is Chinese, accounting for 14 percent of the population. Other minority groups included Malays (4 percent of the population) and the Mon, who are descended from the residents of Myanmar (formerly Burma). Small groups of Mon people are scattered throughout Thailand, but the largest concentration is found immediately west of Bangkok near the Gulf of Thailand.

Smaller groups include the Khmer people, who live in the east near the border with Cambodia; the Karen, who speak a variety of Sino-Tibetan languages; and the Lawa, who are thought to be the ancient inhabitants of the delta plain but have been since driven to the hills where they live in a voluntary isolation. In addition, there are the Semang people, also primitive, who continue to hunt with blowpipes and spears.

Religions

Thailand's people are overwhelmingly Buddhist; in the 2010 census about roughly 93 percent of the population claimed to be followers. There are also small groups of Muslims (just over 5 percent of the population) and Christians (less than 1 percent).

Climate

Thailand's climate is characterized as a Southeast Asian tropical monsoon zone. The monsoon seasons lasts from May until September. In November, the monsoon winds reverse direction until February, bringing cooler, drier air.

The actual amount of rain depends on region and topography. For instance, the Ranong province, located on the peninsula, can receive up to 4,000 millimeters (160 inches) of rain annually, while Hua Hin, on the east coast, may receive only 1,000 millimeters (40 inches). The Songkhla province, in the southernmost area of the peninsula, has a true tropical rainforest climate, experiencing heavy rains during the rest of the country's cool, dry season.

Temperatures in Thailand are fairly consistent, remaining between 25° and 29° Celsius (77° and 84° Fahrenheit) throughout the year. There is occasional frost, but usually only in December in the northern mountains.

ENVIRONMENT & GEOGRAPHY

Topography

Thailand is bordered by Laos on the north and east, Myanmar on the northwest and west, and Cambodia on the southeast. Thailand's southern peninsula connects the country to Malaysia, and is flanked by the Gulf of Thailand and the Andaman Sea.

Thailand's topography is diverse, encompassing mountains, plains, fertile alluvial soils, wet rice paddies, and tropical beaches. The northern and western regions are mountainous, with granite ridges formed by volcanoes. The average elevation in these areas is 1,585 meters (5,200 feet) above sea level. The peak of Doi Inthanon, in the north, is the country's highest point at 2,600 meters (8,530 feet) above sea level.

The eastern part of the country is dominated by the Khorat Plateau, through which flows the Mekong River. To the south lies the Cambodian plain, which gradually turns to rolling hills toward the southern peninsula.

The central Chao Phraya River basin dominates the landscape, accounting for one-third of the country's area. The river is Thailand's most important waterway. The basin's lowland area is the country's most fertile region, sometimes referred to as the "rice bowl."

The capital of Bangkok is located on the flood plains flanking both sides of the Chao Phraya. The heart of the city lies on the Chao Phraya's eastern bank. Here, in the area called Ratanakosin (the Old City), Bangkok's most important palace, temples, and museums attract throngs of tourists. East of Ratanakosin is Dusit, seat of many Thai government offices. To the south lies Chinatown, one of the oldest parts of Bangkok. To the southeast of Chinatown are Sathorn and Bangrak, Bangkok's major financial and business districts.

Thailand has many islands, some of which are home to tourist resorts. The country's largest island, Phuket, lies off the southeastern coast in the Andaman Sea.

Plants & Animals

Although roughly half of Thailand's area was once forested, half of the country's natural forests have been lost to logging and deforestation since the 1970s. Most of the remaining trees are palm trees or hardwoods, such as teak. With commercial planting, the country now has 37.2 percent of its land covered with forests.

Approximately 20 percent of the land is covered with grasses and swampland. Many typical Southeast Asian plants are common in Thailand, including rattan ferns, bamboo, lotuses, and water lilies.

There are few wild animal species remaining in Thailand. Domesticated animals include cattle, mules, horses, buffalo, and elephant, but even these have been largely replaced by machinery. Reptiles are common throughout Thailand, including lizards, crocodiles, and snakes. Silkworms are also prevalent.

Many of Thailand's animal species, such as rhinoceroses and tapirs, have been endangered by deforestation. The government has increased its wildlife conservation efforts and outlawed the sale of these animals. Over-fishing threatens the country's fish and marine life.

CUSTOMS & COURTESIES

Greetings

Like many aspects of Thai culture, greetings in Thailand rely heavily on social hierarchies. As a general rule, those who are older, wealthier and/or more educated are treated as superiors, while younger people and those in service roles are generally subservient. Generally, "Sawadee" is the most commonly used greeting, meaning "Hello" or "Goodbye." It is commonly followed by "Ka" or "Krap," the female and male terms of politeness, respectively.

The traditional greeting in Thailand is called the wai, a slight bow with palms pressed together as in prayer. The depth of the bow and the placement of a person's hands depend on who is being greeted. The most common polite wai has the fingers placed at nose-level, while greeting a monk or other person of high rank requires the fingers to be placed at the forehead. A deeper bow indicates a higher level of respect. Close friends and peers will often place palms at chest-level. A wai from a child, server, or shop vendor should be responded to with a polite nod and smile. Additionally, in business interactions, handshakes are commonly used.

In another demonstration of social hierarchy, Thais typically address their elders with "P'" preceding their name, while younger people's names are preceded with "Nong." This applies even among friends with age differences, since discussing age is not typically a source of embarrassment in Thai culture. There are several other addresses that are used, indicating the nuances of age and social stature. For example, "Noo," literally meaning "mouse," is used for someone much younger, while "Taan" is a very formal show of respect.

Gestures & Etiquette

The head is considered the most sacred part of the body in Thailand, while the feet are considered low and dirty. Consequently, it is considered extremely rude to touch a Thai person's head or to point one's feet at someone. Furthermore, it is important to avoid stepping over people or belongings. When sitting down, particularly on the floor, legs should either be crossed or folded to the side and feet tucked under. These positions are especially important to keep in mind when facing an image of Buddha.

Thai culture values the suppression of anger and emotion, praising calm people as jai yen (cool heart) and criticizing those who display aggression as jai ron (hot heart). Inconveniences and problems are often responded to with "Mai bpen rai," meaning "It doesn't matter" or "Everything is OK." Even crying is discouraged because it is a clear display of emotion. Additionally, the concept of "saving face" is also integral to Thai culture. This is embodied in the term greng jai, which is respect for others, consideration for others' feelings, and helping others save face. It is a complex value that defines much social interaction in Thailand. In general, confrontation is avoided in order to maintain civil relationships.

Eating/Meals

Meals in Thailand are typically eaten with a fork and spoon, though it is considered impolite to put the fork in your mouth. The fork is used to push food onto the spoon, while chopsticks are used to eat noodle dishes, derived from Chinese cuisine. Thai meals are often eaten family style, a communal arrangement with various meat and vegetable platters placed in the middle of the table. Stir-fried dishes are served either on top of rice or on a separate plate, to be shared. Thais take a few spoonfuls at a time of each dish instead of serving themselves all dishes at once.

Restaurants and eateries in Thailand generally serve food as soon as it is ready, so it is not impolite to begin eating before others receive their food. Leaving a bit of food on the plate is an indication of fullness; if the plate is left completely clean, the host may worry that the guest has not eaten enough. It is also customary for the eldest or wealthiest person at the table to pay the bill.

Restaurants vary immensely in type and size in Thailand. Streets are often filled with food carts and small, makeshift restaurants. Food is cooked and served quickly, with everything from a small snack to a full meal available. Meal times are generally adhered to, meaning that most street stands and food carts will close by mid-afternoon, and perhaps reopen for dinnertime. Noodle soup and various snacks are commonly available past midnight.

Visiting

In Thailand, it is customary to remove shoes before entering someone's home. Shoes are usually left either outside the door or in the entryway. One should be sure to step over the threshold when entering a house, as stepping on the threshold is thought to disrespect the spirit residing there. In addition, gifts such as desserts, flowers or alcohol are graciously accepted from visitors. Likewise, visitors should accept food or drink offered to them. Refusal of all offerings may be viewed as a display of greng jai, and the food or drink will be served regardless. In this case, it is important to eat or drink in order to be courteous.

LIFESTYLE

Family

The family is traditionally considered the core of Thai society. Though modernization has provoked changes in family structures, family life is still more tightly knit than in Western cultures. A sense of hierarchy is strongly instilled at a young age, and children are taught to display a deep level of respect for their parents and other elders. Children are expected to take care of their parents when they grow old, and family members are expected to help each other meet financial obligations.

Modernization has, however, led to a decreasing number of families living with a few generations under one roof. It is now common for a husband and wife to live alone instead of in the home of one set of parents, though rural lifestyles tend to accommodate more traditional ways.

Housing

The traditional Thai house was a simple structure that accounted for local lifestyle, climate and available materials and resources. Wood was available in abundance, making it the obvious choice for construction. In particular, strong teakwood became a more luxurious option.

To counter heat and humidity, doors and windows were typically placed for optimal air circulation. Roofs were often peaked upward to allow for additional airflow, and to allow heat to rise. In addition, houses were often elevated to avoid flooding during the monsoon season and to offer further air circulation. The space beneath these elevated houses was often used for livestock or storage, catering to the needs of a largely agricultural society.

Urban housing in modern Thailand is dominated by town houses, apartment blocks and condominiums. Due to restrictions on foreign ownership of Thai land, foreigners can only purchase condominiums, resulting in a surge of construction within and outside of Bangkok. The relatively high socio-economic status among Bangkok residents has generated a local need for condominiums, though these buildings cater to foreigners as well. Low-rise apartment blocks offer simple studio rooms for students and other low-income residents, while middle-class Thais tend to favor houses.

Food

Thai cuisine varies greatly by region, with rice, chilies, and naam plaa (fish sauce) as standard staples nationwide. Food from southern Thailand is distinctly spicier than other cuisines, as it calls for a lot of chilies. There is a wide assortment of curries that are popular in the south, often made with seafood and served with rice. Yam thalay (seafood salad) is commonly served as an appetizer. Other typical southern ingredients include sataw (a type of green pod) and med riang (similar to a bean sprout), which are cooked with curries, meats or chili sauce.

Northern food tends to use more pork, and ingredients are based on what is readily available. Different types of gaeng (curry soup) are popular, such as gaeng panaeng (Panang curry), which is of Indian origin. Other specialties include roasted or fried meats, chili sauces and local vegetables. Sticky rice (steamed glutinous rice) is the staple of northern and northeastern dishes. A meal widely available at markets throughout northern Thailand is sai oua (a type of sausage) served with naam prik noom (a chili sauce), sticky rice, and kep moo (fried pork skin). Generally, northeastern cuisine draws from Laotian dishes, such as minced spiced meat called laab, a lengthy list of fried meats that may include anything from pork to snake to insects, and the popular som tam (papaya salad).

Food in central Thailand combines the various regional cuisines, though it tends to be milder and sweeter in taste. Gaen kiowaan (green curry) is typical of central Thai food, with a slightly sweet flavor created by the coconut milk in which it is cooked.

Life's Milestones

According to Buddhist tradition, any Thai male of at least twenty years of age must be ordained as a monk at some point in his life, whether he chooses to spend four months, four years or a lifetime in the monastery. This period of ordainment is an opportunity for the man to show his gratitude to his parents and provide them a chance to make merit. Earning merit by doing good deeds is a significant aspect of Buddhism in Thailand. Many males choose to spend the three months of Phansa (Buddhist Lent) as monks, though ordainment can be done at any time.

CULTURAL HISTORY

Art

Traditional and classical Thai art is often referred to as Buddhist art since the creation of art throughout Thailand's history has been largely influenced by Buddhism. As such, worship and protection have long been the main motivations to create art, which often included images and sculptures of Buddha. Artistic value was not a primary concern, revealing a key difference with much of Western art. Additionally, traditional Thai art was also influenced by the many different kingdoms, creating a variety of styles that reveal much of Thailand's history. Classic or traditional Thai arts include manuscript illustrations, sculpture, ceramics, and decorative engravings.

Religious art, especially images of Buddha developed different styles under various ancient Thai kingdoms, each style displaying its own distinct features. The earliest Buddhist art in Thailand is dated to the Dvaravati kingdom of the sixth to 11th centuries. This work is influenced by art in India, the birthplace of Buddhism. Depictions of the Buddha during this period feature a flat nose and thick lips. This gradually evolved to embrace Lopburi art, which employed the Khmer style of a broad face, a wide mouth betraying a hint of a smile, and shoulder-length earlobes. Lopburi was a provincial capital of the Khmer Empire, an ancient kingdom in Southeast Asia that flourished between the ninth and 15th centuries. This style was prominent from central Thailand to northeast Thailand.

Meanwhile, art in the Thai peninsula was heavily influenced by the Sri-Vijaya kingdom. At its height in 1000 CE, this kingdom included southern Thailand, Sumatra, and Malaysia. This style is often indistinguishable from Malay art from the same period, with the Buddha displaying the same rounded chin and soft mouth. The beginning of the Kingdom of Siam in the 13th century is sometimes regarded as the beginning of "true" Thai art. In northern Thailand, the similar Chiang Saen and Lanna styles were dominant since the 11th century, showing the first signs of Burmese (Myanmar) influence. Early art from this period shows a rounder, fatter Buddha, though the style transformed with the influence of the Sukhothai Kingdom in the 13th century. These later sculptures displayed differences in the hair, robe and sitting position of the Buddha.

The Sukhothai period (1238–1438) is regarded as Thailand's golden age, during which the Thai kingdom became powerful and prosperous. Sculptures from this period show the Buddha prior to achieving enlightenment, and in a complete state of relaxation. The four postures typically shown were walking, sitting, standing and reclining. The walking Buddha was a distinct feature of this period, along with an oval face, a slightly hooked nose and a small waist. Thai painting also began to progress during this period, and by the end of the Sukhothai reign, painting had become more colorful and stylized.

The next significant art school developed under the Ayutthaya kingdom (1350–1767). These four centuries allowed for the evolution of deeply developed artistic styles that are highly respected in Thai art. Although the sculptures share many features with the Sukhothai period, positions are less fluid and the Buddha's face is often expressionless. In later years, the crowned Buddha image and other ornate additions were commonly portrayed.

In addition, the Ayutthaya period also impacted Thai art and craft with the development of the Krom Chang Sip Mu (Organization of the Ten Crafts). This organization was created under the patronage of royalty to teach Thai craftsmen. These crafts were later divided in the Bangkok, or Ratanakosin, period in the 18th century. They were classified as drawing, which included painters and manuscript illustrators; engraving, including woodcarving and metalwork; sculpting; modeling, including puppetry; figure making; molding, which included metal casting; plastering; lacquering (decorative varnishing of objects); and beating, or metal finishing. In addition, sculpture in this period drew largely from past styles, though artists aimed to humanize the Buddha figure. Painting during the Bangkok period embodied all the advances of previous schools, giving the art of painting a firm foothold in Thai art.

Architecture

Thai architecture is best embodied by the wat (temple), which comprises various structures and areas of worship, and the chedi (stupa), a domed structure built to contain holy and royal relics. The structure of chedi evolved with the different kingdoms, with styles ranging from rounded to square, and one-tiered to multi-tiered. The pillars, roofs and walls of temples are usually ornately decorated with murals, engravings, and gold leaf. Sculptures of mythical creatures, such as the naga serpent, often guard the entrance to the temple, which houses one or more Buddha images.

Other important structures of Thai architecture include the prasat (castle), which typically features rounded spires and a central domed sanctuary, and the bot, or ubosot, an ordination or meditation hall for monk similar to an assembly hall. In addition, a prasat can serve as a royal palace or shrine. Thai architecture reached its zenith during the Sukhothai and Ayutthaya periods, with Western and Chinese architectural elements being incorporated in later periods.

Drama

The theatrical art form known as likeh is popular in the central and south central regions of the country. Likeh, which originated in the early 20th century, is a blended art form, featuring folk and classical music, as well as dramatic costumes, comedy, and social and political commentary.

Dance

Traditional Thai dance is a true form of dramatic story telling. It is known as ramthai, and mostly characterized as either classical dance or folk dance. Most classical dances were originally developed for performance in royal courts, but have expanded to public performances in contemporary culture. Classical dance forms include lakhon, khon, and fawn thai, which are danced with elaborate costumes, sometimes including six-inch false fingernails. The movements are typically characterized as precise, graceful and symbolic, and hand movements are especially notable for their complex twists and undulations.

Music

Classical Thai music has its roots in the country's 13th-century royal courts and is divided into three styles: piphat, the most common in modern-day Thailand; khruang sai, used to accompany puppetry; and mahori, traditionally performed by women. Traditional orchestras that usually accompany traditional Thai dances include various types of Thai instruments. Many of these traditional instruments were first developed with the influence of Indian instruments. Several types of flutes, gongs and stringed instruments create a unique sound that some musicians have attempted to record and preserve with Western musical notation, though the musical systems differ greatly.

Literature

The first known Thai literature was recorded in the 13th century, mostly as stone inscriptions describing life during the Sukhothai period. Verse did not appear until the Ayutthaya period, when religious stories began to surface alongside romance and war tales. *Lilit phra Lo* ("The Story of Prince Lo") is one of Thailand's most celebrated traditional poetic pieces. The nirat genre, developed in the 17th century, comprises works about faraway loves and long journeys. The best-known poem from this period is *Nirat khlong kamsuan* ("A Mournful Journey"), Si Prat's epic tale of his exile. In addition, contemporary Thai poetry is rooted in the works of Sunthon Phu (1787–1855). His epic, *Phra Aphaimani,* named for the central figure, is often considered the country's most recognized work of literature.

Thai literature suffered a severe loss with the destruction of Ayutthaya by the Burmese, so the new kingdom spent much energy in rewriting. The *Ramakian*, the Thai version of the Indian *Ramayana* tale, is an honored adaptation. The twentieth century began with a strong focus on translations of Western literature, but by the 1920s, Thai writers began composing original works of fiction and social commentary.

The 1950s and 1960s represented a silent era for Thai literature, as freedom of speech was harshly limited. Literary production was limited in subsequent years, until a new, more liberal government in 1977 allowed for more freedom. Suchart Sawatsi (1945–) introduced Thailand's first literary journal in 1977, *Lok nangsu'* ("Book World"), which gave a promising boost to the world of words. This new momentum increased both literary production and media attention to Thai books, granting contemporary writers a more solid place in the art world.

CULTURE

Arts & Entertainment

Modernization in Thailand has caused a significant generational gap to form, which is apparent in contemporary arts. Traditional art forms, which largely served as decorations for temples and other religious purposes, are not often commissioned today. Instead, royal patronage and public funds are more likely invested in the maintenance and construction of infrastructure, notably roads, buildings or railways. The influence of Western modernization has also changed the pace of life in Thailand, as younger generations are living in a different environment and struggling to understand new identities. These changes are naturally manifested in Thai modern art; though religious images may persist, the process and style of creation have transformed. Though a Thai avant-garde, or unorthodox, style did exist in the 20th century, visual arts that conformed to conservative ideals of Thai identity were more commonplace.

The advent of art competitions and opportunities to study abroad slowly changed the contemporary art scene in Thailand. By the 1960s, abstract painting was becoming increasingly popular, though more traditional imagery prevailed. Artists struggled with changing ideas of Thai identity and how to portray the traditional identity in a modern context. Student uprisings and protests were tragically ended with a massacre of protestors by the military dictatorship on October 14, 1973, creating deeper confusion about national identity.

Though Thai politics continued to fluctuate, the art scene was able to expand as more exhibition venues opened. It was not until the mid-1980s that modern Thai art became an established presence not only in Thai society, but in international circles as well. A growing economy, expansion of the middle class, and increased art patronage encouraged a new realm of experimentation in Thai art. In addition, contemporary Thai art suffered after the economic crisis of 1997. Momentum has since been regained, though Thai artists are increasingly moving toward independence, rather than associating themselves with certain institutions.

The classical music of Thailand is closely associated with the music of Cambodia and Laos. Traditional Thai music includes luk thung, a type of country music, and mor lam, characterized by its distinctive vocal performances. Contemporary music in Thailand has incorporated the influence of pop and rock and roll music from the United States and Europe, resulting in a vibrant music scene that is highly popular with youth. Technological advances in recent years have also increased exposure to global music and films, namely through wider availability of the Internet and DVDs. Also, the popularity of karaoke has contributed to the wide appreciation and dissemination of music videos.

In regards to Thai cinema, pure entertainment drives the production of most Thai films, with popular actors starring in movies about romance, jealousy, tragedy, comedy and everything in between. These movies are typically successful at the box offices, while films featuring social commentary tend to be less popular.

The native martial art known as Muay Thai, or Thai boxing, is the country's most popular sport; its popularity has also grown throughout the world in recent years. Other popular sports include soccer, tennis, and takraw, which combines elements of volleyball and soccer.

Cultural Sites & Landmarks

The most obvious cultural attractions in Thailand are its temples—there are over 30,000—which demonstrate some of the country's finest art and architecture. Typically, these temples are categorized as either royal or common temples. Among the most famous of the 200 royal temples include Wat Suthat and Wat Arun, both located in Bangkok. The Wat Arun, in particular, features a tower decorated with pieces of porcelain from China.

The elaborately decorated Grand Palace is also in Bangkok. Adorned with glittering gold, imposing statues, and intricate murals; it was constructed by King Rama V (1853–1910) in 1877 to serve as his royal residence. Within the palace complex is the Wat Phra Kaew (Temple of the Emerald Buddha), celebrated for its highly revered 14th-century image of the Buddha, carved from a single block of emerald.

The 16th-century Wat Pho, also located in Bangkok, is renowned for its 46-meter-long (150 feet) statue of the reclining Buddha. During the reign of King Rama III (1788–1851), Wat Pho was an important learning center. Today it serves as a respected massage school, and the temple still boasts a set of marble tablets engraved with anatomical and medical instructions. Outside of Bangkok, the ancient city of Sukhothai offers a broader view of Thai history. In the 13th and 14th centuries, Sukhothai served as the Kingdom of Siam's first capital. Today, the remains are designated as a United Nations Educational, Scientific and Cultural Organization (UNESCO) World Heritage Site, a testament to the historical architecture of the temples and monuments.

Ayutthaya is another UNESCO World Heritage site; it succeeded Sukhothai as the capital of Siam. Built in the 14th century, Ayutthaya was a thriving city until the Burmese army destroyed much of it in the 18th century. The level of destruction forced the Thai kingdom to build a new capital in Thonburi, on the outskirts of what is modern-day Bangkok. Despite the devastation of Ayutthaya, numerous impressive statues and chedis (stupas) remain. The specific style of chedi in Ayutthaya, also known to be a Khmer style, is called a prang. Thailand's three other World Heritage Sites include the Thungyai and Huai Kha Khaeng Wildlife Sanctuaries, the forest complexes of Dong Phayayen and Khao Yai, and the Ban Chiang Archaeological Site.

Chiang Mai, the largest city of northern Thailand, boasts more than 300 temples. The most famous temple, Wat Phrathat Doi Suthep, overlooks the city from a mountain on the northwest side of town. The gold-plated chedi of this 14th-century temple holds holy Buddha relics. Wat Chedi Luang is another 14th-century temple, located in the city center and known for its massive chedi. Other notable temples include the 14th-century Wat Suan Dok, the 13th-century Wat Umong set in the forest, and the 14th-century Wat Phra Sing.

Libraries & Museums

Bangkok is home to several noteworthy museums. The National Museum, housed in an 18th-century palace, holds the country's largest collection of Thai art as well as many examples of traditional Southeast Asian weapons, ceramics, clothing, woodcarvings, and musical instruments. Kamthieng House, a restored teak house that originally belonged to a rice farmer, offers visitors a glimpse into what daily life was like for ordinary 19th-century Thais. The Jim Thompson House, formerly owned by an American who played an instrumental role in founding the Thai silk industry, houses a significant collection of Asian art. The Royal Barge Museum has on display several of the elaborately gilded teak boats used in royal processions. The Queen's Gallery, opened in 2003, promotes contemporary Thai artists.

Two of Bangkok's offbeat but popular attractions include the Royal Thai Air Force Museum, which houses one of the world's finest collections of rare and antique military aircraft, and the Forensic Museum, located at Siriraj Hospital but open to the general public as well as medical students. Visitors are greeted at the entranceway by the skeleton of the museum's founder, Songkran Niyomsane, the father of forensic medicine in Thailand, who died in 1970.

Holidays

Most of the holidays celebrated in Thailand revolve around Buddhist ceremonies, such as Mahka Bucha, Wisakha Bucha, and the holy season of Khao Phansa. Songkran, or Thai New Year, is celebrated for several days in mid-April. Chakri Day (April 13) celebrates the founding of the present dynasty in 1782. Other official holidays include Chulalongkorn Day (October 23), in honor of King Rama V, and Constitution Day (December 10). The birthdays of the ruling monarchs, as well as the date of their coronation, are also celebrated as national holidays.

Youth Culture

Cultural values are shifting for Thailand's youth, as society modernizes. Generally, Thai youth today are less connected to their Buddhist identities than previous generations. Young Thai women are more likely to have sex before marriage than older generations were, highlighting this change in cultural norms.

Thai youth are on par with their Western counterparts in embracing technology. Mobile phones are popular for communicating, and computer games are a prevalent leisure activity. In fact, a survey conducted in 2007 found that about a quarter of Thai youth play computer games on a daily or almost-daily basis, while another 21 percent play three to four days per week. In 2013, more than half of the online minutes for people in Thailand, were by those in the 15–24 age group. Additionally, Thai youth enjoy most of the same popular music and trends of Western culture, and often use their mobile phones to access the latest songs. Karaoke booths are also a popular destination for young Thais.

SOCIETY

Transportation

Buses are the main mode of public transport in Thailand, especially for longer distances. Prices and amenities vary greatly, as buses range from old, third class buses to new "VIP class" buses. About fifteen cities and towns are connected by Thailand's national railway system, which stretches more than 4,000 kilometers (2,485 miles). Bangkok, the capital, is the only city with a metro system, and it also boasts the modern and efficient Skytrain system. Other modes of public transport include three-wheeled tuk-tuk vehicles, motorcycle taxis and songthaew, which are covered pick-up trucks.

Drivers use the left-hand side of the road in Thailand; however, it should be noted that motorcycles and other smaller motorized vehicles tend to illegally travel against the flow of traffic.

Transportation Infrastructure

An extensive highway system connects all areas of Thailand, covering more than 180,000 kilometers (over 110,000 miles). Individual transportation includes a high percentage of motorbikes and an increasing number of cars and sport utility vehicles (SUVs). In 2010, motorcycles represented over 60 percent of registered vehicles in Thailand. Generally, traffic is notoriously congested, especially in Bangkok. In addition, there are several international airports in Thailand, the most well-known ones located in Bangkok, Chiang Mai and Phuket.

Media & Communications

Most print media in Thailand are privately run, while the government and military run the majority of national television networks and many radio networks. Radio remains a highly popular medium, with over sixty stations operating in the Bangkok area alone. Additionally, there are over 500 hundred radio stations nationwide. Cable and satellite TV are also prevalent. Prominent newspapers include the *Thai Rath*, the *Daily News*, and the *Khao Sod*.

Thailand censors Internet content that is deemed to be against the monarchy or against the government, and also censors pornographic material. Censorship made international news in 2007, when YouTube was temporarily blocked in Thailand. Again, in December, 2014, the government ordered the internet providers to remove anything the government deemed undesirable. Additionally, although journalists have freedom of speech when it comes to criticizing government policies and actions, most media outlets choose to self-censor criticism of the monarchy and military.

SOCIAL DEVELOPMENT

Standard of Living

The country ranked 89th out of 187 countries on the 2013 Human Development Index.

Water Consumption

The main sources for water in Thailand are surface and ground water. It is estimated that approximately 75 percent of water used for domestic purposes comes from groundwater reserves. In 2012, a study using World Health Organization standards, found that, in rural areas, 44 percent of surface water and 80 percent of the ground water supplied to households had pollutants exceeding WHO standards. A previous study in 2003, found that 60 percent of the water was suitable for both agricultural and general uses, while 40 percent of the surface water was found to be of poor or very poor quality. Surface water in the northeast part of the country was found to be of the overall highest quality in the country, while surface water in the eastern regions was considered to be of fair quality.

Education

Six years of primary education are compulsory for Thai children. Since 1997, all Thai children are entitled to twelve years of free education. Secondary education is not required, and a small minority of students progress to this level. Secondary school lasts for six years, in lower and upper divisions. English is the language of instruction in the country's secondary schools, and is also widely spoken among the upper classes.

There are many colleges and universities throughout Thailand. Silpakorn University provides fine arts training, and its architects go on to design government buildings and temples. Other universities include the Chula Longkorn University, the country's oldest, founded in 1917 in Bangkok, and Ramkhamaeng University, founded in 1971. Thailand's average literacy rate is high, over 93 percent (95 percent among men and 91 percent among women) in 2005.

The 2014 Global Gender Gap Report, published by the World Economic Forum, ranked countries according to their attainment of gender equality in areas such as education, economic opportunities, and health. Thailand ranked 61st out of 142 countries; however, in the category of educational attainment, the country ranked a bit lower, at 6rth out of 142.

Women's Rights

Thai women garner respect chiefly through their roles as mother-nurturers in a society that is essentially patriarchal. The traditional Thai ideal or concept of kulasatrii (virtuous woman) glorifies women who are domestic, graceful, and sexually conservative. However, Thai women do not generally view this role as restrictive, but rather as honorable. These traditional values are more ingrained in rural settings, but modern women living in cities hold great respect for them as well.

Women have acquired a significant presence in the workforce, though gender discrimination persists. In 2014, women formed 45 percent of the nonagricultural labor force, though in managerial or high-level positions only 28 percent were filled by women. Employers are required by the government to provide equal pay to men and women, but jobs held by women are concentrated in the lower-paying areas.

Domestic violence has recently become an increasingly important issue, as studies point out its prevalence. A study on domestic violence by the World Health Organization (WHO) in 2005 revealed that 29.9 percent of Thai women surveyed had reported instances of forced sex with an intimate partner. The study was a crucial step in revealing the hidden problem of domestic abuse. However, authorities have been slow to address domestic abuse as a legal issue instead of as a personal one. In 2007, the first Protection Against Domestic Violence Act was introduced, recognizing the need to place this crime in a category of its own. Critics lament that loose law enforcement renders legislation against sexual violence ineffective, and so NGO-supported resources offer counseling, emergency hot lines and temporary shelters to supplement the underfunded government crisis centers. As of 2010, incidents of domestic violence had increased further and a 2012 survey found that 63 percent of the population thought husbands hitting wives was acceptable. At that time, Thailand ranked second highest in domestic violence among the forty-nine nations studied.

The Human Trafficking Act was also introduced in 2007, addressing the sensitive issue of forced sex work. Minority groups, such as the various hill tribe communities that are denied citizenship by the Thai government, are especially vulnerable to trafficking. Specific data is difficult to gather, but the law penalizes those involved in human trafficking, prostitution, forced labor, and trade of human organs.

Though prostitution is illegal, it is a widespread practice that caters more to Thais than to foreigners, contrary to popular belief. High demand and the protection of local officials have helped prostitution remain a visible presence in Thai society. The Prostitution Prevention and Suppression Act of 1996 was a progressive move to decriminalize sex workers and penalize customers and agents.

Polygamy was legal until 1935, though the practice of having "minor wives" endures. Men with the financial means to support more than one family may take on a mia noi (minor wife), though the practice is much less accepted in contemporary times. Visiting sex workers is also common among married men. Thai women are much more likely today than in the past to divorce a husband who has a mia noi, but many women also choose to suffer in silence. A pervasive belief that men have insatiable sexual appetites leads many women to believe that sex workers are necessary, but the HIV/AIDS epidemic has raised new concerns of infection. (It was estimated that in 2012, 440,000 people in Thailand were living with HIV/AIDS.) Thai women often struggle with the dilemma of accepting or fighting against husbands' infidelity, which reflects the contemporary ambivalence toward the kulasatrii ideal.

Health Care

Thailand's health care system is not sufficient to meet the needs of the population. Facilities are inadequate, and Thai doctors often leave to practice in other countries, where they can make more money. Most of the country's modern medical facilities are located in the Bangkok metropolitan area. Although there are regional health centers throughout the country, many rural residents must rely on mobile medical units.

Thailand's infant mortality rate remains high, at nearly 10 deaths per 1,000 live births. The use of midwives in childbirth is common in Thailand. The average life expectancy is seventy-four years; seventy-seven years for women and seventy-one years for men.

Malaria, once prevalent in the country, has been curbed due to increased use of pesticides. HIV/AIDS is a growing problem in the country, with approximately 20,800 HIV/AIDS related deaths occurring in 2012.

GOVERNMENT

Structure

Thailand's modern government can be traced to 1932, when a military coup overthrew the monarchy. A constitution was established and since then, the country has wavered between governments installed by the military and those elected democratically. The country now functions as a stable constitutional monarchy; its current constitution was adopted in 2007.

The king remains the head of state and of the armed forces, and is considered sacred. The royal family is the center of Thailand's national life, functioning as a symbol of the country's strength and unity. The king appoints a prime minister, who functions along with a cabinet as the executive authority of the country.

The bicameral National Assembly is comprised of a Senate, whose members are popularly elected to six-year terms, and a House of Representatives, whose members are elected to four-year terms. Under the rules established by the military, individuals seeking election to the Senate cannot be a member of a political party.

Voting is compulsory for those 18 and older, though citizens can only vote for members of the legislative branch.

Political Parties

Thailand's political climate in the early 21st century has been fraught with turmoil and crisis. There are two socioeconomic groups, the rural poor and the urban middle- and upper-middle classes, that form the basis of the two conflicting political ideologies of Thailand.

In 2001 and 2005, Thaksin Shinawatra of the Thai Rak Thai Party was elected prime minister of the country, and his institution of universal health care and poverty reduction made him quote popular with the country's poor. However, Thaksin and his government were accused of corruption by the opposition, the People's Alliance for Democracy (PAD).

After PAD-staged protests in 2006, Thaksin was deposed in a coup d'état while abroad by a military junta that came to be known as the Council for National Security (CNS). The CNS disbanded the Thai Rak Thai Party (TRT) and banned its members from seeking political office. Shortly thereafter, many former TRT members joined the People's Power Party (PPP), which led a coalition government after the 2007 election. The PPP was slated to make several constitutional amendments, an act that was opposed by the People's Alliance for Democracy. However, the Constitutional Court of Thailand disbanded the PPP in 2008, citing election fraud. (It was also widely known that the PPP had become the de facto Thai Rak Thai Party, which had been banned two years earlier.)

Immediately following the dissolution of the PPP, the political party Pheu Thai, or For Thais Party, was founded. While the For Thais Party was appointing its leaders, the House of Representatives nominated Abhisit Vejjajiva of the Democrat Party as prime minister; he assumed office in December 2008.

In April 2010, 21 people were killed and hundreds more wounded during anti-government protests. Protestors of Vejjajiva's government are referred to as "red shirts," made up of poor, rural Thais whose allegiance can be traced back to former Prime Minister Thaksin and the Thai Rak Thai Party. Those in favor of the Democrat Party and Prime Minister Vejjajiva, as well as the PAD, are generally urban, middle- and upper-middle class Thais who are referred to as "yellow shirts." After four years of weak governments, including one headed by Thaksin's sister, Yingluck Shinawatra, the military declared martial law in May 2014, and later stated that elections would be held in October 2015, although some later said 2016. This was the 12th coup since 1932.

Local Government

Thailand is divided into 76 provinces (changwat), each with its own popularly elected local government of mayors and councilors. The provinces are divided into districts, which are headed by district officers. Districts are further divided into sub-districts, or "tambon," of which there were over 7,000 in 2009. Tambon are further divided into villages, or "muban," of which there were over 69,000 in 2009.

Judicial System

Thai law is based on the Hindu code Manusmrti, which has been tempered by the influence of Western law since the late 19th century. At the provincial level exist juvenile and family courts, as well as magistrates' courts, while there are nine regional courts of appeal. The Supreme Court (or Sandika) and the highest Court of Appeal are located in Bangkok. There are no juries in Thai courts; rather, outcomes are determined by a judge or set of judges.

Taxation

The highest income tax rate in Thailand is 35 percent, while the highest corporate tax rate is 20 percent. Other levied taxes include value-added tax (VAT) and property tax.

Armed Forces

Thailand's Armed Forces comprises an army, navy, marine corps, and an air force. In 2005, the Thai Armed Forces comprised just over 300,000 soldiers.

Foreign Policy

The 2006 bloodless coup d'état (sudden overthrow of government) that deposed the Prime Minister Thaksin Shinawatra provoked calls from the international community to swiftly restore democracy. Though Thailand had been viewed as one of the most stable democracies in the region, the 2006 coup was a reminder of the country's long history of political instability. Democracy was reestablished in 2007, however, two prime ministers were forced out of office in 2008, one in 2009, and elections were held in 2011. After trying five cabinet configurations, new elections were called in 2014, the outcome of which resulted in the military coup.

A driving force in Thailand's foreign policy is the Association of Southeast Asian Nations (ASEAN), of which Thailand has been a member since its inception in 1967. Current foreign policy aims to maintain and improve diplomatic relations with other ASEAN members, especially as Thailand began an 18-month chairmanship of ASEAN in July 2008. Thailand is also a member of the World Trade Organization (WTO) and a member of the UN since 1946.

Though Thailand mostly enjoys good relations with other ASEAN member countries, border issues with Myanmar (Burma) and Cambodia in particular have been problematic. Fighting between ethnic minorities and the junta of Myanmar in border areas has created tension when the conflict has spilled over into Thailand. Thailand has also been criticized for repatriating refugees from Myanmar and Laos. However, although the international community constantly condemns the oppressive junta of Myanmar, Thailand remains Myanmar's biggest trading partner.

Economically, Thailand is heavily dependent on foreign trade and investment. Thailand's top trading partners in the early 21st century include Japan, the US, Singapore, Malaysia and China. As of 2012, Thailand's three largest export markets were China, Japan, and the United States. The three largest counties sending imports were Japan, China, and the United Arab Emirates. Thailand is a long-time ally of the U.S. In 2002–03, Thailand sent troops to help rebuild Afghanistan and Iraq. (Thailand also supported the UN peacekeeping mission in East Timor by supplying troops). In 2003, the US designated Thailand as a major non-NATO ally, which allows Thailand military and economic benefits from the US.

Human Rights Profile

International human rights law insists that states respect civil and political rights, and also promote an individual's economic, social and cultural rights. The United Nations Universal Declaration on Human Rights (UDHR) is recognized as the standard for international human rights. Its authors sought the counsel of the world's great thinkers, philosophers, and religious leaders, and were careful to create a document that reflects the core values shared by every world culture. To read this document or view the articles relating to cultural human rights, click here: http://www.udhr.org/UDHR/default.htm.

Although Thailand is praised for providing refuge to those escaping conflict or persecution in neighboring countries, a lack of transparency has provoked criticism of the government's treatment of ethnic minorities, refugees and migrant workers.

Article 2 of the Universal Declaration of Human Rights states that all citizens must be equally granted the rights of the declaration. Thailand does not fully conform to this article, as the process of designating "refugee" or "Person of Concern" status is criticized by many international watchdogs for inefficiency and lack of transparency. Although Thailand is not a member of the 1951 Convention Relating to the Status of Refugees, the international humanitarian law of non-refoulment (protection of refugees) dictates that no refugee should be forcibly repatriated if they are at risk of persecution.

In May 2007, the Thai government urged the UN High Commissioner for Refugees (UNHCR) to stop the determination of refugee status. Since the Thai government has taken over the process of determination, several incidents have elicited international criticism. In particular, two incidents in 2008 drew international attention to the unacceptable conditions of many refugees and migrants in Thailand.

In June 2008, the Thai government deported 837 Lao Hmong (an ethnic minority group) after a mass protest at the camp where they were being held in Thailand. UNHCR expressed concern that the repatriations may have been forced, and may have endangered people who deserved refugee status. Thailand considered this group of Lao Hmong to be illegal economic migrants, rather than refugees, and as such has not acted to protect them.

Similarly, increased restrictions on the rights of migrant workers have perpetuated the cycle of illegal migrant workers who are unable to attain legal status, yet are at great risk of exploitation and deportation. One incident occurred in April 2008, when 54 migrants from Myanmar (Burma) suffocated in an unventilated truck as they were being transferred to a new work site in southern Thailand. The surviving migrants in the truck were detained for illegal entry, highlighting the lack of protection for migrants in Thailand.

As of June 25, 2008, Thailand's nine refugee camps were housing an estimated 123,584 people seeking refuge and/or asylum. Since resettlement of refugees recommenced in January 2005, over 30,000 refugees from Myanmar (Burma) had been resettled in third countries. These resettlements are viewed positively by the international community, though they are marred by the accusations of unfair treatment of many other refugees. Since the 2014 coup, tighter restrictions have been implemented which have reduced the number of refugees in Thailand.

The Thai government's treatment of ethnic minorities within the country is another example of disregard for Article 2. The minority ethnic groups living in the highlands are known as hill tribes. The Thai government recognizes nine groups, though several others exist without official recognition. The Thai government has discriminated against these groups for decades, and at least half of the hill tribe population has not been offered Thai citizenship.

In addition, families that have lived in Thailand for generations can be deported or arrested if they do not have citizenship or permanent residency status, and even temporary status affords them little freedom. They have no protection by labor laws, no social welfare and cannot own land. Additionally, children born of parents with no official status are considered stateless. The process of granting citizenship is muddled by unnecessary complexities and corruption, making it even more difficult for hill tribe people to obtain legal status. These hardships make hill tribe youth particularly vulnerable to labor exploitation and human trafficking.

Human trafficking, especially of women and children into the sex trade, remains a critical issue in Thailand and its border areas. Though legislation and the work of non-governmental organizations (NGOs) in the region have made some progress, extreme poverty and the conditions of stateless people continue to make for a vulnerable population in northern Thailand.

The right to freedom of religion as stated in Article 18 is supported by the Thai government. Government statistics state the Thai population is 94 percent Buddhist and 5 percent Muslim, though other groups have released figures with a higher estimate of Muslim citizens. Though the government respects freedom of religion, the separatist insurgency in predominantly Muslim provinces of southern Thailand has provoked further division between the two religious groups. The suspected militants, mostly of ethnic Muslim Malay descent, have killed over 5,000 civilians—mostly Buddhist—since January 2004.

Freedom of opinion and expression, as outline by Article 19, is protected by the Thai constitution. However, charges of lèse-majesté, or insulting the monarchy, have increased since the 2006 coup d'état. Print media is generally self-censored, though the military junta that ruled until January 2008 exercised ample censorship with the Internet and broadcast radio. This was in an attempt to bar any news of ousted Prime Minister Thaksin Shinawatra and also to censor any criticism of the monarchy. For example, the popular YouTube video website was banned for five months in 2007 after the release of an anti-monarchy video. While freedom expression increased under the democratically elected governments, there were still strict restrictions in certain areas. Since the 2014 coup, more restrictions, on both political and social speech, have been imposed.

Migration

As of 2014, there were more than 2 million migrant works in Thailand. The government grants migrants work permits on a year-to-year basis, but, in January 2010, announced that for migrants to obtain work permits, they must verify their nationality with the Thai government, return to their home countries to register with their government, and return to Thailand legally. The Thai government threatened to deport migrant workers who refused to enroll in the program. At least half of the workers in the country at that time elected to stay as undocumented aliens. International organizations such as Human Rights Watch have criticized this decision as the majority of migrant workers in Thailand have fled the military dictatorship of Myanmar (also referred to as Burma) and may face reprisal upon returning to their home country. By March 2010, over 500,000 migrant workers from Myanmar had gone underground (ostensibly in Thailand) rather than submit to a nationality verification that would require them to return to their home countries. However, after the 2014 coup, increased fear of the government led more than 200,000 Cambodian workers left Thailand.

ECONOMY

Overview of the Economy

Thailand has one of fastest-growing economies in Southeast Asia. A currency crisis in 1997 slowed growth, and the tourism industry experienced a downturn in 2003 and 2004, due to fears over the Severe Acute Respiratory Syndrome (SARS) epidemic and the Indian Ocean tsunami. The economy is recovering, and relies on foreign investment and the export of manufactured goods and food products. However, the 2014 coup has once again reduced the appeal of Thailand as a place to do business.

In 2013, Thailand's gross domestic product (GDP) was officially estimated to be $400.9 billion USD, although $673 billion (USD) in purchasing power and its per capita GDP was estimated to be $9,900 (USD). Approximately 13 percent of the population was living below the poverty line in 2011. In 2013, the unemployment rate was 0.7 percent of a labor force of more than 39 million. The average inflation rate of Thailand between 1977 and 2015 was

4.5 percent. However, the first quarter of 2015 was a period of deflation at a rate of about 0.4 percent.

The capital of Bangkok is the main trading center for both Thailand and Southeast Asia. In addition to its massive import-export business, the local economy also features a significant manufacturing base.

Industry

Most manufacturing activity in Thailand focuses on textiles, machinery, electrical components, and automobiles. Smaller industries include food processing, craftwork, and small-scale oil production.

Bangkok is the country's chief industrial center. Mineral and food processing takes place in the southeastern region.

Labor

In 2013, the unemployment rate was 0.7 percent and the labor force comprised over 39 million people. An estimated 38 percent of the labor force works in the agricultural sector, while 14 percent works in the industrial sector, and 48 percent works in the services industry.

Energy/Power/Natural Resources

Arable land is Thailand's most important resource, and the country's fertile soils are watered by two major rivers (the Mekong and the Chao Phraya) and the reoccurring monsoon season. The flooding of the Chao Phraya delta benefits rice cultivation. Although the Mekong's high salt content inhibits agriculture, there is a salt deposit mining operation in the river's valley.

Most of Thailand's electricity comes from natural gas and coal, though there are a handful of hydroelectric plants.

Forestry

Due to the rapid economic growth in the 1980s and 1990s, many of Thailand's natural resources became depleted. Logging from natural forests was banned around 1990, and in the early 21st century, woods such as teak, rubberwood, and acacia are harvested from planted forests.

Mining/Metals

The southern peninsula is rich in tin, another valuable natural resource. Other mineral resources include coal, zinc, limestone, and tungsten. There is also a flourishing gemstone industry, which produces rubies and sapphires.

Agriculture

Approximately 38 percent of Thailand's labor force is employed in the agricultural sector, though it accounts for about 12 percent of GDP. Roughly 40 percent of the land is used for farming.

As in other Asian countries, rice is the largest crop, grown everywhere from the Chao Phraya River basin to the Khorat Plateau. A high duty is charged on rice exports, in order to ensure a consistent supply for the local population. Other important crops include cassava, corn, sugarcane, tobacco, vegetables, and tropical fruit.

Thailand is the world's largest exporter of natural rubber. The rubber plantations are mostly in the southeast and on the peninsula. Small-scale agriculture is also practiced throughout Thailand. The upland Hmong people grow opium, while the Karen grow rice in terraced fields. Tea and coffee are cultivated in the lowlands.

Animal Husbandry

Thailand is one of the world's largest exporters of chickens. In 2012, it was estimated that the country's livestock industry broke the 1 billion mark in the number of chickens produced. Farm-raised seafood, especially shrimp, is one of the country's top agricultural exports.

Tourism

Thailand is one of the top tourist destinations in Southeast Asia. Tourists are drawn the country's beautiful mountain vistas, tropical beaches, the urban excitement of Bangkok, the many historic Buddhist temples, and the resort islands off the Andaman coast.

The busiest tourism season is during the dry season between October and March, though the country is so popular it remains crowded year-round. However, there are safety considerations when traveling in Thailand. The southern provinces have been the target of occasional terrorist bombings, and the border with Myanmar is also dangerous due to landmines and bandits.

The tourism industry was damaged in 2003 due to fears over an outbreak of Severe Acute Respiratory Syndrome (SARS), despite the fact that no cases of the virus were recorded in the country. Thailand's popular Andaman coast was damaged in the tsunami that struck in December 2004, though it is expected that tourists will return once the coastal area is rebuilt. Restrictions imposed by the military government after the 2014 coup (such as making it illegal to have a beach umbrella) have dampened the prospects for growth in the tourist industry.

The political instability which began in early 2010 negatively affected tourism as over forty countries issued travel warnings to their citizens regarding Thailand. The Federation of Thai Industries estimated that the political unrest in 2010 cost the tourism industry about $1 billion USD, and the unrest and coup in 2014 cost 2.7 billion USD in potential tourism revenue.

Zoë Westhof, Barrett Hathcock, Beverly Ballaro

DO YOU KNOW?

- Thailand remains the only country in Southeast Asia that was never occupied by a European power. The mouth of the Chao Phraya River grows by several feet every year due to the sediment collected in the Gulf of Thailand.
- Bangkok's ceremonial name of Krung Thep is an abbreviated form of "Thep Mahanakhon Amon Rattanakosin Mahinthara Ayuthaya Mahadilok Phop Noppharat Ratchathani Burirom Udomratchaniwet Mahasathan Amon Piman Awatan Sathit Sakkathattiya Witsanukam Prasit," or "The city of angels, the great city, the residence of the Emerald Buddha, the impregnable city (of Ayutthaya) of God Indra, the grand capital of the world endowed with nine precious gems, the happy city, abounding in an enormous Royal Palace that resembles the heavenly abode where reigns the reincarnated god, a city given by Indra and built by Vishnukarn."
- To disguise the value of art from invading armies, craftsmen have been known to cover Bangkok's golden Buddha statues with stucco and plaster.

Bibliography

Baker, Chris and Pasuk Phongpaichit. *A History of Thailand.* 3rd ed. Cambridge, UK: Cambridge University Press, 2014.

Bangkok Post: <http://www.bangkokpost.com>.

Handley, Paul M. *The King Never Smiles: A Biography of Thailand's Bhumibol Adulyadej.* New Haven, CT: Yale University Press, 2006.

Jones, Roger S. *Thailand–Culture Smart!: A quick guide to customs and etiquette.* London: Kuperard, 2014.

Lonely Planet, China Williams, Mark Beales, Time Bewer, and Celeste Brash. *Lonely Planet Thailand.* Oakland, CA: Lonely Planet, 2014.

Mac Donald, Phil. *National Geographic Traveler: Thailand.* 2nd ed. National Geographic, 2006.

Osborne, Milton. *Southeast Asia: An Introductory History.* 11th ed. Sydney: Allen & Unwin, 2013.

Poomsan Becker, Benjawan. *Thai for Beginners.* Bangkok: Paiboon Publishing, 1995.

Stevenson, William. *The Revolutionary King.* London: Robinson Publishing, 2001.

Terwiel, B.J. *Thailand's Political History: From the Fall of Ayutthaya to Recent Times.* Bangkok: River Books Press Dist A/C, 2006.

Wyatt, David K. *Thailand: A Short History.* 2nd ed. New Haven, CT: Yale University Press, 2003.

Works Cited

"6 Decades of Thai Art Exhibition" http://www.rama9art.org/artisan/6decade/index.html

"An Overview of U.S.-East Asia Policy." *U.S. Department of State.* http://www.state.gov/p/eap/rls/rm/2004/33064.htm

Charuwan Chareonla, “Buddhist Arts of Thailand.” http://www.chiangmai-chiangrai.com/art_of_thai_dance.html
“Cultural Roots of Thai Behaviour.” http://www.thaicoach.com/new/eng_column.php?info_id=55
“Dance of Thailand”: http://en.wikipedia.org/wiki/Dance_of_Thailand
DEPDC: http://depdc.org/index.html
“Fascinating Aspects of the Thai Style House.” http://www.jimthompsonhouse.com/museum/fascinat.asp
“Laos’ forgotten exiles seek refugee status in Thailand.” *AlertNet.* http://www.alertnet.org/db/an_art/52132/2008/06/9-113652-1.html
“List of Cities in Thailand by Population.” http://en.wikipedia.org/wiki/List_of_cities in Thailand by population
“Ordination of a Buddhist Monk in Thailand.” http://www.thaibuddhist.com/ordination.html
“Resettlement of Myanmar refugees from Thailand tops 30,000.”
“Thai Architectural Style.” http://www.jimthompsonhouse.com/museum/architec.asp
“Thai art, architecture, music and dance.” http://www.1stopchiangmai.com/culture/art/
“Thai Food from the Central Region.” http://www.enjoythaifood.com/food_central.php
“Thai Food from the Northeastern Region.” http://www.enjoythaifood.com/food_northeastern.php
“Thai Food from the Northern Region.” http://www.enjoythaifood.com/food_north.php
“Thai Food from the Southern Region.” http://www.enjoythaifood.com/food southern.php
“Thai Highway Network.” http://en.wikipedia.org/wiki/Thai_highway_network
“Thai Literature.” http://www.britannica.com/EBchecked/topic/589615/Thai-literature
“Thailand: Country Reports on Human Rights Practices.” Bureau of Democracy, Human Rights, and Labor. *U.S. Department of State*. 2007. <http://www.state.gov/g/drl/rls/hrrpt/2007/100539.htm>
“Thailand Discusses the ASEAN Charter and Cooperation with Its ASEAN Partners.” http://www.boi.go.th/thai/how/press_releases_detail.asp?id=2333
“Thailand: UNHCR concerned over return of Lao Hmong.” http://www.unhcr.org/news/NEWS/4864b8b04.html
“Thailand World Report 2008-Human Rights Watch.” http://facthai.wordpress.com/2008/02/02/thailand-world-report-2008-human-rights-watch/
“The Arts” and “The Land and its People.” http://www.mahidol.ac.th/thailand/
“The Thai Buddha Image.” http://www.buddhanet.net/e-learning/history/buddhist-art/thaiart.html
“Top UNHCR official finds “progress overall” on visit to Thailand, Laos."
“Transport in Thailand.” http://en.wikipedia.org/wiki/Transport_in_Thailand
“Hmong Refugees in Thailand: A Population in Danger.” *Doctors without Borders.* http://www.doctorswithoutborders.org/news/article.cfm?id=2075
“Landmark Study on Domestic Violence.” *World Health Organization*. 24 Nov. 2005. <http://www.who.int/mediacentre/news/releases/2005/pr62/en/index.html>
“The ancient city of Ayutthaya - explorations in virtual reality. *GIS Development.*
http://thailandforvisitors.com/thaihist.html
“Thailand: Beheadings, Burnings in Renewed Terror Campaign.” *Human Rights Watch.* http://hrw.org/english/docs/2008/07/07/thaila19274.htm
“Thailand: Migrants’ Deaths Spotlight Exploitation.” *Human Rights Watch.* http://hrw.org/english/docs/2008/04/11/thaila18527.htm
“Thailand in 2007.” Institute of Public Policy Studies. 2007. *Institute of Public Policy Studies*. <http://www.fpps.or.th/news.php?detail=n1201025132.news>
“Thailand’s Role in the Stability of ASEAN.” *Ministry of Foreign Affairs, Kingdom of Thailand.* http://www.mfa.go.th/web/2654.php?id=19991
Taywaditep, Kittiwut Jod, and Eli Coleman and Pacharin Dumronggittigule. “Thailand.” *The International Encyclopedia of Sexuality*. <http://www2.hu-berlin.de/sexology/IES/thailand.html>
“Thai youth hooked on computer games.” *The Nation.* http://www.nationmultimedia.com/2007/07/26/national/national_30042584.php
“Bangkok Guide.” *Tourism Thailand.* http://www.tourismthailand.org/destination-guide/bangkok-10-1-1.html
“Thailand.” *U.S. Department of State.* http://www.state.gov/g/drl/rls/irf/2007/90155.htm
UNESCO: http://whc.unesco.org/en/statesparties/th/
“Thailand: Background.” *UNICEF.* http://www.unicef.org/infobycountry/Thailand_1022.html
Vanaspong, Chitraporn. “Thailand Has Made Progress in Law to Promote Women’s Rights.” *Asian Women’s Resource Exchange.* 26 Oct. 1999 <http://www.aworc.org/bpfa/gov/escap/26oct03.html>
“World Report 2002: Women’s Human Rights.” *Human Rights Watch.* 2002. <http://www.hrw.org/wr2k2/women.html>
www.apmforum.com/news/ap110500.html
www.buddhanet.net/pdf_file/budartthai2.pdf
www.gisdevelopment.net/application/archaeology/general/archg0007.html
www.unhcr.org/news/NEWS/463a00964.html
www.unhcr.org/news/NEWS/486242242.html

Harvesting salt in Vietnam/Stock photo © dzalcman

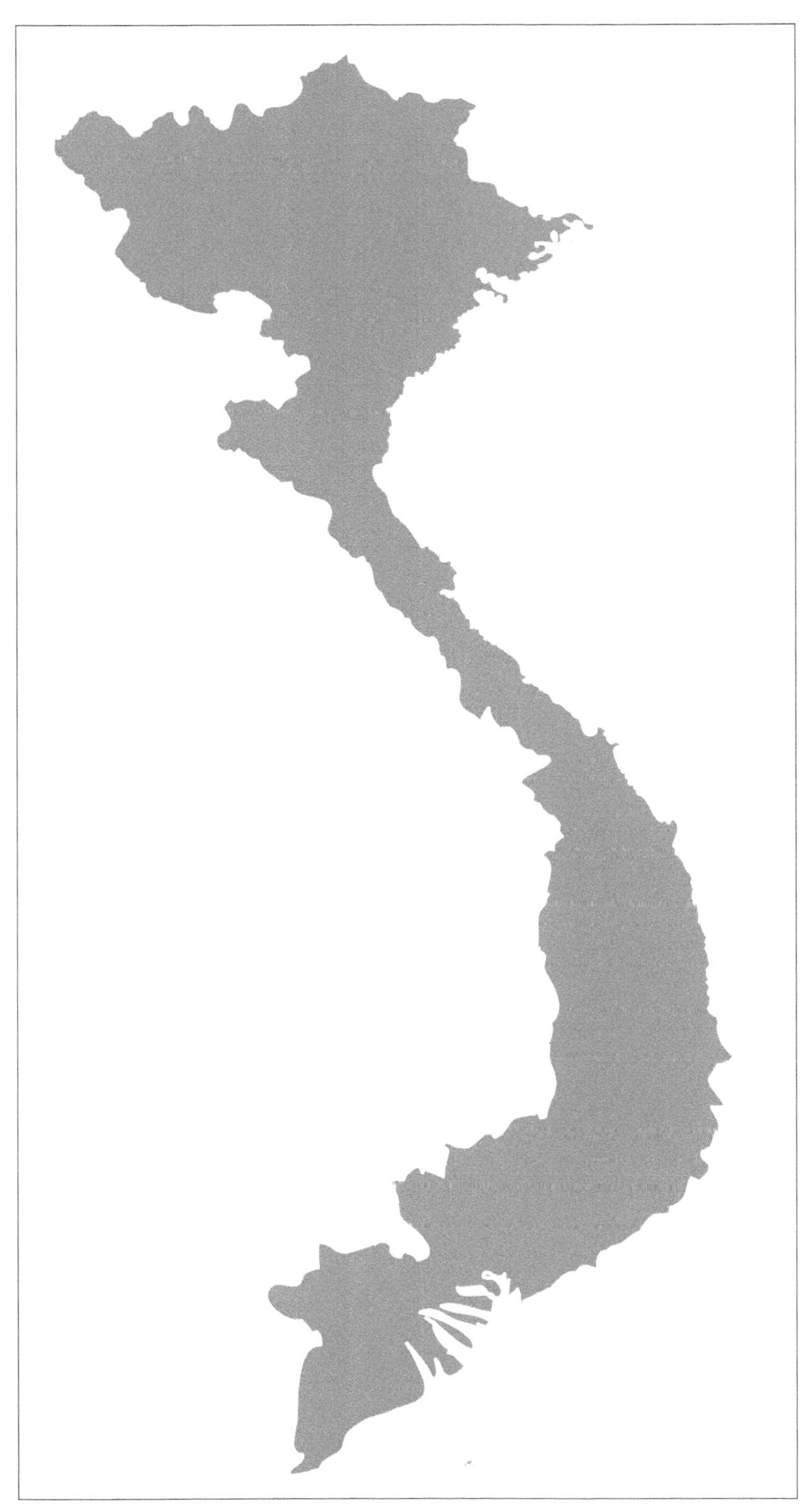

VIETNAM

Introduction

The Socialist Republic of Vietnam is located in southeastern Asia. Before it was colonized by France, Vietnam had nine centuries of independent history behind it. The French colonial period was painful for the country and culminated in North Vietnam repelling the French and establishing communist rule. After years of brutal conflict, involving first France and then the United States, Vietnam was united in 1976, and the North's communist government gained control of the entire country.

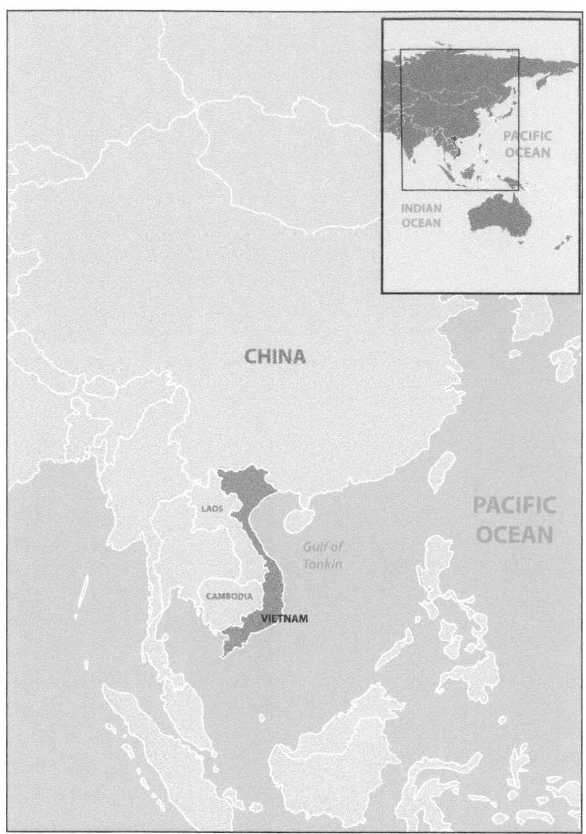

GENERAL INFORMATION

Official Language: Vietnamese
Population: 93,421,835 (2014 estimate)
Currency: Dong
Coins: Vietnamese currency has five coin denominations: 200; 500; 1,000; 2,000; and 5,000.
Land Area: 310,070 square kilometers (119,687 square miles)
Water Area: 21,140 square kilometers (8,160 square miles)
National Motto: "Doc lap, tu do, hanh phuc" ("Independence, liberty, and happiness")
National Anthem: "Tien Quan Ca" ("The Army March")
Capital: Hanoi
Time Zone: GMT +7
Flag Description: The flag of Vietnam is red and features a five-point yellow star in its center.

Population

As of 2014, Vietnam has an estimated 93,421,835 people, with a population growth rate of 1 percent. The median age is just over 29 years old. Approximately 32 percent of the population lives in urban areas.

Though the average population density is 301 persons per square kilometers (780 per square mile), most of the population is concentrated in the river deltas, such as the Mekong River Delta in the southwestern region of the country, which is home to approximately 17.5 million people. Approximately 68 percent of the population is rural, a figure that is continuing to diminish annually. Ho Chi Minh City has the largest population, with 7.8 million people; Hanoi has 2.9 million people. Danang and Haiphong are other important urban centers.

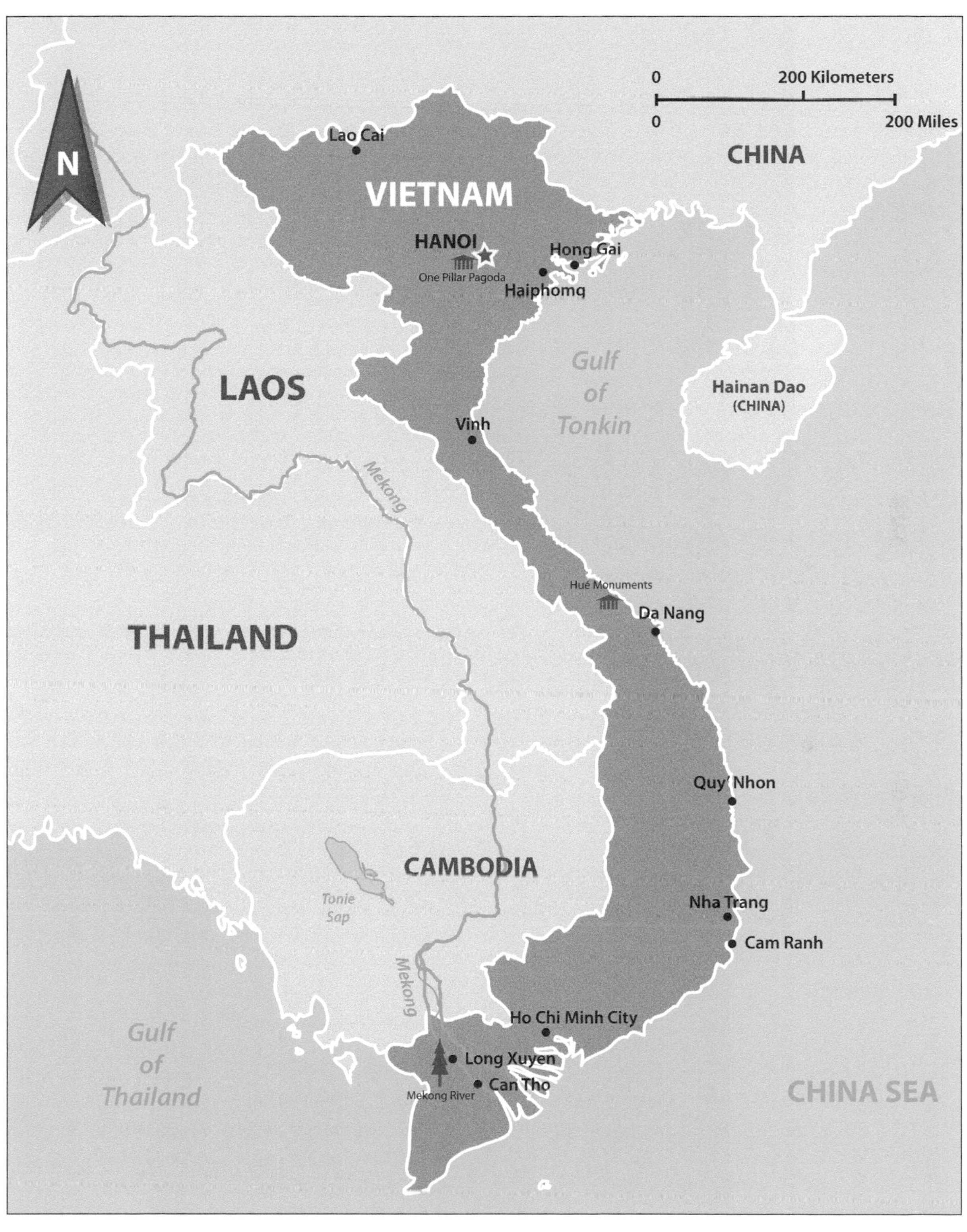

0
200 Kilometers
0
200 Miles
N
CHINA
Lao Cai
VIETNAM
HANOI
One Pillar Pagoda
Hong Gai
Haiphomq
LAOS
Gulf of Tonkin
Hainan Dao (CHINA)
Vinh
Mekong
Hué Monuments
Da Nang
THAILAND
Quy Nhon
CAMBODIA
Tonie Sap
Nha Trang
Cam Ranh
Mekong
Ho Chi Minh City
Long Xuyen
Can Tho
Mekong River
Gulf of Thailand
CHINA SEA

Principal Cities by Population (2013 estimates):

- Ho Chi Minh City (7,818,200)
- Hanoi (2,955,000)
- Haiphong (925,000)
- Da Nang (834,000)
- Can Tho (759,000)
- Bien Hoa (749,000)
- Nha Trang (392,279)
- Hue (333,715)
- Phan Thiet (255,000)
- Ba Ria (122,424)

Languages

Vietnamese is the official language of the country; it is also a common second language for ethnic minorities in Vietnam. The Vietnamese language is part of the Austro-Asiatic language family, and for centuries, it was written with Chinese characters. By the 17th century, its written form changed to Quoc Ngu, which was developed by European missionaries and featured Roman characters. Like Chinese, Vietnamese semantics depend on the tone of speech. The language also features a large number of vowels. English is becoming an increasingly popular second language in Vietnam in the early 21st century and is widely taught in the country's schools.

Native People & Ethnic Groups

As of 2014, ethnic Vietnamese, known as Viet or Kinh, account for over 87 percent of the population. The Tay ethnic group constitutes around two percent of the country's population, and approximately 1.7 percent identifies as Thai. Other ethnic groups are the Khmer (1.3 percent) and Chinese (1.1 percent). The Montagnards, the tribal peoples who live in the central highlands, can be divided into as many as 50 ethnic groups. It is estimated that more than one million Montagnards reside in Vietnam as of 2010.

The various ethnic groups in Vietnam have co-existed peacefully for the most part. However, the tribes of the central highlands, collectively known as the Montagnards, have resisted government control. The central government, fearing a secessionist movement, has clamped down on their protests. In 2004, the Vietnamese government acknowledged that at least part of the dispute between it and the Montagnards stems from the government use of central highland forest for industrial crops, as well as for allowing large numbers of Kinh (the majority ethnic group) to migrate to the central highlands. In 2006, the organization Human Rights Watch issued a report on various human rights violations of the Montagnards, claiming the group's political and religious freedoms were violated by the Vietnamese government in 2005 and 2006. Similar reports were given in 2011 and 2014.

Religions

There is some discrepancy regarding religious statistics in Vietnam. The United States Department of State, in its 2013 report on religious freedom in Vietnam, stated that approximately 50 percent of the country's population is Buddhist. In contrast, the Vietnamese Office of Religious Affairs states that, according to the country's 1999 census, roughly 11 percent of the country is Buddhist and again understated religion in the nation in 2014 giving the total of all religions in the country at 25 percent. It is generally accepted that the most common form of Buddhism practiced is Mahayana Buddhism. A 2014 report from a UN visit, documented the lack of religious freedom in Vietnam. As of that time, all of the recognized religious groups were heavily regulated by the government, while many others were refused recognition and the ability to practice their faith openly.

According to the 2013 U.S. Department of State report, there were between 6 and 7 million Roman Catholics in Vietnam; however, the Vietnamese government has stated that, in the early 21st century, there are just over five million Catholics in the country. The Vietnamese government also states there are approximately 421,000 Protestants, but the 2013 Department of State report gave the number as between 950,000 and 1.8 million Protestants in Vietnam.

Minority religions include Cao Dai, of which the government estimates there are 2.2 million, while others claim there are as many as four million; Hoa Hao, of which the government estimates there are 1.3 million while the State Department asserts there are could be up to three million; and Islam, of which there are an estimated 680,000 adherents. Non-sanctioned religions are not allowed freedom of worship in Vietnam.

Climate

Vietnam has a hot, humid and wet climate. Temperatures average between 5° and 37° Celsius (41° and 99° Fahrenheit); the southern delta and the central coast experience the hottest temperatures while the northern plains, where the seasons are more pronounced, become cold at night.

Annual precipitation averages between 1,200 and 3,000 millimeters (47 and 118 inches). Rainfall is heavier in the south and along the central coast, and the Mekong Delta area experiences the longest rainy season, lasting from May to October. Outside of the monsoon season, the country is typically dry.

The central coast is prone to typhoons between May and January. The typhoons can cause loss of life and extensive flooding, especially of the river deltas, where arable land and property are often destroyed.

ENVIRONMENT & GEOGRAPHY

Topography

Vietnam is bordered by Cambodia, Laos, and China. The South China Sea forms its long coastline. Vietnam is long and narrow, with mountains in the north, central highlands, tropical lowlands in the south, and river deltas in the south and northeast. The northern mountains, which are part of the Yunnan Plateau of China, contain the country's highest point: Fan Si Pan, at an elevation of 3,143 meters (10,312 feet). The central highlands, known as the Giai Truong Son, are densely covered with rainforest, and are sparsely populated.

In the northeast, along the Gulf of Tonkin, is the Red River Delta, a heavily cultivated area of alluvial soils. The other major delta, the Mekong River Delta, dominates the southern lowlands and provides equally rich agricultural land. These two deltas are the major geographical features of Vietnam's 3,444 kilometers (2,140 miles) of coastline. The Red River and the Mekong River are Vietnam's most important rivers. Both are navigable and serve as important shipping routes. Minor rivers include the Thai Binh, the Ca, the Ma, the Han, and the Dong Nai.

Plants & Animals

Vietnam's lush environment contains many plants and trees, and forest accounts for 28 percent of the country's total area. In the mountain forests, both deciduous and evergreen trees are found, including ebony, teak, and pine. Some forests are made even denser by woody vines and broad-leafed plants. In the lower areas, palms, fruit trees, bamboo, grass and brush predominate; mangroves are commonly found in delta areas. Much of the terrain in Vietnam has been cleared for the intense agriculture in which many Vietnamese are involved.

The forests provide habitats for an array of animals. Elephants, tapirs, tigers, leopards, wild oxen, bears, deer, wild boar and numerous smaller mammals such as monkeys and squirrels are all found. Large populations of birds and reptiles also flourish.

Deforestation, poaching, and illegal smuggling threaten many animal species. Among them are bears, several primates, elephants, and large cats. Some animals which were thought to be extinct or not known to exist have been found in Vietnam in recent years. These include the sao la, similar to the cow, and the Java rhinoceros.

CUSTOMS & COURTESIES

Greetings

A typical Vietnamese greeting is "Xin chao" ("Hello"), which is pronounced "seen chow." Men usually shake hands upon greeting and parting, while women are more inclined to bow their heads slightly in respect. It is considered polite to bow one's head to the elderly, who will not typically extend a hand to be shaken. Greetings are typically very formal when conducting business, and politeness is considered a must. Traditionally, businessmen will shake hands upon greeting each other, unless conducting business with a woman.

Young adults usually greet each other in the same manner as adults, sometimes shaking both hands. Children are expected to bow to elders, and are never touched on the head by anyone other than an elder relative.

Gestures & Etiquette

In Vietnam, there are accepted codes of behavior in public. For example, men and women do not show affection in public, including embracing or holding hands. However, it is acceptable for members of the same sex to hold hands while walking. It is also acceptable to eat in public while walking down a street, and for men to spit in public.

Gestures are important in Vietnamese culture. Typically, the Vietnamese beckon to someone by extending an arm—palm down—and moving the fingers in a scratching motion. To beckon with an index finger is considered rude. Similarly, pointing with an index finger is considered inappropriate. Instead, the whole hand should be used, with fingers closed. In addition, standing with one's hands on the hips is considered very impolite in Vietnam, as is crossing one's arms across the chest. Generally, all conversation should be conducted in a quiet and reserved manner, with minimal gestures.

Eating/Meals

The Vietnamese typically eat three meals a day, with noodles and rice the staples of the national diet. Often, lunch is eaten on the street, but dinner is always eaten with the family. Eating with the family in Vietnam is usually an informal affair, even with guests present. (Dining out, on the other hand, is a more formal affair, with the host expected to pay for the meal.) Typically, food is served in a communal fashion (placed in the middle of the table, with everyone serving themselves). Food is commonly eaten with chopsticks, which are kept on the table or a chopstick rest when not being used. In addition, rice bowls are typically held in the hand, so as not to appear lazy, and soupspoons should be held in the left hand while eating soup.

Generally, the elderly are seated first, whereupon the host will then direct the rest of the guests to their seating. Tea may be offered before the meal. Traditionally, the serving of tea is a ritual of hospitality, and should not be refused. At the conclusion of a meal, it is customary for drinks to be served. Also, the Vietnamese may linger for a long time at the table, especially when dining out or in the interests of business.

Visiting

When visiting in Vietnamese culture, it is considered respectful to remove one's shoes. It is also customary to bring a gift. Typically, this gift should be for the woman of the house, but gifts are often brought for any children or elderly parents in the home as well. Gifts are usually wrapped in colorful paper, and usually consist of household items, such as designer soaps, cosmetics, sweets, fruits, incense or photos for the home. Gifts that typically aren't given include anything black or handkerchiefs, as both are considered bad omens. Additionally, flowers are only given from men to women.

LIFESTYLE

Family

Traditionally, Vietnamese families are very close, both emotionally and physically, and the extended family often works and lives together. This extended family unit can include parents, grandparents, siblings, aunts and uncles, and even first, second or third cousins. In general, the welfare of the family unit is more important than that of any individual member. Each member of the family has a specific duty to the whole.

Typically, the father is the provider for the whole family, with the eldest brother being responsible for the family when the father is unavailable. The wife is traditionally expected to submit to her husband and show respect for his parents, and children are expected to obey their parents and respect each other. In addition, good choices reflect well on the family, while poor choices and behavior shame everyone in the family. Therefore, important decisions are usually made with the input of the entire family.

Another important family custom in traditional Vietnamese culture is ancestor worship. Many Vietnamese believe that the souls of relatives are still present on earth, and that the living are able to maintain a spiritual connection with them. Often, the anniversary of a relative or ancestor's death is a special and observed occasion.

Housing

Homes in Vietnam are generally smaller than residences in most Western countries. In rural areas, homes are usually made of native materials such as bamboo trees, dry rice plants, straw and mud. It is also common for rural homes along rivers and in the mountains to be built on stilts. This is due to flooding and for the accommodation of animals and other agricultural necessities.

Homes in urban areas are typically constructed of brick, cement, or imported building materials, except for high-rise apartments and other modern commercial buildings. Apartments in high-rises are also generally small, and typically mimic their detached counterparts as far as interior design. In recent years, overcrowding and lack of housing have become major issues in urban areas, particularly large cities. This is reflected in the urban sprawl of informal residences and horizontal architecture (the addition of more stories to buildings).

Traditionally, Vietnamese houses have one room that is reserved for worship, and may contain an ancestor altar. This is where the Vietnamese worship their ancestors. Vietnamese houses also contain another room or two for living space, one of which includes a kitchen area. It is also common to see beds made of either wood or bamboo and covered with a reed mat.

Food

Vietnamese food relies heavily on rice, wheat, legumes, fresh herbs and vegetables. Meat is treated as a condiment, and oil is used minimally. Although cuisine varies widely between areas, there are some similarities. In the north, salty and stir-fried dishes are popular. In the south, spicy, sweet and curried dishes are common. Rice plays an essential role, but noodles are the popular choice. Noodles can be eaten hot or cold, wet or dry, placed in soup or alone, and are commonly consumed at all meals. In addition, the cuisines of China, Thailand and Cambodia have all been influential in shaping the Vietnamese diet.

An average meal for a Vietnamese family would include rice, a meat or seafood dish with vegetables, another stand-alone vegetable dish, soup, and a fish or soy sauce for dipping. All dishes would be in shared containers other than individual bowls of rice. Phở is probably the most popular noodle dish. It is a traditional rice-noodle soup, served in clear beef broth with cuts of beef. It is served with garnishes such as green onions, cilantro, lemon wedges, and bean sprouts.

Street food is popular throughout Vietnam. Typical lunch items include bánh mì, a sandwich of meat (usually grilled beef, pork, or cold cuts) garnished with cilantro and pickled vegetables. Served on a French baguette, the sandwich is a good example of the blending of native and colonial influences. Bánh xèo is a type of crepe made with rice flour and coconut milk, and filled with meat, shrimp, vegetables, and bean sprouts. Pieces of the crepe are typically eaten wrapped in lettuce leaves.

Bánh chung is a rice cake that is extremely meaningful and popular for the Vietnamese. Eaten during Tet (New Year), the cakes are made with sticky rice and stuffed with a buttery bean filling made from beans, pork, and peppers. After stuffing, the rice cake is wrapped in banana leaf and boiled for up to 12 hours, which tints the outer rice green. They can be eaten warm, at room temperature, or fried.

Life's Milestones

In Vietnamese culture, age is synonymous with wisdom, and the elderly are viewed with esteem and pride. For this reason, the Vietnamese honor the elderly with a celebration of longevity. In the past, this celebration was held when a person turned 40 years old. Nowadays, as life expectancy has increased, this celebration is held when parents or grandparents reach the ages of 70, 80, or 90 years.

These ceremonies of longevity are usually organized by children or grandchildren, and are held on birthdays or during the spring days of Tet, which is the Vietnamese New Year celebration. Old men are typically invited to sit on red mats, and women are offered red dresses. Food is generally served, and ancestors are honored and remembered. The purpose of the ceremony is to show devotion and respect to the elderly, and to show the family's joy and pride in having a relative who has been able to live a long and prosperous life.

CULTURAL HISTORY

Art

Traditional crafts such as ceramics and pottery started to show signs of artistic flair during the Neolithic Era (c. 7000–3300 BCE), although some pottery has been dated back to the Stone Age (prior to 10,000 BCE). However, it was not until the Bronze Age (1000 BCE–300 CE) that Vietnamese art began to fully emerge, and pottery and ceramics were increasingly adorned with colored coatings, similar to enamel. Confucianism, Buddhism, and Taoism all continued to have an influence on ceramics and pottery, and most notably on sculpture. Other traditional handicrafts that flourished in Vietnam included embroidery, bamboo crafts, lacquer ware, jewelry making and copper casting. The latter was used to make brass drums and statues.

The golden age of Vietnamese art began during the Ly Dynasty in the 12th century. Ceramics created during this time became famous across Southeast Asia, and were known for the use of three subdued colors in unusual designs and patterns. Woodblock carving was also popular and figured prominently in Vietnamese folk painting. Generally, folk painting in Vietnam was represented by two main types: religious paintings and paintings associated with Tet, the Vietnamese New Year. Several well-known styles of Vietnamese folk painting include Dung Ho paintings, which emerged in the Red River Delta region, and Hang Trong paintings, typically painted on large sheets of paper with brilliant colors. During the subsequent Tran Dynasty (1225–1400 CE), more subdued forms of art were practiced.

During the early part of the 15th century, when Vietnam was ruled by the Chinese Ming Dynasty, Chinese culture was widely promoted. Consequently, Vietnamese writing and art were suppressed or removed to China. Therefore, art created during this time was predominantly in the style of the Ming Dynasty. When the Ming Dynasty ended its reign in 1427 with the rise of the Later Le Dynasty (1428–1788), a renewed and sustained interest in creating traditional Vietnamese art developed, including ceramics and performing arts.

With the emergence of French colonialism in the 19th century, Vietnamese art adopted European artistic influences and traditions. By the early 20th century, numerous French art schools were established. In particular, Vietnamese artists began to use French techniques with silk and embroidered paintings, lacquer ware, and ceramics. Modern Vietnamese art continues to reflect this blend of French influences and traditional Vietnamese and other Asian styles, including minimal and subdued use of color, and the use of ancient Chinese design.

Architecture

One of the earliest architectural traditions to develop in Vietnam was the construction of stilt houses. This type of architecture dates back to prehistoric times. Typically, stilt houses were dwellings built on stilts, or pilings, over a body of water. The Vietnamese stilt houses were similar to the stilt houses of Thailand, and were constructed of bamboo and wood, with angled roofs. These simplistic houses were the predominant style until the reign of the Chinese Han Dynasty (206 BCE-220 CE), which marked the beginning of 1,000 years of Chinese rule.

Following the establishment of Chinese rule in Vietnam, Chinese architecture became the greatest influence on all types of Vietnamese buildings. This was especially true for buildings designed for worship and royalty, such as pagodas and palaces. General characteristics of this Chinese influence included intricate carvings, embellished motifs and tiled and ornamental roofs—typically supported by pillars rather than weight-bearing walls. However, in contrast with the traditions of Chinese architecture, the colors typically used in Vietnamese architectural styles were much more subdued and muted, reflecting the native preferences. Examples of this architecture include the Temple of Literature (Văn Miếu), located in Hanoi and built during the Ly Dynasty (1009–1225 CE), and the Imperial City, a walled palace which was built to mimic the Forbidden City in Beijing, China.

During the 19th century, as France began to colonize Vietnam, French architecture became a predominate influence. However this colonial French architecture continued to reflect the climate, resulting in its own unique style. Many examples of this distinctive style are evident in government buildings and houses built for the aristocracy, including the Opera House and various mansions located in the capital of Hanoi.

Drama

There are four major types of traditional drama in Vietnam. The first type of traditional drama, Cai luong, originated as folk opera from South Vietnam. Largely developed in the early 20th century, this opera is known for using extensive vibrato and remains a popular stage performance in modern Vietnam.

The second type of drama is the most widespread of all forms of traditional Vietnamese music and dance, and is often referred to as Vietnamese popular theater. The Hat chèo, or Cheo opera as it is more commonly called, is a complex performance involving folk songs, pantomime, instrumental music, dances, interpretive storytelling, acrobatic scenes and even magic tricks. The blending of tragedy and comedy is a popular theme in this style of drama. The play is typically heralded by the Cheo drum, which calls the audience to view it.

Classical opera in Vietnam is known as Tuong, or hát bội in the south. It originated during the Ly and Tran dynasties, and was a theatre form largely influenced and adapted from Chinese opera. Originally performed for the royal court, it was taken up by traveling troops who performed for villagers. This opera typically features the same characters in different situations.

One particular theater tradition largely unique to Vietnam is mua roi nuoc, or Vietnamese water puppetry (mua roi nuoc means "puppets that dance on water"). This style of puppetry is typically performed in standing water, with the puppeteers behind a screen. The tradition is believed to date back as far as the 10th century in northern Vietnam, particularly in the Red River Delta, an area characterized by its many rivers and humid climate. It is believed water puppetry evolved from ceremonies related to the harvest and fishing, and storylines usually involve traditional scenes of Vietnamese life. Overall, Vietnam has a long tradition of puppetry, and the use of hand puppets were an important part of religious ceremonies and festivals in ancient times.

Music

Traditional Vietnamese music varies widely from region to region, with some genres better known than others. These include quan ho, which is sung without accompaniment and often in an improvised style. Quan ho has a long history of being used in courtships rituals. Imperial court music consisted of a wide variety of traditional instruments, including the t'rung (bamboo xylophone) and dàn bầu (monochord zither), as well as lavishly costumed musicians and dancers.

Ca trù originated in the imperial court as a type of chamber music. Usually performed by beautiful women as a form of entertainment for the male aristocracy, it was condemned by the Vietnamese government in the 20th century, but has seen a revival in popularity due to its cultural significance. Another significant style of court music was nha nhac, a refined and scholarly style of music that came to Vietnam during the Ho Dynasty (1400–1407). The cultural significance of this style of royal music was recognized in 2003 when the United Nations Educational, Scientific and Cultural Organization (UNESCO) designated nha nhac as an Intangible Cultural Heritage. The same consideration is now being given to ca trù.

Literature

Early Vietnamese literature, although created largely by Vietnamese speaking people, was written in classical Chinese (Han) due to the long history of Chinese rule in the country. Around the 10th century, a new style of writing developed, called chu nom. This style of writing allowed writers to compose in Vietnamese using modified Chinese characters.

One of the most famous of all authors who wrote in chu nom was a poet named Ho Xuan Huong (1772–1822). Her work has been since translated and remains popular today. By the early 20th century, quoc ngu (a romanticized Vietnamese writing system) became popular after the French mandated its use. Famous works of literature written in quoc ngu by Vietnamese authors include *The Tale of Kieu* by Nguyen Du (1765–1820) and *Luc Van Tien* by Nguyen Dinh Chieu (1822–1888). Vietnamese literature particularly developed during the war years (1945–1975), and typically featured themes of realism and heroism.

Film

Vietnamese cinema began during the French colonial era, and early filmmaking largely consisted of government propaganda and newsreels and documentary-style films. In 1959, the Hanoi Film School was established. That same year, the Democratic Republic of Vietnam's first feature film, *Chung một Dòng sông* ("Together on the Same River"), was released. During this period, Vietnamese cinema began to fully emerge, particularly as it became focused on documenting the Vietnam War (1959–1975). The reunification of North and South Vietnam in 1975, and the emergence of social realism as a cinematic movement in Vietnamese filmmaking, helped mark the shift to contemporary cinema in Vietnam. In 1979, the Vietnam Film Institute (VFI) was established.

However, film production in Vietnam has witnessed a significant decline since the late twentieth century. Today, most features are commercial in nature – romantic comedy is among the most popular genres. Tran Anh Hung (1962–) is the most well-known director abroad and has produced several acclaimed features. Not all of his films, however, have been screened in his native country.

CULTURE

Arts & Entertainment

The state of contemporary art in Vietnam has been one of constant struggle. Traditional Vietnamese art forms have been protected by the government as significant cultural resources. However, these art forms have not adequately reflected the modern advances—including rapid economic growth—that have been made in other areas of Vietnamese culture. Rather, they reflect the ancient and traditional values and customs of the past.

Prior to the 1990s, Vietnamese art had not been allowed to evolve. The government censored any art that was not conservative, and controlled performance art by requiring approval before it was performed. Art schools in Vietnam still taught the classic French forms, which left contemporary artists struggling to learn new techniques on their own. In addition, Vietnam did not have a supportive professional artist community, and it was difficult for contemporary artists to procure funds or even persuade the few art critics in the cities to take their work seriously. Furthermore, art galleries reserved their space for traditional Vietnamese art, which was more desirable and profitable.

Things began to change in the late 20th century. Private and small exhibitions of contemporary art, often held at private residences, became increasingly popular. As a result, the first contemporary art studio in Hanoi, called the House on Stilts (Nha San Studio), was established in 1998. This contemporary art center has since taken a lead role in promoting and supporting Vietnam's contemporary art scene. Despite the government's new liberal attitude toward art, Vietnamese art does not seek to shock, nor would it be considered innovative by European standards. In fact, there has been a renewed interest in the use of traditional techniques among Vietnamese artists, perhaps inspired by the government's recent efforts to renovate historical sites in the country.

In literature, several authors and works stand out for their influence and popularity. Poetry remains the most respected literary form, and "Kim Van Kieu," a philosophical poem by Nguyen Du (1765–1820), is one of the most widely known works. The contemporary novelist and short story writer Nguyen Huy Thiep (1950–) has taken advantage of the liberalizing trend to depict Vietnamese society in frank, realistic detail rather than in a Socialist Realist style.

The Vietnamese also practice many traditional arts, including woodblock printing, wood carving and inlay, lacquer work, silk painting, religious sculpture, weaving, and ceramics. In their leisure time, Vietnamese enjoy playing cards or mahjongg. Football (soccer), volleyball, and cycling are popular sports. Many people practice tai chi or tha cuc guyen, activities that stress overall fitness and breathing through series of movements.

Cultural Sites & Landmarks

Vietnam's patriotic and distinct culture, with its various foreign influences, is reflected in the country's countless cultural sites and landmarks. In addition, Vietnam's natural attractions and climate have shaped the country's cultural heritage. The importance of these influences on Vietnamese culture is represented by the five World Heritage Sites recognized in Vietnam, as designated by UNESCO. They include the Hué Monuments, the ancient town of Hoi An, the Hindu Temple complex of My Son, the Ha Long Bay and Phong Nha-Ke Bang National Park.

The Complex of Hué Monuments, located in central Vietnam on the banks of the Perfume River, is a collection of historic monuments. This former feudal capital of Vietnam, established in 1802, features the Capital City, the Imperial City, the Forbidden Purple City and the Inner City, as well as the tombs of numerous emperors. The government is currently refurbishing these historic monuments in order to preserve them. On the coast of south-central Vietnam is the ancient town of Hoi An, an important trading port from the 15th through the 19th centuries. The town was preserved as a World Heritage Site for its blend of architectural and urban influences. Similar to Hoi An, the My Son Hindu Temple complex was recognized by UNESCO for its significant display of cultural interchange. It also marks the introduction of Hindu architecture into Southeast Asia.

Ha Long Bay, in the Gulf of Tonkin, consists of over 2,000 towering limestone islands and islets, most of which are uninhabited by humans. Some of the islands have been given names, such as elephant or fighting cock, based on their shapes. Many are hollow and filled with caves. Some of the islands are home to floating villages, mostly populated with fishermen who fish for over 200 species of fish and 450 different kinds of mollusks. The islands of Ha Long Bay are also home to hundreds of different species of island wildlife and flora, including bantams, antelopes, monkeys, and iguanas. Some of these species struggle to survive the tourist traffic.

The Phong Nha-Ke Bang National Park was designated as a World Heritage Site for its geographical importance and the insight it provides into the history of the planet. In particular, the park is famous for its limestone forest, karst landscapes (formed by the dissolution of soluble rocks) and artificial caves. In addition, Phong Nha is home to the longest underground river in the world, as well as the largest caverns. There is a wide variety of florae and faunae in the park.

The cultural influence of Chinese rule and French colonialism, particularly architecture, is evident in Hanoi, the capital of Vietnam. In this urban center, old colonial buildings are commonly interspersed with modern high-rise buildings and commercial architecture. In addition, various temples are found throughout the city, and the center of the city features numerous historic monuments. The One Pillar Pagoda is one of the most ancient structures in Hanoi. It was designed by Emperor Ly Thai To (974–1029), who is said to have had a dream that the Goddess of Mercy was sitting on a Lotus flower offering him a son. Other cultural attractions and landmarks include Hoan Kiem Lake ("Lake of the Returned Sword"), located in the city's historic center, the National Museum of Vietnamese History and the Museum of Fine Arts, the Hanoi Opera House and the Thang Long Water Puppets Theatre.

Libraries & Museums

The National Museum of Vietnamese History and the Vietnam Fine Arts Museum are both located in Hanoi. Other museums include the Vietnam Museum of Ethnology, the Museum of Cham Sculpture (in Danang), the Nam Bo Women's Museum (in Saigon), and several city or regional museums, as well as a wealth of war monuments and memorials. The National Library of Vietnam and the Library for Social and Human Sciences are also located in Hanoi.

Holidays

Religious holidays and festivals in Vietnam follow the lunar calendar; the major holidays are celebrated throughout the country, whereas many minor holidays are celebrated only at the provincial or town level. Tet, in late January or early February, is the Vietnamese New Year and the country's most important festival. Resolutions for the new year are made, families gather for feasts, and children receive small gifts of money in the week-long celebrations. On the third day, families visit the graves of their ancestors to leave food for them. A similar spiritual idea informs Thanh Minh (April), which commemorates dead family members, and Trung Nguyen (August), when people offer food and gifts to the forgotten dead.

The following national holidays are also marked: the Foundation of the Communist Party (February 3), the Liberation of Saigon (April 30), the Defeat of the French at Dien Bien Phu (May 7) and the anniversary of Ho Chi Minh's birth (May 19) and death (September 3).

Youth Culture

The Vietnamese youth of the 21st century are the first generation to experience a true youth culture. In the past, young adults were expected to mimic their elders in beliefs, lifestyle, and behavior. In today's culture, youth are pulling away from that tradition and shaping their own values, identity, symbols and language.

However, teenagers in Vietnam are more cautious than their Western counterparts. They are, for the most part, apolitical, modest, polite, and are largely focused on educating themselves to be savvy consumers and world citizens. In addition, rather than focusing on Western countries, Vietnamese youth tend to adopt the trends of youth in Japan and South Korea, including hairstyles, fashion, music and technology. In many ways, the youth of Vietnam, although beginning to define their place in the world, are considered 15 to 20 years behind their counterparts in South Korea and Japan.

Education in Vietnam is available to all, but the curriculum remains a subject of consistent controversy in the early 21st century, particularly regarding health education. No drug or sex education is taught, and research shows that the average age of first sexual activity among Vietnamese teens is 19.7 years of age, according to an international study. Generally, Internet access and cable TV is restricted to privileged urban youth, although Internet use has grown rapidly from 2005 to 2015. However, there is internet censorship and the cables supporting the service have had frequent outages.

SOCIETY

Transportation

Drivers in Vietnam use the right side of the road. Bicycles and motorcycles, which are common, frequently move in the opposite direction of oncoming traffic, although this practice is illegal. According to the U.S. State Department, traffic accidents are the leading cause of injury and death to foreign visitors.

Vietnam's system of expressways is not very well maintained. One issue affecting roads, particularly in rural areas, are landslides. Although taxis are available in the cities, it is recommended that travelers and tourists alike conduct business with only reputable companies.

The main mode of transportation is by motorbike. Most Vietnamese use motorbikes (or traditional bikes) to transport themselves to and from work, as well as for carrying groceries, other items, and even passengers. It is common to see motorbikes and bikes parked throughout urban areas.

Transportation Infrastructure

Vietnam's transportation system is still very much a work in progress. The nation's infrastructure, including its ports, state-run airports and aircraft, and road conditions, are generally outdated. However, the government has recently made arrangements to purchase airplanes from the United States and Europe. Large goods are transported by barge via Vietnam's many rivers and canals.

International airports include Noi Bai International Airport in Hanoi, Tan Son Nhat International Airport in Ho Chi Minh City, and Da Nang International Airport in Danang.

Media & Communications

All forms of media in Vietnam are regulated by the government, which considers the press to be a tool for government information and propaganda. Certain forms of media are more tightly regulated than others, such as newspapers. The government also regulates the programming of state-controlled radio and television stations. Satellite television and foreign broadcasting are increasingly being allowed in hotels, clubs, government offices and even private residences in major cities. It is estimated that up to 90 percent of all households in Vietnam have some kind of television service.

The Internet, unlike print media, is not strongly regulated. As such, no obvious restrictions are in place, although anti-government sites and blogs are typically blocked, and citizens who host or create such sites are often subject to arrest. In fact, the government generally perceives the advent of Internet use and technology as necessary for the country's advancement in the world. While the nation has not met its Internet penetration goals, as of 2014, 42 percent of the population has access to the Internet, a nine percent increase from the previous year.

SOCIAL DEVELOPMENT

Standard of Living

Vietnam is ranked 121st out of 187 countries on the 2013 Human Development Index.

Water Consumption

Over half of the domestic water supply in Vietnam comes from groundwater, which is used by one-third of the urban populations and two-thirds of the rural. As of 2011, over 98 percent of the country's urban population has access to clean water. In rural areas, this was about 93 percent. However, the UN water quality index for 2010 was 64.9, on a scale were 100 was a water supply meeting all pollution and cleanliness standards.

Education

Since the French colonial period, education in Vietnam has been based on modern principles. These were later combined with communist ideology and Vietnamese history and culture. In limited ways, the communist ideology has begun giving ground to broader ideas.

Though the literacy rate is high, averaging 93 percent in 2011, the levels of overall education are quite low in Vietnam. Schooling is free and compulsory for five years, but attendance drops off dramatically after primary school, with the figure of 65 percent given by the World Bank in 2010. Families must pay for secondary school and post-secondary education, and many cannot afford to continue their children's education. In rural areas, where there are shortages of facilities and educational materials, many children do not progress beyond the third grade.

In 2014, there were over 234 universities and 185 junior colleges in Vietnam. It was estimated that, during that during 2004, approximately two percent of the population studied at the post-graduate level. This was seen as insufficient by the government, which has doubled the number of graduate students in the last decade. The major Vietnamese cities have universities, with those in Hanoi and Ho Chi Minh City being the largest and most prestigious. There are also numerous vocational schools for post-secondary studies.

The 2014 Global Gender Gap Report, published by the World Economic Forum, ranked countries according to their attainment of gender equality in areas such as education, economic opportunities, and health. Vietnam was ranked 76th out of 142 countries for overall gender equity; however, in terms of education, the country has improved to a rating of 95 out of 100 in the equality of educational opportunities for women versus men.

Women's Rights

The Vietnamese constitution guarantees equal rights for women. However, poor legal enforcement of Vietnamese laws, which prohibit gender trafficking and discrimination, leave a large number of women subject to rights abuses such as domestic violence, rape, and low rates of education. Although Vietnam's national assembly has one of the highest proportions of female representatives in any Asian country, the government has yet to figure out a workable solution to the problem of discrimination against women. The trafficking of women and children for forced prostitution, domestic services, and marriage remains a serious problem.

Almost half of all adult women in Vietnam work outside the home. However, a large percentage of those do not have an education beyond primary schooling. As such, the female workforce is largely concentrated in lower status occupations, and earns around 72 percent of male salaries for the same type of work. In the home, women are in charge of the children and all domestic tasks, along with caring for any elderly relatives living in the home. Women are traditionally not involved in the family decision-making process.

While women are allowed to hold joint title to ownership of land, in most cases only the husband's name is represented on the title. This is especially common in rural areas. Also common in these areas of Vietnam are forced marriages. This is prohibited by Vietnamese law, but the practice is largely ignored by authorities.

Additionally, Vietnam stated a goal of reducing the birthrate of the country so that by the year 2015, all families will have only two children. This population and family planning strategy, adopted in 1993, includes incentives and birth reduction policies, which have led to a rise in intrauterine device (IUD) use, sterilization and a high rate of abortion. The pressure placed on women to undergo these procedures, along with other forms of birth control, has been criticized as a violation of the reproductive rights. As a result of these actions, the fertility rate for Vietnamese women in 2014 was 1.85 percent.

Health Care

The quality and reach of health care has declined over the last two decades because of inadequate government spending. There is a significant discrepancy between rural and urban medical services, and a shortage of staff and facilities throughout the system. Many Vietnamese cannot afford medical expenses and rely more on traditional medical practices.

As a result of underfunding, diseases which could be prevented still compromise the health of the Vietnamese. These include dengue fever, malaria, cholera, typhoid fever, and tuberculosis; in recent years, the HIV-infection rate has also steadily increased, and malnutrition remains a problem in rural areas. These problems aside, life expectancy levels are high and infant mortality levels low.

GOVERNMENT

Structure

Vietnam was united in 1976, and the North's communist system was imposed on the entire country. Though some liberalization has taken hold over the last few decades, the media is strictly controlled and dissent from the official line is punished. The most recent constitution adopted in 1992 and amended in 2001 and 2013 takes into account the changes that the government has allowed.

The executive branch is presided over by a president, a prime minister, and a general secretary. They are chosen from among the fifteen-member cabinet by the National Assembly. The president is the head of state, and the prime minister is the chief of state. The general secretary serves as both head of the Vietnamese Communist Party (VCP) and the National Assembly. Every senior minister must be a member of the VCP, the country's only legal party.

Vietnam's unicameral legislature is presided over by the National Assembly, which consists of 500 directly elected deputies; their term lasts five years. They meet biannually and are responsible for approving legislation initiated by the executive branch, among other duties.

Political Parties

The Vietnamese Communist Party (VCP) is the country's only legal party. Other political parties in Vietnam not recognized by the government include the People's Action Party of Vietnam (PAP), an anti-communist party founded in 1991 and based in the U.S., and the pro-democracy Vietnam Progression Party.

The Vietnam Populist Party (VNPP), formed in 2006, is another pro-democracy party that supports the rights of ethnic minorities in Vietnam. Its Liaison Office is located in Houston, Texas, and the identities of its members and officials within Vietnam are not publicized for safety reasons.

In the 2011 parliamentary elections, the government allowed non-Communist Party individuals to run, after they had been approved by the government. Forty-two of these individuals won seats versus 458 Communist Party members.

Local Government

Vietnam's 58 provinces and five municipalities are strictly controlled by the central government. The provinces are composed of municipalities, then districts, towns and villages. At each level there is a directly elected council.

Judicial System

The Supreme People's Court, the highest court of the judicial branch, is presided over by a procurator-general. The National Assembly elects the Supreme Court members to five-year terms. District courts operate at the provincial level. Their judges and assessors are elected by the local governments. The judiciary is not fully independent of the executive branch. There are also courts at the district and provincial levels, as well as labor courts, administrative courts, economic courts, and military tribunals.

Taxation

In 2014, the highest personal income tax in Vietnam rate was 35 percent (20 percent for non-residents) and corporate taxes of 22 percent were scheduled to be reduced to 20 percent in 2016. Other taxes levied include healthcare, retirement, property, and value-added taxes.

Armed Forces

The Vietnam People's Army includes a ground forces division, a navy, an air force, and a coast guard. In 2015, it was estimated that the armed forces of Vietnam comprised just over 410,000 active troops, with another five million in the reserves.

Foreign Policy

Since the latter half of the 20th century, Vietnam has shifted its foreign policy away from isolationism, solidarity, and association with communist countries. It has proactively established ties with the West, and has improved relations with China and its Southeast Asian neighbors. However, after a period of cooperation with China, the multi-lateral dispute over control of the South China Sea has created increased tensions between Vietnam and China during the second decade of this century. In particular, Vietnam's new strategy of positive and overseas foreign relation on the diplomatic stage is rooted in economic development, and the need to secure foreign investment.

As of 2009, Vietnam had diplomatic relations with over 170 nations. It joined the UN in 1977 and the Association of South-East Asian Nations (ASEAN) in 1995. In addition, Vietnam is a member of the Asia-Pacific Economic Cooperation (APEC) and the ASEAN Free Trade Area (AFTA), which supports local industries, and has signed a framework agreement with the European Union (EU). In 2006, Vietnam was granted admission to the World Trade Organization, and in 2008 it won a temporary seat on the UN Security Council (UNSC). A key component of Vietnamese foreign policy is independence in foreign affairs, and Vietnam is also a member of the Non-Aligned Movement (NAM).

Although Vietnam has recently strengthened its relations with the U.S., America's refusal to pay compensation to citizens said to be suffering aftereffects of Agent Orange—which was used by American forces during the Vietnam War—remains an issue. However, the two countries, which established formal diplomatic ties in 1995, recently signed a bilateral trade agreement and solidified permanent trade relations. These improved relations also included the first historic visit of President Nguyen Minh Triet to the U.S. in July 2007. About the time tensions increased over the South China Sea, the U.S. reached an agreement with Vietnam for the U.S. to assist Vietnam in strengthening their coastal patrol capabilities. From 1985 to 2013, trade between Vietnam and the U.S. increased from about $450 million to $35 billion (USD), making the U.S. Vietnam's leading market for exports.

Vietnam has been careful in its foreign relations with China. Although there has been increasing disagreement in the dispute over who owns the Spratly and Paracel Islands (archipelagoes in the South China Sea), Vietnam has been a supporter of China's claim of Taiwan. Hanoi and Beijing are working to finish the demarcation of their land borders. Relations between Cambodia and Vietnam have improved since the late 1990s. Both countries have opened trade between their borders and are working to increase bilateral trade.

Human Rights Profile

International human rights law insists that states respect civil and political rights, and also promote an individual's economic, social and cultural rights. The United Nations Universal Declaration on Human Rights (UDHR) is recognized as the standard for international human rights. Its authors sought the counsel of the world's great thinkers, philosophers, and religious leaders, and were careful to create a document that reflects the core values shared by every world culture. (To read this document or view the articles relating to cultural human rights, visit: http://www.udhr.org/UDHR/default.htm.)

The fundamental rights and duties of citizens of Vietnam are outlined in chapter five of Vietnam's constitution, which was revised and adopted in 1992. The chapter was written to reflect the fundamental human rights as defined in the UDHR. However, the human rights record in Vietnam, as regarded by international agencies and other countries, is generally poor. In particular, the censoring of the media, the banning of certain religions or associations, and discrimination against dissenters and certain ethnicities are ongoing issues.

Article 53 of Vietnam's constitution declares all citizens equal before the law, which agrees with Article 2 of the UDHR. However, Article 51 states that the government guarantees the rights of the citizen as long as the citizen is fulfilling his duties to the state and society. This article allows the rights of Vietnamese citizens to be restricted if the government deems their actions to be a threat to the state or society in general.

Articles 6 through 11 of the UDHR outline the rights of a person pertaining to arrest, trial and presumption of innocence. Vietnam's constitution protects these rights "in accordance with the provisions of the law." Vietnamese law authorizes arbitrary detention without trial. Ordinance 44 authorizes placing those suspected of threatening national security under house arrest or in detention indefinitely, without trial, in special rehabilitation camps (known as social protection centers), or even in mental hospitals.

Article 18 of the UDHR outlines freedom of religion. Although Vietnam's constitution declares all religions to be equal and protected, Vietnamese law mandates that all religious groups must register with the government. The law also bans any religious activities that might cause public disorder or harm national security. Certain religious institutions have also been banned, such as the Unified Buddhist Church of Vietnam. Further, Thích Quang Do, a Buddhist monk and government critic associated with the church, has been detained and imprisoned on several occasions for his critical views.

The rights to freedom of speech and expression in Vietnam, as outlined in Article 19 of the UDHR, are subject to government control. All media in Vietnam are owned and censored by the state. Any publication, website or Internet users thought to disseminate information that is a threat to the government or society are made to suffer criminal charges and penalties, including being jailed without trial.

The right to assemble, outlined in Article 20, is also supported in the Vietnamese constitution, only to be contradicted by law. Decree 38 forbids any public gatherings in front of places where any governmental conferences are held, and any gathering at all requires organizers to obtain advance permission from the government. In addition, a 2004 public demonstration by the Degar people, indigenous to Vietnam, ended in a violent and fatal confrontation with the government, resulting in at least 10 deaths.

Migration

Approximately 40,000 indigenous Vietnamese of the central highlands, known as the Montagnards, sided with U.S. forces during the Vietnam War. After U.S. forces pulled out of Vietnam, approximately 2,000 Montagnards were relocated to the US state of North Carolina. Thousands more Montagnards fled to neighboring Cambodia, seeking asylum. In 2002, just over 900 Montagnards who had recently sought asylum in Cambodia were resettled in the U.S.. There have been several instances in the early 21st century of the Cambodian government forcibly returning Montagnards to Vietnam, a move that organizations such as Human Rights Watch have criticized.

ECONOMY

Overview of the Economy

Long, devastating wars, and a centrally planned economy stifled economic growth, but in the late 1980s, the government began implementing more liberal economic policies. As a result, the Vietnamese economy has improved remarkably, though there have been periods of downturn.

Between 2006 and 2008, the average inflation rate was just over 18 percent. Vietnam has slowly been getting inflation under control and in 2013 it was down to 6.8 percent. In 2013, the gross domestic product (GDP) of the country was $358.9 billion (USD), and the per capita GDP that same year was $4,000 (USD).

Industry

Industry accounts for 38.5 percent of the GDP and employs 21 percent of the labor force. Food processing, steel productions, and the manufacture of cigarettes, textiles, chemicals, paper, building materials, and electrical goods are the key sectors. Mining is also important in the north and produces large quantities of coal, among other minerals. Oil, which is extracted from offshore deposits, has become the country's most important export.

Labor

With a labor force of 53 million, Vietnam's unemployment rate was 1.3 percent in 2013.

Energy/Power/Natural Resources

Vietnam has deposits of coal, bauxite, manganese, copper, gold, iron, silver, zinc, and oil. Other natural resources include timber, hydropower, and fish.

Decades of land mismanagement, population growth, and war have created several environmental problems. Intensive cultivation of the land and timber cutting has led to deforestation and soil erosion. Over-fishing has depleted stocks of marine animals. In the largest urban centers, air and water pollution and inadequate waste treatment have reached critical levels.

Use of the defoliant known as Agent Orange by the United States military has contaminated the environment and still causes illnesses and birth defects. Moreover, there are numerous, unexploded landmines littered across the country. They kill or injure an estimated 180 people each month. Forty years after the end of the Vietnam War, Vietnam still is 10th on the list of nations with the most landmines deployed within its borders.

Fishing

Vietnam's fishing industry remains a productive sector and is growing; however, a lack of capital to develop and improve the infrastructure of the fishing industry has limited its growth. Farm-raised catfish are a popular export, as are shrimp.

Forestry

Intensive timber cutting has led to deforestation in Vietnam. Common tree species in the country include teak, mahogany, oak, and ironwood. Timber exports brought in an estimated $4.5 billion (USD) in 2014, with projections for a 12 percent growth in 2015.

Mining/Metals

Mining is important in northern Vietnam and produces large quantities of coal. Vietnam also has deposits of bauxite, manganese, copper, gold, iron, silver, and zinc.

Agriculture

Vietnam developed as an agrarian society, and agriculture remains an essential sector of the economy, accounting for 19 percent of the GDP in 2013, and employing almost 48 percent of the labor force.

Wet rice, cultivated mostly in the river deltas, is the major cash crop. Fruits, vegetables, cotton, coffee, rubber, and sugarcane are other important crops. The fishing industry remains a productive sector and is growing. Water buffalo, cattle, and poultry are the most commonly raised livestock.

Animal Husbandry

Water buffalo, hogs, cattle, and poultry are Vietnam's most commonly raised livestock.

Tourism

Tourism started becoming a major sector in the Vietnamese economy in the early 1990s, and has grown at one of the fastest rates in the world. In 2003, 2.6 million international tourists visited the country, in addition to 13 million local visitors, generating $1.5 billion (USD). In 2007, the tourism industry brought in an estimated $3 billion (USD), increasing to over $7 billion (USD) in 2013. Most tourists hail from China, South Korea, and the United States.

From mountains and tropical forests to beaches and river deltas, Vietnam offers spectacular natural landscapes. Culturally, there are religious buildings honoring Buddha scattered throughout the country. The Royal Tombs of the Nguyen Dynasty in the former imperial city of Hue is one of the most visited sites in the country. Ho Chi Minh City and Hanoi are popular with tourists, who visit the cities' markets, parks, and museums.

April Sanders, Michael Aliprandini,
Micah L. Issitt

DO YOU KNOW?

- At its narrowest point, Vietnam is only 50 kilometers (31 miles) wide.
- The Red River Delta in northern Vietnam is the world's most densely populated agricultural region.
- Ho Chi Minh City is named for the leader (1890–1969) who led the Vietnamese communist movement in its drive for independence.
- The name "Ha Noi" may be translated as "bend of the river," a reference to the city's proximity to the Red River Delta and its tributaries. Fishing and agriculture remain pillars of the local economy.
- Street vendors selling food, electronics, jewelry, and other goods are routinely found throughout Hanoi. Street vending is a major industry and has grown with the expansion of the city's tourism industry.

Bibliography

Kalman, Bobbie. *Vietnam: The Culture (Lands, Peoples and Cultures).* New York: Crabtree Publishing Company, 2002.

Lonely Plant and Iain Steward. *Vietnam.* 12th ed. London: Lonely Planet 2014.

McKay, Susan. *Vietnam (Festivals of the World).* Chicago: Gareth Stevens Publishing, 1997.

Murray, Geoffrey. *Vietnam—Culture Smart! A Quick Guide to Customs and Etiquette.* London: Kuperard, 2005.

Rough Guide. *The Rough Guide to Vietnam.* 8th ed. New York: Penguin Group (USA) LLC, 2015.

Sheen, Barbara. http://www.amazon.com/Vietnam-Enchantment-World-Second-Willis/dp/0516221507/ref=sr_1_8?ie=UTF8&s=books&qid=1222754347&sr=1-8http://www.amazon.com/Taste-Culture-Foods-Vietnam/dp/0737734523/ref=sr_1_12?ie=UTF8&s=books&qid=1222754644&sr=1-12*A Taste of Culture - Foods of Vietnam* (A Taste of Culture). Farmington Hills, MI: Kidhaven Press, 2006. <http://www.britannica.com/EBchecked/topic/359754/Vietnam>.

Willis, Terry. *Vietnam (Enchantment of the World Second Series).* London: Watts Publishing, 2002.

Woods, Shelton. *The Story of Vietnam: From Prehistory to the Present.* Ann Arbor, MI: Association for Asian Studies, 2013.

Works Cited

"2005 Population Estimates for Cities in Vietnam." *Mongabay.com.* 12 Sept. 2008 <http://www.mongabay.com/igapo/2005_world_city_populations/Vietnam.html>.

Mydans, Seth. "The World; Vietnam's Youth Stage A Gentler Revolution." *NYTimes.com.* 12 Nov. 2000. 14 Sept 2008 <http://query.nytimes.com/gst/fullpage.html?res=9D00E6DE1238F931A25752C1A9669C8B63>.

Nguyen, Thuy. "Teenagers Criticize Lack of Sex Education in Vietnam." *Pearl.iearn.org.* 15 August 2007. 14 Sept 2008 <http://www.pearl.iearn.org/pearlnews/content/view/97/37/>.

"Vietnam." *AsianRecipes.com.* 14 Sept. 2008 <http://www.asiarecipe.com/vietnam.html>.

"Vietnam." *Britannica.com.* 16 Sept. 2008 <http://www.britannica.com/EBchecked/topic/359754/Vietnam>.

"Vietnam: Country & People" *Vietnamtourism.com.* Vietnam National Administration of Tourism. 2 April 2015. < http://www.vietnamtourism.com/en/index.php/about/cat/01 >.

"Vietnam." *Ediplomat.com.* 16 Sept 2008 <http://www.ediplomat.com/np/cultural_etiquette/ce_vn.htm>.

"Vietnamese Customs." *Vietnam-Culture.com.* 12 Sept. 2008 < http://www.vietnam-culture.com/zones-3-1/Vietnamese-Customs.aspx>.

"Vietnamese Etiquette." *Asiarooms.com.* TUI Travel PLC. 12 Sept. 2008 < http://www.asiarooms.com/travel-guide/vietnam/culture-of-vietnam/vietnamese-etiquette.html>.

"Vietnam: Events of 2007." 16 Sept. 2008. *Human Rights Watch World Report 2008.* Hwr.org. < http://hrw.org/englishwr2k8/docs/2008/01/31/vietna17630.htm >.

"World Heritage List." *UNESCO.org.* 26 July 2008. <http://whc.unesco.org/en/list>.

Appendix One: World Governments

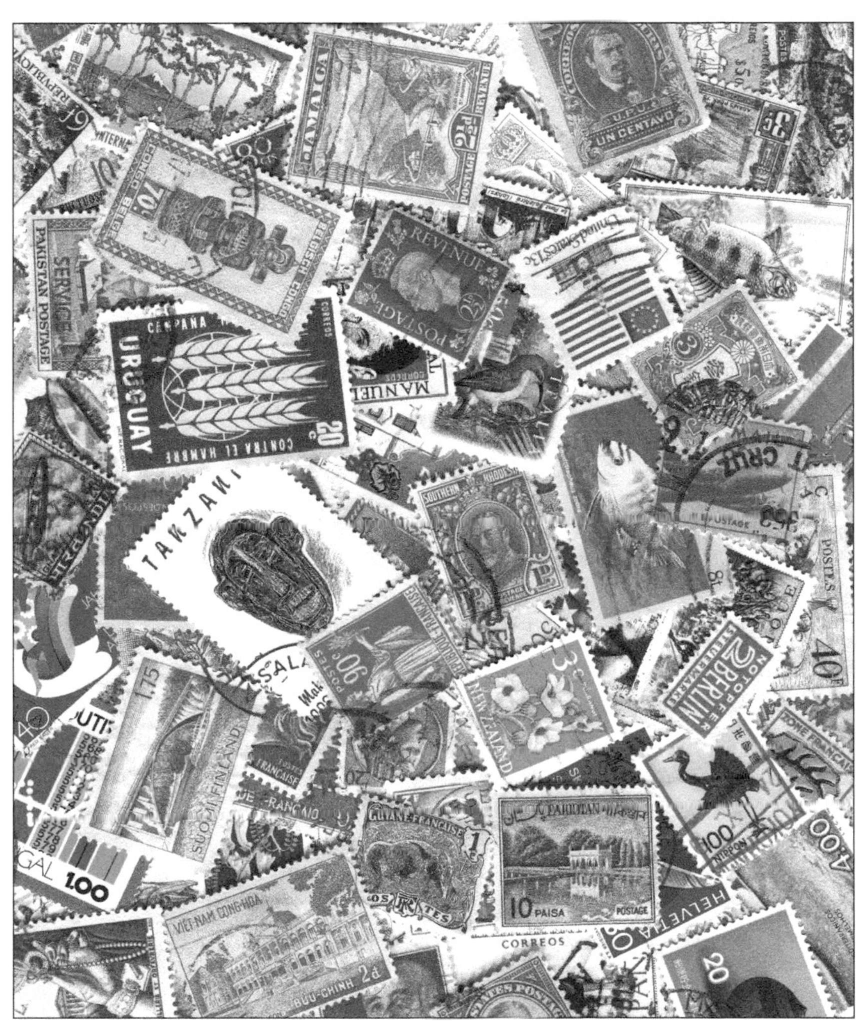

Commonwealth

Guiding Premise

A commonwealth is an organization or alliance of nations connected for the purposes of satisfying a common interest. The participating states may retain their own governments, some of which are often considerably different from one another. Although commonwealth members tend to retain their own sovereign government institutions, they collaborate with other members to create mutually agreeable policies that meet their collective interests. Some nations join commonwealths to enhance their visibility and political power on the international stage. Others join commonwealths for security or economic reasons. Commonwealth members frequently engage in trade agreements, security pacts, and other programs. Some commonwealths are regional, while others are global.

Typical Structure

A commonwealth's structure depends largely on the nature of the organization and the interests it serves. Some commonwealths are relatively informal in nature, with members meeting on a periodic basis and participating voluntarily. This informality does not undermine the effectiveness of the organization, however—members still enjoy a closer relationship than that which exists among unaffiliated states. Commonwealths typically have a president, secretary general, or, in the case of the Commonwealth of Nations (a commonwealth that developed out of the British Empire), a monarch acting as the leader of the organization. Members appoint delegates to serve at summits, committee meetings, and other commonwealth events and programs.

Other commonwealths are more formal in structure and procedures. They operate based on mission statements with very specific goals and member participation requirements. These organizations have legislative bodies that meet regularly. There are even joint security operations involving members. The African Union, for example, operates according to a constitution and collectively addresses issues facing the entire African continent, such as HIV/AIDS, regional security, environmental protection, and economic cooperation.

One of the best-known commonwealths in modern history was the Soviet Union. This collective of communist states was similar to other commonwealths, but the members of the Soviet Union, although they retained their own sovereign government institutions, largely deferred to the organization's central leadership in Moscow, which in turn deferred to the Communist Party leadership. After the collapse of the Soviet Union, a dozen former Soviet states, including Russia, reconnected as the Commonwealth of Independent States. This organization features a central council in Minsk, Belarus. This council consists of the heads of state and heads of government for each member nation, along with their cabinet ministers for defense and foreign affairs.

Commonwealth structures and agendas vary. Some focus on trade and economic development, as well as using their respective members' collective power to address human rights, global climate change, and other issues. Others are focused on regional stability and mutual defense, including prevention of nuclear weapons proliferation. The diversity of issues for which commonwealths are formed contributes to the frequency of member meetings as well as the actions carried out by the organization.

Role of the Citizen

Most commonwealths are voluntary in nature, which means that the member states must choose to join with the approval of their respective governments. A nation with a democratic government, therefore, would need the sanction of its popularly elected legislative and executive bodies in order to proceed. Thus, the role of the private citizen with regard to a commonwealth is indirect—the people may have the power to vote for or against a legislative or executive candidate based on his or her position concerning membership in a commonwealth.

Some members of commonwealths, however, do not feature a democratic government, or their respective governmental infrastructures are not yet in place. Rwanda, for instance, is a developing nation whose 2009 decision to join the Commonwealth of Nations likely came from the political leadership with very little input from its citizens, as Rwandans have very limited political freedom.

While citizens may not directly influence the actions of a commonwealth, they may work closely with its representatives. Many volunteer nonprofit organizations—having direct experience with, for example, HIV/AIDS, certain minority groups, or environmental issues—work in partnership with the various branches of a commonwealth's central council. In fact, such organizations are frequently called upon in this regard to implement the policies of a commonwealth, receiving financial and logistical support when working in impoverished and/or war-torn regions. Those working for such organizations may therefore prove invaluable to the effectiveness of a commonwealth's programs.

Michael Auerbach
Marblehead, Massachusetts

Examples

African Union
Commonwealth of Independent States
Commonwealth of Nations
Northern Mariana Islands (and the United States)
Puerto Rico (and the United States)

Bibliography

"About Commonwealth of Independent States." *Commonwealth of Independent States*. CIS, n.d. Web. 17 Jan. 2013.

"AU in a Nutshell." *African Union*. African Union Commission, n.d. Web. 17 Jan. 2013.

"The Commonwealth." *Commonwealth of Nations*. Nexus Strategic Partnerships Limited, 2013. Web. 17 Jan. 2013.

Communist

Guiding Premise

Communism is a political and economic system that seeks to eliminate private property and spread the benefits of labor equally throughout the populace. Communism is generally considered an outgrowth of socialism, a political and economic philosophy that advocates "socialized" or centralized ownership of the economy and the means of production.

Communism developed largely from the theories of Karl Marx (1818–83), who believed that a revolution led by the working class must occur before the state could achieve the even distribution of wealth and property and eliminate the class-based socioeconomic system of capitalist society. Marx believed that a truly equitable society required centralized control of credit, transportation, education, communication, agriculture, and industry, along with eliminating the rights of individuals to inherit or to own land.

Russia (formerly the Soviet Union) and China are the two largest countries to have been led by communist governments during the twentieth and twenty-first centuries. In both cases, the attempt to bring about a communist government came by way of violent revolutions in which members of the former government and ruling party were executed. Under Russian leader Vladimir Lenin (1870–1924) and Chinese leader Mao Zedong (1893–1976), strict dictatorships were instituted, curtailing individual rights in favor of state control. Lenin sought to expand communism into developing nations to counter the global spread of capitalism. Mao, in his form of communism, considered ongoing revolution within China a necessary aspect of communism. Both gave their names to their respective versions of communism, but neither Leninism nor Maoism managed to achieve the idealized utopia envisioned by Marx and other communist philosophers.

The primary difference between modern socialism and communism is that communist groups believe that a social revolution is necessary to create the idealized state without class structure, where socialists believe that the inequities of class structure can be addressed and eliminated through gradual change.

Typical Structure

Most modern communist governments define themselves as "socialist," though a national communist party exerts control over all branches of government. The designation of a "communist state" is primarily an external definition for a situation in which a communist party controls the government.

Among the examples of modern socialist states operating under the communist model are the People's Republic of China, the Republic of Cuba, and the Socialist Republic of Vietnam. However, each of these governments in fact operates through a mixed system of socialist and capitalist economic policies, allowing private ownership in some situations and sharply enforcing state control in others.

Typically, a communist state is led by the national communist party, a political group with voluntary membership and members in all sectors of the populace. While many individuals may join the communist party, the leadership of the party is generally selected by a smaller number of respected or venerated leaders from within the party. These leaders select a ruling committee that develops the political initiatives of the party, which are thereafter distributed throughout the government.

In China, the Communist Party elects both a chairperson, who serves as executive of the party, and a politburo, a standing committee that makes executive decisions on behalf of the party. In Cuba, the Communist Party selects individuals who sit for election to the National Assembly of People's Power, which then serves directly as the state's sole legislative body.

In the cases of China, Cuba, and Vietnam, the committees and leaders chosen by the communist party then participate directly in electing leaders to serve in the state judiciary. In addition, the central committees typically appoint individuals to serve as heads of the military and to lower-level, provincial, or municipal government positions. In China, the populace elects individuals to local, regional, and provincial councils that in turn elect representatives to sit on a legislative body known as the National People's Congress (NPC), though the NPC is generally considered a largely ceremonial institution without any substantial power to enact independent legislation.

In effect, most modern communist states are controlled by the leadership of the national communist party, though this leadership is achieved by direct and indirect control of lesser legislative, executive, and judicial bodies. In some cases, ceremonial and symbolic offices created under the communist party can evolve to take a larger role in state politics. In China, for instance, the NPC has come to play a more important role in developing legislation in the twenty-first century.

Role of the Citizen

In modern communist societies, citizens have little voice in selecting the leadership of the government. In many communist states, popular elections are held at local and national levels, but candidates are chosen by communist party leadership and citizens are not given the option to vote for representatives of opposing political parties.

In most cases, the state adopts policies that give the appearance of popular control over the government, while in actuality, governmental policies are influenced by a small number of leaders chosen from within the upper echelons of the party. Popularly elected leaders who oppose party policy are generally removed from office.

All existing communist states have been criticized for human rights violations in terms of curtailing the freedoms available to citizens and of enacting dictatorial and authoritarian policies. Cuba, Vietnam, and China, for instance, all have laws preventing citizens from opposing party policy or supporting a political movement that opposes the communist party. Communist governments have also been accused of using propaganda and misinformation to control the opinion of the populace regarding party leadership and therefore reducing the potential for popular resistance to communist policies.

Micah Issitt
Philadelphia, Pennsylvania

Examples

China
Cuba
Laos
North Korea
Vietnam

Bibliography

Caramani, Daniele. *Comparative Politics*. New York: Oxford UP, 2008. Print.

Priestland, David. *The Red Flag: A History of Communism*. New York: Grove, 2009. Print.

Service, Robert. *Comrades! A History of World Communism*. Cambridge: Harvard UP, 2007. Print.

Confederation/Confederacy

Guiding Premise

A confederation or confederacy is a loose alliance between political units, such as states or cantons, within a broader federal government. Confederations allow a central, federal government to create laws and regulations of broad national interest, but the sovereign units are granted the ultimate authority to carry out those laws and to create, implement, and enforce their own laws as well. Confederate governments are built on the notion that a single, central government should not have ultimate authority over sovereign states and populations. Some confederate governments were born due to the rise of European monarchies and empires that threatened to govern states from afar. Others were created out of respect for the diverse ideologies, cultures, and ideals of their respective regions. Confederations and confederacies may be hybrids, giving comparatively more power to a federal government while retaining respect for the sovereignty of their members. True confederate governments are rare in the twenty-first century.

Typical Structure

Confederate governments are typically characterized by the presence of both a central government and a set of regional, similarly organized, and sovereign (independent) governments. For example, a confederate government might have as its central government structure a system that features executive, legislative, and judicial branches. Each region that serves as members of the confederation would have in place a similar system, enabling the efficient flow of lawmaking and government services.

In some confederations, the executive branch of the central government is headed by a president or prime minister, who serves as the government's chief administrative officer, overseeing the military and other government operations. Meanwhile, at the regional level, another chief executive, such as a governor, is charged with the administration of that government's operations.

Legislative branches are also similarly designed. Confederations use parliaments or congresses that, in most cases, have two distinct chambers. One chamber consists of legislators who each represent an entire state, canton, or region. The other chamber consists of legislators representing certain populations of voters within that region. Legislatures at the regional level not only have the power to create and enforce their own laws, but also have the power to refuse to enact or enforce any laws handed down by the national government.

A confederation's judiciary is charged with ensuring that federal and regional laws are applied uniformly and within the limits of the confederation's constitutional framework. Central and regional governments both have such judicial institutions, with the latter addressing those legal matters administered in the state or canton and the former addressing legal issues of interest to the entire country.

Political parties also typically play a role in a confederate government. Political leadership is achieved by a party's majority status in either the executive or the legislative branches. Parties also play a role in forging a compromise on certain matters at both the regional and national levels. Some confederations take the diversity of political parties and their ideologies seriously enough to create coalition governments that can help avoid political stalemates.

Role of the Citizen

The political role of the citizen within a confederate political system depends largely on the constitution of the country. In some confederacies, for example, the people directly elect their legislative and executive leaders by popular vote. Some legislators are elected to open terms—they may technically be reelected, but this election is merely a formality, as they are allowed to stay in office until they decide to leave or they die—while others may be subject to term limits or other reelection rules. Popularly elected legislators and executives in turn draft, file, and pass new laws and regulations that ideally are favorable to the voters. Some confederate systems give popularly elected legislators the ability to elect a party leader to serve as prime minister or president.

Confederations are designed to empower the regional government and avoid the dominance of a distant national government. In this manner, citizens of a confederate government, in some cases, may enjoy the ability to put forth new legislative initiatives. Although the lawmaking process is expected to be administered by the legislators and executives, in such cases the people are allowed and even encouraged to connect and interact with their political representatives to ensure that the government remains open and accessible.

Michael Auerbach
Marblehead, Massachusetts

Examples

European Union
Switzerland
United States under the Articles of Confederation (1781–89)

Bibliography

"Government Type." *The World Factbook.* Central Intelligence Agency, n.d. Web. 17 Jan. 2013.

"Swiss Politics." *SwissWorld.org.* Federal Department of Foreign Affairs Presence Switzerland, n.d. Web. 17 Jan. 2013.

Constitutional Monarchy

Guiding Premise

A constitutional monarchy is a form of government in which the head of state is a monarch (a king or queen) with limited powers. The monarch has official duties, but those responsibilities are defined in the nation's constitution and not by the monarch. Meanwhile, the power to create and rescind laws is given to a legislative body. Constitutional monarchies retain the ceremony and traditions associated with nations that have long operated under a king or queen. However, the constitution prevents the monarch from becoming a tyrant. Additionally, the monarchy, which is typically a lifetime position, preserves a sense of stability and continuity in the government, as the legislative body undergoes periodic change associated with the election cycle.

Typical Structure

The structure of a constitutional monarchy varies from nation to nation. In some countries, the monarchy is predominantly ceremonial. In such cases, the monarch provides a largely symbolic role, reminding the people of their heritage and giving them comfort in times of difficulty. Such is the case in Japan, for example; the emperor of that country was stripped of any significant power after World War II but was allowed to continue his legacy in the interest of ensuring that the Japanese people would remain peaceful. Today, that nation still holds its monarchical family in the highest regard, but the government is controlled by the Diet (the legislature), with the prime minister serving in the executive role.

In other countries, the sovereign plays a more significant role. In the United Kingdom, the king or queen does have some power, including the powers to appoint the prime minister, to open or dissolve Parliament, to approve bills that have been passed by Parliament, and to declare war and make peace. However, the monarch largely defers to the government on these acts. In Bahrain, the king (or, until 2002, emir or hereditary ruler) was far more involved in government in the late twentieth and early twenty-first centuries than many other constitutional monarchs. In 1975, the emir of Bahrain dissolved the parliament, supposedly to run the government more effectively. His son would later implement a number of significant constitutional reforms that made the government more democratic in nature.

The key to the structure of this type of political system is the constitution. As is the case in the United States (a federal republic), a constitutional monarchy is carefully defined by the government's founding document. In Canada, for example, the king or queen of England is still recognized as the head of state, but that country's constitution gives the monarch no power other than ceremonial responsibilities. India, South Africa, and many other members of the Commonwealth of Nations (the English monarch's sphere of influence, spanning most of the former British colonies) have, since gaining their independence, created constitutions that grant no power to the English monarch; instead, they give all powers to their respective government institutions and, in some cases, recognize their own monarchs.

A defining feature of a constitutional monarchy is the fact that the monarch gives full respect to the limitations set forth by the constitution (and rarely seeks to alter such a document in his or her favor). Even in the United Kingdom itself—which does not have a written constitution, but rather a series of foundational documents—the king or queen does not step beyond the bounds set by customary rules. One interesting exception is in Bahrain, where Hamad bin Isa Al-Khalifa assumed the throne in 1999 and immediately implemented a series of reforms to the constitution in order to give greater definition to that country's democratic institutions, including resuming parliamentary elections in 2001. During the 2011 Arab Spring uprisings, Bahraini protesters called for further democratic reforms to be enacted, and tensions between the ruler and his opposition continue.

Role of the Citizen

In the past, monarchies ruled nations with absolute power; the only power the people had was the ability to unify and overthrow the ruling sovereign. Although the notion of an absolute monarchy has largely disappeared from the modern political landscape, many nations have retained their respective kings, queens, emperors, and other monarchs for the sake of ceremony and cultural heritage. In the modern constitutional monarchy, the people are empowered by their nation's foundational documents, which not only define the rights of the people but the limitations of their governments and sovereign as well. The people, through their legislators and through the democratic voting process, can modify their constitutions to expand or shrink the political involvement of the monarchy.

For example, the individual members of the Commonwealth of Nations, including Canada and Australia, have different constitutional parameters for the king or queen of England. In England, the monarch holds a number of powers, while in Canada, he or she is merely a ceremonial head of state (with all government power centered in the capital of Ottawa). In fact, in 1999, Australia held a referendum (a general vote) on whether to abolish its constitutional monarchy altogether and replace it with a presidential republic. In that case, the people voted to retain the monarchy, but the proposal was only narrowly defeated. These examples demonstrate the tremendous power the citizens of a constitutional monarchy may possess through the legislative process and the vote under the constitution.

Michael Auerbach
Marblehead, Massachusetts

Examples

Bahrain
Cambodia
Denmark
Japan
Lesotho
Malaysia
Morocco
Netherlands
Norway
Spain
Sweden
Thailand
United Kingdom

Bibliography

Bowman, John. "Constitutional Monarchies." *CBC News*. CBC, 4 Oct. 2002. Web. 17 Jan. 2013.

"The Role of the Monarchy." *Royal.gov.uk*. Royal Household, n.d. Web. 17 Jan. 2013.

Constitutional Republic

Guiding Premise

A constitutional republic is a governmental system in which citizens are involved in electing or appointing leaders who serve according to rules formulated in an official state constitution. In essence, the constitutional republic combines the political structure of a republic or republican governmental system with constitutional principles.

A republic is a government in which the head of state is empowered to hold office through law, not inheritance (as in a monarchy). A constitutional republic is a type of republic based on a constitution, a written body of fundamental precedents and principles from which the laws of the nation are developed.

Most constitutional republics in the modern world use a universal suffrage system, in which all citizens of the nation are empowered to vote for or against individuals who attempt to achieve public office. Universal suffrage is not required for a nation to qualify as a constitutional republic, and some nations may only allow certain categories of citizens to vote for elected leaders.

A constitutional republic differs from other forms of democratic systems in the roles assigned to both the leaders and the citizenry. In a pure democratic system, the government is formed by pure majority rule, and this system therefore ignores the opinions of any minority group. A republic, by contrast, is a form of government in which the government's role is limited by a written constitution aimed at promoting the welfare of all individuals, whether members of the majority or a minority.

Typical Structure

To qualify as a constitutional republic, a nation must choose a head of state (most often a president) through elections, according to constitutional law. In some nations, an elected president may serve alongside an appointed or elected individual who serves as leader of the legislature, such as a prime minister, often called the "head of government." When the president also serves as head of government, the republic is said to operate under a presidential system.

Typically, the executive branch consists of the head of state and the executive offices, which are responsible for enforcing the laws and overseeing relations with other nations. The legislative branch makes laws and has overlapping duties with the executive office in terms of economic and military developments. The judicial branch, consisting of the courts, interprets the law and the constitution and enforces adherence to the law.

In a constitutional republic, the constitution describes the powers allotted to each branch of government and the means by which the governmental bodies are to be established. The constitution also describes the ways in which governmental branches interact in creating, interpreting, and enforcing laws. For instance, in the United States, the executive and legislative branches both have roles in determining the budget for the nation, and neither body is free to make budgetary legislation without the approval of the other branch.

Role of the Citizen

In a constitutional republic, the citizens have the power to control the evolution of the nation through the choice of representatives who serve on the government. These representatives can, generally through complicated means, create or abolish laws and even change the constitution itself through reinterpretations of constitutional principles or direct amendments.

Citizens in a republic are empowered, but generally not required, to play a role in electing leaders. In the United States, both state governments and the federal government function according to a republican system, and citizens are therefore allowed to take part in the election of leaders to both local and national offices. In addition, constitutional systems generally allow individuals to join political interest groups to further common political goals.

In a constitutional democratic republic such as Guatemala and Honduras, the president, who serves as chief of state and head of government, is elected directly by popular vote. In the United States, a constitutional federal republic, the president is elected by the Electoral College, whose members are selected according to the popular vote within each district. The Electoral College is intended to provide more weight to smaller states, thereby balancing the disproportionate voting power of states with larger populations. In all constitutional republics, the citizens elect leaders either directly or indirectly through other representatives chosen by popular vote. Therefore, the power to control the government is granted to the citizens of the constitutional republic.

Micah Issitt
Philadelphia, Pennsylvania

Examples

Guatemala
Honduras
Iceland
Paraguay
Peru
United States
Uruguay

Bibliography

Baylis, John, Steve Smith, and Patricia Owens. *The Globalization of World Politics: An Introduction to International Relations*. New York: Oxford UP, 2010. Print.

Caramani, Daniele. *Comparative Politics*. New York: Oxford UP, 2008. Print.

Garner, Robert, Peter Ferdinand, and Stephanie Lawson. *Introduction to Politics*. 2nd ed. Oxford: Oxford UP, 2009. Print.

Hague, Rod, and Martin Harrop. *Comparative Government and Politics: An Introduction*. New York: Palgrave, 2007. Print.

Democracy

Guiding Premise

Democracy is a political system based on majority rule, in which all citizens are guaranteed participatory rights to influence the evolution of government. There are many different types of democracy, based on the degree to which citizens participate in the formation and operation of the government. In a direct democratic system, citizens vote directly on proposed changes to law and public policy. In a representative democracy, individuals vote to elect representatives who then serve to create and negotiate public policy.

The democratic system of government first developed in Ancient Greece and has existed in many forms throughout history. While democratic systems always involve some type of majority rule component, most modern democracies have systems in place designed to equalize representation for minority groups or to promote the development of governmental policies that prevent oppression of minorities by members of the majority.

In modern democracies, one of the central principles is the idea that citizens must be allowed to participate in free elections to select leaders who serve in the government. In addition, voters in democratic systems elect political leaders for a limited period of time, thus ensuring that the leadership of the political system can change along with the changing views of the populace. Political theorists have defined democracy as a system in which the people are sovereign and the political power flows upward from the people to their elected leaders.

Typical Structure

In a typical democracy, the government is usually divided into executive, legislative, and judicial branches. Citizens participate in electing individuals to serve in one or more of these branches, and elected leaders appoint additional leaders to serve in other political offices. The democratic system, therefore, involves a combination of elected and appointed leadership.

Democratic systems may follow a presidential model, as in the United States, where citizens elect a president to serve as both head of state and head of government. In a presidential model, citizens may also participate in elections to fill other governmental bodies, including the legislature and judicial branch. In a parliamentary democracy, citizens elect individuals to a parliament, whose members in turn form a committee to appoint a leader, often called the prime minister, who serves as head of government.

In most democratic systems, the executive and legislative branches cooperate in the formation of laws, while the judicial branch enforces and interprets the laws produced by the government. Most democratic systems have developed a system of checks and balances designed to prevent any single branch of government from exerting a dominant influence over the development of governmental policy. These checks and balances may be instituted in a variety of ways, including the ability to block governmental initiatives and the ability to appoint members to various governmental agencies.

Democratic governments generally operate on the principle of political parties, which are organizations formed to influence political development. Candidates for office have the option of joining a political party, which can provide funding and other campaign assistance. In some democratic systems—called dominant party or one-party dominant systems—there is effectively a single political party. Dominant party systems allow for competition in democratic elections, but existing power structures often prevent opposing parties from competing successfully. In multiparty democratic systems, there are two or more political parties with the ability to compete for office, and citizens are able to choose among political parties during elections. Some countries only allow political parties to be active at the national level, while other countries allow political parties to play a role in local and regional elections.

Role of the Citizen

The citizens in a democratic society are seen as the ultimate source of political authority. Members of the government, by contrast, are seen as servants of the people, and are selected and elected to serve the people's interests. Democratic systems developed to protect and enhance the freedom of the people; however, for the system to function properly, citizens must engage in a number of civic duties.

In democratic nations, voting is a right that comes with citizenship. Though some democracies—Australia, for example—require citizens to vote by law, compulsory participation in elections is not common in democratic societies. Citizens are nonetheless encouraged to fulfill their voting rights and to stay informed regarding political issues. In addition, individuals are responsible for contributing to the well-being of society as a whole, usually through a system of taxation whereby part of an individual's earnings is used to pay for governmental services.

In many cases, complex governmental and legal issues must be simplified to ease understanding among the citizenry. This goal is partially met by having citizens elect leaders who must then explain to their constituents how they are shaping legislation and other government initiatives to reflect constituents' wants and needs. In the United States, citizens may participate in the election of local leaders within individual cities or counties, and also in the election of leaders who serve in the national legislature and executive offices.

Citizens in democratic societies are also empowered with the right to join political interest groups and political parties in an effort to further a broader political agenda. However, democratic societies oppose making group membership a requirement and have laws forbidding forcing an individual to join any group. Freedom of choice, especially with regard to political affiliation and preference, is one of the cornerstones of all democratic systems.

Micah Issitt
Philadelphia, Pennsylvania

Examples

Denmark
Sweden
Spain
Japan
Australia
Costa Rica
Uruguay
United States

Bibliography

Barington, Lowell. *Comparative Politics: Structures and Choices*. Boston: Wadsworth, 2012. Print.

Caramani, Daniele. *Comparative Politics*. New York: Oxford UP, 2008. Print.

Przeworski, Adam. *Democracy and the Limits of Self Government*, New York: Cambridge UP, 2010. Print.

Dictatorship/Military Dictatorship

Guiding Premise

Dictatorships and military dictatorships are political systems in which absolute power is held by an individual or military organization. Dictatorships are led by a single individual, under whom all political control is consolidated. Military dictatorships are similar in purpose, but place the system under the control of a military organization comprised of a single senior officer, or small group of officers. Often, dictatorships and military dictatorships are imposed as the result of a coup d'état in which the regime in question directly removes the incumbent regime, or after a power vacuum creates chaos in the nation. In both situations, the consolidation of absolute power is designed to establish a state of strict law and order.

Typical Structure

Dictatorships and military dictatorships vary in structure and nature. Some come about through the overthrow of other regimes, while others are installed through the democratic process, and then become a dictatorship as democratic rights are withdrawn. Still others are installed following a complete breakdown of government, often with the promise of establishing order.

Many examples of dictatorships can be found in the twentieth century, including Nazi Germany, Joseph Stalin's Soviet Union, and China under Mao Tse-tung. A number of dictatorships existed in Africa, such as the regimes of Idi Amin in Uganda, Charles Taylor in Liberia, and Mu'ammar Gadhafi in Libya. Dictatorships such as these consolidated power in the hands of an individual leader. A dictator serves as the sole decision-maker in the government, frequently using the military, secret police, or other security agencies to enforce the leader's will. Dictators also have control over state institutions like legislatures. A legislature may have the ability to develop and pass laws, but if its actions run counter to the dictator's will, the latter can—and frequently does—dissolve the body, replacing its members with those more loyal to the dictator's agenda.

Military dictatorships consolidate power not in the hands of a civilian but in an individual or small group of military officers—the latter of which are often called "juntas." Because military dictatorships are frequently installed following a period of civil war and/or a coup d'état, the primary focus of the dictatorship is to achieve strict order through the application of military force. Military dictatorships are often installed with the promise of an eventual return to civilian and/or democratic control once the nation has regained stability. In the case of North Korea, one-party communist rule turned into a communist military dictatorship as its leader, Kim Il-Sung, assumed control of the military and brought its leadership into the government.

In the late twentieth and early twenty-first centuries, dictatorships and military dictatorships are most commonly found in developing nations, where poverty rates are high and regional stability is tenuous at best. Many are former European colonies, where charismatic leaders who boast of their national heritage have stepped in to replace colonial governments. National resources are typically directed toward military and security organizations in an attempt to ensure security and internal stability, keeping the regime in power and containing rivals. Human rights records in such political systems are typically heavily criticized by the international community.

Role of the Citizen

Dictatorships and military dictatorships are frequently installed because of the absence of viable democratic governments. There is often a disconnect, therefore, between the people and their leaders in a dictatorship. Of course, many dictatorships are identified as such by external entities and not by their own people. For example, the government of Zimbabwe is technically identified as a parliamentary democracy, with Robert Mugabe—who has been the elected leader of the country since 1980—as its president. However, the international community has long complained that Mugabe "won" his positions through political corruption, including alleged ballot stuffing. In 2008, Mugabe lost his first reelection campaign, but demanded a recount. While the recount continued, his supporters attacked opposition voters, utilizing violence and intimidation until his opponent, Morgan Tsvangirai, withdrew his candidacy, and Mugabe was restored as president.

By definition, citizens do not have a role in changing the course of a dictatorship's agenda. The people are usually called upon to join the military in support of the regime, or cast their vote consistently in favor of the ruling regime. Freedom of speech, the press, and assembly are virtually nonexistent, as those who speak out against the ruling regime are commonly jailed, tortured, or killed.

Michael Auerbach
Marblehead, Massachusetts

Examples

Belarus (dictatorship)
Fiji (military dictatorship)
North Korea (military dictatorship)
Zimbabwe (dictatorship)

Bibliography

Clayton, Jonathan. "China Aims to Bring Peace through Deals with Dictators and Warlords." *Times* [London]. Times Newspapers, 31 Jan. 2007. Web. 6 Feb. 2013.

"Robert Mugabe—Biography." *Biography.com*. A+E Television Networks, 2013. Web. 6 Feb. 2013.

Ecclesiastical

Guiding Premise

An ecclesiastical government is one in which the laws of the state are guided by and derived from religious law. Ecclesiastical governments can take a variety of forms and can be based on many different types of religious traditions. In some traditions, a deity or group of deities are considered to take a direct role in the formation of government, while other traditions utilize religious laws or principles indirectly to craft laws used to manage the state.

In many cultures, religious laws and tenets play a major role in determining the formation of national laws. Historically, the moral and ethical principles derived from Judeo-Christian tradition inspired many laws in Europe and North America. Few modern governments operate according to an ecclesiastical system, but Vatican City, which is commonly classified as a city-state, utilizes a modernized version of the ecclesiastical government model. All states utilizing an ecclesiastical or semi-ecclesiastical system have adopted a single state religion that is officially recognized by the government.

In some predominantly Islamic nations, including the Sudan, Oman, Iran, and Nigeria, Islamic law, known as sharia, is the basis for most national laws, and government leaders often must obtain approval by the leaders of the religious community before being allowed to serve in office. Most modern ecclesiastical or semi-ecclesiastical governments have adopted a mixed theocratic republic system in which individuals approved by religious authorities are elected by citizens to hold public office.

Typical Structure

In an ecclesiastical government, the church or recognized religious authority is the source of all state law. In a theocracy, which is one of the most common types of ecclesiastical governments, a deity or group of deities occupies a symbolic position as head of state, while representatives are chosen to lead the government based on their approval by the prevailing religious authority. In other types of ecclesiastical governments, the chief of state may be the leading figure in the church, such as in Vatican City, where the Catholic Pope is also considered the chief of state.

There are no modern nations that operate on a purely ecclesiastical system, though some Islamic countries, like Iran, have adopted a semi-ecclesiastical form of republican government. In Iran, the popularly elected Assembly of Experts—comprised of Islamic scholars called mujtahids—appoints an individual to serve as supreme leader of the nation for life, and this individual has veto power over all other governmental offices. Iranian religious leaders also approve other individuals to run as candidates for positions in the state legislature. In many cases, the citizens will elect an individual to serve as head of government, though this individual must conform to religious laws.

In an ecclesiastical government, those eligible to serve in the state legislature are generally members of the church hierarchy or have been approved for office by church leaders. In Tibet, which functioned as an ecclesiastical government until the Chinese takeover of 1951, executive and legislative duties were consolidated under a few religious leaders, called lamas, and influential citizens who maintained the country under a theocratic system. Most modern nations separate governmental functions between distinct but interrelated executive, legislative, and judicial branches.

Many modern semi-ecclesiastical nations have adopted a set of state principles in the form of a constitution to guide the operation of government and the establishment of laws. In mixed constitutional/theocratic systems, the constitution may be used to legitimize religious authority by codifying a set of laws and procedures that have been developed from religious scripture.

In addition, the existence of a constitution facilitates the process of altering laws and governmental procedures as religious authorities reinterpret religious scriptures and texts.

Role of the Citizen

Citizens in modern ecclesiastical and semi-ecclesiastical governments play a role in formulating the government though national and local elections. In some cases, religious authorities may approve more than one candidate for a certain position and citizens are then able to exercise legitimate choice in the electoral process. In other cases, popular support for one or more candidates may influence religious authorities when it comes time to nominate or appoint an individual to office.

In ecclesiastical governments, the freedoms and rights afforded to citizens may depend on their religious affiliation. Christians living in a Christian ecclesiastical government, for instance, may be allowed to run for and hold government office, while representatives of other religions may be denied this right. In addition, ecclesiastical governments may not recognize religious rights and rituals of other traditions and may not offer protection for those practicing religions other than the official state religion.

Though religious authority dominates politics and legislative development, popular influence is still an important part of the ecclesiastical system. Popular support for or against certain laws may convince the government to alter official policies. In addition, the populace may join local and regional religious bodies that can significantly affect national political developments. As local and regional religious groups grow in numbers and influence, they may promote candidates to political office, thereby helping to influence the evolution of government.

Micah Issitt
Philadelphia, Pennsylvania

Examples

Afghanistan
Iran
Nigeria
Oman
Vatican City

Bibliography

Barrington, Lowell. *Comparative Politics: Structures and Choices*. Boston: Wadsworth, 2012. Print.

Hallaq, Wael B. *An Introduction to Islamic Law*. New York: Cambridge UP, 2009. Print.

Hirschl, Ran. *Constitutional Theocracy*. Cambridge, MA: Harvard UP, 2010. Print.

Failed State

Guiding Premise

A failed state is a political unit that at one point had a stable government that provided basic services and security to its citizens, but then entered a period marked by devastating conflict, extreme poverty, overwhelming political corruption, and/or unlivable environmental conditions. Often, a group takes hold of a failed state's government through military means, staving off rivals to fill in a power vacuum. The nominal leadership of a failed state frequently uses its power to combat rival factions, implement extreme religious law, or protect and advance illicit activities (such as drug production or piracy). Failed states frequently retain their external borders, but within those borders are regions that may be dominated by a particular faction, effectively carving the state into disparate subunits, with some areas even attaining relative stability and security—a kind of de facto independence.

Typical Structure

Failed states vary in appearance based on a number of factors. One such factor is the type of government that existed prior to the state's collapse. For example, a failed state might have originally existed as a parliamentary democracy, with an active legislature and executive system that developed a functioning legal code and administered to the needs of the people. However, that state may not have adequately addressed the needs of certain groups, fostering a violent backlash and hastening the country's destabilization. An ineffectual legislature might have been dissolved by the executive (a prime minister or president), and in the absence of leadership, the government as a whole ceased to operate effectively.

Another major factor is demographics. Many states are comprised of two or more distinct ethnic, social, or religious groups. When the ruling party fails to effectively govern and/or serve the interests of a certain segment of the population, it may be ousted or simply ignored by the marginalized faction within the state. If the government falls, it creates a power vacuum that rival groups compete to fill. If one faction gains power, it must remain in a constant state of vigilance against its rivals, focusing more on keeping enemies in check than on rebuilding crippled government infrastructure. Some also seek to create theocracies based on extreme interpretations of a particular religious doctrine. Frequently, these regimes are themselves ousted by rivals within a few years, leaving no lasting government and keeping the state in chaos.

Failed states are also characterized by extreme poverty and a lack of modern technology. Potable water, electricity, food, and medicine are scarce among average citizens. In some cases, these conditions are worsened by natural events. Haiti, for example, was a failed state for many years before the devastating 2010 earthquake that razed the capitol city of Port au Prince, deepening the country's poverty and instability. Afghanistan and Ethiopia—with their harsh, arid climates—are also examples of failed states whose physical environments and lack of resources exacerbated an already extreme state of impoverishment.

Most failed states' conditions are also worsened by the presence of foreigners. Because their governments are either unable or unwilling to repel terrorists, for example, failed states frequently become havens for international terrorism. Somalia, Afghanistan, and Iraq are all examples of states that failed, enabling terrorist organizations to set up camp within their borders. As such groups pose a threat to other nations, those nations often send troops and weapons into the failed states to engage the terrorists. In recent years, NATO, the United Nations, and the African Union have all entered failed states to both combat terrorists and help rebuild government.

Role of the Citizen

Citizens of a failed state have very little say in the direction of their country. In most cases, when a faction assumes control over the government, it installs strict controls that limit the rights of citizens, particularly such rights as freedom of speech, freedom of assembly, and freedom of religion. Some regimes allow for "democratic" elections, but a continued lack of infrastructure and widespread corruption often negates the legitimacy of these elections.

Citizens of failed states are often called upon by the ruling regime (or a regional faction) to serve in its militia, helping it combat other factions within the state. In fact, many militias within failed states are comprised of people who were forced to join (under penalty of death) at a young age. Those who do not join militias are often drawn into criminal activity such as piracy and the drug trade.

Some citizens are able to make a difference by joining interest groups. Many citizens are able to achieve a limited amount of success sharing information about women's rights, HIV/AIDS and other issues. In some situations, these groups are able to gain international assistance from organizations that were unable to work with the failed government.

Michael Auerbach
Marblehead, Massachusetts

Examples

Chad
Democratic Republic of the Congo
Somalia
Sudan
Zimbabwe

Bibliography

"Failed States: Fixing a Broken World." *Economist*, 29 Jan. 2009. Web. 6 Feb. 2012.

"Failed States." Global Policy Forum, 2013. Web. 6 Feb. 2012.

"Somalia Tops Failed States Index for Fifth Year." *CNN.com*. Turner Broadcasting System, 18 June 2012. Web. 6 Feb. 2012.

Thürer, Daniel. (1999). "The 'Failed State' and International Law." *International Review of the Red Cross*. International Committee of the Red Cross, 31 Dec. 1999. Web. 6 Feb. 2012.

Federal Republic

Guiding Premise

A federal republic is a political system that features a central government as well as a set of regional subunits such as states or provinces. Federal republics are designed to limit the power of the central government, paring its focus to only matters of national interest. Typically, a greater degree of power is granted to the regional governments, which retain the ability to create their own laws of local relevance. The degree to which the federal and regional governments each enjoy authority varies from nation to nation, based on the country's interpretation of this republican form of government. By distributing authority to these separate but connected government institutions, federal republics give the greatest power to the people themselves, who typically vote directly for both their regional and national political representation.

Typical Structure

A federal republic's structure varies from nation to nation. However, most federal republics feature two distinct governing entities. The first is a central, federal government, usually based in the nation's capital city. The federal government's task is to address issues of national importance. These issues include defense and foreign relations, but also encompass matters of domestic interest that must be addressed in uniform fashion, such as social assistance programs, infrastructure, and certain taxes.

A federal republic is comprised of executive, legislative, and judicial branches. The executive is typically a president or prime minister—the former selected by popular vote, the latter selected by members of the legislature—and is charged with the administration of the federal government's programs and regulations. The legislature—such as the US Congress, the Austrian Parliament, or the German Bundestag—is charged with developing laws and managing government spending. The judiciary is charged with ensuring that federal and state laws are enforced and that they are consistent with the country's constitution.

The federal government is limited in terms of its ability to assert authority over the regions. Instead, federal republics grant a degree of sovereignty to the different states, provinces, or regions that comprise the entire nation. These regions have their own governments, similar in structure and procedure to those of the federal government. They too have executives, legislatures, and judiciaries whose foci are limited to the regional government's respective jurisdictions.

The federal and regional segments of a republic are not completely independent of one another, however. Although the systems are intended to distribute power evenly, federal and regional governments are closely linked. This connectivity ensures the efficient collection of taxes, the regional distribution of federal funds, and a rapid response to issues of national importance. A federal republic's greatest strength, therefore, is the series of connections it maintains between the federal, regional, and local governments it contains.

Role of the Citizen

A federal republic is distinguished by the limitations of power it places on the national government. The primary goal of such a design was to place the power of government in the hands of the people. One of the ways the citizens' power is demonstrated is by participating in the electoral process. In a federal republic, the people elect their legislators. In some republics, the legislators in turn elect a prime minister, while in others, the people directly elect a president. The electoral process is an important way for citizens to influence the course of their government, both at the regional and federal levels. They do so by placing people who truly represent their diverse interests in the federal government.

The citizen is also empowered by participating in government as opposed to being subjected to it. In addition to taking part in the electoral process, the people are free to join and become active in a political party. A political party serves as a proxy for its members, representing their viewpoint and interests on a local and national level. In federal republics like Germany, a wide range of political parties are active in the legislature, advancing the political agendas of those they represent.

Michael Auerbach
Marblehead, Massachusetts

Examples

Austria
Brazil
Germany
India
Mexico
Nigeria
United States

Bibliography

"The Federal Principle." *Republik Österreich Parlament.* Republik Österreich Parlament, 8 Oct. 2010. Web. 6 Feb. 2013.

"The Federal Republic of Germany." *Deutscher Bundestag.* German Bundestag, 2013. Web. 6 Feb. 2013.

Collin, Nicholas. "An Essay on the Means of Promoting Federal Sentiments in the United States." *Friends of the Constitution: Writings of the "Other" Federalists, 1787–1788.* Ed. Colleen A. Sheehan and Gary L. McDowell. Online Library of Liberty, 2013. Web. 6 Feb. 2013.

Federation

Guiding Premise

A federation is a nation formed from the unification of smaller political entities. Federations feature federal governments that oversee nationwide issues. However, they also grant a degree of autonomy to the regional, state, or other local governments within the system. Federations are often formed because a collective of diverse regions find a common interest in unification. While the federal government is installed to address those needs, regions with their own distinct ethnic, socioeconomic, or political characteristics remain intact. This "separate but united" structure allows federations to avoid conflict and instability among their regions.

Typical Structure

The primary goal of a federation is to unify a country's political subunits within a national framework. The federal government, therefore, features institutions comprised of representatives from the states or regions. The representatives are typically elected by the residents of these regions, and some federal systems give the power to elect certain national leaders to these representatives. The regions themselves can vary considerably in size. The Russian Federation, for example, includes forty-six geographically large provinces as well as two more-concentrated cities as part of its eighty-three constituent federation members.

There are two institutions in which individuals from the constituent parts of a federation serve. The first institution is the legislature. Legislatures vary in appearance from nation to nation. For example, the US Congress is comprised of two chambers—the House of Representatives and the Senate—whose directly elected members act on behalf of their respective states. The German Parliament, on the other hand, consists of the directly elected Bundestag—which is tasked with electing the German federal chancellor, among other things—and the state-appointed Bundesrat, which works on behalf of the country's sixteen states.

The second institution is the executive. Here, the affairs of the nation are administered by a president or similar leader. Again, the structure and powers of a federal government's executive institutions varies from nation to nation according to their constitutional framework. Federal executive institutions are charged with management of state affairs, including oversight of the military, foreign relations, health care, and education. Similarly diverse is the power of the executive in relation to the legislative branch. Some prime ministers, for example, enjoy considerably greater power than the president. In fact, some presidents share power with other leaders, or councils thereof within the executive branch, serving as the diplomatic face of the nation but not playing a major role in lawmaking. In India, for example, the president is the chief executive of the federal government, but shares power with the prime minister and the Council of Ministers, headed by the prime minister.

In order to promote continuity between the federal government and the states, regions, or other political subunits in the federation, those subunits typically feature governments that largely mirror that of the central government. Some of these regional governments are modified according to their respective constitutions. For example, whereas the bicameral US Congress consists of the Senate and House of Representatives, Nebraska's state legislature only has one chamber. Such distinctive characteristics of state/regional governments reflect the geographic and cultural interests of the region in question. It also underscores the degree of autonomy given to such states under a federation government system.

Role of the Citizen

Federations vary in terms of both structure and distribution of power within government institutions. However, federal systems are typically democratic in nature, relying heavily on the participation of the electorate for installing representatives in those institutions. At the regional level, the people vote for their respective legislators and executives either directly or through political parties. The executive in turn appoints cabinet officials, while the legislators select a chamber leader. In US state governments, for example, such a leader might be a Senate president or speaker of the House of Representatives.

The people also play an important role in federal government. As residents of a given state or region, registered voters—again, through either a direct vote or through political parties—choose their legislators and national executives. In federations that utilize a parliamentary system, however, prime ministers are typically selected by the legislators and/or their political parties and not through a direct, national vote. Many constitutions limit the length of political leaders' respective terms of service and/or the number of times they may seek reelection, fostering an environment in which the democratic voting process is a frequent occurrence.

Michael Auerbach
Marblehead, Massachusetts

Examples

Australia
Germany
India
Mexico
Russia
United States

Bibliography

"Federal System of India." *Maps of India*. MapsOfIndia.com, 22 Sep. 2011. Web. 7 Feb. 2013.
"Political System." *Facts about Germany*. Frankfurter Societäts-Medien, 2011. Web. 7 Feb. 2013.
"Russia." *CIA World Factbook*. Central Intelligence Agency, 5 Feb. 2013. Web. 7 Feb. 2013.

Monarchy

Guiding Premise

A monarchy is a political system based on the sovereignty of a single individual who holds actual or symbolic authority over all governmental functions. The monarchy is one of the oldest forms of government in human history and was the most common type of government until the nineteenth century. In a monarchy, authority is inherited, usually through primogeniture, or inheritance by the eldest son.

In an absolute monarchy, the monarch holds authority over the government and functions as both head of state and head of government. In a constitutional monarchy, the role of the monarch is codified in the state constitution, and the powers afforded to the monarch are limited by constitutional law. Constitutional monarchies generally blend the inherited authority of the monarchy with popular control in the form of democratic elections. The monarch may continue to hold significant power over some aspects of government or may be relegated to a largely ceremonial or symbolic role.

In most ancient monarchies, the monarch was generally believed to have been chosen for his or her role by divine authority, and many monarchs in history have claimed to represent the will of a god or gods in their ascendancy to the position. In constitutional monarchies, the monarch may be seen as representing spiritual authority or may represent a link to the country's national heritage.

Typical Structure

In an absolute monarchy, a single monarch is empowered to head the government, including the formulation of all laws and leadership of the nation's armed forces. Oman is one example of a type of absolute monarchy called a sultanate, in which a family of leaders, called "sultans," inherits authority and leads the nation under an authoritarian system. Power in the Omani sultanate remains within the royal family. In the event of the sultan's death or incapacitation, the Royal Family Council selects a successor by consensus from within the family line. Beneath the sultan is a council of ministers, appointed by the sultan, to create and disseminate official government policy. The sultan's council serves alongside an elected body of leaders who enforce and represent Islamic law and work with the sultan's ministers to create national laws.

In Japan, which is a constitutional monarchy, the Japanese emperor serves as the chief of state and symbolic representative of Japan's culture and history. The emperor officiates national ceremonies, meets with world leaders for diplomatic purposes, and symbolically appoints leaders to certain governmental posts. Governmental authority in Japan rests with the Diet, a legislative body of elected officials who serve limited terms of office and are elected through popular vote. A prime minister is also chosen to lead the Diet, and the prime minister is considered the official head of government.

The Kingdom of Norway is another example of a constitutional monarchy wherein the monarch serves a role that has been codified in the state constitution. The king of Norway is designated as the country's chief of state, serving as head of the nation's executive branch. Unlike Japan, where the monarch's role is largely symbolic, the monarch of Norway has considerable authority under the constitution, including the ability to veto and approve all laws and the power to declare war. Norway utilizes a parliamentary system, with a prime minister, chosen from individuals elected to the state parliament, serving as head of government. Though the monarch has authority over the executive functions of government, the legislature and prime minister are permitted the ability to override monarchical decisions with sufficient support, thereby providing a system of control to prevent the monarch from exerting a dominant influence over the government.

Role of the Citizen

The role of the citizen in a monarchy varies depending on whether the government is a constitutional or absolute monarchy. In an absolute monarchy, citizens have only those rights given to them by the monarch, and the monarch has the power to extend and retract freedoms and rights at will. In ancient monarchies, citizens accepted the authoritarian role of the monarch, because it was widely believed that the monarch's powers were derived from divine authority. In addition, in many absolute monarchies, the monarch has the power to arrest, detain, and imprison individuals without due process, thereby providing a strong disincentive for citizens to oppose the monarchy.

In a constitutional monarchy, citizens are generally given greater freedom to participate in the development of governmental policies. In Japan, Belgium, and Spain, for instance, citizens elect governmental leaders, and the elected legislature largely controls the creation and enforcement of laws. In some countries, like the Kingdom of Norway, the monarch may exert significant authority, but this authority is balanced by that of the legislature, which represents the sovereignty of the citizens and is chosen to promote and protect the interests of the public.

The absolute monarchies of medieval Europe, Asia, and Africa held power for centuries, but many eventually collapsed due to popular uprisings as citizens demanded representation within the government. The development of constitutional monarchies may be seen as a balanced system in which the citizens retain significant control over the development of their government while the history and traditions of the nation are represented by the continuation of the monarch's lineage. In the United Kingdom, the governments of Great Britain and Northern Ireland are entirely controlled by elected individuals, but the continuation of the monarchy is seen by many as an important link to the nation's historic identity.

Micah Issitt
Philadelphia, Pennsylvania

Examples

Belgium
Bhutan
Japan
Norway
Oman
United Kingdom

Bibliography

Barrington, Lowell. *Comparative Politics: Structures and Choices*. Boston: Wadsworth, 2012. Print.
Dresch, Paul, and James Piscatori, eds. *Monarchies and Nations: Globalisation and Identity in the Arab States of the Gulf*. London: Tauris, 2005. Print.
Kesselman, Mark, et al. *European Politics in Transition*. New York: Houghton, 2009. Print.

Parliamentary Monarchy

Guiding Premise

A parliamentary monarchy is a political system in which leadership of the government is shared between a monarchy, such as a king or queen, and the members of a democratically elected legislative body. In such governments, the monarch's role as head of state is limited by the country's constitution or other founding document, preventing the monarch from assuming too much control over the nation. As head of state, the monarch may provide input during the lawmaking process and other operations of government. Furthermore, the monarch, whose role is generally lifelong, acts as a stabilizing element for the government, while the legislative body is subject to the periodic changes that occur with each election cycle.

Typical Structure

Parliamentary monarchies vary in structure and distribution of power from nation to nation, based on the parameters established by each respective country's constitution or other founding document. In general, however, parliamentary monarchies feature a king, queen, or other sovereign who acts as head of state. In that capacity, the monarch's responsibilities may be little more than ceremonial in nature, allowing him or her to offer input during the lawmaking process, to approve the installation of government officials, and to act as the country's international representative. However, these responsibilities may be subject to the approval of the country's legislative body. For example, the king of Spain approves laws and regulations that have already been passed by the legislative branch; formally appoints the prime minister; and approves other ministers appointed by the prime minister. Yet, the king's responsibilities in those capacities are subject to the approval of the Cortes Generales, Spain's parliament.

In general, parliamentary monarchies help a country preserve its cultural heritage through their respective royal families, but grant the majority of government management and lawmaking responsibilities to the country's legislative branch and its various administrative ministries, such as education and defense. In most parliamentary monarchies, the ministers of government are appointed by the legislative body and usually by the prime minister. Although government ministries have the authority to carry out the country's laws and programs, they are also subject to criticism and removal by the legislative body if they fail to perform to expectations.

The legislative body itself consists of members elected through a democratic, constitutionally defined process. Term length, term limit, and the manner by which legislators may be elected are usually outlined in the country's founding documents. For example, in the Dutch parliament, members of the House of Representatives are elected every four years through a direct vote, while the members of the Senate are elected by provincial government councils every four years. By contrast, three-quarters of the members of Thailand's House of Representatives are elected in single-seat constituencies (smaller districts), while the remaining members are elected in larger, proportional representation districts; all members of the House are elected for four-year terms. A bare majority of Thailand's senators are elected by direct vote, with the remainder appointed by other members of the government.

Role of the Citizen

While the kings and queens of parliamentary monarchies are the nominal heads of state, these political systems are designed to be democratic governments. As such, they rely heavily on the input and involvement of the citizens. Participating in legislative elections is one of the most direct ways in which the citizen is empowered. Because the governments of such systems are subject to legislative oversight, the people—through their respective votes for members of parliament—have influence over their government.

Political parties and organizations such as local and municipal councils also play an important role in parliamentary monarchies. Citizens' participation in those organizations can help shape parliamentary agendas and build links between government and the public. In Norway, for example, nearly 70 percent of citizens are involved in at least one such organization, and consequently Norway's Storting (parliament) has a number of committees that are tied to those organizations at the regional and local levels. Thus, through voting and active political involvement at the local level, the citizens of a parliamentary monarchy help direct the political course of their nation.

Michael Auerbach
Marblehead, Massachusetts

Examples

Netherlands
Norway
Spain
Sweden
Thailand
United Kingdom

Bibliography

"Form of Government." *Norway.org*. Norway–The Official Site in the United States, n.d. Web. 17 Jan. 2013.

"Issues: Parliament." *Governmentl.nl*. Government of the Netherlands, n.d. Web. 17 Jan. 2013.

"King, Prime Minister, and Council of Ministers." *Country Studies: Spain*. Lib. of Congress, 2012. Web. 17 Jan. 2013.

"Thailand." *International Foundation for Electoral Systems*. IFES, 2013. Web. 17 Jan. 2013.

Parliamentary Republic

Guiding Premise

A parliamentary republic is a system wherein both executive and legislative powers are centralized in the legislature. In such a system, voters elect their national representatives to the parliamentary body, which in turn appoints the executive. In such an environment, legislation is passed more quickly than in a presidential system, which requires a consensus between the executive and legislature. It also enables the legislature to remove the executive in the event the latter does not perform to the satisfaction of the people. Parliamentary republics can also prevent the consolidation of power in a single leader, as even a prime minister must defer some authority to fellow legislative leaders.

Typical Structure

Parliamentary republics vary in structure from nation to nation, according to the respective country's constitution or other governing document. In general, such a system entails the merger of the legislature and head of state such as a president or other executive. The state may retain the executive, however. However, the executive's role may be largely ceremonial, as is the case in Greece, where the president has very little political authority. This "outsider" status has in fact enabled the Greek president to act as a diplomatic intermediary among sparring parliamentary leaders.

While many countries with such a system operate with an executive—who may or may not be directly elected, and who typically has limited powers—the bulk of a parliamentary republic's political authority rests with the legislature. The national government is comprised of democratically elected legislators and their appointees. The length of these representatives' respective terms, as well as the manner by which the legislators are elected, depend on the frameworks established by each individual nation. Some parliamentary republics utilize a constitution for this purpose, while others use a set of common laws or other legal precepts. In South Africa, members of the parliament's two chambers, the National Assembly and the National Council of Provinces, are elected differently. The former's members are elected directly by the citizens in each province, while the latter's members are installed by the provincial legislatures.

Once elected to parliament, legislators are often charged with more than just lawmaking. In many cases, members of parliament oversee the administration of state affairs as well. Legislative bodies in parliamentary republics are responsible for nominating an executive—typically a prime minister—to manage the government's various administrative responsibilities. Should the executive not adequately perform its duties, parliament has the power to remove the executive from office. In Ireland, for example, the Dail Eireann (the House of Representatives) is charged with forming the country's executive branch by nominating the Taoiseach (prime minister) and approving the prime minister's cabinet selections.

Role of the Citizen

A parliamentary republic is a democratic political system that relies on the involvement of an active electorate. This civic engagement includes a direct or indirect vote for representatives to parliament. While the people do not vote for an executive as well, by way of their vote for parliament, the citizenry indirectly influences the selection of the chief executive and the policies he or she follows. In many countries, the people also indirectly influence the national government by their votes in provincial government. As noted earlier, some countries' parliaments include chambers whose members are appointed by provincial leaders.

Citizens may also influence the political system through involvement in political parties. Such organizations help shape the platforms of parliamentary majorities as well as selecting candidates for prime minister and other government positions. The significance of political parties varies from nation to nation, but such organizations require the input and involvement of citizens.

Michael Auerbach
Marblehead, Massachusetts

Examples

Austria
Greece
Iceland
Ireland
Poland
South Africa

Bibliography

"About the Oireachtas." *Oireachtas.ie*. Houses of the Oireachtas, n.d. Web. 7 Feb. 2013.
"Our Parliament." *Parliament.gov*. Parliament of the Republic of South Africa, n.d. Web. 7 Feb. 2013.
Tagaris, Karolina, and Ingrid Melander. "Greek President Makes Last Push to Avert Elections." *Reuters*. Thomson Reuters, 12 May 2012. Web. 7 Feb. 2013.

Presidential

Guiding Premise

A presidential system is a type of democratic government in which the populace elects a single leader—a president—to serve as both head of state and the head of government. The presidential system developed from the monarchic governments of medieval and early modern Europe, in which a royal monarch, holder of an inherited office, served as both head of state and government. In the presidential system, the president does not inherit the office, but is chosen by either direct or indirect popular vote.

Presidential systems differ from parliamentary systems in that the president is both the chief executive and head of state, whereas in a parliamentary system another individual, usually called the "prime minister," serves as head of government and leader of the legislature. The presidential system evolved out of an effort to create an executive office that balances the influence of the legislature and the judiciary. The United States is the most prominent example of a democratic presidential system.

Some governments have adopted a semi-presidential system, which blends elements of the presidential system with the parliamentary system, and generally features a president who serves only as head of state. In constitutional governments, like the United States, Mexico, and Honduras, the role of the president is described in the nation's constitution, which also provides for the president's powers in relation to the other branches of government.

Typical Structure

In most modern presidential governments, power to create and enforce laws and international agreements is divided among three branches: the executive, legislative, and judicial. The executive office consists of the president and a number of presidential advisers—often called the cabinet—who typically serve at the president's discretion and are not elected to office. The terms of office for the president are codified in the state constitution and, in most cases, the president may serve a limited number of terms before he or she becomes ineligible for reelection.

The president serves as head of state and is therefore charged with negotiating and administering international treaties and agreements. In addition, the president serves as head of government and is therefore charged with overseeing the function of the government as a whole. The president is also empowered, in most presidential governments, with the ability to deploy the nation's armed forces. In some governments, including the United States, the approval of the legislature is needed for the country to officially declare war.

The legislative branch of the government proposes new laws, in the form of bills, but must cooperate with the executive office to pass these bills into law. The legislature and the executive branch also cooperate in determining the government budget. Unlike prime ministers under the parliamentary system, the president is not considered a member of the legislature and therefore acts independently as the chief executive, though a variety of governmental functions require action from both branches of government. A unique feature of the presidential system is that the election of the president is separate from the election of the legislature.

In presidential systems, members of the legislature are often less likely to vote according to the goals of their political party and may support legislation that is not supported by their chosen political party. In parliamentary systems, like the government of Great Britain, legislators are more likely to vote according to party policy. Presidential systems are also often marked by a relatively small number of political parties, which often allows one party to achieve a majority in the legislature. If this majority coincides with the election of a president from the same party, that party's platform or agenda becomes dominant until the next election cycle.

The judicial branch in a presidential system serves to enforce the laws among the populace. In most modern presidential democracies, the president appoints judges to federal posts, though in some governments, the legislature appoints judges. In some cases, the president may need the approval of the legislature to make judicial appointments.

Role of the Citizen

In a democratic presidential system, citizens are empowered with the ability to vote for president and therefore have ultimate control over who serves as head of government and head of state. Some presidential governments elect individuals to the presidency based on the result of a popular vote, while other governments use an indirect system, in which citizens vote for a party or for individuals who then serve as their representatives in electing the president. The United States utilizes an indirect system called the Electoral College.

Citizens in presidential systems are also typically allowed, though not required, to join political parties in an effort to promote a political agenda. Some governmental systems that are modeled on the presidential system allow the president to exert a dominant influence over the legislature and other branches of the government. In some cases, this can lead to a presidential dictatorship, in which the president may curtail the political rights of citizens. In most presidential systems, however, the roles and powers of the legislative and executive branches are balanced to protect the rights of the people to influence their government.

In a presidential system, citizens are permitted to vote for a president representing one political party, while simultaneously voting for legislators from other political parties. In this way, the presidential system allows citizens to determine the degree to which any single political party is permitted to have influence on political development.

Micah Issitt
Philadelphia, Pennsylvania

Examples

Benin
Costa Rica
Dominican Republic
Guatemala
Honduras
Mexico
United States
Venezuela

Bibliography

Barington, Lowell. *Comparative Politics: Structures and Choices*. Boston: Wadsworth, 2012. Print.

Caramani, Daniele. *Comparative Politics*. New York: Oxford UP, 2008. Print.

Garner, Robert, Peter Ferdinand, and Stephanie Lawson. *Introduction to Politics*. 2nd ed. Oxford: Oxford UP, 2009. Print.

Republic

Guiding Premise

A republic is a type of government based on the idea of popular or public sovereignty. The word "republic" is derived from Latin terms meaning "matters" and "the public." In essence, a republic is a government in which leaders are chosen by the public rather than by inheritance or by force. The republic or republican governmental system emerged in response to absolute monarchy, in which hereditary leaders retained all the power. In contrast, the republican system is intended to create a government that is responsive to the people's will.

Most modern republics operate based on a democratic system in which citizens elect leaders by popular vote. The United States and Mexico are examples of countries that use a democratic republican system to appoint leaders to office. However, universal suffrage (voting for all) is not required for a government to qualify as a republic, and it is possible for a country to have a republican government in which only certain categories of citizens, such as the wealthy, are allowed to vote in elections.

In addition to popular vote, most modern republics are further classified as constitutional republics, because the laws and rules for appointing leaders have been codified in a set of principles and guidelines known as a "constitution." When combined with universal suffrage and constitutional law, the republican system is intended to form a government that is based on the will of the majority while protecting the rights of minority groups.

Typical Structure

Republican governments are typically led by an elected head of state, generally a president. In cases where the president also serves as the head of government, the government is called a "presidential republic." In some republics, the head of state serves alongside an appointed or elected head of government, usually a prime minister. This mixed form of government blends elements of the republic system with the parliamentary system found in countries such as the United Kingdom or India.

The president is part of the executive branch of government, which represents the country internationally and heads efforts to make and amend international agreements and treaties. The laws of a nation are typically created by the legislative branch, which may also be composed of elected leaders. Typically, the legislative and executive branches must cooperate on key initiatives, such as determining the national budget.

In addition to legislative and executive functions, most republics have a judiciary charged with enforcing and interpreting laws. The judicial branch may be composed of elected leaders, but in many cases, judicial officers are appointed by the president and/or the legislature. In the United States (a federal republic), the president, who leads the executive branch, appoints members to the federal judiciary, but these choices must be approved by the legislature before they take effect.

The duties and powers allotted to each branch of the republican government are interconnected with those of the other branches in a system of checks and balances. For instance, in Mexico (a federal republic), the legislature is empowered to create new tax guidelines for the public, but before legislative tax bills become law, they must first achieve majority support within the two branches of the Mexican legislature and receive the approval of the president. By creating a system of separate but balanced powers, the republican system seeks to prevent any one branch from exerting a dominant influence over the government.

Role of the Citizen

The role of the citizen in a republic depends largely on the type of republican system that the country has adopted. In democratic republics, popular elections and constitutional law give the public significant influence over governmental development and establish the people as the primary source of political power. Citizens in democratic republics are empowered to join political groups and to influence the development of laws and policies through the election of public leaders.

In many republican nations, a powerful political party or other political group can dominate the government, preventing competition from opposing political groups and curtailing the public's role in selecting and approving leaders. For instance, in the late twentieth century, a dominant political party maintained control of the Gambian presidency and legislature for more than thirty years, thereby significantly limiting the role of the citizenry in influencing the development of government policy.

In general, the republican system was intended to reverse the power structure typical of the monarchy system, in which inherited leaders possess all of the political power. In the republican system, leaders are chosen to represent the people's interests with terms of office created in such a way that new leaders must be chosen at regular intervals, thereby preventing a single leader or political entity from dominating the populace. In practice, popular power in a republic depends on preventing a political monopoly from becoming powerful enough to alter the laws of the country to suit the needs of a certain group rather than the whole.

Micah Issitt
Philadelphia, Pennsylvania

Examples

Algeria
Argentina
Armenia
France
Gambia
Mexico
San Marino
South Sudan
Tanzania
United States

Bibliography

Caramani, Daniele. *Comparative Politics*. New York: Oxford UP, 2008. Print.

Przeworski, Adam. *Democracy and the Limits of Self-Government*. New York: Cambridge UP, 2010. Print.

Socialist

Guiding Premise

Socialism is a political and economic system that seeks to elevate the common good of the citizenry by allowing the government to own all property and means of production. In the most basic model, citizens cooperatively elect members to government, and the government then acts on behalf of the people to manage the state's property, industry, production, and services.

In a socialist system, communal or government ownership of property and industry is intended to eliminate the formation of economic classes and to ensure an even distribution of wealth. Most modern socialists also believe that basic services, including medical and legal care, should be provided at the same level to all citizens and not depend on the individual citizen's ability to pay for better services. The origins of socialism can be traced to theorists such as Thomas More (1478–1535), who believed that private wealth and ownership led to the formation of a wealthy elite class that protected its own wealth while oppressing members of lower classes.

There are many different forms of socialist philosophy, some of which focus on economic systems, while others extend socialist ideas to other aspects of society. Communism may be considered a form of socialism, based on the idea that a working-class revolution is needed to initiate the ideal socialist society.

Typical Structure

Socialism exists in many forms around the world, and many governments use a socialist model for the distribution of key services, most often medical and legal aid. A socialist state is a government whose constitution explicitly gives the government powers to facilitate the creation of a socialist society.

The idealized model of the socialist state is one in which the populace elects leaders to head the government, and the government then oversees the distribution of wealth and goods among the populace, enforces the laws, and provides for the well-being of citizens. Many modern socialist governments follow a communist model, in which a national communist political party has ultimate control over governmental legislation and appointments.

There are many different models of socialist states, integrating elements of democratic or parliamentary systems. In these cases, democratic elections may be held to elect the head of state and the body of legislators. The primary difference between a socialist democracy and a capitalist democracy can be found in the state's role in the ownership of key industries. Most modern noncommunist socialist states provide state regulation and control over key industries but allow some free-market competition as well.

In a socialist system, government officials appoint leaders to oversee various industries and to regulate prices based on public welfare. For instance, if the government retains sole ownership over agricultural production, the government must appoint individuals to manage and oversee that industry, organize agricultural labor, and oversee the distribution of food products among the populace. Some countries, such as Sweden, have adopted a mixed model in which socialist industry management is blended with free-market competition.

Role of the Citizen

All citizens in a socialist system are considered workers, and thus all exist in the same economic class. While some citizens may receive higher pay than others—those who work in supervisory roles, for instance—limited ownership of private property and standardized access to services places all individuals on a level field with regard to basic welfare and economic prosperity.

The degree to which personal liberties are curtailed within a socialist system depends upon the type of socialist philosophy adopted and the degree to which corruption and authoritarianism play a role in government. In most modern communist governments, for instance, individuals are often prohibited from engaging in any activity seen as contrary to the overall goals of the state or to the policies of the dominant political party. While regulations of this kind are common in communist societies, social control over citizens is not necessary for a government to follow a socialist model.

Under democratic socialism, individuals are also expected to play a role in the formation of their government by electing leaders to serve in key positions. In Sri Lanka, for instance, citizens elect members to serve in the parliament and a president to serve as head of the executive branch. In Portugal, citizens vote in multiparty elections to elect a president who serves as head of state, and the president appoints a prime minister to serve as head of government. In both Portugal and Sri Lanka, the government is constitutionally bound to promote a socialist society, though both governments allow private ownership and control of certain industries.

Citizens in a socialist society are also expected to provide for one another by contributing to labor and by forfeiting some ownership rights to provide for the greater good. In the Kingdom of Sweden, a mixed parliamentary system, all citizens pay a higher tax rate to contribute to funds that provide for national health care, child care, education, and worker support systems. Citizens who have no children and require only minimal health care benefits pay the same tax rate as those who have greater need for the nation's socialized benefits.

Micah Issitt
Philadelphia, Pennsylvania

Examples

China
Cuba
Portugal
Sri Lanka
Venezuela
Zambia

Bibliography

Caramani, Daniele. *Comparative Politics*. New York: Oxford UP, 2008. Print.

Heilbroner, Robert. "Socialism." *Library of Economics and Liberty*. Liberty Fund, 2008. Web. 17 Jan. 2013.

Howard, Michael Wayne. *Socialism*. Amherst, NY: Humanity, 2001. Print.

Sultanate/Emirate

Guiding Premise

A sultanate or emirate form of government is a political system in which a hereditary ruler—a monarch, chieftain, or military leader—acts as the head of state. Emirates and sultanates are most commonly found in Islamic nations in the Middle East, although others are found in Southeast Asia as well. Sultans and emirs frequently assume titles such as president or prime minister in addition to their royal designations, meshing the traditional ideal of a monarch with the administrative capacities of a constitutional political system.

Typical Structure

A sultanate or emirate combines the administrative duties of the executive with the powers of a monarch. The emir or sultan acts as the head of government, appointing all cabinet ministers and officials. In Brunei, a sultanate, the government was established according to the constitution (set up after the country declared autonomy from Britain in 1959). The sultan did assemble a legislative council in order to facilitate the lawmaking process, but this council has consistently remained subject to the authority of the sultan and not to a democratic process. In 2004, there was some movement toward the election of at least some of the members of this council. In the meantime, the sultan maintains a ministerial system by appointment and also serves as the nation's chief religious leader.

In some cases, an emirate or sultanate appears similar to a federal system. In the United Arab Emirates (UAE), for example, the nation consists of not one but seven emirates. This system came into being after the seven small regions achieved independence from Great Britain. Each emirate developed its own government system under the leadership of an emir. However, in 1971, the individual emirates agreed to join as a federation, drafting a constitution that identified the areas of common interest to the entire group of emirates. Like Brunei, the UAE's initial government structure focused on the authority of the emirs and the various councils and ministries formed at the UAE's capital of Abu Dhabi. However, beginning in the early twenty-first century, the UAE's legislative body, the Federal National Council, has been elected by electoral colleges from the seven emirates, thus further engaging various local areas and reflecting their interests.

Sultanates and emirates are at times part of a larger nation, with the sultans or emirs answering to the authority of another government. This is the case in Malaysia, where the country is governed by a constitutional monarchy. However, most of Malaysia's western political units are governed by sultans, who act as regional governors and, in many cases, religious leaders, but remain subject to the king's authority in Malaysia's capital of Kuala Lumpur.

Role of the Citizen

Sultanates and emirates are traditionally nondemocratic governments. Like those of other monarchs, the seats of emirs and sultans are hereditary. Any votes for these leaders to serve as prime minister or other head of government are cast by ministers selected by the emirs and sultans. Political parties may exist in these countries as well, but these parties are strictly managed by the sultan or emir; opposition parties are virtually nonexistent in such systems, and some emirates have no political parties at all.

As shown in the UAE and Malaysia, however, there are signs that the traditional sultanate or emirate is increasingly willing to engage their respective citizens. For example, the UAE, between 2006 and 2013, launched a series of reforms designed to strengthen the role of local governments and relations with the people they serve. Malaysia may allow sultans to continue their regional controls, but at the same time, the country continues to evolve its federal system, facilitating multiparty democratic elections for its national legislature.

Michael Auerbach
Marblehead, Massachusetts

Examples

Brunei
Kuwait
Malaysia
Qatar
United Arab Emirates

Bibliography

"Brunei." *The World Factbook*. Central Intelligence Agency, 2 Jan. 2013. Web. 17 Jan. 2013.

"Malaysia." *The World Factbook*. Central Intelligence Agency, 7 Jan. 2013. Web. 17 Jan. 2013.

"Political System." *UAE Interact*. UAE National Media Council, n.d. Web. 17 Jan. 2013.

Prime Minister's Office, Brunei Darussalam. Prime Minister's Office, Brunei Darussalam, 2013. Web. 17 Jan. 2013.

Theocratic Republic

Guiding Premise

A theocratic republic is a type of government blending popular and religious influence to determine the laws and governmental principles. A republic is a governmental system based on the concept of popular rule and takes its name from the Latin words for "public matter." The defining characteristic of a republic is that civic leaders hold elected, rather than inherited, offices. A theocracy is a governmental system in which a supreme deity is considered the ultimate authority guiding civil matters.

No modern nations can be classified as pure theocratic republics, but some nations, such as Iran, maintain a political system largely dominated by religious law. The Buddhist nation of Tibet operated under a theocratic system until it was taken over by Communist China in the early 1950s.

In general, a theocratic republic forms in a nation or other governmental system dominated by a single religious group. The laws of the government are formed in reference to a set of religious laws, either taken directly from sacred texts or formulated by religious scholars and authority figures. Most theocratic governments depend on a body of religious scholars who interpret religious scripture, advise all branches of government, and oversee the electoral process.

Typical Structure

In a typical republic, the government is divided into executive, legislative, and judicial branches, and citizens vote to elect leaders to one or more of the branches of government. In most modern republics, voters elect a head of state, usually a president, to lead the executive branch. In many republics, voters also elect individuals to serve as legislators. Members of the judiciary may be elected by voters or may be appointed to office by other elected leaders. In nontheocratic republics, the citizens are considered the ultimate source of authority in the government.

In a theocratic republic, however, one or more deities are considered to represent the ultimate governmental authority. In some cases, the government may designate a deity as the ultimate head of state. Typically, any individual serving as the functional head of state is believed to have been chosen by that deity, and candidates for the position must be approved by the prevailing religious authority.

In some cases, the religious authority supports popular elections to fill certain governmental posts. In Iran, for instance, citizens vote to elect members to the national parliament and a single individual to serve as president. The Iranian government is ultimately led by a supreme leader, who is appointed to office by the Assembly of Experts, the leaders of the country's Islamic community. Though the populace chooses the president and leaders to serve in the legislature, the supreme leader of Iran can overrule decisions made in any other branch of the government.

In a theocratic republic, the power to propose new laws may be given to the legislature, which works on legislation in conjunction with the executive branch. However, all laws must conform to religious law, and any legislation produced within the government is likely to be abolished if it is deemed by the religious authorities to violate religious principles. In addition, religious leaders typically decide which candidates are qualified to run for specific offices, thereby ensuring that the citizens will not elect individuals who are likely to oppose religious doctrine.

In addition, many modern nations that operate on a partially theocratic system may adopt a set of governmental principles in the form of a constitution, blended with religious law. This mixed constitutional theocratic system has been adopted by an increasing number of Islamic nations, including Iraq, Afghanistan, Mauritania, and some parts of Nigeria.

Role of the Citizen

Citizens in a theocratic republic are expected to play a role in forming the government through elections, but they are constrained in their choices by the prevailing religious authority. Citizens are also guaranteed certain freedoms, typically codified in a constitution, that have been formulated with reference to religious law. All citizens must adhere to religious laws, regardless of their personal religious beliefs or membership within any existing religious group.

In many Middle Eastern and African nations that operate on the basis of an Islamic theocracy, citizens elect leaders from groups of candidates chosen by the prevailing religious authority. While the choices presented to the citizens are more limited than in a democratic, multiparty republic, the citizens nevertheless play a role in determining the evolution of the government through their voting choices.

The freedoms and rights afforded to citizens in a theocratic republic may depend, in part, on the individual's religious affiliation. For instance, Muslims living in Islamic theocracies may be permitted to hold political office or to aspire to other influential political positions, while members of minority religious groups may find their rights and freedoms limited. Religious minorities living in Islamic republics may not be permitted to run for certain offices, such as president, and must follow laws that adhere to Islamic principles but may violate their own religious principles. Depending on the country and the adherents' religion, the practice of their faith may itself be considered criminal.

Micah Issitt
Philadelphia, Pennsylvania

Examples

Afghanistan
Iran
Iraq
Pakistan
Mauritania
Nigeria

Bibliography

Cooper, William W., and Piyu Yue. *Challenges of the Muslim World: Present, Future and Past*. Boston: Elsevier, 2008. Print.

Hirschl, Ran. *Constitutional Theocracy*. Cambridge: Harvard UP, 2010. Print.

Totalitarian

Guiding Premise

A totalitarian government is one in which a single political party maintains absolute control over the state and is responsible for creating all legislation without popular referendum. In general, totalitarianism is considered a type of authoritarian government where the laws and principles used to govern the country are based on the authority of the leading political group or dictator. Citizens under totalitarian regimes have limited freedoms and are subject to social controls dictated by the state.

The concept of totalitarianism evolved in fascist Italy in the 1920s, and was first used to describe the Italian government under dictator Benito Mussolini. The term became popular among critics of the authoritarian governments of Fascist Italy and Nazi Germany in the 1930s. Supporters of the totalitarian philosophy believed that a strong central government, with absolute control over all aspects of society, could achieve progress by avoiding political debate and power struggles between interest groups.

In theory, totalitarian regimes—like that of Nazi Germany and modern North Korea—can more effectively mobilize resources and direct a nation toward a set of overarching goals. Adolf Hitler was able to achieve vast increases in military power during a short period of time by controlling all procedural steps involved in promoting military development. In practice, however, pure totalitarianism has never been achieved, as citizens and political groups generally find ways to subvert complete government control.

Totalitarianism differs from authoritarianism in that a totalitarian government is based on the idea that the highest leader takes total control in order to create a flourishing society for the benefit of the people. By contrast, authoritarian regimes are based on the authority of a single, charismatic individual who develops policies designed to maintain personal power, rather than promote public interest.

Typical Structure

In a fully realized totalitarian system, a single leader or group of leaders controls all governmental functions, appointing individuals to serve in various posts to facilitate the development of legislation and oversee the enforcement of laws. In Nazi Germany, for instance, Adolf Hitler created a small group of executives to oversee the operation of the government. Governmental authority was then further disseminated through a complex network of departments, called ministries, with leaders appointed directly by Hitler.

Some totalitarian nations may adopt a state constitution in an effort to create the appearance of democratic popular control. In North Korea, the country officially operates under a multiparty democratic system, with citizens guaranteed the right to elect leaders to both the executive and legislative branches of government. In practice, the Workers' Party of North Korea is the only viable political party, as it actively controls competing parties and suppresses any attempt to mount political opposition. Under Supreme Leader Kim Il-sung, the Workers' Party amended the constitution to allow Kim to serve as the sole executive leader for life, without the possibility of being removed from office by any governmental action.

In some cases, totalitarian regimes may favor a presidential system, with the dictator serving officially as president, while other totalitarian governments may adopt a parliamentary system, with a prime minister as head of government. Though a single dictator generally heads the nation with widespread powers over a variety of governmental functions, a cabinet or group of high-ranking ministers may also play a prominent role in disseminating power throughout the various branches of government.

Role of the Citizen

Citizens in totalitarian regimes are often subject to strict social controls exerted by the leading political party. In many cases, totalitarian governments restrict the freedom of the press, expression, and speech in an effort to limit opposition to the government. In addition, totalitarian governments may use the threat of police or military action to prevent protest movements against the leading party. Totalitarian governments maintain absolute control over the courts and any security agency, and the legal/judicial system therefore exists only as an extension of the leading political party.

Totalitarian governments like North Korea also attempt to restrict citizens' access to information considered subversive. For instance, North Korean citizens are not allowed to freely utilize the Internet or any other informational source, but are instead only allowed access to government-approved websites and publications. In many cases, the attempt to control access to information creates a black market for publications and other forms of information banned by government policy.

In some cases, government propaganda and restricted access to information creates a situation in which citizens actively support the ruling regime. Citizens may honestly believe that the social and political restrictions imposed by the ruling party are necessary for the advancement of society. In other cases, citizens may accept governmental control to avoid reprisal from the military and police forces. Most totalitarian regimes have established severe penalties, including imprisonment, corporal punishment, and death, for criticizing the government or refusing to adhere to government policy.

Micah Issitt
Philadelphia, Pennsylvania

Examples

Fascist Italy (1922–1943)
Nazi Germany (1933–1945)
North Korea
Stalinist Russia (1924–1953)

Bibliography

Barrington, Lowell. *Comparative Politics: Structures and Choices*. Boston: Wadsworth, 2012. Print.

Gleason, Abbot. *Totalitarianism: The Inner History of the Cold War*. New York: Oxford UP, 1995. Print.

McEachern, Patrick. *Inside the Red Box: North Korea's Post Totalitarian Regime*. New York: Columbia UP, 2010. Print.

Treaty System

Guiding Premise

A treaty system is a framework within which participating governments agree to collect and share scientific information gathered in a certain geographic region, or otherwise establish mutually agreeable standards for the use of that region. The participants establish rules and parameters by which researchers may establish research facilities and travel throughout the region, ensuring that there are no conflicts, that the environment is protected, and that the region is not used for illicit purposes. This system is particularly useful when the region in question is undeveloped and unpopulated, but could serve a number of strategic and scientific purposes.

Typical Structure

A treaty system of government is an agreement between certain governments that share a common interest in the use of a certain region to which no state or country has yet laid internationally recognized claim. Participating parties negotiate treaty systems that, upon agreement, form a framework by which the system will operate. Should the involved parties be United Nations member states, the treaty is then submitted to the UN Secretariat for registration and publication.

The agreement's founding ideals generally characterize the framework of a treaty. For example, the most prominent treaty system in operation today is the Antarctic Treaty System, which currently includes fifty nations whose scientists are studying Antarctica. This system, which entered into force in 1961, focuses on several topics, including environmental protection, tourism, scientific operations, and the peaceful use of that region. Within these topics, the treaty system enables participants to meet, cooperate, and share data on a wide range of subjects. Such cooperative activities include regional meetings, seminars, and large-scale conferences.

A treaty system is not a political institution in the same manner as state governments. Rather, it is an agreement administered by delegates from the involved entities. Scientists seeking to perform their research in Antarctica, for example, must apply through the scientific and/or government institutions of their respective nations. In the case of the United States, scientists may apply for grants from the National Science Foundation. These institutions then examine the study in question for its relevance to the treaty's ideals.

Central to the treaty system is the organization's governing body. In the case of the Antarctic Treaty, that body is the Antarctic Treaty Secretariat, which is based in Buenos Aires, Argentina. The Secretariat oversees all activities taking place under the treaty, welcomes new members, and addresses any conflicts or issues between participants. It also reviews any activities to ensure that they are in line with the parameters of the treaty. A treaty system is not a sovereign organization, however. Each participating government retains autonomy, facilitating its own scientific expeditions, sending delegates to the treaty system's main governing body, and reviewing the treaty to ensure that it coincides with its national interests.

Role of the Citizen

Although treaty systems are not sovereign government institutions, private citizens can and frequently do play an important role in their function and success. For example, the Antarctic Treaty System frequently conducts large-scale planning conferences, to which each participating government sends delegates. These teams are comprised of qualified scientists who are nominated and supported by their peers during the government's review process. In the United States, for example, the State Department oversees American participation in the Antarctic

Treaty System's events and programs, including delegate appointments.

Another area in which citizens are involved in a treaty system is in the ratification process. Every nation's government—usually through its legislative branch—must formally approve any treaty before the country can honor the agreement. This ratification is necessary for new treaties as well as treaties that must be reapproved every few years. Citizens, through their elected officials, may voice their support or disapproval of a new or updated treaty.

While participating governments administer treaty systems and their secretariats, those who conduct research or otherwise take part in activities in the region in question are not usually government employees. In Antarctica, for example, university professors, engineers, and other private professionals—supported by a combination of private and government funding—operate research stations.

Michael Auerbach
Marblehead, Massachusetts

Example

Antarctic Treaty System

Bibliography

"Antarctic." *Ocean and Polar Affairs.* US Department of State, 22 Mar. 2007. Web. 8 Feb. 2013.

"About Us." *Antarctic Treaty System.* Secretariat of the Antarctic Treaty, n.d. Web. 8 Feb. 2013.

"United Nations Treaty Series." *United Nations Treaty Collection.* United Nations, 2013. Web. 8 Feb. 2013.

"Educational Opportunities and Resources." *United States Antarctic Program.* National Science Foundation, 2013. Web. 8 Feb. 2013.

Appendix Two: World Religions

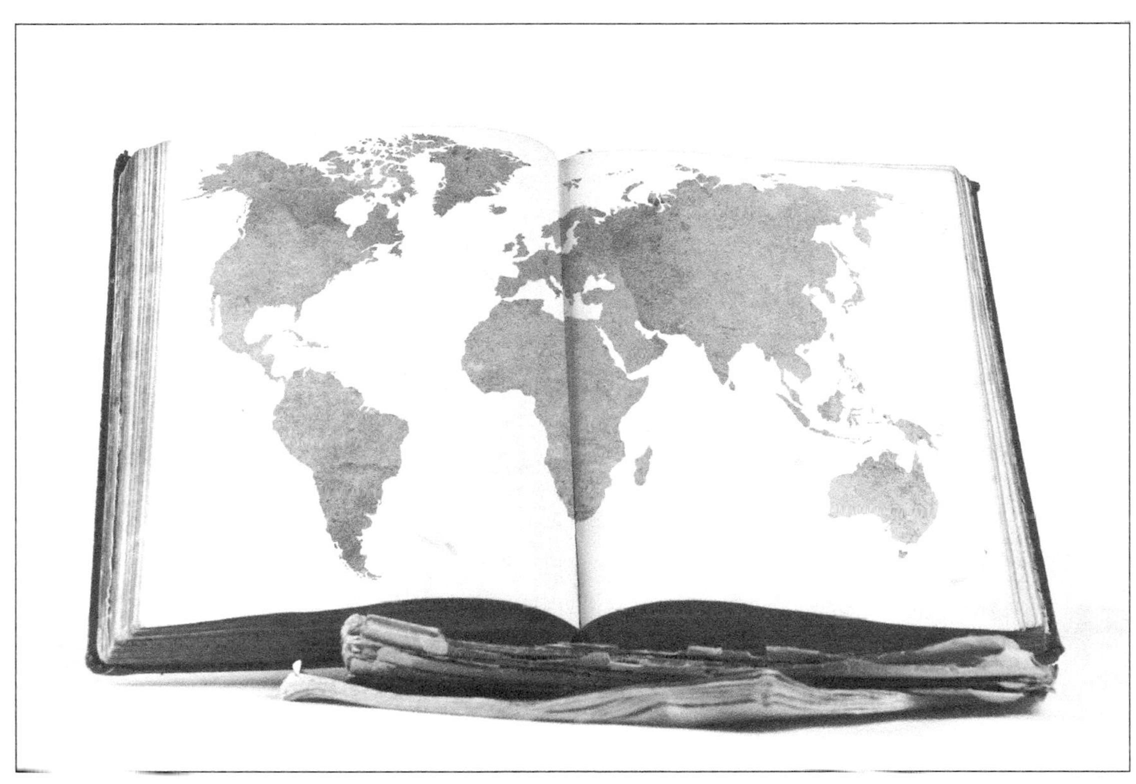

African Religious Traditions

General Description

The religious traditions of Africa can be studied both religiously and ethnographically. Animism, or the belief that everything has a soul, is practiced in most tribal societies, including the Dogon (people of the cliffs), an ethnic group living primarily in Mali's central plateau region and in Burkina Faso. Many traditional faiths have extensive mythologies, rites, and histories, such as the Yoruba religion practiced by the Yoruba, an ethnic group of West Africa. In South Africa, the traditional religion of the Zulu people is based on a creator god, ancestor worship, and the existence of sorcerers and witches. Lastly, the Ethiopian or Abyssinian Church (formally the Ethiopian Orthodox Union Church) is a branch of Christianity unique to the east African nations of Ethiopia and Eritrea.

Number of Adherents Worldwide

Some 63 million Africans adhere to traditional religions such as animism. One of the largest groups practicing animism is the Dogon, who number about six hundred thousand. However, it is impossible to know how many practice traditional religion. In fact, many people practice animism alongside other religions, particularly Islam. Other religions have spread their adherence and influence through the African diaspora. In Africa, the Yoruba number between thirty-five and forty million and are located primarily in Benin, Togo and southwest Nigeria. The Zulu, the largest ethnic group in South Africa, total over eleven million. Like Islam, Christianity has affected the number of people who still hold traditional beliefs, making accurate predictions virtually impossible. The Ethiopian or Abyssinian Church has over thirty-nine million adherents in Ethiopia alone.

Basic Tenets

Animism holds that many spiritual beings have the power to help or hurt humans. The traditional faith is thus more concerned with appropriate rituals rather than worship of a deity, and focuses on day-to-day practicalities such as food, water supplies, and disease. Ancestors, particularly those most recently dead, are invoked for their aid. Those who practice animism believe in life after death; some adherents may attempt to contact the spirits of the dead. Animists acknowledge the existence of tribal gods. (However, African people traditionally do not make images of God, who is thought of as Spirit.)

The Dogon divide into two caste-like groups: the inneomo (pure) and innepuru (impure). The hogon leads the inneomo, who may not sacrifice animals and whose leaders are forbidden to hunt. The inneomo also cannot prepare or bury the dead. While the innepuru can do all of the above tasks, they cannot take part in the rituals for agricultural fertility. Selected young males called the olubaru lead the innepuru. The status of "pure" or "impure" is inherited. The Dogon have many gods. The chief god is called Amma, a creator god who is responsible for creating other gods and the earth.

The Dogon have a three-part concept of death. First the soul is sent to the realm of the dead to join the ancestors. Rites are then performed to remove any ritual polluting. Finally, when several members of the village have died, a rite known as dama occurs. In the ritual, a sacrifice is made to the Great Mask (which depicts a large wooden serpent and which is never actually worn) and dancers perform on the housetops where someone has died to scare off any lingering souls. Often, figures of Nommo (a worshipped ancestral spirit) are put near funeral pottery on the family shrine.

The Yoruba believe in predestination. Before birth, the ori (soul) kneels before Olorun, the wisest and most powerful deity, and selects a destiny. Rituals may assist the person in achieving his or her destiny, but it cannot be altered. The Yoruba, therefore, acknowledge a need for ritual and sacrifice, properly done according to the oracles.

Among the Yoruba, the shaman is known as the babalawo. He or she is able to communicate with ancestors, spirits and deities. Training for this work, which may include responsibility as a doctor, often requires three years. The shaman is consulted before major life decisions. During these consultations, the shaman dictates the right rituals and sacrifices, and to which gods they are to be offered for maximum benefit. In addition, the Yoruba poetry covers right conduct. Good character is at the heart of Yoruba ethics.

The Yoruba are polytheistic. The major god is Olorun, the sky god, considered all-powerful and holy, and a father to 401 children, also gods. He gave the task of creating human beings to the deity Obatala (though Olorun breathed life into them). Olorun also determines the destiny of each person. Onlie, the Great Mother Goddess, is in some ways the opposite of Olorun. Olorun is the one who judges a soul following death. For example, if the soul is accounted worthy, it will be reincarnated, while the unworthy go to the place of punishment. Ogun, the god of hunters, iron, and war, is another important god. He is also the patron of blacksmiths. The Yoruba have some 1,700 gods, collectively known as the Orisa.

The Yoruba believe in an afterlife. There are two heavens: one is a hot, dry place with potsherds, reserved for those who have done evil, while the other is a pleasant heaven for persons who have led a good life. There the ori (soul) may choose to "turn to be a child" on the earth once more.

In the Zulu tradition, the king was responsible for rainmaking and magic for the benefit of the nation. Rainmakers were also known as "shepherds of heaven." They performed rites during times of famine, drought or war, as well as during planting season, invoking royal ancestors for aid. Storms were considered a manifestation of God.

The Zulu are also polytheistic. They refer to a wise creator god who lives in heaven. This Supreme Being has complete control of everything in the universe, and is known as Unkulunkulu, the Great Oldest One. The Queen of heaven is a virgin who taught women useful arts; light surrounds her, and her glory is seen in rain, mist, and rainbows.

The Ethiopian Church incorporates not only Orthodox Christian beliefs, but also aspects of Judaism. The adherents distinguish between clean and unclean meats, practice circumcision, and observe the seventh-day Sabbath. The Ethiopian (or Abyssinian) Church is monotheistic and believes in the Christian God.

Sacred Text

Traditional religions such as animism generally have no written sacred texts. Instead, creation stories and other tales are passed down orally. The Yoruba do have some sacred poetry, in 256 chapters, known as odus. The text covers both right action in worship and ethical conduct. The Ethiopian Church has scriptures written in the ancient Ge'ez language, which is no longer used, except in church liturgy.

Major Figures

A spiritual leader, or hogon, oversees each district among the Dogon. There is a supreme hogon for the entire country. Among the Yoruba, the king, or oba, rules each town. He is also considered sacred and is responsible for performing rituals. Isaiah Shembe is a prophet or messiah among the Zulu. He founded the Nazareth Baptist Church (also called the amaNazaretha Church or Shembe Church), an independent Zulu Christian denomination. His son, Johannes Shembe, took the title Shembe II. In the Ethiopian Church, now fully independent, the head of the church is the Patriarch. Saint Frumentius, the first bishop of Axum in northern Ethiopia, is credited with beginning the Christian tradition during the fourth century. King Lalibela, noted for authorizing construction of monolithic churches carved underground, was a major figure in the twelfth century.

Major Holy Sites

Every spot in nature is sacred in animistic thinking. There is no division between sacred and profane—all of life is sacred, and Earth is Mother. Sky and mountains are often regarded as sacred space.

For the Yoruba of West Africa, Osogbo in Nigeria is a forest shrine. The main goddess is Oshun, goddess of the river. Until she arrived, the work done by male gods was not succeeding. People seeking to be protected from illness and women wishing to become pregnant seek Osun's help. Ilé-Ifè, an ancient Yoruba city in Nigeria, is another important site, and considered the spiritual hub of the Yoruba. According to the Yoruba creation myth, Olorun, god of the sky, set down Odudua, the founder of the Yoruba, in Ilé-Ifè. Shrines within the city include one to Ogun. The shrine is made of stones and wooden stumps.

Mount Nhlangakazi (Holy Mountain) is considered sacred to the Zulu Nazareth Baptist Church (amaNazaretha). There Isaiah Shembe built a High Place to serve as his headquarters. It is a twice-yearly site of pilgrimage for amaNazarites.

Sacred sites of the Ethiopian Church include the Church of St. Mary of Zion in Axum, considered the most sacred Ethiopian shrine. According to legend, the church stands adjacent to a guarded chapel which purportedly houses the Ark of the Covenant, a powerful biblical relic. The Ethiopian Church also considers sacred the eleven monolithic (rock-hewn) churches, still places of pilgrimage and devotion, that were recognized as a collective World Heritage Site by the United Nations Educational, Scientific and Cultural Organization.

Major Rites & Celebrations

Most African religions involve some sacrifice to appease or please the gods. Among the Yoruba, for example, dogs, which are helpful in both hunting and war, are sacrificed to Ogun. In many tribes, including the Yoruba, rites of passage for youth exist. The typical pattern is three-fold: removal from the tribe, instruction, and return to the tribe ready to assume adult responsibilities. In this initiation, the person may be marked bodily through scarification or circumcision. The Yoruba also have a yearly festival re-enacting the story of Obatala and Oduduwa (generally perceived as the ancestor of the Yorubas). A second festival, which resembles a passion play, re-enacts the conflict between the grandsons of these two legendary figures. A third festival celebrates the heroine Moremi, who led the Yoruba to victory over the enemy Igbo, an ethnicity from southeastern Nigeria, and who ultimately reconciled the two tribes.

Yoruba death rites include a masked dancer who comes to the family following a death, assuring them of the ancestor's ongoing care for the family. If the person was important in the village, a mask will be carved and named for them. In yearly festivals, the deceased individual will then appear with other ancestors.

Masks are also used in a Dogon funeral ritual, the dama ceremony, which is led by the Awa, a secret society comprised of all adult Dogon males of the innepuru group. During ceremonial times, the hogon relinquishes control and the Awa control the community. At the end of the mourning period the dama ceremony begins when the Awa leave the village and return with both the front and back of their heads masked. Through rituals and dances, they lead the spirit of the deceased to the next world. Control of the village reverts to the hogon at that point. The Wagem rites govern contact with the ancestors. Following the dama ceremony, the eldest male descendant, called the ginna bana, adds a vessel to the family shrine in the name of the deceased. The spirit of the ancestor is persuaded to return to the descendents through magic and sacrificial offerings, creating a link from the living to the first ancestors.

Ethiopian Christians observe and mark most typical Christian rites, though some occur on different dates because of the difference in the Ethiopian and Western calendars. For example, Christmas in Ethiopia is celebrated on January 7.

ORIGINS

History & Geography

The Dogon live along the Bandiagara Cliffs, a rocky and mountainous region. (The Cliffs of Bandiagara, also called the Bandiagara Escarpment, were recognized as a UNESCO World Heritage Site due to the cultural landscape, including the ancient traditions of the Dogon and their architecture.) This area is south of the Sahara in a region called the Sahel, another region prone to drought (though not a desert). The population of the villages in the region is typically a thousand people or less. The cliffs of the Bandiagara have kept the Dogon separate from other people.

Myths of origin regarding the Dogon differ. One suggestion is that the Dogon came from Egypt, and then lived in Libya before entering the the region of what is now Burkina Faso, Mauritania, or Guinea. Near the close of the fifteenth century, they arrived in Mali.

Among the Yoruba, multiple myths regarding their origin exist. One traces their beginnings to Uruk in Mesopotamia or to Babylon, the site of present-day Iraq. Another story has the Yoruba in West Africa by 10,000 BCE.

After the death of the Zulu messiah Isaiah Shembe in 1935, his son Johannes became the leader of the Nazareth Baptist Church. He lacked the charisma of his father, but did hold the church together. His brother, Amos, became regent in 1976 when Johannes died. Johannes's son Londa split the church in 1979 when Amos refused to give up power. Tangled in South African politics, Londa was killed in 1989.

The Ethiopian Orthodox Church is the nation's official church. A legend states that Menelik, supposed to have been the son of the Queen of Sheba and King Solomon, founded the royal line. When Jesuits arrived in the seventeenth century, they failed to change the church, and the nation closed to missionary efforts for several hundred years. By retaining independence theologically and not being conquered politically, Ethiopia is sometimes considered a model for the new religious movements in Africa.

Founder or Major Prophet

The origins of most African traditional religions or faiths are accounted for through the actions of deities in creation stories rather than a particular founder. One exception, however, is Isaiah Shembe, who founded the Nazareth Baptist Church, also known as the Shembe Church or amaNazarite Church, in 1910 after receiving a number of revelations during a thunderstorm. Shembe was an itinerant Zulu preacher and healer. Through his influence and leadership, amaNazarites follow more Old Testament regulations than most Christians, including celebrating the Sabbath on Saturday rather than Sunday. They also refer to God as Jehovah, the Hebrew name for God. Shembe was regarded as the new Jesus Christ for his people, adapting Christianity to Zulu practice. He adopted the title Nkosi, which means king or chief.

The Ethiopian Orthodox church was founded, according to legend, by preaching from one of two New Testament figures—the disciple Matthew or the unnamed eunuch mentioned in Acts 8. According to historical evidence, the church began when Frumentius arrived at the royal court. Athanasius of Alexandria later consecrated Frumentius as patriarch of the church, linking it to the Christian church in Egypt.

Creation Stories

The Dogon believe that Amma, the sky god, was also the creator of the universe. Amma created two sets of twins, male and female. One of the males rebelled. To restore order, Amma sacrificed the other male, Nommo, strangling and scattering him to the four directions, then restoring him to life after five days. Nommo then became ruler of the universe and the children of his spirits became the Dogon. Thus the world continually moves between chaos and order, and the task of the Dogon is to keep the world in balance through rituals. In a five-year cycle, the aspects of this creation myth are re-enacted at altars throughout the Dogon land.

According to the Yoruba, after one botched attempt at creating the world, Olorun sent his son Obatala to create earth upon the waters. Obatala tossed some soil on the water and released a five-toed hen to spread it out. Next, Olorun told Obatala to make people from clay. Obatala grew bored with the work and drank too much wine. Thereafter, the people he made were misshapen or defective (handicapped). In anger, Olorun relieved him of the job and gave it to Odudua to complete. It was Odudua who made the Yoruba and founded a kingdom at Ilé-Ifè.

The word *Zulu* means "heaven or sky." The Zulu people believe they originated in heaven. They also believe in phansi, the place where spirits live and which is below the earth's surface.

Holy Places

Osun-Osogbo is a forest shrine in Nigeria dedicated to the Yoruba river goddess, Osun. It may be the last such sacred grove remaining among the Yoruba. Shrines, art, sculpture, and sanctuaries are part of the grove, which became a UNESCO World Heritage site in 2005.

Ilé-Ifè, regarded as the equivalent of Eden, is thought to be the site where the first Yoruba was placed. It was probably named for Ifa, the god associated with divination. The palace (Afin) of the spiritual head of the Yoruba, the oni, is located there. The oni has the responsibility to care for the staff of Oranmiyan, a Benin king. The staff, which is eighteen feet tall, is made of granite and shaped like an elephant's tusk.

Axum, the seat of the Ethiopian Christian Church, is a sacred site. The eleven rock-hewn churches of King Lalibela, especially that of Saint George, are a pilgrimage site. According to tradition, angels helped to carve the churches. More than 50,000 pilgrims come to the town of Lalibela at Christmas. After the Muslims captured Jerusalem in 1187, King Lalibela proclaimed his city the "New Jerusalem" because Christians could no longer go on pilgrimage to the Holy Land.

AFRICAN RELIGIONS IN DEPTH

Sacred Symbols

Because all of life is infused with religious meaning, any object or location may be considered or become sacred in traditional African religions. Masks, in particular, have special meaning and may be worn during ceremonies. The mask often represents a god, whose power is passed to the one wearing the mask.

Sacred Practices & Gestures

The Yoruba practice divination in a form that is originally Arabic. There are sixteen basic figures—combined, they deliver a prophecy that the diviner is not to interpret. Instead, he or she recites verses from a classic source. Images may be made to prevent or cure illness. For example, the Yoruba have a smallpox spirit god that can be prayed to for healing. Daily prayer, both morning and evening, is part of life for most Yoruba.

In the amaNazarite Church, which Zulu Isaiah Shembe founded, singing is a key part of the faith. Shembe himself was a gifted composer of hymns. This sacred music was combined with dancing, during which the Zulu wear their traditional dress.

Rites, Celebrations & Services

The Dogon have three major cults. The Awa are associated with dances, featuring ornately carved masks, at funerals and on the anniversaries of deaths. The cult of the Earth god, Lebe, concerns itself with the agricultural cycles and fertility of the land; the hogon of the village guards the soil's purity and presides at ceremonies related to farming. The third cult, the Binu, is involved with communication with spirits, ancestor worship, and sacrifices. Binu shrines are in many locations. The Binu priest makes sacrifices of porridge made from millet and blood at planting time and also when the help of an ancestor is needed. Each clan within the Dogon community has a totem animal spirit—an ancestor spirit wishing to communicate with descendents may do so by taking the form of the animal.

The Dogon also have a celebration every fifty years at the appearing of the star Sirius B between two mountains. (Sirius is often the brightest star in the nighttime sky.) Young males leaving for three months prior to the sigui, as it is called, for a time of seclusion and speaking in private language. This celebration is rooted in the Dogon belief that amphibious creatures, the Nommo, visited their land about three thousand years ago.

The Yoruba offer Esu, the trickster god, palm wine and animal sacrifices. Because he is a trickster, he is considered a cheater, and being on his good side is important. The priests in Yoruba traditional religion are responsible for installing tribal chiefs and kings.

Among the Zulu, families determine the lobola, or bride price. They believe that a groom will respect his wife more if he must pay for her. Further gifts are then exchanged, and the bride's family traditionally gives the groom a goat or sheep to signify their acceptance of him. The groom's family provides meat for the wedding feast, slaughtering a cow on the morning of the wedding. The families assemble in a circle and the men, in costume, dance. The bride gives presents, usually mats or blankets, to members of her new family, who dance or sing their thanks. The final gift, to the groom, is a blanket, which is tossed over his head. Friends of the bride playfully beat him, demonstrating how they will respond if he mistreats his new wife. After the two families eat together, the couple is considered one.

In the traditional Zulu religion, ancestors three generations back are regarded as not yet settled in the afterlife. To help them settle, offerings of goats or other animals are made and rituals to help them settle into the community of ancestors are performed.

Christmas is a major celebration in Ethiopian Christianity. Priests rattle an instrument derived from biblical times, called the sistra, and chant to begin the mass. The festivities include drumming and a dance known as King David's dance.

Judy A. Johnson, MTS

Bibliography

A, Oladosu Olusegun. "Ethics and Judgement: A Panacea for Human Transformation in Yoruba Multireligious Society." *Asia Journal of Theology* 26.1 (2012): 88–104. Print.

Barnes, Trevor. *The Kingfisher Book of Religions*. New York: Kingfisher, 1999. Print.

Dawson, Allan Charles, ed. *Shrines in Africa: history, politics, and society*. Calgary: U of Calgary P, 2009. Print.

Doumbia, Adama, and Naomi Doumbia. *The Way of the Elders: West African Spirituality*. St. Paul: Llewellyn, 2004. Print.

Douny, Laurence. "The Role of Earth Shrines in the Socio-Symbolic Construction of the Dogon Territory: Towards a Philosophy of Containment." *Anthropology & Medicine* 18.2 (2011): 167–79. Print.

Friedenthal, Lora, and Dorothy Kavanaugh. *Religions of Africa*. Philadelphia: Mason Crest, 2007. Print.

Hayes, Stephen. "Orthodox Ecclesiology in Africa: A Study of the 'Ethiopian' Churches of South Africa." *International Journal for the Study of the Christian Church* 8.4 (2008): 337–54. Print.

Lugira, Aloysius M. *African Religion*. New York: Facts on File, 2004. Print.

Mbiti, John S. *African Religions and Philosophy*. 2nd ed. Oxford: Heinemann, 1991. Print.

Monteiro-Ferreira, Ana Maria. "Reevaluating Zulu Religion." *Journal of Black Studies* 35.3 (2005): 347–63. Print.

Peel, J. D. Y. "Yoruba Religion as a Global Phenomenon." *Journal of African History* 5.1 (2010): 107–8. Print.

Ray, Benjamin C. *African Religions*. 2nd ed. Upper Saddle River: Prentice, 2000. Print.

Thomas, Douglas E. *African Traditional Religion in the Modern World*. Jefferson: McFarland, 2005. Print.

Bahá'í Faith

General Description

The Bahá'í faith is the youngest of the world's religions. It began in the mid-nineteenth century, offering scholars the opportunity to observe a religion in the making. While some of the acts of religious founders such as Buddha or Jesus cannot be substantiated, the modern founders of Bahá'í were more contemporary figures.

Number of Adherents Worldwide

An estimated 5 to 7 million people follow the Bahá'í faith. Although strong in Middle Eastern nations such as Iran, where the faith originated, Bahá'í has reached people in many countries, particularly the United States and Canada.

Basic Tenets

The Bahá'í faith has three major doctrines. The first doctrine is that there is one transcendent God, and all religions worship that God, regardless of the name given to the deity. Adherents believe that religious figures such as Jesus Christ, the Buddha, and the Prophet Muhammad were different revelations of God unique to their time and place. The second doctrine is that there is only one religion, though each world faith is valid and was founded by a ""manifestation of God" who is part of a divine plan for educating humanity. The third doctrine is a belief in the unity of all humankind. In light of this underlying unity, those of the Bahá'í faith work for social justice. They believe that seeking consensus among various groups diffuses typical power struggles and to this end, they employ a method called consultation, which is a nonadversarial decision-making process.

The Bahá'í believe that the human soul is immortal, and that after death the soul moves nearer or farther away from God. The idea of an afterlife comprised of a literal "heaven" or "hell" is not part of the faith.

Sacred Text

The Most Holy Book, or the Tablets, written by Baha'u'llah, form the basis of Bahá'í teachings. Though not considered binding, scriptures from other faiths are regarded as "Divine Revelation."

Major Figures

The Bab (The Gate of God) Siyyad 'Ali Mohammad (1819–50), founder of the Bábí movement that broke from Islam, spoke of a coming new messenger of God. Mirza Hoseyn 'Ali Nuri (1817–92), who realized that he was that prophet, was given the title Baha'u'llah (Glory of God). From a member of Persia's landed gentry, he was part of the ruling class, and is considered the founder of the Bahá'í faith. His son, 'Abdu'l-Bahá (Servant of the Glory of God), who lived from 1844 until 1921, became the leader of the group after his father's death in 1892. The oldest son of his eldest daughter, Shogi Effendi Rabbani (1899–1957), oversaw a rapid expansion, visiting Egypt, America, and nations in Europe. Tahirih (the Pure One) was a woman poet who challenged stereotypes by appearing unveiled at meetings.

Major Holy Sites

The Bahá'í World Center is located near Haifa, Israel. The burial shrine of the Bab, a pilgrimage site, is there. The Shrine of Baha'u'llah near Acre, Israel, is another pilgrimage site. The American headquarters are in Wilmette, Illinois. Carmel in Israel is regarded as the world center of the faith.

Major Rites & Celebrations

Each year, the Bahá'í celebrate Ridvan Festival, a twelve-day feast from sunset on April 20 to sunset on May 2. The festival marks Baha'u'llah's declaration of prophethood, as prophesized by the Bab, at a Baghdad garden. (Ridvan means Paradise.) The holy days within that feast are the first (Baha'u'llah's garden arrival), ninth (the arrival of his family), and twelfth (his departure from Ridvan Garden)—on these days, the Bahá'í do not work. During this feast, people attend social events and meet for devotions. Baha'u'llah referred to it as the King of Festivals and Most Great Festival. The Bahá'í celebrate several other events, including World Religion Day and Race Unity Day, both founded by Bahá'í, as well as days connected with significant events in the life of the founder. Elections to the Spiritual Assemblies, and the national and local administrations; international elections are held every five years.

ORIGINS

History & Geography

Siyyad 'Ali Muhammad was born into a merchant family of Shiraz in 1819. Both his parents were descendents of the Prophet Muhammad, Islam's central figure. Like the Prophet, the man who became the Bab lost his father at an early age and was raised by an uncle. A devout child, he entered his uncle's business by age fifteen. After visiting Muslim holy cities, he returned to Shiraz, where he married a distant relative named Khadijih.

While on pilgrimage in 1844 to the black stone of Ka'bah, a sacred site in Islam, the Bab stood with his hand on that holy object and declared that he was the prophet for whom they had been waiting. The Sunni did not give credence to these claims. The Bab went to Persia, where the Shia sect was the majority. However, because Muhammad had been regarded as the "Seal of the Prophets," and the one who spoke the final revelation, Shia clergy viewed his claims as threatening, As such, nothing further would be revealed until the Day of Judgment. The authority of the clergy was in danger from this new movement.

The Bab was placed under house arrest, and then confined to a fortress on the Russian frontier. That move to a more remote area only increased the number of converts, as did a subsequent move to another Kurdish fortress. He was eventually taken to Tabriz in Iran and tried before the Muslim clergy in 1848. Condemned, he was caned on the soles of his feet and treated by a British doctor who was impressed by him.

Despite his treatment and the persecution of his followers—many of the Bab's eighteen disciples, termed the "Letters of the Living," were persistently tortured and executed—the Bab refused to articulate a doctrine of jihad. The Babis could defend themselves, but were forbidden to use holy war as a means of religious conquest. In three major confrontations sparked by the Shia clergy, Babis were defeated. The Bab was sentenced as a heretic and shot by a firing squad in 1850. Lacking leadership and grief-stricken, in 1852 two young Babis fired on the shah in 1852, unleashing greater persecutions and cruelty against those of the Bahá'í faith.

A follower of the Bab, Mirza Hoseyn 'Ali Nuri, announced in 1863 that he was the one who was to come (the twelfth imam of Islam), the "Glory of God," or Baha'u'llah. Considered the founder of the Bahá'í Faith, he was a tireless writer who anointed his son, 'Abdu'l-Bahá, as the next leader. Despite deprivations and imprisonments, Baha'u'llah lived to be seventy-five years old, relinquishing control of the organization to 'Abdu'l-Bahá before the time of his death.

'Abdu'l-Bahá, whom his father had called "the Master," expanded the faith to the nations of Europe and North America. In 1893, at the Parliament of Religions at the Chicago World's Fair, the faith was first mentioned in the United States. Within a few years, communities of faith were established in Chicago and Wisconsin. In 1911, 'Abdu'l-Bahá began a twenty-eight month tour of Europe and North America to promote the Bahá'í faith. Administratively, he established the spiritual assemblies that were the forerunner of the Houses of Justice that his father had envisioned.

During World War I, 'Abdu'l-Bahá engaged in humanitarian work among the Palestinians in the Holy Land, where he lived. In recognition of his efforts, he was granted knighthood by the British government. Thousands of people, including many political and religious dignitaries, attended his funeral in 1921.

'Abdu'l-Bahá conferred the role of Guardian, or sole interpreter of Bahá'í teaching, to his eldest grandson, Shoghi Effendi Rabbani. To him, all questions regarding the faith were to be addressed. Shoghi Effendi Rabbani was a descendent of Baha'u'llah through both parents. He headed the Bahá'í faith from 1921 to 1963, achieving four major projects: he oversaw the physical development of the World Centre and expanded the administrative order; he carried out the plan his father had set in motion; and he provided for the translating and interpreting of Bahá'í teachings, as the writings of both the Bab and those of Baha'u'llah and 'Abdu'l-Bahá have been translated and published in more than eight hundred languages.

Beginning in 1937, Shoghi Effendi Rabbani began a series of specific plans with goals tied to deadlines. In 1953, during the second seven-year plan, the house of worship in Wilmette, Illinois, was completed and dedicated.

Although the beliefs originated in Shi'ite Islam, the Bahá'í Faith has been declared a new religion without connections to Islam. To followers of Islam, it is a heretical sect. During the reign of the Ayatollah Khomeini, a time when Iran was especially noted as intolerant of diverse views, the Bahá'í faced widespread persecution.

Founder or Major Prophet

Mirza Husayn Ali Nuri, known as Baha'u'llah, was born into privilege in 1817 in what was then Persia, now present-day Iran. At twenty-two, he declined a government post offered at his father's death. Although a member of a politically prestigious family, he did not follow the career path of several generations of his ancestors. Instead, he managed the family estates and devoted himself to charities, earning the title "Father of the Poor."

At twenty-seven, he followed the Babis's movement within Shia Islam, corresponding with the Bab and traveling to further the faith. He also provided financial support. In 1848, he organized and helped to direct a conference that explained the Bab's teaching. At the conference, he gave symbolic names to the eighty-one followers who had attended, based on the spiritual qualities he had observed.

Although he managed to escape death during the persecutions before and after the Bab's death, a fact largely attributed to his upbringing, Baha'u'llah was imprisoned several times. During a four-month stay in an underground dungeon in Tehran, he realized from a dream that he was the one of whom the Bab had prophesied. After being released, he was banished from Persia and had his property confiscated by the shah. He went to Baghdad, refusing the offer of refuge that had come from Russia. Over the following three years a small band of followers joined him, including members of his family. When his younger brother attempted to take over the leadership of the Babis, Baha'u'llah spent two years in a self imposed exile in the Kurdistan wilderness. In 1856, with the community near anarchy as a result of his brother's failure of leadership, Baha'u'llah returned to the community and restored its position over the next seven years.

Concerned by the growing popularity of the new faith, the shah demanded that the Babis move further away from Persia. They went to Constantinople where, in 1863, Baha'u'llah revealed to the whole group that he was "He Whom God Will Make Manifest." From there the Bahá'í were sent to Adrianople in Turkey, and at last, in 1868, to the town of Acre in the Holy Land. Baha'u'llah was imprisoned in Acre and survived severe prison conditions. In 1877, he moved from prison to a country estate, then to a mansion. He died in 1892 after a fever.

Philosophical Basis

The thinking of Shia Muslims contributed to the development of Bahá'í. The writings incorporate language and concepts from the Qur'an (Islam's holy book). Like Muslims, the Bahá'í believe that God is one. God sends messengers, the Manifestations of God, to instruct people and benefit society. These have included Jesus Christ, the Buddha, the Prophet Muhammad, Krishna, and the Bab. Bahá'í also goes further than Islam in accepting all religions—not just Judaism, Christianity, and Islam—as being part of a divinely inspired plan.

Shia Muslims believe that Muhammad's descendents should lead the faithful community. The leaders, known as imams, were considered infallible. The Sunni Muslims believed that following the way (sunna) of Muhammad was sufficient qualification for leadership. Sunni dynasties regarded the imams as a threat and executed them, starting with two of Muhammad's grandsons, who became Shia martyrs.

In Persia, a state with a long tradition of divinely appointed rulers, the Shia sect was strong. When the Safavids, a Shia dynasty, came to power in the sixteenth century, the custom of the imamate was victorious. One tradition states that in 873, the last appointed imam, who was still a child, went into hiding to avoid being killed. For the following sixty-nine years, this twelfth imam communicated through his deputies to the faithful. Each of the deputies was called bab, or gate, because they led to the "Hidden Imam." Four babs existed through 941, and the last one died without naming the next bab. The Hidden Imam is thought to emerge at the end of time to bring in a worldwide reign of justice. From this tradition came the expectation of a Mahdi (Guided One) to lead the people.

During the early nineteenth century, many followers of both the Christian and Islamic faiths expected their respective messiahs to return. Shia teachers believed that the return of the Mahdi imam was near. In 1843, one teacher, Siyyid Kázim, noted that the Hidden Imam had disappeared one thousand lunar years earlier. He urged the faithful to look for the Mahdi imam.

The following year in Shiraz, Siyyad 'Ali Mohammad announced that he was the Mahdi. (*Siyyad* is a term meaning descended from Muhammad.) He referred to himself as the Bab, though he expanded the term's meaning. Eighteen men, impressed with his ability to expound the Qur'an, believed him. They became the Letters of the Living, and were sent throughout Persia (present-day Iran) to announce the dawning of the Day of God.

In 1853, Mirza Husayn Ali Nuri experienced a revelation that he was "He Whom God Shall Make Manifest," the one of whom the Bab prophesied. Accepted as such, he began writing the words that became the Bahá'í scriptures. Much of what is known of the early days of the faith comes from a Cambridge academic, Edward Granville Browne, who first visited Baha'u'llah in the 1890. Browne wrote of his meeting, introducing this faith to the West.

The emphasis of the Bahá'í faith is on personal development and the breaking down of barriers between people. Service to humanity is important and encouraged. Marriage, with a belief in the equality of both men and women, is also encouraged. Consent of both sets of parents is required prior to marrying.

Holy Places

The shrine of the Bab near Haifa and that of Baha'u'llah near Acre, in Israel, are the two most revered sites for those of the Bahá'í faith. In 2008, the United Nations Educational, Scientific, and Cultural Organization (UNESCO) recognized both as World Heritage Sites. They are the first such sites from a modern religious tradition to be added to the list of sites. Both sites are appreciated for the formal gardens surrounding them that blend design elements from different cultures. For the Bahá'í, Baha'u'llah's shrine is the focus of prayer, comparable to the significance given to the Ka'bah in Mecca for Muslims or to the Western Wall for Jews.

As of 2013, there are seven Bahá'í temples in the world; an eighth temple is under construction in Chile. All temples are built with a center dome and nine sides, symbolizing both diversity and world unity. The North American temple is located in Wilmette, Illinois. There, daily prayer services take place as well as a Sunday service.

THE BAHÁ'Í FAITH IN DEPTH

Governance

Elected members of lay councils at international, national, and local levels administer the work of the faith. The Universal House of Justice in Haifa, Israel, is the location of the international nine-member body. Elections for all of these lay councils are by secret ballot, and do not include nominating, candidates, or campaigns. Those twenty-one and older are permitted to vote. The councils make decisions according to a process of collective decision-making called consultation. They strive to serve as a model for governing a united global society.

Personal Conduct

In addition to private prayer and acts of social justice, those of the Bahá'í faith are encouraged to have a profession, craft, or trade. They are also asked to shun and refrain from slander and partisan politics. Homosexuality and sexual activity outside marriage are forbidden, as is gambling.

The Bahá'í faith does not have professional clergy, nor does it engage in missionary work. However, Bahá'í may share their faith with others and may move to another country as a "pioneer." Pioneers are unlike traditional missionaries, and are expected to support themselves through a career and as a member of the community.

Avenues of Service

Those of the Bahá'í Faith place a high value on service to humanity, considering it an act of worship. This can be done through caring for one's own family or through one's choice of vocation. Within the local community, people may teach classes for children, mentor youth groups, host devotional programs, or teach adult study circles. Many are engaged in economic or social development programs as well. Although not mandated, a year or two of service is often undertaken following high school or during college.

United Nations Involvement

Beginning in 1947, just one year after the United Nations (UN) first met, the Bahá'í Faith was represented at that body. In 1948, the Bahá'í International Community was accredited by the UN as an international nongovernmental organization (NGO). In 1970, the faith received special consultative status with the UN Economic and Social Council (ECOSOC). Following World War I, a Bahá'í office opened in Geneva, Switzerland, where the League of Nations was headquartered. Thus the Bahá'í Faith has a long tradition of supporting global institutions.

Money Matters

The International Bahá'í Fund exists to develop and support the growth of the faith, and the Universal House of Justice oversees the distribution of the money. Contributions are also used to maintain the Bahá'í World Center. No money is accepted from non-Bahá'í sources. National and local funds, administered by National or Local Spiritual Assemblies, are used in supporting service projects, publishing endeavors, schools, and Bahá'í centers. For the Bahá'í, the size of the donation is less important than regular contributions and the spirit of sacrifice behind them.

Food Restrictions

Bahá'í between fifteen and seventy years of age **fast** nineteen days a year, abstaining from food and drink from sunrise to sunset. Fasting occurs the first day of each month of the Bahá'í calendar, which divides the year into nineteen months of nineteen days each. The Bahá'í faithful do not drink alcohol or use narcotics, because these will deaden the mind with repeated use.

Rites, Celebrations & Services

Daily prayer and meditation is recommended in the Bahá'í faith. During services there are mediations and prayers, along with the reading of Bahá'í scriptures and other world faith traditions. There is no set ritual, no offerings, and no sermons. Unaccompanied by musical instruments, choirs also sing. Light refreshments may be served afterwards.

Bahá'í place great stress on marriage, the only state in which sex is permitted. Referred to as "a fortress for well-being and salvation," a monogamous, heterosexual marriage is the ideal. To express the oneness of humanity, interracial marriages are encouraged. After obtaining the consent of their parents, the couple takes the following vow: "We will all, verily, abide by the will of God." The remainder of the service may be individually crafted and may also include dance, music, feasting, and ceremony. Should a couple choose to end a marriage, they must first complete a year of living apart while trying to reconcile differences. Divorce is discouraged, but permitted after that initial year.

Judy A. Johnson, MTS

Bibliography

Albertson, Lorelei. *All about Bahá'í Faith*. University Pub., 2012. E-book.

Bowers, Kenneth E. *God Speaks Again: an Introduction to the Bahá'í Faith*. Wilmette: Bahá'í, 2004. Print.

Buck, Christopher. "The Interracial 'Bahá'í Movement' and the Black Intelligentsia: The Case of W. E. B. Du Bois." *Journal of Religious History* 36.4 (2012): 542–62. Print.

Cederquist, Druzelle. *The Story of Baha'u'llah*. Wilmette: Bahá'í, 2005. Print.

Echevarria, L. *Life Stories of Bahá'í Women in Canada: Constructing Religious Identity in the Twentieth Century*. Lang, 2011. E-book.

Garlington, William. *The Bahá'í Faith in America*. Lanham: Rowman, 2008. Print.

Hartz, Paula R. *Bahá'í Faith*. New York. Facts on File, 2006. Print.

Hatcher, William S. and J. Douglas Martin. *The Bahá'í Faith: The Emerging Global Religion*. Wilmette: Bahá'í, 2002. Print.

Karlberg, Michael. "Constructive Resilience: The Bahá'í Response to Oppression." *Peace & Change* 35.2 (2010): 222–57. Print.

Lee, Anthony A. *The Bahá'í Faith in Africa: Establishing a New Religious Movement, 1952–1962*. Brill NV, E-book.

Momen, Moojan. "Bahá'í Religious History." *Journal of Religious History* 36.4 (2012): 463–70. Print.

Momen, Moojan. *The Bahá'í Faith: A Beginner's Guide*. Oxford: Oneworld, 2007. Print.

Smith, Peter. *The Bahá'í Faith*. Cambridge: Cambridge UP, 2008. Print.

Wilkinson, Philip. *Religions*. New York: DK, 2008. Print.

Buddhism

General Description

Buddhism has three main branches: Theravada (Way of the Elders), also referred to as Hinayana (Lesser Vehicle); Mahayana (Greater Vehicle); and Vajrayana (Diamond Vehicle), also referred to as Tantric Buddhism. Vajrayana is sometimes thought of as an extension of Mahayana Buddhism. These can be further divided into many sects and schools, many of which are geographically based. In Buddhism, these different divisions or schools are regarded as alternative paths to enlightenment (Wilkinson 2008).

Number of Adherents Worldwide

An estimated 474 million people around the world are Buddhists. Of the major sects, Theravada Buddhism is the oldest, developed in the sixth century BCE. Its adherents include those of the Theravada Forest Tradition. From Mahayana Buddhism, which developed in the third to second centuries BCE, came several offshoots based on location. In what is now China, Pure Land Buddhism and Tibetan Buddhism developed in the seventh century. In Japan, Zen Buddhism developed in the twelfth century, Nichiren Buddhism developed a century later, and Soka Gakkai was founded in 1937. In California during the 1970s, the Serene Reflection Meditation began as a subset of Sōtō Zen. In Buddhism, these different divisions or schools are regarded as alternative paths to enlightenment.

Basic Tenets

Buddhists hold to the Three Universal Truths: impermanence, the lack of self, and suffering. These truths encompass the ideas that everything is impermanent and changing and that life is not satisfying because of its impermanence and the temporary nature of all things, including contentment. Buddhism also teaches the Four Noble Truths: All life is suffering (Dukkha). Desire and attachment cause suffering (Samudaya). Ceasing to desire or crave conceptual attachment ends suffering and leads to release (Nirodha). This release comes through following the Noble Eightfold Path—right understanding (or view), right intention, right speech, right conduct, right occupation, right effort, right mindfulness, and right concentration (Magga).

Although Buddhists do not believe in an afterlife as such, the soul undergoes a cycle of death and rebirth. Following the Noble Eightfold Path leads to the accumulation of good karma, allowing one to be reborn at a higher level. Karma is the Buddhist belief in cause-effect relationships; actions taken in one life have consequences in the next. Ultimately, many refer to the cessation or elimination of suffering as the primary goal of Buddhism.

Buddhists do not believe in gods. Salvation is to be found in following the teachings of Buddha, which are called the Dharma (law or truth). Buddhism does have saint-like bodhisattvas (enlightened beings) who reject ultimate enlightenment (Nirvana) for themselves to aid others.

Sacred Text

Buddhism has nothing comparable to the Qur'an (Islam's holy book) or the Bible. For Theravada Buddhists, an important text is the Pāli Canon, the collection of Buddha's teachings. Mahayana Buddhists recorded their version of these as sutras, many of them in verse. The Lotus Sutra is among the most important. The Buddhist scriptures are written in two languages of ancient India, Pali and Sanskrit, depending on the tradition in which they were developed. Some of these words, such as karma, have been transliterated into English and gained common usage.

Major Figures

Siddhartha Gautama (ca. 563 to 483 BCE) is the founder of Buddhism and regarded as the Buddha or Supreme Buddha. He is the most highly regarded historical figure in Buddhism.

He had two principle disciples: Sariputta and Mahamoggallana (or Maudgalyayana). In contemporary Buddhism, the fourteenth Dalai Lama, Tenzin Gyatso, is a significant person. Both he and Aung San Suu Kyi, a Buddhist of Myanmar who was held as a political prisoner for her stand against the oppressive regime of that nation, have been awarded the Nobel Peace Prize.

Major Holy Sites

Buddhist holy sites are located in several places in Asia. All of those directly related to the life of Siddhartha Gautama are located in the northern part of India near Nepal. Lumbini Grove is noted as the birthplace of the Buddha. He received enlightenment at Bodh Gaya and first began to teach in Sarnath. Kusinara is the city where he died.

In other Asian nations, some holy sites were once dedicated to other religions. Angkor Wat in Cambodia, for example, was constructed for the Hindu god Vishnu in the twelfth century CE. It became a Buddhist temple three hundred years later. It was once the largest religious monument in the world and still attracts visitors. In Java's central highlands sits Borobudur, the world's largest Buddhist shrine. The name means "Temple of Countless Buddhas." Its five terraces represent what must be overcome to reach enlightenment: worldly desires, evil intent, malicious joy, laziness, and doubt. It was built in the eighth and ninth centuries CE, only to fall into neglect at about the turn of the millennium; it was rediscovered in 1815. The complex has three miles of carvings illustrating the life and teachings of the Buddha. In Sri Lanka, the Temple of the Tooth, which houses what is believed to be one of the Buddha's teeth, is a popular pilgrimage site.

Some of the holy sites incorporate gifts of nature. China has four sacred Buddhist mountains, symbolizing the four corners of the universe. These mountains—Wǔtái Shān, Éméi Shān, Jiǔhuá Shān, and Pǔtuó Shān—are believed to be the homes of bodhisattvas. In central India outside Fardapur, there are twenty-nine caves carved into the granite, most of them with frescoes based on the Buddha's life. Ajanta, as the site is known, was created between 200 BCE and the fifth century CE. Five of the caves house temples.

The Buddha's birthday, his day of death, and the day of his enlightenment are all celebrated, either as one day or several. Different traditions and countries have their own additional celebrations, including Sri Lanka's Festival of the Tooth. Buddhists have a lunar calendar, and four days of each month are regarded as holy days.

ORIGINS

History & Geography

Buddhism began in what is now southern Nepal and northern India with the enlightenment of the Buddha. Following his death, members of the sangha, or community, spread the teachings across northern India. The First Buddhist Council took place in 486 BCE at Rajagaha. This council settled the Buddhist canon, the Tipitaka. In 386 BCE, a little more than a century after the Buddha died, a second Buddhist Council was held at Vesali. It was at this meeting that the two major schools of Buddhist thought—Theravada and Mahayana—began to differ.

Emperor Asoka, who ruled most of the Indian subcontinent from around 268 to 232 BCE, converted to Buddhism. He sent missionaries across India and into central parts of Asia. He also set up pillars with Buddhist messages in his own efforts to establish "true dharma" in the kingdom, although he did not create a state church. His desire for his subjects to live contently in this life led to promoting trade, maintaining canals and reservoirs, and the founding a system of medical care for both humans and animals. Asoka's son Mahinda went to southern Indian and to Sri Lanka with the message of Buddhism.

Asoka's empire fell shortly after his death. Under the following dynasties, evidence suggests Buddhists in India experienced persecution. The religion continued to grow, however, and during the first centuries CE, monasteries and monuments were constructed with support from local rulers. Some additional support came from women within the royal courts. Monastic centers also grew in number. By the fourth century CE, Buddhism had become one of the chief religious traditions in India.

During the Gupta dynasty, which lasted from about 320 to 600 CE, Buddhists and Hindus began enriching each other's traditions. Some Hindus felt that the Buddha was an incarnation of Vishnu, a Hindu god. Some Buddhists showed respect for Hindu deities.

Also during this era, Mahavihara, the concept of the "Great Monastery," came to be. These institutions served as universities for the study and development of Buddhist thinking. Some of them also included cultural and scientific study in the curriculum.

Traders and missionaries took the ideas of Buddhism to China. By the first century CE, Buddhism was established in that country. The religion died out or was absorbed into Hinduism in India. By the seventh century, a visiting Chinese monk found that Huns had invaded India from Central Asia and destroyed many Buddhist monasteries. The religion revived and flourished in the northeast part of India for several centuries.

Muslim invaders reached India in the twelfth and thirteenth centuries. They sacked the monasteries, some of which had grown very wealthy. Some even paid workers to care for both the land they owned and the monks, while some had indentured slaves. Because Buddhism had become monastic rather than a religion of the laity, there was no groundswell for renewal following the Muslim invasion.

Prominent in eastern and Southeast Asia, Buddhism is the national religion in some countries. For example, in Thailand, everyone learns about Buddhism in school. Buddhism did not begin to reach Western culture until the nineteenth century, when the Lotus Sutra was translated into German. The first Buddhist temple in the United States was built in 1853 in San Francisco's Chinatown.

Chinese Communists took control of Tibet in 1950. Nine years later, the fourteenth Dalai Lama left for India, fearing persecution. The Dalai Lama is considered a living teacher (lama) who is to instruct others. (The term *dalai* means "great as the ocean.") In 1989, he received the Nobel Peace Prize.

Buddhism experienced a revival in India during the twentieth century. Although some of this new beginning was due in part to Tibetan immigrants seeking safety, a mass conversion in 1956 was the major factor. The year was chosen to honor the 2,500th anniversary of the Buddha's death year. Buddhism was chosen as an alternative to the strict caste structure of Hinduism, and hundreds of thousands of people of the Dalit caste, once known as untouchables, converted in a ceremony held in Nagpur.

Founder or Major Prophet

Siddhartha Gautama, who became known as the "Enlightened One," or Buddha, was a prince in what is now southern Nepal, but was then northern India during the sixth century BCE. The name Siddhartha means "he who achieves his aim." He was a member of the Sakya tribe of Nepal, belonging to the warrior caste. Many legends have grown around his birth and early childhood. One states that he was born in a grove in the woods, emerging from his mother's side able to walk and completely clean.

During Siddhartha's childhood, a Brahmin, or wise man, prophesied that he would grow to be a prince or a religious teacher who would help others overcome suffering. Because the life of a sage involved itinerant begging, the king did not want this life for his child. He kept Siddhartha in the palace and provided him with all the luxuries of his position, including a wife, Yashodhara. They had a son, Rahula.

Escaping from the palace at about the age of thirty, Gautama first encountered suffering in the form of an old man with a walking stick. The following day, he saw a man who was ill. On the third day, he witnessed a funeral procession. Finally he met a monk, who had nothing, but who radiated happiness. He determined to leave his privileged life, an act called the Great Renunciation. Because hair was a sign of vanity in his time, he shaved his head. He looked for enlightenment via an ascetic life of little food or sleep. He followed this path for six years, nearly starving to death. Eventually, he determined on a Middle Way, a path neither luxurious as he had known in the palace, nor ascetic as he had attempted.

After three days and nights of meditating under a tree at Bodh Gaya, Siddhartha achieved his goal of enlightenment, or Nirvana. He escaped fear of suffering and death.

The Buddha began his preaching career, which spanned some forty years, following his enlightenment. He gave his first sermon in northeast India at Sarnath in a deer park. The first five followers became the first community, or sangha. Buddha died around age eighty, in 483 BCE after he had eaten poisoned food. After warning his followers not to eat the food, he meditated until he died.

Buddhists believe in many enlightened ones. Siddhartha is in one tradition regarded as the fourth buddha, while other traditions hold him to have been the seventh or twenty-fifth buddha.

His disciples, who took the ideas throughout India, repeated his teachings. When the later Buddhists determined to write down the teachings of the Buddha, they met to discuss the ideas and agreed that a second meeting should occur in a century. At the third council, which was held at Pataliputta, divisions occurred. The two major divisions—Theravada and Mahayana—differ over the texts to be used and the interpretation of the teachings. Theravada can be translated as "the Teachings of the Elders," while Mahayana means "Great Vehicle."

Theravada Buddhists believe that only monks can achieve enlightenment through the teachings of another buddha, or enlightened being. Thus they try to spend some part of their lives in a monastery. Buddhists in the Mahayana tradition, on the other hand, feel that all people can achieve enlightenment, without being in a monastery. Mahayanans also regard some as bodhisattvas, people who have achieved the enlightened state but renounce Nirvana to help others achieve it.

Philosophical Basis

During Siddhartha's lifetime, Hinduism was the predominant religion in India. Many people, especially in northern India, were dissatisfied with the rituals and sacrifices of that religion. In addition, as many small kingdoms expanded and the unity of the tribes began to break down, many people were in religious turmoil and doubt. A number of sects within Hinduism developed.

The Hindu belief in the cycle of death and rebirth led some people to despair because they could not escape from suffering in their lives. Siddhartha was trying to resolve the suffering he saw in the world, but many of his ideas came from the Brahmin sect of Hinduism, although he reinterpreted them. Reincarnation, dharma, and reverence for cows are three of the ideas that carried over into Buddhism.

In northeast India at Bodh Gaya, he rested under a bodhi tree, sometimes called a bo tree. He meditated there until he achieved Nirvana, or complete enlightenment, derived from the freedom of fear that attached to suffering and death. As a result of his being enlightened, he was known as Buddha, a Sanskrit word meaning "awakened one." Wanting to help others, he began teaching his Four Noble Truths, along with the Noble Eightfold Path that would lead people to freedom from desire and suffering. He encouraged his followers to take Triple Refuge in the Three Precious Jewels: the Buddha, the teachings, and the sangha, or monastic community. Although at first Buddha was uncertain about including women in a sangha, his mother-in-law begged for the privilege.

Greed, hatred, and ignorance were three traits that Buddha felt people needed to conquer. All three create craving, the root of suffering. Greed and ignorance lead to a desire for things that are not needed, while hatred leads to a craving to destroy the hated object or person.

To the Four Noble Truths and Eightfold Path, early devotees of Buddhism added the Five Moral Precepts. These are to avoid taking drugs and alcohol, engaging in sexual misconduct, harming others, stealing, and lying.

The precepts of the Buddha were not written down for centuries. The first text did not appear for more than 350 years after the precepts were first spoken. One collection from Sri Lanka written in Pāli during the first century BCE is known as Three Baskets, or Tipitaka. The three baskets include Buddha's teaching (the Basket of Discourse), commentary on the sayings (the Basket of Special Doctrine), and the rules for monks to follow (the Basket of Discipline). The name Three Baskets refers to the fact that the sayings were first written on leaves from a palm tree that were then collected in baskets.

Holy Places

Buddhists make pilgrimages to places that relate to important events in Siddhartha's life. While Lumbini Grove, the place of Siddhartha's birth, is a prominent pilgrimage site, the primary site for pilgrimage is Bodh Gaya, the location where Buddha received enlightenment. Other pilgrimage sites include Sarnath, the deer park located in what is now Varanasi (Benares) where the Buddha first began to teach, and Kusinara, the city where he died. All of these are in the northern part of India near Nepal.

Other sites in Asia that honor various bodhisattvas have also become pilgrimage destinations. Mountains are often chosen; there are four in China, each with monasteries and temples built on them. In Japan, the Shikoku pilgrimage covers more than 700 miles and involves visits to eighty-eight temples along the route.

BUDDHISM IN DEPTH

Sacred Symbols

Many stylized statue poses of the Buddha exist, each with a different significance. One, in which the Buddha has both hands raised, palms facing outward, commemorates the calming of an elephant about to attack the Buddha. If only the right hand is raised, the hand symbolizes friendship and being unafraid. The teaching gesture is that of a hand with the thumb and first finger touching.

In Tibetan Buddhism, the teachings of Buddha regarding the cycle of rebirth are symbolized in the six-spoke wheel of life. One may be reborn into any of the six realms of life: hell, hungry spirits, warlike demons called Asuras, animals, humans, or gods. Another version of the wheel has eight spokes rather than six, to represent the Noble Eightfold Path. Still another wheel has twelve spokes, signifying both the Four Noble Truths and the Noble Eightfold Path.

Tibetan Buddhists have prayer beads similar to a rosary, with 108 beads representing the number of desires to be overcome prior to reaching enlightenment. The worshipper repeats the Triple Refuge—Buddha, dharma, and sangha—or a mantra.

The prayer wheel is another device that Tibetan Buddhists use. Inside the wheel is a roll of paper on which the sacred mantra—Hail to the jewel in the lotus—is written many times. The lotus is a symbol of growing spiritually; it grows in muddied waters, but with the stems and flowers, it reaches toward the sun. By turning the wheel and spinning the mantra, the practitioner spreads blessings. Bells may be rung to wake the hearer out of ignorance.

In Tantric Buddhism, the mandala, or circle, serves as a map of the entire cosmos. Mandalas may be made of colored grains of sand, carved or painted. They are used to help in meditation and are thought to have a spiritual energy.

Buddhism recognizes Eight Auspicious Symbols, including the banner, conch shell, fish, knot, lotus, treasure vase, umbrella, and wheel. Each has a particular significance. A conch shell, for example, is often blown to call worshippers to meetings. Because its sound travels far, it signifies the voice of Buddha traveling throughout the world. Fish are fertility symbols because they have thousands of offspring. In Buddhist imagery, they are often in facing pairs and fashioned of gold. The lotus represents spiritual growth, rooted in muddy water but flowering toward the sun. The umbrella symbolizes protection, because servants once used them to protect royalty from both sun and rain.

Sacred Practices & Gestures

Two major practices characterize Buddhism: gift-giving and showing respect to images and relics of the Buddha. The first is the transaction between laity and monks in which laypersons present sacrificial offerings to the monks, who in return share their higher state of spiritual being with the laity. Although Buddhist monks are permitted to own very little, they each have a begging bowl, which is often filled with rice.

Buddhists venerate statues of the Buddha, bodhisattvas, and saints; they also show respect to his relics, housed in stupas. When in the presence of a statue of the Buddha, worshippers have a series of movements they repeat three times, thus dedicating their movements to the Triple Refuge. It begins with a dedicated body: placing hands together with the palms cupped slightly and fingers touching, the devotee raises the hands to the forehead. The second step symbolizes right speech by lowering the hands to just below the mouth. In the third movement, the hands are lowered to the front of the chest, indicating that heart—and by extension, mind—are also dedicated to the Triple Refuge. The final movement is prostration. The devotee first gets on all fours, then lowers either the entire body to the floor or lowers the head, so that there are five points of contact with the floor.

Statues of the Buddha give a clue to the gestures held important to his followers. The gesture of turning the hand towards the ground indicates that one is observing Earth. Devotees assume a lotus position, with legs crossed, when in meditation.

Allowing the left hand to rest in the lap and the right hand to point down to Earth is a gesture used in meditation. Another common gesture is to touch thumb and fingertips together while the palms of both hands face up, thus forming a flat triangular shape. The triangle signifies the Three Jewels of Buddhism.

Food Restrictions

Buddhism does not require one to be a vegetarian. Many followers do not eat meat, however, because to do so involves killing other creatures. Both monks and laypersons may choose not to eat after noontime during the holy days of each month.

Rites, Celebrations, & Services

Ancient Buddhism recognized four holy days each month, known as *uposatha*. These days included the full moon and new moon days of each lunar month, as well as the eighth day after each of these moons appeared. Both monks and members of the laity have special religious duties during these four days. A special service takes place in which flowers are offered to images of the Buddha, precepts are repeated, and a sermon is preached. On these four days, an additional three precepts may be undertaken along with the five regularly observed. The three extra duties are to refrain from sleeping on a luxurious bed, eating any food after noon, and adorning the body or going to entertainments.

In Theravada nations, three major life events of the Buddha—birth, enlightenment, and entering nirvana—are celebrated on Vesak, or Buddha Day. In temples, statues of Buddha as a child are ceremonially cleaned. Worshippers may offer incense and flowers. To symbolize the Buddha's enlightenment, lights may be illuminated in trees and temples. Because it is a day of special kindness, some people in Thailand refrain from farm work that could harm living creatures. They may also seek special merit by freeing captive animals.

Other Buddhist nations that follow Mahayana Buddhism commemorate these events on three different days. In Japan, Hana Matsuri is the celebration of Buddha's birth. On that day, people create paper flower gardens to recall the gardens of Lumbini, Siddhartha's birthplace. Worshippers also pour perfumed tea over statues of Buddha; this is because, according to tradition, the gods provided scented water for Siddhartha's first bath.

Poson is celebrated in Sri Lanka to honor the coming of Buddhism during the reign of Emperor Asoka. Other holy persons are also celebrated in the countries where they had the greatest influence. In Tibet, for instance, the arrival of

Padmasambhava, who brought Buddhism to that nation, is observed.

Buddhists also integrate their own special celebrations into regular harvest festivals and New Year activities. These festivities may include a performance of an event in the life of any buddha or bodhisattva. For example, troupes of actors in Tibet specialize in enacting Buddhist legends. The festival of the Sacred Tooth is held in Kandy, Sri Lanka. According to one legend, a tooth of Buddha has been recovered, and it is paraded through the streets on this day. The tooth has been placed in a miniature stupa, or sealed mound, which is carried on an elephant's back.

Protection rituals have been common in Buddhism from earliest days. They may be public rituals meant to avoid a collective danger, such as those held in Sri Lanka and other Southeast Asia nations. Or they may be designed for private use. The role of these rituals is greater in Mahayana tradition, especially in Tibet. Mantras are chanted for this reason.

Customs surrounding death and burial differ between traditions and nations. A common factor, however, is the belief that the thoughts of a person at death are significant. This period may be extended for three days following death, due to a belief in consciousness for that amount of time after death. To prepare the mind of the dying, another person may read sacred texts aloud.

Judy A. Johnson, MTS

Bibliography

Armstrong, Karen. *Buddha*. New York: Penguin, 2001. Print.

Barnes, Trevor. *The Kingfisher Book of Religions*. New York: Kingfisher, 1999. Print.

Chodron, Thubten. *Buddhism for Beginners*. Ithaca: Snow Lion, 2001. Print.

Eckel, Malcolm David. *Buddhism*. Oxford: Oxford UP, 2002. Print.

Epstein, Ron. "Application of Buddhist Teachings in Modern Life." *Religion East & West* Oct. 2012: 52–61. Print.

Harding, John S. *Studying Buddhism in Practice*. Routledge, 2012. E-book. Studying Religions in Practice.

Harvey, Peter. *An Introduction to Buddhism: Teachings, History and Practices*. 2nd ed. Cambridge UP, 2013. E-book.

Heirman, Ann. "Buddhist Nuns: Between Past and Present." *International Review for the History of Religions* 58.5/6 (2011): 603–31. Print.

Langley, Myrtle. *Religion*. New York: Knopf, 1996. Print.

Low, Kim Cheng Patrick. "Three Treasures of Buddhism & Leadership Insights." *Culture & Religion Review Journal* 2012.3 (2012): 66–72. Print.

Low, Patrick Kim Cheng. "Leading Change, the Buddhist Perspective." *Culture & Religion Review Journal* 2012.1 (2012): 127–45. Print.

McMahan, David L. *Buddhism in the Modern World*. Routledge, 2012. E-book.

Meredith, Susan. *The Usborne Book of World Religions*. London: Usborne, 1995. Print.

Morgan, Diane. *Essential Buddhism: A Comprehensive Guide to Belief and Practice*. Praeger, 2010. E-book.

Wilkinson, Philip. *Buddhism*. New York: DK, 2003.Print.

Wilkinson, Philip. *Religions*. New York: DK, 2008. Print.

Christianity

General Description

Christianity is one of the world's major religions. It is based on the life and teachings of Jesus of Nazareth, called the Christ, or anointed one. It is believed that there are over thirty thousand denominations or sects of Christianity worldwide. Generally, most of these sects fall under the denominational families of Catholicism, Protestant, and Orthodox. (Anglican and Oriental Orthodox are sometimes added as separate branches.) Most denominations have developed since the seventeenth-century Protestant Reformation.

Number of Adherents Worldwide

Over 2.3 billion people around the world claim allegiance to Christianity in one of its many forms. The three major divisions are Roman Catholicism, Eastern Orthodox, and Protestant. Within each group are multiple denominations. Roman Catholics number more than 1.1 billion followers, while the Eastern Orthodox Church has between 260 and 278 million adherents. An estimated 800 million adherents follow one of the various Protestant denominations, including Anglican, Baptist, Lutheran, Presbyterian, and Methodist. Approximately 1 percent of Christians, or 28 million adherents, do not belong to one of the three major divisions

There are a number of other groups, such as the Amish, with an estimated 249,000 members, and the Quakers, numbering approximately 377,000. Both of these churches—along with Mennonites, who number 1.7 million—are in the peace tradition (their members are conscientious objectors). Pentecostals have 600 million adherents worldwide. Other groups that are not always considered Christian by more conservative groups include Jehovah's Witnesses (7.6 million) and Mormons (13 million) (Wilkinson, p. 104-121).

Basic Tenets

The summaries of the Christian faith are found in the Apostles Creed and Nicene Creed. In addition, some churches have developed their own confessions of faith, such as Lutheranism's Augsburg Confession. Christianity is a monotheistic tradition, although most Christians believe in the Trinity, defined as one God in three separate but equal persons—Father, Son, and Holy Spirit. More modern, gender-neutral versions of the Trinitarian formula may refer to Creator, Redeemer, and Sanctifier. Many believe in the doctrine of original sin, which means that the disobedience of Adam and Eve in the Garden of Eden has been passed down through all people; because of this sin, humankind is in need of redemption. Jesus Christ was born, lived a sinless life, and then was crucified and resurrected as a substitute for humankind. Those who accept this sacrifice for sin will receive eternal life in a place of bliss after death. Many Christians believe that a Second Coming of Jesus will inaugurate a millennial kingdom and a final judgment (in which people will be judged according to their deeds and their eternal souls consigned to heaven or hell), as well as a resurrected physical body.

Sacred Text

The Bible is the sacred text of Christianity, which places more stress on the New Testament. The canon of the twenty-six books of the New Testament was finally determined in the latter half of the fourth century CE.

Major Figures

Christianity is based on the life and teachings of Jesus of Nazareth. His mother, Mary, is especially revered in Roman Catholicism and the Eastern Orthodox tradition, where she is known as Theotokos (God-bearer). Jesus spread his teachings through the twelve apostles, or disciples, who he himself chose and named. Paul (Saint Paul or Paul the Apostle), who became the first missionary to the Gentiles—and whose writings comprise a bulk of the New Testament—is a key figure for the theological treatises embedded in his letters to early churches. His conversion occurred after Jesus' crucifixion. All of these figures are biblically represented.

Under the Emperor Constantine, Christianity went from a persecuted religion to the state religion. Constantine also convened the Council of Nicea in 325 CE, which expressed the formula defining Jesus as fully God and fully human. Saint Augustine (354–430) was a key thinker of the early church who became the Bishop of Hippo in North Africa. He outlined the principles of just war and expressed the ideas of original sin. He also suggested what later became the Catholic doctrine of purgatory.

In the sixth century, Saint Benedict inscribed a rule for monks that became a basis for monastic life. Martin Luther, the monk who stood against the excesses of the Roman Catholic Church, ignited the seventeenth-century Protestant Reformation. He proclaimed that salvation came by grace alone, not through works. In the twentieth century, Pope John XXIII convened the Vatican II Council, or Second Vatican Council, which made sweeping changes to the liturgy and daily practice for Roman Catholics.

Major Holy Sites

The key events in the life of Jesus Christ occurred in the region of Palestine. Bethlehem is honored as the site of Jesus's birth; Jerusalem is especially revered as the site of Jesus's crucifixion. The capital of the empire, Rome, also became the center of Christianity until the Emperor Constantine shifted the focus to Constantinople. Rome today is the seat of the Vatican, an independent city-state that houses the government of the Roman Catholic Church. Canterbury, the site of the martyrdom of Saint Thomas Becket and seat of the archbishop of the Anglican Communion, is a pilgrimage site for Anglicans. There are also many pilgrimage sites, such as Compostela and Lourdes, for other branches of Christianity. In Ethiopia, Lalibela is the site of eleven churches carved from stone during the twelfth century. The site serves as a profound testimony to the vibrancy of the Christian faith in Africa.

Major Rites & Celebrations

The first rite of the church is baptism, a water-related ritual that is traditionally administered to infants or adults alike through some variant of sprinkling or immersion. Marriage is another rite of the church. Confession is a major part of life for Roman Catholics, although the idea is also present in other branches of Christianity.

The celebration of the Eucharist, or Holy Communion, is a key part of weekly worship for the liturgical churches such as those in the Roman Catholic or Anglican traditions. Nearly all Christians worship weekly on Sunday; services include readings of scripture, a sermon, singing of hymns, and may include Eucharist. Christians honor the birth of Jesus at Christmas and his death and resurrection at Easter. Easter is often considered the most significant liturgical feast, particularly in Orthodox branches.

Many Christians follow a calendar of liturgical seasons. Of these seasons, perhaps the best known is Lent, which is immediately preceded by Shrove Tuesday, also known as Mardi Gras. Lent is traditionally a time of fasting and self-examination in preparation for the Easter feast. Historically, Christians gave up rich foods. The day before Lent was a time for pancakes—to use up the butter and eggs—from which the term Mardi Gras (Fat Tuesday) derives. Lent begins with Ash Wednesday, when Christians are marked with the sign of the cross on their foreheads using ashes, a reminder that they are dust and will return to dust.

ORIGINS

History & Geography

Christianity was shaped in the desert and mountainous landscapes of Palestine, known as the Holy Land. Jesus was driven into the wilderness following his baptism, where he remained for forty days of fasting and temptation. The Gospels record that he often went to the mountains for solitude and prayer. The geography of the deserts and mountains also shaped early Christian spirituality, as men and women went into solitude to pray, eventually founding small communities of the so-called desert fathers and mothers.

Christianity at first was regarded as a sect within Judaism, though it differentiated itself early in the first century CE by breaking with the code of laws that defined Judaism, including the need for circumcision and ritual purity. Early Christianity then grew through the missionary work of the apostles, particularly Paul the Apostle, who traveled throughout the Mediterranean world and beyond the Roman Empire to preach the gospel (good news) of Jesus. (This is often called the Apostolic Age.)

Persecution under various Roman emperors only served to strengthen the emerging religion. In the early fourth century, the Emperor Constantine (ca. 272-337) made Christianity the official religion of the Roman Empire. He also convened the Council of Nicea in 325 CE to quell the religious controversies threatening the Pax Romana (Roman Peace), a time of stability and peace throughout the empire in the first and second centuries.

In 1054 the Great Schism, which involved differences over theology and practice, split the church into Eastern Orthodox and Roman Catholic branches. As Islam grew stronger, the Roman Catholic nations of Europe entered a period of Crusades—there were six Crusades in approximately 175 years, from 1095-1271—that attempted to take the Holy Land out of Muslim control.

A number of theologians became unhappy with the excesses of the Roman church and papal authority during the fifteenth and sixteenth centuries. The Protestant Reformation, originally an attempt to purify the church, was led by several men, most notably Martin Luther (1483-1546), whose ninety-five theses against the Catholic Church sparked the Reformation movement. Other leaders of the Protestant Reformation include John Knox (ca. 1510-1572), attributed as the founder of the Presbyterian denomination, John Calvin (1509-1564), a principle early developer of Calvinism, and Ulrich Zwingli (1484-1531), who initially spurred the Reformation in Switzerland. This period of turmoil resulted in the founding of a number of church denominations: Lutherans, Presbyterians, and Anglicans. These groups were later joined by the Methodists and the Religious Society of Friends (Quakers).

During the sixteenth and seventeenth centuries, the Roman Catholic Church attempted to stem this wave of protest and schism with the Counter-Reformation. Concurrently, the Inquisition, an effort to root out heresy and control the rebellion, took place. There were various inquisitions, including the Spanish Inquisition, which was led by Ferdinand II of Aragon and Isabella I of Castile in mid-fifteenth century and sought to "guard" the orthodoxy of Catholicism in Spain. There was also the Portuguese Inquisition, which began in 1536 in Portugal under King John III, and the Roman Inquisition, which took place in the late fifteenth century in Rome under the Holy See.

During the modern age, some groups became concerned with the perceived conflicts between history (revealed through recent archaeological findings) and the sciences (as described by Charles Darwin and Sigmund Freud) and the literal interpretation of some biblical texts. Fundamentalist Christianity began at an 1895 meeting in Niagara Falls, New York, with an attempt to define the basics (fundamentals) of Christianity. These were given as the inerrant nature of the Bible, the divine nature of Jesus, his literal virgin birth, his substitutionary death and literal physical resurrection, and his soon return. Liberal Christians, on the other hand, focused more on what became known as the Social Gospel, an attempt to relieve human misery.

Controversies in the twenty-first century throughout Christendom focused on issues such as abortion, homosexuality, the ordination of women and gays, and the authority of the scriptures. An additional feature is the growth of Christianity in the Southern Hemisphere. In Africa, for example, the number of Christians grew from 10 million in 1900 to over 506 million a century later. Initially the result of empire-building and colonialism, the conversions in these nations have resulted in a unique blend of native religions and Christianity. Latin America has won renown for its liberation theology, which was first articulated in 1968 as God's call for justice and God's preference for the poor, demonstrated in the ministry and teachings of Jesus Christ. Africa, Asia, and South America are regions that are considered more morally and theologically conservative. Some suggest that by 2050, non-Latino white persons will comprise only 20 percent of Christians.

Founder or Major Prophet

Jesus of Nazareth was born into a peasant family. The date of his birth, determined by accounts in the Gospels of Matthew and Luke, could be as early as 4 or 5 BCE or as late as 6 CE. Mary, his mother, was regarded as a virgin; thus, Jesus' birth was a miracle, engendered by the Holy Spirit. His earthly father, Joseph, was a carpenter.

At about age thirty, Jesus began an itinerant ministry of preaching and healing following his baptism in the Jordan River by his cousin, John the Baptist. He selected twelve followers, known as apostles (sent-ones), and a larger circle of disciples (followers). Within a short time, Jesus' ministry and popularity attracted the negative attention of both the Jewish and Roman rulers. He offended the Jewish leaders with his emphasis on personal relationship with God rather than obedience to rules, as well as his claim to be coequal with God the Father.

For a period of one to three years (Gospel accounts vary in the chronology), Jesus taught and worked miracles, as recorded in the first four books of the New Testament, the Gospels of Matthew, Mark, Luke, and John. On what has become known as Palm Sunday, he rode triumphantly into Jerusalem on the back of a donkey while crowds threw palm branches at his feet. Knowing that his end was near, at a final meal with his disciples, known now to Christians as the Last Supper, Jesus gave final instructions to his followers.

He was subsequently captured, having been betrayed by Judas Iscariot, one of his own twelve apostles. A trial before the Jewish legislative body, the Sanhedrin, led to his being condemned for blasphemy. However, under Roman law, the Jews did not have the power to put anyone to death. A later trial under the Roman governor, Pontius Pilate, resulted in Jesus being crucified, although Pilate tried to prevent this action, declaring Jesus innocent.

According to Christian doctrine, following the crucifixion, Jesus rose from the dead three days later. He appeared before many over a span of forty days and instructed the remaining eleven apostles to continue spreading his teachings. He then ascended into heaven. Ultimately, his followers believed that he was the Messiah, the savior who was to come to the Jewish people and deliver them. Rather than offering political salvation, however, Jesus offered spiritual liberty.

Philosophical Basis

Jesus was a Jew who observed the rituals and festivals of his religion. The Gospels reveal that he attended synagogue worship and went to Jerusalem for celebrations such as Passover. His teachings both grew out of and challenged the religion of his birth.

The Jews of Jesus' time, ruled by the Roman Empire, hoped for a return to political power. This power would be concentrated in a Messiah, whose coming had been prophesied centuries before. There were frequent insurrections in Judea, led in Jesus' time by a group called the Zealots. Indeed, it is believed that one of the twelve apostles was part of this movement. Jesus, with his message of a kingdom of heaven, was viewed as perhaps the one who would usher in a return to political ascendancy.

When challenged to name the greatest commandment, Jesus answered that it was to love God with all the heart, soul, mind, and strength. He added that the second was to love one's neighbor as one's self, saying that these two commands summarized all the laws that the Jewish religion outlined.

Jewish society was concerned with ritual purity and with following the law. Jesus repeatedly flouted those laws by eating with prostitutes and tax collectors, by touching those deemed unclean, such as lepers, and by including

Gentiles in his mission. Women were part of his ministry, with some of them providing for him and his disciples from their own purses, others offering him a home and a meal, and still others among those listening to him teach.

Jesus's most famous sermon is called the Sermon on the Mount. In it, he offers blessings on those on the outskirts of power, such as the poor, the meek, and those who hunger and thirst for righteousness. While not abolishing the law that the Jews followed, he pointed out its inadequacies and the folly of parading one's faith publicly. Embedded in the sermon is what has become known as the Lord's Prayer, the repetition of which is often part of regular Sunday worship. Much of Jesus' teaching was offered in the form of parables, or short stories involving vignettes of everyday life: a woman adding yeast to dough or a farmer planting seeds. Many of these parables were attempts to explain the kingdom of heaven, a quality of life that was both present and to come.

Holy Places

The Christian church has many pilgrimage sites, some of them dating back to the Middle Ages. Saint James is thought to have been buried in Compostela, Spain, which was a destination for those who could not make the trip to the Holy Land. Lourdes, France, is one of the spots associated with healing miracles. Celtic Christians revere places such as the small Scottish isle of Iona, an early Christian mission. Assisi, Italy, is a destination for those who are attracted to Saint Francis (1181-1226), founder of the Franciscans. The Chartres Cathedral in France is another pilgrimage destination from the medieval period.

Jerusalem, Rome, and Canterbury are considered holy for their associations with the early church and Catholicism, as well as with Anglicanism. Within the Old City of Jerusalem is the Church of the Holy Sepulchre, an important pilgrimage site believed to house the burial place of Jesus. Another important pilgrimage site is the Church of the Nativity in Bethlehem. It is built on a cave believed to be the birthplace of Jesus, and is one of the oldest operating churches in existence.

CHRISTIANITY IN DEPTH

Sacred Symbols

The central symbol of Christianity is the cross, of which there are many variant designs. Some of them, such as Celtic crosses, are related to regions of the world. Others, such as the Crusader's cross, honor historic events. The dove is the symbol for the Holy Spirit, which descended in that shape on the gathered disciples at Pentecost after Jesus's ascension.

Various symbols represent Jesus. Candles allude to his reference to himself as the Light of the World, while the lamb stands for his being the perfect sacrifice, the Lamb of God. The fish symbol that is associated with Christianity has a number of meanings, both historic and symbolic. A fish shape stands for the Greek letters beginning the words Jesus Christ, Son of God, Savior; these letters form the word *ichthus*, the Greek word for "fish." Fish also featured prominently in the scriptures, and the early apostles were known as "fishers of man." The crucifixion symbol is also a popular Catholic Christian symbol.

All of these symbols may be expressed in stained glass. Used in medieval times, stained glass often depicted stories from the Bible as an aid to those who were illiterate.

Sacred Practices & Gestures

Roman Catholics honor seven sacraments, defined as outward signs of inward grace. These include the Eucharist, baptism, confirmation, marriage, ordination of priests, anointing the sick or dying with oil, and penance. The Eastern Orthodox Church refers to these seven as mysteries rather than sacraments.

Priests in the Roman Catholic Church must remain unmarried. In the Eastern Orthodox, Anglican, and Protestant denominations, they may marry. Both Roman Catholic and Eastern Orthodox refuse to ordain women to the priesthood.

The Orthodox Church practices a rite known as chrismation, anointing a child with oil following its baptism. The "oil of gladness," as it is known, is placed on the infant's head, eyes, ears, and mouth. This is similar to the practice of confirmation in some other denominations. Many Christian denominations practice anointing the sick or dying with oil, as well as using the oil to seal those who have been baptized.

Many Christians, especially Roman Catholics, use a rosary, or prayer beads, when praying. Orthodox believers may have icons, such as small paintings of God, saints or biblical events, as part of their worship. There may be a font of water that has been blessed as one enters some churches, which the worshippers use to make the sign of the cross, touching fingers to their forehead, heart, right chest, and left chest. Some Christians make the sign of the cross on the forehead, mouth, and heart to signify their desire for God to be in their minds, on their lips, and in their hearts.

Christians may genuflect, or kneel, as they enter or leave a pew in church. In some churches, particularly the Catholic and Orthodox, incense is burned during the service as a sweet smell to God.

In some traditions, praying to or for the dead is encouraged. The rationale for this is known as the communion of saints—the recognition that those who are gone are still a part of the community of faith.

Catholic, Orthodox, and some branches of other churches have monastic orders for both men and women. Monks and nuns may live in a cloister or be engaged in work in the wider world. They generally commit to a rule of life and to the work of prayer. Even those Christians who are not part of religious orders sometimes go on retreats, seeking quiet and perhaps some spiritual guidance from those associated with the monastery or convent.

Food Restrictions

Historically, Christians fasted during Lent as preparation for the Easter celebration. Prior to the Second Vatican Council in 1962, Roman Catholics did not eat meat on Fridays. Conservative Christians in the Evangelical tradition tend to eliminate the use of alcohol, tobacco, and drugs.

Rites, Celebrations & Services

For churches in the liturgical tradition, the weekly celebration of the Eucharist is paramount. While many churches celebrate this ritual feast with wine and a wafer, many Protestant churches prefer to use grape juice and crackers or bread.

Church services vary widely. Quakers sit silently waiting for a word from God, while in many African American churches, hymns are sung for perhaps an hour before the lengthy sermon is delivered. Some churches have a prescribed order of worship that varies little from week to week. Most services, however, include prayer, a sermon, and singing, with or without musical accompaniment.

A church's architecture often gives clues as to the type of worship one will experience. A church with the pulpit in the center at the front generally is a Protestant church with an emphasis on the Word of God being preached. If the center of the front area is an altar, the worship's focus will be on the Eucharist.

Christmas and Easter are the two major Christian celebrations. In liturgical churches, Christmas is preceded by Advent, a time of preparation and quiet to ready the heart for the coming of Christ. Christmas has twelve days, from the birth date of December 25 to the Epiphany on January 6. Epiphany (to show) is the celebration of the arrival of the Magi (wise men) from the East who came to worship the young Jesus after having seen his star. Their arrival is believed to have been foretold by the Old Testament prophet Isaiah, who said "And the Gentiles shall come to thy light, and kings to the brightness of thy rising" (Isaiah 60:3). Epiphany is the revealing of the Messiah to the Gentiles.

In the early church, Easter was preceded by a solemn period of fasting and examination, especially for candidates for baptism and penitent sinners wishing to be reconciled. In Western churches, Lent begins with Ash Wednesday, which is six and half weeks prior to Easter. By excluding Sundays from the fast, Lent thus gives a forty-day fast, imitating that of Jesus in the wilderness. Historically forbidden foods during the fast included eggs, butter, meat, and fish. In the Eastern Church, dairy products, oil, and wine are also forbidden.

The week before Easter is known as Holy Week. It may include extra services such as Maundy Thursday, a time to remember Jesus's new commandment (*maundy* is etymologically related to *mandate*) to love one another. In some Catholic areas, the crucifixion is reenacted in a Passion play (depicting the passion—trial, suffering, and death—of Christ). Some churches will have an Easter vigil the Saturday night before or a sunrise service on Easter morning.

Judy A. Johnson, MTS

Bibliography

Bakker, Janel Kragt. "The Sister Church Phenomenon: A Case Study of the Restructuring of American Christianity against the Backdrop of Globalization." *International Bulletin of Missionary Research* 36.3 (2012): 129–34. Print.

Bandak, Andreas and Jonas Adelin Jørgensen. "Foregrounds and Backgrounds—Ventures in the Anthropology of Christianity." *Ethos: Journal of Anthropology* 77.4 (2012): 447–58. Print.

Barnes, Trevor. *The Kingfisher Book of Religions*. New York: Kingfisher, 1999. Print.

Chandler, Daniel Ross. "Christianity in Cross-Cultural Perspective: A Review of Recent Literature." *Asia Journal of Theology* 26.2 (2012): 44–57. Print.

Daughrity, Dyron B. "Christianity Is Moving from North to South—So What about the East?" *International Bulletin of Missionary Research* 35.1 (2011): 18–22. Print.

Kaatz, Kevin. *Voices of Early Christianity: Documents from the Origins of Christianity*. Santa Barbara: Greenwood, 2013. E-book.

Langley, Myrtle. *Religion*. New York: Alfred A. Knopf, 1996.

Lewis, Clive Staples. *Mere Christianity*. New York: Harper, 2001. Print.

McGrath, Alistair. *Christianity: An Introduction*. Hoboken, New Jersey: Wiley, 2006. Print.

Meredith, Susan. *The Usborne Book of World Religions*. London: Usborne, 1995. Print.

Ripley, Jennifer S. "Integration of Psychology and Christianity: 2022." *Journal of Psychology & Theology* 40.2 (2012): 150–54. Print.

Stefon, Matt. *Christianity: History, Belief, and Practice*. New York: Britannica Educational, 2012. E-book.

Wilkinson, Philip. *Christianity*. New York: DK, 2003. Print.

Wilkinson, Philip. *Religions*. New York: DK, 2008. Print.

Zoba, Wendy Murray. *The Beliefnet Guide to Evangelical Christianity*. New York: Three Leaves, 2005. Print.

East Asian Religions

General Description

East Asian religious and philosophical traditions include, among others, Confucianism, Taoism, and Shintoism. Confucianism is a philosophy introduced by the Chinese philosopher Confucius (Kongzi; 551–479 BCE) in the sixth century BCE, during the Zhou dynasty. Taoism, which centers on Tao, or "the way," is a religious and philosophical tradition that originated in China about two thousand years ago. Shinto, "the way of the spirits," is a Japanese tradition of devotion to spirits and rituals.

Number of Adherents Worldwide

Between 5 and 6 million people, the majority of them in China, practice Confucianism, once the state religion of China. About 20 million people identify as Taoists. Most of the Taoist practitioners are in China as well. In Japan, approximately 107 million people practice Shintoism, though many practitioners also practice Buddhism. Sects of Shinto include Tenrikyo (heavenly truth), founded in 1838, with nearly 2 million devotees. Shukyo Mahikari (divine light) is another, smaller sect founded in the 1960s. Like other sects, it is a blend of different religious traditions (Wilkinson 332–34).

Basic Tenets

Confucianism is a philosophy of life and does concerns itself not with theology but with life conduct. Chief among the aspects of life that must be tended are five key relationships, with particular focus on honoring ancestors and showing filial piety. Confucianism does not take a stand on the existence of God, though the founder, Confucius, referred to "heaven." Except for this reference, Confucianism does not address the question of life after death.

Taoists believe that Tao (the way or the flow) is in everything. Taoism teaches that qi, or life energy, needs to be balanced between yin and yang, which are the female and male principles of life, respectively. With its doctrine of the evil of violence, Taoism borders on pacifism, and it also preaches simplicity and naturalness. Taoists believe in five elements—wood, earth, air, fire and water—that need to be in harmony. The five elements lie at the heart of Chinese medicine, particularly acupuncture. In Taoism, it is believed that the soul returns to a state of nonbeing after death.

Shinto emphasizes nature and harmony, with a focus on lived experience rather than doctrine. Shinto, which means "the way of the gods," is a polytheistic religion; Amaterasu, the sun goddess, is the chief god. At one point in Japan's history, the emperor was believed to be a descendant of Amaterasu and therefore divine. In Tenrikyo Shinto, God is manifested most often as Oyakami, meaning "God the parent."

Shinto teaches that some souls can become kami, a spirit, following death. Each traditional home has a god-shelf, which honors family members believed to have become kami. An older family member tends to the god-shelf, placing a bit of food and some sake (rice wine) on the shelf. To do their work, kami must be nourished. The Tenrikyo sect includes concepts from Pure Land Buddhism, such as an afterlife and the idea of salvation.

Sacred Texts

Five classic texts are sacred to the Confucians. These include the I Ching, or Book of Changes; the Book of Odes; the Book of History; the Book of Rites; and the Annals of Spring and Autumn. The Analects, a collection of Confucius's sayings, is another revered classic. The Tao Te Ching (The Way of Power) is the most sacred book of the Taoists. Those who practice Shinto hold sacred two works: the Kojiki (Record of Ancient Matters) and the Nihon-gi (Chronicles of Japan). Both texts, which contain legends and creation myths, were written during the eighth century.

Major Figures

Confucius, who lived during the sixth century, was the first great philosopher of China. Mengzi (Meng-tzu; 371–289 BCE), known in the West as Mencius, developed Confucius's teachings about the higher power guiding human life. Another ancient Chinese philosopher, Laozi(or Lao-tzu), is the founder of Taoism. He is believed to have been a contemporary of Confucius's in the central region of China. Modern scholars are not certain he ever existed, though one account includes the story of Confucius visiting Laozi. Chuang Tzu wrote of Laozi and his ideas during the fourth and third centuries BCE. Shinto's major figures include Ō no Yasumaro (d. 723), the compiler of the Kokiji who acted under the orders of Empress Gemmei and consulted a bard known to have an infallible memory; the scholar Motoori Norinaga (1730–1800), whose work led to a revived interest in ancient Shinto texts; and Nakayama Miki (1798–1887), the farmer's wife who founded Tenrikyo.

Major Holy Sites

Most Confucian sacred places are located within private homes, where an ancestral shrine and an altar to gods and spirits are maintained. In China's Shandong Province is Qufu, the site of Confucius's family mansion, temple, and cemetery. The temple was built in 478 BCE, only a year after Confucius's death, and has been maintained and enlarged. In addition to its status as a holy site, the United Nations Educational, Scientific, and Cultural Organization (UNESCO) has placed it on their World Heritage List.

Taoists regard mountains as a way to communicate with Earth's primeval powers and with those who are immortal. Five of the nine sacred mountains in China are associated with Taoism: Hengshan in both the north and the south, Songshan in the south, Taishan in the east, and Huashan in the west. The holiest of the five is Taishan, which symbolizes stability, prevents natural disasters, and ensures fertility.

Shintoism has a high regard for natural beauty. As such, Shinto shrines are everywhere, particularly in mountains or near waterfalls. Mountains in particular are regarded as homes of the gods. Mount Fuji is the holiest Shinto mountain, and climbing it to reach the shrine on its peak is an act of worship. More than forty thousand shrines are dedicated to Inari, the rice god.

Shinto was formalized during the Yamato period (the name for ancient Japan), and because the emperor of the imperial dynasty was from the Yamato area and was considered divine, the whole region is revered. At Ise, located near the coast in Mie Prefecture, southeast of Nara, the shrine has been rebuilt every twenty years for at least fourteen centuries. This rebuilding ensures that Toyouke-Ōmikami (the harvest goddess) and Amaterasu (the sun goddess) are renewed in vigor, which in turn invigorates both the rice crop and the imperial line. Those who have died in war are revered as kami in Japan. In Tokyo, a shrine called Yasukuni is dedicated to them. However, there is controversy surrounding the place because of its association with Japan's extreme nationalism prior to World War II.

Sacred Texts

Five classic texts are sacred to the Confucians. These include the I Ching, or Book of Changes; the Book of Odes; the Book of History; the Book of Rites; and the Annals of Spring and Autumn. The Analects, a collection of Confucius's sayings, is another revered classic. The Tao te Ching (The Way of Power) is the most sacred book of the Taoists. Those who practice Shinto hold sacred two works: the Kojiki (Record of Ancient Matters) and the Nihon-gi (Chronicles of Japan). Both texts, which contain legends and creation myths, were written during the eighth century.

Major Figures

Confucius, who lived during the sixth century, was the first great philosopher of China. Mengzi (Meng-tzu; 371–289 BCE), known in the West as Mencius, developed Confucius's teachings about the higher power guiding human life. Another ancient Chinese philosopher, Laozi,(or Lao-tzu) is the founder of Taoism. He is believed to have been a contemporary of Confucius in the central region of China. Modern scholars are not certain he ever existed, though one account includes the story of Confucius visiting Laozi. Chuang Tzu wrote of Laozi and his ideas during the fourth and third centuries BCE. Shinto's major figures include Ō no Yasumaro, the compiler of the Kokiji who acted under the orders of Empress Gemmei and consulted a bard known to have an infallible memory; the scholar Motoori Norinaga (1730–1800), whose work led to a revived interest in ancient Shinto texts; and Nakayama Miki (1798–1887), the farmer's wife who founded Tenrikyo.

Major Holy Sites

Most Confucian sacred places are located within private homes, where an ancestral shrine and an altar to gods and spirits are maintained. In China's Shandong Province is Qufu, the site of Confucius's family mansion, temple and cemetery. The temple was built in 478 BCE, only a year after Confucius's death, and has been maintained and enlarged. In addition to being a holy site, the United Nations Educational, Scientific, and Cultural Organization (UNESCO) has placed it on their World Heritage List.

Taoists consider mountains as a way to communicate with Earth's primeval powers and with those who are immortal. Five of the nine sacred mountains in China are associated with Taoism. They are Hengshan in both the north and south, Songshan in the south, Taishan in the east, and Huashan in the west. The holiest of the five is Taishan, which symbolizes stability, prevents natural disasters, and ensures fertility.

Shintoism has a high regard for natural beauty. As such, Shinto shrines are everywhere, particularly in mountains or near waterfalls. Mountains in particular are regarded as homes of the gods. Mount Fuji is the holiest Shinto mountain, and climbing it to reach the shrine on its peak is an act of worship. More than forty thousand shrines are dedicated to Inari, the rice god.

Shinto was formalized during the Yamato period (the name for ancient Japan), and because the emperor of the imperial dynasty is from the Yamato area, and was considered divine, the whole region is revered. At Ise, located near the coast in the Mie prefecture southeast of Nara, the shrine has been rebuilt every twenty years for at least fourteen centuries. This rebuilding ensures that Toyouke-Ōmikami (the harvest goddess) and Amaterasu (the sun goddess) are renewed in vigor, which in turn invigorates both the rice crop and the imperial line. Those who have died in war are revered as kami in Japan. In Tokyo, a shrine called Yasukuni is dedicated to them. However, there is controversy surrounding the place because of its association with Japan's extreme nationalism prior to World War II.

Major Rites & Celebrations

Confucian celebrations have to do with honoring people rather than gods. At Confucian temples, the philosopher's birthday is celebrated each September. In Taiwan, this day is called "Teacher's Day." Sacrifices, music and dance are part of the event.

Taoism has a jiao (offering) festival near the winter solstice. It celebrates the renewal of the yang force at this turning of the year. During the festival priests, who have been ritually purified, wear lavish clothing. The festival includes music and dancing, along with large effigies of the gods which are designed to frighten away the evil spirits. Yang's renewal is also the focus of New Year celebrations, which is a time for settling debts and cleaning house. Decorations in the yang warm colors of gold, orange and red abound.

Many of the Shinto festivals overlap with Buddhist ones. There are many local festivals and rituals, and each community has an annual festival at the shrine dedicated to the kami of the region. Japanese New Year, which is celebrated for three days, is a major feast. Since the sixteenth century, the Gion Festival has taken place in Kyoto, Japan. Decorated floats are part of the celebration of the shrine.

ORIGINS

History & Geography

During the Zhou dynasty (1050–256 BCE) in China, the idea of heaven as a force that controlled events came to the fore. Zhou rulers believed that they ruled as a result of the "Mandate of Heaven," viewing themselves as morally superior to those of the previous dynasty, the Shang dynasty (1600-1046 BCE). They linked virtue and power as the root of the state.

By the sixth century the Zhou rulers had lost much of their authority. Many schools of thought developed to restore harmony, and were collectively known as the "Hundred Schools." Confucius set forth his ideas within this historical context. He traveled China for thirteen years, urging rulers to put his ideas into practice and failing to achieve his goals. He returned home to teach for the rest of his life and his ideas were not adopted until the Han dynasty (206 BCE–220 CE). During the Han period, a university for the nation was established, as well as the bureaucratic civil service that continued until the twentieth century. When the Chinese Empire fell in 1911, the Confucian way became less important.

Confucianism had influenced not only early Chinese culture, but also the cultures of Japan, Korea, and Vietnam. The latter two nations also adopted the bureaucratic system. In Japan, Confucianism reached its height during the Tokugawa age (1600–1868 CE). Confucian scholars continue to interpret the philosophy for the modern period. Some regard the ideas of Confucius as key to the recent economic booms in the so-called "tiger" economies of East Asia (Hong Kong, Singapore, South Korea, Taiwan, and Thailand). Confucianism continues to be a major influence on East Asian nations and culture.

Taoism's power (te) manifests itself as a philosophy, a way of life, and a religion. Philosophically, Taoism is a sort of self-help regimen, concerned with expending power efficiently by avoiding conflicts and friction, rather than fighting against the flow of life. In China, it is known as School Taoism. As a way of life, Taoism is concerned with increasing the amount of qi available through what is eaten and through meditation, yoga, and tai chi (an ancient Chinese martial art form). Acupuncture and the use of medicinal herbs are outgrowths of this way of life. Church Taoism, influenced by Buddhism and Tao Chiao (religious Taoism), developed during the second century. This church looked for ways to use power for societal and individual benefit.

By the time of the Han dynasty (206–220 CE), Laozi had been elevated to the status of divine. Taoism found favor at court during the Tang dynasty (618–917 CE), during which the state underwrote temples. By adapting and encouraging people to study the writings of all three major faiths in China, Taoism remained relevant into the early twentieth century. During the 1960s and 1970s, Taoist books were burned and their temples were destroyed in the name of the Cultural Revolution (the Great Proletarian Cultural Revolution). Taoism remains popular and vital in Taiwan.

Shinto is an ancient religion, and some of its characteristics appeared during the Yayoi culture (ca. 300 BCE–300 CE). The focus was on local geographic features and the ancestry of local clan leaders. At first, women were permitted to be priests, but that equality was lost due to the influence of Confucian paternalism. The religion declined, but was revived in 1871 following the Meiji Restoration of the emperor. Shoguns (warlords) had ruled Japan for more than 250 years, and Shinto was the state religion until 1945. It was associated with the emperor cult and contributed to Japan's militarism. After the nation's defeat in World War II, the 1947 constitution forbade government involvement in any religion. In contemporary Shinto, women are permitted to become priests and girls, in some places, are allowed to carry the portable shrines during festivals.

Founder or Major Prophet

Confucius, or Kongzi ("Master Kong"), was a teacher whose early life may have included service in the government. He began traveling throughout the country around age fifty, attempting and failing to interest rulers in his ideas for creating a harmonious state. He returned to his home state after thirteen years, teaching a group of disciples who spread his ideas posthumously.

According to legend, Taoism's founder, Laozi, lived during the sixth century. Laozi may be translated as "Grand Old Master," and may be simply a term of endearment. He maintained the archives and lived simply in a western state of China. Weary of people who were uninterested in natural goodness and perhaps wanting greater solitude in his advanced years, he determined to leave China, heading for Tibet on a water buffalo. At the border, a gatekeeper wanted to persuade him to stay, but could not do so. He asked Laozi to leave behind his teachings. For three days Laozi transcribed his teachings, producing the five-thousand-word Tao Te Ching. He then rode off and was never heard of again. Unlike most founders of religions, he neither preached nor promoted his beliefs. Still, he was held with such regard that some emperors claimed descent from him.

No one is certain of the origin of Shinto, which did not have a founder or major prophet. Shinto—derived from two Chinese words, *shen* (spirit) and *dao* (way)—has been influenced by other religions, notably Confucianism and Buddhism.

Philosophical Basis

Confucianism sought to bring harmony to the state and society as a whole. This harmony was to be rooted in the Five Constant Relationships: between parents and children; husbands and wives; older and younger siblings; older and younger friends; and rulers and subjects. Each of these societal relationships existed to demonstrate mutual respect, service, honor, and love, resulting in a healthy society. The fact that three of the five relationships exist within the family highlights the importance of honoring family. Ritual maintains the li, or rightness, of everything, and is a way to guarantee that a person performed the correct action in any situation in life.

Taoism teaches that two basic components—yin and yang—are in all things, including health, the state, and relationships. Yin is the feminine principle, associated with soft, cold, dark, and moist things. Yang is the masculine principle, and is associated with hard, warm, light, and dry things. By keeping these two aspects of life balanced, harmony will be achieved. Another concept is that of wu-wei, action that is in harmony with nature, while qi is the life force in all beings. The Tao is always in harmony with the universe. Conflict is to be avoided, and soldiers are to go as if attending a funeral, solemnly and with compassion. Taoism also teaches the virtues of humility and selflessness.

Shinto is rooted in reverence for ancestors and for the spirits known as kami, which may be good or evil. By correctly worshipping the kami, Shintoists believe that they are assisting in purifying the world and aiding in its functioning.

Holy Places

Confucianism does not always distinguish between sacred and profane space. So much of nature is considered a holy place, as is each home's private shrine. In addition, some Confucian temples have decayed while others have been restored. Temples do not have statues or images. Instead, the names of Confucius and his noted followers are written on tablets. Like the emperor's palace, temples have the most important halls placed on the north-south axis of the building. Temples are also internally symmetrical, as might be expected of a system that honors order. In Beijing, the Temple of Heaven, just south of the emperor's palace, was one of the holiest places in imperial China.

Taoism's holy places are often in nature, particularly mountains. The holiest of the five sacred mountains in China is Taishan, located in the east. Taoism also reveres grottoes, which are caves thought to be illuminated by the light of heaven.

In the Shinto religion, nature is often the focus of holy sites. Mount Fuji is the most sacred mountain. Near Kyoto the largest shrine of Inari, the rice god, is located. The Grand Shrines at Ise are dedicated to two divinities, and for more than one thousand years, pilgrims have come to it. The Inner Shrine (Naiku) is dedicated to Amaterasu, the sun goddess, and is Shinto's most holy location. The Outer Shrine (Geku) is dedicated to

Toyouke, the goddess of the harvest. Every twenty years, Ise is torn down and rebuilt, thus renewing the gods. Shinto shrines all have torii, the sacred gateway. The most famous of these is built in the sea near the island of Miyajima. Those going to the shrine on this island go by boat through the torii.

EAST ASIAN RELIGIONS IN DEPTH

Sacred Symbols

Water is regarded as the source of life in Confucianism. The water symbol has thus become an unofficial symbol of Confucianism, represented by the Japanese ideogram or character for water, the Mizu, which somewhat resembles a stick figure with an extra leg. Other sacred symbols include the ancestor tablets in shrines of private homes, which are symbolic of the presence of the ancestor to whom offerings are made in hopes of aid.

While not a sacred symbol as the term is generally used, the black and white symbol of yin and yang is a common Taoist emblem. Peaches are also of a symbolic nature in Taoism, and often appear in Asian art. They are based on the four peaches that grew every three thousand years and which the mother of the fairies gave to the Han emperor Wu Ti (140–87 BCE). They are often symbolic of the Immortals.

The Shinto stylized sun, which appears on the Japanese flag, is associated with Amaterasu, the sun goddess. The torii, the gateway forming an entrance to sacred space, is another symbol associated with Shinto.

Sacred Practices & Gestures

Confucian rulers traditionally offered sacrifices honoring Confucius at the spring and autumnal equinoxes. Most of the Confucian practices take place at home shrines honoring the ancestors.

Taoists believe that one can reach Tao (the way) through physical movements, chanting, or meditation. Because mountains, caves, and springs are often regarded as sacred sites, pilgrimages are important to Taoists. At a Taoist funeral, a paper fairy crane is part of the procession. After the funeral, the crane, which symbolizes a heavenly messenger, is burned. The soul of the deceased person is then thought to ride to heaven on the back of the crane.

Many Shinto shrines exist throughout Japan. Most of them have a sacred arch, known as a torii. At the shrine's entrance, worshippers rinse their mouths and wash their hands to be purified before entering the prayer hall. Before praying, a worshipper will clap twice and ring a bell to let the kami know they are there. Only priests may enter the inner hall, which is where the kami live. During a festival, however, the image of the kami is placed in a portable shrine and carried in a procession through town, so that all may receive a blessing.

Rites, Celebrations & Services

Early Confucianism had no priests, and bureaucrats performed any rituals that were necessary. When the Chinese Empire fell in 1911, imperial ceremonies ended as well. Rituals have become less important in modern times. In contemporary times the most important rite is marriage, the beginning of a new family for creating harmony. There is a correct protocol for each aspect of marriage, from the proposal and engagement to exchanging vows. During the ceremony, the groom takes the bride to his family's ancestor tablets to "introduce" her to them and receive a blessing. The couple bows to the ancestors during the ceremony.

After a death occurs, mourners wear coarse material and bring gifts of incense and money to help defray the costs. Added to the coffin holding are food offerings and significant possessions. A willow branch symbolizing the deceased's soul is carried with the coffin to the place of burial. After the burial, family members take the willow branch to their home altar and perform a ritual to add the deceased to the souls at the family's shrine.

Confucians and Taoists celebrate many of the same Chinese festivals, some of which originated before either Confucianism or Taoism began and reflect aspects of both traditions. While some festivals are not necessarily Taoist, they may be led by Taoist priests. During the Lantern Festival, which occurs on the first full moon of the New Year, offerings are made to the gods. Many of the festivals are tied to calendar events. Qingming (Clear and Bright) celebrates the coming of spring and is a time to remember the dead. During this time, families often go to the family gravesite for a picnic. The Double Fifth is the midsummer festival that occurs on the fifth day of the fifth month, and coincides with the peak of yang power. To protect themselves from too much of the male force, people don garments of the five colors—black, blue, red, white, and yellow—and with the five "poisons"—centipede, lizard, scorpion, snake, and toad—in the pattern of their clothes and on amulets. The gates of hell open at the Feast of the Hungry Ghosts. Priests have ceremonies that encourage the escaped evil spirits to repent or return to hell.

Marriage is an important rite in China, and thus in Taoism as well. Astrologers look at horoscopes to ensure that the bride and groom are well matched and to find the best day for the ceremony. The groom's family is always placed at the east (yang) and the bride's family to the west (yin) to bring harmony. When a person dies, the mourners again sit in the correct locations, while the head of the deceased points south. White is the color of mourning and of yin. At the home of the deceased, white cloths cover the family altar. Mourners may ease the soul's journey with symbolic artifacts or money. They may also go after the funeral to underground chambers beneath the temples to offer a sacrifice on behalf of the dead.

In the Shinto religion, rites exist for many life events. For example, pregnant women ask at a shrine for their children to be born safely, and the mother or grandmother brings a child who is thirty-two or thirty-three-days-old to a shrine for the first visit and blessing. A special festival also exists for children aged three, five or seven, who go to the shrine for purifying. In addition, a bride and groom are purified before the wedding, usually conducted by Shinto priests. Shinto priests may also offer blessings for a new car or building. The New Year and the Spring Festival are among the most important festivals, and shrine virgins, known as miko girls, may dance to celebrate life's renewal. Other festivals include the Feast of the Puppets, Boys' Day, the Water Kami Festival, the Star Feast, the Festival of the Dead, and the autumnal equinox.

Judy A. Johnson, MTS

Bibliography

Barnes, Trevor. *The Kingfisher Book of Religions*. New York: Kingfisher, 1999. Print.

Bell, Daniel A. "Reconciling Socialism and Confucianism? Reviving Tradition in China." *Dissent* 57.1 (2010): 91–99. Print.

Chang, Chung-yuan. *Creativity and Taoism: A Study of Chinese Philosophy, Art and Poetry*. London: Kingsley, 2011. E-book.

Coogan, Michael D., ed. *Eastern Religions*. New York: Oxford UP, 2005. Print.

Eliade, Mircea, and Ioan P. Couliano. *The Eliade Guide to World Religions*. New York: Harper, 1991. Print.

Lao Tzu. *Tao Te Ching*. Trans. Stephen Mitchell. New York: Harper, 1999. Print.

Li, Yingzhang. *Lao-tzu's Treatise on the Response of the Tao*. Trans. Eva Wong. New Haven: Yale UP, 2011. Print.

Littlejohn, Ronnie. *Confucianism: An Introduction*. New York: Tauris, 2011. E-book.

Littleton, C. Scott. *Shinto*. Oxford: Oxford UP, 2002. Print.

Mcvay, Kera. *All about Shinto*. Delhi: University, 2012. Ebook.

Merton, Thomas. *The Way of Chuang Tzu*. New York: New Directions, 1965. Print.

Oldstone-Moore, Jennifer. *Confucianism*. Oxford: Oxford UP, 2002. Print.

Poceski, Mario. *Chinese Religions: The EBook*. Providence, UT: Journal of Buddhist Ethics Online Books, 2009. E-book.

Van Norden, Bryan W. *Introduction to Classical Chinese Philosophy*. Indianapolis: Hackett, 2011. Print.

Wilkinson, Philip. *Religions*. New York: DK, 2008. Print.

Hinduism

General Description

Hinduism; modern Hinduism is comprised of the devotional sects of Vaishnavism, Shaivism, and Shaktism (though Smartism is sometimes listed as the fourth division). Hinduism is often used as umbrella term, since many point to Hinduism as a family of different religions.

Number of Adherents Worldwide

Between 13.8 and 15 percent of the world's population, or about one billion people, are adherents of Hinduism, making it the world's third largest religion after Christianity and Islam. The predominant sect is the Vaishnavite sect (Wilkinson, p. 333).

Basic Tenets

Hinduism is a way of life rather than a body of beliefs. Hindus believe in karma, the cosmic law of cause and effect that determines one's state in the next life. Additional beliefs include dharma, one's religious duty.

Hinduism has no true belief in an afterlife. Rather, it teaches a belief in reincarnation, known as samsara, and in moksha, the end of the cycle of rebirths. Different sects have different paths to moksha.

Hinduism is considered a polytheist religion. However, it is also accurate to say that Hinduism professes a belief in one God or Supreme Truth that is beyond comprehension (an absolute reality, called Brahman) and which manifests itself in many forms and names. These include Brahma, the creator; Vishnu, the protector; and Shiva, the re-creator or destroyer. Many sects are defined by their belief in multiple gods, but also by their worship of one ultimate manifestation. For example, Shaivism and Vaishnavism are based upon the recognition of Shiva and Vishnu, respectively, as the manifestation. In comparison, Shaktism recognizes the Divine Mother (Shakti) as the Supreme Being, while followers of Smartism worship a particular deity of their own choosing.

Major Deities

The Hindu trinity (Trimurti) is comprised of Brahma, the impersonal and absolute creator; Vishnu, the great preserver; and Shiva, the destroyer and re-creator. The goddesses corresponding to each god are Sarasvati, Lakshimi, and Parvati. Thousands of other gods (devas) and goddesses (devis) are worshipped, including Ganesha, Surya, and Kali. Each is believed to represent another aspect of the Supreme Being.

Sacred Texts

Hindus revere ancient texts such as the four Vedas, the 108 Upanishads, and others. No single text has the binding authority of the Qur'an (Islam's holy book) or Bible. Hindu literature is also defined by Sruti (revealed truth), which is heard, and Smriti (realized truth), which is remembered. The former is canonical, while the latter can be changing. For example, the Vedas and the Upanishads constitute Sruti texts, while epics, history, and law books constitute the latter. The Bhagavad Gita (The Song of God) is also considered a sacred scripture of Hinduism, and consists of a philosophical dialogue.

Major Figures

Major figures include: Shankara (788–820 CE), who defined the unity of the soul (atman) and absolute reality (Brahman); Ramanuja (1077–1157 CE), who emphasized bhakti, or love of God; Madhva (1199–1278 CE), scholar and writer, a proponent of dualism; Ramprahsad Sen (1718–1775 CE), composer of Hindu songs of devotion, poet, and mystic who influenced goddess worship in the; Raja Rammohun Roy (1772–1833 CE), abolished the custom of suttee, in which widows were burned on the funeral pyres of their dead husbands, and decried polygamy, rigid caste systems, and dowries; Rabindranath Tagore (1861–1941 CE), first Asian to win the Nobel Prize in Literature; Dr. Babasaheb R. Ambedkar (1891–1956 CE), writer of India's constitution and leader of a mass conversion to Buddhism; Mohandas K. Gandhi (1869–1948 CE), the "great soul" who left a legacy of effective use of nonviolence.

Major Holy Sites

The major holy sites of Hinduism are located within India. They include the Ganges River, in whose waters pilgrims come to bathe away their sins, as well as thousands of tirthas (places of pilgrimage), many of which are associated with particular deities. For example, the Char Dham pilgrimage centers, of which there are four—Badrinath (north), Puri (east), Dwarka (west) and Rameshwaram (south)—are considered the holy abodes or sacred temples of Vishnu. There are also seven ancient holy cities in India, including Ayodhya, believed to be the birthplace of Rama; Varanasi (Benares), known as the City of Light; Dwarka; Ujjian; Kanchipuram; Mathura; and Hardwar.

Major Rites & Celebrations

Diwali, the Festival of Lights, is a five-day festival that is considered a national holiday in India. Holi, the Festival of Colors, is the spring festival. Krishna Janmashtmi is Krishna's birthday. Shivaratri is Shiva's main festival. Navaratri, also known as the Durga festival or Dasserah, celebrates one of the stories of the gods and the victory of good over evil. Ganesh Chaturthi is the elephant-headed god Ganesha's birthday. Rathayatra, celebrated at Puri, India, is a festival for Jagannath, another word for Vishnu.

ORIGINS

History & Geography

Hinduism, which many people consider to be the oldest world religion, is unique in that it has no recorded origin or founder. Generally, it developed in the Indus Valley civilization several thousand years before the Common Era. The faith blends the Vedic traditions of the Indus Valley civilization and the invading nomadic tribes of the Aryans (prehistoric Indo-Europeans). Most of what is known of the Indus Valley civilization comes from archaeological excavations at Mohenjo-Daro (Mound of the Dead) and Harappa. (Because Harappa was a chief city of the period, the Indus Valley civilization is also referred to as the Harappan civilization.) The Vedas, a collection of ancient hymns, provides information about the Aryan culture.

The ancient Persian word *hind* means Indian, and for centuries, to be Indian was to be Hindu. Even now, about 80 percent of India's people consider themselves Hindu. The root word alludes to flowing, as a river flows. It is also etymologically related to the Indus River. At first, the term Hindu was used as an ethnic or cultural term, and travelers from Persia and Greece in the sixteenth century referred to those in the Indus Valley by that name. British writers coined the term *Hinduism* during the early part of the nineteenth century to describe the culture of India. The Hindus themselves often use the term Sanatana Dharma, meaning eternal law.

The Rigveda, a collection of hymns to various gods and goddesses written around 1500 BCE, is the first literary source for understanding Hinduism's history. The Vedas were chanted aloud for centuries before being written down around 1400 CE. The Rigveda is one of four major collections of Vedas, or wisdom: Rigveda, Yajurveda, Samaveda, and Atharvaveda. Together these four are called Samhitas.

Additionally, Hinduism relies on three other Vedic works: the Aranyakas, the Brahamans, and the Upanishads. The Upanishads is a philosophical work, possibly written down between 800 and 450 BCE, that attempts to answer life's big questions. Written in the form of a dialogue between a teacher (guru) and student (chela), the text's name means "to sit near," which describes the relationship between the two. Along with the Samhitas, these four are called Sruti (heard), a reference to their nature as revealed truth. The words in these texts cannot be altered.

Remaining works are called Smriti, meaning "remembered," to indicate that they were composed by human writers. The longer of the Smriti epics is the Mahabharata, the Great Story of the Bharatas. Written between 300 and 100 BCE, the epic is a classic tale of two rival, related families, including teaching as well as story. It is considered the longest single poem in existence, with about 200,000 lines. (A film made of it lasts for twelve hours.)

The Bhagavad Gita, or Song of the Lord, is the sixth section of the Mahabharata, but is often read as a stand-alone narrative of battle and acceptance of one's dharma. The Ramayana is the second, shorter epic of the Mahabharata, with about fifty thousand lines. Rama was the seventh incarnation, or avatar, of Vishnu. The narrative relates the abduction of his wife, Sita, and her rescue, accomplished with the help of the monkey god, Hanuman. Some have regarded the Mahabharata as an encyclopedia, and the Bhagavad Gita as the Bible within it.

Although many of the practices in the Vedas have been modified or discontinued, sections of it are memorized and repeated. Some of the hymns are recited at traditional ceremonies for the dead and at weddings.

Hinduism has affected American life and culture for many years. For example, the nineteenth-century transcendental writers Margaret Fuller and Ralph Waldo Emerson were both influenced by Hindu and Buddhist literature, while musician George Harrison, a member of the Beatles, adopted Hinduism and explored his new faith through his music, both with and without the Beatles. In 1965, the International Society for Krishna Consciousness (ISKCON), or the Hare Krishna movement, came to the Western world. In addition, many people have been drawn to yoga, which is associated with Hinduism's meditative practices.

Founder or Major Prophet

Hinduism has no founder or major prophet. It is a religion that has developed over many centuries and from many sources, many of which are unknown in their origins.

Philosophical Basis

Hinduism recognizes multiple ways to achieve salvation and escape the endless cycle of rebirth. The way of devotion is the most popular. Through worship of a single deity, the worshipper hopes to attain union with the divine. A second path is the way of knowledge, involving the use of meditation and reason. The third way is via action, or correctly performing religious observances in hope of receiving a blessing from the gods by accomplishing these duties.

Hinduism is considered the world's oldest religion, but Hindus maintain that it is also a way of living, not just a religion. There is great diversity as well as great tolerance in Hinduism. While Hinduism does not have a set of dogmatic formulations, it does blend the elements of devotion, doctrine, practice, society, and story as separate strands in a braid.

During the second century BCE, a sage named Patanjali outlined four life stages, and the fulfilled responsibilities inherent in each one placed one in harmony with dharma, or right conduct. Although these life stages are no longer observed strictly, their ideas still carry weight. Traditionally, these codes applied to men, and only to those in the Brahman caste; members of the warrior and merchant classes could follow them, but were not obligated. The Shudra and Dalit castes, along with women, were not part of the system. Historically, women were thought of as protected by fathers in their childhood, by husbands in their youth and adulthood, and by sons in old age. Only recently have women in India been educated beyond the skills of domestic responsibility and child rearing.

The earliest life stage is the student stage, or brahmacharya, a word that means "to conduct oneself in accord with Brahman." From ages twelve to twenty-four, young men were expected to undertake learning with a guru, or guide. During these twelve years of studying the Veda they were also expected to remain celibate.

The second stage, grihastha, is that of householder. A Hindu man married the bride that his parents had chosen, sired children, and created a livelihood on which the other three stages depended.

Vanaprastha is the third stage, involving retirement to solitude. Historically, this involved leaving the house and entering a forest dwelling.

A man's wife had the option to go with him or to remain. This stage also involved giving counsel to others and further study.

At the final stage of life, sannyasis, the Hindu renounces material goods, including a home of any sort. He may live in a forest or join an ashram, or community. He renounces even making a fire, and lives on fruit and roots that can be foraged. Many contemporary Hindus do not move to this stage, but remain at vanaprastha.

Yoga is another Hindu practice, more than three millennia old, which Patanjali codified. The four forms of yoga corresponded to the Hindu avenues of salvation. Hatha yoga is the posture yoga seeking union with god through action. Jnana yoga is the path to god through knowledge. Bhakti yoga is the way of love to god. Karma yoga is the method of finding god through work. By uniting the self, the practitioner unites with God. Yoga is related etymologically to the English word *yoke*—it attempts to yoke the individual with Brahman. All forms of yoga include meditation and the acceptance of other moral disciplines, such as self-discipline, truthfulness, nonviolence, and contentment.

Aryan society was stratified, and at the top of the social scale were the priests. This system was the basis for the caste system that had long dominated Hinduism. Caste, which was determined by birth, affected a person's occupation, diet, neighborhood, and marriage partner. Vedic hymns allude to four varnas, or occupations: Brahmins (priests), Kshatriyas (warriors), Vaishyas (merchants and common people), and Shudras (servants). A fifth class, the Untouchables, later known as Dalit (oppressed), referred to those who were regarded as a polluting force because they handled waste and dead bodies. The belief was that society would function properly if each group carried out its duties. These varnas later became wrongly blended with castes, or jatis, which were smaller groups also concerned with a person's place in society.

The practice of Hinduism concerns itself with ritual purity; even household chores can be done in a ritualistic way. Some traditions demand ritual purity before one can worship. Brahmin priests, for example, may not accept water or food from non-Brahmins. Refusal to do so is not viewed as classism, but an attempt to please the gods in maintaining ritual purity.

Mohandas Gandhi was one of those who refused to use the term *Untouchable*, using the term *harijan*(children of God), instead. Dr. Babasaheb R. Ambedkar, who wrote India's constitution, was a member of this class. Ambedkar and many of his supporters became Buddhists in an attempt to dispel the power of caste. In 1947, following India's independence from Britain, the caste system was officially banned, though it has continued to influence Indian society.

Ahimsa, or dynamic harmlessness, is another deeply rooted principle of Hinduism. It involves six pillars: refraining from eating all animal products; revering all of life; having integrity in thoughts, words, and deeds; exercising self-control; serving creation, nature, and humanity; and advancing truth and understanding.

Holy Places

In Hinduism, all water is considered holy, symbolizing the flow of life. For a Hindu, the Ganges River is perhaps the most holy of all bodies of water. It was named for the goddess of purification, Ganga. The waters of the Ganges are said to flow through Shiva's hair and have the ability to cleanse sin. Devout Hindus make pilgrimages to bathe in the Ganges. They may also visit fords in the rivers to symbolize the journey from one life to another.

Pilgrimages are also made to sites associated with the life of a god. For example, Lord Rama was said to have been born in Ayodhya, one of the seven holy cities in India. Other holy sites are Dwarka, Ujjian, Kanchipuram, Mathura, Hardwar, and Varanasi, the City of Light.

After leaving his mountain home, Lord Shiva was thought to have lived in Varanasi, or Benares, considered the holiest city. Before the sixth century, it became a center of education for Hindus. It has four miles of palaces and temples along the river. One of the many pilgrimage circuits covers thirty-five miles, lasts for five days, and includes prayer at 108 different shrines. Because of the river's sacred nature, Hindus come to bathe from its many stone steps, called ghats, and to drink the water. It is also the place where Hindus desire to be at their death or to have their ashes scattered. Because Varanasi is regarded as a place of crossing between earth and heaven, dying there is thought to free one from the cycle of rebirth.

The thirty-four Ellora Caves at Maharashtra, India, are known for their sculptures. Built between 600 and 1000 CE, they were cut into a tufa rock hillside on a curve shaped like a horseshoe, so that the caves go deeply into the rock face. Although the one-mile site includes temples for Buddhist, Jain, and Hindu faiths, the major figure of the caves is Shiva, and the largest temple is dedicated to Shiva.

Lastly, Hindu temples, or mandirs, are regarded as the gods' earthly homes. The buildings themselves are therefore holy, and Hindus remove their shoes before entering.

HINDUISM IN DEPTH

Sacred Symbols

The wheel of life represents samsara, the cycle of life, death and rebirth. Karma is what keeps the wheel spinning. Another circle is the hoop of flames in which Shiva, also known as the Lord of the Dance, or Natraja, is shown dancing creation into being. The flames signify the universe's energy and Shiva's power of both destruction and creation. Shiva balances on his right foot, which rests on a defeated demon that stands for ignorance.

The lotus is the symbol of creation, fertility, and purity. This flower is associated with Vishnu because as he slept, a lotus flower bloomed from his navel. From this lotus Brahma came forth to create the world. Yoga practitioners commonly assume the lotus position for meditation.

Murtis are the statues of gods that are found in both temples and private homes. They are often washed with milk and water, anointed with oil, dressed, and offered gifts of food or flowers. Incense may also be burned to make the air around the murti sweet and pure.

One of Krishna's symbols is the conch shell, a symbol of a demon he defeated. A conch shell is blown at temples to announce the beginning of the worship service. It is a visual reminder for followers of Krishna to overcome ignorance and evil in their lives.

For many years, the Hindus used the swastika as a holy symbol. (*Swastika* is a Sanskrit word for good fortune and well-being.) The four arms meet at a central point, demonstrating that the universe comes from one source. Each arm of the symbol represents a path to God and is bent to show that all paths are difficult. It is used at a time of new beginnings, such as at a wedding, where it is traditionally painted on a coconut using a red paste called kum kum. The symbol appears as a vertical gash across the horizontal layers on the southern face of Mount Kailas, one of the Himalayas's highest peaks, thought to have been the home of Shiva. The mountain is also near the source of the Ganges and the Indus Rivers. The use of the swastika as a symbol for Nazi Germany is abhorrent to Hindus.

Some Hindus use a mala, or rosary, of 108 wooden beads when they pray. As they worship, they repeat the names of God.

Sacred Practices & Gestures

Many homes have private altars or shrines to favorite gods. Statues or pictures of these deities are offered incense, flowers and food, as well as prayers. This daily devotion, known as puja, is generally the responsibility of women, many of whom are devoted to goddesses such as Kali or Sita. A rich family may devote an entire room of their house to the shrine.

Om, or Aum, a sacred syllable recorded first in the Upanishads, is made up of three Sanskrit letters. Writing the letter involves a symbol resembling the Arabic number three. Thus, it is a visual reminder of the Trimurti, the three major Hindu gods. The word is repeated at the beginning of all mantras or prayers.

Each day the Gayatri, which is perhaps the world's oldest recorded prayer, is chanted during the fire ritual. The prayer expresses gratitude to the sun for its shining and invokes blessings of prosperity on all. The ritual, typically done at large consecrated fire pits, may be done using burning candles instead.

Holy Hindu men are known as sadhus. They lead ascetic lives, wandering, begging, and living in caves in the mountains. Regarded as having greater spiritual power and wisdom, they are often consulted for advice.

Food Restrictions

Many Hindus are vegetarians because they embrace ahimsa (reverence for and protection of all life) and oppose killing. In fact, Hindus comprise about 70 percent of the world's vegetarians. They are generally lacto-vegetarians, meaning that they include dairy products in their diets. However, Hindus residing in the cold climate of Nepal and Tibet consume meat to increase their caloric intake.

Whether a culture practices vegetarianism or not, cows are thought to be sacred because Krishna acted as a cowherd as a young god. Thus cows are never eaten. Pigs are also forbidden, as are red foods, such as tomatoes or red lentils. In addition, garlic and onions are also not permitted. Alcohol is strictly forbidden.

Purity rituals before eating include cleaning the area where the food is to be eaten and reciting mantras or praying while sprinkling water around the food. Other rituals include Annaprasana, which celebrates a child's eating of solid food—traditionally rice—for the first time. In addition, at funerals departed souls are offered food, which Hindus believe will strengthen the soul for the journey to the ancestors' world.

Serving food to those in need also generates good karma. Food is offered during religious ceremonies and may later be shared with visiting devotees of the god.

To show their devotion to Shiva, many Hindus fast on Mondays. There is also a regular fast, known as agiaras, which occurs on the eleventh day of each two-week period. On that day, only one meal is eaten. During the month of Shravan, which many consider a holy month, people may eat only one meal, generally following sunset.

Rites, Celebrations & Services

Many Hindu celebrations are connected to the annual cycle of nature and can last for many days. In addition, celebrations that honor the gods are common. Shiva, one of the three major gods, is honored at Shivaratri in February or March. In August or September, Lord Krishna is honored at Krishnajanmashtmi. Prayer and fasting are part of this holiday.

During the spring equinox and just prior to the Hindu New Year, Holi is celebrated. It is a time to resolve disputes and forgive or pay debts. During this festival, people often have bonfires and throw objects that represent past impurity or disease into the fire.

Another festival occurs in July or August, marking the beginning of the agricultural year in northern India. Raksha Bandhan (the bond of protection) is a festival which celebrates sibling relationships. During the festivities, Hindus bind a bauble with silk thread to the wrists of family members and friends.

To reenact Rama's defeat of the demon Ravana, as narrated in the Ramayana, people make and burn effigies. This festival is called Navaratri in western India, also known as the Durgapuja in Bengal, and Dasserah in northern India. It occurs in September or October each year as a festival celebrating the victory of good over evil. September is also time to celebrate the elephant-headed god Ganesha's birthday at the festival of Ganesh Chaturthi.

Diwali, a five-day festival honoring Lakshmi (the goddess of good fortune and wealth), occurs in October or November. This Festival of Lights is the time when people light oil lamps and set off fireworks to help Rama find his way home after exile. Homes are cleaned in hopes that Lakshmi will come in the night to bless it. People may use colored rice flour to make patterns on their doorstep. Competitions for designs of these patterns, which are meant to welcome God to the house, frequently take place.

Jagannath, or Vishnu, is celebrated during the festival Rathayatra. A large image of Jagannath rides in a chariot pulled through the city of Puri.

The temple for Hindus is the home of the god. Only Brahmin priests may supervise worship there. The inner sanctuary of the building is called the garbhagriha, or womb-house; there the god resides. Worshippers must be ritually pure before the worship starts. The priest recites the mantras and reads sacred texts. Small lamps are lit, and everyone shares specially prepared and blessed food after the service ends.

Judy A. Johnson, MTS

Bibliography

Barnes, Trevor. *The Kingfisher Book of Religions*. New York: Kingfisher, 1999. Print.

Harley, Gail M. *Hindu and Sikh Faiths in America*. New York: Facts on File, 2003. Print.

Iyengar, B. K. S. and Noelle Perez-Christiaens. *Sparks of Divinity: The Teachings of B. K. S. Iyengar from 1959 to 1975*. Berkeley: Rodmell, 2012. E-book.

"The Joys of Hinduism." *Hinduism Today* Oct./Dec. 2006: 40–53. Print.

Langley, Myrtle. *Religion*. New York: Knopf, 1996. Print.

Meredith, Susan. *The Usborne Book of World Religions*. London: Usborne, 1995. Print.

Rajan, Rajewswari. "The Politics of Hindu 'Tolerance.'" *Boundary 2* 38.3 (2011): 67–86. Print.

Raman, Varadaraja V. "Hinduism and Science: Some Reflections." *Journal of Religion & Science* 47.3 (2012): 549–74. Print.

Renard, John. *Responses to 101 Questions on Hinduism*. Mahwah: Paulist, 1999. Print.

Siddhartha. "Open-Source Hinduism." *Religion & the Arts* 12.1–3 (2008): 34–41. Print.

Shouler, Kenneth and Susai Anthony. *The Everything Hinduism Book*. Avon: Adams, 2009. Print.

Soherwordi, Syed Hussain Shaheed. "'Hinduism'—A Western Construction or an Influence?" *South Asian Studies* 26.1 (2011): 203–14. Print.

Theodor, Ithamar. *Exploring the Bhagavad Gita: Philosophy, Structure, and Meaning*. Farnham and Burlington: Ashgate, 2010. E-book.

Whaling, Frank. *Understanding Hinduism*. Edinburgh: Dunedin, 2010. E-book.

Wilkinson, Philip. *Religions*. New York: DK, 2008. Print.

Islam

General Description

The word *Islam* derives from a word meaning "submission," particularly submission to the will of Allah. Muslims, those who practice Islam, fall into two major groups, Sunni and Shia (or Shi'i,) based on political rather than theological differences. Sunni Muslims follow the four Rightly Guided Caliphs, or Rashidun and believe that caliphs should be elected. Shia Muslims believe that the Prophet's nearest male relative, Ali ibn Abi Talib, should have ruled following Muhammad's death, and venerate the imams (prayer leaders) who are directly descended from Ali and the Prophet's daughter Fatima.

Number of Adherents Worldwide

Approximately 1.6 billion people, or 23 percent of the world's population, are Muslims. Of that total, between 87 and 90 percent of all Muslims are Sunni Muslims and between 10 and 13 percent of all Muslims are Shia. Followers of the Sufi sect, noted for its experiential, ecstatic focus, may be either Sunni or Shia.

Basic Tenets

Islam is a monotheistic faith; Muslims worship only one God, Allah. They also believe in an afterlife and that people are consigned to heaven or hell following the last judgment.

The Islamic faith rests on Five Pillars. The first pillar, Shahadah is the declaration of faith in the original Arabic, translated as: "I bear witness that there is no god but God and Muhammad is his Messenger." The second pillar, Salah, are prayers adherents say while facing Mecca five times daily at regular hours and also at the main service held each Friday at a mosque. Zakat, "the giving of a tax," is the third pillar and entails giving an income-based percentage of one's wealth to help the poor without attracting notice. The fourth pillar is fasting, or Sawm, during Ramadan, the ninth month of the Islamic calendar. Certain groups of people are excused from the fast, however. The final pillar is the Hajj, the pilgrimage to Mecca required of every able-bodied Muslim at least once in his or her lifetime.

Sacred Text

The Qur'an (Koran), meaning "recitation," is the holy book of Islam.

Major Figures

Muhammad, regarded as the Prophet to the Arabs—as Moses was to the Jews—is considered the exemplar of what it means to be a Muslim. His successors—Abu Bakr, Umar, Uthman, and Ali—were known as the four Rightly Guided Caliphs.

Major Holy Sites

Islam recognizes three major holy sites: Mecca, home of the Prophet; Medina, the city to which Muslims relocated when forced from Mecca due to persecution; and the Dome of the Rock in Jerusalem, believed to be the oldest Islamic building in existence. Muslims believe that in 621 CE Muhammad ascended to heaven (called the Night Journey) from a sacred stone upon which the Dome was constructed. Once in heaven, God instructed Muhammad concerning the need to pray at regular times daily...

There are also several mosques which are considered primary holy sites. These include the al-Aqsa Mosque in the Old City of Jerusalem, believed by many to be the third holiest site in Islam. The mosque, along with the Dome of the Rock, is located on Judaism's holiest site, the Temple Mount, where the Temple of Jerusalem is believed to have stood. Muslims also revere the Mosque of the Prophet (Al-Masjid al-Nabawi) in Medina, considered the resting place of the Prophet Muhammad and the second largest mosque in the world; and the Mosque of the Haram (Masjid al-Haram or the Sacred or Grand Mosque) in Mecca, thought to be the largest mosque in the world and site of the Ka'bah, "the sacred house," also known as "the Noble Cube," Islam's holiest structure.

Major Rites & Celebrations

Two major celebrations mark the Islamic calendar. 'Id al-Adha, the feast of sacrifice—including animal sacrifice—held communally at the close of the Hajj (annual pilgrimage), commemorates the account of God providing a ram instead of the son Abraham had been asked to sacrifice. The second festival, 'Id al-Fitr, denotes the end of Ramadan and is a time of feasting and gift giving.

ORIGINS

History & Geography

In 610 CE, a forty-year-old businessman from Mecca named Muhammad ibn Abdullah, from the powerful Arab tribe Quraysh, went to Mount Hira to meditate, as he regularly did for the month of Ramadan. During that month, an entire group of men, the hanif, retreated to caves. The pagan worship practiced in the region, as well as the cruelty and lack of care for the poor, distressed Muhammad. As the tribe to which he belonged had become wealthy through trade, it had begun disregarding traditions prescribed by the nomadic code.

The archangel Jibra'il (Gabriel) appeared in Muhammad's cave and commanded him to read the words of God contained in the scroll that the angel showed him. Like most people of his time, Muhammad was illiterate, but repeated the words Jibra'il said. Some followers of Islam believe that this cave at Jebel Nur, in what is now Saudi Arabia, is where Adam, the first human Allah created, lived.

A frightened Muhammad told only his wife, Khadija, about his experience. For two years, Muhammad received further revelations, sharing them only with family and close friends. Like other prophets, he was reluctant about his calling, fearing that he was—or would be accused of being—possessed by evil spirits or insane. At one point, he tried to commit suicide, but was stopped by the voice of Jibra'il affirming his status as God's messenger.

Muhammad recalled the words spoken to him, which were eventually written down. The Qur'an is noted for being a book of beautiful language, and Muhammad's message reached many. The Prophet thus broke the old pattern of allegiance to tribe and forged a new community based on shared practice.

Muhammad considered himself one who was to warn the others of a coming judgment. His call for social justice and denunciation of the wealthy disturbed the powerful Arab tribe members in Mecca. These men stood to lose the status and income derived from the annual festival to the Ka'bah. The Prophet and his followers were persecuted and were the subject of boycotts and death threats. In 622 CE, Muslim families began a migration (hijrah) to Yathrib, later known as Medina. Two years earlier, the city had sent envoys seeking Muhammad's leadership for their own troubled society. The hijrah marks the beginning of the Islamic calendar.

The persecutions eventually led to outright tribal warfare, linking Islam with political prowess through the victories of the faithful. The Muslims moved from being an oppressed minority to being a political force. In 630 CE, Muhammad and ten thousand of his followers marched to Mecca, taking the city without bloodshed. He destroyed the pagan idols that were housed and worshipped at the Ka'bah, instead associating the hajj with the story of Abraham sending his concubine Hagar and their son Ishmael (Ismail in Arabic) out into the wilderness. With this victory, Muhammad ended centuries of intertribal warfare.

Muhammad died in 632, without designating a successor. Some of the Muslims believed that his nearest male relative should rule, following the custom of the tribes. Ali ibn Abi Talib, although a pious Muslim, was still young. Therefore, Abu Bakr, the Prophet's father-in-law, took the title khalifah, or caliph, which means successor or deputy. Within two years Abu Bakr had stabilized Islam. He was followed by three additional men whom Muhammad had known. Collectively, the four are known as the Four Rightly Guided Caliphs, or the Rashidun. Their rule extended from 632 until 661. Each of the final three met a violent death.

Umar, the second caliph, increased the number of raids on adjacent lands during his ten-year rule, which began in 634. This not only increased wealth, but also gave Umar the authority he needed, since Arabs objected to the idea of a monarchy. Umar was known as the commander of the faithful. Under his leadership, the Islamic community marched into present-day Iraq, Syria, and Egypt and achieved victory over the Persians in 637.

Muslims elected Uthman ibn Affan as the third caliph after Umar was stabbed by a Persian prisoner of war. He extended Muslim conquests into North Africa as well as into Iran, Afghanistan, and parts of India. A group of soldiers mutinied in 656, assassinating Uthman.

Ali, Muhammad's son-in-law, was elected caliph of a greatly enlarged empire. Conflict developed between Ali and the ruler in Damascus whom Uthman had appointed governor of Syria. The fact that the governor came from a rival tribe led to further tensions. Increasingly, Damascus rather than Medina was viewed as the key Muslim locale. Ali was murdered in 661 during the internal struggles.

Within a century after Muhammad's death, Muslims had created an empire that stretched from Spain across Asia to India and facilitated the spread of Islam. The conquerors followed a policy of relative, though not perfect, tolerance toward adherents of other religions. Christians and Jews received special status as fellow "People of the Book," though they were still required to pay a special poll tax in exchange for military protection. Pagans, however, were required to convert to Islam or face death. Later, Hindus, Zoroastrians, and other peoples were also permitted to pay the tax rather than submit to conversion. Following the twelfth century, Sufi mystics made further converts in Central Asia, India, sub-Saharan Africa, and Turkey. Muslim traders also were responsible for the growth of Islam, particularly in China, Indonesia, and Malaya.

The Muslim empire continued to grow until it weakened in the fourteenth century, when it was replaced as a major world power by European states. The age of Muslim domination ended with the 1683 failure of the Ottoman Empire to capture Vienna, Austria.

Although lacking in political power until recent years, a majority of nations in Indonesia, the Middle East, and East and North Africa are predominately Islamic. The rise of Islamic fundamentalists who interpret the Qur'an literally and seek victory through acts of terrorism began in the late twentieth century. Such extremists do not represent the majority of the Muslim community, however.

Like Judaism and Christianity, Islam has been influenced by its development in a desert climate. Arabia, a region three times the size of France, is a land of steppe and desert whose unwelcoming climate kept it from being mapped with any precision until the 1950s. Because Yemen received monsoon rains, it could sustain agriculture and became a center for civilization as early as the second millennium BCE. In the seventh century CE, nomads roamed the area, guarding precious wells and oases. Raiding caravans and other tribes were common ways to obtain necessities.

Mecca was a pagan center of worship, but it was located not far from a Christian kingdom, Ethiopia, across the Red Sea. Further north, followers of both Judaism and Christianity had influenced members of Arab tribes. Jewish tribes inhabited Yathrib, the city later known as Medina. Neither Judaism nor Christianity was especially kind to those they considered pagans. According to an Arabian tradition, in 570 the Ethiopians attacked Yemen and attempted an attack on Mecca. Mecca was caught between two enemy empires—Christian Byzantine and Zoroastrian Persia—that fought a lengthy war during Muhammad's lifetime.

The contemporary clashes between Jews and Muslims are in part a result of the dispersion of Muslims who had lived in Palestine for centuries. More Jews began moving into the area under the British Mandate; in 1948, the state of Israel was proclaimed. Historically, Jews had been respected as a People of the Book.

Founder or Major Prophet

Muslims hold Allah to be the founder of their religion and Abraham to have been the first Muslim. Muhammad is God's prophet to the Arabs. The instructions that God gave Muhammad through the archangel Jibra'il and through direct revelation are the basis for the Islamic religion. These revelations were given over a period of twenty-one years. Because Muhammad and most of the Muslims were illiterate, the teachings were read publicly in chapters, or suras.

Muhammad did not believe he was founding a new religion. Rather, he was considered God's final Prophet, as Moses and Jesus had been prophets. His task was to call people to repent and to return to the straight path of God's law, called Sharia. God finally was sending a direct revelation to the Arab peoples, who had sometimes been taunted by the other civilizations as being left out of God's plan.

Muhammad, who had been orphaned by age six, was raised by an uncle. He became a successful businessman of an important tribe and married Khadija, for whom he worked. His integrity was such that he was known as al-Amin, the trusted one. He and Khadija had six children; four daughters survived. After Khadija's death, Muhammad married several women, as was the custom for a great chief. Several of the marriages were political in nature.

Muhammad is regarded as the living Qur'an. He is sometimes referred to as the perfect man, one who is an example of how a Muslim should live. He was ahead of his time in his attitudes toward women, listening to their counsel and granting them rights not enjoyed by women in other societies, including the right to inherit property and to divorce. (It should be noted that the Qur'an does not require the seclusion or veiling of all women.)

Islam has no religious leaders, especially those comparable to other religions. Each mosque has an imam to preach and preside over prayer at the Friday services. Although granted a moral authority, the imam is not a religious leader with a role comparable to that of rabbis or priests.

Philosophical Basis

Prior to Muhammad's receiving the Qur'an, the polytheistic tribes believed in Allah, "the god." Allah was far away and not part of worship rituals, although he had created the world and sustained it. He had three daughters who were goddesses.

Islam began pragmatically—the old tribal ways were not working—as a call for social justice, rooted in Muhammad's dissatisfaction with the increasing emphasis on accumulating wealth and an accompanying neglect of those in need. The struggle (jihad) to live according to God's desire for humans was to take place within the community, or the ummah. This effort was more important than dogmatic statements or beliefs about God. When the community prospered, this was a sign of God's blessing.

In addition, the revelation of the Qur'an gave Arab nations an official religion. The Persians around them had Zoroastrianism, the Romans and Byzantines had Christianity, and the Jews of the Diaspora had Judaism. With the establishment of Islam, Arabs finally could believe that they were part of God's plan for the world.

Four principles direct Islam's practice and doctrine. These include the Qur'an; the traditions, or sunnah; consensus, or ijma'; and individual thought, or ijtihad. The term sunnah, "well-trodden path," had been used by Arabs before Islam to refer to their tribal law.

A fifth important source for Islam is the Hadith, or report, a collection of the Prophet's words and actions, intended to serve as an example. Sunni Muslims refer to six collections made in the ninth century, while Shia Muslims have a separate Hadith of four collections.

Holy Places

Mecca was located just west of the Incense Road, a major trade route from southern Arabia to Palestine and Syria. Mecca was the Prophet's home and the site where he received his revelations. It is also the city where Islam's holiest structure, the Ka'bah, "the sacred house," was located. The Ka'bah was regarded as having been built by Abraham and his son Ishmael. This forty-three-foot gray stone cube was a center for pagan idols in the time of Muhammad. In 628 the Prophet removed 360 pagan idols—one for each day of the Arabic lunar year—from inside the Ka'bah.

When the followers of Muhammad experienced persecution for their beliefs, they fled to the city of Medina, formerly called Yathrib. When his uncle Abu Talib died, Muhammad lost the protection from persecution that his uncle had provided. He left for Ta'if in the mountains, but it was also a center for pagan cults, and he was driven out. After a group of men from Yathrib promised him protection, Muhammad sent seventy of his followers to the city, built around an oasis about 215 miles north. This migration, called the hijra, occurred in 622, the first year of the Muslim calendar. From this point on, Islam became an organized religion rather than a persecuted and minority cult. The Prophet was buried in Medina in 632, and his mosque in that city is deeply revered.

Islam's third holiest site is the Dome of the Rock in Jerusalem. Muslims believe that the Prophet Muhammad ascended to heaven in 621 from the rock located at the center of this mosque. During this so-called night journey, Allah gave him instructions about prayer. In the shrine at the Dome of the Rock is a strand of hair that Muslims believe was Muhammad's.

Shia Muslims also revere the place in present-day Iraq where Ali's son, Husayn, was martyred. They regard the burial place of Imam Ali ar-Rida in Meshed, Iran, as a site of pilgrimage as well.

ISLAM IN DEPTH

Sacred Symbols

Muslims revere the Black Stone, a possible meteorite that is considered a link to heaven. It is set inside the Ka'bah shrine's eastern corner. The Ka'bah is kept covered by the kiswa, a black velvet cloth decorated with embroidered calligraphy in gold. At the hajj, Muslims walk around it counterclockwise seven times as they recite prayers to Allah.

Muslim nations have long used the crescent moon and a star on their flags. The crescent moon, which the Ottomans first adopted as a symbol during the fifteenth century, is often placed on the dome of a mosque, pointing toward Mecca. For Muhammad, the waxing and waning of the moon signified the unchanging and eternal purpose of God. Upon seeing a new moon, the Prophet confessed his faith in God. Muslims rely on a lunar calendar and the Qur'an states that God created the stars to guide people to their destinations.

Islam forbids the making of graven images of animals or people, although not all Islamic cultures follow this rule strictly. The decorative arts of Islam have placed great emphasis on architecture and calligraphy to beautify mosques and other buildings. In addition, calligraphy, floral motifs, and geometric forms decorate some editions of the Qur'an's pages, much as Christian monks once decorated hand-copied scrolls of the Bible. These elaborate designs can also be seen on some prayer rugs, and are characteristic of Islamic art in general.

Sacred Practices & Gestures

When Muslims pray, they must do so facing Mecca, a decision Muhammad made in January 624 CE. Prior to that time, Jerusalem—a holy city for both Jews and Christians—had been the geographic focus. Prayer involves a series of movements that embody submission to Allah.

Muslims sometimes use a strand of prayer beads, known as subhah, to pray the names of God. The beads can be made of bone, precious stones, or wood. Strings may have twenty-five, thirty-three or 100 beads.

Food Restrictions

Those who are physically able to do so fast from both food and drink during the daylight hours of the month Ramadan. Although fasting is not required of the sick, the aged, menstruating or pregnant women, or children, some children attempt to fast, imitating their parents' devotion. Those who cannot fast are encouraged to do so the following Ramadan. This fast is intended to concentrate the mind on Allah. Muslims recite from the Qur'an during the month.

All meat must be prepared in a particular way so that it is halal, or permitted. While slaughtering the animal, the person must mention the name of Allah. Blood, considered unclean, must be allowed to drain. Because pigs were fed garbage, their meat was considered unclean. Thus Muslims eat no pork, even though in modern times, pigs are often raised on grain.

In three different revelations, Muslims are also forbidden to consume fermented beverages. Losing self-control because of drunkenness violates the Islamic desire for self-mastery.

Rites, Celebrations, and Services

The **mosque** is the spiritual center of the Muslim community. From the minaret (a tower outside the mosque), the call to worship occurs five times daily—at dawn, just past noon, at midafternoon, at sunset, and in the evening. In earliest times, a muezzin, the official responsible for this duty, gave the cry. In many modern countries, the call now comes over a speaker system. Also located outside are fountains to provide the necessary water for ritual washing before prayer. Muslims wash their face, hands, forearms, and feet, as well as remove their shoes before beginning their prayers. In the absence of water, ritual cleansing may occur using sand or a stone.

Praying involves a series of movements known as rak'ah. From a standing position, the worshipper recites the opening sura of the Qur'an, as well as a second sura. After bowing to demonstrate respect, the person again stands, then prostrates himself or herself to signal humility. Next, the person assumes a sitting posture in silent prayer before again prostrating. The last movement is a greeting of "Peace be with you and the mercy of Allah." The worshipper looks both left and right before saying these words, which are intended for all persons, present and not.

Although Muslims stop to pray during each day when the call is given, Friday is the time for communal prayer and worship at the mosque. The prayer hall is the largest space within the mosque. At one end is a niche known as the mihrab, indicating the direction of Mecca, toward which Muslims face when they pray. At first, Muhammad instructed his followers to pray facing Jerusalem, as the Jewish people did. This early orientation was also a way to renounce the pagan associations of Mecca. Some mosques serve as community centers, with additional rooms for study.

The hajj, an important annual celebration, was a custom before the founding of Islam. Pagan worship centered in Mecca at the Ka'bah, where devotees circled the cube and kissed the Black Stone that was embedded in it. All warfare was forbidden during the hajj, as was argument, speaking crossly, or killing even an insect.

Muslims celebrate the lives of saints and their death anniversaries, a time when the saints are thought to reach the height of their spiritual life. Mawlid an-Nabi refers to "the birth of the Prophet." Although it is cultural and not rooted in the Qur'an, in some Muslim countries this is a public holiday on which people recite the Burdah, a poem that praises Muhammad. Muslims also celebrate the night that the Prophet ascended to heaven, Lailat ul-Miraj. The Night of Power is held to be the night on which Allah decides the destiny of people individually and the world at large.

Like Jews, Muslims practice circumcision, a ceremony known as khitan. Unlike Jews, however, Muslims do not remove the foreskin when the male is a baby. This is often done when a boy is about seven, and must be done before the boy reaches the age of twelve.

Healthy adult Muslims fast between sunrise and sunset during the month of Ramadan. This commemorates the first of Muhammad's revelations. In some Muslim countries, cannons are fired before the beginning of the month, as well as at the beginning and end of each day of the month. Some Muslims read a portion of the Qur'an each day during the month.

Judy A. Johnson, MTS

Bibliography

Al-Saud, Laith, Scott W. Hibbard, and Aminah Beverly. *An Introduction to Islam in the 21st Century*. Wiley, 2013. E-book.

Armstrong, Lyall. "The Rise of Islam: Traditional and Revisionist Theories." *Theological Review* 33.2 (2012): 87–106. Print.

Armstrong, Karen. *Islam: A Short History*. New York: Mod. Lib., 2000. Print.

Aslan, Reza. *No god but God: The Origins, Evolution, and Future of Islam*. New York: Random, 2005. Print.

Badawi, Emran El-. "'For All Times and Places': A Humanistic Reception of the Qur'an." *English Language Notes* 50.2 (2012): 99–112. Print.

Barnes, Trevor. *The Kingfisher Book of Religions*. New York: Kingfisher, 1999. Print.

Ben Jelloun, Tahar. *Islam Explained*. Trans. Franklin Philip. New York: New, 2002. Print.

Esposito, John L. *Islam: the Straight Path*. New York: Oxford UP, 1988. Print.

Glady, Pearl. *Criticism of Islam*.Library, 2012. E-book.

Holland, Tom. "Where Mystery Meets History." *History Today* 62.5 (2012): 19–24. Print.

Langley, Myrtle. *Religion*. New York: Knopf, 1996. Print.

Lunde, Paul. *Islam: Faith, Culture, History*. London: DK, 2002. Print.

Nasr, Seyyed Hossein. *Islam: Religion, History, and Civilization*. New York: Harper, 2002. Print.

Pasha, Mustapha Kamal. "Islam and the Postsecular." *Review of International Studies* 38.5 (2012): 1041–56. Print.

Sayers, Destini and Simone Peebles. *Essence of Islam and Sufism*. College, 2012. E-book.

Schirmacher, Christine. "They Are Not All Martyrs: Islam on the Topics of Dying, Death, and Salvation in the Afterlife." *Evangelical Review of Theology* 36.3 (2012): 250–65. Print.

Wilkinson, Philip. *Islam*. New York: DK, 2002. Print.

Wilkinson, Philip. *Religions*. New York: DK, 2008. Print.

Jainism

General Description

Jainism is one of the major religions of India. The name of the religion itself is believed to be based on the Sanskrit word *ji*, which means "to conquer or triumph," or *jina*, which means "victor or conqueror." The earliest name of the group was Nirgrantha, meaning bondless, but it applied to monks and nuns only. There are two sects: the Svetambaras (the white clad), which are the more numerous and wear white clothing, and the Digambaras (the sky clad), the most stringent group; their holy men or monks do not wear clothing at all.

Number of Adherents Worldwide

Jainism has about five million adherents, most of them in India (in some estimates, the religion represents approximately 1 percent of India's population). Because the religion is demanding in nature, few beyond the Indian subcontinent have embraced it. Jainism has spread to Africa, the United States, and nations in the Commonwealth (nations once under British rule) by virtue of Indian migration to these countries.

Basic Tenets

The principle of nonviolence (ahimsa) is a defining feature of Jainism. This results in a pacifist religion that influenced Mohandas Gandhi's ideas on nonviolent resistance. Jains believe that because all living creatures have souls, harming any of those creatures is wrong. They therefore follow a strict vegetarian diet, and often wear masks so as to not inhale living organisms. The most important aspect of Jainism is perhaps the five abstinences: ahimsa, satya (truthfulness), asteya (refrain from stealing), brahmacarya (chaste living), and aparigraha (refrain from greed).

A religion without priests, Jainism emphasizes the importance of the adherents' actions. Like Buddhists and Hindus, Jainists believe in karma and reincarnation. Unlike the Buddhist and Hindu idea of karma, Jainists regard karma as tiny particles that cling to the soul as mud clings to shoes, gradually weighing down the soul. Good deeds wash away these particles. Jainists also believe in moksha, the possibility of being freed from the cycle of death and rebirth. Like many Indian religions, Jainism does not believe in an afterlife, but in a cycle of death and rebirth. Once freed from this cycle, the soul will remain in infinite bliss.

While Jains do not necessarily believe in and worship God or gods, they believe in divine beings. Those who have achieved moksha are often regarded by Jains in the same manner in which other religions regard deities. These include the twenty-four Tirthankaras (ford makers) or jinas (victors), those who have escaped the cycle of death and rebirth, and the Siddhas, the liberated souls without physical form. The idea of a judging, ruling, or creator God is not present in Jainism.

Jainists believe that happiness is not found in material possessions and seek to have few of them. They also stress the importance of environmentalism. Jainists follow the Three Jewels: Right Belief, Right Knowledge, and Right Conduct. To be completely achieved, these three must be practiced together. Jainists also agree to six daily obligations (avashyaka), which include confession, praising the twenty-four Tirthankaras (the spiritual leaders), and calm meditation.

Sacred Text

The words of Mahavira were passed down orally, but lost over a few centuries. During a famine in the mid-fourth century BCE, many monks died. The texts were finally written down, although the Jain sects do not agree as to whether they are Mahavira's actual words. There are forty-five sacred texts (Agamas), which make up the Agam Sutras, Jainism's canonical literature. They were probably written down no earlier than 300 BCE. Two of the primary texts are the Akaranga

Sutra, which outlines the rule of conduct for Jain monks, and the Kalpa Sutra, which contains biographies of the last two Tirthankara. The Digambaras, who believe that the Agamas were lost around 350 BCE, have two main texts and four compendia written between 100 and 800 CE by various scholars.

Major Figures

Jainism has no single founder. However, Mahavira (Great Hero) is one of the Tirthankaras or jinas (pathfinders). He is considered the most recent spiritual teacher in a line of twenty-four. Modern-day Jainism derives from Mahavira, and his words are the foundation of Jain scriptures. He was a contemporary of Siddhartha Gautama, who was revered as the Buddha. Both Mahavira and Rishabha (or Adinatha), the first of the twenty-four Tirthankaras, are attributed as the founder of Jainism, though each Tirthankara maintains founding attributes.

Major Holy Sites

The Jain temple at Ranakpur is located in the village of Rajasthan. Carved from amber stone with marble interiors, the temple was constructed in the fifteenth century CE. It is dedicated to the first Tirthankara. The temple has twenty-nine large halls and each of the temple's 1,444 columns has a unique design with carvings.

Sravanabegola in Karnataka state is the site of Gomateshwara, Lord Bahubali's fifty-seven-foot statue. It was constructed in 981 CE from a single chunk of gneiss. Bahubali is considered the son of the first Tirthankara. The Digambara sect believes him to have been the first human to be free from the world.

Other pilgrimage sites include the Palitana temples in Gujarat and the Dilwara temples in Rajasthan. Sometimes regarded as the most sacred of the many Jain temples, the Palitana temples include 863 marble-engraved temples. The Jain temples at Dilwara were constructed of marble during the eleventh and thirteenth centuries CE. These five temples are often considered the most beautiful Jain temples in existence.

Major Rites & Celebrations

Every twelve years, the festival of Mahamastakabhisheka (anointing of the head) occurs at a statue of one of Jain's holy men, Bahubali, the second son of the first Tirthankara. The statue is anointed with milk, curd, and ghee, a clarified butter. Nearly a million people attend this rite. Jainists also observe Diwali, the Hindu festival of lights, as it symbolizes Mahavira's enlightenment.

The solemn festival of Paryusana marks the end of the Jain year for the Svetambaras (also spelled Shvetambaras). During this eight-day festival, all Jains are asked to live as an ascetic (monk or nun) would for one day. Das Laxana, a ten-day festival similar to that of Paryusana, immediately follows for the Digambara sect. During these special religious holidays, worshippers are involved in praying, meditating, fasting, forgiveness, and acts of penance. These holy days are celebrated during August and September, which is monsoon season in India. During the monsoons, monks prefer to remain in one place so as to avoid killing the smallest insects that appear during the rainy season. The Kalpa Sutra, one of the Jain scriptures, is read in the morning during Paryusana.

The feast of Kartaki Purnima follows the four months of the rainy season. It is held in the first month (Kartik) according to one calendar, and marked by a pilgrimage to the Palitana temples. Doing so with a pure heart is said to remove all sins of both the present and past life. Those who do so are thought to receive the final salvation in the third or fifth birth.

ORIGINS

History & Geography

In the eastern basin of the Ganges River during the seventh century BCE, a teacher named Parshvanatha (or Parshva) gathered a community founded on abandoning earthly concerns. He is considered to be the twenty-third Tirthankara (ford-maker), the one who makes a path for salvation. During the following century, Vardhamana, called Mahavira (Great Hero), who was considered the twenty-fourth and final spiritual teacher of the age, formulated most Jain doctrine and practice. By the time of Mahavira's death, Jains numbered around 36,000 nuns and 14,000 monks.

A division occurred within Jainism during the fourth century CE. The most extreme ascetics, the Digambaras (the sky-clad), argued that even clothing showed too great an attachment to the world, and that laundering them in the river risked harming creatures. This argument applied only to men, as the Digambaras denied that a soul could be freed from a woman's body. The other group, the Svetambaras (the white-clad), believed that purity resided in the mind.

In 453 or 456 CE, a council of the Svetambara sect at Saurashtra in western India codified the canon still used. The split between the Digambaras, who did not take part in the meeting, and Svetambaras thus became permanent. Despite the split, Jainism's greatest flowering occurred during the early medieval age. After that time, Hindu sects devoted to the Hindu gods of Vishnu and Shiva flourished under the Gupta Empire (often referred to as India's golden age), slowing the spread of Jainism. Followers migrated to western and central India and the community became stronger.

The Digambaras were involved in politics through several medieval dynasties, and some Jain monks served as spiritual advisers. Royalty and high-ranking officials contributed to the building and maintenance of temples. Both branches of Jainism contributed a substantial literature. In the late medieval age, Jain monks ceased to live as ascetic wanders. They chose instead to don orange robes and to live at temples and other holy places.

The Muslims invaded India in the twelfth century. The Jains lost power and fractured over the next centuries into subgroups, some of which repudiated the worship of images. The poet and Digambara layman Banarsidas (1586-1643) played a significant role in a reform movement during the early 1600s. These reforms focused on the mystical side of Jainism, such as spiritual exploration of the inner self (meditation), and denounced the formalized temple ritual. The movement, known as the Adhyatma movement, resulted in the Digambara Terapanth, a small Digambara sect.

The Jainists were well positioned in society following the departure of the British from India. Having long been associated with the artisan and merchant classes, they found new opportunities. As traditional Indian studies grew, spurred by Western interest, proponents of Jainism began to found publications and places of study (In fact, Jain libraries are believed to be the oldest in India.) The first Jain temple outside India was consecrated in Britain during the 1960s after Jains had gone there in the wake of political turmoil.

The Jains follow their typical profession as merchants. They publish English-language periodicals to spread their ideas on vegetarianism, environmentalism, and nonviolence (ahimsa). The ideas of ahimsa were formative for Mohandas Gandhi, born a Hindu. Gandhi used nonviolence as a wedge against the British Empire in India. Eventually, the British granted independence to India in 1947.

Virchand Gandhi (1864–1901) is believed to be the first Jain to arrive in America when he came over in 1893. He attended the first Parliament of World Religions, held in Chicago. Today North America has more than ninety Jain temples and centers. Jains in the West often follow professions such as banking and business to avoid destroying animal or plant life.

Founder or Major Prophet

Mahavira was born in India's Ganges Basin region. By tradition, he was born around 599 BCE, although some scholars think he may have lived a century later. His story bears a resemblance to that of the Buddha, with whom he was believed to have been a contemporary. His family was also of the Kshatriya (warrior) caste, and his father was a ruler of his clan. One tradition states that Mahavira's mother was of the Brahman (priestly) caste, although another places her in the Kshatriya.

Because he was not the eldest son, Mahavira was not in line for leadership of the clan.

He married a woman of his own caste and they had a daughter. Mahavira chose the life of a monk, with one garment. Later, he gave up wearing even that. He became a wandering ascetic around age thirty, with some legends stating that he tore out his hair before leaving home. He sought shelter in burial grounds and cremation sites, as well as at the base of trees. During the rainy season, however, he lived in towns and villages.

He followed a path of preaching and self-denial, after which he was enlightened (kevala). He spent the next thirty years teaching. Eleven disciples, all of whom were of the Brahman caste, gathered around him. At the end of his life, Mahavira committed Santhara, or ritual suicide through fasting.

Philosophical Basis

Like Buddhists and the Brahmin priests, the Jains believe in human incarnations of God, known as avatars. These avatars appear at the end of a time of decline to reinstate proper thinking and acting. Such a person was Mahavira. At the time of Mahavira's birth, India was experiencing great societal upheaval. Members of the warrior caste opposed the priestly caste, which exercised authority based on its supposed greater moral purity. Many people also opposed the slaughter of animals for the Vedic sacrifices.

Jainists share some beliefs with both Hinduism and Buddhism. The Hindu hero Rama, for example, is co-opted as a nonviolent Jain, while the deity Krishna is considered a cousin of Arishtanemi, the twenty-second Tirthankara. Like Buddhism, Jainism uses a wheel with twelve spokes; however, Jainism uses the wheel to explain time. The first half of the circle is the ascending stage, in which human happiness, prosperity, and life span increase. The latter half of the circle is the descending stage, involving a decrease of life span, prosperity, and happiness. The wheel of time is always in motion.

For Jainists, the universe is without beginning or ending, and contains layers of both heaven and hell. These layers include space beyond, which is without time, matter, or soul. The cosmos is depicted in art as a large human. The cloud layers surrounding the upper world are called universe space. Above them is the base, Nigoda, where lowest life forms live. The netherworld contains seven hells, each with a different stage of punishment and misery. The middle world contains the earth and remainder of the universe—mankind is located near the waist. There are thirty heavens in the upper world, where heavenly beings reside. In the supreme abode at the apex of the universe, liberated souls (siddha) live.

Jainism teaches that there are six universal entities. Only consciousness or soul is a living substance, while the remaining five are non-living. They include matter, medium of rest, medium of motion, time, and space. Jainism also does not believe in a God who can create, destroy, or protect. Worshipping goddesses and gods to achieve personal gain or material benefit is deemed useless.

Mahavira outlined five basic principles (often referred to as abstinences) for Jainist life, based on the teachings of the previous Tirthankara. They are detachment (aparigraha); the conduct of soul, primarily in sexual morality (brahmacharya); abstinence from stealing (asteya); abstinence from lying (satya); and non-violence in every realm of the person (ahimsa).

Like other Indian religions, Jainism perceives life as four stages. The life of a student is brahmacharya-ashrama; the stage of family life is gruhasth-ashrama; in vanaprasth-ashrama, the Jainist concentrates on both family and aiding others through social services; and the final stage is sanyast-ashrama, a time of renouncing the world and becoming a monk.

Like many religions, Jainism has a bias toward males and toward the rigorous life of monks and nuns. A layperson cannot work off bad karma, but merely keeps new bad karma from accruing. By following a path of asceticism, however, monks and nuns can destroy karma. Even members of the laity follow eight rules of behavior and take twelve vows. Physical austerity is a key concept in Jainism, as a saint's highest ideal is to starve to death.

Holy Places

There are four major Jain pilgrimage sites: the Dilwara temples near Rajasthan; the Palitana temples; the Ranakpur temple; and Shravan Begola, the site of the statue of Lord Bahubali. In addition, Jains may make pilgrimages to the caves of Khandagiri and Udayagiri, which were cells for Jain monks carved from rock. The spaces carved are too short for a man to stand upright. They were essentially designed for prayer and meditation. Udayagiri has eighteen caves and Khandagiri has fifteen. The caves are decorated with elaborate carvings.

JAINISM IN DEPTH

Sacred Symbols

The open palm (Jain Hand) with a centered wheel, sometimes with the word *ahimsa* written on it, is a prominent Jain symbol. Seen as an icon of peace, the open palm symbol can be interpreted as a call to stop violence, and also means "assurance." It appears on the walls of Jain temples and in their publications. Jainism also employs a simple swastika symbol, considered to be the holiest symbol. It represents the four forms of worldly existence, and three dots above the swastika represent the Three Jewels. The Jain emblem, adopted in 1975, features both the Jain Hand (the open palm symbol with an inset wheel) and a swastika. This year was regarded as the 2,500th anniversary of Mahavira being enlightened.

Sacred Practices & Gestures

Jains may worship daily in their homes at private shrines. The Five Supreme Beings stand for stages in the path to enlightenment. Rising before daybreak, worshippers invoke these five. In addition, devout Jainists set aside forty-eight minutes daily to meditate.

To demonstrate faithfulness to the five vows that Jains undertake, there are four virtuous qualities that must be cultivated. They are compassion (karuna), respect and joy (pramoda), love and friendship (maitri), and indifference toward and noninvolvement with those who are arrogant (madhyastha). Mahavira stressed that Jains must be friends to all living beings. Compassion goes beyond mere feeling; it involves offering both material and spiritual aid. Pramoda carries with it the idea of rejoicing enthusiastically over the virtues of others. There are contemplations associated with these virtues, and daily practice is suggested to attain mastery.

Some Jainists, both men and women, wear a dot on the forehead. This practice comes from Hinduism. During festivals, Jains may pray, chant, fast, or keep silent. These actions are seen as removing bad karma from the soul and moving the person toward ultimate happiness.

Food Restrictions

Jainists practice a strict vegetarian way of life (called Jain vegetarianism) to avoid harming any creature. They refuse to eat root vegetables, because by uprooting them, the entire plant dies. They prefer to wait for fruit to drop from trees rather than taking it from the branches. Starving to death, when ready, is seen as an ideal.

Rites, Celebrations & Services

Some festivals are held annually and their observances are based on a lunar calendar. Mahavir Jayanti is an example, as it celebrates Mahavira's birthday.

Jains may worship, bathe, and make offerings to images of the Tirthankaras in their home or in a temple. Svetambaras Jains also clothe and decorate the images. Because the Tirthankaras have been liberated, they cannot respond as a deity granting favors might. Although Jainism rejects belief in gods in favor of worshipping Tirthankaras, in actual practice, some Jainists pray to Hindu gods.

When Svetambara monks are initiated, they are given three pieces of clothing, including a small piece of white cloth to place over the mouth. The cloth, called a mukhavastrika, is designed to prevent the monk from accidentally eating insects.

Monks take great vows (mahavratas) at initiation. These include abstaining from lying, stealing, sexual activity, injury to any living thing, and personal possessions. Monks own a broom to sweep in front of where they are going to walk so that no small creatures are injured, along with an alms bowl and a robe. The Digambara monks practice a more stringent lifestyle, eating one meal a day, for which they beg.

Nuns in the Svetambaras are three times more common than are monks, even though they receive less honor, and are required to defer to the monks. In Digambara Jainism, the nuns wear robes and accept that they must be reborn as men before progressing upward.

The observance of Santhara, which is religious fasting until death, is a voluntary fasting undertaken with full knowledge. The ritual is also known as Sallekhana, and is not perceived as suicide by Jains, particularly as the prolonged nature of the ritual provides ample time for reflection. It is believed that at least one hundred people die every year from observing Santhara.

Judy A. Johnson, MTS

Bibliography

Aristarkhova, Irina. "Thou Shall Not Harm All Living Beings: Feminism, Jainism, and Animals." *Hypatia* 27.3 (2012): 636–50. Print.

Aukland, Knut. "Understanding Possession in Jainism: A Study of Oracular Possession in Nakoda." *Modern Asian Studies* 47.1 (2013): 103–34. Print.

Barnes, Trevor. *The Kingfisher Book of Religions*. New York: Kingfisher, 1999. Print.

Langley, Myrtle. *Religion*. New York: Knopf, 1996. Print.

Long, Jeffery. *Jainism: An Introduction*. London: I. B. Tauris, 2009. Print.

Long, Jeffrey. "Jainism: Key Themes." *Religion Compass* 5.9 (2011): 501–10. Print.

Rankin, Aidan. *The Jain Path*. Berkeley: O Books, 2006. Print.

Shah, Bharat S. *An Introduction to Jainism*. Great Neck: Setubandh, 2002. Print.

Titze, Kurt. *Jainism: A Pictorial Guide to the Religion of Non-Violence*. Delhi: Motilal Banarsidass, 2001. Print.

Tobias, Michael. *Life Force: the World of Jainism* Berkeley:Asian Humanities, 1991. E-book, print.

Wiley, Kristi L. *The A to Z of Jainism*. Lanham: Scarecrow, 2009. Print.

Wiley, Kristi L. *Historical Dictionary of Jainism*. Lanham: Scarecrow, 2004. Print.

Wilkinson, Philip. *Religions*. New York: DK, 2008. Print.

Judaism

General Description

In modern Judaism, the main denominations (referred to as movements) are Orthodox Judaism (including Haredi and Hasidic Judaism); Conservative Judaism; Reform (Liberal) Judaism; Reconstructionist Judaism; and to a lesser extent, Humanistic Judaism. In addition, the Jewry of Ethiopia and Yemen are known for having distinct or alternative traditions. Classical Judaism is often organized by two branches: Ashkenazic (Northern Europe) and Sephardic Jews (Spain, Portugal, and North Africa).

Number of Adherents Worldwide

Judaism has an estimated 15 million adherents worldwide, with roughly 41 percent living in Israel and about 41 percent living in the United States. Ashkenazi Jews represent roughly 75 percent, while Sephardic Jews represent roughly 25 percent, with the remaining 5 percent split among alternative communities. Within the United States, a 2000-01 survey stated that 10 percent of American Jews identified as Orthodox (with that number increasing), 35 percent as Reform, 26 percent as Conservative, leaving the remainder with an alternative or no affiliation. [Source: Wilkinson, 2008]

Orthodox Judaism, which was founded around the thirteenth century BCE, has 3 million followers. Members of Reform Judaism, with roots in nineteenth-century Germany, wanted to live peacefully with non-Jews. Therefore, they left the laws that prevented this vision of peace and downplayed the idea of a Jewish state. Reform Judaism, also known as Progressive or Liberal Judaism, allows women rabbis and does not require its adherents to keep kosher. About 1.1 million Jews are Reform; they live primarily in the United States. When nonkosher food was served at the first graduation ceremony for Hebrew Union College, some felt that the Reform movement had gone too far. Thus the Conservative movement began in 1887. A group of rabbis founded the Jewish Theological Seminary in New York City, wanting to emphasize biblical authority above moral choice, as the Reform tradition stressed. Currently about 900,000 Jews practice this type of Judaism, which is theologically midway between Orthodox and Reform. The Hasidim, an ultra-conservative group, began in present-day Ukraine around 1740. There are 4.5 million Hasidic Jews.

Basic Tenets

Though there is no formal creed (statement of faith or belief), Jews value all life, social justice, education, generous giving, and the importance of living based on the principles and values espoused in the Torah (Jewish holy book). They believe in one all-powerful and creator God, Jehovah or Yaweh, a word derived from the Hebrew letters "YHWH," the unpronounceable name of God. The word is held to be sacred; copyists were required to bathe both before and after writing the word. Jews also believe in a coming Messiah who will initiate a Kingdom of Righteousness. They follow a complex law, composed of 613 commandments or mitzvot. Jews believe that they are God's Chosen People with a unique covenant relationship. They have a responsibility to practice hospitality and to improve the world.

The belief in the afterlife is a part of the Jewish faith. Similar to Christianity, this spiritual world is granted to those who abide by the Jewish faith and live a good life. Righteous Jews are rewarded in the afterlife by being able to discuss the Torah with Moses, who first received the law from God. Furthermore, certain Orthodox sects believe that wicked souls are destroyed or tormented after death.

Sacred Text

The complete Hebrew Bible is called the Tanakh. It includes the prophetic texts, called the Navi'im, the poetic writings, the Ketubim, and the Torah, meaning teaching, law, or guidance. Torah may refer to the entire body of Jewish law or to the first five books of the Hebrew Bible, known as the Pentateuch (it is the Old Testament in the Christian Bible). Also esteemed is the Talmud, made up of the Mishnah, a written collection of oral traditions, and Gemara, a commentary on the Mishnah. The Talmud covers many different subjects, such as law, stories and legends, medicine, and rituals.

Major Figures

The patriarchs are held to be the fathers of the faith. Abraham, the first patriarch, was called to leave his home in the Fertile Crescent for a land God would give him, and promised descendents as numerous as the stars. His son Isaac was followed by Jacob, whom God renamed Israel, and whose twelve sons became the heads of the twelve tribes of Israel. Moses was the man who, along with his brother Aaron, the founder of a priestly line, and their sister Miriam led the chosen people out of slavery in Egypt, where they had gone to escape famine. The Hebrew Bible also details the careers of a group of men and women known as judges, who were really tribal rulers, as well as of the prophets, who called the people to holy lives. Chief among the prophets was Elijah, who confronted wicked kings and performed many miracles. Several kings were key to the biblical narrative, among them David, who killed the giant Goliath, and Solomon, known for his wisdom and for the construction of a beautiful temple.

Major Holy Sites

Most of Judaism's holy sites are within Israel, the Holy Land, including Jerusalem, which was the capital of the United Kingdom of Israel under kings David and Solomon; David captured it from a Canaanite tribe around 1000 BCE. Within the Old City of Jerusalem is the Temple Mount (where the Temple of Jerusalem was built), often considered the religion's holiest site, the Foundation Stone (from which Judaism claims the world was created), and the Western (or Wailing) Wall. Other sites include Mount Sinai in Egypt, the mountain upon which God gave Moses his laws.

Major Rites & Celebrations

The Jewish calendar recognizes several important holidays. Rosh Hashanah, literally "first of the year," is known as the Jewish New Year and inaugurates a season of self-examination and repentance that culminates in Yom Kippur, the Day of Atonement. Each spring, Passover commemorates the deliverance of the Hebrew people from Egypt. Shavuot celebrates the giving of the Torah to Moses, while Sukkot is the harvest festival. Festivals celebrating deliverance from enemies include Purim and Hanukkah. Young adolescents become members of the community at a bar or bat mitzvah, held near the twelfth or thirteenth birthday. The Sabbath, a cessation from work from Friday at sundown until Saturday when the first star appears, gives each week a rhythm.

ORIGINS

History & Geography

Called by God perhaps four thousand years ago, Abraham left from Ur of the Chaldees, or the Fertile Crescent in Mesopotamia in present-day Iraq, to go the eastern Mediterranean, the land of Canaan. Several generations later, the tribe went to Egypt to escape famine. They were later enslaved by a pharaoh, sometimes believed to have been Ramses II (ca. 1279–1213 BCE), who was noted for his many building projects. The Israelites returned to Canaan under Moses several hundred years after their arrival in Egypt. He was given the law, the Ten Commandments, plus the rest of the laws governing all aspects of life, on Mount Sinai about the thirteenth century BCE. This marked the beginning of a special covenant relationship between the new nation, known as Israel, and God.

Following a period of rule by judges, kings governed the nation. Major kings included David, son-in-law to the first king, Saul, and David's son, Solomon. The kingdom split at the beginning of the reign of Solomon's son

Rehoboam, who began ruling about 930 BCE. Rehoboam retained the ten northern tribes, while the two southern tribes followed a military commander rather than the Davidic line.

Rehoboam's kingdom was known as Israel, after the name Jehovah gave to Jacob. Judah was the name of the southern kingdom—one of Jacob's sons was named Judah. Prophets to both nations warned of coming judgment unless the people repented of mistreating the poor and other sins, such as idolatry. Unheeding, Israel was taken into captivity by the Assyrians in 722 BCE. and the Israelites assimilated into the nations around them.

The Babylonians captured Judah in 586 BCE. After Babylon had been captured in turn by Persians, the Jewish people were allowed to return to the land in 538 BCE. There they began reconstructing the temple and the walls of the city. In the second century BCE, Judas Maccabeus led a rebellion against the heavy taxes and oppression of the Greek conquerors, after they had levied high taxes and appointed priests who were not Jewish. Judas Maccabeus founded a new ruling dynasty, the Hasmoneans, which existed briefly before the region came under the control of Rome.

The Jewish people revolted against Roman rule in 70 CE, leading to the destruction of the second temple. The final destruction of Jerusalem occurred in 135 under the Roman Emperor Hadrian. He changed the city's name to Aelia Capitolina and the name of the country to Palaestina. With the cultic center of their religion gone, the religious leaders developed new methods of worship that centered in religious academies and in synagogues.

After Christianity became the official state religion of the Roman Empire in the early fourth century, Jews experienced persecution. They became known for their scholarship, trade, and banking over the next centuries, with periods of brutal persecution in Europe. Christians held Jews responsible for the death of Jesus, based on a passage in the New Testament. The Blood Libel, begun in England in 1144, falsely accused Jews of killing a Christian child to bake unleavened bread for Passover. This rumor persisted for centuries, and was repeated by Martin Luther during the Protestant Reformation. England expelled all Jews in 1290; they were not readmitted until 1656 under Oliver Cromwell, and not given citizenship until 1829. Jews were also held responsible for other catastrophes—namely poisoning wells and rivers to cause the Black Death in 1348—and were often made to wear special clothing, such as pointed hats, or badges with the Star of David or stone tablets on them.

The relationship between Muslims and Jews was more harmonious. During the Muslim Arab dominance, there was a "golden age" in Spain due to the contributions of Jews and Muslims, known as Moors in Spain. This ideal and harmonious period ended in 1492, when both Moors and Jews were expelled from Spain or forced to convert to Christianity.

Jews in Russia suffered as well. An estimated two million Jews fled the country to escape the pogroms (a Russian word meaning devastation) between 1881 and 1917. The twentieth-century Holocaust, in which an estimated six million Jews perished at the hands of Nazi Germany, was but the culmination of these centuries of persecution. The Nazis also destroyed more than six hundred synagogues.

The Holocaust gave impetus to the creation of the independent state of Israel. The Zionist movement, which called for the founding or reestablishment of a Jewish homeland, was started by Austrian Jew Theodor Herzl in the late nineteenth century, and succeeded in 1948. The British government, which had ruled the region under a mandate, left the area, and Israel was thus established. This ended the Diaspora, or dispersion, of the Jewish people that had begun nearly two millennia before when the Romans forced the Jews to leave their homeland.

Arab neighbors, some of whom had been removed forcibly from the land to create the nation of Israel, were displeased with the new political reality. Several wars have been fought, including the War of Independence in 1948, the Six-Day War in 1967, and the Yom Kippur War in 1973. In addition, tension between Israel and its neighboring Arab states is almost constant.

When the Jewish people were dispersed from Israel, two traditions began. The Ashkenazi Jews settled in Germany and central Europe. They spoke a mixture of the Hebrew dialect and German called Yiddish. Sephardic Jews lived in the Mediterranean countries, including Spain; their language, Ladino, mixed Hebrew and old Spanish.

Founder or Major Prophet

Judaism refers to three major patriarchs: Abraham, his son Isaac, and Isaac's son Jacob. Abraham is considered the first Jew and worshipper in Judaism, as the religion began through his covenant with God. As the forefather of the religion, he is often associated as the founder, though the founder technically is God, or Yahweh (YHWH). Additionally, the twelve sons of Jacob, who was also named Israel, became the founders of the twelve tribes of Israel.

Moses is regarded as a major prophet and as the Lawgiver. God revealed to Moses the complete law during the forty days that the Jewish leader spent on Mount Sinai during the wilderness journey from Egypt to Canaan. Thus, many attribute Moses as the founder of Judaism as a religion.

Philosophical Basis

Judaism began with Abraham's dissatisfaction with the polytheistic worship of his culture. Hearing the command of God to go to a land that would be shown to him, Abraham and his household obeyed. Abraham practiced circumcision and hospitality, cornerstones of the Jewish faith to this day. He and his descendents practiced a nomadic life, much like that of contemporary Bedouins. They migrated from one oasis or well to another, seeking pasture and water for the sheep and goats they herded.

The further development of Judaism came under the leadership of Moses. A Jewish child adopted by Pharaoh's daughter, he was raised and educated in the palace. As a man, he identified with the Jewish people, killing one of the Egyptians who was oppressing a Jew. He subsequently fled for his life, becoming a shepherd in the wilderness, where he remained for forty years. Called by God from a bush that burned but was not destroyed, he was commissioned to lead the people out of slavery in Egypt back to the Promised Land. That forty-year pilgrimage in the wilderness and desert of Arabia shaped the new nation.

Holy Places

The city of Jerusalem was first known as Salem. When King David overcame the Jebusites who lived there, the city, already some two thousand years old, became the capital of Israel. It is built on Mount Zion, which is still considered a sacred place. David's son Solomon built the First Temple in Jerusalem, centering the nation's spiritual as well as political life in the city. The Babylonians captured the city in 597 BCE and destroyed the Temple. For the next sixty years, the Jews remained in exile, until Cyrus the Persian conqueror of Babylon allowed them to return. They rebuilt the temple, but it was desecrated by Antiochus IV of Syria in 167 BCE. In 18 BCE, during a period of Roman occupation, Herod the Great began rebuilding and expanding the Temple. The Romans under the general Titus destroyed the Temple in 70 CE, just seven years after its completion.

The city eventually came under the rule of Persia, the Muslim Empire, and the Crusaders before coming under control of Britain. In 1948 an independent state of Israel was created. The following year, Jerusalem was divided between Israel, which made the western part the national capital, and Jordan, which ruled the eastern part of the city. The Western or Wailing Wall, a retaining wall built during Herod's time, is all that remains of the Second Temple. Devout Jews still come to the Wailing Wall to pray, sometimes placing their petitions on paper and folding the paper into the Wall's crevices. The Wall is known as a place where prayers are answered and a reminder of the perseverance of the Jewish people and faith. According to tradition, the Temple will be rebuilt when Messiah comes to inaugurate God's Kingdom.

The Temple Mount, located just outside Jerusalem on a natural acropolis, includes the Dome of the Rock. This shrine houses a rock held sacred by both Judaism and Islam. Jewish tradition states that it is the spot from which the world was created and the spot on which Abraham was asked to sacrifice his son Isaac. Muslims believe that from this rock Muhammad ascended for his night journey to heaven. Much of Jerusalem, including this holy site, has been and continues to be fought over by people of three faiths: Judaism, Islam, and Christianity.

Moses received the law from God on Mount Sinai. It is still regarded as a holy place.

JUDAISM IN DEPTH

Sacred Symbols

Observant Jewish men pray three times daily at home or in a synagogue, a center of worship, from the word meaning "meeting place." They wear a tallis, or a prayer shawl with tassles, during their morning prayer and on Yom Kippur, the Day of Atonement. They may also cover their heads as a sign of respect during prayer, wearing a skullcap known as a kippah or yarmulka. They find their prayers and blessings in a siddur, which literally means "order," because the prayers appear in the order in which they are recited for services. Jewish daily life also includes blessings for many things, including food.

Tefillin or phylacteries are the small black boxes made of leather from kosher animals that Jewish men wear on their foreheads and their left upper arms during prayer. They contain passages from the Torah. Placing the tefillin on the head reminds them to think about the Torah, while placing the box on the arm puts the Torah close to the heart.

The Law of Moses commands the people to remember the words of the law and to teach them to the children. A mezuzah helps to fulfill that command. A small box with some of the words of the law written on a scroll inside, a mezuzah is hung on the doorframes of every door in the house. Most often, the words of the Shema, the Jewish recitation of faith, are written on the scroll. The Shema is repeated daily. "Hear, O Israel: the Lord your God, the Lord is one. . . . Love the Lord your God with all your heart, and with all your soul, and with all your might."

Jews adopted the Star of David, composed of two intersecting triangles, during the eighteenth century. There are several interpretations of the design. One is that it is the shape of King David's shield. Another idea is that it stands for daleth, the first letter of David's name. A third interpretation is that the six points refer to the days of the work week, and the inner, larger space represented the day of rest, the Sabbath, or Shabot. The Star of David appears on the flag of Israel. The flag itself is white, symbolizing peace and purity, and blue, symbolizing heaven and reminding all of God's activity.

The menorah is a seven-branch candlestick representing the light of the Torah. For Hanukkah, however, an eight-branched menorah is used. The extra candle is the servant candle, and is the one from which all others are lit.

Because the Torah is the crowning glory of life for Jewish people, a crown is sometimes used on coverings for the Torah. The scrolls of Torah are stored in a container, called an ark, which generally is covered with an ornate cloth called a mantle. The ark and mantle are often elaborately decorated with symbols, such as the lion of Judah. Because the Torah scroll, made of parchment from a kosher animal, is sacred and its pages are not to be touched, readers use a pointed stick called a yad. Even today, Torahs are written by hand in specially prepared ink and using a quill from a kosher bird. Scribes are trained for seven years.

A shofar is a ram's horn, blown as a call to repentance on Rosh Hashanah, the Jewish New Year. This holiday is the beginning of a ten-day preparation for the Day of Atonement, which is the most holy day in the Jewish calendar and a time of both fasting and repentance.

Sacred Practices & Gestures

Sacred practices can apply daily, weekly, annually, or over a lifetime's events. Reciting the Shema, the monotheistic creed taken from the

Torah, is a daily event. Keeping the Sabbath occurs weekly. Each year the festivals described above take place. Circumcision and bar or bat mitzvah are once-in-a-lifetime events. Each time someone dies, the mourners recite the Kaddish for seven days following death, and grieve for a year.

Food Restrictions

Kosher foods are those that can be eaten based on Jewish law. Animals that chew the cud and have cloven hooves, such as cows and lamb, and domestic poultry are considered kosher. Shellfish, pork, and birds of prey are forbidden. Keeping kosher also includes the method of preparing and storing the food. This includes animals which are slaughtered in a way to bring the least amount of pain and from which all blood is drained. In addition, dairy and meat products are to be kept separate, requiring separate refrigerators in the homes of the Orthodox.

Rites, Celebrations & Services

Sabbath is the weekly celebration honoring one of the Ten Commandments, which commands the people to honor the Sabbath by doing no work that day. The practice is rooted in the Genesis account that God rested on the seventh day after creating the world in six days. Because the Jewish day begins at sundown, the Sabbath lasts from Friday night to Saturday night. Special candles are lit and special food—included the braided egg bread called challah—for the evening meal is served. This day is filled with feasting, visiting, and worship.

Boys are circumcised at eight days of age. This rite, B'rit Milah, meaning "seal of the covenant," was first given to Abraham as a sign of the covenant. A trained circumciser, or mohel, may be a doctor or rabbi. The boy's name is officially announced at the ceremony. A girl's name is given at a special baby-naming ceremony or in the synagogue on the first Sabbath after she is born.

A boy becomes a "son of the commandment," or bar mitzvah, at age thirteen. At a special ceremony, the young man reads a portion of Torah that he has prepared ahead of time. Most boys also give a speech at the service. Girls become bat mitzvah at age twelve. This ceremony developed in the twentieth century. Not all Orthodox communities will allow this rite. Girls may also read from the Torah and give a sermon in the synagogue, just as boys do.

When a Jewish person dies, mourners begin shiva, a seven-day mourning period. People usually gather at the home of the deceased, where mirrors are covered. In the home, the Kaddish, a collection of prayers that praise God and celebrate life, is recited. Traditionally, family members mourn for a full year, avoiding parties and festive occasions.

The Jewish calendar offers a series of feasts and festivals, beginning with Rosh Hashanah, the Jewish New Year. At this time, Jews recall the creation. They may also eat apples that have been dipped into honey and offer each other wishes for a sweet New Year. The next ten days are a time of reflection on the past year, preparing for Yom Kippur.

This Day of Atonement once included animal sacrifice at the Temple. Now it includes an all-day service at the synagogue and a twenty-five-hour fast. A ram's horn, called a shofar, is blown as a call to awaken to lead a holier life. The shofar reminds Jewish people of the ram that Abraham sacrificed in the place of his son, Isaac.

Passover, or Pesach, is the spring remembrance of God's deliverance of the people from slavery in Egypt. In the night that the Jewish people left Egypt, they were commanded to sacrifice a lamb for each household and sprinkle the blood on the lintels and doorposts. A destroying angel from God would "pass over" the homes with blood sprinkled. During the first two nights of Passover, a special meal is served known as a Seder, meaning order. The foods symbolize different aspects of the story of deliverance, which is told during the meal by the head of the family.

Shavuot has its origins as a harvest festival. This celebration of Moses receiving the Torah on Mount Sinai occurs fifty days after the second day of Passover. To welcome the first fruits of the season, the synagogue may be decorated with fruit and flowers. Traditionally, the Ten Commandments are read aloud in the synagogue.

Purim, which occurs in February or March, celebrates the deliverance of the Jews during their captivity in Persia in the fifth century BCE. The events of that experience are recorded in the Book of Esther in the Hebrew Bible (Tanakh). The book is read aloud during Purim.

Sukkot, the feast celebrating the end of the harvest, occurs in September or October. Jews recall God's provision for them in the wilderness when they left Egypt to return to Canaan. Traditionally, huts are made and decorated with flowers and fruits. The conclusion of Sukkot is marked by a synagogue service known as Simchat Torah, or Rejoicing in the Law. People sing and dance as the Torah scrolls are carried and passed from person to person.

Hanukkah, known as the Festival of Lights, takes place over eight days in December. It celebrates the rededicating of the Temple under the leader Judas Maccabeus, who led the people in recapturing the structure from Syria in 164 BCE. According to the story, the Jews had only enough oil in the Temple lamp to last one day, but the oil miraculously lasted for eight days, after which Judas Maccabeus re-dedicated the Temple. On each day of Hanukkah, one of the eight candles is lit until all are burning. The gift-giving custom associated with Hanukkah is relatively new, and may derive from traditional small gifts of candy or money. The practice may also have been encouraged among those integrated with communities that exchange gifts during the Christmas season.

Judy A. Johnson, MTS

Bibliography

Barnes, Trevor. *The Kingfisher Book of Religions*. New York: Kingfisher, 1999. Print.

"A Buffet to Suit All Tastes." *Economist* 28 Jul. 2012: Spec. section 4–6. Print.

Charing, Douglas. *Judaism*. London: DK, 2003. Print.

Coenen Snyder, Saskia. *Building a Public Judaism: Synagogues and Jewish Identity in Nineteenth-Century Europe*. Cambridge: Harvard UP, 2013. E-book.

Diamant, Anita. *Living a Jewish Life*. New York: Collins, 1996. Print.

Exler, Lisa and Rabbi Jill Jacobs. "A Judaism That Matters." *Journal of Jewish Communal Service* 87.1/2 (2012): 66–76. Print.

Gelernter, David Hillel. *Judaism: A Way of Being*. New Haven: Yale UP, 2009. E-book.

Kessler, Edward. *What Do Jews Believe?* New York: Walker, 2007. Print.

Krieger, Aliza Y. "The Role of Judaism in Family Relationships." *Journal of Multicultural Counseling & Development* 38.3 (2010): 154–65. Print.

Langley, Myrtle. *Religion*. New York: Knopf, 1996. Print.

Madsen, Catherine. "A Heart of Flesh: Beyond 'Creative Liturgy.'" *Cross Currents* 62.1 (2012): 11–20. Print.

Meredith, Susan. *The Usborne Book of World Religions*. London: Usborne, 1995. Print.

Schoen, Robert. *What I Wish My Christian Friends Knew About Judaism*. Chicago: Loyola, 2004. Print.

Stefnon, Matt. *Judaism: History, Belief, and Practice*. New York: Britannica Educational, 2012. E-book.

Wertheimer, Jack. "The Perplexities of Conservative Judaism." *Commentary* Sept. 2007: 38–44. Print.

Wilkinson, Philip. *Religions*. New York: DK, 2008. Print.

Sikhism

General Description

The youngest of the world religions, Sikhism has existed for only about five hundred years. Sikhism derives from the Sanskrit word *sishyas*, which means "disciple"; in the Punjabi language, it also means "disciple."

Number of Adherents Worldwide

An estimated 24.5 million people follow the Sikh religion. Most of the devotees live in Asia, particularly in the Punjab region of India (Wilkinson, p. 335).

Basic Tenets

Sikhism is a monotheistic religion. The deity is God, known as Nam, or Name. Other synonyms include the Divine, Ultimate, Ultimate Reality, Infinity, the Formless, Truth, and other attributes of God.

Sikhs adhere to three basic principles. These are hard work (kirt kao), worshipping the Divine Name (nam japo), and sharing what one has (vand cauko). Meditating on the Divine Name is seen as a method of moving toward a life totally devoted to God. In addition, Sikhs believe in karma, or moral cause and effect. They value hospitality to all, regardless of religion, and oppose caste distinctions. Sikhs delineate a series of five stages that move upward to gurmukh, total devotion to God. This service is called Seva. Sahaj, or tranquility, is practiced as a means of being united with God as well as of generating external good will. Sikhs are not in favor of external routines of religion; they may stop in their temple whenever it is convenient during the day.

Sikhism does not include a belief in the afterlife. Instead, the soul is believed to be reincarnated in successive lives and deaths, a belief borrowed from Hinduism. The goal is then to break this karmic cycle, and to merge the human spirit with that of God.

Sacred Text

The Guru Granth Sahib (also referred to as the Aad Guru Granth Sahib, or AGGS), composed of Adi Granth, meaning First Book, is the holy scripture of Sikhism. It is a collection of religious poetry that is meant to be sung. Called shabads, they were composed by the first five gurus, the ninth guru, and thirty-six additional holy men of northern India. Sikhs always show honor to the Guru Granth Sahib by carrying it above the head when in a procession.

A second major text is the Dasam Granth, or Tenth Book, created by followers of Guru Gobind Singh, the tenth guru. Much of it is devoted to retelling the Hindu stories of Krishna and Rama. Those who are allowed to read and care for the Granth Sahib are known as granthi. Granthi may also look after the gurdwara, or temple. In the gurdwara, the book rests on a throne with a wooden base and cushions covered in cloths placed in a prescribed order. If the book is not in use, it is covered with a cloth known as a rumala. When the book is read, a fan called a chauri is fanned over it as a sign of respect, just as followers of the gurus fanned them with chauris. At Amritsar, a city in northwestern India that houses the Golden Temple, the Guru Granth Sahib is carried on a palanquin (a covered, carried bed). If it is carried in the city, a kettle drum is struck and people welcome it by tossing rose petals.

Major Figures

Guru Nanak (1469–1539) is the founder of Sikhism. He was followed by nine other teachers, and collectively they are known as the Ten Gurus. Each of them was chosen by his predecessor and was thought to share the same spirit of that previous guru. Guru Arjan (1581–1606), the fifth guru, oversaw completion of the Golden Temple in Amritsar, India. Guru Gobind Singh (1675–1708) was the tenth and last human guru. He decreed that the True Guru henceforth would be the Granth Sahib, the scripture of the Sikhs. He also founded the Khalsa, originally a military order of male Sikhs willing to die for the faith; the term is now used to refer to all baptized Sikhs.

Major Holy Sites

Amritsar, India, is the holy city of Sikhism. Construction of the city began under Guru Ram Das (1574–1581), the fourth guru, during the 1570s. One legend says that the Muslim ruler, Emperor Akbar, gave the land to the third guru, Guru Amar Das (1552–74). Whether or not that is true, Amar Das did establish the location of Amritsar. He chose a site near a pool believed to hold healing water.

When construction of the Golden Temple began, only a small town existed. One legend says that a Muslim saint from Lahore, India, named Mian Mir laid the foundation stone of the first temple. It has been demolished and rebuilt three times. Although pilgrimage is not required of Sikhs, many come to see the shrines and the Golden Temple. They call it Harmandir Sahib, God's Temple, or Darbar Sahib, the Lord's Court. When the temple was completed during the tenure of the fifth guru, Arjan, he placed the first copy of the Guru Granth Sahib inside.

Every Sikh temple has a free kitchen attached to it, called a langar. After services, all people, regardless of caste or standing within the community, sit on the floor in a straight line and eat a simple vegetarian meal together. As a pilgrimage site, the langar serves 30,000–40,000 people daily, with more coming on Sundays and festival days. About forty volunteers work in the kitchen each day.

Major Rites & Celebrations

In addition to the community feasts at temple langars, Sikhs honor four rites of passage in a person's life: naming, marriage, initiation in Khalsa (pure) through the Amrit ceremony, and death.

There are eight major celebrations and several other minor ones in Sikhism. Half of them commemorate events in the lives of the ten gurus. The others are Baisakhi, the new year festival; Diwali, the festival of light, which Hindus also celebrate; Hola Mahalla, which Gobind Singh created as an alternative to the Hindu festival of Holi, and which involves military parades; and the installing of the Guru Granth Sahib.

ORIGINS

History & Geography

The founder of Sikhism, Nanak, was born in 1469 CE in the Punjab region of northeast India, where both Hinduism and Islam were practiced. Both of these religions wanted control of the region. Nanak wanted the fighting between followers of these two traditions to end and looked for solutions to the violence.

Nanak blended elements of both religions and also combined the traditional apparel of both faiths to construct his clothing style. The Guru Granth Sahib further explains the division between Sikhs and the Islamic and Muslim faiths:

Nanak would become the first guru of the Sikh religion, known as Guru Nanak Dev. A Muslim musician named Bhai Mardana, considered the first follower, accompanied Nanak in his travels around India and Asia. Guru Nanak often sang, and singing remains an important part of worship for Sikhs. Before his death, Nanak renamed one of his disciples Angad, a word meaning "a part of his own self." He became Guru Angad Dev, the second guru, thus beginning the tradition of designating a successor and passing on the light to that person.

Guru Baba Ram Das, the fourth guru, who lived in the sixteenth century, began constructing Amritsar's Golden Temple. The structure was completed by his successor, Guru Arjan Dev, who also collected poems and songs written by the first four gurus and added his own. He included the work of Kabir and other Hindu and Muslim holy men as well. This became the Adi Granth, which he placed in the Golden Temple.

Guru Arjan was martyred in 1606 by Jehangir, the Muslim emperor. His son Hargobind became the sixth guru and introduced several important practices and changes. He wore two swords, representing both spiritual and worldly authority. Near the Golden Temple he had a building known as Akal Takht, or Throne of the Almighty, erected. In it was a court of justice as well as a group of administrators. Even today, orders and decisions enter the community from Akal Takht. Guru Hargobind was the last of the gurus with a direct link to Amritsar. Because of conflict with the Muslim rulers, he and all subsequent gurus moved from the city.

The tenth guru, Gobind Singh, created the Khalsa, the Community of the Pure, in 1699. The members of the Khalsa were to be known by five distinctive elements, all beginning with the letter *k*. These include kes, the refusal to cut the hair or trim the beard; kangha, the comb used to keep the long hair neatly combed in contrast to the Hindu ascetics who had matted hair; kaccha, shorts that would allow soldiers quick movement; kara, a thin steel bracelet worn to symbolize restraint; and kirpan, a short sword not to be used except in self-defense. Among other duties, members of this elite group were to defend the faith. Until the middle of the nineteenth century, when the British created an empire in India, the Khalsa remained largely undefeated.

In 1708, Guru Gobind Singh announced that he would be the final human guru. All subsequent leadership would come from the Guru Granth Sahib, now considered a living guru, the holy text Arjan had begun compiling more than a century earlier.

Muslim persecution under the Mughals led to the defeat of the Sikhs in 1716. The remaining Sikhs headed for the hills, re-emerging after decline of Mughal power. They were united under Ranjit Singh's kingdom from 1820 to 1839. They then came under the control of the British.

The British annexed the Punjab region, making it part of their Indian empire in 1849, and recruited Sikhs to serve in the army. The Sikhs remained loyal to the British during the Indian Mutiny of 1857–1858. As a result, they were given many privileges and land grants, and with peace and prosperity, the first Singh Sabha was founded in 1873. This was an educational and religious reform movement.

During the early twentieth century, Sikhism was shaped in its more modern form. A group known as the Tat Khalsa, which was more progressive, became the dominant way of understanding the faith.

In 1897, a group of Sikh musicians within the British Army was invited to attend the Diamond Jubilee of Queen Victoria in England. They also traveled to Canada and were attracted by the nation's prairies, which were perfect for farming. The first group of Sikhs came to Canada soon after. By 1904, more than two hundred Sikhs had settled in British Columbia. Some of them later headed south to Washington, Oregon, and California in the United States. The first Sikh gurdwara in the United States was constructed in Stockton, California, in 1912. Sikhs became farmers, worked in lumber mills, and helped to construct the Western Pacific railroad. Yuba City, California, has one of the world's largest Sikh temples, built in 1968.

Sikh troops fought for Britain in World War I, achieving distinction. Following the war, in 1919, however, the British denied the Sikhs the right to gather for their New Year festival. When the Sikhs disobeyed, the British troops fired without warning on 10,000 Sikhs, 400 of whom were killed. This became known as the first Amritsar Massacre.

The British government in 1925 did give the Sikhs the right to help manage their own shrines. A fragile peace ensued between the British and the Sikhs, who again fought for the British Empire during World War II.

After the war ended, the Sikh hope for an independent state was dashed by the partition of India and Pakistan in 1947. Pakistan was in the Punjab region; thus, 2.5 million Sikhs lived in a Muslim country where they were not welcome. Many of them became part of the mass internal migration that followed Indian independence.

In 1966, a state with a Sikh majority came into existence after Punjab boundaries were redrawn. Strife continued throughout second half of twentieth century, however, as a result of continuing demands for Punjab autonomy. A second massacre at Amritsar occurred in 1984, resulting in the death of 450 Sikhs (though some estimates of the death toll are higher). Indian troops, under orders from Indian Prime Minister Indira Gandhi, fired on militant leaders of Sikhs, who had gone to the Golden Temple for refuge. This attack was considered a desecration of a sacred place, and the prime minister was later assassinated by her Sikh bodyguards in response. Restoration of the Akal Takht, the administrative headquarters, took fifteen years. The Sikh library was also burned, consuming ancient manuscripts.

In 1999, Sikhs celebrated the three-hundredth anniversary of the founding of Khalsa. There has been relative peace in India since that event. In the United States, however, Sikhs became the object of slander and physical attack following the acts of terrorism on September 11, 2001, as some Americans could not differentiate between Arab head coverings and Sikh turbans.

Founder or Major Prophet

Guru Nanak Dev was born into a Hindu family on April 15, 1469. His family belonged to the merchant caste, Khatri. His father worked as an accountant for a Muslim, who was also a local landlord. Nanak was educated in both the Hindu and Islamic traditions. According to legends, his teachers soon realized they had nothing further to teach him. After a direct revelation from Ultimate Reality that he received as a young man, Nanak proclaimed that there was neither Muslim nor Hindu. God had told Nanak "Rejoice in my Name," which became a central doctrine of Sikhism.

Nanak began to preach, leaving his wife and two sons behind. According to tradition, he traveled not only throughout India, but also eventually to Iraq, Saudi Arabia, and Mecca. This tradition and others were collected in a volume known as Janamsakhis. A Muslim servant of the family, Mardana, who also played a three-stringed musical instrument called the rebec, accompanied him, as did a Hindu poet, Bala Sandhu, who had been a friend from childhood (though the extent of his importance or existence is often considered controversial).

Nanak traveled as an itinerant preacher for a quarter century and then founded a village, Kartarpur, on the bank of Punjab's Ravi River. Before his death he chose his successor, beginning a tradition that was followed until the tenth and final human guru.

Philosophical Basis

When Guru Nanak Dev, the first guru, began preaching in 1499 at about age thirty, he incorporated aspects of both Hinduism and Islam. From Hinduism, he took the ideas of karma and reincarnation. From Islam, he borrowed the Ultimate as the name of God. Some scholars see the influence of the religious reformer and poet Kabir, who lived from 1440 until 1518. Kabir merged the Bhakti (devotional) side of Hinduism with the Islamic Sufis, who were mystics.

Within the Hindu tradition in northern India was a branch called the Sants. The Sants believed that God was both with form and without form, unable to be represented concretely. Most of the Sants were illiterate and poor, but created poems that spoke of the divine being experienced in all things. This idea also rooted itself in Sikhism.

Guru Nanak Dev, who was raised as a Hindu, rejected the caste system in favor of equality of all persons. He also upheld the value of women, rejecting the burning of widows and female infanticide. When eating a communal meal, first begun as a protest against caste, everyone sits in a straight line and shares karah prasad (a pudding), which is provided by those of all castes. However, Sikhs are expected to marry within their caste. In some cases, especially in the United Kingdom, gurdwaras (places of worship) for a particular caste exist.

Holy Places

Amritsar, especially the Golden Temple, which was built in the sixteenth century under the supervision of the fifth guru, Guru Arjan, is the most sacred city.

Ram Das, the fourth guru, first began constructing a pool on the site in 1577. He called it

Amritsar, the pool of nectar. This sacred reflecting pool is a pilgrimage destination. Steps on the southern side of the pool allow visitors to gather water in bottles, to drink it, to bathe in it, or to sprinkle it on themselves.

SIKHISM IN DEPTH

Sacred Symbols

The khanda is the major symbol of Sikhism. It features a two-edged sword, representing justice and freedom, in the center. It is surrounded by a circle, a symbol of both balance and of the unity of God and humankind. A pair of curved swords (kirpans) surrounds the circle. One sword stands for religious concerns, the other for secular concerns. The khanda appears on Sikh flags, which are flown over every temple.

Members of the Khalsa have five symbols. They do not cut their hair, and men do not trim their beards. This symbol, kes, is to indicate a harmony with the ways of nature. To keep the long hair neat, a comb called a kangha is used. The third symbol is the kara, a bracelet usually made of steel to represent continuity and strength. When the Khalsa was first formed, soldiers wore loose-fitting shorts called kaccha. They were worn to symbolize moral restraint and purity. The final symbol is a short sword known as a kirpan, to be used only in self-defense. When bathing in sacred waters, the kirpan is tucked into the turban, which is worn to cover the long hair. The turban, which may be one of many colors, is wound from nearly five yards of cloth.

Sacred Practices & Gestures

Sikhs use Sat Sri Akal (truth is timeless) as a greeting, putting hands together and bowing toward the other person. To show respect, Sikhs keep their heads covered with a turban or veil. Before entering a temple, they remove their shoes. Some Sikhs may choose to wear a bindhi, the dot on the forehead usually associated with Hinduism.

When Guru Gobind Singh initiated the first men into the Khalsa, he put water in a steel bowl and added sugar, stirring the mixture with his sword and reciting verses from the Guru Granth as he did so. He thus created amrit (immortal), a holy water also used in baptism, or the Amrit ceremony. The water represents mental clarity, while sugar stands for sweetness. The sword invokes military courage, and the chanting of verses brings a poetic spirituality.

The Sikh ideal of bringing Ultimate Reality into every aspect of the day is expressed in prayers throughout the day. Daily morning prayer (Bani) consists of five different verses, most of them the work of one of the ten gurus; there are also two sets of evening prayers. Throughout the day, Sikhs repeat the Mul Mantra, "Ikk Oan Kar" (There is one Being). This is the first line of a brief creedal statement about Ultimate Reality.

Food Restrictions

Sikhs are not to eat halal meat, which is the Muslim equivalent of kosher. Both tobacco and alcohol are forbidden. Many Sikhs are vegetarians, although this is not commanded. Members of the Khalsa are not permitted to eat meat slaughtered according to Islamic or Hindu methods, because they believe these means cause pain to the animal.

Rites, Celebrations, & Services

The Sikhs observe four rite of passage rituals, with each emphasizing their distinction from the Hindu traditions. After a new mother is able to get up and bathe, the new baby is given a birth and naming ceremony in the gurdwara. The child is given a name based on the first letter of hymn from the Guru Granth Sahib at random. All males are additionally given the name Singh (lion); all females also receive the name Kaur (princess).

The marriage ceremony (anand karaj) is the second rite of passage. Rather than circle a sacred fire as the Hindus do, the Sikh couple walks four times around a copy of the Guru Granth Sahib, accompanied by singing. The bride often wears red, a traditional color for the Punjabi.

The amrit initiation into the Khalsa is considered the most important rite. It need not take place in a temple, but does require that five

Sikhs who are already Khalsa members conduct the ceremony. Amrit initiation may occur any time after a child is old enough to read the Guru Granth and understand the tenets of the faith. Some people, however, wait until their own children are grown before accepting this rite.

The funeral rite is the fourth and final rite of passage. A section of the Guru Granth is read. The body, dressed in the Five "K's," is cremated soon after death.

Initiation into the Khalsa is now open to both men and women. The earliest gurus opposed the Hindu custom of sati, which required a widow to be burned on her husband's funeral pyre. They were also against the Islamic custom of purdah, which required women to be veiled and covered in public. Women who are menstruating are not excluded from worship, as they are in some religions. Women as well as men can be leaders of the congregation and are permitted to read from the Guru Granth and recite sacred hymns.

The Sikh houses of worship are known as gurdwaras and include a langar, the communal dining area. People remove their shoes and cover their heads before entering. They touch their foreheads to the floor in front of the scripture to show respect. The service itself is in three parts. The first segment is Kirtan, singing hymns (kirtans) accompanied by musical instruments, which can last for several hours. It is followed by a set prayer called the Ardas, which has three parts. The first and final sections cannot be altered. In the first, the virtues of the gurus are extolled. In the last, the divine name is honored. In the center of the Ardas is a list of the Khalsa's troubles and victories, which a prayer leader recites in segments and to which the congregation responds with Vahiguru, considered a word for God. At the end of the service, members eat karah prasad, sacred food made of raw sugar, clarified butter, and coarse wheat flour. They then adjourn for a communal meal, Langar, the third section of worship.

Sikhism does not have a set day for worship similar to the Jewish Sabbath or Christian Sunday worship. However, the first day of the month on the Indian lunar calendar, sangrand, and the darkest night of the month, masia, are considered special days. Sangrand is a time for praying for the entire month. Masia is often considered an auspicious time for bathing in the holy pool at the temple.

Four of the major festivals that Sikhs observe surround important events in the lives of the gurus. These are known as gurpurabs, or anniversaries. Guru Nanak's birthday, Guru Gobind Singh's birthday, and the martyrdoms of the Gurus Arjan and Tegh Bahadur comprise the four main gurpurabs. Sikhs congregate in the gurudwaras to hear readings of the Guru Granth and lectures by Sikh scholars.

Baisakhi is the Indian New Year, the final day before the harvest begins. On this day in 1699, Guru Gobind Singh formed the first Khalsa, adding even more importance to the day for Sikhs. Each year, a new Sikh flag is placed at all temples.

Diwali, based on a word meaning string of lights, is a Hindu festival. For Sikhs, it is a time to remember the return of the sixth guru, Hargobind, to Amritsar after the emperor had imprisoned him. It is celebrated for three days at the Golden Temple. Sikhs paint and whitewash their houses and decorate them with candles and earthenware lamps.

Hola Mohalla, meaning attack and place of attack, is the Sikh spring festival, which corresponds to the Hindu festival Holi. It is also a three-day celebration and a time for training Sikhs as soldiers. Originally, it involved military exercises and mock battles, as well as competitions in archery, horsemanship, and wrestling. In contemporary times, the festival includes athletic contests, discussion, and singing.

Judy A. Johnson, MTS

Bibliography

Barnes, Trevor. *The Kingfisher Book of Religions*. New York: Kingfisher, 1999. Print.

Dhanjal, Beryl. *Amritsar*. New York: Dillon, 1993. Print.

Dhavan, Purnima. *When Sparrows Became Hawks: The Making of the Sikh Warrior Tradition, 1699–1799*. Oxford: Oxford UP, 2011. Print.

Eraly, Abraham, et. al. *India*. New York: DK, 2008. Print.
Harley, Gail M. *Hindu and Sikh Faiths in America*. New York: Facts on File, 2003. Print.
Jakobsh, Doris R. *Sikhism and Women: History, Texts, and Experience*. Oxford, New York: Oxford UP, 2010. Print.
Jhutti-Johal, Jagbir. *Sikhism Today*. London, New York: Continuum, 2011. Print.
Langley, Myrtle. *Religion*. New York: Knopf, 1996. Print.
Mann, Gurinder Singh. *Sikhism*. Upper Saddle River: Prentice, 2004. Print.
Meredith, Susan. *The Usborne Book of World Religions*. London: Usborne, 1995. Print.
Sidhu, Dawinder S. and Neha Singh Gohil. *Civil Rights in Wartime: The Post-9/11 Sikh Experience*. Ashgate, 2009. E-book.
Singh, Nikky-Guninder Kaur. *Sikhism*. New York: Facts on File, 1993. Print.
Singh, Nikky-Guninder Kaur. *Sikhism: An Introduction*. Tauris, 2011. E-book.
Singh, Surinder. *Introduction to Sikhism and Great Sikhs of the World*. Gurgaon: Shubhi, 2012. Print.
Wilkinson, Philip. *Religions*. New York: DK, 2008. Print.

Index